THE BRAVES
ENCYCLOPEDIA

In the series

Baseball Encyclopedias of North America

edited by Richard Westcott

Also in the series:

The New Phillies Encyclopedia, by Richard Westcott
and Frank Bilovsky, 1993

The Cleveland Indians Encyclopedia, by Russell
Schneider, in press

The White Sox Encyclopedia, by Richard Lindberg,
forthcoming

Gary Caruso

THE BRAVES ENCYCLOPEDIA

Temple University Press | Philadelphia

Temple University Press, Philadelphia, PA 19122
Copyright © 1995 by Temple University
All rights reserved
Published 1995

Printed in the United States of America

Library of Congress Cataloging-in-Publication Data

Caruso, Gary.
    The Braves encyclopedia / Gary Caruso.
      p.   cm.
    ISBN 1-56639-384-1
      1. Atlanta Braves (Baseball team)—History.   I. Title.
GV875.A8C37   1995
796.357′64′09758231—dc20   95–23207

Contents

Foreword

Dear Braves Fans:

Braves fans and all baseball fans should find *The Braves Encyclopedia* to be very enjoyable and really informative. It's by far the most thorough book ever written about the Braves.

What I really like is the way all the information is broken down by year, player, and manager and into various other categories. This format makes the book easy and fun to read, whether you've only got a few minutes or several hours. It's brought back a lot of wonderful memories for me about my Braves career and taught me a lot I didn't know about the team and baseball in general.

When I was playing for the Braves, it was impossible to see my career in perspective with the big picture of this historic franchise. Now *The Braves Encyclopedia* has given me the opportunity to learn so much about the team and the role my teammates and I played in this fascinating story.

I especially enjoyed reading about Rabbit Maranville and the "Miracle" Braves of 1914 and the great Milwaukee teams of the 1950s. And I can tell you this—I'm sure glad I never had to hit in mammoth Braves Field!

All the team's personalities are here, from Hall of Famers such as Hank Aaron, Eddie Mathews, Warren Spahn, Babe Ruth, Cy Young, and Casey Stengel to the more recent guys like Phil Niekro, David Justice, Ron Gant, Tom Glavine, Greg Maddux, Terry Pendleton, and Fred McGriff. You can even find a little about me.

Gary Caruso has been following the Braves as a writer and editor for the last 20 years. In fact, he first interviewed me in 1976 when I was still at Richmond. I know he's put an incredible amount of work into this book, but I also know he's loved every minute of it. And I think you will, too.

Dale Murphy
National League MVP 1982, 1983

Prologue, 1995

As *The Braves Encyclopedia* went to press, Atlanta was bearing down on the playoffs—the new, two-tiered version. For the first time in history, a team would have to win seven postseason games against two opponents just to reach the World Series. . . .

Ah, yes, the Series. The Braves had not won it since 1957 in Milwaukee, but 1995 looks promising. By the time you read this, Bobby Cox's team might even be World Series champions, a fitting way to celebrate the Braves' 30th season in Atlanta and 125 years of franchise history.

But whether or not the Braves finally bring the Series title to the South for the first time, 1995 will stand as yet another dynamic chapter in the franchise's success story of the 1990s.

The regular season didn't begin until April 26 and was shortened to 144 games by continued labor-management discord. However, the Braves quickly served notice there was good reason for their favorite's role in the National League East. Behind the pitching of Greg Maddux and two home runs by Fred McGriff, they whipped San Francisco, 12–5, on opening day.

Buoyed by the spring acquisition of center fielder Marquis Grissom from Montreal and the return of rookie Chipper Jones, who missed all of 1994 due to a knee injury, Atlanta appeared well-suited for a run at the pennant. Indeed, when the Braves won six of their first seven games, it seemed like it might be all too easy. But baseball seldom works that way, and 1995 was no different.

The Phillies surprised everyone by playing extremely well the first two months while the Braves struggled at times and fell as many as five games off the pace in late June. But just prior to the All-Star Game, the Braves got hot, winning their last nine games before the break and 13 out of 15. Atlanta suddenly found itself with a four-game lead at the midseason intermission and never looked back. At the same time, the Phillies went into a dive, allowing the Braves to coast into the stretch with a comfortable lead in double figures.

Still, it wasn't easy. It was almost as if the Braves wanted to tease their fans, playing nearly every game ridiculously close, then often coming from behind to win in the last inning. In fact, they were leading the majors in number of wins in the last at bat. Fans hoped it was the trademark of a championship team, but nevertheless it was both nerve-wracking and exhilarating.

The reasons for the Braves' late-season lock on first place were many, but they began with the remarkable Greg Maddux. A personal 10-game winning streak vaulted the machine-like Maddux into position for a run at an unprecedented fourth straight Cy Young Award.

Pitching, as usual, was the key to the Braves' success, especially in '95 with the team batting average mysteriously hovering near the bottom of the league. While Steve Avery struggled and Kent Mercker was inconsistent, the indomitable Tom Glavine rolled efficiently along in Maddux's shadow and John Smoltz, strengthened by elbow surgery, was pitching as well as ever.

The most significant development of the season was the emergence of Mark Wohlers as not only the Braves' closer but as one of the game's most-dominant last-inning specialists. And the rest of the bullpen, led by rookie Brad Clontz and veteran Greg McMichael, suddenly became a strength rather than a liability.

With Jeff Blauser in a lengthy slump and David Justice and McGriff hitting below their normal levels, it was the youngsters—Ryan Klesko, Javy Lopez, and Jones—who were keeping the offense afloat. Taking over as the regular left fielder, Klesko often displayed awesome power. A year of experience worked wonders for Lopez at the plate and behind it. And Jones was playing a new position, third base, like he'd been there his entire life and also was making a surprising challenge for the team lead in home runs.

The conclusion to the season had yet to be played out, but it offered the potential of drama, intrigue, and even the ultimate achievement.

—Gary Caruso, August 1995

Introduction

This is the story of the oldest continuously operating professional sports franchise in America. As such, it's not only a story of wins and losses, ballplayers, managers, and stadiums, but also a history of the birth and development of baseball from the very inception of professional league play.

It's the story of the Braves and their ancestors—the Red Stockings, Beaneaters, Doves, Rustlers, and Bees—and their wanderings from Boston to Milwaukee to Atlanta, weaving a sometimes warped but always rich and colorful heritage that is unique in the annals of pro sports.

On January 20, 1871, the Boston Red Stockings were incorporated. Two months later, they became one of nine charter members of the National Association of Professional Base Ball Players, the first professional league and the forerunner of the National League. That pioneer franchise, now known as the Atlanta Braves, is the only one of today's 28 big league organizations to have fielded a team every season professional league baseball has been in existence.

Following the exploits of this franchise from the Red Stockings to the Braves is like taking a 125-year ride on the world's largest roller coaster, one with the highest peaks and deepest valleys a baseball team is capable of exploring. This ride starts and ends at the same place—the top. The modern Braves have established themselves as one of the finest teams in the game, and so, too, were the original Red Stockings one of the most dominant clubs in the sport's early history.

From 1991 to 1993, Bobby Cox's Braves won three division titles and two pennants and lost two heart-stopping World Series in a period of unequaled popularity for the franchise. Similarly, the Red Stockings of manager Harry Wright won six of the first eight pennants in history—National Association flags in 1872–75 and National League championships in 1877–78.

The Red Stockings, who played the first National League game ever and became known as the Beaneaters in 1883, won eight of the first 23 National League pennants from 1876 to 1898 in what was easily the most successful era in franchise history. But, as all but beginning Braves fans know, the team also has experienced life in the pits. As recently as 1990, Atlanta had the worst record (65–97) in baseball, setting the stage for the improbable "Worst to First" scenario that stunned the sports world in 1991 and thrilled thousands of tomahawk-chopping fans from coast to coast.

Even at their worst, the Braves have been interesting and entertaining. In fact, the 1935 season, which was the lowest ebb in franchise history (38–115, .248) also provides one of the more intriguing chapters in this saga. For it was in 1935 that Babe Ruth played the last 28 games of his career in a Braves uniform.

Ironically, Ruth hit his last six home runs as a Brave, establishing the milestone of 714 career homers that stood until April 8, 1974, when a Brave of considerably longer and more distinguished service named Hank Aaron ascended to the throne of the all-time home run king.

Not only does the all-time Braves honor roll include Aaron, who hit more home runs from the right side of the plate than anyone else, and Ruth, the left-handed champ, but it also boasts Warren Spahn, the winningest left-hander in history, and Cy Young, the right-hander who won more games than any other pitcher in history. Young, like Ruth, just stopped by for a brief good-bye on his way to retirement. And Spahn, like his longtime teammate Aaron, graced the Braves uniform for most of his remarkable career.

There have been 46 Hall of Famers to play, manage, and coach for the Braves. They range from Harry Wright, the "father of professional baseball" who organized the first Boston Red Stockings, to Rabbit Maranville and Johnny Evers, heroes of the "Miracle" Braves of 1914, and Aaron, Spahn, and Eddie Mathews, icons of the great Milwaukee teams in the 1950s. Two more Cooperstown immortals, Christy Mathewson and John Montgomery Ward, served the franchise as president.

Greg Olson's leap into John Smoltz's arms began the improbable 1991 division-clinching celebration and signaled the arrival of the most successful period in Braves history since the 1950s.

But the history of the Braves isn't just a story of Hall of Famers. Of the nearly 1,500 men to have played for the club, many of the lesser names such as "Hurricane" Hazle, Nippy Jones, Francisco Cabrera, Greg Olson, and Pascual Perez and certainly the modern stars such as Dale Murphy, Phil Niekro, Terry Pendleton, David Justice, Greg Maddux, and Tom Glavine are just as entrenched in the overall picture as are the Hall of Famers.

Braves managers have included George Stallings, the only individual in baseball history called "Miracle Man"; Frank Selee, who guided Boston to five pennants in 12 years; the great Casey Stengel before he was great; and Judge Emil Fuchs, an owner who moved into the dugout for the 1929 season, 48 years before Ted Turner tried the same thing for one game.

The Braves have known both the long and short of baseball history.

In 1920, Boston played Brooklyn to a 1–1 tie that was called due to darkness after 26 innings, a major league record. Both pitchers, Joe Oeschger of the Braves and Brooklyn's Leon Cadore, worked the entire 26 innings.

Then there was the 19-inning marathon that began July 4, 1985, and ended July 5. That 16–13 Mets victory was extended in the 18th by pitcher Rick Camp's two-strike, two-out home run, perhaps the most improbable homer in franchise history.

On the short end of things, right-hander Red Barrett used just 58 pitches to beat Cincinnati, 2–0, on August 10, 1944. The game was completed in 75 minutes, the shortest night game in history.

When it comes to power hitting, the Braves have put on some of the most awesome slugging displays of all time. Only 12 men have ever hit four home runs in a game, and three of them were Braves. Bobby Lowe was the first player to accomplish the feat in 1894. Joe Adcock chipped in a double with his four homers for a major league record 18 total bases in 1954. And Bob Horner managed to become the first player to hit four homers in a losing cause in 1986, providing a fitting representation of the team's play for much of that decade.

In 1961, Mathews, Aaron, Adcock, and Frank Thomas hit a major league record four consecutive home runs—and still the Braves lost.

The 1953 Milwaukee Braves put on a slugging display at Pittsburgh's Forbes Field that may never be equaled considering the scarcity of doubleheaders today. With Hank Aaron still in the minors, the Braves hit eight home runs in the first game, tying the major league record and setting a National League single-game record. They also set National League records with 12 homers and 73 total bases in the doubleheader. And they won both games, too.

In 1930, Boston's Wally Berger set National League rookie records with 38 home runs and 119 RBIs. His home run total stood as a major league record until 1987 when Mark McGwire hit 49 for Oakland.

The 1965 Braves, the last to play in Milwaukee, set a National League record with six players—Aaron, Mathews, Joe Torre, Felipe Alou, Mack Jones, and Gene Oliver—hitting 20 or more home runs. And the 1973 team set a major league record with three players—Aaron, Dave Johnson, and Darrell Evans—hitting 40 or more, firmly establishing Atlanta Stadium's nickname as "The Launching Pad."

Braves pitchers have always been proficient with their bats, too. Spahn holds the National League record with 35 career home runs. In 1942, right-handed knuckleballer Jim Tobin hit three home runs in one game, the only 20th-century pitcher ever to accomplish the feat. Two years later, Tobin became the first man to pitch a no-hitter and homer in the same game. In 1947, Johnny Sain hit safely in 14 straight games and batted .346.

But the most notable slugging feat by a Braves pitcher came in 1966, the team's first season in Atlanta, when right-hander Tony Cloninger became the first and only man in National League history to hit two grand slams in the same game. He also drove in a ninth run with a double, tying the single-game RBI record for a pitcher.

The Braves have even hit home runs that weren't home runs. In 1965 at Busch Stadium in St. Louis, Aaron hit what he thought was a home run, only to circle the bases and discover he'd been called out for stepping out of the front of the batter's box when he swung.

And the most famous home run that wasn't came off the bat of Adcock in 1959 at Milwaukee County Stadium. It cleared the fence and ruined Harvey Haddix's masterpiece of 12 perfect innings but was ruled a double because Adcock "passed" Aaron on the bases.

Besides Aaron's 715th home run, the greatest hit in franchise history belongs to Cabrera. Then a relatively unknown and little-used pinch hitter, he sent the Braves to the World Series in 1992 with a two-out, two-run single to beat Pittsburgh in the ninth inning of Game 7 in the National League Championship Series.

Hugh Duffy, a 5–7, 168-pound outfielder, established a standard in 1894 that will never be surpassed—the all-time National League batting average high of .440 (listed in some record books as .438).

In 1945, Boston right fielder Tommy Holmes put together a 37-game hitting streak that stood as the modern National League record until Pete Rose surpassed it in 1978. But the Braves got their revenge on Rose for knocking Holmes out of the record book. It was rookie left-hander Larry McWilliams and veteran reliever Gene Garber who teamed in Atlanta to end Rose's streak at 44 games.

Early and modern Braves history is linked in a number of ways, including stadium fires and aggressive player acquisition techniques.

The team's first home, the South End Grounds in Boston, burned to the ground in 1894. And today's fans remember the 1993 fire which gutted a portion of the club level behind home plate at Atlanta–Fulton County Stadium.

Arthur Soden, who served as franchise president for three decades, was one of the more important executives in baseball's formative years. It was Soden who in 1879 wrote the controversial "reserve clause" that bound players to their teams until the advent of free agency in 1976. It was also under Soden that early Boston clubs initiated the practice of buying players. The Beaneaters astonished other clubs by purchasing "King" Kelly from Chicago for $10,000 in 1887 and John Clarkson for the same price and from the same team a year later. Kelly and Clarkson, two of the premier players of the era, are now in the Hall of Fame.

Once the reserve clause was overturned in 1976, Ted Turner immediately became one of the leaders in pursuing free agents. In fact, he signed the first one—Andy Messersmith—and proceeded to assign the right-hander uniform number 17 and the nickname "Channel" to advertise his television station on the pitcher's jersey.

Braves of three different eras also have pulled off three of the greatest second-half rallies in baseball history. The best-known, of course, was accomplished by the 1914 Braves, who were in last place on July 18, only to win the pennant and the World Series.

But more than 30 years earlier, the 1883 Beaneaters had a similar season. They lost 11 of their first 15 games and were in seventh place in June before righting themselves and winning the pennant.

And the 1993 Braves were 10 games behind the Giants on July 22 before mounting a second-half offensive that produced a franchise-record 104 wins and a third-straight division title.

That 1993 division clinching didn't come until the final day of the season, but the Beaneaters of 1891 had what surely ranks as the latest pennant clinching in history. Boston put on a spirited finish that season, winning 23 of the last 30 games, including 18 in a row at one point, to win the pennant by 3½ games. Runner-up Chicago was so distraught it filed a protest alleging that the eastern teams had conspired to help Boston win. Not until November 11 was the protest denied and the pennant officially awarded to the Beaneaters.

As good as the division race was between Atlanta and San Francisco in 1993, the 1897 pennant race between the Beaneaters and Baltimore was just as electrifying. Boston played franchise-record .705 ball (93–39) yet won by only two games.

Tragedy has been an all-too-frequent part of Braves history. Within a decade, two of the team's best players—Red Schoendienst in 1959 and Rico Carty in 1968—missed full seasons due to tuberculosis.

In 1894, popular catcher Charlie Bennett lost both legs when they slipped under the wheels of a moving train he was trying to board. In 1900, catcher Marty Bergen used an ax and a razor to kill his wife, two young children, and himself. Tony Boeckel, the third baseman who drove in the Braves' only run in the 26-inning game, lost his life in an auto mishap in 1924. And Bill Lucas, who became the game's highest-ranking black in 1976 when he was named director of player personnel, died just over two years later of a massive brain hemorrhage at 43 years of age.

Such misfortune makes the Braves' many on-field disasters seem almost comedic, which many of them are in retrospect.

For instance, only two teams in the 20th century have had four 20-game losers—the Beaneaters of 1905 *and* 1906. The 1962 Braves may have hit the all-time high in embarrassment when they lost a May doubleheader to the original New York Mets, the worst team in history.

In 1910, right-hander Cliff Curtis lost his last 18 decisions of the year, still a National League single-season record.

The Braves have had their share of streaks. The most stirring came at the start of the 1982 season when manager Joe Torre's team won its first 13 games to set a major league record. That team also lost 19 of 21 yet still managed to win the division title.

The 1992 Braves won 13 in a row, too, thanks to a game-saving play known simply as "The Catch" by center fielder Otis Nixon.

On the other end of streaking was a 19-game losing skid in 1906 and the 17-game dive of 1977, the latter punctuated by Turner's one-game managerial career.

Braves' pitchers have spun 14 no-hitters. Among them was the 1914 effort of George "Iron" Davis, who was enrolled in Harvard Law School at the time and won only seven games in his big league career. Kent Mercker, Mark Wohlers, and Alejandro Pena pitched the only combined no-hitter in National League history in 1991.

In 1937, Boston rookies Jim "Milkman" Turner and Lou Fette both won 20 games, the only time in history two rookies on the same team have each won 20.

Among the finest pitching efforts in franchise history is "Fidgety" Lou Burdette's three victories against the Yankees in the 1957 World Series, the last Series won by the Braves. Within 72 hours, Burdette shut out the powerful Yankees in Games 5 and 7.

The 1914 World Series hero was catcher Hank Gowdy, who hit .545 in the four-game sweep of Philadelphia compared to .243 in the regular season.

The Braves have spent many years in financial trouble, as evidenced by the fact that in 1935 the National League basically took over the team. The other club owners loaned the franchise $7,500 for spring-training expenses, then took out a lease on Braves Field and sublet it to the team at a greatly reduced price.

Braves Field is one of only four stadiums the franchise has used as a permanent residence, and it's certainly the most unique. It was the largest ballpark in the nation when it opened in 1915, and that distinction didn't just apply to the 43,500 seating capacity. It wasn't until 1925—nearly 10 full years after the park's opening—when a home run was finally hit over the left-field fence, which was 402 feet down the line and opened quickly to 550 in center.

In 1946, many of the opening day customers at Braves Field went home with green paint all over their clothes because fresh paint on the seats had yet to dry.

Milwaukee County Stadium was the first ballpark built entirely with public funds and also the first to be constructed with lights. And Atlanta Stadium was finished in record time for a facility of its size—51 weeks.

Braves history is the defensive excellence of the "Heavenly Twins," the nickname given to 19th-century outfielders Hugh Duffy and Tommy McCarthy. It's also "Spahn and Sain and pray for rain," as the 1948 team did en route to a pennant. It's Rabbit Maranville's mischief and "vest-pocket" catches.

It's Mathewson, one of the greatest pitchers of all time, and Percy Haughton, the greatest football coach in Harvard history, serving as team presidents. It's Olympic hero Jim Thorpe, the "world's greatest athlete," playing for Boston in 1919.

Braves history also is president Bob Quinn trying to change the team's luck by holding a contest to rename it in 1936. "Bees" won but lasted only five seasons, during which the team's play remained frightful. It's another president, James Gaffney, originally naming the team Braves in 1912, not in recognition of the spirit of the Indian race but rather to honor a group of politicians, of all things.

It's shortstop-manager Dave "Beauty" Bancroft being leveled by a punch from Pittsburgh catcher Earl Smith as he was crossing the plate in 1927. It's Johnny Bates in 1906 becoming the first rookie in modern history to hit a home run in his first at bat. And it's rookie shortstop Ernie Padgett making the first unassisted triple play in modern National League history in only his second game in 1923.

Braves history is Ernie Lombardi, Rogers Hornsby, Buzz Capra, Felix Mantilla, and Felix Millan. It's Bob "Mr. Team" Elliott, Ralph "Roadrunner" Garr, and Al "The Mad Hungarian" Hrabosky. And it's Sam Jethroe, Carl Willey, Lonnie Smith, Max Surkont, Bob Didier, Billy Bruton, Sibby Sisti, and Wes Covington.

In 1990, the Braves were the laughingstock of baseball. The team finished last for the third straight season and the fourth time in five years. Commissioner Fay Vincent said he feared Braves baseball was on the verge of becoming a "studio sport."

"The issue in Atlanta is the Superstation and the very poor attendance," Vincent said.

Los Angeles Times columnist Mike Downey called the Braves "the team that is to major league baseball what Gomer Pyle was to the U.S. Marines."

Even the team's announcers were making cracks. When Skip Caray left the booth one evening, partner Don Sutton asked, "Did Skip just refuse to watch or what?"

But look at the Braves now. The team's astounding success on the field has quieted the "studio sport" talk and the wisecracks. Attendance in 1993 approached 3.9 million. It took the players' strike of 1994 to interrupt the momentum that had been building since 1991.

Only time will tell where the franchise will go from here. A new stadium, already under construction, will await the team in 1997. There's plenty of promising young talent at both the major league and minor league levels, giving reason for optimism. But baseball can be painfully, as well as joyfully, surprising. No team knows that better than the Braves, the oldest continuously operating professional sports franchise in America.

Down Through the Seasons

The beginning of Braves baseball is directly and indisputably linked to the 1869 Cincinnati Red Stockings, universally accepted as baseball's first team composed entirely of openly professional players.

Harry Wright, the "Father of Professional Baseball," founded and managed those Red Stockings. The club traveled extensively and dominated its competition, winning all 89 games it played until mid-June of 1870 when the Red Stockings were beaten in Brooklyn by the Atlantics, 8–7, in 11 innings.

At the same time, the popularity of baseball was growing in Boston, where various forms of the game had been played for years. When the Red Stockings visited the city in 1870 and beat local teams by lopsided scores, a businessman named Ivers Whitney Adams was so impressed that he became interested in building a Boston team of the same caliber as Wright's famed nine.

The problem was that Wright had cornered the market on the most-talented players. It would be difficult for Adams to assemble a Boston team capable of competing with the Cincinnati pros. Or so everyone thought.

But just as in modern times when a team can go from last place to first in a single season—witness the 1991 Atlanta Braves—it also was possible in the early days of baseball for history to be altered almost overnight.

Two important events were on baseball's horizon. Together they brought about the birth of what today is the Atlanta Braves franchise and the creation of the game's first dynasty.

The first circumstance was the temporary disappearance of the Cincinnati Red Stockings from the professional baseball scene. Even as that team was losing for the first time in 90 games, the end of their historic contribution was at hand. The second situation was the impending formation of the first professional league.

The Red Stockings, beset with financial difficulties and dissension, reverted to amateur status following the 1870 campaign. Suddenly, Adams knew where he could find the players it would take to build the strong Boston club he envisioned.

Professional baseball had arrived, and Wright wasn't about to sit back and watch his innovation take shape without participating. He was the obvious solution to Adams' needs, and both men realized it.

The first meeting of the Boston Red Stockings Club was held January 20, 1871, at Boston's Parker House. The club was incorporated with $15,000 and Adams as president. Both Harry Wright and his younger brother George attended. Harry's charge was to sign players for Boston's first pro team. He and George, crucial members of the Cincinnati team, would both play for Boston, and they brought along two of their teammates, Charlie Gould and Cal McVey, as well as the Red Stockings nickname.

Though Cincinnati was stepping out of the picture, professional baseball was bursting onto the sports scene in several cities, thanks in large part to the interest the touring Red Stocking created in 1869 and '70. Amateur and professional factions were bickering over control of the sport, prompting the formation on March 17, 1871, of the National Association of Professional Base Ball Players.

The Boston Red Stockings were one of 10 charter members of the National Association. The others were the Philadelphia Athletics, Forest Cities of Rockford, Chicago White Stockings, Forest Cities of Cleveland, Troy Unions, New York Mutuals, Washington Olympics, Washington Nationals, and Fort Wayne Kekiongas. The membership fee was $10 per team.

The only club of the 10 to play continuously through the five-year history of the National Association, then join its successor, the National League, in its inaugural season of 1876 and field a team every season since was the Boston entry. Today, that very same organization lives on as the Atlanta Braves.

Harry Wright managed the first openly professional team, the 1869 Cincinnati Red Stockings, prior to moving to Boston two years later.

No other man has had as much impact on Braves history as has the all-time home run king, Henry Louis Aaron.

The Braves were born in 1871 when Harry Wright assembled these Boston Red Stockings to play in the first professional league—the National Association.

The Braves, then, are the only franchise in modern Major League Baseball to have fielded a team every season of professional league play. Not only are they the oldest continuously operating club, but they also have one of the richest traditions.

Adams leased the Union Base Ball Ground at Boston's South End for the Red Stockings to play their home games. New seats were built, and there even was a roof over the best ones. Harry Wright designed the uniform, which wasn't much different from what teams wear today other than the material. It consisted of a white flannel suit—shirt and knee breeches—worn with a cap, a red belt, and, of course, red stockings to the knees. "Boston" appeared in red across the chest. There were no numbers on the shirts and certainly no individual names.

The Red Stockings had a successful first season, winning 20 of 30 games but finishing in second place, two games behind Philadelphia. That was the only National Association pennant Wright's team didn't win.

Boston finished first each of the next four seasons. From 1872 to 1875, they were a combined 205–50 (.804). Pitcher Al Spalding, who later would make a fortune in the sporting goods business, won 186 of those 205 games.

The Red Stockings capped that four-year run in 1875, the year the catcher's mask was introduced, by winning 71 of 79 games (.899) and finishing 15 games ahead of Philadelphia. They compiled a 26-game winning streak and won all 38 home games. Boston had four of the league's top five hitters, not to mention Spalding, who was 55–5 including a 24-game winning streak.

The competition, completely demoralized, had seen enough. Of the 13 teams that started the season, just six finished. The National Association was about to fold . . . and the National League was being conceived.

Not only did the National Association suffer from competitive imbalance, but financial woes were mounting and players were constantly jumping teams for better deals. The league had no stability.

After the 1875 season, four members of the Red Stockings, including Spalding, announced they would play for Chicago in 1876. Spalding complained that winning pennants in Boston had become monotonous. This created such a disturbance in Boston that the defectors, also including second baseman Ross Barnes, catcher Cal McVey, and outfielder/catcher Jim White, became known as the "Four Seceders." That label was serious scorn in the post–Civil War era.

At the same time, Chicago White Stockings president William A. Hulbert was leading a reform movement to establish a league better designed for club owner success than was the National Association. On February 2, 1876, Hulbert persuaded seven team presidents, including Boston's Nathaniel T. Apollonio, to join him in forming the National League of Professional Base Ball Clubs.

The annual membership fee was $100, and among other things, teams were urged to draw up strict player contracts to discourage jumping clubs. The initial cities represented were Philadelphia, Boston, Chicago, Cincinnati, Hartford, Louisville, New York, and St. Louis.

Following is a year-by-year summary of the first 119 National League seasons of the franchise which has called Boston, Milwaukee, and Atlanta home and answered to numerous nicknames, including Red Stockings, Beaneaters, Doves, Rustlers, Bees, and, of course, Braves.

Note: An asterisk next to an item in the statistical tables indicates the player led the league in that category for the year.

Al Spalding pitched the Red Stockings to four straight National Association pennants and later founded a sporting goods empire which still bears his name.

1876

Record: 39–31
Finish: Fourth
Games Behind: 15
Manager: Harry Wright

The first game in National League history was played April 22, 1876, at Philadelphia. The Boston Red Stockings picked up where they left off in the National Association by scoring twice in the ninth to beat the Athletics, 6–5.

Philadelphia made 13 errors to "only" seven for Boston. Red Stockings centerfielder Jim O'Rourke was credited with the first hit in NL history, a single to left. Boston catcher Tim McGinley scored the first run, which was driven in by right-fielder Jack Manning with a sacrifice fly to left.

A crowd of about 3,000 paid 50 cents apiece to watch the proceedings on the grounds at 25th and Jefferson streets. Harry Wright captained the Red Stockings, who included Wright's brother George at shortstop.

Despite the opening day victory, the Red Stockings just weren't the same without the "Four Seceders" who'd jumped to Chicago. Particularly missed was pitcher Al Spalding.

To replace Spalding, Wright signed Philadelphia's Joseph Borden to a three-year contract for $2,000 per season. Though he pitched a no-hitter against Chicago in the National Association, Borden was considered a flop. Sportswriters christened him "Josephus the Phenomenal."

Borden was 11–12, and on May 23, he shut out Cincinnati, 8–0. Lee Allen, the late historian for the Hall of Fame, believed Borden should have been credited with the National League's first no-hitter in that game. His research showed that two walks issued by Borden were scored as the game's only two hits. However, the game has never been officially recognized as a no-hitter.

Nevertheless, Borden's work couldn't compare to the standard Spalding had established in Boston. The frustrated Red Stockings demoted him to groundskeeper so he'd do something for his salary. Eventually, they paid him off in a lump sum.

The greatest excitement of the season came May 30 when the White Stockings and the "Four Seceders" made their first visit to Boston's South End Grounds. The crowd literally tore down the fences to see Spalding whip his former team, 5–1.

Chicago beat the Red Stockings nine times in 10 tries en

In 1876, the National League began play with these Boston Red Stockings, still managed by Harry Wright, as one of eight teams.

route to the first National League pennant, and Boston's run of four consecutive championships was broken with a fourth-place finish.

	G	AB	R	H	2B	3B	HR	RBI	AVG
Lew Brown (C)	45	195	23	41	6	6	2	21	.210
Andy Leonard (OF)	64	303	53	85	10	2	0	27	.281
Jack Manning (OF)	70	288	52	76	13	0	2	25	.264
Tim McGinley	9	40	5	6	0	0	0	2	.150
John Morrill (2B)	66	278	38	73	5	2	0	26	.263
Tim Murnane (1B)	69	308	60	87	4	3	2	34	.282
Jim O'Rourke (OF)	70	312	61	102	17	3	2	43	.327
Bill Parks	1	4	0	0	0	0	0	0	.000
Harry Schafer (3B)	70	286	47	72	11	0	0	35	.252
Frank Whitney	34	139	27	33	7	1	0	15	.237
George Wright (SS)	70	335	72	100	18	6	1	34	.299
Harry Wright	1	3	0	0	0	0	0	0	.000
Sam Wright	2	8	0	1	0	0	0	0	.125
	70	2,722	471	723	96	24	9*		.266

	W	L	G	GS	CG	IP	H	BB	SO	ERA
Joe Borden	11	12	29	24	16	218½	257	51	34	2.89
Foghorn Bradley	9	10	22	21	16	173½	201	16	16	2.49
Jack Manning	18	5	34	20	13	197½	213	32	24	2.14
Dick McBride	0	4	4	4	3	33	53	5	2	2.73
Tricky Nichols	1	0	1	1	1	9	7	0	0	1.00
George Wright	0	0	1	0	0	1	1	0	1	0.00
	39	31		70	49	632	732	104	77	2.51

Shutouts—Borden (2), Bradley
Saves—Manning (5*), Borden, Bradley

1877

Record: 42–18
Finish: First
Games Ahead: 7
Manager: Harry Wright

Al Who?

There's no official record of that question circulating among Red Stockings fans in 1877, but someone surely must have uttered it. The mourning over the loss of pitcher Al Spalding to Chicago lasted but a year. The reason was the signing of 21-year-old Irishman Tommy Bond. The young right-hander had won 31 and lost 13 for Hartford in 1876, and he was just the pitcher Wright needed to help Boston return to its pennant-winning ways.

Bond led the National League in wins (40), percentage (.702), shutouts (6), strikeouts (170), and ERA (2.11) in his first season with the Red Stockings. Boston responded by winning its first National League pennant and its fifth flag in six years.

This proved one of the most significant seasons in franchise and league history because of the influential new owners who purchased the Red Stockings.

Arthur H. Soden headed a three-man group that took control of the club from Nathaniel T. Apollonio. Soden would serve as president of the team for 30 years during which he and partners William Conant and James Billings became known as the Triumvirs, after the Triumvirs of ancient Rome—Caesar, Pompey, and Crassus. The team won eight pennants during Soden's reign, and he became a powerful figure in the National League.

Among other contributions, Soden is the man who wrote the "reserve clause" into the league's bylaws. For nearly a century, it bound players to their club, preventing them from jumping teams for a better salary as was common in the early years of the pro game and as is the case today under free agency.

But Soden had not yet come up with the reserve clause when Wright decided Bond was the man to do what pitcher-turned-groundskeeper Joseph Borden could not do.

"Deacon" Jim White, one of the "Four Seceders," also returned to Boston and nearly won the Triple Crown. The first baseman/outfielder led the league in batting average (.387) and RBIs (49), but his two home runs were two short of the league lead.

Another crucial acquisition was infielder Ezra Sutton, who was picked up from Philadelphia. Wright inserted him into the lineup at shortstop and moved his brother, George Wright, to second base for the only season in his career. Sutton, who had a long career with the team, proved to be one of the Red Stockings' best clutch hitters, driving in 39 runs, third in the league.

It was not a particularly good season for the young National League. Only Boston and Chicago showed a profit. Philadelphia was expelled for its failure to make a road trip, and Cincinnati was dismissed for not paying its dues.

	G	AB	R	H	2B	3B	HR	RBI	AVG
Lew Brown (C)	58	221	27	56	12	8	1	31	.253
Andy Leonard (OF)	58	272	46	78	5	0	0	27	.287
John Morrill (3B)	61	242	47	73	5	1	0	28	.302
Tim Murnane (OF)	35	140	23	39	7	1	1	15	.279
Jim O'Rourke (OF)	61	265	68*	96	14	4	0	23	.362
Harry Schafer	33	141	20	39	5	2	0	13	.277
Ezra Sutton (SS)	58	253	43	74	10	6	0	39	.292
Deacon White (1B)	59	266	51	103*	14	11*	2	49*	.387*
George Wright (2B)	61	290	58	80	15	1	0	35	.276
Harry Wright	1	4	0	0	0	0	0	0	.000
	61	2,368	419*	700*	91*	37*	4		.296*

	W	L	G	GS	CG	IP	H	BB	SO	ERA
Tommy Bond	40*	17	58	58	58	521	530	36	170*	2.11*
Will White	2	1	3	3	3	27	27	2	7	3.00
	42*	18		61	61	548	557	38	177*	2.15*

Shutouts—Bond (6*), White
Saves—None

1878

Record: 41–19
Finish: First
Games Ahead: 4
Manager: Harry Wright

The 1878 Red Stockings may have been the original hitless wonders. They won their second straight National League pennant despite finishing next to last in team batting average (.241) and slugging percentage (.300) and dead last in on-base percentage (.253).

Boston also was last in hits and walks. Of course, no one was generating a lot of offense in this era—only 23 home runs were hit the entire season. But the Red Stockings were near the bottom of the barrel in all offensive categories.

Their leading hitter was "Orator" Jim O'Rourke, who batted just .278. The big difference in the offense between 1877 and '78 was the defection of Jim White to Cincinnati. Harry Wright's club finished just four games ahead of White and his new team.

How does a team win a pennant despite having such an anemic offense? It has to have strong pitching and defense, of course, and the 1878 Red Stockings had both.

Tommy Bond posted his second consecutive 40-win season, leading the league in victories and several other departments, including innings, strikeouts, shutouts, and an incredible 57 complete games. He started 59 of the team's 60 games in an era when pitchers weren't allowed to raise their arms above waist level, thus making the strain much less than when overhand pitching was approved in 1884.

Wright decided to move brother George back to shortstop from second base and Ezra Sutton from short to third base. The move paid off with George leading the league's shortstops in defense (.947) for the only time in his Hall of Fame career.

The Red Stockings led the league in team fielding (.914) and double plays (48). They also placed second in ERA (2.32) to Cincinnati.

The Red Stockings were winning, and there was a new rival in the league that captured the fans' imagination. Providence not only joined the National League but also made a strong showing, finishing third. The geographical proximity of Boston and Providence (50 miles) made it possible for special trains to transport fans between the two cities when the clubs played.

	G	AB	R	H	2B	3B	HR	RBI	AVG
Jack Burdock (2B)	60	246	37	64	12	6	0	25	.260
Andy Leonard (OF)	60	262	41	68	8	5	0	16	.260
Jack Manning (OF)	60	248	41	63	10	1	0	23	.254
John Morrill (1B)	60	233	26	56	5	1	0	23	.240
Jim O'Rourke (OF)	60	255	44	71	17	7	1	29	.278
Harry Schafer	2	8	0	1	0	0	0	0	.125
Pop Snyder (C)	60	226	21	48	5	0	0	14	.212
Ezra Sutton (3B)	60	239	31	54	9	3	1	29	.226
George Wright (SS)	59	267	35	60	5	1	0	12	.225
	60	2,220	298	535	75	25	2		.241

	W	L	G	GS	CG	IP	H	BB	SO	ERA
Tommy Bond	40*	19	59*	59	57*	532⅔	571	33	182*	2.06
Jack Manning	1	0	3	1	1	11⅓	24	5	2	14.29
	41*	19		60	58	544	595	38	184	2.32

Shutouts—Bond (9*)
Saves—None

1879

Record: 54–30
Finish: Second
Games Behind: 5
Manager: Harry Wright

The Red Stockings had enjoyed quite a run under Harry Wright, winning two of the first three National League championships and six pennants in seven years, including the four straight National Association flags in 1872–75.

But this dynasty began to crumble in 1879, and in the process the fate of major league ballplayers for the next century was determined to a great extent.

It's quite common for a younger brother to want to escape from the shadow cast by a successful older brother. Such was the case with George Wright, one of the most accomplished players of baseball's early years who nevertheless had to play second fiddle to Harry Wright, 12 years his senior and the "Father of Professional Baseball."

Harry and George worked side by side for a decade shaping the fabric of the game, which was quickly capturing the imagination of a nation and would grow to proportions they never could have envisioned. But in 1879, the two temporarily parted ways with some unexpected and far-reaching results.

Providence, eager to dethrone its Boston rival from atop the National League, decided to raid the neighbor's kitchen. And they hit the Red Stockings where it hurt most, splitting the Wright brothers.

The younger Wright was so popular in Boston that he was referred to as "Our George" by fans and writers. But George, like all working men, had a price as well as an ego. When Providence approached him about captaining their pennant quest in 1879, he was forced to listen. When he liked what he heard, he bolted for Rhode Island and took the versatile Jim O'Rourke, Boston's best hitter, and catcher/outfielder Lew Brown with him.

O'Rourke's decision to jump ship was influenced by a feud with management. He refused to sign a contract, becoming one of the game's first holdouts, because the club was charging players $20 a season for uniforms and 50 cents a day for travel expenses. Neither side would budge, so fans took up a collection to pay the fees. O'Rourke, however, still departed.

If the fans were provoked when the "Four Seceders" jumped ship to Chicago in 1876, they were positively outraged at losing three players, two of them stars, to upstart Providence. Then Providence proceeded to rub it in by winning the pennant.

The two teams entered a season-ending six-game series against each other with Providence holding a four-game edge. The Red Stockings needed to win five of the six in order to tie, but Providence left no such opening, winning four of the games. George's team beat his older brother's club eight times in 12 meetings during the season en route to keeping Boston from its accustomed pennant for only the second time in eight years.

Even without O'Rourke, Boston's offense showed considerable improvement over the previous season. John O'Rourke, a one-year wonder and no relation to "Orator" Jim, led the team in hitting (.341) and the league in slugging percentage (.521). Outfielder Charley Jones led the league in home runs (9), and he and O'Rourke tied for the league lead in RBIs (62).

However, Providence easily had the best offense in the league, hitting 22 points higher than Boston.

The clubs had equally successful pitching, Boston's ERA being 2.19 and Providence's 2.18. Boston's Tommy Bond had another big season with 43 wins, 11 shutouts, and a league-best 1.96 ERA. However, the Red Stockings' stingy pitching wasn't enough to offset the offensive advantage owned by Providence.

Charley Jones led the league in home runs in 1879 and a year later became the first man to hit two homers in the same inning.

It was the last full season of George Wright's playing career. The advent of curveball pitching took a toll on his batting average. It also was the only season he managed. To this day, he owns the distinction of being the lone man in big league history to manage just one year and win a league championship. Additionally, this was the last time two brothers managed in the majors during the same season until 1994 when Rene Lachemann managed the Florida Marlins and brother Marcel Lachemann directed the California Angels.

Yet, it remained for Red Stockings president Arthur H. Soden to write the epilogue on the 1879 season.

Incensed over George Wright's decision to join Providence, Soden was able to get the "reserve clause" written into the National League bylaws. For most of the next century, it bound players to their teams from year to year, even when their contract had expired. The reserve clause played a major role in stabilizing the game in its early years.

	G	AB	R	H	2B	3B	HR	RBI	AVG
Jack Burdock (2B)	84	359	64	86	10	3	0	36	.240
Ed Cogswell (1B)	49	236	51	76	8	1	1	18	.322
Curry Foley	35	146	16	46	3	1	0	17	.315
Bill Hawes	38	155	19	31	3	3	0	9	.200
Sadie Houck (OF)	80	356	69	95	24	9	2	49	.267
Charley Jones (OF)	83	355	85*	112	22	10	9*	62*	.315
John Morrill (3B)	84	348	56	98	18	5	0	49	.282
John O'Rourke (OF)	72	317	69	108	17	11	6	62*	.341
Pop Snyder (C)	81	329	42	78	16	3	2	35	.237
Ezra Sutton (SS)	84	339	54	84	13	4	0	34	.248
	84	3,217	562	883	138	51	20*		.274

	W	L	G	GS	CG	IP	H	BB	SO	ERA
Tommy Bond	43	19	64	64	59	555⅓	543	24	155	1.96*
Curry Foley	9	9	21	16	16	161⅔	175	15	57	2.51
Lee Richmond	1	0	1	1	1	9	4	1	11	2.00
Jim Tyng	1	2	3	3	3	27	35	6	7	5.00
	54	30		84	79	753	757	46	230	2.19

Shutouts—Bond (11*), Foley
Saves—None

1880

Record: 40–44
Finish: Sixth
Games Behind: 27
Manager: Harry Wright

Harry Wright's glory years in Boston were over, but no one knew it. The Red Stockings would require new leadership to regain their lofty status in the National League. However, they had to suffer for a couple of seasons with the also-rans before returning to elite status.

Boston, finishing sixth among eight teams, endured three significant humiliations in 1880. The team failed to win at least half its games for the first time in its 10-year history and also finished in the second division for the first time. To make matters worse, the Red Stockings were subjected to the embarrassment of being no-hit for the first time. Chicago's Larry Corcoran held them hitless August 19 in a 6–0 decision. Boston had to wait another dozen years to be on the right side of a no-hitter.

Lack of pitching was the culprit in Boston's slide. The staff

ERA of 3.08 sounds pretty good today. But back then, it was horrendous. It barely beat Buffalo's 3.09, which was the worst in the league. More importantly, it was over a full run higher than the ERAs posted by the three top teams, who gave up less than two earned runs per game.

Bond was practically worn out, and no wonder. He appeared in 63 games (57 starts), giving him an average of 61 in four seasons with Boston. He still won 26 games in 1880, but that was 15 less than he'd averaged the previous three years. More significantly, he lost 29 times. Since he started two-thirds of the Red Stockings' games, his sub-.500 pitching meant the team was trying to climb uphill all season.

There were some interesting offensive bursts for Wright's team. "Orator" Jim O'Rourke found his way back to Boston—if only for a year—and hit four home runs in the space of two games. That's a pretty good feat today, but back then it was incredible. Consider that O'Rourke hit but six all season—and that figure led the league and was more than the total posted by three entire teams.

The rest of the league must have thought there was something in Boston's water. The Red Stockings pounded 20 home runs during the season, and no other club hit more than eight.

The other individual outburst of note came June 10. That's when outfielder Charley Jones, who led the league in home runs the previous year, hit two in the same inning—the first National Leaguer to do so.

	G	AB	R	H	2B	3B	HR	RBI	AVG
John Bergh	11	40	2	8	3	0	0	0	.200
Jack Burdock (2B)	86	356	58	90	17	4	2	35	.253
Steve Dignan	8	34	4	11	1	0	0	4	.324
Curry Foley (OF)	80	332	44	97	13	2	2	31	.292
Sadie Houck	12	47	2	7	0	0	0	2	.149
Charley Jones (OF)	66	280	44	84	15	3	5	37	.300
John Morrill (1B)	86	342	51	81	16	8	2	44	.237
Dan O'Leary	3	12	1	3	2	0	0	1	.250
Jim O'Rourke (3B)	86	363	71	100	20	11	6*	45	.275
John O'Rourke (OF)	81	313	30	86	22	8	3	36	.275
Phil Powers (C)	37	126	11	18	5	0	0	10	.143
John Richmond	32	129	12	32	3	1	0	9	.248
Denny Sullivan	1	4	1	1	0	0	0	1	.250
Ezra Sutton (SS)	76	288	41	72	9	2	0	25	.250
Sam Trott	39	125	14	26	4	1	0	9	.208
George Wright	1	4	2	1	0	0	0	0	.250
	86	3,080	416	779	134	41	20*		.253

	W	L	G	GS	CG	IP	H	BB	SO	ERA
Tommy Bond	26	29	63	57	49	493	559	45	118	2.67
Curry Foley	14	14	36	28	21	238	264	40	68	3.89
Jack Leary	0	1	1	1	0	3	8	0	1	15.00
John Morrill	0	0	3	0	0	10⅔	9	1	0	0.84
	40	44		86	70	744⅔	840	86	187	3.08

Shutouts—Bond (3), Foley
Saves—None

1881

Record: 38–45
Finish: Sixth
Games Behind: 17½
Manager: Harry Wright

Harry Wright managed for a long time in the National League, but this was his last season in Boston. The man

most responsible for the city's brilliant start in professional baseball was run out of town like so many other managers after a second consecutive sixth-place finish.

By winning six pennants in eight years, Wright established high standards that eventually came back to cost him his job. The 1881 Red Stockings were even worse than the 1880 team. They finished 9½ games closer to first than they had in 1880, but their winning percentage (.458) dropped to a franchise low for the second straight season.

The year marked the arrival of Tommy Bond's successor as the workhorse of the pitching staff. Bond made just three starts, all defeats, before yielding to 23-year-old right-hander "Grasshopper" Jim Whitney.

Wright knew a strong arm when he saw one, and he didn't hesitate to use it. Whitney earned his pay as a rookie, working a league-leading 552⅓ innings. He also led the league with 57 complete games and 31 victories. Unfortunately, he lost 33 times, too.

Boston's biggest problem, though, was an anemic offense. The Red Stockings scored 349 runs, last in the league. Jim O'Rourke and Charley Jones, the two big offensive forces from 1880, no longer were with the team. Soon, Wright wasn't either.

	G	AB	R	H	2B	3B	HR	RBI	AVG
Ross Barnes (SS)	69	295	42	80	14	1	0	17	.271
Jack Burdock (2B)	73	282	36	67	12	4	1	24	.238
Bill Crowley (OF)	72	279	33	71	12	0	0	31	.254
Pat Deasley	43	147	13	35	5	2	0	8	.238
Joe Hornung (OF)	83	324	40	78	12	8	2	25	.241
Fred Lewis (OF)	27	114	17	25	6	0	0	9	.219
Bobby Mathews	19	71	2	12	2	0	0	4	.169
John Morrill (1B)	81	311	47	90	19	3	1	39	.289
—— Quinn	1	4	0	0	0	0	0	0	.000
John Richmond	27	98	13	27	2	2	1	12	.276
Pop Snyder (C)	62	219	14	50	8	0	0	16	.228
Ezra Sutton (3B)	83	333	43	97	12	4	0	31	.291
Jim Whitney	75	282	37	72	17	3	0	32	.255
George Wright	7	25	4	5	0	0	0	0	.200
Sam Wright	1	4	0	1	0	0	0	0	.250
	83	2,916	349	733	121	27	5		.251

	W	L	G	GS	CG	IP	H	BB	SO	ERA
Tommy Bond	0	3	3	3	2	25⅓	40	2	2	4.26
John Fox	6	8	17	16	12	124⅓	144	39	30	3.33
Bobby Mathews	1	0	5	1	1	23	22	11	5	2.35
John Morrill	0	1	3	0	0	5⅔	9	1	0	6.35
Jim Whitney	31*	33	66*	63	57*	552⅓*	548	90	162	2.48
	38	45		83	72	730⅔	763	143	199	2.71

Shutouts—Whitney (6)
Saves—Mathews (2*), Morrill

1882

Record: 45–39
Finish: Tie–Third
Games Behind: 10
Manager: John Morrill

Honest John Morrill already had taken over for one of the Wright brothers, thus Red Stockings president Arthur Soden figured Morrill could replace the other one, too. The result was the first of many managerial changes in franchise history.

A Boston native and a member of the team since the formation of the National League in 1876, Morrill was quite popular with Red Stockings fans. He became team captain when George Wright left for Providence in 1879, so it was a logical step for him to succeed Harry Wright as manager in 1882.

A versatile performer, Morrill played all nine positions at some point during his 13 years with the team. He also was a good enough manager to win one pennant in seven seasons directing the Red Stockings.

Morrill didn't work any miracle in his first season, but he did get the club back over the .500 hump and into a tie for third place with Buffalo.

The star of the team was "Grasshopper" Jim Whitney. Not only was he the team's top pitcher and one of the better ones in the league, but he also played first base and outfield and was among the league leaders in numerous offensive categories.

Whitney pitched less frequently than he had the previous year as a rookie, but he still won 24 games. He also batted .323, fifth in the league, and ranked third in both on-base percentage (.382) and slugging average (.510).

Control artist Bobby Mathews was brought in as a number-two pitcher and won 19 games. Together, Whitney and Mathews gave the Red Stockings quite a one-two punch. However, their supporting cast was mediocre at best—the reason Boston still finished 10 games back of pennant-winning Chicago.

	G	AB	R	H	2B	3B	HR	RBI	AVG
Charlie Buffinton	15	50	5	13	1	0	0	4	.260
Jack Burdock (2B)	83	319	36	76	6	7	0	27	.238
Pat Deasley (C)	67	264	36	70	8	0	0	29	.265
Joe Hornung (OF)	85	388	67	117	14	11	1	50	.302
Pete Hotaling (OF)	84	378	64	98	16	5	0	28	.259
Bobby Mathews	45	169	17	38	6	0	0	13	.225
Hal McClure	2	6	1	2	0	0	0	0	.333
John Morrill (1B)	83	349	73	101	19	11	2	54	.289
Ed Rowen (OF)	83	327	36	81	7	4	1	43	.248
Ezra Sutton (3B)	81	319	44	80	8	1	2	38	.251
Jim Whitney	61	251	49	81	18	7	5	48	.323
Sam Wise (SS)	78	298	44	66	11	4	4	34	.221
	85	3,118	472	823	114	50	15		.264

	W	L	G	GS	CG	IP	H	BB	SO	ERA
Charlie Buffinton	2	3	5	5	4	42	53	14	17	4.07
Bobby Mathews	19	15	34	32	31	285	278	22	153	2.87
John Morrill	0	0	1	0	0	2	3	0	2	0.00
Jim Whitney	24	21	49	48	46	420	404	41	180	2.64
	45	39		85	81	749	738	77	352	2.80

Shutouts—Whitney (3), Buffinton
Saves—None

1883

Record: 63–35
Finish: First
Games Ahead: 4
Managers: Jack Burdock, John Morrill

Today's Braves fans will never forget the race for the 1993 division title in which Atlanta overcame a 10-game deficit on July 22, winning a franchise-record 104 games to nose out San Francisco by one game on the final day of the season.

It was indeed one of the most exciting and rewarding stretch drives in team history—but certainly not the only one that was accomplished against seemingly insurmountable odds.

The most famous example of a second-half rally in history

took place in 1914 when the "Miracle Braves" came from dead last on July 18 to win the National League pennant and the World Series.

But it was the 1883 Beaneaters (as the Red Stockings were now called to tie their identity to Boston and avoid confusion with the Cincinnati Reds of the American Association) who set the precedent for stirring, never-say-die forced marches to championships. In seventh place in June, the Beaneaters righted themselves to win their third National League pennant in the league's eight-year history.

It wasn't easy. "Honest" John Morrill turned over leadership of the team to Jack Burdock, and the team did not respond well to the change. The club started slowly, losing 11 of its first 15 games. No one could say Burdock wasn't trying his best, though. One day at Detroit, he grabbed the opponent's catcher to prevent him from catching the pop foul he'd hit. The umpire fined Burdock $20 on the spot.

Boston began to climb gradually, finally getting to 30–24 (.556) under Burdock. But on July 22, the Triumvirs put Morrill back in charge. Under "Honest John," the Beaneaters caught fire, winning 33 of their last 44 games (a .750 clip) and 14 of their final 15. They clinched the pennant September 27 with four days left in the season.

There were many memorable moments in the season. The club played the first game ever against the Giants in New York, losing 7–5 before a crowd that included General Ulysses S. Grant.

Boston may have gained the confidence and momentum it needed June 9 when it fell behind Detroit, 5–2, in the second inning, then rallied to win, 30–8. "Grasshopper" Jim Whitney got five hits and set what was then a record by scoring six times.

On June 20, Boston took advantage of 21 Philadelphia errors for a 29–4 victory. Shortstop Sam Wise had six hits, four for extra bases. The Beaneaters were on a roll.

Boston knocked Providence out of first place August 7 with a 6–4 decision. The Beaneaters finally moved into first place September 4 when Whitney beat the Giants, 8–2. Next came a temporary setback in the form of two defeats against Providence. That set up what was to prove to be the decisive series of the season against torrid Chicago.

The White Stockings came to Boston September 10 sporting an 11-game winning streak. However, the Beaneaters stunned Cap Anson's team by sweeping the four-game series. After a 4–2 victory in the first game, Boston rallied with two in the ninth of the second game for a 3–2 victory. That win allowed Morrill's team to regain a grip on first place it would not relinquish. The team received a huge ovation after the game, and fans showered the field with hats and cushions. Chicago was demoralized and would not recover.

When the pennant was finally won, the players received true hero treatment from an adoring city. They were presented rings, watches, and engraved mustache cups. President Arthur Soden gave each man a $100 bonus. The team set an attendance record, drawing 138,000, an average of 2,760 per game. The fans usually went home happy, too. The Beaneaters were 42–8 (.840) at the South End Grounds.

Burdock led Boston in hitting. His .330 average was fourth in the league. Morrill, who played six different positions, was second in the league in total bases and slugging percentage.

Whitney and Charlie Buffinton formed a neat tag team, alternating between pitching (a combined 62 wins) and playing center field (83 RBIs between them). Whitney, who batted cleanup even when pitching, ranked third in the league in wins and ERA.

	G	AB	R	H	2B	3B	HR	RBI	AVG
Lew Brown	14	54	5	13	4	1	0	9	.241
Charlie Buffinton	86	341	28	81	8	3	1	26	.238
Jack Burdock (2B)	96	400	80	132	27	8	5	88	.330
Mert Hackett	46	179	20	42	8	6	2	24	.235
Mike Hines (C)	63	231	38	52	13	1	0	16	.225
Joe Hornung (OF)	98	446	107*	124	25	13	8	66	.278
John Morrill (1B)	97	404	83	129	33	16	6	68	.319
Paul Radford (OF)	72	258	46	53	6	3	0	14	.205
Edgar Smith (OF)	30	115	10	25	5	3	0	16	.217
Ezra Sutton (3B)	94	414	101	134	28	15	3	73	.324
Jim Whitney	96	409	78	115	27	10	5	57	.281
Sam Wise (SS)	96	406	73	110	25	7	4	58	.271
	98	3,657	669	1,010	209	86*	34*		.276

	W	L	G	GS	CG	IP	H	BB	SO	ERA
Charlie Buffinton	25	14	43	41	34	333	346	51	188	3.03
John Morrill	1	0	2	1	1	13	15	4	5	2.77
Jim Whitney	37	21	62	56	54	514	492	35	345*	2.24
	63*	35		98	89	860	853	90	538*	2.55

Shutouts—Buffinton (4), Whitney
Saves—Whitney (2*), Buffinton

1884

Record: 73–38
Finish: Second
Games Behind: 10½
Manager: John Morrill

When the 1993 Braves won a franchise-record 104 games to capture the National League West by one game over San Francisco, they had a winning percentage of .642. In 1884, the Beaneaters played better than that (.658) but still finished second—by 10½ games!

Whether or not the best team won the National League pennant that year may have been a matter of debate, but there was no questioning the fact that the best man won it. You see, 1884 was the year of Charley "Old Hoss" Radbourn. When the season was over, all the Beaneaters could do was tip their caps to the great Providence right-hander.

As late as July 31, Boston was in first place and looking as if it might successfully defend its National League championship. Little did the Beaneaters know they were about to be sidetracked by an individual performance that still ranks as one of the most incredible feats in sports history.

Radbourn was the premier pitcher of the 19th century, but Boston had a couple of aces of its own in Charlie Buffinton and "Grasshopper" Jim Whitney. It made for an interesting rivalry—at least until Radbourn kicked into high gear.

On June 6, the Beaneaters held a one-game lead over Providence when Whitney and Radbourn hooked up in a classic duel that ended in a 1–1 tie after 16 innings.

The next day, Charlie Sweeney of Providence struck out 19 Beaneaters in a 2–1 victory that allowed the Grays to take first place by percentage points. Sweeney's 19 strikeouts stood as the major league record for a nine-inning game (though it was tied) until Roger Clemens struck out 20 in 1986.

On June 30, Boston moved back into first with an 11–2 victory over Detroit. The two clubs battled back and forth through much of July until the critical event of the season July 22. Sweeney, pitching for Providence against Philadelphia, refused to leave the mound for right field with a big lead in the ninth inning. He was suspended without pay and jumped to St. Louis of the Union Association, leaving the Grays with but one pitcher—Radbourn.

It could have been the break Boston needed to win the pennant, but it proved to be their undoing. The Beaneaters had a two-game lead entering August, only to see Radbourn embark on a two-month sprint.

"Old Hoss" agreed to pitch nearly every game for the rest of the season. In fact, he pitched the last 27 games—and won 26 of them. Boston, even with two good pitchers, was helpless in trying to keep up with that pace. Radbourn finished the season 59–12, working 678⅔ innings, completing all 73 of his starts, and finishing with a 1.38 ERA. All, of course, were league-leading totals.

Boston had better hitting and better defense than Providence, but the Grays had Radbourn.

On the bright side, Boston third baseman Ezra Sutton had a big year, leading the league in hits (162), finishing third in batting average (.346), and leading his position in fielding percentage (.908).

It was a great season, but not quite good enough. Only six teams in franchise history have had a better winning percentage than the 1884 Beaneaters, and all six won pennants.

	G	AB	R	H	2B	3B	HR	RBI	AVG
Bill Annis	27	96	17	17	2	0	0	3	.177
Marty Barrett	3	6	0	0	0	0	0	0	.000
Charlie Buffinton	87	352	48	94	18	3	1	39	.267
Jack Burdock (2B)	87	361	65	97	14	4	6	49	.269
Bill Crowley (OF)	108	407	50	110	14	6	6	61	.270
Tom Gunning	12	45	4	5	1	1	0	2	.111
Mert Hackett (C)	72	268	28	55	13	2	1	20	.205
Mike Hines	35	132	16	23	3	0	0	3	.174
Joe Hornung (OF)	115	518	119	139	27	10	7	51	.268
Jim Manning (OF)	89	345	52	83	8	6	2	35	.241
Gene Moriarity	4	16	1	1	0	0	0	0	.063
John Morrill (1B)	111	438	80	114	19	7	3	61	.260
Ezra Sutton (3B)	110	468	102	162*	28	7	3	61	.346
Jim Whitney	66	270	41	70	17	5	3	40	.259
Sam Wise (SS)	114	426	60	91	15	9	4	41	.214
	116	4,189	684	1,063	179*	60	36		.254

	W	L	G	GS	CG	IP	H	BB	SO	ERA
Charlie Buffinton	48	16	67	67	63	587	506	76	417	2.15
John Connor	1	4	7	7	7	60	70	18	29	3.15
Daisy Davis	1	3	4	4	3	31	50	8	13	7.84
John Morrill	0	1	7	1	1	23	34	6	13	7.43
Jim Whitney	23	14	38	37	35	336	272	27	270	2.09
	73	38		116	109	1,037	932	135	742*	2.47

Shutouts—Buffinton (8), Whitney (6)
Saves—Morrill (2*)

1885

Record: 46–66
Finish: Fifth
Games Behind: 41
Manager: John Morrill

Talk about a dropoff. The 1885 Beaneaters fell off a cliff. The team's .411 winning percentage was the worst in its history up to that point, and the difference in the club's record from the previous year represented a slide of 27½ games.

John Morrill's team didn't hit very well, didn't pitch particularly well, and didn't play very good defense. Boston finished just eight games ahead of last-place St. Louis.

The Beaneaters were next-to-last in the league in errors and tied for last in fielding percentage. They were fifth in team batting and sixth in team pitching.

Jim Whitney and Charlie Buffinton, the mainstays of the 1884 team, both lost more than they won and had higher ERAs than usual, but it was clear their main problem was lack of support.

Whitney's 32 losses were an indication that he was on the downside of his career, but he certainly deserved to win more than 18. Buffinton, who tied for fourth in the league with six shutouts, still had a lot of good innings left. Unfortunately, few of them would be worked in Boston.

The hitting was atrocious all season. Third baseman Ezra Sutton had another productive year, batting .313 and finishing fourth in the league with 143 hits.

Buffinton and Whitney continued to contribute offensively as much as just about anybody on the team. In late May, Buffinton pitched a six-hitter against Detroit and also collected five hits himself.

finished fifth for the second straight season. However, they did play better, winding up just five games under .500. That record didn't meet Boston standards, but at least there was some improvement.

With "Grasshopper" Jim Whitney released to Kansas City and Charlie Buffinton suffering from a sore arm, Boston was in dire need of pitching. They knew just where to turn, remembering what Charley "Old Hoss" Radbourn had done to them two years earlier.

Showing signs of deterioration at age 32—and no wonder— Radbourn was released by Providence to Boston. The Beaneaters agreed to pay the great righthander $4,500, and he responded reasonably well considering how his arm had been abused in the previous five years.

Though he finished four games under .500, quite in line with the team's performance, "Old Hoss" was as tenacious as ever. He was among the league leaders in several categories, including second in complete games and innings.

Radbourn's pitching mate was "Cannon Ball" Bill Stemmeyer, a hard-throwing young right-hander who would burn out as quickly as he arrived on the scene. Just 21 years old, Stemmeyer was 22–18. He was one of the toughest pitchers in the league to hit and also one of the most erratic.

Stemmeyer was fifth in the league in strikeouts. However, he set a major league record with 64 wild pitches in just 41 games.

On May 3, Boston catcher Patrick Dealy was charged with a National League record 10 passed balls in a 12–11 loss to Washington. It was no coincidence that Stemmeyer happened to be pitching that day and contributed five wild pitches.

	G	AB	R	H	2B	3B	HR	RBI	AVG
Charlie Buffinton	82	338	26	81	12	3	1	33	.240
Jack Burdock (2B)	45	169	18	24	5	0	0	7	.142
Bill Coliver	1	4	0	0	0	0	0	0	.000
Pat Dealy	35	130	18	29	4	1	1	9	.223
Tom Gunning (C)	48	174	17	32	3	0	0	15	.184
Mert Hackett	34	115	9	21	7	1	0	4	.183
Walter Hackett	35	125	8	23	3	0	0	9	.184
Mike Hines	14	56	11	13	4	0	0	4	.232
Joe Hornung	25	109	14	22	4	1	1	7	.202
Dick Johnston	26	111	17	26	6	3	1	23	.234
Jim Manning (OF)	84	306	34	63	8	9	2	27	.206
Tommy McCarthy (OF)	40	148	16	27	2	0	0	11	.182
John Morrill (1B)	111	394	74	89	20	7	4	44	.226
Billy Nash	26	94	9	24	4	0	0	11	.255
Tom Poorman (OF)	56	227	44	54	5	3	3	25	.238
Blondie Purcell	21	87	9	19	1	1	0	3	.218
Ezra Sutton (3B)	110	457	78	143	23	8	4	47	.313
Pop Tate	4	13	1	2	0	0	0	2	.154
Gurdon Whiteley	33	135	14	25	2	2	1	7	.185
Jim Whitney	72	290	35	68	8	4	0	36	.234
Sam Wise (SS)	107	424	71	120	20	10	4	46	.283
	113	3,950	528	915	144	53	22		.232

	W	L	G	GS	CG	IP	H	BB	SO	ERA
Charlie Buffinton	22	27	51	50	49	434⅓	425	112	242	2.88
Daisy Davis	5	6	11	11	10	94⅓	110	28	30	4.29
Bill Stemmeyer	1	1	2	2	2	11	7	11	8	0.00
Jim Whitney	18	32	51	50	50	441⅓	503	37	200	2.98
	46	66		113	111*	981	1,045	188	480	3.03

Shutouts—Buffinton (6), Whitney (2), Davis, Stemmeyer
Saves—None

	G	AB	R	H	2B	3B	HR	RBI	SB	AVG
Myron Allen	1	3	0	0	0	0	0	0	0	.000
Charlie Buffinton	44	176	27	51	4	1	1	30	3	.290
Jack Burdock (2B)	59	221	26	48	6	1	0	25	3	.217
Con Daily (C)	50	180	25	43	4	2	0	21	2	.239
Pat Dealy	15	46	9	15	1	1	0	3	5	.326
Tom Gunning	27	98	15	22	2	1	0	7	3	.224
Joe Hornung (OF)	94	424	67	109	12	2	2	40	16	.257
Dick Johnston (OF)	109	413	48	99	18	9	1	57	11	.240
John Morrill (SS)	117	430	86	106	25	6	7	69	9	.247
Billy Nash (3B)	109	417	61	117	11	8	1	45	16	.281
Tom Poorman (OF)	88	371	72	97	16	6	3	41	31	.261
Charley Radbourn	66	253	30	60	5	1	2	22	5	.237
Ezra Sutton	116	499	83	138	21	6	3	48	18	.277
Pop Tate	31	106	13	24	3	1	0	3	0	.226
Sam Wise (1B)	96	387	71	112	19	12	4	72	31	.289
	118	4,180	657	1,085	151	59	24		156	.260

	W	L	G	GS	CG	IP	H	BB	SO	ERA
Charlie Buffinton	7	10	18	17	16	151	203	39	47	4.59
John Morrill	0	0	1	0	0	4	5	0	2	0.00
Charlie Parsons	0	2	2	2	2	16	20	4	5	3.94
Charley Radbourn	27	31	58	58	57	509⅓	521	111	218	3.00
Bill Stemmeyer	22	18	41	41	41	348⅔	300	144	239	3.02
	56	61		118	116	1,029	1,049	298	511	3.24

Shutouts—Radbourn (3)
Saves—None

1886

Record: 56–61
Finish: Fifth
Games Behind: 30½
Manager: John Morrill

The 1886 Beaneaters went through a changing of the guard. It did them no good in the standings, where they

1887

Record: 61–60
Finish: Fifth
Games Behind: 16½
Managers: King Kelly, John Morrill

This was a landmark season in franchise history, certainly not for a third consecutive fifth-place finish, but rather for the acquisition of one of the most celebrated players of all time.

Mike "King" Kelly was the Babe Ruth of the 19th century. He was a great showman as well as an excellent player, and he unquestionably was the most popular player of this period. Primarily an outfielder and catcher, Kelly was talented enough that he could—and did—play all positions. He was a good enough hitter to have won two National League batting titles by the time he joined the Beaneaters, but he probably was best known for his daring and inventive baserunning, not to mention his carousing.

Distraught over finishing under .500 for two straight years, team president Arthur Soden was desperate to turn around the club's fortunes. One of Soden's partners, James Billings, proposed that they approach Chicago White Stockings president Al Spalding about buying Kelly.

Such a player purchase had never taken place, but Billings proceeded to contact Spalding by telegram to see if Chicago was interested in such a deal. The Beaneaters proposed a price of $5,000. Spalding said he'd think about it—for twice as much. The Chicago president also asked Kelly how he would receive such a deal. True to his modern-day legacies, Kelly, who made $3,000 in 1886, said he'd go anywhere for the right price.

So, Billings met Kelly to discuss salary. The maximum allowed at the time by league rules was $2,000, but there were ways to get around that. Kelly said he wanted $5,000, and Billings eventually conceded. They drew up a contract for $2,000 plus an additional $3,000 Kelly would receive for "posing for a picture."

The sports world was stunned, and Boston fans were ecstatic. The Beaneaters met Spalding's asking price; thus Kelly was called the "$10,000 Beauty." By making this move, the Boston owners greatly escalated the commercial implications of the game and initiated the practice of buying and selling players.

Kelly, 29, didn't play his best in his first year with the Beaneaters, but he was quite productive. His .322 average was 66 points less than his league-leading .388 of the previous year.

Of more significance, however, was the dissension Kelly's presence created. Though John Morrill retained the title of manager, Kelly was given the more prestigious title of captain and actually ran the club. The players were confused about who really was in charge. Late in the season, the Triumvirs recognized the error of their ways and gave the title of captain back to Morrill, but the damage had been done.

Still, the team climbed over .500, if only by a game. It was a lack of pitching which kept the Beaneaters in fifth place. Radbourn struggled to a 24–23 finish and his 4.55 ERA was the highest of his stellar 11-year career. "Cannon Ball" Stemmeyer was a bust. Only the surprising contribution (21–14)

of 20-year-old rookie left-hander Kid Madden kept Boston from diving in the standings.

The offense was respectable. One of the highlights of the season came on June 17 when the Beaneaters exploded for 10 in the 10th inning to beat New York, 19–9.

The most publicized event, however, was Kelly's first visit to Chicago, which received tremendous coverage in newspapers. "King" bet a silver service on the outcome of the first game with White Stockings great Cap Anson and lost.

	G	AB	R	H	2B	3B	HR	RBI	SB	AVG
Jack Burdock (2B)	65	237	36	61	6	0	0	29	19	.257
Con Daily	36	120	12	19	5	0	0	13	7	.158
Joe Hornung (OF)	98	437	85	118	10	6	5	49	41	.270
Dick Johnston (OF)	127	507	87	131	13	20	5	77	52	.258
King Kelly (OF)	116	484	120	156	34	11	8	63	84	.322
John Morrill (1B)	127	504	79	141	32	6	12	81	19	.280
Billy Nash (3B)	121	475	100	140	24	12	6	94	43	.295
Tom O'Rourke	22	78	12	12	3	0	0	10	4	.154
Charley Radbourn	51	175	25	40	2	2	1	24	6	.229
Ezra Sutton	77	326	58	99	14	9	3	46	17	.304
Pop Tate (C)	60	231	34	60	5	3	0	27	7	.260
Bobby Wheelock	48	166	32	42	4	2	2	15	20	.253
Sam Wise (SS)	113	467	103	156	27	17	9	92	43	.334
	127	4,531	831	1,255	185	94	53		373	.277

	W	L	G	GS	CG	IP	H	BB	SO	ERA
Dick Conway	9	15	26	26	25	222⅓	249	86	45	4.66
King Kelly	1	0	3	0	0	13	17	14	0	3.46
Kid Madden	21	14	37	37	36	321	317	122	81	3.79
Charley Radbourn	24	23	50	50	48	425	505	133	87	4.55
Bill Stemmeyer	6	8	15	14	14	119⅓	138	41	41	5.20
	61	60		127	123	1,100⅔	1,226	396	254	4.41

Shutouts—Madden (3), Radbourn
Saves—Stemmeyer (1*)

1888

Record: 70–64
Finish: Fourth
Games Behind: 15½
Manager: John Morrill

Ted Turner has shown many times that he's willing to pay virtually whatever it takes to bring top-name ballplayers to Atlanta. Sometimes, his purchases have worked, and sometimes they haven't. Either way, he's following a pattern set by the partners known as the Triumvirs who owned the franchise for three decades in its early history.

In 1887, the Triumvirs brought "King" Kelly to Boston, purchasing him from Chicago for the sum that earned him recognition as the "$10,000 Beauty." The Beaneaters still didn't win the pennant with Kelly in the lineup, though, so the Triumvirs got out the checkbook again. This time, they forked out another $10,000 to the White Stockings to purchase pitching great John Clarkson.

Together, Kelly and Clarkson formed Boston's "$20,000 Battery." Beaneaters fans were elated. Not only did their team now have two of the game's biggest stars, but as a bonus, Clarkson was a local product, hailing from across the Charles River in Cambridge. In 1887, he'd led National League pitchers in numerous departments, including wins with 38.

To help accommodate Boston fans wanting to see Clarkson and Kelly, the Triumvirs added a double-decked pavilion

The purchase of John Clarkson from the White Stockings in 1888 gave Boston the highly celebrated "$20,000 Battery" of Clarkson and King Kelly.

	G	AB	R	H	2B	3B	HR	RBI	SB	AVG
Tom Brown (OF)	107	420	62	104	10	7	9	49	46	.248
Jack Burdock	22	79	5	16	0	0	0	4	1	.203
Ed Glenn	20	65	8	10	0	2	0	3	0	.154
Bill Higgins	14	54	5	10	1	0	0	4	1	.185
Mike Hines	4	16	3	2	0	1	0	2	0	.125
Joe Hornung (OF)	107	431	61	103	11	7	3	53	29	.239
Dick Johnston (OF)	135	585	102	173	31	18*	12	68	35	.296
King Kelly (C)	107	440	85	140	22	11	9	71	56	.318
Billy Klusman	28	107	9	18	4	0	2	11	3	.168
John Morrill (1B)	135	486	60	96	18	7	4	39	21	.198
Billy Nash (3B)	135	526	71	149	18	15	4	75	20	.283
Tom O'Rourke	20	74	3	13	0	0	0	4	2	.176
Joe Quinn (2B)	38	156	19	47	8	3	4	29	12	.301
Irv Ray	50	206	26	51	2	3	2	26	7	.248
Pete Sommers	4	13	1	3	1	0	0	0	0	.231
Ezra Sutton	28	110	16	24	3	1	1	16	10	.218
Pop Tate	41	148	18	34	7	1	1	6	3	.230
Nick Wise	1	3	0	0	0	0	0	0	0	.000
Sam Wise (SS)	105	417	66	100	19	12	4	40	33	.240
	137	4,834	669	1,183	167	89	56		293	.245

	W	L	G	GS	CG	IP	H	BB	SO	ERA
John Clarkson	33	20	54	54	53	483½*	448	119	223	2.76
Dick Conway	4	2	6	6	6	53	49	8	12	2.38
Kid Madden	7	11	20	18	17	165	142	24	53	2.95
Charley Radbourn	7	16	24	24	24	207	187	45	64	2.87
Bill Sowders	19	15	36	35	34	317	278	73	132	2.07
	70	64		137	134	1,225½	1,104	269	484	2.61

Shutouts—Clarkson (3), Sowders (2), Madden, Radbourn
Saves—None

1889

Record: 83–45
Finish: Second
Games Behind: 1
Manager: Jim Hart

Many managers in history have lost their jobs because of friction caused by the presence of a temperamental superstar. "Honest" John Morrill probably was the first to fall into that category.

The Beaneaters' ownership was becoming disenchanted with Morrill, who was extremely popular with the team's fans. He batted just .198 in 1888 yet demanded a raise for '89.

The Triumvirs signed him, but problems arose at the annual preseason Fast Day exhibition game. Morrill was asked to captain the "picked nine" of local players, while Kelly captained the Beaneaters. Morrill saw it as an insult and refused. The next day he was sold to Washington.

Morrill was replaced by Jim Hart, who managed in the minors the previous year. Hart inherited a talented ball club that had been enriched by the purchase of several players from Detroit, which had folded. Those acquisitions included future Hall of Fame first baseman Dan Brouthers.

It was an exciting but ultimately disappointing year for the Beaneaters, who lost the pennant by one game on the last day of the season. The second-place finish came despite remarkable seasons from Brouthers, who led the league in hitting (.373), and Clarkson, who led in wins (49) and ERA (2.73).

at the South End Grounds. A crowd of 12,000 turned out for the home opener, but Boston lost to the Phillies, 4–1.

The Beaneaters' two high-priced superstars didn't guarantee a pennant, though. In early June, Clarkson lost the longest game of the season, tiring in the 16th inning of an 11–5 Detroit victory. Later in the month, the Beaneaters got just one hit in a 7–0 defeat to the Phillies and old teammate Charlie Buffinton.

Clarkson led the league in innings but won "only" 33 games, his lowest total in four years.

Kelly had another fine season, finishing third in the league in batting average (.318) and fourth in slugging percentage (.480). There were two other big sticks on the team. Outfielder Dick Johnston led the league in triples (18). Third baseman Billy Nash was second to Chicago great Cap Anson in RBIs (75).

At the end of August, Boston held a two-game lead over New York. The margin was still two games on September 12 when Clarkson pitched and won both ends of a doubleheader with Cleveland, 3–2 and 5–0. But by the end of the month, the Beaneaters and Giants were virtually deadlocked. Boston, with a 79–42 record, trailed 80–43 New York by three percentage points.

On October 1, Boston won and New York lost, giving the Beaneaters a one-game edge. But in many ways, the pennant was decided the next day in Cleveland when the Spiders beat Boston, 7–1, while New York was winning.

Kelly showed up drunk and was on the bench in street clothes when the game began. He soon was ejected for arguing with the umpire and had to be escorted from the field by police. Hart was blamed for allowing Kelly to get in such a state.

Still, the race came down to the final day with New York holding the lead by a scant two percentage points. Before the game, the publisher of the *Boston Globe* promised the Beaneaters a $1,000 bonus if they won the pennant.

But New York won and Boston lost. It was a bitter way to end a great season. However, the *Globe* lessened the disappointment by giving the players the $1,000 bonus anyway.

	G	AB	R	H	2B	3B	HR	RBI	SB	AVG
Charlie Bennett (C)	82	247	42	57	8	2	4	28	7	.231
Dan Brouthers (1B)	126	485	105	181	26	9	7	118	22	.373*
Tom Brown (OF)	90	362	93	84	10	5	2	24	63	.232
Charlie Ganzel	73	275	30	73	3	5	1	43	13	.265
Jerry Hurley	1	4	0	0	0	0	0	0	0	.000
Dick Johnston (OF)	132	539	80	123	16	4	5	67	34	.228
King Kelly (OF)	125	507	120	149	41*	5	9	78	68	.294
Billy Nash (3B)	128	481	84	132	20	2	3	76	26	.274
Joe Quinn (SS)	112	444	57	116	13	5	2	69	24	.261
Charley Radbourn	35	122	17	23	1	0	1	13	3	.189
Irv Ray	9	33	8	10	1	0	0	2	1	.303
Hardy Richardson (2B)	132	536	122	163	33	10	6	79	47	.304
Pop Smith	59	208	21	54	13	4	0	32	11	.260
	133	4,628	826	1,251	196	54	42		331*	.270

	W	L	G	GS	CG	IP	H	BB	SO	ERA
John Clarkson	49*	19	73*	72	68*	620*	589	203	284*	2.73*
Bill Daley	3	3	9	7	4	48	34	43	40	4.31
Kid Madden	10	10	22	19	18	178	194	71	64	4.40
Billy Nash	0	0	1	0	0	1	0	1	0	0.00
Charley Radbourn	20	11	33	31	28	277	282	72	99	3.67
Bill Sowders	1	2	7	4	3	42	53	23	10	5.14
	83*	45		133	121	1,166	1,152	413	497	3.36*

Shutouts—Clarkson (8*), Madden, Radbourn
Saves—Sowders (2*), Clarkson, Madden

1890

Record: 76–57
Finish: Fifth
Games Behind: 12
Manager: Frank Selee

The Beaneaters had a disappointing 1890, finishing fifth, but it was not a lost season by any stretch of the imagination. In fact, it served as a prelude to the most prosperous period in franchise history.

The labor problems in modern baseball are not a new phenomenon to the game. In 1890 the players were so upset with the owners that they started their own league, and in the process, the Beaneaters were decimated.

Protesting the reserve clause and salary limit of $2,000, the players started the National Brotherhood of Base Ball Players, or simply the Players League. "King" Kelly left the Beaneaters to manage and captain the rival Boston entry in the league. Nine other Beaneaters signed with the new league, including Dan Brouthers, who'd just won the batting title the previous year, and Charley "Old Hoss" Radbourn, who was near the end of his career but was still coming off a 20-victory season.

Imagine what state the 1993 Braves would have been in had they lost, say, Tom Glavine, Terry Pendleton, David Justice, and seven other players just prior to the season. That's what faced the 1890 Beaneaters.

Boston's Players League entry was well stocked and finished in first place. The Beaneaters, meanwhile, played remarkably well under the circumstances but still dropped out of the first division.

The club was able to play as well as it did because the owners signed several quality players. They also made a significant managerial change. Jim Hart, who became the scapegoat for losing the 1889 pennant—and for Kelly's drunkenness—was fired. He was replaced by Frank Selee, a reserved 30-year-old who'd never managed or played in the majors but who was quickly gaining a reputation for assessing ballplayers.

One of those players was a 20-year-old right-hander named Charles "Kid" Nichols who pitched for Selee the previous season at Omaha. All Nichols did as a rookie was win 27 games, lead the league in shutouts (7), finish second in ERA (2.23), and complete all 47 games he started. And "Kid" would prove to be anything but a one-year wonder.

Other significant new players included first baseman Tommy Tucker, shortstop Herman Long, who hit two home runs in his debut, and outfielder Bobby Lowe. Like Nichols, these players would prove very instrumental in the Beaneaters' future.

	G	AB	R	H	2B	3B	HR	RBI	SB	AVG
Charlie Bennett (C)	85	281	59	60	17	2	3	40	6	.214
Steve Brodie (OF)	132	514	77	152	19	9	0	67	29	.296
Patsy Donovan	32	140	17	36	0	0	0	9	10	.257
Charlie Ganzel	38	163	21	44	7	3	0	24	1	.270
Lou Hardie	47	185	17	42	8	0	3	17	4	.227
Paul Hines (OF)	69	273	41	72	12	3	2	48	9	.264
Herman Long (SS)	101	431	95	108	15	3	8	52	49	.251
Bobby Lowe	52	207	35	58	13	2	2	21	15	.280
Chippy McGarr (3B)	121	487	68	115	12	7	1	51	39	.236
Al Schellhase	9	29	1	4	0	0	0	1	0	.138
Pop Smith (2B)	134	463	82	106	16	12	1	53	39	.229
Marty Sullivan (OF)	121	505	82	144	19	7	6	61	33	.285
Tommy Tucker (1B)	132	539	104	159	17	8	1	62	43	.295
	134	4,722	763	1,220	175	62	31		285	.258

	W	L	G	GS	CG	IP	H	BB	SO	ERA
John Clarkson	26	18	44	44	43	383	370	140	138	3.27
Charlie Getzien	23	17	40	40	39	350	342	82	140	3.19
Al Lawson	0	1	1	1	1	9	12	4	1	4.00
Kid Nichols	27	19	48	47	47	424	374	112	222	2.23
John Taber	0	1	2	1	1	13	11	8	3	4.15
Tony Von Fricken	0	1	1	1	1	8	23	8	2	10.13
	76	57		134	132*	1,187	1,132	354	506	2.93

Shutouts—Nichols (7*), Getzien (4), Clarkson (2)
Saves—Taber

1891

Record: 87–51
Finish: First
Games Ahead: 3½
Manager: Frank Selee

The Beaneaters, under second-year manager Frank Selee, were about to embark on a decade of achievement unparalleled in franchise history and equaled by very few teams in any era. It began with one of the most hotly disputed pennants in baseball history—one that wasn't formally decided until nearly Thanksgiving!

The Players League was dissolved, but the team still faced head-to-head competition for Boston fans from a very talented club in the American Association. In fact, for most of the season, it seemed that the American Association team was more likely to win a pennant than the Beaneaters. In the end, Boston experienced the joy of having two championship teams.

Selee's club opened the season in New York with a 4–3 victory over the Giants before 17,355, the largest opening-day crowd in the league. However, the Beaneaters trailed Chicago in the race most of the season.

Though Boston didn't have a .300 hitter, it did have a balanced attack. More importantly, though, Selee had the league's best pitching staff and its tightest defense.

Herman or "Germany" Long was just launching a long career as one of the league's best shortstops. Long could hit as well as field. On June 11, with Selee's team floundering around .500, Long put a charge in his teammates with a 6-for-6 performance that sparked a 14–6 victory over the Chicago Colts.

In August, with Chicago still leading the league, the Beaneaters stunned everyone by again signing "King" Kelly, taking him away from the city's rival American Association franchise. Though Kelly was virtually finished, the Triumvirs agreed to pay him what was then the incredible sum of $25,000 for the last month of 1891 and all of the following season.

Kelly didn't play a significant role on this team, but after his arrival, Selee's club embarked on a stretch drive that would rival any other in franchise history. In September and October, the Beaneaters won 23 of 30—including 18 in a row—to wrest the pennant from Chicago.

As with all long winning streaks, there was more than solid play involved in this one. There were a few doses of luck, and even, some complained, a little conspiracy in Boston's torrid sprint to the National League pennant.

The winning streak reached 10 on September 25 when Philadelphia third baseman Ed Mayer made three errors to help the Beaneaters escape, 6–3.

Three days later, the Giants, a strong team but out of the pennant picture, came to Boston for a five-game series that included two makeup games. New York did not bring its two best pitchers, Amos Rusie and John Ewing, nor its top hitter, Roger Connor. Chicago, trying to hang on to the league lead, was suspicious.

When the Beaneaters completed a sweep of the five games on September 30 and moved into first place with three days to go, Chicago president Jim Hart—who preceded Selee as Boston manager—filed a protest. Hart and some sportswriters felt eastern teams had collaborated to help one of their own win the pennant.

Boston clinched the title October 1, beating Philadelphia, 6–1, for its 17th straight victory. For good measure, the Beaneaters made it a franchise-record 18 wins in a row the next day.

Not until November 11 did the pennant become official, though. That's when the National League met to review charges by Chicago that the eastern teams assisted Boston in winning the championship. However, Hart's protest was denied.

Boston's 2.76 ERA was easily the best in the league and nearly three-quarters of a run better than Chicago's. The Beaneaters committed fewer errors than any other team in the league. They led the league in runs scored, and their .255 team batting average, only third in the league, was still better than Chicago's. Clearly, Selee had the superior team. It just didn't peak until September.

John Clarkson and Nichols, both on the way to Cooperstown, combined for 63 of Boston's 87 victories. Nichols was second in the league in ERA and shutouts. But Harry Staley, picked up from last-place Pittsburgh early in the season, actually pitched better than his two celebrated teammates, winning 20 of his 28 decisions after joining the Beaneaters.

Long's .287 average was the highest on the team, and his 60 steals ranked fourth in the league. Outfielder Harry Stovey, obtained from Boston's defunct Players League entry, was the big run producer. He tied for the league lead in home runs (16) and led in both total bases (271) and slugging percentage (.498). Stovey and third baseman Billy Nash tied for second in the league with 95 RBIs apiece.

	G	AB	R	H	2B	3B	HR	RBI	SB	AVG
Charlie Bennett (C)	75	256	35	55	9	3	5	39	3	.215
Steve Brodie (OF)	133	523	84	136	13	6	2	78	25	.260
Charlie Ganzel	70	263	33	68	18	5	1	29	7	.259
Joe Kelley	12	45	7	11	1	1	0	3	0	.244
King Kelly	16	52	7	12	1	0	0	5	6	.231
Fred Lake	5	7	1	1	0	0	0	0	0	.143
Herman Long (SS)	139	577	129	163	21	11	10	76	60	.282
Bobby Lowe (OF)	125	497	92	129	19	5	6	74	43	.260
Billy Nash (3B)	140	537	92	148	24	9	5	95	28	.276
Joe Quinn (2B)	124	508	70	122	8	10	3	63	24	.240
George Rooks	5	16	1	2	0	0	0	0	0	.125
Harry Stovey (OF)	134	544	118	152	31	20*	16*	95	57	.279
Marty Sullivan	17	67	15	15	1	0	2	7	7	.224
Tommy Tucker (1B)	140	548	103	148	16	5	2	69	26	.270
	140	4,956	847*	1,264	181	80	54		289	.255

	W	L	G	GS	CG	IP	H	BB	SO	ERA
Tod Brynan	0	1	1	1	0	1	4	3	0	54.00
John Clarkson	33	19	55	51	47	460⅔	435	154	141	2.79
Charlie Getzien	4	5	11	9	7	89	112	23	29	3.84
John Kiley	0	1	1	1	1	8	13	5	1	6.75
Bobby Lowe	0	0	1	0	0	1	3	1	0	9.00
Kid Nichols	30	17	52	48	45	425⅓	413	103	240	2.39
Cyclone Ryan	0	0	1	0	0	3	2	1	0	0.00
Harry Staley	20	8	31	30	26	252⅓	236	69	114	2.50
Jim Sullivan	0	0	1	0	0	⅓	2	5	0	81.00
Tommy Tucker	0	0	1	0	0	1	3	0	0	9.00
	87*	51		140	126*	1,241⅔	1,223	364	525	2.76*

Shutouts—Nichols (5), Clarkson (3), Staley
Saves—Clarkson (3*), Nichols (3*)

1892

Record: 102–48
Finish: First
Games Ahead: 8½
Manager: Frank Selee

This was one of the greatest seasons in franchise history. The National League expanded to 12 teams and adopted a split-season, 154-game format. But when all was said and done, the Beaneaters were still the class of the league.

In fact, manager Frank Selee's team was so good it was able to release pitching great John Clarkson at midseason.

With Kid Nichols, Harry Staley, and newcomer Jack Stivetts, who was picked up from the defunct American Association, Boston had a formidable pitching staff, even without Clarkson. They combined for 92 victories, 35 apiece for Stivetts and Nichols.

There was plenty of offense, too, and 1892 marked the first pairing of Hugh Duffy and Tommy McCarthy, who became known as the "Heavenly Twins" in the outfield for their angelic defense.

In short, Boston had it all—and the King, too. "King" Kelly was in his last season with the club. His contributions would be infrequent, but a song inspired by his baserunning exploits debuted. Early in the year, "Slide, Kelly, Slide" by George Gaskin became the first baseball song to make the pop music chart.

The Beaneaters wasted no time in displaying their superiority, winning 11 of their first 13 games.

Clarkson may have been near the end in Boston, but he still could pitch. On opening day, he beat Washington, 14–4, and chipped in a home run. On May 6, he pitched 14 scoreless innings against Cincinnati, giving up just four hits, but had to settle for a scoreless tie. Later in the month, he held Louisville without a hit for 8⅔ innings before Hughie Jennings, starting a Hall of Fame career of his own, singled.

Yet in July, Clarkson found himself pitching for Cleveland. That's how good this Boston team was.

With the first-half title in hand July 11, the Beaneaters—led, of course, by the irrepressible Kelly—came on the field in Chicago wearing fake beards and outlandish costumes. The crowd loved it, and Boston didn't play like clowns, winning, 3–2, to finish 2½ games ahead of Brooklyn in the first-half standings.

Perhaps lacking incentive, Selee's team started slowly in the second half and finished second by three games to Cleve-

land despite a very respectable 50–26 record. The team's overall .680 winning percentage remains fifth best in franchise history, and its combined record for both halves was 8½ games better than runner-up Cleveland.

The National League owners knew what they were doing with the split-season format. Without it, Boston's clear superiority would have left no suspense in September.

Though Selee's club did not win the second-half title, it certainly provided quite a few highlights for the fans to remember.

"Happy" Jack Stivetts probably was never happier than he was August 5–6. On August 5, Stivetts, a versatile player, was subbing in left field and hit a two-run homer in the 12th to break up a scoreless game and beat Brooklyn. The next day, he pitched the first official no-hitter in franchise history, beating Brooklyn's Bridegrooms, 11–0.

Stivetts, a 24-year-old right-hander from the Pennsylvania coal mines, wasn't through. On September 5, he pitched and won both ends of a doubleheader against Louisville. He won the first game, 2–1, in 11 innings, and the second, 5–2.

The season also produced quite an offensive explosion by Nichols. On September 19, the great pitcher hit a grand slam in the fifth inning. The next inning, he added a bases-loaded triple. With seven RBIs, he had to leave the game in the bottom of the sixth after being hit with a batted ball.

The winning teams from each half met in a best-of-nine championship series. The first three games were scheduled in Cleveland, the next three in Boston, and the last three, if needed, on a neutral field. The talented Beaneaters spared the league the necessity of finding a neutral site.

Stivetts and the great Cy Young opposed each other in a classic duel in Game 1. After 11 scoreless innings, the game had to be called. King Kelly, who batted just .189 in the regular season, as usual found a way to make his presence felt, even from the bench. In the ninth inning, when the Cleveland catcher was chasing a pop foul, Kelly called for the Spiders' first baseman to make the play. The two collided, and the ball dropped. Boston, however, couldn't take advantage of Kelly's gamesmanship and failed to score. "King," by the way, was fined $10.

In Game 2, the Beaneaters beat the Spiders, 4–3, with Staley defeating his old teammate, Clarkson. In Game 3, Stivetts beat Young, 3–2, even though he walked eight.

Thus, the series moved to Boston with the Beaneaters holding a 2–0 advantage. Nichols proceeded to pitch a seven-hit shutout, winning 4–0.

It appeared Cleveland would finally get on the board in Game 5 when the Spiders jumped off to a 6–0 lead behind a three-run homer by Clarkson. However, the former Boston pitcher fell apart, allowing the Beaneaters to rally for a 12–7 victory.

It remained for Nichols to put the Spiders out of their misery in Game 6. He beat Young, 8–3, giving Selee's team a sweep.

Duffy, who led Boston with a .302 average during the regular season, also was the club's best batter in the playoff, collecting 12 hits.

The 1892 Beaneaters were a good example of a true *team*. They didn't lead the league in any major offensive, defensive, or pitching category except shutouts (15). But, of course, they were near the top in virtually all departments.

Likewise, no Beaneater led the league in any major statistic.

Duffy was third in runs and hits and fifth in total bases. Even the pitchers weren't very prominent in the final stats. Clarkson, who was released at midseason to Cleveland, actually finished third in the league with a 2.48 ERA, which was better than any of Boston's big three of Nichols, Stivetts, and Staley.

	G	AB	R	H	2B	3B	HR	RBI	SB	AVG
Charlie Bennett	35	114	19	23	4	0	1	16	6	.202
Dan Burke	1	4	0	0	0	0	0	0	0	.000
Joe Daly	1	0	0	0	0	0	0	0	0	—
Hugh Duffy (OF)	147	612	125	184	28	12	5	81	51	.301
Charlie Ganzel	54	198	25	53	9	3	0	25	7	.268
King Kelly (C)	78	281	40	53	7	0	2	41	24	.189
Herman Long (SS)	151	646	115	181	33	6	6	78	57	.280
Bobby Lowe (OF)	124	475	79	115	16	7	3	57	36	.242
Tommy McCarthy (OF)	152	603	119	146	19	5	4	63	53	.242
Billy Nash (3B)	135	526	94	137	25	5	4	95	31	.260
Joe Quinn (2B)	143	532	63	116	14	1	1	59	17	.218
Jack Stivetts	71	240	40	71	14	2	3	36	8	.296
Harry Stovey	38	146	21	24	8	1	0	12	20	.164
Tommy Tucker (1B)	149	542	85	153	15	7	1	62	22	.282
	152	5,301	862	1,324	203	51	34		338	.250

	W	L	G	GS	CG	IP	H	BB	SO	ERA
Dad Clarkson	1	0	1	1	1	7	5	3	0	1.29
John Clarkson	8	6	16	16	15	145⅔	115	60	48	2.35
King Kelly	0	0	1	0	0	6	8	4	0	1.50
Kid Nichols	35	16	53	51	49	453	404	121	187	2.84
Harry Staley	22	10	37	35	31	299⅔	273	97	93	3.03
Jack Stivetts	35	16	54	48	45	415⅔	346	171	180	3.03
Lee Viau	1	0	1	1	1	9	5	4	1	0.00
	102*	48		152	142	1,336	1,156	460	509	2.86

Shutouts—Nichols (5), J.Clarkson (4), Staley (3), Stivetts (3)
Saves—Stivetts

1893

Record: 86–43
Finish: First
Games Ahead: 5
Manager: Frank Selee

Another year, another pennant. The Braves of 1991–93 came close to winning three consecutive National League championships, only to have a 1993 playoff loss to Philadelphia spoil that bid. But a century earlier, their ancestors accomplished the rare feat of winning three consecutive pennants. These victories also gave Boston a remarkable six of the first 18 National League flags.

The split-season format of 1892 was dropped after one year, and the pitching distance was moved back five feet to 60 feet, 6 inches in 1893. The Beaneaters played as if they barely noticed the changes. By late July, they assumed the league lead for good. Frank Selee's team was so set that not a single player was released during the season, a National League first.

One of the more unusual events in franchise history occurred early in the season. Boston and Brooklyn played to a scoreless tie through eight innings May 19. Brooklyn appeared headed to a victory after scoring three times in the top of the ninth. However, Boston mounted a rally in the bottom of the inning, too. Third baseman Billy Nash started it by hitting a ball over the left-field fence. Instead of running around the bases, though, Nash stopped at third, settling for a triple so he could "bother the pitcher." Sure enough, Boston got three runs to tie the game.

Both clubs scored a run in the 10th, the Beaneaters' run coming on another fence-clearing hit by Nash. This time, he circled the bases. Boston finally won the game, 5–4, in 12 innings.

Pitcher Harry Staley hit two home runs June 1 in a 15–4 rout of Louisville. On July 22, first baseman Tommy Tucker tied a major league record with four doubles, including two in an inning, during a 7–2 victory against New York. Two days later, in the midst of a nine-game winning streak, the Beaneaters beat Baltimore, 6–2, taking a league lead they would not relinquish.

Boston's chief competition for the pennant was Pittsburgh, and some bad blood developed between the two clubs. One indication of that took place in the second inning of the August 19 game at Pittsburgh when four Boston batters were hit by pitches.

When the two clubs met the following month, the Beaneaters were on the verge of wrapping up the pennant. Selee's players had not forgotten serving as targets for Pittsburgh pitchers, which may have been the impetus behind Boston shortstop Herman Long crashing into Pittsburgh catcher Connie Mack at the plate, breaking his leg. Long was scoring from third on a single, and there was no play being made on him. Mack, who was destined for the Hall of Fame as a manager, was out for the rest of the season.

One of the many interesting sidelights to the season was Boston's progressive offense. At a time when other teams often played for one run at a time, using the sacrifice bunt to advance runners on a regular basis, the Beaneaters were perfecting the hit-and-run and playing for big innings.

Tommy McCarthy, half of the "Heavenly Twins" outfielders and one of the most imaginative players in the game, frequently was responsible for coordinating the hit-and-run with his "Twin," Duffy. McCarthy also was behind another practice the Beaneaters developed of stealing the catcher's signals when on second base and relaying them to the batter with signals of their own.

Billy Nash started a memorable rally in 1893 when he hit an apparent home run but chose to stay at third so he could rattle the pitcher.

These techniques are taken for granted in modern baseball, but they were new then and perfected by the Braves' ancestors.

Nichols, as usual, was among the league's pitching leaders in most departments. His ERA rose as a result of the increase in pitching distance, but his effectiveness in relation to other pitchers didn't change a bit. He reached the 30-victory level for the third consecutive season, finishing tied for second in the league with 34 wins. Throwing an extra five feet didn't cause him to beg off any work either. He finished 43 of the 44 games he started.

Perhaps Giants manager John Montgomery Ward best summed up the league's feelings about the Beaneaters' strength when he said, "The Bostons could have beaten any all-star nine the league could have put together this season."

	G	AB	R	H	2B	3B	HR	RBI	SB	AVG
Charlie Bennett (C)	60	191	34	40	6	0	4	27	5	.209
Cliff Carroll (OF)	120	438	80	98	7	5	2	54	29	.224
Hugh Duffy (OF)	131	560	147	203	23	7	6	118	44	.363
Charlie Ganzel	73	281	50	75	10	2	1	48	6	.267
Herman Long (SS)	128	552	149*	159	22	6	6	58	38	.288
Bobby Lowe (2B)	126	526	130	157	19	5	14	89	22	.298
Tommy McCarthy (OF)	116	462	107	160	28	6	5	111	46	.346
Bill Merritt	39	141	30	49	6	3	3	26	3	.348
Billy Nash (3B)	128	485	115	141	27	6	10	123	30	.291
Jack Stivetts	50	172	32	51	5	6	3	25	6	.297
Tommy Tucker (1B)	121	486	83	138	13	2	7	91	8	.284
Bill Van Dyke	3	12	2	3	1	0	0	1	1	.250
	131	4,678	1,008	1,358	178	50	65		243	.290

	W	L	G	GS	CG	IP	H	BB	SO	ERA
Bill Coyle	0	1	2	1	0	8	14	3	2	9.00
Jim Garry	0	1	1	0	0	1	5	4	2	63.00
Hank Gastright	12	4	19	18	16	156	179	76	27	5.13
Kid Nichols	34	14	52	44	43	425	426	118	94	3.52
Bill Quarles	2	1	3	3	3	27	31	5	6	4.67
Harry Staley	18	10	36	31	23	263	344	81	61	5.13
Jack Stivetts	20	12	38	34	29	283⅔	315	115	61	4.41
	86*	43		131	114*	1,163⅔	1,314	402	253	4.43

Shutouts—Nichols, Stivetts
Saves—Nichols, Stivetts

1894

Record: 83–49
Finish: Third
Games Behind: 8
Manager: Frank Selee

The Beaneaters were favored to win yet another pennant in 1894. Not only did they fail to do so, but they also suffered through one of the most tragic seasons in franchise history.

The year started with one of the most dreadful accidents ever to befall a major league player. Charlie Bennett, an outstanding defensive catcher, lost both legs January 9 when he slipped under the wheels of a train in Kansas.

Bennett's fate was a severe blow to both the players and the fans. But an even more shocking setback came after the disappointing season.

On November 8, Mike "King" Kelly, the most popular player of the 19th century and a major figure in the franchise's early history, died of pneumonia at age 36.

Yet another misfortune, minor in comparison, came May 16 when fire destroyed the club's South End Grounds. The Beaneaters were in the third inning of a game with Baltimore when the fire erupted in the right-field bleachers.

Some of the remaining home games were played on the road, but most were shifted to the old Brotherhood League Grounds on Congress Street adjacent to Boston Harbor.

Between and around these ill-fated incidents, the team did manage to play ball, and for most of the season, they played very well.

On July 30, manager's Frank Selee's club completed a three-game sweep of Baltimore to open a four-game lead. As late as August 29, Boston was still in first place. But the Beaneaters fell behind Baltimore by a half game entering September. Down the stretch, Boston won only 14 of 25 games and fell to third place. Baltimore sprinted to the pennant by winning 20 of 23.

The season was filled with highs and lows. Selee probably knew he was in trouble when the Beaneaters entered the ninth inning of an early season game against Baltimore with a 3–1 lead, only to lose, 15–3. And shortstop Herman Long had to miss several games in May after getting hot ashes from his cigar in his eye. It was that sort of season.

Among the bright spots was Bobby Lowe's performance May 30 when he became the first major leaguer to hit four home runs in the same game.

The Beaneaters had the most potent offense in the league. They led all teams in runs, home runs, and slugging percentage. The best example of the team's capabilities occurred in a three-game sweep of Cleveland in early July. Boston outscored the Spiders by a combined score of 57–23 and had a total of 69 hits. Every Boston starter had at least one hit in each of the three games.

And on August 7, outfielder Jimmy Bannon hit two grand slams in the same game, the first major leaguer to do so.

Some of the offense has to be attributed to a lively ball. Only one team, second-place New York (3.83), had an ERA under 4.97.

The biggest beneficiary of the juiced ball was Boston outfielder Hugh Duffy. An excellent hitter throughout the 17-year career that took him to the Hall of Fame, Duffy exceeded even his own standards in 1894. He led the league with a .440 average, which still stands as the all-time National League record.

A 5–7, 168-pounder, Duffy also led the league in home runs (18), RBIs (145), hits (237), doubles (51), total bases (374), and slugging percentage (.694). Lively ball or not, it was a phenomenal season.

Seven Beaneaters scored 100 runs, and the club set a record with its 1,220 runs. Boston was not shut out the entire season.

Pitching was a problem, though, and Bennett's loss left a void behind the plate, too. Selee got so desperate that he tried a left-handed catcher out of Brown University, Fred Tenney.

	G	AB	R	H	2B	3B	HR	RBI	SB	AVG
Jimmy Bannon (OF)	128	494	130	166	29	10	13	114	47	.336
Frank Connaughton	46	171	42	59	9	2	2	33	3	.345
Hugh Duffy (OF)	125	539	160	237*	51*	16	18*	145*	48	.440*
Charlie Ganzel (C)	70	266	51	74	7	6	3	56	1	.278
Herman Long (SS)	104	475	136	154	28	11	12	79	24	.324
Bobby Lowe (2B)	133	613	158	212	34	11	17	115	23	.346
Tommy McCarthy (OF)	127	539	118	188	21	8	13	126	43	.349
Bill Merritt	10	26	3	6	1	0	0	6	0	.231
Billy Nash (3B)	132	512	132	148	23	6	8	87	20	.289
Jack Ryan	53	201	39	54	12	7	1	29	3	.269
Jack Stivetts	68	244	55	80	12	7	8	64	3	.328
Fred Tenney	27	86	23	34	7	1	2	21	6	.395
Tommy Tucker (1B)	123	500	112	165	24	6	3	100	18	.330
	133	5,011	1,220*	1,658	272*	94	103*		241	.331

	W	L	G	GS	CG	IP	H	BB	SO	ERA
Jimmy Bannon	0	0	1	0	0	2	4	1	0	0.00
Scott Hawley	0	1	1	1	1	7	10	7	1	7.71
George Hodson	4	4	12	11	8	74	103	35	12	5.84
Henry Lampe	0	1	2	1	0	5⅓	17	7	1	11.81
Tom Lovett	8	6	15	13	10	104	155	36	23	5.97
Tommy McCarthy	0	0	1	0	0	2	1	3	0	4.50
Kid Nichols	32	13	50	46	40	407	488	121	113	4.75
Tom Smith	0	0	2	0	0	6	8	6	2	15.00
Harry Staley	12	10	27	21	18	208⅔	305	61	32	6.81
Jack Stivetts	26	14	45	39	30	338	429	127	76	4.90
George Stultz	1	0	1	1	1	9	4	5	1	0.00
Frank West	0	0	1	0	0	3	5	2	1	9.00
	83	49		133	108	1,166	1,529	411	262	5.41

Shutouts—Nichols (3*)
Saves—Smith

1895

Record: 71–60
Finish: Tie–Fifth
Games Behind: 16½
Manager: Frank Selee

The Beaneaters had their first spring training in the South in 1895. They held a preseason camp at Columbia, South Carolina, and when they headed home to start the schedule, Frank Selee's players felt they were ready to regain the National League pennant after a one-year hiatus from the throne.

Indeed, the Beaneaters were in the pennant race for the first half. They moved past Pittsburgh and into first place on June 11 by whipping Louisville, 11–0. They dropped out of the lead July 3. At that point, the race was a toss-up between Selee's club, Baltimore, Chicago, and Pittsburgh. On July 8, only one game separated the four teams.

However, Boston died quickly after that. The result was the team's worst record in Selee's six years as manager. A tie for fifth—just a half game ahead of seventh-place Pittsburgh—was not what anyone associated with the team had in mind.

Boston's defense was sound, but the offense and the pitching were mediocre at best.

After his dazzling 1894, Hugh Duffy saw his average drop 88 points to .352, his homers from 18 to 9 and his RBIs from 145 to 100. Obviously, Duffy still had a fine season, yet he wasn't even among the league leaders in any of the categories he dominated a year earlier.

Tommy McCarthy's average dived 59 points to .290; he hit just two home runs compared to 13 in 1894; and his RBIs dropped from 126 to 73. He was sold to Brooklyn after the season.

Even Kid Nichols couldn't escape the team's problems. He failed to win 30 games for the first time in five years. It was the only season in the eight-year period 1891–98 he didn't win 30.

	G	AB	R	H	2B	3B	HR	RBI	SB	AVG
Jimmy Bannon (OF)	123	489	101	171	35	5	6	74	28	.350
Jimmy Collins	11	38	10	8	3	0	1	8	0	.211
Cozy Dolan	26	83	12	20	4	1	0	7	3	.241
Hugh Duffy (OF)	130	531	110	187	30	6	9	100	42	.352
Charlie Ganzel (C)	80	277	38	73	2	5	1	52	1	.264
Joe Harrington	18	65	21	18	0	2	2	13	3	.277
Herman Long (SS)	124	535	109	169	23	10	9	75	35	.316
Bobby Lowe (2B)	99	412	101	122	12	7	7	62	24	.296
Tommy McCarthy (OF)	117	452	90	131	13	2	2	73	18	.290
Billy Nash (3B)	132	508	97	147	23	6	10	108	18	.289
Charlie Nyce	9	35	7	8	5	0	2	9	0	.229
Jack Ryan	49	189	22	55	7	0	0	18	3	.291
Jack Stivetts	46	158	20	30	6	4	0	24	1	.190
Fred Tenney	49	173	35	47	9	1	1	21	6	.272
Tommy Tucker (1B)	125	462	87	115	19	6	3	73	15	.249
John Warner	3	7	2	1	0	0	0	1	0	.143
	132	4,715	907	1,369	197	57	54		199	.290

	W	L	G	GS	CG	IP	H	BB	SO	ERA
Jimmy Bannon	0	0	1	0	0	3	4	2	1	6.00
Cozy Dolan	11	7	25	21	18	198½	215	67	47	4.27
Kid Nichols	26	16	47	42	42	379¾	417	86	140	3.41
Frank Sexton	1	5	7	5	4	49	59	22	14	5.69
Jack Stivetts	17	17	38	34	30	291	341	89	111	4.64
Otis Stocksdale	2	2	4	4	1	23	31	8	2	5.87
Jim Sullivan	11	9	21	19	16	179½	236	58	46	4.82
Zeke Wilson	2	4	6	6	4	45	54	27	5	5.20
Bill Yerrick	1	0	1	1	1	7	7	4	4	0.00
	71	60		132	116	1,175½	1,364	363	370	4.27

Shutouts—Dolan (3), Nichols
Saves—Nichols (3*), Dolan

1896

Record: 74–57
Finish: Fourth
Games Behind: 17
Manager: Frank Selee

The Beaneaters suffered another disappointing season in 1896, but they experienced an influx of new talent that was about to help them embark on yet another chapter of the club's amazing 19th-century success story.

One of those new players was "Slidin' Billy" Hamilton, already a 30-year-old veteran outfielder with four National League stolen-base titles on his résumé. An ideal leadoff man, Hamilton topped the league in walks (110) and on-base percentage (.477) in his first season with Boston and stole 83 bases, third in the league and still an all-time franchise record. His .365 batting average was the best on the team.

Another player working his way into the picture was Fred Tenney, the Brown University product who broke in as a left-handed catcher two years earlier. Manager Frank Selee, still trying to decide where to play Tenney, farmed him out to Springfield early in the season to work at first base and outfield, as well as catcher. On Memorial Day, Tenney played for Springfield at Providence in the morning, then was recalled and rushed to Boston to play against Cleveland that very afternoon. Mainly an outfielder then, Tenney soon found his home at first base.

The team started well before slumping in May and July. On April 20, an overflow crowd of 18,033 at Boston created need for a ground rule that any ball hit into the standing mass was a single. The Beaneaters took full advantage of the rule (and perhaps the fans pushed forward when the home team was at bat), equaling the major league record of 28 singles in a 21–8 victory against Baltimore.

On May 13, Selee's team won by forfeit against Chicago. When the Beaneaters scored six in the top of the 11th to take a 10–4 lead, Chicago stalled in the bottom of the inning, hoping to get the game called because of darkness, negating Boston's rally. However, umpire Tim Keefe refused to let the home team get away with the tactic and awarded the victory to the Beaneaters.

Most of the rest of the season was a gradual downhill slide, though. One exception was a 28–7 win over St. Louis on September 3. Boston had 30 hits, including two home runs by Hugh Duffy, who'd been named the team's captain, and five hits apiece from Hamilton, Tenney, and Jimmy Collins. It was an indication that new blood was about to turn around the Beaneaters' fortunes.

The phenomenal Kid Nichols just kept rolling along, tying for the league lead in victories (30) and finishing second in ERA and third in games.

	G	AB	R	H	2B	3B	HR	RBI	SB	AVG
Jimmy Bannon (OF)	89	343	52	86	9	5	0	50	16	.251
Marty Bergen (C)	65	245	39	66	6	4	4	37	6	.269
Jimmy Collins (3B)	84	304	48	90	10	9	1	46	10	.296
Hugh Duffy (OF)	131	527	97	158	16	8	5	113	39	.300
Charlie Ganzel	47	179	28	47	2	0	1	18	2	.263
Billy Hamilton (OF)	131	523	152	191	24	9	3	52	83	.365
Joe Harrington	54	198	25	39	5	3	1	25	2	.197
Herman Long (SS)	120	501	105	172	26	8	6	100	36	.343
Bobby Lowe (2B)	73	305	59	98	11	4	2	48	15	.321
Dan McGann	43	171	25	55	6	7	2	30	2	.322
Jack Ryan	8	32	2	3	1	0	0	0	0	.094
Jack Stivetts	67	221	42	76	9	6	3	49	4	.344
Fred Tenney	88	348	64	117	14	3	2	49	18	.336
Tommy Tucker (1B)	122	474	74	144	27	5	2	72	6	.304
George Yeager	2	5	1	1	0	0	0	0	0	.200
	132	4,717	860	1,416	175	74	36		241	.300

	W	L	G	GS	CG	IP	H	BB	SO	ERA
Cozy Dolan	1	4	6	5	3	41	55	27	14	4.83
Fred Klobedanz	6	4	10	9	9	80⅔	69	31	26	3.01
Ted Lewis	1	4	6	5	4	41⅔	37	27	12	3.24
Willard Mains	3	2	8	5	3	42⅔	43	31	13	5.48
Kid Nichols	30*	14	49	43	37	372⅓	387	101	102	2.83
Jack Stivetts	22	14	42	36	31	329	353	99	71	4.10
Jim Sullivan	11	12	31	26	21	225⅓	268	68	33	4.03
Bill Yerrick	0	3	4	3	2	23	42	13	6	10.57
	74	57		132	110	1,155⅔	1,254	397	277	3.78

Shutouts—Nichols (3), Stivetts (2), Sullivan
Saves—Mains, Nichols, Sullivan

1897

Record: 93–39
Finish: First
Games Ahead: 2
Manager: Frank Selee

The 1897 Beaneaters were the best team of record in franchise history. Their .705 winning percentage has never been equaled—and probably never will be matched.

A team would have to win 115 games in a 162-game schedule to better that percentage. Considering that the 104 games won by the 1993 Braves, who played to a .642 percentage, is the franchise record for victories, it's clear just how difficult it would be to win 115.

In spite of playing at such a torrid pace, Frank Selee's 1897 team had its hands full winning the pennant. In fact, Boston didn't clinch until September 30, and the Beaneaters finished just a scant two games ahead of Baltimore.

What a formidable pair of adversaries these two teams made for each other! The Beaneaters had four players headed for the Hall of Fame. The Orioles, who'd won the

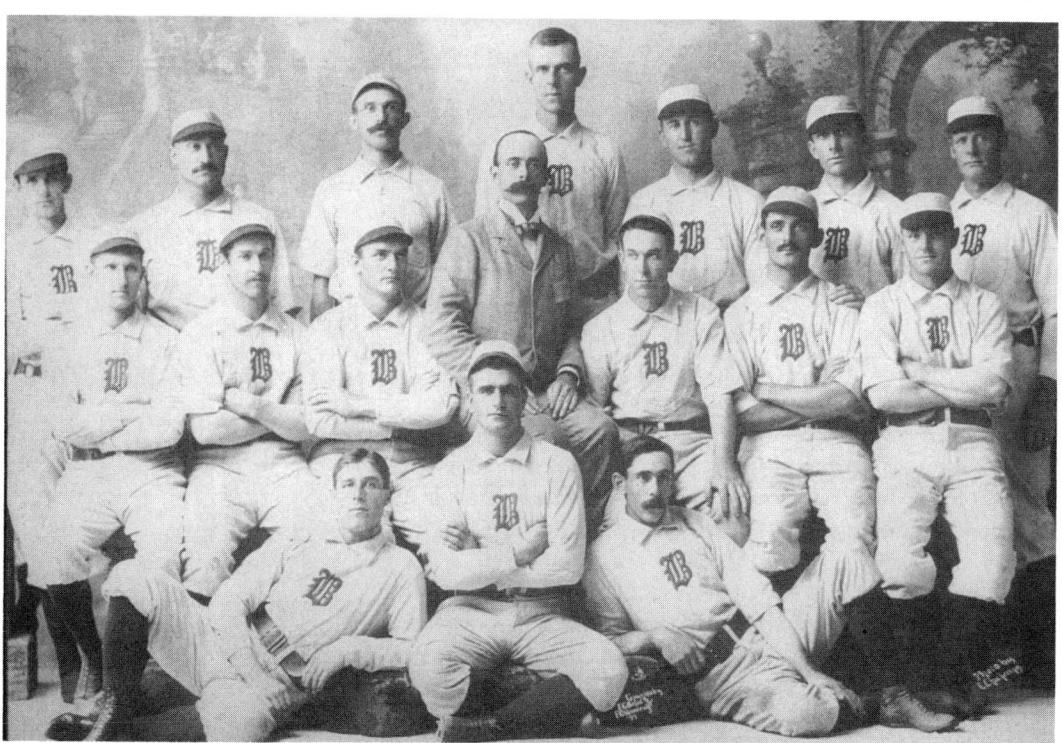

Frank Selee's Beaneaters of 1897 played to a .705 percentage, the best record in franchise history.

three previous pennants, had five, two who would get to Cooperstown more for their managerial accomplishments than for their playing deeds.

Boston had Jimmy Collins, the premier third baseman of the day, incomparable pitcher Kid Nichols, and outfielders Hugh Duffy and "Slidin' Billy" Hamilton.

Baltimore's future immortals were third baseman John McGraw and catcher Wilbert Robinson, solid players who would gain greater fame as managers; shortstop Hughie Jennings; left fielder Joe Kelley, who broke in with Boston in 1891; and outfielder "Wee Willie" Keeler, who "hit 'em where they weren't" in the first 44 games of the season.

Along with Collins at third, Boston also had first baseman Fred Tenney, second baseman Bobby Lowe, and shortstop Herman Long in a strong defensive infield. Duffy was in left, Hamilton in center, and talented rookie Chick Stahl in right, forming an outfield in which no one would hit less than .340. The pitching staff, of course, was led by Nichols, a perennial 30-game winner. He was followed by Ted Lewis and Fred Klobedanz, second-year pitchers who would have short but prosperous careers.

When the team started rather slowly—it was in sixth place on May 15—Selee made a move that wasn't popular with veterans but may have been what the Beaneaters needed to start them on a blistering pace for the rest of the season.

The Boston manager shifted Tenney from right field to first, benching longtime first baseman Tommy Tucker, and inserted Stahl in right. Some of the veterans brooded and referred to Tenney as "the spoiled collegian." To avoid prolonged discord, Selee sent Tucker to Washington.

Boston began to come to life in late May. On May 31, paced by Tenney's 6-for-8 performance, the Beaneaters used 29 hits to whip St. Louis, 25–5. On June 7, Selee's team moved into second place with a 4–0 win against Cincinnati.

Two weeks later, Boston won its 17th straight game, beating Brooklyn, 11–6, to take first place. The Beaneaters lost the next day, falling one shy of the club record 18 straight victories set in 1891. However, they had served notice to Baltimore that the battle had been joined.

On July 6, Boston won for the 28th time in 30 games, yet Baltimore and even Cincinnati were close on the Beaneaters' heels. All summer, the Beaneaters and Orioles went back and forth, sliding in and out of first place, never by more than a game or two.

On August 6 the Beaneaters beat the Orioles, 6–5, when Duffy threw out the tying run at the plate in the ninth inning. Boston beat Baltimore again the next day, but on August 27 the Orioles returned the favor, sweeping a doubleheader from Selee's club. Thus Baltimore moved back into first place by four percentage points—.683 to .679.

They continued to slug it out with each other through the first three weeks of September. On September 22, Boston won its last home game of the season, finishing 52–13 (.800) at the South End Grounds. But Baltimore still held first place by a percentage point, .707 to .706, setting the stage for the biggest series of the season, three games at Baltimore.

On September 24, the Beaneaters took over first place with a 6–4 victory in front of 13,000 Baltimore partisans. Nichols barely escaped with the win. The game ended when Keeler, batting with the bases loaded, lined to Long for a double play.

The next day, the Orioles won, 6–3, and regained the lead.

After an off day on Sunday, a paid crowd of 25,390 turned

out for the decisive game of the series. Another 1,500 people got in by breaking down a fence, and an estimated 5,000 others watched from nearby rooftops. Some people were sitting within 20 feet of home plate, and many overflowed into the outfield.

The pitching matchup was Nichols against Joe Corbett, a one-year wonder who finished the season with 24 victories. Because of the crowd squeezing the playing field, there were 15 doubles in the slugfest, won by Boston, 19–10.

Three days later, the Beaneaters clinched Selee's fourth pennant by beating Brooklyn, 12–3, while Baltimore was losing to Washington, 9–3.

The players and the team's fans were elated. They had played a full season of some of the best baseball imaginable, returned the National League pennant to Boston, and dethroned a talented team that had won the last three flags. They couldn't ask for more—but there was more ball to be played.

In 1894, Pittsburgh sportsman William C. Temple put up a trophy for the winner of a postseason series between the top two regular-season teams. The Temple Cup died after four years due to lack of interest, but it remained for the Beaneaters and Orioles to play the final series of the ill-fated competition.

Boston won the opener, 13–12, of what was no more than an exhibition. But Baltimore won the next four by scores of 13–11, 8–3, 12–11, and 9–3.

"We didn't have any interest in the series in 1897 after winning the pennant as we did in the last week," Tenney said years later. "We had beaten Baltimore in the competition that counted, and this was just something extra."

Duffy led the league in home runs (11) and was third in RBIs (129). Hamilton led in runs and walks and was third in steals. Collins was runner-up in RBIs (132).

Nichols led the league's pitchers in wins (31) and innings for the second straight season and was second in ERA (2.64). Klobedanz, a 26-year-old left-hander who had but 10 games of big league experience entering the season, led the league in winning percentage (.788) and was third in victories (26).

	G	AB	R	H	2B	3B	HR	RBI	SB	AVG
Bob Allen	34	119	33	38	5	0	1	24	1	.319
Marty Bergen (C)	87	327	47	81	11	3	2	45	5	.248
Jimmy Collins (3B)	134	529	103	183	28	13	6	132	14	.346
Hugh Duffy (OF)	134	550	130	187	25	10	11*	129	41	.340
Charlie Ganzel	30	105	15	28	4	3	0	14	2	.267
Billy Hamilton (OF)	127	507	152*	174	17	5	3	61	66	.343
Fred Lake	19	62	2	15	4	0	0	5	2	.242
Herman Long (SS)	107	450	89	145	32	7	3	69	22	.322
Bobby Lowe (2B)	123	499	87	154	24	8	5	106	16	.309
Mike Mahoney	2	2	1	1	0	0	0	1	0	.500
Chick Stahl (OF)	114	469	112	166	30	13	4	97	18	.354
Jack Stivetts	61	199	41	73	9	9	2	37	2	.367
Fred Tenney (1B)	132	566	125	180	24	3	1	85	34	.318
Tommy Tucker	4	14	0	3	2	0	0	4	0	.214
George Yeager	30	95	20	23	2	3	2	15	2	.242
	135	4,937	1,025*	1,574	230	83	45*		233	.319

	W	L	G	GS	CG	IP	H	BB	SO	ERA
Charlie Hickman	0	0	2	0	0	7⅔	10	5	0	5.87
Fred Klobedanz	26	7	38	37	30	309⅓	344	125	92	4.60
Ted Lewis	21	12	38	34	30	290	316	125	65	3.85
Mike Mahoney	0	0	1	0	0	1	3	1	1	18.00
Kid Nichols	31*	11	46*	40	37	368*	362	68	127	2.64
Jack Stivetts	11	4	18	15	10	129⅓	147	43	27	3.41
Jim Sullivan	4	5	13	9	8	89	91	26	17	3.94
	93*	39		135	115	1,194⅓	1,273	393	329	3.65

Shutouts—Klobedanz (2), Lewis (2), Nichols (2), Sullivan
Saves—Nichols (3*), Sullivan (2), Hickman, Lewis

1898

Record: 102–47
Finish: First
Games Ahead: 6
Manager: Frank Selee

The 1898 Beaneaters weren't quite as good, percentage-wise, as the 1897 team, but they were plenty good enough.

Boston won nine more games than it had the previous year, but its percentage (.685) wasn't quite as high since the National League returned to a 154-game schedule. The 102 victories tied Frank Selee's 1892 pennant winners for the franchise record, which stood until Bobby Cox's Braves won 104 (of 162) in 1993.

It was the fifth pennant in eight years for Boston and its eighth in the National League's 23-year history.

In spite of the team's high level of play, the route to the league championship was somewhat rocky, just as it had been the previous season.

An indication that there would be periodic trouble came early when the Beaneaters suffered the embarrassment of a no-hitter April 22. The pitcher was Baltimore's Jim Hughes, who was making just the second start of his short but successful major league career, and the score was 8–0.

Two and a half months later, on July 8, Boston was on the wrong end of yet another no-hitter, this one by Philadelphia's Frank Donahue by a 5–0 score.

Some championship team!

There was more than no-hitters to worry about, too. Hugh Duffy, a perennial .300 hitter, struggled most of the year and was dropped to eighth in the order. Only a September blitz got him to .298. However, he still finished fourth in the league in RBIs.

In late August, first baseman Fred Tenney missed two weeks with a leg injury, and the Beaneaters dropped nine of 12 games. Cincinnati, which led the league most of the season anyway, was able to slip back into first during the Boston slump. Duffy said the players were getting soft, and president Arthur Soden complained about the team's play.

Expectations were high, and the team wasn't delivering—but it would.

With Tenney back in the lineup, the team warmed to the challenge of winning another championship.

On September 5, the Beaneaters swept a Labor Day doubleheader against Washington. Rookie Vic Willis won the first game, 2–1, and Kid Nichols got credit for the second victory, 6–2, behind a home run from Jimmy Collins.

Cincinnati was dropping out of contention in a hurry, but Baltimore mounted a 12-game winning streak to put yet one more scare into Selee's club. The Orioles pulled within 2½ games on September 22, but they couldn't get any closer. Boston won nine of its last 11 games to pull away for its final six-game margin.

The team was 61–15 (.803) at home. Among the other season highlights were a couple of pitching performances by Ted Lewis, who would soon abandon baseball for a career in education that culminated with the presidency of two universities.

On May 17, only a ninth-inning single by opposing pitcher Joe Yeager of Brooklyn kept Lewis from authoring the second no-hitter in franchise history.

Then, on June 22, he turned in one of the finest relief performances in franchise history. With three runs in and two men on base with one out in the first inning against Chicago, Lewis replaced Willis and quickly got a double play to end the inning. Lewis then dueled the Orphans' Walter Woods over the next 13 innings, giving up just two runs and winning, 6–5, in the 14th.

The top offensive exploits included a 24-run outburst, the biggest in the league that year, in a 24–4 whipping of Louisville September 20. And on September 29, Collins hit two homers, one a grand slam, in an 11–10 victory. The Boston third baseman led the league with 15 homers, five more than his closest competitors. He also was second in RBIs (111).

Despite a knee injury, Hamilton had a big year, finishing second to Baltimore's Willie Keeler in the batting race (.369).

The key to the success of this team was pitching, though. And, as usual, that started with Nichols. If not for a tie between victories 9 and 10, "Kid" would have had a 16-game winning streak. He finished with his seventh 30-win season in eight years, leading the league in victories (31) for the third consecutive season.

What a staff Selee had, especially with the arrival of Willis, who won 25 as a freshman. With Lewis winning 26 and leading the league in percentage (.765) and Klobedanz adding 19 wins, the Beaneaters boasted what was then the finest four-man staff the game had seen.

	G	AB	R	H	2B	3B	HR	RBI	SB	AVG
Marty Bergen (C)	120	446	62	125	16	5	3	60	9	.280
Kitty Bransfield	5	9	2	2	0	1	0	1	0	.222
Jimmy Collins (3B)	152	597	107	196	35	5	15*	111	12	.328
Hugh Duffy (OF)	152	568	97	169	13	3	8	108	29	.298
Billy Hamilton (OF)	110	417	110	154	16	5	3	50	54	.369
Charlie Hickman	19	58	4	15	2	0	0	7	0	.259
Bill Keister	10	30	5	5	2	0	0	4	0	.167
Hi Ladd	1	4	1	1	0	0	0	0	0	.250
Herman Long (SS)	144	589	99	156	21	10	6	99	20	.265
Bobby Lowe (2B)	147	559	65	152	11	7	4	94	12	.272
Dave Pickett	14	43	3	12	1	0	0	3	2	.279
Stub Smith	3	10	1	1	0	0	0	0	0	.100
Chick Stahl (OF)	125	467	72	144	21	8	3	52	6	.308
Jack Stivetts	41	111	16	28	1	1	2	16	1	.252
Fred Tenney (1B)	117	488	106	160	25	5	0	62	23	.328
George Yeager	68	221	37	59	13	1	3	24	1	.267
	152	5,276	872	1,531	190	55	53*		172	.290

	W	L	G	GS	CG	IP	H	BB	SO	ERA
Charlie Hickman	1	2	6	3	3	33	22	13	9	2.18
Fred Klobedanz	19	10	35	33	25	270⅔	281	99	51	3.89
Ted Lewis	26	8	41	33	29	313⅓	267	109	72	2.90
Kid Nichols	31*	12	50*	42	40	388	316	85	138	2.13
Jack Stivetts	0	1	2	1	1	12	17	7	1	8.25
Mike Sullivan	0	1	3	2	0	12	19	9	1	12.00
Vic Willis	25	13	41	38	29	311	264	148	160	2.84
	102*	47		152	127	1,340	1,186	470	432	2.98

Shutouts—Nichols (5), Hickman, Lewis, Willis
Saves—Nichols (4*), Hickman (2), Lewis (2)

1899

Record: 95–57
Finish: Second
Games Behind: 8
Manager: Frank Selee

By looking at the statistics of the 1899 Beaneaters, it is difficult to imagine that the team didn't win a third consecutive pennant or at least make a better run at Brooklyn, which finished eight games ahead of Boston.

Brooklyn did have a strong team, since Baltimore owner Harry B. Von der Horst bought control of that team and transferred many of his better players to what became known as the Superbas.

However, the Beaneaters had a formidable team of their own. They again had the best pitching and the best defense in the league. Kid Nichols finally began to show the wear and tear of an incredible decade of pitching, but Vic Willis took over as perhaps the best pitcher in the league.

The offensive production of Billy Hamilton, Hugh Duffy, and Jimmy Collins all fell off significantly, but Fred Tenney and Chick Stahl had their best seasons and helped take up the slack. Boston scored nearly as many runs as Brooklyn, hit more home runs, and batted only four points lower (.287 to .291).

Though Nichols won "only" 21 games, he still was one of the better pitchers in the league. On July 14, he pitched a one-hitter against Pittsburgh, the lone hit coming off the bat of opposing pitcher Jack Chesbro, a future Hall of Famer making just his second appearance.

On August 7, Willis pitched the second no-hitter in franchise history, beating Washington, 7–1. Willis's unique "drop" pitch was so effective that later in the season, he worked a complete game against Pittsburgh without a single putout being made by the Boston outfield.

Tenney, the popular first baseman, had his best season, and right fielder Stahl also was among the league leaders in several departments.

Collins may have lost 51 points off his batting average and two-thirds of his home run total (15 to 5) from the previous year, but he remained the best third baseman in the league. He set a record for chances at his position (601).

	G	AB	R	H	2B	3B	HR	RBI	SB	AVG
Marty Bergen (C)	72	260	32	67	11	3	1	34	4	.258
Boileryard Clarke	60	223	25	50	3	2	2	32	2	.224
Jimmy Collins (3B)	151	599	98	166	28	11	5	92	12	.277
Hugh Duffy (OF)	147	588	103	164	29	7	5	102	26	.279
Charlie Frisbee	42	152	22	50	4	2	0	20	10	.329
Billy Hamilton (OF)	84	297	63	92	7	1	1	33	19	.310
Mike Hickey	1	3	0	1	0	0	0	0	0	.333
Charlie Hickman	19	63	15	25	2	7	0	15	1	.397
Charlie Kuhns	7	18	2	5	0	0	0	3	0	.278
Herman Long (SS)	145	578	91	153	30	8	6	100	20	.265
Bobby Lowe (2B)	152	559	81	152	5	9	4	88	17	.272
Bill Merritt	1	2	0	0	0	0	0	0	0	.000
Chick Stahl (OF)	148	576	122	202	23	19	7	52	33	.351
Billy Sullivan	22	74	10	20	2	0	2	12	2	.270
Fred Tenney (1B)	150	603	115	209	19	17	1	67	28	.347
George Yeager	3	8	1	1	0	0	0	0	0	.125
	153	5,290	858	1,517	178	90	39		185	.287

	W	L	G	GS	CG	IP	H	BB	SO	ERA
Harvey Bailey	6	4	12	11	8	86⅔	83	35	26	3.95
Billy Ging	1	0	1	1	1	8	5	5	2	1.13
Charlie Hickman	6	0	11	9	5	66⅓	52	40	14	4.48
Frank Killen	7	5	12	12	11	99⅓	108	26	23	4.26
Fred Klobedanz	1	4	5	5	4	33⅓	39	9	8	4.86
Ted Lewis	17	11	29	25	23	234⅔	245	73	60	3.49
Jouett Meekin	7	6	13	13	12	108	111	23	23	2.83
Kid Nichols	21	19	42	37	37	343⅓	326	82	108	2.99
Chick Stahl	0	0	1	0	0	2	2	3	0	9.00
Oscar Streit	1	0	2	1	1	14⅔	15	15	0	6.75
Mike Sullivan	1	0	1	1	1	9	10	4	1	5.00
Vic Willis	27	8	41	38	35	342⅔	277	117	120	2.50*
	95	57		153	138	1,348	1,273	432	385	3.26

Shutouts—Willis (5*), Nichols (4), Hickman (2), Lewis (2)
Saves—Willis (2), Hickman, Nichols

1900

Record: 66–72
Finish: Fourth
Games Behind: 17
Manager: Frank Selee

During the 1899 season, several players were so upset by the moodiness of catcher Marty Bergen that they said they wouldn't play with him in 1900. They didn't have to do so.

On January 19, Bergen's father discovered a brutal scene at the catcher's farm in Massachusetts. Bergen had used a razor and an ax to kill his wife, their three-year old son and baby daughter, and then himself.

Not only did Boston experience its first losing season since 1886, but the club also finished a weak fourth, closer to last place than to third.

There was reason to believe 1900 would be much better than that. Not only was the nucleus back from 1899, but the Beaneaters also picked up outfielder/first baseman Buck Freeman, the reigning National League home run king, and pitcher Bill Dinneen from Washington when that team sold its players and folded.

Dinneen won 20 games, but Freeman's home run output plummeted from 25 to 6. They were not enough to offset the simple fact that many of the team's stars were over the hill.

Shortstop Herman Long did lead the league in home runs (12), but Hugh Duffy played in only 55 games due to injury and had but 31 RBIs after driving in 100 or more for the previous seven years. Billy Hamilton, though still a better-than-average player, was just a year away from the end of his career. Boileryard Clarke replaced Bergen behind the plate and led the league's catchers with 27 errors. Fred Tenney's batting average dropped 68 points to .279.

Kid Nichols led the league with four shutouts but failed to win half his games, and Vic Willis, who still had six more 20-victory seasons in him, could win but 10 times.

Marty Bergen's dark moods of 1899 were a precursor of one of the grimmest tragedies in franchise history in 1900.

On July 7, Nichols beat Chicago, 11–4. It was the 300th victory of his career and came two months before his 31st birthday, the earliest any pitcher in history has reached that level.

	G	AB	R	H	2B	3B	HR	RBI	SB	AVG
Shad Barry	81	254	40	66	10	7	1	37	9	.260
Boileryard Clarke (C)	81	270	35	85	5	2	1	30	0	.315
Jack Clements	16	42	6	13	1	0	1	10	0	.310
Jimmy Collins (3B)	142	586	104	178	25	5	6	95	23	.304
Joe Connor	7	19	2	4	0	0	0	4	1	.211
Hugh Duffy	55	181	27	55	5	4	2	31	11	.304
Buck Freeman (OF)	117	418	58	126	19	13	6	65	10	.301
Billy Hamilton (OF)	136	520	103	173	20	5	1	47	32	.333
Herman Long (SS)	125	486	80	127	19	4	12*	66	26	.261
Bobby Lowe (2B)	127	474	65	132	11	5	3	71	15	.278
Chick Stahl (OF)	136	553	88	163	23	16	5	82	27	.295
Billy Sullivan	72	238	36	65	6	0	8	41	4	.273
Fred Tenney (1B)	112	437	77	122	13	5	1	56	17	.279
	142	4,952	778	1,403	163	68	48*		182	.283

	W	L	G	GS	CG	IP	H	BB	SO	ERA
Harvey Bailey	0	0	4	1	0	20	24	11	9	4.95
Jerome Chambers	0	0	1	0	0	4	5	5	2	11.25
Nig Cuppy	8	4	17	13	9	105⅓	107	24	23	3.08
Bill Dinneen	20	14	40	37	33	320⅔	304	105	107	3.12
Ted Lewis	13	12	30	22	19	209	215	86	66	4.13
Kid Nichols	13	16	29	27	25	231⅓	215	72	53	3.07
Togie Pittinger	2	9	18	13	8	114	135	54	27	5.13
Vic Willis	10	17	32	29	22	236	258	106	53	4.19
	66	72		142	116	1,240⅓	1,263	463	340	3.72

Shutouts—Nichols (4*), Willis (2), Dinneen, Lewis
Saves—Chambers, Cuppy

1901

Record: 69–69
Finish: Fifth
Games Behind: 20½
Manager: Frank Selee

This season marked the beginning of the so-called modern era of baseball. It was the year the American League was born, if on hostile terms, providing the basic structure for the major leagues we know today.

Unfortunately for the Beaneaters, it meant the club once again had competition for the Boston fans. The city's American League franchise was called the Somersets.

While the battle at the box office was a definite concern for the club, its performance on the field was even more of a problem, so much so that Frank Selee's 12-year reign as manager would end with a fifth-place finish. In those dozen seasons, he won five pennants and established standards for winning that probably will never be equaled.

The start-up of the American League hurt the Beaneaters in more ways than one. Two of the club's best players, Hugh Duffy and Jimmy Collins, departed to manage in the new league. Duffy directed Milwaukee, and Collins stayed in town to manage the Somersets. Collins also persuaded outfielder Chick Stahl, slugger Buck Freeman, and pitcher Ted Lewis to follow him. Catcher Billy Sullivan left the Beaneaters, too, to play for the Chicago entry in the new league.

The Beaneaters' owners did not fight to keep players, and that decision proved costly. By mid-June, they were trailing the Somersets in attendance and were forced to drop admission from 50 cents to a quarter to match the American

Chick Stahl jumped from the Beaneaters to Boston's new American League franchise in 1901 and found himself in the first World Series two years later.

League team. Nevertheless, the Somersets, who finished second by just four games, drew some 200,000 more fans for the year than the fifth-place Beaneaters.

How quickly the mighty had fallen! Three years earlier, the Beaneaters were the toast of Boston and the entire National League. Now, they were playing second fiddle to the new guys in town.

Selee had a decent pitching staff but a puny offense. The club had the worst batting average (.249) in the league and scored the fewest runs.

Vic Willis tied for the league lead in shutouts (6) and should have had at least one more. On September 21, he worked 16 scoreless innings, only to lose, 1–0, in the 17th to Chicago's Tom Hughes.

Kid Nichols, Bobby Lowe, and "Slidin' Billy" Hamilton all played their last season with the team. Memories of the great clubs of 1897 and '98 remained, but that was about all.

	G	AB	R	H	2B	3B	HR	RBI	SB	AVG
Shad Barry	11	40	3	7	2	0	0	6	1	.175
Fred Brown	7	14	1	2	0	0	0	2	0	.143
Pat Carney	13	55	6	16	2	1	0	6	0	.291
Duff Cooley (OF)	63	240	27	62	13	3	0	27	5	.258
Fred Crolius	49	200	22	48	4	1	1	13	6	.240
Gene DeMontreville (2B)	140	577	83	173	14	4	5	72	25	.300
Daff Gammons	28	93	10	18	0	1	0	10	5	.194
George Grossart	7	26	4	3	0	0	0	1	0	.115
Billy Hamilton (OF)	102	348	71	100	11	2	3	38	20	.287
John Hinton	4	13	0	1	0	0	0	0	0	.077
Mal Kittredge (C)	114	381	24	96	14	0	2	40	2	.252
Herman Long (SS)	138	518	54	112	14	6	3	68	20	.216
Bobby Lowe (3B)	129	491	47	125	11	1	3	47	22	.255
Billy Lush	7	27	2	5	1	1	0	3	0	.185
Pat Moran	52	180	12	38	5	1	2	18	3	.211
Frank Murphy	45	176	13	46	5	3	1	18	6	.261
Joe Rickert	13	60	6	10	1	2	0	1	1	.167
Jimmy Slagle (OF)	66	255	35	69	7	0	0	7	14	.271
Elmer Smith	16	57	5	10	2	1	0	3	2	.175
Fred Tenney (1B)	115	451	66	127	13	1	1	22	15	.282
	140	4,746	531	1,180	135	36	28	449	158	.249

	W	L	G	GS	CG	IP	H	BB	SO	ERA
Bill Dinneen	15	18	37	34	31	309⅓	295	77	141	2.94
Bob Lawson	2	2	6	4	4	46	45	28	12	3.33
Kid Nichols	19	16	38	34	33	321	306	90	143	3.22
Togie Pittinger	13	16	34	33	27	281⅓	288	76	129	3.01
Vic Willis	20	17	38	35	33	305⅓	262	78	133	2.36
	69	69		140	128	1,263	1,196	349	558	2.90

Shutouts—Willis (6*), Nichols (4), Pittinger
Saves—Willis (2)

	W	L	G	GS	CG	IP	H	BB	SO	ERA
Pat Carney	0	1	2	1	0	5	6	3	3	9.00
Sam Curran	0	0	1	0	0	6⅔	6	0	3	1.35
Bob Dresser	0	1	1	1	1	9	12	0	8	3.00
Mal Eason	9	11	27	26	20	206½	237	59	50	2.75
Dad Hale	1	4	8	6	3	47	69	18	12	6.32
Fred Klobedanz	1	0	1	1	1	8	9	2	4	1.13
Red Long	0	0	1	1	1	8	4	3	5	1.13
John Malarkey	8	10	21	19	17	170⅓	158	58	39	2.59
Togie Pittinger	27	16	46	40	36	389⅓	360	128*	174	2.52
Vic Willis	27	20	51*	46*	45*	410*	372*	101	225*	2.20
	73	64		142	124	1,259⅔	1,233	372*	523	2.61

Shutouts—Pittinger (7), Willis (4), Eason (2), Malarkey
Saves—Willis (3*), Malarkey

1902

Record: 73–64
Finish: Third
Games Behind: 29
Manager: Al Buckenberger

The 1902 season began with Frank Selee, who'd built the Beaneaters into a powerhouse, managing Chicago's National League club. The dismissal of Selee was not a popular move with the players or with many other people in baseball who felt the team's owners made him the scapegoat for their failure to fend off American League competition.

Selee's replacement was Al Buckenberger, who'd managed Pittsburgh (1892–94) and St. Louis (1895) but who had been in the minors at Rochester most recently. He was only 41 years old but had been managing since he was 23.

Many of the Beaneaters' stars were gone. Second baseman Bobby Lowe went to Chicago with Selee. Pitcher Bill Dinneen jumped to Boston's American League team. Kid Nichols was released, as was Billy Hamilton.

Buckenberger brought his first Boston team in third, its best finish since 1899. However, that was deceiving because the Beaneaters were closer to last place than they were to first. The National League in 1902 was made up of Pittsburgh, who won the pennant by 27½ games, and then everyone else.

The Beaneaters led the league in defense (.959) and fewest errors and placed third in staff ERA (2.61). However, they were sixth in team hitting (.249) and had very little power.

Togie Pittinger and Vic Willis won 27 games apiece, tying for second in the league behind Jack Chesbro's 28 for Pittsburgh. Pittinger's seven shutouts tied for third in the league and set a modern franchise record that has been equaled but not broken.

Herman Long was still around, and though he wasn't much of an offensive threat, he led the league's shortstops in defense (.946) for the second straight year.

	G	AB	R	H	2B	3B	HR	RBI	SB	AVG
Fred Brown	2	6	1	2	1	0	0	0	0	.333
Pat Carney (OF)	137	522	75	141	17	4	2	65	27	.270
Dick Cooley (OF)	135	548	73	162	26	8	0	58	27	.296
Ernie Courtney	48	165	23	36	3	0	0	17	3	.218
Gene DeMontreville (2B)	124	481	51	125	16	5	0	53	23	.260
Charlie Dexter	48	183	33	47	3	0	1	18	16	.257
Ed Gremminger (3B)	140	522	55	134	20	12	1	65	7	.257
Mal Kittredge (C)	80	255	18	60	7	0	2	30	4	.235
Herman Long (SS)	120	439	40	101	11	0	2	44	24	.230
Billy Lush (OF)	120	413	68	92	8	1	2	19	30	.223
Pat Moran	80	251	22	60	5	5	1	24	6	.239
Fred Tenney (1B)	134	489	88	154	18	3	2	30	21	.315
	142	4,728	572	1,178	142	39	14	453	189	.249

1903

Finish: Sixth
Record: 58–80
Games Behind: 32
Manager: Al Buckenberger

The first modern World Series was played in 1903. A Boston team, managed by former Beaneaters third-base great Jimmy Collins, won it. But, the Beaneaters were not one of the participating teams.

In fact, only once before in their history did the franchise finish with a worse percentage or further from first place than it did in 1903. That was in 1885, when John Morrill's club was 46–66 and came in 41 games behind pennant-winning Chicago.

It was the Boston Pilgrims, with former Beaneaters Chick Stahl and Bill Dinneen, who represented the American League in the first World Series, beating Pittsburgh in the best-of-nine matchup, 5–3 in games.

And things would get much worse for the Beaneaters before they'd get their first World Series berth. As bad as the 1903 club was, the franchise was far from bottoming out.

Shortstop Herman Long was smart enough to skip town before the season, jumping to the New York Highlanders, where the powers of the game allowed him to stay even though the leagues had made peace and were no longer raiding each other. Fred Tenney took his place as captain and hit .313.

But Tenney couldn't do it all by himself, especially since the Beaneaters were the worst defensive team (361 errors) and the worst offensive team (.245 average) in the league, a bad combination in any season.

The pitching wasn't that bad, but the support was horrendous. Poor Wiley Piatt, in his only season with the club and his last in the majors, was saddled with the distinction of losing two complete games in the same day, the only man ever to do so in the 20th century. He lost to Pittsburgh, 1–0 and 5–3, June 25.

Most of the season carried a similar theme. Vic Willis, upset that the game's powers hadn't allowed him to escape to the American League (and who could blame him?), won but 12 times despite a 2.98 ERA. Togie Pittinger was third in the league in innings and fourth in strikeouts and probably was lucky to be only four games under .500 (18–22).

Pittsburgh's staff pitched a record six straight shutouts in June—three were against Boston. And New York's "Iron Man" Joe McGinnity pitched and won three doubleheaders in August—one was against the Beaneaters.

Surely, when part of the left-field bleachers in Philadelphia collapsed during a doubleheader, killing 12 and injuring 282, it was no surprise that the visiting team was Boston. It was that kind of season.

	G	AB	R	H	2B	3B	HR	RBI	SB	AVG
Ed Abbaticchio (2B)	136	489	61	111	18	5	1	46	23	.227
Harry Aubrey (SS)	96	325	26	69	8	2	0	27	7	.212
Frank Bonner	48	173	11	38	5	0	1	10	2	.220
Pat Carney (OF)	110	392	37	94	12	4	1	49	10	.240
Duff Cooley (OF)	138	553	76	160	26	10	1	70	27	.289
Charlie Dexter (OF)	123	457	82	102	15	1	3	34	32	.223
Ed Gremminger (3B)	140	511	57	135	24	9	5	56	12	.264
Mal Kittredge	32	99	10	21	2	0	0	6	1	.212
Tom McCreery	23	83	15	18	2	1	1	10	6	.217
Pat Moran (C)	109	389	40	102	25	5	7	54	8	.262
Joe Stanley	86	308	40	77	12	5	1	47	10	.250
Fred Tenney (1B)	122	447	79	140	22	3	3	41	21	.313
	140	4,682	578	1,145	176	47	25	479	159	.245

	W	L	G	GS	CG	IP	H	BB	SO	ERA
Pat Carney	4	5	10	9	9	78	93	31	29	4.04
John Malarkey	11	16	32	27	25	253	266	96	98	3.09
Wiley Piatt	9	14	25	23	18	181	198	61	100	3.18
Togie Pittinger	18	22*	44	39	35	351⅓	396*	143*	140	3.48
Joe Stanley	0	0	1	0	0	4	4	4	4	9.00
Pop Williams	4	5	10	10	9	83	97	37	20	4.12
Vic Willis	12	18	33	32	29	278	256	88	125	2.98
	58	80		140	125	1,228⅔	1,310	460*	516	3.34

Shutouts—Willis (2), Malarkey (2), Williams
Saves—Pittinger

1904

Record: 55–98
Finish: Seventh
Games Behind: 51
Manager: Al Buckenberger

The crumbling of the franchise continued in 1904 with its worst record and finish in the 29-year history of the National League. One of the Beaneaters' three partners, James Billings, left, selling his shares to Arthur Soden and William Conant.

Once again, the Beaneaters were made to look even worse in Boston by the fact that the Pilgrims repeated as American League champions. Former Beaneater Bill Dinneen had a big season for the Pilgrims, pitching an American League record 37 consecutive complete games and helping to douse a hotel fire to earn recognition as a hero.

It was to be Al Buckenberger's last season as the Beaneaters'

Kaiser Wilhelm was a 20-game loser in both seasons he pitched for Boston and had an unsightly .115 winning percentage in 1905.

manager, though time would prove that the club's woes ran much deeper than his work.

The team was every bit as bad as its record indicated. It had three 20-game losers (Vic Willis, Togie Pittinger, and Irvin "Kaiser" Wilhelm) and the worst staff ERA (3.43) in the league. Willis somehow led the league in complete games.

The team batting average (.237) was second-worst in the league, as was the defense, which was only slightly better than it had been the previous year. Shortstop Ed Abbaticchio made 78 errors, perhaps in large part because he was out of position. In 1908 with Pittsburgh, he led National League second basemen in fielding.

On the final day of the season, the team committed 10 errors against Cleveland. Everyone was happy just to reach the off-season alive.

	G	AB	R	H	2B	3B	HR	RBI	SB	AVG
Ed Abbaticchio (SS)	154	579	76	148	18	10	3	54	24	.256
George Barclay	24	93	5	21	3	1	0	10	3	.226
Rip Cannell (OF)	100	346	32	81	5	1	0	18	10	.234
Pat Carney	78	279	24	57	5	2	0	11	6	.204
Duff Cooley (OF)	122	467	41	127	18	7	5	70	14	.272
Jim Delahanty (3B)	142	499	56	142	27	8	3	60	16	.285
Phil Geier (OF)	149	580	70	141	17	2	1	27	18	.243
Bill Lauterborn	20	69	7	19	2	0	0	2	1	.275
Doc Marshall	13	43	3	9	0	1	0	2	2	.209
Gene McAuliffe	1	2	0	1	0	0	0	0	0	.500
Pat Moran	113	398	26	90	11	3	4	34	10	.226
Tom Needham (C)	84	269	18	70	12	3	4	19	3	.260
Kid O'Hara	8	29	3	6	0	0	0	0	1	.207
Fred Raymer (2B)	114	419	28	88	12	3	1	27	17	.210
Joe Stanley	3	8	0	0	0	0	0	0	0	.000
Andy Sullivan	1	1	0	0	0	0	0	0	0	.000
Fred Tenney (1B)	147	533	76	144	17	9	1	37	17	.270
John White	1	5	1	0	0	0	0	0	0	.000
	155	5,135	491	1,217	153	50	24	394	143	.237

	W	L	G	GS	CG	IP	H	BB	SO	ERA
Pat Carney	0	4	4	2	1	26⅓	40	12	5	5.81
Jim Delahanty	0	0	1	0	0	3⅓	5	1	0	0.00
Tom Fisher	6	16	31	21	19	214	257	82	84	4.25
Ed McNichol	2	12	17	15	12	122	120	74	39	4.28
Togie Pittinger	15	21	38	38	35	335⅓	298	144*	146	2.66
Joe Stewart	0	0	2	0	0	9⅓	12	4	1	9.64
Kaiser Wilhelm	14	20	39	36	30	288	316	74	73	3.69
Vic Willis	18	25*	43	43	39*	350	357	109	196	2.85
	55	98		155	136	1,348⅓	1,405	500*	544	3.43

Shutouts—Pittinger (5), Wilhelm (3), Fisher (2), Willis (2), McNichol
Saves—None

1905

Record: 51–103
Finish: Seventh
Games Behind: 54½
Manager: Fred Tenney

The Beaneaters continued to reach new depths in 1905. Ownership didn't do local favorite Fred Tenney any favor by naming him manager to replace Al Buckenberger. But at least Tenney knew what he was getting into.

At this point, club president Arthur Soden and partner William Conant were interested in only one thing—getting out. They told Tenney not to worry about losing games, only money, and offered him a bonus if he avoided red ink. Tenney took them seriously, climbing into the stands to retrieve balls and getting into a fight with Hall of Fame umpire Bill Klem, whom Tenney accused of keeping balls. And Tenney got his bonus.

The Beaneaters found what kind of season it was going to be on opening day when they lost to the Giants, 10–1, at the Polo Grounds. It never got any better, especially for starting pitcher "Kaiser" Wilhelm who would lose 22 more times. He had plenty of company, though.

Vic Willis, Irv "Young Cy" Young, and Chick Fraser all lost 20 or more, Willis dropping a modern record 29 decisions. It was the veteran right-hander's last year in Boston, but he was far from through. Once he got out of town, he strung together four straight 20-victory seasons for Pittsburgh.

This was the first time a team had four 20-game losers, and it would happen only one more time in history. The Beaneaters got that honor, too, only a year later.

Young seemed to be quite a find. A 28-year-old rookie left-hander, he led the league in complete games and innings and was second to Hall of Famer Christy Mathewson in shutouts with six. He may have lost 21, but he also managed to win 20 with a very bad team.

For years, Young was a fireman on the Boston and Maine Railroad, pitching only on weekends until a scout named Billy Hamilton, who'd served the franchise quite well as a player, signed him in 1904. Young was being compared to Cy himself, and late in the season, Pittsburgh tried to buy him for $7,500. The Beaneaters should have taken the deal. "Young Cy" fizzled quickly.

Pat Moran, who led the league's catchers in defense, performed a rarity August 10 when he had three of his five triples for the season. He's the last catcher to triple thrice in the same game.

Besides managing and chasing foul balls, Tenney still played a pretty good first base. His 152 assists for the season stood as a record at the position until 1986 when it was broken by Sid Bream, then of the Pirates.

	G	AB	R	H	2B	3B	HR	RBI	SB	AVG
Ed Abbaticchio (SS)	153	610*	70	170	25	12	3	41	30	.279
George Barclay	29	108	5	19	1	0	0	7	2	.176
Rip Cannell (OF)	154	567	52	140	14	4	0	36	17	.247
Jim Delahanty (OF)	125	461	50	119	11	8	5	55	12	.258
Cozy Dolan (OF)	112	433	44	119	11	7	3	48	21	.275
Bill Lauterborn	67	200	11	37	1	1	0	9	1	.185
Bill McCarthy	1	3	0	0	0	0	0	0	0	.000
Pat Moran (C)	85	267	22	64	11	5	2	22	3	.240
Dave Murphy	3	11	0	2	0	0	0	1	0	.182
Tom Needham	83	271	21	59	6	1	2	17	3	.218
Fred Raymer (2B)	137	498	26	105	14	2	0	31	15	.211
Bud Sharpe	46	170	8	31	3	2	0	11	0	.182
Gabby Street	3	12	0	2	0	0	0	0	1	.167
Allie Strobel	5	19	1	2	0	0	0	2	0	.105
Fred Tenney (1B)	149	549	84	158	18	3	0	28	17	.288
Harry Wolverton (3B)	122	463	38	104	15	7	2	55	10	.225
	156	5,190	468	1,217	148	52	17	387	132	.234

	W	L	G	GS	CG	IP	H	BB	SO	ERA
Jim Delahanty	0	0	1	1	0	2	5	0	0	4.50
Cozy Dolan	0	1	2	0	0	4	7	1	1	9.00
Chick Fraser	14	21	39	38	35	334⅓	320	149*	130	3.28
Dick Harley	2	5	9	4	4	65⅔	72	19	19	4.66
Frank Hershey	0	1	1	1	0	4	5	2	1	6.75
Fred Tenney	0	0	1	0	0	2	5	1	0	4.50
Jake Volz	0	2	3	2	0	8⅔	12	8	1	10.38
Kaiser Wilhelm	3	23	34	27	23	242⅓	287	75	76	4.53
Vic Willis	12	29*	41	41	36	342	340*	107	149	3.21
Irv Young	20	21	43	42*	41*	378*	337	71	156	2.90
	51	103		156	139*	1,383	1,390	433	533	3.52

Shutouts—Young (6), Willis (4), Fraser (2), Harley
Saves—None

1906

Record: 49–102
Finish: Eighth
Games Behind: 66½
Manager: Fred Tenney

Last in hitting, last in pitching, last in fielding, and last in the National League. That was the 1906 Beaneaters, who finished further from first place than any other team in franchise history.

The first edition of the club ever to finish last, Fred Tenney's team had a batting average of .226, a staff ERA of 3.14, and a composite fielding percentage of .947. None of the other seven teams in the league could do worse in any of the three departments. And, for the second straight year, Boston had four 20-game losers.

But things didn't look so glum on opening day. Johnny Bates, a rookie outfielder, became the first player in modern history to hit a home run in his first big league at bat. And Irv Young pitched a one-hitter, beating Brooklyn, 2–0.

If only they could have quit right there. Instead, they went about embarrassing themselves for the next six months.

From May 17 to June 8, the Beaneaters lost a franchise-record 19 in a row. Among other distinctions, they were shut out 28 times, including four straight games in May. The Pirates alone shut them out 10 times. Third baseman Dave Brain made five errors on June 11, a modern record, and it rubbed off on the other players. The team was charged with 11 errors for the day.

Tenney was so desperate he'd try anything. In this case, that meant "Happy" Jack Cameron, a sign painter "discovered" in a sandlot game on Boston Common.

An outfielder who couldn't hit, Cameron was given a chance to pitch. After a scoreless five-inning relief appearance, he started against the Cardinals September 26. He gave up a leadoff single, then was struck in the head by a line drive off the bat of Al Burch. The ball caromed back to catcher Jack O'Neill, who caught it and threw to Tenney at first, doubling off the runner. Cameron never played another game in the majors, abandoning a career ERA of 0.00 to protect his cranial well-being.

The other "tryouts" included Gene Good, a 5–6, 126-pound musician, actor, and wannabe outfielder who somehow managed to get 119 at bats and just 18 hits—all singles.

At the end of the season, Arthur Soden and William Conant finally unloaded their burden. The purchaser was John Harris, a Pittsburgh businessman, but he allowed the Dovey brothers, George and John, to run the franchise. Tenney helped negotiate the transaction, thus discovering the only way a manager could keep his job after such a miserable season.

	G	AB	R	H	2B	3B	HR	RBI	SB	AVG
Johnny Bates (OF)	140	504	52	127	21	5	6	54	9	.252
Dave Brain (3B)	139	525	43	131	19	5	5	45	11	.250
Al Bridwell (SS)	120	459	41	104	9	1	0	22	6	.227
Sam Brown	71	231	12	48	6	1	0	20	4	.208
Jack Cameron	18	61	3	11	0	0	0	4	0	.180
Frank Connaughton	12	44	3	9	0	0	0	1	1	.205
Ernie Diehl	3	11	1	5	0	1	0	0	0	.455
Cozy Dolan (OF)	152	549	54	136	20	4	0	39	17	.248
Gene Good	34	119	4	18	0	0	0	0	2	.151
Del Howard (OF)	147	545	46	142	19	8	1	54	17	.261
Tommy Madden	4	15	1	4	0	0	0	0	0	.267
Tom Needham (C)	83	285	11	54	8	2	1	12	3	.189
Jack O'Neill	61	167	14	30	5	1	0	4	0	.180
Big Jeff Pfeffer	60	158	10	31	3	3	1	11	4	.196
Jack Schulte	2	7	0	0	0	0	0	0	0	.000
Chet Spencer	8	27	1	4	1	0	0	0	0	.148
Allie Strobel (2B)	100	317	28	64	10	3	1	24	2	.202
Fred Tenney (1B)	143	544	61	154	12	8	1	28	17	.283
	152	4,925	408	1,115	136	43	16	330	93	.226

	W	L	G	GS	CG	IP	H	BB	SO	ERA
Jack Cameron	0	0	2	1	0	6	4	6	2	0.00
Cozy Dolan	0	1	2	0	0	12	12	6	7	4.50
Gus Dorner	8	25*	34	32	29	273⅓	264	103	104	3.65
Vive Lindaman	12	23	39	37	32	307⅓	303	90	115	2.43
Bill McCarthy	0	0	1	0	0	2	2	3	0	9.00
Jim Moroney	0	3	3	3	3	27	28	12	11	5.33
Big Jeff Pfeffer	13	22	35	35	33	302⅓	270	114	158	2.95
Roy Witherup	0	3	8	3	3	46	59	19	14	6.26
Irv Young	16	25*	43	41*	37*	358⅓*	349*	83	151	2.91
	49	102*		152	137*	1,334⅓	1,291*	436	562	3.14

Shutouts—Pfeffer (4), Young (4), Lindaman (2)
Saves—None

Ginger Beaumont led the league in hits in 1907, the first of his three years with Boston.

1907

Record: 58–90
Finish: Seventh
Games Behind: 47
Manager: Fred Tenney

If you can't beat 'em, change your nickname. That's a policy that was followed a few times in franchise history, including 1907. Entrenched in a string of miserable seasons but with new ownership offering a ray of hope, the team became known as the Doves, rather than Beaneaters, after the Dovey brothers who operated the club.

The Doveys appeased the fans temporarily by making a couple of improvements in the South End Grounds. They added a new scoreboard and cushioned seats in the right-field bleachers. Several good players would have been a better idea.

Tragedy preceded the season. On March 29, outfielder Cozy Dolan died of typhoid fever in Louisville. The team canceled the remainder of its training camp.

Things would get better, but barely.

On May 8, Frank "Big Jeff" Pfeffer, who won just 31 games in a six-year career, pitched the third no-hitter in franchise history, beating Cincinnati, 6–0.

In 1990, Pirates fans named a group of their stars, including Barry Bonds, Bobby Bonilla, Sid Bream, and Jay Bell, the "Killer B's" en route to a division title. The 1907 Doves should have beaten them to it considering the work of outfielder Ginger Beaumont, third baseman Dave Brain, and shortstop Al Bridwell. Beaumont led the league in hits, Brain

led it in home runs (10), and Bridwell led all shortstops in fielding.

However, the net effect was strictly superficial. The team endured a 16-game losing streak, and though it managed to get out of the cellar and climb 19½ games closer to first than in 1906, 47 games out was still a long way from being competitive.

Thus, in December, the Doveys ended Fred Tenney's ill-fated three-year managerial term by sending him to the Giants in an eight-player trade.

	G	AB	R	H	2B	3B	HR	RBI	SB	AVG
Tom Asmussen	2	5	0	0	0	0	0	0	0	.000
Jim Ball	10	36	3	6	2	0	0	3	0	.167
Johnny Bates (OF)	126	447	52	116	18	12	2	49	11	.260
Ginger Beaumont (OF)	150	580	67	187*	19	14	4	62	25	.322
Dave Brain (3B)	133	509	60	142	24	9	10*	56	10	.279
Al Bridwell (SS)	140	509	49	111	8	2	0	26	17	.218
Sam Brown	70	208	17	40	6	0	0	14	0	.192
Bob Brush	2	2	0	0	0	0	0	0	0	.000
Frank Burke	43	129	6	23	0	1	0	8	3	.178
Izzy Hoffman	19	86	17	24	3	1	0	3	2	.279
Del Howard	50	187	20	51	4	2	1	13	11	.273
Joe Knotts	3	8	0	0	0	0	0	0	0	.000
Tom Needham (C)	86	260	19	51	6	2	1	19	4	.196
Jess Orndorff	5	17	0	2	0	0	0	0	0	.118
Newt Randall (OF)	75	258	16	55	6	3	0	15	4	.213
Claude Ritchey (2B)	144	499	45	127	17	4	2	51	8	.255
Bill Sweeney	58	191	24	50	2	0	0	18	8	.262
Fred Tenney (1B)	150	554	83	151	18	8	0	26	15	.273
Oscar Westerberg	2	6	0	2	0	0	0	1	0	.333
	152	5,020*	502	1,222	142	61	22	395	118	.243

	W	L	G	GS	CG	IP	H	BB	SO	ERA
Frank Barberich	1	1	2	2	1	12⅓	19	5	1	5.84
Jake Boultes	5	9	24	12	11	139⅔	140	50	49	2.71
Rube Dessau	0	1	2	2	1	9⅓	13	10	1	10.61
Gus Dorner	12	16	36	31	24	271⅓	253	92	85	3.12
Patsy Flaherty	12	15	27	25	23	217	197	59	34	2.70
Sam Frock	1	2	5	3	3	33⅓	28	11	12	2.97
Vive Lindaman	11	15	34	28	24	260	252	108	90	3.63
Ernie Lindemann	0	0	1	1	0	6⅓	6	4	3	5.68
Big Jeff Pfeffer	6	8	19	16	12	144	129	61	65	3.00
Irv Young	10	23	40	32	22	245⅓	287	58	86	3.96
	58	90		152	121	1,338⅔	1,324*	458	426	3.33

Shutouts—Young (3), Dorner (2), Lindaman (2), Frock, Pfeffer
Saves—Lindaman, Young

1908

Record: 63–91
Finish: Sixth
Games Behind: 36
Manager: Joe Kelley

The Dovey brothers decided on Joe Kelley to replace Fred Tenney as manager. A Hall of Famer with a .317 lifetime batting average, Kelley debuted with Boston in 1891, appearing in just 12 games. He'd have been better off if he'd never returned, even if he was a native of Cambridge, located just across the Charles River from Boston.

Kelley previously was a player-manager in Cincinnati for three-plus seasons, always finishing over .500 but never getting higher than third place.

Under Kelley, the Doves advanced to sixth place, which was the club's best finish since 1903 and would be as high as they would get for several more seasons. Nevertheless, they were still 28 games under .500 and 20 games out of the first division.

The team had respectable hitting and defense, leading the league in double plays, but it was burdened with the league's worst pitching staff. The team ERA (2.79) was the highest in the league.

The season marked the exit of Irv "Young Cy" Young, the 1905 rookie wonder, and the debut of Harley "Cy the Third" Young. They crossed paths in a trade with Pittsburgh, and neither stayed around long.

The Doves were no-hit by Brooklyn's Nap Rucker on September 5. In November, the Doveys asked Kelley to resign. Another one had bitten the dust.

	G	AB	R	H	2B	3B	HR	RBI	SB	AVG
Jim Ball	6	15	1	1	0	0	0	0	0	.067
Johnny Bates (OF)	127	445	48	115	14	6	1	29	25	.258
Ginger Beaumont (OF)	125	476	66	127	20	6	2	52	13	.267
Beals Becker	43	171	13	47	3	1	0	7	7	.275
Frank Bowerman (C)	86	254	16	58	8	1	1	25	4	.228
George Browne (OF)	138	536	61	122	10	6	1	34	17	.228
Bill Dahlen (SS)	144	524	50	125	23	2	3	48	10	.239
Peaches Graham	75	215	22	59	5	0	0	22	4	.274
Jack Hannifin	90	257	30	53	6	2	2	22	7	.206
Joe Kelley	73	228	25	59	8	2	2	17	5	.259
Dan McGann (1B)	135	475	52	114	8	5	2	55	9	.240
Herbie Moran	8	29	3	8	0	0	0	2	1	.276
Claude Ritchey (2B)	121	421	44	115	10	3	2	36	7	.273
Harry Smith	41	130	13	32	2	2	1	16	2	.246
Fred Stem	20	72	9	20	0	1	0	3	1	.278
Bill Sweeney (3B)	127	418	44	102	15	3	0	40	17	.244
Walt Thomas	5	13	2	2	0	0	0	1	2	.154
	156	5,131*	537	1,228	137	43	17	426	134	.239

	W	L	G	GS	CG	IP	H	BB	SO	ERA
Jake Boultes	3	5	17	5	1	74⅔	80	8	28	3.01
Bill Chappelle	2	4	13	7	3	70⅓	60	17	23	1.79
Gus Dorner	8	19	38	28	14	216⅓	176	77	41	3.54
George Ferguson	11	11	37	20	13	208	168	84	98	2.47
Patsy Flaherty	12	18	31	31	21	244	221	81	50	3.25
Vive Lindaman	12	16	43	30	21	270⅓	246	70	68	2.36
Charlie Maloney	0	0	1	0	0	2	3	1	0	4.50
Al Mattern	1	2	5	3	1	30⅓	30	6	8	2.08
Tom McCarthy	7	3	14	11	7	94	77	28	27	1.63
Big Jeff Pfeffer	0	0	4	0	0	10	18	8	3	12.60
Tom Tuckey	3	3	8	8	3	72	60	20	26	2.50
Harley Young	0	1	6	2	1	27⅓	29	4	12	3.29
Irv Young	4	9	16	11	7	85	94	19	32	2.86
	63	91		156	92	1,404⅔	1,262*	423	416	2.79

Shutouts—Dorner (3), Ferguson (3), Lindaman (2), McCarthy (2), Chappelle, Mattern, Tuckey, I. Young
Saves—Lindaman

1909

Record: 45–108
Finish: Eighth
Games Behind: 65½
Managers: Frank Bowerman, Harry Smith

As bad as the previous six seasons were, the next four were even worse. It would be the only time the team finished last in four consecutive seasons until the Atlanta Braves did so in the six-team National League West in 1976–79.

Frank Bowerman, a catcher/first baseman who came to the Doves from the Giants in 1908, was the next poor soul to attempt to manage the team. He wanted the job badly, and his politicking helped lead to Joe Kelley's ouster. However, he was gone by midseason.

Distressed by the club's poor play, Bowerman was sent home to rest for a few days. Shortstop Bill Dahlen handled the team in his absence. When Bowerman returned, he resigned with a 23–55 (.295) record. He was replaced in mid-July by catcher Harry Smith. There was no discernible difference in the team's play.

The team also sustained a shock when club president George Dovey died suddenly June 19 at age 48 on a scouting trip to Ohio. His brother John replaced him as president of the club.

On the field, the team lost 13 straight at home and played to an overall .294 percentage. They lost 21 of 22 to Chicago and 20 of 21 to Pittsburgh. The team batting average of .223 is an all-time franchise low. And its .274 slugging percentage is a National League record low.

	G	AB	R	H	2B	3B	HR	RBI	SB	AVG
Chick Autry	65	199	16	39	4	0	0	13	5	.196
Johnny Bates	63	236	27	68	15	3	1	23	15	.288
Ginger Beaumont (OF)	123	407	35	107	11	4	0	60	12	.263
Fred Beck	96	334	20	66	4	6	3	27	5	.198
Beals Becker (OF)	152	562	60	138	15	6	6	24	21	.246
Frank Bowerman	33	99	6	21	2	0	0	4	0	.212
Jack Coffey (SS)	73	257	21	48	4	4	0	20	2	.187
Bill Dahlen	69	197	22	46	6	1	2	16	4	.234
Bill Dam	1	2	1	1	1	0	0	0	0	.500
Ernie Diehl	1	4	1	2	1	0	0	0	0	.500
Gus Getz	40	148	6	33	2	0	0	9	2	.223
Peaches Graham (C)	92	267	27	64	6	3	0	17	7	.240
Herbie Moran	8	31	8	7	1	0	0	0	0	.226
Bill Rariden	13	42	1	6	1	0	0	1	1	.143
Claude Ritchey	30	87	4	15	1	0	0	3	1	.172
Al Shaw	18	41	1	4	0	0	0	0	0	.098
Dave Shean (2B)	75	267	32	66	11	4	1	29	14	.247

	G	AB	R	H	2B	3B	HR	RBI	SB	AVG
Hosea Siner	10	23	1	3	0	0	0	1	0	.130
Harry Smith	43	113	9	19	4	1	0	4	3	.168
Charlie Starr	61	216	16	48	2	3	0	6	7	.222
Fred Stem (1B)	73	245	13	51	2	3	0	11	5	.208
Bill Sweeney (3B)	138	493	44	120	19	3	1	36	25	.243
Roy Thomas (OF)	82	281	36	74	9	1	0	11	5	.263
	155	5,017	435	1,121	124	43	15	338	135	.223

	W	L	G	GS	CG	IP	H	BB	SO	ERA
Jake Boultes	0	0	1	0	0	8	9	0	1	6.75
Buster Brown	4	8	18	17	8	123⅓	108	56	32	3.14
Bill Chappelle	1	1	5	3	2	29	31	11	8	1.86
Bill Cooney	0	0	3	0	0	6⅓	4	2	3	1.42
Cliff Curtis	4	5	10	9	8	83	53	30	22	1.41
Gus Dorner	1	2	5	2	0	24⅔	17	17	7	2.55
Chick Evans	0	3	4	3	1	21⅔	25	14	11	4.57
George Ferguson	5	23*	36	30	19	226⅔	235	83	87	3.73
Vive Lindaman	1	6	15	6	6	66	75	28	13	4.64
Al Mattern	15	21	47	32	24	316⅓	322*	108*	98	2.85
Tom McCarthy	0	5	8	7	3	46⅓	47	28	11	3.50
Forrest More	1	5	10	4	3	48⅔	47	20	10	4.44
Lew Richie	7	7	22	13	9	131⅔	118	44	42	2.32
Tom Tuckey	0	9	17	10	4	90⅔	104	22	16	4.27
Kirby White	6	13	23	19	11	148⅓	134	80	53	3.22
	45	108*		155	98	1,370⅔	1,329	543*	414	3.20

Shutouts—Ferguson (3), Brown (2), Curtis (2), Mattern (2), Richie (2), Lindaman
Saves—Mattern (3), Richie (2), Dorner

1910

Record: 53–100
Finish: Eighth
Games Behind: 50½
Manager: Fred Lake

The landmark of the 1910 season came May 19. The Doves—what an appropriately peaceful nickname—beat Pittsburgh for the first time in 26 tries. The team had another new manager, its fifth in four seasons, but the same last-place address as the year before.

Fred Lake, a catcher of little distinction with Boston in 1891 and again on the 1897 pennant winner, took over the club under rather unique circumstances. He'd just managed the Red Sox to a third-place finish in 1909 and asked for a raise because it was the team's first visit to the first division in four years. The Sox didn't agree with Lake and promoted scout Patsy Donovan to manager.

Perhaps thinking he could score a coup with the fans, Doves president John Dovey hired Lake, the team's fifth manager in four years. Harry Smith, who'd managed the club the second half of 1909, was content to simply catch in 1910. Smith, obviously, was a smart man.

This was the season right-hander Cliff Curtis lost 18 straight games, his last 18 decisions of the year, still a National League record for one season. Curtis's name was prominent on the sports pages in 1992–93 when the Mets' Anthony Young was in the process of losing 27 straight. Buster Brown wasn't far behind Curtis, losing 14 in a row. Together, they lost 47 games.

Al Mattern, a right-hander with a short and undistinguished career, somehow must have been inspired in the midst of all the ineptitude surrounding him. He set a modern Boston record by appearing in 51 games, but more significantly, he tied for the league lead with six shutouts. He had only three other shutouts in his career, none after 1910.

Another unexpected twist to the season came from outfielder/first baseman Fred Beck, who tied for the league lead with 10 home runs. He hit just 24 others in his five-year career.

The Doves seemed to have a promising rookie in Bill Collins, who stole 36 bases and led the league's outfielders with a .977 defensive percentage. He stole only six more bases in his career, though, and soon was out of the game.

The Doves were last in runs scored, errors, and defensive percentage. They were next to last in runs allowed, batting average, and ERA. They were awful.

On December 17, John Harris sold the franchise to a syndicate headed by William Hepburn Russell, a New York lawyer and city official, for approximately $100,000.

	G	AB	R	H	2B	3B	HR	RBI	SB	AVG
Ed Abbaticchio	52	178	20	44	4	2	0	10	2	.247
Fred Beck (OF)	154	571	52	157	32	9	10*	64	8	.275
Joe Burg	13	46	7	15	0	1	0	10	5	.326
Bill Collins (OF)	151	584	67	141	6	7	3	40	36	.241
Bill Cooney	8	12	2	3	0	0	0	1	0	.250
Rowdy Elliott	3	2	0	0	0	0	0	0	0	.000
Gus Getz	54	144	14	28	0	1	0	7	2	.194
Wilbur Good	23	86	15	29	5	4	0	11	5	.337
Peaches Graham (C)	110	291	31	82	13	2	0	21	5	.282
Buck Herzog (3B)	106	380	51	95	20	3	3	32	13	.250
Art Kruger	1	1	0	0	0	0	0	0	0	.000
Fred Lake	3	1	0	0	0	0	0	0	0	.000
Fred Liese	5	4	0	0	0	0	0	0	0	.000
Doc Martel	10	31	0	4	0	0	0	1	0	.129
Doc Miller (OF)	130	482	48	138	27	4	3	55	17	.286
Herbie Moran	20	67	11	8	0	0	0	3	6	.119
Bill Rariden	49	137	15	31	5	1	1	14	1	.226
Jimmy Riley	1	1	0	0	0	0	0	0	0	.000
Rube Sellers	12	32	3	5	0	0	0	2	1	.156
Bud Sharpe (1B)	115	439	30	105	14	3	0	29	4	.239
Dave Shean (2B)	150	543	52	130	12	7	3	36	16	.239
Harry Smith	70	147	8	35	4	0	1	15	5	.238
Bill Sweeney (SS)	150	499	43	133	22	4	5	46	25	.267
	157	5,123	495	1,260	173	49	31	421	152	.246

	W	L	G	GS	CG	IP	H	BB	SO	ERA
Buster Brown	9	23	46	29	16	263	251	94	88	2.67
Billy Burke	1	0	19	1	1	64	68	29	22	4.08
Cliff Curtis	6	24	43	37	12	251	251	124	75	3.55
Chick Evans	1	1	13	1	0	31	28	27	12	5.23
George Ferguson	7	7	26	14	10	123	110	58	40	3.80
Sam Frock	12	19	45	29	13	255⅓	245	91	170	3.21
Ralph Good	0	0	2	0	0	9	6	2	4	2.00
Al Mattern	16	19	51*	37	17	305	288	121	94	2.98
Jiggs Parson	0	2	10	4	0	35⅓	35	26	7	3.82
Lew Richie	0	3	4	2	0	16⅓	20	9	7	2.76
Lefty Tyler	0	0	2	0	0	11⅓	11	6	6	2.38
Kirby White	1	2	3	3	3	26	15	12	6	1.38
	53	100*		157	72	1,390⅓	1,328	599*	531	3.22

Shutouts—Mattern (6*), Curtis (2), Frock (2), Brown, Ferguson
Saves—Brown (2), Curtis (2), Evans (2), Frock (2), Mattern

1911

Record: 44–107
Finish: Eighth
Games Behind: 54
Manager: Fred Tenney

Club president William Russell bought out the last year of Fred Lake's contract and asked a familiar name, Fred Tenney, to manage the team. Tenney, who already had been through a miserable experience at the job in 1905–07, declined, because he said the club was "rotten."

No one argued, but Russell persuaded Tenney to take the position anyway by offering to buy some stock in the team that Tenney had been trying to get rid of for several years.

Russell also gave Tenney permission to make the changes necessary to turn around the club's fortunes.

Tenney revitalized the offense, but the pitching and defense were repulsive. Cliff Curtis, who entered the season with 18 straight defeats, lost his first five decisions for 23 in a row. On June 10, with a 1–8 record, he was traded to the Cubs in a seven-player deal.

The team, by the way, was now known as the Rustlers after Russell. Tenney made a lot of changes and shuffled players on and off the roster. Still, the Rustlers played to a .291 percentage—a club record at the time but one that actually would be surpassed. They lost 14 in a row at home in May and lost 16 straight later in the season.

Bill Sweeney was moved from shortstop to second base and had an excellent season, putting together a 31-game hitting streak that stood as the club record until Tommy Holmes' set what was then a modern National League record of 37 in 1945.

A pleasant surprise was outfielder Doc Miller, obtained from Chicago as a rookie in 1910. He led the league with 192 hits and lost the batting title by just one point to the great Honus Wagner. Wagner went on to the Hall of Fame, and Miller was never heard from again.

Late in the season, with attendance lagging, and for good reason, club treasurer Fred Murphy thought it would be a good idea for the team to sign 44-year-old Cy Young, who had been released by Cleveland. After all, the team once had Irv "Young Cy" Young and Harley "Cy the Third" Young; it might as well take a shot at the original. Besides already owning 507 victories, Young was popular in Boston, since he had spent eight seasons with the American League franchise.

Young didn't have much left, but he gave the fans a couple of thrills. On September 7, he hooked up in a duel with a sensational rookie named Grover Cleveland Alexander but lost, 1–0.

Five days later, Young was matched against Christy Mathewson of the Giants in a game that attracted 10,000 fans,

Boston's largest crowd of the season. New York routed Young early, and Mathewson, with a big lead, was lifted after two innings to save his arm for the pennant race.

On September 22, Young got it together one more time, beating Pittsburgh, 1–0, for victory number 511, the last of his incomparable career.

In December, Russell died. New Yorkers James E. Gaffney, a political contractor, and John Montgomery Ward, a lawyer and a great pitcher in the early years of the National League, bought 945 of 1,000 existing shares for $177,000. They were brave men.

	G	AB	R	H	2B	3B	HR	RBI	SB	AVG
Al Bridwell	51	182	29	53	5	0	0	10	2	.291
Art Butler	27	68	11	12	2	0	0	2	0	.176
Josh Clarke	32	120	16	28	7	3	1	4	6	.233
Bill Collins	17	44	8	6	1	1	0	8	4	.136
Mike Donlin (OF)	56	222	33	70	16	1	2	34	7	.315
Patsy Flaherty	38	94	9	27	3	2	2	20	2	.287
Wilbur Good	43	165	21	44	9	3	0	15	3	.267
Hank Gowdy	29	97	9	28	4	2	0	16	2	.289
Peaches Graham	33	88	7	24	6	1	0	12	2	.273
Buck Herzog (SS)	79	294	53	91	19	5	5	41	26	.310
Ben Houser	20	71	11	18	1	0	1	9	2	.254
Scotty Ingerton (3B)	136	521	63	130	24	4	5	61	6	.250
George Jackson	39	147	28	51	11	2	0	25	12	.347
Bill Jones	24	51	6	11	2	1	0	3	1	.216
Al Kaiser (OF)	66	197	20	40	5	2	2	15	4	.203
Jay Kirke	20	89	9	32	5	5	0	12	3	.360
Johnny Kling (C)	75	241	32	54	8	1	2	24	0	.224
Ed McDonald	54	175	28	36	7	3	1	21	11	.206
Doc Miller (OF)	146	577	69	192*	36	3	7	91	32	.333
Bill Rariden	70	246	22	56	9	0	0	21	3	.228
Harry Spratt	62	154	22	37	4	4	2	13	1	.240
Harry Steinfeldt	19	63	5	16	4	0	1	8	1	.254
Bill Sweeney (2B)	137	523	92	164	33	6	3	63	33	.314
Fred Tenney (1B)	102	369	52	97	13	4	1	36	5	.263
Bert Weeden	1	1	0	0	0	0	0	0	0	.000
Herman Young	9	25	2	6	0	0	0	0	0	.240
	156	5,308*	699	1,417*	249*	54	37	594	169	.267

	W	L	G	GS	CG	IP	H	BB	SO	ERA
Buster Brown	8	18	42	25	13	241	258	116	76	4.29
Billy Burke	0	1	2	1	0	3⅓	6	5	1	18.90
Cliff Curtis	1	8	12	9	5	77	79	34	23	4.44
Ed Donnelly	3	2	5	4	4	36⅔	33	9	16	2.45
George Ferguson	1	3	6	3	0	24	40	12	4	9.75
Patsy Flaherty	0	2	4	2	1	14	21	8	0	7.07
Sam Frock	0	1	4	1	1	16	29	5	8	5.63
Hank Griffin	0	6	15	6	1	82⅔	96	34	30	5.23
Brad Hogg	0	3	8	3	2	25⅔	33	14	8	6.66
Al Mattern	4	15	33	21	11	186⅓	228	63	51	4.97
Bill McTigue	0	5	14	8	0	37	37	49	23	7.05
Jiggs Parson	0	1	7	0	0	25	36	15	7	6.48
Hub Perdue	6	10	24	19	9	137⅓	180	41	40	4.98
Big Jeff Pfeffer	7	5	26	6	4	97	116	57	24	4.73
Fuller Thompson	0	0	3	0	0	4¾	5	2	0	3.86
Lefty Tyler	7	10	28	20	10	165⅓	150	109	90	5.06
Orlie Weaver	3	12	27	17	4	121	140	84	50	6.47
Cy Young	4	5	11	11	8	80	83	15	35	3.71
	44	107*		156	73	1,374	1,570*	672	486	5.08

Shutouts—Young (2), Donnelly, Pfeffer, Tyler
Saves—Brown (2), Pfeffer (2), Curtis, Hogg, Perdue

1912

Record: 52–101
Finish: Eighth
Games Behind: 52
Manager: Johnny Kling

For the first time in its history, the franchise was known as the Braves. The name stemmed from partner James Gaffney's political ties with the Tammany Hall regime in New York. The Tammany politicos were often referred to as

Cy Young didn't have much left when he got to Boston in 1911 yet he still managed the last four of his all-time record 511 victories.

"braves" because the Tammany Society was named after a Delaware Indian chief. The profile of an Indian chief replaced the old English *B* on the team's uniform jerseys.

Fred Tenney still had a year to go on his contract, but with a new nickname and new uniforms, the new owners figured they might as well have a new manager, too. Johnny Kling, a veteran catcher who came to the team from the Cubs the year before in the Cliff Curtis deal, was named Tenney's replacement.

Everything was new except the way the team played. Cy Young reported to spring training but left after three weeks, admitting his arm was shot. The Braves won eight more games than the Rustlers of 1911, but when a team is that bad, it's difficult to notice.

The ultimate disgrace came June 20 when the Giants set a modern record by stealing 11 bases against the Braves. New York led 14–2 after eight innings, then added seven more runs in the ninth. Boston came back with 10 in the bottom of the inning for a 21–12 final score. The 17 runs scored by the two teams in the ninth set a modern record.

Things were so bad that the Braves, trying to rally in the ninth from a 9–8 deficit to Brooklyn, got four hits and a walk but didn't score. Vin Campbell got a one-out single but was picked off first. Bill Sweeney and Jay Kirke singled, and John Titus walked to load the bases. Ben Houser then hit a grounder that struck Titus, resulting in a hit for Houser but ending the game.

The Braves led the league in most errors and highest staff ERA (4.17), yet there were some interesting individual performances.

Somehow, Buster Brown was just 4–15 but was fourth in the league in opponents' batting average (.239) and fifth in fewest hits per nine innings (7.81).

Second baseman Bill Sweeney had the best year of his career, finishing second in the league in batting average (.344), hits, and RBIs (100) and fourth in total bases. He also set a record for putouts at second (459) which lasted for 21 years.

Bill Sweeney strung together a 31-game hitting streak in 1911 and finished second to Hall of Famer Honus Wagner for the RBI title in 1912.

	G	AB	R	H	2B	3B	HR	RBI	SB	AVG
Al Bridwell	31	106	6	25	5	1	0	14	2	.236
Vin Campbell (OF)	145	624*	102	185	32	9	3	48	19	.296
Art Devlin	124	436	59	126	18	8	0	54	11	.289
Mike Gonzalez	1	2	0	0	0	0	0	0	0	.000
Hank Gowdy	44	96	16	26	6	1	3	10	3	.271
Ben Houser (1B)	108	332	38	95	17	3	8	52	1	.286
George Jackson (OF)	110	397	55	104	13	5	4	48	22	.262
Bill Jones	3	2	0	1	0	0	0	2	0	.500
Al Kaiser	4	13	0	0	0	0	0	0	0	.000
Jay Kirke	103	359	53	115	11	4	4	62	7	.320
Johnny Kling (C)	81	252	26	80	10	3	2	30	3	.317
Rabbit Maranville	26	86	8	18	2	0	0	8	1	.209
Ed McDonald (3B)	121	459	70	119	23	6	2	34	22	.259
Doc Miller	51	201	26	47	8	1	2	24	6	.234
Frank O'Rourke (SS)	61	196	11	24	3	1	0	16	1	.122
Bill Rariden	79	247	27	55	3	1	1	14	3	.223
Joe Schultz	4	12	1	3	1	0	0	4	0	.250
Art Schwind	1	2	0	1	0	0	0	0	0	.500
Dave Shean	4	10	1	3	0	0	0	0	0	.300
Harry Spratt	27	89	6	23	3	2	3	15	2	.258
Bill Sweeney (2B)	153	593	84	204	31	13	1	100	27	.344
John Titus (OF)	96	345	56	112	23	6	2	48	5	.325
Gil Whitehouse	2	3	0	0	0	0	0	0	0	.000
	153	5,361*	693	1,465	227	68	35	605	137	.273

	W	L	G	GS	CG	IP	H	BB	SO	ERA
Bill Brady	0	0	1	0	0	1	2	0	0	0.00
King Brady	0	0	2	0	0	2⅔	5	3	0	20.25
Buster Brown	4	15	31	21	12	168⅓	146	66	68	4.01
Walt Dickson	3	19	36	20	9	189	233	61	47	3.86
Ed Donnelly	5	10	37	18	10	184⅓	225	72	67	4.35
Hank Griffin	0	0	3	0	0	1⅔	3	3	0	27.00
Otto Hess	12	17	33	31	21	254	270	90	80	3.76
Brad Hogg	1	1	10	1	0	31	37	16	12	6.97
Rube Kroh	0	0	3	1	0	6⅓	8	6	1	5.68
Al Mattern	0	1	2	1	0	6⅓	10	1	3	7.11
Bill McTigue	2	0	10	1	1	34⅔	39	18	17	5.45
Hub Perdue	13	16	37	30	20	249	295	54	101	3.80
Lefty Tyler	12	22*	42	29	15	256⅓	262	126	144	4.18
Steve White	0	0	3	0	0	6	9	5	2	6.00
	52	101*		153	88	1,390⅔*	1,544*	521	542	4.17

Shutouts—Brown, Dickson, Hess, Perdue
Saves—Perdue (3), Dickson, Hogg

1913

Record: 69–82
Finish: Fifth
Games Behind: 31½
Manager: George Stallings

The value of a manager and how much difference he can make in a team is a subject often debated among those who closely follow the game. It is one of those arguments—like who's the greatest player of all time—that baseball people thrive on but that doesn't have a concrete answer.

Or does it?

Anyone familiar with the work George Tweedy Stallings—a native Georgian—did with the Braves might point to it as proof positive that a manager can have a major impact on a team's won-loss record. And, it would be next to impossible to argue that what was about to transpire in Braves history would have taken place without him.

When Stallings took over the Braves in 1913, he was the team's eighth manager in seven seasons. No one had held the job two years in a row since Fred Tenney was chasing balls in the stands in 1906–07.

The team Stallings inherited had finished last in four consecutive seasons, averaging 104 losses and 55½ games out of first. But with shrewd maneuvering of personnel and constant cajoling of his troops, Stallings improved the Braves by three places and 20½ games in the standings in 1913. The team's fifth-place finish was its highest in 11 years. It was quite a testament to his managerial skill.

Stallings used 46 players in 1913. They came and went with remarkable frequency. On August 25, third baseman Art Devlin got the game-winning hit in the ninth inning and immediately was shipped to Rochester, never to play in the majors again.

Key acquisitions in 1913 included outfielders Joe Connolly and Les Mann, first baseman Butch Schmidt and pitchers Dick Rudolph, Bill James, and George Davis. None were particularly accomplished, but Stallings knew how to get the most out of them.

Rudolph, for example, was a 26-year-old right-hander obtained from the Giants for whom he'd yet to win a game. He immediately became a solid starter for Boston on a pitching staff which improved its ERA by a run over 1912.

Handling pitchers was Stallings' specialty. Lefty Tyler, one of the few players from 1912 who survived under Stallings, continued his development, pitching a one-hitter against the Giants and leading the league in complete games.

Hap Myers, a well-traveled first baseman, stopped through for his lone season in a Braves uniform and finished second in the league in steals (57), setting a modern franchise record which stood until Otis Nixon came along in 1991. Myers, though, jumped to the Federal League in 1914 and missed the fun that was to come.

The Braves still had the worst defense in the league, and the offense wasn't a whole lot better. The team batting average of .256 was seventh among eight teams. As the season progressed, the team slowly showed improvement, climbing from the nether regions of the standings to fifth place by late August.

	G	AB	R	H	2B	3B	HR	RBI	SB	AVG
Drummond Brown	15	34	3	11	1	0	1	2	0	.324
Art Bues	2	1	0	0	0	0	0	0	0	.000
Bill Calhoun	6	13	0	1	0	0	0	0	0	.077
Otis Clymer	14	37	4	12	3	1	0	6	2	.324
Wilson Collins	16	3	3	1	0	0	0	0	0	.333
Joe Connolly (OF)	126	427	79	120	18	11	5	57	18	.281
Charlie Deal	10	36	6	11	1	0	0	3	1	.306
Art Devlin (3B)	73	210	19	48	7	5	0	12	8	.229
Rex DeVogt	3	6	0	0	0	0	0	0	0	.000
Oscar Dugey	5	8	1	2	0	0	0	0	0	.250
Hank Gowdy	3	5	0	3	1	0	0	2	0	.600
Tommy Griffith	37	127	16	32	4	1	1	12	1	.252
George Jackson	3	10	2	3	0	0	0	0	0	.300
Jay Kirke	18	38	3	9	2	0	0	3	0	.237
Bris Lord	73	235	22	59	12	1	6	26	7	.251
Les Mann (OF)	120	407	54	103	24	7	3	51	7	.253
Rabbit Maranville (SS)	143	571	68	141	13	8	2	48	25	.247
Jeff McCleskey	2	3	0	0	0	0	0	0	0	.000
Tex McDonald	62	145	24	52	4	4	0	18	4	.359
Bill McKechnie	1	4	1	0	0	0	0	0	0	.000
Bill McTigue	1	0	0	0	0	0	0	0	0	—
Fred Mitchell	4	3	0	1	0	0	0	0	0	.333
Hap Myers (1B)	140	524	74	143	20	1	2	50	57	.273
Bill Rariden (C)	95	246	31	58	9	2	3	30	5	.236
Butch Schmidt	22	78	6	24	2	2	1	14	1	.308
Joe Schultz	9	18	2	4	0	0	0	1	0	.222
Cy Seymour	39	73	2	13	2	0	0	10	2	.178
Fred Smith	92	285	35	65	9	3	0	27	7	.228
Bill Sweeney (2B)	139	502	65	129	17	6	0	47	18	.257
John Titus (OF)	87	269	33	80	14	2	5	38	4	.297
Walt Tragesser	2	0	0	0	0	0	0	0	0	—
Bert Whaling	79	211	22	51	8	2	0	25	3	.242
Guy Zinn	36	138	15	41	8	2	1	15	3	.297
	154	5,145	641	1,318	191	60	32	533	177	.256

	W	L	G	GS	CG	IP	H	BB	SO	ERA
Buster Brown	0	0	2	0	0	13⅓	19	3	3	4.73
Gene Cocreham	0	1	1	1	0	8⅓	13	4	3	7.56
George Davis	0	0	2	0	0	8	7	5	3	4.50
Walt Dickson	6	7	19	15	8	128	118	45	47	3.23
Lefty Gervais	0	1	5	2	1	15⅔	18	4	1	5.74
Otto Hess	7	17	29	27	19	218⅓	231	70	80	3.83
Bill James	6	10	24	14	10	135⅔	134	57	73	2.79
Win Noyes	0	0	11	0	0	20⅔	22	6	5	4.79
Hub Perdue	16	13	38	32	16	212½	201	39	91	3.26
Jack Quinn	4	3	8	7	6	56⅓	55	7	33	2.40
Dick Rudolph	14	13	33	22	17	249½	258	59	109	2.92
Paul Strand	0	0	7	0	0	17	22	12	6	2.12
Lefty Tyler	16	17	39	34	28*	290⅓	245	108	143	2.79
	69	82		154	105*	1,373⅓	1,343	419	597	3.19

Shutouts—Tyler (4), Perdue (3), Hess (2), James, Quinn, Rudolph
Saves—Tyler (2), Perdue

1914

Record: 94–59
Finish: First
Games Ahead: 10½
Manager: George Stallings

The history of a century and a quarter of professional league baseball is filled with hundreds of chapters of captivating stories and oft-unbelievable feats by individual players and teams. However, there is no other chapter quite like the story of the 1914 season.

The adventure of the "Miracle Braves of 1914" is one of the most treasured legends in all sports history. Unlike many legends, though, it is all true.

As much as the deeds of George Stallings' team have been glorified through the years, the fact is that the 1914 Braves were dead last in the eight-team National League on July 18. By going 51–16 (.761) in the second half and winning 34 of their last 44 (.773), the Braves not only sprinted from last place to a pennant clinching in little more than two months, but they wound up leading the league by 10½ games. This band of scrappy, unheralded overachievers then took four straight from Connie Mack's highly favored Philadelphia Athletics to complete the first four-game sweep in World Series history.

Stallings was proclaimed the "Miracle Man," and his team, forever after, was known as the "Miracle Braves."

Boston fans could barely believe how much the team changed from 1912 to 1914 under Stallings. Only four players—shortstop Rabbit Maranville, catcher Hank Gowdy, pitcher Lefty Tyler, and Swiss-born reserve outfielder Otto Hess—made it through the purge of 1913.

Probably the single most important event, other than the hiring of Stallings, that made the "miracle" possible occurred during the winter when Johnny Evers, of Tinkers-to-Evers-to-Chance fame, opted to leave the Cubs. The hard-driving second baseman served as player-manager for the Cubs in 1913, bringing the team to a respectable third-place finish. However, he was dismissed as manager for losing the city series with the White Sox.

Since he was unwilling to stay with the team just as a player, Evers was traded to the Braves for Bill Sweeney and cash. The Federal League was being formed at the time of the deal, and Evers used it as leverage to squeeze a $25,000 bonus out of the Braves. It probably was the best $25,000 the franchise ever spent. Knowing a leader when he saw one, Stallings installed Evers as captain.

"Anybody that comes to this team will either hustle with the rest of us, or we'll drive him off the team," Evers told sports writer Grantland Rice.

Spring training was held at Macon in middle Georgia. When the team broke camp for Boston, not even Stallings thought he had a pennant winner. However, he did tell the players that the Giants, who'd won the last three pennants, were the only club they had to worry about. That, in itself, must have been pretty heady stuff considering the franchise hadn't finished higher than fifth since 1902.

Of course, these players knew little of the club's history. They were young, inexperienced, and full of themselves. They were a perfect group for Stallings to mold.

But the pitching was erratic early. Stallings, a master psychologist, complained, "I have 16 pitchers, all of them rotten."

On top of that, Evers was sick, and Maranville had tonsillitis. When Boston lost 18 of its first 22, Stallings grumbled, "This bunch of mine is the worst looking ball club I've ever seen. They can't do anything right. I've never seen such luck. But don't think we're a tail-end team. It'll take us a month to get back in shape, but then we're going to be hard to beat."

It took more than a month, but in the end, Stallings surprised even himself with the accuracy of his prophecy. He and Evers were made for each other. They wouldn't let the players back down an inch. They kept them scratching and clawing until, little by little, the pieces started to come together.

Evers and Maranville were a perfect tandem around second base, enabling the Braves to lead the league in double plays (143) by a wide margin. Tyler, Dick Rudolph, and Bill James settled in to give Boston a solid starting rotation. The midseason purchase of third baseman Red Smith, an Atlanta product, from Brooklyn added some needed power to the lineup.

On July 3, the Braves were 26–40 and trailed the first-place Giants by 15 games. Boston lost an Independence Day doubleheader to Brooklyn, and Evers recalled, "Not only were we in last place on the Fourth of July, but just after the holi-

day, we lost an exhibition game to a soap manufacturing team. That's how bad we were."

But the tide was turning.

The Braves were still last on July 15, the halfway point of the season. But all eight teams were tightly bunched, with only 11½ games separating the top and bottom of the league.

On July 19, Boston climbed out of the cellar for good by sweeping a doubleheader at Cincinnati with a stirring rally in the ninth inning of the second game. The Braves were down 2–0 entering the ninth, only to score three times to win. They celebrated wildly on the field and jumped all over Stallings, who said, "Now we'll catch New York. We're playing 30 percent better ball than any team in the league. They won't be able to stop us."

From Cincinnati, the team went to Pittsburgh, where Maranville demonstrated to what extent the Braves would go to win a ball game. With the bases loaded and Boston batting in a scoreless tie, the impish shortstop took one for the team—literally. He leaned into a pitch which hit him in the forehead and knocked him to the ground. Umpire Charlie Moran said, "If you can walk to first base, I'll let you get away with it." Rabbit staggered down the line and, when he got to the bag, was replaced by a pinch runner. The Braves won, 1–0, and were on their way.

Since the teams were so closely bunched, the Braves were able to reach fourth three days after exiting the National League basement. They got only one hit in a loss to St. Louis, then reeled off nine straight victories, their longest winning streak of the season.

On August 10, they moved into second, and the Giants were hearing footsteps. The Braves went to the Polo Grounds for three games and won them all, Tyler outdueling the great Christy Mathewson, 2–0, in 10 innings in the final game.

On August 23, five weeks after they'd been in last place, the Braves moved into a tie for first. However, they didn't stay long and dropped to third for a few days. On September 2, the Giants dropped completely out of the lead for the first time when they lost to Brooklyn while the Braves were winning a doubleheader in Philadelphia.

But when the Braves returned home from a 16–6 road trip

The "Miracle" Braves of 1914 were in last place on July 18 yet won the pennant by 10½ games and swept highly favored Philadelphia in the World Series.

One of the most popular players in Braves history, Rabbit Maranville would go to any extent to win a game or to entertain the fans.

for a Labor Day doubleheader with the Giants, the two teams were tied. The Red Sox offered the use of Fenway Park for the remainder of the Braves' home games. A total of some 75,000 people packed Fenway for the Labor Day extravaganza, 35,000 in the morning and 40,000 in the afternoon.

The Braves trailed Mathewson, 4–3, in the bottom of the ninth in the morning game when Evers delivered a two-run double that made Rudolph a winner and sent the players and the crowd into a celebration. The Giants, however, brought them back to earth in the afternoon game, 10–1.

The rubber game was played the next afternoon before 17,000, and Boston got a three-hit performance from James for an 8–3 victory. The Braves led by one game—and they would not be headed the rest of the way. The Giants faded, and the Braves kept rolling.

The next day, Boston took a doubleheader from Philadelphia. In the second game, right-hander George "Iron" Davis, a Harvard law student, pitched the fourth no-hitter in franchise history, winning 7–0. Davis won only seven games in his career, six in three years with the Braves. The no-hitter was his only shutout.

When you're hot, you're hot.

Boston clinched the pennant September 29 by beating the Cubs. However, on the final day of the season, the Braves suffered what appeared to be a major setback when Smith, one of the team's few power hitters, broke his leg sliding. Stallings named defensive specialist Charlie Deal to play third in the World Series against Philadelphia.

How did the Braves do it? With strong pitching, tight de-

fense, timely hitting, a strong will to win, and the genius of Stallings.

Of the team's 19 shutouts, only one was pitched before the Fourth of July. The opposition didn't get much to work with in the second half.

Rudolph and James tied for second in the league in victories (26), just one win behind Grover Cleveland Alexander—and two ahead of Mathewson. They ranked high in many other categories, too, including complete games where they finished 2, 3, respectively, behind Alexander.

The Braves were second in the league in runs scored—only 15 behind the Giants. But left-fielder Joe Connolly was Boston's lone .300 hitter.

Stallings, who had morning practice for his team every day except Sunday, was praised for two methods in particular. He proved a team could win with a small pitching staff, and he demonstrated the benefits of platooning.

Three of his pitchers—Rudolph, Tyler, and James—combined to win 68 games. And never satisfied with his outfield, Stallings alternated players in center and right, using left-handed hitters against right-handed pitchers and vice versa. Only Connolly, a left-handed batter, played regularly.

Evers and Maranville were the heart of the team. Maranville was steady, if not spectacular, on both offense and defense. It was his first full season in the majors on the way to a legendary career now immortalized at Cooperstown.

There were those who felt Maranville was even the team's most valuable player, though it was the veteran Evers who received official recognition as such. Evers led the league's second basemen in fielding, had a fine season offensively, and provided the on-field leadership this team needed.

For his work, Evers received the equivalent of today's MVP award. He was presented the Chalmers Award—a Chalmers automobile—by winning a vote of sportswriters. The Braves dominated the voting, with Maranville finishing second and James third.

"Every man did his share," Stallings said. "It was team play that won. Stars couldn't have done it. There's no substitute in baseball for fighting spirit, and this team had it."

They may have had more of it than any other team in baseball history.

	G	AB	R	H	2B	3B	HR	RBI	SB	AVG
Ted Cather	50	145	19	43	11	2	0	27	7	.297
Wilson Collins	27	35	5	9	0	0	0	1	0	.257
Joe Connolly (OF)	120	399	64	122	28	10	9	65	12	.306
Charlie Deal (3B)	79	257	17	54	13	2	0	23	4	.210
Josh Devore	51	128	22	29	4	0	1	5	2	.227
Oscar Dugey	58	109	17	21	2	0	1	10	10	.193
Johnny Evers (2B)	139	491	81	137	20	3	1	40	12	.279
Larry Gilbert (OF)	72	224	32	60	6	1	5	25	3	.268
Hank Gowdy (C)	128	366	42	89	17	6	3	46	14	.243
Tommy Griffith	16	48	3	5	0	0	0	1	0	.104
Clarence Kraft	3	3	0	1	0	0	0	0	0	.333
Les Mann (OF)	126	389	44	96	16	11	4	40	9	.247
Rabbit Maranville (SS)	156	586	74	144	23	6	4	78	28	.246
Bill Martin	1	3	0	0	0	0	0	0	0	.000
Jack Martin	33	85	10	18	2	0	0	5	0	.212
Herbie Moran	41	154	24	41	3	1	0	4	4	.266
Jim Murray	39	112	10	26	4	2	0	12	2	.232
Butch Schmidt (1B)	147	537	67	153	17	9	1	71	14	.285
Red Smith	60	207	30	65	17	1	3	37	4	.314
Fred Tyler	6	19	2	2	0	0	0	2	0	.105
Bert Whaling	60	172	18	36	7	0	0	12	2	.209
Possum Whitted	66	218	36	57	11	4	2	31	10	.261
	158	5,206*	657	1,307	213	60	35	502*	139	.251

	W	L	G	GS	CG	IP	H	BB	SO	ERA
Gene Cocreham	3	4	15	3	1	44⅔	48	27	15	4.84
Ensign Cottrell	0	1	1	1	0	1	2	3	1	9.00
Dick Crutcher	5	7	33	15	5	158⅔	169	66	48	3.46
George Davis	3	3	9	6	4	55⅔	42	26	26	3.40
Otto Hess	5	6	14	11	7	89	89	33	24	3.03
Tom Hughes	2	0	2	2	1	17	14	4	11	2.65
Bill James	26	7	46	37	30	332⅓	261	118	156	1.90
Dolf Luque	0	1	2	1	1	8⅔	5	4	1	4.15
Hub Perdue	2	5	9	9	2	51	60	11	13	5.82
Dick Rudolph	26	10	42	36	31	336⅓	288	61	138	2.35
Paul Strand	6	2	16	3	1	55⅓	47	23	33	2.44
Lefty Tyler	16	13	38	34	21	271⅓	247	101	140	2.69
	94*	59		158	104*	1,421	1,272	477	606	2.74

Shutouts—Rudolph (6), Tyler (5), James (4), Crutcher, Davis, Hess
Saves—James (2), Tyler (2), Hess

1915

Record: 83–69
Finish: Second
Games Behind: 7
Manager: George Stallings

Because of the nature of the Braves team that won the 1914 pennant and World Series, many cynics suggested during the off-season that the effort was a fluke. Though the team did not repeat as champions in 1915, it did prove its legitimacy.

Boston finished a solid second, and if not for injury and illness, George Stallings' club probably would have put some serious pressure on the pennant-winning Phillies.

Johnny Evers, the league's MVP in 1914, hurt his ankle sliding April 18 and had to be carried off the field. He missed more than two months, a critical blow to the team.

Right-hander "Seattle Bill" James, who led the league in winning percentage the previous year on the way to 26 victories, got ill and had to spend a good portion of the season at home. James pitched in 33 fewer games and won 21 less than he did in the championship effort. At age 23, his career was over. He would appear in only one more big league game.

During the off-season, the Braves obtained outfielder Sherry Magee, one of the better hitters in the league, from Philadelphia for Possum Whitted. During spring training, Magee fell and injured his shoulder and was never again the same hitter.

Those three setbacks were more than enough to hamper the team in the early going.

On July 15, the Braves were in last place, just as they had been at the same point in 1914, bringing speculation that Stallings might work yet another "miracle." And, indeed, Boston did make steady progress, reaching second on September 24. They couldn't overtake the Phillies, but at least they showed they still had their spunk.

Dick Rudolph remained one of the best pitchers in the league, but he suffered from lack of support, winning only three more than he lost. Lefty Tyler had a similar problem.

The pitching staff had the second best ERA in the league, and the defense was the league's tightest. However, the team batting average of .240 was last in the league. Joe Connolly's .298 led the club.

On August 18, club president James Gaffney welcomed a

A hero of the 1914 team, Dick Rudolph beat the Cardinals, 3–1, in the first game ever played at Braves Field.

throng estimated as high as 56,000 to the team's new 43,500-seat home, Braves Field. Several thousand more were turned away from what was then the largest ballpark in the nation.

The Braves, behind Rudolph's pitching, beat the Cardinals, 3–1, in the first game at Braves Field. Gaffney had hoped the new park would host the World Series in its inaugural season—and it did. Unfortunately, the Braves were spectators. The Red Sox, who allowed the Braves to use Fenway Park in the 1914 Series, played their "home" Series games there to take advantage of more seats. And they won the Series, too.

	G	AB	R	H	2B	3B	HR	RBI	SB	AVG
Earl Blackburn	3	6	0	1	0	0	0	0	0	.167
Ted Cather	40	102	10	21	3	1	2	18	2	.206
Zip Collins	5	14	3	4	1	1	0	0	1	.286
Pete Compton	35	116	10	28	7	1	1	12	4	.241
Joe Connolly (OF)	104	305	48	91	14	8	0	23	13	.298
Dick Egan	83	220	20	57	9	1	0	21	3	.259
Johnny Evers (2B)	83	278	38	73	4	1	1	22	7	.263
Ed Fitzpatrick	105	303	54	67	19	3	0	24	13	.221
Larry Gilbert	45	106	11	16	4	0	0	4	4	.151
Hank Gowdy (C)	118	316	27	78	15	3	2	30	10	.247
Fletcher Low	1	4	1	1	0	1	0	1	0	.250
Sherry Magee (OF)	156	571	72	160	34	12	2	87	15	.280
Rabbit Maranville (SS)	149	509	51	124	23	6	2	43	18	.244
Herbie Moran (OF)	130	419	59	84	13	5	0	21	16	.200
Butch Schmidt (1B)	127	458	46	115	26	7	2	60	3	.251
Joe Shannon	5	10	3	2	0	0	0	1	0	.200
Red Shannon	1	3	0	0	0	0	0	0	0	.000
Red Smith (3B)	157	549	66	145	34	4	2	65	10	.264
Fred Snodgrass	23	79	10	22	2	0	0	9	0	.278
Paul Strand	24	22	3	2	0	0	0	2	0	.091
Walt Tragesser	7	7	1	0	0	0	0	0	0	.000
Bert Whaling	72	190	10	42	6	2	0	13	0	.221
	157	5,070	582	1,219	231*	57	17	496	121	.240

	W	L	G	GS	CG	IP	H	BB	SO	ERA
Jesse Barnes	3	0	9	3	2	45⅓	41	10	16	1.39
Gene Cocreham	0	0	1	0	0	1⅔	3	0	0	5.40
Dick Crutcher	2	2	14	4	1	43¾	50	16	17	4.33
George Davis	3	3	15	9	4	73⅓	85	19	26	3.80
Otto Hess	0	1	4	1	1	14	16	6	5	3.86
Tom Hughes	16	14	50*	25	17	280½	208	58	171	2.12
Bill James	5	4	13	10	4	68⅓	68	22	23	3.03
Dolf Luque	0	0	2	1	0	5	6	4	3	3.60
Art Nehf	5	4	12	10	6	78⅓	60	21	39	2.53
Pat Ragan	16	12	33	26	13	227	208	59	81	2.46
Dick Rudolph	22	19*	44	43*	30	341⅓	304*	64	147	2.37
Paul Strand	1	1	6	2	2	22⅔	26	3	13	2.38
Lefty Tyler	10	9	32	24	15	204⅔	182	84	89	2.86
	83	69		157	95	1,405⅔	1,257	366	630	2.57

Shutouts—Hughes (4), Nehf (4), Ragan (3), Rudolph (3), Tyler
Saves—Hughes (9*), Crutcher (2), Rudolph, Strand

1916

Record: 89–63
Finish: Third
Games Behind: 4
Manager: George Stallings

The World Series was back at Braves Field in 1916, but once again, it was the Red Sox who were hosting the games.

For a while, though, it appeared there might be an all-Beantown Series. The Braves were in first place as late as September 4 and made a strong enough run at the pennant that they were given permission to print World Series tickets. Though George Stallings' team finished third, it wasn't eliminated until October 2, two days before the end of the season.

The year began with the team being sold by James Gaffney to a Boston syndicate for $500,000. Former Harvard football coach Percy Haughton was elected president.

Haughton was new to baseball and professional sports. He started his regime by lecturing the players during spring training about swearing. He told them to say "nice" or "good" when they were upset rather than using profanity.

That day, a grounder to first took a bad hop past Sherry Magee, allowing a run to score. He shouted "good" over and over until he got to the bench at the end of the inning. Stallings exploded, and profanity was quickly reinstated in the team's protocol.

The strength of the 1916 team was pitching and defense. The Braves gave up fewer runs and made fewer errors than any other team in the league. Rabbit Maranville led the league's shortstops in fielding percentage (.947) for the first of five times in his career.

Tom Hughes, who relieved in more games than he started, led the league in winning percentage (.842) and also pitched the fifth no-hitter in franchise history. On June 16, he held Pittsburgh hitless and struck out future Hall of Famer Honus Wagner to end the 2–0 game. However, Hughes suffered a broken hand late in the season, a hindrance to the stretch drive.

Dick Rudolph had another excellent season, though it would be the last time he was really on top of his game. He won 10 in a row at one point. He and Hughes combined for 16 shutout innings against Cincinnati June 3, only to settle for a scoreless tie. The Braves managed but three hits, a familiar theme to the season.

The consummate showman, Rabbit Maranville demonstrates his famous "vest-pocket" catch.

Lefty Tyler tied for second in the league with six shutouts. As a team, the Braves had 21 shutouts—nine of them were 1–0 victories.

Hitting was another matter. For the second straight year, Boston was last in the league in team batting average (.233). Newly acquired first baseman Ed Konetchy (Butch Schmidt stayed in Baltimore to tend his butcher shop) led the regulars in hitting with a paltry .260 average.

Johnny Evers played in just 71 games because of an arm injury. His career was all but over, but since he had two more years on his contract at $10,000 per, he was in no hurry to retire.

	G	AB	R	H	2B	3B	HR	RBI	SB	AVG
Fred Bailey	6	10	0	1	0	0	0	1	0	.100
Earl Blackburn	47	110	12	30	4	4	0	7	2	.273
Larry Chappell	20	53	4	12	1	1	0	9	1	.226
Zip Collins	93	268	39	56	1	6	1	18	4	.209
Pete Compton	34	98	13	20	2	0	0	8	5	.204
Joe Connolly	62	110	11	25	5	2	0	12	5	.227
Dick Egan	83	238	23	53	8	3	0	16	2	.223
Johnny Evers (2B)	71	241	33	52	4	1	0	15	5	.216
Ed Fitzpatrick	83	216	17	46	8	0	1	18	5	.213
Hank Gowdy (C)	118	349	32	88	14	1	1	34	8	.252
Ed Konetchy (1B)	158	566	76	147	29	13	3	70	13	.260
Sherry Magee (OF)	122	419	44	101	17	5	3	54	10	.241
Rabbit Maranville (SS)	155	604	79	142	16	13	4	38	32	.235
Joe Mathes	2	0	0	0	0	0	0	0	0	—
Art Rico	4	4	0	0	0	0	0	0	0	.000
Red Smith (3B)	150	509	48	132	16	10	3	60	13	.259
Fred Snodgrass (OF)	112	382	33	95	13	5	1	32	14	.249
Walt Tragesser	41	54	3	11	1	0	0	4	0	.204
Joe Wilhoit (OF)	116	383	44	88	13	4	2	38	18	.230
	158	5,075	542	1,181	166	73	22	472	141	.233

	W	L	G	GS	CG	IP	H	BB	SO	ERA
Frank Allen	8	2	19	14	7	113	102	31	63	2.07
Jesse Barnes	6	15	33	18	9	163	154	37	55	2.37
Tom Hughes	16	3	40	14	7	161	121	51	97	2.35
Elmer Knetzer	0	2	2	0	0	5	11	2	2	7.20
Art Nehf	7	5	22	12	6	121	110	20	36	2.01
Pat Ragan	9	9	28	23	14	182	143	47	94	2.08
Ed Reulbach	7	6	21	11	6	109⅓	99	41	47	2.47
Dick Rudolph	19	12	41	38	27	312	266	38	133	2.16
Lefty Tyler	17	9	34	28	21	249⅓	200	58	117	2.02
	89	63		158	97*	1,415⅔	1,206	325	644*	2.19

Shutouts—Tyler (6), Rudolph (5), Barnes (3), Ragan (3), Allen (2), Hughes, Nehf
Saves—Hughes (5), Rudolph (3), Allen, Barnes, Tyler

1917

Record: 72–81
Finish: Sixth
Games Behind: 25½
Manager: George Stallings

The United States entered World War I in 1917, and the Boston Braves began a stretch of futility that would endure even beyond World War II. As bad as the franchise was in the early 1900s and in much of the 1970s and '80s, it was nothing compared to the funk of 1917–45.

Only three times in those 29 years did the team finish in the first division. In just six of those years did Boston win at least half of its games. Eight times the club won fewer than 40 percent of its games, and 12 times it finished 35 or more games out of first place.

In 1917, the Braves were expected to be contenders after finishing just four games out the previous season. However, they didn't get above fifth after May and finished sixth, their worst showing since 1912.

At least they led the way in patriotism. Catcher Hank Gowdy, the hero of the 1914 World Series, was the first major leaguer to enlist in the armed services.

Johnny Evers played in only 24 games before he was released to the Phillies. Tom Hughes couldn't pitch until August because of a hand injury.

The pitching and defense kept the club afloat, and the offense again was among the weakest in the league.

The highlight of the season was left-hander Art Nehf coming into his own. He strung together 40 consecutive scoreless innings late in the year.

	G	AB	R	H	2B	3B	HR	RBI	SB	AVG
Fred Bailey	50	110	9	21	2	1	1	5	3	.191
Larry Chappell	4	2	0	0	0	0	0	1	0	.000
Zip Collins	9	27	3	4	0	1	0	2	0	.148
Sam Covington	17	66	8	13	2	0	1	10	1	.197
Johnny Evers	24	83	5	16	0	0	0	0	1	.193
Ed Fitzpatrick	63	178	20	45	8	4	0	17	4	.253
Hank Gowdy	49	154	12	33	7	0	0	14	2	.214
Fred Jacklitsch	1	0	0	0	0	0	0	0	0	—
Joe Kelly (OF)	116	445	41	99	9	8	3	36	21	.222
Ed Konetchy (1B)	130	474	56	129	19	13	2	54	16	.272
Sherry Magee	72	246	24	63	8	4	1	29	7	.256
Rabbit Maranville (SS)	142	561	69	146	19	13	3	43	27	.260
Mike Massey	31	91	12	18	0	0	0	2	2	.198
Chief Meyers	25	68	5	17	4	4	0	4	0	.250
Ray Powell (OF)	88	357	42	97	10	4	4	30	12	.272
Johnny Rawlings (2B)	122	371	37	95	9	4	2	31	12	.256
Wally Rehg (OF)	87	341	48	92	12	6	1	31	13	.270
Art Rico	13	14	1	4	1	0	0	2	0	.286
Hank Schreiber	2	7	1	2	0	0	0	0	0	.286
Red Smith (3B)	147	505	60	149	31	6	2	62	16	.295
Walt Tragesser (C)	98	297	23	66	10	2	0	25	5	.222
George Twombly	32	102	8	19	1	1	0	9	4	.186
Lefty Tyler	61	134	8	31	4	0	0	11	0	.231
Joe Wilhoit	54	186	20	51	5	0	1	10	5	.274
	157	5,201	536	1,280	169	75	22	452	155	.246

	W	L	G	GS	CG	IP	H	BB	SO	ERA
Frank Allen	3	11	29	14	2	112	124	47	56	3.94
Jesse Barnes	13	21*	50	33	27	295	261	50	107	2.68
Cal Crum	0	0	1	0	0	1	1	1	0	0.00
Tom Hughes	5	3	11	8	6	74	54	30	40	1.95
Art Nehf	17	8	38	23	17	233⅓	197	39	101	2.16
Pat Ragan	6	9	30	13	5	147⅔	138	35	61	2.93
Ed Reulbach	0	1	5	2	0	22⅓	21	15	9	2.82
Dick Rudolph	13	13	31	30	22	242⅔	252	54	96	3.41
Jack Scott	1	2	7	3	3	39⅔	36	5	21	1.82
Lefty Tyler	14	12	32	28	22	239	203	86	98	2.52
Ed Walsh	0	1	4	3	1	18	22	9	4	3.50
	72	81		157	105*	1,424⅔	1,309	371	593	2.77

Shutouts—Nehf (5), Rudolph (5), Tyler (4), Barnes (2), Hughes (2), Ragan
Saves—Barnes, Ragan, Tyler

1918

Record: 53–71
Finish: Seventh
Games Behind: 28½
Manager: George Stallings

The Braves temporarily lost the heart of their team in 1918 when Rabbit Maranville enlisted in the navy. The spunky shortstop didn't forget his teammates, though. He got a 10-day leave and returned to hit .316 in 11 games. Even more remarkable, he didn't strike out in 38 at bats.

Boston, like other teams, had several players serve during the war. One, seldom-used outfielder Larry Chappell, didn't return, dying of influenza at an army camp that winter at age 27.

Because of the war, both leagues voted in July to end the season on Labor Day, September 2. The Braves probably were glad to go home early, even though they finally beat the Giants in their last game after losing 15 in a row to them.

Scoring runs remained the team's biggest problem. They were next to last in the league in that department. No better example existed than the August 1 game against Pittsburgh which the Pirates won, 2–0 in 21 innings. Poor Art Nehf, who led the league in complete games, worked a then-record 20 consecutive scoreless innings and still got a loss.

The war, the shortened season, and the team's performance kept total attendance at a Boston record low 84,938.

	G	AB	R	H	2B	3B	HR	RBI	SB	AVG
Fred Bailey	4	4	1	1	0	0	0	0	0	.250
Doc Bass	2	1	1	1	0	0	0	0	1	1.000
Chet Chadbourne	27	104	9	27	2	1	0	6	5	.260
Rip Conway	14	24	4	4	0	0	0	2	1	.167
Sam Covington	3	3	0	1	0	0	0	0	0	.333
Doc Crandall	14	28	1	8	0	0	0	2	0	.286
John Henry	43	102	6	21	2	0	0	4	0	.206
Buck Herzog (2B)	118	473	57	108	12	6	0	26	10	.228
Joe Kelly	47	155	20	36	2	4	0	15	12	.232
Ed Konetchy (1B)	119	437	33	103	15	5	2	56	5	.236
Rabbit Maranville	11	38	3	12	0	1	0	3	0	.316
Red Massey (OF)	66	203	20	59	6	2	0	18	1	.291
Tom Miller	2	2	0	0	0	0	0	0	1	.000
Buzz Murphy	9	32	6	12	2	3	1	9	0	.375
Ray Powell (OF)	53	188	31	40	7	5	0	20	2	.213
Johnny Rawlings (SS)	111	410	32	85	7	3	0	21	10	.207
Wally Rehg	40	133	6	32	5	1	1	12	3	.241
Jimmy Smith	34	102	8	23	3	4	1	14	1	.225
Red Smith (3B)	119	429	55	128	20	3	2	65	8	.298
Bob Taggert	35	146	19	48	1	4	0	4	4	.329
Zeb Terry	28	105	17	32	2	2	0	8	1	.305
Walt Tragesser	7	1	0	0	0	0	0	0	0	.000
Bill Wagner	13	47	2	10	0	0	1	7	0	.213
Al Wickland (OF)	95	332	55	87	7	13	4	32	12	.262
Art Wilson (C)	89	280	15	69	8	2	0	19	5	.246
	124	4,162	424	1,014	107	59	13	353	83	.244

	W	L	G	GS	CG	IP	H	BB	SO	ERA
Hugh Canavan	0	4	11	3	3	46⅔	70	15	18	6.36
Doc Crandall	1	2	5	3	3	34	39	4	4	2.38
Cal Crum	0	1	1	1	0	2⅓	6	3	0	15.43
Dana Fillingim	7	6	14	13	10	113	99	28	29	2.23
Lefty George	1	5	9	5	4	54⅓	56	21	22	2.32
Bunny Hearn	5	6	17	12	9	126⅓	119	29	30	2.49
Tom Hughes	0	2	3	3	1	18⅓	17	6	9	3.44
Ed Konetchy	0	1	1	1	1	8	14	2	3	6.75
Hugh McQuillan	1	0	1	1	1	9	7	5	1	3.00
Art Nehf	15	15	32	31	28*	284⅓	274*	76	96	2.69
Jake Northrop	5	1	7	4	4	40	26	3	4	1.35
Pat Ragan	8	17	30	25	15	206⅓	212	54	68	3.23
Dick Rudolph	9	10	21	20	15	154	144	30	48	2.57
Bill Upham	1	1	3	2	2	20⅔	28	1	8	5.23
	53	71*		124	96*	1,117⅓	1,111	277	340	2.90

Shutouts—Fillingim (4), Rudolph (3), Nehf (2), Ragan (2), Hearn, Northrop
Saves—None

1919

Record: 57–82
Finish: Sixth
Games Behind: 38½
Manager: George Stallings

How bad were the 1919 Braves? So bad that they acquired the "world's greatest athlete," Olympic champion Jim Thorpe, and still finished sixth.

Jim Thorpe, winner of the Olympic decathlon in 1912, took his last swings in the majors for the Braves in 1919 then turned his attention to pro football.

Thorpe, of course, was no baseball player. Boston got him on May 21 from the Giants for the $1,500 waiver price. Playing outfield and first base, Thorpe actually hit the best of his brief career. However, the curveball remained a mystery to him, and he didn't play again after 1919, turning his full attention to pro football.

The Braves were under new ownership. George Washington Grant bought the club from Percy Haughton's syndicate.

The season marked the return of Hank Gowdy from army duty, and a day was held in his honor May 23 when he played in his first game in two years. He singled on the first pitch thrown to him.

Rabbit Maranville was back from the navy, too, but not even the great shortstop could make a significant difference on this team. It was easy to see why the Braves were near the bottom of the league. That's where they fell in all major statistical categories. They were glad to see the schedule coming to an end, as they proved September 21 when they lost to the Cubs, 3–0, in just 58 minutes.

	G	AB	R	H	2B	3B	HR	RBI	SB	AVG
Gene Bailey	4	6	0	2	0	0	0	1	1	.333
Lena Blackburne	31	80	5	21	3	1	0	4	3	.262
Tony Boeckel (3B)	95	365	42	91	11	5	1	26	10	.249
Dixie Carroll	15	49	10	13	3	1	0	7	5	.265
Lloyd Christenbury	7	31	5	9	1	0	0	4	0	.290
Walton Cruise (OF)	73	241	23	52	7	0	1	21	8	.216
Hod Ford	10	28	4	6	0	1	0	3	0	.214
Hank Gowdy (C)	78	219	18	61	8	1	1	22	5	.279
Buck Herzog (2B)	73	275	27	77	8	5	1	25	16	.280
Walter Holke (1B)	137	518	48	151	14	6	0	48	19	.292
Joe Kelly	18	64	3	9	1	0	0	3	2	.141
Lee King	2	1	0	0	0	0	0	0	0	.000
Les Mann	40	145	15	41	6	4	3	20	7	.283
Rabbit Maranville (SS)	131	480	44	128	18	10	5	43	12	.267
Tom Miller	7	6	2	2	0	0	0	0	0	.333
Dizzy Nutter	18	52	4	11	0	0	0	3	1	.212
Mickey O'Neil	11	28	3	6	0	0	0	1	0	.214
Charlie Pick	34	114	12	29	1	1	1	7	4	.254
Ray Powell (OF)	123	470	51	111	12	12	2	33	16	.236
Johnny Rawlings	77	275	30	70	8	2	1	16	10	.255
Joe Riggert (OF)	63	240	34	68	8	5	4	17	9	.283
Red Smith	87	241	24	59	6	0	1	25	6	.245
Jim Thorpe	60	156	16	51	7	3	1	25	7	.327
Walt Tragesser	20	40	3	7	2	0	0	3	1	.175
Sam White	1	1	0	0	0	0	0	0	0	.000
Art Wilson	71	191	14	49	8	1	0	16	2	.257
	140	4,746	465	1,201	142	62	24	399	145	.253

	W	L	G	GS	CG	IP	H	BB	SO	ERA
Red Causey	4	5	10	10	3	69	81	20	14	4.57
Larry Cheney	0	2	8	2	0	33	35	15	13	3.55
Al Demaree	6	6	25	13	6	128	147	35	34	3.80
Dana Fillingim	6	13	32	19	9	186⅓	185	39	50	3.38
Bill James	0	0	1	0	0	5⅓	6	2	1	3.38
Ray Keating	7	11	22	13	9	136	129	45	48	2.98
Hugh McQuillan	2	3	16	7	2	60	66	14	13	3.45
Art Nehf	8	9	22	19	13	168⅔	151	40	53	3.09
Jake Northrop	1	5	11	3	2	37⅓	43	10	9	4.58
Joe Oeschger	4	2	7	7	4	56⅔	63	21	16	2.54
Pat Ragan	0	2	4	3	0	12⅔	16	4	3	7.11
Dick Rudolph	13	18*	37	32	24	273⅔	282*	54	76	2.17
Jack Scott	6	6	19	12	7	103⅔	109	39	44	3.13
	57	82		140	79	1,270⅓	1,313	337	374	3.17

Shutouts—Rudolph (2), Keating, Nehf, Oeschger
Saves—Demaree (3), Fillingim (2), Rudolph (2), McQuillan, Scott

1920

Record: 62–90
Finish: Seventh
Games Behind: 30
Manager: George Stallings

The "Miracle Man" had long since run out of miracles. George Stallings was frustrated and disgusted with the state of the team and particularly with what he felt was a lack of support from the new ownership to build a contending team.

That his stay in Boston had to end on such a sour note was unfortunate, but his 1920 swan song was the worst team he fielded in his eight seasons as Braves manager.

This pitiful crew led the league in errors, scored fewer runs than any other team, and was seventh in staff ERA and total runs allowed. Boston finished just a half game ahead of last-place Philadelphia, and only because the Phillies played one more game, a loss.

Nevertheless, this Braves team produced one of the most memorable games in history. On a cold, damp May 1 at Braves Field, Joe Oeschger, who came to Boston the year before in the Art Nehf trade, hooked up with Brooklyn's Leon Cadore in one of the most incredible pitching duels ever.

The Robins scored a run in the fifth on a walk, an infield out, and a single. Boston tied it in the sixth when Walt Cruise tripled and Tony Boeckel singled.

Twenty innings later, it was still 1–1, and the game was called due to darkness.

Oeschger's 21 consecutive scoreless innings set a single-game record. In 16 of the 26 innings, he retired Brooklyn in order. He struck out seven, walked four, and gave up just nine hits, none for extra bases. The Braves had 12 hits and five walks.

It remains the longest major league game ever played in terms of innings. However, it took just 3 hours, 50 minutes—and only three balls were used.

Perhaps buoyed by playing nearly three games in one and not losing, the Braves were able to stay as high as third into mid-May. But they skidded fast after that. On September 17, Boston pitchers gave up 12 straight hits against St. Louis.

Stallings was fit to be tied. A month after the season, he resigned, never to manage in the majors again.

	W	L	G	GS	CG	IP	H	BB	SO	ERA
Eddie Eayrs	1	2	7	3	0	26⅓	36	12	7	5.47
Dana Fillingim	12	21	37	30	22	272	292	79	66	3.11
Bunny Hearn	0	3	11	4	2	43	54	11	9	5.65
Johnny Jones	1	0	3	1	0	9⅔	16	5	6	6.52
Hugh McQuillan	11	15	38	27	17	225⅔	230	70	53	3.55
Joe Oeschger	15	13	38	30	20	299	294	99	80	3.46
Al Pierotti	1	1	6	2	2	25	23	9	12	2.88
Dick Rudolph	4	8	18	12	3	89	104	24	24	4.04
Jack Scott	10	21	44	32	22	291	308	85	94	3.53
Ira Townsend	0	0	4	1	0	6⅔	10	2	1	1.35
Leo Townsend	2	2	7	1	1	24⅓	18	2	0	1.48
Mule Watson	5	4	13	10	4	74⅔	79	17	16	3.62
	62	90		153	93	1,386⅓	1,464	415	368	3.54

Shutouts—Oeschger (5), Scott (3), Fillingim (2), Watson (2), McQuillan
Saves—McQuillan (5), Scott

	G	AB	R	H	2B	3B	HR	RBI	SB	AVG
Gene Bailey	13	24	2	2	0	0	0	0	0	.083
Tony Boeckel (3B)	153	582	70	156	28	5	3	62	18	.268
Lloyd Christenbury	65	106	17	22	2	2	0	14	0	.208
Walton Cruise (OF)	91	288	40	80	7	5	1	21	5	.278
Oscar Dugey	5	0	2	0	0	0	0	0	0	—
Eddie Eayrs	87	244	31	80	5	2	1	24	4	.328
Hod Ford	88	257	16	62	12	5	1	30	3	.241
Hank Gowdy	80	214	14	52	11	2	0	18	6	.243
Walter Holke (1B)	144	551	53	162	15	11	3	64	4	.294
Les Mann (OF)	115	424	48	117	7	8	3	32	7	.276
Rabbit Maranville (SS)	134	493	48	131	19	15	1	43	14	.266
Mickey O'Neil (C)	112	304	19	86	5	4	0	28	4	.283
Charlie Pick (2B)	95	383	34	105	16	6	2	28	10	.274
Ray Powell (OF)	147	609	69	137	12	12	6	29	10	.225
Johnny Rawlings	5	3	0	0	0	0	0	2	0	.000
John Sullivan	81	250	36	74	14	4	1	28	3	.296
Red Torphy	3	15	1	3	2	0	0	2	0	.200
Tom Whelan	1	1	0	0	0	0	0	0	0	.000
Art Wilson	16	19	0	1	0	0	0	0	0	.053
	153	5,218	523	1,358	168	86	23	456	88	.260

1921

Record: 79–74
Finish: Fourth
Games Behind: 15
Manager: Fred Mitchell

Perhaps Fred Mitchell should be known as "Miracle Man" in Braves history rather than George Stallings. How else to explain the 1921 season?

Not that fourth place and five games over .500 is that great, but it came on the heels of three positively miserable seasons and was followed by perhaps the longest stretch of wretched baseball in franchise history. It stands almost as an oasis in the midst of a vast desert where victories would not materialize.

Stallings called Mitchell his "right eye." When Stallings got the job in 1913, he immediately hired Mitchell, who had the dual responsibility of coaching the pitchers and directing traffic at third base. He left the Braves to coach Harvard in 1916, then managed the Cubs from 1917 until returning to Boston in 1921.

The key to the Braves' success, however, was not as much Mitchell as it was an off-season trade that sent the immensely popular Rabbit Maranville to Pittsburgh. In return, Boston got three players who proved quite productive and $15,000.

One of the acquisitions in the Maranville deal was outfielder Billy Southworth, who one day would manage the Braves during an important chapter in their history. Southworth gave Boston what it most needed, offense, as did the other two players obtained in the trade.

Fred Nicholson, another outfielder, and Walter Barbare, who replaced Maranville at short, both had career years in 1921. Though Barbare couldn't play defense like Maranville, the Braves obtained three .300 hitters (at least in 1921) for a player who'd yet to hit .270 in a full season.

Almost overnight, the anemic Braves became the third-most-potent offense in the league, both in runs scored and in team batting (.290, a modern franchise record to that point).

Of course, offense was up everywhere. This season marked the beginning of the lively ball era that enabled Babe Ruth to become the most celebrated man in sports.

Mitchell's team hit 61 home runs, fourth in the league, but the most by a Boston National League club since 1894. Outfielder Ray Powell, who paced the team with 12 home runs, also led the league in triples with a modern club record 18.

The real tipoff that the ball was wound tighter came when hitters started challenging the distant fence at Braves Field. Walt Cruise hit one into the right field Jury Box August 16, only the second to fall there since the park was built in 1915. The space beyond the left-field fence was still virgin territory, but on August 25, Austin McHenry of St. Louis became the first player to hit the fence on the fly.

Other highlights included Joe Oeschger's 20 victories; Walter Holke's league-leading and club-record .997 fielding at first; and John "Mule" Watson pitching and winning both ends of a doubleheader against Philadelphia, 4–3 and 8–0.

	G	AB	R	H	2B	3B	HR	RBI	SB	AVG
Walter Barbare (SS)	134	550	66	166	22	7	0	49	11	.302
Tony Boeckel (3B)	153	592	93	185	20	13	10	84	20	.313
Lloyd Christenbury	62	125	34	44	6	2	3	16	3	.352
Walton Cruise (OF)	108	344	47	119	16	7	8	55	10	.346
Hod Ford (2B)	152	555	50	155	29	5	2	61	2	.279
Frank Gibson	63	125	14	33	5	4	2	13	0	.264
Hank Gowdy	64	164	17	49	7	2	2	17	2	.299
Walter Holke (1B)	150	579	60	151	15	10	3	63	8	.261
Fred Nicholson	83	245	36	80	11	7	5	41	5	.327
Al Nixon	55	138	25	33	6	3	1	9	3	.239
Mickey O'Neil (C)	98	277	26	69	9	4	2	29	2	.249
Ray Powell (OF)	149	624	114	191	25	18*	12	74	6	.306
Billy Southworth (OF)	141	569	86	175	25	15	7	79	22	.308
John Sullivan	5	5	0	0	0	0	0	0	0	.000
	153	5,385	721	1,561	209	100	61	630	94	.290

	W	L	G	GS	CG	IP	H	BB	SO	ERA
Garland Braxton	1	3	17	2	0	37⅓	44	17	16	4.82
Johnny Cooney	0	1	8	1	0	20⅔	19	10	9	3.92
Eddie Eayrs	0	0	2	0	0	4⅔	9	9	1	17.36
Dana Fillingim	15	10	44	22	11	239⅔	249	56	54	3.45
Hugh McQuillan	13	17	45	31	13	250	284	90	94	4.00
Cy Morgan	1	1	17	0	0	30⅓	37	17	8	6.53
Joe Oeschger	20	14	46	36	19	299	303	97*	68	3.52
Al Pierotti	0	1	2	0	0	1⅔	3	3	1	21.60
Jack Scott	15	13	47*	29	16	233⅓	258	57	83	3.70
Ira Townsend	0	0	4	0	0	7⅓	11	4	0	6.14
Leo Townsend	0	1	1	1	0	1⅓	2	3	0	27.00
Mule Watson	14	13	44	31	15	259⅓	269	57	48	3.85
	79	74		153	74	1,385	1,488	420*	382	3.90

Shutouts—Fillingim (3*), Oeschger (3*), McQuillan (2), Scott (2), Watson
Saves—McQuillan (5), Scott (3), Watson (2), Fillingam, Morgan

1922

Record: 53–100
Finish: Eighth
Games Behind: 39½
Manager: Fred Mitchell

Fred Toney knew a bad team when he saw one, and he wanted no part of the 1922 Braves. On July 30, the Giants, headed for another pennant, sent the veteran right-hander, along with pitching prospect Larry Benton and $100,000, to Boston for right-hander Hugh McQuillan. Toney refused to report to the Braves, who were headed for last place, and sat out the rest of the season.

He undoubtedly couldn't get the image out of his mind of his former Giants teammates circling the bases for four—yes, four—inside-the-park home runs at Braves Field in April.

Toney didn't want to take a chance that the same thing might happen while he was on the mound.

Though the Braves weren't a good team, they probably didn't deserve to finish last either. But injuries and illness cost them 365 playing days. Manager Fred Mitchell proved not to be a miracle worker after all, since his team never got above seventh place all year.

Billy Southworth, a key ingredient in the surprising fourth-place showing the previous season, suffered a dislocated knee and missed most of the season.

Without Southworth, the Braves' offense was so bad its .263 team batting average was 19 points lower than the next-worst club. And with the second-highest team ERA in the league (4.37), the pitching certainly couldn't overcome the hitting deficiencies.

	G	AB	R	H	2B	3B	HR	RBI	SB	AVG
Walter Barbare	106	373	38	86	5	4	0	40	2	.231
Tony Boeckel (3B)	119	402	61	116	19	6	6	47	14	.289
Lloyd Christenbury	71	152	22	38	5	2	1	13	2	.250
Walton Cruise (OF)	104	352	51	98	15	10	4	46	4	.278
Hod Ford (SS)	143	515	58	140	23	9	2	60	2	.272
Gil Gallagher	7	22	1	1	1	0	0	2	0	.045
Frank Gibson	66	164	15	49	7	2	3	20	4	.299
Hank Gowdy	92	221	23	70	11	1	1	27	2	.317
Snake Henry	18	66	5	13	4	1	0	5	2	.197
Walter Holke (1B)	105	395	35	115	9	4	0	46	6	.291
Larry Kopf (2B)	126	466	59	124	6	3	1	37	8	.266
Fred Nicholson	78	222	31	56	4	5	2	29	5	.252
Al Nixon (OF)	86	318	35	84	14	4	2	22	6	.264
Mickey O'Neil (C)	83	251	18	56	5	2	0	26	1	.223
Ray Powell (OF)	142	550	82	163	22	11	6	37	3	.296
Bunny Roser	32	113	13	27	3	4	0	16	2	.239
Billy Southworth	43	158	27	51	4	4	4	18	4	.323
	154	5,161	596	1,355	162	73	32	509	67	.263

	W	L	G	GS	CG	IP	H	BB	SO	ERA
Garland Braxton	1	2	25	4	2	66⅔	75	24	15	3.38
Johnny Cooney	1	2	4	3	1	25	19	6	7	2.16
Dana Fillingim	5	9	25	12	5	117	143	37	25	4.54
Joe Genewich	0	2	6	2	1	23	29	11	4	7.04
Harry Hulihan	2	3	7	6	2	40	40	26	16	3.15
Gene Lansing	0	1	15	1	0	40⅔	46	22	14	5.98
Rube Marquard	11	15	39	24	7	198	255	66	57	5.09
Joe Matthews	0	1	3	1	0	10	5	6	0	3.60
Tim McNamara	3	4	24	5	4	70⅔	55	26	16	2.42
Hugh McQuillan	5	10	28	17	7	136	154	56	33	4.24
Frank Miller	11	13	31	23	14	200	213	60	65	3.51
Cy Morgan	0	0	2	0	0	1⅓	8	2	0	27.00
Joe Oeschger	6	21	46	23	10	195⅔	234	81	51	5.06
Dick Rudolph	0	2	3	3	1	16	22	5	3	5.06
Mule Watson	8	14	41	29	8	201	262	59	53	4.70
Al Yeargin	0	1	1	1	1	7	5	2	1	1.29
	53	100*		154	63	1,348	1,565	489*	360	4.37

Shutouts—McNamara (2), Miller (2), Fillingim, Oeschger, Watson
Saves—Fillingam (2), Marquard, Miller, Oeschger, Watson

1923

Record: 54–100
Finish: Seventh
Games Behind: 41½
Manager: Fred Mitchell

Throughout their history, the Braves franchise made a habit of picking up star players who were on their last legs. Babe Ruth and Cy Young are the two best examples. If only the front office could have moved a little faster on these guys . . .

Well, the Braves really dragged their feet on Christy Mathewson. Only Young and Walter Johnson won more games in their careers than Mathewson, but the immortal Giants right-hander had been retired for six seasons when the Braves finally brought him into their fold—as president.

George Washington Grant sold the team in February to one of the most colorful men ever to sit in the franchise's boardroom. Judge Emil Fuchs, a New York attorney, was the Ted Turner of his time. Fuchs agreed to buy the team on the condition that Mathewson would serve as president. "Matty" was battling a lung disorder but said he would take the job.

Too bad Mathewson didn't have a couple of games left in his arm. It's a wonder Fred Mitchell, who was retained as manager, didn't try to persuade the 42-year-old great to put on a uniform in spite of his failing health. Mitchell needed all the help he could find. In fact, he even let 35-year-old coach Dick Rudolph, who supposedly was retired and hadn't pitched effectively since 1919, make a brief comeback.

Rudolph didn't last long, making just four starts, but he did provide some excitement. He shut out the Pirates and Wilbur Cooper, 1–0, in 10 innings for his only victory. He also shut down a 25-game hitting streak by Pittsburgh first baseman Charlie Grimm, who one day would manage the Braves.

The Braves were essentially the same club that lost 100 games the previous season; hence they lost 100 again.

There wasn't a winning pitcher on the team. Only the Phillies, who won the battle for last place, had a worse staff statistically. But offensively, the Braves were clearly at the bottom of the league with the worst batting average (.273), the fewest home runs (32), and the lowest total of runs scored.

Billy Southworth returned from his knee injury to have a fine offensive season, finishing fourth in the league in triples. First baseman Stuffy McInnis, a nice waiver pickup from Cleveland, joined Southworth in the .300 club. But otherwise the offense often was nonexistent.

At least the Braves gave their fans something to remember over the long winter. On the final day of the season, rookie shortstop Ernie Padgett, playing in his second game, made the first unassisted triple play in the National League since 1878.

Stuffy McInnis provided much of the Braves' limited offensive spark in 1923.

	W	L	G	GS	CG	IP	H	BB	SO	ERA
Jesse Barnes	10	14	31	23	12	195⅓	204	43	41	2.76
Joe Batchelder	1	0	4	1	1	9	12	1	2	7.00
Larry Benton	5	9	35	9	1	128	141	57	42	4.99
Johnny Cooney	3	5	23	8	5	98	92	22	23	3.31
Dana Fillingim	1	9	35	12	1	100⅓	141	36	27	5.20
Joe Genewich	13	14	43	24	12	227⅓	272	46	54	3.72
Rube Marquard	11	14	38	29	11	239	265	65	78	3.73
Tim McNamara	3	13	32	16	3	139⅓	185	29	32	4.91
Frank Miller	0	3	8	6	0	39⅓	54	11	6	4.58
Joe Oeschger	5	15	44	19	6	166⅓	227	54	33	5.68
Dick Rudolph	1	2	4	4	1	19⅓	27	10	3	3.72
Mule Watson	1	2	11	4	1	31⅓	42	20	10	5.17
	54	100		155	54	1,392⅔	1,662	394	351	4.21

Shutouts—Barnes (5), Marquard (3), Cooney (2), Genewich, Oeschger, Rudolph
Saves—Barnes (2), Oeschger (2), Genewich, Miller, Watson

1924

Record: 53–100
Finish: Eighth
Games Behind: 40
Manager: Dave Bancroft

Fred Tenney somehow survived as Boston manager in 1907 after consecutive 100-loss seasons, but Fred Mitchell couldn't do the same in 1924. He was made a scout and was replaced by Dave "Beauty" Bancroft, one of the great shortstops of the era.

Known for his sharp baseball mind, Bancroft came to the Braves from the Giants along with an eccentric outfielder

	G	AB	R	H	2B	3B	HR	RBI	SB	AVG
Bill Bagwell	56	93	8	27	4	2	2	10	0	.290
Tony Boeckel (3B)	148	568	72	169	32	4	7	79	11	.298
Jocko Conlon	59	147	23	32	3	0	0	17	0	.218
Johnny Cooney	42	66	7	25	1	0	0	3	0	.379
Dee Cousineau	1	2	1	2	0	0	0	2	0	1.000
Walton Cruise	21	38	4	8	2	0	0	0	1	.211
Bob Emmerich	13	24	3	2	0	0	0	0	1	.083
Gus Felix (OF)	139	506	64	138	17	2	6	44	8	.273
Hod Ford (2B)	111	380	27	103	16	7	2	50	1	.271
Frank Gibson	41	50	13	15	1	0	0	5	0	.300
Hank Gowdy	23	48	5	6	1	1	0	5	1	.125
Snake Henry	11	9	1	1	0	0	0	2	0	.111
Al Hermann	31	93	2	22	4	0	0	11	3	.237
Larry Kopf	39	138	15	38	3	1	0	10	0	.275
Stuffy McInnis (1B)	154	607	70	191	23	9	2	95	7	.315
Al Nixon	88	321	53	88	12	4	0	19	2	.274
Mickey O'Neil (C)	96	306	29	65	7	4	0	20	3	.212
Ernie Padgett	4	11	3	2	0	0	0	0	0	.182
Ray Powell (OF)	97	338	57	102	20	4	4	38	1	.302
Bob Smith (SS)	115	375	30	94	16	3	0	40	4	.251
Earl Smith	72	191	22	55	15	1	3	19	0	.288
Billy Southworth (OF)	153	611	95	195	29	16	6	78	14	.319
	155	5,329	636	1,455	213	58	32	569	57	.273

named Casey Stengel and Bill Cunningham, another outfielder, in exchange for Billy Southworth and Joe Oeschger.

The franchise was rocked by yet another tragedy prior to the season. Tony Boeckel, who'd been the club's third baseman since mid-1919, was killed in an auto mishap.

The Braves played reasonably well until Bancroft had an appendectomy July 1. By late in the month, the club had fallen to the bottom of the league en route to its third consecutive season of exactly 100 losses.

Boston was ridiculously inept offensively, finishing last in batting average, runs, and home runs by remarkably large margins in all three departments.

The Braves couldn't hit anyone. On July 17, the Cardinals' Jesse Haines, headed for the Hall of Fame, pitched a no-hitter against them. Two days later, a rookie named Hi Bell, who would win but 32 games in an eight-year career, pitched and won a doubleheader against them, allowing a total of just six hits.

	G	AB	R	H	2B	3B	HR	RBI	SB	AVG
Dave Bancroft	79	319	49	89	11	1	2	21	4	.279
Johnny Cooney	55	130	10	33	2	1	0	4	0	.254
Dee Cousineau	3	2	0	0	0	0	0	0	0	.000
Walton Cruise	9	9	4	4	1	0	1	3	0	.444
Bill Cunningham (OF)	114	437	44	119	15	8	1	40	8	.272
Gus Felix	59	204	25	43	7	1	1	10	0	.211
Frank Gibson	90	229	25	71	15	6	1	30	1	.310
Al Hermann	1	1	0	0	0	0	0	0	0	.000
John Kelleher	1	1	0	0	0	0	0	0	0	.000
Hunter Lane	7	15	0	1	0	0	0	0	0	.067
Wade Lefler	1	1	0	0	0	0	0	0	0	.000
Les Mann	32	102	13	28	7	4	0	10	1	.275
Stuffy McInnis (1B)	146	581	57	169	23	7	1	59	9	.291
Mickey O'Neil (C)	106	362	32	89	4	1	0	22	4	.246
Ernie Padgett (3B)	138	502	42	128	25	9	1	46	4	255
Eddie Phillips	3	3	0	0	0	0	0	0	0	.000
Ray Powell	74	188	21	49	9	1	1	15	1	.261
Marty Shay	19	68	4	16	3	1	0	2	2	.235
Bob Smith (SS)	106	347	32	79	12	3	2	38	5	.228
Earl Smith	33	59	1	16	3	0	0	8	0	.271
Ed Sperber	24	59	8	17	2	0	1	12	3	.288
Casey Stengel (OF)	131	461	57	129	20	6	5	39	13	.280
Herb Thomas	32	127	12	28	4	1	1	8	5	.220
Cotton Tierney (2B)	136	505	38	131	16	1	6	58	11	.259
Frank Wilson (OF)	61	215	20	51	7	0	1	15	3	.237
	154	5,283	520	1,355	194	52	25	459	74	.256

	W	L	G	GS	CG	IP	H	BB	SO	ERA
Jesse Barnes	15	20*	37	32	21	267⅔	292	53	49	3.23
Joe Batchelder	0	0	3	0	0	4⅔	4	2	2	3.86
Larry Benton	5	7	30	13	4	128	129	64	41	4.15
Johnny Cooney	8	9	34	19	12	181	176	50	67	3.18
Dinty Gearin	0	1	1	1	0	0	3	2	0	∞
Joe Genewich	10	19	34	27	11	200⅓	258	65	43	5.21
Skinny Graham	0	4	5	4	1	33	33	11	15	3.82
Ike Kamp	0	1	1	1	0	7	9	5	4	5.14
Red Lucas	1	4	27	4	1	83⅔	112	18	30	5.16
Rube Marquard	1	2	6	6	1	36	33	13	10	3.00
Tim McNamara	8	12	35	21	6	179	242	31	35	5.18
Joe Muich	0	0	3	0	0	9	19	5	1	11.00
Lou North	1	2	9	4	1	35⅓	45	19	11	5.35
Dutch Stryker	3	8	20	10	2	73⅓	90	22	22	6.01
Al Yeargin	1	11	32	12	6	141⅓	162	42	34	5.09
	53	100*		154	66	1,379⅓	1,607	402	364	4.46

Shutouts—Barnes (4*), Cooney (2), Genewich (2), McNamara (2)
Saves—Cooney (2), Benton, Genewich

1925

Record: 70–83
Finish: Fifth
Games Behind: 25
Manager: Dave Bancroft

The conquering of the left-field fence at Braves Field finally occurred in 1925. Since the park opened in August 1915, no player had hit a home run to left, not even in practice.

But with the ball wound tighter than ever, Bernie Neis, a 160-pound outfielder who hit but 25 homers in an eight-year career, hit one over the left-field fence in batting practice a few days before opening day. Then on May 28, Giants catcher Pancho Snyder, not much of a slugger himself, hit the first official home run to left off Larry Benton.

It took nearly 10 full years for someone to do what Ty Cobb said no one would ever do when he first gazed at the green expanse of Braves Field. Then, six weeks later, Neis hit one that counted, the second to go out in left. Baseball was changing.

The Braves batted .292, still the highest team average in modern history, yet it ranked just fifth in the league. Pittsburgh led at .307.

Dave Bancroft's team was considerably improved—at least it didn't even approach 100 defeats. Much of the improvement was directly related to the play and direction of Bancroft, who bounced back from his appendectomy to lead the league's shortstops in fielding, hit .319, and finish sixth in the MVP voting.

Each city hosted a Golden Jubilee Day in recognition of the National League's 50th season. George Wright, who helped start the franchise 55 years before in the National Association, was on hand.

Though the club finished fifth, it was just 2½ games ahead of last-place Chicago. That and the 16 losses in 22 games to the seventh-place Phillies indicated the Braves were still a long way from climbing back into contention.

The day the World Series began, team president Christy Mathewson died of tuberculosis at age 45.

	G	AB	R	H	2B	3B	HR	RBI	SB	AVG
Dave Bancroft (SS)	128	479	75	153	29	8	2	49	7	.319
Dick Burrus (1B)	152	588	82	200	41	4	5	87	8	.340
Johnny Cooney	54	103	17	33	7	0	0	13	1	.320
Dee Cousineau	1	0	0	0	0	0	0	0	0	—
Gus Felix (OF)	121	459	60	141	25	7	2	66	5	.307
Doc Gautreau (2B)	68	279	45	73	13	3	0	23	11	.262
Frank Gibson (C)	104	316	36	88	23	5	2	50	3	.278
Dave Harris	92	340	49	90	8	7	5	36	6	.265
Andy High	60	219	31	63	11	1	4	28	3	.288
Shanty Hogan	9	21	2	6	1	1	0	3	0	.286
Abie Hood	5	21	2	6	2	0	1	2	0	.286
Hod Kibbie	11	41	5	11	2	0	0	2	0	.268
Red Lucas	6	20	1	3	0	0	0	2	0	.150
Les Mann	60	184	27	63	11	4	2	20	6	.342
Bill Marriott (3B)	103	370	37	99	9	1	1	40	3	.268
Bernie Neis (OF)	106	355	47	101	20	2	5	45	8	.285
Mickey O'Neil	70	222	29	57	6	5	2	30	1	.257
Ernie Padgett	86	256	31	78	9	7	0	29	3	.305
Oscar Siemer	16	46	5	14	0	1	1	6	0	.304
Bob Smith	58	174	17	49	9	4	0	23	2	.282
Ed Sperber	2	2	0	0	0	0	0	0	0	.000
Casey Stengel	12	13	0	1	0	0	0	2	0	.077
Herb Thomas	5	17	2	4	0	1	0	0	0	.235
Jimmy Welsh (OF)	122	484	69	151	25	8	7	63	7	.312
Frank Wilson	12	31	3	13	1	1	0	0	2	.419
	153	5,365	708	1,567	260	70	41	643	77	.292

	W	L	G	GS	CG	IP	H	BB	SO	ERA
Bill Anderson	0	0	2	0	0	2⅔	5	2	1	10.13
Jesse Barnes	11	16	32	28	17	216⅓	255	63	55	4.53
Joe Batchelder	0	0	4	0	0	7	10	1	2	5.14
Larry Benton	14	7	31	21	16	183⅓	170	70	49	3.09
Johnny Cooney	14	14	31	29	20	245⅔	267	50	65	3.48
Foster Edwards	0	0	1	0	0	2	6	1	1	9.00
Joe Genewich	12	10	34	21	10	169	185	41	34	3.99
Kyle Graham	7	12	34	23	5	157	177	62	32	4.41
Ike Kamp	2	4	24	4	1	58⅓	68	35	20	5.09
Rube Marquard	2	8	26	8	0	72	105	27	19	5.75
Tim McNamara	0	0	1	0	0	⅔	6	2	1	81.00
Joe Ogrodowski	0	0	1	0	0	1	6	3	0	54.00
Rosy Ryan	2	8	37	7	1	122⅔	152	52	48	6.31
Bob Smith	5	3	13	10	6	92⅔	110	36	19	4.47
Bill Vargus	1	1	11	2	1	36⅓	45	13	5	3.96
	70	83		153	77	1,366⅔	1,567	458	351	4.39

Shutouts—Benton (2), Cooney (2)
Saves—Ryan (2), Benton, Graham

1926

Record: 66–86
Finish: Seventh
Games Behind: 22
Manager: Dave Bancroft

The slight improvement the team seemed to show in 1925 was nothing but a mirage. The 1926 Braves lost three more games than the previous year and dropped two places in the standings.

On July 22, the Reds feasted on Boston pitching for 11 runs in the second inning of a 13–3 game. Apparently the frustration hadn't worn off three days later.

On July 25, Cincinnati third baseman Babe Pinelli brushed against Braves coach Art Devlin, who had been harassing him, coming off the field in the third inning. Devlin took a swing at Pinelli, inciting a major brawl between the two clubs. The police had to be called to restore order, and in the process, they arrested Boston outfielder Frank Wilson, who slugged an officer.

The fisticuffs resumed in the next inning when Boston's Jimmy Welsh collided with Cincinnati catcher Val Picinich on a play at the plate. Picinich took a swing at Welsh, for which he was ejected, but not before both benches cleared again.

At least no one could say Dave Bancroft didn't have a scrappy bunch.

The sensation of the season was "Glass Arm" Eddie Brown, an outfielder acquired from Brooklyn in a six-player trade. Brown led the league in hits (201) and nearly won the batting title, finishing third (.328), eight points less than Paul Waner.

Bancroft, 35, had another excellent season as a player. Johnny Werts, a 28-year-old right-hander called up from Worcester, was the team's lone winning pitcher, but he was never productive again. The team hit but 16 home runs, its lowest total since 1918.

	G	AB	R	H	2B	3B	HR	RBI	SB	AVG
Dave Bancroft (SS)	127	453	70	141	18	6	1	44	3	.311
Eddie Brown (OF)	153	612	71	201*	31	8	2	84	5	.328
Dick Burrus (1B)	131	486	59	131	21	1	3	61	4	.270
Johnny Cooney	64	126	17	38	3	2	0	18	6	.302
Doc Gautreau (2B)	79	266	36	71	9	4	0	8	17	.267
Frank Gibson	24	47	3	16	4	0	0	7	0	.340
Andy High (3B)	130	476	55	141	17	10	2	66	4	.296
Shanty Hogan	4	14	1	4	1	1	0	5	0	.286
Jimmy Johnston	23	57	7	14	1	0	1	5	2	.246
Les Mann	50	129	23	39	8	2	1	20	5	.302
Eddie Moore	54	184	17	49	3	2	0	15	6	.266
Bernie Neis	30	93	16	20	5	2	0	8	4	.215
Harry Riconda	4	12	1	2	0	0	0	0	0	.167
Oscar Siemer	31	73	3	15	1	0	0	5	0	.205
Jack Smith (OF)	96	322	46	100	15	2	2	25	11	.311
Eddie Taylor	92	272	37	73	8	2	0	33	4	.268
Zack Taylor (C)	125	432	36	110	22	3	0	42	1	.255
Jimmy Welsh (OF)	134	490	69	136	18	11	3	57	6	.278
Frank Wilson	87	236	22	56	11	3	0	23	3	.237
Sid Womack	1	3	0	0	0	0	0	1	0	.000
	153	5,216	624	1,444	209	62	16	560	81	.277

	W	L	G	GS	CG	IP	H	BB	SO	ERA
Larry Benton	14	14	43	27	12	231⅔	244	81	103	3.85
Johnny Cooney	3	3	19	8	3	83⅓	106	29	23	4.00
Foster Edwards	2	0	3	3	1	25	20	13	4	0.72
Joe Genewich	8	16	37	26	12	216	239	63	59	3.88
Hal Goldsmith	5	7	19	15	5	101	135	28	16	4.37
Skinny Graham	3	3	15	4	1	36⅓	54	19	7	7.93
Bunny Hearn	4	9	34	12	3	117⅓	121	56	40	4.22
George Mogridge	6	10	39	10	2	142	173	36	46	4.50
Rosy Ryan	0	2	7	2	0	19	29	7	1	7.58
Bob Smith	10	13	33	23	14	201⅓	199	75	44	3.75
Bill Vargus	0	0	4	0	0	3	4	1	0	3.00
Johnny Werts	11	9	32	23	7	189⅓	212	47	65	3.28
	66	86		153	60	1,365½	1,536	455	408	4.01

Shutouts—Smith (4), Genewich (2), Benton, Cooney, Werts
Saves—Mogridge (3), Genewich (2), Hearn (2), Benton, Smith

1927

Record: 60–94
Finish: Seventh
Games Behind: 34
Manager: Dave Bancroft

This was Dave Bancroft's last season as Braves manager, and it was a rough one—in more ways than one.

His team was lousy, but on June 18 at Pittsburgh, that wasn't Bancroft's biggest headache. As the Boston manager was crossing home plate, he exchanged words with Pittsburgh catcher Earl Smith, who promptly decked Bancroft with a right to the jaw. The Braves manager had to be carried off the field.

When Smith played with the Braves in 1924, he was fined $500 by Bancroft for throwing a hotel chair. It seems he'd never gotten over it. But by slugging Bancroft, Smith drew another $500 fine and a 30-day suspension.

When the Pirates visited Boston later in the season, Bancroft attempted to have a warrant served on Smith. But the catcher climbed over the back fence at Braves Field and escaped, spraining an ankle in the process.

The Braves and Cubs played two extra-inning games within 72 hours that lasted a total of 40 innings, and Boston lost both—7–2 in 18 innings and 4–3 in 22 innings. In the latter, converted infielder Bob Smith pitched all 22 innings for the Braves, holding Chicago scoreless from the fifth inning until the 22nd when he finally gave up the decisive run. The Braves also lost 15 in a row on the road at one point.

Maybe the Braves weren't talented, but they were spunky. In September, tiny second baseman Doc Gautreau stole home twice in the same game against Brooklyn, tying a major league record that wouldn't be duplicated for 37 years.

Eddie Brown finished the season with a streak of 575 consecutive games played, then a modern National League record. He deserved a medal for playing every day with this team.

After the season, Judge Fuchs told Bancroft he would not be retained as manager. Bancroft never managed again. Perhaps, after four seasons with the Braves, he never had the desire.

	G	AB	R	H	2B	3B	HR	RBI	SB	AVG
Dave Bancroft (SS)	111	375	44	91	13	4	1	31	5	.243
Eddie Brown (OF)	155	558	64	171	35	6	2	75	11	.306
Dick Burrus	72	220	22	70	8	3	0	32	3	.318
Earl Clark	13	44	6	12	1	0	0	3	0	.273
Johnny Cooney	10	1	3	0	0	0	0	0	0	.000
Doc Farrell	110	424	44	124	13	2	1	58	4	.292
Jack Fournier (1B)	122	374	55	106	18	2	10	53	4	.283
Doc Gautreau (2B)	87	236	38	58	12	2	0	20	11	.246
Frank Gibson	60	167	7	37	1	2	0	19	2	.222
Sid Graves	7	20	5	5	1	1	0	2	1	.250
Andy High (3B)	113	384	59	116	15	9	4	46	4	.302
Shanty Hogan (C)	71	229	24	66	17	1	3	32	2	.288
Les Mann	29	66	8	17	3	1	0	6	2	.258
Dinny McNamara	11	9	3	0	0	0	0	0	0	.000
Eddie Moore	112	411	53	124	14	4	1	32	5	.302
Lance Richbourg (OF)	115	450	57	139	12	9	2	34	24	.309
Jack Smith	84	183	27	58	6	4	1	24	8	.317
Zack Taylor	30	96	8	23	2	1	1	14	0	.240
Herb Thomas	24	74	11	17	6	1	0	6	2	.230
Luke Urban	35	111	11	32	5	0	0	10	1	.288
Jimmy Welsh (OF)	131	497	72	143	26	7	9	54	11	.288
	155	5,370	651	1,498	216	61	37	582	100	.279

	W	L	G	GS	CG	IP	H	BB	SO	ERA
Larry Benton	4	2	11	10	3	60½	72	27	25	4.48
Foster Edwards	2	8	29	11	1	92	95	45	37	4.99
Joe Genewich	11	8	40	19	7	181	199	54	38	3.83
Hal Goldsmith	1	3	22	5	1	71⅓	83	26	13	3.52
Kent Greenfield	11	14	27	26	11	190	203	59	59	3.84
Bunny Hearn	0	2	8	0	0	12⅔	16	9	5	4.26
Jack Knight	0	0	3	0	0	3	6	2	0	15.00
Hugh McQuillan	3	5	13	11	2	78	109	24	17	5.54
Art Mills	0	1	15	1	0	37⅓	41	18	7	3.82
George Mogridge	6	4	20	1	0	48⅔	48	15	26	3.70
Guy Morrison	1	2	11	3	1	34⅓	40	15	6	4.46
Charlie Robertson	7	17	28	22	6	154⅓	188	46	49	4.72
Dick Rudolph	0	0	1	0	0	1⅓	1	1	0	0.00
Bob Smith	10	18	41	32	16	260⅔	297	75	81	3.76
Johnny Werts	4	10	42	15	4	164⅓	204	52	39	4.55
	60	94		155	52	1,390*	1,602	468	402	4.22

Shutouts—Greenfield, Smith
Saves—Mogridge (5), Smith (3), Genewich, Goldsmith, Werts

1928

Record: 50–103
Finish: Seventh
Games Behind: 44½
Managers: Jack Slattery, Rogers Hornsby

Thank goodness for the Phillies. They saved the Braves from more than one last-place finish, including 1928.

Boston, with 103 losses, certainly was deserving of the National League basement, but the Braves just couldn't keep up

with the Phillies, who lost 109 games, playing to a .283 percentage.

The 1928 Braves never had a chance—at least not after Judge Fuchs hired a college coach, Jack Slattery, as manager, then two days later acquired the tempestuous Rogers Hornsby in a trade.

Slattery coached under Boston manager George Stallings in 1918 and 1919. He went on to coach at Tufts College, Boston College, and Harvard and was popular with the sports writers, who were quite influential with Fuchs.

Hornsby was one of the game's biggest stars with an ego to match. He'd already won six batting titles. He also was difficult to get along with, as evidenced by the fact that the Braves were his third team in three years. He was coming off a .361 season, yet the Giants parted with him for Shanty Hogan, a promising young catcher, and Jimmy Welsh, an adequate outfielder.

Besides being a great player, Hornsby had managed the Cardinals to the pennant two years earlier. He was not hesitant to talk about the way Slattery was running the club in spring training, creating speculation about who was directing the team and who was best for the job.

On May 23, with the team off to a slow start, Slattery resigned and was replaced by Hornsby. Little did it matter. The team played .355 under Slattery and .320 for Hornsby.

Regardless of the circumstances, though, Hornsby could hit. He won the National League batting title and set a modern Braves record with his .387 average.

Home runs were more frequent at Braves Field because Fuchs had stands built that cut the left-field line from 402 feet to 353 and reduced the center-field distance from 550 to 387. Left-center was a mere 330. The problem was that opponents were better equipped than the Braves to take advantage of the new home run target. After Fuchs saw the er-

George Sisler's eyes may have been weakened by the time he joined the Braves, but he still batted over .300 in each of his three seasons in Boston.

ror of his ways in mid-June, he had a 30-foot canvas erected in front of the new bleachers to cut down cheap homers.

In May, the Braves purchased future Hall of Fame first baseman George Sisler from Washington. His vision supposedly was suffering from an eye infection. Too bad he couldn't give it to his teammates. He only finished fourth in the league in batting average (.340).

Despite having three of the league's best hitters in Hornsby, Sisler, and outfielder Lance Richbourg (.337), the Braves finished sixth in team hitting (.275), quite a feat.

Richbourg was known more for speed than power, but he got six of his season's 52 RBIs in one three-inning stretch against St. Louis during which he homered in the first, doubled with the bases full in the second, and delivered a two-run triple in the third.

Another noteworthy accomplishment came July 2 when third baseman Les Bell became the first franchise player in the modern era to hit three home runs in a game.

The team was seventh in the league in ERA (4.83). Rookie Ed Brandt pitched the club's lone shutout. Even Eddie Brown's record consecutive-games-played streak was snapped at 618 in June when Hornsby benched him.

As if this team didn't have enough misery, circumstances forced the Braves to play a record nine consecutive doubleheaders from September 4 to 15. They lost five of them—but still finished ahead of the Phillies.

In 1928, third baseman Les Bell became the first Brave of the modern era to hit three home runs in a game.

After the season, Hornsby was sent to the Cubs for $200,000 and five players. It was his fourth team in four years.

	G	AB	R	H	2B	3B	HR	RBI	SB	AVG
Les Bell (3B)	153	591	58	164	36	7	10	91	1	.277
Eddie Brown (OF)	142	523	45	140	28	2	2	59	6	.268
Dick Burrus	64	137	15	37	6	0	3	13	1	.270
Earl Clark	28	112	18	34	9	1	0	10	0	.304
Jimmy Cooney	18	51	2	7	0	0	0	3	1	.137
Bill Cronin	3	2	1	0	0	0	0	0	0	.000
Doc Farrell (SS)	134	483	36	104	14	2	3	43	3	.215
Charlie Fitzberger	7	7	0	2	0	0	0	0	0	.286
Howard Freigau	52	109	11	28	8	1	1	17	1	.257
Doc Gautreau	23	18	3	5	0	1	0	1	1	.278
Dave Harris	7	17	2	2	1	0	0	0	0	.118
Rogers Hornsby (2B)	140	486	99	188	42	7	21	94	5	.387*
Dinny McNamara	9	4	2	1	0	0	0	0	0	.250
Eddie Moore	68	215	27	51	9	0	2	18	7	.237
Heinie Mueller	42	151	25	34	3	1	0	19	1	.225
Lance Richbourg (OF)	148	612	105	206	26	12	2	52	11	.337
George Sisler (1B)	118	491	71	167	26	4	4	68	11	.340
Jack Smith (OF)	96	254	30	71	9	2	1	32	6	.280
Al Spohrer	51	124	15	27	3	0	0	9	1	.218
Zack Taylor (C)	125	399	36	100	15	1	2	30	2	.251
Luke Urban	15	17	0	3	0	0	0	2	0	.176
Earl Williams	3	2	0	0	0	0	0	0	0	.000
	153	5,228	631	1,439	241	41	52	577	60	.275

	W	L	G	GS	CG	IP	H	BB	SO	ERA
Virgil Barnes	2	7	16	10	1	60⅓	86	26	7	5.82
Ray Boggs	0	0	4	0	0	5	2	7	0	5.40
Ed Brandt	9	21*	38	31	12	225⅓	234	109	84	5.07
Ben Cantwell	3	3	22	9	3	90	112	36	18	5.10
Bill Clarkson	0	2	19	1	0	34⅔	53	22	8	6.75
Johnny Cooney	3	7	24	6	2	89⅔	106	31	18	4.32
Art Delaney	9	17	39	22	8	192⅓	197	56	45	3.79
Foster Edwards	2	1	21	3	2	49⅓	67	23	17	5.66
Joe Genewich	3	7	13	11	4	80⅔	88	18	15	4.13
Hal Goldsmith	0	0	4	0	0	8⅓	14	1	1	3.24
Kent Greenfield	3	11	32	23	5	143⅔	173	60	30	5.32
Bunny Hearn	1	0	7	0	0	10	6	8	8	6.30
Bonnie Hollingsworth	0	2	7	2	0	22⅓	30	13	10	5.24
Art Mills	0	0	4	0	0	7⅔	17	8	0	12.91
Guy Morrison	0	0	1	0	0	3	4	3	0	12.00
Emilio Palmero	0	1	3	1	0	6⅔	14	2	0	5.40
Charlie Robertson	2	5	13	7	3	59⅓	73	16	17	5.31
George Sisler	0	0	1	0	0	1	0	1	0	0.00
Bob Smith	13	17	38	25	14	244⅓	274	74	59	3.87
Clay Touchstone	0	0	5	0	0	8	15	2	1	4.50
Johnny Werts	0	2	10	2	0	18⅓	31	8	5	10.31
	50	103		153	54	1,360	1,596	524	343	4.83

Shutouts—Brandt
Saves—Delaney (2), Smith (2), Cooney, Robertson

1929

Record: 56–98
Finish: Eighth
Games Behind: 43
Manager: Emil Fuchs

When Ted Turner pulled on a uniform and stepped into the dugout to manage the Braves in 1977, he wasn't the first owner in franchise history to pull such a stunt. In fact, although Turner lasted only one game at the job, Judge Emil Fuchs is credited with managing the entire 1929 season.

The Braves were bad, no matter how you cut it and no matter who was calling the shots. Under Fuchs, an attorney and former magistrate, the team actually won six more games than it had in 1928. However, it also slipped into last place for the first time since 1924.

Hoping to recapture the magic of 1914, Fuchs brought back Maranville, who helped St. Louis to the 1928 pennant. He even signed World Series hero Hank Gowdy as a player-coach, even though Gowdy had little to offer as a 39-year-old catcher.

When the Braves won seven of their first nine, Fuchs thought he was onto something. But as soon as reality set in during May, he headed to New York for a court case, leaving "assistant manager" Johnny Evers in charge. Fuchs made periodic returns to the dugout during the course of the season and continued to hold the title of manager, but Evers ran the team most of the time.

On August 19, Boston dipped into the cellar and never left.

Besides Fuchs' decision to manage, the other landmark event of the season was the birth of Sunday baseball, leaving Pennsylvania as the only state prohibiting it. Voters approved Sunday play only at ballparks located at least 1,000 feet from a church, with the result that games couldn't be played at Fenway Park. Therefore, the Braves allowed the Red Sox to play their Sunday games at Braves Field.

The Braves were last in the league in runs scored, team batting, home runs, errors, and defensive percentage. They were seventh in ERA and sixth in opponents' runs. It was ugly.

In October, Fuchs decided to get a real manager, signing Bill McKechnie to a four-year contract. Then he used half the $200,000 he got for Rogers Hornsby to buy a minor league outfielder named Wally Berger who was trapped in the Cubs farm system.

	G	AB	R	H	2B	3B	HR	RBI	SB	AVG
Red Barron	10	21	3	4	1	0	0	1	2	.190
Les Bell (3B)	139	483	58	144	23	5	9	72	4	.298
Buzz Boyle	17	57	8	15	2	1	1	2	2	.263
Earl Clark (OF)	84	279	43	88	13	3	1	30	6	.315
Pat Collins	7	5	1	0	0	0	0	2	0	.000
Johnny Cooney	41	72	10	23	4	1	0	6	1	.319
Bill Cronin	6	9	0	1	0	0	0	0	0	.111
Jack Cummings	3	6	0	1	0	0	0	1	0	.167
Joe Dugan	60	125	14	38	10	0	0	15	0	.304
Bill Dunlap	10	29	6	12	0	1	1	4	0	.414
Johnny Evers	1	0	0	0	0	0	0	0	0	—
Doc Farrell	5	8	0	1	0	0	0	2	0	.125
Hank Gowdy	10	16	1	7	0	0	0	3	0	.438
George Harper (OF)	136	457	65	133	25	5	10	68	5	.291
Bernie James	46	101	12	31	3	2	0	9	3	.307
Lou Legett	39	81	7	13	2	0	0	6	2	.160
Freddie Maguire (2B)	138	496	54	125	26	8	0	41	8	.252
Rabbit Maranville (SS)	146	560	87	159	26	10	0	55	13	.284
Heinie Mueller	46	93	10	19	2	1	0	11	2	.204
Henry Peploski	6	10	1	2	0	0	0	1	0	.200
Lance Richbourg (OF)	139	557	76	170	24	13	3	56	7	.305
Gene Robertson	8	28	1	8	0	0	0	6	1	.286
George Sisler (1B)	154	629	67	205	40	8	2	79	6	.326
Jack Smith	19	20	2	5	0	0	0	2	0	.250
Al Spohrer (C)	114	342	42	93	21	8	2	48	1	.272
Zack Taylor	34	101	8	25	7	0	0	10	0	.248
Phil Voyles	20	68	9	16	0	2	0	14	0	.235
Jimmy Welsh	53	186	24	54	8	7	2	16	1	.290
Al Weston	3	3	0	0	0	0	0	0	0	.000
	154	5,291	657	1,481	252	77	33	598	65	.280

	W	L	G	GS	CG	IP	H	BB	SO	ERA
Ed Brandt	8	13	26	21	13	167⅔	196	83	50	5.53
Ben Cantwell	4	13	27	20	8	157	171	52	25	4.47
Bill Clarkson	0	1	2	1	0	7	16	4	0	10.29
Johnny Cooney	2	3	14	2	1	45	57	22	11	5.00
Bruce Cunningham	4	6	17	8	4	91⅓	100	32	22	4.52
Art Delaney	3	5	20	8	3	75	103	35	17	6.12
Kent Greenfield	0	0	6	2	0	15⅔	33	15	7	10.91
Bunny Hearn	2	0	10	1	0	18⅓	18	9	12	4.42
Percy Jones	7	15	35	22	11	188⅓	219	84	69	4.64
Dixie Leverett	3	7	24	12	3	97⅓	135	30	28	6.36
Red Peery	0	1	9	1	0	44	53	9	3	5.11
Socks Seibold	12	17	33	27	16	205⅔	228	80	54	4.73
Bob Smith	11	17	34	29	19	231	256	71	65	4.68
Clay Touchstone	0	0	1	0	0	2⅔	6	0	1	16.88
Johnny Werts	0	0	4	0	0	6	13	4	2	10.50
	56	98*		154	78	1,352⅔	1,604	530	366	5.12

Shutouts—Delaney, Jones, Seibold, Smith
Saves—Cooney (3), Smith (3), Cantwell (2), Cunningham, Leverett, Seibold, Werts

1930

Record: 70–84
Finish: Sixth
Games Behind: 22
Manager: Bill McKechnie

It was hard to argue with Judge Fuchs' selection of Bill McKechnie as Braves manager. McKechnie won a pennant and a World Series managing Pittsburgh in 1925 and a pennant with St. Louis in 1928. After he left Boston, he won a pennant and a World Series for Cincinnati in 1940.

But in eight years in Boston, McKechnie couldn't get the Braves higher than fourth. In 1930, he brought the team in sixth, its best finish in five years, testimony to his managing expertise.

McKechnie's troops included a 24-year-old rookie outfielder named Wally Berger and the sprightly 38-year-old Rabbit Maranville.

Berger was a big, raw-boned right-handed slugger who couldn't even be tamed by spacious Braves Field. His deeds were legendary.

On successive days in late May, Berger hit balls over the outside fence at Braves Field where no one hit a ball in the first decade of the park's existence. In 1930 alone, he hit five game-winning home runs to beat the Giants by one run. On one of those occasions, New York pitcher Joe Genewich knocked down Berger with a pitch, and the young Brave got up and hit the next pitch for a game-winning homer.

The Giants, by the way, finished third—five games behind first-place St. Louis.

Berger's 38 home runs and 119 RBIs in 1930 still stand as National League rookie records. His home run total was a major league record until Oakland's Mark McGwire broke it in 1987.

Maranville was far from being a rookie, but he played with the spark of one, leading the league's shortstops in fielding for the fourth time and hitting .281, 33 points higher than his career average.

Six of the teams in the league had batting averages over .300, but the Braves weren't one of them. And despite Berger's 38 home runs, which ranked third in the league, Boston still was last in team home runs (66).

The hitting exploits of powerful rookie Wally Berger in 1930 have never been equaled in the National League.

1931

Record: 64–90
Finish: Seventh
Games Behind: 37
Manager: Bill McKechnie

The 1931 season was another of many forgettable campaigns in this bleak period of Braves history. But at least there were Rabbit Maranville and Wally Berger.

At 39, Maranville was showing remarkably few signs of slowing down. He didn't lead the league's shortstops in fielding as he had the year before, but he did have a solid season at bat and in the field and played every day.

The Braves played reasonably well until August and September when they went into a 17–43 (.283) swoon. But Berger's exploits made the club well worth following. Though his power numbers were off quite a bit from his rookie year, Berger improved his batting average and was still quite a sight to behold. He finished second in the league in doubles, third in home runs (19), and fourth in total bases.

On April 27, Berger tied the modern record for outfielders with four assists, preserving a 2–0 victory for Socks Seibold against the Phillies. Then on May 30, he became the first player since 1922 to hit a ball over the stadium wall at Philadelphia's Baker Bowl.

In spite of Berger's fine work, the Braves were last in the league in batting average (.258), runs scored, slugging percentage (.341), and on-base percentage (.309).

Left-hander Ed Brandt, who won his first eight decisions, began a string of four consecutive productive seasons but was the club's only dependable pitcher.

	G	AB	R	H	2B	3B	HR	RBI	SB	AVG
Wally Berger (OF)	151	555	98	172	27	14	38	119	3	.310
Buzz Boyle	1	1	0	0	0	0	0	0	0	.000
Buster Chatham (3B)	112	404	48	108	20	11	5	56	8	.267
Earl Clark	82	233	29	69	11	3	3	28	3	.296
Bill Cronin	66	178	19	45	9	1	0	17	0	.253
Bill Dunlap	16	29	3	2	1	0	0	0	0	.069
Hank Gowdy	16	25	0	5	1	0	0	2	0	.200
Bernie James	8	11	1	2	1	0	0	1	0	.182
Owen Kahn	1	0	1	0	0	0	0	0	0	—
Freddie Maguire (2B)	146	516	54	138	21	5	0	52	4	.267
Rabbit Maranville (SS)	142	558	85	157	26	8	2	43	9	.281
Randy Moore	83	191	24	55	9	0	2	34	3	.288
Johnny Neun	81	212	39	69	12	2	2	23	9	.325
Billy Rhiel	20	47	3	8	4	0	0	4	0	.170
Lance Richbourg (OF)	130	529	81	161	23	8	3	54	13	.304
Gene Robertson	21	59	7	11	1	0	0	7	0	.186
Red Rollings	52	123	10	29	6	0	0	10	2	.236
George Sisler (1B)	116	431	54	133	15	7	3	67	7	.309
Al Spohrer (C)	112	356	44	113	22	8	2	37	3	.317
Jimmy Welsh (OF)	113	422	51	116	21	9	3	36	5	.275
	154	5,356	693	1,503	246	78	66	631	69	.281

	W	L	G	GS	CG	IP	H	BB	SO	ERA
Ed Brandt	4	11	41	13	4	147⅓	168	59	65	5.01
Bob Brown	0	0	3	0	0	6	10	8	1	10.50
Ben Cantwell	9	15	31	21	10	173⅓	213	45	43	4.88
Johnny Cooney	0	0	2	0	0	7	16	3	1	18.00
Bruce Cunningham	5	6	36	6	2	106⅔	121	41	28	5.48
Fred Frankhouse	7	6	27	11	3	110⅔	138	43	30	5.61
Burleigh Grimes	3	5	11	9	1	49	72	22	15	7.35
Ken Jones	0	1	8	1	0	19⅔	28	4	4	5.95
Socks Seibold	15	16	36	33	20	251	288	85	70	4.12
Bill Sherdel	6	5	21	14	7	119½	131	30	26	4.75
Bob Smith	10	14	38	24	14	219⅔	247	85	84	4.26
Tom Zachary	11	5	24	22	10	151⅓	192	50	57	4.58
	70	84		154	71	1,361	1,624	475	424	4.91

Shutouts—Smith (2), Brandt, Frankhouse, Seibold, Zachary
Saves—Smith (5), Cantwell (2), Seibold (2), Brandt, Sherdel

	G	AB	R	H	2B	3B	HR	RBI	SB	AVG
Wally Berger (OF)	156	617	94	199	44	8	19	84	13	.323
Al Bool	49	85	5	16	1	0	0	6	0	.188
Buster Chatham	17	44	4	10	1	0	1	3	0	.227
Earl Clark	16	50	8	11	2	0	0	4	1	.220
Bill Cronin	51	107	8	22	6	1	0	10	0	.206
Bill Dreesen	48	180	38	40	10	4	1	10	1	.222
Bill Hunnefield	11	21	2	6	0	0	0	1	0	.286
Freddie Maguire (2B)	148	492	36	112	18	2	0	26	3	.228
Rabbit Maranville (SS)	145	562	69	146	22	5	0	33	9	.260
Randy Moore	83	192	19	50	8	1	3	34	1	.260
Johnny Neun	79	104	17	23	1	3	0	11	2	.221
Lance Richbourg	97	286	32	82	11	6	2	29	9	.287
Johnny Scalzi	2	1	0	0	0	0	0	0	0	.000
Wes Schulmerich (OF)	95	327	36	101	17	7	2	43	0	.309
Earl Sheely (1B)	147	538	30	147	15	2	1	77	0	.273
Al Spohrer (C)	114	350	23	84	17	5	0	27	2	.240
Billy Urbanski (3B)	82	303	22	72	13	4	0	17	3	.238
Pat Veltman	1	1	0	0	0	0	0	0	0	.000
Bucky Walters	9	38	2	8	2	0	0	0	0	.211
Charlie Wilson	16	58	7	11	4	0	1	11	0	.190
Red Worthington (OF)	128	491	47	143	25	10	4	44	1	.291
	156	5,296	533	1,367	221	59	34	490	46	.258

	W	L	G	GS	CG	IP	H	BB	SO	ERA
Ed Brandt	18	11	33	29	23	250	228	77	112	2.92
Bob Brown	0	1	3	1	0	6⅓	9	3	2	8.53
Ben Cantwell	7	9	33	16	9	156½	160	34	32	3.63
Bruce Cunningham	3	12	33	16	6	136⅔	157	54	32	4.48
Fred Frankhouse	8	8	26	15	6	127½	125	43	50	4.03
Hal Haid	0	2	27	0	0	56	59	16	20	4.50
Bill McAfee	0	1	18	1	0	29⅔	39	10	9	6.37
Ray Moss	1	3	12	5	0	45	56	16	14	4.60
Socks Seibold	10	18	33	29	10	206½	226	65	50	4.67
Bill Sherdel	6	10	27	16	8	137½	163	35	34	4.25
Tom Zachary	11	15	33	28	16	229	243	53	64	3.10
	64	90		156	78	1,380½	1,465	406	419	3.90

Shutouts—Brandt (3), Seibold (3), Zachary (3), Cantwell (2), Cunningham
Saves—Brandt (2), Cantwell (2), Zachary (2), Cunningham, Frankhouse, Haid

1932

Record: 77–77
Finish: Fifth
Games Behind: 13
Manager: Bill McKechnie

The summer of 1932 was a trying one for Braves pitchers. What they wouldn't have given for a few more runs. Just a little more offense, and Bill McKechnie's team might have been a serious contender.

As it was, the club started well and was in second place on the Fourth of July. On May 22, they drew a crowd of 47,123 to Braves Field for a doubleheader against Philadelphia. The rest of the league wasn't very strong, and the Boston pitching was respectable enough to keep them in the hunt for a while.

The main reason was Bob Brown, a 21-year-old right-hander who was in his first full season with the Braves. In seven seasons, he would win just 16 games—all but two of those came in 1932 when he was one of the toughest pitchers to hit in the league.

Additionally, Huck Betts, who'd never before won more than seven games in a season, nearly doubled that figure with 13 victories; and Tom Zachary equaled his career high with 12 wins.

Their pitching benefited from a defense that set a league record at the time with a .976 fielding average. At age 40, Rabbit Maranville moved from shortstop to second base and led the league in defense at the position.

Thanks to pitching and defense, it was the first season since 1921 that the Braves didn't have a losing record.

Wally Berger's power numbers took a dip for the second straight year, though he did lead the league's outfielders in defensive average.

	G	AB	R	H	2B	3B	HR	RBI	SB	AVG
Bill Akers	36	93	8	24	3	1	1	17	0	.258
Wally Berger (OF)	145	602	90	185	34	6	17	73	5	.307
Earl Clark	50	44	11	11	2	0	0	4	1	.250
Ox Eckhardt	8	8	1	2	0	0	0	1	0	.250
Hod Ford	40	95	9	26	5	2	0	6	0	.274
Pinky Hargrave	82	217	20	57	14	3	4	33	1	.263
Dutch Holland	39	156	15	46	11	1	1	18	0	.295
Buck Jordan	49	212	27	68	12	3	2	29	1	.321
Fritz Knothe (3B)	89	344	45	82	19	1	1	36	5	.238
Fred Leach	84	223	21	55	9	2	1	29	1	.247
Rabbit Maranville (2B)	149	571	67	134	20	4	0	37	4	.235
Randy Moore	107	351	41	103	21	2	3	43	1	.293
Wes Schulmerich (OF)	119	404	47	105	22	5	11	57	5	.260
Johnny Schulte	10	9	1	2	0	0	1	2	0	.222
Art Shires (1B)	82	298	32	71	9	3	5	30	1	.238
Al Spohrer (C)	104	335	31	90	12	2	0	33	2	.269
Billy Urbanski (SS)	136	563	80	153	25	8	8	46	8	.272
Bucky Walters	22	75	8	14	3	1	0	4	0	.187
Red Worthington (OF)	105	435	62	132	35	8	8	61	1	.303
	155	5,506	649	1,460	262	53	63	594	36	.265

	W	L	G	GS	CG	IP	H	BB	SO	ERA
Huck Betts	13	11	31	27	16	221⅔	229	35	32	2.80
Ed Brandt	16	16	35	31	19	254	271	57	79	3.97
Bob Brown	14	7	35	28	9	213	187	104	110	3.30
Ben Cantwell	13	11	37	9	3	146	133	33	33	2.96
Bruce Cunningham	1	0	18	3	0	47	50	19	21	3.45
Fred Frankhouse	4	6	37	6	3	108⅔	113	45	35	3.56
Leo Mangum	0	0	7	0	0	10⅓	17	0	3	5.23
Hub Pruett	1	5	18	7	4	63	76	30	27	5.14
Socks Seibold	3	10	28	20	6	136⅔	173	41	33	4.68
Bill Sherdel	0	0	1	0	0	1⅔	3	1	0	0.00
Tom Zachary	12	11	32	24	12	212	231	55	67	3.10
	77	77		155	72	1,414*	1,483	420	440	3.53

Shutouts—Betts (3), Brandt (2), Cantwell, Seibold, Zachary
Saves—Cantwell (5), Betts, Brandt, Brown

Huck Betts surprised everyone with 13 wins in 1932.

1933

Record: 83–71
Finish: Fourth
Games Behind: 9
Manager: Bill McKechnie

Using the familiar combination of pitching and defense, the Braves continued to improve under the direction of Bill McKechnie in 1933. In fact, the team actually was in the pennant race most of the season and finished with its best record since 1921.

The nation was still feeling the effects of the depression, but many Bostonians were forgetting their financial woes, at least temporarily, by getting caught up in the exploits of the Braves.

Wally Berger, whose power numbers if not his overall performance had declined since his rookie season, was back pounding home runs again. He was selected as the team's

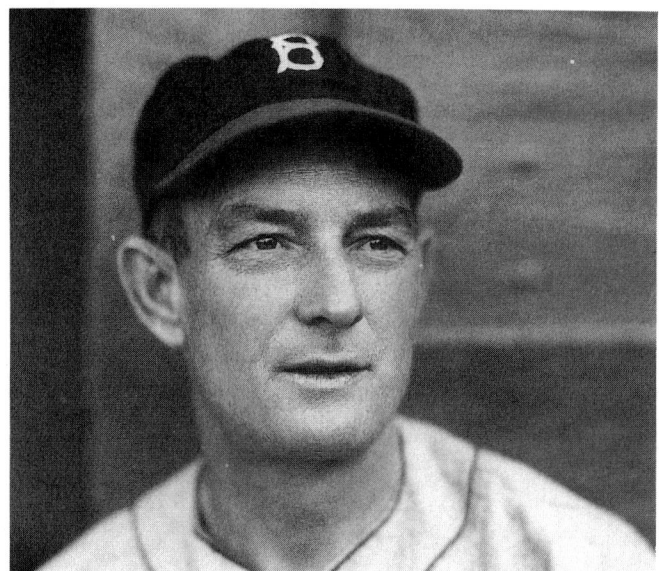

One of the best managers ever to direct the Braves, Bill McKechnie won pennants in three cities but couldn't get Boston higher than fourth.

lone representative in the first All-Star Game held July 6 at Chicago's Comiskey Park.

When the regular season resumed, McKechnie's team caught fire, climbing from fifth place on the Fourth of July to second in late August with a 22–6 run. Not surprisingly, there was even talk of another "miracle."

On August 31, the first-place Giants came to Boston for a six-game series with the home team six games off the pace. In the series opener, Berger hit his 25th home run of the season to back Ben Cantwell's pitching in a 7–3 victory. A serious run at the top seemed feasible.

However, in that game, right fielder Randy Moore, in the midst of his finest season and a real factor in the club's success, sustained a hand injury and missed the remainder of the series. The Braves didn't win again until the Giants left town, and pennant fever was little more than a memory. Still, the series drew 150,000 to Braves Field, including a record 51,465 for the doubleheader.

The suspense was reduced to Berger's battle with Philadelphia's Chuck Klein for the home run title. Even that suffered a severe setback when the Boston slugger came down with pneumonia on a road trip and had to miss three weeks of the season, spending most of it in a Pittsburgh hospital.

On the day Berger was discharged, the Phillies were playing the Pirates in Pittsburgh. The season was about over, but he stopped by Forbes Field on his way out of town and saw a youngster named Reggie Grabowski pitching for Philadelphia. It proved to be a fruitful scouting mission.

Berger returned to Boston with little thought of playing again until 1934. On the final day of the season, he sat on the bench in street clothes until the third inning when he put on his uniform. It so happened that Grabowski was shutting out the Braves, 1–0, on three hits through seven innings. With two runners on and two outs in the seventh, Grabowski walked catcher Shanty Hogan intentionally to get to Rabbit Maranville. McKechnie looked down the bench and asked

the weakened Berger if he could pinch-hit. He did, delivering a grand slam that became one of the most famous home runs in the franchise's Boston era.

It was Berger's 27th home run, leaving him one short of Klein for the league lead. However, the Braves' 4–1 victory was the difference between fourth and fifth place. It became known as the $7,100 home run, the bonus the team received for finishing in the first division, one-half game ahead of St. Louis. It amounted to just $242.82 per man, but in 1933, that was enough for a nice shopping spree.

The 517,803 fans who visited Braves Field that year represented a franchise record that stood until 1946.

With a .978 fielding average, the Braves led the league in defense for the second straight season, breaking the NL record they'd set the previous year. Cantwell led the league in percentage (.667), winning 20 for the only time in his career and finishing tied for second in victories with Dizzy Dean. He was the club's first 20-game winner since Joe Oeschger in 1921. However, Bob Brown, who'd won 14 the year before, appeared in just five games due to an injury sustained playing badminton.

In spite of his illness, Berger finished among the league leaders in several departments, including second in RBIs (106), total bases, and slugging average to Klein, who won the Triple Crown.

	G	AB	R	H	2B	3B	HR	RBI	SB	AVG
Wally Berger (OF)	137	528	84	165	37	8	27	106	2	.313
Earl Clark	7	23	3	8	1	0	0	1	0	.348
Hod Ford	5	15	0	1	0	0	0	1	0	.067
Dick Gyselman	58	155	10	37	6	2	0	12	0	.239
Pinky Hargrave	45	73	5	13	0	0	0	6	1	.178
Shanty Hogan (C)	96	328	15	83	7	0	3	30	0	.253
Dutch Holland	13	31	3	8	3	0	0	3	1	.258
Buck Jordan (1B)	152	588	77	168	29	9	4	46	4	.286
Fritz Knothe	44	158	15	36	5	2	1	6	1	.228
Hal Lee (OF)	88	312	32	69	15	9	1	28	1	.221
Rabbit Maranville (2B)	143	478	46	104	15	4	0	38	2	.218
Randy Moore (OF)	135	497	64	150	23	7	8	70	3	.302
Joe Mowry	86	249	25	55	8	5	0	20	1	.221
Wes Schulmerich	29	85	10	21	6	1	1	13	0	.247
Al Spohrer	67	184	11	46	6	1	1	12	3	.250
Tommy Thompson	24	97	6	18	1	0	0	6	0	.186
Billy Urbanski (SS)	144	566	65	142	21	4	0	35	4	.251
Pinky Whitney (3B)	100	382	42	94	17	2	8	49	2	.246
Red Worthington	17	45	3	7	4	0	0	0	0	.156
Al Wright	4	1	0	1	0	0	0	0	0	1.000
	156	5,243	552	1,320	217	56	54	511	25	.252

	W	L	G	GS	CG	IP	H	BB	SO	ERA
Huck Betts	11	11	35	26	17	242	225	55	40	2.79
Ed Brandt	18	14	41	32	23	287⅔	256	77	104	2.60
Bob Brown	0	0	5	0	0	6⅔	6	3	3	2.70
Ben Cantwell	20	10	40	29	18	254⅔	242	54	57	2.62
Ed Fallenstein	2	1	9	4	1	35	43	13	5	3.60
Fred Frankhouse	16	15	43	30	14	244⅔	249	77	83	3.16
Leo Mangum	4	3	25	5	2	84	93	11	28	3.32
Socks Seibold	1	4	11	5	1	36⅔	43	14	10	3.68
Bob Smith	4	3	14	4	3	58⅔	68	7	16	3.22
Ray Starr	0	1	9	1	0	28	32	9	15	3.86
Tom Zachary	7	9	26	20	6	125	134	35	22	3.53
	83	71	156		85	1,403	1,391	355	383	2.96

Shutouts—Brandt (3), Betts (2), Cantwell (2), Frankhouse (2), Zachary (2), Fallenstein, Mangum, Smith
Saves—Betts (4), Brandt (4), Cantwell (2), Frankhouse (2), Zachary (2), Seibold, Smith

1934

Record: 78–73
Finish: Fourth
Games Behind: 16
Manager: Bill McKechnie

At age 42, Rabbit Maranville was still playing a solid second base, though his offensive production was sliding as he began his 24th season. He long ago had become a Boston landmark and a bit of a national institution as well.

But on March 28, 1934, his career essentially came to an end when he sustained a broken leg sliding home on a double steal in an exhibition game against the Yankees.

The leg was set while Rabbit lay on the field smoking a cigarette. The injury didn't heal properly, and Maranville not only missed the entire season but would play just 23 more games in his career.

Will Rogers was so moved as to write in the Boston Globe, "When Rabbit Maranville breaks a leg right at the opening of the season, that constitutes America's greatest crisis, and if anybody reading this had to ask who Rabbit is, then you should be made to show your citizenship papers."

At least spiritually, Maranville's loss was a blow to the team and even more so to the fans, who stayed away in droves after turning out in record numbers a year earlier. A "day" was held for the injured hero in September, but bad weather held the turnout to just 22,000.

Once again, Wally Berger's exploits were the primary source of entertainment. And for the second straight year,

Fred Frankhouse was the first Brave other than Wally Berger to represent the franchise in the All-Star Game.

he missed the home run title by one, trailing Mel Ott and Ripper Collins, who tied for the lead with 35.

Flint Rhem, a right-hander acquired from St. Louis early in the season, pitched a near no-hitter against Brooklyn in July. He gave up only a bunt single in a 1–0 victory. Fred Frankhouse was among the league's best pitchers and went to the All-Star Game, along with Berger. Hal Lee, an outfielder/second baseman, hit three of his eight home runs in one game, the second Brave to do so in the 20th century.

	G	AB	R	H	2B	3B	HR	RBI	SB	AVG
Wally Berger (OF)	150	615	92	183	35	8	34	121	2	.298
Elbie Fletcher	8	4	4	2	0	0	0	0	1	.500
Dick Gyselman	24	36	7	6	1	1	0	4	0	.167
Shanty Hogan	92	279	20	73	5	2	4	34	0	.262
Buck Jordan (1B)	124	489	68	152	26	9	2	58	3	.311
Hal Lee (OF)	139	521	70	152	23	6	8	79	3	.292
Les Mallon	42	166	23	49	6	1	0	18	0	.295
Dan McGee	7	22	2	3	0	0	0	1	0	.136
Marty McManus (2B)	119	435	56	120	18	0	8	47	5	.276
Randy Moore	123	422	55	120	21	2	7	64	2	.284
Joe Mowry	25	79	9	17	3	0	1	4	0	.215
Al Spohrer (C)	100	265	25	59	15	0	0	17	1	.223
Tommy Thompson (OF)	105	343	40	91	12	3	0	37	2	.265
Johnnie Tyler	3	6	0	1	0	0	0	1	0	.167
Billy Urbanski (SS)	146	605	104	177	30	6	7	53	4	.293
Pinky Whitney (3B)	146	563	58	146	26	2	12	79	7	.259
Red Worthington	41	65	6	16	5	0	0	6	0	.246
	152	5,370	683	1,460	233	44	83	649	30	.272

	W	L	G	GS	CG	IP	H	BB	SO	ERA
Dick Barrett	1	3	15	3	0	32⅓	50	12	14	6.68
Huck Betts	17	10	40	27	10	213	258	42	69	4.06
Ed Brandt	16	14	40	28	20	255	249	83	106	3.53
Bob Brown	1	3	16	8	2	58⅓	59	36	21	5.71
Ben Cantwell	5	11	27	19	6	143⅓	163	34	45	4.33
Jumbo Elliott	1	1	7	3	0	15⅓	19	9	6	5.87
Fred Frankhouse	17	9	37	31	13	233⅔	239	77	78	3.20
Leo Mangum	5	3	29	3	1	94⅓	127	23	28	5.72
Clarence Pickrel	0	0	10	1	0	16	24	7	9	5.06
Flint Rhem	8	8	25	20	5	152⅔	164	38	56	3.60
Bob Smith	6	9	39	5	3	121⅔	133	36	26	4.66
Tom Zachary	1	2	5	4	2	24	27	8	4	3.38
	78	73		152	62	1,359⅔	1,512	405	462	4.11

Shutouts—Brandt (3), Betts (2), Frankhouse (2), Rhem (2), Brown, Cantwell, Zachary
Saves—Brandt (5), Cantwell (5), Smith (5), Betts (3), Frankhouse, Mangum

1935

Record: 38–115
Finish: Eighth
Games Behind: 61½
Manager: Bill McKechnie

Baseball history is filled with many stories of ineptitude. Contemporary fans usually think of the original 1962 Mets, who lost 120 games, when the subject is incompetence. But before the exploits of Casey Stengel's amazing expansion team graced the National League, the bumbling Braves of 1935 set the post-1900 standard for inferior play and all-around disgracefulness.

Before the year was over, the team would sign Babe Ruth, apply for a license to stage dog racing at Braves Field, see Ruth retire, and be taken over by the league because of its strapped financial state.

Team president Judge Emil Fuchs had been slowly sinking into debt and decided dog racing was the ticket out of his financial hole. The league, however, was horrified and re-

jected Fuchs' plan. The estate of former owner James Gaffney, which still controlled Braves Field, then stepped in and
threatened to kick the team out on the street and stage the
dog races anyway.

To solve the team's financial dilemma, the league agreed
to loan the franchise $7,500 for spring training expenses and
to take over the lease on Braves Field, subletting it to Fuchs
at a reduced price.

It was only a temporary fix, and Fuchs realized it. He knew
he had to find a way to make enough money to pay off
$79,000 he'd borrowed against his stock from vice president
Charles F. Adams.

Fuchs found what he thought was the solution in the presence of George Herman Ruth. The Babe was 40 years old and
out of shape. He was set on managing, but the Yankees
weren't interested in his services as either a player or manager.

Ruth was still the game's biggest draw, and he was quite
popular in Boston, where he had begun his career with the
Red Sox. Fuchs approached the Yankees, who were willing to
release Ruth so the Braves could sign him. The Braves president then pitched an offer to Ruth to become a player, assistant manager, and second vice president for $25,000 and a
share of profits.

Fans were thrilled at the announcement, some 3,000
greeting Ruth when he arrived in Boston February 27 via
train. Fuchs thought he'd remedied his problems, especially when a record opening day crowd of 25,000 showed
up at Braves Field. Ruth had a home run and double off
Carl Hubbell, leading the Braves to a 4–2 victory over the
Giants.

But the thrill faded quickly. Ruth's presence caused dissension because he had his own set of rules and appeared a
constant threat to Bill McKechnie's job. His opening day offensive flourish was a mirage, too. The Bambino's skills were
gone, as were those of Rabbit Maranville.

At 43, Maranville returned May 9 after missing the entire
1934 season with a broken leg. He set a National League
record by appearing in his 23rd season, but, like Ruth, he
had nothing left.

The Babe's last hurrah came May 25 at Pittsburgh when
he hit three home runs. The third was No. 714 of his career
and the first ever to clear the right-field roof at Forbes Field.
Remarkably, it was only the second time in his career that
Ruth homered three times in the same game.

Babe Ruth, shown here with the Dean brothers, Dizzy (L) and Paul (R),
had little to smile about in his brief Braves career.

Guy Bush was pitching for Pittsburgh against the Braves when he gave
up Babe Ruth's last home run, then he joined Boston for a brief tour in
1936–37.

But on June 2, Ruth announced his retirement. He played
in just 28 games as a Brave, hitting six home runs—which was
still second on the team at the end of the season.

At the same time, Fuchs' fate was sealed. With a lousy
team and without Ruth to draw crowds, he had no hope of
paying off his debt. On July 31, he forfeited his majority
share of the team, and 14 months later he filed for bankruptcy.

The team was last from May 22 to the end of the season. It
lost 15 in a row on the road in July and then went 2–28 from
mid-August to mid-September. On September 22, the Braves
lost for the 110th time to set the modern NL record that
stood until the '62 Mets came along. Boston's 115 losses for
the year were the most in the league since the 1899 Cleveland Spiders lost 134.

But through it all, Wally Berger had perhaps his finest season, leading the league in both home runs (34) and RBIs
(130) and hitting three grand slams. On August 11, he had a
home run, triple, and two doubles to tie what was then the
modern record of 11 total bases in a game. His 130 RBIs set
a modern franchise record that stood until broken by Eddie
Mathews in 1953.

The team's .248 percentage remains an all-time franchise
low. The 61½-game deficit was the worst since 1909 and ranks
as the third worst in club history.

After the season, the league temporarily took over the
team until it could be reorganized financially with Adams as
the majority stockholder and former Red Sox boss Bob
Quinn as president.

	G	AB	R	H	2B	3B	HR	RBI	SB	AVG
Wally Berger (OF)	150	589	91	174	39	4	34*	130*	3	.295
Joe Coscarart	86	284	30	67	11	2	1	29	2	.236
Art Doll	3	10	0	1	0	0	0	0	0	.100
Elbie Fletcher	39	148	12	35	7	1	1	9	1	.236
Shanty Hogan	59	163	9	49	8	0	2	25	0	.301
Buck Jordan (1B)	130	470	62	131	24	5	5	35	3	.279
Hal Lee (OF)	112	422	49	128	18	6	0	39	0	.303
Bill Lewis	6	4	1	0	0	0	0	0	0	.000
Les Mallon (2B)	116	412	48	113	24	2	2	25	3	.274
Rabbit Maranville	23	67	3	10	2	0	0	5	0	.149
Randy Moore (OF)	125	407	42	112	20	4	4	42	1	.275
Ed Moriarty	8	34	4	11	2	1	1	1	0	.324
Joe Mowry	81	136	17	36	8	1	1	13	0	.265
Ray Mueller	42	97	10	22	5	0	3	11	0	.227
Babe Ruth	28	72	13	13	0	0	6	12	0	.181
Al Spohrer (C)	92	260	22	63	7	1	1	16	0	.242
Tommy Thompson	112	297	34	81	7	1	4	30	2	.273
Johnnie Tyler	13	47	7	16	2	1	2	11	0	.340
Billy Urbanski (SS)	132	514	53	118	17	0	4	30	3	.230
Pinky Whitney (3B)	126	458	41	125	23	4	4	60	2	.273
	153	5,309	575	1,396	233	33	75	544	20	.263

	W	L	G	GS	CG	IP	H	BB	SO	ERA
Larry Benton	2	3	29	0	0	72	103	24	21	6.88
Huck Betts	2	9	44	19	2	159⅔	213	40	40	5.47
Al Blanche	0	0	6	0	0	17⅓	14	5	4	1.56
Ed Brandt	5	19	29	25	12	174⅔	224	66	61	5.00
Bob Brown	1	8	15	10	2	65	79	36	17	6.37
Ben Cantwell	4	25*	39	24	13	210⅔	235	44	34	4.61
Fred Frankhouse	11	15	40	29	10	230⅔	278	81	64	4.76
Danny MacFayden	5	13	28	20	7	151⅔	200	34	46	5.10
Leo Mangum	0	0	3	0	0	4⅔	6	2	0	3.86
Flint Rhem	0	5	10	6	0	40½	61	11	10	5.36
Bob Smith	8	18	46	20	8	203⅓	232	61	58	3.94
	38	115*		153	54	1,330	1,645	404	355	4.93

Shutouts—Smith (2), Betts, Brown, Frankhouse, MacFayden
Saves—Smith (5)

1936

Record: 71–83
Finish: Sixth
Games Behind: 21
Manager: Bill McKechnie

New club president Bob Quinn probably thought long and hard about how to alter the negative image surrounding the franchise after the disastrous 1935 season. His solution was to change the team's nickname.

Though the franchise had been known as the Braves since 1912, Quinn decided to conduct a fan poll to choose a replacement. The most-popular submissions were turned over to a panel of sportswriters who made the final choice. The most appropriate suggestion may have been the Bankrupts, but the judges chose Bees. The name of Braves Field was even changed to National League Park—or more commonly, the Beehive.

Whether it was the nickname or just the restoration of general order to the franchise, manager Bill McKechnie fielded one of the most improved teams in history. Not that it was good—just improved.

The Bees won 33 more games than in 1935, moved up two notches in the standings, and finished 41½ games closer to first place. More than anything else, this record simply showed how pathetic the '35 Braves were.

Wally Berger, playing his last full season in Boston, had another fine year. Though his numbers were down, he still tied for third in the league in home runs (25).

As usual, the club relied mainly on pitching and defense, finishing dead last in team batting average and runs scored despite the spark of newcomers Tony Cuccinello at second and Gene Moore in the outfield. Moore led the league's outfielders with 31 assists in his first full season in the majors.

Tony Cuccinello (second from left) had to get on his toes in the spring of 1936 to pose with teammate Al Blance and Yankees (L-R) Tony Lazzeri, Frank Crosetti, and rookie Joe DiMaggio.

The Beehive hosted the fourth All-Star Game, which also was the first won by the National League, 4–3. However, only 25,556 turned out to witness it.

	G	AB	R	H	2B	3B	HR	RBI	SB	AVG
Wally Berger (OF)	138	534	88	154	23	3	25	91	1	.288
Joe Coscarart (3B)	104	367	28	90	11	2	2	44	0	.245
Tony Cuccinello (2B)	150	565	68	174	26	3	7	86	1	.308
Art Doll (C)	1	2	0	0	0	0	0	0	0	.000
Mickey Haslin	36	104	14	29	1	2	2	11	0	.279
Buck Jordan (1B)	138	555	81	179	27	5	3	66	2	.323
Swede Larsen	3	1	0	0	0	0	0	0	0	.000
Hal Lee (OF)	152	565	46	143	24	7	3	64	4	.253
Bill Lewis	29	62	11	19	2	0	0	3	0	.306
Al Lopez (C)	128	426	46	103	12	5	7	50	1	.242
Gene Moore (OF)	151	637	91	185	38	12	13	67	6	.290
Ed Moriarty	6	6	1	1	0	0	0	0	0	.167
Ray Mueller	24	71	5	14	4	0	0	5	0	.197
Andy Pilney	3	2	0	0	0	0	0	0	0	.000
Tommy Thompson	106	266	37	76	9	0	4	36	3	.286
Billy Urbanski (SS)	122	494	55	129	17	5	0	26	2	.261
Rabbit Warstler	74	304	27	64	6	0	0	17	2	.211
Pinky Whitney	10	40	1	7	0	0	0	5	0	.175
	157	5,480	631	1,450	207	45	67	594	23	.265

	W	L	G	GS	CG	IP	H	BB	SO	ERA
John Babich	0	0	3	0	0	6	11	6	1	10.50
Ray Benge	7	9	21	19	2	115	161	38	32	5.79
Al Blanche	0	1	11	0	0	16	20	8	4	6.19
Bob Brown	0	2	2	2	0	8⅓	10	3	5	5.40
Guy Bush	4	5	15	11	5	90⅓	98	20	28	3.39
Ben Cantwell	9	9	34	12	4	133⅓	127	35	42	3.04
Tiny Chaplin	10	15	40	31	14	231⅔	273	62	86	4.12
Art Doll	0	1	1	1	0	8	11	2	2	3.38
Gene Ford	0	0	2	1	0	2	2	3	0	13.50
Fabian Kowalik	0	1	1	1	1	9	18	2	0	8.00
Johnny Lanning	7	11	28	20	3	153	154	55	33	3.65
Danny MacFayden	17	13	37	31	21	266⅔	268	66	86	2.87
Jim McCloskey	0	0	4	1	0	8	14	3	2	11.25
Ambrose Murray	0	0	4	1	0	11	15	3	2	4.09
Wayne Osborne	1	1	5	3	0	20	31	9	8	5.85
Bobby Reis	6	5	35	5	3	138⅔	152	74	25	4.48
Bob Smith	6	7	35	11	5	136	142	35	36	3.77
Hal Weafer	0	0	1	0	0	3	6	3	0	12.00
Bill Weir	4	3	12	7	3	57⅓	53	24	29	2.83
	71	83		157	61	1,413⅓*	1,566	451	421	3.94

Shutouts—MacFayden (2), Smith (2), Weir (2), Lanning
Saves—Smith (8), Cantwell (2), Chaplin (2), Blanche

1937

Record: 79–73
Finish: Fifth
Games Behind: 16
Manager: Bill McKechnie

The Bees showed continued improvement in 1937, and the reasons were Jim Turner and Lou Fette.

Few Boston fans had heard of either Turner or Fette when the season began, but by October, the pitchers were the talk of the city and the entire National League.

Neither Turner, a 33-year-old right-hander, nor Fette, a 30-year-old right-hander, had ever appeared in a major league game prior to 1937. All they did as rookies—old ones at that—was win 20 games apiece with the weakest offensive club in the league. Their story is one of the most interesting sagas in the annals of the franchise.

Turner was the oldest rookie in the majors. The Bees bought him from Indianapolis for $1,000. They got Fette, a youngster compared to Turner, from St. Paul for $3,000. Both were primarily curveball specialists who relied on ex-

The oldest rookie in the majors in 1937 at age 33, Jim Turner baffled hitters on his way to 20 victories and a league-leading 2.38 ERA.

cellent control. They prospered with the handling of catcher Al Lopez and Bill McKechnie's acclaimed knowledge of pitchers.

Only two other National League pitchers won 20 in 1937, and both, the great Carl Hubbell and rookie left-hander Cliff Melton, worked for the pennant-winning Giants.

Turner, who also became the third rookie ever to lead a league in ERA (2.38), wouldn't have even made the club if not for Vic Frasier's homesickness. Frasier was sent home to Texas, and Turner became a sensation. Among other things, he led the league in complete games (24) and tied with Fette and Cincinnati's Lee Grissom for the most shutouts (5).

Fette was just as successful, finishing second in complete games, third in percentage, and fifth in ERA and innings.

Neither man would ever again pitch with the same efficiency.

The other notable event in the season was the June 15 deal that sent Wally Berger to the Giants. New president Bob Quinn basically gave away the slugging outfielder. In exchange, the Bees received $30,000 and a pitcher named Frank Gabler who never amounted to anything. Though Berger was off to a slow start and was taking abuse from the fans, it's difficult to justify the deal despite the fact he never regained the form that made him the team's centerpiece for seven years.

Rookie Vince DiMaggio debuted with the club, leading the league in strikeouts (111) and quickly proving he was not to be mistaken for brother Joe.

Just how bad was the offense? The Bees led the league in both staff ERA (3.22) and fielding percentage (.975) yet still finished fifth.

The Sporting News was impressed, naming McKechnie the National League Manager of the Year "for his managerial skill and his ability in handling men, especially pitchers, enabling him to pilot a mediocre team to a fifth place finish."

But worn down by eight years of fighting an uphill battle, McKechnie signed to manage Cincinnati in 1938. Within two years, he was back in the World Series.

	G	AB	R	H	2B	3B	HR	RBI	SB	AVG
Wally Berger	30	113	14	31	9	1	5	22	0	.274
Tony Cuccinello (2B)	152	575	77	156	36	4	11	80	2	.271
Vince DiMaggio (OF)	132	493	56	126	18	4	13	69	8	.256
Gil English (3B)	79	269	25	78	5	2	2	37	3	.290
Elbie Fletcher (1B)	148	539	56	133	22	4	1	38	3	.247
Debs Garms (OF)	125	478	60	124	15	8	2	37	2	.259
Roy Johnson	85	260	24	72	8	3	3	22	5	.277
Buck Jordan	8	8	1	2	0	0	0	0	0	.250
Al Lopez (C)	105	334	31	68	11	1	3	38	3	.204
Eddie Mayo	65	172	19	39	6	1	1	18	1	.227
Beauty McGowan	9	12	0	1	0	0	0	0	0	.083
Gene Moore (OF)	148	561	88	159	29	10	16	70	11	.283
Ray Mueller	64	187	21	47	9	2	2	26	1	.251
Bobby Reis	45	86	10	21	5	0	0	6	2	.244
Johnny Riddle	2	3	0	0	0	0	0	0	0	.000
Tommy Thevenow	21	34	5	4	0	1	0	2	0	.118
Billy Urbanski	1	1	0	0	0	0	0	0	0	.000
Rabbit Warstler (SS)	149	555	57	124	20	0	3	36	4	.223
Link Wasem	2	1	0	0	0	0	0	0	0	.000
	152	5,124	579	1,265	200	41	63	534	45	.247

	W	L	G	GS	CG	IP	H	BB	SO	ERA
Guy Bush	8	15	32	20	11	180⅔	201	48	56	3.54
Lou Fette	20	10	35	33	23	259	243	81	70	2.88
Vic Frasier	0	0	3	0	0	8	12	1	2	5.63
Frank Gabler	4	7	19	9	2	76	84	16	19	5.09
Ira Hutchinson	4	6	31	8	1	91⅓	99	35	29	3.73
Johnny Lanning	5	7	32	11	4	116⅔	107	40	37	3.93
Danny MacFayden	14	14	32	32	16	246	250	60	70	2.93
Bobby Reis	0	0	4	0	0	5	3	5	0	1.80
Milt Shoffner	3	1	6	5	3	42⅔	38	9	13	2.53
Bob Smith	0	1	18	0	0	44	52	6	14	4.09
Jim Turner	20	11	33	30	24*	256⅔	228	52	69	2.38*
Bill Weir	1	1	10	4	1	33	27	19	8	3.82
	79	73		152	85*	1,359½	1,344	372	387	3.22*

Shutouts—Fette (5*), Turner (5*), MacFayden (2), Bush, Gabler, Lanning, Shoffner
Saves—Smith (3), Gabler (2), Lanning (2), Bush, Shoffner, Turner

In two years with the Bees, Vince DiMaggio twice broke the National League record for strikeouts in a season.

1938

Record: 77–75
Finish: Fifth
Games Behind: 12
Manager: Casey Stengel

Casey Stengel served the franchise as a player and manager, neither with much success, but he left behind a wealth of amusing stories.

Jim Turner and Lou Fette both lost more games than they won in 1938, and they combined for 15 fewer victories than they had as rookies. Nevertheless, Casey Stengel's first Boston team won just two fewer games than Bill McKechnie's last one.

It could have been a sign that Stengel was about to lead the franchise back to respectability; however, that was anything but the case.

Stengel was a long way from managerial fame. He'd managed Brooklyn in 1934–36, never finishing above fifth, and he wouldn't see the first division in six seasons with Boston either.

Bees fans had mixed emotions about their new manager, who spent the last two seasons of his 14-year career as an outfielder with the club in 1924 and 1925. However, he was well thought of by team president Bob Quinn, and of course, he was popular with the writers because he was so colorful and entertaining.

But Stengel, like McKechnie, couldn't do much to help the team's offensive production. The Bees scored just 11 more runs than last-place Philadelphia, finishing fifth only on the strength of the second-best team ERA (3.40) in the league.

Turner and Fette still were effective, but the staff ace became 33-year-old right-hander Danny MacFayden, who had his third straight season of 14 or more wins and finished second in the league in shutouts (5) and fourth in ERA.

On June 11, Cincinnati's Johnny Vander Meer, once

Boston property, pitched the first of his record two consecutive no-hitters against the Bees, winning 4–0. Four days later, he no-hit Brooklyn. In his next start, he again faced the Bees but had his bid for a third straight no-hitter broken up with two out in the fourth by a Debs Garms single.

The season was not without a few offensive highlights, though. In April, Gene Moore and Harl Maggert hit grand slams in a 16–11 victory over Philadelphia. In July, Tony Cuccinello, Max West, and Elbie Fletcher hit successive home runs on just four pitches from Carl Hubbell. And against Vander Meer, rookie Max West hit a three-run homer with two outs and two strikes in the ninth to turn a 3–1 deficit into a 4–3 victory.

Late in the season, a hurricane blew into Boston during a game with the Cardinals. Umpire Beans Reardon said he wouldn't call the game until the outfield advertising signs were blown down. He changed his mind when Cuccinello called for a pop-up behind second base and catcher Al Lopez eventually caught it against the backstop.

The wind could have resulted from Vince DiMaggio's

Debs Garms broke up Johnny Vander Meer's bid for a third consecutive no-hitter.

bat flailing through the air. He broke the National League strikeout record for the second straight year, this time with 134.

	G	AB	R	H	2B	3B	HR	RBI	SB	AVG
Johnny Cooney (OF)	120	432	45	117	25	5	0	17	2	.271
Tony Cuccinello (2B)	147	555	62	147	25	2	9	76	4	.265
Vince DiMaggio (OF)	150	540	71	123	28	3	14	61	11	.228
Art Doll (C)	3	1	0	1	0	0	0	0	0	1.000
Gil English	53	165	17	41	6	0	2	21	1	.248
Elbie Fletcher (1B)	147	529	71	144	24	7	6	48	5	.272
Debs Garms	117	428	62	135	19	1	0	47	4	.315
Jim Hitchcock	28	76	2	13	0	0	0	7	1	.171
Roy Johnson	7	29	2	5	0	0	0	1	1	.172
Bob Kahle	8	3	2	1	0	0	0	0	0	.333
Tom Kane	2	2	0	0	0	0	0	0	0	.000
Al Lopez	71	236	19	63	6	1	1	14	5	.267
Harl Maggert	66	89	12	25	3	0	3	19	0	.281
Eddie Mayo	8	14	2	3	0	0	1	4	0	.214
Ralph McLeod	6	7	1	2	1	0	0	0	0	.286
Gene Moore	54	180	27	49	8	3	3	19	1	.272
Ray Mueller (C)	83	274	23	65	8	6	4	35	3	.237
Bobby Reis	34	49	6	9	0	0	0	4	1	.184
Johnny Riddle	19	57	6	16	1	0	0	2	0	.281
Joe Stripp (3B)	59	229	19	63	10	0	1	19	2	.275
Butch Sutcliffe	4	4	1	1	0	0	0	2	0	.250
Joe Walsh	4	8	0	0	0	0	0	0	0	.000
Rabbit Warstler (SS)	142	467	37	108	10	4	0	40	3	.231
Max West (OF)	123	418	47	98	16	5	10	63	5	.234
	153	5,251	561	1,312	199	39	54	519	49	.250

	W	L	G	GS	CG	IP	H	BB	SO	ERA
Mike Balas	0	0	1	0	0	1⅓	3	0	0	6.75
Art Doll	0	0	3	0	0	4	4	3	1	2.25
Tom Earley	1	0	2	1	1	11	8	1	4	3.27
Dick Errickson	9	7	34	10	6	122⅔	113	56	40	3.15
Lou Fette	11	13	33	32	17	239⅔	235	79	83	3.15
Frank Gabler	0	0	1	0	0	⅓	3	1	0	81.00
Ira Hutchinson	9	8	36	12	4	151	150	61	38	2.74
Art Kenney	0	0	2	0	0	2⅓	3	8	2	15.43
Johnny Lanning	8	7	32	18	4	138	146	52	39	3.72
Danny MacFayden	14	9	29	29	19	219⅔	208	64	58	2.95
Hiker Moran	0	0	1	0	0	3	1	1	0	0.00
John Niggeling	1	0	2	0	0	2	4	1	1	9.00
Bobby Reis	1	6	16	2	1	57⅔	61	41	20	4.99
Tommy Reis	0	0	4	0	0	6⅓	8	1	4	7.11
Milt Shoffner	8	7	26	15	9	139⅔	147	36	49	3.54
Jim Turner	14	18	35	34	22	268	267	54	71	3.46
Bill Weir	1	0	5	0	0	13⅓	14	6	3	6.75
	77	75		153	83*	1,380	1,375	465	413	3.40

Shutouts—MacFayden (5), Fette (3), Turner (3), Errickson, Hutchinson, Lanning, Shoffner
Saves—Errickson (6), Hutchinson (4), Fette, Shoffner

1939

Record: 63–88
Finish: Seventh
Games Behind: 32½
Manager: Casey Stengel

At least the 1939 Bees didn't have to worry about finishing last. They ended the season 18 games ahead of the dreadful Phillies. But that was about all you could say for Casey Stengel's second team, which finished 32½ games back of Cincinnati and a manager named Bill McKechnie.

About the only thing Boston led the league in was double plays. That achievement was due primarily to two things: a lot of base runners for the opposition and a slick 22-year-old shortstop named Eddie Miller. The Bees got Miller from Kansas City, a Cincinnati farm club, for Vince DiMaggio and four other players.

Miller made a quick impression but missed the second half of the season when he suffered a broken ankle in a collision with teammate and future Hall of Fame outfielder Al Simmons, who was just passing through Boston.

On June 27 the Bees entertained Brooklyn at the Beehive in a 23-inning extravaganza that was called because of darkness with the score 2–2 after 5 hours, 15 minutes. The game probably would have ended in the 13th if Boston pinch runner Otto Huber hadn't slipped and fallen rounding third with the winning run. Huber blamed his shoes, and for the rest of the season, Stengel checked a player's shoes before using him as a pinch runner.

Lou Fette won only 10 games, but six were shutouts to lead the league. Jim Turner won just four times, partly because he took a line drive on the nose and missed a month.

Hall of Famer Al Simmons made little impact in Boston, except to break shortstop Eddie Miller's ankle in a collision.

Otto Huber slipped and fell in 1939 and Casey Stengel never trusted a pinch-runner's shoes again.

But newly acquired Bill Posedel helped keep the team afloat by winning 15, tying for second in the league with five shutouts, and finishing fifth in complete games.

New first baseman Buddy Hassett led the club in hitting (.308) and was fifth in the league with 13 steals but provided no power.

And speaking of power, there was veteran Johnny Cooney, who had played 15 years without hitting a single home run until September 24. He hit his second the next day, then played the final five years of his career without hitting another.

The ultimate statement about the season and the frustration Bees fans were feeling came July 22 when Al Lopez dropped his second pop-up of the game. A fan charged out of the stands and punched the usually dependable catcher.

	W	L	G	GS	CG	IP	H	BB	SO	ERA
George Barnicle	2	2	6	1	0	18⅓	16	8	15	4.91
Joe Callahan	1	0	4	1	1	17½	17	3	8	3.12
Tom Earley	1	4	14	2	0	40	49	19	9	4.72
Dick Errickson	6	9	28	11	3	128⅓	143	54	33	4.00
Lou Fette	10	10	27	26	11	146	123	61	35	2.96
Fred Frankhouse	0	2	23	0	0	38	37	18	12	2.61
Johnny Lanning	5	6	37	6	3	129	120	53	45	3.42
Danny MacFayden	8	14	33	28	8	191⅓	221	59	46	3.90
Al Moran	1	1	6	2	1	20	21	11	4	4.50
Bill Posedel	15	13	33	29	18	220⅔	221	78	73	3.92
Milt Shoffner	4	6	25	11	7	132½	133	42	51	3.13
Joe Sullivan	6	9	31	11	7	113⅔	114	50	46	3.64
Jim Turner	4	11	25	22	9	157⅔	181	51	50	4.28
Al Veigel	0	1	2	2	0	2⅔	3	5	1	6.75
Bill Weir	0	0	2	0	0	2⅔	1	1	2	0.00
	63	88		152	68	1,358⅓	1,400	513	430	3.71

Shutouts—Fette (6*), Posedel (5)
Saves—Frankhouse (4), Lanning (4), MacFayden (2), Sullivan (2), Earley, Errickson, Shoffner

	G	AB	R	H	2B	3B	HR	RBI	SB	AVG
Stan Andrews	13	26	1	6	0	0	0	1	0	.231
Red Barkley	12	11	1	0	0	0	0	0	0	.000
Chet Clemens	9	23	2	5	0	0	0	1	1	.217
Johnny Cooney (OF)	118	368	39	101	8	1	2	27	2	.274
Tony Cuccinello (2B)	81	310	42	95	17	1	2	40	5	.306
Elbie Fletcher	35	106	14	26	2	0	0	6	1	.245
Debs Garms (OF)	132	513	68	153	24	9	2	37	2	.298
Buddy Hassett (1B)	147	590	72	182	15	3	2	60	13	.308
Oliver Hill	2	2	1	1	1	0	0	0	0	.500
Ralph Hodgin	32	48	4	10	1	0	0	4	0	.208
Otto Huber	11	22	2	6	1	0	0	3	0	.273
Al Lopez (C)	131	412	32	104	22	1	8	49	1	.252
Hank Majeski (3B)	106	367	35	100	16	1	7	54	2	.272
Phil Masi	46	114	14	29	7	2	1	14	0	.254
Eddie Miller (SS)	77	296	32	79	12	2	4	31	4	.267
Jimmy Outlaw	65	133	15	35	2	0	0	5	1	.263
Chet Ross	11	31	4	10	1	1	0	0	0	.323
Bama Rowell	21	59	5	11	2	2	0	6	0	.186
Bill Schuster	2	3	0	0	0	0	0	0	0	.000
Al Simmons	93	330	39	93	17	5	7	43	0	.282
Sibby Sisti	63	215	19	49	7	1	1	11	4	.228
Rabbit Warstler	114	342	34	83	11	3	0	24	2	.243
Max West (OF)	130	449	67	128	26	6	19	82	1	.285
Whitey Wietelmann	23	69	2	14	1	0	0	5	1	.203
	152	5,286	572	1,395	199	39	56	534	41	.264

1940

Record: 65–87
Finish: Seventh
Games Behind: 34½
Manager: Casey Stengel

Everyone, it seemed, had installed lights except the Bees. Maybe it's a good thing. Boston played the first night game at the Polo Grounds May 24 and lost to the Giants, 8–1. A week and a half later, Casey Stengel's club helped the Pirates switch on the electric at Forbes Field and lost, 14–2.

The only park other than the Beehive without lights was Wrigley Field in Chicago. At least the Bees weren't in danger of being the last to host night games.

It mattered little whether the 1940 club played by daylight or artificial light, however. The Bees were just as atrocious as they'd been in 1939. Thankfully, the Phillies again were even worse and claimed last place by a wide margin.

The story of the 1940 season was 39-year-old Johnny Cooney, a pitcher turned outfielder turned coach who wasn't even expected to play. But when it became evident the team was simply too thin to get along without him, Cooney took over as the regular center fielder. His .318 average led the club.

There were a lot of names from the 1939 team missing, including Debs Garms, who batted .355 for Pittsburgh. Jim Turner joined Bill McKechnie in Cincinnati, where he helped pitch the Reds to a pennant. Lou Fette was sold to Brooklyn. Al Lopez and Danny MacFayden were sent to Pittsburgh, and Tony Cuccinello became a Giant. The turnover made little difference, since the team's record was nearly identical to the previous season's.

Buddy Hassett, the Bees' steady-hitting first baseman, tied the National League record with 10 consecutive hits over three games in June yet batted .234—50 points lower than in any other season during his career.

Another record setter was shortstop Eddie Miller, who recovered from his broken ankle in 1939 to string together 241 errorless chances over 42 consecutive games. His .970 fielding average for the season set a league record for shortstops.

Manny Salvo, in his first year with the club, won 10 games, half of which were shutouts to tie for the league lead.

Rookie outfielder Chet Ross struck out 127 times, just short of Vince DiMaggio's league record, but led the team in home runs (17) and RBIs (89). He proved to be another flash in the pan, though, hitting just six homers the rest of his career, which was plagued by injuries.

One unexpected source of pride for the franchise was outfielder Max West, the club's lone representative in the All-Star Game at Sportsman's Park in St. Louis. West, who hit but seven home runs all season, was inserted into the starting lineup when Giants great Mel Ott was scratched. He responded with a three-run homer in the first inning of a 4–0 National League victory.

	G	AB	R	H	2B	3B	HR	RBI	SB	AVG
Stan Andrews	19	33	1	6	0	0	0	2	1	.182
Ray Berres (C)	85	229	12	44	4	1	0	14	0	.192
Siggy Broskie	11	22	1	6	1	0	0	4	0	.273
Johnny Cooney (OF)	108	365	40	116	14	3	0	21	4	.318
Tony Cuccinello	34	126	14	34	9	0	0	19	1	.270
Al Glossop	60	148	17	35	2	1	3	14	1	.236
Buddy Gremp	4	9	0	2	0	0	0	2	0	.222
Buddy Hassett (1B)	124	458	59	107	19	4	0	27	4	.234
Bobby Loane	13	22	4	5	3	0	0	1	2	.227
Al Lopez	36	119	20	35	3	1	2	17	1	.294
Hank Majeski	3	3	0	0	0	0	0	0	0	.000
Don Manno	3	7	1	2	0	0	1	4	0	.286
Phil Masi	63	138	11	27	4	1	0	14	0	.196
Eddie Miller (SS)	151	569	78	157	33	3	14	79	8	.276
Gene Moore	103	363	46	106	24	1	5	39	2	.292
Mel Preibisch	11	40	3	9	2	0	0	5	0	.225
Chet Ross (OF)	149	569	84	160	23	14	17	89	4	.281
Bama Rowell (2B)	130	486	46	148	19	8	3	58	12	.305
Les Scarsella	18	60	7	18	1	3	0	8	2	.300
Sibby Sisti (3B)	123	459	73	115	19	5	6	34	4	.251
Rabbit Warstler	33	57	6	12	0	0	0	4	0	.211
Max West (OF)	139	524	72	137	27	5	7	72	2	.261
Whitey Wietelmann	35	41	3	8	1	0	0	1	0	.195
Claude Wilborn	5	7	0	0	0	0	0	0	0	.000
	152	5,329	623	1,366	219	50	59	558	48	.256

	W	L	G	GS	CG	IP	H	BB	SO	ERA
George Barnicle	1	0	13	2	1	32⅔	28	31	11	7.44
Joe Callahan	0	2	6	2	0	15	20	13	3	10.20
Dick Coffman	1	5	31	0	0	48½	63	11	11	5.40
Tom Earley	2	0	4	1	1	16⅓	16	3	5	3.86
Dick Errickson	12	13	34	29	17	236½	241	90	34	3.16
Lou Fette	0	5	7	5	0	32⅓	38	18	2	5.57
Al Javery	2	4	29	4	1	83⅓	99	36	42	5.51
Art Johnson	0	1	2	1	0	6	10	3	1	10.50
Frank Lamanna	1	0	5	1	1	13⅓	13	8	3	4.73
Al Piechota	2	5	21	8	2	61	68	41	18	5.75
Bill Posedel	12	17	35	32	18	233	263	81	86	4.13
Manny Salvo	10	9	21	20	14	160⅔	151	43	60	3.08
Nick Strincevich	4	8	32	14	5	128⅔	142	63	54	5.53
Joe Sullivan	10	14	36	22	7	177⅓	157	89	64	3.55
Bill Swift	1	1	4	0	0	9⅓	12	7	7	2.89
Jim Tobin	7	3	15	11	9	96⅓	102	24	29	3.83
Bob Williams	0	0	5	0	0	9	21	12	5	16.00
	65	87		152	76	1,359	1,444	573	435	4.36

Shutouts—Salvo (5*), Errickson (3), Earley
Saves—Errickson (4), Coffman (3), Javery, Posedel, Strincevich, Sullivan, Swift

1941

Record: 62–92
Finish: Seventh
Games Behind: 38
Manager: Casey Stengel

Finally realizing that the team nickname had nothing to do with its miserable performance, the franchise scrapped Bees and returned to Braves. And Casey Stengel proved he could bring the team in seventh, regardless of what it was called.

A new syndicate, still headed by Bob Quinn, bought the team from the estate of Charles F. Adams. Among the stockholders was contractor Lou Perini. His entrance into the picture would prove to be one of the major events in franchise history, though it would take a few years for that fact to be recognized.

Max West wasn't an All-Star Game hero as he was in 1940. In fact, only Eddie Miller made the National League team. However, West still provided one of the season's most memorable moments, one quite fitting for this team.

Eddie Miller was one of the finest defensive shortstops in franchise history and set a league fielding record at the position in 1940.

Starting in place of the great Mel Ott, Max West hit a home run in the 1940 All-Star Game, but a year later, a boner and a sip of water cost him some teeth.

One day after making an infield out, West was returning to the dugout when he noticed a loose ball rolling up to his feet. Assuming it was a foul ball, he picked it up and flipped it to Phillies catcher Mickey Livingston, who turned and tagged out Braves runner Frank Demaree, who was trying to score on a passed ball.

Babe Dahlgren's power could have helped the '41 Braves if he hadn't been sold to Cincinnati in June.

The embarrassed West retreated to the water fountain to quench his thirst while awaiting what certainly would have been a memorable line from Stengel. But before the quick-witted manager could react, a foul ball by Paul Waner hit West in the mouth, breaking some teeth and sending him to the hospital.

Prior to the season, the Braves bought first baseman Babe Dahlgren from the Yankees. But in June they turned around and sold him to the Cubs. He wound up fifth in the league in home runs—a department in which Boston finished last.

The only player with his act together, once again, was 40-year-old Johnny Cooney. He was among the league leaders in hitting and also led outfielders with a .996 fielding average. One of his hits was a ninth-inning single to break up a no-hit bid by New York's Bill Lohrman. Not bad for someone who was supposed to be content to sit on the bench as a coach two years earlier.

	G	AB	R	H	2B	3B	HR	RBI	SB	AVG
Earl Averill	8	17	2	2	0	0	0	2	0	.118
Ray Berres (C)	120	279	21	56	10	0	1	19	2	.201
Buster Bray	4	11	2	1	1	0	0	1	0	.091
Johnny Cooney (OF)	123	442	52	141	25	2	0	29	3	.319
Babe Dahlgren	44	166	20	39	8	1	7	30	0	.235
Frank Demaree	48	113	20	26	5	2	2	15	2	.230
John Dudra	14	25	3	9	3	1	0	3	0	.360
Buddy Gremp	37	75	7	18	3	0	0	10	0	.240
Buddy Hassett (1B)	118	405	59	120	9	4	1	33	10	.296
Hank Majeski	19	55	5	8	5	0	0	3	0	.145
Don Manno	22	30	2	5	1	0	0	4	0	.167
Phil Masi	87	180	17	40	8	2	3	18	4	.222
Eddie Miller (SS)	154	585	54	140	27	3	6	68	8	.239
Al Montgomery	42	52	4	10	1	0	0	4	0	.192
Gene Moore (OF)	129	397	42	108	17	8	5	43	5	.272
Mel Preibisch	5	4	0	0	0	0	0	0	0	.000
Skippy Roberge	55	167	12	36	6	0	0	15	0	.216
Chet Ross	29	50	1	6	1	0	0	4	0	.120
Bama Rowell (2B)	138	483	49	129	23	6	7	60	11	.267
Sibby Sisti (3B)	140	541	72	140	24	3	1	45	7	.259
Lloyd Waner	19	51	7	21	1	0	0	4	1	.412
Paul Waner	95	294	40	82	10	2	2	46	1	.279
Max West (OF)	138	484	63	134	28	4	12	68	5	.277
Whitey Wietelmann	16	33	1	3	0	0	0	0	0	.091
	156	5,414	592	1,357	231	38	48	552	61	.251

	W	L	G	GS	CG	IP	H	BB	SO	ERA
George Barnicle	0	1	1	1	0	6⅔	5	4	2	6.75
Eddie Carnett	0	0	2	0	0	1⅓	4	3	2	20.25
Tom Earley	6	8	33	13	6	138⅔	120	46	54	2.53
Dick Errickson	6	12	38	23	5	165⅔	192	62	45	4.78
Wes Ferrell	2	1	4	3	1	14	13	9	10	5.14
Johnny Hutchings	1	6	36	7	1	95¾	110	22	36	4.14
Al Javery	10	11	34	23	9	160⅔	181	65	54	4.31
Art Johnson	7	15	43	18	6	183⅓	189	71	70	3.53
Frank Lamanna	5	4	35	4	0	72⅔	77	56	23	5.33
Al Piechota	0	0	1	0	0	1	0	1	0	0.00
Bill Posedel	4	4	18	9	3	57⅓	61	30	10	4.87
Manny Salvo	7	16	35	27	11	195	192	93	67	4.06
Nick Strincevich	0	0	3	0	0	3⅓	7	6	1	10.80
Joe Sullivan	2	2	16	2	0	52⅓	60	26	11	4.13
Jim Tobin	12	12	33	26	20	238	229	60	61	3.10
	62	92		156	62	1,385⅔	1,440	554	446	3.95

Shutouts—Tobin (3), Errickson (2), Salvo (2), Earley, Hutchings, Javery
Saves—Earley (3), Hutchings (2), Errickson, Javery, Johnson, Lamanna

1942

Record: 59–89
Finish: Seventh
Games Behind: 44
Manager: Casey Stengel

Considering that the Braves finished seventh for the fourth consecutive season, 1942 still was an eventful year for the club.

Boston made two major offensive acquisitions in catcher Ernie Lombardi and outfielder Tommy Holmes. Yet the Braves still had one of the weakest attacks in the league—unless knuckleball specialist Jim Tobin was pitching.

Acquired from Pittsburgh two years earlier, Tobin was a better-than-average right-hander who was just as likely to win a game with his bat as he was with his arm. On May 12, Casey Stengel called on Tobin to pinch-hit, and Tobin responded with a home run. He was just finding his groove, though.

The next day against the Cubs, Tobin hit three home runs and pitched a 6–5 victory. He is the only pitcher to accomplish that feat in the 20th century. Tobin finished the year with six homers, one for every 19 at bats. The league leader, Hall of Famer Mel Ott with 30, hit one every 18.3 at bats.

Tobin led the league in complete games and innings pitched despite being 12–21. Stengel, understandably, never felt he had to lift Tobin for a pinch hitter.

Lombardi, who was purchased from Cincinnati, played his only season in Boston and won the batting title (.330). He was the first batting champ produced by the franchise since Rogers Hornsby in 1928, and like Hornsby, Lombardi was gone the following season.

Paul Waner, yet another Hall of Famer who was passing through town at the end of his career, reached a major offensive milestone, too. He collected his 3,000th career hit June 19.

Though Ernie Lombardi (C) batted .330 in 1942 and was awarded the batting title, he teamed with Max West (L) and Chet Ross (R) to account for just 32 home runs between them.

Eddie Miller continued to play a dazzling shortstop, leading the league in fielding average (.983) for the third straight year, breaking his own record.

	G	AB	R	H	2B	3B	HR	RBI	SB	AVG
Johnny Cooney	74	198	23	41	6	0	0	7	2	.207
Tony Cuccinello	40	104	8	21	3	0	1	8	1	.202
Frank Demaree	64	187	18	42	5	0	3	24	2	.225
Ducky Detweiler	12	44	3	14	2	1	0	5	0	.318
Nanny Fernandez (3B)	145	577	63	147	29	3	6	55	15	.255
Buddy Gremp	72	207	12	45	11	0	3	19	1	.217
Tommy Holmes (OF)	141	558	56	155	24	4	4	41	2	.278
Clyde Kluttz	72	210	21	56	10	1	1	31	0	.267
Ernie Lombardi (C)	105	309	32	102	14	0	11	46	1	.330*
Phil Masi	57	87	14	19	3	1	0	9	2	.218
Frank McElyea	7	4	2	0	0	0	0	0	0	.000
Eddie Miller (SS)	142	534	47	130	28	2	6	47	11	.243
Skippy Roberge	74	172	10	37	7	0	1	12	1	.215
Chet Ross (OF)	76	220	20	43	7	2	5	19	0	.195
Mike Sandlock	2	1	1	1	0	0	0	0	0	1.000
Sibby Sisti (2B)	129	407	50	86	11	4	4	35	5	.211
Paul Waner (OF)	114	333	43	86	17	1	1	39	2	.258
Max West (1B)	134	452	54	115	22	0	16	56	4	.254
Whitey Wietelmann	13	34	4	7	2	0	0	0	0	.206
	150	5,077	515	1,216	210	19	68	479	49	.240

Warren Spahn got his big league baptism in 1942, prompting Casey Stengel to predict the left-hander would not succeed.

Paul Waner played most of his career with Pittsburgh, but he got his 3,000th hit with the Braves in 1942.

	W	L	G	GS	CG	IP	H	BB	SO	ERA
George Diehl	0	0	1	0	0	3⅔	2	2	0	2.45
Bill Donovan	3	6	31	10	2	89⅓	97	32	23	3.43
Tom Earley	6	11	27	18	6	112⅔	120	55	28	4.71
Dick Errickson	2	5	21	4	0	59⅓	76	20	15	5.01
Jim Hickey	0	1	1	1	0	1⅓	4	2	0	20.25
Johnny Hutchings	1	0	20	3	0	65⅔	66	34	27	4.39
Al Javery	12	16	42	37*	19	261	251	78	85	3.03
Art Johnson	0	0	4	0	0	6⅓	4	5	0	1.42
Frank Lamanna	0	1	5	0	0	6⅔	5	3	2	5.40
Johnny Sain	4	7	40	3	0	97	79	63	68	3.90
Manny Salvo	7	8	25	14	6	130⅔	129	41	25	3.03
Warren Spahn	0	0	4	2	1	15⅔	25	11	7	5.74
Jim Tobin	12	21*	37	33	28*	287⅔*	283	96	71	3.97
Lou Tost	10	10	35	22	5	147⅔	146	52	43	3.53
Jim Wallace	1	3	19	3	1	49⅓	39	24	20	3.83
	59	89		150	68	1,334	1,326	518	414	3.76

Shutouts—Javery (5), Donovan, Salvo, Tobin, Tost
Saves—Sain (6), Earley, Errickson

1943

Record: 68–85
Finish: Sixth
Games Behind: 36½
Manager: Casey Stengel

Casey Stengel finally proved he could bring the Braves in some place other than seventh . . . or did he?

After four consecutive sevenths, the Braves moved all the way up to sixth, but they did it with their manager in the hospital much of the season.

Two days before the opener, Stengel was hit by a car and suffered a broken leg. He was in traction for two months. Some said he did it on purpose so he wouldn't have to watch his team. However, a Boston newspaper obviously felt the club was better off without Stengel, because it nominated the driver for "sportsman of the year." Coaches George Kelly and Bob Coleman ran the team until Stengel returned.

Under wartime restrictions, the Braves trained in Wallingford, Connecticut, and many of the club's players enlisted or were drafted. When 1942 batting champ Ernie Lombardi held out in the spring, he was traded to the Giants for Connie Ryan and Hugh Poland.

The talent was so thin that when first baseman Johnny McCarthy broke his leg in midseason, the Braves had to replace him for the rest of the year with pitcher Kerby Farrell.

Al Javery, a tall right-hander, had his best season, leading the club in victories (17–16) and the league in innings. Newcomer Nate Andrews finished fifth in the league in ERA (2.57) yet still lost 20 games. Such was the state of Braves baseball.

The team batting average of .233 was last in the league by a wide margin and the club's worst since 1916.

	G	AB	R	H	2B	3B	HR	RBI	SB	AVG
Bill Brubaker	13	19	3	8	3	0	0	1	0	.421
Joe Burns	52	135	12	28	3	0	1	5	2	.207
Connie Creedon	5	4	0	1	0	0	0	1	0	.250
Tony Cuccinello	13	19	0	0	0	0	0	2	0	.000
Buck Etchison	10	19	2	6	3	0	0	2	0	.316
Kerby Farrell	85	280	11	75	14	1	0	21	1	.268
Sam Gentile	8	4	1	1	1	0	0	0	0	.250
Ben Geraghty	8	1	2	0	0	0	0	0	0	.000
Heinie Heltzel	29	86	6	13	3	0	0	5	0	.151
Tommy Holmes (OF)	152	629*	75	170	33	10	5	41	7	.270
Eddie Joost (3B)	124	421	34	78	16	3	2	20	5	.185
Clyde Kluttz	66	207	13	51	7	0	0	20	0	.246
Phil Masi (C)	80	238	27	65	9	1	2	28	7	.273
Johnny McCarthy (1B)	78	313	32	95	24	6	2	33	1	.304
Butch Nieman (OF)	101	335	39	85	15	8	7	46	4	.251
Hugh Poland	44	141	5	27	7	0	0	13	0	.191
Chet Ross	94	285	27	62	12	2	7	32	1	.218
Connie Ryan (2B)	132	457	52	97	10	2	1	24	7	.212
Whitey Wietelmann (SS)	153	534	33	115	14	1	0	39	9	.215
Chuck Workman (OF)	153	615	71	153	17	1	10	67	12	.249
	153	5,196	465	1,213	202	36	39	431	56	.233

	W	L	G	GS	CG	IP	H	BB	SO	ERA
Nate Andrews	14	20*	36	34	23	283⅔	253	75	80	2.57
Red Barrett	12	18	38	31	14	255	240	63	64	3.18
Ben Cardoni	0	0	11	0	0	28	38	14	5	6.43
John Dagenhard	1	0	2	1	1	11	9	4	2	0.00
George Diehl	0	0	1	0	0	4	4	3	1	4.50
Bill Donovan	1	0	7	0	0	14⅔	17	9	1	1.84
Kerby Farrell	0	1	5	0	0	23	24	9	4	4.30
Al Javery	17	16	41	35	19	303*	288*	99	134	3.21
George Jeffcoat	1	2	8	1	0	17⅔	15	10	10	3.06
Carl Lindquist	0	2	2	2	0	13	17	4	1	6.23
Danny MacFayden	2	1	10	1	0	21⅓	31	9	5	5.91
Ray Martin	0	0	2	0	0	3⅓	3	1	1	8.10
Dave Odom	0	3	22	3	1	54⅔	54	30	17	5.27
Manny Salvo	5	7	21	14	5	98⅔	99	31	26	3.46
Allyn Stout	1	0	9	0	0	9⅓	17	4	3	6.75
Roy Talcott	0	0	1	0	0	⅔	1	2	0	27.00
Jim Tobin	14	14	33	30	24	250	241	69	52	2.66
Lou Tost	0	1	3	1	0	6⅔	10	4	3	5.40
	68	85		153	87	1,397⅔	1,361	441	409	3.25

Shutouts—Javery (5), Andrews (3), Barrett (3), Salvo, Tobin
Saves—Odom (2), Cardoni, Stout

1944

Record: 65–89
Finish: Sixth
Games Behind: 40
Manager: Bob Coleman

A new era in franchise history began in 1944 when Lou Perini and partners Guido Rugo and Joseph Maney purchased controlling interest in the club from the syndicate headed by Bob Quinn, who was retained as president.

The wealthy Boston contractors were nicknamed the "Three Little Steam Shovels," and one of their first moves in remodeling the Braves was to oust Casey Stengel. They replaced him with coach Bob Coleman, who had a lot of minor league managing experience but none in the majors.

Though the team finished sixth, it was only 3½ games out of last and was just as wretched as it had been for several years. Perini had big plans for the franchise, but he would move slowly during the war years.

The story of the season was 31-year-old knuckleball artist and occasional slugger Jim Tobin, one of the most unhittable pitchers in the league.

In a span of three starts over nine days in April, Tobin gave up only four hits but won just two of the three games.

The streak began when he lost a three-hitter against the Giants, 2–1. In his next start, Tobin beat Philadelphia with a one-hitter. Then, four days later on April 27, he pitched the sixth no-hitter in franchise history and the first since 1916. Tobin beat Brooklyn, 2–0, allowing only two walks to Paul Waner. For good measure, he also hit a home run in the eighth inning, making him the first pitcher ever to combine a no-hitter and a home run.

But Tobin wasn't through. On June 22, he beat Philadelphia, 7–0, in the second game of a doubleheader that was called after five innings due to darkness. Though he held the Phillies hitless and the game was regarded as a no-hitter at the time, current rules do not recognize it as such.

Tobin finished the year fifth in the league in victories yet was still a game below .500 (18–19). He led the league in complete games (28), and he was second in innings and third in shutouts (5). He was the Phil Niekro of the '40s but a better hitter.

As fate would have it, Tobin also was victimized by a no-hitter. Cincinnati's Clyde Shoun, normally a reliever, made his first start of the year a game to remember. In holding the Braves hitless May 15, he beat Tobin, 1–0. The only Brave to reach base, you might guess, was Tobin, who drew a walk.

However, a pitching performance even more incredible than any of these came August 10. Red Barrett, in the midst of an otherwise unspectacular season, beat Cincinnati, 2–0, by throwing only 58 pitches, a major league record. The game took just 75 minutes, a record for a night game.

	G	AB	R	H	2B	3B	HR	RBI	SB	AVG
Pat Capri	7	1	1	0	0	0	0	0	0	.000
Chet Clemens	19	17	7	3	1	1	0	2	0	.176
Dick Culler	8	28	2	2	0	0	0	0	0	.071
Frank Drews	46	141	14	29	9	1	0	10	0	.206
Buck Etchison (1B)	109	308	30	66	16	0	8	33	1	.214
Ben Geraghty	11	16	3	4	0	0	0	0	0	.250
Roland Gladu	21	66	5	16	2	1	1	7	0	.242
Stew Hofferth	66	180	14	36	8	0	1	26	0	.200
Tommy Holmes (OF)	155	631	93	195	42	6	13	73	4	.309
Warren Huston	33	55	7	11	1	0	0	1	0	.200
Clyde Kluttz	81	229	20	64	12	2	2	19	0	.279
Max Macon	106	366	38	100	15	3	3	36	7	.273
Phil Masi (C)	89	251	33	69	13	5	3	23	4	.275
Butch Nieman (OF)	134	468	65	124	16	6	16	65	5	.265
Gene Patton	1	0	0	0	0	0	0	0	0	—
Damon Phillips (3B)	140	489	35	126	30	1	1	53	1	.258
Hugh Poland	8	23	1	3	1	0	0	2	0	.130
Chet Ross	54	154	20	35	9	2	5	26	1	.227
Connie Ryan (2B)	88	332	56	98	18	5	4	25	13	.295
Mike Sandlock	30	30	1	3	0	0	0	2	0	.100
Steve Shemo	18	31	3	9	2	0	0	1	0	.290
Whitey Wietelmann (SS)	125	417	46	100	18	1	2	32	0	.240
Chuck Workman (OF)	140	418	46	87	18	3	11	53	1	.208
Ab Wright	71	195	70	50	9	0	7	35	0	.256
	155	5,282	593	1,299	250	39	79	558	37	.246

	W	L	G	GS	CG	IP	H	BB	SO	ERA
Nate Andrews	16	15	37	34	16	257⅓	263	74	76	3.22
Red Barrett	9	16	42	30	11	230⅓	257	63	54	4.06
Ben Cardoni	0	6	22	5	1	75⅔	83	37	24	3.93
Jim Hickey	0	0	8	0	0	9⅓	15	5	3	4.82
Johnny Hutchings	1	4	14	7	1	56⅔	55	26	26	3.97
Ira Hutchinson	9	7	40	8	1	119⅔	136	53	22	4.21
Al Javery	10	19	40	33	11	254	248	118	137	3.54
Stan Klopp	1	2	24	0	0	46⅓	47	33	17	4.27
Carl Lindquist	0	0	5	0	0	8⅔	8	2	4	3.12
Max Macon	0	0	1	0	0	3	10	1	1	21.00
Harry MacPherson	0	0	1	0	0	1	0	1	1	0.00
Woody Rich	1	1	7	2	1	25	32	12	6	5.76
Jim Tobin	18	19	43	36	28*	299⅓	271	97	83	3.01
George Woodend	0	0	3	0	0	2	5	5	0	13.50
	65	89	155	70		1,388⅓	1,430	527	454	3.67

Shutouts—Tobin (5), Javery (3), Andrews (2), Barrett, Hutchinson
Saves—Tobin (3), Javery (3), Andrews (2), Barrett (2), Hutchings, Hutchinson

1945

Record: 67–85
Finish: Sixth
Games Behind: 30
Managers: Bob Coleman, Del Bissonette

The 1945 season proved an eventful, if unsuccessful one. It also served to show that under the ownership of Lou Perini and partners, the franchise would not continue to stagger without efforts to stabilize it.

In February, Bob Quinn resigned as president on his 75th birthday, and his son John replaced him.

Then in May the "Three Little Steam Shovels" served notice they were intent on making significant changes in the Boston baseball landscape. They sent Red Barrett and $60,000 to the Cardinals for pitcher Mort Cooper, who'd won 65 games the three previous seasons. The deal was a flop because Cooper had a bum elbow and Barrett prospered, but Perini would not be deterred.

While the Braves were settling into their familiar sixth-place slot in the standings for the third straight year, a little outfielder who didn't have enough power to make it as a Yankee was rewriting the club and National League record books.

On June 6, Tommy Holmes began a 37-game hitting streak that would stand as the modern National League record until Pete Rose broke it in 1978. On July 6, Holmes hit safely in both ends of a doubleheader with Pittsburgh to tie and break Rogers Hornsby's record of 33 games. On July 8, the popular Boston right fielder hit in his 37th straight game, then the majors took a break from the schedule for the All-Star Game.

Mort Cooper was a big winner for the Cardinals, but he struggled with a bad arm for the Braves.

In the first game after the break, the streak ended when the Cubs' Hank Wyse pitched a three-hitter against Boston.

During the streak, Holmes batted .433. For the season, he hit .352, finishing just three points behind Phil Cavaretta for the batting title, but led the league in hits (224), doubles (47), home runs (28), total bases, and slugging percentage. The line-drive hitter was second in RBIs (117) and third in runs. His most remarkable statistic, though, was nine strikeouts in 636 at bats.

Shortly after Holmes' streak ended, the Braves dropped a doubleheader and fell to seventh place. It was more than Bob Coleman could stand, and he resigned. Coach Del Bissonette finished the season as manager but made little, if any, headway with the club.

A shortened right-field fence at Braves Field helped boost the power numbers of the left-handed-hitting Holmes, but he wasn't the only one to benefit. Third baseman/outfielder Chuck Workman, also a left-handed batter, hit a career-high 25 homers, second to Holmes in the league. Of the 25, 19 came at home. The fence was moved back in 1946.

In November, Perini made his boldest maneuver yet. He approached the Cardinals for permission to talk with highly regarded manager Billy Southworth and proceeded to use a lucrative three-year contract offer to hire the man who'd led St. Louis to three pennants and two World Series titles in 1942–44.

1946

Record: 81–72
Finish: Fourth
Games Behind: 15½
Manager: Billy Southworth

The war was over, and Lou Perini and his partners kicked their efforts to rejuvenate the franchise into high gear. Lights finally were added to Braves Field, along with neon foul poles, and the team was outfitted with special satin jerseys just for night games.

The team was promoted, special ticket packages were developed, buses were run from nearby towns, and fans were even flown in from Cape Cod.

More importantly, players were imported. Billy Southworth picked up a couple of his former Cardinals, first baseman/outfielder Johnny Hopp and first baseman Ray Sanders, to start the season. And the team continued to wheel and deal throughout the year, spending thousands of dollars to acquire players in a massive shopping spree. Among the acquisitions were a pair of significant "futures," shortstop Al Dark, who cost $40,000, and first baseman Earl Torgeson, who carried a $50,000 price tag.

Additionally, Johnny Sain returned from the service, and Warren Spahn would soon follow.

Southworth instilled new discipline in the team and built up morale. The result was a hustling, determined team, if not the most talented group of players in the league. Perini gave the team a boost by offering cash prizes for shutouts and new suits for home runs.

The first night game at Braves Field was played May 11. Though the Braves lost to the Giants, 5–1, more than 30,000 fans turned out for the event. It was evident that night baseball and active ownership were a hit with the fans because the club almost doubled its previous attendance record, falling just short of 1 million for the year.

	G	AB	R	H	2B	3B	HR	RBI	SB	AVG
Morrie Aderholt	31	102	15	34	4	0	2	11	3	.333
Dick Culler (SS)	136	527	87	138	12	1	2	30	7	.262
Frank Drews	49	147	13	30	4	1	0	19	0	.204
Carden Gillenwater (OF)	144	517	74	149	20	2	7	72	13	.288
Stew Hofferth	50	170	13	40	2	0	3	15	1	.235
Tommy Holmes (OF)	154	636	125	224*	47*	6	28*	117	15	.352
Eddie Joost	35	141	16	35	7	1	0	9	0	.248
Clyde Kluttz	25	81	9	24	4	1	0	10	0	.296
Joe Mack	66	260	30	60	13	1	3	44	1	.231
Phil Masi (C)	114	371	55	101	25	4	7	46	9	.272
Joe Medwick	66	218	17	62	13	0	0	26	3	.284
Tom Nelson	40	121	6	20	2	0	0	6	1	.165
Butch Nieman (OF)	97	247	43	61	15	0	14	56	11	.247
Bill Ramsey	78	137	16	40	8	0	1	12	1	.292
Steve Shemo	17	46	4	11	1	0	0	7	0	.239
Vince Shupe (1B)	78	283	22	76	8	0	0	15	3	.269
Mike Ulisney	11	18	4	7	1	0	1	4	0	.389
Norm Wallen	4	15	1	2	0	1	0	1	0	.133
Stan Wentzel	4	19	3	4	0	1	0	6	1	.211
Whitey Wietelmann (2B)	123	428	53	116	15	3	4	33	4	.271
Chuck Workman (3B)	139	514	77	141	16	2	25	87	9	.274
	154	5,441	721	1,453	229	25	101	668	82*	.267

	W	L	G	GS	CG	IP	H	BB	SO	ERA
Nate Andrews	7	12	21	19	8	137⅔	160	52	26	4.58
Red Barrett	2	3	9	5	2	38	43	16	13	4.74
Ben Cardoni	0	0	3	0	0	4	6	3	5	9.00
Mort Cooper	7	4	20	11	4	78	77	27	45	3.35
Charlie Cozart	1	0	5	0	0	8	10	15	4	10.13
Tom Earley	2	1	11	2	1	41	36	19	4	4.61
Lou Fette	0	2	5	1	0	11	16	7	4	5.73
Don Hendrickson	4	8	37	2	1	73⅓	74	39	14	4.91
Joe Heving	1	0	3	0	0	5⅓	5	3	1	3.38
Johnny Hutchings	7	6	57	12	3	185	173	75	99	3.75
Ira Hutchinson	2	3	11	0	0	28⅔	33	8	4	5.02
Al Javery	2	7	17	14	2	77½	92	51	18	6.28
Bill Lee	6	3	16	13	6	106⅓	112	36	12	2.79
Bob Logan	7	11	34	25	6	187	213	53	53	3.18
Ewald Pyle	0	1	4	2	0	13⅓	16	18	10	7.24
Hal Schacker	0	1	6	0	0	15½	14	9	6	5.28
Elmer Singleton	1	4	7	5	1	37⅓	35	14	14	4.82
Jim Tobin	9	14	27	25	16	196⅔	220	56	38	3.84
Jim Wallace	1	0	5	3	1	20	18	9	4	4.50
Bob Whitcher	0	2	6	3	0	15⅔	12	12	6	2.87
Whitey Wietelmann	0	0	1	0	0	1	6	2	0	54.00
Ed Wright	8	3	15	12	7	111⅓	104	33	24	2.51
	67	85		154	57	1,391⅔	1,474	557	404	4.04

Shutouts—Hutchings (2), Cooper, Javery, Lee, Logan, Wright
Saves—Hendrickson (5), Hutchings (3), Barrett (2), Cooper, Hutchinson, Logan

First baseman Earl Torgeson was a solid all-around player who could steal bases, play good defense and hit for power.

Only a popup single kept Johnny Sain from pitching a perfect game in 1946.

On the wrong end of a no-hitter by Brooklyn's Ed Head in April, the Braves nearly got it back in July when Sain pitched a near-perfect game against Cincinnati. The lone base runner came in the first inning when three players stood and watched Grady Hatton's pop-up behind third fall for a single.

Sain, a 28-year-old right-hander from Havana, Arkansas, was a sensation, though. He finished second in the league in victories (20–14) and ERA (2.21), led in complete games (24), and was third in strikeouts and innings. Spahn joined the team in June and gave indications that he was ready to blossom, too.

Hopp batted .333, second in the league to Stan Musial, and Holmes had another fine season, finishing second in doubles, fourth in hits, and fifth in batting average (.310) and total bases. The team batting average of .264 was a point behind pennant-winning St. Louis, a far cry from the anemic offense Braves fans were used to watching.

As satisfying as it was for the team to finish in the first division for the first time since 1934 and with its best percentage (.529) since 1933, things could have been even better. Southworth had to manage around numerous injuries and still brought the team in just one game behind the third-place Cubs.

Even when the season ended, the Braves didn't relax. After making 14 trades during the season, the club acquired third baseman Bob Elliott from Pittsburgh in a six-player deal.

	G	AB	R	H	2B	3B	HR	RBI	SB	AVG
Johnny Barrett	24	43	3	10	3	0	0	6	0	.233
Bob Brady	3	5	0	1	0	0	0	0	0	.200
Dick Culler (SS)	134	482	70	123	15	3	0	33	7	.255
Alvin Dark	15	13	0	3	3	0	0	1	0	.231
Ducky Detweiler	1	1	0	0	0	0	0	0	0	.000
Nanny Fernandez (3B)	115	372	37	95	15	2	2	42	1	.255
Carden Gillenwater (OF)	99	224	30	51	10	1	1	14	3	.228
Billy Herman	75	252	32	77	23	1	3	22	1	.306
Stew Hofferth	20	58	3	12	1	1	0	10	0	.207
Tommy Holmes (OF)	149	568	80	176	35	6	6	79	7	.310
Johnny Hopp	129	445	71	148	23	8	3	48	21	.333
Danny Litwhiler	79	247	29	72	12	2	8	38	1	.291
Phil Masi (C)	133	397	52	106	17	5	3	62	5	.267
Johnny McCarthy	2	7	0	1	0	0	0	1	0	.143
Mike McCormick	59	164	23	43	6	2	1	16	0	.262
Tommy Neill	13	45	8	12	2	0	0	7	0	.267
Ken O'Dea	12	32	4	7	0	0	0	2	0	.219
Don Padgett	44	98	6	25	3	0	2	21	0	.255
Damon Phillips	2	2	0	1	0	0	0	0	0	.500
Hugh Poland	4	6	0	1	1	0	0	0	0	.167
Skippy Roberge	48	169	13	39	6	2	2	20	1	.231
Bama Rowell (OF)	95	293	37	82	12	6	3	31	5	.280
Connie Ryan (2B)	143	502	55	121	28	8	1	48	7	.241
Ray Sanders (1B)	80	259	43	63	12	0	6	35	0	.243
Sibby Sisti	1	0	0	0	0	0	0	0	0	—
Max West	1	1	0	0	0	0	0	0	0	.000
Whitey Wietelmann	44	78	7	16	0	0	0	5	0	.205
Chuck Workman	25	48	5	8	2	0	2	7	0	.167
	154	5,225	630	1,377	238	48	44	596	60	.264

	W	L	G	GS	CG	IP	H	BB	SO	ERA
Frank Barrett	2	4	23	0	0	35⅓	35	17	12	5.09
Mort Cooper	13	11	28	27	15	199	181	39	83	3.12
Don Hendrickson	0	1	2	0	0	2	4	2	2	4.50
Johnny Hutchings	0	1	1	1	0	3	5	1	1	9.00
Al Javery	0	1	2	1	0	3⅓	5	5	0	13.50
Si Johnson	6	5	28	12	5	127	134	35	41	2.76
Jim Konstanty	0	1	10	1	0	15⅓	17	7	9	5.28
Bill Lee	10	9	25	21	8	140	148	45	32	4.18
Dick Mulligan	1	0	4	0	0	15⅓	6	9	4	2.35
Johnny Niggeling	2	5	8	8	3	58	54	21	24	3.26
Bill Posedel	2	0	19	0	0	28⅓	34	13	9	6.99
Earl Reid	1	0	2	0	0	3	4	3	2	3.00
Steve Roser	1	1	14	1	0	35	33	18	18	3.60
Johnny Sain	20	14	37	34	24*	265	225	87	129	2.21
Elmer Singleton	0	1	15	2	0	33¾	27	21	17	3.74
Warren Spahn	8	5	24	16	8	125⅔	107	36	67	2.94
Jim Wallace	3	3	27	8	2	75⅓	76	31	27	4.18
Ernie White	0	1	12	1	0	23¾	22	12	8	4.18
Whitey Wietelmann	0	0	3	0	0	6⅔	9	4	2	8.10
Bob Williams	0	0	1	0	0	0	1	1	0	—
Ed Wright	12	9	36	21	9	176½	164	71	44	3.52
	81	72		154	73	1,371	1,291	478	566	3.35

Shutouts—Cooper (3), Sain (3), Wright (2), Johnson
Saves—Posedel (4), Sain (2), Barrett, Cooper, Johnson, Roser, Singleton, Spahn

Johnny Hopp finished second to Stan Musial in the 1946 batting race.

1947

Record: 86–68
Finish: Third
Games Behind: 8
Manager: Billy Southworth

If anyone thought the Braves' drastic improvement in 1946 under Billy Southworth was a fluke, they quickly found that wasn't the case. The 1947 Braves posted the franchise's best winning percentage (.558) since 1916 and finished closer to first than any club since that same 1916 team of "Miracle Man" George Stallings.

Finally, the team had both good hitting and good pitching. The Braves led the league with a .275 team batting average and ranked second in staff ERA (3.62).

Warren Spahn and Johnny Sain provided Boston with the best pitching tandem in the league. They tied for second in victories (21), just one win behind Cincinnati's Ewell Blackwell, who pitched a no-hitter against Boston in June. And Spahn, who won his first eight games and led the league with seven shutouts, became the second Brave in the 20th century to lead in ERA (2.33).

Bob Elliott, who'd been a solid player for Pittsburgh, making three National League All-Star teams, developed into a superstar at age 31 with Boston. Though he didn't lead the league in any major offensive department, he was second in batting average (.317) and doubles and led all third baseman in fielding average.

Elliott's all-around excellence drove the Braves upward in the standings and earned him the league's Most Valuable Player Award. He was the first third baseman to win the honor, as well as the first Brave to receive it under the modern voting system.

Tommy Holmes was as steady as ever, leading the league in hits (191) for the second time in three years. Rookie first

Phil Masi was one of the game's best defensive catchers in the 1940s.

baseman Earl Torgeson provided considerable power and run production in spite of being platooned with Mike McCormick. Together, they combined for 19 home runs and 114 RBIs.

One of the team's best hitters, however, was Sain. He hit safely in 14 straight games and batted a robust .346 for the year.

And Phil Masi led the league's catchers in defensive percentage (.989).

It was quite a season for a team that had barely seen the first division for the past 30 years. And for the second straight season, an attendance record was set. The Braves went over 1 million for the first time in their history on August 20 and gave away two cars to fans. The final attendance was 1,277,361. What the "Three Little Steam Shovels" and Southworth had accomplished was the talk of baseball.

All Bob Elliott did in his first year with the Braves was win the National League MVP award.

	G	AB	R	H	2B	3B	HR	RBI	SB	AVG
Bob Brady	1	1	0	0	0	0	0	0	0	.000
Hank Camelli	52	150	10	29	8	1	1	11	0	.193
Dick Culler (SS)	77	214	20	53	5	1	0	19	1	.248
Bob Elliott (3B)	150	555	93	176	35	5	22	113	3	.317
Nanny Fernandez	83	209	16	43	4	0	2	21	2	.206
Tommy Holmes (OF)	150	618	90	191*	33	3	9	53	3	.309
Johnny Hopp (OF)	134	430	74	124	20	2	2	32	13	.288
Danny Litwhiler	91	226	38	59	5	2	7	31	1	.261
Max Macon	1	1	0	0	0	0	0	0	0	.000
Phil Masi (C)	126	411	54	125	22	4	9	50	7	.304
Frank McCormick	81	212	24	75	18	2	2	43	2	.354
Mike McCormick	92	284	42	81	13	7	3	36	1	.285
Danny Murtaugh	3	8	0	1	0	0	0	0	0	.125
Tommy Neill	7	10	1	2	0	1	0	0	0	.200
Bama Rowell (OF)	113	384	48	106	23	2	5	40	7	.276
Connie Ryan (2B)	150	544	60	144	33	5	5	69	5	.265
Sibby Sisti	56	153	22	43	8	0	2	15	2	.281
Earl Torgeson (1B)	128	399	73	112	20	6	16	78	11	.281
	154	5,254	701	1,444	265*	42	85	645	58	.275*

	W	L	G	GS	CG	IP	H	BB	SO	ERA
Red Barrett	11	12	36	30	12	210⅔	200	53	53	3.55
Johnny Beazley	2	0	9	2	2	28⅔	30	19	12	4.40
Mort Cooper	2	5	10	7	2	46⅔	48	13	15	4.05
Glenn Elliott	0	1	11	0	0	19	18	11	8	4.74
Si Johnson	6	8	36	10	3	112⅔	124	34	27	4.23
Andy Karl	2	3	27	0	0	35	41	13	5	3.86
Walt Lanfranconi	4	4	36	4	1	64	65	27	18	2.95
Johnny Lanning	0	0	3	0	0	3⅔	4	6	0	9.82
Max Macon	0	0	1	0	0	2	1	1	1	0.00
Ray Martin	1	0	1	1	1	9	7	4	2	1.00
Dick Mulligan	0	0	1	0	0	2	4	1	1	9.00
Johnny Sain	21	12	38	35	22	266	265*	79	132	3.52
Clyde Shoun	5	3	26	3	1	73⅔	73	21	23	4.40
Warren Spahn	21	10	40	35	22	289⅔*	245	84	123	2.33*
Bill Voiselle	8	7	22	20	7	131½	146	51	59	4.32
Ernie White	0	0	1	1	0	4	1	1	1	0.00
Ed Wright	3	3	23	6	1	64⅔	80	35	14	6.40
	86	68		154	74*	1,362⅔	1,342	453	494	3.62

Shutouts—Spahn (7*), Barrett (3), Sain (3), Shoun
Saves—Karl (3), Spahn (3), Johnson (2), Barrett, Elliott, Lanfranconi, Sain, Shoun

1948

Record: 91–62
Finish: First
Games Ahead: 6½
Manager: Billy Southworth

This was the year that long-suffering Braves fans finally were rewarded. It was the year of "Spahn and Sain and pray for rain." It was the year the Braves won their first pennant since 1914, and it was nearly the year of an all-Boston World Series.

The team's success in 1948 was the result of several factors coming together at the same time.

The development of a championship team began when Lou Perini and his partners lured manager Billy Southworth from the Cardinals in 1946. At the same time, the "Three Little Steam Shovels" were making significant player acquisitions, shelling out cash to sign unproven names such as first baseman Earl Torgeson and shortstop Al Dark. Warren Spahn and Johnny Sain were coming back from the war, too, and in 1947 third baseman Bob Elliott was acquired in a big trade with Pittsburgh.

The finishing touches were put together for the '48 season with a new middle infield. Dark was promoted from the Braves' Milwaukee farm club to play short, and Eddie "The Brat" Stanky was acquired by trade from Brooklyn to play second. Two other significant additions to the club were outfielder Jeff Heath, who was purchased from the Browns, and rookie right-hander Vern Bickford, who was promoted from Milwaukee. Nels Potter, acquired from the Athletics in June, also made quite a contribution as a reliever.

It was an incredibly exciting season for Boston baseball fans, since the Red Sox also were in a pennant race. The prospect of an all-Boston World Series piqued the interest of even those Bostonians never before intrigued by the game.

After losing six of their first seven games of the year, the Braves quickly established themselves as contenders. They reached .500 on May 13 and climbed into first place for the first time on June 11. That was just in time for the team's first televised game from Braves Field, a 6–3 win over the Cubs June 15.

On July 8, Stanky, who was hitting over .300 and playing excellent defense, broke an ankle crashing into Brooklyn's

Rookie shortstop Al Dark and veteran second baseman Eddie Stanky were major players on the 1948 pennant-winning team.

Bruce "The Bull" Edwards at third base. With the rookie Dark at short, the loss of Stanky could have crippled the Braves' infield. However, Sibby Sisti stepped in and played some of the best baseball of his career.

Remarkably, the Braves continued to play just as well as before Stanky's injury. At the All-Star break, Boston held a 5½-game lead over Pittsburgh, and they increased it to eight games on July 18.

August, however, was a disaster. By the middle of the month, the Braves' lead was down to two games, and on August 28 they fell from first place for the first time in 10 weeks. Billy Southworth's team righted itself quickly, regaining first place four days later and keeping it for the remainder of the year.

Pitching was the biggest reason for the Braves' success, and in September, it was Spahn and Sain who wrapped up the pen-

Sibby Sisti's play at second after Eddie Stanky broke his ankle was a key to winning the 1948 pennant.

nant. In the process, the phrase "Spahn and Sain and pray for rain" was born as part of baseball lore. Though the Braves' pitching depth wasn't as bad as that slogan would indicate, the team's fans, starving for a pennant, could hardly be blamed for wanting their two aces on the mound all the time.

In one of the more important days of the season, Spahn and Sain combined for a doubleheader victory against the Dodgers and showed why they deserved their popularity.

On September 6 at Braves Field, Spahn pitched a masterful 14-inning, 2–1 victory against Brooklyn, allowing just five hits and picking Jackie Robinson off base twice. Earl Torgeson doubled in the winning run.

In the second game, called after seven innings, Sain shut out the Dodgers, 4–0.

Beginning September 3, Spahn and Sain started 16 of 26 games. Sain was 8–1 with a 2.19 ERA in nine starts. Spahn won four games in 13 days and had an ERA of 1.22 in that stretch.

The pennant clincher wasn't pitched by either Sain or Spahn, though. It came September 26 when Bickford beat the Giants, 3–2, on the strength of a three-run homer by Elliott in the first inning.

Elliott didn't have quite as good a season as he had the year before when he was the league's MVP, but he still was quite productive. "Mr. Team," as he was known throughout Boston, was second in the league to Stan Musial in on-base percentage (.423) and reached the century mark in RBIs for the second straight season.

Though Elliott didn't get a lot of votes for a repeat MVP, Sain made a strong run, finishing second to Musial. And Dark, who finished fourth in the batting race (.322), was third in the MVP balloting. The 26-year-old shortstop was a runaway winner for Rookie of the Year, even though there was only one award for both leagues at the time. He also had a 23-game hitting streak that tied the league's rookie record at the time.

Tommy Holmes was his usual steady self in right field and at the plate. He was third in the batting race (.325) to Musial and Richie Ashburn and second in hits. Led by Holmes, the Braves topped the league in hitting (.275), hits, and doubles.

Heath had an excellent season in left, filling a void in only his first year with the club. He was productive at the plate and led the league's outfielders in defense. However, four days before the end of season, he broke his ankle sliding at Brooklyn.

Torgeson at first and Phil Masi at catcher gave the Braves two of the best defensive players in the league. Torgeson didn't hit as much as the Braves thought he would, but surprisingly, he did finish fifth in the league in steals (19) and was safe on his first 14 attempts.

The pitching staff posted the best team ERA (3.37) in the league by a wide margin.

Sain, who had his third straight 20-win season, led the league in victories (24), complete games (28), and innings. He also tied for second in shutouts (4) and was third in ERA (2.60) and strikeouts. The Cy Young Award had yet to be created or Sain most certainly would have won it.

The World Series wound up being a twofold letdown. For starters, the Red Sox didn't make it, finishing the regular season in a tie with Cleveland and losing the first playoff in American League history. Then the Braves, weakened by the loss of Heath, also lost to Cleveland.

Still, it was a superb season for a franchise that only three

Acquired from Cleveland, left-fielder Jeff Heath proved invaluable in 1948, but a late-season broken ankle quickly ended his career.

seasons earlier was mired in an agonizing stretch among the league's also-rans. Attendance was a record 1,455,439.

	G	AB	R	H	2B	3B	HR	RBI	SB	AVG
Paul Burris	2	4	0	2	0	0	0	0	0	.500
Clint Conatser	90	224	30	62	9	3	3	23	0	.277
Alvin Dark (SS)	137	543	85	175	39	6	3	48	4	.322
Bob Elliott (3B)	151	540	99	153	24	5	23	100	6	.283
Jeff Heath (OF)	115	364	64	116	26	5	20	76	2	.319
Tommy Holmes (OF)	139	585	85	190	35	7	6	61	1	.325
Danny Litwhiler	13	33	0	9	2	0	0	6	0	.273
Phil Masi (C)	113	376	43	95	19	0	5	44	2	.253
Frank McCormick	75	180	14	45	9	2	4	34	0	.250
Mike McCormick (OF)	115	343	45	104	22	7	1	39	1	.303
Marv Rickert	3	13	1	3	0	1	0	2	0	.231
Jim Russell	89	322	44	85	18	1	9	54	4	.264
Connie Ryan	51	122	14	26	3	0	0	10	0	.213
Bill Salkeld	78	198	26	48	8	1	8	28	1	.242
Ray Sanders	5	4	0	1	0	0	0	2	0	.250
Sibby Sisti	83	221	30	54	6	2	0	21	0	.244
Eddie Stanky (2B)	67	247	49	79	14	2	2	29	3	.320
Bobby Sturgeon	34	78	10	17	3	1	0	4	0	.218
Earl Torgeson (1B)	134	438	70	111	23	5	10	67	19	.253
	154	5,297	739	1,458*	272*	49	95	695	43	.275*

	W	L	G	GS	CG	IP	H	BB	SO	ERA
Johnny Antonelli	0	0	4	0	0	4	2	3	0	2.25
Red Barrett	7	8	34	13	3	128⅓	132	28	40	3.65
Johnny Beazley	0	1	3	2	0	16	19	7	4	4.50
Vern Bickford	11	5	33	22	10	146	125	63	60	3.27
Glenn Elliott	1	0	1	1	0	3	5	1	2	3.00
Bobby Hogue	8	2	40	1	0	86⅓	88	19	43	3.23
Al Lyons	1	0	7	0	0	12⅔	17	8	5	7.82
Ray Martin	0	0	2	0	0	2⅓	0	1	0	0.00
Nelson Potter	5	2	18	7	3	85	77	8	47	2.33
Jim Prendergast	1	1	10	2	0	16⅔	30	5	3	10.26
Johnny Sain	24*	15	42	39*	28*	314⅔*	297*	83	137	2.60
Clyde Shoun	5	1	36	2	1	74	77	20	25	4.01
Warren Spahn	15	12	36	35	16	257	237	77	114	3.71
Bill Voiselle	13	13	37	30	9	215⅓	226	90	89	3.63
Ernie White	0	2	15	0	0	23	13	17	8	1.96
Ed Wright	0	0	3	0	0	4⅔	9	2	2	1.93
	91*	62		154	70*	1,389⅓	1,354	430	579	3.37*

Shutouts—Sain (4), Spahn (3), Voiselle (2), Bickford
Saves—Shoun (4), Hogue (2), Potter (2), Voiselle (2), White (2), Antonelli, Bickford, Prendergast, Sain, Spahn

1949

Record: 75–79
Finish: Fourth
Games Behind: 22
Manager: Billy Southworth

Since the 1948 National League champions were composed mainly of veterans, many of whom had quite a bit of mileage on them, there wasn't much talk of the pennant spawning a Braves dynasty. Still, it was surprising just how quickly and completely they deteriorated.

Ever the taskmaster, manager Billy Southworth made sure his players weren't entering the 1949 season as fat cats. He drove them in strict two-a-day workouts during spring training. The six-hour-per-day regimen may have been good for

the Braves' physically, but it didn't help the team's mental outlook. In fact, Southworth's discipline irritated the veterans and led to dissension.

The club's unrest certainly was a contributing factor to its demise, but injuries probably played the biggest role in the disappointing fourth-place finish. In fact, the team was in first place June 4 until injuries began to take their toll.

The biggest problem was Johnny Sain's sore arm. Though he continued to pitch regularly, making just three fewer starts than in 1948, he clearly wasn't the same man. At times during the pennant-winning season, he came as close to carrying a team as a pitcher could, so much so that he nearly won the league's MVP award. But he won 14 fewer games in 1949, more than 60 percent of the Braves' deficit in the final standings.

Warren Spahn, on the other hand, replaced Sain as the best pitcher in the league. The stylish southpaw led the league in victories (21), complete games (25), innings, and strikeouts.

However, the pitching staff as a whole dropped from the league lead in ERA in 1948 to fifth place (3.99). Likewise, the team batting average (.258) fell from first in the league to sixth, due in large part to Al Dark's encounter with the "sophomore jinx." The shortstop's average plummeted 46 points (.276).

Besides Sain's bum arm, the Braves also had to endure significant time lost to injury by left fielder Jeff Heath and first baseman Earl Torgeson.

Heath, one of the club's top hitters in 1948, had difficulty recovering from the broken ankle that had kept him out of the World Series, and he played in just 36 games—the last 36 of his career. Torgeson sustained a shoulder separation May 14 sliding into Jackie Robinson. Just when

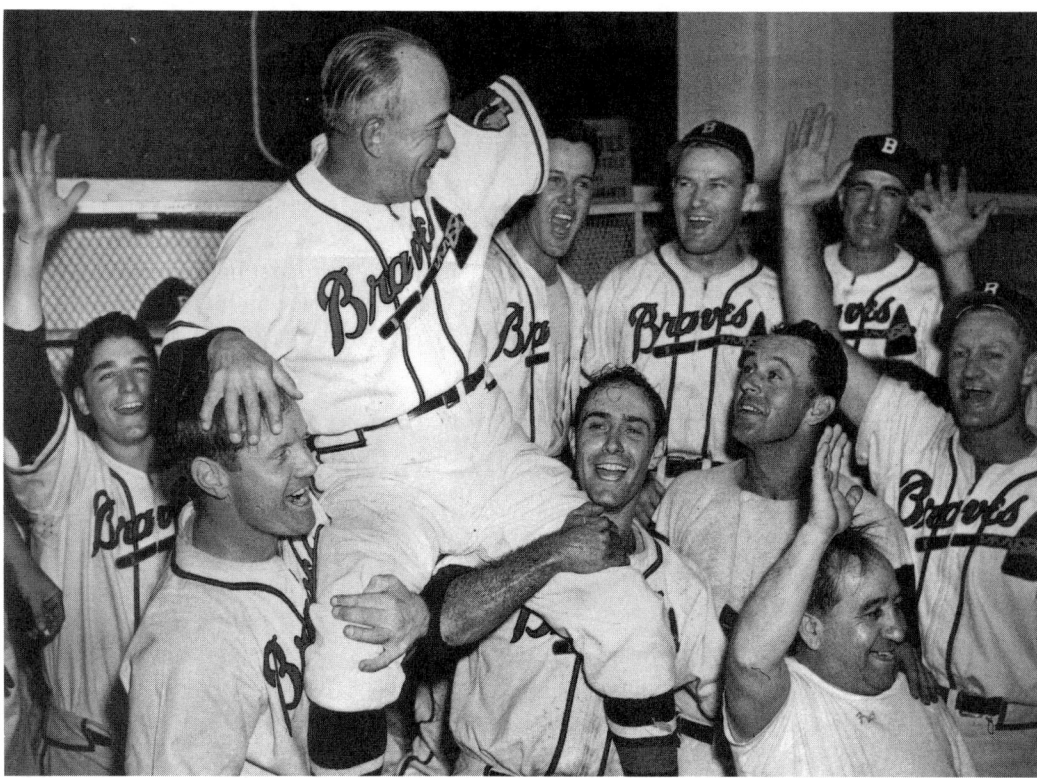

Billy Southworth was riding high after he led the Braves to the 1948 pennant, but his relationship with his players quickly soured.

he was ready to return in August, he broke his thumb in a fight with teammate Jim Russell and appeared in only 25 games.

The sorry state of affairs got to the hard-driving Southworth more than anyone else. So tense he seemingly bordered on a breakdown, the manager was sent home to rest on August 16, with coach Johnny Cooney taking over the club.

A strong indication of the anti-Southworth sentiment on the team surfaced at the end of the year when the players voted him only half a share of their fourth-place money. Commissioner Happy Chandler stepped in and restored it to a full share, though. It was a turbulent season, to say the least.

Sam "Jet" Jethroe integrated the Braves in 1950, led the league in stolen bases, and was named the league's Rookie of the Year.

	G	AB	R	H	2B	3B	HR	RBI	SB	AVG
Clint Conatser	53	152	10	40	6	0	3	16	0	.263
Del Crandall (C)	67	228	21	60	10	1	4	34	2	.263
Alvin Dark (SS)	130	529	74	146	23	5	3	53	5	.276
Bob Elliott (3B)	139	482	77	135	29	5	17	76	0	.280
Elbie Fletcher (1B)	122	413	57	108	19	3	11	51	1	.262
Jeff Heath	36	111	17	34	7	0	9	23	0	.306
Tommy Holmes (OF)	117	380	47	101	20	4	8	59	1	.266
Steve Kuczek	1	1	0	1	1	0	0	0	0	1.000
Al Lakeman	3	6	0	1	0	0	0	0	0	.167
Mickey Livingston	28	64	6	15	2	1	0	6	0	.234
Phil Masi	37	105	13	22	2	0	0	6	1	.210
Pete Reiser	84	221	32	60	8	3	8	40	3	.271
Marv Rickert (OF)	100	277	44	81	18	3	6	49	1	.292
Jim Russell (OF)	130	415	57	96	22	1	8	54	3	.231
Connie Ryan	85	208	28	52	13	1	6	20	1	.250
Bill Salkeld	66	161	17	41	5	0	5	25	1	.255
Ray Sanders	9	21	0	3	1	0	0	0	0	.143
Ed Sauer	79	214	26	57	12	0	3	31	0	.266
Sibby Sisti	101	268	39	69	12	0	5	22	1	.257
Eddie Stanky (2B)	138	506	90	144	24	5	1	42	3	.285
Don Thompson	7	11	0	2	0	0	0	0	0	.182
Earl Torgeson	25	100	17	26	5	1	4	19	4	.260
	157	5,336	706	1,376	246	33	103	654	28	.258

	W	L	G	GS	CG	IP	H	BB	SO	ERA
Johnny Antonelli	3	7	22	10	3	96	99	42	48	3.56
Red Barrett	1	1	23	0	0	44⅓	58	10	17	5.68
Johnny Beazley	0	0	1	0	0	2	0	0	0	0.00
Vern Bickford	16	11	37	36	15	230⅔	246	106	101	4.25
Glenn Elliott	3	4	22	6	1	68⅓	70	27	15	3.95
Bob Hall	6	4	31	6	2	74⅓	77	41	43	4.36
Bobby Hogue	2	2	33	0	0	72	78	25	23	3.13
Nelson Potter	6	11	41	3	1	96⅔	99	30	57	4.19
Johnny Sain	10	17	37	36	16	243	285	75	73	4.81
Clyde Shoun	0	0	1	0	0	1	1	0	0	0.00
Warren Spahn	21*	14	38	38*	25*	302⅓	283	86	151*	3.07
Bill Voiselle	7	8	30	22	5	169⅓	170	78	63	4.04
	75	79		157	68*	1,400	1,466*	520	591	3.99

Shutouts—Spahn (4), Voiselle (4), Bickford (2), Antonelli, Sain
Saves—Potter (7), Hogue (3), Voiselle

1950

Record: 83–71
Finish: Fourth
Games Behind: 8
Manager: Billy Southworth

Since Billy Southworth had three years left on his contract calling for $50,000 per season, there was no question he would return as manager in 1950.

On the other hand, shortstop Al Dark and second baseman Eddie Stanky, major contributors to the 1948 pennant, were sent packing in an attempt to reformulate the team's chemistry.

Of the four players the Braves received from the Giants in the trade for Dark and Stanky, only left fielder Sid Gordon was a big contributor. And while the Braves struggled to stay in the first division, the Giants were contenders in 1950 and pennant winners the next year with Dark and Stanky anchoring their infield.

Meanwhile, the biggest baseball news in Boston was generated by the integration of the Braves. Speedy center fielder Sam Jethroe was the team's first black. A strong offensive player who homered in his first game, Jethroe led the league in stolen bases (35) and became the second Brave in three years to be named Rookie of the Year.

The Braves had plenty of talent in certain spots, just not enough overall producers throughout the team. The pitching was an excellent example. Warren Spahn, Johnny Sain, and Vern Bickford were three of the best pitchers in the league, yet the arms dropped off drastically after that.

Only Bickford of the threesome failed to reach 20, and then just by one win. However, he pitched the seventh no-hitter in franchise history—the first at night—on August 11 when he beat the Dodgers, 7–0. It was the only no-hitter of the season in the majors.

Spahn, Sain, and Bickford ranked 1–2–4 in the league in victories. They also controlled the top three spots in complete games and three of the top four positions in innings. Spahn led the league in strikeouts for the second straight year.

That pitching helped the Braves stay in the race during the first half. They even worked themselves into a tie for first place on July 18. However, they slumped badly in August and never got back into the race in September.

After missing nearly all of 1949, Earl Torgeson bounced back to realize the potential the Braves had seen in him. He led the league in runs and produced the best power numbers of his young career.

After an off season in 1949, Bob Elliott recovered with numbers comparable to his first two seasons with the Braves. And the newly acquired Gordon was an excellent addition, finishing fourth in the league in slugging average (.557) and contributing a major-league-record-tying four grand slams. Gordon and Elliott paced the club to a new franchise home run record of 148.

However, attendance dropped below 1 million for the first time in four years. Boston fans had begun an abandonment of the team that soon would reach epidemic proportions.

Sid Gordon tied a major league record with four grand slams in 1950.

	G	AB	R	H	2B	3B	HR	RBI	SB	AVG
Bob Addis	16	28	7	7	1	0	0	2	1	.250
Paul Burris	10	23	1	4	1	0	0	3	0	.174
Walker Cooper (C)	102	337	52	111	19	3	14	60	1	.329
Del Crandall	79	255	21	56	11	0	4	37	0	.220
Bob Elliott (3B)	142	531	94	162	28	5	24	107	2	.305
Sid Gordon (OF)	134	481	78	146	33	4	27	103	2	.304
Roy Hartsfield (2B)	107	419	62	116	15	2	7	24	7	.277
Tommy Holmes (OF)	105	322	44	96	20	1	9	51	0	.298
Sam Jethroe (OF)	141	582	100	159	28	8	18	58	35*	.273
Buddy Kerr (SS)	155	507	45	115	24	6	2	46	0	.227
Walt Linden	3	5	0	2	1	0	0	0	0	.400
Willard Marshall	105	298	38	70	10	2	5	40	1	.235
Gene Mauch	48	121	17	28	5	0	1	15	1	.231
Luis Olmo	69	154	23	35	7	1	5	22	3	.227
Pete Reiser	53	78	12	16	2	0	1	10	1	.205
Connie Ryan	20	72	12	14	2	0	3	6	0	.194
Sibby Sisti	69	105	21	18	3	1	2	11	1	.171
Earl Torgeson (1B)	156	576	120*	167	30	3	23	87	15	.290
Emil Verban	4	5	1	0	0	0	0	0	0	.000
	156	5,363	785	1,411	246	36	148	726	71	.263

	W	L	G	GS	CG	IP	H	BB	SO	ERA
Johnny Antonelli	2	3	20	6	2	57⅔	81	22	33	5.93
Vern Bickford	19	14	40	39*	27*	311⅔*	293	122	126	3.47
Bob Chipman	7	7	27	12	4	124	127	37	40	4.43
Dave Cole	0	1	4	0	0	8	7	3	8	1.13
Dick Donovan	0	2	10	3	0	29⅔	28	34	9	8.19
Mickey Haefner	0	2	8	2	1	24	23	12	10	5.63
Bob Hall	0	2	21	4	0	50⅓	58	33	22	6.97
Bobby Hogue	3	5	36	1	0	62⅔	69	31	15	5.03
Ernie Johnson	2	0	16	1	0	20⅔	37	13	15	6.97
Dick Manville	0	0	1	0	0	2	0	3	2	0.00
Norm Roy	4	3	19	6	2	59⅔	72	39	25	5.13
Johnny Sain	20	13	37	37	25	278⅓	294*	70	96	3.94
Warren Spahn	21*	17	41	39*	25	293	248	111	191*	3.16
Max Surkont	5	2	9	6	2	55⅔	63	20	21	3.23
Murray Wall	0	0	1	0	0	4	6	2	2	9.00
Bucky Walters	0	0	1	0	0	4	5	2	0	4.50
	83	71		156	88*	1,385⅓	1,411	554	615	4.14

Shutouts—Sain (3), Bickford (2), Antonelli, Spahn
Saves—Hogue (7), Chipman, Roy, Spahn

1951

Record: 76–78
Finish: Fourth
Games Behind: 20½
Managers: Billy Southworth, Tommy Holmes

The Braves and the Red Sox were waging a war for Boston's baseball fans, and the Braves were not faring well. Both teams broadcast all of their games on radio for the first time in 1951, but it paid off only for the Red Sox.

For the sixth straight season, the Sox attracted in excess of 1.3 million fans to Fenway Park. The Braves, however, saw their attendance nearly cut in half from 1950 to 1951. It fell from 944,391 to 487,475, the lowest level in six years.

And though the Red Sox weren't winning pennants, they were a much stronger contender than the Braves and included the spectacular hitting of Ted Williams among their attractions. They finished in third place in 1951, 20 games over .500, and led the American League in runs scored, while the Braves were never a factor in the National League race.

In early May, they were victimized, 3–0, in a no-hitter by Pittsburgh's Cliff Chambers, who issued eight walks in the game. Chambers didn't even survive the season with the Pirates.

Things were so bad that on June 19, Billy Southworth finally resigned as manager even though he had a year and a half left on his contract. Popular Tommy Holmes, who began the season as manager of the Braves' farm club at Hartford, was promoted to replace Southworth.

The change didn't make a significant difference in the team's play. The Braves were in fifth place, three games under .500, when Southworth departed. They played one game over .500 for Holmes and managed to advance to fourth by the end of the year.

On August 11, the Braves earned the distinction of winning the first major league game telecast in color, beating Brooklyn, 8–1. But with the team out of the pennant race on August 28 and few fans showing interest, the Braves sent Johnny Sain, who was struggling, to the Yankees for $50,000 and a young right-hander, Lou Burdette.

With Sain gone, it became increasingly difficult for Holmes to fill the starting rotation. On September 15, he sent 21-year-old right-hander Dave Cole out against the Cardinals. Cole walked the first three batters, then hit Enos Slaughter to force in a run. Braves pitchers wound up issuing 11 walks in the 10–1 loss.

The pitching discovery of the year was 20-year-old left-hander Chet Nichols, who split time as a starter and reliever, leading the league in ERA (2.88). Nichols finished second to a Giants outfielder named Willie Mays for National League Rookie of the Year, then left for military duty. He returned in 1954 but never was as effective as he was in his freshman season.

Warren Spahn had another typically outstanding year, falling one win short (22) of the league lead but topping the league in complete games (26), shutouts (7), and strikeouts. He was second in innings and third in ERA (2.98).

Sam Jethroe led the league in steals (35) for the second straight season, and Earl Torgeson was fourth. They allowed the Braves to finish second in the league in that department.

Sid Gordon had one of the finest seasons of his career and tied for second in the league in RBIs (109). Walker Cooper, in his first full season with the Braves, also had a productive year. In his final season as a Brave, Bob Elliott had the lowest home run and RBI totals of his five years with the club.

	G	AB	R	H	2B	3B	HR	RBI	SB	AVG
Bob Addis	85	199	23	55	7	0	1	24	3	.276
Walker Cooper (C)	109	342	42	107	14	1	18	59	1	.313
Bob Elliott (3B)	136	480	73	137	29	2	15	70	2	.285
Sid Gordon (OF)	150	550	96	158	28	1	29	109	2	.287
Roy Hartsfield (2B)	120	450	63	122	11	2	6	31	7	.271
Tommy Holmes	27	29	1	5	2	0	0	5	0	.172
Sam Jethroe (OF)	148	572	101	160	29	10	18	65	35*	.280
Buddy Kerr (SS)	69	172	18	32	4	0	1	18	0	.186
Johnny Logan	62	169	14	37	7	1	0	16	0	.219
Luis Marquez	68	122	19	24	5	1	0	11	4	.197
Willard Marshall (OF)	136	469	65	132	24	7	11	62	0	.281
Gene Mauch	19	20	5	2	0	0	0	1	0	.100
Ray Mueller	28	70	8	11	2	0	1	9	0	.157
Luis Olmo	21	56	4	11	1	1	0	4	0	.196
Ebba St. Claire	72	220	22	62	17	2	1	25	2	.282
Sibby Sisti	114	362	46	101	20	2	2	38	4	.279
Bob Thorpe	2	2	1	1	0	1	0	1	0	.500
Earl Torgeson (1B)	155	581	99	153	21	4	24	92	20	.263
	155	5,293	723	1,385	234	37	130	683	80	.262

	W	L	G	GS	CG	IP	H	BB	SO	ERA
Vern Bickford	11	9	25	20	12	164⅔	146	76	76	3.12
Lou Burdette	0	0	3	0	0	4⅓	6	5	1	6.23
Bob Chipman	4	3	33	0	0	52	59	19	17	4.85
Dave Cole	2	4	23	7	1	67⅔	64	64	33	4.26
Blix Donnelly	0	1	6	0	0	7⅓	8	6	3	7.36
Dick Donovan	0	0	8	2	0	13⅔	17	11	4	5.27
George Estock	0	1	37	1	0	60⅓	56	37	11	4.33
Bobby Hogue	0	0	3	0	0	5	4	3	0	5.40
Chet Nichols	11	8	33	19	12	156	142	69	71	2.88*
Phil Paine	2	0	21	0	0	35⅓	36	20	17	3.06
Johnny Sain	5	13	26	22	6	160⅓	195	45	63	4.21
Sid Schacht	0	2	5	0	0	4⅔	6	2	1	1.93
Warren Spahn	22	14	39	36	26*	310⅔	278	109*	164*	2.98
Max Surkont	12	16	37	33	11	237	230	89	110	3.99
Jim Wilson	7	7	20	15	5	110	131	40	33	5.40
	76	78		155	73*	1,389	1,378	595	604	3.75

Shutouts—Spahn (7*), Bickford (3), Nichols (3), Surkont (2), Sain
Saves—Chipman (4), Estock (3), Nichols (2), Sain, Surkont, Wilson

1952

Record: 64–89
Finish: Seventh
Games Behind: 32
Managers: Tommy Holmes, Charlie Grimm

The 1952 season was both the end and, in many ways, the beginning for the Braves. It marked the conclusion of the franchise's 82-year history in Boston (77 in the National League). But in retrospect, it also could be viewed as the start of an exciting and successful new era in Braves history.

The move to Milwaukee was a year away, yet the foundation for a 13-year stay in Wisconsin that would produce two pennants, a World Series championship, and nary a single losing season was beginning to take shape.

Warren Spahn, of course, was already entrenched on the Braves staff as one of the finest pitchers in the game. However, in 1952, he was joined full-time by Lou Burdette. Spahn and Burdette would give the Braves one of the most successful pitching tandems in the game.

Also in 1952, Johnny Logan took over as the Braves' regular shortstop, a job he would hold with distinction for nearly a decade. A young third baseman by the name of Eddie Mathews burst onto the scene to tie Sid Gordon for fourth in the league in home runs (25). He also became the first rookie in history to hit three homers in the same game.

And on June 14, scout Dewey Griggs signed Hank Aaron to a Braves contract. Before long, Aaron and Mathews would develop into the greatest fence-busting teammates in history.

But first, the Braves had to get through 1952, which was quite an ordeal for the players and the few fans who bothered to watch the proceedings.

Only 4,694 fans showed up for the home opener, which Spahn lost to Brooklyn, 3–2. It was the beginning of a poor start from which the Braves never recovered. In fact, the club failed to reach .500 or the first division at any point.

The immensely popular Tommy Holmes, who was too close to the players and too accommodating, was replaced as manager by Charlie Grimm on May 31. But the Braves played only marginally better under Grimm, who was promoted from the organization's Milwaukee farm club.

Spahn remained one of the best pitchers in the league, but his record suffered from lack of support. On the way to leading the league in strikeouts for the fourth consecutive season, he tied the National League record with 18 strikeouts in a 15-inning game against the Cubs June 14. Typical of the season, though, the Braves lost, 3–1, and their lone run was a home run by Spahn.

The end of the Braves' Boston era went like this:
They were mathematically eliminated August 31.

The 1952 Braves were the last to represent Boston, ending a run of 82 years, 77 in the National League, in the city.

On September 21, the Braves played their last game at Braves Field, losing to the Dodgers, 8–2. The attendance of 8,822 was the second-largest crowd of the year. Just four years after a franchise record in excess of 1.45 million watched the team, the season total was a pitiful 281,278.

After 10 losses in a row, the final Boston victory came September 27 when Mathews had his three-homer game in an 11–3 victory against Brooklyn. The last game came the next day at Brooklyn and was called after 12 innings in a 5–5 tie.

In spite of the lack of support for the team, there was no immediate indication that the Braves were going to leave town. The team was an integral part of Boston's history, and franchise shifts were all but without precedent.

But on November 26, the Perini brothers announced they had purchased the 45 percent of the club owned by minority stockholders. President Lou Perini said the reason was that he wanted to be able to act on matters without consulting others. Still, no one was reading between the lines.

Perini promised the people of Milwaukee, where the Braves' top farm club was located, that he would help them get a major league team. However, everyone thought that team would be the struggling St. Louis Browns.

Throughout the winter, it remained business as usual for the Braves. Not until the spring of 1953 did the fans of Boston and Milwaukee discover the fate of the only franchise to field a team every season of professional league baseball.

	G	AB	R	H	2B	3B	HR	RBI	SB	AVG
Paul Burris	55	168	14	37	4	0	2	21	0	.220
Buzz Clarkson	14	25	3	5	0	0	0	1	0	.200
Walker Cooper (C)	102	349	33	82	12	1	10	55	1	.235
George Crowe	73	217	25	56	13	1	4	20	0	.258
Jack Cusick	49	78	5	13	1	0	0	6	0	.167
Jack Daniels	106	219	31	41	5	1	2	14	3	.187
Jack Dittmer (2B)	93	326	26	63	7	2	7	41	1	.193
Sid Gordon (OF)	144	522	69	151	22	2	25	75	0	.289
Roy Hartsfield	38	107	13	28	4	3	0	4	0	.262
Sam Jethroe (OF)	151	608	79	141	23	7	13	58	28	.232
Billy Klaus	7	4	3	0	0	0	0	0	0	.000
Johnny Logan (SS)	117	456	56	129	21	3	4	42	1	.283
Willard Marshall	21	66	5	15	4	1	2	11	0	.227
Eddie Mathews (3B)	145	528	80	128	23	5	25	58	6	.242
Bill Reed	15	52	4	13	0	0	0	0	0	.250
Ebba St. Claire	39	108	5	23	2	0	2	4	0	.213
Sibby Sisti	90	245	19	52	10	1	4	24	2	.212
Bob Thorpe (OF)	81	292	20	76	8	2	3	26	3	.260
Earl Torgeson (1B)	122	382	49	88	17	0	5	34	11	.230
Pete Whisenant	24	52	3	10	2	0	0	7	1	.192
	155	5,221	569	1,214	187	31	110	530	58	.233

	W	L	G	GS	CG	IP	H	BB	SO	ERA
Vern Bickford	7	12	26	22	7	161⅓	165	64	62	3.74
Lou Burdette	6	11	45	9	5	137	138	47	47	3.61
Bob Chipman	1	1	29	0	0	41⅓	28	20	16	2.81
Dave Cole	1	1	22	3	0	44⅔	38	42	22	4.03
Gene Conley	0	3	4	3	0	12⅔	23	9	6	7.82
Dick Donovan	0	2	7	2	0	13	18	12	6	5.54
Dick Hoover	0	0	2	0	0	4⅔	8	3	0	7.71
Virgil Jester	3	5	19	8	4	73	80	23	25	3.33
Ernie Johnson	6	3	29	10	2	92	100	31	45	4.11
Sheldon Jones	1	4	39	1	0	70	81	31	40	4.76
Warren Spahn	14	19	40	35	19	290	263	73	183*	2.98
Max Surkont	12	13	31	29	12	215	201	76	125	3.77
Bert Thiel	1	1	4	0	0	7	11	4	6	7.71
Jim Wilson	12	14	33	33	14	234	234	90	104	4.23
	64	89		155	63	1,396	1,388	525	687	3.78

Shutouts—Spahn (5), Surkont (3), Bickford, Jester, Johnson
Saves—Burdette (7), Spahn (3), Donovan, Johnson, Jones

1953

Record: 92–62
Finish: Second
Games Behind: 13
Manager: Charlie Grimm

There's probably never been as much excitement surrounding the opening of a baseball season as there was in Milwaukee in the spring of 1953. It was almost as if the entire city won a lottery jackpot.

A month before the start of the season, citizens were admiring their new Milwaukee County Stadium, which was nearing completion. They fully expected the ballpark would be home to the American Association's Brewers, the Braves' top farm club.

But on March 13, Braves owner Lou Perini, faced with declining attendance in Boston and the prospect of being pressured to relinquish his Milwaukee territorial rights to the St. Louis Browns, shook up Sudsville. He announced his intent to move the club from Boston to Milwaukee for the 1953 schedule, pending the approval of National League owners. Five days later, at the Vinoy Park Hotel in St. Petersburg, Florida, the owners voted unanimously to allow the Braves—then in the midst of spring training in Bradenton—to leave their home of 82 years.

It was the first significant franchise shift in the history of pro sports. The moving of the Baltimore American League franchise to New York in 1903 after only two years on the Chesapeake Bay hardly qualifies for comparison.

The news, coming without warning and so close to the start of the season, sent Milwaukee into a state of wild celebration. In spite of the Braves' seventh-place finish in 1952 and a long history of losing, the town welcomed them like heroes.

The team arrived a few days before the season opener to a rousing reception. A crowd estimated at 12,000 greeted the Braves at the train station, and some 60,000 watched a parade that put the club on public display for the first time. Players and team officials received all sorts of free services and merchandise, ranging from dry cleaning to automobiles. Tickets sold like bratwurst and beer.

Manager Charlie Grimm led the Braves at signing in at the Press Club when the team arrived to much festivity in Milwaukee.

The Braves' starting rotation in 1953 included (L-R) Max Surkont, Warren Spahn, and Johnny Antonelli.

Buoyed by the acquisition of outfielder Andy Pafko and first baseman Joe Adcock, the promotion of Billy Bruton from Triple-A Milwaukee to major league Milwaukee, and the discharge of Del Crandall, Johnny Antonelli, and Bob Buhl from the military, the '53 Braves barely resembled the pathetic seventh-place team of the previous season. And Charlie Grimm's club undoubtedly got a boost from the excitement generated by its wildly enthusiastic fans.

The Braves opened with a 2–0 victory at Cincinnati behind Max Surkont's three-hitter, then came to Milwaukee for the home opener. A standing-room crowd of 34,357 turned out April 14 to officially christen County Stadium. And the Braves cooperated, even though it took them 10 innings to subdue the Cardinals and Stan Musial.

Warren Spahn had a 2–1 lead with two outs and none on in the ninth, only to allow the Cardinals to tie it. However, in the bottom of the 10th, Bruton hit his only home run of the year for a 3–2 victory.

Home runs would be a big part of the Braves' Milwaukee story. They were few and far between at gigantic Braves Field, but a bevy of sluggers and a more conventional ballpark combined to change the club's offensive personality drastically.

One of those sluggers was Adcock, who came to the Braves during the off season from Cincinnati. A part-time player for the Reds, Adcock quickly warmed to being a regular, and on April 29, he struck fear in the hearts of National League pitchers by hitting the first home run ever to reach the center-field bleachers at the Polo Grounds, 475 feet from home plate.

Few Braves responded as well to the new environment as Surkont, a mediocre pitcher most of his career but a world-beater the first half of 1953. On May 25, the hefty right-hander raised his record to 6–0 and also set a major league record at the time by striking out eight consecutive Reds in a 10–3 decision.

Young third baseman Eddie Mathews, in only his second big league season, cemented his reputation as one of the brightest young stars in the game by leading the majors in home runs (47). He also set modern club records for home runs and RBIs (135) that still stand.

Three of Mathews' home runs came August 30 in an explosive doubleheader victory at Pittsburgh. In the first game, outfielder Jim Pendleton became only the second rookie in history to hit three home runs in a game (Mathews was the first a year earlier). The Braves hit five more in the 19–4 win to tie the Yankees' record of eight in a game. Milwaukee then

hit four more homers in the second game, an 11–5 victory, to set a record with 12 in a doubleheader.

Spahn had his fifth 20-win season and tied for the league lead with 23. He pitched a nearly perfect game August 1 against Philadelphia when the lone base runner was Richie Ashburn, who reached on an infield single in the fourth.

It was a talented, exciting team, one that looked like a pennant contender through the All-Star break. But the Dodgers were simply too strong, winning 105 games in a 154-game schedule. Grimm's team couldn't keep pace in the second half and finished a distant, but solid, second.

Milwaukee had the best pitching staff in the league, leading in ERA (3.30). The Braves also had the league's top base stealer in Bruton (26), and they set a franchise record in home runs (156).

Without the benefit of off-season sales, the Braves set an all-time National League attendance record of 1,826,297, breaking the standard set by Brooklyn in 1947. They surpassed the entire 1952 season attendance in Boston on May 20, the 13th home date of the season, and broke the Braves' franchise record, set in 1948, on September 4.

	G	AB	R	H	2B	3B	HR	RBI	SB	AVG
Joe Adcock (1B)	157	590	71	168	33	6	18	80	3	.285
Bill Bruton (OF)	151	613	82	153	18	14	1	41	26*	.250
Paul Burris	2	1	0	0	0	0	0	0	0	.000
Walker Cooper	53	137	12	30	6	0	3	16	1	.219
Del Crandall (C)	116	382	55	104	13	1	15	51	2	.272
George Crowe	47	42	6	12	2	0	2	6	0	.286
Jack Dittmer (2B)	138	504	54	134	22	1	9	63	1	.266
Sid Gordon (OF)	140	464	67	127	22	4	19	75	1	.274
Harry Hanebrink	51	80	8	19	1	1	1	8	1	.237
Billy Klaus	2	2	1	0	0	0	0	1	0	.000
Johnny Logan (SS)	150	611	100	167	27	8	11	73	2	.273
Eddie Mathews (3B)	157	579	110	175	31	8	47*	135	1	.302
Andy Pafko (OF)	140	516	70	153	23	4	17	72	2	.297
Jim Pendleton	120	251	48	75	12	4	7	27	6	.299
Mel Roach	5	2	1	0	0	0	0	0	0	.000
Ebba St. Claire	33	80	7	16	3	0	2	5	0	.200
Sibby Sisti	38	23	8	5	1	0	0	4	0	.217
Bob Thorpe (OF)	27	37	1	6	1	0	0	5	0	.162
	157	5,349	738	1,422	227	52	156	691	46	.266

Johnny Logan led the league's shortstops in defense three straight seasons from 1952–54.

	W	L	G	GS	CG	IP	H	BB	SO	ERA
Johnny Antonelli	12	12	31	26	11	175½	167	71	131	3.18
Vern Bickford	2	5	20	9	2	58	60	35	25	5.28
Bob Buhl	13	8	30	18	8	154½	133	73	83	2.97
Lou Burdette	15	5	46	13	6	175	177	56	58	3.24
Dave Cole	0	1	10	0	0	14⅔	17	14	13	8.59
Joey Jay	1	0	3	1	1	10	6	5	4	0.00
Virgil Jester	0	0	2	0	0	2	4	4	0	22.50
Ernie Johnson	4	3	36	1	0	81	79	22	36	2.67
Dave Jolly	0	1	24	0	0	38⅓	34	27	23	3.52
Don Liddle	7	6	31	15	4	128⅔	119	55	63	3.08
Warren Spahn	23*	7	35	32	24	265⅔	211	70	148	2.10*
Max Surkont	11	5	28	24	11	170	168	64	83	4.18
Jim Wilson	4	9	20	18	5	114	107	43	71	4.34
	92	62		157	72	1,387*	1,282	539	738	3.30*

Shutouts—Spahn (5), Buhl (3), Antonelli (2), Surkont (2), Burdette, Jay
Saves—Burdette (8), Spahn (3), Liddle (2), Antonelli, Bickford

1954

Record: 89–65
Finish: Third
Games Behind: 8
Manager: Charlie Grimm

The Braves thought they needed a power-hitting outfielder for 1954 in order to make up ground on Brooklyn, who ran away with the pennant a year earlier by hitting 52 more home runs than Milwaukee. They got one, but in the process unwittingly shifted the balance of power in the National League to the Giants.

In 1951, Bobby Thomson hit the "shot heard 'round the world" to win the pennant for the Giants in the decisive game of a playoff with the Dodgers. He'd driven in over 100 runs in four of the last five years when the Braves pried him away from New York in January 1954 in a six-player deal that sent promising left-hander Johnny Antonelli to the Giants.

During spring training, Thomson broke an ankle sliding into third base and was lost until midseason. Meanwhile, Antonelli pitched the Giants to the World Series championship, winning 21 games and leading the league in several categories, including ERA (2.30).

In the spring of 1954, the Braves' offense was built around (L-R) Joe Adcock, Andy Pafko, Bobby Thomson, and Eddie Mathews, but when Thomson broke his ankle, a rookie by the name of Hank Aaron was thrust into the picture.

All was not lost, however. The Braves elected to replace Thomson in left with 20-year-old rookie Hank Aaron. On April 23 at Sportsman's Park in St. Louis, Aaron connected for his first big league home run off Vic Raschi, helping the Braves to a 7–5 victory. It was a story line that would be repeated quite frequently over the ensuing two decades.

However, Braves fans had no way of knowing just what Aaron would accomplish. But they could visualize what a force Milwaukee would have been with a pitching staff consisting of Warren Spahn, Lou Burdette, rookie Gene Conley, and Antonelli—not that this disappointment kept them at home or dampened their enthusiasm.

With the seating capacity at County Stadium increased to 43,340, the Braves drew a record 2,131,388, becoming the first team in the league to surpass 2 million. And despite winning three fewer games than in 1953 and dropping to third place, Charlie Grimm actually brought the team in five games closer to first than in its Milwaukee debut.

The end result might have been even better if not for a season-long barrage of injuries that culminated September 5 when Aaron broke an ankle sliding. Two weeks later, the Giants clinched the pennant.

Still, the Braves had come a long way since their last dismal year in Boston. They played poorly in April but climbed into first by late May, only to drop to .500 at the All-Star break. Shortly after the break, however, they went on a binge, winning 41 of 54 games to climb into second place in early September. During that period, Spahn put together an 11-game winning streak.

But when Aaron was lost, followed in six days by Adcock's wrist being broken by a Don Newcombe pitch, the wheels came off the offense.

The season was filled with memorable events. That Jim Wilson would provide one of those highlights was a major shock. The Braves actually tried to waive the 32-year-old right-hander in May, but no one claimed him.

Because of a doubleheader, Wilson was given an unusual start June 6 and shut out Pittsburgh. Grimm decided to start him again June 12 against Robin Roberts and the Phillies, and Wilson responded with the franchise's first no-hitter since 1950, the first ever at County Stadium. The Braves won, 2–0, and Wilson was rolling on what would be an eight-game winning streak that landed him in the All-Star Game. However, he wouldn't win another game for the team once the streak ended.

On July 31, Adcock put on a slugging display the likes of which the game had never seen nor which has ever been duplicated. He single-handedly dismantled the Dodgers at Ebbets Field with four home runs and a double. The 18 total bases in the 15–7 victory established a major league record that still stands.

The previous day, Adcock had seven total bases. His two-day total of 20 tied a record set by Ty Cobb. However, when the Braves began bombing the Dodgers again a day later, Clem Labine beaned the Braves' first baseman. Adcock had to be carried from the field but was not seriously injured.

Not to be deterred, Adcock hit his ninth homer of the season at Ebbets Field on September 10, setting a National League record for home runs in an opponent's park. Of course, the next day Newcombe struck back, snuffing Adcock's season and the Braves' pennant hopes with one pitch.

Milwaukee led the league in team defense (.981) and was

Joe Adcock hammered the Dodgers in 1954, but on September 12, he suffered a broken wrist when hit by a pitch from Brooklyn's Don Newcombe.

second in ERA (3.19). Billy Bruton led the league in steals (34) for the second straight season, and Mathews had another monster season.

Spahn was second in the league in wins (21). Burdette, in his first full season as a starter, finished second in the league in ERA (2.76), and Conley, the tall rookie, was fifth in ERA (2.96).

	G	AB	R	H	2B	3B	HR	RBI	SB	AVG
Hank Aaron (OF)	122	468	58	131	27	6	13	69	2	.280
Joe Adcock (1B)	133	500	73	154	27	5	23	87	1	.308
Bill Bruton (OF)	142	567	89	161	20	7	4	30	34*	.284
Sam Calderone	22	29	3	11	2	0	0	5	0	.379
Del Crandall (C)	138	463	60	112	18	2	21	64	0	.242
Jack Dittmer	66	192	22	47	8	0	6	20	0	.245
Johnny Logan (SS)	154	560	66	154	17	7	8	66	2	.275
Eddie Mathews (3B)	138	476	96	138	21	4	40	103	10	.290
Catfish Metkovich	68	123	7	34	5	1	1	15	0	.276
Danny O'Connell (2B)	146	541	61	151	28	4	2	37	2	.279
Andy Pafko (OF)	138	510	61	146	22	4	14	69	1	.286
Jim Pendleton	71	173	20	38	3	1	1	16	2	.220
Billy Queen	3	2	0	0	0	0	0	0	0	.000
Mel Roach	3	4	0	0	0	0	0	0	0	.000
Sibby Sisti	9	0	2	0	0	0	0	0	0	—
Roy Smalley	25	36	5	8	0	0	1	7	0	.222
Bobby Thomson	43	99	7	23	3	0	2	15	0	.232
Charlie White	50	93	14	22	4	0	1	8	0	.237
	154	5,261	670	1,395	217	41	139	636	54	.265

	W	L	G	GS	CG	IP	H	BB	SO	ERA
Bob Buhl	2	7	31	14	2	110⅓	117	65	57	4.00
Lou Burdette	15	14	38	32	13	238	224	62	79	2.76
Gene Conley	14	9	28	27	12	194⅓	171	79	113	2.96
Ray Crone	1	0	19	2	1	49	44	19	33	2.02
Charlie Gorin	0	1	5	0	0	9⅔	5	6	12	1.86
Joey Jay	1	0	15	1	0	18	21	16	13	6.50
Ernie Johnson	5	2	40	4	1	99⅓	77	34	68	2.81
Dave Jolly	11	6	47	1	0	111⅓	87	64	62	2.43
Dave Koslo	1	1	12	0	0	17⅓	13	9	7	3.12
Chet Nichols	9	11	35	20	5	122⅓	132	65	55	4.41
Phil Paine	1	0	11	0	0	14	14	12	11	3.86
Warren Spahn	21	12	39	34	23	283⅓	262	86	136	3.14
Jim Wilson	8	2	27	19	6	127⅔	129	36	52	3.52
	89	65		154	63	1,394⅔*	1,296	553	698	3.19

Shutouts—Burdette (4), Wilson (4), Conley (2), Buhl, Nichols, Spahn
Saves—Jolly (10), Buhl (3), Spahn (3), Johnson (2), Crone, Koslo, Nichols

1955

Record: 85–69
Finish: Second
Games Behind: 13½
Manager: Charlie Grimm

In 1955, the Braves put together their third consecutive solid season in as many years in Milwaukee—but once again, it wasn't good enough. The Dodgers won their first 10 games and 22 of their first 24. So much for a pennant race.

The Braves were second most of the year but failed to make a serious run at Brooklyn, who clinched on September 8, a National League record for a 154-game season. Once again, injuries played a big role in Milwaukee's shortcomings, though the Dodgers would have been tough to catch under any circumstances.

Home runs were up throughout baseball, and the Braves took advantage of the trend to set a club record with 182, still 19 fewer than Brooklyn.

Milwaukee's first home run of the season came under unusual circumstances. On opening day, in the eighth inning, rookie Chuck Tanner pinch-hit for Warren Spahn and hit the first pitch he saw for a home run. Tanner, who became manager of the team in 1986, hit just eight more home runs in his brief playing career with the club.

The real slugging continued to be done by third baseman Eddie Mathews, though. Despite being walked a league-high

In 1955, Chuck Tanner, who would manage the Braves 31 years later, made his major league debut as a pinch-hitter and hit a home run on the first pitch he saw.

(L-R) Joe Adcock, Ernie Johnson, and Bobby Thomson ham it up after a victory.

109 times and missing two weeks with an appendectomy, he finished fifth in home runs (41), reaching the 40-homer level for the third consecutive year.

Young Hank Aaron also showed signs that he had a little pop in his bat. Playing just his second season in the majors, Aaron tied teammate Johnny Logan for the league lead in doubles and more than doubled his rookie-year home run total. An infielder before making the majors, Aaron played 27 games at second base during the season in an attempt to shore up one of the team's weaknesses.

Fully recovered from his broken leg, Bobby Thomson assumed the left-field job and started like the Thomson of old, driving in 17 runs in the first 10 games. But he sustained a shoulder injury in early May and never really returned to his old form.

Other significant injuries occurred to Gene Conley and Joe Adcock. Conley was selected for the All-Star Game, hosted by the Braves, and struck out the side in the 12th inning to earn the win. However, he hurt his shoulder shortly afterward and basically was through for the year.

Adcock, the Louisiana Strongman, had his arm broken by a Jim Hearn pitch on July 31 and missed the remainder of the season.

Spahn failed to win 20 games for the first time in three years. He did, however, finish fourth in the league in ERA, one spot behind teammate Bob Buhl. Billy Bruton won his third straight stolen base title (25).

Gene Conley struck out the side in the 12th inning to win the 1955 All-Star Game at Milwaukee County Stadium.

	W	L	G	GS	CG	IP	H	BB	SO	ERA
Bob Buhl	13	11	38	27	11	201⅓	168	109	117	3.21
Lou Burdette	13	8	42	33	11	230	253	73	70	4.03
Gene Conley	11	7	22	21	10	158	152	52	107	4.16
Ray Crone	10	9	33	15	6	140⅓	117	42	76	3.46
John Edelman	0	0	5	0	0	5⅔	7	8	3	11.12
Charlie Gorin	0	0	2	0	0	⅓	1	3	0	54.00
Joey Jay	0	0	12	1	0	19	23	13	3	4.74
Ernie Johnson	5	7	40	2	0	92	81	55	43	3.42
Dave Jolly	2	3	36	0	0	58⅓	58	51	23	5.71
Dave Koslo	0	1	1	0	0	0	1	0	0	∞
Chet Nichols	9	8	34	21	6	144	139	67	44	4.00
Phil Paine	2	0	15	0	0	25⅓	20	14	26	2.49
Humberto Robinson	3	1	13	2	1	38	31	25	19	3.08
Warren Spahn	17	14	39	32	16	245⅔	249	65	110	3.26
Roberto Vargas	0	0	25	0	0	24⅔	39	14	13	8.76
	85	69		154	61*	1,383	1,339	591	654	3.85

Shutouts—Burdette (2), Buhl, Crone, Spahn
Saves—Johnson (4), Robinson (2), Vargas (2), Buhl, Jolly, Nichols, Spahn

	G	AB	R	H	2B	3B	HR	RBI	SB	AVG
Hank Aaron (OF)	153	602	105	189	37*	9	27	106	3	.314
Joe Adcock	84	288	40	76	14	0	15	45	0	.264
Bill Bruton (OF)	149	636*	106	175	30	12	9	47	25*	.275
Del Crandall (C)	133	440	61	104	15	2	26	62	2	.236
George Crowe (1B)	104	303	41	85	12	4	15	55	1	.281
Jack Dittmer	38	72	4	9	1	1	1	4	0	.125
Johnny Logan (SS)	154	595	95	177	37*	5	13	83	3	.297
Eddie Mathews (3B)	141	499	108	144	23	5	41	101	3	.289
Danny O'Connell (2B)	124	453	47	102	15	4	6	40	2	.225
Andy Pafko	86	252	29	67	3	5	5	34	1	.266
Jim Pendleton	8	10	0	0	0	0	0	0	0	.000
Del Rice	27	71	5	14	0	1	2	7	0	.197
Bob Roselli	6	9	1	2	1	0	0	0	0	.222
Chuck Tanner	97	243	27	60	9	3	6	27	0	.247
Bennie Taylor	12	10	2	1	0	0	0	0	0	.100
Bobby Thomson (OF)	101	343	40	88	12	3	12	56	2	.257
Charlie White	12	30	3	7	1	0	0	4	0	.233
	154	5,277	743	1,377	219	55	182	699	42	.261

1956

Record: 92–62
Finish: Second
Games Behind: 1
Managers: Charlie Grimm, Fred Haney

Looking back, it's difficult to understand why the 1956 Braves didn't win the pennant. They certainly had the horses.

Basically, the team had the same personnel as the year before, but individually and collectively, that talent seemed to perform at a higher level than that of any other club. Make no mistake, the Dodgers were strong, although they weren't the same team that ran away with the 1955 title. But in the end—the very end—the Braves were looking up at Brooklyn, if only by a single game.

The 1956 pennant race was one of the best in National League history, with just two games separating the top three teams in the final standings. A slugging Cincinnati team finished third, one game behind Milwaukee.

Any fan who looked at the final statistics for the season without knowing the outcome in the standings most certainly would surmise that the Braves won the pennant. There would be many reasons for such an assumption, the most obvious being an incredible pitching staff that led the league in ERA (3.11) by nearly half a run. And it's not like this team couldn't hit and field. The Braves were third in runs, home runs, batting average, and fielding average.

Charlie Grimm had quite an array of talent, including the batting champ, Hank Aaron (.328), and the ERA leader (2.70), Lou Burdette, and runner-up, Warren Spahn.

Yet something was missing, a fact that became painfully obvious when the club got off slowly, costing the popular Grimm his job. On June 16, the Braves were 24–22. They were just four games out of first but had lost nine of their last 13 to drop to fifth place. At that point, Grimm announced he was resigning. Coach Fred Haney, who'd had unsuccessful managing tours with the St. Louis Browns and the Pirates, was put in charge.

Did Haney have the answers Grimm didn't possess, or was Grimm's exit simply the wakeup call the team needed? For whatever reason, the Braves proceeded to win their first 11 games under Haney and move to the top of the standings.

The streak started at Ebbets Field, Joe Adcock's favorite playground, with the big first baseman hitting three home runs to spur a doubleheader sweep of the Dodgers. Adcock hit a ninth-inning, game-winning homer in the first game that was the only ball ever to reach the left-field roof, 350 feet from home and 83 feet high.

The Braves had leveled off by the All-Star break and dropped to second place. But after the break, they proceeded to win 15 of 17, bursting into a 5½-game lead over Cincinnati and six games ahead of Brooklyn. It looked as if Milwaukee was capable of running away from the rest of the league, but such was not the case.

Haney's club held onto first place into September, but Brooklyn and Cincinnati were making up ground. The Braves were slowed somewhat when Bob Buhl was hit on the right hand by a line drive. He continued to pitch but wasn't nearly as effective as he'd been before the accident.

On September 15, Milwaukee fell out of first place by percentage points for the first time since July 13. Nevertheless, they fought back and held a one-game lead going into the final weekend, a three-game series at St. Louis. Haney had Spahn, Burdette, and Buhl lined up to pitch, and the Braves needed only to win two out of three in order to guarantee at least a tie. At the same time, the Dodgers were playing three with Pittsburgh.

The Braves lost the opener, 5–4, and the Dodgers were rained out, cutting the Milwaukee lead to a half game. The following day, Spahn pitched brilliantly but suffered an excruciating loss, 2–1, in 12 innings. At the same time, the Dodgers took two from Pittsburgh, giving Brooklyn a one-game lead entering the final game of the season.

Lou Burdette led the league in ERA and shutouts in 1956.

Burdette beat the Cardinals, 4–2, in the finale, but at the same time, the Dodgers completed a sweep of the Pirates and repeated as National League champions.

The club's failure to win the pennant should not be attributed in any way to the work of Adcock. For starters, he led the league's first baseman in fielding for the first of four times. But, of course, it was his bat that did the real damage to opponents. He tied for second in the league in home runs (38) with Frank Robinson, and he finished second in RBIs (103) to Stan Musial. His ratio of one home run for every 11.9 at bats was the best in the league.

There are many examples throughout Adcock's career of the devastating power he possessed, and one of his most sustained efforts came in mid-July when he hit 10 home runs in 13 games. Included in that streak was his July 19 performance against New York in which he drove in eight runs with a grand slam, a three-run homer, and an RBI single. He also doubled—all before he was taken out of the game after six innings of a 13–3 win.

Aaron led the league in hits (200), doubles, and total bases, as well as average, and finished one behind Billy Bruton in triples. Mathews finished fourth in home runs, just one behind Adcock.

Buhl, Burdette, and Spahn were second, third, and fifth, respectively, in winning percentage, and Burdette led in shutouts (6). Spahn, at age 35, recorded his 200th career victory.

It was a team loaded with superstars who all had seasons worthy of their reputations. However, the Braves still came up one game short of their goal. Attendance exceeded 2 million for the third straight year.

	G	AB	R	H	2B	3B	HR	RBI	SB	AVG
Hank Aaron (OF)	153	609	106	200*	34*	14	26	92	2	.328*
Joe Adcock (1B)	137	454	76	132	23	1	38	103	1	.291
Toby Atwell	15	30	2	5	1	0	2	7	0	.167
Bill Bruton (OF)	147	525	73	143	23	15*	8	56	8	.272
Wes Covington	75	138	17	39	4	0	2	16	1	.283
Del Crandall (C)	112	311	37	74	14	2	16	48	1	.238
Jack Dittmer	44	102	8	25	4	0	1	6	0	.245
Earl Hersh	7	13	0	3	3	0	0	0	0	.231
Johnny Logan (SS)	148	545	69	153	27	5	15	46	3	.281
Felix Mantilla	35	53	9	15	1	1	0	3	0	.283
Eddie Mathews (3B)	151	552	103	150	21	2	37	95	6	.272
Danny O'Connell (2B)	139	498	71	119	17	9	2	42	3	.239
Andy Pafko	45	93	15	24	5	0	2	9	0	.258
Jim Pendleton	14	11	0	0	0	0	0	0	0	.000
Del Rice	71	188	15	40	9	1	3	17	0	.213
Bob Roselli	4	2	1	1	0	0	1	1	0	.500
Chuck Tanner	60	63	6	15	2	0	1	4	0	.238
Bobby Thomson (OF)	142	451	59	106	10	4	20	74	2	.235
Frank Torre	111	159	17	41	6	0	0	16	1	.258
	155	5,207	709	1,350	212	54	177	667	29	.259

	W	L	G	GS	CG	IP	H	BB	SO	ERA
Bob Buhl	18	8	38	33	13	216⅔	190	105	86	3.32
Lou Burdette	19	10	39	35	16	256⅓	234	52	110	2.70*
Gene Conley	8	9	31	19	5	158⅓	169	52	68	3.13
Ray Crone	11	10	35	21	6	169⅔	173	44	73	3.87
Ernie Johnson	4	3	36	0	0	51	54	21	26	3.71
Dave Jolly	2	3	29	0	0	45⅔	39	35	20	3.74
Red Murff	0	0	14	1	0	24⅓	25	7	18	4.44
Chet Nichols	0	1	2	0	0	4	9	3	2	6.75
Phil Paine	0	0	1	0	0	0	3	0	0	∞
Taylor Phillips	5	3	23	6	3	87⅔	69	33	36	2.26
Humberto Robinson	0	0	1	0	0	2	1	2	0	0.00
Lou Sleater	2	2	25	1	0	45⅔	42	27	32	3.15
Warren Spahn	20	11	39	35	20	281⅓	249	52	128	2.78
Bob Trowbridge	3	2	19	4	1	50⅔	38	34	40	2.66
	92	62		155	64*	1,393⅓*	1,295	467	639	3.11*

Shutouts—Burdette (6*), Spahn (3), Buhl (2), Conley
Saves—Jolly (7), Johnson (6), Conley (3), Spahn (3), Crone (2), Phillips (2), Sleater (2), Burdette, Murff

1957

Record: 95–59
Finish: First
Games Ahead: 8
Manager: Fred Haney

It was career home run No. 109, though no one was counting at the time, and came on September 23, 1957. Because of Hank Aaron's all-around excellence, he wasn't even thought of as a true "home run hitter." It would be years before the notion would enter anyone's mind that this magnificent ballplayer might someday break Babe Ruth's career home run record. But even though Aaron would hit 646 more home runs, it was this one—No. 109—which the Braves' great outfielder has always called his "most memorable."

Playing at home, the Braves were locked in a 2–2 tie with St. Louis in the 11th inning. With Johnny Logan at first and two outs, the 23-year-old Aaron lined a pitch from Billy Muffett over the center-field fence, causing County Stadium, the city of Milwaukee, and most of the state of Wisconsin to erupt in the biggest celebration since the Braves arrived in 1953. Aaron's teammates mobbed him at home plate and carried him off the field.

The Braves were National League champions and headed to the World Series for the first time since 1948. After three second-place finishes and a strong third in their four previous years in Milwaukee, the Braves had finally proven they were more than just a collection of talented individuals. They were the best team in the league.

And Fred Haney's club had to pull together in order to win the pennant, because there were plenty of problems to overcome. The Braves were in first place much of the year and never were more than 3½ games out of the lead, but that was more a tribute to their tenaciousness than to the ease with which they won the pennant.

The turning point in the season was the June 15 trading deadline. That's when general manager John Quinn repaired the team's most obvious weakness by acquiring second baseman Red Schoendienst from New York for outfielder Bobby Thomson, second baseman Danny O'Connell, and pitcher Ray Crone.

Schoendienst solidified the infield and provided more offense at second than the team had enjoyed since Rogers Hornsby in 1928. Without him, it is doubtful the Braves could have played through the setbacks that awaited them and still maintained control of their destiny.

On June 23, the heart of the batting order was torn out when Joe Adcock broke his right leg sliding. By the time he returned in September, the pennant was well within reach. Adcock's replacement, Frank Torre, did a creditable job. He led the league's first basemen in defense, but though he was steady with the bat, he wasn't in Adcock's league when it came to power.

Milwaukee sustained yet another injury, one that would

The 1957 Milwaukee Braves were the last franchise representative to win the World Series.

The mid-season acquisition of second baseman Red Schoendienst, chatting here with Cincinnati's Gus Bell, was critical to Milwaukee's success in 1957.

The bat of Bob "Hurricane" Hazle was nearly unstoppable the last two months of 1957.

have crippled a lesser team, on July 11 when center fielder and leadoff hitter Billy Bruton was lost for the remainder of the year. Bruton and shortstop Felix Mantilla collided in short center while chasing a pop fly. Bruton damaged knee ligaments, and Mantilla suffered a knee injury that caused him to miss nearly three weeks.

Aaron thus became the Braves' center fielder for the rest of the season, a fact that made his splendid offensive statistics for the year even more impressive, considering he'd never before played the demanding position.

The 1957 Braves were too deep in talent to let injuries ruin their mission, though.

Outfielders Wes Covington and Bob Hazle and reliever Don McMahon were virtual unknowns when the season began. Hazle and McMahon had never worn Milwaukee uniforms and opened the season in the minors. Covington had limited experience with the Braves but was farmed out in May. However, their collective contributions proved invaluable.

Covington was recalled when Thomson was traded and wound up starting more games in left than anyone else. His power production went a long way toward helping the club overcome Adcock's loss.

McMahon, a hard-throwing, 27-year-old right-hander, also was called up in late June to begin what would be a long and prosperous career as a closer, even though that term had yet to become part of baseball jargon. Relief had been a bit of an Achilles heel for the Braves since arriving in Milwaukee, but McMahon shored up that department in a hurry. He was nearly impeccable in 32 appearances.

And all Hazle did was take the league by storm for two months, earning the nickname "Hurricane" and lasting recognition as a franchise hero.

Hazle arrived in the early stages of what would prove to be Milwaukee's biggest surge of the season. And before the team cooled off, the 26-year-old left-handed hitter played a major role in supplying much of the momentum needed to carry the Braves to the pennant. In his first nine games, Hazle had a four-hit game and three three-hit games. He was

"unconscious," hitting over .500 in August and contributing seven of his lifetime nine home runs in the final two months.

Starting July 16, Milwaukee won 17 of 19 and 24 of 29 games to open an 8½-game lead. Just when it looked like the Braves could go on cruise control, they lost eight of 11 and saw their lead dwindle to 2½ games over St. Louis on September 15. Not about to let their hard work go to waste in the final two weeks, Haney's club mustered one last burst, winning seven in a row—culminating with Aaron's pennant-winning home run to eliminate the Cardinals September 23.

The Braves led the league in home runs with a then-franchise-record 199 and also boasted league-leading totals in runs, triples, and slugging percentage. The defense was ranked second by a mere percentage point. The pitching staff led in complete games and fewest home runs allowed and was second in ERA (3.47).

The league's individual statistical leaders were heavily populated with Braves, the most prominent being Aaron, who won two-thirds of the Triple Crown. He won the first of his four career league championships in both home runs (44) and RBIs (132). He also finished fourth in batting average (.322).

Aaron led the league in runs and total bases and was second in hits and third in slugging average. No wonder he was named the league's Most Valuable Player in a close battle with Stan Musial. Schoendienst, who didn't join the team until mid-June, finished third in the MVP race and led the league in hits (200).

Warren Spahn, who was fifth in the MVP voting, won the Cy Young Award at a time when there was only one such honor to cover both leagues. The indestructible left-hander led the league in wins (21) and complete games (18), was second in shutouts and innings, tied for second in ERA (2.69), and was third in winning percentage.

Bob Buhl, despite late-season shoulder woes, led the league in percentage (.720) and placed third in victories and fourth in ERA. Eddie Mathews had his lowest power numbers since his rookie year yet still finished fifth in total bases. And Lou Burdette, who saved his best work for the Yankees in the World Series, tied for fourth in the league in victories.

(L–R) Ernie Johnson, Frank Torre, Don McMahon, Joe Adcock, and Andy Pafko revel in the Braves' clubhouse after clinching the '57 pennant.

The list of heroes included nearly everyone who wore the tomahawk across his chest that year. Team captain Del Crandall continued as the league's top defensive catcher, had a steady season offensively, and even played a little first base and right field to help cover during injuries. Johnny Logan had another solid season in the midst of a long run as the team's regular shortstop, making the All-Star team for the second time in his career.

And Haney, who held the team together for six months, was named Manager of the Year in his first full season directing the Braves.

Altogether, it was a sensational effort by what many experts and historians regard as one of the finest teams ever assembled. Attendance was a franchise-record 2,215,404. Things couldn't have been better for an organization that five years earlier had been a disgrace.

Owner Lou Perini joins Hank Aaron for the '57 pennant celebration.

	G	AB	R	H	2B	3B	HR	RBI	SB	AVG
Hank Aaron (OF)	151	615	118*	198	27	6	44*	132*	1	.322
Joe Adcock	65	209	31	60	13	2	12	38	0	.287
Bill Bruton (OF)	79	306	41	85	16	9	5	30	11	.278
Dick Cole	15	14	1	1	0	0	0	0	0	.071
Wes Covington (OF)	96	328	51	93	4	8	21	65	4	.284
Del Crandall (C)	118	383	45	97	11	2	15	46	1	.253
John DeMerit	33	34	8	5	0	0	0	1	1	.147
Harry Hanebrink	6	7	0	2	0	0	0	0	0	.286
Bob Hazle	41	134	26	54	12	0	7	27	1	.403
Nippy Jones	30	79	5	21	2	1	2	8	0	.266
Johnny Logan (SS)	129	494	59	135	19	7	10	49	5	.273
Bobby Malkmus	13	22	6	2	0	1	0	0	0	.091
Felix Mantilla	71	182	28	43	9	1	4	21	2	.236
Eddie Mathews (3B)	148	572	109	167	28	9	32	94	3	.292
Danny O'Connell	48	183	29	43	9	1	1	8	1	.235
Andy Pafko	83	220	31	61	6	1	8	27	1	.277
Del Rice	54	144	15	33	1	1	9	20	0	.229
Mel Roach	7	6	1	1	0	0	0	0	0	.167
Carl Sawatski	58	105	13	25	4	0	6	17	0	.238
Red Schoendienst (2B)	93	394	56	122	23	4	6	32	2	.310
Ray Shearer	2	2	1	1	0	0	0	0	0	.500
Chuck Tanner	22	69	5	17	3	0	2	6	0	.246
Hawk Taylor	7	1	2	0	0	0	0	0	0	.000
Bobby Thomson	41	148	15	35	5	3	4	23	2	.236
Frank Torre (1B)	129	364	46	99	19	5	5	40	0	.272
	155	5,458	772*	1,469	221	62*	199*	722	35	.269

	W	L	G	GS	CG	IP	H	BB	SO	ERA
Bob Buhl	18	7	34	31	14	216⅔	191	121	117	2.74
Lou Burdette	17	9	37	33	14	256⅔	260	59	78	3.72
Gene Conley	9	9	35	18	6	148	133	64	61	3.16
Ray Crone	3	1	11	5	2	42⅓	54	15	15	4.46
Joey Jay	0	0	1	0	0	⅔	0	0	0	0.00
Ernie Johnson	7	3	30	0	0	65	67	26	44	3.88
Dave Jolly	1	1	23	0	0	37⅔	37	21	27	5.02
Don McMahon	2	3	32	0	0	46⅔	33	29	46	1.54
Red Murff	2	2	12	1	0	26	31	11	13	4.85
Phil Paine	0	0	1	0	0	2	1	3	2	0.00
Taylor Phillips	3	2	27	6	0	73	82	40	36	5.55
Juan Pizarro	5	6	24	10	3	99⅓	99	51	68	4.62
Warren Spahn	21*	11	39	35	18*	271	241	78	111	2.69
Bob Trowbridge	7	5	32	16	3	126	118	52	75	3.64
	95*	59		155	60*	1,411*	1,347	570	693	3.47

Shutouts—Spahn (4), Buhl (2), Burdette, Conley, Trowbridge
Saves—McMahon (9), Johnson (4), Spahn (3), Murff (2), Phillips (2), Conley, Jay, Jolly, Trowbridge

1958

Record: 92–62
Finish: First
Games Ahead: 8
Manager: Fred Haney

Champions come and champions go. But the true test of greatness is a team's ability to sustain from year to year, to repeat as the best the league has to offer in two or more seasons.

The Braves won a pennant in Boston in 1948, then barely made the first division in 1949. George Stallings' Braves pulled off a "miracle" in 1914 but finished a rather distant second in 1915. Not since 1897–98 had the Braves franchise won consecutive National League championships.

That's the challenge which faced the 1958 Braves, and they responded in the fashion of the true greatness they represented by repeating as pennant winners.

With basically the same roster as the 1957 World Series champs, Fred Haney's team was heavily favored to repeat, especially with the prospect of Joe Adcock and Billy Bruton returning in good health. But though Milwaukee beat Pittsburgh by a comfortable 8-game margin, the successful title defense was not a cakewalk. The primary reason, once again, was a rash of injuries that served to equalize the club's talented lineup.

Red Schoendienst, the glue of the 1957 team, was not the same player he had been the year before. He appeared in just 106 games, and though he led the league's second basemen in defensive percentage, his offensive numbers were down across the board. The reason, it was discovered after the season, was that he was weakened by the early stages of tuberculosis, which would sideline him virtually all of 1959.

Mel Roach, 25, filled in well when Schoendienst was on the bench, but he simply couldn't offer the savvy and leadership of the seasoned veteran.

Wes Covington, who was sensational at times in '57, suffered a knee injury in spring training. When he played, he was even more extraordinary, at least offensively, but Haney had to nurse him along in order to get him in 90 games.

Bruton, still recovering from his 1957 knee injury, wasn't ready until late May, and Bob Hazle was gone by then. On May 6, "Hurricane" was beaned and had to be carried off the field. Later in the month, the phenom of the 1957 stretch drive was sold to Detroit.

Sore-armed Bob Buhl and Gene Conley won just five games between them. But youngsters Carlton Willey, Joey Jay, and Juan Pizarro and veteran Bob Rush, acquired from the Cubs, combined to pick up the slack.

Though the Braves tied for the league lead with a .266 team batting average, pitching was unquestionably the strength of the club thanks primarily to the continued excellence of the incomparable Warren Spahn and his cohort, Lou Burdette. Milwaukee's 3.21 staff ERA was easily the best in the league. Braves pitchers gave up fewer hits and runs than any other team and also led the league in complete games and shutouts.

The offensive power was still there, as evidenced on May 31 when Hank Aaron, Eddie Mathews, and Covington homered on three successive pitches in an 8–3 victory at Pittsburgh. Haney's offense was geared to such displays of power.

Milwaukee stole a league-low 26 bases and set a record by being caught stealing just eight times.

The Braves spent much of the first half in and out of first place, always struggling to keep command. It wasn't until July 30, when Spahn beat the Dodgers, 4–3, that Milwaukee finally moved into the penthouse for the remainder of the season.

It wouldn't have happened that soon if not for the arrival of Willey, who was recalled from Wichita in late May. He made his first start June 23 and shut out a strong San Francisco lineup, 7–0. It was one of a league-high four shutouts Willey threw en route to being named the league's Rookie of the Year by *The Sporting News*.

Jay, the bonus baby the club had been waiting for to mature since 1953, finally showed signs of developing in July. He won five games, two by shutout, to be selected the league's Player of the Month.

The turning point of the season came the first week of August when the Giants, who had moved to the West Coast with the Dodgers this year, came to County Stadium for a four-game series. They trailed the Braves by a single game, but only until Haney's club swept the series to open a five-game bulge. Burdette, who hit two home runs in a game in July, picked up one of the victories and went on to win six more times in the month. He was named Player of the Month to help the Braves put the rest of the league far back.

The pennant clinching came September 21, but all doubt about a return to the World Series was long gone by then.

One of the individual highlights of the season was Spahn reaching the 20-victory level for the ninth time, establishing a major league record for a left-hander.

Spahn led the league in wins (22), percentage, complete games, and innings and was second in strikeouts and fourth in ERA. Burdette, the best control pitcher in the league, finished second in percentage and innings and third in victories (20), ERA, and complete games.

There still was only one Cy Young Award being given for both leagues, and Spahn and Burdette fractured the National League returns, allowing the Yankees' Bob Turley to win by one vote over Spahn and two over Burdette.

Spahn also was a strong fifth in the National League MVP voting, won by the Cubs' Ernie Banks. Aaron finished third after another typically excellent all-around season. He was third in total bases, runs, hits, and slugging percentage, fourth in batting average (.326), and fifth in doubles and home runs (30).

The team hit 32 fewer home runs than in 1957. Mathews tied for third in the league (31), but his average and RBI total declined for the third consecutive season.

Covington was the player most likely to hit one over the fence—when he could play. He averaged a home run every 12.2 at bats.

Don McMahon, in only his second year in the majors, was picked for the All-Star Game. He was quickly being recognized as one of the best relievers in the game.

	G	AB	R	H	2B	3B	HR	RBI	SB	AVG
Hank Aaron (OF)	153	601	109	196	34	4	30	95	4	.326
Joe Adcock	105	320	40	88	15	1	19	54	0	.275
Bill Bruton (OF)	100	325	47	91	11	3	3	28	4	.280
Wes Covington (OF)	90	294	43	97	12	1	24	74	0	.330
Del Crandall (C)	131	427	50	116	23	1	18	63	4	.272
John DeMerit	3	3	1	2	0	0	0	0	0	.667
Eddie Haas	9	14	2	5	0	0	0	1	0	.357
Harry Hanebrink	63	133	14	25	3	0	4	10	0	.188
Bob Hazle	20	56	6	10	0	0	0	5	0	.179
Joe Koppe	16	9	3	4	0	0	0	0	0	.444
Johnny Logan (SS)	145	530	54	120	20	0	11	53	1	.226
Felix Mantilla	85	226	37	50	5	1	7	19	2	.221
Eddie Mathews (3B)	149	546	97	137	18	1	31	77	5	.251
Andy Pafko	95	164	17	39	7	1	3	23	0	.238
Del Rice	43	121	10	27	7	0	1	8	0	.223
Mel Roach	44	136	14	42	7	0	3	10	0	.309
Bob Roselli	1	1	0	0	0	0	0	0	0	.000
Carl Sawatski	10	10	1	1	0	0	0	1	0	.100
Red Schoendienst (2B)	106	427	47	112	23	1	1	24	3	.262
Hawk Taylor	4	8	1	1	1	0	0	0	0	.125
Frank Torre (1B)	138	372	41	115	22	5	6	55	2	.309
Casey Wise	31	71	8	14	1	0	0	0	1	.197
	154	5,225	675	1,388	221	21	167	641	26	.266*

	W	L	G	GS	CG	IP	H	BB	SO	ERA
Bob Buhl	5	2	11	10	3	73	74	30	27	3.45
Lou Burdette	20	10	40	36	19	275⅓	279	50	113	2.91
Gene Conley	0	6	26	7	0	72	89	17	53	4.88
Joey Jay	7	5	18	12	6	96⅔	60	43	74	2.14
Ernie Johnson	3	1	15	0	0	23⅓	35	10	13	8.10
Dick Littlefield	0	1	4	0	0	6⅓	7	1	7	4.26
Don McMahon	7	2	38	0	0	58⅔	50	29	37	3.68
Juan Pizarro	6	4	16	10	7	96⅔	75	47	84	2.70
Humberto Robinson	2	4	19	0	0	41⅓	30	13	26	3.02
Bob Rush	10	6	28	20	5	147½	142	31	84	3.42
Warren Spahn	22*	11	38	36	23*	290*	257	76	150	3.07
Bob Trowbridge	1	3	27	4	0	55	53	26	31	3.93
Carlton Willey	9	7	23	19	9	140	110	53	74	2.70
	92*	62		154	72*	1,376	1,261	426	773	3.21*

Shutouts—Willey (4*), Burdette (3), Jay (3), Rush (2), Spahn (2), Pizarro
Saves—McMahon (8), Conley (2), Buhl, Johnson, Littlefield, Pizarro, Robinson, Spahn, Trowbridge

1959

Record: 86–70
Finish: Second
Games Behind: 2
Manager: Fred Haney

The 1959 season was one of the most bitterly disappointing in franchise history. Much was expected of Fred Haney's two-time defending National League champions, and rightfully so. The team had three superstars—Hank Aaron, Warren Spahn, and Eddie Mathews—bound for the Hall of Fame, and a supporting cast of talented veteran players, many of whom were stars in their own right.

The Braves were again favored to win the pennant, but somehow, they didn't.

In spite of leading the league in home runs, complete games, shutouts, and fewest home runs allowed . . . in spite of Spahn and Burdette tying for the league lead in victories (21) and dominating most pitching departments . . . and in spite of Mathews and Aaron finishing first (46) and third (39) in home runs and dominating most offensive categories, the best Milwaukee could do was finish the regular season 18 games over .500—and in a dead heat with the Dodgers.

The tie came after a torrid pennant race in which the Dodgers and Braves, as well as the Giants, entered the final day

of the season with a chance to win the title. San Francisco needed to sweep a doubleheader from the Cardinals while the Braves and Dodgers were losing to create a three-way tie. However, the Giants lost two, and both Milwaukee and Los Angeles won, necessitating a best-of-three playoff for a trip to the World Series.

The first game was played in Milwaukee, and Haney had to start Carlton Willey, since Spahn and Burdette were in need of rest. The Dodgers got a run in the first, but the Braves rallied for two in the second, causing Los Angeles manager Walter Alston to lift starter Danny McDevitt for Larry Sherry. The Dodgers tied the game in the third, and John Roseboro hit a solo homer in the sixth to give Los Angeles a 3–2 edge. That's the way it stayed, with Sherry working 7⅔ shutout innings of relief for the victory.

The scene shifted to the Los Angeles Coliseum for the second game, which featured a pitching matchup suited for such an occasion. This time, the Braves matched Burdette against Don Drysdale, a 17-game winner and the league leader in strikeouts.

The Braves jumped on Drysdale for two in the first on a walk to Mathews and doubles by Aaron and Frank Torre. Los Angeles scored one in the first, but Milwaukee made it 3–1 in the second on singles by Logan and Burdette and a throwing error by Duke Snider.

Charlie Neal hit a solo homer for the Dodgers in the fourth, and Mathews matched it in the fifth, making the score 4–2.

In the bottom of the seventh, Dodgers left fielder Norm Larker barreled into Johnny Logan in an attempt to break up a double play. Though the Braves got the double play, they lost Logan, who had to be carried off on a stretcher. He was replaced by Felix Mantilla, who shifted from second base, a move that proved to be fateful.

Milwaukee got another run in the eighth to give Burdette a 5–2 advantage entering the ninth. Since the Dodgers hadn't gotten a runner past first since Neal's homer in the fourth, a third game seemed inevitable.

However, the Dodgers rallied for three in the ninth against Burdette, McMahon, Spahn, and Joey Jay to tie the score. And only a sensational catch by Aaron, who crashed into the fence in the right-field corner to corral the final out, enabled the Braves to send the game into extra innings.

The game was 5–5 in the bottom of the 12th with two outs when further disaster struck. Bob Rush walked Gil Hodges, and Joe Pignatano singled, Hodges stopping at second. Carl Furillo then hit a high bouncer up the middle that Mantilla, now at shortstop, gloved and threw off balance to first. The throw was wide, sailing past Torre and enabling Hodges to score the pennant-winning run.

The Dodgers advanced to the World Series, and the Braves returned home. It would be a long time before they'd get that close to a pennant again.

Five days after the playoff loss, Haney resigned. In three and two-thirds seasons as Braves manager, he won two pennants and a World Series and lost one pennant on the last day of the season and yet another in a playoff. He never managed again.

The 1959 season had been filled with so much promise that its wrenching finish was difficult to accept. Nothing seemed capable of keeping this team from a third straight Series berth. It was that talented. Plus, anytime a club is held without a single base runner for 12 innings and still wins, it figures that fate is on its side.

That's what happened on May 26 at County Stadium when Pittsburgh left-hander Harvey Haddix put on the most remarkable display of pitching in history. Working against one of the more potent lineups ever assembled in the National League, Haddix retired the first 36 Braves he faced, pitching 12 perfect innings and using but 104 pitches. He was the first National League pitcher since 1880 to work nine perfect innings. No one had ever done it for 12.

However, the Pirates couldn't score against Burdette either. The crafty right-hander gave up 12 hits but refused to yield. In the bottom of the 13th, a throwing error by Pittsburgh third baseman Don Hoak, a sacrifice bunt by Mathews, and an intentional walk to Aaron set up a bizarre conclusion to Haddix's masterpiece.

Joe Adcock hit a pitch from Haddix over the right-center fence, ending the game. The final score is listed as 1–0 because Aaron failed to circle the bases, leaving the field and causing Adcock to pass him.

Surely a team this lucky and this talented couldn't help but win the pennant.

The Braves started well and had a 4½-game lead on May 19. However, that was the biggest lead they had all season. For much of the year, they were treading water at best and occasionally bobbing below the surface. In July and August, they spent considerable time in third place behind the Dodgers and Giants.

It wasn't until after Labor Day that the Braves finally seemed to figure out that they'd better kick it in gear or be left behind in October. They won 13 of 16 to reclaim first place with a week to go, only to duel the Dodgers to a standoff.

The "dynasty" died quickly, but there still was much about the season to admire.

The power of Mathews and Aaron was so devastating it must have been scary for even the most courageous pitchers. And Spahn and Burdette were so consistently excellent it was a surprise when either lost.

Mathews, who had been on a moderate but noticeable three-year slide, bounced back with one of the finest seasons of his career. Besides hitting a career-high .306 and leading the majors in home runs (46), he finished in the top five in nearly every major offensive category. He was second to Aaron in total bases, and the awesome twosome combined for 752 total bases. Mathews was runner-up to Ernie Banks for MVP, and Aaron placed third.

Aaron won his second, and last, batting championship (.355) and led the league in hits and slugging, too. His career-high 223 hits were 18 more than anyone else in baseball.

Spahn's 21 victories gave him 267 for his career. At age 38, he led the league in wins for the third straight year and the sixth overall. He also led in complete games and innings, tied for the lead in shutouts, and was fourth in ERA.

Bob Buhl nearly rivaled Spahn and Burdette for pitching excellence, equaling their shutout production with four and finishing third in the league in ERA. And Don McMahon led the league in saves (15).

Yet somehow, the Braves played to just a .551 percentage, including the two playoff losses, which was their worst record since the move to Milwaukee. Admittedly, Red Schoendienst missed virtually the entire season with tuberculosis, and the pitching staff could have used Gene Conley, who was traded to Philadelphia. But this was a team that should have won more than 86 games—especially when 87 would have been enough.

Eddie Mathews led the league in home runs with 46 in 1959.

	G	AB	R	H	2B	3B	HR	RBI	SB	AVG
Hank Aaron (OF)	154	629	116	223*	46	7	39	123	8	.355*
Joe Adcock (1B)	115	404	53	118	19	2	25	76	0	.292
Bobby Avila	51	172	29	41	3	2	3	19	3	.238
Ray Boone	13	15	3	3	0	0	1	2	0	.200
Bill Bruton (OF)	133	478	72	138	22	6	6	41	13	.289
Chuck Cottier	10	24	1	3	1	0	0	1	0	.125
Wes Covington (OF)	103	373	38	104	17	3	7	45	0	.279
Del Crandall (C)	150	518	65	133	19	2	21	72	5	.257
John DeMerit	11	5	4	1	0	0	0	0	0	.200
Johnny Logan (SS)	138	470	59	137	17	0	13	50	1	.291
Stan Lopata	25	48	2	5	0	0	0	4	0	.104
Felix Mantilla (2B)	103	251	26	54	5	0	3	19	6	.215
Eddie Mathews (3B)	148	594	118	182	16	8	46*	114	2	.306
Lee Maye	51	140	17	42	5	1	4	16	2	.300
Joe Morgan	13	23	2	5	1	0	0	1	0	.217
Johnny O'Brien	44	116	16	23	4	0	1	8	0	.198
Andy Pafko	71	142	17	31	8	2	1	15	0	.218
Jim Pisoni	9	24	4	4	1	0	0	0	0	.167
Del Rice	13	29	3	6	0	0	0	1	0	.207
Mel Roach	19	31	1	3	0	0	0	0	0	.097
Red Schoendienst	5	3	0	0	0	0	0	0	0	.000
Enos Slaughter	11	18	0	3	0	0	0	1	0	.167
Al Spangler	6	12	3	5	0	1	0	0	1	.417
Frank Torre	115	263	23	60	15	1	1	33	0	.228
Mickey Vernon	74	91	8	20	4	0	3	14	0	.220
Casey Wise	22	76	11	13	2	0	1	5	0	.171
	157	5,388*	724	1,426	216	36	177*	683	41	.265

	W	L	G	GS	CG	IP	H	BB	SO	ERA
Bob Buhl	15	9	31	25	12	198	181	74	105	2.86
Lou Burdette	21*	15	41	39*	20	289⅔	312*	38	105	4.07
Bob Giggie	1	0	13	0	0	20	24	10	15	4.05
Bob Hartman	0	0	3	0	0	1⅓	6	2	1	27.00
Joey Jay	6	11	34	19	4	136⅓	130	64	88	4.09
Don McMahon	5	3	60	0	0	80⅔	81	37	55	2.57
Juan Pizarro	6	2	29	14	6	133⅓	117	70	126	3.77
Bob Rush	5	6	31	9	1	101⅓	102	23	64	2.40
Warren Spahn	21*	15	40	36	21*	292*	282	70	143	2.96
Bob Trowbridge	1	0	16	0	0	30⅓	45	10	22	5.93
Carlton Willey	5	9	26	15	5	117	126	31	51	4.15
	86	70		157	69*	1,400⅓	1,406	429	775	3.51

Shutouts—Buhl (4*), Burdette (4*), Spahn (4*), Pizarro (2), Willey (2), Jay, Rush
Saves—McMahon (15*), Burdette, Giggie, Trowbridge

1960

Record: 88–66
Finish: Second
Games Behind: 7
Manager: Charlie Dressen

In 1959, 88 wins would have won the pennant, but in 1960, 88 wins didn't even allow the Braves to make a serious run at National League champion Pittsburgh.

In spite of more extraordinary performances by the big four—Warren Spahn, Hank Aaron, Eddie Mathews, and Lou Burdette—Milwaukee finished an uninspired second under new manager Charlie Dressen.

The Braves plucked Dressen from the Dodgers coaching staff to replace Fred Haney. Dressen was confident he could win with this team of aging but talented superstars, but he found it was a tougher assignment than he anticipated.

There really were no significant changes in the team from the year before. Red Schoendienst returned from his bout with tuberculosis and opened the season at second base, but at age 37, he was not nearly the player who led the Braves to the 1957 pennant.

Still basically a power team, the Braves led the National League in home runs for the second straight year and finished just 10 behind the Pirates in runs scored.

But though Spahn, Burdette, and Bob Buhl had excellent seasons, the rest of the pitching staff was in shambles. Carlton Willey, Joey Jay, and Juan Pizarro continued to be inconsistent as starters. Even ace reliever Don McMahon was largely ineffective. The staff ERA (3.76) was fifth in the league, easily its lowest ranking since that last miserable year in Boston.

The Braves were playing only .500 ball entering June, and though they eventually climbed into first place briefly in late July, they never could sustain enough momentum to overcome that slow start. Pittsburgh reclaimed first place on July 25 and kept it for the rest of the year. The Braves fell as low as fourth place at one point.

Aaron, Mathews, Del Crandall, and Joe Adcock comprised half of the National League's starting lineup for the All-Star Game, but that dominance didn't translate into victories for the Braves.

Aaron and Mathews finished 1–2 in the league in RBIs and 2–3 in the home run race to Ernie Banks. Just 28 years old, Mathews became the second-youngest man in history to join the 300-home run club. Only Jimmie Foxx got there at an earlier age.

Billy Bruton had his finest season, leading the league in runs and triples, finishing fourth in hits and fifth in steals, and reaching double figures in home runs for the first time. Adcock had another excellent year at the plate and led the league's first basemen in defense. Crandall continued as the class of catchers and had perhaps his finest offensive season.

Wes Covington was hobbled with injuries much of the year, creating problems in left field, but it still was an awesome lineup—at least on paper.

Both Spahn and Burdette reached landmarks in their careers by pitching no-hitters.

Spahn led the league in victories (21) for the seventh time and had his 11th 20-win season and fifth in a row. On September 16, the 39-year-old marvel pitched the first no-hitter of his career, beating the Phillies, 4–0. In the process, he also set a franchise record for strikeouts in a nine-inning game

Billy Bruton led the league in runs and triples in 1960 but was traded to Detroit after the season.

with 15. The only two base runners came via walks in the fourth and fifth innings, and neither got past first.

Less than a month earlier, the 33-year-old Burdette no-hit the Phillies, 1–0. Burdette faced the minimum of 27 batters. The only Philadelphia base runner came in the fifth when Burdette hit Tony Gonzalez with a pitch, then erased him with a double play.

It was an eventful season, to say the least, but so much more was expected. Proof came in the turnstile count, which dropped to just under 1.5 million, a Milwaukee low for the second straight year.

	G	AB	R	H	2B	3B	HR	RBI	SB	AVG
Hank Aaron (OF)	153	590	102	172	20	11	40	126*	16	.292
Joe Adcock (1B)	138	514	55	153	21	4	25	91	2	.298
Ray Boone	7	12	3	3	1	0	0	4	0	.250
Bill Bruton (OF)	151	629	112*	180	27	13*	12	54	22	.286
Chuck Cottier (2B)	95	229	29	52	8	0	3	19	1	.227
Wes Covington (OF)	95	281	25	70	16	1	10	35	1	.249
Del Crandall (C)	142	537	81	158	14	1	19	77	4	.294
Alvin Dark	50	141	16	42	6	2	1	18	0	.298
Len Gabrielson	4	3	1	0	0	0	0	0	0	.000
Eddie Haas	32	32	4	7	2	0	1	5	0	.219
Mike Krsnich	4	9	0	3	1	0	0	2	0	.333
Charlie Lau	21	53	4	10	2	0	0	2	0	.189
Johnny Logan (SS)	136	482	52	118	14	4	7	42	1	.245
Stan Lopata	7	8	0	1	0	0	0	0	0	.125
Felix Mantilla	63	148	21	38	7	0	3	11	3	.257
Eddie Mathews (3B)	153	548	108	152	19	7	39	124	7	.277
Lee Maye	41	83	14	25	6	0	0	2	5	.301
Mel Roach	48	140	12	42	12	0	3	18	0	.300
Red Schoendienst	68	226	21	58	9	1	1	19	1	.257
Al Spangler	101	105	26	28	5	2	0	6	6	.267
Frank Torre	21	44	2	9	1	0	0	5	0	.205
Joe Torre	2	2	0	1	0	0	0	0	0	.500
	154	5,263	724	1,393	198	48	170*	681	69	.265

	W	L	G	GS	CG	IP	H	BB	SO	ERA
George Brunet	2	0	17	6	0	49⅔	53	22	39	5.07
Bob Buhl	16	9	36	33	11	238⅔	202	103*	121	3.09
Lou Burdette	19	13	45	32	18*	275⅔	277*	35	83	3.36
Terry Fox	0	0	5	0	0	8⅓	6	6	5	4.32
Bob Giggie	0	0	3	0	0	4⅓	5	4	5	4.15
Joey Jay	9	8	32	11	3	133⅓	128	59	90	3.24
Ken MacKenzie	0	1	9	0	0	8⅓	9	3	9	6.48
Don McMahon	3	6	48	0	0	63⅔	66	32	50	5.94
Don Nottebart	1	0	5	1	0	15⅓	14	15	8	4.11
Ron Piche	3	5	37	0	0	48	48	23	38	3.56
Juan Pizarro	6	7	21	17	3	114⅔	105	72	88	4.55
Bob Rush	2	0	10	0	0	15	24	5	8	4.20
Warren Spahn	21*	10	40	33	18*	267⅔	254	74	154	3.50
Carlton Willey	6	7	28	21	2	144⅔	136	65	109	4.35
	88	66		154	55*	1,387⅓	1,327	518	807	3.76

Shutouts—Burdette (4), Spahn (4), Buhl (2), Willey
Saves—McMahon (10), Piche (9), Burdette (4), Spahn (2), Jay, Nottebart, Rush

1961

Record: 83–71
Finish: Fourth
Games Behind: 10
Managers: Charlie Dressen, Birdie Tebbetts

If there was any doubt remaining about whether the star-studded Braves would ever return to their championship form of 1957–58, it was put to rest in 1961. The "dynasty" was in deep decline.

The team had its worst record since leaving Boston, and it eventually cost Charlie Dressen his job. Of utmost significance was the team's attendance, which barely exceeded 1.1 million, less than half the high-water mark of 1957.

It's not like the Braves were that bad. It's just that expectations in Milwaukee were raised so high, so soon that the natives had difficulty accepting anything short of a championship.

There certainly continued to be many reasons to go to County Stadium. There wasn't a lack of excitement, at least not for anyone who appreciated power hitting or the work of the consummate master craftsman, Warren Edward Spahn.

For the third consecutive year, the Braves led the National League in home runs. And at the age of 40, Spahn was as good as ever—perhaps even better.

On April 28 in Milwaukee, five days after his 40th birthday, Spahn became what was then the second-oldest man in history (next to Cy Young) to pitch a no-hitter. He humbled the potent San Francisco Giants, 1–0, allowing only a pair of walks that were erased by double plays. After going nearly 16 seasons without a no-hitter, Spahn had pitched two within a span of six starts. Additionally, it was the great left-hander's 290th career victory, setting up the countdown to the coveted 300 club.

Spahn's 300th came August 11 in Milwaukee when he beat the Cubs, 2–1, with a six-hitter. He was just the third left-hander to reach 300 victories and only the 13th pitcher overall.

Besides the aforementioned, all Spahn did in 1961 was lead the league in victories (21) for the eighth time with his 12th 20-win season and sixth in a row. He also led the league in ERA (3.02), complete games (21), and shutouts (4).

As for the team's propensity for hitting home runs, it often was a breathtaking sight to behold.

On June 8, Eddie Mathews and Hank Aaron knocked out Cincinnati's Jim Maloney with back-to-back home runs in the

seventh inning. Marshall Bridges replaced Maloney, and Joe Adcock and Frank Thomas greeted him with successive homers, giving the Braves a major-league-record four in a row. The only problem was, Milwaukee lost, 10–8, providing a perfect synopsis of the season.

That game started a three-game spree in which the Braves clubbed 14 homers to tie the National League record. The next day, they hit two more to tie the four-game record of 16. And a week after that, Aaron, Adcock, and Thomas hit three consecutive home runs against Los Angeles—and the Braves won this time, 10–2.

Perhaps to prove that this offense wasn't entirely one-dimensional, Aaron, Adcock, and Joe Torre teamed on one of the true oddities of the season in July when they pulled a triple steal against the Reds, Aaron stealing home. What made it so bizarre was that Adcock and Torre rank as two of the most classic station-to-station players in franchise history.

There were plenty of thrills, just not enough victories.

The club was retooled to some extent with a new double-play combination of weak-hitting shortstop Roy McMillan and second baseman Frank Bolling. The Braves gave up on Joey Jay and Juan Pizarro, both of whom prospered in new surroundings, Jay with the Reds and Pizarro with the White Sox. Thomas replaced Covington in left, and Torre broke in behind the plate with Del Crandall missing most of the season with a shoulder injury. Center fielder Billy Bruton and shortstop Johnny Logan, popular mainstays of the team, were traded.

The net effect was that the team was in first place only one day of the season—after Spahn's no-hitter April 28.

The Braves rallied in August, winning 20 of 29 to climb into third place, just 6½ games out with 27 to play. But it wasn't

On August 11, 1961, 40-year-old Warren Spahn beat the Cubs, 2-1, to become the 13th 300-game winner in history.

The acquisition of shortstop Roy McMillan in 1961 was supposed to help retool the Braves, but manager Charlie Dressen still lost his job.

enough to save Dressen. On September 2, he was dismissed and replaced by executive vice president Birdie Tebbetts.

	G	AB	R	H	2B	3B	HR	RBI	SB	AVG
Hank Aaron (OF)	155	603	115	197	39*	10	34	120	21	.327
Joe Adcock (1B)	152	562	77	160	20	0	35	108	2	.285
Frank Bolling (2B)	148	585	86	153	16	4	15	56	7	.262
Bob Boyd	36	41	3	10	0	0	0	3	0	.244
Neil Chrisley	10	9	1	2	0	0	0	0	0	.222
Gino Cimoli	37	117	12	23	5	0	3	4	1	.197
Wes Covington	9	21	3	4	1	0	0	0	0	.190
Del Crandall	15	30	3	6	3	0	0	1	0	.200
John DeMerit	32	74	5	12	3	0	2	5	0	.162
Mack Jones	28	104	13	24	3	2	0	12	4	.231
Charlie Lau	28	82	3	17	5	0	0	5	1	.207
Johnny Logan	18	19	0	2	1	0	0	1	0	.105
Felix Mantilla	45	93	13	20	3	0	1	5	1	.215
Billy Martin	6	6	1	0	0	0	0	0	0	.000
Eddie Mathews (3B)	152	572	103	175	23	6	32	91	12	.306
Lee Maye (OF)	110	373	68	101	11	5	14	41	10	.271
Roy McMillan (SS)	154	505	42	111	16	0	7	48	2	.220
Mel Roach	13	36	3	6	0	0	1	6	0	.167
Phil Roof	1	0	0	0	0	0	0	0	0	—
Al Spangler	68	97	23	26	2	0	0	6	4	.268
Hawk Taylor	20	26	1	5	0	0	1	1	0	.192
Frank Thomas (OF)	124	423	58	120	13	3	25	67	2	.284
Joe Torre (C)	113	406	40	113	21	4	10	42	3	.278
Sammy White	21	63	1	14	1	0	1	5	0	.222
	155	5,288	712	1,365	199	34	188*	662	70	.258

	W	L	G	GS	CG	IP	H	BB	SO	ERA
Johnny Antonelli	1	0	9	0	0	10⅔	16	3	8	7.59
George Brunet	0	0	5	0	0	5	7	2	0	5.40
Bob Buhl	9	10	32	28	9	188⅓	180	98	77	4.11
Lou Burdette	18	11	40	36	14	272½*	295	33	92	4.00
Tony Cloninger	7	2	19	10	3	84	84	33	51	5.25
Moe Drabowsky	0	2	16	0	0	25⅓	26	18	5	4.62
Bob Hendley	5	7	19	13	3	97	96	39	44	3.90
Ken MacKenzie	0	1	5	0	0	7	8	2	5	5.14
Don McMahon	6	4	53	0	0	92	84	51	55	2.84
Seth Morehead	1	0	12	0	0	15⅓	16	7	13	6.46
Don Nottebart	6	7	38	11	2	126⅓	117	48	66	4.06
ChiChi Olivo	0	0	3	0	0	2	3	5	1	18.00
Ron Piche	2	2	12	1	1	23⅓	20	16	16	3.47
Claude Raymond	1	0	13	0	0	20⅓	22	9	13	3.98
Warren Spahn	21*	13	38	34	21*	262⅔	236	64	115	3.02*
Carlton Willey	6	12	35	22	4	159⅔	147	65	91	3.83
	83	71		155	57*	1,391⅓*	1,357	493	652	3.89

Shutouts—Spahn (4*), Burdette (3), Buhl
Saves—McMahon (8), Nottebart (3), Drabowsky (2), Raymond (2), Piche

1962

Record: 86–76
Finish: Fifth
Games Behind: 15½
Manager: Birdie Tebbetts

It didn't take long to find out that neither Birdie Tebbetts nor several off-season personnel moves were the answer to the Braves' problems.

Starting slowly, which the Braves did by losing eight of their first 10, was one thing. But what Milwaukee did on May 12 was another matter completely and demonstrated that it was going to be a long season for the team and its fans.

The complete, bumbling ineptitude of the 1962 expansion New York Mets is well documented. Yet on May 12 at the Polo Grounds, with the Mets barely old enough to find the clubhouse, the once-proud Braves managed to lose a doubleheader to Casey Stengel's misfits.

Mets reliever Craig Anderson was credited with both victories—the last of his career. He lost his next 19 before retiring

in 1964. Both games were decided with ninth-inning home runs, Hobie Landrith's providing a 3–2 margin for the Mets in game one and Gil Hodges' deciding the second game, 9–8.

Tebbetts, by the way, sold ace reliever Don McMahon to Houston four days earlier because he felt the right-hander had lost his fastball. McMahon finished the year with a 1.69 ERA while the Braves' bullpen often was inadequate.

Eight days after the doubleheader loss to the Mets in New York, the Braves defied all odds by duplicating the feat at County Stadium. Milwaukee blew leads in both games, losing 7–6 and 9–6 to a team that lost a record 120 games that year.

Milwaukee recovered from that embarrassment to regain respectability but not enough to make a run at the pennant-winning Giants. The Braves finished with their lowest winning percentage (.531) since 1952 and were able to claim a first-division finish only because the two expansion clubs swelled the league to 10 teams.

The Braves made several ill-advised personnel changes besides the McMahon deal. They also traded left fielder Frank Thomas to the Mets, for whom he hit 34 homers and drove in 94 runs. There's no telling what he'd have done if he'd been surrounded by the sluggers the Braves possessed.

Tebbetts had a home-run-or-nothing offense. The team hit 181 home runs, second in the league, but ranked eighth in batting average (.252)—its worst since Boston and better than only the two expansion clubs. The team did lead the league in fielding average (.980), and the pitching staff ranked fourth in ERA (3.68). But the run production was simply too sporadic.

No one knew that fact better than Warren Spahn, who was denied 20 wins for the first time since 1955 in spite of leading the league in complete games (22) and posting a very creditable ERA (3.04).

While Spahn was still going strong at 42, Lou Burdette was fading at age 35 and became only a part-time starter. One acquisition that helped overcome Burdette's decline was Bob Shaw, who came from Kansas City to finish second in the league in ERA (2.80) to Sandy Koufax. Shaw's contributions were short-lived, though. The staff also missed Bob Buhl, who was traded to the Cubs April 30 and beat his old teammates four times during the season.

The difficulty the offense had in consistently producing runs had nothing to do with the typically splendid performance of Hank Aaron. Playing mainly in center for the second year in a row with Billy Bruton gone, he was second in the league in home runs (45) and slugging average (.618), third in total bases, fourth in RBIs (128) and runs, and fifth in batting average (.323).

Eddie Mathews, on the other hand, had his lowest batting average since 1958 and failed to hit at least 30 home runs for the first time since he was a rookie in 1952. And Joe Adcock slumped to his lowest average since 1951.

Del Crandall returned after missing nearly all of the previous season to lead the league's catchers in defense and hit for the best average of his career. However, his shoulder injury seemed to have sapped his power.

The fans, probably tipped off early by the humiliation at the hands of the Mets, stayed away from County Stadium in droves. The final count of 766,921 marked the first time the team had failed to attract at least 1.1 million in Milwaukee and signaled a need for some serious change.

Those adjustments started immediately and began at the

top. Five days after the final game, Tebbetts resigned to manage Cleveland. He soon was replaced by Bobby Bragan.

But the big move came November 16 when the Perini Corporation, which had held controlling interest in the team since 1944, sold it for $5.5 million to the LaSalle Corporation, a syndicate of Chicago businessmen headed by Bill Bartholomay.

	G	AB	R	H	2B	3B	HR	RBI	SB	AVG
Hank Aaron (OF)	156	592	127	191	28	6	45	128	15	.323
Tommie Aaron	141	334	54	77	20	2	8	38	6	.231
Joe Adcock (1B)	121	391	48	97	12	1	29	78	2	.248
Ken Aspromonte	34	79	11	23	2	0	0	7	0	.291
Howie Bedell	58	138	15	27	1	2	0	2	1	.196
Gus Bell	79	214	28	61	11	3	5	24	0	.285
Ethan Blackaby	6	13	0	2	1	0	0	0	0	.154
Frank Bolling (2B)	122	406	45	110	17	4	9	43	2	.271
Del Crandall (C)	107	350	35	104	12	3	8	45	3	.297
Lou Johnson	61	117	22	33	4	5	2	13	6	.282
Mack Jones	91	333	51	85	17	4	10	36	5	.255
Lou Klimchock	8	8	0	0	0	0	0	0	0	.000
Mike Krsnich	11	12	0	1	1	0	0	2	0	.083
Eddie Mathews (3B)	152	536	106	142	25	6	29	90	4	.265
Lee Maye (OF)	99	349	40	85	10	0	10	41	9	.244
Roy McMillan (SS)	137	468	66	115	13	0	12	41	2	.246
Denis Menke	50	146	12	28	3	1	2	16	0	.192
Amado Samuel	76	209	16	43	10	0	3	20	0	.206
Hawk Taylor	20	47	3	12	0	0	0	2	0	.255
Joe Torre	80	220	23	62	8	1	5	26	1	.282
Bob Uecker	33	64	5	16	2	0	1	8	0	.250
	162	5,458	730	1,376	204	38	181	685	57	.252

	W	L	G	GS	CG	IP	H	BB	SO	ERA
Bob Buhl	0	1	1	1	0	2	6	4	1	22.50
Lou Burdette	10	9	37	19	6	143⅔	172	23	59	4.89
Cecil Butler	2	0	9	2	1	31	26	9	22	2.61
Tony Cloninger	8	3	24	15	4	111	113	46	69	4.30
Jimmy Constable	1	1	3	2	1	18	14	4	12	2.00
Jack Curtis	4	4	30	5	0	75⅔	82	27	40	4.16
Hank Fischer	2	3	29	0	0	37⅓	43	20	29	5.30
Bob Hendley	11	13	35	29	7	200	188	59	112	3.60
Denny Lemaster	3	4	17	12	4	86⅔	75	32	69	3.01
Don McMahon	0	1	2	0	0	3	3	0	3	6.00
Don Nottebart	2	2	39	0	0	64	64	20	36	3.23
Ron Piche	3	2	14	8	2	52	54	29	28	4.85
Claude Raymond	5	5	26	0	0	42⅔	37	15	40	2.74
Bob Shaw	15	9	38	29	12	225	223	44	124	2.80
Warren Spahn	18	14	34	34	22*	269⅓	248	55	118	3.04
Carlton Willey	2	5	30	6	0	73⅓	95	20	40	5.40
	86	76		162	59	1,434⅔	1,443	407	802	3.68

Shutouts—Shaw (3), Hendley (2), Burdette, Cloninger, Constable, Lemaster
Saves—Raymond (10), Fischer (4), Burdette (2), Nottebart (2), Shaw (2), Constable, Curtis, Hendley, Willey

1963

Record: 84–78
Finish: Sixth
Games Behind: 15
Manager: Bobby Bragan

By 1963, only memories of championships remained with the Braves, and those were fading quickly. There were, however, two spectacular exceptions: Warren Spahn and Hank Aaron.

Bobby Bragan's first team finished with the worst winning percentage (.519) and lowest team batting average (.244) of the franchise's Milwaukee existence and slipped into the second division for the only time in what would be a 13-year tenure in Milwaukee.

Yet Spahn, at age 42, and Aaron, just 29, continued to perform at a level attained by very few men who've ever played

the game. While just about everything around them was crumbling, Spahn and Aaron just kept compiling their Hall of Fame credentials.

Spahn finished tied for third in wins (23), only two behind young bucks Sandy Koufax and Juan Marichal. He equaled his career high in victories, becoming the oldest 20-game winner in history, and reaching 20 for the 13th time.

Spahn led the league in complete games (22), and perhaps most incredible of all, pitched seven shutouts, second in the league to Koufax. His first victory of the year was the 328th of his career, making him the winningest left-hander of all time. He also passed Grover Cleveland Alexander's record for most National League starts in the modern era.

The most memorable game Spahn pitched during the season and one of the most spectacular of his career was actually a loss. It came July 2 at San Francisco; he and 25-year-old Marichal were locked in a scoreless duel in the bottom of the 16th when Willie Mays hit a one-out solo home run to beat Spahn, 1–0.

All Aaron did was make a serious bid at the Triple Crown. He tied Willie McCovey for the league lead in home runs (44), won the RBI title with ease (130), but finished tied for third in average (.319), only seven points behind Willie Davis.

Aaron also led the league in runs, total bases, and slugging percentage (.586) and had a career high in steals (31), too, finishing second only to Maury Wills.

The rest of the Braves, of course, paled in comparison to Spahn and Aaron. Even Mathews was in decline. The biggest reason he led in on-base percentage (.400) was a league-high 124 walks.

The face of the team continued to change drastically. Joe Adcock had been traded to Cleveland before the season, and Lou Burdette was shipped to St. Louis on June 15. Additionally, Del Crandall became a backup to Joe Torre, who was developing into an offensive force.

In games that Spahn didn't pitch, the Braves were 59–70 (.457). Predictably, attendance (773,018) again was poor, almost identical to the previous year's. And St. Louis sports writer Bob Broeg predicted that if the tide wasn't soon turned, the Braves would be off to Atlanta.

	G	AB	R	H	2B	3B	HR	RBI	SB	AVG
Hank Aaron (OF)	161	631	121*	201	29	4	44*	130*	31	.319
Tommie Aaron	72	135	6	27	6	1	1	15	0	.200
Gus Bell	3	3	0	1	0	0	0	0	0	.333
Frank Bolling (2B)	142	542	73	132	18	2	5	43	2	.244
Rico Carty	2	2	0	0	0	0	0	0	0	.000
Ty Cline	72	174	17	41	2	1	0	10	2	.236
Del Crandall	86	259	18	52	4	0	3	28	1	.201
Don Dillard	67	119	9	28	6	4	1	12	0	.235
Len Gabrielson	46	120	14	26	5	0	3	15	1	.217
Mack Jones (OF)	93	228	36	50	11	4	3	22	8	.219
Lou Klimchock	24	46	6	9	1	0	0	1	0	.196
Norm Larker	64	147	15	26	6	0	1	14	0	.177
Eddie Mathews (3B)	158	547	82	144	27	4	23	84	3	.263
Lee Maye (OF)	124	442	67	120	22	7	11	34	14	.271
Roy McMillan (SS)	100	320	35	80	10	1	4	29	1	.250
Denis Menke	146	518	58	121	16	4	11	50	6	.234
Bubba Morton	15	28	1	5	0	0	0	4	0	.179
Gene Oliver (1B)	95	296	34	74	12	2	11	47	4	.250
Amado Samuel	15	17	0	3	1	0	0	0	0	.176
Hawk Taylor	16	29	1	2	0	0	0	0	0	.069
Joe Torre (C)	142	501	57	147	19	4	14	71	1	.293
Bob Uecker	13	16	3	4	2	0	0	0	0	.250
Woody Woodward	10	2	1	0	0	0	0	0	0	.000
	163	5,518	677	1,345	204	39	139	624	75	.244

	W	L	G	GS	CG	IP	H	BB	SO	ERA
Wade Blasingame	0	0	2	0	0	3	7	2	6	12.00
Lou Burdette	6	5	15	13	4	84	71	24	28	3.64
Tony Cloninger	9	11	41	18	4	145⅓	131	63	100	3.78
Hank Fischer	4	3	31	6	1	74⅓	74	28	72	4.96
Frank Funk	3	3	25	0	0	43⅔	42	13	19	2.68
Bob Hendley	9	9	41	24	7	169½	153	64	105	3.93
Denny Lemaster	11	14	46	31	10	237	199	85	190	3.04
Ron Piche	1	1	37	1	0	53	53	25	40	3.40
Claude Raymond	4	6	45	0	0	53⅓	57	27	44	5.40
Bob Sadowski	5	7	19	18	5	116⅔	99	30	72	2.62
Dan Schneider	1	0	30	3	0	43⅔	36	20	19	3.09
Bob Shaw	7	11	48	16	3	159	144	55	105	2.66
Warren Spahn	23	7	33	33	22*	259⅔	241	49	102	2.60
Bobby Tiefenauer	1	1	12	0	0	29⅔	20	4	22	1.21
	84	78		163	56*	1,471⅔*	1,327	489	924	3.27

Shutouts—Spahn (7), Hendley (3), Shaw (3), Cloninger (2), Burdette, Lemaster, Sadowski
Saves—Shaw (13), Raymond (5), Hendley (3), Tiefenauer (2), Cloninger, Lemaster

Outfielder Lee Maye had his best year in 1964, leading the league in doubles with 44.

1964

Record: 88–74
Finish: Fifth
Games Behind: 5
Manager: Bobby Bragan

Even before the 1964 season began, an ominous chord was struck. On March 5, Atlanta mayor Ivan Allen, Jr., said an unnamed major league club had committed to move to the Georgia city in 1965 if a stadium was built. The following day, the city approved an $18 million stadium, and on April 15, work began on the facility.

The handwriting was on the wall, yet Braves officials continued to deny they had plans to move the club. In the meantime, the Braves embarked on their 12th season in Milwaukee.

And what a season it was. The team never made a serious run at the pennant despite finishing just five games back. But the 1964 Braves certainly were entertaining—especially for fans who were partial to offense.

The Braves featured one of the most potent attacks in franchise history—one so explosive that future Hall of Famer Eddie Mathews, one of the game's all-time great sluggers, frequently batted leadoff.

The team batting average of .272 tied for the league lead and was the best by the franchise since the 1948 pennant winners hit .275. No Braves team since has hit for higher average, though the 1983 club also batted .272.

The 1964 Braves also led the league in runs, doubles, on-base percentage, and slugging percentage. They finished just behind San Francisco in home runs (159) and boasted the unique distinction of having five players (Hank Aaron, Eddie Mathews, Rico Carty, Denis Menke, and Joe Torre) with 20 or more homers.

Unfortunately, the pitching was every bit as bad as the hitting was good. Only the pathetic Mets had a higher ERA than Milwaukee's 4.12.

A major reason for the dearth of pitching was the onset of the inevitable downfall of the peerless Warren Spahn. The great left-hander's ERA more than doubled from the previous year, and he eventually was dropped from the starting rotation. He failed to win more than he lost for the first time since 1952, and at age 43, the end finally was at hand. In November, he was sold to the Mets.

Several players of note established themselves during the '64 season, in which the roster was constantly shuffled.

Right-hander Tony Cloninger finally moved into the regular rotation and became the staff ace, and left-hander Denny Lemaster also blossomed, pitching a one-hit shutout against Cincinnati. Center fielder Lee Maye had a big year, leading the league in doubles. Torre finished fourth in the league in RBIs. But most notable was the work of 24-year-old rookie left fielder Rico Carty.

Carty came out of nowhere to finish second (.330) to Roberto Clemente in the batting race.

Aaron had another fine year, though his home run total (24) was his lowest since his rookie year of 1954, and he failed to drive in at least 100 runs for the first time in six years.

Carty (.330), Aaron (.328), and Torre (.321) finished 2–3–4 in the league in hitting.

The Braves won 14 of their last 17 games to pick up nine games on first place and make their final standing look respectable. However, they were never in the race, which St. Louis won when Philadelphia lost 10 straight down the stretch.

Attendance increased to 910,911, but everyone knew the Braves were headed to the South. On October 14, team officials finally admitted they had a lease offer from Atlanta. A week later, the club's board voted to ask the National League for permission to move to Atlanta, and Milwaukee County filed suit to block the move.

On November 7, the National League gave the Braves permission to move to Atlanta—but in 1966, not in 1965.

	G	AB	R	H	2B	3B	HR	RBI	SB	AVG
Hank Aaron (OF)	145	570	103	187	30	2	24	95	22	.328
Sandy Alomar	19	53	3	13	1	0	0	6	1	.245
Felipe Alou	121	415	60	105	26	3	9	51	5	.253
Ed Bailey	95	271	30	71	10	1	5	34	2	.262
Gus Bell	3	3	0	0	0	0	0	0	0	.000
Ethan Blackaby	9	12	0	1	0	0	0	1	0	.083
Frank Bolling (2B)	120	352	35	70	11	1	5	34	0	.199
Rico Carty (OF)	133	455	72	150	28	4	22	88	1	.330
Ty Cline	101	116	22	35	4	2	1	13	0	.302
Mike de la Hoz	78	189	25	55	7	1	4	12	1	.291
Len Gabrielson	24	38	0	7	2	0	0	1	1	.184
Lou Klimchock	10	21	3	7	2	0	0	2	0	.333
Gary Kolb	36	64	7	12	1	0	0	2	3	.188
Eddie Mathews (3B)	141	502	83	117	19	1	23	74	2	.233
Lee Maye (OF)	153	588	96	179	44*	5	10	74	5	.304
Roy McMillan	8	13	1	4	0	0	0	2	1	.308
Denis Menke (SS)	151	505	79	143	29	5	20	65	4	.283
Gene Oliver (1B)	93	279	45	77	15	1	13	49	3	.276
Merritt Ranew	9	17	1	2	0	0	0	0	0	.118
Phil Roof	1	2	0	0	0	0	0	0	0	.000
Bill Southworth	3	7	2	2	0	0	1	2	0	.286
Joe Torre (C)	154	601	87	193	36	5	20	109	2	.321
Woody Woodward	77	115	18	24	2	1	0	11	0	.209
	162	5,591	803*	1,522	274*	32	159	755*	53	.272*

	W	L	G	GS	CG	IP	H	BB	SO	ERA
Wade Blasingame	9	5	28	13	3	116⅔	113	51	70	4.24
John Braun	0	0	1	0	0	2	2	1	1	0.00
Cecil Butler	0	0	2	0	0	4⅓	7	0	2	8.31
Clay Carroll	2	0	11	1	0	20⅓	15	3	17	1.77
Tony Cloninger	19	14	38	34	15	242⅔	206	82	163	3.56
Dave Eilers	0	0	6	0	0	7⅔	11	1	1	4.70
Hank Fischer	11	10	37	28	9	168⅓	177	39	99	4.01
Billy Hoeft	4	0	42	0	0	73⅓	76	18	47	3.80
Dick Kelley	0	0	2	0	0	2	2	3	2	18.00
Frank Lary	1	0	5	2	0	12⅓	15	0	4	4.38
Denny Lemaster	17	11	39	35	9	221	216	75	185	4.15
Phil Niekro	0	0	10	0	0	15	15	7	8	4.80
ChiChi Olivo	2	1	38	0	0	60	55	21	45	3.75
Bob Sadowski	9	10	51	18	5	166⅔	159	56	96	4.10
Dan Schneider	1	2	13	5	0	36⅓	38	13	14	5.45
Jack Smith	2	2	22	0	0	31	28	11	19	3.77
Warren Spahn	6	13	38	25	4	173⅔	204	52	78	5.29
Bobby Tiefenauer	4	6	46	0	0	73	61	15	48	3.21
Arnie Umbach	1	0	1	1	0	8⅓	11	4	7	3.24
	88	74		162	45	1,434⅔	1,411	452	906	4.12

Shutouts—Fischer (5), Cloninger (3), Lemaster (3), Blasingame, Spahn
Saves—Tiefenauer (13), Olivo (5), Sadowski (5), Hoeft (4), Spahn (4), Blasingame (2), Cloninger (2), Fischer (2), Carroll, Lemaster

1965

Record: 86–76
Finish: Fifth
Games Behind: 11
Manager: Bobby Bragan

A new ballpark awaited the Braves in Atlanta in 1965, and the LaSalle Corporation desperately wanted to move there. The franchise owners even offered Milwaukee County $500,000 to let them out of their lease a year early. However, officials turned down the Braves' request by unanimous vote, meaning the team was stuck with playing a lame-duck season in Milwaukee.

No one told the Braves' hitters they were lame ducks, though. It was another banner season for the Milwaukee sluggers, who led the league in home runs (196). A National League record six Braves (Hank Aaron, Eddie Mathews, Mack Jones, Joe Torre, Felipe Alou, and Gene Oliver) hit 20 or more homers.

It wasn't a consistent offense, but when it exploded, it was quite a sight to behold. For example, on June 8 at Chicago, the Braves and Cubs were locked in a 2–2 duel in the 10th inning when Torre, Alou, Aaron, and Oliver erupted with a quartet of home runs for an 8–2 victory.

On August 20, Mathews hit his 28th home run of the year, enabling him and Aaron to pass Babe Ruth and Lou Gehrig as the top home-run-hitting teammates of all time with a total of 794.

The team's pitching was considerably improved. In fact, the Braves were fourth in the league in ERA (3.52) after being ninth the year before. Key additions were reliever Billy O'Dell and starter Ken Johnson. Right-hander Tony Cloninger won a Milwaukee-record 24 games, second in the league, and 21-year-old left-hander Wade Blasingame won 16.

The combination of the volatile offense and adequate pitching nearly made the Braves serious contenders even though no one was coming to County Stadium to see them. At the All-Star break, Milwaukee was in fifth place, just two games over .500. But when the schedule resumed, the Braves quickly embarked on a 10-game winning streak, mainly on the strength of their bats, to quickly reach third place. They

stayed hot, and on August 18 they moved into first place with a 5–3 victory over St. Louis.

However, the Braves lost nine of their next 11 games and fell to fourth place. A brief flurry in September enabled Bragan's club to get within 2½ games of first before the wheels finally came off. The Braves proceeded to lose 14 of their last 21 games, not a particularly memorable way to leave Milwaukee.

The team's last game at County Stadium was played September 22 against the Dodgers. Only 12,577 witnessed it. The Braves built a 6–1 lead behind a Frank Bolling grand slam off Sandy Koufax, only to lose, 7–6, to the eventual National League champions.

Baseball was just a sidelight to the season, though. In August, both Milwaukee County and the state of Wisconsin filed antitrust suits against the Braves and the National League. The issue wasn't resolved until the following year when the team already was playing in Atlanta.

	G	AB	R	H	2B	3B	HR	RBI	SB	AVG
Hank Aaron (OF)	150	570	109	181	40*	1	32	89	24	.318
Tommie Aaron	8	16	1	3	0	0	0	1	0	.188
Sandy Alomar	67	108	16	26	1	1	0	8	12	.241
Felipe Alou (OF)	143	555	80	165	29	2	23	78	8	.297
Jim Beauchamp	4	3	0	0	0	0	0	0	0	.000
John Blanchard	10	10	1	1	0	0	1	2	0	.100
Frank Bolling (2B)	148	535	55	141	26	3	7	50	0	.264
Rico Carty	83	271	37	84	18	1	10	35	1	.310
Ty Cline	123	220	27	42	5	3	0	10	2	.191
Billy Cowan	19	27	4	5	1	0	0	0	0	.185
Mike de la Hoz	81	176	15	45	3	2	2	11	0	.256
Don Dillard	20	19	1	3	0	0	1	3	0	.158
Jesse Gonder	31	53	2	8	2	0	1	5	0	.151
Mack Jones (OF)	143	504	78	132	18	7	31	75	8	.262
Lou Klimchock	34	39	3	3	0	0	0	3	0	.077
Gary Kolb	24	27	3	7	0	0	0	1	0	.259
Eddie Mathews (3B)	156	546	77	137	23	0	32	95	1	.251
Lee Maye	15	53	8	16	2	0	2	7	0	.302
Denis Menke	71	181	16	44	13	1	4	18	1	.243
Gene Oliver (1B)	122	392	56	106	20	0	21	58	5	.270
Frank Thomas	15	33	3	7	3	0	0	1	0	.212
Joe Torre (C)	148	523	68	152	21	1	27	80	0	.291
Woody Woodward (SS)	112	265	17	55	7	4	0	11	2	.208
	162	5,542	708	1,419	243	28	196*	664	64	.256

Eddie Mathews and Hank Aaron walk up the County Stadium tunnel to the clubhouse following the Braves' last game in Milwaukee.

	W	L	G	GS	CG	IP	H	BB	SO	ERA
Wade Blasingame	16	10	38	36	10	224⅔	200	116	117	3.77
Clay Carroll	0	1	19	1	0	34⅔	35	13	16	4.41
Tony Cloninger	24	11	40	38	16	279	247	119*	211	3.29
Dave Eilers	0	0	6	0	0	3⅔	8	0	1	12.27
Hank Fischer	8	9	31	19	2	122⅔	126	39	79	3.89
Ken Johnson	13	8	29	26	8	179⅔	165	37	123	3.21
Dick Kelley	1	1	21	4	0	45	37	20	31	3.00
Denny Lemaster	7	13	32	23	4	146⅓	140	58	111	4.43
Phil Niekro	2	3	41	1	0	74⅔	73	26	49	2.89
Billy O'Dell	10	6	62	1	0	111⅓	87	30	78	2.18
ChiChi Olivo	0	1	8	0	0	13	12	5	11	1.38
Dan Osinski	0	3	61	0	0	83	81	40	54	2.82
Bob Sadowski	5	9	34	13	3	123	117	35	78	4.32
Bobby Tiefenauer	0	1	6	0	0	7	8	3	7	7.71
	86	76		162	43	1,447⅔	1,336	541	966	3.52

Shutouts—Blasingame, Cloninger, Johnson, Lemaster
Saves—O'Dell (18), Niekro (6), Osinski (6), Sadowski (3), Johnson (2), Blasingame, Carroll, Cloninger

1966

Record: 85–77
Finish: Fifth
Games Behind: 10
Managers: Bobby Bragan, Billy Hitchcock

Even as the Braves broke spring camp in 1966 and headed to Atlanta for a welcoming parade similar to the one they'd received 13 years earlier in Milwaukee, the battle to keep them in Wisconsin was being waged in courtrooms. In fact, Milwaukee even prepared County Stadium for the season—just in case.

The Braves, of course, never went back to Milwaukee, but their fate hung in the balance throughout the season and into the winter. After a series of injunctions, rulings, reversals, and appeals, the United States Supreme Court, on December 12, refused to hear the final appeal by the state of Wisconsin, upholding baseball's exemption from antitrust laws and ending the legal brawl it took to move the Braves to Atlanta.

The Braves retained their personality in the move to the South. Their home run bats weren't affected in the least by the change of scenery. In fact, they hit a franchise-record 207 home runs to lead the league and they also led in runs scored. Atlanta Stadium, it seemed, was very much to their liking.

Unfortunately, opposing hitters quickly grew comfortable in the new park, too. Whether it was the atmosphere in Atlanta, the cozy makeup of the park, or simply Braves pitching, Atlanta Stadium quickly gained a reputation around the league as the "Launching Pad" for the seeming ease with which balls were put into orbit.

The Atlanta Braves played their first regular-season game April 12 at Atlanta Stadium. The opponents for the first major league game played in the South were the Pittsburgh Pirates. The first lineup the team presented to its Atlanta fans was Felipe Alou, CF; Eddie Mathews, 3B; Hank Aaron, RF; Rico Carty, LF; Joe Torre, C; Denis Menke, SS; Lee Thomas, 1B; Frank Bolling, 2B; and Tony Cloninger, P.

A near-capacity crowd of 50,671 saw the Pirates beat the Braves, 3–2, in 13 innings in spite of a great pitching performance by Cloninger, who went the distance, striking out 12, walking three, and giving up 10 hits.

All five runs in the game were the result of home runs. Torre hit a solo homer in the fifth off Pirates left-hander Bob Veale, then Pittsburgh's Jim Pagliaroni matched it in the

President John McHale and chairman Bill Bartholomay wave to Little Leaguers during the parade which preceded the Braves' first game in Atlanta.

eighth. The score remained 1–1 until the top of the 13th when future Hall of Famer Willie Stargell hit a two-run home run. Torre hit his second homer of the evening in the bottom of the inning to account for the final 3–2 score.

Manager Bobby Bragan, who would not survive the season, was criticized for allowing Cloninger to work 13 innings so early in the year. And statistics show that the big right-hander, who won a Milwaukee-record 24 games the previous season, was never quite the same pitcher after his Atlanta debut.

However, Cloninger did tie for the team lead in victories (14) and left an even bigger impression with his bat. On July 3 at Candlestick Park in San Francisco, he became the first and only man in National League history to hit two grand slams in the same game, a 17–3 rout of the Giants. Cloninger also drove in a ninth run with a double, allowing him to tie the one-game RBI record for a pitcher. One of his Braves ancestors, Harry Staley, is the only other National League pitcher with nine RBIs in a game, and he did it for Boston way back in 1893.

Inconsistent pitching haunted the Braves, who were 13½ games out of first at the All-Star break. Shortly thereafter, Bragan was fired and replaced on August 9 by popular first base coach Billy Hitchcock. That night, the Braves were hosting the Dodgers and Sandy Koufax, who was scheduled to pitch against Atlanta left-hander Denny Lemaster. An overflow crowd of more than 52,000, some standing behind the outfield fence, turned out for what proved to be a classic pitching duel.

Alou homered in the first to give the Braves a 1–0 lead. It stayed that way through a two-hour rain delay and into the eighth, with Lemaster retiring 19 straight Dodgers at one point. However, Jim Lefebvre homered in the eighth to tie the game. In the bottom of the ninth, a struggling Mathews, who had been benched by Bragan but reinstated by Hitch-cock, hit an 0–2 pitch from Koufax over the right-field fence to end the game. A wild celebration followed, but it was one of the few the team and its fans had that season.

The Braves rallied under Hitchcock, winning 19 of 21 at one point, but it was only enough to get them out of the second division.

Braves were prominent in the league's final offensive statistics, but noticeably absent in the pitching stats. Aaron won two-thirds of the Triple Crown—home runs (44) and RBIs (127)—and Alou would have won the other third if not for his brother, Matty, who won the batting title by 15 points over runner-up Felipe (.327), who still led in hits (218), runs, and total bases.

Carty was third in the batting race (.326), and Torre was fourth in home runs (36).

It was quite an offensive powerhouse, but the other components of a winning team were missing. Still, attendance was 1,539,801, not as good as the first year in Milwaukee but still the best draw by the club since 1959.

	G	AB	R	H	2B	3B	HR	RBI	SB	AVG
Hank Aaron (OF)	158	603	117	168	23	1	44*	127*	21	.279
Sandy Alomar	31	44	4	4	1	0	0	2	0	.091
Felipe Alou (1B)	154	666*	122*	218*	32	6	31	74	5	.327
Lee Bales	12	16	4	1	0	0	0	0	0	.063
Frank Bolling	75	227	16	48	7	0	1	18	1	.211
Rico Carty (OF)	151	521	73	170	25	2	15	76	4	.326
Ty Cline	42	71	12	18	0	0	0	6	2	.254
Mike de la Hoz	71	110	11	24	3	0	2	7	0	.218
Adrian Garrett	4	3	0	0	0	0	0	0	0	.000
Gary Geiger	78	126	23	33	5	3	4	10	0	.262
John Herrnstein	17	18	2	4	0	0	0	1	0	.222
Mack Jones (OF)	118	417	60	110	14	1	23	66	16	.264
Marty Keough	17	17	1	1	0	0	0	1	0	.059
George Kopacz	6	9	1	0	0	0	0	0	0	.000
Eddie Mathews (3B)	134	452	72	113	21	4	16	53	1	.250
Denis Menke (SS)	138	454	55	114	20	4	15	60	0	.251
Felix Millan	37	91	20	25	6	0	0	5	3	.275
Gene Oliver	76	191	19	37	9	1	8	24	2	.194
Bill Robinson	6	11	1	3	0	1	0	3	0	.273
Eddie Sadowski	3	9	1	1	0	0	0	1	0	.111
Lee Thomas	39	126	11	25	1	1	6	15	1	.198
Joe Torre (C)	148	546	83	172	20	3	36	101	0	.315
Woody Woodward (2B)	144	455	46	120	23	3	0	43	2	.264
	163	5,617	782*	1,476	220	32	207*	734*	59	.263

	W	L	G	GS	CG	IP	H	BB	SO	ERA
Ted Abernathy	4	4	38	0	0	65⅓	58	36	42	3.86
Wade Blasingame	3	7	16	12	0	67⅔	71	25	34	5.32
Clay Carroll	8	7	73*	3	0	144⅓	127	29	67	2.37
Tony Cloninger	14	11	39	38	11	257⅔	253	116*	178	4.12
Hank Fischer	2	3	14	8	0	48⅓	55	14	22	3.91
Herb Hippauf	0	1	3	0	0	2⅔	6	1	1	13.50
Pat Jarvis	6	2	10	9	3	62⅓	46	12	41	2.31
Joey Jay	0	4	9	8	0	29⅔	39	20	19	7.89
Ken Johnson	14	8	32	31	11	215⅔	213	46	105	3.30
Dick Kelley	7	5	20	13	2	81	75	21	50	3.22
Denny Lemaster	11	8	27	27	10	171	170	41	139	3.74
Phil Niekro	4	3	28	0	0	50⅓	48	23	17	4.11
Billy O'Dell	2	3	24	0	0	41⅓	44	18	20	2.40
ChiChi Olivo	5	4	47	0	0	66	59	19	41	4.23
Ron Reed	1	1	2	2	0	8⅓	7	4	6	2.16
Jay Ritchie	0	1	22	0	0	35⅓	32	12	33	4.08
Dan Schneider	0	0	14	0	0	26⅓	35	5	11	3.42
Don Schwall	3	3	11	8	0	45⅓	44	19	27	4.37
Arnie Umbach	0	2	22	3	0	40⅔	40	18	23	3.10
Cecil Upshaw	0	0	1	0	0	3	0	3	2	0.00
Charley Vaughan	1	0	1	1	0	7	8	3	6	2.57
	85	77	163	37	1,469⅓	1,430	485	884	3.68	

Shutouts—Lemaster (3), Johnson (2), Kelley (2), Cloninger, Jarvis
Saves—Carroll (11), Olivo (7), O'Dell (6), Abernathy (4), Ritchie (4), Niekro (2), Cloninger, Jay

1967

Record: 77–85
Finish: Seventh
Games Behind: 24½
Managers: Billy Hitchcock, Ken Silvestri

The 1967 season began without Eddie Mathews in a Braves uniform for the first time since 1952. The only Brave to play in all three cities the franchise has called home, Mathews was traded to Houston. He hit 493 home runs as a Brave and departed tied with Lou Gehrig for seventh place on the all-time list.

Billy Hitchcock returned as manager even though he was only intended as an "interim" replacement when Bobby Bragan was fired in 1966. However, the team played so well under him that he was given a contract for 1967. Like all managers, though, Hitchcock was indeed "interim" and was replaced for the final three games of the season by coach Ken Silvestri.

The Braves had their worst year since the Boston exit in 1952, finishing with their first losing record in 15 seasons. They managed to outplay only the expansion teams, New York and Houston, as well as the Dodgers.

The team's performance was severely hindered by injuries to three key players, Felipe Alou, Joe Torre, and Tony Cloninger. A hairline fracture of the wrist in May caused Alou's average to plummet 53 points. A sprained ankle in June hobbled Torre for most of the second half. And Cloninger spent much of the year incapacitated with a sore arm and a virus that affected his vision.

The Braves were 67–64 through August despite a no-hitter at the hands of Houston's Don Wilson. They won just 10 of their final 31 games, though, prompting Hitchcock's dismissal.

However, there were some individual accomplishments of note.

It was a breakthrough season for Phil Niekro, who had been bouncing back and forth between the minors and majors and had been utilized mainly as a reliever in the first three years of his career. Given a chance to start, the 28-year-old knuckleball specialist led the league in ERA (1.87).

The Braves' pitching also got a much-needed boost from stocky right-hander Pat Jarvis, who developed into the ace of the staff in spite of not getting a single start during the first month of the schedule.

Clete Boyer, acquired from the Yankees to replace Mathews, led the league's third basemen in defense (.980).

For the third consecutive year, the Braves led the league in home runs. But their 158 homers represented a big drop from the 207 of the previous season. The offense was generally down, across the board, and the team batting average (.240) was third-worst in the league.

The one man who kept up his end of the bargain, of course, was Hank Aaron. He led the league in home runs (39) for the fourth and final time of his career.

	G	AB	R	H	2B	3B	HR	RBI	SB	AVG
Hank Aaron (OF)	155	600	113*	184	37	3	39*	109	17	.307
Felipe Alou (1B)	140	574	76	157	26	3	15	43	6	.274
Jim Beauchamp	4	3	0	0	0	0	0	1	0	.000
Clete Boyer (3B)	154	572	63	140	18	3	26	96	6	.245
Rico Carty (OF)	134	444	41	113	16	2	15	64	4	.255
Glen Clark	4	4	0	0	0	0	0	0	0	.000
Ty Cline	10	8	0	0	0	0	0	0	0	.000
Mike de la Hoz	74	143	10	29	3	0	3	14	1	.203
Tito Francona	82	254	28	63	5	1	6	25	1	.248
Cito Gaston	9	25	1	3	0	1	0	1	1	.120
Gary Geiger	69	117	17	19	1	1	1	5	1	.162
Angel Hermoso	11	26	3	8	0	0	0	0	1	.308
Mack Jones (OF)	140	454	72	115	23	4	17	50	10	.253
Charlie Lau	52	45	3	9	1	0	1	5	0	.200
Mike Lum	9	26	1	6	0	0	0	1	0	.231
Marty Martinez	44	73	14	21	2	1	0	5	0	.288
Denis Menke (SS)	129	418	37	95	14	3	7	39	5	.227
Felix Millan	41	136	13	32	3	3	2	6	0	.235
Dave Nicholson	10	25	2	5	0	0	0	1	0	.200
Gene Oliver	17	51	8	10	2	0	3	6	0	.196
Joe Torre (C)	135	477	67	132	18	1	20	68	2	.277
Bob Uecker	62	158	14	23	2	0	3	13	0	.146
Woody Woodward (2B)	136	429	30	97	15	2	0	25	0	.226
	162	5,450	631	1,307	191	29	158*	596	55	.240

	W	L	G	GS	CG	IP	H	BB	SO	ERA
Wade Blasingame	1	0	10	4	0	25⅓	27	21	20	4.62
Jim Britton	0	2	2	2	0	13⅓	15	2	4	6.08
Bob Bruce	2	3	12	7	1	38⅔	42	15	22	4.89
Clay Carroll	6	12	42	7	1	93	111	29	35	5.52
Tony Cloninger	4	7	16	16	1	76⅔	85	31	55	5.17
Ramon Hernandez	0	2	46	0	0	51⅔	60	14	28	4.18
Pat Jarvis	15	10	32	30	7	194	195	62	118	3.66
Ken Johnson	13	9	29	29	6	210⅓	191	38	85	2.74
Dick Kelley	2	9	39	9	1	98	88	42	75	3.77
Denny Lemaster	9	9	31	31	8	215⅓	184	72	148	3.34
Phil Niekro	11	9	46	20	10	207	164	55	129	1.87*
Ed Rakow	3	2	17	3	0	39½	36	15	25	5.26
Claude Raymond	4	1	28	0	0	34⅓	33	11	14	2.62
Ron Reed	1	1	3	3	0	21⅓	21	3	11	2.95
Jay Ritchie	4	6	52	0	0	82⅓	75	29	57	3.17
Don Schwall	0	0	1	0	0	⅔	0	1	0	0.00
George Stone	0	0	2	1	0	7⅓	8	1	5	4.91
Cecil Upshaw	2	3	30	0	0	45⅓	42	8	31	2.58
	77	85		162	35	1,454	1,377	449	862	3.47

Shutouts—Lemaster (2), Jarvis, Kelley, Niekro
Saves—Niekro (9), Upshaw (8), Hernandez (5), Raymond (5), Kelley (2), Ritchie (2), Bruce

1968

Record: 81–81
Finish: Fifth
Games Behind: 16
Manager: Luman Harris

In 1968, the Braves had their best staff ERA (2.92) since 1918 and one that hasn't been equaled in the 26 seasons since. But all it got them was a break-even record.

There were two reasons for the club's inability to capitalize on this pitching windfall under new manager Luman Harris. First, it was the year of the pitcher throughout the league. Bob Gibson had a 1.12 ERA to lead St. Louis to the pennant. And second, the Braves were so bogged down with injuries and players having off years that they simply didn't score runs the way they had in recent years.

In fact, the team that averaged 187 home runs in leading the league the three previous years hit but 80—sixth in the league.

The lineup suffered a severe blow before the club even got

Luman Harris' 1968 pitching staff included (L-R) Dick Kelley, Pat Jarvis and Ken Johnson.

out of spring training when it was discovered that Rico Carty had tuberculosis and would have to sit out the season.

New shortstop Sonny Jackson, obtained from Houston, was supposed to be the speed player who would help the Braves modernize their style of play. Instead, he was hampered by injuries and stole just 16 bases.

Slick-fielding third baseman Clete Boyer missed the second half with an injury sustained when he was hit by a Don Drysdale pitch. Second baseman Felix Millan and catcher Joe Torre were hampered by injuries, too. Torre's power production was particularly disappointing.

Hank Aaron had his worst season, statistically, since his rookie year. But in relation to the rest of the league, it really wasn't that bad. He still was fifth in the league in home runs (29), second in total bases, and fourth in slugging percentage. The 34-year-old Aaron also hit his 500th career home run in July.

Felipe Alou bounced back from an injury-plagued season to tie Pete Rose for the league lead in hits (210). He also was third in the batting race (.317), although his power production continued to lag.

The unexpected pitching prowess came from several sources. Phil Niekro, almost exclusively a starter except when he occasionally relieved during a crisis, was effective for the second straight year. Pat Jarvis led the club in victories (16), and Ron Reed made the All-Star team. Milt Pappas and George Stone won more than they lost, too, and Cecil Upshaw developed into one of the league's better relievers.

Another "pitching" addition was 62-year-old Satchel Paige, who was signed to a contract August 11 so he could qualify for a pension. He originally was called an "assistant trainer" but later was classified as a coach.

On June 1, the Braves were tied for first place with St. Louis. It was the first time the team had been on top of the standings since coming to Atlanta, but it lasted just a day. Harris's team played under .500 the rest of the season.

	G	AB	R	H	2B	3B	HR	RBI	SB	AVG
Hank Aaron (OF)	160	606	84	174	33	4	29	86	28	.287
Tommie Aaron	98	283	21	69	10	3	1	25	3	.244
Felipe Alou (OF)	160	662*	72	210*	37	5	11	57	12	.317
Dusty Baker	6	5	0	2	0	0	0	0	0	.400
Clete Boyer (3B)	71	273	19	62	7	2	4	17	2	.227
Wayne Causey	16	37	2	4	0	1	1	4	0	.108
Tito Francona	122	346	32	99	13	1	2	47	3	.286
Ralph Garr	11	7	3	2	0	0	0	0	1	.286
Gil Garrido	18	53	5	11	0	0	0	2	0	.208
Walt Hriniak	9	26	0	9	0	0	0	3	0	.346
Sonny Jackson (SS)	105	358	37	81	8	2	1	19	16	.226
Bob Johnson	59	187	15	49	5	1	0	11	0	.262
Deron Johnson (1B)	127	342	29	71	11	1	8	33	0	.208
Mike Lum (OF)	122	232	22	52	7	3	3	21	3	.224
Marty Martinez	113	356	34	82	5	3	0	12	6	.230
Felix Millan (2B)	149	570	49	165	22	2	1	33	6	.289
Mike Page	20	28	1	5	0	0	0	1	0	.179
Bob Tillman	86	236	16	52	4	0	5	20	1	.220
Joe Torre (C)	115	424	45	115	11	2	10	55	1	.271
Sandy Valdespino	36	86	8	20	1	0	1	4	0	.233
Woody Woodward	12	24	2	4	1	0	0	1	1	.167
	163	5,552	514	1,399	179	31	80	480	83	.252

	W	L	G	GS	CG	IP	H	BB	SO	ERA
Jim Britton	4	6	34	9	2	90	81	34	61	3.10
Clay Carroll	0	1	10	0	0	22⅓	26	6	10	4.84
Tony Cloninger	1	3	8	1	0	19	15	11	7	4.26
Ted Davidson	0	0	4	0	0	6⅔	10	4	3	6.75
Skip Guinn	0	0	3	0	0	5	3	3	4	3.60
Pat Jarvis	16	12	34	34	14	256	202	50	157	2.60
Ken Johnson	5	8	31	16	1	135	145	25	57	3.47
Dick Kelley	2	4	31	11	1	98	86	45	73	2.76
Rick Kester	0	0	5	0	0	6⅓	8	3	9	5.68
Stu Miller	0	0	2	0	0	1⅓	1	4	1	27.00
Phil Niekro	14	12	37	34	15	257	228	45	140	2.59
Milt Pappas	10	8	22	19	3	121⅓	111	22	75	2.37
Claude Raymond	3	5	36	0	0	60⅓	56	18	37	2.83
Ron Reed	11	10	35	28	6	201⅔	189	49	111	3.35
Al Santorini	0	1	1	1	0	3	4	0	0	0.00
George Stone	7	4	17	10	2	75	63	19	52	2.76
Cecil Upshaw	8	7	52	0	0	116⅔	98	24	74	2.47
	81	81		163	44	1,474⅔	1,326	362	871	2.92

Shutouts—Niekro (5), Britton (2), Jarvis, Kelley, Pappas, Reed
Saves—Upshaw (13), Raymond (10), Britton (3), Niekro (2), Kelley

1969

Record: 93–69
Finish: First (West)
Games Ahead: 3
Manager: Luman Harris

It would be a while before Atlanta and the South were exposed to the excitement of hosting a World Series, but thanks to the advent of divisional play in 1969, Braves fans got their first taste of postseason action. Winning the first "minititle" in National League history was a welcome accomplishment for a franchise that had been having difficulty finishing in the first division for several years.

Luman Harris's club had to come from behind to win the West division, and they did so by simply outplaying their chief contenders, Cincinnati and San Francisco, down the stretch.

On August 19, the Cubs' Ken Holtzman pitched a no-hitter against the Braves without the benefit of a single strikeout, dropping Atlanta to fifth place in the six-team division. Though the Braves had been in and out of first place earlier, at this point a division title seemed quite unlikely.

But the Braves quickly righted themselves and climbed back in the race. On September 9, Phil Niekro beat the

The late-season acquisition of knuckleball reliever Hoyt Wilhelm enabled the Braves to win the West in 1969, the first year of division play.

Dodgers, 2–1, for his 20th victory. The win put the Braves in third place, just 1½ games out of first. Three days later, Atlanta moved on top with a 4–3 victory against Houston.

For the next week, the Giants, Reds, and Braves jostled for position, then Atlanta embarked on a 10-game winning streak that gave the other teams no margin for error. On September 30, the Braves clinched the division by beating Cincinnati, 3–2, before 46,357 at Atlanta Stadium. Niekro got his 23rd victory, and another knuckleball artist, Hoyt Wilhelm, saved it by getting the last six outs. Rico Carty's sacrifice fly in the eighth inning drove in Felix Millan with the decisive run.

The victory set off a raucous celebration in Atlanta, of which *Atlanta Journal* sports editor Furman Bisher wrote, "I grant you, it was the first time the South has ever won the West. I grant you that it was the greatest sports event that ever happened in the city of Atlanta. I also grant you that I never saw such behavior in my life. I don't deplore it. I just never saw anything like it."

Including the clinching victory, Harris's club won 17 of 20 games and 27 of 37 to get the franchise in postseason play for the first time since 1958.

Besides leading the league in fielding percentage (.981), the Braves weren't particularly outstanding in any area. They simply stayed close all year and got hot at the right time. There were practically as many heroes as there were roster spots.

The inspiration for turning a consistently mediocre team into a winning one came in the March trade that sent Joe Torre to St. Louis in exchange for veteran first baseman Orlando Cepeda. Though Torre blossomed into an MVP in St. Louis and gave the Cardinals much more service than Atlanta got from the gimpy Cepeda, it seemed that "Cha Cha's" leadership and enthusiasm helped the Braves gain the confidence they needed to win.

Cepeda had been on two pennant winners in St. Louis and

The spiritual leader of the 1969 team was first baseman Orlando Cepeda.

another in San Francisco. He was the 1967 National League MVP for the Cardinals, and his mere presence was as important to the '69 Braves as was his hitting, which was timely and strong, especially in the early stages of the season. The Braves won four of their first five games, and Cepeda had the game-winning hit in three of those.

Niekro had what was probably the finest season of his career. He was second in the league in victories (23), only two behind Tom Seaver.

Niekro's success was partly attributed to the work of 20-year-old rookie catcher Bob Didier, who did an outstanding job of corralling the elusive knuckleball. The switch-hitting Didier also did a respectable job with the bat but was never a regular again after 1969 and was finished by age 25.

Hank Aaron was second to Willie McCovey in home runs, matching his uniform number of 44 in homers for the fourth and final time of his career. Aaron made a big move on the all-time home run chart in 1969, too, finishing the year in third place with 554.

Carty came back from a year off with tuberculosis to hit like he'd never been gone. After sustaining shoulder separations on three occasions, he was particularly strong down the stretch and finished with a .342 average, which would have been third in the league if he'd had enough at bats to qualify.

Millan led the club in hits and developed into an All-Star second baseman, leading the league in defense (.980). Clete Boyer led all third basemen in defense (.965) for the second time as a Brave and was one of the most timely hitters in the Atlanta lineup. Sonny Jackson and Gil Garrido shared shortstop with efficiency.

Regular center fielder Felipe Alou did not have one of his better seasons but was more than adequate, and a weakness in left field was filled very capably June 12 when general manager Paul Richards obtained Tony Gonzalez from San Diego.

The other acquisition Richards made during the season that helped get the team over the hump was the purchase of 46-year-old Wilhelm from California for the waiver price. The September 8 move was made too late to get Wilhelm on the postseason roster, but he was almost perfect in eight appearances, picking up two wins and four saves and taking some of the strain off bullpen ace Cecil Upshaw.

After Niekro, Ron Reed was easily the most effective starter.

He had his best year with the Braves and won nine of his last 11 decisions to contribute heavily during the stretch drive. George Stone and Pat Jarvis also were effective members of the starting rotation.

Reserve outfielder Mike Lum and backup catcher Bob Tillman, who had a three-home-run game, were among the major contributors off the bench.

	G	AB	R	H	2B	3B	HR	RBI	SB	AVG
Hank Aaron (OF)	147	547	100	164	30	3	44	97	9	.300
Tommie Aaron	49	60	13	15	2	0	1	5	0	.250
Felipe Alou (OF)	123	476	54	134	13	1	5	32	4	.282
Bob Aspromonte	82	198	16	50	8	1	3	24	0	.253
Dusty Baker	3	7	0	0	0	0	0	0	0	.000
Clete Boyer (3B)	144	496	57	124	16	1	14	57	3	.250
Jim Breazeale	2	1	1	0	0	0	0	0	0	.000
Oscar Brown	7	4	2	1	0	0	0	0	0	.250
Rico Carty	104	304	47	104	15	0	16	58	0	.342
Orlando Cepeda (1B)	154	573	74	147	28	2	22	88	12	.257
Bob Didier (C)	114	352	30	90	16	1	0	32	1	.256
Darrell Evans	12	26	3	6	0	0	0	1	0	.231
Tito Francona	51	88	5	26	1	0	2	22	0	.295
Ralph Garr	22	27	6	6	1	0	0	2	1	.222
Gil Garrido	82	227	18	50	5	1	0	10	0	.220
Tony Gonzalez (OF)	89	320	51	94	15	2	10	50	3	.294
Walt Hriniak	7	7	0	1	0	0	0	0	0	.143
Sonny Jackson (SS)	98	318	41	76	3	5	1	27	12	.239
Mike Lum	121	168	20	45	8	0	1	22	0	.268
Felix Millan (2B)	162	652	98	174	23	5	6	57	14	.267
Bob Tillman	69	190	18	37	5	0	12	29	0	.195
	162	5,460	691	1,411	195	22	141	640	59	.258

	W	L	G	GS	CG	IP	H	BB	SO	ERA
Jim Britton	7	5	24	13	2	88	69	49	60	3.78
Paul Doyle	2	0	36	0	0	39	31	16	25	2.08
Garry Hill	0	1	1	1	0	2⅓	6	1	2	15.43
Pat Jarvis	13	11	37	33	4	217½	204	73	123	4.43
Ken Johnson	0	1	9	2	0	29	32	9	20	4.97
Rick Kester	0	0	1	0	0	2	5	0	2	13.50
Larry Maxie	0	0	2	0	0	3	1	1	1	3.00
Mike McQueen	0	0	1	1	0	3	2	3	3	3.00
Gary Neibauer	1	2	29	0	0	57⅔	42	31	42	3.90
Phil Niekro	23	13	40	35	21	284⅓	235	57	193	2.56
Milt Pappas	6	10	26	24	1	144	149	44	72	3.63
Bob Priddy	0	0	1	0	0	2	1	1	1	0.00
Claude Raymond	2	2	33	0	0	48	56	13	15	5.25
Ron Reed	18	10	36	33	7	241⅓	227	56	160	3.47
George Stone	13	10	36	20	3	165⅓	166	48	102	3.65
Cecil Upshaw	6	4	62	0	0	105⅓	102	29	57	2.91
Charley Vaughan	0	0	1	0	0	1	1	3	1	18.00
Hoyt Wilhelm	2	0	8	0	0	12⅓	5	4	14	0.73
	93	69		162	38	1,445	1,334	438	893	3.53

Shutouts—Niekro (4), Britton, Jarvis, Reed
Saves—Upshaw (27), Doyle (4), Wilhelm (4), Stone (3), Britton, Johnson, Niekro, Raymond

1970

Record: 76–86
Finish: Fifth (West)
Games Behind: 26
Manager: Luman Harris

The 1970 season was doomed before it even got started. Phil Niekro underwent an emergency appendectomy just before spring training and never resembled the 23-game winner of the previous season. Ron Reed, an 18-game winner in 1969, tripped over first base and broke his collarbone in spring training, causing him to miss the first nine weeks of the season. And relief ace Cecil Upshaw missed the entire season after severing his right ring finger in a freak accident in which he caught the finger on an awning.

Just like that, the Braves pitching staff—not the strong point of the team anyway—was in deep trouble.

Atlanta finished ninth in the league in ERA (4.33), its highest since 1940 when Casey Stengel was manager. Not even a team with as much offensive punch as the 1970 Braves could win with such a pitching staff.

And Atlanta could hit. The Braves tied for the league lead with a .270 batting average. They had three .300 hitters, including the league leader, three players with at least 25 home runs, and three with 100 or more RBIs.

Rico Carty's .366 average not only led the league but was the highest average in the majors since 1957 when Ted Williams batted .388. Felix Millan and Orlando Cepeda joined Carty in the .300 club.

Early in the season, Carty strung together an Atlanta-record 31-game hitting streak during which he batted .451. On May 31, shortly after the streak ended, Carty hit three homers off three different Philadelphia pitchers and also singled, driving in six runs in a 9–1 victory. He was hitting .436 at the time and kept his average over .400 through mid-June.

Hank Aaron was fifth in the league in RBIs and had yet another fine season, finishing with 592 lifetime home runs. One of the biggest moments of Aaron's fabulous career took place May 17 at Cincinnati's Crosley Field when he got his 3,000th hit off Wayne Granger. He was the ninth man to reach that level but the first to do so with 500 home runs.

Yet another milestone reached by a Brave came when 46-year-old reliever Hoyt Wilhelm became the first man to pitch in 1,000 games. Orlando Cepeda and Mike Lum both had three-home-run games, and Millan had a 6-for-6 outing.

But it all came down to pitching, and the Braves simply didn't have enough of it. In the off-season, they acquired Jim Nash, a rookie sensation in 1966, from Oakland. Though he pitched well at times, he wasn't enough to enable the team to overcome the setbacks to Reed and Niekro, the latter of whom was eventually relegated to the bullpen and then sent to the Instructional League in the off-season.

	W	L	G	GS	CG	IP	H	BB	SO	ERA
Steve Barber	0	1	5	2	0	14⅔	17	5	11	4.91
Don Cardwell	2	1	16	2	1	23	31	13	16	9.00
Aubrey Gatewood	0	0	3	0	0	2	4	2	0	4.50
Pat Jarvis	16	16	36	34	11	254	240	72	173	3.61
Larry Jaster	1	1	14	0	0	22⅓	33	8	9	6.85
Rick Kester	0	0	15	0	0	32⅓	36	19	20	5.57
Ron Kline	0	0	5	0	0	6⅓	9	2	3	7.11
Mike McQueen	1	5	22	8	1	66	67	31	54	5.59
Jim Nash	13	9	34	33	6	212⅓	211	90	153	4.07
Julio Navarro	0	0	17	0	0	26⅓	24	1	21	4.10
Gary Neibauer	0	3	7	0	0	12⅔	11	8	9	4.97
Phil Niekro	12	18	34	32	0	229⅔	222	68	168	4.27
Milt Pappas	2	2	11	3	1	35⅓	44	7	25	6.06
Bob Priddy	5	5	41	0	0	73	75	24	32	5.42
Ron Reed	7	10	21	18	6	134⅔	140	39	68	4.41
George Stone	11	11	35	30	9	207½	218	50	131	3.86
Hoyt Wilhelm	6	4	50	0	0	78⅓	69	39	67	3.10
	76	86		162	45	1,430⅔	1,451	478	960	4.33

Shutouts—Niekro (3), Nash (2), Stone (2), Cardwell, Jarvis
Saves—Wilhelm (13), Priddy (8), Kline, McQueen, Navarro

1971

Record: 82–80
Finish: Third (West)
Games Behind: 8
Manager: Luman Harris

Oh, what Luman Harris would have given for just a little more pitching. As it was, the 1971 Braves slugged their way back to respectability with very little of that precious commodity. With a couple of more arms, they could have been serious contenders.

There were plenty of offensive highlights, as was becom-

	G	AB	R	H	2B	3B	HR	RBI	SB	AVG
Hank Aaron (OF)	150	516	103	154	26	1	38	118	9	.298
Tommie Aaron	44	63	3	13	2	0	2	7	0	.206
Bob Aspromonte	62	127	5	27	3	0	0	7	0	.213
Dusty Baker	13	24	3	7	0	0	0	4	0	.292
Clete Boyer (3B)	134	475	44	117	14	1	16	62	2	.246
Oscar Brown	28	47	6	18	2	1	1	7	0	.383
Rico Carty (OF)	136	478	84	175	23	3	25	101	1	.366*
Orlando Cepeda (1B)	148	567	87	173	33	0	34	111	6	.305
Bob Didier	57	168	9	25	2	1	0	7	1	.149
Darrell Evans	12	44	4	14	1	1	0	9	0	.318
Ralph Garr	37	96	18	27	3	0	0	8	5	.281
Gil Garrido	101	367	38	97	5	4	1	19	0	.264
Tony Gonzalez (OF)	123	430	57	114	18	2	7	55	3	.265
Jimmie Hall	39	47	7	10	2	0	2	4	0	.213
Sonny Jackson (SS)	103	328	60	85	14	3	0	20	11	.259
Hal King	89	204	29	53	8	0	11	30	1	.260
Mike Lum	123	291	25	74	17	2	7	28	3	.254
Felix Millan (2B)	142	590	100	183	25	5	2	37	16	.310
Bob Tillman	71	223	19	53	5	0	11	30	0	.238
Earl Williams	10	19	4	7	4	0	0	5	0	.368
	162	5,546	736	1,495	215	24	160	692	58	.270*

The American League MVP for Minnesota in 1965, Zoilo Versalles couldn't help the Braves in 1971.

ing an Atlanta trademark. The Braves finished second in the league in home runs, just one behind Pittsburgh, and Hank Aaron had the biggest home run total (47) of his career.

Aaron hit No. 600 of his career April 27 against San Francisco's Gaylord Perry. By moving to first base regularly for the first time, Aaron seemed to get an extra burst at age 37. He finished just one homer behind league leader Willie Stargell. Aaron also was fifth in the league in batting average (.327) and third in RBIs (118). At the end of the year, he had closed the gap on Babe Ruth to 76 home runs.

For the second time in four years, the Braves had to play without the gifted bat of left fielder Rico Carty. During a winter league game in the Dominican Republic, Carty, who owned a .322 career batting average, suffered a fractured knee and ligament damage. During his rehabilitation, Carty also was involved in an altercation with Atlanta police in which he was beaten and sustained eye damage.

Rookie Earl Williams did his best to help the club overcome the loss of Carty. Williams, who had no previous experience at catcher, nevertheless spent the season behind the plate and was named National League Rookie of the Year. Of course, it was his 33 home runs, tied for fifth in the league, that did more to get him the honor than his defense.

Yet another welcome addition to the lineup was the speedy Ralph Garr, who was finally able to move into left field because of Carty's injury. In his first full season in the majors, Garr finished second (.343) to Joe Torre in the batting race. Not known for power, Garr still tied a major league record for home runs in extra innings by hitting one in the 10th inning and one in the 12th of a 4–3 victory against the Mets. He also set an Atlanta record with 30 steals.

Earl Williams hit 33 home runs in 1971 en route to being selected the National League Rookie of the Year.

Some of the new blood on the team didn't fare so well, though. Shortstop Leo Foster made one of the most dreadful debuts in big league history July 9 against Pittsburgh. He made an error on his first chance, hit into a double play in the fifth inning, and hit into a triple play in the seventh.

Two infielders, Darrell Evans at third and Marty Perez at shortstop, began long stints as regulars. Perez teamed with steady second baseman Felix Millan to help the Braves set a club record with 180 double plays, leading the league.

Phil Niekro bounced back well from his poor showing in 1970, but the big comeback of the season was Cecil Upshaw's. The sidearming right-hander, who nearly lost a finger on his pitching hand the year before, finished fifth in the league in saves (17).

	G	AB	R	H	2B	3B	HR	RBI	SB	AVG
Hank Aaron (1B)	139	495	95	162	22	3	47	118	1	.327
Tommie Aaron	25	53	4	12	2	0	0	3	0	.226
Dusty Baker	29	62	2	14	2	0	0	4	0	.226
Clete Boyer	30	98	10	24	1	0	6	19	0	.245
Jim Breazeale	10	21	1	4	0	0	1	3	0	.190
Oscar Brown	27	43	4	9	4	0	0	5	0	.209
Orlando Cepeda	71	250	31	69	10	1	14	44	3	.276
Bob Didier	51	155	9	34	4	1	0	5	0	.219
Darrell Evans (3B)	89	260	42	63	11	1	12	38	2	.242
Leo Foster	9	10	1	0	0	0	0	0	0	.000
Ralph Garr (OF)	154	639	101	219	24	6	9	44	30	.343
Gil Garrido	79	125	8	27	3	0	0	12	0	.216
Sonny Jackson (OF)	149	547	58	141	20	5	2	25	7	.258
Hal King	86	198	14	41	9	0	5	19	0	.207
Tony LaRussa	9	7	1	2	0	0	0	0	0	.286
Mike Lum (OF)	145	454	56	122	14	1	13	55	0	.269
Felix Millan (2B)	143	577	65	167	20	8	2	45	11	.289
Marty Perez (SS)	130	410	28	93	15	3	4	32	1	.227
Marv Staehle	22	36	5	4	0	0	0	1	0	.111
Zoilo Versalles	66	194	21	37	11	0	5	22	2	.191
Earl Williams (C)	145	497	64	129	14	1	33	87	0	.260
	162	5,575	643	1,434	192	30	153	597	57	.257

	W	L	G	GS	CG	IP	H	BB	SO	ERA
Steve Barber	3	1	39	3	0	75	92	25	40	4.80
Ron Herbel	0	1	25	0	0	51⅔	61	23	22	5.23
Tom House	1	0	11	1	0	20⅔	20	3	11	3.05
Pat Jarvis	6	14	35	23	3	162⅓	162	51	68	4.10
Tom Kelley	9	5	28	20	5	143	140	69	68	2.96
Mike McQueen	4	1	17	3	0	56	47	23	38	3.54
Jim Nash	9	7	32	19	2	133	166	50	65	4.94
Gary Neibauer	1	0	6	1	0	21	14	9	6	2.14
Phil Niekro	15	14	42	36	18	268⅔	248	70	173	2.98
Bob Priddy	4	9	40	0	0	64	71	44	36	4.22
Ron Reed	13	14	32	32	8	222⅓	221	54	129	3.72
George Stone	6	8	27	24	4	172⅔	186	35	110	3.60
Cecil Upshaw	11	6	49	0	0	82	95	28	56	3.51
Hoyt Wilhelm	0	0	3	0	0	2⅓	6	1	1	15.43
	82	80		162	40	1,474⅔*	1,529*	485	823	3.75

Shutouts—Niekro (4), Jarvis (3), Stone (2), Reed
Saves—Upshaw (17), Priddy (4), Barber (2), Nash (2), Niekro (2), Herbel, Jarvis, McQueen, Neibauer

1972

Record: 70–84
Finish: Fourth (West)
Games Behind: 25
Managers: Luman Harris, Eddie Mathews

The 1972 Braves were a sorry lot. Once again, the club could hit, but pitching and fielding were a mystery to it. The staff ERA (4.27) was half a run worse than that of any other team in the league, and the club's defensive average (.974) tied for last. It made for an ugly combination.

Turned off by the Braves' low caliber of play and a players' strike that delayed the start of the season by a week, fans were reluctant to purchase tickets. Attendance dropped by a quarter of a million from 1971, and the total of 752,973 was easily the lowest in Atlanta history.

Of course, the team's ugly new "mod" uniforms might have kept a few fans at home, too. Adorned with a feather that looked more like a tulip on the sleeves, the uniforms—especially the powder-blue road version—made the Braves look like a slow-pitch softball team. Considering the way they played, that was appropriate.

Atlanta was the only member of the six-team National League West not to spend at least one day in first place, and the franchise's .455 winning percentage was its worst since 1952.

There was plenty of change, as usually accompanies such a season. On June 29, the club made a rather useless swap of over-the-hill players, sending Orlando Cepeda to Oakland in exchange for washed-up former 30-game winner Denny McLain.

Eddie Robinson was promoted from minor league director to general manager, pushing aside vice president Paul Richards, who retained his title but no power. And on August 7, Robinson fired manager Luman Harris, a buddy of Richards', and replaced him with former third base great Eddie Mathews, who had been a coach.

Though the pitching and defense were morbid, the offense supplied numerous highlights.

On June 10, Hank Aaron hit his 14th career grand slam, tying Gil Hodges for the National League record. It also was home run No. 649 of Aaron's career, moving him ahead of Willie Mays and into second place on the all-time list.

Though it didn't count in his pursuit of Babe Ruth, a home run Aaron hit July 25 was one of the more memorable of his career. It came at Atlanta Stadium in the sixth inning of the All-Star Game, thrilling the capacity crowd and helping the National League to a 4–3 victory.

Aaron passed another milestone August 6, the day before Mathews took over the club, by hitting home runs No. 660 and 661, the most ever by a player with one franchise. Though Aaron's batting average (.265) dropped 62 points from the previous season, he still was fourth in the league in home runs (34) and ended the year just 42 behind Babe Ruth.

Perhaps the best example of the team's pitching deficiency came August 1 when the Braves lost a doubleheader at home to San Diego by the scores of 9–0 and 11–7. The Padres' Nate Colbert tied a major league record with five homers and set another record with 13 RBIs.

But on the right day, the Braves were capable of similar outbursts. On September 20, they routed Houston, 13–6, scoring all their runs in the second inning.

Ralph Garr, who finished second in the league in hitting (.325), Earl Williams, and Darrell Evans were major contributors to the offense, as was center fielder Dusty Baker, who in his first full season with the club finished third in the league in hitting (.321).

	G	AB	R	H	2B	3B	HR	RBI	SB	AVG
Hank Aaron (1B)	129	449	75	119	10	0	34	77	4	.265
Dusty Baker (OF)	127	446	62	143	27	2	17	76	4	.321
Larvell Blanks	33	85	10	28	5	0	1	7	0	.329
Jim Breazeale	52	85	10	21	2	0	5	17	0	.247
Oscar Brown	76	164	19	37	5	1	3	16	0	.226
Rico Carty (OF)	86	271	31	75	12	2	6	29	0	.277
Paul Casanova	49	136	8	28	3	0	2	10	0	.206
Orlando Cepeda	28	84	6	25	3	0	4	9	0	.298
Bob Didier	13	40	5	12	2	1	0	5	0	.300
Darrell Evans (3B)	125	418	67	106	12	0	19	71	4	.254
Ralph Garr (OF)	134	554	87	180	22	0	12	53	25	.325
Gil Garrido	40	75	11	20	1	0	0	7	1	.267
Rod Gilbreath	18	38	2	9	1	0	1	1	1	.237
Sonny Jackson	60	126	20	30	6	3	0	8	1	.238
Mike Lum	123	369	40	84	14	2	9	38	1	.228
Felix Millan (2B)	125	498	46	128	19	3	1	38	6	.257
Rowland Office	2	5	1	2	0	0	0	0	0	.400
Marty Perez (SS)	141	479	33	109	13	1	1	28	0	.228
Earl Williams (C)	151	565	72	146	24	2	28	87	0	.258
	155	5,278	628	1,363	186	17	144	593	47	.258

	W	L	G	GS	CG	IP	H	BB	SO	ERA
Steve Barber	0	0	5	0	0	15⅔	18	6	6	5.74
Jimmy Freeman	2	2	6	6	1	36	40	22	18	6.00
Jim Hardin	5	2	26	9	1	79⅓	93	24	25	4.41
Joe Hoerner	1	3	25	0	0	23⅓	34	8	19	6.56
Tom House	0	0	8	0	0	9⅓	7	6	7	2.89
Pat Jarvis	11	7	37	6	0	98¾	94	44	56	4.10
Larry Jaster	1	1	5	1	0	12⅓	12	8	6	5.11
Tom Kelley	5	7	27	14	2	116⅓	122	65	59	4.56
Denny McLain	3	5	15	8	2	54	60	18	21	6.50
Mike McQueen	0	5	23	7	1	78⅓	79	44	40	4.60
Jim Nash	1	1	11	4	0	31⅓	35	25	10	5.46
Gary Neibauer	0	0	8	0	0	17⅓	27	6	8	7.27
Phil Niekro	16	12	38	36	17	282⅓	254	53	164	3.06
Ron Reed	11	15	31	30	11	213	222	60	111	3.93
Ron Schueler	5	8	37	18	3	144⅔	122	60	96	3.67
George Stone	6	11	31	16	2	111	143	44	63	5.51
Cecil Upshaw	3	5	42	0	0	53⅔	50	19	23	3.69
	70	84		155	40	1,377	1,412*	512	732	4.27

Shutouts—Kelley, Niekro, Reed, Stone

Saves—Upshaw (13), Hardin (2), Hoerner (2), House (2), Jarvis (2), Schueler (2), McLain, McQueen, Nash, Stone

1973

Record: 76–85
Finish: Fifth (West)
Games Behind: 22½
Manager: Eddie Mathews

The 1973 Braves scored more runs than any other team in the National League—however, they also gave up more runs than anyone else. That combination made for yet another dismal season. However, Hank Aaron's pursuit of Babe Ruth and the team's record overall firepower made for plenty of thrills along the way to fifth place.

Believe it or not, the '73 Braves were so explosive that Aaron's accomplishments were almost overshadowed at times. In fact, despite an extraordinary season by the 39-year-old Aaron, he didn't even finish first or second on the team in home runs.

The Braves became the first—and only—team in history to have three men hit 40 or more home runs in the same season. Joining Aaron in the 40-home-run club were third baseman Darrell Evans (41) and second baseman Dave Johnson (43), the most unlikely 40-homer man in history.

During the off-season, the Braves obtained Johnson from Baltimore in a deal designed primarily to bolster the Atlanta pitching staff. Earl Williams and Taylor Duncan were sent to Baltimore in exchange for veteran pitcher Pat Dobson, strong-armed Roric Harrison, catcher Johnny Oates, and Johnson. Dobson, Harrison, and Oates contributed little, but Johnson, who hit five homers the year before and never previously hit more than 18 in a season, suddenly was transformed—if only for a year—into a virtual home-run machine.

All but one of Johnson's home runs came as a second baseman, allowing him to tie one of the oldest major league records in the books, Rogers Hornsby's for most home runs in a season (1922) by a second baseman.

Johnson fell just one home run shy of future Hall of Famer Willie Stargell for the league lead. Evans was third, two back of Johnson, and then came Aaron in fourth place with 40.

On July 21 at Atlanta, Aaron hit No. 700 against the Phillies' Ken Brett. Unfortunately, it came in an 8–4 loss, characteristic of all too many of his homers that year.

Aaron finished the season with 713 home runs, setting up a winter of tremendous buildup for his certain ascent to the all-time home run throne in 1974.

The Braves led the league in home runs with a total that was just one short of the franchise-record 207 in 1966. Atlanta also led the league in hits, RBIs, batting average (.266), on-base percentage (.341), and slugging percentage (.427).

But though general manager Eddie Robinson made several attempts to shore up the pitching—adding Harrison, Dobson, Gary Gentry, Carl Morton, and Danny Frisella—it remained miserable. The bullpen was particularly weak, as evidenced by the club's losing 30 games in which it was ahead or tied after seven innings.

One notable exception to the pitching woes took place August 5 in Atlanta when Phil Niekro pitched the first no-hitter in the team's history in the South. He beat San Diego, 9–0, for the first no-hitter by a Brave since Warren Spahn in 1961.

Even with Aaron in hot pursuit of an "unbreakable" record, attendance didn't nudge over 800,000 until the last home date of the season.

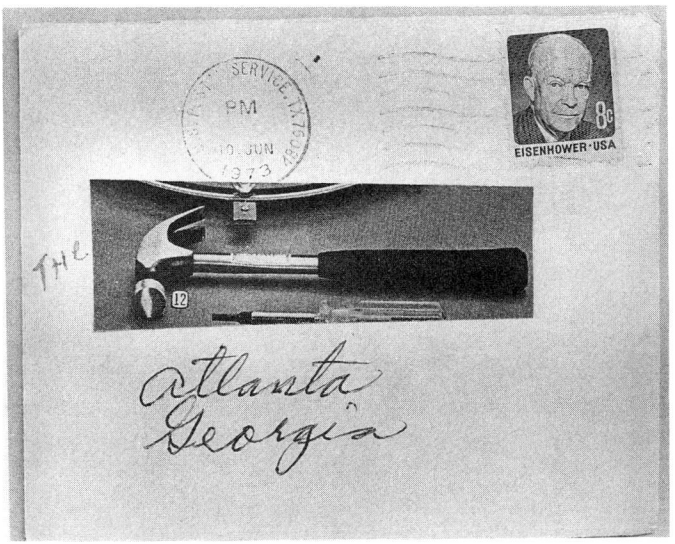

With Hank Aaron's pursuit of 714 at its peak, this piece of mail had no trouble finding its way to "The Hammer."

	G	AB	R	H	2B	3B	HR	RBI	SB	AVG
Hank Aaron (OF)	120	392	84	118	12	1	40	96	1	.301
Dusty Baker (OF)	159	604	101	174	29	4	21	99	24	.288
Larvell Blanks	17	18	1	4	0	0	0	0	0	.222
Oscar Brown	22	58	3	12	3	0	0	0	0	.207
Paul Casanova	82	236	18	51	7	0	7	18	0	.216
Dick Dietz	83	139	22	41	8	1	3	24	0	.295
Darrell Evans (3B)	161	595	114	167	25	8	41	104	6	.281
Leo Foster	3	6	1	1	1	0	0	0	0	.167
Ralph Garr (OF)	148	668	94	200	32	6	11	55	35	.299
Rod Gilbreath	29	74	10	21	2	1	0	2	2	.284
Chuck Goggin	64	90	18	26	5	0	0	7	0	.289
Larry Howard	4	8	0	1	0	0	0	0	0	.125
Sonny Jackson	117	206	29	43	5	2	0	12	6	.209
Dave Johnson (2B)	157	559	84	151	25	0	43	99	5	.270
Mike Lum (1B)	138	513	74	151	26	6	16	82	2	.294
Norm Miller	9	8	2	3	1	0	1	6	0	.375
Johnny Oates (C)	93	322	27	80	6	0	4	27	1	.248
Joe Pepitone	3	11	0	4	0	0	0	1	0	.364
Marty Perez (SS)	141	501	66	125	15	5	8	57	2	.250
Jack Pierce	11	20	0	1	0	0	0	0	0	.050
Frank Tepedino	74	148	20	45	5	0	4	29	0	.304
Freddy Velazquez	15	23	2	8	1	0	0	3	0	.348
	162	5,631*	799*	1,497*	219	34	206*	758*	84	.266*

	W	L	G	GS	CG	IP	H	BB	SO	ERA
Dave Cheadle	0	1	2	0	0	2	2	3	2	18.00
Alan Closter	0	0	4	0	0	4⅓	7	4	2	14.54
Adrian Devine	2	3	24	1	0	32⅓	45	12	15	6.40
Pat Dobson	3	7	12	10	1	57⅔	73	19	23	4.99
Wenty Ford	1	2	4	2	1	16⅓	17	8	4	5.51
Jimmy Freeman	0	2	13	5	0	37⅓	50	25	20	7.71
Danny Frisella	1	2	42	0	0	45	40	23	27	4.20
Gary Gentry	4	6	16	14	3	86⅔	74	35	42	3.43
Roric Harrison	11	8	38	22	3	177⅓	161	98	130	4.16
Joe Hoerner	2	2	20	0	0	12⅔	17	4	10	6.39
Tom House	4	2	52	0	0	67⅓	58	31	42	4.68
Tom Kelley	0	1	7	0	0	12⅔	13	7	5	2.84
Max Leon	2	2	12	1	1	27	30	9	18	5.33
Carl Morton	15	10	38	37	10	256⅓	254	70	112	3.41
Gary Neibauer	2	1	16	1	0	21⅓	24	19	9	7.17
Joe Niekro	2	4	20	0	0	24	23	11	12	4.13
Phil Niekro	13	10	42	30	9	245	214	89	131	3.31
Jim Panther	2	3	23	0	0	30⅔	45	9	8	7.63
Ron Reed	4	11	20	19	2	116⅓	133	31	64	4.41
Ron Schueler	8	7	39	20	4	186	179	66	124	3.87
Cecil Upshaw	0	1	5	0	0	3⅔	8	2	3	9.82
	76	85		162	34	1,462	1,467	575	803	4.25

Shutouts—Morton (4), Schueler (2), Dobson, P. Niekro

Saves—Frisella (8), Harrison (5), Devine (4), House (4), P. Niekro (4), J. Niekro (3), Hoerner (2), Schueler (2), Freeman, Gentry, Reed

1974

Record: 88–74
Finish: Third (West)
Games Behind: 14
Managers: Eddie Mathews, Clyde King

After an off-season dominated with talk of Hank Aaron's impending ascent to the title of all-time home run king, the changing of the guard took place with magnificent efficiency but not without a bit of controversy.

The Braves were due to open the season in Cincinnati, and both the club and Aaron wanted Atlanta fans to have the opportunity to witness the historic homers, if at all possible. The decision was made to withhold Aaron from the lineup for the three games in Cincinnati. However, Commissioner Bowie Kuhn ruled that Aaron had to play.

Therefore, on the afternoon of April 4, in the traditional National League opener, manager Eddie Mathews penciled Aaron into the lineup. After all, Aaron had never hit a home run on opening day before, so what were the odds he would do it this time with the weight of so much public attention on his shoulders?

But in the first inning, with Ralph Garr and Mike Lum on base, Aaron took his first swing of the season at a 3–1 pitch from Jack Billingham and deposited it over the left-field wall to tie Babe Ruth at 714.

Mathews elected not to play Aaron in the second game of the series, then was ordered by Kuhn to put him in the lineup for the final game. However, Aaron didn't come close to hitting No. 715, going hitless in three at bats.

The Braves returned to Atlanta for their home opener April 8 against the Dodgers. A standing-room-only crowd of 53,775 turned out on a chilly evening in hope of seeing history unfold. And Aaron did not disappoint them and a national television audience.

In his first at bat, Aaron drew a walk on five pitches, and the fans booed Los Angeles pitcher Al Downing. But in the bottom of the fourth, with Darrell Evans on first, Aaron took his first swing of the year in Atlanta on a 1–0 pitch and sent the ball sailing over the left-field fence for No. 715.

Afterward, Aaron admitted he was happy to have "The Chase" behind him. Besides the tremendous media pressure he faced, Aaron had been targeted with hate mail and even death threats. He had a full-time bodyguard with him around the clock throughout the ordeal.

The distraction created by Aaron's pursuit of history quickly out of the way, the 1974 Braves settled in to play surprisingly good baseball.

After having the worst pitching in the league for the past two seasons, Atlanta suddenly had one of the best staffs. The Braves finished a close second to the West division champion Dodgers in staff ERA (3.05). The team also tied the then-franchise record for shutouts originally set in 1916 with a league-leading 21.

One of the biggest reasons for the sudden reversal was the unexpected performance of Buzz Capra, a 26-year-old right-hander who was picked up from the Mets for the waiver price. Capra, who'd never won more than three games in a season, was inserted in the starting rotation May 19. He responded by beating the Dodgers, 4–2, in Los Angeles and proceeded to become one of the biggest surprises in the majors. He won nine in a row at one point, made the All-Star team, and led both leagues in ERA (2.28).

Though Capra proved to be a one-year wonder, he brought a breath of fresh air to a pitching staff in need.

Phil Niekro had the second 20-victory season of his career, led the league in complete games (18) and innings, was second to Capra in ERA, and also finished second in shutouts.

Carl Morton and Ron Reed also were effective starters, and Tom House had an excellent season anchoring a dependable bullpen, which included Max Leon.

However, the Braves still couldn't put it all together. This offensive juggernaut suddenly forgot how to hit. The home run production was third in the league, but Atlanta slipped to eighth in runs scored.

The only player who hit up to expectations was 28-year-old outfielder Ralph Garr. After twice being runner-up in the batting race, the speedy left fielder led the league in average (.353) by a whopping 32-point margin over Pittsburgh's Al Oliver. Garr also led the league in hits (214) and triples.

The heart of the order, namely Darrell Evans, Dusty Baker,

Clyde King replaced Eddie Mathews as manager in 1974 and was the beneficiary of excellent pitching by Phil Niekro and Buzz Capra (R).

and Dave Johnson, all had off years, and Aaron, who played less than he had in any previous season, naturally produced less in what everyone expected would be his final season.

The lack of offense resulted in a slow start and eventually cost Eddie Mathews his job. The Braves rallied in mid-May to win 26 of 34 through June 21. However, they immediately went into a dive, falling to fourth place, 14 games back.

On July 21, with the club only one game over .500, Mathews was fired, and superscout Clyde King replaced him. It was the fourth managerial change in nine years in Atlanta. The Braves played to a .603 pace over the final 63 games under King to finish a solid third but 10 games behind second-place Cincinnati.

A fitting climax to the season and to Aaron's career as a Brave came on October 2. In his last at bat in the National League, Aaron hit home run No. 733 against Cincinnati's Rawly Eastwick to aid a 13–0 rout of the Reds.

Aaron had indicated he would retire at the end of the season, but he changed his mind. On November 2, he was returned to Milwaukee, the city where he began his major league

Ralph Garr, who won the 1974 batting title, presents an All-Star ballot to then-Georgia Governor Jimmy Carter who won a big election of his own.

career. In exchange, the Braves got outfielder Dave May and minor league pitcher Roger Alexander from the Brewers.

	G	AB	R	H	2B	3B	HR	RBI	SB	AVG
Hank Aaron (OF)	112	340	47	91	16	0	20	69	1	.268
Dusty Baker (OF)	149	574	80	147	35	0	20	69	18	.256
Larvell Blanks	3	8	0	2	0	0	0	1	0	.250
Paul Casanova	42	104	5	21	0	0	0	8	0	.202
Vic Correll	73	202	20	48	15	1	4	29	0	.238
Darrell Evans (3B)	160	571	99	137	21	3	25	79	4	.240
Leo Foster	72	112	16	22	2	0	1	5	1	.196
John Fuller	3	3	1	1	0	0	0	0	0	.333
Ralph Garr (OF)	143	606	87	214*	24	17*	11	54	26	.353*
Rod Gilbreath	3	6	2	2	0	0	0	0	0	.333
Sonny Jackson	5	7	0	3	0	0	0	0	0	.429
Dave Johnson (1B)	136	454	56	114	18	0	15	62	1	.251
Mike Lum	106	361	50	84	11	2	11	50	0	.233
Norm Miller	42	41	1	7	1	0	1	5	0	.171
Ivan Murrell	73	133	11	33	1	1	2	12	0	.248
Johnny Oates (C)	100	291	22	65	10	0	1	21	2	.223
Rowland Office	131	248	20	61	16	1	3	31	5	.246
Marty Perez (2B)	127	447	51	116	20	5	2	34	2	.260
Jack Pierce	6	9	1	1	0	0	0	0	0	.111
Craig Robinson (SS)	145	452	52	104	4	6	0	29	11	.230
Frank Tepedino	78	169	11	39	5	1	0	16	1	.231
	163	5,533	661	1,375	202	37	120	599	72	.249

	W	L	G	GS	CG	IP	H	BB	SO	ERA
Jack Aker	0	1	17	0	0	16⅔	17	9	7	3.78
Mike Beard	0	0	6	0	0	9⅓	5	1	7	2.89
Buzz Capra	16	8	39	27	11	217	163	84	137	2.28*
Jamie Easterly	0	0	3	0	0	2⅔	6	4	0	16.88
Danny Frisella	3	4	36	1	0	41⅔	37	28	27	5.18
Gary Gentry	0	0	3	1	0	6⅔	4	2	0	1.35
Roric Harrison	6	11	20	20	3	126	148	49	46	4.71
Tom House	6	2	56	0	0	102⅔	74	27	64	1.93
Lew Krausse	4	3	29	4	0	66⅔	65	32	27	4.18
Max Leon	4	7	34	2	1	75	68	14	38	2.64
Carl Morton	16	12	38	38	7	274⅔	293*	89	113	3.15
Joe Niekro	3	2	27	2	0	43	36	18	31	3.56
Phil Niekro	20*	13	41	39	18*	302⅓*	249	88	195	2.38
Ron Reed	10	11	28	28	6	186	171	41	78	3.39
Mike Thompson	0	0	1	1	0	4	7	2	2	4.50
	88	74		163	46	1,474⅓*	1,343	488	772	3.05

Shutouts—P. Niekro (6), Capra (5), Reed (2), Leon, Morton
Saves—House (11), Frisella (6), Leon (3), Capra, P. Niekro

1975

Record: 67–94
Finish: Fifth (West)
Games Behind: 40½
Managers: Clyde King, Connie Ryan

You had to go back to 1942 to find a Braves team that was worse than the one Clyde King fielded in 1975. That '42 club of manager Casey Stengel played to a .399 percentage and finished 44 games out of first. Thirty-three years later, King's Braves played only 17 percentage points better and finished just 3½ games closer to first.

Don't think Atlanta didn't notice. Attendance plunged to 534,672, still the worst in the franchise's history in the South. A very dark era in Braves history was under way.

As is the case with almost any team this bad, the Braves could neither hit, pitch, field, nor run. They were last, or close to it, in nearly every major team statistical department. It's a wonder they were able to finish three games ahead of Houston, who was last in the West.

King, who was presented a two-year contract as manager after rescuing the team the year before, was fired August 30, the day the club was mathematically eliminated. Coach Connie Ryan stepped in to finish the season.

The pitching, which bordered on brilliant in 1974, fell apart quickly, mainly because of injuries. After leading the league in ERA the year before, Buzz Capra experienced shoulder woes. Phil Niekro barely broke even, due in large part to a bad back. Reliever Max Leon also had a bad shoulder. Ron Reed and Roric Harrison were traded. Carl Morton was the club's biggest winner for the second time in three years, but his record suffered from lack of support.

The once-proud offense finished with the worst batting average (.244) in the league. Outfielder Rowland Office led the regulars at just .290. Ralph Garr's average dropped 75 points.

Some of the offensive inadequacy might have been averted if an off-season deal had gone off as planned. The Braves acquired—or so they thought—slugger Richie Allen from the White Sox for Jim Essian and cash. However, Allen refused to report, and on May 7, Atlanta sent him to Philadelphia, along with Johnny Oates, in exchange for Barry Bonnell, Essian, and cash.

Darrell Evans committed 36 errors at third base, and Larvell Blanks made 25 at shortstop.

If there was a highlight, it came September 5 when the organization honored Niekro in a pregame ceremony as the last of the original Atlanta Braves. Three nights later, only 737 people paid to get into the stadium.

	G	AB	R	H	2B	3B	HR	RBI	SB	AVG
Dusty Baker (OF)	142	494	63	129	18	2	19	72	12	.261
Bob Beall	20	31	2	7	2	0	0	1	0	.226
Rob Belloir	43	105	11	23	2	1	0	9	0	.219
Larvell Blanks (SS)	141	471	49	110	13	3	3	38	4	.234
Vic Correll (C)	103	325	37	70	12	2	11	39	0	.215
Darrell Evans (3B)	156	567	82	138	22	2	22	73	12	.243
Ralph Garr (OF)	151	625	74	174	26	11*	6	31	14	.278
Cito Gaston	64	141	17	34	4	0	6	15	1	.241
Rod Gilbreath	90	202	24	49	3	1	2	16	5	.243
Ed Goodson	47	76	5	16	2	0	1	8	0	.211
Dave Johnson	1	1	0	1	1	0	0	1	0	1.000
Mike Lum	124	364	32	83	8	2	8	36	2	.228
Dave May	82	203	28	56	8	0	12	40	1	.276
Joe Nolan	4	4	0	1	0	0	0	0	0	.250
Johnny Oates	8	18	0	4	1	0	0	0	0	.222
Rowland Office (OF)	126	355	30	103	14	1	3	30	2	.290
Marty Perez (2B)	120	461	50	127	14	2	2	34	2	.275
Biff Pocoroba	67	188	15	48	7	1	1	22	0	.255
Craig Robinson	10	17	1	1	0	0	0	0	0	.059
Frank Tepedino	8	7	0	0	0	0	0	0	0	.000
Earl Williams (1B)	111	383	42	92	13	0	11	50	0	.240
	161	5,424	583	1,323	179	28	107	541	55	.244

	W	L	G	GS	CG	IP	H	BB	SO	ERA
Mike Beard	4	0	34	2	0	70⅓	71	28	27	3.20
Buzz Capra	4	7	12	12	5	78⅓	77	28	35	4.25
Bruce DalCanton	2	7	26	9	0	67	63	24	38	3.36
Adrian Devine	1	0	5	2	0	16⅓	19	7	8	4.41
Jamie Easterly	2	9	21	13	0	68⅔	73	42	34	4.98
Gary Gentry	1	1	7	2	0	20	25	8	10	4.95
Preston Hanna	0	0	4	0	0	5⅔	7	5	2	1.59
Roric Harrison	3	4	15	7	2	54⅔	58	19	22	4.77
Tom House	7	7	58	0	0	79⅓	79	36	36	3.18
Frank LaCorte	0	3	3	2	0	13⅔	13	6	10	5.27
Max Leon	2	1	50	1	0	85	90	33	53	4.13
Carl Morton	17	16	39	39	11	277⅔	302*	82	78	3.50
Phil Niekro	15	15	39	37	13	275⅔	285	72	144	3.20
Blue Moon Odom	1	7	15	10	0	56	78	28	30	7.07
Ron Reed	4	5	10	10	1	74⅔	93	16	40	4.22
Ray Sadecki	2	3	25	5	0	66⅓	73	21	24	4.21
Elias Sosa	2	2	43	0	0	62⅓	70	29	31	4.48
Mike Thompson	0	6	16	10	0	51⅔	60	32	42	4.70
Pablo Torrealba	0	1	6	0	0	6⅔	7	3	5	1.35
	67	94		161	32	1,430	1,543*	519	669	3.91

Shutouts—Morton (2), Niekro
Saves—House (11), Leon (6), DalCanton (3), Sosa (2), Harrison, Sadecki

1976

Record: 70–92
Finish: Sixth (West)
Games Behind: 32
Manager: Dave Bristol

The Braves got a new owner, a new manager, a new name for their home ballpark, a new pitching ace, and a new place in the National League standings in 1976. Not all were good.

The owner, of course, was the indomitable R. E. Turner III. The manager was Dave Bristol. Atlanta Stadium was renamed Atlanta–Fulton County Stadium. The pitcher was two-time 20-game winner and free-agent maverick Andy Messersmith. And the place in the standings was last, where the franchise hadn't finished since 1935. It was not a pretty way to celebrate the 100th anniversary of the National League.

Atlantan Ted Turner bought the club from the LaSalle Corporation for $10 million, the terms for which he said were "nothing down and easy payments." At the time, Turner was owner of WTBS, Channel 17, a UHF television station that broadcast Braves games. The Superstation had not been invented, and most of the nation had no idea who this guy with the thin mustache and squeaky voice was. It didn't take them long to find out that baseball had never before had an owner quite like this one.

Turner found more ways to get attention than the greatest players the game has known. At 37, he was baseball's youngest team president and easily the most outrageous. When he was introduced with the team on opening day, he jumped out of his seat and onto the field, sprinting to the mound. The fans loved him immediately.

Turner sat by the Braves dugout chewing tobacco, drinking beer, and even taking off his shirt on hot afternoons. Among his stunts were sweeping off the bases between innings, participating in a motorized bathtub race, and pushing a baseball around the bases with his nose. The pathetic Braves needed fan support, and Turner would go to any length to bring a few extra patrons through the gate.

One of Turner's first bold moves was the signing of Messersmith, who had found a way to beat the reserve clause and become the game's first big-name free agent. He played the 1975 season without a contract with the Dodgers, then was ruled a free agent in a decision by arbitrator Peter Seitz that was upheld by a federal judge.

Coming off a 19-win season in which he led the league in complete games, shutouts, innings, and opponents' batting average, Messersmith was a hot commodity, though many owners were hesitant to pursue him for fear of opening a series of bidding wars for players. But Turner didn't hesitate, signing the 30-year-old right-hander to a "lifetime" contract for $1 million. The money was big news in 1976.

To help Turner maximize his investment, Messersmith agreed to wear the number 17 on his uniform and the "nickname" Channel above it. The baseball lords, who quickly banned Messersmith's jersey, were suddenly wondering just

Jerry Royster never provided the consistent spark the Braves thought they were getting when they acquired him from the Dodgers.

what they had allowed to buy into their ultraconservative, tradition-rich institution.

However, the new manager, brought in to play sort of a ringleader in this developing circus, was indeed quite conservative. Dave Bristol was out of the old school of managing, the fiery sort. His two previous managerial stints, neither particularly successful, were in Cincinnati and Milwaukee.

The team Bristol was given to work with barely resembled the 1975 Braves. Five of the eight regulars were new to Atlanta.

Third baseman Jerry Royster and left fielder Jimmy Wynn were obtained in a six-player exchange that sent Dusty Baker to the Dodgers. Shortstop Darrel Chaney, a Bristol favorite, was picked up from Cincinnati for Mike Lum. Right fielder Ken Henderson came from the White Sox in a four-player deal that sent Ralph Garr to the American League. And two months into the schedule, Atlanta got first baseman Willie Montanez from San Francisco in a six-player trade that sent Darrell Evans and Marty Perez to the Giants.

The flurry of activity was useless, though. The Braves won three more games than in '75 and finished 8½ games closer to first place. But the bottom line was last place.

Injuries played a significant role in the club's disappointing season. Leading the list of the wounded was Messersmith, who was reduced to a .500 pitcher by a hamstring pull and a sore shoulder. Center fielder Rowland Office, who put together an early 29-game hitting streak, suffered a mid-July knee injury that made him almost useless the rest of the way.

But even good health wouldn't have made this a good team. The Braves lost 13 in a row at one point, the franchise's longest losing streak since 1906.

The highlights were the play of newcomer Montanez and the pitching of old standby Phil Niekro. The flamboyant Montanez with 206 hits for two teams was second in the league to Pete Rose, and he batted .321 as a Brave. Niekro, fifth in the league in strikeouts, managed to finish six games over .500, quite a feat considering the support he usually received. On May 29, Niekro gave up a particularly memorable home run—it was the only one his brother Joe, then a pitcher for Houston, ever hit in his career.

	W	L	G	GS	CG	IP	H	BB	SO	ERA
Al Autry	1	0	1	1	0	5	4	3	3	5.40
Mike Beard	0	2	30	0	0	33⅔	38	14	8	4.28
Rick Camp	0	1	5	1	0	11⅓	13	2	6	6.35
Buzz Capra	0	1	5	0	0	9⅓	9	6	4	8.68
Bruce DalCanton	3	5	42	1	0	73⅓	67	42	36	3.56
Adrian Devine	5	6	48	1	0	73	72	26	48	3.21
Jamie Easterly	1	1	4	4	0	22	23	13	11	4.91
Preston Hanna	0	0	5	0	0	8	11	4	3	4.50
Frank LaCorte	3	12	19	17	1	105⅓	97	53	79	4.70
Max Leon	2	4	30	0	0	36	32	15	16	2.75
Mike Marshall	2	1	24	0	0	36⅔	35	14	17	3.19
Andy Messersmith	11	11	29	28	12	207⅓	166	74	135	3.04
Roger Moret	3	5	27	12	1	77½	84	27	30	5.00
Carl Morton	4	9	26	24	1	140½	172	45	42	4.17
Phil Niekro	17	11	38	37	10	270⅔	249	101	173	3.29
Dick Ruthven	14	17*	36	36	8	240⅓	255	90	142	4.19
Elias Sosa	4	4	21	0	0	35⅓	41	13	32	5.35
Pablo Torrealba	0	2	36	0	0	53	67	22	33	3.57
	70	92		162	33	1,438	1,435	564	818	3.86

Shutouts—Ruthven (4), Messersmith (3), Niekro (2), Morton
Saves—Devine (9), Marshall (6), Leon (3), Sosa (3), Torrealba (2) Beard, DalCanton, Messersmith, Moret

Rowland Office put together a 29-game hitting streak in 1976, but few fans came out to see him or his teammates.

In the final home game of the season, San Francisco's John Montefusco pitched a no-hitter, beating the Braves, 9–0. But not even that put a damper on the season for Turner, who toasted the 1,369 fans in attendance with a post-game champagne party.

	G	AB	R	H	2B	3B	HR	RBI	SB	AVG
Brian Asselstine	11	33	2	7	0	0	1	3	0	.212
Rob Belloir	30	60	5	12	2	0	0	4	0	.200
Darrel Chaney (SS)	153	496	42	125	20	8	1	50	5	.252
Vic Correll (C)	69	200	26	45	6	2	5	16	0	.225
Terry Crowley	7	6	0	0	0	0	0	1	0	.000
Mike Eden	5	8	0	0	0	0	0	1	0	.000
Darrell Evans	44	139	11	24	0	0	1	10	3	.173
Cito Gaston	69	134	15	39	4	0	4	25	1	.291
Rod Gilbreath (2B)	116	383	57	96	11	8	1	32	7	.251
Ken Henderson (OF)	133	435	52	114	19	0	13	61	5	.262
Lee Lacy	50	180	25	49	4	2	3	20	2	.272
Dave May	105	214	27	46	5	3	3	23	5	.215
Willie Montanez (1B)	103	420	52	135	14	0	9	64	0	.321
Junior Moore	20	26	1	7	1	0	0	2	0	.269
Dale Murphy	19	65	3	17	6	0	0	9	0	.262
Rowland Office (OF)	99	359	51	101	17	1	4	34	2	.281
Tom Paciorek	111	324	39	94	10	4	4	36	2	.290
Marty Perez	31	96	12	24	4	0	1	6	0	.250
Biff Pocoroba	54	174	16	42	7	0	0	14	1	.241
Craig Robinson	15	17	4	4	0	0	0	3	0	.235
Pat Rockett	4	5	0	1	0	0	0	0	0	.200
Jerry Royster (3B)	149	533	65	132	13	1	5	45	24	.248
Pete Varney	5	10	0	1	0	0	0	0	0	.100
Earl Williams	61	184	18	39	3	0	9	26	0	.212
Jimmy Wynn (OF)	148	449	75	93	19	1	17	66	16	.207
	162	5,345	620	1,309	170	30	82	586	74	.245

1977

Record: 61–101
Finish: Sixth (West)
Games Behind: 37
Managers: Dave Bristol, Ted Turner

The era of free agency was upon baseball, and Ted Turner wasn't about to let Andy Messersmith's injury-plagued, so-so performance in 1976 slow him down in pursuing players.

Because of his zeal, the colorful owner once again wound up being more of a story than the team.

After trading five players, including pitcher Carl Morton, and tossing in $250,000 to obtain slugger Jeff Burroughs, the 1974 American League MVP, from Texas, Turner opened his checkbook for free-agent outfielder Gary Matthews.

In the process, Turner got himself and the Braves in hot water with the Commissioner's office. Turner signed Matthews to a $1.2 million contract for five years. However, the Giants, Matthews' former employer, cried foul. A member of the Braves organization first approached Matthews when he was under contract to San Francisco in 1976. Turner also openly flaunted his intention to sign Matthews in front of Giants owner Bob Lurie.

Two tampering charges cost the Braves $10,000 and their first-round picks in the January and June drafts. Turner also was suspended for a year. The Braves filed a suit against Commissioner Bowie Kuhn over the severity of the penalty, and during the legal process, in which a federal court upheld Kuhn's punishment of Turner but returned the team's draft picks, the Braves owner was able to resume his association with the club.

Turner took advantage of the temporary leave from baseball jail to stir up even more trouble—or fun—depending on your perspective.

On May 11, with the Braves having lost 16 in a row, Turner suddenly sent manager Dave Bristol on a "scouting assignment" and took over the team himself. He pulled on a uniform, stuck a wad of tobacco in his cheek, and sat in the dugout as "manager" for a game against Pittsburgh so he "could find out what's wrong." The Braves lost, 2–1, and Turner's managerial stint ended as quickly as it started. National League president Chub Feeney, citing an obscure rule prohibiting a manager from having a financial stake in the team, ordered Turner out of the dugout.

Bristol returned the next day, and the Braves beat the Pirates, 6–1. Still, the Atlanta-record 17-game losing streak left the team at 9–22. It was a deep hole, and one that would only get deeper as this miserable season continued.

The final tally of 101 losses was the worst showing by the franchise since 1935. Atlanta pitchers gave up more runs than any other team in baseball; the offense scored fewer runs than all but one other team in the division; the Braves were 11th in the league in steals; and only two teams in the league made more errors.

Messersmith underwent arm surgery, and another key member of the pitching staff, Dick Ruthven, had to have tendons in his heel repaired after slipping on a wet base in St. Louis. But healthy or wounded, this was not a good team.

Phil Niekro became the first 20-game loser in Atlanta history, though he did lead the league in strikeouts, innings, and complete games.

The only real excitement was provided by Burroughs, who finished second in the league in home runs (41) and fourth in RBIs (114) in his first season with the team.

Bristol, who had a year remaining on his contract, was fired. Turner used the time off under suspension for a successful defense of the America's Cup. Unfortunately, his knowledge of sailing was of no use in turning around his baseball team.

	G	AB	R	H	2B	3B	HR	RBI	SB	AVG
Brian Asselstine	83	124	12	26	6	0	4	17	1	.210
Rob Belloir	6	1	2	0	0	0	0	0	0	.000
Barry Bonnell	100	360	41	108	11	0	1	45	7	.300
Jeff Burroughs (OF)	154	579	91	157	19	1	41	114	4	.271
Darrel Chaney	74	209	22	42	7	2	3	15	0	.201
Vic Correll	54	144	16	30	7	0	7	16	2	.208
Cito Gaston	56	85	6	23	4	0	3	21	1	.271
Rod Gilbreath (2B)	128	407	47	99	15	2	8	43	3	.243
Gary Matthews (OF)	148	555	89	157	25	5	17	64	22	.283
Willie Montanez (1B)	136	544	70	156	31	1	20	68	1	.287
Junior Moore (3B)	112	361	41	94	9	3	5	34	4	.260
Dale Murphy	18	76	5	24	8	1	2	14	0	.316
Joe Nolan	62	82	13	23	3	0	3	9	1	.280
Rowland Office (OF)	124	428	42	103	13	1	5	39	2	.241
Tom Paciorek	72	155	20	37	8	0	3	15	1	.239
Biff Pocoroba (C)	113	321	46	93	24	1	8	44	3	.290
Craig Robinson	27	29	4	6	1	0	0	1	0	.207
Pat Rockett (SS)	93	264	27	67	10	0	1	24	1	.254
Jerry Royster	140	445	64	96	10	2	6	28	28	.216
Larry Whisenton	4	4	1	1	0	0	0	1	0	.250
	162	5,534	678	1,404	218	20	139	638	82	.254

	W	L	G	GS	CG	IP	H	BB	SO	ERA
Mike Beard	0	0	4	0	0	4⅔	14	2	1	9.64
Larry Bradford	0	0	2	0	0	2⅔	3	0	1	3.38
Rick Camp	6	3	54	0	0	78⅔	89	47	51	4.00
Dave Campbell	0	6	65	0	0	88⅔	78	33	42	3.05
Buzz Capra	6	11	45	16	0	139⅓	142	80	100	5.36
Don Collins	3	9	40	6	0	70⅔	82	41	27	5.09
Mike Davey	0	0	16	0	0	16	19	9	7	5.06
Jamie Easterly	2	4	22	5	0	58⅔	72	30	37	6.14
Preston Hanna	2	6	17	9	1	60	69	34	37	4.95
Steve Hargan	0	3	16	5	0	36⅓	49	16	18	6.87
Bob Johnson	0	1	15	0	0	22⅓	24	14	16	7.25
Steve Kline	0	0	16	0	0	20⅓	21	12	10	6.64
Frank LaCorte	1	8	14	7	0	37	67	29	28	11.68
Max Leon	4	4	31	9	0	81⅓	89	25	44	3.97
Mickey Mahler	1	2	5	5	0	23	31	9	14	6.26
Mike Marshall	1	0	4	0	0	6	12	2	6	9.00
Joey McLaughlin	0	0	3	2	0	6	10	3	0	15.00
Andy Messersmith	5	4	16	16	1	102⅓	101	39	69	4.40
Phil Niekro	16	20*	44	43*	20*	330⅓*	315*	164*	262*	4.03
Dick Ruthven	7	13	25	23	6	151	158	62	84	4.23
Eddie Solomon	6	6	18	16	0	88⅔	110	34	54	4.57
Duane Theiss	1	1	17	0	0	20⅓	26	16	7	6.53
	61	101*		162	28	1,445⅓	1,581*	701*	915	4.85

Shutouts—Niekro (2)
Saves—Campbell (13), Camp (10), Collins (2), Davey (2), Easterly, Hanna, Kline, Leon

1978

Record: 69–93
Finish: Sixth (West)
Games Behind: 26
Manager: Bobby Cox

Just because the Braves were in annual contention for the title "worst team in baseball" during this gloomy period of their history didn't mean they were boring. In fact, they usually had more going on to attract attention than the average pennant contender. There was no better example than the events of the 1978 season.

It was the year of Bobby Cox, Dale Murphy, Bob Horner, Pete Rose, Gene Garber, Larry McWilliams, and Jim Bouton.

To replace Dave Bristol as manager, the Braves sifted through numerous candidates, including 39-year-old Phil Niekro, who applied to be pitcher-manager.

The other four finalists for the job were former National League MVP Ken Boyer, Hank Aaron's brother Tommie, Hall of Fame catcher Yogi Berra, and Cox, easily the least known of the group to Atlanta fans, who was the Yankees' first base coach in 1977.

A former major league infielder of no distinction, the 36-year-old Cox had managed in the minors but not in the majors. Nevertheless, Ted Turner decided to make him the youngest manager in baseball, putting him in charge of the organization's youth movement.

The Braves sold Andy Messersmith to the Yankees, traded Willie Montanez to Texas and jettisoned a host of other players to make room for prospects such as 22-year-old Murphy. A catcher who had developed a block on throwing accurately, Murphy was installed as the team's regular first baseman. Though he led the league with 20 errors at the position, he immediately displayed the offensive potential that would make him one of the team's all-time greats.

Another youngster with considerable offensive capability was Horner, who was playing for Arizona State when the season began. He set a single-season NCAA record with 25 home runs and was taken by the Braves as the first player in the June draft.

When Horner signed his contract on June 13, it was expected that he would go to the minors to develop like other players. However, he asked general manager Bill Lucas for the opportunity to play immediately in Atlanta. To everyone's amazement, Lucas consented, and on June 16, Horner—less than two months from his 21st birthday—started at third base.

In one of the most stunning individual accomplishments in the team's Atlanta history, Horner hit a home run in his third at bat against Pittsburgh veteran Bert Blyleven. That was only the beginning. Horner went on to be named National League Rookie of the Year, the only man ever to win that honor and College Player of the Year in the same season.

In June, the Braves acquired the services of Garber, one of the better relievers in the league, from Philadelphia in exchange for Dick Ruthven. Though Garber wasn't particularly enthralled with the deal, he filled a big void in the Atlanta bullpen and helped play out the most dramatic event of the season.

On July 31, Rose brought a 43-game hitting streak to Atlanta–Fulton County Stadium in an attempt to break "Wee Willie" Keeler's all-time National League record of 44. The Cincinnati great tied Keeler's record with a single off Niekro. On August 1, Cox sent out McWilliams, a 24-year-old rookie left-hander, to try and prevent Rose from breaking Keeler's record.

In his second at bat of the evening, Rose lined a ball up the middle that McWilliams somehow caught with a behind-the-back stab. Later, with the Braves on the verge of a 16–4 victory, it remained for Garber to get the final out of the ninth against a hitless Rose. The sidearming right-hander struck out Rose with a 2–2 change-up, ending the immense

buildup that had begun for a possible assault on Joe DiMaggio's all-time 56-game hitting streak.

The season also included Jeff Burroughs' unlikely quest for the batting title. An April spree in which he was 14-for-18 pushed his average to .413, and he kept the league lead until September. At season's end, he still led the league in on-base percentage and was fifth in slugging average.

Niekro fell just short of his third 20-victory season when the Braves were shut out in his final three starts. However, he led the league in complete games and innings, was second in strikeouts and shutouts, and was presented a $100,000 bonus by Turner.

The sideshow that always seemed to accompany Turner's teams back then reached a peak in September. That's when 39-year-old *Ball Four* author Jim Bouton, who hadn't pitched in the majors since 1970 but had been attempting a "comeback" in the minors, used a knuckleball to humiliate the Giants, 4–1. It was the only victory of his final big league fling.

	G	AB	R	H	2B	3B	HR	RBI	SB	AVG
Brian Asselstine	39	103	11	28	3	3	2	13	2	.272
Bob Beall	108	185	29	45	8	0	1	16	4	.243
Rob Belloir	2	1	0	1	1	0	0	0	0	1.000
Bruce Benedict	22	52	3	13	2	0	0	1	0	.250
Barry Bonnell	117	304	36	73	11	3	1	16	12	.240
Jeff Burroughs (OF)	153	488	72	147	30	6	23	77	1	.301
Darrel Chaney (SS)	89	245	27	55	9	1	3	20	1	.224
Cito Gaston	60	118	5	27	1	0	1	9	0	.229
Rod Gilbreath	116	326	22	80	13	3	3	31	7	.245
Bob Horner (3B)	89	323	50	86	17	1	23	63	0	.266
Glenn Hubbard	44	163	15	42	4	0	2	13	2	.258
Jerry Maddox	7	14	1	3	0	0	0	1	0	.214
Gary Matthews (OF)	129	474	75	135	20	5	18	62	8	.285
Eddie Miller	6	21	5	3	1	0	0	2	3	.143
Dale Murphy (1B)	151	530	66	120	14	3	23	79	11	.226
Joe Nolan	95	213	22	49	7	3	4	22	3	.230
Rowland Office (OF)	146	404	40	101	13	1	9	40	8	.250
Tom Paciorek	5	9	2	3	0	0	0	0	0	.333
Biff Pocoroba (C)	92	289	21	70	8	0	6	34	0	.242
Pat Rockett	55	142	6	20	2	0	0	4	1	.141
Jerry Royster (2B)	140	529	67	137	17	8	2	35	27	.259
Chico Ruiz	18	46	3	13	3	0	0	2	0	.283
Hank Small	1	4	0	0	0	0	0	0	0	.000
Larry Whisenton	6	16	1	3	1	0	0	2	0	.188
	162	5,381	600	1,313	191	39	123	558	90	.244

	W	L	G	GS	CG	IP	H	BB	SO	ERA
Tommy Boggs	2	8	16	12	1	59	80	26	21	6.71
Jim Bouton	1	3	5	5	0	29	25	21	10	4.97
Rick Camp	2	4	42	4	0	74⅓	99	32	23	3.75
Dave Campbell	4	4	53	0	0	69⅓	67	49	45	4.80
Mike Davey	0	0	3	0	0	2⅔	1	1	0	0.00
Adrian Devine	5	4	31	6	0	65⅓	84	25	26	5.92
Jamie Easterly	3	6	37	6	0	78	91	45	42	5.65
Gene Garber	4	4	43	0	0	78⅓	58	13	61	2.53
Preston Hanna	7	13	29	28	0	140½	132	93	90	5.13
Frank LaCorte	0	1	2	2	0	14⅔	9	4	7	3.68
Max Leon	0	0	5	0	0	5⅔	6	4	1	6.35
Mickey Mahler	4	11	34	21	1	134⅔	130	66	92	4.68
Larry McWilliams	9	3	15	15	3	99⅓	84	35	42	2.81
Phil Niekro	19	18*	44	42*	22*	334⅓*	295*	102	248	2.88
Dick Ruthven	2	6	13	13	2	81	78	28	45	4.11
Craig Skok	3	2	43	0	0	62	64	27	28	4.35
Eddie Solomon	4	6	37	8	0	106	98	50	64	4.08
Duane Theiss	0	0	3	0	0	6½	3	3	3	1.42
	69	93		162	29	1,440⅓	1,404	624*	848	4.08

Shutouts—Niekro (4), Boggs, McWilliams, Ruthven
Saves—Garber (22), Devine (3), Skok (2), Solomon (2), Campbell, Easterly, Niekro

Gene Garber ended Pete Rose's 44-game hitting streak with a ninth-inning strikeout.

1979

Record: 66–94
Finish: Sixth (West)
Games Behind: 23½
Manager: Bobby Cox

The Braves maintained their viselike grip on last place in the West in 1979, but their biggest loss came off the field.

On May 1, general manager Bill Lucas collapsed at home from a massive cerebral hemorrhage brought on by an undetected aneurysm. He died the following day.

Lucas was the highest-ranking black official in the game and was well liked by the young players in the Braves organization, many of whom he had developed when he was farm director.

Lucas had been under enormous strain, though there was no way to correlate that with his death. In the off-season, he'd constantly been in the middle of a bitter contract dispute between Bob Horner and Ted Turner in which Horner's agent, Bucky Woy, attempted to have his client declared a free agent.

Although Horner failed to win free agency in a June arbitration hearing, he wound up becoming the highest-paid player in franchise history when he signed a three-year contract for $1.2 million.

Adding to Lucas's woes was a poor start by the team. Horner, the league's Rookie of the Year the previous season, injured his ankle opening night and missed the next 32 games. The following day, Houston's Ken Forsch beat Atlanta, 6–0, with a no-hitter.

Matters only got worse as the season progressed, but the Braves never stopped fighting. In fact, on May 9, they were involved in four bench-clearing brawls with Pittsburgh. Atlanta's Gary Matthews and Pittsburgh's John Milner traded grand slams in the Pirates' 17–9 victory, which included the ejection of five players, both managers, and three coaches.

Dale Murphy was one of the few Braves who started well. He had 13 home runs and 36 RBIs in May when he tore cartilage in his knee and had to undergo surgery. Bobby Cox had moved Murphy back behind the plate in an attempt to get Mike Lum's bat in the lineup at first base. Murphy returned late in the season but didn't regain his timing. He never caught again, and the knee injury was the first of a series of knee problems that eventually brought Murphy's great career to a premature end.

Horner returned from his injury to have an excellent season, finishing fourth in the league in home runs (33) and fifth in batting average (.314). Gary Matthews had his best year as a Brave, establishing career highs in several departments. Jerry Royster, who played third and second, tied the Atlanta record for steals (35) and had his best all-around season.

Niekro continued to roll along at age 40. He got his 20th win September 26, beating Houston and younger brother Joe, 9–4. The brothers tied for the league lead in victories and were the only two 20-game winners in the league. They became the second pair of brothers to win 20 in the same season, joining the Perrys, Gaylord and Jim, who did so in 1970.

Bob Horner and Dale Murphy provided the Braves with one of the best one-two offensive punches in baseball.

Unfortunately, Niekro also lost 20, becoming the first National Leaguer to win and lose 20 in the same season since 1905. The only Brave to win in double figures in 1979, Niekro picked up a $20,000 bonus from Turner.

After two excellent seasons with the Braves, Jeff Burroughs dropped off significantly in all offensive categories. Glenn Hubbard began a long run as the team's regular second baseman but contributed little with his bat.

Pitching remained the team's biggest—of many—problem areas. The Atlanta staff had the highest ERA (4.18) in the league. The Braves also had the league's worst defense, committing 20 more errors than anyone else.

	G	AB	R	H	2B	3B	HR	RBI	SB	AVG
Brian Asselstine	8	10	1	1	0	0	0	0	0	.100
Bob Beall	17	15	1	2	2	0	0	1	0	.133
Bruce Benedict (C)	76	204	14	46	11	0	0	15	1	.225
Barry Bonnell	127	375	47	97	20	3	12	45	8	.259
Jeff Burroughs (OF)	116	397	49	89	14	1	11	47	2	.224
Darrel Chaney	63	117	15	19	5	0	0	10	2	.162
Pepe Frias (SS)	140	475	41	123	18	4	1	44	3	.259
Bob Horner (3B)	121	487	66	153	15	1	33	98	0	.314
Glenn Hubbard	97	325	34	75	12	0	3	29	0	.231
Mike Lum	111	217	27	54	6	0	6	27	0	.249
Mike Macha	6	13	2	2	0	0	0	1	0	.154
Gary Matthews (OF)	156	631	97	192	34	5	27	90	18	.304
Eddie Miller	27	113	12	35	1	0	0	5	15	.310
Dale Murphy (1B)	104	384	53	106	7	2	21	57	6	.276
Joe Nolan	89	230	28	57	9	3	4	21	1	.248
Rowland Office (OF)	124	277	35	69	14	2	2	37	5	.249
Biff Pocoroba	28	38	6	12	4	0	0	4	1	.316
Jerry Royster (2B)	154	601	103	164	25	6	3	51	35	.273
Charlie Spikes	66	93	12	26	8	0	3	21	0	.280
Jim Wessinger	10	7	2	0	0	0	0	0	0	.000
Larry Whisenton	13	37	3	9	2	1	0	1	1	.243
	160	5,422	669	1,389	220	28	126	626	98	.256

	W	L	G	GS	CG	IP	H	BB	SO	ERA
Tommy Boggs	0	2	3	3	0	12⅔	21	4	1	6.39
Larry Bradford	1	0	21	0	0	19	11	10	11	0.95
Tony Brizzolara	6	9	20	19	2	107⅓	133	33	64	5.28
Adrian Devine	1	2	40	0	0	66⅔	84	25	22	3.24
Jamie Easterly	0	0	4	0	0	2⅔	7	3	3	13.50
Gene Garber	6	16	68	0	0	106	121	24	56	4.33
Preston Hanna	1	1	6	4	0	24½	27	15	15	2.96
Frank LaCorte	0	0	6	0	0	8⅓	9	5	6	7.56
Mickey Mahler	5	11	26	18	1	100	123	47	71	5.85
Rick Mahler	0	0	15	0	0	22	28	11	12	6.14
Rick Matula	8	10	28	28	1	171⅓	193	64	67	4.15
Bo McLaughlin	1	1	37	1	0	49⅔	63	16	45	4.89
Joey McLaughlin	5	3	37	0	0	69	54	34	40	2.48
Larry McWilliams	3	2	13	13	1	66⅔	69	22	32	5.56
Phil Niekro	21*	20*	44	44*	23*	342⅓	311*	113*	208	3.39
Craig Skok	1	3	44	0	0	54½	58	17	30	3.98
Eddie Solomon	7	14	31	30	4	186	184	51	96	4.21
	66	94		160	32	1,407⅔	1,496	494	779	4.18

Shutouts—Niekro
Saves—Garber (25), J. McLaughlin (5), Bradford (2), Skok (2)

1980

Record: 81–80
Finish: Fourth (West)
Games Behind: 11
Manager: Bobby Cox

At long last, the Braves showed some noticeable improvement in 1980. They climbed out of the National League West basement for the first time under Ted Turner's ownership, and they finished over .500 for the first time since 1974.

A lot of organizations would have been disappointed with fourth place, but it was a refreshing break for the Braves, who hadn't ended a season that high in six years.

Some significant off-season acquisitions helped Bobby Cox finally get his team moving upward in the standings. The most significant addition was first baseman Chris Chambliss, who was obtained from Toronto in a five-player deal. He provided veteran leadership to a young team, as well as steady play offensively and defensively.

Another benefit of Chambliss's presence was that it enabled Cox to shift Dale Murphy from first base to center field, where he prospered, making his first National League All-Star team.

The Braves also picked up a pair of veteran pitchers, right-hander Doyle Alexander and left-handed reliever Al "Mad Hungarian" Hrabosky. Alexander, acquired from Texas, helped stabilize the starting rotation. Hrabosky, however, proved to be another in a long line of ill-advised free-agent signings for Turner. The Braves gave Hrabosky a five-year contract for $2.2 million, but he was well past his prime and played only three seasons.

Third baseman Bob Horner missed 35 of the first 61 games with various ailments, and the team even tried to send him to Richmond in April because of a slow start. But he fought off the demotion and went on a binge, mostly in July, in which he hit 15 home runs in 23 games. Horner was named the league's Player of the Month for July after hitting 14 homers, one shy of the major league record, and driving in 33 runs.

At age 41, Phil Niekro struggled and finished three games below .500 (15–18) in spite of winning seven in a row late in the season. However, talented young right-hander Tommy Boggs finally showed signs of reaching his potential, winning seven of his last eight decisions.

The surprise of the year was right-hander Rick Camp, who missed all of 1979 with elbow surgery. The Braves didn't know if Camp would even pitch again, but he won a spot on the team as a nonroster player in spring training and became the ace of the bullpen. He set a franchise record with 77 appearances.

	G	AB	R	H	2B	3B	HR	RBI	SB	AVG
Brian Asselstine	87	218	18	62	13	1	3	25	1	.284
Bruce Benedict (C)	120	359	18	91	14	1	2	34	3	.253
Larvell Blanks	88	221	23	45	6	0	2	12	1	.204
Jeff Burroughs (OF)	99	278	35	73	14	0	13	51	1	.263
Chris Chambliss (1B)	158	602	83	170	37	2	18	72	7	.282
Gary Cooper	21	2	3	0	0	0	0	0	2	.000
Luis Gomez (SS)	121	278	18	53	6	0	0	24	0	.191
Terry Harper	21	54	3	10	2	1	0	3	2	.185
Bob Horner (3B)	124	463	81	124	14	1	35	89	3	.268
Glenn Hubbard (2B)	117	431	55	107	21	3	9	43	7	.248
Mike Lum	93	83	7	17	3	0	0	5	0	.205
Gary Matthews (OF)	155	571	79	159	17	3	19	75	11	.278
Eddie Miller	11	19	3	3	0	0	0	0	1	.158
Dale Murphy (OF)	156	569	98	160	27	2	33	89	9	.281
Bill Nahorodny	59	157	14	38	12	0	5	18	0	.242
Joe Nolan	17	22	2	6	1	0	0	2	0	.273
Biff Pocoroba	70	83	7	22	4	0	2	8	1	.265
Rafael Ramirez	50	165	17	44	6	1	2	11	2	.267
Jerry Royster	123	392	42	95	17	5	1	20	22	.242
Chico Ruiz	25	26	3	8	2	1	0	2	0	.308
Charlie Spikes	41	36	6	10	1	0	0	2	0	.278
	161	5,402	630	1,352	226	22	144	597	73	.250

	W	L	G	GS	CG	IP	H	BB	SO	ERA
Doyle Alexander	14	11	35	35	7	231⅔	227	74	114	4.20
Tommy Boggs	12	9	32	26	4	192⅓	180	46	84	3.42
Larry Bradford	3	4	56	0	0	55⅓	49	22	32	2.44
Rick Camp	6	4	77	0	0	108⅓	92	29	33	1.91
Gene Garber	5	5	68	0	0	82⅓	95	24	51	3.83
Preston Hanna	2	0	32	2	0	79⅓	63	44	35	3.18
Al Hrabosky	4	2	45	0	0	59⅔	50	31	31	3.62
Rick Mahler	0	0	2	0	0	3⅔	2	0	1	2.45
Rick Matula	11	13	33	30	3	176⅔	195	60	62	4.58
Larry McWilliams	9	14	30	30	4	163⅔	188	39	77	4.95
Phil Niekro	15	18*	40	38*	11	275	256	85	176	3.63
	81	80		161	29	1,428	1,397	454	696	3.77

Shutouts—Boggs (3), Niekro (3), Alexander, Matula, McWilliams
Saves—Camp (22), Garber (7), Bradford (4), Hrabosky (3), Niekro

1981

Record: 50–56
Finish: Fourth (first half)
Fifth (second half)
Games Behind: 9½ (first half)
7½ (second half)
Manager: Bobby Cox

A players' strike interrupted the 1981 season and the Braves' quest for respectability. The result was that Bobby Cox lost his job . . . though he would return.

The schedule was split into prestrike and poststrike halves, with the winners meeting in a playoff to get into the National League Championship Series. The Braves didn't come close to contending in either half, but they helped create quite a controversy on October 3 when they beat the Reds, 4–3, behind two home runs by Bob Horner.

The defeat cost Cincinnati the second-half title and a post-season berth despite the fact that the Reds had the best over-all record in the majors.

Owner Ted Turner continued his relentless pursuit of free agents, signing outfielder Claudell Washington to a five-year contract and 42-year-old pitcher Gaylord Perry to a one-year deal. The Braves also rid themselves of a couple of out-fielders, Jeff Burroughs and Gary Matthews, who'd been key members of the team.

The roster shuffling saddled Cox with a team that couldn't hit. It's .243 average was last in the division and 11th in the league. Bob Horner, Dale Murphy, and Chris Chambliss all had off years, making it difficult for the Braves to generate any consistent offense. Horner did lead the team in home runs for the fourth straight year even though he missed 32 games with a broken wrist.

The Braves didn't have a .300 hitter and had no one with more than 15 homers, 51 RBIs, or 23 steals. Even with a short-ened season, those were low numbers.

The pitching, on the other hand, was surprisingly re-spectable at times. The staff ERA of 3.45 ranked fifth in the league, and it was 2.81 in the second half when Phil Niekro was particularly effective.

Rick Camp had his second consecutive excellent season as a reliever, finishing fourth in the league in saves (17) and leading the team in wins (9). Tommy Boggs, who looked so promising a year earlier, lost a club-record nine straight games. In six of those games, the Braves failed to give Boggs a run to work with, a testament to Atlanta's biggest problem all season. Unheralded rookie Rick Mahler showed promise by leading the team in ERA. And had it not been for the strike, Perry might have recorded his 300th victory, but he ended the season with 297 and was not re-signed.

Gaylord Perry hoped to win his 300th game with the Braves, but a mid-season strike in 1981 prevented it.

Cox broke in several young players, including catcher Bruce Benedict and shortstop Rafael Ramirez, who were about to help raise the franchise from its doldrums. How-ever, on October 7, Turner fired Cox, who quickly landed the manager's job in Toronto. Shortly thereafter, Turner hired former Braves catcher Joe Torre to try to get the Braves back on the road to improvement. He was the team's eighth manager since the move to Atlanta in 1966.

	G	AB	R	H	2B	3B	HR	RBI	SB	AVG
Brian Asselstine	56	86	8	22	5	0	2	10	1	.256
Bruce Benedict (C)	90	295	26	78	12	1	5	35	1	.264
Brett Butler	40	126	17	32	2	3	0	4	9	.254
Chris Chambliss (1B)	107	404	44	110	25	2	8	51	4	.272
Luis Gomez	35	35	4	7	0	0	0	1	0	.200
Albert Hall	6	2	1	0	0	0	0	0	0	.000
Terry Harper	40	73	9	19	1	0	2	8	5	.260
Bob Horner (3B)	79	300	42	83	10	0	15	42	2	.277
Glenn Hubbard (2B)	99	361	39	85	13	5	6	33	4	.235
Brook Jacoby	11	10	0	2	0	0	0	1	0	.200
Rufino Linares (OF)	78	253	27	67	9	2	5	25	8	.265
Mike Lum	10	11	1	1	0	0	0	0	0	.091
Eddie Miller	50	134	29	31	3	1	0	7	23	.231
Dale Murphy (OF)	104	369	43	91	12	1	13	50	14	.247
Bill Nahorodny	14	13	0	3	1	0	0	2	0	.231
Larry Owen	13	16	0	0	0	0	0	0	0	.000
Biff Pocoroba	57	122	4	22	4	0	0	8	0	.180
Bob Porter	17	14	2	4	1	0	0	4	0	.286
Rafael Ramirez (SS)	95	307	30	67	16	2	2	20	7	.218
Jerry Royster	64	93	13	19	4	1	0	9	7	.204
Paul Runge	10	27	2	7	1	0	0	2	0	.259
Matt Sinatro	12	32	4	9	1	1	0	4	1	.281
Ken Smith	5	3	0	1	1	0	0	0	0	.333
C. Washington (OF)	85	320	37	93	22	3	5	37	12	.291
Larry Whisenton	9	5	1	1	0	0	0	0	0	.200
	107	3,642	395	886	148	22	64	366	98	.243

	W	L	G	GS	CG	IP	H	BB	SO	ERA
Jose Alvarez	0	0	1	0	0	2	0	0	2	0.00
Steve Bedrosian	1	2	15	1	0	24⅓	15	15	9	4.44
Tommy Boggs	3	13	25	24	2	142⅔	140	54	81	4.10
Larry Bradford	2	0	25	0	0	26⅔	26	12	14	3.71
Rick Camp	9	3	48	0	0	76	68	12	47	1.78
Gene Garber	4	6	35	0	0	58¾	49	20	34	2.61
Luis Gomez	0	0	1	0	0	1	3	2	0	27.00
Preston Hanna	2	1	20	1	0	35⅓	45	23	22	6.37
Al Hrabosky	1	1	24	0	0	33¾	24	9	13	1.07
Rick Mahler	8	6	34	14	1	112⅓	109	43	54	2.80
Rick Matula	0	0	5	0	0	7	8	2	0	6.43
Larry McWilliams	2	1	6	5	2	37⅔	31	8	23	3.11
John Montefusco	2	3	26	9	0	77⅓	75	27	34	3.49
Phil Niekro	7	7	22	22	3	139⅓	120	56	62	3.10
Gaylord Perry	8	9	23	23	3	150⅔	182*	24	60	3.94
Bob Walk	1	4	12	8	0	43⅓	41	23	16	4.57
	50	56		107	11	968	936	330	471	3.45

Shutouts—Niekro (3), McWilliams
Saves—Camp (17), Garber (2), Mahler (2), Bradford, Hrabosky, Montefusco

1982

Record: 89–73
Finish: First (West)
Games Ahead: 1
Manager: Joe Torre

When Bobby Cox was fired after the 1981 season, he said, "Believe me, this team is awfully close."

Few people, Cox included, would have guessed the Braves were as "close" as they proved to be.

Ted Turner thought his team could use another weapon, so he wooed free agent Reggie Jackson. The brash owner didn't get his man, but it wouldn't matter.

Seldom—perhaps never before—has a team responded to a new manager the way the 1982 Braves took to Joe Torre. At least that's the way it seemed.

The team's 18–6 exhibition record in Florida gave reason for optimism . . . but it was just spring training. However, the Braves played even better once the season began. In fact, they played better than any team in history had ever played the first two weeks of the season, setting the tone for their second division title in 14 years.

Even with 43-year-old Phil Niekro on the disabled list for the first time in his career after being hit in the ribs by a Rick Mahler batting-practice line drive during spring training, the Braves opened their 17th season in Atlanta with more optimism than usual. Mahler, taking advantage of the injury he'd inflicted on the club's elder statesman, drew the opening day assignment at San Diego.

Using a roster that included seven rookies—Steve Bedrosian, Brett Butler, Joe Cowley, Randy Johnson, Matt Sinatro, Ken Smith, and Larry Whisenton—Atlanta opened with a 1–0 victory behind a two-hitter by Mahler. Glenn Hubbard drove in the only run in the fifth with a double that was one of just four hits the Braves got in the game.

The next night, Dale Murphy hit his first home run of the season, and Butler drove in the winning run. Bob Walk took advantage of the offensive support to beat San Diego, 6–4.

After a day off, the Braves returned to Atlanta for the home opener and jumped on Houston for five first-inning runs en route to a 6–2 victory. Murphy hit his second home run, and Tommy Boggs and Al Hrabosky did the pitching.

The Braves again struck early in their next game, scoring five in the first two innings to beat the Astros, 8–6, and move to 4–0 for the season. Murphy made a spectacular catch, and Butler scored three times.

On April 11, Mahler, who'd never pitched a shutout before 1982, pitched his second in two starts. Murphy, on his way to being named league Player of the Month, and Bob Horner homered in the 5–0 win over Houston.

As the Braves left for Cincinnati, fans were starting to believe there might be something special about this team. The series against the Reds began with a 6–1 victory after which unimpressed Cincinnati shortstop Dave Concepcion predicted, "They're not going to win the division."

The streak reached seven with a come-from-behind effort. The Braves scored three in the seventh inning for an 8–5 vic-

tory in which Claudell Washington was beaned in the first inning. His replacement, Rufino Linares, went 4-for-4.

The Braves completed a sweep of the Reds with a 5–2, 10-inning victory. Atlanta got a run in the ninth to tie and three in the 10th to move to 8–0 for the season.

In the ninth game of the season, the Braves trailed Houston, 3–0, through five innings, and Nolan Ryan was pitching a one-hitter. But the Braves got five runs in the sixth and hung on to win, 5–3. The nine straight victories matched the 1888 Boston Beaneaters for the best start in franchise history. "The way we came back tonight, especially against Ryan, there's no telling when we'll lose," proclaimed Rick Camp.

On April 17, the Braves tied the National League record for consecutive season-opening wins with 10. Bob Horner doubled in two runs in the first, and strong relief work made those runs hold up for a 2–1 victory. Gene Garber retired the last nine Astros without letting a ball leave the infield.

In victory No. 11, Biff Pocoroba's two-run, pinch-hit double in the eighth beat Houston, 6–5. The win tied Oakland's major league record of 11 consecutive victories to open the 1981 season. A crowd estimated at 5,000 greeted the team when it returned to the Atlanta airport. One sign read, "Torre! Torre! Torre!—162–0."

Not quite, but what the Braves were doing seemed nearly as unbelievable. And the team's perfection was stirring up interest in Atlanta like never before.

On April 20, the Braves set the major league record by going to 12–0 with a 4–2 victory against Cincinnati before a crowd of 37,270. Washington, playing for the first time since his beaning, tripled home the winning run.

The following evening, the streak reached 13 with what was the most improbable victory of the streak. The Braves trailed Cincinnati, 3–2, with two outs in the bottom of the ninth when Washington delivered a bases-loaded single to

Rick Mahler was 4–0 and unscored upon in opening day assignments during the 1980s.

Claudell Washington delivered the decisive hits in the final two games of the record 13-game winning streak the Braves compiled to open the 1982 season.

center for two RBIs and a 4–3 win. The crowd of 22,153 gave the team a five-minute standing ovation.

The Reds finally beat the Braves, 2–1, on April 22, ending "The Streak," as it had become known, at 13. Torre's team played just three games over .500 (76–73) after those first 13 games, but it was good enough—barely—to produce the West division title.

The Braves quickly proved they weren't invincible, losing the next five after their 13 straight wins and dropping out of first place by percentage points. They quickly regained the division lead, though, and stayed there until jousting with the Dodgers began in September.

Atlanta's jump start was accomplished without Niekro, who didn't win his first game until May 3 when he beat Pittsburgh, 10–4. He was in the heat of the fray after that, though, finishing 17–4 to lead the majors in percentage (.810) by a wide margin.

It was "Knucksie" who refused to let the young team knuckle under in its first meeting with the chief division rival, the Dodgers. With a three-run homer from Murphy and a save from Steve Bedrosian, Niekro beat Los Angeles, 4–3, at Dodger Stadium June 7. In retrospect, it was one of the more crucial victories of the season, because the Braves proceeded to sweep the three-game series, firmly establishing themselves in the domain of their chief nemesis.

Though the Braves were winning, their pitching was less than stable. After two excellent seasons in the bullpen, Rick Camp was struggling. His difficulties prompted Torre to try him in the starting rotation, where Camp found himself. Another important move for the pitching staff came June 30 when the Braves traded left-hander Larry McWilliams to Pittsburgh for minor leaguer Pascual Perez. Since McWilliams was struggling and Perez was sent to Richmond, little thought was given to the deal at the time.

But fans were paying attention to the Braves for a change. Attendance surpassed 1 million two days before the All-Star break, the earliest in the team's Atlanta history. The Braves had a 51–33 record at the break, two games better than San Diego and seven games ahead of the Dodgers.

By July 29, it appeared the Braves had made a mockery of the West division race. They led the Padres by 10 and the Dodgers by 10½. But three days later, the Dodgers had pulled within 6½ by sweeping a four-game series in Atlanta. Suddenly, there was concern. Mahler was demoted to the bullpen as Torre continued his season-long juggling of the rotation. Washington was benched for "personal problems," and a slumping Murphy actually tossed his batting helmet.

By August 8, Braves fans—if not the Braves—were in a state of panic. Everything that went right in the first two weeks of the season was falling apart. The Dodgers swept four from Atlanta in Los Angeles and pulled within 1½ games of the lead. The Braves had dropped 10 of 11 and seemed to be in a fatal spin with no signs of pulling out.

They moved on to San Francisco and lost three more, then to San Diego where the losing reached 11 in a row and 15 of 16 before a 6–5 victory over the Padres on August 14. By this time, the Dodgers had ascended to first place, ending the Braves' 104-day run at the top. When the win in San Diego was followed by four more losses, making it 19 defeats in 21 games, it seemed as if the team had thrown in the towel.

After a 12–2 spanking by Montreal on August 18, Atlanta was four games behind the Dodgers and just one-half game ahead of the Padres. The skid was being referred to in some quarters as one of the biggest "chokes" in history.

Then fate intervened to lift the black veil of tension that had closed in around the Atlanta clubhouse.

Perez, who in late July was summoned from Richmond where he was 5–0, drew the starting assignment for the August 19 game against Montreal. However, after getting his driver's license that morning, Perez tried to drive to the ballpark by himself for the first time and got lost. He completely circled Atlanta "two or three times" on I-285, the perimeter highway, and didn't get to Atlanta–Fulton County Stadium until 10 minutes after the game had begun. Niekro started in his place, and the Braves rallied from a 4–3 deficit to a 5–4 victory.

The team found comic relief in Perez's adventure, which seemed to help the players forget the anxiety of the past three weeks. Perez got to the park on time the next night and pitched 9⅔ innings of the Braves' 2–1, 10-inning victory over the Mets. The tide had turned.

Atlanta reeled off six straight victories and won nine of 10 and 13 of 15 to reclaim first place. During that stretch, the team broke the attendance record set in its first season in Atlanta, released reliever Al Hrabosky, and on September 5, began to sell playoff tickets.

Catcher Bruce Benedict hit one of the biggest home runs of the season September 6, a grand slam off Fernando Valenzuela, to spur a 10–3 rout of the Dodgers and give the Braves a 1½-game lead.

But by September 17, Atlanta was in another dive, falling 3½ games back of the Dodgers. The next night, the Braves won, but Horner fell in a rundown and suffered a hyperextended elbow. The team captain was lost for the final two weeks.

On September 22, after a 2–4 road trip, Torre's club trailed the Dodgers by three games with only 10 to play. The chances of winning the division were remote, at best.

But while the Braves won four of their next five, the Dodgers dropped five straight. It didn't seem possible, yet the Braves found themselves holding a one-game lead with five to play.

The division leaders split two games in Los Angeles, so the Braves led by one as they headed to San Diego for the final three games of the schedule. At the same time, the stumbling Dodgers had to go to San Francisco to play their most-hated rival.

On October 1, Niekro, who earlier recorded his 250th career win, pitched his second straight shutout and hit a home run to beat the Padres, 4–0. However, the Dodgers also won. Both teams won the next day, too, so it came down to the final day with Atlanta holding a one-game edge.

The Braves began October 3 in control of their own destiny. All they needed to do in order to advance to the postseason for the first time since 1969 was win. But when the Padres beat them, 5–1, a one-game playoff was staring them in the face if the Dodgers could beat San Francisco. But with the Giants and Dodgers locked at 2–2 in the bottom of the seventh, 39-year-old future Hall of Famer Joe Morgan hit a three-run homer that sealed a 5–3 loss for Los Angeles and a division title for Atlanta.

Chris Chambliss's power and leadership were crucial to the Braves in winning the 1982 West division title.

	W	L	G	GS	CG	IP	H	BB	SO	ERA
Jose Alvarez	0	0	7	0	0	7⅔	8	2	6	4.70
Steve Bedrosian	8	6	64	3	0	137⅔	102	57	123	2.42
Tommy Boggs	2	2	10	10	0	46½	43	22	29	3.30
Rick Camp	11	13	51	21	3	177⅓	199	52	68	3.65
Joe Cowley	1	2	17	8	0	52½	53	16	27	4.47
Ken Dayley	5	6	20	11	0	71⅓	79	25	34	4.54
Carlos Diaz	3	2	19	0	0	25⅓	31	9	16	4.62
Gene Garber	8	10	69	0	0	119⅓	100	32	68	2.34
Preston Hanna	3	0	20	1	0	36	36	28	17	3.75
Tom Hausman	0	0	3	0	0	3⅔	6	4	2	4.91
Al Hrabosky	2	1	31	0	0	37⅓	41	17	20	5.54
Rick Mahler	9	10	39	33	5	205½	213	62	105	4.21
Larry McWilliams	2	3	27	2	0	37⅔	52	20	24	6.21
Donnie Moore	3	1	16	0	0	27⅔	32	7	17	4.23
Phil Niekro	17	4	35	35	4	234⅓	225	73	144	3.61
Pascual Perez	4	4	16	11	0	79½	85	17	29	3.06
Bob Walk	11	9	32	27	3	164½	179	59	84	4.87
	89	73		162	15	1,463	1,484	502	813	3.82

Shutouts—Mahler (2), Niekro (2), Walk
Saves—Garber (30), Bedrosian (11), Camp (5), Hrabosky (3), Diaz, Moore

Murphy, only 26, had a monster season and was named National League MVP. He tied for the league lead in RBIs (109), and finished one back of Dave Kingman for the home run title with 36. He also won a Gold Glove for his defense and stole 23 bases.

Horner was fourth in the league in home runs (32) despite missing 22 games. Torre called utility man Jerry Royster, who hit .326 the last two months, the team MVP in the second half for the way he filled in at four positions, especially third base in Horner's absence.

Other keys to the Braves' success: Garber set a team record for saves (30); Chris Chambliss reached a career high in home runs (20); shortstop Rafael Ramirez and second baseman Glenn Hubbard helped the Braves turn a major-league-high 186 double plays; the team set a then-Atlanta record for steals (151); and the Braves led the league in home runs (146).

The season's attendance of 1.8 million was the franchise's best since 1958, and because of Turner's cable Superstation, the Braves became tremendously popular, coast to coast.

	G	AB	R	H	2B	3B	HR	RBI	SB	AVG
Bruce Benedict (C)	118	386	34	95	11	1	3	44	4	.246
Brett Butler	89	240	35	52	2	0	0	7	21	.217
Chris Chambliss (1B)	157	534	57	144	25	2	20	86	7	.270
Albert Hall	5	0	1	0	0	0	0	0	0	—
Terry Harper	48	150	16	43	3	0	2	16	7	.287
Bob Horner (3B)	140	499	85	130	24	0	32	97	3	.261
Glenn Hubbard (2B)	145	532	75	132	25	1	9	59	4	.248
Randy Johnson	27	46	5	11	5	0	0	6	0	.239
Rufino Linares (OF)	77	191	28	57	7	1	2	17	5	.298
Dale Murphy (OF)	162	598	113	168	23	3	36	109*	23	.281
Larry Owen	2	3	1	1	1	0	0	0	0	.333
Biff Pocoroba	56	120	5	33	7	0	2	22	0	.275
Bob Porter	24	27	1	3	0	0	0	0	0	.111
Rafael Ramirez (SS)	157	609	74	169	24	4	10	52	27	.278
Jerry Royster	108	261	43	77	13	2	2	25	14	.295
Paul Runge	4	2	0	0	0	0	0	0	0	.000
Matt Sinatro	37	81	10	11	2	0	1	4	0	.136
Ken Smith	48	41	6	12	1	0	0	3	0	.293
C. Washington (OF)	150	563	94	150	24	6	16	80	33	.266
Bob Watson	57	114	16	28	3	1	5	22	1	.246
Larry Whisenton	84	143	21	34	7	2	4	17	2	.238
Paul Zuvella	2	1	0	0	0	0	0	0	0	.000
	162	5,507	739*	1,411	215	22	146*	687	151	.256

1983

Record: 88–74
Finish: Second (West)
Games Behind: 3
Manager: Joe Torre

Atlanta, slow to embrace the Braves when they were mediocre or worse, showed in 1983 it would support an exciting team by turning out in record numbers for the second straight year. With a contending team and interesting players to watch, Atlanta fans broke their attendance record with a final count of 2,119,935, the Braves' best draw since the World Series championship season of 1957.

After winning a division title in 1982, the World Series is exactly what the team and its fans had in mind in 1983, too. And for much of the season, that seemed a plausible goal, so much so that the city formed a World Series task force in the late summer.

The Braves won seven of their first eight games and 13 of 16. Behind the power hitting of Dale Murphy and Bob Horner, they had the best record in baseball through much of the summer, standing at 71–46 on August 13, 6½ games ahead of the Dodgers.

In fact, August 13 was the date of the most memorable game of the season. The Dodgers jumped off to an 8–2 lead in the fourth inning at Atlanta. But Glenn Hubbard and Claudell Washington hit three-run homers to tie the game through seven innings. In the ninth, Greg Brock homered off Steve Bedrosian for a 9–8 Dodgers' lead. In the bottom of the inning, though, Bob Watson batted for Washington and hit a two-run, game-ending home run that sent a packed stadium into ecstasy.

But two days later, Horner broke his right wrist sliding into second base. He was hitting .303 with 20 home runs and 68 RBIs, and his loss took a big chunk out of the lineup for the remainder of the season. The Braves went into an immediate slide and never recovered. By the end of the month, they were in second place and on the way to losing 28 of their final 45 games.

Murphy would not be deterred from the finest season of his career, though. The 27-year-old outfielder raised his batting average (.302) 21 points from 1982, led the league in RBIs (121) and slugging average, and finished second in home runs (36), total bases, and runs. His 131 runs scored set a modern Braves record, and he played in all 162 games for the second straight season. Additionally, he stole 30 bases to become only the sixth 30–30 (home runs–steals) man in history.

Murphy was named the league's MVP for the second consecutive year, receiving 21 of 24 first-place votes and winning by an even bigger margin than he did in 1982. He joined Ernie Banks, Joe Morgan, and Mike Schmidt as the only players to win the honor in successive seasons, though Barry Bonds has since joined them.

Offense was the team's strength. The bullpen was inconsistent, and starting pitching was Atlanta's biggest weakness.

The Braves led the league in runs, batting average (an Atlanta-record .272), and on-base percentage (.344). Shortstop Rafael Ramirez, second baseman Hubbard, and catcher Bruce Benedict had career years at the plate to make the high team average possible.

The bullpen led the league with 48 saves, due in large part to the off-season acquisition of left-hander Terry Forster. However, Gene Garber and Bedrosian weren't as reliable as they'd been in 1982 and were particularly ineffective down the stretch.

The starting rotation got a big boost from right-hander Craig McMurtry, who was named the league's Rookie Pitcher of the Year. Pascual Perez, also in his first full year in the majors, had a fine season and was second in the league in winning percentage.

However, the veteran starters did not fare quite so well. Phil Niekro struggled, finishing with more hits than innings for the first time in eight years and winning only one more than he lost.

Niekro was 44 years old, and the prevailing sentiment in the organization was that he was finished. He was given his

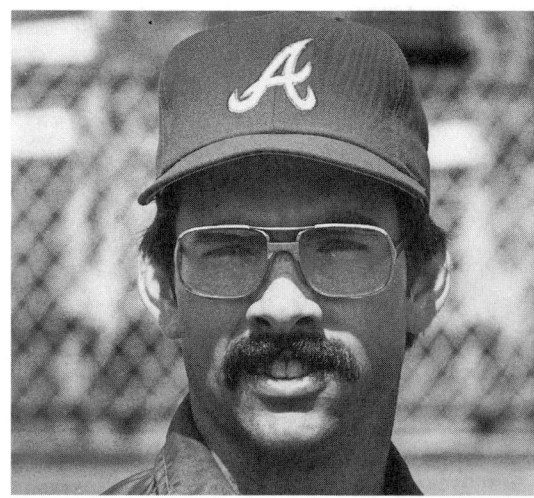

Craig McMurtry won 15 games as a rookie.

unconditional release, a decision that created a lot of controversy among Braves followers. The veteran knuckleball specialist won 268 games in 20 seasons as a Brave, and he was extremely popular with fans.

In an attempt to bolster the starting pitching for a stretch run at the pennant, the Braves made a controversial late-season trade. They obtained right-hander Len Barker from Cleveland in exchange for pitcher Rick Behenna, $150,000, and two players to be named, who turned out to be popular center fielder Brett Butler and third baseman Brook Jacoby. Barker failed to contribute in 1983 or thereafter, but Butler and Jacoby became All-Stars.

Even with all their problems, the Braves weren't eliminated until September 30 and finished just three games back of the Dodgers.

	G	AB	R	H	2B	3B	HR	RBI	SB	AVG
Bruce Benedict (C)	134	423	43	126	13	1	2	43	1	.298
Brett Butler (OF)	151	549	84	154	21	13*	5	37	39	.281
Chris Chambliss (1B)	131	447	59	125	24	3	20	78	2	.280
Albert Hall	10	8	2	0	0	0	0	0	1	.000
Terry Harper	80	201	19	53	13	1	3	26	6	.264
Bob Horner (3B)	104	386	75	117	25	1	20	68	4	.303
Glenn Hubbard (2B)	148	517	65	136	24	6	12	70	3	.263
Brook Jacoby	4	8	0	0	0	0	0	0	0	.000
Randy Johnson	86	144	22	36	3	0	1	17	1	.250
Mike Jorgensen	57	48	5	12	1	0	1	8	0	.250
Brad Komminsk	19	36	2	8	2	0	0	4	0	.222
Dale Murphy (OF)	162	589	131	178	24	4	36	121*	30	.302
Larry Owen	17	17	0	2	0	0	0	1	0	.118
Gerald Perry	27	39	5	14	2	0	1	6	0	.359
Biff Pocoroba	55	120	11	32	6	0	2	16	0	.267
Rafael Ramirez (SS)	152	622	82	185	13	5	7	58	16	.297
Jerry Royster	91	268	32	63	10	3	3	30	11	.235
Paul Runge	5	8	0	2	0	0	0	1	0	.250
Matt Sinatro	7	12	0	2	0	0	0	2	0	.167
Ken Smith	30	12	2	2	0	0	1	2	1	.167
C. Washington (OF)	134	496	75	138	24	8	9	44	31	.278
Bob Watson	65	149	14	46	9	0	6	37	0	.309
Paul Zuvella	3	5	0	0	0	0	0	0	0	.000
	162	5,472	746*	1,489	218	45	130	691*	146	.272*

Dale Murphy's popularity soared when he won back-to-back Most Valuable Players Awards in 1982–83.

Bob Watson provided a memorable home run in the 1983 pennant race, but the Braves still came up short.

	W	L	G	GS	CG	IP	H	BB	SO	ERA
Len Barker	1	3	6	6	0	33	31	14	21	3.82
Steve Bedrosian	9	10	70	1	0	120	100	51	114	3.60
Rick Behenna	3	3	14	6	0	37⅓	37	12	17	4.58
Tommy Boggs	0	0	5	0	0	6⅓	8	1	5	5.68
Tony Brizzolara	1	0	14	0	0	20⅓	22	6	17	3.54
Rick Camp	10	9	40	16	1	140	146	38	61	3.79
Ken Dayley	5	8	24	16	0	104⅔	100	39	70	4.30
Jeff Dedmon	0	0	5	0	0	4	10	0	3	13.50
Pete Falcone	9	4	33	15	2	106⅔	102	60	59	3.63
Terry Forster	3	2	56	0	0	79⅓	60	31	54	2.16
Gene Garber	4	5	43	0	0	60⅔	72	23	45	4.60
Rick Mahler	0	0	10	0	0	14⅓	16	9	7	5.02
Craig McMurtry	15	9	36	35	6	224⅔	204	88	105	3.08
Donnie Moore	2	3	43	0	0	68⅔	72	10	41	3.67
Phil Niekro	11	10	34	33	2	201⅓	212	105	128	3.97
Pascual Perez	15	8	33	33	7	215⅓	213	51	144	3.43
Bob Walk	0	0	1	1	0	3⅔	7	2	4	7.36
	88	74		162	18	1,440⅔	1,412	540	895	3.67

Shutouts—McMurtry (3), Perez
Saves—Bedrosian (19), Forster (13), Garber (9), Moore (6), Brizzolara

1984

Record: 80–82
Finish: Tie–Second (West)
Games Behind: 12
Manager: Joe Torre

The 1984 Braves embarked on a new course in franchise history: Life without Phil Niekro. At age 45, Niekro was a New York Yankee after spending two decades on the Braves staff. He won 16 games with his new team, a figure no one on his old team could match.

Starting pitching wasn't the biggest problem Atlanta had in Joe Torre's third year as manager, but it was a contributor to the club's very disappointing sub-.500 record.

Unlike Torre's first two Braves teams, this one did not sprint out of the starting gate. In fact, it was 9–12 in April and didn't creep above .500 until May 11. Then a nine-game winning streak, which lasted through June 7, vaulted the club into first place by 1½ games. But just when it appeared as if the team was adjusting well to life without Niekro, the bottom fell out. The Braves lost five in a row and 11 of 16 and were never again a threat. After that June 7 perch atop the West, the Braves were 13 under .500 (46–59) the rest of the way.

The decline, following two seasons at or near the top of the division, prompted impatient owner Ted Turner to fire Torre, sending the organization spinning in misdirection for several seasons.

Dale Murphy upheld his end of the bargain, playing all 162 games and hitting 36 home runs for the third consecutive season. Murphy tied Mike Schmidt for the league lead in homers, led the league in total bases and slugging percentage (.547), and finished third in RBIs.

However, Murphy's partner in power, Bob Horner, missed the remainder of the season after breaking his wrist diving for a ball May 29. As the Braves had already discovered, they weren't the same team without their productive but injury-prone third baseman.

After leading the league in runs scored in 1983, the Braves fell to eighth in that department. They also fell from third in opponents' runs to seventh. It was a combination which made for a very uninspiring season that concluded far behind San Diego in a second-place tie with Houston.

The top winner on the pitching staff was Pascual Perez, who got a late start because of his January arrest in the Dominican Republic for cocaine possession and a suspension through May 6. He won two fewer games (14) than Niekro did with the Yankees. Rick Mahler, the Braves' next best starter, checked in three wins behind Niekro, and the rest of the staff wasn't even in contention. Len Barker, for whom the Braves had mortgaged the future the year before, appeared in just three games after the All-Star break because of a bum elbow.

The biggest reason for the Braves' decline—and for Torre's firing—was the lack of production from young players such as outfielder Brad Komminsk and first baseman/outfielder Gerald Perry. Veteran Chris Chambliss also failed to produce up to his norm, and catcher Bruce Benedict and infielders Rafael Ramirez and Glenn Hubbard didn't hit at all in the second half of the season.

The team's frustration at failing to live up to expectations boiled over August 12 during a 5–3 victory against San Diego at Atlanta–Fulton County Stadium. Perez drilled the Padres' Alan Wiggins in the back with the first pitch of the game, and events quickly deteriorated from there.

San Diego pitchers threw at Perez all four times he batted. There were two bench-clearing brawls, the second of which included several fans. There were a total of 19 ejections. Padres manager Dick Williams received a 10-day suspension and a $10,000 fine, and Torre and five of his players got three-day suspensions.

Pascual Perez is the victim of a wayward pitch in the August 12, 1984 game against San Diego that featured two brawls, one including fans, and 19 ejections and led to seven suspensions.

	G	AB	R	H	2B	3B	HR	RBI	SB	AVG
Bruce Benedict (C)	95	300	26	67	8	1	4	25	1	.223
Chris Chambliss (1B)	135	389	47	100	14	0	9	44	1	.257
Albert Hall	87	142	25	37	6	1	1	9	6	.261
Terry Harper	40	102	4	16	3	1	0	8	4	.157
Bob Horner	32	113	15	31	8	0	3	19	0	.274
Glenn Hubbard (2B)	120	397	53	93	27	2	9	43	4	.234
Randy Johnson (3B)	91	294	28	82	13	0	5	30	4	.279
Mike Jorgensen	31	26	4	7	1	0	0	5	0	.269
Brad Komminsk (OF)	90	301	37	61	10	0	8	36	18	.203
Rufino Linares	34	58	4	12	3	0	1	10	0	.207
Dale Murphy (OF)	162	607	94	176	32	8	36*	100	19	.290
Ken Oberkfell	50	172	21	40	8	1	1	10	1	.233
Gerald Perry	122	347	52	92	12	2	7	47	15	.265
Biff Pocoroba	4	2	1	0	0	0	0	0	0	.000
Rafael Ramirez (SS)	145	591	51	157	22	4	2	48	14	.266
Jerry Royster	81	227	22	47	13	2	1	21	6	.207
Paul Runge	28	90	5	24	3	1	0	3	5	.267
Matt Sinatro	2	4	0	0	0	0	0	0	0	.000
Milt Thompson	25	99	16	30	1	0	2	4	14	.303
Alex Trevino	79	266	36	65	16	0	3	28	5	.244
C. Washington (OF)	120	416	62	119	21	2	17	61	21	.286
Bob Watson	49	85	4	18	4	0	2	12	0	.212
Paul Zuvella	11	25	2	5	1	0	0	1	0	.200
	162	5,422	632	1,338	234	27	111	578	140	.247

	W	L	G	GS	CG	IP	H	BB	SO	ERA
Len Barker	7	8	21	20	1	126⅓	120	38	95	3.85
Steve Bedrosian	9	6	40	4	0	83⅔	65	33	81	2.37
Tony Brizzolara	1	2	10	4	0	29	33	13	17	5.28
Rick Camp	8	6	31	21	1	148⅔	134	63	69	3.27
Ken Dayley	0	3	4	4	0	18⅔	28	6	10	5.30
Jeff Dedmon	4	3	54	0	0	81	86	35	51	3.78
Pete Falcone	5	7	35	16	2	120	115	57	55	4.13
Terry Forster	2	0	25	0	0	26⅓	30	7	10	2.70
Gene Garber	3	6	62	0	0	106	103	24	55	3.06
Rick Mahler	13	10	38	29	9	222	209	62	106	3.12
Craig McMurtry	9	17	37	30	0	183⅓	184	102	99	4.32
Donnie Moore	4	5	47	0	0	64⅓	63	18	47	2.94
Mike Payne	0	1	3	1	0	5⅔	7	3	3	6.35
Pascual Perez	14	8	30	30	4	211⅓	208	51	145	3.74
Zane Smith	1	0	3	3	0	20	16	13	16	2.25
	80	82		162	17	1,447	1,401	525	859	3.57

Shutouts—Falcone, Mahler, Perez
Saves—Moore (16), Bedrosian (11), Garber (11), Forster (5), Dedmon (4), Falcone (2)

1985

Record: 66–96
Finish: Fifth (West)
Games Behind: 29
Managers: Eddie Haas, Bobby Wine

When Joe Torre was hired to manage the Braves in 1982, it was because owner Ted Turner overruled the prevailing sentiment in the front office and bypassed Eddie Haas, a long-time player, coach, scout, and manager in the organization. So, when Torre was jettisoned, Turner finally acquiesced, giving Haas a shot at handling the young players he'd helped to develop in the Braves' farm system.

In spite of 27 years of service to the organization, Haas failed to survive even one season as major league manager. That's how bad 1985 was for the Braves, who discovered they were a long way from even being competitive in the National League West.

Once again, considerable optimism preceded the season. Not only did the Braves have one of the game's top offensive performers in Dale Murphy, but they also picked up the services of Bruce Sutter, the league's most dominating closer, thanks to another well-intentioned but ill-fated shopping spree on the free agent market by Turner.

Murphy had another outstanding season, but Sutter, like most of his new teammates, failed to excel with any degree of consistency, finally yielding to a sore shoulder. The Braves rose above fifth place for only one day after May 7, and when the team lost 12 of 13 to fall 21 games below .500 on August 26, Haas was fired. Coach Bobby Wine called the shots the rest of the way.

Murphy, at age 29, played every game for the fourth straight year and won his first and only outright home run title (37) after sharing it with Mike Schmidt the year before. He also led the league in runs and walks and was second in RBIs (111). In April alone, Murphy drove in 29 runs, tying Ron Cey's 1977 record for the month.

Bob Horner, who was moved to first base June 10, played his highest number of games since 1982 and produced solid power numbers. However, after Murphy and Horner, the offense was severely lacking. Atlanta finished 10th in the league in both runs and team hitting (.246).

Two of the biggest disappointments were Brad Komminsk, who opened the season in left, and first baseman/outfielder Gerald Perry. They were supposed to prosper under the tutelage of Haas, as they did in the minors, but they wound up as major contributors to his demise.

For the third time in four years, Atlanta led the league in double plays, thanks to the glove work of shortstop Rafael Ramirez and second baseman Glenn Hubbard. However, the Braves continued to get little offense from the middle infield and catching positions, and their poor team speed was reflected in finishing next-to-last in the league in steals.

There wasn't much to recommend the pitching either. Rick Mahler won his first seven decisions then went 10–15 the rest of the way to finish with just one more victory (17) than 46-year-old Phil Niekro had in reaching 300 career wins with the Yankees. The Braves' staff had the highest ERA (4.19) in the league.

	W	L	G	GS	CG	IP	H	BB	SO	ERA
Len Barker	2	9	20	18	0	73⅔	84	37	47	6.35
Steve Bedrosian	7	15	37	37	0	206⅔	198	111	134	3.83
Rick Camp	4	6	66	2	0	127⅔	130	61	49	3.95
Jeff Dedmon	6	3	60	0	0	86	84	49	41	4.08
Terry Forster	2	3	46	0	0	59½	49	28	37	2.28
Gene Garber	6	6	59	0	0	97½	98	25	66	3.61
Joe Johnson	4	4	15	14	1	85⅔	95	24	34	4.10
Rick Mahler	17	15	39	39*	6	266⅔	272*	79	107	3.48
Craig McMurtry	0	3	17	6	0	45	56	27	28	6.60
Pascual Perez	1	13	22	22	0	95⅓	115	57	57	6.14
Dave Schuler	0	0	9	0	0	10⅔	19	3	10	6.75
Steve Shields	1	2	23	6	0	68	86	32	29	5.16
Zane Smith	9	10	42	18	2	147	135	80	85	3.80
Bruce Sutter	7	7	58	0	0	88⅓	91	29	52	4.48
	66	96		162	9	1,457⅓	1,512*	642*	776	4.19

Shutouts—Smith (2), Mahler
Saves—Sutter (23), Camp (3), Forster, Garber, McMurtry

Rick Camp wasn't much of a hitter, but on July 5, 1985, he sent one into the night . . . rather the morning.

The most memorable game of the season occurred July 4 . . . and 5. The annual Fireworks Night game at Atlanta-Fulton County Stadium lasted 6 hours, 10 minutes plus two rain delays, ending at 3:55 A.M. in a 16–13 victory by the Mets.

New York took a 10–8 lead in the 13th, only to see the Braves tie it. The Mets went ahead 11–10 in the 18th, but with two outs and two strikes on pitcher Rick Camp, who was batting only because there were no position players left to hit for him, the .060 career hitter connected for a home run to tie the game. In the 19th, the Mets scored five off Camp, and the Braves responded with only two.

It was far too late to celebrate Independence Day, but at 4:01 A.M., they finally set off the fireworks—much to the alarm of neighbors—to celebrate the end of the marathon.

In October, deposed Pittsburgh manager Chuck Tanner was hired to replace Haas, and former Braves manager Bobby Cox resigned as Toronto's manager to return to the Braves as general manager.

	G	AB	R	H	2B	3B	HR	RBI	SB	AVG
Bruce Benedict	70	208	12	42	6	0	0	20	0	.202
Rick Cerone (C)	96	282	15	61	9	0	3	25	0	.216
Chris Chambliss	101	170	16	40	7	0	3	21	0	.235
Albert Hall	54	47	5	7	0	1	0	3	1	.149
Terry Harper (OF)	138	492	58	130	15	2	17	72	9	.264
Bob Horner (1B)	130	483	61	129	25	3	27	89	1	.267
Glenn Hubbard (2B)	142	439	51	102	21	0	5	39	4	.232
Brad Komminsk	106	300	52	68	12	3	4	21	10	.227
Dale Murphy (OF)	162	616	118*	185	32	3	37*	111	10	.300
Ken Oberkfell (3B)	134	412	30	112	19	4	3	35	1	.272
Larry Owen	26	71	7	17	3	0	2	12	0	.239
Gerald Perry	110	238	22	51	5	0	3	13	9	.214
Johnny Rabb	3	2	0	0	0	0	0	0	0	.000
Rafael Ramirez (SS)	138	568	54	141	25	4	5	58	2	.248
Paul Runge	50	87	15	19	3	0	1	5	0	.218
Andres Thomas	15	18	6	5	0	0	0	2	0	.278
Milt Thompson	73	182	17	55	7	2	0	6	9	.302
C. Washington (OF)	122	398	62	110	14	6	15	43	14	.276
Paul Zuvella	81	190	16	48	8	1	0	4	2	.253
	162	5,526	632	1,359	213	28	126	598	72	.246

1986

Record: 72–89
Finish: Sixth (West)
Games Behind: 23½
Manager: Chuck Tanner

How bad were the 1986 Braves?

So bad that Bob Horner hit four home runs against the Expos July 6 and the Braves still lost, 11–8. Horner was the 11th man in history to hit four home runs in a game and the first to do so in a losing cause.

How bad were the '86 Braves?

So bad that on July 22, Ken Griffey hit three home runs and the Braves lost to the Phillies, 5–4, in 11 innings.

How bad was Chuck Tanner's first Braves team?

So bad that on September 14, they were beaten by San Francisco, 7–6, even though Giants catcher-turned-third-baseman Bob Brenly committed a major league record four errors in one inning.

The Braves finished under .500 for the third consecutive year and fell into the National League West basement for the first time since 1979 when Bobby Cox was the manager rather than the general manager. On the positive side, Atlanta actually had a better winning percentage than it posted the year before and finished 5½ games closer to first place. But any way you cut it, it was the Braves' fifth last-place finish in 11 years of ownership by Ted Turner.

For the first three months, the Braves looked like they might be a contending team, but it was just a mirage. On July 3, Atlanta was only 1½ games behind San Francisco. However, Tanner's club dropped 14 of its next 16, beginning an agonizing second half.

The formula for the Braves' failure: last in the division (11th in the league) in runs scored and next to last (10th in the league) in runs allowed. Atlanta ranked last in the league in steals, 11th in team hitting (.250), and 10th in team pitching (3.97). The only positive team statistic was 181 double plays, the fourth time in five years the Braves led the league in that department.

Even Dale Murphy slipped at age 30. On July 9, his consecutive games played streak was halted at 740, 12th all-time, when he missed a game for the first time since September

1981. Though he was fourth in the league in home runs (29) and total bases, Murphy's offensive statistics were lower across the board than they'd been since the strike-shortened 1981 season.

Horner played more than ever before in his injury-riddled career, and though he had a productive year, it wasn't as fruitful as was expected of him if he ever played close to a full season.

But if Murphy and Horner were somewhat disappointing, the rest of the offense was rather pathetic. Other than Griffey's contributions after he was picked up from the Yankees in a midseason deal, anemia was the norm throughout the other spots in the lineup. The best chance for a big hit often came from the bench, where Ted Simmons led the "Bomb Squad" of pinch hitters who combined for a .277 average with seven homers and 53 RBIs. But on June 23, the Braves still tied a league record for a nine-inning game by stranding 18 runners in a 6–5 loss to the Dodgers.

The pitching staff was a makeshift group that generally lacked consistency. Pascual Perez, Len Barker, Terry Forster, and Rick Camp were released. Bruce Sutter was lost to rotator cuff surgery, and Rick Mahler led the league in losses (18).

	G	AB	R	H	2B	3B	HR	RBI	SB	AVG
Bruce Benedict	64	160	11	36	10	1	0	13	1	.225
Chris Chambliss	97	122	13	38	8	0	2	14	0	.311
Ken Griffey (OF)	80	292	36	90	15	3	12	32	12	.308
Albert Hall	16	50	6	12	2	0	0	1	8	.240
Terry Harper	106	265	26	68	12	0	8	30	3	.257
Bob Horner (1B)	141	517	70	141	22	0	27	87	1	.273
Glenn Hubbard (2B)	143	408	42	94	16	1	4	36	3	.230
Brad Komminsk	5	5	1	2	0	0	0	1	0	.400
Omar Moreno (OF)	118	359	46	84	18	6	4	27	17	.234
Darryl Motley	5	10	1	2	1	0	0	0	0	.200
Dale Murphy (OF)	160	614	89	163	29	7	29	83	7	.265
Ken Oberkfell (3B)	151	503	62	136	24	3	5	48	7	.270
Gerald Perry	29	70	6	19	2	0	2	11	0	.271
Rafael Ramirez	134	496	57	119	21	1	8	33	19	.240
Paul Runge	7	8	1	2	0	0	0	0	0	.250
Billy Sample	92	200	23	57	11	0	6	14	4	.285
Ted Simmons	76	127	14	32	5	0	4	25	1	.252
Andres Thomas (SS)	102	323	26	81	17	2	6	32	4	.251
Ozzie Virgil (C)	114	359	45	80	9	0	15	48	1	.223
Claudell Washington	40	137	17	37	11	0	5	14	4	.270
	161	5,384	615	1,348	241	24	138	575	93	.250

	W	L	G	GS	CG	IP	H	BB	SO	ERA
Jim Acker	3	8	21	14	0	95	100	26	37	3.79
Doyle Alexander	6	6	17	17	2	117⅓	135	17	74	3.84
Paul Assenmacher	7	3	61	0	0	68⅓	61	26	56	2.50
Jeff Dedmon	6	6	57	0	0	99⅔	90	39	58	2.98
Gene Garber	5	5	61	0	0	78	76	20	56	2.54
Joe Johnson	6	7	17	15	2	87	101	35	49	4.97
Rick Mahler	14	18*	39	39	7	237⅔	283*	95	137	4.88
Craig McMurtry	1	6	37	5	0	79⅔	82	43	50	4.74
Ed Olwine	0	0	37	0	0	47⅔	35	17	37	3.40
David Palmer	11	10	35	35	2	209⅔	181	102	170	3.65
Charlie Puleo	1	2	5	3	1	24⅓	13	12	18	2.96
Steve Shields	0	0	6	0	0	12⅔	13	7	6	7.11
Zane Smith	8	16	38	32	3	204⅔	209	105	139	4.05
Cliff Speck	2	1	13	1	0	28⅓	25	15	21	4.13
Bruce Sutter	2	0	16	0	0	18⅔	17	9	16	4.34
Duane Ward	0	1	10	0	0	16	22	8	8	7.31
	72	89		161	17	1,424⅔	1,443	576	932	3.97

Shutouts—Smith, Mahler
Saves—Garber (24), Assenmacher (7), Dedmon (3), Sutter (3), Olwine, Smith

1987

Record: 69–92
Finish: Fifth (West)
Games Behind: 20½
Manager: Chuck Tanner

How strange was the 1987 season for the Braves?

So strange that Bob Horner played in Japan. So strange that Rick Mahler—of all people—pitched a league-record third opening-day shutout. So strange that Albert Hall—of all people—hit for the cycle. And so strange that Phil Niekro, a year and a half from his 50th birthday, was brought back after a four-year absence to start the last home game of the season as a "tribute."

Only in Atlanta . . . home of the Braves, and in those days, home of the bizarre.

But while the Braves of old were dwindling in fifth place, a new generation was being born. Tom Glavine, Ron Gant, Jeff Blauser, and Pete Smith made their major league debuts, and John Smoltz was obtained from Detroit in an August trade for Doyle Alexander. Help was on the way, though it would take a while to mature.

Chuck Tanner's second Braves team was three games worse than his first one, but at least Atlanta managed to get out of the West basement, thanks to San Diego's generosity. Unlike the 1986 Braves, this team could score runs; however, its pitching staff was considerably worse than its predecessor. The Braves were fifth in the league and third in the West in runs scored. However, they were dead last in ERA (4.63), which was the team's worst since 1977 and second-worst since 1935.

The Braves and, by no coincidence, all major league teams showed little interest in free agents during the previous winter. Horner and Alexander were two of several players who found no suitors on the open market, a fact later attributed to collusion among the owners. Though Alexander returned to the Braves in May, Horner sold his services to the Yakult Swallows.

But even without the Blond Bomber, the Atlanta offense was rather substantial. Dale Murphy, after a disappointing 1986, bounced back with a career high in home runs (44), including the 300th of his career. He finished second to Andre Dawson in that department.

Spurred by the rejuvenation of Murphy, the Braves scored more runs than they had in any season since 1973.

The sparkplug of the offense and one of the biggest surprises of the season in the National League was center fielder Dion James, who had been acquired from Milwaukee for Brad Komminsk. James finished fifth in the league batting race (.312) and led the club in doubles. On May 2, James and Graig Nettles both hit grand slams in a 12–4 rout of Houston, the first time the Braves had hit two bases-loaded homers in the same game since pitcher Tony Cloninger did it in 1966. James also led the league's outfielders with a .996 fielding average.

Other major contributors to the offense were catcher Ozzie Virgil, who had a career high in home runs, and first baseman Gerald Perry, who finally developed into the player the club had been expecting. Among his other accomplishments, Perry stole an Atlanta-record 42 bases. He and Hall gave the team its best base-stealing tandem in years.

Hall, a part-time outfielder, hit for the cycle (single, double, triple, home run) September 23 in a 5–4 victory against Houston, becoming the first Brave in 77 years—and the last—to accomplish this rare feat.

Centerfielder Dion James had a big season with both the bat and the glove in 1987.

	W	L	G	GS	CG	IP	H	BB	SO	ERA
Jim Acker	4	9	68	0	0	114⅔	109	51	68	4.16
Doyle Alexander	5	10	16	16	3	117⅔	115	27	64	4.13
Paul Assenmacher	1	1	52	0	0	54⅔	58	24	39	5.10
Joe Boever	1	0	14	0	0	18⅓	29	12	18	7.36
Chuck Cary	1	1	13	0	0	16⅔	17	4	15	3.78
Marty Clary	0	1	7	1	0	14⅔	20	4	7	6.14
Kevin Coffman	2	3	5	5	0	25⅓	31	22	14	4.62
Jeff Dedmon	3	4	53	3	0	89⅔	82	42	40	3.91
Gene Garber	8	10	49	0	0	69⅓	87	28	48	4.41
Tom Glavine	2	4	9	9	0	50⅓	55	33	20	5.54
Rick Mahler	8	13	39	28	3	197	212	85	95	4.98
Larry McWilliams	0	1	9	2	0	20⅓	25	7	13	5.75
Phil Niekro	0	0	1	1	0	3	6	6	0	15.00
Ed Olwine	0	1	27	0	0	23⅓	25	8	12	5.01
Randy O'Neal	4	2	16	10	0	61	79	24	33	5.61
David Palmer	8	11	28	28	0	152⅓	169	64	111	4.90
Charlie Puleo	6	8	35	16	1	123⅓	122	40	99	4.23
Pete Smith	1	2	6	6	0	31⅓	39	14	11	4.83
Zane Smith	15	10	36	36*	9	242	245	91	130	4.09
Steve Ziem	0	1	2	0	0	2⅓	4	1	0	7.71
	69	92		161	16	1,427⅔	1,529*	587	837	4.63

Shutouts—Z. Smith (3), Mahler
Saves—Acker (14), Garber (10), Dedmon (4), Assenmacher (2), Cary, Olwine

But even with the offense the Braves generated, the pitching staff still managed to give up 82 more runs than the team scored. After Mahler's opening-day 6–0 victory against Philadelphia, Atlanta pitchers blanked the opposition only three more times, a league low. Mahler didn't record another shutout, won only seven more games, and barely kept his ERA under 5.00.

The lone bright spot in the rotation was Zane Smith, who won more games (15) than any Braves left-hander since Denny Lemaster won 17 for Milwaukee in 1964. The bullpen was even worse.

With the season long since a lost cause and perhaps thinking the pitching couldn't get any worse, the Braves invited 48-year-old Niekro, who had been released by Toronto and Cleveland earlier in the year, to pitch against San Francisco September 27. In his final major league appearance, Niekro gave up six hits, six walks, and five runs in three innings but managed not to get charged with the 15–6 loss.

	G	AB	R	H	2B	3B	HR	RBI	SB	AVG
Terry Bell	1	1	0	0	0	0	0	0	0	.000
Bruce Benedict	37	95	4	14	1	0	1	5	0	.147
Jeff Blauser	51	165	11	40	6	3	2	15	7	.242
Trench Davis	6	3	0	0	0	0	0	0	0	.000
Mike Fischlin	1	0	0	0	0	0	0	0	0	—
Ron Gant	21	83	9	22	4	0	2	9	4	.265
Ken Griffey (OF)	122	399	65	114	24	1	14	64	4	.286
Albert Hall	92	292	54	83	20	4	3	24	33	.284
Glenn Hubbard (2B)	141	443	69	117	33	2	5	38	1	.264
Dion James (OF)	134	494	80	154	37	6	10	61	10	.312
Darryl Motley	6	8	0	0	0	0	0	1	0	.000
Dale Murphy (OF)	159	566	115	167	27	1	44	105	16	.295
Graig Nettles	112	177	16	37	8	1	5	33	1	.209
Ken Oberkfell (3B)	135	508	59	142	29	2	3	48	3	.280
Gerald Perry (1B)	142	533	77	144	35	2	12	74	42	.270
Rafael Ramirez	56	179	22	47	12	0	1	21	6	.263
Gary Roenicke	67	151	25	33	8	0	9	28	0	.219
Paul Runge	27	47	9	10	1	0	3	8	0	.213
Ted Simmons	73	177	20	49	8	0	4	30	1	.277
Andres Thomas (SS)	82	324	29	75	11	0	5	39	6	.231
Ozzie Virgil (C)	123	429	57	106	13	1	27	72	0	.247
	161	5,428	747	1,401	284	24	152	696	135	.258

1988

Record: 54–106
Finish: Sixth (West)
Games Behind: 39½
Managers: Chuck Tanner, Russ Nixon

The Braves' ineptitude reached a new low in 1988. Never before in its Atlanta history had the club been so wretched, nor had it been subjected to so much absolute humiliation. Not since 1935 in Boston had the franchise fielded a worse team.

Supposedly in the midst of a rebuilding program but with an eye on contending, the Braves had no competition for the booby prize as the worst team in the National League. They were an incredible 27 games worse than fifth-place Houston in the West and 10½ games worse than the last-place Phillies in the East.

The only team in baseball to manage a worse record than the Braves—and then by just a half game—were the Baltimore Orioles, who opened the season with a record 21-game losing streak. The Braves, who lost a National League record 10 games to start the year, were neck and neck with the Orioles all season in a match of incompetence, though Baltimore easily outplayed Atlanta after April.

In finishing last for the sixth time in 13 years, the Braves scored the fewest runs in the league and allowed the most, had the worst on-base percentage, stole the fewest bases, had the fewest saves, and made the most errors. Only two teams hit fewer home runs. If that's not a horrible team, there's never been one.

Chuck Tanner survived only the first 39 games before he was fired in the midst of a season for the first time in his career. The team played only slightly better under his replacement, Russ Nixon, who was promoted from Atlanta's Double-A farm club at Greenville.

The change of command came nine days after the Braves put their offensive futility on display in a 19-inning victory over St. Louis. When the Cardinals ran out of pitchers, infielder Jose Oquendo pitched three scoreless innings before Atlanta finally solved him with two runs for a 7–5 win.

Even Dale Murphy, who had averaged 36 homers and 105

RBIs the previous six seasons, was caught up amid the Braves' offensive inadequacy. His batting average dropped to its lowest level since his first full season in the majors in 1978, and his home runs and RBIs were fewer than they'd been in a full season since 1979. The fact that there were no productive power hitters around him in the lineup contributed greatly to Murphy's struggles, since he rarely saw good pitches.

Gerald Perry was the only veteran Brave to have a productive season at the plate. He finished fifth in the league batting race but had to ask off the last day of the season to ensure his average would stay at .300.

Ron Gant, shaky on defense with 26 errors at second base, led all major league rookies in home runs, RBIs, runs, triples, and extra-base hits.

The Braves continued to bring along several young pitchers. John Smoltz made his major league debut. Pete Smith was the only Brave to pitch a shutout by himself. Tom Glavine's record wasn't much, but his ERA showed continued improvement.

The veteran pitchers contributed little. No one on the team won in double figures. A seemingly positive sign was Bruce Sutter's return from shoulder surgery to lead the team in saves (14). He became only the third man to save 300 career games; however, his arm was not healed, and he never pitched again.

Gerald Perry asked to sit out the final game of the 1988 season so he could keep his batting average at .300.

	G	AB	R	H	2B	3B	HR	RBI	SB	AVG
Bruce Benedict	90	236	11	57	7	0	0	19	0	.242
Jeff Blauser	18	67	7	16	3	1	2	7	0	.239
Terry Blocker	66	198	13	42	4	2	2	10	1	.212
Jody Davis	2	8	2	2	0	0	1	3	0	.250
Ron Gant (2B)	146	563	85	146	28	8	19	60	19	.259
Damaso Garcia	21	60	3	7	1	0	1	4	1	.117
Tommy Gregg	11	29	1	10	3	0	0	4	0	.345
Ken Griffey	69	193	21	48	5	0	2	19	1	.249
Albert Hall (OF)	85	231	27	57	7	1	1	15	15	.247
Dion James (OF)	132	386	46	99	17	5	3	30	9	.256
Mark Lemke	16	58	8	13	4	0	0	2	0	.224
Jim Morrison	51	92	6	14	2	0	2	13	0	.152
Dale Murphy (OF)	156	592	77	134	35	4	24	77	3	.226
Ken Oberkfell (3B)	120	422	42	117	20	4	3	40	4	.277
Gerald Perry (1B)	141	547	61	164	29	1	8	74	29	.300
Gary Roenicke	49	114	11	26	5	0	1	7	0	.228
Jerry Royster	68	102	8	18	3	0	0	1	0	.176
Paul Runge	52	76	11	16	5	0	0	7	0	.211
Ted Simmons	78	107	6	21	6	0	2	11	0	.196
Lonnie Smith	43	114	14	27	3	0	3	9	4	.237
Andres Thomas (SS)	153	606	54	153	22	2	13	68	1	.252
Ozzie Virgil (C)	107	320	23	82	10	0	9	31	2	.256
	160	5,440	555	1,319	228	28	96	527	95	.242

	W	L	G	GS	CG	IP	H	BB	SO	ERA
Jim Acker	0	4	21	1	0	42	45	14	25	4.71
Jose Alvarez	5	6	60	0	0	102⅓	88	53	81	2.99
Paul Assenmacher	8	7	64	0	0	79⅓	72	32	71	3.06
Kevin Blankenship	0	1	2	2	0	10⅔	7	7	5	3.38
Joe Boever	0	2	16	0	0	20⅓	12	1	7	1.77
Chuck Cary	0	0	7	0	0	8⅓	8	4	7	6.48
Kevin Coffman	2	6	18	11	0	67	62	54	24	5.78
Gary Eave	0	0	5	0	0	5	7	3	0	9.00
Juan Eichelberger	2	0	20	0	0	37⅓	44	10	13	3.86
Tom Glavine	7	17*	34	34	1	195⅓	201	63	84	4.56
German Jimenez	1	6	15	9	0	55⅔	65	12	26	5.01
Rick Mahler	9	16	39	34	5	249	279*	42	131	3.69
Jim Morrison	0	0	3	0	0	3⅔	3	2	1	0.00
Ed Olwine	0	0	16	0	0	18⅔	22	4	5	6.75
Charlie Puleo	5	5	53	3	0	106⅓	101	47	70	3.47
Pete Smith	7	15	32	32	5	195⅓	183	88	124	3.69
Zane Smith	5	10	23	22	3	140⅓	159	44	59	4.30
John Smoltz	2	7	12	12	0	64	74	33	37	5.48
Bruce Sutter	1	4	38	0	0	45¼	49	11	40	4.76
	54	106*		160	14	1,446	1,481	524	810	4.09

Shutouts—P. Smith (3)
Saves—Sutter (14), Assenmacher (5), Alvarez (3), Boever, Olwine, Puleo

1989

Record: 63–97
Finish: Sixth (West)
Games Behind: 28
Manager: Russ Nixon

In retrospect, you can see something positive was starting to develop in 1989. But at the time, it all blended into a dismal bottom line that read: Last place.

The National League pitching statistics for 1989 were dotted with two names that meant little to Braves fans then but who would soon help lead the team's march to prominence.

John Smoltz, a 22-year-old right-hander, and Tom Glavine, a 23-year-old left-hander, somehow found a way to post winning records for a team that finished 34 games under .500. Those records should have been strong enough indications that Smoltz and Glavine would be around for a while, but if they weren't, the league's final pitching stats provided even more evidence.

Smoltz, who made the All-Star team, was ranked third in the league in lowest opponents' batting average (.212) and fourth in fewest hits per nine innings (6.92), two of the more telling indicators of a pitcher's effectiveness. Glavine tied for third in shutouts (4) and was fifth in fewest walks per nine innings (1.94).

It would take more than just two pitchers to turn the Braves into champions, but it was a good start.

For the time being, though, the team and its fans had to deal with a second straight last-place finish, its third in four years, and the seventh in 14 seasons. For the second consecutive year, the Braves had the worst record in the National League and the second-worst percentage in baseball.

Atlanta had the worst batting average (.234) in the league and its lowest since 1952. Nixon's club was 11th in runs scored and stolen bases. The pitching staff ranked 10th in ERA (3.70), and the bullpen blew 23 save opportunities.

Another problem was the continuing struggle of 33-year-old Dale Murphy, once the cornerstone of the team. His average stayed in the .220s for the second straight year, and his home runs declined for the third consecutive season. In July, Murphy did manage two home runs and six RBIs in the sixth inning of a 10–1 romp over the Giants. He was the first Brave to hit two homers in an inning since Bobby Lowe in 1894, and his six RBIs tied the major league record for an inning.

However, the team's biggest offensive force was the rejuvenated Lonnie Smith. Given up for dead much of 1988 when he was at Richmond, the 33-year-old outfielder bounced back to finish third in the league batting race (.315) behind Tony Gwynn and Will Clark. Smith also had career highs in home runs (21) and RBIs (79) and was named Comeback Player of the Year by *The Sporting News*.

Highly regarded Ron Gant went the opposite direction from Smith, though. After an outstanding rookie season, the young infielder had to be demoted to Class-A Sumter of the South Atlantic League in June when he was hitting just .172. Converted to the outfield, Gant returned to the majors before the end of the season.

	G	AB	R	H	2B	3B	HR	RBI	SB	AVG
Bruce Benedict	66	160	12	31	3	0	1	6	0	.194
Geronimo Berroa	81	136	7	36	4	0	2	9	0	.265
Jeff Blauser (3B)	142	456	63	123	24	2	12	46	5	.270
Terry Blocker	26	31	1	7	1	0	0	1	1	.226
Francisco Cabrera	4	14	0	3	2	0	0	0	0	.214
Jody Davis (C)	78	231	12	39	5	0	4	19	0	.169
Drew Denson	12	36	1	9	1	0	0	5	1	.250
Darrell Evans	107	276	31	57	6	1	11	39	0	.207
Ron Gant	75	260	26	46	8	3	9	25	9	.177
Tommy Gregg	102	276	24	67	8	0	6	23	3	.243
Dion James	63	170	15	44	7	0	1	11	1	.259
David Justice	16	51	7	12	3	0	1	3	2	.235
Mark Lemke	14	55	4	10	2	1	2	10	0	.182
Kelly Mann	7	24	1	5	2	0	0	1	0	.208
Oddibe McDowell (OF)	76	280	56	85	18	4	7	24	15	.304
John Mizerock	11	27	1	6	0	0	0	2	0	.222
Dale Murphy (OF)	154	574	60	131	16	0	20	84	3	.228
Gerald Perry (1B)	72	266	24	67	11	0	4	21	10	.252
Ed Romero	7	19	1	5	1	0	1	1	0	.263
John Russell	74	159	14	29	2	0	2	9	0	.182
Lonnie Smith (OF)	134	482	89	152	34	4	21	79	25	.315
Andres Thomas (SS)	141	554	41	118	18	0	13	57	3	.213
Jeff Treadway (2B)	134	473	58	131	18	3	8	40	3	.277
Jeff Wetherby	52	48	5	10	2	1	1	7	1	.208
Ed Whited	36	74	5	12	3	0	1	4	1	.162
	161	5,463	584	1,281	201	22	128	544	83	.234

	W	L	G	GS	CG	IP	H	BB	SO	ERA
Jim Acker	0	6	59	0	0	97⅔	84	20	68	2.67
Jay Aldrich	1	2	8	0	0	12⅓	7	6	7	2.19
Jose Alvarez	3	3	30	0	0	50⅓	44	24	45	2.86
Paul Assenmacher	1	3	49	0	0	57⅔	55	16	64	3.59
Terry Blocker	0	0	1	0	0	1	0	2	0	0.00
Joe Boever	4	11	66	0	0	82⅓	78	34	68	3.94
Tony Castillo	0	1	12	0	0	9⅓	8	4	5	4.82
Marty Clary	4	3	18	17	2	108⅔	103	31	30	3.15
Gary Eave	2	0	3	3	0	20⅔	15	12	9	1.31
Mark Eichhorn	5	5	45	0	0	68⅓	70	19	49	4.35
Tom Glavine	14	8	29	29	6	186	172	40	90	3.68
Tommy Greene	1	2	4	4	1	26⅓	22	6	17	4.10
Dwayne Henry	0	2	12	0	0	12⅔	12	5	16	4.26
Derek Lilliquist	8	10	32	30	0	165⅔	202	34	79	3.97
Kent Mercker	0	0	2	1	0	4⅓	8	6	4	12.46
Charlie Puleo	1	1	15	1	0	29	26	16	17	4.66
Rusty Richards	0	0	2	2	0	9⅓	10	6	4	4.82
John Russell	0	0	1	0	0	⅓	0	0	0	0.00
Pete Smith	5	14	28	27	1	142	144	57	115	4.75
Zane Smith	1	12	17	17	0	99	102	33	58	4.45
John Smoltz	12	11	29	29	5	208	160	72	168	2.94
Mike Stanton	0	1	20	0	0	24	17	8	27	1.50
Sergio Valdez	1	2	19	1	0	32⅔	31	17	26	6.06
	63	97*		161	15	1,447⅔	1,370	468	966	3.70

Shutouts—Glavine (4), Clary, Greene
Saves—Boever (21), Stanton (7), Acker (2), Alvarez (2), Henry

1990

Record: 65–97
Finish: Sixth (West)
Games Behind: 26
Managers: Russ Nixon, Bobby Cox

Dale Murphy was traded to Philadelphia. David Justice moved into right field. Bobby Cox moved back into the dugout. Greg Olson went from being a minor league castoff to an All-Star catcher. Ron Gant joined the 30–30 club. Mark Lemke became a full-time major leaguer. And Steve Avery and Charlie Leibrandt joined the show.

The 1990 season was an eventful one, especially in light of what has transpired since then.

But, a third straight last-place finish and seventh consecutive sub-.500 performance was nothing to get excited about back in 1990. Even with the continued influx of young players and the truly outstanding accomplishments by some of them, the Braves appeared still to be in turmoil. They had the worst record in either league, they made yet another managerial change, and their big free agent signee was a bust.

Everything started as usual in 1990. Only the Braves could sign the game's most-coveted free agent and get just nine games out of him. The team's big catches had a history of going sour, but the case of Nick Esasky topped them all.

The powerful first baseman had a career year for Boston in 1989, hitting 30 home runs and driving in 108 runs. He signed a three-year deal with the Braves for $5.6 million. But in spring training, the 30-year-old Esasky was stricken with bouts of dizziness. Eventually, he was diagnosed with vertigo. He tried to play but couldn't. Ted Turner had written some

The trade of Dale Murphy to Philadelphia in 1990 enabled David Justice to move to right field, where he immediately prospered.

bad checks before, but never before had he gotten so little return on such a large investment.

Between losing Esasky and 13 of 17 games in April, the season couldn't have started much worse. One early bright spot came May 27 when John Smoltz no-hit the Phillies for 8⅓ innings before Len Dykstra broke it up with a double.

The team continued to flounder, though, and with its record at 25–40, Russ Nixon was fired June 22. Cox came out of the general manager's office to manage, and team president Stan Kasten said a decision would be made after the season about which position—not both—Cox would keep in 1991.

The Braves played to only a slightly better percentage under Cox over the final 97 games. But significant changes continued in the makeup of the club.

Just before Nixon's ouster, Avery, a highly regarded 20-year-old left-hander, made his greatly anticipated major league debut. He was shelled (8 runs in 2⅓ innings), but he would get better.

Then on August 4, Murphy, the two-time MVP, was sent to the Phillies along with Tommy Greene in exchange for Jeff Parrett, Jim Vatcher, and Victor Rosario.

Perhaps the most popular player of the team's Atlanta era, Murphy had been struggling for two and a half years. His exit was an emotional event for the team, its fans, and the entire city. However, it enabled Justice to move from first base to his natural position in right field.

The young power hitter with the picturesque swing responded in robust style. Over the final two months, Justice hit 20 home runs and drove in 50, leading the league with 11 homers in August and again with nine in September. His 23 home runs after the All-Star break tied Detroit's Cecil Fielder for the major league lead. Justice became the first Brave since Bob Horner in 1978 to be named National League Rookie of the Year.

Another of the year's big stories was the play of Olson, a previously unknown catcher who became the Braves' starter through a series of events affecting four players in front of him at the position. He opened the season at Triple-A Richmond but by midseason was the Braves' lone representative in the All-Star Game at Wrigley Field.

Gant, back from his refresher course in the minors as an outfielder, started slowly but caught fire in late May. He became only the 13th member of the 30–30 (home runs–steals) club.

Though the offense appeared to be making strides, with Gant and Justice giving the Braves one of the most exciting tandems of young power hitters in the game, the pitching, supposedly the backbone of the club's revitalization, was lagging. In fact, the staff ERA (4.58) was the worst in baseball.

Smoltz's ERA jumped nearly a run from 1989; Tom Glavine fell under .500 and saw his ERA escalate, too. Avery was just getting his feet wet, and Leibrandt, the veteran brought in to stabilize the staff, had to sit out part of the year with a shoulder injury. The bullpen, too, was shaky as Mike Stanton was sidelined with a bad shoulder and Kent Mercker tried to convert from starter to reliever.

To make matters even worse for the pitchers, the defense led the majors in errors.

Greg Olson went from the minors to the 1990 All-Star Game in half a season.

Kasten decided to keep Cox in the dugout for 1991, and in October, he brought in John Schuerholz from Kansas City as general manager.

	G	AB	R	H	2B	3B	HR	RBI	SB	AVG
Mike Bell	36	45	8	11	5	1	1	5	0	.244
Geronimo Berroa	7	4	0	0	0	0	0	0	0	.000
Jeff Blauser (SS)	115	386	46	104	24	3	8	39	3	.269
Francisco Cabrera	63	137	14	38	5	1	7	25	1	.277
Jody Davis	12	28	0	2	0	0	0	1	0	.071
Nick Esasky	9	35	2	6	0	0	0	0	0	.171
Ron Gant (OF)	152	575	107	174	34	3	32	84	33	.303
Tommy Gregg	124	239	18	63	13	1	5	32	4	.264
Alex Infante	20	28	3	1	1	0	0	0	0	.036
David Justice (1B)	127	439	76	124	23	2	28	78	11	.282
Jimmy Kremers	29	73	7	8	1	1	1	2	0	.110
Mark Lemke	102	239	22	54	13	0	0	21	0	.226
Kelly Mann	11	28	2	4	1	0	1	2	0	.143
Oddibe McDowell	113	305	47	74	14	0	7	25	13	.243
Dale Murphy (OF)	97	349	38	81	14	0	17	55	9	.232
Greg Olson (C)	100	298	36	78	12	1	7	36	1	.262
Jim Presley (3B)	140	541	59	131	34	1	19	72	1	.242
Victor Rosario	9	7	3	1	0	0	0	0	0	.143
Lonnie Smith (OF)	135	466	72	142	27	9	9	42	10	.305
Andres Thomas	84	278	26	61	8	0	5	30	2	.219
Jeff Treadway (2B)	128	474	56	134	20	2	11	59	3	.283
Jim Vatcher	21	27	2	7	1	1	0	3	0	.259
Ernie Whitt	67	180	14	31	8	0	2	10	0	.172
	162	5,504	682	1,376	263	26	162	636	92	.250

	W	L	G	GS	CG	IP	H	BB	SO	ERA
Steve Avery	3	11	21	20	1	99	121	45	75	5.64
Joe Boever	1	3	33	0	0	42⅓	40	35	35	4.68
Tony Castillo	5	1	52	3	0	76⅔	93	20	64	4.23
Marty Clary	1	10	33	14	0	101⅔	128	39	44	5.67
Marvin Freeman	1	0	9	0	0	15⅔	7	3	12	1.72
Tom Glavine	10	12	33	33	1	214⅓	232	78	129	4.28
Mark Grant	1	2	33	1	0	52⅓	61	18	40	4.64
Tommy Greene	1	0	5	2	0	12⅓	14	9	4	8.03
Dwayne Henry	2	2	34	0	0	38⅓	41	25	34	5.63
Joe Hesketh	0	2	31	0	0	31	30	12	21	5.81
Charley Kerfeld	3	1	25	0	0	30⅔	31	23	27	5.58
Charlie Leibrandt	9	11	24	24	5	162⅓	164	35	76	3.16
Derek Lilliquist	2	8	12	11	0	61⅓	75	19	34	6.28
Rick Luecken	1	4	36	0	0	53	73	30	35	5.77
Paul Marak	1	2	7	7	1	39	39	19	15	3.69
Kent Mercker	4	7	36	0	0	48⅓	43	24	39	3.17
Jeff Parrett	1	1	20	0	0	27	27	19	17	3.00
Rusty Richards	0	0	1	0	0	1	2	1	0	27.00
Doug Sisk	0	0	3	0	0	2⅓	1	4	1	3.86
Pete Smith	5	6	13	13	3	77	77	24	56	4.79
John Smoltz	14	11	34	34	6	231⅓	206	90*	170	3.85
Mike Stanton	0	3	7	0	0	7	16	4	7	18.00
Sergio Valdez	0	0	6	0	0	5⅓	6	3	3	6.75
	65	97*		162	17	1,429⅔	1,527*	579	938	4.58

Shutouts—Leibrandt (2), Smoltz (2), Avery, Marak
Saves—Boever (8), Mercker (7), Hesketh (5), Grant (3), Kerfeld (2), Stanton (2), Castillo, Luecken, Parrett

1991

Record: 94–68
Finish: First (West)
Games Ahead: 1
Manager: Bobby Cox

The 1991 Braves were no less a miracle than their ancestors of 1914, who went from last place on July 18 to the World Series championship.

When Ron Gant screamed, "We shook up the world," in the Braves' clubhouse following the clinching of the 1991 West division title, he was not overstating the circumstances one bit. Atlanta had entered the season as the laughingstock of baseball and emerged as one of the great Cinderella teams in all sports history.

"Worst to First."

Never before in modern times, until Bobby Cox's 1991 club, had a team finished one season with the worst record in the game and come back the next year to finish first. The Braves not only were last in 1990, but they were at the bottom of the division in 1989 and 1988, too. In 1991, though, they won the West, beat the Pirates in the National League Championship Series, and took the Minnesota Twins to the 10th inning of the seventh game of a tingling World Series before being subdued.

Atlanta and the South had never experienced anything like it before and probably never will again. The Chop and the Chant were brand new, the thrills came out of nowhere, and hysteria swept over baseball fans throughout the region like a plague of sheer enchantment. There's no time quite like the first time.

There were signs of a few of the franchise's young players beginning to develop and mature in 1990, but no one could have imagined what it would lead to in just one year. But when John Schuerholz arrived as general manager in the fall of 1990 to oversee the continuation of the Braves' rebuilding ef-

fort, he immediately began shopping for the ingredients missing from the developing package Cox turned over to him.

Terry Pendleton, Sid Bream, Juan Berenguer, Rafael Belliard, and Deion Sanders weren't the biggest names on the free agent market. Sanders was only a minor league free agent. The others were accomplished veterans, but by no means superstars. Schuerholz signed them, then just before the start of the season, swung a trade with Montreal for speedy center fielder Otis Nixon. That deal didn't exactly light up Peachtree Street either.

But, in time, all six would prove close to perfect fits for the roles Schuerholz and Cox planned for them.

The events of the season unfolded slowly at first, making the end result even more gripping. The Braves were 8–10 in April, certainly nothing to prompt pennant fever over a team that hadn't finished above .500 since 1983. But May . . . May was a different matter.

Atlanta was 17–9 in May. Tom Glavine was 6–0 with a 1.76 ERA to earn National League Pitcher of the Month. And David Justice was selected Player of the Month for hitting .381 with five home runs and 28 RBIs. Pendleton led the league in hitting for the month, and Ron Gant led it in home runs. The Braves had their first winning month in four years and moved into second place, just one-half game behind the Dodgers. It was pretty heady stuff.

Cox's team came back to earth in June, dropping to third place, 7½ games back, after losing 17 of 29 games. In the last week of the month, Justice, who led the league with 51 RBIs, was lost because of a bad back, and Bream had to undergo knee surgery. In the past, the team would have folded, but in 1991, it rallied.

Terry Pendleton led the league in hitting in 1991 and was named the league's MVP for fueling the Braves' stunning "Worst to First" saga.

Veteran Lonnie Smith and rookies Brian Hunter and Keith Mitchell stepped in to weather the storm in the absence of Justice and Bream. At the All-Star break, the Braves had slipped to third place with a 39–40 record, 9½ games out of first. Apparently refreshed by the three days off, they won nine of their first 11 games at the same time the Dodgers were losing nine of 11. Within 12 days, the Braves went from 9½ games behind to 2½ back. Steve Avery was 4–0 in July, Nixon led the league in hitting for the month, and Pendleton batted .360.

It was still hard to believe, but these were the Braves.

Atlanta refused to fold. Glavine won his 15th on August 13, beating the Giants, 9–2, and moving the Braves within one-half game of the Dodgers again.

Eight days later, a 9–6 loss and a 3½-game deficit was staring them in the face with two outs in the ninth at Cincinnati. But Francisco Cabrera proceeded to hit a three-run homer off Rob Dibble to tie a game the Braves won in the 13th on a double by Justice. It was the sort of magic an underdog team needs to win a championship.

On August 26, the Braves rallied from a 7–1 deficit to Montreal after 4½ innings to win 8–7 behind a grand slam from Jeff Blauser and another homer by Justice. The next night, Atlanta moved into a first-place tie with Los Angeles on the strength of a 13-strikeout performance by red-hot Charlie Leibrandt.

Berenguer, who had become the bullpen ace with 17 saves in 18 tries, was lost August 12 due to a stress fracture in his forearm. But on August 29, Schuerholz picked up Alejandro Pena, who filled the void quite nicely, from the Mets.

In September, the Braves and Dodgers stayed at each other's throats. They changed places seven times and were never separated by more than 2½ games. Notable accomplishments included a combined no-hitter by Kent Mercker, Mark Wohlers, and Pena against San Diego September 11,

and Gant becoming the third man to attain the 30–30 (home runs–steals) club in consecutive seasons.

On September 15, Bream hit a grand slam to help beat the Dodgers, giving the Braves a 1½-game lead. However, the next day it was announced that Nixon, a catalyst of the club, was suspended for 60 days for substance abuse. The Braves lost four of their next five and found themselves 1½ games back. By September 26, they were two games in arrears with only nine to play—the next six on the road.

They swept three at Houston and moved to within a game of the Dodgers with six to go. John Smoltz, rebounding from a 2–11 first half, shut out the Reds, 4–0, but the Dodgers won, too, on the final day of September.

Atlanta's hopes seemed to border on extinction October 1 when Cincinnati jumped to a 6–0 lead through three innings behind the pitching of Jose Rijo. But the Braves fought back to within 6–5 entering the ninth against Dibble. That's when Justice hit a two-run homer to win one of the most memorable games in franchise history.

Even though the Dodgers also won, their one-game lead with four to play suddenly seemed tenuous.

The Braves completed a sweep of Cincinnati the next night and the Dodgers lost. The two teams were tied for first with three games to play. Atlanta returned home to play Houston, while the Dodgers ventured into hostile Candlestick Park to play the Giants.

On October 4, Avery beat the Astros, and the Dodgers lost at San Francisco. Atlanta was one up with two to play.

On the next-to-last day of the season, Smoltz beat Houston, 5–2, for the Braves' eighth straight victory. After the final out, the players huddled in the middle of the field and watched the center-field TV screen, along with thousands of fans still in the stadium, as the Giants again beat the Dodgers. It was all over. The Braves were division champs, and a wild celebration followed.

The Braves were 55–28 (.663) after the All-Star break and won 21 of their last 29 (.724). They set Atlanta records with 94 victories and an attendance of 2,140,217 tomahawk-chopping fans.

Glavine became the first Brave to win the Cy Young Award since Warren Spahn in 1957. Pendleton, who batted .230 with

Juan Berenguer saved 17 games in 18 attempts before suffering a stress fracture in his arm in mid-August.

Bobby Cox and his team watched the final outs of the Dodgers' loss on the center field TV screen before breaking into a full-scale celebration on the next-to-last day of the 1991 season.

St. Louis the year before, won the organization's first National League MVP since Dale Murphy in 1983. He also led the league in hitting, the first Brave to do so since Ralph Garr in 1974, and set a franchise record for third basemen with his .319 average. Cox was honored as the league's Manager of the Year, and Schuerholz as the league's Executive of the Year.

The pitching staff led the league in complete games (18), fewest hits allowed, and opponents' batting average (.240). The pitchers also set an Atlanta record with 969 strikeouts.

Avery, at 21, was third in the league in wins, becoming the youngest 18-game winner in modern Braves history. He beat the Dodgers twice down the stretch and won his last five decisions.

Smoltz went from 2–11 with a 5.16 ERA in the first half to 12–2, 2.62 in the second half. He was 8–1 with a 1.49 ERA in his last 13 starts.

Glavine, the franchise's first 20-game winner since Phil Niekro in 1979, tied for the league lead in victories and complete games, and he was second in innings and third in strikeouts and ERA.

The real hero of the pitching staff may have been Pena, who was 2–0 with 11 saves in as many opportunities with the Braves. In his last 17⅔ innings, he allowed only one earned run.

The Braves were second in the league in runs and tied for third in home runs. They also were third in stolen bases with an Atlanta-record 165.

Rafael Belliard supplied excellent defense at shortstop. Jeff Treadway battled various ailments to give the club its best offense at second base in a long time. Durable Greg Olson did a superb job handling the pitching staff and was one of the team's best clutch hitters. Bream and Hunter were a formidable platoon at first base, combining for 23 homers and 95 RBIs. Even with his season ending early, Nixon set an Atlanta record for steals (72), second in the league.

Gant wound up third in the league in home runs and fifth in RBIs. Pendleton, the team leader on and off the field, topped the league in hits (187) and total bases as well as average and finished third in slugging percentage (.517).

It was an incredible, unforgettable season, one that can never be duplicated or probably even approached for its sheer captivating electricity. But, at the same time, it was only the beginning of one of the most spectacular eras in franchise history.

	G	AB	R	H	2B	3B	HR	RBI	SB	AVG
Mike Bell	17	30	4	4	0	0	1	1	1	.133
Rafael Belliard (SS)	149	353	36	88	9	2	0	27	3	.249
Damon Berryhill	1	1	0	0	0	0	0	0	0	.000
Jeff Blauser	129	352	49	91	14	3	11	54	5	.259
Sid Bream (1B)	91	265	32	67	12	0	11	45	0	.253
Francisco Cabrera	44	95	7	23	6	0	4	23	1	.242
Vinny Castilla	12	5	1	1	0	0	0	0	0	.200
Ron Gant (OF)	154	561	101	141	35	3	32	105	34	.251
Tommy Gregg	72	107	13	20	8	1	1	4	2	.187
Mike Heath	49	139	4	29	3	1	1	12	0	.209
Danny Heep	14	12	4	5	1	0	0	3	0	.417
Brian Hunter	97	271	32	68	16	1	12	50	0	.251
David Justice (OF)	109	396	67	109	25	1	21	87	8	.275
Mark Lemke	136	269	36	63	11	2	2	23	1	.234
Keith Mitchell	48	66	11	21	0	0	2	5	3	.318
Otis Nixon	124	401	81	119	10	1	0	26	72	.297
Greg Olson (C)	133	411	46	99	25	0	6	44	1	.241
Terry Pendleton (3B)	153	586	94	187*	34	8	22	86	10	.319*
Rico Rossy	5	1	0	0	0	0	0	0	0	.000
Deion Sanders	54	110	16	21	1	2	4	13	11	.191
Lonnie Smith (OF)	122	353	58	97	19	1	7	44	9	.275
Jeff Treadway (2B)	106	306	41	98	17	2	3	32	2	.320
Jerry Willard	17	14	1	3	0	0	1	4	0	.214
	162	5,456	749	1,407	255	30	141	704	165	.258

	W	L	G	GS	CG	IP	H	BB	SO	ERA
Steve Avery	18	8	35	35	3	210⅓	189	65	137	3.38
Juan Berenguer	0	3	49	0	0	64⅓	43	20	53	2.24
Mike Bielecki	0	0	2	0	0	1⅔	2	2	3	0.00
Tony Castillo	1	1	7	0	0	8⅔	13	5	8	7.27
Jim Clancy	3	2	24	0	0	34⅔	36	14	17	5.71
Marvin Freeman	1	0	34	0	0	48	37	13	34	3.00
Tom Glavine	20*	11	34	34	9*	246⅔	201	69	192	2.55
Charlie Leibrandt	15	13	36	36	1	229⅔	212	56	128	3.49
Rick Mahler	1	1	13	2	0	28⅔	33	13	10	5.65
Kent Mercker	5	3	50	4	0	73⅓	56	35	62	2.58
Jeff Parrett	1	2	18	0	0	21⅓	31	12	14	6.33
Alejandro Pena	2	0	15	0	0	19⅓	11	3	13	1.40
Dan Petry	0	0	10	0	0	24⅓	29	14	9	5.55
Armando Reynoso	2	1	6	5	0	23⅓	26	10	10	6.17
Randy St. Claire	0	0	19	0	0	28⅔	31	9	30	4.08
Doug Sisk	2	1	14	0	0	14⅓	21	8	5	5.02
Pete Smith	1	3	14	10	0	48	48	22	29	5.06
John Smoltz	14	13	36	36	5	229⅔	206	77	148	3.80
Mike Stanton	5	5	74	0	0	78	62	21	54	2.88
Mark Wohlers	3	1	17	0	0	19⅔	17	13	13	3.20
	94	68		162	18*	1,452⅔	1,304	481	969	3.49

Shutouts—Avery, Glavine, Leibrandt
Saves—Berenguer (17), Pena (11), Stanton (7), Mercker (6), Clancy (3), Wohlers (2), Freeman

The 1991 National League champion Braves provided fans with unforgettable thrills and brought the World Series to the South for the first time.

1992

Record: 98–64
Finish: First (West)
Games Ahead: 8
Manager: Bobby Cox

The Braves liked their "Last to First" script of 1991 so much that they did it again in 1992.

As late as May 26, Bobby Cox's team was in last place and not looking at all like it was intent on a successful defense of the National League pennant. The Braves had stumbled to a 20–27 record (.426) at that point and were seven games out of first place.

The slow start came in spite of the blistering pace set by Deion Sanders, who opened the year in center field because Otis Nixon had to sit out the first 16 games because his suspension carried over from 1991. Sanders put together a 14-game hitting streak with six triples in the first two weeks during which he batted .407.

However, the team did not follow suit, largely because of bullpen failures. The best example came May 9 at St. Louis. The Braves had leads of 9–0 and 11–3 behind John Smoltz but lost 12–11 when the Cardinals scored 12 times in the final five innings.

On May 24, Smoltz struck out 15, tying a franchise record in a 2–1 victory against Montreal. But the Braves lost the next two, dropping into the division basement. The club had bottomed out at that point and proceeded to embark on an exhilarating climb through the ranks.

For nearly the next three months, Atlanta played one of the most phenomenal sustained stretches of baseball in franchise history. In the process, the Braves all but guaranteed themselves a second consecutive division title.

Between May 27 and August 19, Cox's club was 53–18 (.746), opening a 6½-game lead over Cincinnati, who was favored to win the division. Left-hander Kent Mercker helped stabilize the bullpen, stringing together 25 scoreless innings in 22 appearances in which he was 2–0 with five saves.

Just before the All-Star Game, Atlanta suffered a temporary setback, losing three straight at Cincinnati and falling four games off the pace. But they bounced right back to win the last five games before the break in the schedule. In the final game, a 7–4 victory at Chicago, Jeff Blauser became only the fourth shortstop in history to hit three home runs in a game.

After the three-day All-Star break, the team came back to win another seven in a row, bringing it within one of the modern franchise record of 13 straight.

On July 25 at Atlanta, the Braves were on the brink of equaling that record when they entered the ninth inning protecting a 1–0 lead against the Pirates. However, with a man on, Pittsburgh's Andy Van Slyke hit what appeared to be a potential game-winning home run off Alejandro Pena. Just as the ball was disappearing over the right-center fence, though, Nixon came sprinting from center, leaped, reached over the fence, and managed to pull the ball back in the park with what immediately became known as "The Catch." One out later, the Braves had their 13th straight win and a two-game lead over Cincinnati.

The final serious challenge by Cincinnati came in early August when the Reds, trailing the Braves by just one-half game, came to Atlanta for a three-game series. They left town with a 3½-game deficit.

Damon Berryhill became the everyday catcher when Greg Olson suffered a broken leg on September 19, 1992.

The Braves won the first game of the series, 6–5, on a two-run homer by Terry Pendleton in the ninth. Steve Avery's pitching highlighted a 5–1 victory in the second game, and Smoltz won the final game, 5–3. Atlanta then stood 64–42, the best record in baseball.

On August 19, Tom Glavine beat Montreal for his 13th consecutive victory, the longest by a Braves pitcher in the 20th century. That game moved Atlanta to 28 games over .500 for the first time since 1958 in Milwaukee.

Though the club appeared well prepared for another run at the pennant and possibly a World Series championship, the bullpen remained a question mark. Pena, who was invincible down the stretch in '91, was struggling with illness and arm problems. That prompted John Schuerholz to go shopping once again.

On August 30, the Braves general manager sent two prospects to Boston in exchange for 37-year-old Jeff Reardon, baseball's all-time saves leader at the time. In his first 11 games as a Brave, Reardon was 3–0 with three saves and a 0.69 ERA.

By September 16, the Braves had opened a 10½-game gap on Cincinnati. The clinching didn't come until September 29 because of a nine-game winning streak by the Reds, and during the wait Atlanta suffered a painful loss. On September 19, Houston's Ken Caminiti crashed into Greg Olson, leaving the popular catcher with a broken leg and dislocated

Brian Hunter teamed with Sid Bream to form an effective platoon tandem at first base.

ankle. The loss of Olson made Damon Berryhill, who'd been platooning, the everyday catcher.

The Braves finished with 98 wins, a modern franchise record and the most since Frank Selee's Beaneaters won 102 in 1898. After August 2, they were never out of first place.

There was little lacking from the Atlanta arsenal. Cox's team led the league in home runs (138) and slugging percentage (.388) and was third in runs scored. The pitching staff led the league in ERA (3.14) for the first time since 1958 and also led in shutouts (24).

Pendleton did not win the MVP award, finishing second to Pittsburgh's Barry Bonds, but he actually had a better season than when he won it in 1991. The switch-hitting third baseman set an Atlanta record for doubles (39), tied for the league lead in hits (199), finished second in RBIs (105), and was fourth in total bases.

David Justice and Ron Gant actually had off years by their standards. Nixon had an excellent season after returning from his suspension, and Sanders, who then became the fourth outfielder, led the league in triples.

Mark Lemke, the hero of the 1991 postseason, finally took over as the regular second baseman. The first-base platoon of Sid Bream and Brian Hunter produced 24 homers and 102 RBIs.

The pitching staff was what allowed the Braves to dominate, though.

Smoltz became the first Brave to lead the league in strikeouts since Phil Niekro in 1977 and finished fourth in complete games. Glavine, who lost the Cy Young Award to Greg Maddux of the Cubs, became the first Brave to record consecutive 20-victory seasons since Warren Spahn notched six in a row (1956–61). He tied Maddux for the league lead in victories (20) and also tied for the lead in shutouts (5).

Veteran Charlie Leibrandt had another fine season. The Braves were 22–9 in games he started. Avery's record dropped to .500, largely because of a lack of offensive support. Pete Smith, who opened the year at Richmond, became the fifth starter down the stretch when Mike Bielecki was injured, and the Braves won all 11 games he started.

The franchise attendance record was obliterated. The final count was 3,077,400, a far cry from 1990 when the club failed to draw even 1 million for the third straight year.

	G	AB	R	H	2B	3B	HR	RBI	SB	AVG
Rafael Belliard (SS)	144	285	20	60	6	1	0	14	0	.211
Damon Berryhill	101	307	21	70	16	1	10	43	0	.228
Jeff Blauser	123	343	61	90	19	3	14	46	5	.262
Sid Bream (1B)	125	372	30	97	25	1	10	61	6	.261
Francisco Cabrera	12	10	2	3	0	0	2	3	0	.300
Vinny Castilla	9	16	1	4	1	0	0	1	0	.250
Ron Gant (OF)	153	544	74	141	22	6	17	80	32	.259
Tommy Gregg	18	19	1	5	0	0	1	1	1	.263
Brian Hunter	102	238	34	57	13	2	14	41	1	.239
David Justice (OF)	144	484	78	124	19	5	21	72	2	.256
Ryan Klesko	13	14	0	0	0	0	0	1	0	.000
Mark Lemke (2B)	155	427	38	97	7	4	6	26	0	.227
Javy Lopez	9	16	3	6	2	0	0	2	0	.375
Steve Lyons	11	14	0	1	0	1	0	1	0	.071
Mel Nieves	12	19	0	4	1	0	0	1	0	.211
Otis Nixon (OF)	120	456	79	134	14	2	2	22	41	.294
Greg Olson (C)	95	302	27	72	14	2	3	27	2	.238
Terry Pendleton (3B)	160	640	98	199*	39	1	21	105	5	.311
Deion Sanders	97	303	54	92	6	14*	8	28	26	.304
Lonnie Smith	84	158	23	39	8	2	6	33	4	.247
Jeff Treadway	61	126	5	28	6	1	0	5	1	.222
Jerry Willard	26	23	2	8	1	0	2	7	0	.348
	162	5,480	682	1,391	223	48	138*	641	126	.254

	W	L	G	GS	CG	IP	H	BB	SO	ERA
Steve Avery	11	11	35	35*	2	233⅓	216	71	129	3.20
Juan Berenguer	3	1	28	0	0	33⅓	35	16	19	5.13
Mike Bielecki	2	4	19	14	1	80⅔	77	27	62	2.57
Pedro Borbon	0	1	2	0	0	1⅓	2	1	1	6.75
Mark Davis	1	0	14	0	0	16⅔	22	13	15	7.02
Marvin Freeman	7	5	58	0	0	64⅓	61	29	41	3.22
Tom Glavine	20*	8	33	33	7	225	197	70	129	2.76
Charlie Leibrandt	15	7	32	31	5	193	191	42	104	3.36
Kent Mercker	3	2	53	0	0	68⅓	51	35	49	3.42
David Nied	3	0	6	2	0	23	10	5	19	1.17
Alejandro Pena	1	6	41	0	0	42	40	13	34	4.07
Jeff Reardon	3	0	14	0	0	15⅔	14	2	7	1.15
Armando Reynoso	1	0	3	1	0	7⅔	11	2	2	4.70
Ben Rivera	0	1	8	0	0	15⅓	21	13	11	4.70
Randy St. Claire	0	0	10	0	0	15⅓	17	8	7	5.87
Pete Smith	7	0	12	11	2	79	63	28	43	2.05
John Smoltz	15	12	35	35*	9	246⅔	206	80	215*	2.85
Mike Stanton	5	4	65	0	0	63⅔	59	20	44	4.10
Mark Wohlers	1	2	32	0	0	35⅓	28	14	17	2.55
	98*	64		162	26	1,460	1,321	489	948	3.14*

Shutouts—Glavine (5*), Smoltz (3), Avery (2), Leibrandt (2), Bielecki, Smith
Saves—Pena (15), Stanton (8), Mercker (6), Wohlers (4), Freeman (3), Reardon (3), Berenguer, Reynoso

1993

Record: 104–58
Finish: First (West)
Games Ahead: 1
Manager: Bobby Cox

No, the Braves didn't finally win the World Series in 1993. They didn't even win the National League pennant. But the '93 Braves supplied their fans with an abundance of thrills for the third straight season, and they provided baseball with what may always be remembered as "The Last Great Pennant Race."

The reason Bobby Cox's team fell short of its postseason goals may well have been that it burned itself out during a spectacular two-and-a-half-month crusade to a most improbable third consecutive division title.

On July 22, even the most faithful Braves fans had to be wavering about the team's chances of catching the first-place Giants. And everyone who wasn't a Braves diehard was uttering the same line: "No way!"

The only place where resolve remained was in the Atlanta clubhouse, and even there, the Braves admitted they had their hands full if they were to overcome San Francisco's 10-game lead. They were right—but they did it anyway.

The Braves treaded water early, fighting the effects of an inconsistent offense, the prolonged slump of team leader Terry Pendleton, and the turmoil created by Deion Sanders' month-long sabbatical and a bizarre walkout by Pendleton in the middle of an inning.

Atlanta finished April in third place with a mediocre 12–13 record, alternately looking invincible and uninspired. Cox's club also entered May wondering whether or not Sanders was part of the team. The flashy two-sport star left April 23 to be at the bedside of his terminally ill father, who died shortly after Sanders arrived. When Sanders hadn't returned by April 29, announcing he was doing some soul-searching, the Braves placed him on the disqualified list.

It was obviously a ploy by Sanders to wrangle more playing time and more money out of the Braves—and amazingly, it worked. He finally returned May 22, armed with a new contract, and proceeded to play more frequently than Otis Nixon, who then became disenchanted.

Meanwhile, Pendleton was struggling with his batting average. Through May 4, he was hitting just .148. He also contributed to the uncertainty about where the Braves were headed when he walked off the field and into the clubhouse in the seventh inning May 26 because Marvin Freeman failed to brush back Cincinnati hitters after Sanders had been hit in the sixth. The Braves' unofficial captain received undisclosed disciplinary action from the team. But more importantly, he picked up the pace with his bat.

Pendleton batted .279 in May, and as had been the case for the two previous seasons, the Braves responded to his lead. They won 17 of 27 games yet still lost a game in the standings to the red-hot Giants.

Tom Glavine won his first seven decisions of the season, only the fourth Brave ever to do so. However, reliever Mike Stanton was the big story on the pitching staff. For two years, the Braves' biggest weakness was its bullpen, but Stanton made a strong bid to correct that defect. He became the team's closer by taking over the league lead in saves with 18 through the first two months.

The Braves had signed free-agent pitcher Greg Maddux, the 1992 Cy Young Award winner, prior to the season. His presence, along with that of Glavine, John Smoltz, and Steve Avery, gave Atlanta a starting rotation that was being compared to the great ones in history. Indeed, they were pitching well, too.

Avery strung together eight wins through late June, the longest streak of his career. Smoltz was leading the league in strikeouts. Glavine was halfway to a third straight 20-win season. And though Maddux's record didn't show it (7–6 through June), he was pitching well but suffering from lack of support.

Nevertheless, the Braves couldn't gain on the Giants. In fact, they were losing ground. In winning 15 of 26 games during June, Atlanta fell to 7½ back of San Francisco.

The mid-season trade which brought Fred McGriff to Atlanta from San Diego ignited the Braves on a torrid second-half sprint to their third straight division title.

That trend continued well into July until John Schuerholz made a move that seemingly injected the entire club with a large dose of adrenalin. It came in the bat of first baseman Fred McGriff.

On July 18, Schuerholz sent prospects Melvin Nieves, Vince Moore, and Donnie Elliott to San Diego for McGriff, one of the game's finest power hitters. The evening McGriff debuted, July 20, the press-box area of Atlanta–Fulton County Stadium caught fire, delaying the start of the game nearly two hours. When the game finally began, St. Louis jumped to a 5–0 lead. But a McGriff home run spurred the Braves to a come-from-behind, 8–5 victory in what became a familiar formula for success.

Two nights later, when Atlanta lost at Pittsburgh and San Francisco won again, the Braves fell to 10 games back. The situation couldn't have looked much bleaker. But from that point on, the Braves played .754 ball, winning 49 and losing but 16. As brilliant as that stretch was, it was barely enough.

The Braves were 19–9 in July but still trailed the Giants by 7½, the same margin as when the month began. But the momentum had begun to swing toward the two-time defending division champs.

The way the Giants were playing, the Braves knew they couldn't lose very often. And it almost seemed like they were winning every day. In August, they were 19–7, paced by McGriff's bat (six homers) and Maddux's arm (4–1, 1.53). Atlanta put together a season-high nine-game winning streak August 8–18 yet still trailed the Giants by 7½ when the two clubs met for a three-game series in San Francisco August 23–25.

It was now or never for the Braves, and they responded like true champions. Avery pitched a 5–3, complete-game victory in the series opener. Pendleton, David Justice, and Ron Gant hit home runs in the second game to back Glavine's pitching in a 6–4 win. And in the finale of the series, Maddux won his 15th and got the support of six home runs—two each by McGriff and Justice—in a 9–1 rout. The deficit had suddenly been cut to 4½, and the Giants knew they were in a pennant race.

On September 10 the Braves moved into a tie for first with a 3–2 win at San Diego, and the following night they finally moved atop the division with a 13–1 rout of the Padres. All year long, the Braves had been waiting for the Giants to have a slump, which finally came in mid-September, allowing Atlanta to open a four-game lead by September 16.

To San Francisco's credit, though, they didn't die. Cox's team won its 100th game of the season September 26, but the next night, the Braves lost and allowed the Giants to move back into a tie for first with five games to go.

The race was still tied Sunday, October 3, the final day of the season. Atlanta was hosting the expansion Rockies, who hadn't beaten the Braves all year. The Giants were on the road against the Dodgers, their bitter rival.

With Glavine picking up his 22nd victory and Justice hitting his 40th home run, the Braves beat Colorado, 5–3. Then when the Dodgers beat the Giants later that afternoon, the Braves became the first National League team to win three consecutive division titles.

Since an expanded playoff format in 1994 would allow a second-place team to qualify for the postseason for the first time in history, the classic duel the Braves and Giants staged to the wire was viewed by many as possibly "The Last Great Pennant Race."

The Braves led the majors in victories for the second

Jeff Blauser established himself as one of the game's finest all-around shortstops in 1993.

straight year with a franchise-record 104, surpassing the 102 reached by Frank Selee's Beaneaters in 1892 and again in 1898. Atlanta was 54–19 after the All-Star break, the third-best record in history from that point, and was 51–17 after McGriff arrived in town.

Cox's team won with a variety of weapons. The Braves could bludgeon opponents, as evidenced by their league-high 169 home runs. And they could win with pitching. Their highly touted staff led the league in ERA (3.14) and numerous other departments, including shutouts (16), fewest hits, and fewest home runs. The defense was quite capable, too, finishing tied for second in fielding (.983).

Ron Gant was at his best in the stretch drive, knocking in 25 runs in his last 20 games. He teamed with McGriff and Justice to give Atlanta the first trio of 100-RBI teammates since Hank Aaron, Rico Carty, and Orlando Cepeda in 1970.

Jeff Blauser, who finally worked his way into the regular lineup, became the first Braves shortstop to hit .300 since Al Dark in 1948. He also set a franchise record for a shortstop by scoring 110 runs. Pendleton couldn't match his production of the two previous seasons, but he still finished strong with nine home runs in the last 25 games. He batted .299 after May 4.

Maddux and Glavine gave the Braves two 20-game winners for the first time since 1959 when Warren Spahn and Lou Burdette were in top form. Maddux led the league in ERA (2.36), complete games, and innings. He won 13 of his last 15 decisions en route to his second consecutive Cy Young Award, just the fifth pitcher ever to win the honor twice.

Glavine, who finished third in the Cy Young voting, became the first National League pitcher with three straight 20-win seasons since Ferguson Jenkins posted six in a row in 1967–72.

The work of Avery and Smoltz gave the franchise its first foursome of 15-game winners in the 20th century.

Greg McMichael, who wasn't even supposed to make the club entering spring training, was the surprise of the year. He took over the closer's role in the second half and converted

his first 15 save opportunities. His final save total of 19 was the best showing by a rookie in the league since Todd Worrell's 36 in 1986 and allowed McMichael to finish second to Dodgers catcher Mike Piazza for Rookie of the Year.

Just as amazing as the play of the team was the enthusiasm of the fans. Attendance cracked 3 million for the second straight year and pushed 4 million before settling at a franchise-record 3,884,720.

This phenomenal season capped a three-year period in which the Braves led the majors in victories—14 more than runner-up Toronto.

	G	AB	R	H	2B	3B	HR	RBI	SB	AVG
Rafael Belliard	91	79	6	18	5	0	0	6	0	.228
Damon Berryhill (C)	115	335	24	82	18	2	8	43	0	.245
Jeff Blauser (SS)	161	597	110	182	29	2	15	73	16	.305
Sid Bream	117	277	33	72	14	1	9	35	4	.260
Francisco Cabrera	70	83	8	20	3	0	4	11	0	.241
Ramon Caraballo	6	0	0	0	0	0	0	0	0	—
Ron Gant (OF)	157	606	113	166	27	4	36	117	26	.274
Brian Hunter	37	80	4	11	3	1	0	8	0	.138
Chipper Jones	8	3	2	2	1	0	0	0	0	.667
David Justice (OF)	157	585	90	158	15	4	40	120	3	.270
Ryan Klesko	22	17	3	6	1	0	2	5	0	.353
Mark Lemke (2B)	151	493	52	124	19	2	7	49	1	.252
Javy Lopez	8	16	1	6	1	1	1	2	0	.375
Fred McGriff (1B)	68	255	59	79	18	1	19	55	1	.310
Otis Nixon (OF)	134	461	77	124	12	3	1	24	47	.269
Greg Olson	83	262	23	59	10	0	4	24	1	.225
Bill Pecota	72	62	17	20	2	1	0	5	1	.323
Terry Pendleton (3B)	161	633	81	172	33	1	17	84	5	.272
Deion Sanders	95	272	42	75	18	6	6	28	19	.276
Tony Tarasco	24	35	6	8	2	0	0	2	0	.229
	162	5,515	767	1,444	239	29	169*	712	125	.262

	W	L	G	GS	CG	IP	H	BB	SO	ERA
Steve Avery	18	6	35	35	3	223⅓	216	43	125	2.94
Steve Bedrosian	5	2	49	0	0	49⅔	34	14	33	1.63
Pedro Borbon	0	0	3	0	0	1⅔	3	3	2	21.60
Marvin Freeman	2	0	21	0	0	23⅔	24	10	25	6.08
Tom Glavine	22*	6	36	36*	4	239⅓	236	90	120	3.20
Jay Howell	3	3	54	0	0	58⅓	48	16	37	2.31
Greg Maddux	20	10	36	36*	8*	267*	228	52	197	2.36*
Greg McMichael	2	3	74	0	0	91⅔	68	29	89	2.06
Kent Mercker	3	1	43	6	0	66	52	36	59	2.86
Pete Smith	4	8	20	14	0	90⅔	92	36	53	4.37
John Smoltz	15	11	35	35	3	243¾	208	100	208	3.62
Mike Stanton	4	6	63	0	0	52	51	29	43	4.67
Mark Wohlers	6	2	46	0	0	48	37	22	45	4.50
	104*	58		162	18	1,455	1,297	480	1,036	3.14*

Shutouts—Glavine (2), Avery, Maddux, Smoltz
Saves—Stanton (27), McMichael (19)

1994

Record: 68–46
Finish: Second (East)
Games Behind: 6
Manager: Bobby Cox

The 1994 season began with such promise and ended with such disappointment.

Many prognosticators and fans felt that it might be the season when the Braves finally won their first World Series since 1957, especially with Fred McGriff in the lineup for a full season. And when the team won 13 of its first 14 games, it appeared the preseason predictions might be right on target.

However, the combination of uncommonly inconsistent pitching, a lack of timely hitting, and the emergence of the

Greg Maddux became the first man in history to win three consecutive Cy Young Awards in 1994.

Montreal Expos as one of the game's best teams combined to make the season an uphill struggle for Atlanta.

Perhaps if the full 162 games had been played, the Braves might have rallied for their fourth straight division title. But when the players' strike hit after 114 games, Atlanta was six games behind the Expos in the newly aligned National League East. The schedule wasn't resumed, so that's the way 1994 went into the record books.

The most positive aspect to come out of the season for the Braves was the pitching of Greg Maddux, who became the first man in history to win three consecutive Cy Young Awards and the first Brave to win more than one. In a year that was completely dominated by hitters who would have challenged some of the loftiest offensive records had the full schedule been played, Maddux stood alone as the one pitcher the hitters couldn't solve.

In fact, if the baseball was wound tighter in 1994, as many observers theorized, Maddux clearly was pitching with a stash of old balls he'd been hiding in his locker.

The composite National League ERA in 1994 was 4.21. Maddux's was 1.56. The next closest was Bret Saberhagen's 2.74. The only lower league-leading ERAs in the National League since 1916 were Bob Gibson's 1.12 in 1968 and Dwight Gooden's 1.53 in 1985.

The composite National League batting average was .267. But hitters batted just .207 against Maddux.

What the 28-year-old right-hander did was compile one of the most dominating seasons of any pitcher in history. The difference of 2.65 between his ERA and the league's was the largest differential ever. Even when Gibson compiled the all-time record low ERA of 1.12 in 1968, he was but 1.87 below the league ERA of 2.99.

Maddux's numbers were impressive under any circumstances, but in light of the proliferation of offense throughout baseball, his accomplishments were positively staggering.

Maddux was 16–6, tying Montreal's Ken Hill for the league lead in wins. In his second season as a Brave, Maddux also led the league in innings (202), complete games (10),

and opponents' batting average and tied for first in shutouts (3). He ranked third in strikeouts (156) and fewest walks per nine innings (1.4).

Other highlights of the year included McGriff's seventh consecutive season of 30 or more home runs. The Atlanta first baseman finished fourth in the league with 34 homers to become the ninth man in history to have seven straight years in the 30 club. The others represent some of the great sluggers in history—Jimmie Foxx, Lou Gehrig, Mike Schmidt, Eddie Mathews, Babe Ruth, Mickey Mantle, Ralph Kiner, and Hank Aaron.

The Braves' defensive standout was clearly Mark Lemke, who made just three errors all season and finished with a .994 fielding percentage. That broke Frank Bolling's all-time franchise record for second basemen of .989 set in 1962.

Bobby Cox's team was in first place from opening day through July 10, and even as late as July 21 the Braves had regained a tie with the Expos through 94 games. Over the final 20 games, though, Atlanta was 11–9 and torrid Montreal was 17–3 to open its six-game lead when the strike hit after the games of August 11.

The Braves' blistering 13–1 start was unusual because 10 of the wins came on the road. Included in that streak was a no-hitter by Kent Mercker on April 8 at Los Angeles. The left-hander struck out a career-high 10 in beating the Dodgers, 6–0, for the first complete game he'd ever pitched. He walked four in the Braves' third no-hitter since moving to Atlanta, the 14th in franchise history, and the first ever on the road.

Also in the first two weeks of the season the Braves set an Atlanta record with 19 runs on April 15 at Wrigley Field. That 19–5 victory over the Cubs included three consecutive home runs by McGriff, Terry Pendleton, and Tony Tarasco. Three days later, Ryan Klesko, McGriff, and David Justice repeated the feat in Atlanta.

The season was full of change, starting with the shift from the West division to the East and the loss of several players who'd contributed to the club's recent success.

Catcher Greg Olson was released, first baseman Sid Bream, center fielder Otis Nixon, and catcher Damon Berryhill became free agents and signed elsewhere. Right-hander

Ron Gant's career with the Braves came crashing to an end prior to the 1994 season when he broke his leg in a motorcycle accident.

Pete Smith was traded to the Mets, and 1992 playoff hero Francisco Cabrera went to Japan to play.

In February, starting left fielder Ron Gant suffered two compound fractures of his lower right leg when he was pinned between his off-road motorcycle and a tree during a recreational outing. He was expected to be out three to five months, but the Braves released him to avoid paying most of his $5.5-million salary.

The loss of Gant became even more devastating when rookie Chipper Jones, who was on the verge of winning the left-field job, mangled his left knee trying to avoid a tag late in spring training. The organization's top prospect thus missed the entire season.

Finally, on May 29, general manager John Schuerholz dropped a bomb by trading center fielder Deion Sanders to Cincinnati for Roberto Kelly.

Through it all, Cox was working five talented rookies into the lineup. Catcher Javy Lopez, left fielder Klesko, and third baseman Jose Oliva, who was sensational in a brief callup from Richmond, all made the Topps Major League Rookie All-Star Team. Tarasco and Mike Kelly also played well in the outfield.

	G	AB	R	H	2B	3B	HR	RBI	SB	AVG
Rafael Belliard	46	9	29	7	1	0	9	0	0	.242
Jeff Blauser (SS)	96	380	56	98	21	4	6	45	1	.258
Jarvis Brown	17	15	3	2	1	0	1	1	0	.133
Dave Gallagher	89	152	27	34	5	0	2	14	0	.224
David Justice (OF)	104	352	61	110	16	2	19	59	2	.313
Mike Kelly	30	77	14	21	10	1	2	9	0	.273
Roberto Kelly (OF)	63	255	44	73	15	3	6	24	10	.286
Ryan Klesko (OF)	92	245	42	68	13	3	17	47	1	.278
Mark Lemke (2B)	104	350	40	103	15	0	3	31	0	.294
Javy Lopez (C)	80	277	27	68	9	0	13	35	0	.245
Fred McGriff (1B)	113	424	81	135	25	1	34	94	7	.318
Mike Mordecai	4	4	1	1	0	0	1	3	0	.250
Charlie O'Brien	51	152	24	37	11	0	8	28	0	.243
Jose Oliva	19	59	9	17	5	0	6	11	0	.288
Bill Pecota	64	112	11	24	5	0	2	16	1	.214
Terry Pendleton (3B)	77	309	25	78	18	3	7	30	2	.252
Deion Sanders	46	191	32	55	10	0	4	21	19	.288
Tony Tarasco	87	132	16	36	6	0	5	19	5	.273
	114	3,861	542	1,031	198	18	137	510	48	.267

	W	L	G	GS	CG	IP	H	BB	SO	ERA
Steve Avery	8	3	24	24	1	151⅔	127	55	122	4.04
Steve Bedrosian	0	2	46	0	0	46	41	18	43	3.33
Mike Bielecki	2	0	19	1	0	27	28	12	18	4.00
Tom Glavine	13	9	25	25	2	165⅓	173	70	140	3.97
Milt Hill	0	0	10	0	0	11⅓	18	6	10	7.94
Greg Maddux	16	6	25	25	10	202	150	3	156	1.56
Greg McMichael	4	6	51	0	0	58⅔	66	19	47	3.84
Kent Mercker	9	4	20	17	2	112⅓	90	45	111	3.45
Gregg Olson	0	2	16	0	0	14⅔	19	13	10	9.20
John Smoltz	6	10	21	21	1	134⅔	120	48	113	4.14
Mike Stanton	3	1	49	0	0	45⅔	41	26	35	3.55
Mark Wohlers	7	2	51	0	0	51	51	33	58	4.59
Brad Woodall	0	1	1	1	0	6	5	2	2	4.50
	68	46		114	16	1,026⅓	929	378	865	3.57

Shutouts—Maddux (3), Mercker
Saves—McMichael (21), Stanton (3), Olson, Wohlers

Player Profiles

Players come and players go, but never are they forgotten. Once a man makes his first appearance in a major league game, he becomes an indelible part of the history of his team and of the sport. His accomplishments, or lack of same, are recorded for eternity in box scores and record books, regardless of whether he is a star or a bit player.

This chapter contains profiles of 150 of the nearly 1,500 players who helped chisel the saga of the oldest continuously operating professional sports franchise in America.

The players profiled range from the Braves' all-time greats to others who experienced a wide range of success with the team. However, all 150 own interesting and significant niches in franchise history for reasons as diverse as their playing records. Selections for this section were based solely on each player's career with the Braves and not with other teams.

Aaron, Hank

Braves: 1954–74
Outfielder
Birthplace: Mobile, Alabama

B: February 5, 1934
Batted right, threw right
Ht. 6–0; **Wt.** 180

Hank Aaron

It is virtually impossible to write Hank Aaron's name without using the words "all-time home run king" either directly before or after its first reference. Such is the magnitude of Aaron's place in history. This characterization is, at the same time, both magnificent and mildly upsetting for those who watched this uniquely graceful man carve his unforgettable presence into the game's history.

It is magnificent that a man as talented and as important to the Braves franchise as Aaron has such a majestic record to hang his cap on for generations to admire and respect. Yet it is mildly upsetting for those who watched him in his prime to think that those who gaze upon his plaque at Cooperstown or casually inspect the records probably will not realize the incredible array of talents and achievements represented by his unmatched career.

"All-time home run king." Is there a more royal way for a ballplayer to be remembered? On the surface, probably not. Yet Aaron demands so much more. As breathtaking as 755 home runs is, as monumental as this man's climb to that milestone of all baseball milestones is, there is so much more for which he must be remembered.

Trying to compare players, especially from era to era, is virtually impossible. It's great fun, but there simply are too many variables to make an airtight case for "the best pitcher of all time" or "the best player of all time."

Most historians lean toward Ty Cobb, Babe Ruth, perhaps Willie Mays, or even Joe DiMaggio when they attempt to pinpoint "the greatest player of all time." Certainly, a case can be made for all of them. Exactly where Aaron fits into the equation could be—and will be—argued for decades. The point to be made is that no one in the post–World War II era played better in all nonpitching phases of the game more consistently and for a longer period of time than Henry Louis Aaron.

Besides hitting for power, the all-time home run king also could run, field, throw, hit for average, and hit in the clutch with anyone. He did it, day in and day out, year after year. And he did it in relative anonymity created by his own soft-spokeness and deceivingly smooth style of play, as well as the fate of spending his career in Milwaukee and Atlanta, well off the beaten path of the media mob.

For a player of such diverse and encompassing talent who led his league in home runs just four times in his 23-year career to be remembered as "the all-time home run king" is ironic, to

Each a great pitcher in his own right, Warren Spahn and Johnny Sain were immortalized as a tandem in 1948 when they pitched the Braves to the pennant under the battle cry, "Spahn and Sain and pray for rain!"

Hank Aaron watches the flight of home run No. 713 late in 1973, setting the stage for his swift ascent to the all-time home run throne the following April.

say the least. But it also is the ultimate testament to the prolonged, high-level consistency that stands as the true measure of Aaron's peerless stature at the very top of his profession.

The third of eight children, Aaron was the son of a rivet bucker for a shipbuilding company in Mobile, Alabama. A younger brother, Tommie, also played for the Braves. He was a slick-fielding first baseman but was not a strong hitter. After a brief playing career, he became a highly regarded minor league coach and manager and major league coach for the Braves before an early death from leukemia. Two other Mobile products, Billy Williams and Willie McCovey, would follow Hank to the majors and eventually to the Hall of Fame.

Aaron didn't even play high school baseball, because his school didn't have a team. He was a star football player, though, and began playing semipro baseball for the Mobile Black Bears during his junior year. The Bears played a game against the Indianapolis Clowns, a Negro League team on a barnstorming tour, and the visitors were impressed by the 17-year-old Aaron. The next year, the Clowns signed him for $200 a month. Aaron had gone to a Dodgers tryout camp first, but when someone said he was too small to play, he left before even taking the field.

He departed Mobile to join the Clowns in 1952 carrying only two dollars, two sandwiches his mother made him, and a banged-up suitcase. To show just how raw Aaron was when he started his pro career, he actually batted cross-handed, with the left hand above the right on the handle. Braves scout Dewey Griggs convinced him to change—in the middle of a game, no less—and Aaron went on to lead the Negro American League with a .467 average until he signed with Boston.

Aaron was playing shortstop then, and both the Braves and Giants wanted him. Griggs won the battle, signing him for

$350 a month. The Braves paid the Clowns $10,000 for Aaron's contract, and Clowns owner Syd Pollack gave Aaron a suitcase for his first plane trip from Charlotte, North Carolina, to Eau Claire, Wisconsin, home of the Braves' Class-C team.

Just 18 years old and far from home in a white man's world, a white man's profession, Aaron played as if he were still in the Mobile sandlots. Two weeks after his arrival, he was named to the Northern League All-Star team, and at the end of the year he was selected the league's Rookie of the Year for batting .336 with nine home runs and 61 RBIs in 87 games.

Aaron had an even bigger year in 1953, his second pro season, leading Jacksonville to the Sally League pennant and being named the league's MVP. He led the league in hitting (.362) and RBIs (125). It didn't all come naturally to Aaron, though. He was playing second base and not particularly well. Besides his defense, he had to do a little work on his baserunning. In one game, he stole three bases and each time was tagged out when the second baseman pulled the hidden-ball trick.

The Braves still felt Aaron wasn't ready for the majors despite two highly productive seasons in the minors. During the off-season, they converted him to an outfielder in the Puerto Rican Winter League. And when the Braves obtained outfielder Bobby Thomson in a trade with the Giants, it appeared the club was determined to keep Aaron in the minors for another season. During spring training, though, Thomson broke his ankle sliding into second. Thus, on March 14, 1954, Aaron became Milwaukee's starting left fielder, and he never looked back.

"Magic is the only way to describe it," Thomson said years later about his 20-year-old replacement. "You just had this feeling—even then—that this guy was something special. He was far removed from the ordinary class of ballplayer, like the rest of us. Some of the guys were skeptical. Everybody had said he was bound to be a great one. He'd hit well in the minors, sure, but we figured he'd be like so many other rookies—come to camp with a reputation, really see the curveball for the first time, and bomb out."

Instead of "bombing out," it was bombs away.

Aaron's first home run came in his seventh game against Vic Raschi of the Cardinals at Busch Stadium in St. Louis. He was productive enough as a rookie to finish second to Wally Moon of St. Louis for NL Rookie of the Year. However, his season was abbreviated when he broke his ankle sliding on September 5. Amazingly, he avoided serious injury for the remainder of his career. His 122 games played as a rookie were the fewest he appeared in until 1973 when he was 39 years old.

In 1955, just his second major league season, Aaron established himself as a bona fide star and made the All-Star team for the first time. Thomson returned to play left, so Aaron moved into right field, where he would spend most of his career. He hit .314 with 27 home runs and 106 RBIs at age 21 and led the league in doubles with 37. "Bad Henry" or "Hammerin' Hank" had arrived.

Aaron believes his "Bad Henry" nickname came from Dodgers pitching greats Sandy Koufax and Don Drysdale. And "Hammerin' Hank" is credited to longtime Braves front office executive Donald Davidson. Later in his career, "Hammerin' Hank" became simply "The Hammer."

Aaron's reputation grew quickly throughout the league, even if he was overshadowed in the media and with the public by other stars of the era.

"Throwing a fastball by Henry Aaron is like trying to sneak the sun past a rooster," said St. Louis pitcher Curt Simmons, summing up the frustration of pitchers all over the league.

In 1956, Aaron won the batting title (.328) and led the league in numerous other offensive categories, including hits, total bases, and doubles. In the process, he helped the Braves almost win their first pennant in Milwaukee, though they had to settle for second on the final day of the season.

The talented Braves went all the way in '57, though, and Aaron, of course, was a big reason for that. He hit an 11th-inning home run to beat St. Louis and clinch the pennant on September 23. He also led the league in both home runs (44) and RBIs (132) for the first time en route to being named the National League's MVP.

The Yankees were heavy favorites in the '57 Series, and future Hall of Fame catcher Yogi Berra was so confident he even tried to give Aaron a tip during batting practice.

"Hey kid, you're holding your bat wrong. It's supposed to be with the label up," Berra said to Aaron, who replied, "I didn't come here to read."

But he did come to hit, batting .393 with three home runs and seven RBIs in the Braves' seven-game Series victory, the last winning postseason experience of Aaron's career.

In 1958, Aaron had another typically big year at the plate as the Braves won their second straight pennant. But his defense also began to be recognized. He won the first of three consecutive Gold Gloves.

As with all phases of his game, Aaron's unique defensive style was so smooth and seemingly effortless that he made even the most difficult plays appear considerably easier than they really were.

"When he first joined our team, we held our breath when a fly ball was hit in his direction," said Billy Bruton, who played center field for much of the Braves' stay in Milwaukee. "It was the way he went after the ball, like he was never going to get there. But after we saw him a while and saw the kind of things he could do, we didn't worry anymore."

Every other player ran after balls. Aaron somehow seemed to glide across wide expanses of outfield grass to tuck away potential extra-base hits. It didn't look like he was expending much energy at all, when of course, he was working just as hard as the next guy.

The same held true on the base paths and in the batter's box. Aaron strolled to the plate like he was walking out to pick up the Sunday paper. Even in the box, he was a picture of casual elegance, undoubtedly involved in intense concentration even though he appeared as relaxed as a couch potato except for the wiggling of the bat in his powerful hands.

"He's the only ballplayer I've ever seen who goes to sleep at the plate and wakes up only to swing as the pitch comes in," said Curt Simmons, who Aaron named as the toughest pitcher he ever faced.

And the swing itself was as unique as everything else about the great outfielder. He broke all the "rules," hitting with his weight on his front foot, overstriding, and dragging his back foot—then lashing at the last split second with wrists and forearms equipped with both the power of thunder and the speed of lightning.

Unlike conventional power hitters, Aaron swung down on the ball, especially early in his career. His line drives rocketed off the bat, rising from the backspin, and often causing infielders to think they were catchable before they escaped the ballpark's field of gravity and landed in distant territory inaccessible to outfielders.

Obviously possessed with tremendous natural talent, Aaron also worked hard to develop that potential. And he refused to rely strictly on his physical ability, as he easily could have done. He became a student of the game, particularly of pitchers and their patterns. He admitted to being a "guess hitter," which is a modest way of saying he was a thinking man's hitter. Rather than simply reacting to the pitch, he was always trying to outthink the pitcher, "guessing" what pitch would be thrown and in what location. And he was very good at it.

"Slapping a rattlesnake across the face with the back of your hand is safer than trying to fool Henry Aaron," said Dodgers pitcher Claude Osteen.

In 1959, Aaron won his second batting title with a .355 average and 223 hits, both of which would stand as career highs, as would his league-leading 400 total bases. Year after year, his accomplishments began to pile up, long before anyone could have imagined where it was all leading.

He led the league in RBIs (126) in 1960 for the second of four times in his career. In 1963, he was named National League Player of the Year when he became only the fifth man to enter the 30–30 (home runs–stolen bases) club. Though his 31 steals represented a career high, he most certainly could have reached the 30–30 level several other times had he not played on such power-laden clubs or had he played in an era when stolen bases were more valued. He also led the NL in home runs (44), RBIs (130), and total bases in '63. With a few more points on his batting average Aaron would have won the rare Triple Crown. He hit .319, and Tommy Davis's .326 led the league.

In many ways, 1964 serves to illustrate just how productive Aaron was for so long. It was considered an "off" season for him because he failed to lead the league in any major offensive categories. All he did was hit .328 with 24 home runs, 95 RBIs, and 22 steals. Players become stars with such seasons, but for Aaron, it was a "downer" at age 30.

He led the league in doubles in 1965. The next year, the Braves moved to Atlanta, and Aaron showed his new fans just what he could do by racking up his third home run title and fourth RBI championship (127). It was the third of four seasons he would complete with 44 home runs, the number he wore on his uniform. Early that year, he hit his 400th career home run, too. And he and Eddie Mathews combined to set a major league record for home runs by teammates, passing Ruth and Lou Gehrig, and ultimately reaching 863.

In '67, Aaron won his fourth and final home run title (39), putting together yet another superb all-around season and leading the league in runs and total bases. On July 14, 1968, the "quiet" home run hitter connected for his 500th career home run, still 214 away from Ruth but a number that had been reached by only seven other men.

The Braves won the National League West in 1969, the first year of division play, and Aaron was a big reason with 44 home runs and his eighth and last year of leading the NL in total bases. The division title provided Aaron his first postseason exposure since 1958 and the last of his career. He didn't disappoint. Facing the powerful pitching of Tom Seaver and the Miracle Mets, he batted .357 with a home run in each of the three games but couldn't prevent the Braves from being swept in the best-of-five playoffs.

Early in 1970, May 17 to be exact, Aaron achieved one of his proudest moments. His single at Cincinnati against Wayne Simpson was his 3,000th career hit. Only seven others had ever reached that number then. Aaron tied Musial for getting No. 3,000 the earliest in a career, his 17th season. He also became the first player to combine 3,000 hits with 500 home runs.

In 1970, Aaron set a major league record with his 12th season of 30 or more home runs. The following year, he moved from right field to first base to help relieve some of the wear and tear and preserve his strength for The Chase. He also hit his 600th home run on April 27 against San Francisco's Gaylord Perry. Only Mays remained between Aaron and Ruth.

Aaron reached yet another milestone in '71, though not nearly as significant. Always an underachiever in All-Star Games, he hit his first All-Star home run at Detroit against Vida Blue. It came in his 20th All-Star appearance.

Later in the year, Aaron set a National League record for most seasons with 40 or more home runs (8). He ended the season with 47 home runs, a personal high, and at age 37, he batted a robust .327, his highest since 1964. He also had a career-high slugging percentage of .669, which led the league.

It appeared as if Aaron had been rejuvenated for his pursuit of Ruth.

On June 10, 1972, he hit a grand slam at Philadelphia against Wayne Twitchell. It was the 649th homer of his career, surpassing Mays for second place, and it also was his 14th career grand slam, tying McCovey and Gil Hodges for the league record. Less than three weeks later, Aaron passed Lou Gehrig for second place on the all-time RBI chart.

By this time, it seemed that nearly every week Aaron was reaching a milestone. His 659th career homer, coming on July 19, 1972, tied Ruth for the most homers with a single team.

The Braves hosted the All-Star Game that year, the first time the event had been played in the South. Aaron responded with his second All-Star home run, prompting the third of four rousing ovations he received that evening.

Aaron ended the '72 season with 673 home runs, 41 short of Ruth, creating a media buildup of gigantic proportions as he entered the final stage of his pursuit of a record many experts long felt was unbreakable.

Despite the pressure of an entire nation and much of the world watching his every swing, despite the constant demand for interviews and appearances, despite pitchers concentrating on avoiding his personal hit list, despite hate mail and death threats, despite his advanced age of 39, he hit 40 home runs in 1973, the most ever by a player his age. All winter, he sat at 713, just one short of Ruth's record.

The scrutiny of Aaron was so great in the final stages of his ascent to the home run throne that he couldn't stay with the team on the road, registering in different hotels under an assumed name. He also hired a bodyguard in case the people behind any of the threatening mail and calls materialized.

Though Aaron held up remarkably well under all the attention and duress, he said he'd be glad when it was behind him. And did he ever get the burden off his back in a hurry!

No. 714 came at Cincinnati on opening day 1974, against Jack Billingham in the first inning—on his very first swing of the season. The date was April 4. One down and one to go.

The Braves returned to Atlanta for the home opener April 8. The biggest crowd (53,775) in the history of Atlanta Stadium showed up, along with a horde of media, hundreds of celebrities and dignitaries, Aaron's parents, and assorted other guests of significance in his life. A 45-minute pregame salute to Aaron was staged, and national network TV interrupted programming to report on his at bats. Most men would have melted, but not Aaron, the epitome of cool under any circumstances.

In his first at bat, Aaron never even swung, drawing a walk on five pitches from Dodgers starter Al Downing. Then came the fourth inning. With Los Angeles leading, 3–1, and Dar-

rell Evans on first with no outs, Downing fell behind with a first-pitch ball. On the next pitch, Aaron took his first cut of the game and his first of the year in Atlanta, depositing No. 715 neatly over the left-field fence and into the hands of relief pitcher Tom House.

Pandemonium, of course, ensued. Hank Aaron was the new all-time home run king.

Aaron hit 18 more home runs that year, ending his Braves career with 733. The Braves weren't sure how much playing time they could give Aaron in '75, and he wasn't ready to accept a reserve role. Thus the team sent the greatest player in franchise history back to Milwaukee, where he began his big league career, in exchange for outfielder Dave May and minor league pitcher Roger Alexander.

After two seasons with the Brewers, Aaron retired with 755 home runs and more major league batting records than anyone else in history. His career records include most RBIs (2,297), total bases (6,856), and long hits (1,477). He's also second in lifetime at bats and runs, third in games and hits, ninth in doubles, 11th in singles, and tied for 14th in years of service. He and younger brother Tommie combined for 768 home runs, the most ever by brothers.

An All-Star in every season he played except his first and last, Aaron was incredibly consistent. He hit between 24 and 45 home runs for 19 straight seasons, averaging 33 from 1955 through 1973. He drove in 100 runs 11 times and scored 100 runs 15 times. He won two batting titles and four Gold Gloves.

Aaron returned to the Braves front office after retiring as a player. He spent 13 years as a team vice president and director of player development. Often outspoken about baseball's indifference to promoting racial equality in the game's administration, Aaron protested in 1980 by refusing to accept a special award from Commissioner Bowie Kuhn honoring him for his 715th home run.

In 1989, Aaron was appointed a senior vice president and assistant to Braves president Stan Kasten. He's also a vice president and board member of Turner Broadcasting and is active with various community organizations.

Aaron, Hank

Braves	G	AB	R	H	2B	3B	HR	RBI	SB	AVG	SLG
1954	122	468	58	131	27	6	13	69	2	.280	.447
1955	153	602	105	189	37*	9	27	106	3	.314	.540
1956	153	609	106	200*	34*	14	26	92	2	.328*	.558
1957	151	615	118*	198	27	6	44*	132*	1	.322	.600
1958	153	601	109	196	34	4	30	95	4	.326	.546
1959	154	629	116	223*	46	7	39	123	8	.355*	.636*
1960	153	590	102	172	20	11	40	126*	16	.292	.566
1961	155	603	115	197	39*	10	34	120	21	.327	.594
1962	156	592	127	191	28	6	45	128	15	.323	.618
1963	161	631	121*	201	29	4	44*	130*	31	.319	.586*
1964	145	570	103	187	30	2	24	95	22	.328	.514
1965	150	570	109	181	40*	1	32	89	24	.318	.560
1966	158	603	117	168	23	1	44*	127*	21	.279	.539
1967	155	600	113*	184	37	3	39*	109	17	.307	.573*
1968	160	606	84	174	33	4	29	86	28	.287	.498
1969	147	547	100	164	30	3	44	97	9	.300	.607
1970	150	516	103	154	26	1	38	118	9	.298	.574
1971	139	495	95	162	22	3	47	118	1	.327	.669*
1972	129	449	75	119	10	0	34	77	4	.265	.514
1973	120	392	84	118	12	1	40	96	1	.301	.643
1974	112	340	47	91	16	0	20	69	1	.268	.491
Career	3,076	11,628	2,107	3,600	600	96	733	2,202	240	.310	.567

Adcock, Joe

Braves: 1953–62
First baseman
Birthplace: Coushatta, Louisiana

B: October 30, 1927
Batted right, threw right
Ht. 6–4; **Wt.** 220

Joe Adcock

Joe Adcock was one of the great home run hitters in Braves history. For that matter, he was one of the great home run hitters in history. When he retired in 1966, he ranked 20th on the all-time list (seventh among right-handed hitters) with 336 home runs.

But Adcock spent the prime of his career playing amid a bevy of sluggers, most notably Hank Aaron and Eddie Mathews, so his deeds often were overshadowed by teammates destined for Cooperstown. On Saturday afternoon, July 31, 1954, however, Adcock took center stage with a performance the likes of which may never be matched.

At Brooklyn's Ebbets Field, the then-26-year-old first baseman broke two major league records. His line for the day included four home runs—all off different Dodgers pitchers—and a double. His 18 total bases established a major league record, as did his 13 extra bases.

In the second inning, Adcock, using a borrowed bat because he'd broken his the previous evening, led off with a home run off Don Newcombe. In the third, he doubled and scored against Erv Palica. With Palica still working in the fifth, Adcock hit a three-run homer. A two-run homer off Pete Wojey followed in the seventh. Finally, in the ninth, Adcock hit his fourth homer of the day, this one coming against Johnny Podres.

Adcock drove in seven runs and scored five in Milwaukee's 15–7 victory. One of the most remarkable aspects of his performance is that Brooklyn pitchers made only seven pitches to him all day. You'd think they'd have been more careful . . . but then, they already knew there was little they could do to fool the one-time Louisiana farm boy.

Adcock entered the game hitting .442 for the year against the Dodgers, .467 at Ebbets Field. Just the previous night, he had a home run, double, and single. He finished the '54 season with nine of his 23 homers coming at Ebbets Field, tying a major league record.

The day after his record assault, Adcock doubled in his second at bat following a knockdown pitch by Russ Meyer. On his next trip to the plate, he received a stronger message from the Dodgers in the form of a Clem Labine pitch to the side of the head. Adcock had to be carried off the field, though his helmet prevented serious injury.

But not even a beaning could ruin Adcock's appetite for slugging Dodgers pitching, especially at Ebbets Field. Two years later, he tied an NL record by hitting 13 (of his 38) homers against the Dodgers.

Adcock did quite a bit of damage to other teams, too. In fact, for someone who went to LSU on a basketball scholarship; didn't play organized baseball until college; battled injuries, prolonged slumps, and platooning throughout his career; and never really learned to pull the ball, he had quite a career.

In 1950, Adcock debuted in the majors with Cincinnati. Since the Reds already had Ted Kluszewski, one of the league's most-feared hitters, at first base, Adcock spent most of his first three seasons as a part-timer in left field.

Just before spring training 1953, the Braves participated in a four-team deal with Philadelphia, Cincinnati, and Brooklyn that brought Adcock to the Braves for their inaugural season in Milwaukee. He immediately became the club's regular first baseman, holding the position for the better part of a decade and averaging 24 home runs per season.

Adcock batted a career-high .308 in 1954. His two biggest power seasons were 1956 (38 homers, 103 RBIs) and 1961 (35, 108). A broken arm in 1955 (hit by a Jim Hearn pitch) and a broken leg (sliding into second) in 1957 cost him two half seasons and, most certainly, quite a few home runs. Often injured, he exceeded 138 games in a season only twice in his career.

The fact that he wasn't a pull hitter also cost Adcock a lot of home runs and led to many deep fly outs to center. However, many times not even center field would hold his best shot. Such was the case in 1953 when he became the first man to hit a ball over the center-field fence, 483 feet from home, at the immense Polo Grounds.

Adcock's other memorable blasts included a 500-foot-plus shot in 1960 that was the first by a right-handed batter to clear the scoreboard at Connie Mack Stadium and, in 1956, the first ball to clear the double-decked left-field grandstand at Ebbets Field. He also hit the 13th-inning home run (later ruled a double for passing Aaron on the bases) in 1959 that beat Harvey Haddix after the Pittsburgh left-hander had strung together 12 perfect innings.

As one of the game's best sluggers and as a big, rigid target in the batter's box, Adcock took a few lumps from pitchers upset over damage to their ERAs. He sustained three beanings in his career, and in 1956, he gained the painful distinction of being hit twice in the same at bat by the same pitcher.

Nicked for two runs in the first inning and facing Adcock, who had homered eight times in the last 10 games, Giants pitcher Ruben Gomez hit the Milwaukee first baseman on the wrist to open the second. On his way to first, Adcock yelled at Gomez, who responded in kind. Adcock charged Gomez, who threw the ball at his attacker, drilling him in the left thigh, and then sprinted for the safety of the dugout. The ensuing brawl ended only when the County Stadium organist played the National Anthem.

Adcock appeared in both the 1957 and '58 World Series for the Braves, hitting .250 with no extra-base hits. After the 1962 season, Milwaukee sent the 35-year-old slugger to Cleveland in a five-player deal that brought Ty Cline, Don Dillard, and Frank Funk to the Braves. Fittingly, in his last trip to the plate as a Brave, Adcock hit a home run.

As a part-time player during his last four years with the Indians and Angels, Adcock still averaged over 16 homers per season. He was a fine defensive first baseman, leading the National League in fielding four times and finishing his career with a .994 defensive percentage.

After completing his playing career with California in 1966, Adcock managed Cleveland in 1967 to an eighth-place finish in a 10-team league.

Adcock, Joe

Braves	G	AB	R	H	2B	3B	HR	RBI	SB	AVG	SLG
1953	157	590	71	168	33	6	18	80	3	.285	.453
1954	133	500	73	154	27	5	23	87	1	.308	.520
1955	84	288	40	76	14	0	15	45	0	.264	.469
1956	137	454	76	132	23	1	38	103	1	.291	.597
1957	65	209	31	60	13	2	12	38	0	.287	.541
1958	105	320	40	88	15	1	19	54	0	.275	.506
1959	115	404	53	118	19	2	25	76	0	.292	.535
1960	138	514	55	153	21	4	25	91	2	.298	.500
1961	152	562	77	160	20	0	35	108	2	.285	.507
1962	121	391	48	97	12	1	29	78	2	.248	.506
Career	1,207	4,232	564	1,206	197	22	239	760	11	.285	.511

Alexander, Doyle

Braves: 1980, 1986–87
Pitcher
Birthplace: Cordova, Alabama

B: September 4, 1950
Batted right, threw right
Ht. 6–3; **Wt.** 205

Doyle Alexander's biggest contribution to the Braves was not as a pitcher but rather as trade bait. Late in 1987, with Detroit involved in a heated pennant race in the American League East and the Braves going nowhere under Chuck Tanner, Atlanta general manager Bobby Cox sent the veteran right-hander to the Tigers in exchange for minor league pitching prospect John Smoltz.

Doyle Alexander

Smoltz, of course, developed into a key member of the Braves' championship clubs in the early 1990s. Though Alexander did his part in helping Detroit win its division in '87, Tigers manager Sparky Anderson would frequently bemoan letting Smoltz escape.

That trade ended Alexander's second stint as a Brave. His Atlanta career began following the 1979 season when Texas traded him, along with Larvell Blanks, to the Braves in exchange for Adrian Devine and Pepe Frias. His 14–11 record helped the Braves finish a game over .500 after four consecutive last-place finishes.

But at the end of the season, the Braves sent Alexander packing to San Francisco for pitcher John "The Count" Montefusco.

Owner of a dour personality that brought public outbursts about management and fans, Alexander seldom stayed with one team for an extended period even though he had a long and successful career. He won nearly 200 games but changed teams nine times. In 1983, he had to go on the disabled list due to a self-inflicted injury to his pitching hand caused by punching a concrete wall in frustration. Yankees owner George Steinbrenner was so incensed he released him, leading to a successful stint with Toronto.

Alexander was one of only a handful of pitchers to be successful and well traveled enough to record victories against every team when there were 26 clubs in the majors. He pitched for 19 years, going 194–174, and seemed to improve in the latter stages of his career. His two biggest years were 1984 and 1985 when he had back-to-back 17-victory seasons for Toronto. He led the AL in winning percentage (.739) in '84 and worked the division clincher for the Blue Jays in '85.

But in '86, when Alexander popped off about not being paid what he felt he was worth, the Jays sent him to the Braves—perhaps as punishment—for reliever Duane Ward.

At the time Atlanta traded him to Detroit in 1987, Alexander was only 5–10 with a 4.13 ERA. Seemingly rejuvenated by joining a pennant contender, he went 9–0 with a 1.53 ERA in 11 starts for the Tigers over the last month and a half, earning recognition as AL pitcher of the month in September.

Alexander, Doyle

Braves	W	L	Pct	G	GS	CG	ShO	IP	H	BB	SO	ERA	SV
1980	14	11	.560	35	35	7	1	231⅔	227	74	114	4.20	0
1986	6	6	.500	17	17	2	0	117⅓	135	17	74	3.84	0
1987	5	10	.333	16	16	3	0	117⅔	115	27	64	4.13	0
Career	25	27	.481	68	68	12	1	466⅔	477	118	252	4.09	0

Alou, Felipe

Braves: 1964–69
Outfielder, first baseman
Birthplace: Haina, Dominican Republic

B: May 12, 1935
Batted right, threw right
Ht. 6–0; **Wt.** 195

Few men have ever played for the Braves with the glorious fury of Felipe Alou. A consummate team player, he went about his work with daily devotion and verve rare in any era. A majestic, powerful athlete, he seemingly could play and hit anywhere the Braves put him—in the batting order or on the field. He could hit for average and power, run, field, and throw.

By all rights, Alou should have owned Atlanta in 1966, the year the team moved to the South. In another era, with a

Felipe Alou with general manager Paul Richards

more successful team, he might have been elected mayor. Besides spreading himself around in the outfield and at first base, third base, and even shortstop, Alou finished second in the National League batting race (.327) to—of all people—his brother, Matty, of the Pirates.

Felipe led the league with 218 hits and 122 runs scored. He hit a career-high 31 home runs, and lest you think his 74 RBIs a paltry number for a power hitter, you should know he batted leadoff most of the time. His 355 total bases not only led the NL but still stand as an Atlanta record.

More than any other player, Alou showed the fans of Atlanta the way major league baseball is supposed to be played. While his efforts were appreciated, the magnitude of his effort and composite accomplishments was lost on a fifth-place team and amid his talented offensive surroundings, which included Hank Aaron, Eddie Mathews, Rico Carty, and Joe Torre.

But Alou was not one who craved the spotlight anyway. His unselfishness on the field spoke for his baseball priority, and his deep religious faith kept him at peace off the field.

Alou already was established as an All-Star outfielder and, at age 28, was a veteran of the 1962 World Series when he was traded to the Braves prior to the 1964 season. He was part of a seven-player trade in which Milwaukee sent popular catcher Del Crandall and pitchers Bob Shaw and Bob Hendley to San Francisco for Alou, pitcher Billy Hoeft, catcher Ed Bailey, and utility infielder Ernie Bowman, who never played in the majors again.

Even though Bailey and Hoeft played only one season with Milwaukee, it's a wonder the Braves weren't indicted for grand theft. Crandall was finished, and Shaw and Hendley never accomplished anything to compare with what Alou did for the Braves.

A knee injury slowed Alou in his first season with the Braves; a hairline fracture of the right wrist cut his production in 1967; and an arm injury robbed him of his power in his final year with the club. His effort never wavered, though, and when he was healthy, he was one of the best players in the league.

He made two All-Star teams, led the league in hits in '66 as well as '68, and was the regular center fielder on the '69 division championship club. Alou's four-year composite average

of .302 after the shift from Milwaukee ranks third to Ralph Garr and Rico Carty in Atlanta history. And he is one of just 10 Braves since 1900 to accumulate 200 hits in a season.

Alou signed his first professional contract with the Giants for a mere $200 bonus. He batted .380 in his first pro season to win the Florida State League batting title at Cocoa, providing a preview of his big league capabilities and perhaps providing impetus for the Giants' Dominican scouts to keep track of Alou's two younger brothers.

Eventually, Matty and Jesus Alou signed with the Giants, and all three played briefly for San Francisco at the same time. On September 10, 1963, the three went to bat in the same inning, but none got the ball out of the infield. A couple of weeks later, the Giants started Matty in left, Jesus in center, and Felipe in right for the same game. They combined for four hits—two singles for Jesus and a double and triple for Felipe.

After an off season for the Braves in 1969, Felipe was traded to Oakland for pitcher Jim Nash. He played five more seasons but never regained the productivity he had in his prime with the Braves and Giants. He played briefly for Montreal in 1973, and when his playing career was over, he returned there as a coach and eventually became the Expos' manager, leading that club to baseball's best record in the strike-shortened 1994 season.

Alou, Felipe

Braves	G	AB	R	H	2B	3B	HR	RBI	SB	AVG	SLG
1964	121	415	60	105	26	3	9	51	5	.253	.395
1965	143	555	80	165	29	2	23	78	8	.297	.481
1966	154	666*	122*	218*	32	6	31	74	5	.327	.533
1967	140	574	76	157	26	3	15	43	6	.274	.408
1968	160	662*	72	210*	37	5	11	57	12	.317	.438
1969	123	476	54	134	13	1	5	32	4	.282	.345
Career	841	3,348	464	989	163	20	94	335	40	.295	.440

Antonelli, Johnny

Braves: 1948–50, 1953, 1961
Pitcher
Birthplace: Rochester, New York

B: April 12, 1930
Batted left, threw left
Ht. 6–0; **Wt.** 190

Prior to the 1954 season, Braves general manager John Quinn made a trade that nearly caused a riot in New York and several months later created a wild celebration in the same city.

The two principal parties in the deal were Bobby Thomson, the man who hit the most dramatic home run in history in 1951, and a young left-handed pitcher named Johnny Antonelli.

Desperately in need of a power-hitting outfielder and unaware that the future all-time home run king was about to make his presence known, the Braves decided to part with the 23-year-old Antonelli despite the fact that he had just finished fourth in the National League with a 3.18 ERA in 1953.

New York Giants fans were furious about losing Thomson, a god to many who was still going strong, coming off a 106-RBI season. They cared not about Antonelli's potential. How quickly they changed their tune, though.

Antonelli was 21–7 in 1954, a main force in the Giants winning the National League pennant. He led the league in win-

Johnny Antonelli

ning percentage (.750), shutouts (6), and ERA (2.30), then won another game in the World Series, which the Giants swept in four games with Cleveland.

Thomson, on the other hand, broke his leg in the spring, prompting the team to insert rookie Hank Aaron in the lineup.

The Braves originally signed Antonelli as one of the first "bonus babies" in 1948 for the then-fabulous sum of $65,000. At age 18, he went directly to the majors, pitching little for three years and mostly in relief. With a 5–10 career record through 1950, Antonelli departed for two years of military service. He returned to Milwaukee a man and ready to pitch, at last.

Though he was just 12–12 in 1953, he easily could have won several more games with support, as his excellent ERA showed.

Milwaukee might not have had to wait until 1957 for its first pennant if Antonelli had stayed in town. He was one of the best pitchers in the league over the next five years, winning 20 games in 1956 and 19 in '59. Including 1954, he made five NL All-Star teams and was the winning pitcher in 1959.

When Antonelli, who had excellent control, was on, he could be almost unhittable. He won 126 games in his 12-year career, and 25 (20 percent) were by shutout.

An original Milwaukee Brave, Antonelli returned to the club for a brief swan song in 1961, working only 10⅔ innings. At age 31, his once-bright star had been snuffed. The Braves never knew him at his best.

In 1969, he was named one of four pitchers on the Giants' all-time team—the other three were Hall of Famers Christy Mathewson, Juan Marichal, and Carl Hubbell.

Antonelli, Johnny

Braves	W	L	Pct	G	GS	CG	ShO	IP	H	BB	SO	ERA	SV
1948	0	0	—	4	0	0	0	4	2	3	0	2.25	1
1949	3	7	.300	22	10	3	1	96	99	42	48	3.56	0
1950	2	3	.400	20	6	2	1	57⅔	81	22	33	5.93	0
1953	12	12	.500	31	26	11	2	175⅓	167	71	131	3.18	1
1961	1	0	1.000	9	0	0	0	10⅔	16	3	8	7.59	0
Career	18	22	.450	86	42	16	4	343⅔	365	141	220	3.87	2

Avery, Steve

Braves: 1990–   **B:** April 14, 1970
Pitcher   **Bats left, throws left**
Birthplace: Trenton, Michigan   **Ht.** 6–4; **Wt.** 205

With the exception of the incomparable Warren Spahn, the Braves franchise had not been blessed with quality left-handed starters with staying power until the 1990s. Then, along came two of the finest left-handers in the game, three-time 20-game winner Tom Glavine and the precocious Steve Avery.

In 1994, at age 24, Avery had already moved into fifth place on the Braves' all-time list of winningest left-handers with 58 career victories. Three years earlier, when only 21 years old, he was named Most Valuable Player of the 1991 National League Championship Series against Pittsburgh for stringing together an NLCS-record 16⅓ consecutive scoreless innings.

Avery was the Braves' first-round draft pick in 1988. A much-heralded Michigan schoolboy star, he turned down a scholarship to Stanford in order to sign. Blessed with a talented arm and textbook mechanics taught to him by his father, Ken, Avery blitzed through the Braves' farm system. In fact, 1989 was his only full season in the minors, and he debuted in the majors the following year at age 20, barely two years out of high school.

On June 13, 1990, Avery made his big league debut at age 20 years, 2 months, the youngest Braves pitcher since Mike McQueen in 1969. Though Avery was roughed up by Cincinnati in his first game and struggled often in his first season, he showed flashes of brilliance and also gained valuable experience and confidence. He beat the Dodgers, 4–2, to gain

Steve Avery

his first victory in his third start, and he later picked up his first shutout, beating the Cubs, 3–0, with a six-hitter.

Almost overnight, Avery blossomed into one of the best pitchers in the National League in 1991, just in time to help the Braves pull off a stunning drive to their first pennant since 1958.

Avery's 18 wins in 1991 ranked third in the league, and he became the youngest pitcher to win that many games in modern (post-1900) franchise history. Most importantly, Avery was at his best in the clutch. He won his last five starts and beat the Dodgers twice with complete-game victories September 15 and 20 when Atlanta and Los Angeles were battling for first place down the stretch. For the year, he was 3–0 with an 0.57 ERA against the Dodgers.

Then in the playoffs, Avery beat the Pirates in Games 2 and 6, both times by a 1–0 score and both times at Pittsburgh. In Game 6, he matched veteran Doug Drabek through eight scoreless innings until Braves catcher Greg Olson drove in the game's lone run in the ninth. That victory kept the Braves from being eliminated and enabled them to come back and win the pennant in Game 7.

In the World Series against Minnesota, Avery failed to get a decision though he had a 3.46 ERA in two starts. From August 30 through the end of the Series, Avery was 7–0 with a 1.94 ERA in 12 starts for a display of clutch pitching that is among the best in franchise history.

Avery just managed to split 22 decisions in 1992, though most of his statistics were very similar to those he posted the year before. However, he suffered from poor offensive support. The Braves scored only 25 runs in his 11 defeats.

In a repeat matchup of the Braves and Pirates in the 1992 League Championship Series, Avery extended his consecutive scoreless innings streak to 22⅓ with six shutout innings to start Game 2. That broke the major league record for LCS play previously held by Oakland's Ken Holtzman. After winning that game, 13–5, Avery was knocked out in the first inning of Game 5, the shortest outing of his young career. In the World Series against Toronto, he was 0–1, 3.75 in two starts.

Avery bounced back in 1993 with his best year yet, equaling his career high with 18 victories and posting his best ERA, 2.94. He ended the season with 50 career wins, the youngest Brave to reach that level in the modern era.

Avery also was named to the All-Star team for the first time in 1993, and the Braves enjoyed phenomenal success when he was pitching. They were 28–7 overall when he started.

In the playoffs against Philadelphia, Avery pitched well (2.77 ERA) in Games 1 and 5, but he failed to get a decision in either, both of which Atlanta lost in extra innings.

Despite winning eight of 10 decisions in strike-shortened 1994, Avery struggled most of the year. His problems seemed to be related to the premature birth of his first child. When his son's health improved, Avery's pitching did, too. However, the season ended shortly thereafter.

Baker, Dusty

Braves: 1968–75		**B:** June 15, 1949	
Outfielder		**Batted right, threw right**	
Birthplace: Riverside, California		**Ht.** 6–2; **Wt.** 187	

On two different occasions at the height of the Braves' success in Atlanta, Dusty Baker was a bitter rival of the team's. However, he also was one of the club's better players in the early 1970s before he was sent across the country in a six-player deal.

When the Braves won the National League West in 1982, Baker was a key member of the Dodgers, who finished one game behind Joe Torre's surprisingly potent club.

What Atlanta fans remember most dramatically, though, is Baker sitting in the dugout as the San Francisco Giants' rookie manager in 1993. The Braves had to win 51 of their last 68 games just to edge Baker's spirited team by one game on the final day of the season.

A foe in many battles, Baker nevertheless was a friend at the beginning of his career. He was the Braves' regular center fielder in 1972 and '73. Then, he replaced Hank Aaron in right field for a good portion of 1974 when Aaron cut back his playing time after he hit home run No. 715 and in 1975 when Aaron was traded to Milwaukee.

Baker did make one mistake during his Atlanta career that deprived him of respect of some fans. He created great expectations in '72, his first full season in the majors, by batting a career-high .321, third in the National League. He never approached that average again in three more seasons with the Braves, though he certainly was a productive player. In 1973, he not only batted .288 with 99 RBIs but also joined Aaron in the 20–20 (home runs–stolen bases) club. Until Dale Murphy's first MVP season in 1982, they were the only two Atlanta Braves to achieve that combination of power and speed.

In '74 and '75, Baker's numbers declined, and the team had difficulty reaching a contract agreement with him. General manager Eddie Robinson decided to package him with Ed Goodson in a trade with the Dodgers that brought Jerry Royster, Lee Lacy, Jimmy Wynn, and Tom Paciorek to Atlanta. The move proved to be the best thing that ever happened to Baker, who flourished in Los Angeles as the team's left fielder.

In 1977, Baker joined teammates Ron Cey, Steve Garvey, and Reggie Smith with 30 homers, giving the Dodgers the first 30-homer quartet in history.

Baker was at his best in postseason play, a factor which certainly played a big role in Dodgers fans selecting him to their

Avery, Steve

Braves	W	L	Pct	G	GS	CG	ShO	IP	H	BB	SO	ERA	SV
1990	3	11	.214	21	20	1	1	99	121	45	75	5.64	0
1991	18	8	.692	35	35	3	1	210½	189	65	137	3.38	0
1992	11	11	.500	35	35*	2	2	233⅓	216	71	129	3.20	0
1993	18	6	.750	35	35	3	1	223⅓	216	43	125	2.94	0
1994	8	3	.727	24	24	1	0	151⅔	127	55	122	4.04	0
Career	58	39	.598	150	149	10	5	918	869	279	588	3.57	0

Dusty Baker

100th-anniversary team in 1990. In 1977, he was the MVP of the NLCS, hitting .357 with two home runs in four games against the Phillies. The following year, he set a playoff record by hitting .467, including a grand slam.

Baker, Dusty

Braves	G	AB	R	H	2B	3B	HR	RBI	SB	AVG	SLG
1968	6	5	0	2	0	0	0	0	0	.400	.400
1969	3	7	0	0	0	0	0	0	0	.000	.000
1970	13	24	3	7	0	0	0	4	0	.292	.292
1971	29	62	2	14	2	0	0	4	0	.226	.258
1972	127	446	62	143	27	2	17	76	4	.321	.504
1973	159	604	101	174	29	4	21	99	24	.288	.454
1974	149	574	80	147	35	0	20	69	18	.256	.422
1975	142	494	63	129	18	2	19	72	12	.261	.421
Career	628	2,216	311	616	111	8	77	324	58	.278	.440

Bancroft, Dave

Braves: 1924–27
Shortstop
Birthplace: Sioux City, Iowa
B: April 20, 1891

D: October 9, 1972
Batted both, threw right
Ht. 5–9; **Wt.** 160

Dave Bancroft helped shape the theory that "great players don't make good managers." One of the greatest defensive shortstops in history and good enough at the plate to get 2,004 career hits, the Hall of Famer couldn't coax the Braves out of their doldrums in a four-year stint as player/manager in 1924–27.

Of course, neither could two managers in seven seasons before Bancroft, nor could a host of managers, including Casey Stengel, for nearly two decades after he was relieved.

Bancroft had the misfortune of managing Boston during a prolonged dark period in franchise history. He barely won 40 percent (.407) of his games and never managed again.

But though his best playing days, which came with the Phillies and the New York Giants, were behind him, Bancroft still was a slick fielder when he came to Boston in 1924 at age 33. And in 1925 and '26, he even managed to post the last two of his five career .300 seasons at the plate.

As a rookie in 1915, Bancroft played for the pennant-winning Phillies. He later played on three successive NL championship Giants clubs in 1921–23, hitting over .300 each year. He was at the height of his career when the Giants shipped him to Boston in an interesting five-player deal that may have included more baseball brainpower than any other deal in history, since it involved three future Braves managers.

Bancroft, of course, was named manager at the time of the trade. Also coming with him from New York were two outfielders, journeyman Bill Cunningham and Stengel, who was at the end of a steady but unspectacular playing career.

Stengel would manage Boston from 1938 to 1943 before going on to bigger and better things with the Yankees.

In exchange for that trio, the Braves sent pitcher Joe Oeschger and outfielder Billy Southworth to the Giants. Southworth would later manage St. Louis to World Series championships in 1942 and '44 before returning to Boston to manage the Braves in 1946–51, winning the pennant in 1948.

Two years before coming to Boston, Bancroft set a major league record for chances accepted by a shortstop with 984. Proving he still had his trademark soft hands and quick reflexes, he led NL shortstops in fielding percentage (.945) in 1925 despite the considerable distractions of managing the Braves.

Bancroft, Dave

Braves	G	AB	R	H	2B	3B	HR	RBI	SB	AVG	SLG
1924	79	319	49	89	11	1	2	21	4	.279	.339
1925	128	479	75	153	29	8	2	49	7	.319	.426
1926	127	453	70	141	18	6	1	44	3	.311	.384
1927	111	375	44	91	13	4	1	31	5	.243	.307
Career	445	1,626	238	474	71	19	6	145	19	.292	.370

Barker, Len

Braves: 1983–85
Pitcher
Birthplace: Fort Knox, Kentucky

B: July 7, 1955
Batted right, threw right
Ht. 6–5; **Wt.** 225

Len Barker was supposed to win the division title for the Braves in 1983, but he wound up being nothing but a bust in one of the worst deals in modern franchise history.

A powerful right-hander, Barker pitched a three-hitter against the White Sox in his major league debut for Texas in 1976. Slow to develop, though, he was traded to Cleveland after the 1978 season. There he led the American League in strikeouts in 1980 and '81 and finished second in '82. He won 19 games for the lowly Indians in 1980 and pitched the 12th perfect game in history in 1981 against Toronto.

The Braves won the National League West in 1982 and were trying to repeat the following season. They were attempting to catch the Dodgers down the stretch and felt that acquiring another quality starting pitcher would allow them to successfully defend their title.

Barker was struggling with Cleveland. He was 8–13 with a 5.11 ERA. Basically, his arm had burned out, but the Braves didn't know it. So, they packaged three promising youngsters—Brett Butler, Brook Jacoby, and Rick Behenna—and sent them to the Indians on August 28 in exchange for Barker.

It didn't work. Barker was but 1–3. The Braves not only failed to catch the Dodgers, but they also gave away what could have been a significant part of their future for relatively nothing.

Dave Bancroft

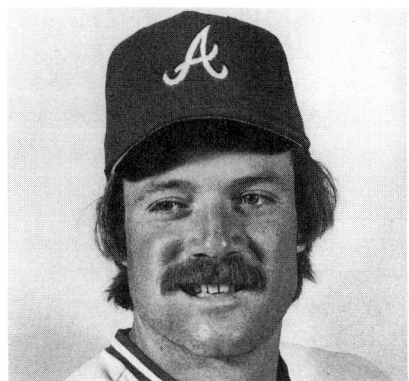

Len Barker

In August 1984, Barker was forced to undergo arm surgery for removal of a bone spur, and he never recovered, pitching ineffectively in parts of two more seasons before his career ended at age 32.

Barker, Len

Braves	W	L	Pct	G	GS	CG	ShO	IP	H	BB	SO	ERA	SV
1983	1	3	.250	6	6	0	0	33	31	14	21	3.82	0
1984	7	8	.467	21	20	1	0	126⅓	120	38	95	3.85	0
1985	2	9	.182	20	18	0	0	73⅔	84	37	47	6.35	0
Career	10	20	.333	47	44	1	0	233	235	89	163	4.64	0

Barrett, Red

Braves: 1943–45, 1947–49
Pitcher
Birthplace: Santa Barbara, California
B: February 14, 1915

D: July 28, 1990
Batted right, threw right
Ht. 5–11; **Wt.** 183

Red Barrett didn't like to fool around on the baseball field— it cut into his time for monkeying around off the field.

Barrett was good at both getting games over in a hurry and at cutting up before and after. The right-hander broke in with brief stints for Cincinnati in four seasons before landing full-time in the majors with the Braves in 1943. The next season, he pitched one of the most incredible games in franchise history, though there is little record of it.

On August 10, 1944, Barrett beat Cincinnati ace Bucky Walters, 2–0, in 1 hour, 15 minutes. It remains the shortest

Red Barrett

night game in history. But the really remarkable facet of the game is that Barrett threw just 58 pitches. That's the easiest any pitcher has ever gotten through nine innings.

Barrett faced just 29 batters, so he averaged only two pitches per hitter. He didn't strike out or walk anyone, he gave up just two hits, and the Braves made no errors.

For years, historians doubted the accuracy of claims that Barrett actually was able to complete a game with 58 pitches. However, in 1993, Joe Dittmar of the Society for American Baseball Research uncovered an article from the *Cincinnati Times-Star* that was written by the game's official scorer and verified the pitch count.

Barrett was quite a character, as well as a decent pitcher. In 1936, his second pro season, he was released by Ponca City of the Western Association. He told the president of Muskogee that if that team would give him a job, the club would win the pennant. He was hired and proceeded to pitch Muskogee to the pennant with 24 victories.

Six years later, Barrett still hadn't been able to establish himself in the majors when the desperate Braves, who'd finished 44 games out of first in 1942, purchased him from Syracuse of the International League.

After two-plus seasons with the Braves during which he failed to post a winning record, Barrett was sent to St. Louis, along with $60,000, for pitcher Mort Cooper on May 23, 1945. Barrett proceeded to win 21 games for manager Billy Southworth. Added to the pair of games he won for Boston before the trade, that gave Barrett a league-leading total of 23 victories.

In 1946, Barrett won just three games for the Cardinals, who sold him right back to the Braves, then being managed by Southworth. In three more seasons with Boston, Barrett never regained his 1945 form.

Eddie Dyer, who managed Barrett at St. Louis in 1946 when Southworth jumped to the Braves, said of his enigmatic pitcher, "If that fellow devoted as much time to his pitching as he does to clowning and making jokes, he would become a very fine pitcher."

One of Barrett's favorite pastimes on the road was to sing with the band at the team's hotel. And when the Braves went to Havana, Cuba, for an exhibition series in the spring of 1947, Barrett somehow managed to get through customs, find the hotel, check in the entire team, and take over the assistant manager's desk before traveling secretary Duffy Lewis arrived.

Barrett, Red

Braves	W	L	Pct	G	GS	CG	ShO	IP	H	BB	SO	ERA	SV
1943	12	18	.400	38	31	14	3	255	240	63	64	3.18	0
1944	9	16	.360	42	30	11	1	230⅓	257	63	54	4.06	2
1945	2	3	.400	9	5	2	0	38	43	16	13	4.74	2
1947	11	12	.478	36	20	12	3	210⅔	200	53	53	3.55	1
1948	7	8	.467	34	13	3	0	128⅓	132	28	40	3.65	0
1949	1	1	.500	23	0	0	0	44⅓	58	10	17	5.68	0
Career	42	58	.420	182	99	42	7	906⅔	930	233	241	3.74	5

Bedrosian, Steve

Braves: 1981–85, 1993–95   **B:** December 6, 1957
Pitcher   **Batted right, threw right**
Birthplace: Methuen, Massachusetts   **Ht.** 6–3; **Wt.** 200

It was always easy to tell when Steve Bedrosian was warming up in the bullpen. He was the one with his pant legs turned up near his knees—where they're supposed to be. In the 1990s, when most players wear their pants at or near the ankle, Bedrosian remained one of the few throwbacks to the game's traditional style.

He also remained a remarkably successful reliever for someone whose career seemingly ended in the 1991 World Series in which he helped Minnesota beat the Braves. Unable to find the cause of numbness in the fingers of his pitching hand, Bedrosian retired in 1992 at age 34. However, after he sat out one entire season, Bedrosian decided to try a comeback after the numbness disappeared.

Since he lived in suburban Atlanta and had a young son battling leukemia, Bedrosian elected to try to make the Braves in spring training so he could play close to home. He not only made the team, but he also regained much of the form that had made him one of the game's top relievers in the 1980s.

Used as a setup man in the Atlanta bullpen, Bedrosian posted a 1.63 ERA in 1993, the best of his career and the lowest on the Braves' staff. He continued to pitch effectively in 1994. At age 36, he actually gained speed on his fastball, and he averaged nearly a strikeout per inning. However, he was forced to retire in August 1995.

The National League Cy Young Award winner in 1987 when he recorded a league-leading 40 saves for Philadelphia, Bedrosian helped the Braves win a division title in 1982 as a rookie. He won eight games and saved 11 for manager Joe Torre that year, sharing the closing duties with Gene Garber.

His 112 strikeouts out of the bullpen were the most in the NL, and he was named the league's Rookie Pitcher of the Year by *The Sporting News*.

Bedrosian put together two more productive seasons in the Atlanta bullpen in 1983 and '84. But in 1985, new manager Eddie Haas attempted to turn him into a starter. The hard-throwing right-hander failed to complete any of his 37 starts, winning just seven times, and the Braves reacted by trading him to the Phillies along with Milt Thompson in exchange for Ozzie Virgil and Pete Smith.

Back in the bullpen, Bedrosian flourished for Philadelphia, winning the Cy Young and saving 103 games in three-plus seasons.

Bedrosian, Steve

Braves	W	L	Pct	G	GS	CG	ShO	IP	H	BB	SO	ERA	SV
1981	1	2	.333	15	1	0	0	24⅓	15	15	9	4.44	0
1982	8	6	.571	64	3	0	0	137⅔	102	57	123	2.42	11
1983	9	10	.474	70	1	0	0	120	100	51	114	3.60	19
1984	9	6	.600	40	4	0	0	83⅔	65	33	81	2.37	11
1985	7	15	.318	37	37	0	0	206⅔	198	111	134	3.83	0
1993	5	2	.714	49	0	0	0	49⅔	34	14	33	1.63	0
1994	0	2	.000	46	0	0	0	46	41	18	43	3.33	0
1995	1	2	.333	29	0	0	0	28	40	12	22	6.11	0
Career	40	45	.471	350	46	0	0	695⅔	595	311	559	3.26	41

Benedict, Bruce

Braves: 1978–89   **B:** August 18, 1955
Catcher   **Batted right, threw right**
Birthplace: Birmingham, Alabama   **Ht.** 6–1; **Wt.** 190

The height of Bruce Benedict's career coincided with the Braves' brief run of success in the early 1980s. Regarded as a good-field/no-hit catcher most of his 12 years in the majors, Benedict blossomed under new manager Joe Torre when the Braves won a division title in 1982 and finished second the following season.

Known as "Eggs" to his teammates, Benedict's real first name often echoed through Atlanta Stadium in the midst of Braves rallies in those two seasons. "Bruuuce . . . Bruuuce," fans yelled, much as they chanted, "Sid . . . Sid" for Sid Bream a decade later.

Benedict responded well to the encouragement. Though

Steve Bedrosian

Bruce Benedict

he batted only .246 in the Braves' division-winning effort of '82, he did most of his hitting in the final five weeks, batting .389 from August 23 to the end of the season. He delivered one of the biggest hits of the year late in the season when he hit a game-winning grand slam against the Dodgers after manager Tom Lasorda ordered Glenn Hubbard intentionally walked to bring Benedict to the plate. The Braves ended the season one game in front of Los Angeles.

Most importantly, Benedict led National League catchers with a .993 fielding percentage that year.

In 1983, the Braves came up three games short of the Dodgers in the standings, but Benedict had his career season, hitting .298—11th in the league—and making the All-Star team for the second and final time of his career.

Benedict never appeared in more than 95 games in a season after that and hit over .225 just once. But considering that he became the team's starting catcher mainly because of Biff Pocoroba's shoulder injury and Dale Murphy's throwing problems, Benedict had a fine career, all of which was spent in Atlanta.

After retiring, he became a catching instructor in the Braves farm system and eventually moved up to become a minor league manager in the organization.

Wally Berger

Benedict, Bruce

Braves	G	AB	R	H	2B	3B	HR	RBI	SB	AVG	SLG
1978	22	52	3	13	2	0	0	1	0	.250	.288
1979	76	204	14	46	11	0	0	15	1	.225	.279
1980	120	359	18	91	14	1	2	34	3	.253	.315
1981	90	295	26	78	12	1	5	35	1	.264	.363
1982	118	386	34	95	11	1	3	44	4	.246	.303
1983	134	423	43	126	13	1	2	43	1	.298	.348
1984	95	300	26	67	8	1	4	25	1	.223	.297
1985	70	208	12	42	6	0	0	20	0	.202	.231
1986	64	160	11	36	10	1	0	13	1	.225	.300
1987	37	95	4	14	1	0	1	5	0	.147	.189
1988	90	236	11	57	7	0	0	19	0	.242	.271
1989	66	160	12	31	3	0	1	6	0	.194	.231
Career	982	2,878	214	696	98	6	18	260	12	.242	.299

Berger, Wally

Braves, Bees: 1930–37
Outfielder
Birthplace: Chicago, Illinois
B: October 10, 1905

D: November 30, 1988
Batted right, threw right
Ht. 6–2; **Wt.** 198

Wally Berger once was considered the heir apparent to Babe Ruth as the game's greatest power hitter. He earned that distinction despite playing in mammoth Braves Field.

Because Berger played in the 1930s when the Braves were positively horrible, he is not as heralded as he deserves to be in the history of either the franchise or the game.

There are Braves fans from the Boston era who contend the organization should have retired uniform number 3 in Berger's honor long before Dale Murphy ever came along. And there are historians who think Berger belongs in the Hall of Fame, since his career statistics match quite favorably with those of Cubs slugger Hack Wilson, who is enshrined at Cooperstown.

A strong-armed center fielder, Berger led the National League in home runs and RBIs in 1935, and he fell one home run short of league titles in both 1933 and '34. However, his

biggest claim to fame was holding the major league record for home runs by a rookie (38 in 1930) for 57 years. Cincinnati's Frank Robinson tied the record in 1956, but it wasn't broken until Oakland's Mark McGwire hit 49 in 1987.

The right-handed slugger would have been a landslide winner for Rookie of the Year had that honor existed in 1930. His 119 RBIs that year still rank as the National League rookie record.

Raised in San Francisco, Berger played on the same high school team as Hall of Famer Joe Cronin. However, Berger dropped out of school as a junior to work on the docks, drive a truck, and play semipro ball. He became a proficient slugger in the Cubs farm system but in 1929 appeared stuck in the minors by the only all-100-RBI outfield in history: Riggs Stephenson, Hack Wilson, and Kiki Cuyler.

After the 1929 season, in which Berger established club records with 40 home runs and 166 RBIs for Los Angeles of the Pacific Coast League, the Cubs traded him to Boston for three players and cash. Berger made the club in the spring of 1930, then proceeded to demonstrate that not even Braves Field could harness his power.

There were more home runs hit in the majors in 1930 than in any previous season, evidence of a livelier ball, but that doesn't detract from Berger's performance. Only two National Leaguers—Wilson and Chuck Klein—hit more homers than the 25-year-old rookie. And the only American Leaguers who hit more were a couple of guys named Ruth and Gehrig.

Berger's home runs were memorable, too. He was noted for long, towering drives. In his rookie season, he hit home runs that were regarded as the longest ever hit at Braves Field and Pittsburgh's huge Forbes Field. *Ripley's Believe It or Not* even recognized him as hitting the longest home run "ever" for one that landed beyond the Braves Field wall in a moving boxcar bound for Chicago.

Berger hit them long, and he hit them in the clutch. In his rookie season alone, he hit five home runs that accounted for the winning run in one-run victories over the Giants, who finished five games out of first. And in 1933, he hit what was known as the "$7,100 home run." On the final day of the season, he delivered a pinch-hit grand slam to beat the Phillies, lifting the Braves into fourth place and their first first-division bonus money in 12 years.

That home run was Berger's 27th of the year, one shy of Philadelphia's Klein. Had Berger not missed the previous three weeks with pneumonia, he likely would have ruined Klein's successful Triple Crown bid.

Berger batted .307 or better in each of his first four seasons and drove in 106 or more runs in four of his first six years. He was the National League's starting center fielder in the very first All-Star Game, which was played at Chicago in 1933. He was the starting center fielder the next year, too, and was selected to the squad in 1935 and '36, as well.

Few hitters have ever been more productive in their first seven seasons than was Berger, whose top salary as a Brave was $12,500. However, he never hit more than 17 home runs or drove in more than 65 in any of the final four years of his short career. He suffered a shoulder injury in 1936 from which he never fully recovered.

Strapped for cash, the Braves traded him to the Giants early in 1937 for $25,000 and pitcher Frank Gabler, who was no more than a throw-in. Though Berger never regained his productivity with the Giants or later with Cincinnati or Philadelphia, he did get to play in two World Series, 1937 with New York and 1939 with the Reds.

He was released by the Phillies in 1940 and retired at age 34 with a career batting average of .300 and 242 lifetime home runs. Berger hit 105 home runs at Braves Field, more than anyone else, and his 130 RBIs in 1935 stood as a modern franchise record until surpassed by Eddie Mathews in 1953.

Besides his offensive accomplishments, Berger was sure-handed enough to lead the league's outfielders with a .993 fielding average in 1932.

Berger, Wally

Braves, Bees	G	AB	R	H	2B	3B	HR	RBI	SB	AVG	SLG
1930	151	555	98	172	27	14	38	119	3	.310	.614
1931	156	617	94	199	44	8	19	84	13	.323	.512
1932	145	602	90	185	34	6	17	73	5	.307	.468
1933	137	528	84	165	37	8	27	106	2	.313	.566
1934	150	615	92	183	35	8	34	121	2	.298	.546
1935	150	589	91	174	39	4	34*	130*	3	.295	.548
1936	138	534	88	154	23	3	25	91	1	.288	.483
1937	30	113	14	31	9	1	5	22	0	.274	.504
Career	1,057	4,153	651	1,263	248	52	199	746	29	.304	.533

Bickford, Vern

Braves: 1948–53
Pitcher
Birthplace: Hellier, Kentucky
B: August 17, 1920

D: May 6, 1960
Batted right, threw right
Ht. 6–0; **Wt.** 185

Vern Bickford had a short but successful career in the majors. But during his six seasons with the Braves, he played a very important role in franchise history.

Only through the fate of a coin toss did the hard-throwing right-hander even wind up as Braves property. Bickford had spent five years in the low minors and three in the military during World War II when he was placed on the roster of Indianapolis, a Braves farm team, in the spring of 1947. The

Vern Bickford

owner of the American Association club, Frank McKinney, then bought controlling interest in the Pittsburgh Pirates.

A dispute arose over whether the Braves or Indianapolis owned the rights to eight players, including Bickford. Braves president Lou Perini and McKinney agreed to flip a coin for the first pick in a "draft" of those eight. Perini won the toss and chose Bickford first.

"I didn't recognize any of the names at first, but all of a sudden the name of Bickford rang a bell," Perini said. "I recalled that Branch Rickey at one time had expressed an interest in him. I figured that if Bickford was good enough for Rickey, he was good enough for the Braves."

Even though Bickford pitched in Class B in 1946, he was immediately assigned to the Braves' Triple-A team at Milwaukee where he pitched a two-hitter in his first game. The following year, 1948, he made the Braves as a reliever. But he was unimpressive and fully expected to be farmed out on the May 20 cutdown date.

Manager Billy Southworth decided to take one more good look at the 27-year-old rookie, though, and gave him a start against Pittsburgh on May 20. Bickford responded with a five-hitter, beating the Pirates, 4–1. He not only kept his job in the big leagues, but he also assumed a critical role in the Braves' march to the team's first pennant since 1914.

"Spahn and Sain and pray for rain" was the battle cry of Braves fans that year, but Bickford also became an effective part of Southworth's starting rotation. He won 11 of 16 decisions, and his .688 percentage was the best on the club. Bickford started Game 3 of the World Series and was charged with a 2–0 loss to Cleveland.

The Braves slid to fourth place in 1949, but it wasn't Bickford's fault. He won 16 games and made the National League All-Star team. Then in 1950, at age 29, Bickford had his finest season. He pitched the seventh no-hitter in franchise history, led the league in complete games and innings, and finished fourth in victories.

On August 11, six days shy of his 30th birthday, Bickford no-hit the Dodgers, 7–0, at Braves Field. He faced only 30 hitters and didn't allow a man to reach second until the ninth inning when he issued two of his four walks. With runners at first and second and one out in the ninth, Bickford induced future Hall of Famer Duke Snider to ground into a game-ending double play.

It was Bickford's 14th victory of the season and the first no-hitter of his pro career. He won five more games that year, but failed six times to win his 20th, a fact he later called the biggest disappointment of his career.

Bickford, known as a tough competitor, was off to a good start again in 1951 when a line drive hit him on his pitching hand, breaking a finger. He missed most of the last three months of the season and was never the same pitcher again.

ries was a one-hitter against his hero—Spahn, who was finishing his brilliant career as an outcast with the Mets.

In 1967, Blasingame's physical problems were supposed to be history, but in June he was just 1–0 with a 4.62 ERA in 10 games. The Braves gave up on him and shipped him to Houston in exchange for French Canadian reliever Claude Raymond.

Bickford, Vern

Braves	W	L	Pct	G	GS	CG	ShO	IP	H	BB	SO	ERA	SV
1948	11	5	.688	33	22	10	1	146	125	63	60	3.27	1
1949	16	11	.593	37	36	15	2	230⅔	246	106	101	4.25	0
1950	19	14	.576	40	39*	27*	2	311⅔*	293	122	126	3.47	0
1951	11	9	.550	25	20	12	3	162⅔	146	76	76	3.12	0
1952	7	12	.368	26	22	7	1	161⅓	165	64	62	3.74	0
1953	2	5	.286	20	9	2	0	58	60	35	25	5.28	1
Career	66	56	.541	181	148	73	9	1,072⅓	1,035	466	450	3.69	2

Blasingame, Wade

Braves: 1963–67
Pitcher
Birthplace: Deming, New Mexico

B: November 22, 1943
Batted left, threw left
Ht. 6–1; **Wt.** 185

There were many baseball experts who thought Wade Blasingame was destined for stardom. That's why the Braves paid him a whopping $100,000 bonus for his autograph on a contract in 1961.

In 1964, "The Blazer" went 9–5, prompting Braves manager Bobby Bragan to say his 20-year-old left-hander had the best curveball in the National League. Bragan was known to make an unsubstantiated comment now and then, but when Blasingame went 16–10 in 1965, it appeared the boisterous Bragan might be right on target.

However, when the Braves moved to Atlanta the next year, Blasingame experienced arm problems and had a broken finger. He was but 3–7. Bragan, by the way, was fired late in the season.

One of a bevy of left-handers to come up through the Braves farm system supposedly capable of being the "next Warren Spahn," Blasingame won only 26 games following his 22nd birthday, after having 25 victories at age 21. He never had another winning season after '65, when one of his victo-

Blasingame, Wade

Braves	W	L	Pct	G	GS	CG	ShO	IP	H	BB	SO	ERA	SV
1963	0	0	.000	2	0	0	0	3	7	2	6	12.00	0
1964	9	5	.643	28	13	3	1	116⅔	113	51	70	4.24	2
1965	16	10	.615	38	36	10	1	224⅔	200	116	117	3.77	1
1966	3	7	.300	16	12	0	0	67⅔	71	25	34	5.32	0
1967	1	0	1.000	10	4	0	0	25⅓	27	21	20	4.62	0
Career	29	22	.569	94	65	13	2	437⅓	418	215	247	4.24	3

Blauser, Jeff

Braves: 1987–
Shortstop, third baseman,
    second baseman, outfielder
Birthplace: Los Gatos, California

B: November 8, 1965
Bats right, throws right
Ht. 6–1; **Wt.** 180

A durable, dependable player, Jeff Blauser blossomed in 1993 when he became the first Braves shortstop since Al Dark in 1948 to hit over .300 (.305). He also came into his own as a defensive player and was named to the National League All-Star team for the first time in his career.

Signed as a shortstop after being the first pick in the secondary draft by the Braves in 1984, Blauser was unable to settle into a position early in his career. He spent a lot of time at second base and third base and even was occasionally used in the outfield. In 1989, his first full season in the majors, Blauser was Atlanta's regular third baseman. His 12 homers were the most by a Brave at that position since Bob Horner hit 20 in 1983.

In 1990, however, Blauser was supplanted at third by Jim Presley and had to split time at second and short. During the pennant-winning 1991 season, he was the backup at shortstop to Rafael Belliard. But in 1992, Blauser gradually overtook Belliard as the everyday shortstop.

Steady on defense, Blauser supplied the Braves with more offense than they were used to getting from their shortstop. On July 12 at Chicago, he became the fourth shortstop in modern history to hit three homers in the same game, join-

Wade Blasingame

Jeff Blauser

ing Ernie Banks, Barry Larkin, and Fred Patek in that department. In August, he got the Braves' first inside-the-park home run in nearly two decades, then he closed the season with a flourish, hitting .326 over his last 43 games.

There was more of the same in 1993. Blauser set an Atlanta record for fielding percentage by a shortstop (.970) and continued to swing a potent bat. His 73 RBIs were the most by a Braves shortstop since Johnny Logan's 83 in 1965. He also set a franchise record for shortstops by scoring 110 runs, passing Billy Urbanski's 104 in 1934. His 161 games played established another franchise record at his position, and he set an Atlanta record by being hit by a pitch a league-leading 16 times.

Blauser, Jeff

Braves	G	AB	R	H	2B	3B	HR	RBI	SB	AVG	SLG
1987	51	165	11	40	6	3	2	15	7	.242	.352
1988	18	67	7	16	3	1	2	7	0	.239	.403
1989	142	456	63	123	24	2	12	46	5	.270	.410
1990	115	386	46	104	24	3	8	39	3	.269	.409
1991	129	352	49	91	14	3	11	54	5	.259	.409
1992	123	343	61	90	19	3	14	46	5	.262	.458
1993	161	597	110	182	29	2	15	73	16	.305	.436
1994	96	380	56	98	21	4	6	45	1	.258	.382
Career	835	2,746	403	744	140	21	70	325	42	.271	.414

Bolling, Frank

Braves: 1961–66
Second baseman
Birthplace: Mobile, Alabama

B: November 16, 1931
Batted right, threw right
Ht. 6–1; **Wt.** 175

After winning consecutive pennants in 1957 and 1958, then losing a playoff to the Dodgers in 1959 and finishing second again in '60, Braves management felt it could get the team back on top quickly with a few moves. One of the areas in need was second base where popular Red Schoendienst was aging and had been weakened by tuberculosis.

The club was able to pick up one of the game's best second basemen that off-season, but had to give up Billy Bruton, a Milwaukee favorite, to do so. In exchange for Bruton, infielder Chuck Cottier, and two minor leaguers, the Braves received 29-year-old Frank Bolling, who led American League second baseman in fielding in 1958.

Capable of providing substantial offense for a second baseman, Bolling helped ease the loss of Bruton with an All-Star season in his National League debut. He led National

League second basemen in fielding in 1961, tied his career-high with 15 home runs, and batted a respectable .262.

For the most part, Bolling continued to play well for the team's final four seasons in Milwaukee. He led the league's second baseman in fielding again in 1962 and '64. However, an aberration in his offensive record occurred in 1964 when he seemed to forget how to hit, batting just .199. To his credit, Bolling didn't let his anemic bat affect his steady glove, and he bounced back in '65 to hit .264.

Bolling's career ended in 1966, the club's first year in Atlanta, when his struggles at the plate returned. In his 12-year career, he never played an inning at any position other than second base, finishing with a lifetime fielding percentage of .982. His .989 fielding in 1962 stood as the franchise record for second basemen until it was broken by Mark Lemke (.994) in 1994.

Bolling, Frank

Braves	G	AB	R	H	2B	3B	HR	RBI	SB	AVG	SLG
1961	148	585	86	153	16	4	15	56	7	.262	.379
1962	122	406	45	110	17	4	9	43	2	.271	.399
1963	142	542	73	132	18	2	5	43	2	.244	.312
1964	120	352	35	70	11	1	5	34	0	.199	.278
1965	148	535	55	141	26	3	7	50	0	.264	.363
1966	75	227	16	48	7	0	1	18	1	.211	.256
Career	755	2,647	310	654	95	14	42	244	12	.247	.341

Bond, Tommy

Red Stockings: 1877–81
Pitcher
Birthplace: Granard, Ireland
B: April 2, 1856

D: January 24, 1941
Batted right, threw right
Ht. 5–7; **Wt.** 160

Tommy Bond was one of the first true heroes in franchise history. A native of Ireland, he pitched the Red Stockings to their first two NL pennants in 1877 and 1878, leading the league in victories with 40 both years.

Most teams used only one starting pitcher in the early years of the game, and Bond was manager Harry Wright's man. He started all but two of the club's 60 games in 1877 and all 59 the following season.

After winning the last four pennants in the National Association, the Red Stockings dropped to fourth place in

Frank Bolling

Tommy Bond

1876, the first year of the National League. Wright knew he needed a pitcher to get back on top, so he proceeded to lure Bond away from Hartford. Only 21 when he joined Boston, Bond won a phenomenal 123 games in his first three seasons with the Red Stockings.

In his first year with Boston, Bond became the first winner of pitching's Triple Crown, leading the league in strikeouts and ERA, as well as wins. He nearly repeated in 1878, leading in wins and strikeouts but finishing fifth in ERA.

Bond is credited with being one of the game's first curveball pitchers. In fact, Wright once used Bond for a demonstration to show skeptics that a ball could be made to curve and that the pitch was not an optical illusion.

In 1878 at Cincinnati, Wright had two fences placed 20 yards apart with a post midway between the two. All three were on the same line. Bond then stood to the left of one fence and made the ball curve around the post so that it passed to the left of the second fence.

Besides his curve, Bond also had a good fastball, and he has been called the "father of modern pitching." Winner of 31 games for Hartford in 1876, Bond notched 180 victories in his first five seasons in the National League. However, at age 24, he was burned out and didn't win another game in the league.

He pitched 35 career shutouts, including a career-high 11 in 1879 when there were only 45 in the entire National League.

After retiring from baseball in 1884, Bond coached at Harvard and was an umpire in the New England League.

Bond, Tommy

Red Stockings	W	L	Pct	G	GS	CG	ShO	IP	H	BB	SO	ERA	SV
1877	40*	17	.702	58	58	58	6*	521	530	36	170*	2.11*	0
1878	40*	19	.678	59*	59	57*	9*	532⅔*	571	33	182*	2.06	0
1879	43	19	.694	64	64	59	11*	555⅓	543	24	155	1.96*	0
1880	26	29	.473	63	57	54	3	493	559	45	118	2.67	0
1881	0	3	.000	3	3	2	0	25⅓	40	2	2	4.26	0
Career	149	87	.631	247	241	230	29	2,127⅓	2,243	140	627	2.21	0

Bouton, Jim

Braves: 1978
Pitcher
Birthplace: Newark, New Jersey

B: March 8, 1939
Batted right; threw right
Ht. 6–0; **Wt.** 185

Jim Bouton is better known as an author than as a pitcher, but because of the nature of his brief tenure with the Braves, he is included in this section.

As a power pitcher, Bouton won 21 games for the Yankees in 1963 and another 18 in '64, when he also won two more in the World Series against St. Louis. Those were his only two successful seasons in his first nine years in the majors. Arm problems robbed him of his speed, but he managed to hang on through 1970.

In 1970, he wrote *Ball Four,* which unveiled the off-field antics of ballplayers, drew scorn from the game's establishment, and became the best-selling sports book of its time. He became a sportscaster and did some acting. Then in 1977, at the age of 38 and seven years removed from the majors, he mounted a comeback attempt with the Class-A Portland Mavericks. His pitching arsenal consisted mainly of change-ups and knuckleballs.

Considered an outcast by many in baseball because of *Ball Four,* Bouton might never have made it all the way back except

Jim Bouton

for Braves owner Ted Turner, himself a maverick in the game's establishment. The Braves purchased Bouton's contract in 1978 and called him up from Double-A Savannah in September when the only suspense in Atlanta was whether or not the team would lose 100 games. San Francisco third baseman Darrell Evans, a former Brave, called the promotion a farce.

But on September 14, Evans and his Giants teammates suffered the humiliation of losing to Bouton, 4–1, in his second start. He pitched six innings and gave up only three bloop hits and an unearned run against the second-place team in the NL West. It was his first big league victory since 1970 when he was with Houston.

San Francisco second baseman Bill Madlock, who'd already won two NL batting titles and would win two more, summed up the Giants' embarrassment by saying of Bouton's offerings, "It's a nothing pitch. This is a double disgrace. It's a disgrace for him to get out there with that stuff, and it's a double disgrace that we let him get away with it."

Madlock even offered to pay Bouton's salary if he would return in 1979. He didn't. Whether Bouton's comeback was legitimate or a stunt, it ended quickly. He'd have been 40 in '79, and after posting a 4.97 ERA in 29 innings for the Braves, he didn't find anyone interested in his pitching services.

Bouton, Jim

Braves	W	L	Pct	G	GS	CG	ShO	IP	H	BB	SO	ERA	SV
1978	1	3	.250	5	5	0	0	29	25	21	10	4.97	0
Career	1	3	.250	5	5	0	0	29	25	21	10	4.97	0

Boyer, Clete

Braves: 1967–71
Third baseman
Birthplace: Cassville, Missouri

B: February 9, 1937
Batted right, threw right
Ht. 6–0; **Wt.** 182

Clete Boyer was one of the finest defensive third basemen in history, as well as a dangerous clutch hitter with occasional power. However, he never made an All-Star team.

In his prime with the Yankees, he played in the shadow of the master third baseman, Baltimore's Brooks Robinson. Once he came to the Braves, he found himself overlooked in

Clete Boyer

favor of such great offensive third basemen as the Cubs' Ron Santo and Cincinnati's Tony Perez.

Nevertheless, Boyer, using a unique, low-to-the-ground set position, led National League third basemen in fielding in 1967 and '69. In '67, his first season in Atlanta, he also compiled career highs with 26 home runs and 96 RBIs. In '69, he played a major role in the Braves winning the NL West. Late that season, mired in a 1-for-17 slump, he was smooched by Morganna, the kissing bandit, and proceeded to deliver an RBI single and eight hits in his next 15 at-bats.

A fun-loving, carefree individual, Boyer came from one of the most productive baseball families. Brother Ken was a seven-time All-Star third baseman with the Cardinals, winning the National League MVP Award in '64. Another brother, Cloyd, had a five-year career as a pitcher with St. Louis and Kansas City in the early '50s and was a Braves coach under Bobby Cox in 1978–81. Two other brothers played in the minors.

In Game 7 of the 1964 World Series, Ken and Clete both hit home runs, Ken's carrying more weight, since the Cardinals beat the Yankees, 7–5. It was the only time brothers have hit home runs in the same Series game.

Boyer appeared in five World Series with the Yankees, hitting .227 in 27 games. He set a Series record, since broken, with 66 assists at third.

The Braves obtained Boyer from the Yankees to replace Eddie Mathews after the club sent the future Hall of Famer to Houston after the '66 season. To get Boyer, the Braves had to give up a good outfield prospect, Bill Robinson, and reliever Chi Chi Olivo.

The end of Boyer's Atlanta career did not come under the best of circumstances. He not only tangled verbally with general manager Paul Richards in 1971, but he also was the subject of a gambling investigation ordered by the commissioner's office.

Boyer complained about enforcement of a midnight curfew, and Richards responded, "For such a lousy player, Boyer does a lot of talking. I'll give him his release if he writes out a check for 60 days of pay."

The basic agreement between the players and owners called for 60 days severance pay. Boyer volunteered to pay $10,000 for his release. However, the move was nullified as a violation of the basic agreement. The Braves wound up paying Boyer $15,000 in severance, and the third baseman still blasted Richards and manager Luman Harris.

Boyer was unable to find another job in the majors. He felt the gambling investigation was the reason. Commissioner Bowie Kuhn fined him $1,000 in June of 1971 for betting on college and pro football in 1968 and 1969.

Whether it was due to the gambling or his run-in with Richards, Boyer indeed seemed to be blackballed from the game. At age 33, he played in 134 games for the Braves in 1970. His fielding percentage slipped to .954, partly because he played several games at shortstop, but he still hit above his career average and with decent power. He was playing just as well through the first 30 games of 1971 when he and the Braves divorced.

When no contract offer came from another club, he signed with Hawaii of the Pacific Coast League. Later that season, he gained the distinction of becoming the first player ever traded to Japan, when Hawaii sent him to the Tayio Whales for John Werhas.

Boyer, Clete

Braves	G	AB	R	H	2B	3B	HR	RBI	SB	AVG	SLG
1967	154	572	63	140	18	3	26	96	6	.245	.423
1968	71	273	19	62	7	2	4	17	2	.227	.311
1969	144	496	57	124	16	1	14	57	3	.250	.371
1970	134	475	44	117	14	1	16	62	2	.246	.381
1971	30	98	10	24	1	0	6	19	0	.245	.439
Career	533	1,914	193	467	56	8	66	251	13	.244	.385

Brandt, Ed

Braves: 1928–35	**D:** November 1, 1944
Pitcher	**Batted left, threw left**
Birthplace: Spokane, Washington	**Ht.** 6–1; **Wt.** 190
B: February 17, 1905	

Everyone who saw Ed Brandt work knew he was an excellent pitcher. Everyone, that is, except Brandt himself.

The talented left-hander suffered from an inferiority complex and bouts of homesickness that kept him from realizing his potential until Braves manager Bill McKechnie finally got through to him. Then from 1931 through 1934, Brandt developed into one of the top left-handers in the game, averaging 17 wins per season.

Called "Dutch" by teammates, Brandt deserted his team several times early in his minor league career. He admitted he didn't think he could succeed and was more comfortable pitching back home in the Spokane city league. But after

Ed Brandt

spending his early years in the minors as a reliever, Brandt got the opportunity to start in 1927 and won 19 games for Seattle of the Pacific Coast League.

The Braves purchased his contract for $20,000. However, when Seattle refused to give him a portion of the purchase price, he once again returned home. During spring training, he finally decided to report and quickly earned a spot in the team's starting rotation.

For three years, Brandt struggled, losing a league-high 21 games as a rookie and a total of 45 in his first three seasons. His ERA was over 5.00 each of those three years, and he was used less and less.

After watching Brandt stagger in 1930, McKechnie, in his first year as Braves manager, had a heart-to-heart with his pitcher.

"What do you do in the winter?" asked McKechnie of Brandt, who replied, "I hunt."

"Do you want to keep on hunting?" queried McKechnie. And when Brandt responded that he did, the Braves manager said, "Then you'd better make up your mind that you're a major league pitcher and not a semipro star. If you do, you can hunt every winter from now on. But if you don't, you'll be asking some friend of your late father to get you a job in a tinsmith shop."

Brandt got the message. He won his first eight decisions in 1931 en route to finishing fourth in the league with 18 wins. He was second in the league in complete games and third in ERA.

Possessor of a fine forkball, Brandt wasn't quite as effective in 1932, but he bounced back in 1933 to win 18 again, finishing fourth in the league in ERA and third in complete games. He had one more productive season before he was traded to Brooklyn in a six-player deal that brought Al Lopez and Tony Cuccinello to Boston.

Brandt was one of the best hitting pitchers in the league. He was called on to pinch-hit at times, and in 1933 he batted .309 to lead all pitchers.

Brandt, Ed

Braves	W	L	Pct	G	GS	CG	ShO	IP	H	BB	SO	ERA	SV
1928	9	21*	.300	38	31	12	1	225⅓	234	109	84	5.07	0
1929	8	13	.381	26	21	13	0	167⅓	196	83	50	5.53	0
1930	4	11	.267	41	13	4	1	147⅓	168	59	65	5.01	1
1931	18	11	.621	33	29	23	3	250	228	77	112	2.92	2
1932	16	16	.500	35	31	19	2	254	271	57	79	3.97	1
1933	18	14	.563	41	32	23	4	287⅔	256	77	104	2.60	4
1934	16	14	.533	40	28	20	3	255	249	83	106	3.53	5
1935	5	19	.208	29	25	12	0	174⅔	224	66	61	5.00	0
Career	94	119	.441	283	210	126	14	1,761⅔	1,826	611	661	4.01	13

Bream, Sid

Braves: 1991–93   **B:** August 3, 1960
First baseman   **Bats left, throws left**
Birthplace: Carlisle, Pennsylvania   **Ht.** 6–4; **Wt.** 220

Sid Bream was greatly instrumental in the Braves' sudden rise to National League prominence in the early 1990s, and he was in the midst of one of the most exciting and memorable plays in franchise history.

When John Schuerholz became general manager of the Braves after the 1990 season, he signed several veteran, mid-

Sid Bream

level free agents to bring leadership to a talented, young team. To play first base, he signed Bream, who was 30 years old and had just helped Pittsburgh win the National League East.

A steady performer, Bream brought to the Braves a sense of professionalism and leadership that had been lacking. Though he had to sit out all of July and most of August with knee problems, Bream was a consistent contributor to the club's unexpected championship season.

Among Bream's accomplishments in 1991 were two grand slams, making him the first Brave since Dale Murphy in 1978 to hit two bases-loaded homers in the same season. His first slam was dramatic because it came against his former Pittsburgh teammates, but his second was even more memorable, since it propelled the Braves to an important September victory against the Dodgers.

In the League Championship Series, Bream hit a three-run homer in Game 3, a 10–3 rout of the Pirates. However, like most of the Braves, he failed to hit well (.125) in the World Series loss to Minnesota.

Bream had a solid season as the Braves regular first baseman in 1992, his third consecutive year playing with a division champion. The biggest moment of his Atlanta career came in the League Championship Series, again versus his former Pittsburgh teammates.

The Braves entered the ninth inning of decisive Game 7 trailing the Pirates, 2–0. In the midst of a rally that narrowed the margin to 2–1, Bream drew a walk. He was perched at second with two outs and the bases full when Bobby Cox decided to send up Francisco Cabrera as a pinch hitter for Jeff Reardon, representing Atlanta's last hope.

On a 2–1 pitch from Stan Belinda, Cabrera hit a hard grounder to the right of shortstop Jay Bell and into left field. David Justice scored from third with the tying run, then Bream—one of the slowest Braves ever because of several knee operations—rounded third and plodded toward home with the potential winning run. As Barry Bonds' throw arrived from left, Bream slid across the plate, narrowly escaping the tag of Mike LaValliere.

Justice immediately leaped on Bream, and the rest of the Braves followed, in the wildest victory celebration ever at Atlanta–Fulton County Stadium. The crowd went berserk, and the entire city and much of the South rocked for hours with unbridled revelry. It was the first time in postseason history that a team went from losing to winning on the final pitch of a series.

Almost as quickly as Bream's name became synonymous with the most famous run ever scored in Atlanta Braves history, he faded into the background. The team's offense was sluggish through the first half of 1993, and though Bream was no more to blame than anyone else, he was the one relegated to the bench when Schuerholz acquired Fred McGriff from San Diego. The new first baseman carried the Braves to a third straight division title.

Bream, still the true pro, accepted his reserve role quietly and became one of the team's better pinch hitters. His contract was up at the end of the season, and the Braves did not re-sign him.

Bream, Sid											
Braves	G	AB	R	H	2B	3B	HR	RBI	SB	AVG	SLG
1991	91	265	32	67	12	0	11	45	0	.253	.423
1992	125	372	30	97	25	1	10	61	6	.261	.414
1993	117	277	33	72	14	1	9	35	4	.260	.415
Career	333	914	95	236	51	2	30	141	10	.258	.417

Brouthers, Dan

Beaneaters: 1889
First baseman
Birthplace: Sylvan Lake, New York
B: May 8, 1858

D: August 2, 1932
Batted left, threw left
Ht. 6–2; **Wt.** 207

One of the many peculiarities in Braves history is that four of the first five National League batting champs produced by the franchise played just that one season with the club.

Dan Brouthers was the second in that line of one-season wonders—not that he or any of the other three (Deacon White in 1877, Rogers Hornsby in 1928, and Ernie Lombardi in 1942) were flukes as batting champs. Brouthers, in fact, had already won two batting crowns (1882 and '83) before he became a Beaneater.

Known as "Big Dan" because of his stature (6–2, 207), which was extraordinary then and would still be considered sizable for a major leaguer, Brouthers was purchased by Boston from Detroit when that franchise folded after the 1888 season. One of the greatest hitters of the 1800s, the mighty first baseman led the Beaneaters nearly to a pennant with his offensive heroics in 1889.

Besides winning the batting title with a .373 average, the 31-year-old Brouthers finished second in the league in hits (181 in 133 games) and RBIs (118). However, Boston still finished one game behind New York in the pennant race.

In 1890 the mustachioed Brouthers jumped to the upstart Players League franchise in Boston. Two years later, in 1892, Brouthers won his fourth and last National League batting title with Brooklyn.

During his 19-year career that spanned four decades, Brouthers compiled a lifetime batting average of .342 in a dead-ball era. He had a string of 14 consecutive seasons in which he hit .307 or better, and he was elected to the Hall of Fame in 1945.

Brouthers, Dan											
Beaneaters	G	AB	R	H	2B	3B	HR	RBI	SB	AVG	SLG
1889	126	485	105	181	26	9	7	118	22	.373*	.507
Career	126	485	105	181	26	9	7	118	22	.373	.507

Brown, Eddie

Braves: 1926–28
Left fielder, first baseman
Birthplace: Milligan, Nebraska
B: July 17, 1891

D: September 10, 1956
Batted right, threw right
Ht. 6–3; **Wt.** 190

Nicknames can be unkind, and they also can tell quite a lot about a player. Such is the case with "Glass Arm Eddie" Brown.

An accomplished contact hitter with above-average speed, Brown could shag fly balls with almost any outfielder. The problem was what he couldn't do after he tracked down the ball. He had a notoriously weak arm, as his nickname sug-

Dan Brouthers

Eddie Brown

gests, and it was quite a hindrance to what otherwise might have been a substantial career.

Saddled with a weak arm, Brown found himself stuck in the farm system of the powerful New York Giants until he was nearly 30 years old. He eventually escaped and became a rather accomplished player for the Braves.

Brown spent one year in the military and bounced around the minors for eight seasons before finally getting some brief time with the Giants in 1920 and '21. But he was sent back to the minors. After hitting .361 in 1923 for Indianapolis of the American Association, he was picked up by Brooklyn and immediately became a regular.

At age 32, he hit .308 in his first full season with the Dodgers in 1924. Though he didn't have much power, he was known as a clutch hitter and drove in a career-high 99 runs in 1925. The Braves then acquired him from Brooklyn in a six-player deal that sent Jesse Barnes to the Dodgers.

"Glass Arm Eddie" continued to hit well in Boston. In 1926, his first season with the Braves, Brown led the league in hits (201) and finished third in the batting race (.328).

In 1927, the Braves began using Brown at first base at times so his weak arm wouldn't be such a potential hindrance. He continued as one of the club's top hitters, posting his fourth consecutive .300 season.

At the same time, Brown was putting together an impressive consecutive games played streak. In 1927, he broke the National League record of 533 held by Fred Luderus, a first baseman with the Phillies. Brown's streak reached 618 games when Braves manager Rogers Hornsby benched him June 7, 1928, just over four years after it began. The streak still ranks 19th on the all-time list.

Brown's brief big league career came to an end in 1928 at age 37 when he retired with a .303 lifetime average.

Brown, Eddie

Braves	G	AB	R	H	2B	3B	HR	RBI	SB	AVG	SLG
1926	153	612	71	201*	31	8	2	84	5	.328	.415
1927	155	558	64	171	35	6	2	75	11	.306	.401
1928	142	523	45	140	28	2	2	59	6	.268	.340
Career	450	1,693	180	512	94	16	6	218	22	.302	.387

Bruton, Billy

Braves: 1953–60
Center fielder
Birthplace: Panola, Alabama

B: December 22, 1925
Batted left, threw right
Ht. 6–0; **Wt.** 169

Billy Bruton was the original Milwaukee Braves hero. He gained that distinction for two reasons. First, he was a star with the Milwaukee Brewers of the American Association in 1952, the year before the Braves moved out of Boston. The city's baseball fans already were familiar with his considerable skills, since he batted .325 that season and led the league with 211 hits and 130 runs scored.

Second, he hit a home run in the bottom of the 10th to give the Braves a 3–2 victory against St. Louis in the team's first game in Milwaukee in 1953.

But the speedy Bruton didn't stop there. He led the National League in steals each of his first three seasons in the majors and was a vital part of the team for eight seasons before being traded to Detroit.

Billy Bruton

One of the more interesting questions about Bruton is just how old he was when he broke in with the Braves in 1953. The son-in-law of William "Judy" Johnson, a great third baseman in the Negro Leagues and a member of the Hall of Fame, he was listed as a 24-year-old rookie. However, various sources say he really was anywhere from 28 to 34.

Scout John Ogden supposedly lied about Bruton's age in order to get the Braves to sign him. But no matter how old he was, he was quite a player.

In the 1953 season opener at Cincinnati, Bruton singled in the first, stole second, and scored the Milwaukee Braves first run, the winning run in a 2–0 victory. Perhaps more importantly, he made three excellent defensive plays in center to help preserve Max Surkont's shutout.

The next day at Milwaukee County Stadium, Bruton robbed Stan Musial of an extra-base, game-breaking hit in the eighth with two on and two out in a 1–1 game. In the bottom of the inning, the Braves center fielder tripled and scored the go-ahead run. However, St. Louis rallied with two out in the ninth against Warren Spahn to tie the game.

With one out and none on in the bottom of the 10th, Bruton homered to right. The ball glanced off Enos Slaughter's glove and over the fence. At first, umpire Lon Warneke ruled the ball had bounced over the fence for a double. But after brief protest from Braves manager Charlie Grimm, the ruling was changed, and Bruton was awarded a home run. He would not hit his next for nearly a year and a half.

But speed, not power, was Bruton's game. He twice led the league in triples and stole 207 career bases. There's no telling how many more of both he might have had if he'd played on a team that wasn't as power-laden as the Braves and if he hadn't suffered a serious knee injury in 1957.

In July 1957 at Pittsburgh's Forbes Field, Bruton and shortstop Felix Mantilla collided chasing a short pop-up behind second base. Bruton sustained ligament damage and didn't play again until late the next May. His injury forced manager Fred Haney to move Hank Aaron to center field for the rest of that pennant-winning season.

Bruton returned in good form to help the Braves win another pennant in 1958. He took it easy on the knee, stealing just four bases, but he hit .280 in 100 games. Furthermore, after missing the '57 Series, he made his presence known this time against the Yankees by leading all players with a .412 average.

In 1959, he became one of only two players to hit two bases-loaded triples in the same game.

Bruton had perhaps his best season in 1960, leading the league in triples (13) and runs scored (112) while hitting .286 with a then-career-high 12 home runs. However, the Braves felt one of their biggest needs to get back on top of the league was a quality second baseman. Therefore, they were willing to send Bruton to Detroit in a six-player deal that brought Frank Bolling to Milwaukee.

Bruton, Billy

Braves	G	AB	R	H	2B	3B	HR	RBI	SB	AVG	SLG
1953	151	613	82	153	18	14	1	41	26*	.250	.330
1954	142	567	89	161	20	7	4	30	34*	.284	.365
1955	149	636*	106	175	30	12	9	47	25*	.275	.403
1956	147	525	73	143	23	15*	8	56	8	.272	.419
1957	79	306	41	85	16	9	5	30	11	.278	.438
1958	100	325	47	91	11	3	3	28	4	.280	.360
1959	133	478	72	138	22	6	6	41	13	.289	.397
1960	151	629	112*	180	27	13*	12	54	22	.286	.428
Career	1,052	4,079	622	1,126	167	79	48	327	143	.276	.391

Buffinton, Charlie

Red Stockings, Beaneaters: 1882–86
Pitcher
Birthplace: Fall River, Massachusetts
B: June 14, 1861

D: September 23, 1907
Batted right, threw right
Ht. 6–1; **Wt.** 180

Charlie Buffinton had been dead for 85 years and was well buried in the Braves record book when his name and his legend resurfaced in the summer of 1992.

It took a 13-game winning streak by Atlanta left-hander Tom Glavine to bring Buffinton's exploits back to life. When Glavine was beaten by Montreal on August 25, his first loss since May 22, his name went into the records alongside Buffinton's as the authors of the two longest winning streaks by Braves pitchers. Buffinton's 13-game streak came in 1884— 108 years before Glavine's.

Buffinton did some pitching in 1884. The Beaneaters played 111 games that season. Buffinton, then 23, started 67 of them—60 percent. He completed 63 of the 67 and worked 587 innings! The team won 73 games, and Charlie won 48 of

those. That total ranks second in franchise history to the 49 won by Hall of Famer John Clarkson in 1889.

In the three-year period 1883–85, Buffinton was a combined 95–57 and averaged more than 451 innings per season. No wonder he later became a labor leader among the players, the equivalent of today's player representative.

Apparently tired from those three seasons as a workhorse, Buffinton worked only 151 innings in 1886, going 7–10. Boston gave up on him and shipped him to Philadelphia, where he proved his right arm still had plenty of life in it. He strung together three consecutive years of 21 or more victories for the Phillies, working as many as 400 innings in 1888.

Buffinton won 233 games in only an 11-year career. True to his role as a labor leader, he held out for the entire 1893 season and never pitched in the majors again.

Buffinton, Charlie

Red Stockings, Beaneaters	W	L	Pct	G	GS	CG	ShO	IP	H	BB	SO	ERA	SV
1882	2	3	.400	5	5	4	1	42	53	14	17	4.07	0
1883	25	14	.641	43	41	34	4	333	346	51	188	3.03	1
1884	48	16	.750	67	67	63	8	587	506	76	417	2.15	0
1885	22	27	.449	51	50	49	6	434½	425	112	242	2.88	0
1886	7	10	.412	18	17	16	0	151	203	39	47	4.59	0
Career	104	70	.598	184	180	166	19	1,547⅓	1,533	292	911	2.83	1

Buhl, Bob

Braves: 1953–62
Pitcher
Birthplace: Saginaw, Michigan

B: August 12, 1928
Batted right, threw right
Ht. 6–2; **Wt.** 190

With a little more luck and less distinguished teammates, Bob Buhl might have been a superstar. As it was, he had to settle for pitching in the extensive shadows cast by Warren Spahn and Lou Burdette, and injuries robbed him of reaching the milestone of 20 victories at least twice.

In 1953, Buhl returned to baseball after a stint as a paratrooper in Korea. He not only made the Braves, but pitched a two-hitter in his first big league start and a shutout in his second start. For the ensuing decade, he helped give Milwaukee what was often the best pitching staff in the league.

A power pitcher with a strong competitive nature, Buhl had a composite .621 winning percentage in his first eight years with the Braves. That was the best of all active pitchers— including Spahn and Burdette—during the period 1953–60.

A fast worker, he won in double figures six times in those eight seasons, topping out with 18 in both 1956 and '57. In the latter year, he led the league in winning percentage (.720).

As good as Buhl was those two seasons, he could have accomplished considerably more—and perhaps taken the Braves to another pennant in '56—had his production not been cut short by injuries.

In August 1956 a line drive off the bat of Pittsburgh's Lee Walls caused a chip fracture of the index finger on Buhl's pitching hand. He missed only one start, but his effectiveness was reduced. He had 14 wins when the injury occurred and managed just four more over the final eight weeks of the season.

Milwaukee lost the pennant by just a single game to Brook-

Charlie Buffinton

Bob Buhl

lyn. A healthy Buhl the last two months could well have meant a league championship.

Buhl made another run at 20 wins in 1957, but he missed a month with a sore shoulder and had to settle for 18 again. He had the fourth-best ERA in the league that season and was third in victories. He made two starts in the World Series but fared badly in both.

In 1958, Buhl appeared in only 11 games and missed the World Series because of a bad shoulder, but he bounced back the next season to tie for the league lead in shutouts and finish third in ERA.

A fast worker with a herky-jerky motion that probably contributed to his shoulder problems, Buhl finished among the league's top 10 in ERA six times in his nine full seasons with Milwaukee. On any given day, he could be close to unhittable, as evidenced by the one-hitter and four two-hitters he pitched for the Braves.

Buhl was a Dodger killer. In 1956 alone, he beat them eight times, and he was 19–8 against them from 1953 to 1959.

Buhl also pitched quite well against another team—the Braves. Traded to the Cubs in April 1962 for Jack Curtis, he beat his former teammates four times that year and had a 2.49 ERA in six starts against them.

Buhl was one of the worst hitters of all time. In 1962, he was 0-for-70, the worst single-season hitless streak ever. It took him until May 8, 1963, to get his first hit in 88 at bats with the Cubs. Buhl's lifetime average was .089, and he struck out in 45 percent of his at bats.

Burdette, Lou

Braves: 1951–63
Pitcher
Birthplace: Nitro, West Virginia

B: November 22, 1926
Batted right, threw right
Ht. 6–2; **Wt.** 190

No examination of Selva Lewis Burdette can begin without addressing the question: Lou or Lew?

Throughout Burdette's outstanding 18-year career, his first name often appeared both ways, on baseball cards and in record books, newspapers, magazines, and official Braves publications.

Considering that Burdette's middle name is Lewis, it would seem the proper shortened version would be Lew. Indeed, that's the way most reference souces list it today. However, Burdette always said he didn't care which way it was spelled. ("I write it however it's spelled on my checks," he once said.) And the fact is that he enrolled himself in the Braves Alumni Association in 1993 as Lou. Since a man's name should be spelled the way he prefers, we have opted to use Lou in this work.

Regardless of how his first name is spelled, Burdette ranks as one of the most accomplished pitchers in Braves history. "Nitro" Lou, after his hometown, or "Fidgety" Lou, because of his nervous mannerisms on the mound, led the National League in victories (21) in 1959; winning percentage (.667) in 1958; shutouts (6) in 1956 and (4) in '59; earned run average (2.70) in 1956; innings (272⅓) in 1961; and complete games (18) in 1960. His 179 victories as a Brave rank fourth on the club's all-time list and second to Phil Niekro among modern-era right-handers.

However, Burdette is best remembered for pitching the Braves to the 1957 World Series championship against the powerful Yankees.

The '57 Yanks, powered by Mickey Mantle, Yogi Berra, Hank Bauer, and Bill Skowron, won a major-league-high 98 games and were shut out just twice. In the Series, Burdette pitched three complete-game victories against them, shutting out the Bronx Bombers in Games 5 and 7 in a span of just four days.

Lou Burdette

Buhl, Bob

Braves	W	L	Pct	G	GS	CG	ShO	IP	H	BB	SO	ERA	SV
1953	13	8	.619	30	18	8	3	154⅓	133	73	83	2.97	0
1954	2	7	.222	31	14	2	1	110⅓	117	65	57	4.00	3
1955	13	11	.542	38	27	11	1	201⅔	168	109	117	3.21	1
1956	18	8	.692	38	33	13	2	216⅔	190	105	86	3.32	0
1957	18	7	.720	34	31	14	2	216⅔	191	121	117	2.74	0
1958	5	2	.714	11	10	3	0	73	74	30	27	3.45	1
1959	15	9	.625	31	25	12	4*	198	181	74	105	2.86	0
1960	16	9	.640	36	33	11	2	238⅔	202	103*	121	3.09	0
1961	9	10	.474	32	28	9	1	188⅓	180	98	77	4.11	0
1962	0	1	.000	1	1	0	0	2	6	4	1	22.50	0
Career	109	72	.602	282	220	83	16	1,599⅔	1,442	782	791	3.27	5

He was named the Series MVP, of course, and etched his name in the record books beside some impressive names and next to some impressive achievements. He was the first pitcher in 37 years (since Cleveland's Stan Coveleski in 1920) to win three complete games in the same Series and the first since the immortal Christy Mathewson (1905) to pitch two shutouts in the same Series.

In Game 5 at Milwaukee, Burdette threw only 87 pitches— and allowed just two fly balls to the outfield. Warren Spahn, winner of Game 4, was supposed to work Game 7 in New York but was ill. Manager Fred Haney elected to use Burdette on short rest, a decision eased by the way the right-hander breezed through Game 5.

After allowing single runs in the second and third innings of Game 2, Burdette finished the Series with 24 consecutive scoreless innings during which he faced only 101 batters.

Burdette's World Series magic continued for a while in 1958, but not quite long enough for the Braves to knock off the Yankees again. He beat New York, 13–5, in Game 2, hitting a home run in the process and giving the Braves a 2–0 edge in games. However, he lost Games 5 (7–0) and 7 (6–2), as Milwaukee blew its 3–1 advantage.

Ironically, Burdette started his career in 1950 with the Yankees. But instead of a promising prospect, the Yanks decided they'd rather have a proven veteran on their staff for the 1951 pennant drive. So, they gave the Braves $50,000 and Burdette for Johnny Sain on August 30.

The Braves easily got the best of the deal. Burdette teamed with Spahn to form one of the great one-two punches in history. The two close friends won a combined 443 games over the ensuing 13 years and pulled off even more practical jokes on teammates and bystanders.

A late bloomer, Burdette didn't hit his stride until age 26, when he was 15–5 in 1953, the Braves' first season in Milwaukee. He opened that season in the bullpen but soon worked his way into the starting rotation, where he remained, for the most part, until he was traded to St. Louis in 1963. In the Braves' first nine seasons in Milwaukee, Burdette averaged better than 17 wins a season.

Burdette was often accused of throwing a spitball, but no one ever figured out exactly how and when he was wetting up the ball, since he went through a disorienting set of contortions and gyrations as he readied for his delivery. His main legal weapons were a slider, a sinker, and excellent control. He led the league in walks-per-innings ratio in 1958, '60, and '61.

Because of his control and frequently good run support, he won a lot of games despite allowing high hit totals. On August 18, 1960, though, the Phillies couldn't scratch against him. The 1–0 victory was the ninth no-hitter in Braves history.

Burdette also was on the winning end of the most famous losing pitching effort in history—Harvey Haddix's 12-inning perfect game on May 26, 1959, at Milwaukee County Stadium. Haddix, of course, lost the perfect game, the no-hitter, the shutout, and the decision in the 13th.

Burdette, who gave up 12 hits but no runs in going the distance in that game, got credit for the victory. That winter, he asked for a $10,000 raise (big money then), reasoning, "I'm the greatest pitcher that ever lived. The greatest game that was ever pitched in baseball wasn't good enough to beat me, so I've got to be the greatest."

Not quite, but he was pretty darn good.

Burdette returned to the Braves as a coach under Luman Harris in 1971 and 1972.

Burdette, Lou

Braves	W	L	Pct	G	GS	CG	ShO	IP	H	BB	SO	ERA	SV
1951	0	0	—	3	0	0	0	4⅓	6	5	1	6.23	0
1952	6	11	.353	45	9	5	0	137	138	47	47	3.61	7
1953	15	5	.750	46	13	6	1	175	177	56	58	3.24	8
1954	15	14	.517	38	32	13	4	238	224	62	79	2.76	0
1955	13	8	.619	42	33	11	2	230	253	73	70	4.03	0
1956	19	10	.655	39	35	16	6*	256⅓	234	52	110	2.70*	1
1957	17	9	.654	37	33	14	1	256⅔	260	59	78	3.72	0
1958	20	10	.667*	40	36	19	3	275⅓	279	50	113	2.91	0
1959	21*	15	.583	41	39*	20	4*	289⅔	312*	38	105	4.07	1
1960	19	13	.594	45	32	18*	4	275¾	277*	35	83	3.36	4
1961	18	11	.621	40	36	14	3	272⅓*	295	33	92	4.00	0
1962	10	9	.526	37	19	6	1	143¾	172	23	59	4.89	2
1963	6	5	.545	15	13	4	1	84	71	24	28	3.64	0
Career	179	120	.599	468	330	146	30	2,638	2,698	557	923	3.53	23

Burroughs, Jeff

Braves: 1977–80
Left fielder
Birthplace: Long Beach, California

B: March 7, 1951
Batted right, threw right
Ht. 6–1; **Wt.** 200

Jeff Burroughs had the misfortune of playing on some truly terrible Braves teams at what should have been the peak of his career. The American League's Most Valuable Player in 1974 with the Texas Rangers, Burroughs came to Atlanta in 1977 in exchange for Ken Henderson, Dave May, Carl Morton, Rogelio Moret, Adrian Devine, and $250,000.

After putting together excellent seasons in his first two years with the Braves, Burroughs saw his production drop significantly in 1979 and '80. Playing on three last-place teams in four years and having a weak supporting cast no doubt contributed to his quick decline and eventual trade to Seattle.

In his first season in the National League, Burroughs batted .271 and finished second in the league with 41 home runs and fourth with 114 RBIs. Yet the Braves managed to lose 101 games.

Undaunted, Burroughs returned in '78 to equal his MVP batting average of .301. His power numbers were significantly lower than in his MVP year, but only because he seldom was given a pitch to hit, evidenced by the fact that he led the league with 117 walks and a .436 on-base percentage. He still managed 23 home runs and 77 RBIs.

When his production dropped the next two seasons, he became a bit of a scapegoat for the team's woes. His lack of

Jeff Burroughs

offense made his slow-footed outfield play more noticeable, and he finally was sent to Seattle for pitcher Carlos Diaz.

The first player taken in the 1969 free agent draft by the old Washington Senators, Burroughs gained quick prominence when Senators manager and Hall of Famer Ted Williams proclaimed him "one of the best young hitters I've ever seen." Burroughs won the MVP at the age of 23 with 25 home runs and 118 RBIs, making Williams appear to be a prophet. Though the stocky outfielder had a fine career, he couldn't live up to the extraordinary expectations Williams' quote and his MVP season created.

In 1992 and '93, Burroughs again found himself in the baseball spotlight, this time as a coach. He led Long Beach, California, to successive Little League World Series championships, a first for an American team since the advent of international play.

Burroughs, Jeff

Braves	G	AB	R	H	2B	3B	HR	RBI	SB	AVG	SLG
1977	154	579	91	157	19	1	41	114	4	.271	.520
1978	153	488	72	147	30	6	23	77	1	.301	.529
1979	116	397	49	89	14	1	11	47	2	.224	.348
1980	99	278	35	73	14	0	13	51	1	.263	.453
Career	522	1,742	247	466	77	8	88	289	8	.268	.472

Cabrera, Francisco

Braves: 1989–93
Catcher
Birthplace: Santo Domingo, Dominican Republic

B: October 10, 1966
Bats right, throws right
Ht. 6–4; **Wt.** 195

With one swing of the bat, Francisco Cabrera became one of the biggest heroes not only in Braves history but also in the annals of major league baseball.

Collared, perhaps unfairly, with the "good hit/no field" tag, the seldom-used catcher came off the bench to deliver the stunning, ninth-inning pinch hit that gave the Braves the 1992 National League pennant. His two-out single to left off Pittsburgh's Stan Belinda in Game 7 drove in David Justice and Sid Bream, wiping out the Pirates' 2–1 lead and ending the '92 National League Championship Series.

Cabrera's bases-loaded hit, which produced the Braves' second straight NL pennant, was the first in history to win a postseason championship for a team that went from losing to winning on the final pitch.

Francisco Cabrera

A reserve who spent most of 1992 at Triple-A Richmond, Cabrera had only 10 major league at bats during the regular season. But one hit brought the Dominican slugger instant stardom and even a key to the City of Atlanta from Mayor Maynard Jackson.

Originally signed by Toronto, Cabrera came to the Braves in a 1989 trade as the "player to be named" in an otherwise insignificant deal. Besides his 1992 pennant-winning hit, he also delivered one of the biggest hits of Atlanta's miraculous stretch drive to the 1991 NL West title. His two-out, three-run homer in the top of the ninth against Cincinnati's Rob Dibble August 21 tied the game, 9–9. The Braves won, 10–9, in 13 innings. The victory was one of the most momentous of the regular season, which ended with Atlanta one game ahead of the Dodgers in the standings.

Cabrera opted to leave the Braves after 1993, going to Japan in hopes of playing more frequently and earning more money. However, he returned to the team a year later, signing a minor league contract. He was released at mid-season.

Cabrera, Francisco

Braves	G	AB	R	H	2B	3B	HR	RBI	SB	AVG	SLG
1989	4	14	0	3	2	0	0	0	0	.214	.357
1990	63	137	14	38	5	1	7	25	1	.277	.482
1991	44	95	7	23	6	0	4	23	1	.242	.432
1992	12	10	2	3	0	0	2	3	0	.300	.900
1993	70	83	8	20	3	0	4	11	0	.241	.422
Career	193	339	31	87	16	1	17	62	2	.257	.460

Camp, Rick

Braves: 1976–85
Pitcher
Birthplace: Trion, Georgia

B: June 10, 1953
Batted right, threw right
Ht. 6–0; **Wt.** 198

One of the most down-to-earth men ever to pitch for the Braves, Rick Camp was a native Georgian who made significant contributions to the team as both a starter and a reliever.

An .074 career hitter, Camp also was one of the most feeble hitters ever to swing a bat in Atlanta. That's what makes one of his last accomplishments for the club so memorable.

It was Camp's home run—the only one he hit in his nine-year career—that was responsible for keeping the Braves, Mets, and a few fans at Atlanta Stadium until close to dawn on July 5, 1985. The game, which began the evening of July 4, officially lasted 6 hours, 10 minutes, the longest in Atlanta history.

The Braves and Mets had been at it through several rain delays and nearly 18 innings when Camp struck his most unlikely blow. It was after 3 A.M., and everyone was looking forward to finally going home. After all, the Mets had the lead and two outs in the bottom of the 18th with Camp due to hit.

Manager Eddie Haas was out of pinch hitters, so he threw in the towel and let Camp bat. Mets pitcher Tom Gorman got two quick strikes on the Atlanta pitcher, but on the next pitch, Camp, figuring he might as well swing, did so and somehow connected. The ball disappeared over the left-field fence, making the score 11–11.

Apparently overwhelmed by his deed, Camp either forgot how to pitch in the 19th or just ran out of gas. The Mets scored five and hung on for a 16–13 victory. Several rain delays pushed the game well into the morning of the 5th, mean-

Rick Camp

Camp, Rick

Braves	W	L	Pct	G	GS	CG	ShO	IP	H	BB	SO	ERA	SV
1976	0	1	.000	5	1	0	0	11⅓	13	2	6	6.35	0
1977	6	3	.667	54	0	0	0	78⅔	89	47	51	4.00	10
1978	2	4	.333	42	4	0	0	74⅓	99	32	23	3.75	0
1980	6	4	.600	77	0	0	0	108⅓	92	29	33	1.91	22
1981	9	3	.750	48	0	0	0	76	68	12	47	1.78	17
1982	11	13	.458	51	21	3	0	177⅓	199	52	68	3.65	5
1983	10	9	.526	40	16	1	0	140	146	38	61	3.79	0
1984	8	6	.571	31	21	1	0	148⅔	134	63	69	3.27	0
1985	4	6	.400	66	2	0	0	127⅔	130	61	49	3.95	3
Career	56	49	.533	414	65	5	0	942⅓	970	336	407	3.37	57

ing the traditional Independence Day postgame fireworks served as an unwelcomed wake-up call for many Atlantans.

Camp still ranks among the club's pitching leaders during its Atlanta tenure in games, saves (57), and ERA (3.37).

In 1976, Camp went to spring training as a nonroster player and surprised the Braves with a strong enough showing to make the team. However, he was on the big league roster for only one day when the club signed free-agent pitcher Andy Messersmith, bumping Camp to Richmond.

After a brief call-up at the end of '76, the right-hander had a good rookie season in '77, winning six and saving 10 in 54 relief appearances.

That off-season, Camp, an avid outdoorsman, jumped into a cold river to save the life of a companion whose boat had overturned.

Following a lukewarm '78 season, Camp was forced to sit out all of 1979 when arm problems threatened to end his career at age 26. But he made the club as a nonroster invitee to spring training in '80 and proceeded to pitch better than ever. His 77 relief appearances that season broke Clay Carroll's club record set in 1966. With 22 saves and six wins, he finished fourth in the NL Relief Man standings.

In 1981, Camp continued to use his sinker and excellent control (1.42 walks per nine innings) to remain one of the league's best relievers. His 1.78 ERA was tops among relief specialists, and his nine relief wins tied for first. He finished just two points behind the Cardinals' Bruce Sutter for the NL Relief Man title.

After two ultrasuccessful seasons, Camp began to struggle early in 1982. In mid-June, manager Joe Torre decided to put him in the starting rotation. It was his first start since 1978 and only the sixth of his career, but he gave up just one run in 5⅔ innings. A month later, he pitched his first complete game, and from there on, he continued as a valuable starter in the Braves' drive to a division title.

In the playoffs, with Atlanta down two games to none against St. Louis, Torre called on the right-hander to start Game 3 of the best-of-five series. However, Camp was KOed in the second inning, and the Braves were eliminated, 6–2.

He spent three more seasons splitting time between starting and relieving but never regained the effectiveness he enjoyed in 1980 and '81.

Cantwell, Ben

Braves, Bees: 1928–36
Pitcher
Birthplace: Milan, Tennessee
B: April 13, 1902

D: December 4, 1962
Batted right, threw right
Ht. 6–1; **Wt.** 168

Ben Cantwell may have been the most unlikely 20-game winner in Braves history. Manager Bill McKechnie was noted for his handling of pitchers, and the mileage he got out of Cantwell no doubt helped enhance that reputation.

Cantwell was a star pitcher at the University of Tennessee, where he earned a degree in commerce. After graduating in 1925, Cantwell began his pro career. In his first full season, 1926, he was 24–5 for Sanford in the Florida State League. The next year, he put together a 13-game winning streak for Jacksonville of the Southeastern League on his way to a 25–5 finish.

Despite those impressive numbers, the major league scouts weren't awed. They didn't think Cantwell could throw hard enough to win in the big leagues. Nevertheless, word of his performance piqued the interest of none other than John McGraw. The famed Giants manager went to Florida to scout Cantwell himself and was impressed enough to purchase his contract from Jacksonville.

However, Cantwell didn't get much of a chance to pitch for New York. In June 1928, he and three other players were traded to the Braves for Joe Genewich.

Ben Cantwell

Splitting time between starting and relieving for Boston, Cantwell stumbled through three and a half rather unimpressive seasons before finding himself in 1932. Mainly working in relief, the right-hander won 12 of his 13 games out of the bullpen to lead the league in relief victories.

Then in 1933, McKechnie decided to use the soft-tossing control artist primarily as a starter. Cantwell responded by pitching a career-high 254⅔ innings and posting a career-low 2.62 ERA. His 20 victories tied for second in the league, and his .667 winning percentage was the best in the league. Cantwell's performance was a big factor in Boston's surprisingly strong fourth-place finish.

Whatever magic Cantwell discovered in 1932 and '33 quickly vanished, though. He dropped to five wins in 1934. Then in 1935, he lost 25 times, including 13 in a row, for a miserable team that lost 115 games and finished 61½ games out of first. Since 1935, no pitcher has lost as many games as Cantwell did that season, and his .138 percentage is the worst in the 20th century among the 19 25-loss seasons in the record book.

Cantwell, Ben

Braves, Bees	W	L	Pct	G	GS	CG	ShO	IP	H	BB	SO	ERA	SV
1928	3	3	.500	22	9	3	0	90	112	36	18	5.10	0
1929	4	13	.235	27	20	8	0	157	171	52	25	4.47	2
1930	9	15	.375	31	21	10	0	173⅓	213	45	43	4.89	2
1931	7	9	.438	33	16	9	2	156⅓	160	34	32	3.63	2
1932	13	11	.542	37	9	3	1	146	133	33	33	2.96	5
1933	20	10	.667	40	29	18	2	254⅔	242	54	57	2.62	2
1934	5	11	.313	27	19	6	1	143⅓	163	34	45	4.34	5
1935	4	25*	.138	39	24	13	0	210⅔	235	44	34	4.61	0
1936	9	9	.500	34	12	4	0	133⅓	127	35	42	3.05	2
Career	74	106	.411	290	159	74	6	1,464⅔	1,556	367	329	3.87	20

Capra, Buzz

Braves: 1974–77
Pitcher
Birthplace: Chicago

B: October 1, 1947
Batted right, threw right
Ht. 5–10; **Wt.** 168

As a team, the 1974 Braves were nothing special. They finished in third place, 14 games back of the division champion Dodgers.

But as a group of individuals, the '74 Braves were one of the more entertaining and memorable clubs in Atlanta history. It was the year, of course, when Hank Aaron broke Babe Ruth's all-time home run record. However, many other stories of individual achievement unfolded that year. One of the best was Buzz Capra, perhaps king of the one-year wonders in Braves history.

Capra came to the Braves at the end of 1974 spring training in a straight cash deal with the New York Mets, for whom he had won but five games in three seasons. The Braves promptly assigned him to the bullpen, and he quickly got his name in two of the biggest box scores in history. He was the losing pitcher on opening day when Aaron hit No. 714. Then a few days later in the Braves' home opener, he was credited with the only save of his Atlanta career in the game in which Aaron hit No. 715.

Buzz Capra

So, at least Capra was getting known quickly. But in five weeks of bullpen duty, he gave no indication of what was to come.

When Ron Reed suffered a broken hand in mid-May, Capra was thrust into the starting rotation. All he did was win 16 of 27 starts, including five by shutout. At one point, he won nine in a row, then an Atlanta record, and he was named to the National League All-Star team. He finished with a 2.28 ERA, the best in the league, and he was the toughest pitcher in the league to hit, yielding an opponents' batting average of just .208.

Late in the season, though, Capra felt a twinge of pain in his right shoulder. It was the signal that the clock had struck midnight on his Cinderella story. The pain worsened in 1975, limiting Capra to just 12 starts. He finally submitted to surgery during the off-season but never really recovered.

Capra, Buzz

Braves	W	L	Pct	G	GS	CG	ShO	IP	H	BB	SO	ERA	SV
1974	16	8	.667	39	27	11	5	217	163	84	137	2.28*	1
1975	4	7	.364	12	12	5	0	78⅓	77	28	35	4.25	0
1976	0	1	.000	5	0	0	0	9⅓	9	6	4	8.68	0
1977	6	11	.353	45	16	0	0	139⅓	142	80	100	5.36	0
Career	26	27	.491	101	55	16	5	444	391	198	276	3.73	1

Carroll, Clay

Braves: 1964–68
Pitcher
Birthplace: Clanton, Alabama

B: May 2, 1941
Batted right, threw right
Ht. 6–1; **Wt.** 200

Clay Carroll experienced a long run as one of the best relievers in the National League. Unfortunately, most of that work was done with the Cincinnati Reds instead of the Braves.

In 1966, the Braves' first season in Atlanta and Carroll's first full season in the majors, the "Hawk" led the National League with 73 appearances. That figure stood as an Atlanta record until broken by Rick Camp in 1980. Carroll won eight games and saved 11 more, and with an excellent 2.37 ERA at age 25, it appeared he would be a vital part of the Braves' pitching staff for quite a while.

He was a big hit in Atlanta and the South, a city and region experiencing their first taste of major league sports. In the off-season, Carroll was made a deputy sheriff in Fulton County, where Atlanta is located. And he was called home to Clanton, Alabama, for "Clay Carroll Day." His colorful wit and a language he called "Clantonese" added to his popularity.

But Carroll came to camp overweight in '67 and struggled the entire season. He was even sent back to Richmond for a short time in midseason and occasionally was used as a starter after his return to Atlanta.

When he started slowly again in '68, general manager Paul Richards entertained trade talks. However, Richards made the mistake of dealing with Bob Howsam, the Cincinnati GM who assembled the most dominant National League team of the 1970s.

Richards sent Carroll, infielder Woody Woodward, and right-hander Tony Cloninger to the Reds in exchange for pitchers Milt Pappas and Ted Davidson and infielder Bob Johnson. It was a steal for Cincinnati.

Carroll blossomed as a workhorse for Reds managers Dave Bristol and Sparky Anderson. The chunky right-hander didn't have a losing season in eight years with the Reds, never appearing in fewer than 53 games. He saved 37 games in 1972, then a record, and was named NL Fireman of the Year. He was named to two National League All-Star teams and appeared in four playoffs and three World Series. In 1975, he

got credit for the Reds' Game 7 victory over Boston in one of the most exciting World Series in history.

Carroll, Clay													
Braves	W	L	Pct	G	GS	CG	ShO	IP	H	BB	SO	ERA	SV
1964	2	0	1.000	11	1	0	0	20⅓	15	3	17	1.77	1
1965	0	1	.000	19	1	0	0	34⅔	35	13	16	4.41	1
1966	8	7	.533	73*	3	0	0	144⅓	127	29	67	2.37	11
1967	6	12	.333	42	7	1	1	93	111	29	35	5.52	0
1968	0	1	.000	10	0	0	0	22⅓	26	6	10	4.84	0
Career	16	21	.432	155	12	1	1	314⅔	314	80	145	3.66	13

Carty, Rico

Braves: 1963–72
Outfielder
Birthplace: San Pedro de Macorís, Dominican Republic

B: September 1, 1939
Batted right, threw right
Ht. 6–3; **Wt.** 200

Rico Carty was one of the greatest hitters ever to wear a Braves uniform. He was known as a "natural hitter" because it seemed he could get a hit almost at will. He made it look so easy. He sat out the entire 1968 season with tuberculosis and returned the following year to hit .342. He was that good.

The big Dominican also was popular with fans. His hitting was part of the reason for his popularity, but much of it stemmed from the bright, infectious smile he always seemed to be wearing. As splendid a hitter as Carty was, he was even better at smiling.

Known as the "Beeg Boy," a nickname he gave himself, Carty still owns Atlanta records for highest single-season batting average (.366 in 1970) and longest hitting streak (31 games in 1970). His career batting average as a Brave was .317, and in 1970 he became the first Atlanta Brave to win the National League batting crown.

A colorful character known for doing things in excess, Carty originally signed contracts with the Braves—and seven other teams. Fortunately, the Braves were the first club to get his autograph. He also liked to invest in lumber, owning 64 bats at one point. His shopping sprees were legendary. He was known to buy six suits, 24 shirts, 15 sweaters, and 25 pairs of shoes at a time.

When Carty, originally a catcher, got to the majors to stay with Milwaukee in 1964, he was a defensive liability, to say the least. However, he worked hard at his outfield play and made significant improvement. Still, he was only adequate at best.

Clay Carroll

Rico Carty

But with a bat in his hands, he was a magnificent sight. His powerful forearms enabled him to lash line drives to all fields, and when those line drives reached high enough altitudes, they frequently left ballparks. He never hit more than 25 home runs in a season as a Brave, but that low total was due only to injuries and the fact that he swung down on the ball rather than up like traditional power hitters.

Make no mistake, though, Carty had plenty of power. In fact, during his brief minor league career, he gained a distinction that may be unique in pro ball—hitting two home runs in the same at bat. Playing for Toronto of the International League at Little Rock in 1963, he hit an apparent home run, only to have the umpire rule that time had been called. So, Carty simply resolved the dispute by hitting the next pitch over the fence, too.

In Carty's rookie season, 1964, he hit .330 with 22 home runs and 88 RBIs. He was runner-up to Pittsburgh's Roberto Clemente (.339) for the batting title and finished second to Philadelphia's Richie Allen for Rookie of the Year. More of the same followed. Carty batted .310 or better in five of his seven full seasons with the Braves.

Carty's cumulative average for his first three seasons in the majors was .323. It took the effects of undiagnosed tuberculosis to drag his average down to .255 in 1967. After spending five months of 1968 in a Florida hospital, Carty returned with a vengeance in '69. Though he suffered three shoulder separations that year, he was a key figure in leading the Braves to the NL West title—hitting .390 in the September pennant drive. He also batted .300 in the playoffs, which Atlanta lost to the Mets.

In 1970, Carty's success and popularity peaked. He led both leagues in hitting and won a starting job on the NL All-Star team by virtue of 552,382 write-in votes. His .366 average was the highest in the majors since Ted Williams hit .388 in 1957.

But tragedy struck again that winter when Carty was involved in an outfield collision during the Dominican winter league. His kneecap was crushed, and he sustained ligament and cartilage damage. He sat out all of 1971, the second full season in four he missed. As Carty was recovering, even more adversity struck. In August, he was arrested and beaten by Atlanta policemen in civilian clothes. Carty sustained damage to one eye. The policemen were suspended, and the Atlanta mayor called the encounter "apparently an incident of blatant brutality."

This time, Carty's comeback was not so dramatic as it was in 1969. He appeared in just 86 games, hitting .277 with then career lows of six home runs and 29 RBIs. The Braves thought he was finished. The fact that Carty had been involved in a couple of well-publicized fights with formidable foes such as the Atlanta police and Hank Aaron during his career contributed to their decision to virtually give him away. He was sent to Texas in exchange for Jim Panther.

Carty did little in '73, hitting a combined .229 for three teams and getting released by the Cubs at the end of the season. At age 34, Carty did indeed appear to be finished, as the Braves had suspected.

However, the Beeg Boy had yet another comeback left in him. He went to the Mexican League and proved he could still hit. He was batting .354 when Cleveland signed him late in the '74 season.

Carty was used mainly as a designated hitter for the next six years. He batted .363 for the Indians in 33 games in '74,

then produced averages of .308 and .310 the next two years. He was named the team's Man of the Year in 1976 and finished second to Kansas City's Hal McRae as the league's outstanding DH. At that time, only Pete Rose had a higher lifetime batting average for active players with 10 or more years experience than Carty's .308.

Cleveland lost Carty to Toronto in the first round of the expansion draft that year but got him back in a trade. He proceeded to lead the Indians in RBIs with 80 in 1977. The following season, playing with Toronto and Oakland, he hit a combined 31 home runs—a career high at age 39.

Carty's career ended in 1979, but even at age 40, he went out swinging. He batted .256 with 12 home runs and 55 RBIs as Toronto's regular DH.

Carty, Rico

Braves	G	AB	R	H	2B	3B	HR	RBI	SB	AVG	SLG
1963	2	2	0	0	0	0	0	0	0	.000	.000
1964	133	455	72	150	28	4	22	88	1	.330	.554
1965	83	271	37	84	18	1	10	35	1	.310	.494
1966	151	521	73	170	25	2	15	76	4	.326	.468
1967	134	444	41	113	16	2	15	64	4	.255	.401
1969	104	304	47	104	15	0	16	58	0	.342	.549
1970	136	478	84	175	23	3	25	101	1	.366*	.584
1972	86	271	31	75	12	2	6	29	0	.277	.402
Career	829	2,746	385	871	137	14	109	451	11	.317	.496

Cepeda, Orlando

Braves: 1969–72
First baseman
Birthplace: Ponce, Puerto Rico

B: September 17, 1937
Batted right, threw right
Ht. 6–2; **Wt.** 210

Joe Torre for Orlando Cepeda was not one of the better trades in Braves history. In fact, some might say it was one of the worst.

However, there's no way to know if Torre would have lost weight and become a more dedicated player, as he did in St. Louis, had he remained in Atlanta. And there's no questioning that Cepeda played a significant role in the Braves' winning the National League West in 1969, nor that in 1970 he had one of the finest seasons of his fabulous career.

Orlando Cepeda

Cepeda helped the Giants win the pennant in 1962 and the Cardinals win pennants in 1967 and '68. In fact, in 11 big league seasons prior to the trade, Cepeda had never played on a losing team. He immediately helped teach the Braves to win in '69. Atlanta opened the season by winning four of its first five games, and Cepeda drove in the winning run in three of the four victories.

Overall, 1969 may not have been one of Cepeda's more productive seasons by the standards he set earlier in his career, but his 22 home runs and 88 RBIs went a long way in helping the Braves reach the postseason for the first time since 1958.

"Cha Cha" saved his best for 1970, though. It was the last truly great season of his 17-year career. He batted over .300 for the ninth time and surpassed 30 home runs and 100 RBIs for the fifth time each. It also was his sixth season with more than 30 doubles.

In 1971 a serious knee injury threatened his career, as it had in 1965. He underwent surgery in August but failed to bounce back in '72. As a result, the Braves traded him to Oakland for another former great who was at the end of his career—Denny McLain, the last pitcher to win 30 games in a season.

Cepeda was born into baseball. His father, "The Bull," was a legendary home run hitter in Puerto Rico. When Cepeda reached the majors in 1958, he showed his good bloodlines by leading the league in doubles and being named NL Rookie of the Year. In 1961, at the age of 24, the "Baby Bull" led the league in home runs (46) and RBIs (142).

After missing most of 1965 with a knee injury, he was named Comeback Player of the Year in '66. Then in 1967, his first full year with St. Louis, he led the league in RBIs (111) and was a unanimous pick as the NL's Most Valuable Player.

Like Mickey Mantle, there's no telling just how much more accomplished Cepeda might have been had it not been for his knee miseries that cost him many games and forced him to play with much pain in many others.

After his playing days, Cepeda was convicted of marijuana smuggling in his homeland and spent some time in prison. He admitted his guilt, and after his release, he did extensive community work to clear his name. He narrowly failed to gain election to Baseball's Hall of Fame in 1994, his final year of eligibility.

flourished and won two MVP awards. (2) At little cost, the club acquired a player who performed well as the regular first baseman for five years and as a backup for two more seasons. (3) Perhaps most importantly, the Braves got a quiet, respected leader who had been with winning teams before and who would be invaluable in the transformation of a young team into a division champion.

To get Chambliss and shortstop Luis Gomez, the Braves sent pitcher Joey McLaughlin, shortstop Pat Rockett, and outfielder Barry Bonnell to Toronto.

Chambliss, who was 31 when the Braves got him, was skilled with both the bat and the glove. In his first season with the club, he tied Hank Aaron's Atlanta record for doubles with 37 (since broken) and tied the franchise record (Ed Konetchy, 1916) by appearing in 158 games at first. Then in 1981, he tied a franchise record for first basemen with a .977 fielding percentage (four errors). Joe Adcock (1962) and Walter Holke (1921) share it.

When the Braves won the National League West in 1982 under new manager Joe Torre, Chambliss was a major contributor, hitting a career-high 20 home runs and driving in 86 runs. He equaled that home run total the next season.

In 1985, Chambliss opened the season at first base but lost his job to Bob Horner. Even in his last season with the Braves, 1986, when he was reduced mainly to pinch hitting, Chambliss continued to deliver. He led the NL in pinch hits with 20 and batted .311.

Chambliss already had many notable accomplishments to his credit before joining the Braves. After being drafted three times, he finally signed with Cleveland in 1970. The next year, he was the American League Rookie of the Year for the Indians.

Traded to the Yankees in 1974, he became a part of that organization's rich lore on October 14, 1976, when he hit one of the most dramatic home runs in history. In the ninth inning of Game 5 in the ALCS, he homered off Kansas City's Mark Littell to break a 6–6 tie and end the Yankees' 12-year pennant drought. In that series, he batted .524 and undoubtedly would have been MVP had the award existed at the time.

Cepeda, Orlando

Braves	G	AB	R	H	2B	3B	HR	RBI	SB	AVG	SLG
1969	154	573	74	147	28	2	22	88	12	.257	.428
1970	148	567	87	173	33	0	34	111	6	.305	.543
1971	71	250	31	69	10	1	14	44	3	.276	.492
1972	28	84	6	25	3	0	4	9	0	.298	.476
Career	401	1,474	198	414	74	3	74	252	21	.281	.486

Chambliss, Chris

Braves: 1980–86　　　　**B:** December 26, 1948
First baseman　　　　　**Batted left, threw right**
Birthplace: Dayton, Ohio　**Ht.** 6–1; **Wt.** 215

The Braves' acquisition of veteran first baseman Chris Chambliss in 1980 was a threefold success. (1) It enabled the team to move Dale Murphy to the outfield, where he

Chris Chambliss

Chambliss, Chris

Braves	G	AB	R	H	2B	3B	HR	RBI	SB	AVG	SLG
1980	158	602	83	170	37	2	18	72	7	.282	.440
1981	107	404	44	110	25	2	8	51	4	.272	.403
1982	157	534	57	144	25	2	20	86	7	.270	.436
1983	131	447	59	125	24	3	20	78	2	.280	.481
1984	135	389	47	100	14	0	9	44	1	.257	.362
1985	101	170	16	40	7	0	3	21	0	.235	.329
1986	97	122	13	38	8	0	2	14	0	.311	.426
Career	886	2,668	319	727	140	9	80	366	21	.272	.422

Clarkson, John

Beaneaters: 1888–92
Pitcher
Birthplace: Cambridge, Massachusetts
B: July 1, 1861

D: February 4, 1909
Batted right, threw right
Ht. 5–10; **Wt.** 155

John Clarkson was the Greg Maddux of his time. He was a true master craftsman who studied hitters and worked their weaknesses with an assortment of pitches. He took a remarkably scientific approach to his job considering the early era when he played. He was far ahead of most 19th-century pitchers in that regard.

Clarkson led the league in victories three times, including 1889 with the Beaneaters, and he pitched Boston to the pennant in 1891 when he won 33 games. His 328 career victories rank 10th all-time and earned him a spot in the Hall of Fame.

In 1887 the Beaneaters forked out what was considered the astronomical sum of $10,000 to buy catcher/outfielder Mike "King" Kelly from Chicago, whom he'd just led to the 1886 pennant by winning the batting title. However, Boston finished fifth even with their "$10,000 Beauty," so the team went shopping again in the off-season.

This time, the Beaneaters purchased Clarkson from the White Stockings for another $10,000. Clarkson, who led the league in victories with 38 in 1887, was promptly dubbed the "$10,000 Wonder." Together, Kelly and Clarkson were known as the "$20,000 Battery."

Clarkson, who used an assortment of breaking pitches, was 26 years old when he joined Boston. He'd already won 138 games, leading the league with 53 wins for Chicago in 1885, a total that ranks second all-time for a single season. His acquisition was quite popular with Beaneaters fans for two reasons. Not only was he an acknowledged star, but he also was a local product, coming from Cambridge.

A control pitcher, Clarkson immediately proved his worth with a fine season in his first year in a Boston uniform. He finished just two wins (33) behind Tim Keefe for the league lead.

Clarkson was considered high-strung and supposedly needed constant encouragement to pitch well. But he didn't seem bothered by the fact that the Beaneaters changed managers in each of his first three seasons with the team. After pitching for John Morrill in 1888, he led the league with 49 victories—fourth all-time—for Jim Hart in 1889. He followed that with 26 and 33 the next two seasons for Frank Selee.

Clarkson's 1889 performance compared favorably with 1885 when he won 53 games for Chicago. In his second year as a Beaneater, he led the league in numerous departments other than wins, including percentage, complete games, shutouts, innings, and strikeouts. He also won the only ERA title of his career. Seldom has any other pitcher so dominated the major statistical categories.

In 1890, Kid Nichols joined the Boston staff. Another future Hall of Famer, Nichols temporarily wrested the role of staff ace from Clarkson. But Clarkson regained his status as the team's ace in 1891, winning three more games (33) than Nichols and finishing in a tie for second in the league in wins. More importantly, the duo accounted for 63 of the team's 87 wins en route to its first pennant since 1883.

The Beaneaters repeated as pennant winners in 1892, but Clarkson played a limited role, since he was traded to Cleveland early in the season.

Besides ranking 10th on the all-time list for wins, Clarkson also is seventh with 487 complete games and 21st in innings. Those are pretty good numbers for someone who became a pitcher in the minors only when he nearly got released as a utility man because he kept dropping fly balls.

Clarkson had two brothers, Dad and Walter, who also pitched in the majors, though with little success. Dad even pitched with the Beaneaters for a brief period in 1892. The three Clarksons combined for 385 career victories, third to the Niekros and Perrys among brothers.

Clarkson, John

Beaneaters	W	L	Pct	G	GS	CG	ShO	IP	H	BB	SO	ERA	SV
1888	33	20	.623	54	54	53	3	483⅓*	448	119	223	2.76	0
1889	49*	19	.721*	73	72	68*	8*	620*	589	203	284*	2.73*	1
1890	26	18	.591	44	44	43	2	383	370	140	138	3.27	0
1891	33	19	.635	55	51	47	3	460⅔	435	154	141	2.79	3*
1892	8	6	.571	16	16	15	4	145⅔	115	60	48	2.35	0
Career	149	82	.645	242	237	226	20	2,092⅔	1,957	676	834	2.82	4

John Clarkson

Cloninger, Tony

Braves: 1961–68
Pitcher
Birthplace: Lincoln, North Carolina

B: August 13, 1940
Batted right, threw right
Ht. 6–0; **Wt.** 210

When the Braves forked out a $100,000 bonus to sign Tony Cloninger off the North Carolina sandlots in 1958, they thought they were getting a pretty good pitching prospect. Little did they know they were getting considerably more than that.

For the period 1964–66, Cloninger was indeed one of the Braves' best pitchers. And on one unbelievable day in 1966, he put on one of the most awesome slugging displays in history.

Tony Cloninger

Cloninger, Tony													
Braves	W	L	Pct	G	GS	CG	ShO	IP	H	BB	SO	ERA	SV
1961	7	2	.778	19	10	3	0	84	84	33	51	5.25	0
1962	8	3	.727	24	15	4	1	111	113	46	69	4.30	0
1963	9	11	.450	41	18	4	2	145⅓	131	63	100	3.78	1
1964	19	14	.576	38	34	15	3	242⅔	206	82	163	3.56	2
1965	24	11	.686	40	38	16	1	279	247	119*	211	3.29	1
1966	14	11	.560	39	38	11	1	257⅔	253	116*	178	4.12	1
1967	4	7	.364	16	16	1	0	76⅔	85	31	55	5.17	0
1968	1	3	.250	8	1	0	0	19	15	11	7	4.26	0
Career	86	62	.581	225	170	54	8	1,215½	1,134	501	834	3.94	5

You can still read about it in the record books: two bases-loaded home runs and nine RBIs. He remains the only man in National League history to hit two grand slams in the same game. His nine RBIs represent a Braves single-game record for any position and a major league record for a pitcher.

Cloninger's fireworks display came on July 3, 1966, at San Francisco's Candlestick Park. In a wild first inning, he hit his first grand slam against Bob Priddy. The second slam came in the fourth off Ray Sadecki, and he added an RBI single in the sixth in the 17–3 whipping of the Giants.

A fluke? Not really. Earlier in the season, Cloninger had another two-home-run game in a 17–1 rout of the Mets. With the July 3 display, he joined Brooklyn's Don Newcombe (1955) as the only pitchers to have two two-homer games in the same season. Cloninger finished the season with five home runs and 23 RBIs. He hit 11 career home runs.

Raised on a North Carolina farm, the muscular Cloninger used his natural strength to his advantage as a pitcher, too. He averaged 19 victories for the three consecutive seasons he was at his peak. And he might have stayed on top even longer if not for the rather unusual demand placed on him by Braves manager Bobby Bragan in the team's first regular-season game at Atlanta Stadium in 1966.

Bragan apparently got carried away in the excitement of the Braves' debut in the South and allowed his ace right-hander to work all 13 innings of a 3–2 loss to Pittsburgh. Only 25 then, Cloninger was coming off a 24–11 season, the team's last in Milwaukee, when he was second in the league in victories to Sandy Koufax. He admitted he pitched with a sore arm the rest of 1966, and he never seemed to be the same pitcher again. He hit like crazy, but his 4.12 ERA was more significant than his .234 batting average.

In '67, Cloninger was plagued by a sore shoulder and a virus that nearly cost him sight in one eye. The following June, he was traded to Cincinnati along with Woody Woodward and Clay Carroll in exchange for Milt Pappas, Ted Davidson, and Bob Johnson. The deal was almost a complete bust for Atlanta but helped Cincinnati win the NL pennant in 1970 when Cloninger was 9–7.

Collins, Jimmy

Beaneaters: 1895–1900
Third baseman, shortstop, outfielder
Birthplace: Buffalo, New York
B: January 16, 1870
D: March 6, 1943
Batted right, threw right
Ht. 5–9; **Wt.** 178

Jimmy Collins was a cross between Brooks Robinson and Terry Pendleton. In other words, he was a sensational defensive third baseman who also could hit.

For someone who was nearly booed out of Boston before he even got his feet on the ground, Collins managed to survive quite nicely, eventually playing for both the Beaneaters and the Red Sox on his way to a place in the Hall of Fame. He is the only pre-1920 third baseman represented at Cooperstown.

Collins debuted at age 25 with the Beaneaters in 1895 as a right fielder, replacing popular Jimmy Bannon. When he didn't produce immediately, the vocal bleacher fans in right and the press tore him apart. Manager Frank Selee promptly sent him down to Louisville for more seasoning.

While at Louisville, Collins learned to play third base, which would prove his ticket to a long and lustrous career. He revolutionized the position, playing off the bag and behind it so that he could cover more ground. Also, in an era when most hitters were constant threats to bunt, Collins perfected the barehand scoop and off-balance throw to first.

Jimmy Collins

The Spalding Guide wrote, "Few bunts were made so skillfully that Collins could not make a play on the ball. With a swoop like that of a chicken hawk, Collins would gather up the ball and throw it accurately to whoever should receive it."

Collins set two defensive records for third basemen that still stand. In 1899, with the Beaneaters, he set the National League record for most chances accepted in a season, 601. And the following year, he set the major league record for most putouts by a third baseman, 252.

He led his league's third basemen in putouts five times, assists four times, and double plays twice. Until Pie Traynor was well into his career in the late 1920s, Collins was considered the greatest third baseman of all time.

Of course, Collins never would have gained such stature if he couldn't have handled the bat, too. A lifetime .294 hitter, he hit over .300 in three of his four full seasons as the Beaneaters' third baseman. In 1897 he helped take Selee's team to a pennant by driving in 132 runs, second in the league, and hitting a career-high .346. He also led the National League in home runs in 1898 with 15 and in total bases. That same year, he ranked second in the league in slugging (.479) and tied for third in doubles. He batted over .300 five times in his career, drove in more than 100 runs twice, and scored more than 100 four times.

Unfortunately, less than half of Collins' outstanding career was with the Beaneaters, though most of his 14 years were spent in Boston. In 1901 he jumped to the new American League club, then known as the Pilgrims, as player-manager. There he continued as one of the game's finest all-around players and also took his team to pennants in 1903 and 1904.

Collins holds the singular distinction of being the first manager to win the World Series. His Pilgrims beat Pittsburgh, five games to three, in the best-of-nine Series of 1903.

Collins, Jimmy

Beaneaters	G	AB	R	H	2B	3B	HR	RBI	SB	AVG	SLG
1895	11	38	10	8	3	0	1	8	0	.211	.368
1896	84	304	48	90	10	9	1	46	10	.296	.398
1897	134	529	103	183	28	13	6	132	14	.346	.482
1898	152	597	107	196	35	5	15*	111	12	.328	.479
1899	151	599	98	166	28	11	5	92	12	.277	.386
1900	142	586	104	178	25	5	6	95	23	.304	.394
Career	674	2,653	470	821	129	43	34	484	71	.309	.429

Conley, Gene

Braves: 1952, 1954–58
Pitcher
Birthplace: Muskogee, Oklahoma

B: November 10, 1930
Batted right, threw right
Ht. 6–8; **Wt.** 225

Gene Conley was a professional two-sport athlete before Deion Sanders was born. Baseball and basketball were his games, and he was a good enough pitcher to make the National League All-Star team three times, twice (1954–55) with the Braves.

A two-time minor league player of the year, Conley became a regular starter for the Braves in 1954 and posted a 14–9 record with a career-best 2.96 ERA. The next year he was 11–7 and was the winning pitcher in the All-Star Game. An arm injury kept him from winning a single game after the All-Star break, however.

Often referred to as "the elongated hurler" during his ca-

Gene Conley

reer, Conley never again won in double figures for the Braves. He did play an important role in the World Series championship season of 1957, though. In one 15-day stretch, from July 28 to August 11, he pitched four consecutive complete game victories, beating four different teams and allowing a total of just six runs. Conley also got credit for the Braves' pennant-winning victory on September 23. He relieved starter Lou Burdette in the 11th inning and was the beneficiary of Hank Aaron's 11th-inning home run that touched off a wild celebration throughout Milwaukee.

After going 0–6 in the pennant-winning season of 1958, Conley was shipped to Philadelphia, where he rebounded with a 12–7 record and selection for his third All-Star Game. However, his performance continued to be rather erratic for the remainder of his career. To some degree, that inconsistency probably was due to his flirtation with basketball, understandable for someone who stood 6–8.

Conley broke into the NBA with the Boston Celtics in 1952–53 when he was still trying to establish himself in baseball. He didn't play again until 1958–59 when he rejoined the Celtics. He continued to play basketball through the 1963–64 season, averaging 5.9 points per game as a reserve forward in six seasons with the Celtics and New York Knicks.

Conley was involved in what may have been the "tallest" trade in baseball history. The Phillies sent him to the Red Sox after the 1960 season for pitcher Frank Sullivan, who at 6–7 was just an inch shorter than Conley.

Conley, Gene

Braves	W	L	Pct	G	GS	CG	ShO	IP	H	BB	SO	ERA	SV
1952	0	3	.000	4	3	0	0	12⅔	23	9	6	7.82	0
1954	14	9	.609	28	27	12	2	194⅓	171	79	113	2.96	0
1955	11	7	.611	22	21	10	0	158	152	52	107	4.16	0
1956	8	9	.471	31	19	5	1	158⅓	169	52	68	3.13	3
1957	9	9	.500	35	18	6	1	148	133	64	61	3.16	1
1958	0	6	.000	26	7	0	0	72	89	17	53	4.88	2
Career	42	43	.494	146	95	33	4	743⅓	737	273	408	3.56	6

Connolly, Joe

Braves: 1913–16
Outfielder
Birthplace: North Smithfield, Rhode Island
B: February 12, 1888

D: September 1, 1943
Batted left, threw right
Ht. 5–7; **Wt.** 165

Joe Connolly's career in professional baseball was short and rather undistinguished. However, he received a great deal of acclaim for being the only .300 hitter on the World Series champion "Miracle" Braves of 1914.

Son of a Rhode Island farmer, Connolly grew up watching his older brother play baseball with Nap Lajoie, who had a Hall of Fame career ahead of him. The young Connolly would retrieve balls for the older boys and developed a love for the game at an early age.

Though his father wanted him to be a farmer, Connolly decided that baseball paid better than farming and was considerably easier. A diminutive left-handed-hitting outfielder, he started his pro career as a right-handed pitcher. But when scouts said he wasn't big enough to pitch in the majors, Connolly talked his way into a job as an outfielder in 1911 with Terre Haute.

In the spring of 1913 he failed to make the Washington roster, and the Braves picked him up on waivers. Boston was coming off four straight last-place finishes, and new manager George Stallings was desperate for help. He liked what he saw of Connolly and made him a regular. The 25-year-old rookie responded by hitting .281. In spite of breaking his ankle sliding and missing the last month, he helped Boston claw its way all the way to fifth place.

Much better things were in store for the Braves and Connolly in 1914.

Stallings, never satisfied with his outfielders, platooned them throughout the season. The only one he showed much confidence in was Connolly, who played against right-handers and most left-handers and produced the best numbers of his career. Besides leading the club in hitting, he finished fourth

in the league in doubles. In the World Series, he had only one hit in the Braves' four-game sweep of the Athletics.

Not many of the Braves played as well in 1915, and Connolly was no exception. His numbers were down across the board, most noticeably in doubles and RBIs. A year later, he was out of the majors.

Connolly, Joe

Braves	G	AB	R	H	2B	3B	HR	RBI	SB	AVG	SLG
1913	126	427	79	120	18	11	5	57	18	.281	.410
1914	120	399	64	122	28	10	9	65	12	.306	.494
1915	104	305	48	91	14	8	0	23	13	.298	.397
1916	62	110	11	25	5	2	0	12	5	.227	.309
Career	412	1,241	202	358	65	31	14	157	48	.288	.425

Cooney, Johnny

Braves, Bees: 1921–30, 1938–42
Outfielder, pitcher, first baseman
Birthplace: Cranston, Rhode Island
B: March 18, 1901

D: July 8, 1986
Batted right, threw left
Ht. 5–10; **Wt.** 165

Johnny Cooney probably had the most unique career of any man who ever played for the Braves.

By no means was he the most accomplished player, though he did lead National League outfielders in fielding percentage twice and compiled a lifetime .286 batting average. However, he gained the distinction of being the only man ever to play in both leagues, coach in both leagues, manage in both leagues, and umpire in one. Not only that, but he did most of it after overcoming an injury and operation that left his throwing arm (his left) three inches shorter than his gloved one.

Cooney was the product of a baseball family. His father, Jimmy, was a shortstop for Hall of Famer Cap Anson and the Chicago White Stockings in 1890–92. And his older brother, also Jimmy, was an infielder for several teams from 1917 to 1928, finishing with the Braves.

Johnny originally was going to sign with the Red Sox in 1921 but balked when he learned he was to be paid by check rather than cash. So, he joined the other team in town and wound up playing there most of his 20-year career.

Cooney was a decent pitcher, winning a career-high 14 games in 1925. He also was an excellent defensive outfielder who could hit for average but not power and never struck out

Joe Connolly

Johnny Cooney

more than once in a game. He was used frequently at both positions and occasionally at first base.

However, in 1926 he suffered an arm injury that threatened his career. Due to paralysis and an operation, his left arm wound up three inches shorter than the right. Cooney was determined to continue playing, but he struggled and eventually was sent to the minors in 1930.

In 1935, he was hitting .371 when Casey Stengel, then managing Brooklyn, brought him back to the majors at the end of the season. The following year, he was a regular outfielder, hitting .282 for the Dodgers and leading NL outfielders with a .994 fielding percentage.

Cooney rejoined the Bees/Braves for five years as a player-coach in 1938 when Stengel came to Boston to manage. Years later, Stengel would compare Cooney favorably to Hall of Famer Joe DiMaggio as a defensive player.

In 20 big league seasons, Cooney hit only two home runs, and they came on back-to-back days with the Bees in 1939. As a regular, Cooney batted .318 in 1940 and .319 the next year.

In 1944, Cooney spent the final 10 games of his career with the Yankees, accounting for his American League playing experience.

When no major league club wanted his services in 1945, he played with Kansas City of the American Association and batted a robust .343. In '46, he was back with the Braves as a coach, a job he held, on and off, through 1955 in Milwaukee. In 1949, he got his National League managerial experience when he replaced Billy Southworth for the final 46 games of the year.

In 1957, he began an eight-year coaching stint in the American League with the White Sox. He managed several games when Al Lopez, himself a former Brave, was away from the club briefly.

As for Cooney's umpiring experience, it came during his playing days with the Braves. The regular umpires were traveling from Boston to New York by boat. When they failed to arrive in time for the game, Cooney umpired behind the plate, and the Giants' Freddy Fitzsimmons worked the bases.

Cooney, Johnny

Braves, Bees	G	AB	R	H	2B	3B	HR	RBI	SB	AVG	SLG
1921	8	5	0	1	0	0	0	0	0	.200	.200
1922	4	8	0	0	0	0	0	0	0	.000	.000
1923	42	66	7	25	1	0	0	3	0	.379	.394
1924	55	130	10	33	2	1	0	4	0	.254	.285
1925	54	103	17	33	7	0	0	13	1	.320	.388
1926	64	126	17	38	3	2	0	18	6	.302	.357
1927	10	1	3	0	0	0	0	0	0	.000	.000
1928	33	41	2	7	0	0	0	0	2	.171	.171
1929	41	72	10	23	4	1	0	6	1	.319	.403
1930	4	3	0	0	0	0	0	0	0	.000	.000
1938	120	432	45	117	25	5	0	17	2	.271	.352
1939	118	368	39	101	8	1	2	27	2	.274	.318
1940	108	365	40	116	14	3	0	21	4	.318	.373
1941	123	442	52	141	25	2	0	29	3	.319	.385
1942	74	198	23	41	6	0	0	7	2	.207	.237
Career	858	2,360	265	676	95	15	2	145	23	.286	.342

Braves	W	L	Pct	G	GS	CG	ShO	IP	H	BB	SO	ERA	SV
1921	0	1	.000	8	1	0	0	20⅔	19	10	9	3.92	0
1922	1	2	.333	4	3	1	0	25	19	6	7	2.16	0
1923	3	5	.375	23	8	5	2	98	92	22	23	3.31	0
1924	8	9	.471	34	19	12	2	181	176	50	67	3.18	2
1925	14	14	.500	31	29	20	2	245⅔	267	50	65	3.48	0
1926	3	3	.500	19	8	3	1	83⅓	106	29	23	4.00	0
1928	3	7	.300	24	6	2	0	89⅔	106	31	18	4.32	1
1929	2	3	.400	14	2	1	0	45	57	22	11	5.00	3
1930	0	0	.000	2	0	0	0	7	16	3	1	18.00	0
Career	34	44	.436	159	76	44	7	795⅓	858	223	224	3.72	6

Covington, Wes

Braves: 1956–61
Outfielder
Birthplace: Laurinburg, North Carolina

B: March 27, 1932
Batted left, threw right
Ht. 6–1; **Wt.** 205

Wes Covington was one of the most gifted hitters ever to come up through the Braves farm system. Unfortunately, injuries and an argumentative nature prohibited him from approaching his full potential.

A good portion of the Braves' ability to win two pennants and a World Series in 1957 and '58 was due to Covington's bat. In those two seasons, the left-handed-hitting outfielder from North Carolina averaged a home run every 13.8 at bats. By comparison, Hank Aaron averaged one homer every 16.4 at bats in the same two-year period—and Aaron won the National League home run title in 1957.

However, Covington never enjoyed similar success again. The Braves waived him early in 1961, and by the end of that season, he had worn four different uniforms. In his 11-year career, he hit 131 home runs, of which over 34 percent came in 1957 and '58.

Covington, a sensational high school football player who turned down several scholarship offers to play baseball, broke in with Milwaukee in 1956 but was used infrequently. He made the club out of spring training in 1957, only to be sent back to

Wes Covington

Wichita May 15 when he complained about Bobby Thomson and then Chuck Tanner playing in front of him. A month later he was recalled, and his bat helped propel the Braves to their first pennant since 1948. Covington became particularly invaluable July 11 when center fielder Billy Bruton was lost for the remainder of the year with a damaged knee.

Covington finished third on the team that year in both home runs (21) and RBIs (65), trailing only Aaron and Eddie Mathews in both categories. Without his bat, Milwaukee probably would not have celebrated a pennant in 1957.

Ironically, Covington was not well regarded as a defensive outfielder. But in the '57 World Series, in which he batted just .208 and drove in only one run, he made two spectacular game-saving catches.

In Game 2 at Yankee Stadium, the score was tied, 1–1, in the bottom of the second. The Yankees, who had won Game 1, had two runners aboard when pitcher Bobby Shantz lined a ball down the left-field line that appeared capable of scoring two runs. However, Covington made a running, backhand catch in the corner, and Milwaukee went on to win, 4–2, behind Lou Burdette.

The Yankees and Braves were tied at two games apiece when Covington saved Burdette once again in Game 5. With the game scoreless in the fourth, New York's Gil McDougald hit a drive to left that appeared headed for extra bases and possibly a home run. But Covington crashed into the fence to make the catch, and the Braves eventually won, 1–0.

Covington hit even better in 1958 than he did in '57 in spite of a late start because of injury. In a spring training game he sprained his knee sliding, and he didn't play again until May 2. But in his second at bat he hit a two-run homer and proceeded to make up for lost time quickly. Still somewhat hobbled, Covington hit four homers in his first eight games and drove in 10 runs in his first six games.

The knee was a constant hindrance throughout the year, but Covington didn't let it affect him at the plate. For the second year in a row, he finished third on the club to Aaron and Mathews in home runs (24) and RBIs. His efficiency was breathtaking. In just 294 at bats, he drove in 74 runs, only three less than Mathews, who had 252 more at bats. He hit just six homers less than Aaron who had 307 more at bats.

In the World Series, Covington failed to get an extra-base hit, but he did lead the Braves with four RBIs in the seven games.

In 1959, Covington continued to have injury problems. He had more at bats than in any other season of his career, yet his production dropped drastically. Then on August 20 he tore a ligament in his ankle and was lost for the rest of the season.

Covington was gimpy the rest of his career, and not much more of it was spent with the Braves. He reported out of shape in 1960 and had his worst season yet. Early in 1961, the once-prized outfielder, now 29, was put on waivers by the Braves and claimed by the White Sox.

Covington, Wes

Braves	G	AB	R	H	2B	3B	HR	RBI	SB	AVG	SLG
1956	75	138	17	39	4	0	2	16	1	.283	.355
1957	96	328	51	93	4	8	21	65	4	.284	.537
1958	90	294	43	97	12	1	24	74	0	.330	.622
1959	103	373	38	104	17	3	7	45	0	.279	.397
1960	95	281	25	70	16	1	10	35	1	.249	.420
1961	9	21	3	4	1	0	0	0	0	.190	.238
Career	468	1,435	177	407	54	13	64	235	6	.284	.473

Crandall, Del

Braves: 1949–63
Catcher
Birthplace: Ontario, California

B: March 5, 1930
Batted right, threw right
Ht. 6–1; **Wt.** 195

When the great Braves teams of the 1950s are discussed, Del Crandall's name usually receives relatively little attention. The reason, of course, is that he played with so many Hall of Famers, superstars, and headline-grabbing personalities that he is easy to overlook. All Crandall did was his job—and he did it consistently better than any other catcher in Braves history.

Crandall wore number 1 on his back, and it was a fitting number for him. Often referred to as "a ballplayer's ballplayer," he was the Braves' captain. Besides being an accomplished defensive player, he was a good hitter with power. Though certainly not in the category of teammates such as Hank Aaron, Eddie Mathews, and Joe Adcock, he hit 20 or more home runs three times and averaged 19 in the eight-year period 1953–60. He also homered in the 1957 and '58 World Series and the first 1960 All-Star Game.

But defense was Crandall's forte. He led National League catchers in fielding percentage four times and won four Gold Gloves. He'd undoubtedly have won more Gold Gloves except that the award wasn't instituted until 1957, and there weren't separate NL and AL teams until '58. By then, Crandall had already led the league in fielding once and had been selected to four of the eight All-Star teams he would make.

In 1959 he appeared in 150 games, the first catcher in five years to do so. He caught three no-hitters (Jim Wilson, Lou Burdette, and Warren Spahn) in his career.

At age 19, Crandall broke in with Boston in 1949 and split the catching with Bill Salkeld. The next year, he was the backup to Walker Cooper. Then it was off for two years of military service.

When Crandall returned to the Braves in 1953, he took over the regular catching chores from Cooper in the team's first year in Milwaukee. Crandall held the job for nine of the next 10 years, yielding only in 1961 when he sustained a shoulder injury April 20 that limited him to pinch hitting the rest of the year. Though he never hit home runs in double figures again, Crandall came back in '62 to reclaim his job, hitting a career-high .297 and making his final All-Star team.

Reduced to a part-time role in '63 when Joe Torre became the regular, Crandall was traded to San Francisco after the season in the seven-player deal in which the Braves acquired

Del Crandall

Felipe Alou. He didn't play regularly again, retiring after the '66 season, his 16th in the majors.

When Aaron, approaching Babe Ruth's home run record, was asked to select an all-time team of the best players he'd competed with or against, he named Crandall his catcher.

Crandall, Del

Braves	G	AB	R	H	2B	3B	HR	RBI	SB	AVG	SLG
1949	67	228	21	60	10	1	4	34	2	.263	.368
1950	79	255	21	56	11	0	4	37	0	.220	.310
1953	116	382	55	104	13	1	15	51	2	.272	.429
1954	138	463	60	112	18	2	21	64	0	.242	.425
1955	133	440	61	104	15	2	26	62	2	.236	.457
1956	112	311	37	74	14	2	16	48	1	.238	.450
1957	118	383	45	97	11	2	15	46	1	.253	.410
1958	131	427	50	116	23	1	18	63	4	.272	.457
1959	150	518	65	133	19	2	21	72	5	.257	.423
1960	142	537	81	158	14	1	19	77	4	.294	.430
1961	15	30	3	6	3	0	0	1	0	.200	.300
1962	107	350	35	104	12	3	8	45	3	.297	.417
1963	86	259	18	52	4	0	3	28	1	.201	.251
Career	1,394	4,583	552	1,176	167	17	170	628	25	.257	.412

Cuccinello, Tony

Bees, Braves: 1936–40, 1942–43
Second baseman, third baseman, shortstop
Birthplace: Long Island City, New York

B: November 8, 1907
Batted right, threw right
Ht. 5–7; **Wt.** 160

Tony "Chick" Cuccinello had a lot of Mark Lemke in him. In baseball parlance, Cuccinello was a "gamer." If Bobby Cox had been managing back in the late 1930s, he might have called Cuccinello "Dirt," just as he often referred to Lemke in the 1990s.

Like Lemke, Cuccinello was a gritty little second baseman who loved to play the game and would do whatever it took to help win. The best example of Cuccinello's vigor may have come in 1939 when he was returning from a six-week layoff that resulted from a knee injury.

Manager Casey Stengel put him right in the starting lineup for a home game against Brooklyn. As early as the sixth inning, Stengel asked Cuccinello if he wanted to come out of the game and rest his knee. The second baseman declined, saying he felt he could go nine innings. At the end of

nine, the game was tied 2–2, and Cuccinello, feeling fine and figuring the game would end soon, told Stengel he wanted to stay in to the end. With the score still tied in the 15th, Stengel once again asked his second baseman if he wanted relief, and once more he was turned down.

The game eventually went 23 innings, lasting 5 hours and 15 minutes before it was called because of darkness with the score still tied 2–2. Cuccinello played every minute.

Originally traded to Boston from Brooklyn with Al Lopez in a six-player exchange prior to the 1936 season, Cuccinello spent more than one-third of his 15-year big league career, during which he compiled a lifetime .280 batting average, with the franchise in two different stints.

Cuccinello had his best season with the Bees in 1936 when he hit .308 and drove in 86 runs. He made the National League All-Star team in 1938.

Cuccinello was known as a clutch hitter, but many of those hits were to no avail. He played on some pretty bad teams.

Cuccinello, Tony

Bees, Braves	G	AB	R	H	2B	3B	HR	RBI	SB	AVG	SLG
1936	150	565	68	174	26	3	7	86	1	.308	.402
1937	152	575	77	156	36	4	11	80	2	.271	.405
1938	147	555	62	147	25	2	9	76	4	.265	.366
1939	81	310	42	95	17	1	2	40	5	.306	.387
1940	34	126	14	34	9	0	0	19	1	.270	.341
1942	40	104	8	21	3	0	1	8	1	.202	.260
1943	13	19	0	0	0	0	0	2	0	.000	.000
Career	617	2,254	271	627	116	10	30	311	14	.278	.378

Curtis, Cliff

Doves, Rustlers: 1909–11
Pitcher
Birthplace: Delaware, Ohio
B: July 3, 1883

D: April 23, 1943
Batted right, threw right
Ht. 6–2; **Wt.** 180

Anthony Young certainly wasn't trying to do anyone a favor, but when he lost his 24th consecutive game in 1993, the New York Mets right-hander finally got Cliff Curtis off the hook he'd been hanging on for 82 years.

That's how long Curtis held the major league record for consecutive games lost, 23.

It all began quite unexpectedly in 1910. The 26-year-old right-hander started 6–6 for the worst team in the National League, one that was on its way to losing 100 games and fin-

Tony Cuccinello

Cliff Curtis

ishing 50½ games out of first. Splitting 12 decisions was quite an accomplishment.

But Curtis didn't win again the rest of the year. He lost his last 18 decisions of the season, still a National League record. The streak continued for Curtis's first five decisions of 1911 before he finally won, halting the streak at 23.

Shortly thereafter, Curtis was traded to the Cubs in an eight-player deal. He pitched through 1913 for the Cubs, Phillies, and Dodgers but never posted a winning record for any team. He finished his career with a horrible 28–61 record, yet his lifetime ERA was a very respectable 3.31.

Curtis's biggest victory for Boston—besides the one that stopped his losing streak—came in 1910 when he shut out Pittsburgh, 1–0. It was Boston's first win against the Pirates in 17 games.

Curtis, Cliff

Doves, Rustlers	W	L	Pct	G	GS	CG	ShO	IP	H	BB	SO	ERA	SV
1909	4	5	.444	10	9	8	2	83	53	30	22	1.41	0
1910	6	24	.200	43	37	12	2	251	251	124	75	3.55	2
1911	1	8	.111	12	9	5	0	77	79	34	23	4.44	1
Career	11	37	.229	65	55	25	4	411	383	188	120	3.28	3

Dark, Al

Braves: 1946, 1948–49, 1960
Shortstop
Birthplace: Comanche, Oklahoma
B: January 7, 1922
Batted right, threw right
Ht. 5–11; **Wt.** 185

One of the most magical seasons in Braves history was 1948, and Al Dark played a major role in the enchantment that enveloped Boston's long-suffering National League fans that summer.

In many ways, Dark was the Deion Sanders of his day . . . perhaps even a more accomplished athlete than the multitalented Atlanta outfielder of the '90s. Dark was a three-sport star at LSU. Besides his obvious baseball skill, he was the high scorer on the basketball team and a good enough backfield player in football to be drafted by the Philadelphia Eagles of the NFL.

After a tour with the Marines, Dark signed with the Braves for a $40,000 bonus. His decision to pursue a baseball career helped the Braves emerge from one of the darkest depres-

Al Dark

sions known by any major league franchise. When he became the team's regular shortstop as a 26-year-old rookie in 1948, the Braves hadn't won a pennant since the "miracle" of 1914 and had finished higher than fourth just once in 31 years.

When a team finally turns the corner, as the '48 team did, it takes a lot of contributors, many of them totally unexpected. And though Dark certainly was considered a good prospect, no one could have envisioned him performing as well as he did as a freshman. He batted .322, fourth in the league, and also was third in doubles (39) and fifth in hits (175). A 23-game hitting streak equaled the modern (post-1900) rookie record.

No Braves shortstop since '48 has matched Dark's batting average. He teamed with second baseman Eddie Stanky (.320) to give Boston one of the most potent combinations of middle infielders in franchise history.

Dark was voted the Major League Rookie of the Year at a time when there was just one rookie award for both leagues.

As brilliant as Dark's rookie season was, he didn't remain a Brave for long. His sophomore average dipped considerably but still was quite respectable at .276. When the team's record fell below .500, though, changes were dictated. The Braves packaged Dark with Stanky in a blockbuster six-man trade with the Giants after the season. Boston received Sid Gordon, Buddy Kerr, Willard Marshall, and Red Webb in the deal.

Dark went on to a long and prosperous career, playing on two pennant winners for the Giants and making three All-Star teams. In 1969 fans voted him the top shortstop in Giants history. A long managing career followed his playing career. In 13 seasons with five clubs, he won a World Series ('74, Oakland), a pennant ('62, San Francisco), and a division title ('75, Oakland).

Dark, Alvin

Braves	G	AB	R	H	2B	3B	HR	RBI	SB	AVG	SLG
1946	15	13	0	3	3	0	0	1	0	.231	.462
1948	137	543	85	175	39	6	3	48	4	.322	.433
1949	130	529	74	146	23	5	3	53	5	.276	.355
1960	50	141	16	42	6	2	1	18	0	.298	.390
Career	332	1,226	175	366	71	13	7	120	9	.299	.395

Davis, George

Braves: 1913–15
Pitcher
Birthplace: Lancaster, New York
B: March 9, 1890
D: June 4, 1961
Batted both, threw right
Ht. 5–10; **Wt.** 175

George "Iron" Davis won but seven games in his career and only six as a Brave. However, he holds unique status in franchise history. One of those six victories was a no-hitter for the "Miracle" Braves of 1914—and Davis was enrolled in Harvard Law School when he pitched it.

The son of a wealthy Buffalo judge, Davis was a star pitcher at Williams College, attracting the attention of pro scouts. However, his father didn't want his son pursuing a career as a professional ballplayer. That objection was overcome when the Yankees offered him what then was an extraordinary bonus of $5,000.

George Davis

Vince DiMaggio

After graduating from Williams in 1912, Davis, 22, joined the Yankees but pitched in only 10 games, once allowing 11 runs in an inning, and winning one of five decisions. He opened the 1913 season in the International League. New Boston manager George Stallings had seen the hard-throwing right-hander work and liked his potential. At Stallings' request, the Braves purchased Davis from Rochester in August.

The Boston manager encouraged Davis to work on a spitball, and he used his young pupil sparingly as a reliever in 1914 during the Braves' frenzied drive from last place to first. However, with doubleheaders stacking up, Stallings gave Davis his first National League start September 9 in the second game of a doubleheader with Philadelphia. The previous day, the Braves had moved into first place to stay, and Davis provided additional momentum for the stretch drive by no-hitting Philadelphia, 7–0. He walked five and struck out four.

The no-hitter was the second in modern Braves history and proved to be the only shutout Davis would pitch in his career. He made five more starts that season but was not used in the World Series.

In 1915, he showed only limited development and was released by Stallings with a career record of 7–10, 4.48. Davis returned to Harvard, finished law school, and became a real estate attorney in Buffalo.

Davis, George

Braves	W	L	Pct	G	GS	CG	ShO	IP	H	BB	SO	ERA	SV
1913	0	0	—	2	0	0	0	8	7	5	3	4.50	0
1914	3	3	.500	9	6	4	1	55⅔	42	26	26	3.40	0
1915	3	3	.500	15	9	4	0	73⅓	85	19	26	3.80	0
Career	6	6	.500	26	15	8	1	137	134	50	55	3.68	0

DiMaggio, Vince

Bees: 1937–38
Outfielder, second baseman
Birthplace: Martinez, California
B: September 6, 1912

D: October 3, 1986
Batted right, threw right
Ht. 5–11; **Wt.** 183

A lot of ballplayers would have liked to be good enough to accomplish some of the things Vince DiMaggio did in his career. However, normal standards don't usually apply when assessing DiMaggio's career because of the prominence of his last name in the game's history.

Thus, the shortcomings of the eldest of the three DiMaggio brothers tend to attract more attention than his successes.

When Vince broke in with the Bees in 1937, younger brother Joe was beginning only his second season in the majors, but he already was well on his way to becoming a legendary Yankee. Dom, the youngest of the three DiMaggios, didn't come along until 1940, but he quickly established himself as a productive outfielder with the Red Sox.

Vince, in the meantime, was still trying to find his niche. In May 1940, he was traded for the second time in just over three years in the majors. Yet he eventually would have a 100-RBI season, make two National League All-Star teams, and hit 125 career home runs. No, he wasn't as good as Joe or Dom, but Vince had a 10-year career that many players would have been proud to claim.

A solid defensive outfielder with a good arm and better-than-average speed, Vince had power, but he also experienced quite a bit of difficulty making contact. He hit 19 home runs in 1936 in the minors, prompting the Bees to acquire him to supplement Wally Berger's power.

In two seasons with Boston, DiMaggio produced decent power numbers, but he also led the league in strikeouts both years. His 134 strikeouts in 1938 was a National League record at the time, and they also got him traded to Cincinnati. The Bees had him fitted for glasses, benched him, and even moved him to second base for a short time, before giving up on him.

DiMaggio had his best seasons with Pittsburgh, posting career highs of 21 homers and 100 RBIs in 1941.

DiMaggio, Vince

Bees	G	AB	R	H	2B	3B	HR	RBI	SB	AVG	SLG
1937	132	493	56	126	18	4	13	69	8	.256	.387
1938	150	540	71	123	28	3	14	61	11	.228	.369
Career	282	1,033	127	249	46	7	27	130	19	.241	.378

Duffy, Hugh

Beaneaters: 1892–1900	**B:** November 26, 1866
Outfielder, second baseman, shortstop,	**D:** October 19, 1954
third baseman, first baseman, catcher	**Batted right, threw right**
Birthplace: Cranston, Rhode Island	**Ht.** 5–7; **Wt.** 168

When the greatest hitters in baseball history—or even in Braves history—are discussed, Hugh Duffy's name won't even draw a mention. Yet Duffy, unquestionably, holds two of the most distinguished honors of any man ever to swing a bat.

His .440 batting average in 1894 (.438 in some books) is the all-time major league season record. The Beaneaters outfielder also led the National League in home runs (18) and RBIs (145) that year, making him one of only 14 men—and the only Brave—ever to win the Triple Crown.

That Duffy ever became such an accomplished hitter surprised a lot of people, not the least of whom was the great Cap Anson, player-manager of the Chicago White Stockings. The future Hall of Famer thought Duffy was too small to be successful. And that misjudgment proved to be the Beaneaters' good fortune.

Duffy actually began his pro career as a catcher in 1886. The following year, the manager of Salem purchased his contract from Springfield for $25. When the owner of the Salem club learned of the transaction, he was furious. He said he would pay Duffy just $5 a week plus room and board and would withhold the $5 if Duffy played poorly.

Under such pressure, Duffy played miserably in his first game, prompting the owner to fire him and the team's manager. But the same evening, the club was sold, and Duffy was given another chance. He played well, and by August,

Hugh Duffy

Chicago and Boston were bidding for his services. He eventually signed with Chicago for the 1888 season, but Anson kept him on the bench most of the first half.

Duffy played two years for the White Stockings, mostly as an outfielder. He then went on the open market for two years, selling his services as a free agent, first in the Players League and then in the American Association. When the latter league consolidated with the National League in 1892, Duffy joined the Beaneaters and soon became one of the early stars of the game.

He immediately was one of the league's top hitters, finishing third in hits and fifth in total bases in 1892 and third in hits and fourth in batting average in 1893, helping Boston win pennants both seasons. Duffy was a proficient base stealer and was known for excellent positioning in the outfield. Playing center field, he teamed with rightfielder Tommy McCarthy to form a tandem so adept defensively that the two were nicknamed the "Heavenly Twins."

But nothing Duffy did his first two years with the club indicated he'd ever hit the way he did in 1894. The ball supposedly was "juiced" that year, and the league's composite .309 batting average indicated that supposition was true. However, everyone hit the same ball, and no one hit it like Duffy did.

Besides leading the league in average, home runs, and RBIs, he also led in hits, doubles, total bases, and slugging percentage (.694). Not bad for someone who was too small to play for Anson.

It has often been said—and quite incorrectly—that Duffy was able to hit .440 because walks counted as hits in 1894. Such was not the case. He was 237-for-539, a true .440.

Statistics weren't constantly updated and publicized back then, and Duffy went into the final game of the season not knowing exactly what he was hitting or by how much he was leading the league. After he got hits in his first two at bats, his teammates encouraged him to take off the rest of the day. However, he declined and proceeded to get three more hits.

He won the race by 33 points, becoming the third batting champ in franchise history. During the off-season, he was feted by fans and teammates alike. The Bleacher Club gave him a banquet and presented him with a gold watch engraved to the "Great Run-Getter." And the Beaneaters gave him a watch charm with five diamonds engraved "Presented to Hugh Duffy, champion batsman of the world, by his fellow players and manager."

Duffy, who lifted his front foot before swinging, never had another season that even approached 1894, nor did he ever lead the league again in batting average or RBIs. He did, however, win the home run crown again in 1897 with 11, and he remained a strong offensive force. In the nine years he played for the Beaneaters, he drove in 100 or more runs seven times.

Pound for pound—or by any other standard—Duffy certainly was one of the game's best hitters. He had 10 .300 seasons and compiled a .324 lifetime average.

Duffy was a Braves scout in 1917–19. He later was a coach for the Red Sox and was one of Ted Williams' first hitting coaches.

Duffy, Hugh											
Beaneaters	G	AB	R	H	2B	3B	HR	RBI	SB	AVG	SLG
1892	147	612	125	184	28	12	5	81	51	.301	.410
1893	131	560	147	203	23	7	6	118	44	.363	.461
1894	125	539	160	237*	51*	16	18*	145*	48	.440*	.694*
1895	130	531	110	187	30	6	9	100	42	.352	.482
1896	131	527	97	158	16	8	5	113	39	.300	.389
1897	134	550	130	187	25	10	11*	129	41	.340	.482
1898	152	568	97	169	13	3	8	108	29	.298	.373
1899	147	588	103	164	29	7	5	102	26	.279	.378
1900	55	181	27	55	5	4	2	31	11	.304	.409
Career	1,152	4,656	996	1,544	220	73	69	927	331	.332	.455

Elliott, Bob

Braves: 1947–51
Third baseman
Birthplace: San Francisco
B: November 26, 1916

D: May 4, 1966
Batted right, threw right
Ht. 6–0; **Wt.** 185

Bob Elliott told the Pirates to put him at third base and forget about him, but they wouldn't listen. Instead, they labeled him a troublemaker and traded him to Boston. He made trouble, okay, but it was for the rest of the league—not for the Braves.

The Pirates discovered Elliott during spring training of 1936 when he was 19 years old. After three years in the low minors, he told the Pirates that if they didn't advance him in their system, he was going to quit so he could support his wife. Pittsburgh sent him to Triple-A, where he was hitting .338 late in 1939 when the Pirates called him to the majors.

Even though Elliott made the All-Star team four times, Pirates manager Frankie Frisch continually moved him back and forth between third base and the outfield. Elliott's objections finally led to his trade to the Braves after an off year at the plate in 1946. The other main player in the six-player deal was Billy Herman, whom Pittsburgh installed as manager.

Braves manager Billy Southworth, who started Elliott at third in the 1944 All-Star Game, coveted him. Southworth did indeed put Elliott at third and forgot about him.

In five seasons with the Braves, Elliott didn't play a single game at another position. He responded by being named the National League MVP in 1947, his first year in Boston, then leading the Braves to a pennant in 1948. In the process, he became known as "Mr. Team" for his all-around contributions to making the Braves a contender.

Bob Elliott

It was as if Elliott was born again as a ballplayer when he joined the Braves at age 30. He could do no wrong in 1947. He led the league's third basemen in fielding percentage (.956), and though he didn't lead in any offensive departments, he was near the top in several. He finished second to Harry Walker in the batting race (.317) and also was second in doubles and fourth in RBIs (113).

The Braves already were an improving team after spending most of the previous 30 years in the depths of the league. However, the addition of Elliott was a major factor in the team's ability to climb to third for the first time since 1916. He was rewarded with the MVP, the first Brave to win the award since Johnny Evers in 1914, by a comfortable margin over Cincinnati's Ewell Blackwell and New York's Johnny Mize.

In 1948, Elliott's average dropped considerably, but he still posted excellent power numbers, driving in 100 runs for the fifth time in six seasons. He led the league in walks and finished second to Stan Musial in on-base percentage to help Boston return to the World Series for the first time in 34 years.

The Braves lost to Cleveland in the World Series, but Elliott was second on the team with a .333 average and led the club with two homers and five RBIs. The home runs and four of the five RBIs came in Game 5 when Boston routed Bob Feller, 11–5.

Elliott had three more solid seasons with the Braves, and in 1950 posted numbers similar to those of his MVP year. In 1951, at age 34, he made the All-Star team for the third time as a Brave and seventh time overall. But the Braves traded him to the Giants prior to the 1952 season, and it proved a wise move. He was finished as a regular and retired after 1953 with a .289 lifetime average and 1,195 RBIs in a 15-year career.

Elliott, Bob											
Braves	G	AB	R	H	2B	3B	HR	RBI	SB	AVG	SLG
1947	150	555	93	176	35	5	22	113	3	.317	.517
1948	151	540	99	153	24	5	23	100	6	.283	.474
1949	139	482	77	135	29	5	17	76	0	.280	.467
1950	142	531	94	162	28	5	24	107	2	.305	.512
1951	136	480	73	137	29	2	15	70	2	.285	.448
Career	718	2,588	436	763	145	22	101	466	13	.295	.485

Esasky, Nick

Braves: 1990
First baseman
Birthplace: Hialeah, Florida

B: February 24, 1960
Batted right, threw right
Ht. 6–3; **Wt.** 215

Beginning with Andy Messersmith in 1976, the Braves went through a horrible run of sour free-agent signings before John Schuerholz became general manager. The last and certainly the most disappointing of the lot was Nick Esasky.

Esasky's case ranks as one of the strangest in the history of sports. In 1989 he had a career season with the Boston Red Sox, batting .277 with 30 home runs and 108 RBIs. The Braves were in need of a power-hitting first baseman for 1990, and Esasky, a free agent, was eager to play in Atlanta, where he already made his home. It was a perfect match, and no one was surprised when the Braves signed the 30-year-old first baseman to a three-year, $5.6 million contract.

Nick Esasky

However, Esasky began to feel ill toward the end of spring training. He first thought he had the flu. He was fatigued and dizzy and suffered from headaches and nausea. He lost weight. Baseballs appeared fuzzy and out of focus to him.

Nine games into the season, Esasky was hitting .171 with no extra-base hits or RBIs, and he had committed five errors. After the Braves' game of April 21, he went to manager Russ Nixon and told him something was wrong.

Esasky's problem was diagnosed as vertigo, a disturbance in the inner ear caused by a viral infection. He consulted specialist after specialist and went through various programs designed to help him overcome the dizziness.

He made enough progress that the Braves sent him to Triple-A Richmond in 1991 on a rehabilitation assignment to see if he could still play. The results were inconclusive. At the end of the rehab stint, the Braves, who had acquired Sid Bream to play first and were in a pennant race, asked Esasky to continue at Richmond. He declined and asked to be traded. Given his condition and his high salary, there were no takers.

Esasky's final line as a Brave read just as it did on April 21, 1990, after only 35 at bats with the team. He never played another game in the majors.

Esasky, Nick											
Braves	G	AB	R	H	2B	3B	HR	RBI	SB	AVG	SLG
1990	9	35	2	6	0	0	0	0	0	.171	.171
Career	9	35	2	6	0	0	0	0	0	.171	.171

Evans, Darrell

Braves: 1969–76, 1989
Third baseman, first baseman
Birthplace: Pasadena, California

B: May 26, 1947
Batted left, threw right
Ht. 6–2; **Wt.** 205

The second most prolific left-handed home run hitter in Atlanta Braves history, Darrell Evans was the club's regular third baseman for the five-year period 1971–75. As a Brave, he peaked in 1973 in only his second full season in the majors. At age 26 he made the National League All-Star team and attained career highs with 41 home runs, 104 RBIs, and a .281 average.

Evans, who started wearing contact lenses that season, combined with Hank Aaron (40) and Dave Johnson (43) to give the Braves the first 40-homer threesome in history. Little good it did, though. The team still finished fifth in Eddie

Mathews' only full season as manager. It was no coincidence that Evans flourished under Mathews' tutelage even though the team didn't.

Evans, drafted by the Braves from the Athletics' farm system, credited Mathews for teaching him to pull the ball. Anyone who saw both men play could see the similarity in their stances and mannerisms at the plate. The 41 homers Evans hit that season even matched the number Mathews wore on his back. There seemed to be plenty of reasons for Braves fans to believe this left-handed-hitting third baseman could prove to be a clone of their manager, who had put together a Hall of Fame career as a player.

However, Mathews was fired late the next season, and even though Evans would go on to an outstanding 21-year career, he was traded by the Braves in 1976 and never again approached the promise he showed in '73.

Usually hitting third, in front of Aaron (he was on first base for No. 715), Evans saw a lot of good pitches, yet his keen eye still enabled him to draw a lot of walks. He led the league in walks in both 1973 and '74. In 1976, he set an all-time franchise record by drawing at least one walk in 15 consecutive games, and he wound up his career ranked 10th all-time in bases on balls.

Though he later became a respectable defensive third baseman, Evans set one other dubious Atlanta record that still stands—most errors in an inning (4) in 1975.

After productive but still disappointing seasons in 1974 and '75, Evans opened 1976 in a deep funk. Perhaps he was being too selective at the plate, as his 15-game walk streak might indicate. But for whatever reason, he was hitting just .173 when the Braves sent him to San Francisco on June 13 along with Marty Perez in exchange for first baseman Willie Montanez, shortstop Craig Robinson, and two other players.

Evans played seven and a half years for the Giants, making the All-Star team in 1983 at age 36, his last season in San Francisco, when he moved from third base to first. Five years with Detroit followed. In 1985, at age 38, he hit 40 home runs to lead the American League. He became the only player to have 40-homer seasons in both leagues, as well as the oldest player to win a home run crown.

Looking for some veteran leadership to help develop a young but promising team, the Braves signed the veteran free-agent slugger for 1989. Ron Gant's demotion to the minors and an injury to Gerald Perry necessitated that Evans

Darrell Evans

play more than planned, and he hit the last 11 of his 414 career home runs as a Brave.

Evans, Darrell

Braves	G	AB	R	H	2B	3B	HR	RBI	SB	AVG	SLG
1969	12	26	3	6	0	0	0	1	0	.231	.231
1970	12	44	4	14	1	1	0	9	0	.318	.386
1971	89	260	42	63	11	1	12	38	2	.242	.431
1972	125	418	67	106	12	0	19	71	4	.254	.419
1973	161	595	114	167	25	8	41	104	6	.281	.556
1974	160	571	99	137	21	3	25	79	4	.240	.419
1975	156	567	82	138	22	2	22	73	12	.243	.406
1976	44	139	11	24	0	0	1	10	3	.173	.194
1989	107	276	31	57	6	1	11	39	0	.207	.355
Career	866	2,896	453	712	98	16	131	424	31	.246	.426

Evers, Johnny

Braves: 1914–17, 1929
Second baseman
Birthplace: Troy, New York
B: July 21, 1881

D: March 28, 1947
Batted left, threw right
Ht. 5–9; **Wt.** 125

Johnny Evers is best known to most baseball fans as the Cubs second baseman who was immortalized in the poem "Tinker to Evers to Chance." But Evers played a big role in Braves history, too. In 1914, he spearheaded the pennant drive of the "Miracle" Braves and consequently became the first man in franchise history to be voted the National League's MVP.

The Most Valuable Player Award, as it is known today, wasn't instituted until 1922. However, from 1911 to 1914, there was a similar honor called the Chalmers Award. The Chalmers Motor Company presented a car to the player from each league who "should prove himself as the most important and useful player to his club and to the league at large in point of deportment and value of services rendered." Baseball writers voted on the Chalmers, just as they do the MVP today.

The Cubs and Braves exchanged second basemen in February 1914, Evers coming to Boston and Bill Sweeney going to Chicago along with some cash. Not a particularly strong hitter, Evers nevertheless was smart, aggressive, and fast, and

Johnny Evers

he played hard. He had played on three pennant winners in Chicago and provided the Braves with the leadership they needed to climb out of the NL cellar in July en route to their stunning World Series championship.

At age 33, Evers was on his last legs in 1914. In fact, it was to be his final season as a major league regular. However, he batted .279, one of the better averages of his career, and led NL second basemen in fielding (.976) for the only time in his 18-year career.

Then in the World Series, he batted a robust .438—second to Braves catcher Hank Gowdy's .545—to help Boston sweep four straight games from Connie Mack's heavily favored Philadelphia Athletics. Evers' two-run single drove in the decisive runs in Boston's 3–1 victory in the final game of the Series.

A part-time player the next two seasons, Evers was sent to Philadelphia in 1917, for all practical purposes the last year of his career. He made a token appearance for the Braves in 1929 when he was serving as "assistant manager" under owner Judge Emil Fuchs. By the end of the season, Evers was running the club himself, but Boston still finished a deep eighth.

Evers continued as assistant manager for the next three years under Bill McKechnie, then became a scout.

Evers, Johnny

Braves	G	AB	R	H	2B	3B	HR	RBI	SB	AVG	SLG
1914	139	491	81	137	20	3	1	40	12	.279	.338
1915	83	278	38	73	4	1	1	22	7	.263	.295
1916	71	241	33	52	4	1	0	15	5	.216	.241
1917	24	83	5	16	0	0	0	0	1	.193	.193
1929	1	0	0	0	0	0	0	0	0	—	—
Career	318	1,093	157	278	28	5	2	77	25	.254	.295

Fette, Lou

Bees, Braves: 1937–40, 1945
Pitcher
Birthplace: Alma, Missouri
B: March 15, 1907

D: January 3, 1981
Batted right, threw right
Ht. 6–1; **Wt.** 200

By 1937, Lou Fette probably thought he'd never pitch in the major leagues. He was 30 years old and had been a consistent winner in the minors for a long time. However, he didn't have a blazing fastball, and big league clubs were hesitant to take a chance on his ability to succeed with just a good curve and control.

But the Bees, hard up for talent as well as the cash to pay proven big leaguers, decided to take a chance on the Missouri farmer. General manager Bob Quinn paid $3,000 to St. Paul of the American Association, for whom Fette had won 25 games in 1936, then listened to skeptics tell him how he'd wasted his precious cash.

Quinn, of course, had the last laugh.

Fette was one of the top pitchers in the league in 1937, combining with fellow geriatric rookie Jim Turner to provide one of the most remarkable stories of the season. Both men won 20 games, tying for second in the league. It was the only time in history that two rookies have won 20 games for the same team, and they were the first rookies to win 20 since Hall of Famer Grover Cleveland Alexander in 1911.

Turner, who was 33, and Fette were both curveball pitchers. Neither smoke nor drank, and they became friends and

Lou Fette

Elbie Fletcher

roommates. They accounted for more than half the team's 79 wins that year and even tied for the league lead with five shutouts apiece. They credited manager Bill McKechnie with giving them the opportunity to pitch and catcher Al Lopez for handling them.

Fette, who used a sidearm delivery and was known for his poise, also finished second in complete games, just one behind Turner's 24, and was third in winning percentage (.667) and fifth in ERA and innings.

"I was no better pitcher when I got to Boston than I was before," Fette said of his late-found success in the majors. "I don't know why they never paid any attention to me. I thought I pitched some right good ball down in the minors, but nobody ever seemed to care. I don't mean to be boasting, but I'm sure I could have pitched up here before this time."

The baby-faced right-hander often is referred to as a "one-year wonder," but he deserves more credit than that. Though Fette never again approached a season like 1937, he was good enough to lead the league in shutouts again in 1939. He won 10 games, six by shutout, before hurting his arm in late July, then never won another game.

In the winter of 1934 the *Boston American* newspaper held a contest seeking the names of young amateur players with big league potential. Readers flooded the newspaper with nominations of Fletcher, and he was rewarded with a trip to spring training in St. Petersburg with the Braves. Fletcher, who hailed from the Boston suburb of Milton, was just 18 years old, but he impressed enough to eventually earn a contract. That September, he made his big league debut, appearing in eight games.

After splitting 1935 between the minors and majors, Fletcher spent a full year at Buffalo of the International League before being called back in 1937 to become the club's starting first baseman at age 21. He replaced Buck Jordan, who was a holdout in the spring and consequently was traded to Cincinnati.

Fletcher wasn't ready to replace Jordan offensively, but he already had developed into a fine defensive first baseman. After two years as a regular, Fletcher, still only 23, was shipped to Pittsburgh for infielder Bill Schuster and cash.

It was a terrible deal for Boston. Schuster never contributed, and Fletcher became an All-Star for the Pirates. A line-drive hitter, he led the league in on-base percentage three straight years, 1940–42, driving in a career-high 104 runs in 1940 and twice leading the league in walks. He also led the league's first basemen in fielding percentage (.996) in 1943, when he was a starter in the All-Star Game.

Fletcher spent 1948 in the minors due to a foot injury, then was picked up by the Braves for his final big league season in 1949.

Fette, Lou

Bees, Braves	W	L	Pct	G	GS	CG	ShO	IP	H	BB	SO	ERA	SV
1937	20	10	.667	35	33	23	5*	259	243	81	70	2.88	0
1938	11	13	.458	33	32	17	3	239⅔	235	79	83	3.15	1
1939	10	10	.500	27	26	11	6*	146	123	61	35	2.96	0
1940	0	5	.000	7	5	0	0	32⅓	38	18	2	5.57	0
1945	0	2	.000	5	1	0	0	11	16	7	4	5.73	0
Career	41	40	.506	107	97	51	14	688	655	246	194	3.17	1

Fletcher, Elbie

Braves, Bees	G	AB	R	H	2B	3B	HR	RBI	SB	AVG	SLG
1934	8	4	4	2	0	0	0	0	1	.500	.500
1935	39	148	12	35	7	1	1	9	1	.236	.318
1937	148	539	56	133	22	4	1	38	3	.247	.308
1938	147	529	71	144	24	7	6	48	5	.272	.378
1939	35	106	14	26	2	0	0	6	1	.245	.264
1949	122	413	57	108	19	3	11	51	1	.262	.402
Career	499	1,739	214	448	74	15	19	152	12	.258	.350

Fletcher, Elbie

Braves, Bees: 1934–35, 1937–39, 1949	**D:** March 9, 1994
First baseman	**Batted left, threw left**
Birthplace: Milton, Massachusetts	**Ht.** 6–0; **Wt.** 180
B: March 18, 1916	

Elbie Fletcher had his best seasons with Pittsburgh, but his formative years in Boston with his hometown team are particularly noteworthy because of the way he became a Brave.

Forster, Terry

Braves: 1983–85	**B:** January 14, 1952
Pitcher	**Batted left, threw left**
Birthplace: Sioux Falls, South Dakota	**Ht.** 6–3; **Wt.** 210

The advent of the TBS Superstation made national television stars out of all the Braves. But Terry Forster took his celebrity status a step further, turning excellent relief pitch-

Terry Forster

<table>
<tr><td colspan="14">Forster, Terry</td></tr>
<tr><th>Braves</th><th>W</th><th>L</th><th>Pct</th><th>G</th><th>GS</th><th>CG</th><th>ShO</th><th>IP</th><th>H</th><th>BB</th><th>SO</th><th>ERA</th><th>SV</th></tr>
<tr><td>1983</td><td>3</td><td>2</td><td>.600</td><td>56</td><td>0</td><td>0</td><td>0</td><td>79⅓</td><td>60</td><td>31</td><td>54</td><td>2.16</td><td>13</td></tr>
<tr><td>1984</td><td>2</td><td>0</td><td>1.000</td><td>25</td><td>0</td><td>0</td><td>0</td><td>26⅔</td><td>30</td><td>7</td><td>10</td><td>2.70</td><td>5</td></tr>
<tr><td>1985</td><td>2</td><td>3</td><td>.400</td><td>46</td><td>0</td><td>0</td><td>0</td><td>59⅓</td><td>49</td><td>28</td><td>37</td><td>2.28</td><td>1</td></tr>
<tr><td>Career</td><td>7</td><td>5</td><td>.583</td><td>127</td><td>0</td><td>0</td><td>0</td><td>165⅓</td><td>139</td><td>66</td><td>101</td><td>2.29</td><td>19</td></tr>
</table>

Frankhouse, Fred

Braves, Bees: 1930–35, 1939
Pitcher
Birthplace: Port Royal, Pennsylvania
B: April 9, 1904

D: August 17, 1989
Batted right, threw right
Ht. 5–11; **Wt.** 175

The 1935 Braves were a sorry lot. They lost a then-modern-record 115 games, finishing with a .248 percentage, the most pathetic in franchise history. Somehow, Fred Frankhouse managed to win 11 games that year and finish with a .423 percentage, surely one of the most notable sub-.500 seasons in history.

That wasn't Frankhouse's best year, by any means, but it stands out on his record because of the miserable circumstances he worked under that season. No other Braves pitcher won more than eight games in 1935, and only one other—Bob Smith—managed to win more than five.

A product of the Cardinals' farm system, Frankhouse began his pro career at age 16. He was an accomplished outfielder as well as an excellent pitcher in the minors.

Promoted to St. Louis late in 1927, Frankhouse attracted the attention of Bill McKechnie, who managed the Cardinals in 1928 and '29. When the Braves hired McKechnie in 1930, he brought Frankhouse with him to Boston in a midseason deal for future Hall of Famer Burleigh Grimes, who helped the Cardinals to a couple of pennants.

Frankhouse, who had good control and a sweeping curve, didn't blossom for the Braves until 1933 when he won 16 games. The next year, he won a career-high 17 (13 by the All-Star

ing and a weight problem into a guest appearance on "Late Night with David Letterman."

The talk show host referred to Forster as a "fat tub of goo" during June 1985, the last season of the left-hander's three-year stint with the Braves. Forster later was invited onto the show to defend himself.

Actually, there wasn't much defense. Forster, who was pitching in the majors at age 19, had developed a considerable weight problem by the time he used free agency to sign with the Braves in 1983.

Forster had three good years in Atlanta—when he was able to pitch. Unfortunately, he spent a lot of time fighting hamstring injuries that undoubtedly were related to the fact that he was carrying extra poundage.

In 1983 he recorded 13 saves to help the Braves in what turned out to be a failed attempt to repeat as division champs.

The hard-throwing reliever could be nearly unhittable at times, as he was during most of the first half of 1984 when he got off to a 2–0 start with a 1.09 ERA until he hurt his right hamstring June 23.

Forster signed with the White Sox out of high school in 1971 and pitched in just 10 games in the minors. In 1972 he won six and saved 29, then a club record, at the age of 20. He also was an accomplished hitter, batting .526 in 1972, the last year before the designated hitter was adopted, and he posted a .397 lifetime average. He was the top reliever in the American League in 1974, and in 1978 he was the first free agent ever signed by the Dodgers.

But Forster gained his greatest celebrity status as a Brave, more for what he did on the scales than for what he could do with a baseball.

Fred Frankhouse

break), made the National League All-Star team, finished fifth in the league in winning percentage, and led Boston in ERA.

After the 1935 season, the Braves sent Frankhouse to Brooklyn, where he pitched a seven-inning no-hitter in 1937 against Cincinnati. He also outdueled Carl Hubbell that year to break the great Giant pitcher's 24-game winning streak.

Frankhouse, Fred

Braves, Bees	W	L	Pct	G	GS	CG	ShO	IP	H	BB	SO	ERA	SV
1930	7	6	.538	27	11	3	1	110⅔	138	43	30	5.61	0
1931	8	8	.500	26	15	6	0	127⅓	125	43	50	4.03	1
1932	4	6	.400	37	6	3	0	108⅔	113	45	35	3.56	0
1933	16	15	.516	43	30	14	2	244⅔	249	77	83	3.16	2
1934	17	9	.654	37	31	13	2	233⅔	239	77	78	3.20	1
1935	11	15	.423	40	29	10	1	230⅔	278	81	64	4.76	0
1939	0	2	.000	23	0	0	0	38	37	18	12	2.61	4
Career	63	61	.508	233	122	49	6	1,093⅔	1,179	384	353	3.87	8

Gant, Ron

Braves: 1987–93
Outfielder, second baseman, third baseman
Birthplace: Victoria, Texas

B: March 2, 1965
Bats right, throws right
Ht. 6–0; **Wt.** 200

Ron Gant was one of the biggest reasons for the Braves' success in 1991–93, but his Atlanta career crashed and burned February 3, 1994, when he broke his right leg in two places in an off-road motorcycle accident.

Gant averaged 28 home runs, 101 RBIs, and 31 steals per season to help the Braves win back-to-back National League pennants in 1991–92 and another division title in '93. He then signed a $5.5-million contract for 1994, the largest one-year deal in history, making him the highest-paid player on the team.

However, the motorbike accident forced the Braves to release him March 15 with 30 days' termination pay of $901,000. The length of Gant's recovery period was in doubt, as was his ability to make a complete comeback. If the team had kept him a day longer, it would have had to pay his full salary whether he contributed that season or not. An addi-

Ron Gant

tional factor in the decision was that Gant would have become eligible for free agency at the end of the season.

Though Gant often fell into prolonged slumps and didn't hit well in postseason play, his contributions to the franchise's remarkable rise in the early '90s cannot be overstated. He had more home runs and RBIs than any other Brave from 1991 to 1993. He was at his best late in 1993 when Atlanta rallied against tremendous odds to overtake San Francisco in the NL West. His accomplishments that year earned him fifth place in the league MVP voting.

But success didn't come easily to the well-conditioned bodybuilder, who pound for pound probably was as strong as anyone in baseball. Originally an infielder, Gant debuted in Atlanta in late 1987 after a strong season at Double-A. He hit his first home run off Nolan Ryan. The next year, he opened at Richmond but earned a quick promotion to Atlanta. He proved himself ready. As the Braves' regular second baseman, he led all major league rookies in home runs (19), RBIs (60), runs (85), extra-base hits (55), and triples (8).

In the off-season, however, it seemed Gant forgot how to hit. Either that, or the switch to third base in 1989 completely unnerved him. In his first 60 games, he batted just .172 and made 16 errors. The Braves responded by sending him all the way back to Class-A Sumter on June 21 and told him to learn to play the outfield. It was a discouraging turn of events for someone who finished fourth for NL Rookie of the Year a few months earlier, but Gant accepted the challenge. After two weeks at Sumter, he was bumped up to Richmond on July 4 and finally to Atlanta on September 6. He returned like a man on a mission.

As the Braves' regular center fielder in 1990, Gant earned recognition as Comeback Player of the Year from both *Sports Illustrated* and *USA Today* when he became just the 13th man in history to join the 30 home runs–30 steals club.

In 1991, Gant proved he was no fluke. He joined Willie Mays and Bobby Bonds as the only three players to post back-to-back 30–30 seasons. His performance, which included a major-league-high 21 game-winning hits, helped spur Atlanta to its shocking National League pennant. For his work, he was awarded a sixth-place finish in the MVP voting and was named to the Silver Slugger team as one of the three best offensive outfielders in the NL.

Gant set a National League Championship Series record with seven stolen bases against Pittsburgh in 1991.

In 1992, Gant moved to left field. He started well and made the NL All-Star team for the first time in his career. However, he adopted a new batting style in which he sacrificed power in an attempt to raise his batting average. It eventually wound up confusing him and sent him spiraling into a deep slump at midseason. From June 8 to September 9, Gant batted only .199 in 72 games. At one point, he went 30 games without a home run. Yet he still managed to become the first player in franchise history to have three straight seasons with 30 steals and 80 RBIs and joined Hank Aaron, Eddie Mathews, Wally Berger, and Dale Murphy as the only Braves since 1900 to have three consecutive 80-RBI seasons.

Despite two home runs, Gant was unimpressive at the plate (.182) in the playoffs against Pittsburgh. Cox benched him in the World Series, where he got only eight at bats and one hit. With a steal in the NLCS and two in the Series, though, he set a postseason record by going 11-for-11 over two years.

Gant returned to his pull-hitting, power style in 1993 and

assembled the best numbers of his career in several categories, including home runs (36) and RBIs (117). Of his 36 homers, 18 gave the Braves the lead or victory. With the Braves needing to win nearly every day down the stretch, he had 25 RBIs in his last 20 games. However, another subpar playoff performance followed. He batted only .185 in the loss to the Phillies, and his postseason stolen base streak was stopped at 11 by Darren Daulton.

Seldom does a player come along with the unique combination of power and speed Gant possesses. However, he often said he didn't feel he received the respect he deserved in Atlanta. That's probably true, because of the streaky nature of his hitting and his unreliability in the postseason.

Perhaps Gant could have overcome that lack of respect in 1994, but his motorbike accident and the economics of the modern game denied him the opportunity. In late 1994 he signed with the Cincinnati Reds. He didn't play in any games in '94 but came back strong in '95.

Gant, Ron

Braves	G	AB	R	H	2B	3B	HR	RBI	SB	AVG	SLG
1987	21	83	9	22	4	0	2	9	4	.265	.386
1988	146	563	85	146	28	8	19	60	19	.259	.439
1989	75	260	26	46	8	3	9	25	9	.177	.335
1990	152	575	107	174	34	3	32	84	33	.303	.539
1991	154	561	101	141	35	3	32	105	34	.251	.496
1992	153	544	74	141	22	6	17	80	32	.259	.415
1993	157	606	113	166	27	4	36	117	26	.274	.510
Career	858	3,192	515	836	158	27	147	480	157	.262	.466

Garber, Gene

Braves: 1978–87
Pitcher
Birthplace: Lancaster, Pennsylvania

B: November 13, 1947
Batted right, threw right
Ht. 5–10; **Wt.** 175

More often than not, the Braves have found themselves searching for an effective closer since moving to Atlanta in 1966. Oh, there have been several that have filled the role successfully for a few weeks or months or even a year or two, relief aces such as Cecil Upshaw, Rick Camp, Alejandro Pena, and Mike Stanton.

But no other Brave has come close to being as good at closing games over an extended period as Gene Garber during his 10 years in Atlanta. The proof is in the record book. Garber recorded 141 saves in an Atlanta uniform. That's almost twice as many as runner-up Upshaw, who had 78.

A right-hander with a sidearm delivery who actually turned his back completely on the hitter before spinning forward in his motion, Garber looked like a farmer going to work when he walked determinedly from the bullpen to the mound. That's probably because he was raised on a dairy farm in eastern Pennsylvania, a business he returned to after retiring from baseball.

Always reticent, Garber was particularly uncommunicative when he learned he'd been traded to the Braves by the Phillies in mid-1978 in exchange for pitcher Dick Ruthven. Not only was he leaving a team he helped pitch to the playoffs the previous two seasons and going to a last-place club, but he also had to depart the area of the country he'd called home his entire life.

Gene Garber

But the bearded reliever didn't let his displeasure with the deal upset his pitching. He saved 22 games over the final three and a half months for the moribund '78 Braves, who still finished last with a 69–93 record. On August 1 of that year, Garber etched a place in the history books by striking out Pete Rose, ending Rose's NL-record hitting streak at 44 games.

"He pitched like it was the seventh game of the World Series," complained Rose, who didn't like the fact that Garber nibbled at the plate rather than challenging him.

"I don't know what it's like to pitch in the seventh game of the World Series," responded Garber. "He gets paid to get hits. I get paid to get outs."

Garber pitched well for bad Braves teams and also for good ones. In 1982, he saved a club-record 30 games, second in the league, to help Atlanta win the National League West. Manager Joe Torre felt so strongly about his reliever's contributions that he said Garber deserved consideration for MVP. The right-hander did tie for seventh in the Cy Young voting and enabled the Braves to win the award for the NL's best bullpen.

In all, Garber led the team in saves four times before he was traded to Kansas City in 1987. He also had his bad times in Atlanta, losing 16 games, then a major league record for a reliever, in 1979, when he also was third in the NL with 25 saves.

Garber, Gene

Braves	W	L	Pct	G	GS	CG	ShO	IP	H	BB	SO	ERA	SV
1978	4	4	.500	43	0	0	0	78⅓	58	13	61	2.53	22
1979	6	16	.273	68	0	0	0	106	121	24	56	4.33	25
1980	5	5	.500	68	0	0	0	82⅓	95	24	51	3.83	7
1981	4	6	.400	35	0	0	0	58⅓	49	20	34	2.61	2
1982	8	10	.444	69	0	0	0	119⅓	100	32	68	2.34	30
1983	4	5	.444	43	0	0	0	60⅔	72	23	45	4.60	9
1984	3	6	.333	62	0	0	0	106	103	24	55	3.06	11
1985	6	6	.500	59	0	0	0	97⅓	98	25	66	3.61	1
1986	5	5	.500	61	0	0	0	78	76	20	56	2.54	24
1987	8	10	.444	49	0	0	0	69⅓	87	28	48	4.41	10
Career	53	73	.421	557	0	0	0	856	859	233	540	3.34	141

Garr, Ralph

Braves: 1968–75
Left fielder
Birthplace: Monroe, Louisiana

B: December 12, 1945
Batted left, threw right
Ht. 5–11; **Wt.** 197

With the nickname "Roadrunner" and a composite batting average of .317 in eight years with Atlanta, Ralph Garr rates as one of the most colorful and talented men ever to wear a Braves uniform.

Few players have burst onto the major league scene the way Garr did in 1971. The speedy, free-swinging outfielder smacked 219 hits and batted .343. Both figures ranked second in the National League to former Brave Joe Torre, who put together an MVP season with St. Louis. The 219 hits is an Atlanta record and represents the fourth-highest total in franchise history. Garr also set a franchise record with 180 singles that year.

Because he spent brief periods with the club the previous three seasons when called up from the minors, Garr wasn't eligible for rookie honors. Yet his first full season in the majors was one of the finest in history and gave Atlanta fans a good taste of what Garr would accomplish in his career.

From 1968 to 1975, Garr batted a composite .317, an Atlanta record he shares with Rico Carty. More significantly, though, in the decade of the 1970s, he ranked as the number-two hitter in baseball with a .314 average. Among hitters with at least 3,000 at bats, only Hall of Famer Rod Carew (.344) posted a higher average for the decade.

The Braves' regular left fielder from 1971 to 1975, Garr compiled three 200-hit seasons, a feat only Hank Aaron equaled in franchise history. He finished second in the National League batting race in '71 and '72 before he finally won it in 1974 with a lusty .353 average—32 points ahead of runner-up Al Oliver of Pittsburgh. His 668 at bats in 1973 also represent a franchise record.

Garr didn't see many pitches he didn't like, so he seldom walked. He came to the plate ready to swing, and he usually made contact, too. There was never any question about Garr's ability to hit. The Braves drafted him out of Grambling State University where he was the NAIA batting champ in 1967 with a .568 average.

Professional pitching didn't faze him much. At Triple-A Richmond in 1969 and '70, he led the International League in hitting both seasons. His .389 average in 1970 was a modern league record.

Not known for his defense, Garr was pretty much limited to left field. His best year was 1974 when he made the NL All-Star team. Besides leading the league in hitting, he also led

in triples (17) and hits (214) and became the first player since 1930 to have 200 hits by the end of August.

With his "Roadrunner" speed, Garr probably was capable of being an accomplished stolen base artist. In fact, the first base he stole in the majors was home. However, the Braves of the early 1970s were a power-laden unit with players such as Hank Aaron, Darrell Evans, Dave Johnson, Earl Williams, and Dusty Baker capable of hitting the ball out of the park at any time. Therefore, Garr's job often was to get on base and then trot around on a home run. He stole a career-high 35 bases in '73, but that total ranked only sixth in the league. In 1971 he was third in the NL with 30 steals.

In 1975, Garr's average tumbled 75 points to .278. The Braves suffered through a miserable season, finishing fifth with a 67–94 record. In the off-season, the team was sold to Ted Turner, and with the club seeking new direction, Garr was put on the trading block. He and Larvell Blanks were sent to the Chicago White Sox for outfielder Ken Henderson, right-hander Dick Ruthven, and minor leaguer Danny Osborn.

Garr is now a scout for the Braves in Texas.

Garr, Ralph

Braves	G	AB	R	H	2B	3B	HR	RBI	SB	AVG	SLG
1968	11	7	3	2	0	0	0	0	1	.286	.286
1969	22	27	6	6	1	0	0	2	1	.222	.259
1970	37	96	18	27	3	0	0	8	5	.281	.313
1971	154	639	101	219	24	6	9	44	30	.343	.441
1972	134	554	87	180	22	0	12	53	25	.325	.430
1973	148	668	94	200	32	6	11	55	35	.299	.415
1974	143	606	87	214*	24	17*	11	54	26	.353*	.503
1975	151	625	74	174	26	11*	6	31	14	.278	.384
Career	800	3,222	470	1,022	132	40	49	247	137	.317	.429

Genewich, Joe

Braves: 1922–28
Pitcher
Birthplace: Elmira, New York
B: January 15, 1897

D: December 21, 1985
Batted right, threw right
Ht. 6–0; **Wt.** 174

Bob Horner created much ado in 1978 when he came straight off the campus of Arizona State to start his pro career at the major league level. Similar excitement surrounded the 1923 Braves owing to the presence of a pitcher named Joe Genewich. But instead of debuting in the majors right out of college, Genewich went directly from pitching for $5 a game on the Elmira, New York, sandlots to pitching for the Braves.

The right-hander was 25 years old when Boston signed him in 1922, but he had no minor league or college experience. He'd served a nine-month tour in the Navy during World War I and returned home to pitch weekend games for mill teams. A no-hitter and 43 consecutive scoreless innings attracted big league scouts.

Genewich signed with the Braves in time to appear in only six games in 1922. But when the following season began, he was a full-fledged member of Boston's starting rotation. It didn't take long for him to make his presence felt. He beat the defending World Series champion New York Giants twice within eight days in April. In fact, two of the Giants' first three losses of the year were to Genewich.

On a terrible team that lost 100 games, Genewich finished

Ralph Garr

Joe Genewich

Tom Glavine

only a game under .500 (13–14) and was third in the league in fewest walks per nine innings (1.82). He was considered the best young pitcher in the game.

That winter the *New York World* wrote, "The son of a Polish mill worker at Elmira becomes, in six short months, the most prominent, the most talked of of all of the ball players in the United States, possibly excepting Babe Ruth and the other men on the two teams which competed for the championship of the world."

It was pretty heady stuff, to say the least. However, Genewich never developed into the pitcher everyone thought he would be after his rookie performance. Part of the reason, of course, was the Braves, who never even made a serious run at .500 during his five-plus seasons with them.

McGraw, thinking all Genewich needed was a better team behind him, acquired him from Boston in June 1928 in exchange for four players, including pitcher Ben Cantwell. And for the remainder of that season, it looked as if McGraw had gotten a steal. Genewich won 11 of 15 decisions and posted a 3.18 ERA, the best of his career, pitching the Giants to within two games of the pennant.

But he pitched just two more seasons, winning a total of but five games.

Genewich, Joe

Braves	W	L	Pct	G	GS	CG	ShO	IP	H	BB	SO	ERA	SV
1922	0	2	.000	6	2	1	0	23	29	11	4	7.04	0
1923	13	14	.481	43	24	12	1	227⅓	272	46	54	3.72	1
1924	10	19	.345	34	27	11	2	200⅓	258	65	43	5.21	1
1925	12	10	.545	34	21	10	0	169	185	41	34	3.99	0
1926	8	16	.333	37	26	12	2	216	239	63	59	3.88	2
1927	11	8	.579	40	19	7	0	181	199	54	38	3.83	1
1928	3	7	.300	13	11	4	0	80⅔	88	18	15	4.13	0
Career	57	76	.429	207	130	57	5	1,097⅓	1,270	298	247	4.18	5

Glavine, Tom

Braves: 1987–ㅤㅤㅤㅤ**B:** March 25, 1966
Pitcherㅤㅤㅤㅤㅤㅤㅤㅤ**Bats left, throws left**
Birthplace: Concord, Massachusettsㅤ**Ht.** 6–1; **Wt.** 185

The Braves had long ago departed New England, passed through Milwaukee, and were about to settle in Atlanta when

Tom Glavine entered the world in the spring of 1966. But a core of Braves fans remained in the franchise's original home of Boston. One of those fans who remembered the days of "Spahn and Sain and pray for rain," was Glavine's father, Fred.

The elder Glavine, a contractor, had been a big fan of Warren Spahn, the stylish Braves pitcher who became the winningest left-hander of all time. When Fred Glavine saw his son's interest in sports and his left-handed tendencies, his thoughts naturally drifted to the prospect of producing another classic left-hander right where the great Spahn had begun his big league career. Though he might have dreamt it, Fred Glavine couldn't possibly have thought his young son would someday become the greatest Braves left-hander since Spahn.

"He told me a lot about Spahn," Tom said of his father's teachings. "He even tried to show me the high leg kick."

Glavine didn't learn the big kick, a Spahn trademark, and he's a long way from climbing into Spahn's class. Yet with a Braves uniform on his back, a Cy Young Award in his trophy case, and three straight 20-win seasons to his credit from 1991 to 1993, Glavine certainly was displaying more Spahn-like tendencies than any other lefty who'd come through the organization since the master himself.

Raised in the Boston suburb of Billerica, Glavine was a superb high school athlete who was drafted by two professional sports teams. The Braves took him in the second round in 1984, and the Los Angeles Kings of the National Hockey League picked him in the fourth round. Fortunately for the Braves, he chose a baseball career.

Glavine climbed quickly through the Braves farm system, spending just two full years in the minors before debuting in the majors in late 1987 at age 21. One of a group of pitchers heralded as the Braves' "Young Guns," Glavine was thrown to the wolves in 1988 as a regular member of the Atlanta rotation. Inexperienced and with a horrible team behind him, he struggled, winning just seven of 24 decisions. But he showed excellent poise and learned from the experience.

In 1989, Glavine managed to finish six games over .500 for a team that was 34 games under .500. He pitched four shutouts, tying Mark Langston for the most by a left-hander in the majors. Four shutouts also represented the most by a Brave since Phil Niekro in 1978 and the most by a Braves lefty since Spahn in 1963.

Statistically, Glavine slid back a little in 1990, yet he still managed to win in double figures (10) for a last-place team and had a winning percentage considerably better than the club's. He also built his arm strength, pitching a career-high number of innings.

In 1991 it all came together for Glavine and the Braves. After three straight seasons in last place, Atlanta climbed to the top of the National League West in one fell swoop. And no one played a bigger role in the turnaround than Glavine.

With the addition of a devastating change-up to his repertoire, the 25-year-old left-hander emerged as one of the game's best pitchers. Glavine became the first Braves 20-game winner since Phil Niekro in 1979 and won more games than any Braves left-hander since Spahn in 1963. He also became the first Atlanta pitcher—and the only Brave besides Spahn in 1957—to win the Cy Young Award.

Glavine tied for the league lead in complete games (9) and finished second in innings and third in strikeouts, ERA (2.55), and opponents' batting average (.222). He was the National League's starting pitcher in the All-Star Game and was named to the Silver Slugger team as the best-hitting pitcher in the league.

In the playoffs against Pittsburgh, Glavine was charged with losses in Games 1 and 5, even though he pitched well, especially in Game 5 when he lost, 1–0. He split two World Series decisions against Minnesota, winning Game 5, 14–5.

The 1992 season was nearly a carbon copy of 1991 for Glavine, except that he finished second in the Cy Young voting to the Cubs' Greg Maddux. He became the only pitcher in the majors to win 20 games each of the previous two seasons and the first Brave to post back-to-back 20-win seasons since you-know-who—Spahn.

From May 27 to August 19, Glavine put together a 13-game winning streak (16 starts), setting a modern Braves record and matching the all-time franchise record of Charlie Buffinton in 1884. Through August 19, Glavine was 19–3, but a cracked rib slowed his pace considerably the rest of the way.

Glavine also tied for the league lead with a career-high five shutouts and started the All-Star Game for the second straight year. Though he was roughed up by the American League and was charged with the loss, he was the first NL pitcher to start All-Star games in consecutive years since Robin Roberts in 1954 and '55.

In the National League Championship Series, Glavine lost Games 3 and 6. But he rebounded in the World Series, beating Toronto's Jack Morris, 3–1, in Game 1 before losing, 2–1, in Game 4. He worked complete games both times, becoming the first left-hander to post two complete games in the same Series since Mickey Lolich in 1968.

Glavine's Spahn-like tendencies continued in 1993 when he became the first National League pitcher to record three straight 20-victory seasons since Ferguson Jenkins in 1967 through 1972. His 22 wins tied for the league lead, yet he slipped to third in the Cy Young voting behind teammate Maddux and San Francisco's Bill Swift.

Though the Braves failed to win their third straight National League pennant, Glavine picked up his first NLCS victory by beating Philadelphia, 9–4, in Game 3.

Glavine was behind his normal pace in 1994 but was still within reach of a fourth straight 20-win season when the players' strike ended the season August 11 with his victory total at 13.

Glavine, Tom

Braves	W	L	Pct	G	GS	CG	ShO	IP	H	BB	SO	ERA	SV
1987	2	4	.333	9	9	0	0	50⅓	55	33	20	5.54	0
1988	7	17*	.292	34	34	1	0	195⅓	201	63	84	4.56	0
1989	14	8	.636	29	29	6	4	186	172	40	90	3.68	0
1990	10	12	.455	33	33	1	0	214⅓	232	78	129	4.28	0
1991	20*	11	.645	34	34	9*	1	246⅔	201	69	192	2.55	0
1992	20*	8	.714	33	33	7	5*	225	197	70	129	2.76	0
1993	22*	6	.786	36	36*	4	2	239⅓	236	90	120	3.20	0
1994	13	9	.591	25	25	2	0	165⅓	173	70	140	3.97	0
Career	108	75	.590	233	233	30	12	1,522⅓	1,467	513	904	3.58	0

Gonzalez, Tony

Braves: 1969–70	**B:** August 28, 1936
Outfielder	**Batted left, threw right**
Birthplace: Central Cunagua, Cuba	**Ht.** 5–9; **Wt.** 170

Tony Gonzalez was one of the most accomplished defensive outfielders in National League history, but his eighth-inning error in Game 1 of the 1969 NL playoffs was one of the more costly mistakes in Braves postseason history.

The Braves were favored to beat the Mets in the first championship series in National League history, but little did the oddsmakers realize that Atlanta was up against a true team of destiny. Luman Harris's club came from behind twice to take a 5–4 lead over the Mets through seven innings of Game 1 in Atlanta. But in the eighth, New York scored five times, thanks in large part to sloppy defense by the Braves.

Gonzalez contributed to the Braves' lead with a home run off Tom Seaver, but he also committed the error that put the

Tony Gonzalez

game out of reach. With two outs and the bases loaded in the eighth, Gonzalez let J. C. Martin's single get past him in center field, clearing the bases. The Braves never recovered, losing the game, 9–5, and getting swept in the best-of-five playoff.

Yet Gonzalez still had a productive three games against the Mets, hitting .357 to tie Hank Aaron for the best average on the club. And, if not for his regular-season contributions, Atlanta quite likely wouldn't have beaten the Giants by three games in the NL West.

Acquired on June 12 from San Diego in exchange for three players of no consequence, Gonzalez batted .294 with 10 home runs and 50 RBIs in just 89 games. He tripled in his first at bat for the Braves and homered twice in his first game in Atlanta. One of his home runs was a grand slam against his former Padres teammates.

Gonzalez played regularly for the Braves in 1970 until California purchased him August 31 for what proved to be a futile run at the AL West title (despite Gonzalez's .304 hitting).

The Cuban-born outfielder's best years were with the Phillies. In 1967 he hit .339, finishing second to Roberto Clemente for the NL batting title.

In 1962, '64, and '67, he led NL outfielders in defensive percentage. In '62, he fielded a perfect 1.000, the first regular center fielder ever to compile an errorless season. He once played 205 consecutive errorless games, a major league record since surpassed.

Star Sid Gordon, a hard-hitting outfielder/third baseman who was extremely popular in New York.

A Brooklyn native, Gordon wasted no time making himself at home in Boston. He finished fourth in the league in slugging percentage (.557) in his first season as a Brave, setting a franchise record that still stands. Though he played in just 134 games, Gordon belted four grand slams, something no other Brave has ever accomplished. His presence played a big role in the team's quick climb back to respectability, too.

In 1951, Gordon led the Braves in home runs (29) and RBIs, tying for second in the league with 109.

Gordon, who had to pay his own expenses just to get a tryout with the Giants back in 1938, had a short but very productive career with the Braves. He already was 32 years old when Boston obtained him. The son of a Russian immigrant, he made two All-Star teams and led National League third basemen in fielding in 1948.

He was primarily a left fielder for the Braves, and a good one, leading the league with a .996 defensive percentage in 1952. He hit 25 or more home runs in three of his four years with the Braves and had two 100-RBI seasons and one .300 campaign.

After the 1953 season, the Braves' first in Milwaukee, they packaged Gordon with five other players, including Max Surkont and Sam Jethroe, to obtain second baseman Danny O'Connell from Pittsburgh.

Gonzalez, Tony

Braves	G	AB	R	H	2B	3B	HR	RBI	SB	AVG	SLG
1969	89	320	51	94	15	2	10	50	3	.294	.447
1970	123	430	57	114	18	2	7	55	3	.265	.365
Career	212	750	108	208	33	4	17	105	6	.277	.400

Gordon, Sid

Braves	G	AB	R	H	2B	3B	HR	RBI	SB	AVG	SLG
1950	134	481	78	146	33	4	27	103	2	.304	.557
1951	150	550	96	158	28	1	29	109	2	.287	.500
1952	144	522	69	151	22	2	25	75	0	.289	.483
1953	140	464	67	127	22	4	19	75	1	.274	.461
Career	568	2,017	310	582	105	11	100	362	5	.289	.500

Gordon, Sid

Braves: 1950–53
Outfielder, third baseman
Birthplace: Brooklyn, New York
B: August 13, 1917

D: June 17, 1975
Batted right, threw right
Ht. 5–10; **Wt.** 185

After the Braves won the National League pennant in 1948, they fell apart in 1949, finishing four games under .500 and 22 games out of first. Changes were imminent, and the biggest was the purge of the middle infield. Shortstop Al Dark and second baseman Eddie Stanky were sent to the Giants for four players, the most prominent of which was All-

Sid Gordon

Gowdy, Hank

Rustlers, Braves: 1911–23, 1929–30
Catcher
Birthplace: Columbus, Ohio
B: August 24, 1889

D: August 1, 1966
Ht. 6–2, **Wt.** 182
Batted right, threw right

The World Series has a way of creating some unusual heroes, and in 1914 it was light-hitting Hank Gowdy who emerged as the offensive star of the "Miracle" Braves' October sweep of the highly favored Philadelphia Athletics.

Gowdy, a 25-year-old catcher who moved into a starting role for the first time that year, batted .243 with three home runs and 46 RBIs during the regular season. But in the Series, Connie Mack's pitching staff found him nearly unstoppable. Gowdy batted .545, the highest on either team, and hit the only home run of the Series. Of his six hits, five were for extra bases. He also drew five walks in the four games.

Gowdy was the Braves' starting catcher only from 1914 through 1916, but he played with the club in all but three of his 17 seasons in the majors. He caught no-hitters by George Davis in 1914 and Tom Hughes in 1916.

In 1917, Gowdy became the first major leaguer to enlist for service in World War I, and he saw considerable action in France. He returned to the Braves in 1919 but never was a regular catcher again. A midseason trade to New York in

Hank Gowdy

1923 enabled him to play in two more World Series, but with much less success than he enjoyed in 1914.

Gowdy, Hank

Rustlers, Braves	G	AB	R	H	2B	3B	HR	RBI	SB	AVG	SLG
1911	29	97	9	28	4	2	0	16	2	.289	.371
1912	44	96	16	26	6	1	3	10	3	.271	.448
1913	3	5	0	3	1	0	0	2	0	.600	.800
1914	128	366	42	89	17	6	3	46	14	.243	.347
1915	118	316	27	78	15	3	2	30	10	.247	.332
1916	118	349	32	88	14	1	1	34	8	.252	.307
1917	49	154	12	33	7	0	0	14	2	.214	.260
1919	78	219	18	61	8	1	1	22	5	.279	.338
1920	80	214	14	52	11	2	0	18	6	.243	.313
1921	64	164	17	49	7	2	2	17	2	.299	.402
1922	92	221	23	70	11	1	1	27	2	.317	.389
1923	23	48	5	6	1	1	0	5	1	.125	.188
1929	10	16	1	7	0	0	0	3	0	.438	.438
1930	16	25	0	5	1	0	0	2	0	.200	.240
Career	852	2,290	216	595	103	20	13	246	55	.260	.338

Hall, Albert

Braves: 1981–88
Outfielder
Birthplace: Birmingham, Alabama

B: March 7, 1958
Batted both, threw right
Ht. 5–11; **Wt.** 158

Hitting for the cycle is one of the rarest and least recognized individual accomplishments in baseball. It actually happens less frequently than a no-hitter, yet it receives much less publicity on the rare occasions when a player collects a single, double, triple and home run in the same game.

Few players have the speed and offensive capability to hit for the cycle. Only four men in Braves history have ever done so—and most Braves fans would be hard pressed to name one. That's because the feat has taken place just once since 1910, and the player who did it isn't exactly one of the franchise's all-time greats.

On September 23, 1987, Albert Hall hit for the cycle against Houston, and he did it the hard way—saving the triple for his last at bat. Hall was the first Brave to accomplish this rare feat since another little-known outfielder, Bill Collins, did so as a rookie for Boston in 1910. The only other Braves to hit for the cycle were John Bates (1907) and Duff Cooley (1904).

Albert Hall

Hall was at his best in 1987, appearing in a career-high 92 games and batting a career-best .284. What makes his cycle especially unusual is that he had only five home runs and eight triples in his entire nine-year career. He was strictly a singles/speed player. A four-time minor league base-stealing champ, he stole 33 bases in 1987, the first Atlanta Brave ever to steal 30 or more while playing in fewer than 100 games.

Ironically, hitting for the cycle was nothing new for Hall. He also did it in 1982 while playing for Triple-A Richmond.

Hall, Albert

Braves	G	AB	R	H	2B	3B	HR	RBI	SB	AVG	SLG
1981	6	2	1	0	0	0	0	0	0	.000	.000
1982	5	0	1	0	0	0	0	0	0	—	—
1983	10	8	2	0	0	0	0	0	1	.000	.000
1984	87	142	25	37	6	1	1	9	6	.261	.338
1985	54	47	5	7	0	1	0	3	1	.149	.191
1986	16	50	6	12	2	0	0	1	8	.240	.280
1987	92	292	54	83	20	4	3	24	33	.284	.411
1988	85	231	27	57	7	1	1	15	15	.247	.299
Career	355	772	121	196	35	7	5	52	64	.254	.337

Hamilton, Billy

Beaneaters: 1896–1901
Center fielder
Birthplace: Newark, New Jersey
B: February 16, 1866

D: December 16, 1940
Batted left, threw right
Ht. 5–6; **Wt.** 165

Because of the differences in baseball today compared to its early years, it's impossible to accurately compare the achievements of players in the modern and pre-1900 eras. But it's reasonably safe to say that Billy Hamilton would be a star now, just as he was in the 1890s when he set base-stealing

Billy Hamilton

Hamilton, Billy

Beaneaters	G	AB	R	H	2B	3B	HR	RBI	SB	AVG	SLG
1896	131	523	152	191	24	9	3	52	83	.365	.463
1897	127	507	152*	174	17	5	3	61	66	.343	.414
1898	110	417	110	154	16	5	3	50	54	.369	.453
1899	84	297	63	92	7	1	1	33	19	.310	.350
1900	136	520	103	173	20	5	1	47	32	.333	.396
1901	102	348	71	100	11	2	3	38	20	.287	.356
Career	690	2,612	651	884	95	27	14	281	274	.338	.412

Hazle, Bob

Braves: 1957–58
Outfielder
Birthplace: Laurens, South Carolina
B: December 9, 1930

D: April 25, 1992
Batted left, threw right
Ht. 6–0; **Wt.** 190

records that stood until Lou Brock and Rickey Henderson came along.

Hamilton, a Hall of Famer known as "Slidin' Billy," is the only player in history to accumulate more lifetime runs scored (1,690) than games played (1,591). Though rules for scoring a stolen base were more liberal in his day, Hamilton held both the career (937) and season (115 in 1891) stolen-base records until they were broken by Brock and then Henderson.

In 1991, Otis Nixon stole 72 bases, setting the modern Braves record. However, he was still 11 shy of the 83 Hamilton swiped in 1896, his first season with the Beaneaters. Though Hamilton didn't join Boston until he was 30 years old and played only six years with the franchise, he also holds the team's career record for steals with 274. Interestingly, he's also the Phillies career leader in steals (508).

Hamilton was a great deal like Nixon as a player with the additional advantage of being a better hitter for average than Nixon. "Slidin' Billy" was an excellent defensive center fielder, ideal leadoff man, and a career .344 hitter who won two batting titles early in his career with Philadelphia. He also led the league in hits four times, including his last two seasons with the Phillies, for whom he had his greatest years. The only reason he was traded to Boston in 1896 was that Phillies ownership was upset because Hamilton wanted a modest raise.

He was a major contributor to Boston's pennants in 1897 and '98, his second and third seasons with the club. In '97 he led the league in walks and runs and was third in steals. The next year he led the league in on-base percentage and was second in batting average and steals, third in walks, and fifth in slugging percentage. That was Hamilton's last really big season, though he continued to play well until he retired from the majors three years later.

The Phillies probably regretted for years that they let him get away because of a disagreement over a few dollars, especially considering that they only got Billy Nash, a fading third baseman, in return.

Hamilton's .344 lifetime average is tied for sixth all-time with Ted Williams and Tris Speaker. He still holds major league records for runs scored in a season, 192 in 1894, and most consecutive games scoring at least one run (24 in 1894). He holds National League records for most years scoring 150 or more runs (four) and most combined hits and walks in a season (346 in 1894). He once put together a 36-game hitting streak, fifth longest in NL history.

The 1957 Milwaukee Braves had a bevy of superstars that included four future Hall of Famers, but if not for an unknown outfielder named Bob Hazle, they might not have won the National League pennant.

The Braves' pennant chances that year were weakened by several injuries, one of the most significant coming July 11 when center fielder Billy Bruton sprained knee ligaments, forcing him to miss the rest of the season.

One of the players manager Fred Haney called on to plug the outfield gap was minor leaguer Hazle, whose previous major league experience amounted to 13 at bats with Cincinnati in 1955. Knee and ankle problems had all but ended Hazle's career, but a chiropractor pieced him together well enough so that he could continue playing.

Obtained with Corky Valentine in April 1956 for George Crowe, Hazle was summoned from the minors and made his first start for the Braves on July 31, 1957. He had a sixth-inning RBI double in a 4–2 victory against Pittsburgh. Little

Bob Hazle

did anyone know just what that double would lead to over the ensuing two months.

In his first nine games, Hazle had a four-hit game and three three-hit games. At the same time, the Braves were in the midst of winning 17 of 19 and 24 of 29. Hazle batted .403 over the final two months with seven homers and 27 RBIs, earning the nickname "Hurricane" by storming through the league. With that added boost, the Braves went on to win the pennant by eight games over St. Louis.

Milwaukee won the World Series, but Hazle returned to earth, hitting just .154 in four games.

In '58, Hazle got off to a poor start. He was hitting well below .200 on May 7 when he was beaned by Larry Jackson of St. Louis. The Braves outfielder had to be carried off the field on a stretcher and was diagnosed with a concussion. He returned in a few days, but on May 24, with his average at .179, he was sold to Detroit. He batted just 58 times for the Tigers that year, mainly as a pinch hitter, and never played again in the majors.

Hazle, Bob

Braves	G	AB	R	H	2B	3B	HR	RBI	SB	AVG	SLG
1957	41	134	26	54	12	0	7	27	1	.403	.649
1958	20	56	6	10	0	0	0	5	0	.179	.179
Career	61	190	32	64	12	0	7	32	1	.337	.511

Holmes, Tommy

Braves: 1942–51	**B:** March 29, 1917
Outfielder	**Batted left, threw left**
Birthplace: Brooklyn, New York	**Ht.** 5–10; **Wt.** 180

When Pete Rose hit in his 38th straight game in 1978 against the Mets to set the modern National League record, a small, trim man in his 60s emerged from behind home plate at Shea Stadium to congratulate him. The man, the Mets' director of community relations, was Tommy Holmes, whose record Rose had just broken.

In 1945, Holmes excited Boston and the entire baseball world, much as Rose did in 1978, with his 37-game hitting streak that broke Rogers Hornsby's modern record of 33 games.

One of the most popular men ever to wear a Braves uniform, Holmes reached near godlike status when he was at his peak in Boston. His name is still prominent in the club's record book, though his deeds have otherwise been swept undercover by the effects of two franchise shifts.

Tommy Holmes

Holmes was a product of the New York Yankees farm system, but he never played a game for that team at the big league level. It certainly wasn't a lack of production that kept him in the minors, though. In five minor league seasons, he hit over .300 five times, setting records and making all-star teams. However, the Yankees were laden with talent, and Holmes did not possess the power that the Bronx Bombers liked in their outfield.

At spring training in 1941, Yankees manager Joe McCarthy told Holmes that with Joe DiMaggio, Tommy Henrich, and Charlie Keller established in the outfield, he would sit on the bench if he stayed in New York. McCarthy told him to go back to the minors, and if the Yankees still couldn't use him in 1942, they'd trade him.

To the Braves' good fortune, that's what happened. They got Holmes from the Yankees for first baseman Buddy Hassett and outfielder Gene Moore, both of whom were at the end of mediocre careers.

Holmes, at age 25, got two hits in his first big league game and established himself immediately with the lackluster Braves. He increased his hit total in each of his first four seasons, and by 1944, his third year, he was among the league's best hitters. He finished third in the league in hits, doubles, and total bases that year.

Then, in 1945, he enjoyed a landmark season, putting together the record hitting streak en route to leading the league in hits (224), doubles, total bases, home runs, and slugging percentage. He was second in RBIs (117) and missed the batting title (.352) by three points to Phil Cavarretta.

Normally a line-drive hitter who didn't produce many home runs, Holmes took advantage of a shortened porch in right field at Braves Field to hit a career-high 28 homers that season. He also led National League regulars in fewest strikeouts, the first and only time in modern history a home run king ever led in that department, too.

Holmes' hitting streak began June 6 in an unusual manner, with the Braves winning four games—a twilight doubleheader followed by an afternoon doubleheader—within 24 hours against the Phillies. He had 10 hits in the four games.

If Holmes felt any pressure from the streak, he didn't show it. He tied Hornsby's record of 33 in the first game of a doubleheader against Pittsburgh with a single, double, and home run. He broke it in the second game by getting three doubles. During the 37 games, he batted .423.

Holmes hit in his 37th straight game July 8, the last game before the All-Star break. When play resumed July 12, he was stopped by the Cubs' Hank Wyse, who pitched a three-hitter against Boston in the midst of what would be a 22-win season.

During the streak, Holmes used a hardened yellow bat that Braves coach Del Bissonette found in his attic. It had belonged to Brooklyn outfielder Johnny Frederick when he and Bissonette were teammates on the Dodgers.

Holmes set several modern club records that year, three of which still stand. The 37-game hitting streak remains in the Braves' book, and so do his 224 hits and 47 doubles. He finished second to Cavarretta in the official Most Valuable Player voting conducted by the Baseball Writers Association of America. However, *The Sporting News* named Holmes its MVP.

At the end of the season, Braves fans chipped in and bought their hero a new car. Holmes was so popular that the fans in the right-field bleachers developed a special ritual for greeting him when he came on the field for each game. They also were such devout supporters that they were capable of dictating the Braves lineup.

Originally a center fielder, Holmes moved to right in 1943 and developed quite a relationship with the fans in the Jury Box. They talked to him, and he talked back. Beginning in 1945, the fans in the Box developed a tradition of falling into silence as Holmes was about to run onto the field. When he got to his position, they cheered wildly, and he'd raise both arms and wave. Then the fans would yell, "How many hits to-day, Tommy?" and he'd hold up one to five fingers.

In 1946 the Braves obtained Johnny Barrett, normally a right fielder, from Pittsburgh. The plan was to move Holmes to left. However, when Holmes headed to left for the first time, the Jury Box fans revolted. They taunted Barrett the entire game to such an extent that afterward he said he wouldn't play right field again. Manager Billy Southworth sent Holmes back to right for the rest of the year.

Holmes had another good year in 1946, but his hitting slipped considerably from the previous season. With the Braves gearing up for a run at the pennant in 1947, Southworth was considering platooning the left-handed-hitting Holmes in right with Mike McCormick. But the fans didn't approve and gave McCormick a rough time in his first game in right. Southworth decided to leave Holmes out there, and he responded by leading the league in hits (191) for the second time in his career and finishing third in doubles.

From 1944 to 1948, Holmes strung together five consecutive seasons in which he hit .309 or better. He made the All-Star team for the second time in 1948 and helped lead the Braves to their first pennant since 1914. Like most of his teammates, he didn't hit well (.192) in the World Series loss to Cleveland, but he did drive in the only run in the Braves' 1–0 victory against Bob Feller in Game 1.

After the 1950 season, with his skills obviously declining, Holmes agreed to go to Hartford, a Braves farm club, to manage. When Southworth was let go in mid-June 1951, Holmes was immediately summoned to take over the club as a player-manager. The Braves played marginally better for him, but he was still too close to most of the players and too mild-mannered to provide strong leadership. The club finished fourth, and when it got off to a slow start in 1952, Holmes was cut loose after 35 games in favor of Charlie Grimm.

Horner, Bob

Braves: 1978–86	**B:** August 6, 1957
Third baseman, first baseman	**Batted right, threw right**
Birthplace: Junction City, Kansas	**Ht.** 6–1; **Wt.** 215

No other player in Atlanta history, perhaps none in Braves history, caused as much commotion throughout his career as Bob Horner did from the moment he signed a professional contract to the day he left the club. Controversy followed the husky third baseman like the number 5 on the back of his uniform.

Basically a calm, matter-of-fact, down-to-earth individual, Horner just had the knack for being at the center of a storm, thanks in large part to his flamboyant agent, Bucky Woy. There were many times in Horner's career when Braves management and the team's fans would have loved to see Woy tarred and feathered.

Only Dale Murphy and Hank Aaron hit more home runs and drove in more runs in an Atlanta uniform than Horner. And only Aaron had a higher slugging percentage than "Horns."

Yet Horner was a constant target of media criticism and taunts from fans for his ongoing contract hassles, threats of leaving the team, the many games he missed because of injury, his blond hair (was it curled/bleached?), and most of all, for his pudgy appearance. He actually had a weight clause in his contract.

It all began when the Braves made Horner the number-one draft pick in the nation in 1978. He came out of Arizona State as one of the most-decorated amateur players of his time. In 1977 he was named the College World Series MVP, and in '78 he was the College Player of the Year. He set what was then the NCAA single-season home run record with 25.

Though the Braves had every intention of starting Horner at their Double-A Savannah farm club, the player and his agent convinced general manager Bill Lucas that the 20-year-old third baseman was ready to step right into the major league lineup even though he hadn't touched a wooden bat in three and a half years. Guess who was right?

All Horner did was hit a home run in the third at bat of his first game off Pittsburgh's Bert Blyleven, one of the game's best pitchers at the time. In the postgame interview, Horner

Holmes, Tommy

Braves	G	AB	R	H	2B	3B	HR	RBI	SB	AVG	SLG
1942	141	558	56	155	24	4	4	41	2	.278	.357
1943	152	629*	75	170	33	10	5	41	7	.270	.378
1944	155	631	93	195	42	6	13	73	4	.309	.456
1945	154	636	125	224*	47*	6	28*	117	15	.352	.577*
1946	149	568	80	176	35	6	6	79	7	.310	.424
1947	150	618	90	191*	33	3	9	53	3	.309	.416
1948	139	585	85	190	35	7	6	61	1	.325	.439
1949	117	380	47	101	20	4	8	59	1	.266	.403
1950	105	322	44	96	20	1	9	51	0	.298	.450
1951	27	29	1	5	2	0	0	5	0	.172	.241
Career	1,289	4,956	696	1,503	291	47	88	580	40	.303	.434

Bob Horner

referred to Blyleven as "Mr. Blyleven." "I can't help it," he said. "Most of these guys are 10 or 15 years older than me."

Though the season was more than two months old when he debuted on June 16, he went on to hit 23 home runs in just 89 games. Veteran baseball experts were comparing him to Hall of Famer Harmon Killebrew. Horner was named National League Rookie of the Year, and his ratio of one home run for every 14.04 at bats was the best of any Rookie of the Year up to that time. He still holds the distinction of being the only player selected College Player of the Year and a major league Rookie of the Year in the same season.

Woy knew he and the Braves had a hot commodity. He was determined to work every angle in getting his client a major raise for 1979, even though second-year players seldom make big gains at the bargaining table because they lack the leverage of free agency. That didn't stop Woy. He told the Braves he wanted a three-year, $1 million contract for Horner and said if he didn't get it, he'd file a grievance for free agency based on a contract technicality.

The two sides argued back and forth all winter in the *Atlanta Journal*. One day they were close to agreement; the next day Woy said the Braves reneged, and Horner demanded to be traded. That's when Braves owner Ted Turner stepped in with the verbal flair he was so noted for in his early years of ownership.

"If his [Horner's] spirit is broken, maybe we'll let him build it back up with some time in the minors," Turner said. "I'm sick and tired of this whole thing. They're trying to browbeat us over a technicality and using the press in trying to intimidate us into doing something that's not right. I'm not a cheapskate . . . ask Phil Niekro and Pete Rose [whom Turner was trying to lure to Atlanta]."

"Horner says his spirit is broken because we're only offering $100,000. Well, I'll give him $300,000 someday when he deserves it. But the only way I'll give him $300,000 this year is if he can make that cute blond hair curl without going to a hairdresser to get a permanent. A freshman in college doesn't run the family. I do like Bob Horner, but we just have to establish who's running the team—Bucky Woy or Lucas and Turner."

Woy's response?

"They've [the Braves] dug their own grave," the agent said. "We'll get out of there one way or another. Bob wants no part of the Braves."

"Judging by the things that have happened, I don't see how I can ever play for the Braves again," Horner said.

Of course, he did. A contract agreement was reached, and Horner played eight more seasons with the Braves. But there was always a sideshow going, whether it had to do with contract negotiations, his numerous games missed with injuries, or his tendency to put on a few pounds.

Horner underwent some shoulder surgery after his rookie season and missed six weeks of his sophomore year with bone chips, but neither seemed to faze him. He batted .314 and had a .552 slugging percentage. Both ranked fifth in the league. He hit 33 home runs, fourth in the league, though he played in just 121 games, and he drove in 98 runs. His 20-game hitting streak was second in the NL.

In 1980, Horner stayed on the attack. His average slipped to .268, but his 35 home runs were second in the league. He got off to a slow start because of injuries, something fans already were starting to moan about, and appeared in just 124 games. But when he played . . . his 14 home runs in July were one short of the major league record held by Hall of Famers Joe DiMaggio and Hank Greenberg and former Braves first baseman Joe Adcock.

Horner managed to play in but 79 of the team's 106 games in the strike-shortened 1981 season, yet his 15 home runs actually led the Braves for the fourth straight year and ranked eighth in the NL. At the age of 24, he hit the 100th home run of his career in September, victimizing Houston's Nolan Ryan.

After the Braves finished six games under .500 and well back in both halves of the 1981 split season, Bobby Cox was fired as manager and replaced by former Brave Joe Torre. Perhaps with an eye on Horner's penchant for missing a lot of games, Torre named him team captain in spring training. Dale Murphy would have been the obvious choice for the honor, but Murphy needed no added motivation to play every day.

It appeared to work. Horner started better than ever in '82, and the young Braves blossomed under Torre, putting together a season-opening 13-game winning streak that propelled them to the division title and established a modern major league record.

Horner was named to the National League All-Star team for the only time in his career and was headed toward career highs in home runs and RBIs until he was felled by yet another injury on September 18 as the Braves were fighting the Dodgers for the NL West title. A hyperextended elbow caused him to miss the last two weeks. Still, Horner's 32 home runs ranked fourth in the league, and his 97 RBIs were one shy of his career high.

In 1983 it was more of the same—great offense when he played, which was not often enough to allow the Braves to repeat as division champs.

The Dodgers beat Atlanta by just three games. Horner's frequent absence easily could have been the difference, since he missed 58 games—10 in June with a bad ankle and the final seven weeks with a broken right wrist. There's no telling where he could have taken the Braves if he'd remained healthy, since he batted .303, hit 20 home runs, and drove in 68 runs in just 386 at bats.

The Braves again finished second in 1984, but this time they were 12 games behind the Padres. It's a wonder they did that well considering Horner appeared in a career-low 32 games. The blond bomber missed 16 games in April and May with a jammed shoulder, then was sidelined for the season May 30 when he re-broke his right wrist. Surgery was required on the twice-broken navicular bone, and it was feared Horner, only 27 years old, would never again be the same hitter.

But he shocked even the most optimistic by reporting early to spring training and being in the lineup on opening day 1985. He rested frequently early in the year to avoid overworking the wrist, but appeared to be the same hitter as always by midseason. He batted .293 in June and .378 in July. His 130 games for the season ranked second in his career to that point. At midseason, he began playing first base regularly and handled the position change well.

Seemingly healthier than ever, Horner played in a personal-high 141 games in 1986. He ranked fifth in the NL with 27 home runs and ninth with 87 RBIs. It was the seventh time in nine seasons he finished with 20 or more homers.

On June 19, two months shy of his 29th birthday, he hit his 200th career home run. And less than a month later, he became only the 11th player in major league history to hit four home runs in a game. On July 6 he connected three times off Montreal's Andy McGaffigan and hit the fourth off Jeff Reardon, though the Braves lost the game.

Eligible for free agency, Horner was in line for a big contract—or so it seemed. He was only 29 years old, owned 215 lifetime home runs, and had just posted more than 500 at bats for the first season in his career. What team in need of a power hitter could pass up the opportunity to sign him?

Apparently all of them. The Braves made an offer, but it was not to Woy's liking. The agent could find no takers—at least not at his asking price. To get Horner what he considered a suitable contract, Woy exported his client to the Far East. No other player of Horner's stature had ever left the major leagues for Japan at the height of his career, but then Woy had never followed the conventional route. Horner agreed to a one-year deal with the Yakult Swallows for $1.3 million plus travel and living expenses.

He debuted with a home run in his first game and three in his second game. He had six homers in his first seven games. Horner could hit in any country. He finished with 31 home runs in only 303 at bats (one every 9.8 at bats).

There have been few players in history with Horner's proclivity for hitting home runs. However, there also have been few who seemed to be so injury-prone. He looked anything but fragile, but that's exactly what he was.

He returned to the majors in 1988, signing a one-year contract with St. Louis. But the shoulder injury that required surgery after his rookie season returned, causing him to struggle through 60 games. His power was gone. He hit just three home runs.

Horner went through two operations and exhaustive rehabilitation to try and keep his career alive. He went to spring training with Baltimore in 1989, but early in the exhibition schedule he realized the shoulder could not hold up to the demands of a baseball schedule. At age 31, he retired.

Horner, Bob

Braves	G	AB	R	H	2B	3B	HR	RBI	SB	AVG	SLG
1978	89	323	50	86	17	1	23	63	0	.266	.539
1979	121	487	66	153	15	1	33	98	0	.314	.552
1980	124	463	81	124	14	1	35	89	3	.268	.529
1981	79	300	42	83	10	0	15	42	2	.277	.460
1982	140	499	85	130	24	0	32	97	3	.261	.501
1983	104	386	75	117	25	1	20	68	4	.303	.528
1984	32	113	15	31	8	0	3	19	0	.274	.425
1985	130	483	61	129	25	3	27	89	1	.267	.499
1986	141	517	70	141	22	0	27	87	1	.273	.472
Career	960	3,571	545	994	160	7	215	652	14	.278	.507

Hornsby, Rogers

Braves: 1928
Second baseman
Birthplace: Winters, Texas
B: April 27, 1896

D: January 5, 1963
Batted right, threw right
Ht. 5–11; **Wt.** 175

Imagine a player talented enough to win the batting title in his first year with a team and controversial enough to be traded at the end of that season. That was Rogers Hornsby.

Only nine men in Braves franchise history have ever led the National League in hitting, and Hornsby was the first in

Rogers Hornsby

the 20th century to do so. After he hit .361, second in the league, in 1927 for the Giants, Hornsby, who already had six batting titles to his credit, was traded to Boston. New York manager John McGraw was afraid Hornsby was undermining him, so he let him go for Shanty Hogan, a promising catcher, and Jimmy Welsh, an adequate outfielder.

The opinionated Hornsby, who managed St. Louis to a World Series championship in 1926, created immediate problems for the Braves, who'd just hired Jack Slattery, a college coach, as manager. Dissension began to crop up in spring training. Though this was not a team that was going to win for any manager, Slattery couldn't handle the heat of a poor start and the presence of Hornsby, who had the added leverage of being team captain. Slattery resigned in late May, and Hornsby managed for the rest of the season.

The team lost 103 games and finished seventh, 44½ games out of first. Hornsby couldn't work any miracles with the Braves, but that didn't slow him down at the plate. He established a modern Braves record by hitting .387 and also led the league in slugging percentage and on-base percentage.

However, at the end of the year, he was traded to the Cubs for five players and $200,000, the cash being a major inducement for the financially strapped Braves. The Cubs were his fourth team in four years despite the fact that he was only 32 and regarded as probably the greatest right-handed hitter in history.

Hornsby batted over .400 three times, including 1924 when he posted a modern record .424 average. In 23 seasons, he had a .358 lifetime average, second only to Ty Cobb. He was a two-time MVP, including 1929, the year after he played for the Braves. To protect his batting eye, Hornsby never watched movies and rarely read. He also didn't smoke or drink, but he was notorious for gambling on horse races and was always in debt.

Hornsby, Rogers

Braves	G	AB	R	H	2B	3B	HR	RBI	SB	AVG	SLG
1928	140	486	99	188	42	7	21	94	5	.387*	.632*
Career	140	486	99	188	42	7	21	94	5	.387	.632

House, Tom

Braves: 1971–75
Pitcher
Birthplace: Seattle

B: April 29, 1947
Batted left, threw left
Ht. 5–11; **Wt.** 190

For a relief pitcher who never saved more than 11 games in a season, Tom House certainly achieved a great deal of fame during his career. As long as sports fans engage in trivia challenges, the bespectacled left-hander will live in tales of the game's richest lore.

Who caught Hank Aaron's 715th home run?

Of course, it was House, who was patrolling the bullpen area behind the left-field fence when Aaron connected off the Dodgers' Al Downing on April 8, 1974, to break Babe Ruth's all-time home run record. He raced to home plate to greet Aaron and presented him the ball amid the wild celebration in progress.

" 'Hammer, here it is,' I said," House said in recounting the moment. "I put the ball in his hand. He said, 'Thanks, Kid,' and touched me on the shoulder. I kept staring at him. And it was then that it was brought home to me what this home run meant, not only to him, but to all of us."

House still refers to his catch as "the highlight of my career." However, he was a pretty good pitcher, too.

Perhaps some of Aaron's magic rubbed off on House in that 1974 encounter, because the 27-year-old reliever went on to have the best season of his career. He was 6–2 with 11 saves, fifth in the league, and had a 1.93 ERA.

In the three-year period 1973–75, House appeared in an average of 55 games per season, and he led the Braves in saves the last two years with 11 in each. In need of a starting pitcher, Atlanta then made the ill-fated decision to part with House, sending him to Boston in exchange for star-crossed left-hander Rogelio Moret.

House, Tom

Braves	W	L	Pct	G	GS	CG	ShO	IP	H	BB	SO	ERA	SV
1971	1	0	1.000	11	1	0	0	20⅔	20	3	11	3.05	0
1972	0	0	—	8	0	0	0	9⅓	7	6	7	2.89	2
1973	4	2	.667	52	0	0	0	67⅓	58	31	42	4.68	4
1974	6	2	.750	56	0	0	0	102⅔	74	27	64	1.93	11
1975	7	7	.500	58	0	0	0	79⅓	79	36	36	3.18	11
Career	18	11	.621	185	1	0	0	279⅓	238	103	160	3.06	28

Tom House

Hrabosky, Al

Braves: 1980–82
Pitcher
Birthplace: Oakland, California

B: July 21, 1949
Batted right, threw left
Ht. 5–11; **Wt.** 185

In his early years as Braves owner, Ted Turner could never pass up the opportunity to shop for high-profile free agents. Pete Rose and Reggie Jackson were two of the biggest names he pursued and failed to lure to Atlanta.

Al Hrabosky certainly didn't fit in the class of Rose and Jackson, but he was an accomplished, much-publicized free agent when he went on the market after the 1979 season. With his famed "Mad Hungarian" persona, he fit right into the profile of the type of player Turner felt would help boost ratings for his TBS Superstation.

In the five seasons leading up to his signing with the Braves, Hrabosky averaged 15 saves per year at St. Louis and Kansas City, leading the National League with 22 in 1975 when he was the league's Fireman of the Year. But though he still put on the same act in Atlanta that he'd become famous for, Hrabosky didn't have the same fastball. Consequently, he never gained the full confidence of the managers he served, and his pitching was limited.

Hrabosky came to Atlanta with his trademark Fu Manchu mustache, which he eventually grew into a full beard. In key situations, he'd "meet" with himself behind the mound, slam the ball into his glove, and whirl around to bolt up the mound and challenge the hitter with a dark glare.

However, neither Bobby Cox in 1980 and '81 nor Joe Torre in '82 gave Hrabosky much of an opportunity to perform his specialty—saving games. He actually pitched fairly well when Cox used him, but he recorded just four saves in his first two seasons as a Brave. Rick Camp was Cox's favorite closer at the time.

Then, when Torre arrived in 1982, Gene Garber returned to form and regained his old job as the closer, leaving Hrabosky out in the cold again. The "Mad Hungarian" did manage three saves that season to help the Braves win the division title, but it was his last year in the majors.

Al Hrabosky

Hrabosky, Al

Braves	W	L	Pct	G	GS	CG	ShO	IP	H	BB	SO	ERA	SV
1980	4	2	.667	45	0	0	0	59⅔	50	31	31	3.62	3
1981	1	1	.500	24	0	0	0	33⅓	24	9	13	1.07	1
1982	2	1	.667	31	0	0	0	37⅓	41	17	20	5.54	3
Career	7	4	.636	100	0	0	0	130⅔	115	57	64	3.51	7

Hubbard, Glenn

Braves: 1978–87
Second baseman
Birthplace: Hahn Air Force Base, Germany

B: September 25, 1957
Batted right, threw right
Ht. 5–7; **Wt.** 180

Hubbard, Glenn

Braves	G	AB	R	H	2B	3B	HR	RBI	SB	AVG	SLG
1978	44	163	15	42	4	0	2	13	2	.258	.319
1979	97	325	34	75	12	0	3	29	0	.231	.295
1980	117	431	55	107	21	3	9	43	7	.248	.374
1981	99	361	39	85	13	5	6	33	4	.235	.349
1982	145	532	75	132	25	1	9	59	4	.248	.350
1983	148	517	65	136	24	6	12	70	3	.263	.402
1984	120	397	53	93	27	2	9	43	4	.234	.380
1985	142	439	51	102	21	0	5	39	4	.232	.314
1986	143	408	42	94	16	1	4	36	3	.230	.304
1987	141	443	69	117	33	2	5	38	1	.264	.381
Career	1,196	4,016	498	983	196	20	64	403	32	.245	.351

Few players in Braves history have fielded their positions as well as Glenn Hubbard did at second base during a 10-year period that included a division title in 1982 and a trip to the All-Star Game in 1983.

A memorable presence on the field because of his short stature (5–7), frequent full beard, and undying hustle, Hubbard also was a threat with the bat, much more so than his .244 career average would indicate. His best year was 1983 when he batted .263 with 12 home runs and 70 RBIs.

Because of his size and limited offensive capabilities, Hubbard had to have a lot of drive to get to the majors and stay there for 12 years—especially considering that he was only a 20th-round draft pick. At the peak of his career, he could turn the double play as well as any second baseman in the majors. He led National League second basemen in double plays in 1983 and led major league second basemen in that category in 1985 and '87.

Hubbard's .988 fielding percentage in 1984 ranks third at his position in franchise history.

In 1987, Hubbard left the Braves when he was on top of his game. He hit a career-high .264 and posted his best-ever numbers in doubles (33) and on-base percentage (.378), also leading major league second basemen in turning DPs. He took advantage of free agency to sign with Oakland.

Jackson, Sonny

Braves: 1968–74
Shortstop, outfielder
Birthplace: Washington, D.C.

B: July 9, 1944
Batted left, threw right
Ht. 5–9; **Wt.** 155

When the Braves acquired Sonny Jackson from Houston for the 1968 season, they thought they had the player who was going to lead them into the new era of speed and defense in the National League. And perhaps that's what a healthy Jackson would have done. But injury after injury during his seven-year Braves career kept him from becoming the force he threatened to be when he stole a National League rookie record 49 bases in 1966 for Houston.

When Jackson's batting average dropped from .292 in his first full season in the majors to .237 in 1967, Houston sent him to Atlanta along with first baseman Chuck Harrison in exchange for pitcher Denny Lemaster and infielder Denis Menke. He was immediately installed as the Braves' regular

Glenn Hubbard

Sonny Jackson

shortstop, replacing Menke. However, he was able to play in only 105 games, mainly because of injuries.

That trend followed Jackson the next two seasons. His nimble legs were particularly susceptible to hamstring pulls. Though he held the regular shortstop job for two more years, he didn't play in more than 103 games either season, and his productivity suffered because of his frequent stays on the bench. He also had an erratic throwing arm.

In 1970, San Francisco's Dick Dietz slid into Jackson at second, cutting the Brave below the left knee and bringing his brief tenure at short to a halt. When he was able to return to the lineup, he alternated at the position with Gil Garrido.

In 1971 the Braves installed Marty Perez at short and converted Jackson to a center fielder. He played in 149 games, the most since his rookie year, but all the injuries had taken a toll on his legs. He batted .258 yet stole just seven bases. Since he had no power (four of his seven career homers were inside-the-park), his game basically had disappeared. He never played regularly again and retired in 1974 at age 30.

Jackson, Sonny

Braves	G	AB	R	H	2B	3B	HR	RBI	SB	AVG	SLG
1968	105	358	37	81	8	2	1	19	16	.226	.268
1969	98	318	41	76	3	5	1	27	12	.239	.289
1970	103	328	60	85	14	3	0	20	11	.259	.320
1971	149	547	58	141	20	5	2	25	7	.258	.324
1972	60	126	20	30	6	3	0	8	1	.238	.333
1973	117	206	29	43	5	2	0	12	6	.209	.252
1974	5	7	0	3	0	0	0	0	0	.429	.429
Career	637	1,890	245	459	56	20	4	111	53	.243	.300

James, Bill

Braves: 1913–15, 1919
Pitcher
Birthplace: Iowa Hill, California
B: March 12, 1892

D: March 10, 1971
Batted right, threw right
Ht. 6–3; **Wt.** 196

Without Bill James, there would have been no "miracle" in 1914 for the Braves. And that statement, sadly, pretty much sums up his career.

A hard thrower with a nasty spitball, James turned pro in 1912 at the age of 20. The Braves acquired him the next season from Seattle, hence his nickname "Seattle Bill." James showed plenty of promise as a rookie, posting a 2.79 ERA while alternating between starting and relieving for a team that finished 13 games under .500.

But no one expected what transpired in 1914 from either James or the Braves. The lanky right-hander quickly developed into quite possibly the best pitcher in the league and teamed with Dick Rudolph and Lefty Tyler to pitch Boston to one of the most unlikely pennants and World Series championships of all time.

James and Rudolph won 26 games apiece, one less than league leader Grover Cleveland Alexander. James also led the league in winning percentage (.788) and was second in ERA, third in complete games and innings, and fifth in strikeouts.

In the Braves' four-game World Series sweep of the heavily favored Athletics, James picked up two victories. He pitched a two-hitter in Game 2, outdueling Eddie Plank, 1–0. Two days

Bill James

later, in Game 3, he worked two hitless and scoreless innings of relief to get credit for a 5–4 victory in 12 innings.

Like many spitball pitchers, though, James developed a sore arm and basically was finished in 1915. He tried a brief comeback in 1919, but to no avail. James won only 11 games besides the 26 victories he posted in 1914.

James, Bill

Braves	W	L	Pct	G	GS	CG	ShO	IP	H	BB	SO	ERA	SV
1913	6	10	.375	24	14	10	1	135⅔	134	57	73	2.79	0
1914	26	7	.788	46	37	30	4	332⅓	261	118	156	1.90	2
1915	5	4	.556	13	10	4	0	68⅓	68	22	23	3.03	0
1919	0	0	—	1	0	0	0	5⅓	6	2	1	3.38	0
Career	37	21	.638	84	61	44	5	541⅓	469	199	253	2.28	2

Jarvis, Pat

Braves: 1966–72
Pitcher
Birthplace: Carlyle, Illinois

B: March 18, 1941
Batted right, threw right
Ht. 5–10; **Wt.** 190

Pat Jarvis didn't look like a pitcher, but he led the Braves in victories in 1967, 1968, and 1970. Relatively short and squat for his position, Jarvis used his tenacity and determination to average 15 victories per season during a four-year period that included a division title for Atlanta in 1969. His appearance and his style earned him the nickname "The Little Bulldog."

Always an underdog, Jarvis had to fight an uphill battle just to get signed. Detroit scout Joe Mathes happened to be passing through Jarvis's hometown of Carlyle, Illinois, in July 1960 on his way to scout another player. He read in the newspaper that an all-star game was being played, so he stopped by, saw Jarvis strike out 18, and signed him for $400 a month and a $1,000 bonus.

The Tigers saw no future for him, though, and traded him to Milwaukee in 1963 for Bruce Brubaker, who pitched a grand total of three innings in the majors. Jarvis, on the other hand, was called to Atlanta in mid-1966 when the Braves were

Pat Jarvis

plagued by a host of sore arms. He lost his first game, then reeled off six consecutive victories before losing his last decision. For his work, he was named the Braves' Rookie of the Year.

Pitching like he'd never heard of the sophomore jinx, Jarvis won 15 times in 1967 to lead the staff despite opening the season in the bullpen.

"Jarvis can win 10 to 15 games a year on his guts," said Braves third baseman Clete Boyer.

And that's what he did with the help of excellent control. When the Braves won the National League West in 1969, Jarvis's victory total slipped to 13, his lowest in the four years he was a consistent winner in the Atlanta rotation.

When the Braves felt his skills were eroding, they traded Jarvis to Montreal in the spring of 1973 for right-hander Carl Morton. It proved to be one of the club's better deals. Jarvis pitched only 39 more innings in the majors, and Morton was one of Atlanta's best pitchers the next three seasons.

Jay, Joey

Braves: 1953–55, 1957–60, 1966	B: August 15, 1935
Pitcher	Batted both, threw right
Birthplace: Middletown, Connecticut	Ht. 6–4; Wt. 228

Joey Jay had two 20-win seasons in his career, two more than most men who ever pitched in the big leagues. However, what he's most remembered for is being the first graduate of Little League baseball to reach the majors. When he was 12 years old, he was so big for his age that parents petitioned, unsuccessfully, to have him barred from Little League.

Jay was one of the big "bonus babies" who eventually led to the birth of the amateur draft. He was signed in an era when there was a wide-open market for amateur players. However, in a failed attempt to keep signing bonuses under control, players who received more than a $6,000 reward for turning pro were prohibited from being sent to the minor leagues for two years.

Therefore, Jay went straight from high school to the majors at age 18 in 1953. He seldom was used in a game, appearing in just three. But in his lone start, he shut out Cincinnati, 3–0.

The next year he pitched only 18 innings, then finally was farmed out in 1955. Not until 1958, at age 23, did Jay return to the majors to stay. Though he still pitched infrequently on a talented staff that would lead the Braves to a second straight pennant, he showed exceptional promise at times. In fact, he pitched three shutouts—tied for second in the league—in just 12 starts. In July he was named National League Player of the Month for going 5–2 with two shutouts.

However, after two more seasons of mixed results, Jay fell victim to the large number of quality starters around him and the Braves' desire to overhaul their infield defense. He and left-hander Juan Pizarro were sent to Cincinnati in exchange for shortstop Roy McMillan prior to the 1961 season.

All Jay did was help pitch the Reds to the pennant, tying former Braves teammate Warren Spahn for the league lead in wins (21) and shutouts (4). He also pitched Cincinnati's lone World Series victory, beating the Yankees, 6–2, in Game 2 at Yankee Stadium.

Jay repeated as a 21-game winner in 1962. Since he was only 27 years old, it appeared he would be one of the game's top pitchers for several more years. However, he never won more than 11 in a season again. He was traded back to the Braves in mid-1966, the team's first season in Atlanta, but he lost all four decisions.

Jarvis, Pat

Braves	W	L	Pct	G	GS	CG	ShO	IP	H	BB	SO	ERA	SV
1966	6	2	.750	10	9	3	1	62⅓	46	12	41	2.31	0
1967	15	10	.600	32	30	7	1	194	195	62	118	3.66	0
1968	16	12	.571	34	34	14	1	256	202	50	157	2.60	0
1969	13	11	.542	37	33	4	1	217⅓	204	73	123	4.43	0
1970	16	16	.500	36	34	11	1	254	240	72	173	3.61	0
1971	6	14	.300	35	23	3	3	162⅓	162	51	68	4.10	1
1972	11	7	.611	37	6	0	0	98⅔	94	44	56	4.10	2
Career	83	72	.535	221	169	42	8	1,244⅔	1,143	364	736	3.59	3

Joey Jay

Jay, Joey

Braves	W	L	Pct	G	GS	CG	ShO	IP	H	BB	SO	ERA	SV
1953	1	0	1.000	3	1	1	1	10	6	5	4	0.00	0
1954	1	0	1.000	15	1	0	0	18	21	16	13	6.50	0
1955	0	0	—	12	1	0	0	19	23	13	3	4.74	0
1957	0	0	—	1	0	0	0	⅔	0	0	0	0.00	1
1958	7	5	.583	18	12	6	3	96⅔	60	43	74	2.14	0
1959	6	11	.353	34	19	4	1	136⅓	130	64	88	4.09	0
1960	9	8	.529	32	11	3	0	133⅓	128	59	90	3.24	1
1966	0	4	.000	9	8	0	0	29⅔	39	20	19	7.89	1
Career	24	28	.462	124	53	14	5	443¾	407	220	291	3.69	3

Jethroe, Sam

Braves: 1950–52
Center fielder
Birthplace: East St. Louis, Illinois

B: January 20, 1922
Batted both, threw right
Ht. 6–1; **Wt.** 178

As the first black ever to play for the Braves, Sam Jethroe holds a significant place in franchise history. He paved the way for such players as Hank Aaron, Billy Bruton, and Wes Covington, who helped make the Braves one of the game's most talented and successful teams in the 1950s.

Jethroe had a distinguished career in the Negro Leagues before joining the Braves in 1950 at age 28. He led the Negro American League in hitting in 1942, '44, and '45 and led the Cleveland Buckeyes to a sweep in the 1945 Negro League Series.

In 1948 the Buckeyes sold the speedy outfielder to the Dodgers, who assigned him to their Montreal farm club. He hit over .300 in two seasons there and set an International League record with 89 steals in 1949.

In 1950 the Braves paid the Dodgers a reported $100,000 for Jethroe, and manager Charlie Grimm installed him as the club's starting center fielder during spring training. When he played his first exhibition game at St. Petersburg against the Cardinals, it was a first at Al Lang Field, and the *New York World Telegram* proclaimed, "Social revolution hits St. Pete."

It was three years after Robinson broke the color barrier with the Dodgers. Jethroe was only the fifth black playing on four major league teams when he debuted. And it would be nine more years before Pumpsie Green integrated Boston's other major league club.

Much like many modern players, Jethroe had a special blend of speed and power. A switch-hitter, he was generally re-

Sam Jethroe

garded as the fastest runner in either league. However, he also had a weak throwing arm and poor eyesight that hindered his defense and ultimately led to a short stay in the majors.

Jethroe's career started promisingly enough. "Jet," as he was called, led the league with 35 steals, more than twice as many as anyone else in the majors in 1950. And he hit for average as well as for power, driving in 58 runs from the leadoff spot. The baseball writers were impressed enough to vote him National League Rookie of the Year by a substantial margin.

In 1951, Jethroe had an even better season, again leading the majors with 35 steals in just 40 attempts. He hit 18 home runs again and improved most of his other offensive statistics.

But in 1952, at age 30, Jethroe's career took a turn for the worse, and he never recovered. He managed 28 steals, second in the league to Pee Wee Reese, but his batting average dropped sharply, and the rest of his statistics followed.

The Braves were about to move to Milwaukee, and they had Bruton, a talented young center fielder, ready and waiting to assume the job in center. Jethroe didn't even make the team in 1953, spending the entire season in the minors and then being traded to Pittsburgh during the winter. He appeared in just two games for the Pirates in 1954.

Jethroe played Triple-A ball for six years before retiring at age 38.

Jethroe, Sam

Braves	G	AB	R	H	2B	3B	HR	RBI	SB	AVG	SLG
1950	141	582	100	159	28	8	18	58	35*	.273	.442
1951	148	572	101	160	29	10	18	65	35*	.280	.460
1952	151	608	79	141	23	7	13	58	28	.232	.357
Career	440	1,762	280	460	80	25	49	181	98	.261	.418

Johnson, Dave

Braves: 1973–75
Second baseman, first baseman
Birthplace: Orlando, Florida

B: January 30, 1943
Batted right, threw right
Ht. 6–1; **Wt.** 180

Every once in a while, an aberration occurs on Earth, an event that defies logic or reasonable explanation. Such an abnormality became part of Braves history in 1973 when the club's newly acquired second baseman stunned the baseball world—and even himself—by hitting 43 home runs.

Prior to 1973, Dave Johnson had never hit more than 18 home runs in a season, and after 1973, he never hit more than 15 in a single year. In his 13-year career, Johnson hit 136 homers, nearly one-third of those in 1973.

The only man in baseball who hit more home runs than Johnson that year was future Hall of Famer Willie Stargell—and he only beat Johnson by one for the National League title.

What made the 30-year-old second baseman's slugging even more remarkable is that it tied one of the oldest records in baseball. Of Johnson's 43 home runs, 42 came while he was playing second (he had one as a pinch hitter), equaling the number hit by Hall of Famer Rogers Hornsby in 1922 for the most ever by a second baseman.

Though Johnson's pursuit of Hornsby's record received a lot of publicity, it was greatly overshadowed by Hank Aaron's quest to become the all-time home run king. Aaron hit 40 and finished the year at 713. Johnson and Aaron were joined in the 40-home-run club by Darrell Evans with 41. The trio

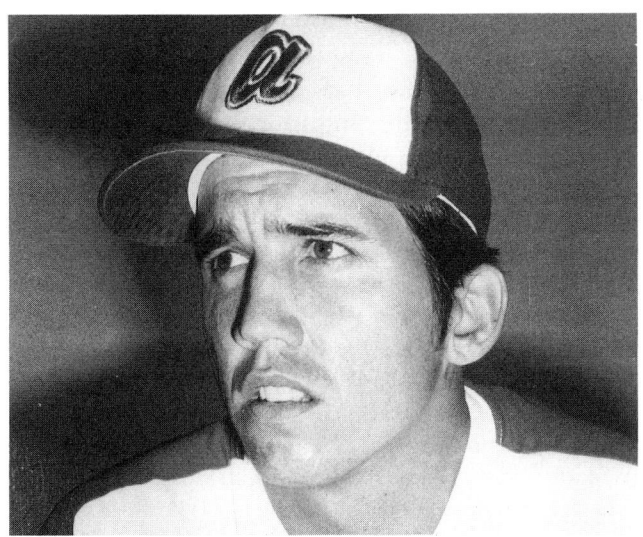

Dave Johnson

finished second, third, and fourth in the league in home runs, and in the process became the first three teammates ever to hit 40 in the same season.

Johnson came to the Braves prior to the 1973 season along with pitchers Pat Dobson and Roric Harrison and catcher Johnny Oates in exchange for slugging catcher Earl Williams and infield prospect Taylor Duncan.

The deal was designed primarily to bolster Atlanta's pitching, not to bring in power. But just the opposite resulted. While Dobson and Harrison didn't pitch as expected, Johnson became an overnight muscle man. He finished third in the league in slugging percentage (.546) and fourth in total bases (305) and fell just one shy of what would have been the only 100-RBI season of his career. His work earned him recognition by *The Sporting News* as Comeback Player of the Year in the National League.

Though he never impressed with his glove in the National League, Johnson came to the Braves with a better defensive reputation than offensive. In fact, he won three Gold Gloves with Baltimore and led American League second basemen in fielding in 1972 (.990) when he batted just .221 and hit a measly five home runs.

In 1974, Johnson dropped back to 15 home runs, and the following year he was released by the Braves.

After his playing career, Johnson went directly into managing in the minors. Then in 1984 he took over the New York Mets, whom he directed to the World Series championship in 1986. He was fired by the Mets in 1990 and was out of baseball until he returned to manage the Cincinnati Reds in 1993.

Johnson, Ernie

Braves: 1950, 1952–58	**B:** June 16, 1924
Pitcher	**Batted right, threw right**
Birthplace: Brattleboro, Vermont	**Ht.** 6–4; **Wt.** 195

Before relief pitching became fashionable, Ernie Johnson carved out a nice spot for himself in the Braves' bullpen. In the process, he paved the way for a postplaying career as a broadcaster in which he became one of the most popular individuals ever associated with the franchise.

Johnson, who is semiretired but still does some Braves telecasts, is a rare three-city Brave. He signed with the club when it was still based in Boston and pitched his first two seasons in the majors prior to the move to Milwaukee in 1953. He continued to pitch with the club through 1958, then later returned to the Braves as a front-office employee. In 1962 he joined the broadcast team, a role he kept when the club moved to Atlanta.

A native of Vermont, Johnson began his pro career with the Braves' farm club at Hartford in 1942. He missed the next three seasons because of active duty with the Marines, then returned to pitch four more years in the minors before getting his first shot at the majors in 1950.

Farmed out again for the entire 1951 season, Johnson finally stuck with Boston in 1952 at age 27.

A tall right-hander with a sidearm delivery, he could be particularly tough on right-handed hitters with his curveball and palm ball.

"I tried the spitter once, and [catcher] Del Crandall told me to forget it. He said it's so slow that it's dry by the time it gets to the plate," said Johnson, who liked to joke about himself.

Spitball or not, he was an important part of the 1957 club, the last Braves team to win the World Series. Johnson won a career-high seven games and saved four more to help Milwaukee win the 1957 pennant. He made three appearances in the World Series against the Yankees and pitched extremely well, even though his only decision was a 3–2 loss in Game 6. Johnson retired 13 of the 15 Yankees he faced in that game but was beaten by Hank Bauer's homer in the seventh inning. It was one of just two hits he gave up in seven innings during the Series, in which he posted a 1.29 ERA.

Johnson, Dave

Braves	G	AB	R	H	2B	3B	HR	RBI	SB	AVG	SLG
1973	157	559	84	151	25	0	43	99	5	.270	.546
1974	136	454	56	114	18	0	15	62	1	.251	.390
1975	1	1	0	1	1	0	0	1	0	1.000	1.000
Career	294	1,014	140	266	44	0	58	162	6	.262	.477

Ernie Johnson

After a poor season in 1958, Johnson was released by the Braves. He was signed by Baltimore and spent his last season in the majors with the Orioles in 1959 before retiring with a 40–23 record and a 3.77 ERA.

Johnson made his home in Milwaukee and did some public speaking for the Braves before joining them in a full-time public relations position and later moving into the broadcast booth.

He was named Georgia Sportscaster of the Year three times. His easygoing, down-home style and knowledge of the game made him a favorite of Braves fans across the nation who listened to him nightly on the TBS Superstation. He retired from full-time broadcasting in 1989 but continues to work an abbreviated schedule of games on TBS and Sport-South, a regional cable network, where he's often paired in the booth with his son, Ernie Jr.

Johnson, Ernie

Braves	W	L	Pct	G	GS	CG	ShO	IP	H	BB	SO	ERA	SV
1950	2	0	1.000	16	1	0	0	20⅔	37	13	15	6.97	0
1952	6	3	.667	29	10	2	1	92	100	31	45	4.11	1
1953	4	3	.571	36	1	0	0	81	79	22	36	2.67	0
1954	5	2	.714	40	4	1	0	99⅓	77	34	68	2.81	2
1955	5	7	.417	40	2	0	0	92	81	55	43	3.42	4
1956	4	3	.571	36	0	0	0	51	54	21	26	3.71	6
1957	7	3	.700	30	0	0	0	65	67	26	44	3.88	4
1958	3	1	.750	15	0	0	0	23⅓	35	10	13	8.10	1
Career	36	22	.621	242	18	3	1	524⅓	530	212	290	3.74	18

Jones, Nippy

Braves: 1957
First baseman, outfielder
Birthplace: Los Angeles

B: June 29, 1925
Batted right, threw right
Ht. 6–1; **Wt.** 185

Nippy Jones played only 30 regular-season games for the Braves, yet he was a central figure in the last World Series won by the team.

Jones was lucky to be playing any baseball at all in 1957. In 1948, at age 22, he was a good enough first base prospect that the Cardinals moved Stan Musial to the outfield to make room for him. He was no Musial, but he did drive in 81 runs that year and batted .300 in 1949.

However, he sustained a herniated disk that required surgery after the 1949 season. He emerged from the surgery paralyzed from the waist down, and it appeared he might never play baseball again. But through extensive rehabilitation, he regained use of his legs in time for spring training.

Except for 1951, he spent most of the next seven-plus years in the minors until the Braves bought him on July 6, 1957, to serve as a backup first baseman to Frank Torre. Joe Adcock was out with a broken leg suffered in late June.

Jones, who had been out of the majors since 1952, played sparingly but did contribute a big home run to the pennant effort. On July 26 the Braves had only a half game lead over St. Louis. They were at home against the Giants and were tied, 3–3, through eight innings. After Torre left for a pinch runner in the eighth, Jones entered the game to play first base in the ninth.

The game remained tied entering the bottom of the 11th. With one out and runners at first and second, Jones came to the plate to face noted soft-toss artist Stu Miller. The unknown substitute suddenly became a hero by hitting a home run down the left-field line to win the game, 6–3. It was his first big league homer since 1952 and enabled Milwaukee to maintain its slim hold on first place.

But it was what happened in Game 4 of the World Series that forever stamped Jones's name in the memories of longtime Braves fans and made him a permanent part of Series lore.

New York had won two of the first three games of the Series and held a 5–4 lead entering the bottom of the 10th inning of Game 4. With Warren Spahn due to lead off the bottom of the 10th, Jones was sent up to pinch-hit. Yankees reliever Tommy Byrne threw an inside pitch that appeared to bounce in the dirt, but Jones claimed it hit him on the foot. Umpire Augie Donatelli disagreed and called a ball. However, Jones argued and asked Donatelli to check the ball. The umpire did so, and when he found a spot of black shoe polish on it, he awarded Jones first base.

Felix Mantilla ran for Jones and eventually scored the tying run on a one-out hit by Johnny Logan. Eddie Mathews followed with a two-run homer, giving the Braves a 7–5 victory and evening the Series at two games apiece.

Jones, Nippy

Braves	G	AB	R	H	2B	3B	HR	RBI	SB	AVG	SLG
1957	30	79	5	21	2	1	2	8	0	.266	.392
Career	30	79	5	21	2	1	2	8	0	.266	.392

Nippy Jones

Justice, David

Braves: 1989–
Outfielder
Birthplace: Cincinnati, Ohio

B: April 14, 1966
Bats left, throws left
Ht. 6–3; **Wt.** 195

When the Braves traded Dale Murphy to Philadelphia on August 4, 1990, and moved David Justice from first base to right field, a lot of people thought Justice would someday be the answer to the trivia question "Who replaced Dale Murphy in right field for the Braves?"

But for all anyone knows, the question could someday be reversed to "Who played right field for the Braves before David Justice?"

Justice still has quite a way to go to put together a career that will rival Murphy's, but he appears talented enough to

David Justice

make a run at it. Murphy had won two National League MVP awards by the time he was 27. The best Justice had done was finish third in the 1993 MVP race when he was 27. However, any player who can hit 40 home runs and drive in 120 runs at age 27, as Justice did, certainly has MVP potential.

A fourth-round pick in the 1985 draft out of Thomas More College in Kentucky, Justice was only 19 when he became a Braves farmhand even though he had three years of college. He accomplished that distinction by skipping both the seventh and eighth grades in school.

After spending most of his first five seasons in the minors, Justice got his first taste of the majors with two brief stints in Atlanta in 1989. The next year he became the club's starting first baseman, but he struggled at the new position. When Murphy was traded in early August, Justice was hitting just .243 with eight home runs and 28 RBIs in 68 games. However, the move back to his natural right-field position seemed to ignite his bat.

Justice was the hottest hitter in the National League the last two months of the season, leading the league with 11 home runs in August and with nine in September. He wound up leading all major league rookies with 28 homers and 78 RBIs for the year and tied Detroit's Cecil Fielder for most home runs after the All-Star break (23).

The result was that Justice was a runaway winner as NL Rookie of the Year, the first Brave to win the honor since Bob Horner in 1978 and the first Braves outfielder to be so honored since Sam Jethroe broke the franchise's racial barrier in 1950.

The following year, Justice missed two crucial months, July and most of August, with a bad back during the Braves' stirring drive to the National League pennant. Yet he still posted formidable statistics and delivered one of the biggest hits of the season.

He was on a tear early in the season and led the league in RBIs with 51 before going on the disabled list June 27. When Justice returned to the lineup in late August, Atlanta was in the heat of an incredible pennant race with the Dodgers. The Braves were 31-14 (.688) with him back in the lineup from August 21 through the end of the season.

On October 1, the Braves were in a virtual "must-win" situation, trailing the Dodgers by a game with only five to play.

When they fell behind Cincinnati's Jose Rijo, 6-0, through three innings, it appeared they'd soon be two games back with four to play.

However, Atlanta closed to within 6-5 after eight innings. In the top of the ninth, Mark Lemke led off with a walk, and with one out, Justice delivered what proved to be a game-winning home run off Reds relief ace Rob Dibble. It was the most dramatic home run in the team's Atlanta history.

Justice was not particularly productive in the League Championship Series against Pittsburgh, but he hit .259 with two home runs and six RBIs in the World Series against Minnesota. In Game 5, he had five RBIs in a 14-5 rout to tie the Series record for a National League player.

In 1992, with the Braves on top of Atlanta if not the entire world, Justice somehow managed to alienate fans and the media. He was on the disabled list in April, and even when he came off, he didn't produce. As late as May 26, he was hitting just .169. The Braves were seven games under .500, and Justice was receiving much of the blame.

But Justice got hot, and so did the Braves. He had 11 home runs and 30 RBIs in the final 43 games, becoming the first Brave since Bob Horner and Murphy in 1978-80 to hit 20 or more home runs in each of his first three full seasons.

Justice had a good League Championship Series against Pittsburgh, hitting .280 with two homers, both in Game 6. He also made what would become a series-saving throw in Game 7 when he nailed Orlando Merced at the plate in the eighth inning to keep the score at 2-0. The Braves then won the game and the playoffs in the ninth.

During the ensuing off-season, Justice married actress Halle Berry, and in 1993 he seemed to be a changed man. He no longer was at odds with the media and fans, he avoided injury, and he played the way the Braves always thought he would perform.

Justice, who finished second in the league in both home runs and RBIs, joined Murphy, Jeff Burroughs, Darrell Evans, and Hank Aaron as the only Atlanta Braves to have at least 40 homers and 100 RBIs. He also became only the third left-handed hitter in franchise history to hit 40 home runs in a season, joining Eddie Mathews and Evans.

The sweet-swinging right fielder's popularity soared on all fronts. The fans voted him a starter on the All-Star team, and managers and coaches selected him for the Silver Slugger team as one of the three top offensive outfielders in the league.

Then in the off-season, he was named one of *People* magazine's 50 most beautiful people, an honor his wife had won the year before. To top it all, he signed a new five-year, $27.5 million contract with the Braves, signifying his stature as the cornerstone of the team's future and one of the game's bright, new superstars.

Justice was in the process of putting together another fine year in 1994 when the season was cut short by the players' strike. His power numbers were down from 1993, but his .313 average was second on the team and easily a career high.

Justice, David

Braves	G	AB	R	H	2B	3B	HR	RBI	SB	AVG	SLG
1989	16	51	7	12	3	0	1	3	2	.235	.353
1990	127	439	76	124	23	2	28	78	11	.282	.535
1991	109	396	67	109	25	1	21	87	8	.275	.503
1992	144	484	78	124	19	5	21	72	2	.256	.446
1993	157	585	90	158	15	4	40	120	3	.270	.515
1994	104	352	61	110	16	2	19	59	2	.313	.531
Career	657	2,307	379	637	101	14	130	419	28	.276	.501

Kelly, King

Beaneaters: 1887–89, 1891–92
Catcher, outfielder, third baseman, first baseman, second baseman, pitcher, shortstop
Birthplace: Troy, New York

B: December 31, 1857
D: November 8, 1894
Batted right, threw right
Ht. 5–10; **Wt.** 170

Mike "King" Kelly is regarded as the Babe Ruth of 19th-century baseball. By no stretch of the imagination was he the slugger Ruth was, but like the Bambino, Kelly captured the imagination of the fans like no other player of his era.

That's why the Beaneaters created the biggest ruckus the game had yet known when they purchased the "King of Baseball" from Chicago in 1887 for the unheard of price of $10,000. Boston fans were ecstatic that they were getting the game's biggest star, who had led the White Stockings to the last two pennants and won the National League batting title two of the previous three seasons. Chicago fans were equally as distraught.

Besides being a great player, Kelly was a showman without equal who was not against modifying the rules to fit the situation, as long as it benefited his team. He was acknowledged as the best base runner of his time, even though some of his best moves included stunts such as cutting across the diamond short of the bases when the one umpire used in those days wasn't watching him.

He was a quick thinker, as evidenced by a stunt he pulled one day while he was sitting on the bench as the Beaneaters' captain. An opposing batter hit a pop foul that Boston catcher Charlie Ganzel couldn't find. Kelly jumped up, yelled, "Kelly now catching for Boston," and caught the ball. The league had yet to pass a rule requiring that substitutions

be announced by the umpire, but Kelly got them thinking along those lines.

A play that best typified the type of player Kelly was occurred during his career in Boston when the Beaneaters trailed Washington by a run going into the ninth inning. Ruth would have hit a game-winning homer, but Kelly won the game with his sheer cunning.

He led off the ninth with a walk, stole second, took third on a short fly to center, and scored the tying run on a grounder to short. The throw to the plate had him beaten easily, but rather than bowling over the catcher—a young man named Connie Mack—Kelly faked to the left and slid to the right, avoiding the confused Mack and barely touching the plate with his hand to tie the score.

The game wound up going 14 innings, and it was Kelly, of course, who drove in the winning run.

He was famous for such daring and aggressive baserunning, and the fans adored it. "Slide, Kelly, Slide!" became a popular phrase in the grandstands and eventually a hit song.

Kelly was known as the "$10,000 Beauty." However, his acquisition did not have the desired effect on the Beaneaters, who still finished fifth in 1887.

Kelly was 29 years old when he came to Boston, and his best years were behind him, thanks in part to his strong inclination to party. Nevertheless, he contributed some good baseball for the Beaneaters, displaying his versatility by playing every position at some point.

In 1887, Kelly was second in the league in doubles, third in steals, fourth in runs, and fifth in on-base percentage. The next season, he was third in the batting race and tied for third in slugging percentage. And in 1889, his last season with Boston during his first tour, he led the league in doubles and was second in steals.

But in 1889, Kelly may well have cost the Beaneaters the pennant he was brought to Boston to win. The Beaneaters held a one-game edge on New York October 1, but the next day Kelly showed up drunk for a game at Cleveland. Boston lost the game, 7–1, and eventually the pennant by one game. That loss and the disruption its circumstances created on the club may have been too much to overcome at that stage of the season.

To add insult to injury, Kelly jumped the club the next year to play with the Boston entry in the new Players League. He returned to the Beaneaters at the end of the 1891 season and for all of 1892, but he was finished and had little to do with the club's winning pennants those two years.

Still, his popularity was unparalleled in Boston and throughout the league in that era. Beaneaters fans often referred to him as "His Royal Highness." John McGraw, the New York Giants Hall of Fame manager, named Kelly as the catcher on his all-time team. Cap Anson, another Hall of Famer, credited Kelly with creating the hit-and-run play.

King Kelly

Kelly, King

Beaneaters	G	AB	R	H	2B	3B	HR	RBI	SB	AVG	SLG
1887	116	484	120	156	34	11	8	63	84	.322	.488
1888	107	440	85	140	22	11	9	71	56	.318	.480
1889	125	507	120	149	41*	5	9	78	68	.294	.448
1891	16	52	7	12	1	0	0	5	6	.231	.250
1892	78	281	40	53	7	0	2	41	24	.189	.235
Career	442	1,764	372	510	105	27	28	258	238	.289	.427

Leibrandt, Charlie

Braves: 1990–92
Pitcher
Birthplace: Chicago

B: October 4, 1956
Batted right, threw left
Ht. 6–3; Wt. 200

Charlie Leibrandt was a major contributor to the Braves' successive National League pennants in 1991 and '92. Unfortunately, many people will remember him more for the role he played in Atlanta's losing the World Series both years.

A 15-game winner as a starter in both pennant-winning seasons, Leibrandt was called on in an unfamiliar relief role during the World Series both years. He failed miserably.

In 1991 the Braves held a 3–2 lead in games and were tied with Minnesota, 3–3, entering the bottom of the 11th inning of Game 6. That's when Bobby Cox summoned Leibrandt to make the first relief appearance of his Atlanta career.

The Twins' Kirby Puckett proceeded to hit a leadoff home run to end the game and tie the Series at three games apiece. Minnesota's Jack Morris pitched a 10-inning, 1–0 shutout the next evening, denying the Braves their first World Series championship since 1957.

"Why not Leibrandt?" Cox said. "We'd be pretty stupid if we were resistant in bringing in a 15-game winner."

The next October, Atlanta trailed Toronto 3–2 in games and was tied, 2–2, through nine innings of Game 6 when Cox called on Leibrandt in relief once again. The crafty left-hander managed to work a scoreless 10th. However, in the 11th, with right-hander Jeff Reardon warmed and waiting in the bullpen, Leibrandt was allowed to pitch to the right-handed-hitting Dave Winfield, whose two-out double drove in the decisive runs of the 4–3 game. The Braves had come up short in the Series for the second straight year.

Leibrandt never pitched for the Braves again. His contract was up at the end of the season, and Atlanta did not try to re-sign him. Instead, they replaced him in the starting rotation by signing 1992 Cy Young Award winner Greg Maddux.

The Braves, however, might never have won those two pennants without Leibrandt, who came to Atlanta from Kansas City in a trade after the 1989 season. He was 17–9 for the World Series champion Royals in 1985.

In 1991, Leibrandt's second year as a Brave, he combined with Steve Avery and Tom Glavine to give Atlanta three left-handers with 15 or more victories, the first team to have such a trio since the 1917 New York Giants. Besides his steady pitching, he also contributed to the club by fostering the development of young pitchers such as Avery, Glavine, and John Smoltz. In watching Leibrandt work, they learned how effective and successful a pitcher can be by outsmarting hitters, rather than overpowering them.

Leibrandt, Charlie												
Braves	W	L	Pct	G	GS	CG	ShO	IP	H	BB	SO	ERA	SV
1990	9	11	.450	24	24	5	2	162⅓	164	35	76	3.16	0
1991	15	13	.536	36	36	1	1	229⅔	212	56	128	3.49	0
1992	15	7	.682	32	31	5	2	193	191	42	104	3.36	0
Career	39	31	.557	92	91	11	5	585	567	133	308	3.35	0

Lemaster, Denny

Braves: 1962–67
Pitcher
Birthplace: Corona, California

B: February 25, 1939
Batted right, threw left
Ht. 6–1; Wt. 185

As a talented left-hander coming through the Braves farm system at the time when the career of Hall of Famer Warren Spahn was winding down, Denny Lemaster was one of several pitchers scrutinized as "the next Spahn." None, of course, ever came close to matching the work of the winningest left-hander in history, but Lemaster was one of the most talented of the lot.

In 1964, Spahn's last year with the Braves, Lemaster won a career-high 17 games. At age 25, he seemed to have "arrived" right on schedule. However, he would never approach 17 victories again and had but two more winning seasons the rest of his career. One of those came in 1966, the Braves' first year in Atlanta.

The Braves' arrival in the South created quite a stir, and the frenzy peaked at Atlanta Stadium on August 9 when Lemaster and Sandy Koufax hooked up in one of the great-

Charlie Leibrandt

Denny Lemaster

est pitching duels the city has ever seen. Koufax was en route to a 27–9 record and his second consecutive Cy Young Award. The two left-handers met earlier in the season at Dodger Stadium, with Koufax winning, 2–1.

The rematch, played before a standing-room-only crowd, had all the drama and emotion of a World Series game. A two-hour rain delay after the fourth inning only heightened the tension. The Braves led, 1–0, and Lemaster had a no-hitter in the eighth until Jim Lefebvre homered to tie the score. In the bottom of the ninth, future Braves Hall of Famer Eddie Mathews hit a home run off Koufax to end the game. Lemaster struck out 16 in the 2–1 victory.

Lemaster finished 11–8 that year, and when he got off to a good start in 1967, he was named to the National League All-Star team for the only time in his career. However, a back injury kept him from participating in the game and put a damper on his season. He finished 9–9 and was traded to Houston immediately after the season. The Braves acquired Sonny Jackson and Chuck Harrison in exchange for Lemaster and Denis Menke.

Lemaster won 23 games in his first two years with the Astros, posting excellent ERAs of 2.81 in 1968 and 3.16 in '69.

Lemaster, Denny

Braves	W	L	Pct	G	GS	CG	ShO	IP	H	BB	SO	ERA	SV
1962	3	4	.429	17	12	4	1	86⅔	75	32	69	3.01	0
1963	11	14	.440	46	31	10	1	237	199	85	190	3.04	1
1964	17	11	.607	39	35	9	3	221	216	75	185	4.15	1
1965	7	13	.350	32	23	4	1	146⅓	140	58	111	4.43	0
1966	11	8	.579	27	27	10	3	171	170	41	139	3.74	0
1967	9	9	.500	31	31	8	2	215⅓	184	72	148	3.34	0
Career	58	59	.496	192	159	45	11	1,077⅓	984	363	842	3.63	2

Lemke, Mark

Braves: 1988–
Second baseman
Birthplace: Utica, New York

B: August 13, 1965
Bats both, throws right
Ht. 5–9; **Wt.** 167

The World Series often has a way of making heroes out of the most unlikely candidates.

That's certainly true of Mark Lemke. He set an all-time franchise defensive record for second basemen in 1994, but Lemke is more famous for nearly winning the 1991 World Series with his bat than he is for anything he's ever done with the glove.

Lemke wasn't even the Braves' regular second baseman in 1991. He was the backup for Jeff Treadway, an accomplished line-drive hitter. However, Treadway was injured the last two weeks of the season when the Braves were driving to upset the Dodgers for the division title. Lemke filled in and put together a nine-game hitting streak, helping the Braves win their first division title since 1982.

The switch-hitting leprechaun lookalike saved his best hitting for the postseason, though. In the League Championship Series against Pittsburgh, he drove in the only run of Game 2 with a sixth-inning double. Then in the eighth inning, he prevented Pittsburgh from scoring the tying run with a diving stop of a grounder up the middle.

In the World Series against Minnesota, Lemke was a one-man wrecking crew. In the 12th inning of Game 3, he singled home David Justice with the winning run of the franchise's

Mark Lemke

first World Series victory since 1958. He finished the Series hitting .417, the best of any regular on either team. He had three triples to tie a Series record, finishing with a team-high .708 slugging percentage.

Lemke was easily the team's best player in the Series but failed to be named MVP because the Braves lost Game 7 to the Twins. Minnesota pitcher Jack Morris won the award instead.

The 1991 postseason was Lemke's coming-out party. He became the Braves' regular second baseman in 1992, and even though he hit just .227, Bobby Cox fell in love with his defense. Once again, Lemke hit better than expected in the postseason. His .333 average in the NLCS against the Pirates was easily the best on the team.

Lemke continued to show improvement in 1993, then had an absolutely banner year in 1994. He made just three errors in the strike-shortened season, and his .994 fielding percentage set an all-time franchise record at second, surpassing Frank Bolling's .989 in 1962 for Milwaukee.

Additionally, Lemke continued improvement at the plate, hitting a career-high .294, third among Braves regulars to Fred McGriff and David Justice.

Lemke, Mark

Braves	G	AB	R	H	2B	3B	HR	RBI	SB	AVG	SLG
1988	16	58	8	13	4	0	0	2	0	.224	.293
1989	14	55	4	10	2	1	2	10	0	.182	.364
1990	102	239	22	54	13	0	0	21	0	.226	.280
1991	136	269	36	63	11	2	2	23	1	.234	.312
1992	155	427	38	97	7	4	6	26	0	.227	.304
1993	151	493	52	124	19	2	7	49	1	.252	.341
1994	104	350	40	103	15	0	3	31	0	.294	.363
Career	678	1,891	200	464	71	9	20	162	2	.245	.324

Lewis, Ted

Beaneaters: 1896–1900
Pitcher
Birthplace: Machynlleth, Wales
B: December 25, 1872

D: May 24, 1936
Batted right, threw right
Ht. 5–10; **Wt.** 158

Ted "Parson" Lewis was one of the most unique individuals ever to play for the Braves, who were known as the

Ted Lewis

Johnny Logan

Beaneaters during his five-year stint with Boston at the turn of the century.

Born in Wales and educated at Marietta (Ohio) College and Williams College, where he earned a master's degree, Lewis was ordained as a minister and served both the University of Massachusetts and the University of New Hampshire as president. He also was an English professor, a friend of famed poet Robert Frost, and a pretty darned good pitcher.

In 1897, Lewis's first full year in the majors, he won 21 games to help Boston win the National League pennant. The following year, he led the league in winning percentage (.765) en route to 26 victories in another pennant-winning effort by the Beaneaters.

In the four-year period 1897–1900, Lewis averaged over 19 victories per year for the Beaneaters. He jumped from the Beaneaters to the new Boston American League franchise in 1901 and pitched the first shutout for the Pilgrims, who later became the Red Sox.

However, after that season, he retired at age 29 because he felt a clergyman shouldn't be a pro ballplayer. He taught English at Columbia University and twice ran unsuccessfully for the Massachusetts legislature before becoming the only major leaguer ever to be president of a major university. He died at age 63, and Frost read from Tennyson and Whitman at his funeral.

Lewis, Ted

Beaneaters	W	L	Pct	G	GS	CG	ShO	IP	H	BB	SO	ERA	SV
1896	1	4	.200	6	5	4	0	41⅓	37	27	12	3.24	0
1897	21	12	.636	38	34	30	2	290	316	125	65	3.85	1
1898	26	8	.765	41	33	29	1	313⅓	267	109	72	2.90	2
1899	17	11	.607	29	25	23	2	234⅔	245	73	60	3.49	0
1900	13	12	.520	30	22	19	1	209	215	86	66	4.13	0
Career	78	47	.624	144	119	105	6	1,088⅔	1,080	420	275	3.53	3

Logan, Johnny

Braves: 1951–61
Shortstop
Birthplace: Endicott, New York

B: March 23, 1927
Batted right, threw right
Ht. 5–11; **Wt.** 175

The Milwaukee Braves of the mid-to-late 1950s were one of the finest teams ever assembled. They nearly won a third consecutive pennant in 1959, and might have if not for the collision between Johnny Logan and Norm Larker in the seventh inning of the second game of the playoff with the Dodgers for the National League championship.

With the Braves leading 4–2 and trying to even the best-of-three playoff, Larker barreled into second attempting to break up a double play and leveled Logan with a shoulder block any football player would have been proud to claim. The blow knocked Logan unconscious, and he had to be carried off on a stretcher.

When the 32-year-old shortstop came to his senses, the first words out of his mouth were "Did we get the guy at first?"

Yes, they did, but in the bottom of the 12th inning, Logan's replacement, Felix Mantilla, made a throwing error that enabled the Dodgers to win, 6–5, and end the Braves' pennant run at two.

But Logan's concern for the team over his own health typified the fighting spirit that made him one of the Braves' most popular players. He was talented enough to lead the league's shortstops in fielding three times, make four All-Star teams, and lead the league in doubles in 1955. However, it was his gutsy, rough-and-tumble style of play that really caught the imagination of the beer-drinking, blue-collar crowd in Milwaukee.

Logan probably also would have led the league in fights if such statistics had been kept. One of his most memorable bouts came with his own teammate, pitcher Vern Bickford, whom Logan pounded to a pulp at a New York restaurant in 1953. The Braves' shortstop didn't back down from anyone. His many opponents included Don Drysdale, Vic Power, Johnny Temple, Hal Jeffcoat, Clint Courtney, and Jim Greengrass.

One of the keys to Logan's success at baseball and fighting were his strong hands, which he claimed came from milking cows as a youth. He said he was a professional milker by age 11.

Nicknamed "Yachta," Ukrainian for John, Logan broke in with the Braves in Boston in 1951. When the Braves played an exhibition game against the Yankees, Logan asked longtime New York shortstop and coach Frank Crosetti to critique him. A few weeks later, Logan got a long list of pointers from Crosetti in the mail and said they were quite beneficial.

Perhaps Crosetti's advice made a big impact, for Logan led the league's shortstops in fielding each of his first three full seasons. Logan spent nine years as the Braves' starting shortstop, and except for the 1959 playoff game, he was extremely durable, rarely missing a game.

Offensively, Logan didn't stack up well with a lot of his teammates, but few players of that era did. He reached double figures in home runs six times, including five straight years from 1955 to 1959. His best offensive season was 1955 when he jumped out with a .364 April, was still at .307 at the All-Star break, and barely missed what would have been the only .300 season of his career.

Logan did not hit well in either the 1957 or '58 World Series. However, he did deliver two clutch hits in the '57 Series. In Game 2, he hit a home run to back Lou Burdette's 4–2 victory, and in Game 4, he doubled home the tying run in the bottom of the 10th inning of the Braves' 7–5 victory.

Logan was finally unseated as Milwaukee's regular shortstop in 1961 when the Braves acquired slick-fielding but light-hitting Roy McMillan from Cincinnati. Two months into the season, a 34-year-old Logan was traded to Pittsburgh for outfielder Gino Cimoli. He never played regularly in the majors again but spent 1964 in Japan.

After returning from Japan, Logan settled in Wisconsin and became a sheriff and a broadcaster, serving on the Milwaukee Brewers announcing team for a while.

Those were appropriate avocations for someone famous for fighting and for his "Loganisms." He once called Stan Musial "one of baseball's great immorals," and he introduced former Commissioner Ford Frick as "my great and good friend, Frick Ford."

Ernie Lombardi

Logan, Johnny

Braves	G	AB	R	H	2B	3B	HR	RBI	SB	AVG	SLG
1951	62	169	14	37	7	1	0	16	0	.219	.272
1952	117	456	56	129	21	3	4	42	1	.283	.368
1953	150	611	100	167	27	8	11	73	2	.273	.398
1954	154	560	66	154	17	7	8	66	2	.275	.373
1955	154	595	95	177	37*	5	13	83	3	.297	.442
1956	148	545	69	153	27	5	15	46	3	.281	.431
1957	129	494	59	135	19	7	10	49	5	.273	.401
1958	145	530	54	120	20	0	11	53	1	.226	.326
1959	138	470	59	137	17	0	13	50	1	.291	.411
1960	136	482	52	118	14	4	7	42	1	.245	.334
1961	18	19	0	2	1	0	0	1	0	.105	.158
Career	1,351	4,931	624	1,329	207	40	92	521	19	.270	.384

Lombardi, Ernie

Braves: 1942
Catcher
Birthplace: Oakland, California
B: April 6, 1908

D: September 26, 1977
Batted right, threw right
Ht. 6–3; **Wt.** 230

The Braves have produced 10 batting champions in their 119-year history . . . or is it only nine?

That depends on what criteria you feel must be met to earn a batting crown. There was debate over who deserved the title in 1942, and to some extent, that controversy still exists. However, the bottom line is that Ernie Lombardi was awarded the 1942 batting championship by National League president Ford Frick, regardless of the fact that the Braves catcher had only 309 at bats.

Most record books list Lombardi as the 1942 batting champ for that reason, but some sources, including *Total Baseball,* give the title to Enos Slaughter, who hit just .318 but had 591 at bats.

In 1940 an unofficial standard of 400 at bats was set to qualify for the batting title. However, it was never written as

a rule. When Frick was questioned about Lombardi's right to the 1942 title, he ruled that the 400 at bat standard did not apply to catchers because of the extra work load required at the position. "To bar such a man from the hitting title would be an injustice," said Frick, displaying the diplomacy that would one day make him commissioner.

It was Lombardi's second batting title, making him the only catcher ever to win two and the last catcher to lead the league in hitting. His first championship was in 1938 for the Reds when he hit .342 in 489 at bats. Today's standard is 502 plate appearances, which include walks, sacrifices, and so on.

The reason Lombardi did not have more at bats in 1942 is that he had to sit out several weeks with a split finger. No one ever questioned whether he was a good enough hitter to win the batting crown. In fact, there were people who swore he was one of the greatest pure hitters of all time—and perhaps the best. However, he also was quite possibly the slowest man ever to play the game. He never got leg hits, and infielders played ridiculously deep on him, robbing him of what would have been countless hits for most other players.

Lombardi was a big, strong man who used a 42-ounce bat, the heaviest of his era. He held it with his hands interlocked, much like a golfer's grip. He wasn't a great home run hitter, but he hit the ball as hard as—or harder than—anyone else. He also had an excellent throwing arm, and in 1938 he won the National League MVP award as well as the batting title.

He was immensely popular with Cincinnati fans, and he caught both of Johnny Vander Meer's back-to-back no-hitters in 1938. But management was not pleased with his annual holdout ritual. When Lombardi had an off season in 1941 because he was injured and out of shape, the Reds decided they'd seen enough of him.

Not many teams were interested because he was 34, out of shape, and coming off a bad year. However, the Braves, annually buried in the standings, had little to lose, so they bought him. Lombardi shocked everyone by reporting in shape for spring training, saying he was determined to prove the Reds had made a mistake.

Except for the finger injury, he had an excellent 1942 season, making his sixth All-Star team. But the next spring, he was a holdout, as usual. He didn't sign until April, and the Braves turned around and traded him to the Giants for Hugh Poland and Connie Ryan.

Lombardi, Ernie

Braves	G	AB	R	H	2B	3B	HR	RBI	SB	AVG	SLG
1942	105	309	32	102	14	0	11	46	1	.330*	.482
Career	105	309	32	102	14	0	11	46	1	.330	.482

Long, Herman

Beaneaters: 1890–1902	**B:** April 13, 1866
Shortstop, outfielder, second baseman,	**D:** September 17, 1909
third baseman, first baseman	**Batted left, threw right**
Birthplace: Chicago	**Ht.** 5–8; **Wt.** 160

Perhaps the most crucial ingredient to the makeup of a truly great team is an outstanding shortstop, one who can tie together the club's defense and also contribute offensively.

That's what Herman "Germany" Long was to the Beaneaters of the 1890s.

In the eight-year period between 1891 and 1898, Boston won five pennants. Only two everyday players—second baseman Bobby Lowe and Long—played on all five pennant winners.

Long was the glue of the Boston defense as well as one of the team's better all-around offensive players. He was brilliant defensively and offered the uncommon combination, especially in his era, of speed and power. He won games with home runs and stolen bases, as well as with his glove and arm.

Long might have won a few games with his mouth, too. He was always talking, taunting the opposition, even leading the crowd in razzing the rival pitcher.

In 1890, Boston purchased Long's contract for $6,500 from Kansas City of the American Association. Manager Frank Selee made him his starting shortstop immediately, and Long held the job for 13 years.

He had outstanding range, as evidenced by the fact that he ranks first all-time in chances accepted by a shortstop, an especially impressive figure considering the small gloves used at that time. He was so athletic that he supposedly practiced deflecting balls with his feet to the second baseman if he couldn't get a glove on them.

Long led National League shortstops in defensive percentage twice, ironically the last two years he played for Boston.

A left-handed hitter, the "Flying Dutchman," as he was sometimes called, batted .300 for four straight years and compiled a .279 lifetime average. He led the league in home runs with 12 in 1900, the only shortstop other than Ernie Banks to lead a league in homers. Long also led the league in runs in 1893. He stole at least 20 bases every year he played for the Beaneaters and ranks 26th all-time in career steals.

Long, Herman

Beaneaters	G	AB	R	H	2B	3B	HR	RBI	SB	AVG	SLG
1890	101	431	95	108	15	3	8	52	49	.251	.355
1891	139	577	129	163	21	11	10	76	60	.282	.409
1892	151	646	115	181	33	6	6	78	57	.280	.378
1893	128	552	149*	159	22	6	6	58	38	.288	.382
1894	104	475	136	154	28	11	12	79	24	.324	.505
1895	124	535	109	169	23	10	9	75	35	.316	.447
1896	120	501	105	172	26	8	6	100	36	.343	.463
1897	107	450	89	145	32	7	3	69	22	.322	.444
1898	144	589	99	156	21	10	6	99	20	.265	.365
1899	145	578	91	153	30	8	6	100	20	.265	.375
1900	125	486	80	127	19	4	12*	66	26	.261	.391
1901	138	518	54	112	14	6	3	68	20	.216	.284
1902	120	439	40	101	11	0	2	44	24	.230	.269
Career	1,646	6,777	1,291	1,900	295	90	89	964	431	.280	.390

Lopez, Al

Bees: 1936–40	**B:** August 20, 1908
Catcher	**Batted right, threw right**
Birthplace: Tampa, Florida	**Ht.** 5–11; **Wt.** 165

Al Lopez was one of the finest defensive catchers in franchise history. Unfortunately, he came along during a bleak period, so his contributions had little impact on the club's success.

The Braves were in such a dismal state when they acquired Lopez in 1936 that they changed their nickname to Bees in a preposterous attempt to alter the club's fortunes.

The son of Spanish immigrants, Lopez already had caught six full seasons for the Dodgers, making the All-Star team in 1934, when Boston obtained him prior to the 1936 season. It was a six-player deal in which the Bees also got infielder Tony Cuccinello and two other players for left-hander Ed Brandt and outfielder Randy Moore. Since Brandt and Moore were

Herman Long

Al Lopez

at the end of their careers, it proved to be a wise move for Boston.

Lopez, who would lead the league's catchers in defense four times, was one of the smartest men ever to play the position. Once with the Bees, he signaled pitcher Danny MacFayden to knock down a hitter even though the count was 3–0. MacFayden shook off the signal three times, then finally did it. Lopez took the inside pitch and rifled the ball to third where he picked off a shocked base runner who represented a big run.

Perhaps the biggest contribution Lopez made to the Braves was the role he played in developing rookies Lou Fette, age 30, and Jim Turner, 33, into 20-game winners in 1937. There's never been another story quite like that of Fette and Turner, and both credited their handling by manager Bill McKechnie and Lopez as major factors in achieving their overnight prestige.

Even with two 20-game winners coming practically out of nowhere, the Bees never got above fifth place while Lopez was with the team. Lopez was traded to Pittsburgh in mid-1940 for catcher Ray Berres and $40,000. The move was strictly economical for Boston, because Berres wasn't even in Lopez's class.

Undersized as catchers go, Lopez nevertheless had a 19-year career in which he set a record for games caught (1,918). The record stood until Bob Boone surpassed it in 1987.

Lopez eventually became a Hall of Famer, but more for his work as a manager than as a catcher. In a 17-year career with the Indians and White Sox, he won pennants for Cleveland in 1954 and Chicago in 1959.

Lopez, Al

Bees	G	AB	R	H	2B	3B	HR	RBI	SB	AVG	SLG
1936	128	426	46	103	12	5	7	50	1	.242	.343
1937	105	334	31	68	11	1	3	38	3	.204	.269
1938	71	236	19	63	6	1	1	14	5	.267	.314
1939	131	412	32	104	22	1	8	49	1	.252	.369
1940	36	119	20	35	3	1	2	17	1	.294	.387
Career	471	1,527	148	373	54	9	21	168	11	.244	.333

Lowe, Bobby

Beaneaters: 1890–1901
Second baseman, outfielder, third baseman, shortstop, first baseman, pitcher
Birthplace: Pittsburgh, Pennsylvania

B: July 10, 1868
D: December 8, 1951
Batted right, threw right
Ht. 5–10; **Wt.** 150

Bobby Lowe hit 71 home runs in his 18-year major league career, reaching double figures in a season just twice. Yet he was the first man in history to accomplish one of the most revered of power-hitting feats.

On May 30, 1894, Lowe, a 25-year-old infielder, hit four home runs in the second game of a morning/afternoon doubleheader against Cincinnati at Boston's Congress Street Grounds. Only 11 other players in history have managed four homers in a game, and Lowe is one of just four to have done it in consecutive at bats.

After the morning game of the Memorial Day doubleheader, Lowe went to a restaurant near Boston harbor and had a meal of fresh seafood. Batting leadoff in the afternoon game, he struck out in the first inning, then led off the third inning

Bobby Lowe

with a home run to start a nine-run rally against Elton "Icebox" Chamberlain. Later in the third, he hit a two-run homer.

Lowe also hit home runs in the fifth and sixth innings. After No. 4, the game was stopped while fans showered him with some $160 in coins, quite a substantial bonus for a day's work in those days. Lowe batted one more time, settling for a single in the eighth inning.

Like most ballplayers even today, Lowe was careful not to change his routine the next day, hoping to maintain his good fortune. He ate the same pregame meal at the same restaurant but failed to get even a hit, let alone a home run.

Lowe hit 13 other home runs that year, finishing second in the league with 17, one behind teammate Hugh Duffy. Both Duffy and Lowe had career years in 1894, finishing first and second, respectively, in the league in total bases. Though it was a record year for offense throughout the league, opposing teams must have wondered if there was something in the water in Boston.

Lowe was primarily a second baseman, though he played quite a bit of outfield early in his career and appeared at every position but catcher at some point. That he weighed just 150 pounds and batted leadoff shows that he wasn't considered a power hitter in spite of what he did in 1894. However, he also tied for third in the league in home runs in 1893.

The Beaneaters won five pennants during the 1890s, and Lowe was one of only three men to play on each of those teams. Pitcher Kid Nichols and shortstop Herman Long were the other two.

Lowe, Bobby

Beaneaters	G	AB	R	H	2B	3B	HR	RBI	SB	AVG	SLG
1890	52	207	35	58	13	2	2	21	15	.280	.391
1891	125	497	92	129	19	5	6	74	43	.260	.354
1892	124	475	79	115	16	7	3	57	36	.242	.324
1893	126	526	130	157	19	5	14	89	22	.298	.433
1894	133	613	158	212	34	11	17	115	23	.346	.520
1895	99	412	101	122	12	7	7	62	24	.296	.410
1896	73	305	59	98	11	4	2	48	15	.321	.403
1897	123	499	87	154	24	8	5	106	16	.309	.419
1898	147	559	65	152	11	7	4	94	12	.272	.338
1899	152	559	81	152	5	9	4	88	17	.272	.335
1900	127	474	65	132	11	5	3	71	15	.278	.342
1901	129	491	47	125	11	1	3	47	22	.255	.299
Career	1,410	5,617	999	1,606	186	71	70	872	260	.286	.382

Maddux, Greg

Braves: 1993–
Pitcher
Birthplace: San Angelo, Texas

B: April 14, 1966
Bats right, throws right
Ht. 6–0; **Wt.** 175

In the first 37 years of its existence, the Cy Young Award was an infrequent visitor to the Braves franchise. Then along came Greg Maddux.

In 1957, Warren Spahn won the second Cy Young ever presented, when there was just one award for both leagues. That was the last time a Brave claimed the ultimate award for pitching excellence until Tom Glavine won it in 1991.

Glavine was the runner-up for the honor in 1992 when Maddux won it with the Chicago Cubs. Then Maddux, who'd become a free agent, signed a five-year contract with the Braves and put a viselike grip on the award like no one else had ever been able to do. He won it in 1993 and again in 1994, becoming the first pitcher ever to win three in a row and doubling the number of Cy Youngs won by Braves.

Originally a second-round draft pick by the Cubs in 1984, Maddux earned a late call to the majors in 1986 at age 20, becoming the youngest Cub since 1967. In 1988, at age 22, he was the youngest Cub ever to make the All-Star team, and a year later, he won 19 games and finished third in the Cy Young voting.

After two 15-win seasons in 1990 and '91, Maddux established himself among the game's elite in 1992, tying Glavine for the league lead in victories (20), finishing third in ERA (2.18), and winning his first Cy Young. That off-season, he turned down a more lucrative contract offer from the Yankees to sign with the Braves because he felt he'd have a better chance to be with a pennant winner.

In 1993, Maddux proceeded to pick up with the Braves where he left off with the Cubs, posting his second straight 20-win season. He and Glavine (22 victories) gave the Braves two 20-game winners for the first time since 1959 when Spahn and Lou Burdette each won 21. Maddux also led the league in ERA (2.36), the first Brave to do so since Buzz Capra in 1974.

As good as Maddux's season was, it could have been much better with a little more offensive support. In his 10 losses, the Braves scored a total of just 15 runs. He won 13 of his last 15 decisions and also led the league in complete games and innings.

It all added up to his second consecutive Cy Young. Maddux became the fifth pitcher to win back-to-back awards, along with Sandy Koufax, Denny McLain, Jim Palmer, and Roger Clemens. He also joined Gaylord Perry as the only men to win Cy Youngs with different clubs.

If the pressure of becoming the first pitcher to win three straight Cy Youngs ever entered Maddux's thinking in 1994, he never showed it. In fact, he had what should go down as one of the greatest seasons of any pitcher in history, even if the schedule was cut short by the players' strike.

In winning the Cy Young, Maddux tied Montreal's Kent Hill for the league lead in victories (16). However, what was most impressive about the work of the 28-year-old right-hander was the manner in which he dominated hitters in a year that was known for offense—not pitching. Maddux easily led the league with an all-time franchise record 1.56 ERA, which was 2.65 runs better than the league ERA of 4.21. That was the largest differential in history. The closest NL pitcher to Maddux, the Mets' Bret Saberhagen, was more than a run higher at 2.74.

When Bob Gibson posted his record 1.12 ERA for St. Louis in 1968, he did so in a season dominated by pitching. The National League ERA was 2.99, and the league's composite batting average was just .243. By comparison, the league's batting average in 1994 was .267 (only a league-low .207 against Maddux), and several of the game's offensive records, including the single-season home run record, were in jeopardy before the strike.

Maddux, Greg

Braves	W	L	Pct	G	GS	CG	ShO	IP	H	BB	SO	ERA	SV
1993	20	10	.667	36	36*	8*	1	267*	228	52	197	2.36*	0
1994	16*	6	.727	25	25	10*	3*	202*	150	31	156	1.56*	0
Career	36	16	.692	61	61	18	4	469	378	83	353	2.01	0

Greg Maddux

Mantilla, Felix

Braves: 1956–61
Second baseman, shortstop, third baseman, outfielder
Birthplace: Isabela, Puerto Rico

B: July 29, 1934
Batted right, threw right
Ht. 6–0; **Wt.** 160

A talented utility man for the Braves' pennant winners in 1957 and '58, Felix Mantilla had an unfortunate knack for being in the wrong place at the wrong time.

Mantilla holds two major distinctions in Braves history: (1) In 1957 he helped turn Hank Aaron unexpectedly into a center fielder, and (2) in 1959, he made the errant throw that ruined hopes of a Braves dynasty and may have cost Milwaukee a third consecutive pennant.

Felix Mantilla

For sure, Mantilla had assistance in those two misadventures, but not many Braves fans shed a tear when he was selected as one of the 22 original New York Mets in the expansion draft following the 1961 season. In fact, most probably felt that was a just reward for him.

On July 11, 1957, with the Braves battling for their first pennant since 1948, Mantilla almost demolished that effort and the career of talented center fielder Billy Bruton in one fell swoop.

Subbing for the slumping Johnny Logan at shortstop, Mantilla raced into short center field in pursuit of a pop-up and crashed into the oncoming Bruton. Both Mantilla and Bruton had to leave the game with knee injuries, and though Mantilla missed three weeks, Bruton was out for nearly a year with ligament damage. Manager Fred Haney was forced to use Aaron in center the rest of the season.

After winning the 1958 pennant, the Braves were favored to make it three in a row in 1959. However, they finished the regular season tied with the Dodgers, forcing a best-of-three playoff. Milwaukee lost the first game and was tied, 5–5, with the Dodgers in the bottom of the 12th inning of the second game. With two on and two out, Mantilla, filling in at short for Logan, who had been injured in the seventh inning, fielded a potential inning-ending grounder and threw wildly past first, permitting the decisive run to score and sending the Dodgers to the World Series.

Maranville, Rabbit

Braves: 1912–20, 1929–33, 1935   **B:** November 11, 1891
Shortstop, second baseman,   **D:** January 5, 1954
  third baseman   **Batted right, threw right**
Birthplace: Springfield, Massachusetts   **Ht.** 5–5; **Wt.** 155

Rabbit Maranville was one of the most colorful and memorable players in Braves history. He also was one of the franchise's greatest players. A Hall of Famer, he was one of the most accomplished defensive shortstops of all time and a prominent member of the "Miracle" Braves of 1914.

Only a .258 lifetime hitter, Maranville never led the league in any major offensive department during his 23-year career. He did, however, lead the National League in defense at his position five times—three of those at shortstop, where he spent most of his career, and twice at second base. He had exceptionally sure hands, quickness, and speed, as well as a quick release on his throws.

Animated and energetic, Maranville, whose given name was Walter, picked up the nickname "Rabbit" when he was still in the minors. A little girl saw him warming up before a game and said, "You jump around just like a rabbit."

The nickname certainly fit. At 5–5, he was one of the smallest major leaguers ever, and his childish appearance and behavior made him a favorite of the fans. He entertained with on-field stunts that wouldn't have been tolerated from anyone else. And off the field he was just as devilish, a characteristic that was accented by his hearty drinking.

Born in Springfield, Massachusetts, Maranville was the son of a policeman who opposed his youngster's desire to become a ballplayer because of the rowdy behavior for which they were known. But his father's opposition didn't keep young Walter from excelling at both baseball and rowdiness.

The Braves were mired in last place for the fourth straight season in 1912 when they brought in Maranville, then 20, for a look in September. He wasn't all that impressive, but the Braves couldn't afford to be picky, and they brought him back the next spring when new manager George Stallings took over the club. The competition for the starting shortstop job was between Maranville and another rookie, Art Bues, who just happened to be Stallings' nephew.

"What chance have I got if I have to fight your whole family?" Maranville asked Stallings. "But I'll tell you one thing, if I ever get in there, you'll never get me out."

Whether it was nepotism or simply a case of poor judgment, Stallings awarded the job to Bues. However, as fate would have it, Bues came down with diphtheria just as the

Mantilla, Felix										
Braves	**G**	**AB**	**R**	**H**	**2B**	**3B**	**HR**	**RBI**	**SB**	**AVG**	**SLG**
1956	35	53	9	15	1	1	0	3	0	.283	.340
1957	71	182	28	43	9	1	4	21	2	.236	.363
1958	85	226	37	50	5	1	7	19	2	.221	.345
1959	103	251	26	54	5	0	3	19	6	.215	.271
1960	63	148	21	38	7	0	3	11	3	.257	.365
1961	45	93	13	20	3	0	1	5	1	.215	.280
Career	402	953	134	220	30	3	18	78	14	.231	.325

Rabbit Maranville

season was about to start. Stallings was forced to go with Maranville.

True to his promise, Maranville quickly became a fixture in the lineup. He went 3-for-4 on opening day against future Hall of Famer Christy Mathewson and held the shortstop job until he volunteered for the navy in 1918. Bues recovered but played in just two games and wound up with the Cubs in 1914.

It's amazing just how quickly Maranville became a fan favorite. In mid-1913, his rookie year, the 21-year old shortstop was feted with a day in his honor at the South End Grounds. His hometown fans presented him with many gifts. Maranville's father attended the game and forgave his son for pursuing a baseball career.

Maranville's popularity stemmed from his playing skill, of course, but also from his pixie appearance and demeanor. He began his playful behavior as a rookie, once pulling a pair of glasses from his pocket and offering them to an umpire. Also that year, several Braves locked Maranville in a room and went to another room to play cards. A few minutes later, he was making faces at them through the window—from his position on a narrow ledge on the 12th floor of the hotel.

His antics throughout his career were legendary. He'd occasionally play to the fans by crawling through the legs of the umpire when he came to the plate to bat. He'd sit on opposing players at second base or crawl through their legs. He'd strut around the infield after making a great play, which was often. On a dare, he once dived, fully clothed, into a goldfish pool in St. Louis.

But Maranville's most famous stunt was his "vest-pocket catch." He caught pop-ups of any height with his hands cupped at his belt buckle. He said he did it so, in the event of a bobble, he could pin the ball against his body.

Late in his career, Maranville did stage shows during which he demonstrated the vest-pocket catch on a "pop-up" thrown by a stagehand. And on a postseason tour of Japan, he tried to teach the Japanese infielders to make the catch. However, after several were hit on the head, he quit.

Of course, Rabbit's act wouldn't have held water if he couldn't play ball. A good indication of the high esteem in which Maranville was held is the fact that he finished a close second to Miracle Braves teammate Johnny Evers for the Chalmers Award in 1914. The Chalmers, named after the automobile given the winner, was the equivalent of the Most Valuable Player Award.

After the Braves' 1914 World Series victory, Stallings said Maranville was the "greatest player to come to the majors since Ty Cobb." Though that statement proved to be a bit much, Rabbit was one of the game's most highly regarded players in his era.

There was no MVP award in the National League from 1915 to 1923 or in 1930. However, in the years of his career when there was such an award, Maranville usually did well in the voting. He finished in the top 10 five times with three different teams—the Braves (1913, 1914, and 1931), Pirates (1924), and Cardinals (1928). As late as 1933, when he was 41 years old and batted just .218 for Boston, Maranville managed to place 12th in the MVP voting.

Make no mistake, Rabbit was one of the great defensive infielders of all time. His fielding percentages don't compare to those of modern players who play on well-manicured infields or carpet and who have much larger and better developed gloves, but he was a wizard in his time, the Ozzie Smith

of his era. He was a regular on two pennant winners, the 1928 Cardinals as well as the 1914 Braves.

Maranville's best full-season batting average came in 1922 when he hit .295 for Pittsburgh. His best years in home runs (5 in 1919), RBIs (78 in 1914), and steals (32 in 1916) all came as a Brave. When the Braves traded him to Pittsburgh in 1921 for three players, including Billy Southworth, and $15,000, Boston fans were not happy.

Only 18 men in history, encompassing all-time greats from Ty Cobb to Hank Aaron and Willie Mays, ever went to bat 10,000 times. Maranville was the fourth player in history to do so, joining Cobb, Honus Wagner, and Tris Speaker in 1933.

Injuries, military service, and booze probably kept Maranville from another couple of thousand at bats. He missed most of 1918 because of World War I, and half of 1925 with a broken leg, and he was released in 1926 because of his drinking. He spent 1927 in the minors proving he had overcome alcohol problems and missed all of 1934 with a broken leg.

In 1926, Maranville was released by the Dodgers, his third team in three years, midway through the season. It appeared his career might be over at age 34 because of his drinking. However, he swore off alcohol and played at Rochester in 1937, hitting .298 and earning a late-season call to St. Louis. The next year, he helped the Cardinals to the pennant and hit .308 in the World Series loss to the Yankees.

Fresh off his triumphant comeback in St. Louis, Maranville returned to Boston in 1929 when the Braves bought him from the Cardinals. Though he was 37, he still had plenty of ability and spunk left. In fact, 1929 and 1930 were two of his better offensive seasons, and he led the league in fielding percentage in 1930 at shortstop and in 1932—when he was 40 years old—at second base.

In the spring of 1934, Maranville suffered a broken leg while sliding home on an attempted double steal in an exhibition game. The injury caused him to miss the entire season and essentially ended his major league career.

Though ill-suited for the job, Maranville served as player-manager with the Cubs for two months in late 1925 at the height of his drinking. He was relieved of his managerial duties in September, and that was the last he managed until 1936 when he returned to the minors with the fire for baseball still burning inside him. Rabbit not only managed Elmira of the New York–Penn League, but he also played 123 games and batted .323 at age 44.

He managed a few more seasons in the minors, then went back in the navy at age 51, serving in World War II. The spirit that helped make him such a great player remained indomitable.

Though Maranville's accomplishments on the field were enough to make him one of the game's immortals, it was his antics on and off the field that carved his larger-than-life legend.

He once swam across Boston's Charles River to get to the ballpark rather than walk a few blocks to get to the bridge. During his stage show, he slid over the footlights and into the orchestra pit while demonstrating his sliding technique. During a trip to Japan, he was arrested for impersonating a soldier in a military review, and he "soaped" Al Simmons' bat, causing the Hall of Fame slugger to foul off pitch after pitch.

The stories are virtually endless. The adventures of Rabbit Maranville represent one of the most prominent, as well as one of the most unique, chapters in Braves history.

Maranville, Rabbit

Braves	G	AB	R	H	2B	3B	HR	RBI	SB	AVG	SLG
1912	26	86	8	18	2	0	0	8	1	.209	.233
1913	143	571	68	141	13	8	2	48	25	.247	.308
1914	156	586	74	144	23	6	4	78	28	.246	.326
1915	149	509	51	124	23	6	2	43	18	.244	.324
1916	155	604	79	142	16	13	4	38	32	.235	.325
1917	142	561	69	146	19	13	3	43	27	.260	.357
1918	11	38	3	12	0	1	0	3	0	.316	.368
1919	131	480	44	128	18	10	5	43	12	.267	.377
1920	134	493	48	131	19	15	1	43	14	.266	.371
1929	146	560	87	159	26	10	0	55	13	.284	.366
1930	142	558	85	157	26	8	2	43	9	.281	.367
1931	145	562	69	146	22	5	0	33	9	.260	.317
1932	149	571	67	134	20	4	0	37	4	.235	.284
1933	143	478	46	104	15	4	0	38	2	.218	.266
1935	23	67	3	10	2	0	0	5	0	.149	.179
Career	1,795	6,724	801	1,696	244	103	23	558	194	.252	.329

Mathews, Eddie

Braves: 1952–66
Third baseman, first baseman, outfielder
Birthplace: Texarkana, Texas

B: October 13, 1931
Batted left, threw right
Ht. 6–1; **Wt.** 200

Some men just look like ballplayers more than others do. No man who has ever worn a Braves uniform looked more like a ballplayer than did Edwin Lee Mathews. And with the exception of Hank Aaron, the franchise hasn't had a better position player over an extended period.

Mathews, the leading left-handed home run hitter in franchise history, carried himself like a star from the moment he joined the Braves. He was muscular, handsome, and athletic. Competitiveness seemed to ooze from his pores. He could run fast and throw well, and he had a classic swing with power to match.

There were those who thought in the early 1950s that Mathews might be capable of hitting 700 home runs. That's the kind of player he was in his early 20s.

Though the slugging Mathews fell a couple of hundred

Eddie Mathews

home runs shy of 700, he still had a fabulous career and ranks as one of the finest third baseman in the game's history. He stands 12th all-time on the career home run list with 512, and Willie McCovey is the only left-handed hitter with more lifetime home runs in the National League than Mathews. His uniform number 41 is one of only five to have been retired by the Braves.

Mathews is the only Brave who played at the big league level in Boston, Milwaukee, and Atlanta, and thus is the only man in history to play for the same franchise in three cities.

There was never any question about Mathews' ability, even as a 17-year-old baseball and football high school star in Santa Barbara, California, in 1949. College football recruiters coveted him, and baseball scouts were swarming all over each other trying to get his name on a contract. Fortunately for the Braves, their scout, Johnny Moore, was the most ingenious of the lot.

Under baseball rules, prospects couldn't be signed until they graduated from high school. Mathews went to his prom after the graduation ceremony, and several scouts followed in hope of getting his signature on a contract that evening. Little did they know just how far they were behind Moore, who'd become friends with the Mathews family. While the other scouts waited for the prom to end, Moore snuck Mathews and his girlfriend, for whom the scout had bought a corsage, out the back door.

Mathews and his father, a Western Union telegraph operator, signed the contract, which called for a bonus of $5,999, one dollar under the level that prevented a player from being sent to the minors. The Dodgers' Branch Rickey had offered Mathews $10,000 plus another $30,000 for his family, but Mathews didn't want to rot on the big league bench for two years. Moore's resourcefulness would pay off big dividends for the Braves for years to come.

One of the reasons Mathews chose the Braves was that he felt their major league third baseman, Bob Elliott, was near the end of his career and would soon need a replacement. It didn't take the youngster long to get that job either.

In his first pro season, Mathews hit .363 with 17 home runs for High Point–Thomasville of the Class-D North Carolina State League—and he didn't even reach his 18th birthday until after the season. He played for the Atlanta Crackers of the Southern League in 1950 and hit 32 home runs.

With the Korean War in progress, Mathews was about to be drafted after the 1950 season, so he enlisted in the navy. However, his father became ill, and since Mathews was an only child, he was discharged late in the 1951 season. Though he played in just 49 games that year with Milwaukee of the American Association and Atlanta, Mathews was handed a regular major league job in 1952.

At the age of 20, he became the Braves' third baseman for their final season in Boston. And he didn't relinquish the position for 15 years.

As a rookie, Mathews wasn't much of a third baseman, but he knew what to do with the bat. He finished tied for fourth in the league with 25 home runs. Three of the homers came on September 27 at Ebbets Field in the next-to-last game of the season, making him the first rookie ever to accomplish that feat.

The Braves moved to Milwaukee in 1953, and Mathews quickly gave the team's new fans someone to worship. Acting as if he'd never heard of the "sophomore jinx," the sweet-swinging 21-year-old led all of baseball with 47 home runs, a total he'd never again reach. He raised his batting average 60 points and also finished second in the National League to Roy Campanella in RBIs and to Duke Snider in total bases and slugging percentage.

The Braves all received immediate celebrity status the moment they arrived in Milwaukee. With his youth, good looks, and success, Mathews was the most revered of the city's new idols.

On August 16, 1954, he was featured on the very first cover of *Sports Illustrated*.

Understandably, but unfortunately, the third baseman was not prepared for all the attention and often didn't handle it well. He drew criticism in the press and boos from the fans for his occasional brooding. He warred with photographers, was fined for missing curfew, and got arrested for reckless driving. But by his 25th birthday, Mathews already had 190 home runs.

While he was slugging his way through the league, Mathews wasn't ignoring the rest of his game. A wild swinger who led the league with 115 strikeouts as a rookie, he learned the strike zone and became disciplined enough to walk 113 times in 1954 and to lead the league in walks four times. He also worked hard on his defense and went from being a poor fielder to being a very good one.

A competitor, Mathews was rarely out of the lineup. In May 1955 he underwent an emergency appendectomy but was back in the lineup 16 days later.

In 1957 and '58, when the Braves won two pennants and a World Series, Mathews actually had two of his poorer seasons, though they weren't bad by most standards. He didn't hit particularly well in either Series but did make some big plays, offensively and defensively, to help Milwaukee beat the Yankees in the '57 Series.

In Game 4, the Yankees led 5–4 in the bottom of the 10th and were on the verge of taking a 3–1 lead in games. However, Johnny Logan doubled to tie the game, then Mathews followed with a two-run homer off Bob Grim for a 7–5 victory, evening the Series in games. In Game 5, he beat out an infield single in the sixth inning and scored the only run in Lou Burdette's 1–0 victory.

Then in Game 7, Milwaukee led, 5–0, in the ninth but the Yankees rallied to load the bases with two outs and Moose Skowron at the plate. Skowron scorched an apparent double down the third-base line, but Mathews made a lunging, backhanded stop and stepped on the bag for the force that produced the last World Series championship in franchise history. It also set off a wild celebration in Milwaukee.

In 1959, Mathews had the best season of his career, leading the majors with 46 home runs. He batted a career-high .306 and combined with Aaron to finish first and second in the league in total bases. Their total of 752 total bases was the highest by two National League teammates since 1930.

The Braves of the 1960s never lived up to the promise of the 1950s, and Mathews was part of the reason. Though he continued to perform at a high level, offensively and defensively, he was not the same slugger he was in his 20s. In fact, a case could be made that he was somewhat burned out by the time he was 30.

At age 29, Mathews had averaged 37.5 home runs in his first nine seasons. He should have been in his prime at that point, but he never hit more than 32 homers in a season again and was down to 16 by age 34. And after driving in 124 runs

in 1960 when he was 28, Mathews never exceeded 95 RBIs again. His statistics would have done most players proud, but they weren't quite up to the standards Mathews had established for himself.

On the last day of the 1964 season, the Braves thought they might be playing their last game at Milwaukee County Stadium. Manager Bobby Bragan decided to sit in the stands for the game against Pittsburgh and turned the club over to Mathews as a possible farewell gesture to the city. The team, however, was forced to play a lame-duck season in Milwaukee in 1965.

In 1966, with the team in Atlanta, Mathews was obviously near the end of the line, struggling at the plate most of the season. However, he provided his new fans with a taste of his old glory on August 8 in one of the most memorable games in the team's Atlanta history. Denny Lemaster and Dodgers immortal Sandy Koufax had dueled to a 1–1 standoff entering the bottom of the ninth when Mathews delivered a game-winning homer.

With the aging superstar seven home runs shy of the coveted 500 mark entering 1967, the Braves traded Mathews to Houston, where he was moved to first base. After getting his 500th home run, Mathews was traded to Detroit late in the year to help the Tigers pursue the American League pennant. He added six home runs to Detroit's cause and wound up taking part in his second World Series championship, if only as a pinch hitter.

One of the greatest third basemen in history, Eddie Mathews led the league with 47 home runs in 1953 when he was just 21 years old and went on to hit 512 in his Hall of Fame career.

Mathews, a nine-time National League All-Star, finished his career with the Tigers in 1968. He retired with 14 seasons of 20 or more home runs, 10 of 30 or more, and four of 40 or more. He and Mike Schmidt share the National League record for most consecutive seasons of 30 or more home runs (9). Mathews averaged just over 30 home runs per season in his 17-year career and also held the major league record for most games played at third base until it was broken by Brooks Robinson. He hit seven homers on opening day, tied for second all-time with Babe Ruth and Willie Mays and one behind Frank Robinson.

Among his franchise records are most RBIs in a season since 1900 (135), most consecutive games with an RBI (8), most career walks (1,444), most home runs on the road in a season (30 in 1953), and tied for most home runs in a season (47) with Aaron.

Mathews and Aaron combined for more home runs (863) than any other teammates in history. And twice Mathews was runner-up for National League MVP, in 1953 to Campanella and 1959 to Ernie Banks.

A heated competitor, Mathews seldom passed up a chance to fight an opponent if the occasion warranted it. One of his better bouts came in 1961 with Cincinnati pitcher Jim O'-Toole. After O'Toole slapped the ball from his hand during a squeeze play, Mathews leveled the Reds pitcher, earning an ejection and instigating a bench-clearing brawl.

In 1971, Mathews rejoined the Braves as a coach under Luman Harris. The following year he replaced Harris as manager late in the season. The Braves finished fifth in 1973, his only full season at the helm, and he was relieved of his duties late the following year.

Mathews served as a scout and minor league instructor for the Milwaukee Brewers for four years until he was elected to the Hall of Fame in 1978. He later scouted for Oakland and was a hitting instructor in the Braves farm system. And in 1994, his *Sports Illustrated* cover was brought out of mothballs to grace the front of the magazine's 40th-anniversary issue.

Mathews, Eddie

Braves	G	AB	R	H	2B	3B	HR	RBI	SB	AVG	SLG
1952	145	528	80	128	23	5	25	58	6	.242	.447
1953	157	579	110	175	31	8	47*	135	1	.302	.627
1954	138	476	96	138	21	4	40	103	10	.290	.603
1955	141	499	108	144	23	5	41	101	3	.289	.601
1956	151	552	103	150	21	2	37	95	6	.272	.518
1957	148	572	109	167	28	9	32	94	3	.292	.540
1958	149	546	97	137	18	1	31	77	5	.251	.458
1959	148	594	118	182	16	8	46*	114	2	.306	.593
1960	153	548	108	152	19	7	39	124	7	.277	.551
1961	152	572	103	175	23	6	32	91	12	.306	.593
1962	152	536	106	142	25	6	29	90	4	.265	.496
1963	158	547	82	144	27	4	23	84	3	.263	.453
1964	141	502	83	117	19	1	23	74	2	.233	.412
1965	156	546	77	137	23	0	32	95	1	.251	.469
1966	134	452	72	113	21	4	16	53	1	.250	.420
Career	2,223	8,049	1,452	2,201	338	70	493	1,388	66	.273	.517

Matthews, Gary

Braves: 1977–80	**B:** July 5, 1950
Outfielder	**Batted right, threw right**
Birthplace: San Fernando, California	**Ht.** 6–3; **Wt.** 190

Gary Matthews had a unique habit of reaching up and knocking off his batting helmet as he approached first base following a hit. He denied even knowing he did it, but it helped create the perception that he was an all-out, hustling ballplayer. He really didn't need to lose his cap to do that, though.

What Matthews lacked in talent—which wasn't a lot—he helped make up for with effort and consistency. He never had a superstar-caliber season, yet he was one of the steadiest and most productive outfielders in the National League for more than a decade.

Many Braves fans will remember Matthews best for getting team owner Ted Turner in hot water. Actually, it was Turner who got himself in trouble, but it was his interest in Matthews that created the situation.

When a court order abolished baseball's reserve clause in the summer of 1976, effectively creating free agency, Matthews was one of the players who went on the open market at the end of the season. Turner, who had just purchased the Braves, was looking for players. He openly courted Matthews during the season. That activity resulted in a "tampering" charge from Commissioner Bowie Kuhn that cost Turner $10,000 and the Braves their first-round draft pick.

At a World Series cocktail party, Turner told Giants owner Bob Lurie he would pay whatever was necessary to sign Matthews, prompting another complaint to Kuhn and an eventual one-year suspension for Turner. Nevertheless, Turner and the Braves got their man.

Was Matthews worth all the trouble? The Braves finished last in each of Matthews' first three seasons with the club and only climbed to fourth in his final year in Atlanta. Not that it was Matthews' fault, but as the old saying goes, "The Braves could have finished last without him."

Matthews batted .288 during his four-year stay with the Braves and averaged 20 home runs and 73 RBIs per season. His best year, in fact the best of his career, came in 1979 when he hit .304 with 27 home runs and 90 RBIs. He also made the National League All-Star team for the only time in his career.

After the 1980 season, Matthews got the biggest break of his career. The Braves traded him to Philadelphia for pitcher Bob Walk. Matthews was instrumental in the Phillies' success in the early 1980s, including winning the National League

Gary Matthews

pennant in 1983. In the National League Championship Series with the Dodgers that year, Matthews hit .429 with three home runs to be named MVP of the playoffs.

Matthews, Gary

Braves	G	AB	R	H	2B	3B	HR	RBI	SB	AVG	SLG
1977	148	555	89	157	25	5	17	64	22	.283	.438
1978	129	474	75	135	20	5	18	62	8	.285	.462
1979	156	631	97	192	34	5	27	90	18	.304	.502
1980	155	571	79	159	17	3	19	75	11	.278	.419
Career	588	2,231	340	643	96	18	81	291	59	.288	.456

McCarthy, Tommy

Beaneaters: 1885, 1892–95
Outfielder, second baseman, shortstop, pitcher
Birthplace: Boston

B: July 24, 1863
D: August 5, 1922
Batted right, threw right
Ht. 5–7; **Wt.** 170

One of the smallest Hall of Famers, Tommy McCarthy was a sensational outfielder who was as smart as he was skilled. He was known for outfoxing base runners with trick plays that forced rule changes, and he teamed with Hugh Duffy to form Boston's vaunted "Heavenly Twins."

A product of the south Boston sandlots, McCarthy had a brief stint with the Beaneaters in 1885. However, he didn't win a regular job in a major league until 1888 with the St. Louis Browns of the American Association.

When that league folded after the 1891 season, McCarthy signed with the Beaneaters. McCarthy in right and Duffy in center were such smooth, speedy outfielders that seldom did a ball drop between them. Boston fans dubbed them the "Heavenly Twins," and for four years they formed an incomparable tandem.

In that era, a runner couldn't advance after a fly out until the outfielder not only had caught the ball but was ready to throw it. One of McCarthy's favorite tricks was to juggle the ball repeatedly after a catch while running toward the infield until he was close enough to throw out any runner trying to advance. Hall of Fame umpire Bill Klem said McCarthy was responsible for the rule change allowing runners to leave as soon as the fielder touches the ball.

Another of McCarthy's tactics was perfecting the trapped ball, conning unsuspecting players into double plays.

If a runner was tagging, McCarthy often let a flyball drop at the last second, enabling him to get a double play. But if the runner suspected such a play and began to run, he'd make the catch and double him off base.

McCarthy and Duffy also formed a clever duo on offense. They were adept at executing the hit-and-run, as well as the fake bunt and the double steal. The two outfielders were even ahead of their time when it came to contract negotiations. They held out jointly, just as Dodgers pitchers Sandy Koufax and Don Drysdale did some 70 years later.

Duffy, who was three years younger than McCarthy, was a better hitter than his "twin," but McCarthy was the stronger of the two defensively. Duffy always said McCarthy was the "heavenly one" of the pair and claimed McCarthy and King Kelly were the two smartest ballplayers he ever saw.

McCarthy didn't have much power, but he had a keen eye and was a good performer in the clutch. Twice he had well over 100 RBIs for Boston. He also averaged 47 steals in his first three full years with the Beaneaters.

McCarthy, Tommy

Beaneaters	G	AB	R	H	2B	3B	HR	RBI	SB	AVG	SLG
1885	40	148	16	27	2	0	0	11	NA	.182	.196
1892	152	603	119	146	19	5	4	63	53	.242	.310
1893	116	462	107	160	28	6	5	111	46	.346	.465
1894	127	539	118	188	21	8	13	126	43	.349	.490
1895	117	452	90	131	13	2	2	73	18	.290	.341
Career	552	2,204	450	652	83	21	24	384	160	.296	.385

McGriff, Fred

Braves: 1993–
First baseman
Birthplace: Tampa, Florida

B: October 31, 1963
Bats left, throws left
Ht. 6–3; **Wt.** 215

Never before in Braves history has a player lit a fire under the team—literally—the way Fred McGriff did when he joined the club July 20, 1993.

The Braves were languishing in second place, nine games behind the Giants, and their offense was stagnant at worst and inconsistent at best through the first 94 games of the season. That's why general manager John Schuerholz attempted to wake up the team's lineup by sending three prospects—Melvin Nieves, Donnie Elliott, and Vince Moore—to liquidation-minded San Diego for McGriff.

The evening McGriff reported to Atlanta–Fulton County Stadium, a fire broke out in the press box area behind home plate during batting practice. The start of the game was delayed two hours, and when it began, the Braves fell behind,

Tommy McCarthy

Fred McGriff

5–0, through 5½ innings. But in the bottom of the sixth, a Mc-Griff home run keyed a five-run rally and led to an eventual 8–5 victory.

McGriff, who replaced Sid Bream in the lineup at first base, seemed to give the team just the boost it needed to catch the Giants, a task many people didn't think was possible. But Atlanta was 51–17 (.750) after McGriff's arrival, just enough to edge San Francisco by one game on the final day of the season for a third straight division title.

For the sixth consecutive season, McGriff hit 30 or more home runs (37), joining an elite group of 11 other players—all Hall of Famers—to have such a streak. He was named to the Silver Slugger team as the top offensive first baseman in the league. He reached 100 RBIs for the third straight year and also scored a career-high 111.

Though the Braves struggled in the League Championship Series against Philadelphia, McGriff was still on fire, hitting .435.

Even with the strike shortening the 1994 season to 114 games, McGriff still managed to reach the 30-homer club for the seventh straight year. Only eight others—Jimmie Foxx, Lou Gehrig, Mike Schmidt, Eddie Mathews, Babe Ruth, Mickey Mantle, Ralph Kiner, and Hank Aaron—have sustained such a stretch of slugging.

McGriff was well on his way to the best year of his career when the strike hit. Besides his 34 homers, he was hitting a career-best .318 with 94 RBIs through August 11 when the players headed for the golf courses. At only 31 years old, McGriff already had 262 career home runs. He also hit a pinch-hit home run to earn recognition as MVP of the All-Star Game.

Originally drafted and signed by the Yankees in 1981, Mc-Griff was traded to Toronto the following year when he was still in the low minors. He debuted in the majors with the Blue Jays in a brief 1986 stint, then spent the next four seasons with Toronto before being traded to San Diego prior to the 1991 season. He played well at all stops, but he never started a fire anywhere else like he did in Atlanta.

McGriff, Fred

Braves	G	AB	R	H	2B	3B	HR	RBI	SB	AVG	SLG
1993	68	255	59	79	18	1	19	55	1	.310	.612
1994	113	424	81	135	25	1	34	94	7	.318	.623
Career	181	679	140	214	43	2	53	149	8	.315	.619

McMahon, Don

Braves: 1957–62
Pitcher
Birthplace: Brooklyn, New York
B: January 4, 1930

D: July 22, 1987
Batted right, threw right
Ht. 6–2; **Wt.** 222

What the Braves of the early 1990s wouldn't have given for a pitcher like Don McMahon! The hard-throwing right-hander was a major contributor to the last World Series championship season enjoyed by the Braves. He was a closer supreme before the term *closer* was even invented.

Originally a third baseman, McMahon was converted to a pitcher because of his strong arm. He floundered around the minor leagues for several years, much of that time as a starter, and spent two years in the military before being summoned to Milwaukee in late June 1957 as a reliever. He already was

Don McMahon

27 years old, and perhaps his age helped him handle the situations manager Fred Haney thrust upon him.

In the midst of a tight pennant race, McMahon stepped into critical relief situations like a proven veteran. In his first six outings covering 10 innings, he was unscored upon and gave up just five hits and a walk, striking out nine.

The rookie's work continued at a high level all season. The role of closer had yet to develop to the point that one pitcher was kept for all "save" situations as is done today. In fact, the save wasn't even an official statistic yet. But in just half the season, McMahon collected nine saves, good enough to rank among the league leaders. He didn't have enough innings to qualify for the ERA title, but his 1.54 mark was more than a full run lower than any pitcher who did qualify.

McMahon was just as baffling to the Yankees in the World Series, too. He worked five scoreless innings over three games.

Though he pitched only four more full seasons with the Braves, McMahon went on to one of the longest and most prosperous careers of any reliever in history. He was still pitching at 44, quite an advanced age for a fastball specialist.

In 1958, McMahon made the All-Star team for the only time in his career. In 1959 he tied for the league lead in saves (15) with the Cardinals' Lindy McDaniel and set what was then a franchise record by appearing in 60 games.

After a horrible season in 1960, the right-hander bounced back strong in 1961, his last full year with Milwaukee. Braves manager Birdie Tebbetts lost his confidence in McMahon and sold him to Houston in May of 1962. Tebbetts' judgment couldn't have been worse. In 76½ innings for Houston, McMahon had a 1.53 ERA, winning five and saving eight.

McMahon, Don

Braves	W	L	Pct	G	GS	CG	ShO	IP	H	BB	SO	ERA	SV
1957	2	3	.400	32	0	0	0	46⅔	33	29	46	1.54	9
1958	7	2	.778	38	0	0	0	58⅔	50	29	37	3.68	8
1959	5	3	.625	60	0	0	0	80⅔	81	37	55	2.57	15*
1960	3	6	.333	48	0	0	0	63⅔	66	32	50	5.94	10
1961	6	4	.600	53	0	0	0	92	84	51	55	2.84	8
1962	0	1	.000	2	0	0	0	3	3	0	3	6.00	0
Career	23	19	.548	233	0	0	0	344⅔	317	178	246	3.34	50

McWilliams, Larry

Braves: 1978–1982, 1987
Pitcher
Birthplace: Wichita, Kansas

B: February 10, 1954
Batted left; threw left
Ht. 6–5; **Wt.** 180

Larry McWilliams was a tall string bean, just barely off the Texas prairie, when he walked to the mound at Atlanta–Fulton County Stadium the night of August 1, 1978. He was making only his fourth major league start for a Braves team destined for a last-place finish in the National League West.

But the 24-year-old left-hander would play a major role that evening in one of the most scintillating dramas of modern major league history. McWilliams, still an obscure name to most Braves fans and unknown to most of the baseball world, was about to become a major factor in stopping Pete Rose's National League record hitting streak at 44 games.

Just two weeks earlier, McWilliams made his big league debut, combining with Gene Garber to shut out the Mets. That same McWilliams-Garber tandem halted Rose's pursuit of Joe DiMaggio's 56-game hitting streak, one of the game's most-hallowed records.

In the first inning, McWilliams walked Rose, bringing a cascade of boos from the Atlanta fans who came to cheer the fierce rival they detested but respected. Then, in the second inning, McWilliams made the play that, more than any other, broke the back of Rose's remarkable streak.

The Cincinnati star lined a shot up the middle that appeared headed for center field. But quicker than Rose could say, "45," McWilliams continued to whirl to his right from the momentum of his follow-through, somehow spearing the ball as it was about to disappear into the history books.

"The ball was behind him," a disappointed Rose said later. "Two inches either way and he doesn't get a glove on it."

Rose grounded routinely to shortstop in the fifth, lined out to third in the seventh, and struck out against Garber in the ninth. It was Garber's strikeout that got the most attention, but it was McWilliams' quick reaction and good fortune on the second-inning line drive that robbed Rose of his best shot at a hit that evening.

In the postgame press conference, Rose was asked if he would recognize McWilliams if he was sitting next to him. The famed batsman admitted he wouldn't, then realized there was a reason for the question. McWilliams was sitting beside him.

"Why the hell did you catch that ball?" Rose demanded good-naturedly.

McWilliams could only smile shyly.

McWilliams might have gone back to Texas and sat around telling his good neighbors about the night he stopped Rose. Instead, he put together a respectable, if not overwhelming, 13-year career with five clubs. His best work, however, was not done in a Braves uniform.

McWilliams was with Atlanta for parts of five seasons, and his rookie year was the high-water mark as a Brave. Besides stopping Rose, he won nine of 12 decisions and posted a career-best 2.81 ERA. Midway through 1982, with McWilliams struggling with a 2–3 record and 6.21 ERA, the Braves decided they'd be better served with another arm. They traded McWilliams to Pittsburgh in exchange for an erratic right-hander named Pascual Perez and a minor leaguer.

McWilliams, Larry

Braves	W	L	Pct	G	GS	CG	ShO	IP	H	BB	SO	ERA	SV
1978	9	3	.750	15	15	3	1	99⅓	84	35	42	2.81	0
1979	3	2	.600	13	13	1	0	66⅓	69	22	32	5.56	0
1980	9	14	.391	30	30	4	1	163⅔	188	39	77	4.95	0
1981	2	1	.667	6	5	2	1	37⅓	31	8	23	3.11	0
1982	2	3	.400	27	2	0	0	37⅔	52	20	24	6.21	0
1987	0	1	.000	9	2	0	0	20⅓	25	7	13	5.75	0
Career	25	24	.510	100	67	10	3	425	449	131	211	4.53	0

Mercker, Kent

Braves: 1989–
Pitcher
Birthplace: Indianapolis, Indiana

B: February 1, 1968
Bats left, throws left
Ht. 6–1; **Wt.** 175

Only one man other than Hall of Famer Warren Spahn has ever pitched in two Braves no-hitters. Kent Mercker may not be the least likely pitcher to fit that description, but he's pretty far down the list.

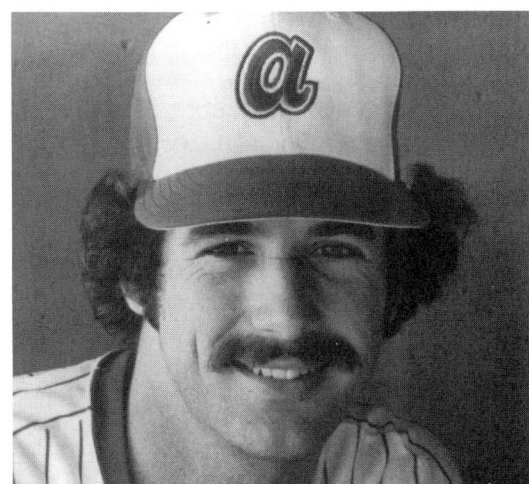

Larry McWilliams

Kent Mercker

Yet the talented young left-hander had two no-hitters—one shared—on his resume by age 26.

A first-round pick by the Braves in the 1986 draft, Mercker broke into the majors in 1989 but didn't stay in Atlanta until a year later. He had difficulty finding a role on the talented pitching staff the club had assembled and wound up as a "utility pitcher." He worked in long relief, middle relief, and short relief and even got an occasional start in his first three-plus seasons in the majors.

On September 11, 1991, with the Braves in the thick of a surprising pennant race with the Dodgers, Mercker made just his second start of the season and the third of his career. Atlanta was at home against the Padres and was trying to protect a half-game lead over the Dodgers.

Through six innings, Mercker did not allow San Diego a hit, and thanks to a Terry Pendleton home run, he led, 1–0. Bobby Cox, more concerned with winning the game than in seeing a no-hitter, feared Mercker was tiring, since he wasn't used to starting. He replaced him with Mark Wohlers, who kept the Padres hitless through the seventh and eighth innings. Cox then turned the 1–0 game over to Alejandro Pena, who got the final three outs.

It was the 13th no-hitter in Braves history and the first since Phil Niekro's in 1973. It also was the first combined no-hitter in National League history.

Nevertheless, Mercker didn't get a single start in 1992. He had to settle for stringing together 25 consecutive scoreless innings in relief, the longest such streak on the team. He continued to work primarily in relief in 1993, though he did get six starts.

Then in 1994, Mercker finally broke into the rotation, supposedly as the "fifth starter" behind Greg Maddux, Tom Glavine, Steve Avery, and John Smoltz. However, he won more games (9–4) than Avery and Smoltz and had a lower ERA than all the other starters except Maddux.

The highlight of his season came April 8 at Los Angeles in his very first start of the year—and just the 12th of his career. He no-hit the Dodgers, 6–0, striking out a career-high 10 in the first complete game of his career. He allowed just four base runners, all on walks, with the last coming in the sixth inning. In the ninth, he struck out Brett Butler and Mike Piazza, then got Eric Karros to tap to the mound for the final out.

Andy Messersmith

Mercker, Kent

Braves	W	L	Pct	G	GS	CG	ShO	IP	H	BB	SO	ERA	SV
1989	0	0	.000	2	1	0	0	4⅓	8	6	4	12.47	0
1990	4	7	.364	36	0	0	0	48⅓	43	24	39	3.17	7
1991	5	3	.625	50	4	0	0	73⅓	56	35	62	2.58	6
1992	3	2	.600	53	0	0	0	68⅓	51	35	49	3.42	6
1993	3	1	.750	43	6	0	0	66	52	36	59	2.86	0
1994	9	4	.692	20	17	2	1	112⅓	90	45	111	3.45	0
Career	24	17	.585	204	28	2	1	372⅔	300	181	324	3.24	19

Messersmith, Andy

Braves: 1976–77
Pitcher
Birthplace: Toms River, New Jersey

B: August 6, 1945
Batted right, threw right
Ht. 6–1; **Wt.** 200

Andy Messersmith changed the course of baseball history in 1976. Unfortunately, he did not alter the course of Braves history, as Ted Turner hoped he would do.

Messersmith, one of the game's better pitchers, was the first player to escape the grasp of baseball's reserve clause—which used to bind players to a team throughout their careers—and become a free agent capable of selling his services to the highest bidder.

Turner, who had just purchased the Braves in 1976, was intent on making a name for himself and letting baseball and Atlanta fans know he would do whatever was possible to improve his team.

The two were a perfect match—the maverick player and the maverick owner.

Messersmith, along with Dave McNally, another pitcher, played without contracts in 1975, Messersmith with the Dodgers and McNally with the Expos. They claimed that since they didn't sign contracts they no longer were bound by the reserve clause and thus were free agents. Baseball contended that the reserve clause restricted them to their teams as long as they played.

The two pitchers took their cases to a three-man arbitration panel set up to handle disputes between players and management. The decisive vote was cast by impartial arbitrator Peter Seitz, who ruled that the reserve clause was no more than a one-year option and that Messersmith and McNally were indeed free agents. Federal Judge John W. Oliver later upheld Seitz's decision.

McNally was at the end of his career and was forced to retire when there were no bidders for his services. If not for Turner, Messersmith might have found the pickings slim, too, for the owners were furious about the state of affairs.

But Turner, who was new to the game and never was one to follow the crowd, was more than up for the change. He signed the 30-year-old right-hander to what he called a "lifetime" contract for $1 million. The deal would be laughed at today, but it was considered lavish at the time, even for someone who'd won 39 games the previous two seasons.

Determined to get his money's worth, Turner had the Braves issue Messersmith uniform number 17, which just happened to be the number designating WTBS, his TV station. And to make sure no one missed the symbolism, Turner "nicknamed" Messersmith "Channel" and had that word sewn above the number where players normally display their names.

Baseball quickly nixed Turner's human billboard idea. The number stayed, but not the nickname.

A three-time All-Star, two-time 20-game winner, and the National League leader in shutouts (7) in 1975, Messersmith certainly appeared to be worth the big contract if anyone was. However, he never lived up to his promise.

Runner-up for the 1974 Cy Young Award, he missed all of spring training in 1976 because of contract negotiations and consequently got off to a poor start. He didn't pick up his first win as a Brave until his seventh start on May 17. However, he was 5–1 in June, improving his overall record to 9–6 and earning a spot on the All-Star team.

Just prior to the All-Star Game, Messersmith suffered a pulled hamstring. That and a sore shoulder hounded him the rest of the season. His second half record was just 2–5, and the Braves wound up in last place for the first time since moving to Atlanta.

In 1977, Messersmith won five of nine decisions before suffering an elbow injury July 3. He had to undergo surgery and missed the remainder of the season. At the end of the year, the Braves sold him to the Yankees.

Messersmith, Andy

Braves	W	L	Pct	G	GS	CG	ShO	IP	H	BB	SO	ERA	SV
1976	11	11	.500	29	28	12	3	207⅓	166	74	135	3.04	1
1977	5	4	.556	16	16	1	0	102⅓	101	39	69	4.40	0
Career	16	15	.516	45	44	13	3	309⅔	267	113	204	3.49	1

Millan, Felix

Braves: 1966–72
Second baseman, shortstop,
   third baseman
Birthplace: Yabucoa, Puerto Rico

B: August 21, 1943
Batted right, threw right
Ht. 5–11; **Wt.** 172

Felix Millan ranks as one of the best second basemen in franchise history and quite possibly the best in the Braves' Atlanta years. A smooth, dependable fielder with quick hands, he also was a steady hitter who annually proved one of the toughest men in baseball to strike out. Comparable defensively to Glenn Hubbard and Mark Lemke, Millan was a better offensive player than the other two premier second baseman of the Atlanta era.

A native of Puerto Rico, Millan became Braves' property

Felix Millan

only when Kansas City, who originally drafted him in 1964, left him unprotected in the minor league draft that winter. After a brief stint with the Braves in 1966, Millan was in line to become Atlanta's regular second baseman in 1967. However, he sustained an ankle injury early and was sent to Richmond, where he was named the International League's top player and helped the Braves' top farm club win the pennant.

In 1968, at age 24, Millan broke through as the Braves' starting second baseman. He was one of the top rookies in baseball, hitting .289 and fielding .980. The following season he played a key role in the Braves' winning the first National League West title. He played in every game and fielded a league-best .980, helping the Braves lead the league in defense (.981). He also posted career highs with six home runs and 57 RBIs, and although Atlanta was swept by the Mets in the playoffs, Millan batted .333.

The stylish second baseman had his best offensive year in 1970, hitting .310. He made the All-Star team for the second of three consecutive seasons, though he couldn't play because of a broken hand. In 1971, Millan teamed with shortstop Marty Perez to enable the Braves to lead the league with a then-club-record 180 double plays.

After the 1972 season, in which the Braves finished 25 games out of first and had a major-league high 4.27 ERA, the club was desperate for pitching. They sent Millan and left-hander George Stone to the Mets in exchange for right-handers Gary Gentry and Danny Frisella in what proved to be one of the worst deals in franchise history.

Millan, Felix

Braves	G	AB	R	H	2B	3B	HR	RBI	SB	AVG	SLG
1966	37	91	20	25	6	0	0	5	3	.275	.341
1967	41	136	13	32	3	3	2	6	0	.235	.346
1968	149	570	49	165	22	2	1	33	6	.289	.340
1969	162	652	98	174	23	5	6	57	14	.267	.345
1970	142	590	100	183	25	5	2	37	16	.310	.380
1971	143	577	65	167	20	8	2	45	11	.289	.362
1972	125	498	46	128	19	3	1	38	6	.257	.313
Career	799	3,114	391	874	118	26	14	221	56	.281	.349

Montanez, Willie

Braves: 1976–77
First baseman
Birthplace: Cataño, Puerto Rico

B: April 1, 1948
Batted left; threw left
Ht. 6–1; **Wt.** 193

The Braves have had some flashy players over the years . . . and then they've had Willie Montanez.

The Puerto Rican first baseman had a show that even Deion Sanders couldn't match on a baseball field. The fans and the media called Montanez a "hot dog," and he proudly agreed with them. He had the most stylish home run trot of the 1970s. When he caught pop-ups, he literally snapped them out of the air, as if he were slapping at a pesky fly. And as he strutted to the plate for each at bat, he'd bounce his bat off the turf and flip it, acting almost like a featured twirler.

The Braves acquired Montanez from the Giants in a six-player deal in which Darrell Evans and Marty Perez went to San Francisco in mid-1976. Then 28 years old, Montanez was a proven talent. In 1971, his first full season in the majors, he hit 30 home runs and drove in 99 runs for the Phillies. The

Willie Montanez

Dale Murphy

following year he led the National League with 39 doubles, and in 1975 he drove in 101 runs splitting time with the Phillies and Giants.

Montanez was excited about being traded to Atlanta because it was considerably warmer than Philadelphia and San Francisco. And he played well for the Braves, hitting .321 for the remainder of the 1976 season. In 1977 he batted .287 with 20 home runs and was the lone Brave named to the National League All-Star team.

But the Braves were in a state of turmoil. Following a second straight last-place finish in 1977, the club tried to find more pitching. Montanez was one of the few tradable commodities, and he was shipped to Texas for right-handers Adrian Devine and Tommy Boggs and speedy outfielder Eddie Miller.

Montanez, Willie

Braves	G	AB	R	H	2B	3B	HR	RBI	SB	AVG	SLG
1976	103	420	52	135	14	0	9	64	0	.321	.419
1977	136	544	70	156	31	1	20	68	1	.287	.458
Career	239	964	122	291	45	1	29	132	1	.302	.441

Murphy, Dale

Braves: 1976–90
Outfielder, first baseman, catcher
Birthplace: Portland, Oregon

B: March 12, 1956
Batted right, threw right
Ht. 6–5; **Wt.** 215

The late Bill Lucas, the first black general manager in baseball history, loved to talk about prospects coming up through the Braves farm system in the late 1970s. He was convinced they were about to turn the Braves into contenders.

During the winter between the 1977 and '78 seasons, he returned from a scouting mission to the Dominican winter league with a story he'd been told by former Brave Rico Carty, the self-proclaimed "Beeg Boy."

"Rico pointed to the scoreboard in left field and said, 'The Beeg Boy hit one over there last night,' " Lucas reported with a big grin. "Then he pointed to the field beyond the scoreboard and said, "But the Beeg Donkey hit one way over there."

Lucas burst out laughing. The "Beeg Donkey" Carty was referring to was Dale Murphy, the pride of the Atlanta farm system. He was one of the few prospects who would live up to his potential, eventually helping the Braves win a division title in 1982, three years after Lucas's premature death.

Lucas, who was the Braves' farm director when Murphy signed as the club's number-one draft pick (fifth overall) in 1974, would have delighted, perhaps more than anyone else, in the success Murphy enjoyed in a long and productive career that culminated in the Braves' retirement of his uniform number 3 in 1994.

Though he was a tremendous prospect, even as a high school player in Portland, Oregon, Murphy did not achieve stardom and win two consecutive National League MVP awards without working through considerable adversity.

Once regarded as "the next Johnny Bench," Murphy possessed the rifle arm and offensive capabilities to be a truly great major league catcher. In fact, he broke into the majors with brief call-ups as a catcher in 1976 and '77. However, he suddenly developed a mental block on throwing the ball back to the pitcher or to second base. Tosses to the pitcher were subject to sailing into center field, and throws to second often endangered the well-being of pitchers who sometimes sprawled on the ground to avoid his errant projectiles.

The short-term solution was to move Murphy to first base, where he seldom had to throw. The dilemma was lessened but still cropped up occasionally during 1978 and '79, his first two full years in the majors. Murphy still caught, but only occasionally. His problems behind the plate weren't limited to throwing either. In one of the last games he caught, Murphy committed five passed balls—of course, the fact that Phil Niekro was serving his knuckleball that game was a major contributing factor.

The long-term answer, however, came in 1980 when manager Bobby Cox decided to try his promising 24-year-old slugger in the outfield.

Perhaps it was just coincidence, or maybe the switch to center field was what Murphy needed to put his mind at ease. Whatever the reason, he blossomed into an All-Star in 1980 and soon was one of the game's most respected players. At the same time, he was becoming known as one of the most genuinely humble, charitable, and respected men in baseball history.

Murphy adapted to the outfield like he was a natural. He was speedy enough to run down balls in the gaps, and his strong throwing arm was perfect for the position—especially since accuracy no longer was a problem for him.

A slugger who hit 30 or more home runs six times in his career, durable Dale Murphy also was an excellent defensive outfielder and a threat to steal bases in his prime.

In 1980, Murphy finished third in the league in home runs (33), trailing only leader Mike Schmidt and Braves teammate Bob Horner. He also was third in runs scored and slugging percentage (.510) and fifth in total bases.

The strike-split 1981 season seemed to throw off Murphy's timing, but in 1982 he began a run of offensive production and overall excellence and durability seldom approached by anyone else in franchise history.

During the Braves' 1982 division-winning effort, Murphy tied for the league lead in RBIs (109), finished second in home runs (36) and runs scored, and was third in total bases and fourth in walks. For good measure, he added 23 steals and played in all 162 games, the first Brave to appear in every game since Felix Millan in 1969. Murphy won a Gold Glove for defensive excellence and easily outpolled the Cardinals' Lonnie Smith as the league MVP.

The 1983 season was nearly a carbon copy of 1982 for Murphy, except that the Braves finished second in the NL West. The 27-year-old outfielder attained career highs in RBIs (121) and batting average (.302), leading the league in the former. He also led the league in slugging percentage (.540); was second in home runs (36), total bases, and runs; and was third in on-base percentage (.396) and fourth in walks. He played in every game again, won another Gold Glove, and became just the fourth National Leaguer to join the elite 30–30 (home runs–steals) club.

In the MVP voting, Murphy won by a substantial margin over Montreal's Andre Dawson. He thus became the youngest player ever to win back-to-back MVPs and, at the time, just the fourth to win it two years in a row and the fourth Brave to receive the honor.

Murphy posted a third very similar season in 1984, hitting 36 home runs for the third straight year but tying Schmidt for the league lead this time. He also led the league in slugging (.547) and total bases and hit his only All-Star Game home run. However, he finished well back in the MVP voting, largely because the Braves dropped two games under .500.

In 1985, Atlanta fell to fifth place, but Murphy continued to play like he was in a pennant race. He kept his consecutive games streak alive, had his second .300 season, and finally got off the 36 mark in home runs, finishing with 37 and his second straight league title. He won his fourth of five straight Gold Gloves and led the league in runs scored and walks, too. He also was runner-up in RBIs (111) and total bases and was third in slugging percentage and fifth in hits.

Murphy's nationwide popularity was evident from the fact that he led all players in All-Star votes received in 1985.

On April 29, 1986, it appeared Murphy's consecutive games streak was finally at an end at 676 games. After making a running catch of a fly ball against the Mets, he caught the palm of his hand in a seam in the fence at Atlanta–Fulton County Stadium, opening a cut that required nine stitches. The prognosis was that he would miss at least a week and possibly more. In fact, he was on the bench the following night. However, in a moment that was vintage Murphy, he came off the bench to deliver a pinch-hit home run in the fifth inning against Dwight Gooden. The crowd erupted with a standing ovation for one of the most spine-tingling moments in Braves history.

Murphy returned to the regular lineup the next day, but his streak did end later that year. He finally took a day off July 9 after playing in 740 consecutive games, 12th all-time. It was his first game on the bench since September 27, 1981.

After four straight seasons of 36 or more home runs and 100 or more RBIs, Murphy failed to approach either of those levels in 1986, though he was still fourth in the league in home runs (29) and had a very productive season at age 30.

In 1987 he bounced back with yet another MVP-caliber season even though the Braves lost 92 games under manager Chuck Tanner. Murphy was named team captain during spring training and was moved from center field to right. The changes couldn't have fit him any better. He finished second in the league with a career-high 44 homers and also was third in total bases and walks and fifth in runs, slugging percentage, and on-base percentage.

Murphy's batting average took a mysterious tumble into the low .200s in 1988 and never fully recovered the rest of his career, even though his power numbers remained respectable for another couple of seasons. He was one of only three players, the others being Eddie Murray and Dwight Evans, to hit 20 or more home runs nine times in the 1980s.

In 1989, Murphy hit two three-run home runs in the sixth inning against the Giants July 27, tying the modern major league record for RBIs, as well as home runs, in an inning. He was the first Brave to hit two home runs in an inning since Bobby Lowe in 1894. It was Murphy's last real blaze of glory in an Atlanta uniform. He went on to lead the team in RBIs (84) for the eighth straight season but failed to lead the club in home runs (20) for the first time since 1981.

On August 4, 1990, Murphy's 15-year Braves career came to an end when he was traded to Philadelphia, along with Tommy Greene, for Jeff Parrett, Jim Vatcher, and Victor Rosario. Murphy remained productive through 1991 (.252, 18, 81), but knee problems limited him to 18 games in 1992 and forced him into retirement in 1993 at age 37 after only two months with Colorado.

A seven-time National League All-Star, Murphy hit 398 career home runs. He holds 10 Atlanta Braves career records, including most home runs, RBIs, hits, games, and runs. His uniform number is one of five to be retired and displayed on the outfield wall at Atlanta–Fulton County Stadium. The others are Hank Aaron (44), Eddie Mathews (41), Phil Niekro (35), and Warren Spahn (21).

Though Murphy ranks as one of the greatest players in franchise history and may someday be voted into the Hall of Fame, it actually is his personality and off-field contributions for which he is most revered.

Murphy's community and charitable work earned him the Lou Gehrig Memorial Award in 1985 and the Roberto Clemente Award in 1988. He remained active in community work after his retirement. Devoutly religious, he and his wife are the parents of seven sons and a daughter. They live in Utah.

In 1994, Murphy worked as a spring training instructor for former Braves manager Joe Torre and the St. Louis Cardinals.

"Murphy is the closest thing there is to the all-American boy," Torre once said. No truer words were ever spoken.

Murphy, Dale

Braves	G	AB	R	H	2B	3B	HR	RBI	SB	AVG	SLG
1976	19	65	3	17	6	0	0	9	0	.262	.354
1977	18	76	5	24	8	1	2	14	0	.316	.526
1978	151	530	66	120	14	3	23	79	11	.226	.394
1979	104	384	53	106	7	2	21	57	6	.276	.469
1980	156	569	98	160	27	2	33	89	9	.281	.510
1981	104	369	43	91	12	1	13	50	14	.247	.390
1982	162	598	113	168	23	3	36	109*	23	.281	.507
1983	162	589	131	178	24	4	36	121*	30	.302	.540*
1984	162	607	94	176	32	8	36*	100	19	.290	.547*
1985	162	616	118*	185	32	3	37*	111	10	.300	.539
1986	160	614	89	163	29	7	29	83	7	.265	.477
1987	159	566	115	167	27	1	44	105	16	.295	.580
1988	156	592	77	134	35	4	24	77	3	.226	.421
1989	154	574	60	131	16	0	20	84	3	.228	.361
1990	97	349	38	81	14	0	17	55	9	.232	.418
Career	1,926	7,098	1,103	1,901	306	37	371	1,143	160	.268	.478

Nichols, Kid

Beaneaters: 1890–1901
Pitcher
Birthplace: Madison, Wisconsin
B: September 14, 1869

D: April 11, 1953
Batted both, threw right
Ht. 5–10; **Wt.** 175

When Charles Augustus Nichols was a mere teenager, his fate was being shaped by the powers of the National League who were tinkering with the rules of how a pitcher could deliver a baseball.

In 1884 overhand pitching was allowed for the first time, and youngsters like Nichols who were devoted to the game immediately began practicing the new technique. Few did it as well as the young right-hander from the Midwest, who within a few years would be well on his way to becoming one of the greatest pitchers of all time.

At age 20, "Kid" Nichols broke into the majors with the Beaneaters in 1890 after three years of seasoning in the minors. It was the team's first season under manager Frank Selee, who would lead the franchise out of a seven-year pennant drought and into renewed prominence as the dominant club of the 1890s. No one would be more responsible for Boston's decade of success, which included five pennants, than Nichols.

Selee directed Omaha to the Western Association championship in 1889, in large part because Nichols went 36–12. So, when Selee was hired to replace Jim Hart as Boston's manager, he advised the Beaneaters to purchase Nichols. The price was $3,500.

Nichols was viewed as Boston's number-two starter behind

Kid Nichols

John Clarkson, who won 49 games in 1889. However, Clarkson had only a couple of productive seasons left in what proved to be a Hall of Fame career.

As a rookie, Nichols quickly established himself as one of the best pitchers in the league. Relying mainly on an excellent fastball and superb control, he won 27 games, one more than Clarkson and sixth in the league. He led the league in shutouts (7), was second in ERA (2.23), and finished third in strikeouts. Nichols also demonstrated quite a knack for finishing what he started, a trait that would become a trademark. He made 47 starts in 1890 and completed them all.

The modern rules of baseball still hadn't been completely established. Though pitchers were allowed to throw overhand, they were but 50 feet from home plate. Hitters, understandably, were having a tough time. The pitching distance didn't change to 60 feet, 6 inches until 1893. The added distance drove some pitchers out of the game, but Nichols had no difficulty adjusting.

In the eight-year period 1891–98, Nichols won 30 or more games seven times and averaged just over 31 victories per season. It was a stretch of success unequaled by any other overhanded pitcher in history and ended only when Nichols had pretty much burned out his arm.

In 1891, Nichols won 30 games, three less than Clarkson, and the duo pitched Boston to its first pennant in eight years. Besides ranking fourth in the league in victories, Nichols was second in ERA (2.39) and shutouts (5). His formula for success was evident in the fact that he was the league's top control pitcher (2.18 walks per game) and yet still ranked second in strikeouts per game (5.08).

The Beaneaters repeated as pennant winners in 1892 even though Clarkson was released to Cleveland early in the season. Nichols won a career-high 35 games, tying teammate Jack Stivetts for third in the league in the last season before the pitching distance was lengthened.

Selee's club won a third consecutive pennant in 1893, and though Nichols' ERA climbed more than half a run, he still won 34 games, tying Cy Young for second in the league. He also worked over 400 innings for the fourth of what would be a stretch of five consecutive years.

Boston failed to win the pennant the next three seasons,

though Nichols proceeded with business as usual. He was third in the league in wins (32) in 1894, and after slipping to only 26 victories the next year, bounced back with 30 in 1896 to lead the league for the first of three straight seasons. He topped the league with 31 wins in both 1897 and '98, pitching the club to its last two pennants before the "miracle" of 1914.

Though Nichols remained an effective major league pitcher for Boston the next three seasons, averaging nearly 18 victories per year, he was no longer the dominating force he'd been during his first nine seasons—and no wonder, considering that his average workload from 1890 through 1898 was 404 innings per year.

After winning only 19 games in 1901, Nichols was released by the Beaneaters. He purchased part interest in the Kansas City club of the Western Association and, apparently intent on proving he could still pitch, became player-manager. He was effective, too, winning 48 games in two seasons and earning another shot at the majors.

Pitching for St. Louis in 1904, Nichols went 21–13 in one final burst of glory at age 35. He tied for fourth in the league in victories, finished fifth with a 2.02 ERA, and also managed the club to a fifth-place finish. He was relieved of his managerial duties early in 1905 and went to the Phillies, where he won the last 10 games of his illustrious career.

A Hall of Famer, Nichols won 361 lifetime games, sixth all-time. The only men to win more are Young, Walter Johnson, Christy Mathewson, Grover Cleveland Alexander, and Warren Spahn. No one ever won 300 games quicker than Nichols, who was only 23 days past his 30th birthday when he reached that level.

Nichols' seven 30-win seasons is a major league record. He completed 531 games, tied for fourth all-time. He actually completed nearly 95 percent of his career starts, failing to go the distance just 30 times in 561 starts.

After his baseball career, Nichols was involved in numerous pursuits. Among other things, he became a championship bowler and also coached the Missouri Valley College baseball team.

Nichols, Kid

Beaneaters	W	L	Pct	G	GS	CG	ShO	IP	H	BB	SO	ERA	SV
1890	27	19	.587	48	47	47	7*	424	374	112	222	2.23	0
1891	30	17	.638	52	48	45	5	425⅓	413	103	240	2.39	3*
1892	35	16	.686	53	51	49	5	453	404	121	187	2.84	0
1893	34	14	.708	52	44	43	1	425	426	118	94	3.52	1
1894	32	13	.711	50	46	40	3*	407	488	121	113	4.75	0
1895	26	16	.619	47	42	42	1	379⅔	417	86	140	3.41	3*
1896	30*	14	.682	49	43	37	3	372⅓	387	101	102	2.83	1
1897	31*	11	.738	46*	40	37	2	368*	362	68	127	2.64	3*
1898	31*	12	.721	50*	42	40	5	388	316	85	138	2.13	4*
1899	21	19	.525	42	37	37	4	343⅓	326	82	108	2.99	1
1900	13	16	.448	29	27	25	4*	231⅓	215	72	53	3.07	0
1901	19	16	.543	38	34	33	4	321	306	90	143	3.22	0
Career	329	183	.643	556	501	475	44	4,538	4,434	1,159	1,667	3.00	16

Niekro, Phil

Braves: 1964–83, 1987 **B:** April 1, 1939
Pitcher **Batted right, threw right**
Birthplace: Blaine, Ohio **Ht.** 6–1; **Wt.** 180

Bob Uecker didn't contribute much to the Braves as a catcher, but he did leave quite a legacy with his wit, from which he makes a much better living than he ever did as a career .200 hitter.

One of the assignments Uecker drew during his minor league and major league stint in the Braves organization was catching—or trying to catch—Phil Niekro's elusive knuckleball. Using that unique perspective and his knack for humor, Uecker summed up his own shortcomings and Niekro's fascinating talent by describing what it was like attempting to hem in the darting butterfly pitch.

"It was great. I got to meet a lot of important people. They all sit behind home plate," Uecker joked of his constant scampers to the backstop.

Niekro's specialty pitch, taught to him as a child by his father, who was an Ohio Valley coal miner, earned him 318 victories and even more humorous attempts at describing the somewhat freakish nature of his phenomenal success.

"Trying to hit him is like trying to eat Jell-O with chopsticks," said former Giant and Cub Bobby Murcer.

Rick Monday, who tried to hit Niekro's knuckler for 13 seasons with the Cubs and Dodgers, described the pitch by saying, "It actually giggles at you as it goes by."

Perhaps no other pitcher in history has left so many hitters feeling so helpless and frustrated as Niekro, the only man to reach the prestigious 300-victory club relying almost exclusively on the knuckleball. Few others ever used the mysterious pitch in their repertoire, let alone mastered it.

Initially, the knuckleball, which would allow Niekro to pitch until he was nearly 50 years old, was a hindrance to his career. It baffled almost as many catchers as it did opposing hitters. Consequently, he bounced around the minors for most of six years, learning to control the pitch better and waiting for Braves management to gain confidence that he could win in the majors with the flutterball.

Even after he earned his first shot at the majors in 1964 when the Braves were still in Milwaukee, the team failed to see his value as a starter and used him primarily in relief for three more years, demoting him to the minors for more seasoning in 1966.

Then in 1967, at age 28, he finally made the big league club to stay. And even if the Braves weren't sure how to utilize him, Niekro forged ahead at carving one of the finest pitching careers in franchise history. Splitting time between the bullpen and the starting rotation, he led the league in ERA by a substantial margin. Niekro's 1.87 ERA was the all-time franchise record until surpassed by Greg Maddux in 1994.

National League hitters would long regret that the soft-tossing right-hander finally established himself in the majors. Beginning in 1967, he reached double figures in victories for 14 straight years and 19 of 20 seasons, falling short only in strike-shortened 1981 during that two-decade span.

Though the Braves had little success as a team in that period, he usually gave them their best chance of winning and helped lead them to division titles in 1969 and 1982. He also

Phil Niekro

established Atlanta records in most career and season pitching categories, became one of the most beloved players ever to wear the franchise's uniform in the South, and eventually had a statue erected in his honor outside Atlanta–Fulton County Stadium.

Niekro grew up in a highly industrial area along the Ohio River that produced many quality athletes who were eager to escape the mines and mills where their fathers and grandfathers worked.

One of Niekro's high school teammates at Bridgeport (Ohio) High was John Havlicek, who went on to become one of the greatest players in NBA history with the Boston Celtics. Niekro's younger brother Joe also had a distinguished career as a big league pitcher. And the only pitcher to beat Phil in a high school game was Bill Mazeroski from nearby Tiltonsville. Mazeroski had an illustrious career as a second baseman with the Pittsburgh Pirates and hit one of the most famous home runs in history to beat the Yankees in the ninth inning of Game 7 of the 1960 World Series.

Niekro turned down a college baseball scholarship to sign with the Braves in 1959. His reward was splitting the season between the distant outposts of Wellsville, New York, and McCook, Nebraska. He slowly advanced through the Braves farm system as a reliever until 1963, which he spent in the military. Back from active duty in 1964, he made the big league club in spring training but pitched most of the season at Denver of the American Association.

He spent all of 1965 with the Braves, the club's last season in Milwaukee, and picked up his first two big league victories. His 2.89 ERA showed the difficulty hitters were having with the knuckleball, but his 74⅔ innings showed that manager Bobby Bragan wasn't all that comfortable with Niekro in the game.

After a stint with Richmond in 1966, Niekro's development and the Braves' lack of pitching combined in 1967 to force manager Billy Hitchcock to find a way to utilize his knuckleball specialist. In a situation he would become all too familiar with, Niekro pitched brilliantly with a poor team, one destined for seventh place and its worst showing since 1952 in Boston. In spite of leading the league in ERA for the only time in his career and finishing fourth in fewest hits per nine innings (7.13), "Knucksie" barely won half his decisions (11–9).

As well as Niekro pitched in 1967, he couldn't save Hitchcock's job. Under Luman Harris in 1968, the 29-year-old Niekro was used as a starter all season for the first time in his pro career. It was the "year of the pitcher" in which Bob Gibson of St. Louis posted an incredible 1.12 ERA, and Niekro fit right in with his 2.59 ERA. His most impressive achievement that year may have been his 1.58 walks per nine innings, fifth in the league and unusually low for a knuckleball pitcher.

But the true blossoming of Niekro didn't occur until 1969, the first year of division play. The Braves won the National League West to earn their first postseason berth since 1958, and Niekro was a major factor in the club's reaching that milestone.

His career-high 23 victories, including two 1–0 wins, established an Atlanta record that still stands and were second in the league to Tom Seaver's 25. Niekro won 15 games before the All-Star break and made the All-Star team for the first of five times in his career. He also finished second to Juan Marichal in walks per nine innings (1.80) and was fourth in opponents' on-base percentage (.264) and fifth in complete games. He was the only pitcher other than Seaver to be recognized in the voting for the league's Cy Young Award.

In the playoffs against the "Miracle" Mets, Niekro was charged with the loss in Game 1 when New York reached him for five unearned runs in the eighth on the way to a three-game sweep of Atlanta.

In many ways, 1969 was one of Niekro's finest seasons, yet he remained the Braves' pitching ace for most of the next 14 years. But 1970 was a bitter disappointment for both Niekro and the Braves. The team dipped to fifth place, and Niekro's ERA ballooned to 4.27, the highest he would post in a full big league season until 1986 when he was 47 years old.

Always an intense competitor, Niekro bounced back strong in 1971 with 15 victories and a 2.98 ERA. Including '71, he led the club in wins nine times in the 12-year period through 1982. The Braves finished on the plus side of .500 just three times in those dozen seasons and finished last four times.

On a team that finished 14 games under .500 in 1972, Niekro managed 16 victories. He was third in the league in innings and fewest walks per game (1.69) and was fourth in lowest on-base percentage allowed (.275).

One of the highlights of his magnificent career came in 1973 when he pitched a no-hitter to beat San Diego, 9–0, August 5 at Atlanta Stadium. It was the Braves' first no-hitter since Warren Spahn's in 1961.

In 1974, Niekro had his second 20-victory season, tying Andy Messersmith for the league lead in wins. He finished third to Mike Marshall and Messersmith, both Dodgers, in the Cy Young voting. Across the board, Niekro's statistics were as impressive as any in the league. He led in complete games and innings and finished second in ERA and shutouts.

The 1974 season also signaled Niekro's emergence as the premier workhorse in the league. In the seven seasons from 1974 through 1980, he led the league in innings four times and never finished out of the top five in that department.

Niekro had a mediocre season in 1975, splitting 30 decisions with a fifth-place club. However, on September 5 he was honored as the last original Atlanta Brave in a ceremony attended by many of his family members and friends. There probably were those in attendance who felt Niekro, at age 36, was near the end of his career. Certainly no one—except possibly Niekro himself—would have guessed he'd more than double the 145 career victories he'd own by season's end.

The Braves finished 22 games under .500 in 1976, Ted Turner's first year of ownership. Niekro, however, somehow managed to finish six games over .500 with his 17–11 record. On the last day of the season, he spun a one-hitter, beating the division champion Reds, 3–0.

The 1977 Braves were one of the worst clubs in franchise history, once losing 17 in a row en route to 101 defeats, the most since Boston dropped 115 in 1935. Niekro got more than his share of those losses, 20 to be exact, and his ERA climbed over 4.00 for the first time since 1970. However, the fact that he also managed to win 16 said something about his staying power. He led the league in strikeouts for the only time in his career and also was first in innings and complete games.

When the Braves fired manager Dave Bristol at the end of the 1977 season, Niekro shocked everyone by applying for the job. He had no plans to stop pitching at age 39. He simply wanted to manage, too. Though Turner and general manager Bill Lucas gave Niekro serious consideration, they chose Bobby Cox instead.

The 1978 Braves were only marginally better than the previous year's club and still finished last. However, Niekro got his ERA back down to 2.88 and somehow managed to win 19 games, which was third in the league. He led in complete games and innings once again, and also was second in strikeouts behind Houston's J. R. Richard and tied for second in shutouts.

Niekro turned 40 in style in 1979. He won 21 games, the third and last 20-win season of his career. Two things were particularly significant about those 21 victories. First, they came with a last-place club. And second, they tied for the league lead with none other than his brother, Joe, who was pitching for Houston. Early in the season, Phil got his 200th career win and received a $20,000 bonus from Turner for the achievement.

In 1980, the Braves had their first winning season since 1974, but Niekro struggled at 15–18. Then in 1981, when the season was shortened by a players strike, Niekro won just seven games, though his ERA was a very respectable 3.10.

The 1982 season began in unusual fashion for both Niekro and the Braves. The 43-year-old right-hander was struck in the ribs by a line drive off the bat of fellow pitcher Rick Mahler in spring training and was placed on the disabled list for the first time in his career. Thus he had to sit and watch as the Braves put together a major league record 13-game winning streak to open the season.

But when he returned, Niekro, perhaps smelling a last chance at the pennant he always wanted for Atlanta, pitched like he was in his prime, winning 17 of 21 decisions. His .810 winning percentage was the best in both leagues and established an Atlanta record.

In the playoffs against St. Louis, Niekro held a 1–0 lead at St. Louis in Game 1, only to see his effort rained out in the fifth inning. He returned to pitch well again in Game 2 but got no decision in Atlanta's 4–3 setback on the way to being swept by the Cardinals.

A talented, young team fresh off a division title, the 1983 Braves were expected to win the West again. When they fell three games short, they looked for reasons. At age 44, Niekro won just 11 games, only one more than he lost. The prevailing sentiment in the organization was that he probably was finished with 268 career wins. And even if he wasn't, he didn't fit on a team that pictured itself one of the best young clubs in the game. Thus the Braves did not offer Niekro a contract, allowing him to become a free agent. They soon discovered they'd quit on him too soon.

At 45, Niekro could still pitch and could still be a big winner. He had 300 victories in his sight and figured a two-year contract with the Yankees just might get him there. His calculation couldn't have been better.

In 1984, Niekro made the American League All-Star team on his way to a 16-victory season, while the Braves failed to win even half their games. He duplicated that win total in 1985, the last one coming October 8 with a four-hit, 8–0 victory against Toronto. Not only did that make Niekro the 18th man to win 300 games, but it also made him the oldest pitcher ever to record a shutout.

Niekro pitched for two more seasons, winning 18 games for Cleveland and pitching briefly for Toronto before being brought back to Atlanta for a three-inning "curtain call," ending the 1987 season and his 24-year career.

Niekro once said his biggest thrill was winning the game that allowed him and brother Joe to pass the Perrys, Gaylord and Jim, for most victories by brothers. The Niekros hold that record with 539 wins.

Phil and Joe, Braves teammates in 1973–74, had nine decisions against each other. Joe held the advantage, 5–4, but his biggest coup on his older brother came in 1976 when he hit his only big league home run against Phil.

Niekro was not just an accomplished pitcher, but a fine all-around player. He had one of the best right-handed pickoff moves in the game and won five Gold Gloves for defensive excellence. He also was a good bunter and got many clutch hits in his own behalf.

He also was heavily involved in charitable and community work in the Atlanta area. He won the Brian Piccolo Award in 1977, the Lou Gehrig Memorial Award in 1979, and the Roberto Clemente Award in 1980 for his skills, character, and off-field contributions. His uniform number 35 is one of five to be retired by the Braves.

Niekro managed Atlanta's top farm club at Richmond in 1991 before parting ways with the organization over a difference in philosophies. But in 1992 he returned to Atlanta–Fulton County Stadium to pitch batting practice before Game 6 of the National League Championship Series in order to give the Braves a chance to hit against the knuckler they would face that night from Pittsburgh's Tim Wakefield.

In 1994, Niekro managed the Silver Bullets women's professional baseball team and became part-owner of an Atlanta restaurant bearing his name.

Though he ranks 14th all-time with 318 victories, Niekro failed to be elected to the Hall of Fame in his first three years of eligibility. However, no 300-game winner has ever failed to be inducted eventually, and Niekro has shown he shouldn't be counted out too soon.

Niekro, Phil

Braves	W	L	Pct	G	GS	CG	ShO	IP	H	BB	SO	ERA	SV
1964	0	0	—	10	0	0	0	15	15	7	8	4.80	0
1965	2	3	.400	41	1	0	0	74⅔	73	26	49	2.89	6
1966	4	3	.571	28	0	0	0	50⅓	48	23	17	4.11	2
1967	11	9	.550	46	20	10	1	207	164	55	129	1.87*	9
1968	14	12	.560	37	34	15	5	257	228	45	140	2.59	2
1969	23	13	.639	40	35	21	4	284⅓	235	57	193	2.56	1
1970	12	18	.400	34	32	10	3	229⅔	222	68	168	4.27	0
1971	15	14	.517	42	36	18	4	268⅔	248	70	173	2.98	2
1972	16	12	.571	38	36	17	1	282⅓	254	53	164	3.06	0
1973	13	10	.565	42	30	9	1	245	214	89	131	3.31	4
1974	20*	13	.606	41	39	18*	6	302⅓*	249	88	195	2.38	1
1975	15	15	.500	39	37	13	1	275⅔	285	72	144	3.20	0
1976	17	11	.607	38	37	10	2	270⅔	249	101	173	3.29	0
1977	16	20*	.444	44	43*	20*	2	330⅓*	315*	164*	262*	4.03	0
1978	19	18*	.514	44	42*	22*	4	334⅓*	295*	102	248	2.88	1
1979	21*	20*	.512	44	44*	23*	1	342*	311*	113*	208	3.39	0
1980	15	18*	.455	40	38*	11	3	275	256	85	176	3.63	1
1981	7	7	.500	22	22	3	3	139⅓	120	56	62	3.10	0
1982	17	4	.810	35	35	4	2	234⅓	225	73	144	3.61	0
1983	11	10	.524	34	33	2	0	201⅔	212	105	128	3.97	0
1987	0	0	—	1	1	0	0	3	6	6	0	15.00	0
Career	268	230	.538	740	595	226	43	4,622⅔	4,224	1,458	2,912	3.20	29

Nixon, Otis

Braves: 1991–93
Center fielder
Birthplace: Evergreen, North Carolina

B: January 9, 1959
Bats both, throws right
Ht. 6–2; **Wt.** 180

O tis Nixon was one of the catalysts of the Braves' success in 1991–93. The defining moment of his three years with the club will forever be known to Braves fans as "The Catch."

In the pennant-winning season of 1992, the Braves played a rather uninspired first half and were six games out of first place through 81 games on July 7. It seemed as if the first game of the second half served as a signal for the club to get its act together. The Braves won 12 consecutive games and moved into first place for the first time since early April.

On July 25 the winning streak seemingly disappeared for a brief moment, then Nixon magically brought it back to life. Atlanta led Pittsburgh, 1–0, with one out and one on in the

top of the ninth when Andy Van Slyke hit a drive toward the right-center wall at Atlanta–Fulton County Stadium. Nixon sprinted toward the same spot, and as the ball was exiting the playing field, he leaped from a dead run, reached over the top of the wall and turned a home run into one of the most exciting outs in team history by snatching the ball as it was about to vanish. After Kent Mercker got one more out, the winning streak was 13, and the Braves mobbed Nixon. The team held first place all but two days the rest of the season.

Nixon pursued free agency after '93, signing with Boston. For a time late in 1991 he was regarded with complete disdain by many Braves fans, but he left the club as one of the most beloved players as a result of the three-year reign of success he helped create.

A week before the start of the 1991 season, the Braves acquired Nixon from Montreal in one of the best trades in Atlanta history, giving up only two minor leaguers. Nixon filled the much-needed role of leadoff hitter with success no one could have predicted. A career .228 hitter when he arrived, Nixon proceeded to bat .297, complete with a 20-game hitting streak, and steal 72 bases.

On June 16 he tied a major league record with six steals against his former Montreal teammates. His season total of 72 steals was second in the league and broke the modern Braves record of 57 set by Hap (Ralph) Myers in 1913. You had to go back to "Slidin'" Billy Hamilton in 1896 to find a Brave with more steals (83).

Nixon might even have challenged Hamilton's record had he not received a 60-day suspension on September 16 for violating the commissioner's drug policy and aftercare program. The Braves were in the midst of a torrid pennant race with the Dodgers at the time. Fan and media reaction to Nixon was vengeful. The general feeling was that he had let down the team and the city at the moment he was most needed. Besides missing the last two weeks of the season, he was ineligible for the postseason and the beginning of '92.

But Nixon rebounded to win back the hearts of Braves fans, not only with his performance but also with his conduct as a citizen in the community. He apologized, went through an aftercare program, and became a prominent spokesman in the war against drug use.

On the field, he came back from his suspension and picked up where he left off the previous year. He batted .294 in 1992 and stole 41 bases, becoming the first Brave to produce back-to-back 40-steal seasons in the 20th century. And don't forget "The Catch."

In the National League Championship Series against Pittsburgh, he had four hits in Game 4 to tie an NLCS record, and he strung together five consecutive hits over two games to tie another record. In the World Series against Toronto, his five steals tied a record for a six-game Series. His clutch two-out, two-strike hit in the bottom of the ninth of Game 6 enabled the Braves to tie the Blue Jays, 2–2. However, Atlanta lost, 4–3, in the 11th when Nixon failed by a step to beat out a bunt, ending the game and the Series.

Otis Nixon

Nixon, Otis

Braves	G	AB	R	H	2B	3B	HR	RBI	SB	AVG	SLG
1991	124	401	81	119	10	1	0	26	72	.297	.327
1992	120	456	79	134	14	2	2	22	41	.294	.346
1993	134	461	77	124	12	3	1	24	47	.269	.315
Career	378	1,318	237	377	36	6	3	72	160	.286	.329

Olson, Greg

Braves: 1990–93
Catcher
Birthplace: Marshall, Minnesota

B: September 6, 1960
Batted right, threw right
Ht. 6–0; **Wt.** 200

Greg Olson wasn't even supposed to make the big leagues, let alone become one of the more popular players to emerge from the Braves' success of the early 1990s. He is truly one of the most remarkable rags-to-riches stories in franchise history.

Prior to 1990, Olson had two major league at bats. Even when the Braves signed him as a six-year minor league free agent for the 1990 season, his career appeared to be going nowhere, considering that he was 29 years old.

But a chain reaction among the organization's catching corps vaulted Olson into the starting job in late April and sent him to the All-Star Game that year.

Olson actually opened 1990 at Triple-A Richmond and was ranked fifth at catcher on the organization's depth chart. But when the Braves acquired Phil Lombardi from the Mets just before opening day to be the number-three catcher, John Russell refused assignment to Richmond and became a free agent. Then Lombardi abruptly retired. When the Braves' top two catchers, Jody Davis and Ernie Whitt, got off to horrendous starts, the team had little choice but to stick Olson in the lineup.

Olson made his debut on April 22 and gave the impression he was going to make people forget Johnny Bench. He batted .371 in his first 16 games and remained hot through most of the first half. At midseason, he became the first Braves rookie to be named to the NL All-Star team since Ron Reed in 1968.

Though that was the height of his individual success, Olson continued to be a major player in the team's surge to two NL pennants and three division titles in the next three seasons. He provided many clutch hits in the Braves' worst-to-first drive of 1991 and caught all but two innings in a stretch of 32 consecutive games that culminated when Atlanta finally eliminated the Dodgers from the division race on the next-to-last day of the season.

The image of Olson that will remain with Braves fans for years and will be part of the franchise's lore for eternity is the catcher jumping into John Smoltz's arms following the final out on the day the team clinched the 1991 division title. In that year's NLCS against Pittsburgh, he tied for the team lead in batting average (.333) and RBIs (4) and hit a two-run homer in Game 3.

With the acquisition of Damon Berryhill, Olson had to share the catching duties in 1992. He continued to provide solid defense and clutch hitting until a chilling injury ended his season and jeopardized his career. On September 18, Houston's Ken Caminiti bowled over Olson at the plate, buckling the catcher's right leg underneath his body. He suffered a fractured leg and dislocated ankle and had to be carried from the field on a stretcher.

For the remainder of the season and during the postseason, Olson, wearing a thigh-to-ankle cast in the dugout, was a constant source of inspiration to his teammates and fans. When the team rushed onto the field to celebrate winning the pennant, Deion Sanders carried the burly catcher around on his back. During the World Series, the full cast was removed and replaced by a walking cast.

With the Braves trailing Toronto three games to one in the Series, the old cast was flown to Toronto for good luck in Game 5. The Braves won, returning the Series to Atlanta for Game 6, which was won by the Blue Jays.

Against tremendous odds, Olson not only recovered for 1993, but was ready to go at full speed on opening day. He continued to share the catching chores with Berryhill but found himself behind the plate less and less in the second half. The Braves didn't offer him a contract for '94.

Olson, Greg

Braves	G	AB	R	H	2B	3B	HR	RBI	SB	AVG	SLG
1990	100	298	36	78	12	1	7	36	1	.262	.379
1991	133	411	46	99	25	0	6	44	1	.241	.345
1992	95	302	27	72	14	2	3	27	2	.238	.328
1993	83	262	23	59	10	0	4	24	1	.225	.309
Career	411	1,273	132	308	61	3	20	131	5	.242	.342

Pafko, Andy

Braves: 1953–59
Outfielder, third baseman
Birthplace: Boyceville, Wisconsin

B: February 25, 1921
Batted right, threw right
Ht. 6–0; **Wt.** 190

Not knowing how their new fans would receive them in Milwaukee, the Braves made a wise decision in January 1953 as they plotted to leave Boston. The announcement of the franchise shift had yet to be made, but inquiring minds might have gotten a hint of the events about to unfold when Wisconsin native Andy Pafko was sent from Brooklyn to the Braves in exchange for Roy Hartsfield and $50,000.

Nothing like a hometown boy to help a migratory team gain acceptance in a new home.

As it turned out, the Braves probably didn't need Pafko to help win the fans of Wisconsin—but he sure helped anyway.

With his best seasons behind him, Pafko was 32 years old when the Braves moved to Milwaukee, and he was a regular only the first two years there. However, he was immensely popular, partially because of his local ties and Slovak ancestry, but also because of his tenacious style of play. Famous for his belly-flop catches in the outfield and head-first slides on the base paths, Pafko was a clutch hitter and a big fan favorite throughout his seven seasons as a Brave.

In spite of playing amid a bevy of superstars, Pafko won a contest in 1953 when he was voted "The Best of the Braves" in a poll of fans. He had a fine season, but it certainly didn't

Greg Olson

Andy Pafko

Alejandro Pena

compare with the performances of several of his teammates, including Eddie Mathews, who led the league in home runs, and Warren Spahn, who led it in victories and ERA. But as far as the fans were concerned, Pafko was "the best." He received a new Cadillac and $5,000 for a charity from the Blatz Brewing Company, who sponsored the contest.

At the time he was traded to the Braves, Pafko wasn't too excited about leaving a pennant winner for a team that finished seventh in 1952. However, it didn't take him long to warm to playing in front of familiar fans, especially when the Braves quickly became a dominating team.

Pafko's playing time decreased significantly in 1955 after two seasons as the starting right fielder, but he continued to be a key reserve. In 1955 he even played third base, where he had little experience, for two weeks when Mathews underwent an emergency appendectomy.

Pafko batted a combined .261 in limited duty during the 1957 and '58 World Series. His 17-year career ended in 1959 with a .285 lifetime batting average and 213 home runs.

Pafko, Andy

Braves	G	AB	R	H	2B	3B	HR	RBI	SB	AVG	SLG
1953	140	516	70	153	23	4	17	72	2	.297	.455
1954	138	510	61	146	22	4	14	69	1	.286	.427
1955	86	252	29	67	3	5	5	34	1	.266	.377
1956	45	93	15	24	5	0	2	9	0	.258	.376
1957	83	220	31	61	6	1	8	27	1	.277	.423
1958	95	164	17	39	7	1	3	23	0	.238	.348
1959	71	142	17	31	8	2	1	15	0	.218	.324
Career	658	1,897	240	521	74	17	50	249	5	.275	.411

Pena, Alejandro

Braves: 1991–92, 1995
Pitcher
Birthplace: Cambiaso, Dominican Republic

B: June 25, 1959
Bats right, throws right
Ht. 6–1; **Wt.** 205

The one thing missing from the successful Braves teams of the early 1990s was a consistent closer. Consequently, general manager John Schuerholz had to swing a couple of late-season deals to help get the club into postseason play.

Late in 1991, with the team stunning the sports world in its spirited bid to overcome the highly favored Dodgers in the National League West, Schuerholz acquired veteran Alejandro Pena from the Mets on August 29. It proved to be the move that gave the Braves the added edge they needed to clinch the division on the next-to-last day of the season and to reach the World Series for the first time since 1958.

A starter early in his career with Los Angeles, Pena had been a reliever since undergoing shoulder surgery in 1985. He had a reputation of not being able to work on successive days, but he was a picture of both hard work and perfection for Atlanta in '91. To say there would not have been a division title and a pennant without him is an understatement.

In the final five weeks of the season he was 2–0 with 11 saves in 11 opportunities. After giving up two runs in his first game as a Brave, he yielded only one more run in his final 14 games. On September 11 he even pitched the last inning of a combined no-hitter (Kent Mercker and Mark Wohlers) against San Diego. It was the first combined no-hitter in National League history.

Pena continued his dominating work in the playoffs. He appeared in four games against Pittsburgh, picking up three saves and not allowing a run. He finally lost at the most inopportune time—the seventh game of the World Series. It was Pena who yielded the one-out, bases-loaded single to Minnesota's Gene Larkin in the 10th inning. The hit drove in the only run of the game and ended the Series.

In '92, Pena was plagued with illness and arm problems, spending two extended periods on the disabled list. He still managed 15 saves in 18 opportunities, but the club elected not to re-sign him for '93. However, he was re-acquired in late August 1995.

Pena, Alejandro

Braves	W	L	Pct	G	GS	CG	ShO	IP	H	BB	SO	ERA	SV
1991	2	0	1.000	15	0	0	0	19⅓	11	3	13	1.40	11
1992	1	6	.143	41	0	0	0	42	40	13	34	4.07	15
Career	3	6	.333	56	0	0	0	61⅓	51	16	47	3.23	26

Pendleton, Terry

Braves: 1991–94	**B:** July 16, 1960
Third baseman	**Bats both, throws right**
Birthplace: Los Angeles	**Ht. 5–9; Wt.** 195

No other player in history made such a huge impact on the Braves in such a short period of time as Terry Pendleton did in the four years he played for the team.

In 1914 the Braves acquired Johnny Evers in a trade and he immediately led them to a "miracle" World Series championship. In the process, he won the Chalmers Award, the equivalent of today's Most Valuable Player Award.

Pendleton did much the same thing in 1991. He used free agency to become a Brave that season and proceeded to lead the club to a pennant that was every bit as miraculous as the one in 1914. He also won the National League batting title and was named the league's MVP.

But unlike Evers, who was at the end of his career, Pendleton didn't stop after one season. The switch-hitting third baseman led the Braves to another pennant in 1992 with a performance worthy of a second straight MVP. However, he finished second to Pittsburgh's Barry Bonds.

Pendleton continued to play a significant role in 1993 when Atlanta won a third consecutive division title, then he struggled in the strike-shortened 1994 season, his last as a Brave.

Only two teams—the Yankees and the Braves—showed interest in Pendleton when he became a free agent after the 1990 season. He was 30 years old and coming off the poorest year of his career (.230, 6, 58) with the Cardinals. The Yankees offered more money, but Pendleton took the Braves' four-year, $10.6 million contract because he felt his family would like Atlanta better than New York.

Terry Pendleton

Before long, Braves president Stan Kasten was calling the acquisition of Pendleton "the greatest free agent signing in history." And no one argued the point.

Coming off three straight last-place finishes and baseball's worst record in 1990, Atlanta vaulted to a division title and the pennant in 1991 before suffering a seventh-game defeat in a scintillating World Series. Without a doubt, Pendleton was the leader of the Braves' surge, both on and off the field.

Besides presiding as the team's unofficial captain, he became the first Brave to be named MVP since Dale Murphy in 1983. He also was the first Brave to win the batting title (.319) and lead the league in hits (187) since Ralph Garr claimed that double in 1974. Both his average and hit total established franchise highs for a third baseman.

The increase of 89 points in Pendleton's batting average over the previous season tied for the third-biggest increase in major league history. He batted 60 points over his career average and set a career high with 22 home runs despite playing with a bum knee that required arthroscopic surgery after the season.

Pendleton was just what the young Braves needed. A two-time Gold Glove winner in St. Louis who'd played in two World Series, he helped tighten the defense behind Atlanta's talented pitching staff and also showed a group of inexperienced players how to win.

With the Braves seemingly in a must-win situation nearly every day down the stretch, he was at his best. He hit .353 over his last 28 games and batted .347 with runners in scoring position after May 15. He hit a solo home run to provide the only run in the combined no-hitter by Kent Mercker, Mark Wohlers, and Alejandro Pena over San Diego on September 11.

The praise for Pendleton clearly demonstrated his role in the Braves' rise.

General manager John Schuerholz called him "the anchor of our team."

"We needed somebody to come in with a winning attitude and lead by example, and that's exactly what Terry did," said pitcher Steve Avery.

And second baseman Jeff Treadway summed up Pendleton's contributions by saying, "He showed the rest of the team how to act in a pennant race."

Though he was throttled by Pittsburgh in the National League Championship Series (.167), Pendleton had a big World Series, hitting .367 with two home runs against Minnesota.

Best of all, Pendleton came back in 1992 with a performance that was every bit as strong as his MVP effort of 1991. Among the highlights were the third Gold Glove of his career and a league-leading average of .387 with runners in scoring position. His 105 RBIs were a career high. He became the first Braves third baseman since 1900 to post consecutive .300 seasons and only the third Atlanta Brave (Garr and Lonnie Smith) to perform the feat.

Pendleton also set an Atlanta record with 39 doubles, tied for the league lead in hits (199), and was second in RBIs and sixth in average. Though he hit just .233 in the playoffs against Pittsburgh, he doubled to ignite the thrilling, ninth-inning rally in Game 7 that enabled the Braves to win consecutive pennants for the first time since 1957–58. He batted .240 in the World Series against Toronto.

In his first two seasons with the Braves, Pendleton missed a total of just 11 games, and despite a series of nagging injuries in 1993, he missed only one game. His offensive production was down, a big reason for the Braves' slow start, but he finished strong to help the club overcome the Giants on the last day of the season with a franchise-record 104 victories.

Pendleton batted just .148 through May 4 but then hit .299 over his final 133 games. He hit nine of his 17 home runs in the 25-game stretch from August 24 to October 1 when the Braves were in a mad dash to catch San Francisco.

Though Atlanta failed to win a third straight pennant, it wasn't Pendleton's fault. He continued his strong finish at the plate, hitting safely in all six games of the NLCS against the Phillies for a .346 average and five RBIs. He set NLCS records with 129 career at bats and 32 games and established another NLCS standard with 31 consecutive errorless games at third base.

As in 1993, Pendleton got off to a slow start in 1994, but unlike the previous season, he never got fully untracked this time. Many of the third baseman's woes were due to early-season injuries, including a bad back, which forced him to miss 37 games—three times as many as he missed in his first three seasons as a Brave combined.

After the season the Braves elected not to offer Pendleton a contract for 1995 for economic reasons. That decision brought an abrupt end to the Atlanta career of one of the most respected and most popular players in franchise history.

Pendleton, Terry

Braves	G	AB	R	H	2B	3B	HR	RBI	SB	AVG	SLG
1991	153	586	94	187*	34	8	22	86	10	.319*	.517
1992	160	640	98	199*	39	1	21	105	5	.311	.473
1993	161	633	81	172	33	1	17	84	5	.272	.408
1994	77	309	25	78	18	3	7	30	2	.252	.398
Career	551	2,168	298	636	124	13	67	305	22	.293	.455

Perez, Marty

Braves: 1971–76
Shortstop, second baseman
Birthplace: Visalia, California

B: February 28, 1947
Batted right, threw right
Ht. 5–11; **Wt.** 160

Marty Perez never led the league in anything, but he was an integral part of the Braves' middle infield from 1971 to 1975. Once a highly touted prospect in the California Angels farm system, Perez was traded to the Braves in '71 before he had a chance to establish himself with the American League club.

Known as "Taco" to teammates and fans, Perez moved right in as the team's regular shortstop in his first full season in the majors. He replaced Sonny Jackson, who was shifted to center field after three years at short. Perez batted just .227, but he teamed with second baseman Felix Millan to form an effective double-play combination—something the Braves always seemed to be seeking. In fact, Perez and Millan worked so well together that they helped the club set a franchise record with a league-leading 180 double plays.

Perez remained Atlanta's regular shortstop for two more years, then was moved to second base in mid-1974 by manager Eddie Mathews. Craig Robinson was tried at shortstop, and though he didn't last, Perez got comfortable at second quickly. He tied Houston's Tommy Helms for the best fielding percentage (.985) among the league's second basemen in '74 and was the starter there for two seasons.

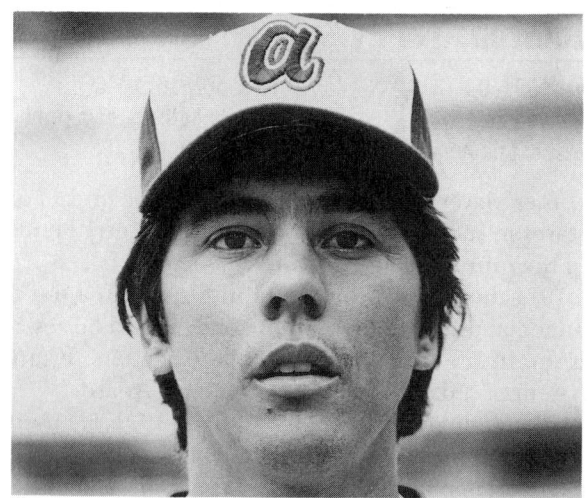
Marty Perez

Never a strong hitter, Perez nevertheless improved steadily at the plate in Atlanta, going from .227 in his first season to .275 in 1975. At one point in '75, he hit in 41 of 47 games and had his average in the .280s before breaking his thumb in August.

A disagreement over salary in 1976 led general manager Eddie Robinson to trade Perez early in the season. He and Darrell Evans were sent to San Francisco in exchange for Willie Montanez, Craig Robinson, and throw-ins Mike Eden and Jake Brown.

Perez, Marty

Braves	G	AB	R	H	2B	3B	HR	RBI	SB	AVG	SLG
1971	130	410	28	93	15	3	4	32	1	.227	.307
1972	141	479	33	109	13	1	1	28	0	.228	.265
1973	141	501	66	125	15	5	8	57	2	.250	.347
1974	127	447	51	116	20	5	2	34	2	.260	.340
1975	120	461	50	127	14	2	2	34	2	.275	.328
1976	31	96	12	24	4	0	1	6	0	.250	.323
Career	690	2,394	240	594	81	16	18	191	7	.248	.318

Perez, Pascual

Braves: 1982–85
Pitcher
Birthplace: San Cristóbal, Dominican Republic

B: May 17, 1957
Batted right, threw right
Ht. 6–2; **Wt.** 163

Mention Pascual Perez to anyone who was a Braves fan in 1982, and the first thing out of the person's mouth probably will be "I-285."

Interstate 285 is the perimeter highway that circles Atlanta. It leads nowhere but 'round and 'round the city. It certainly doesn't lead to Atlanta Stadium. Perez discovered that fact the afternoon and evening of August 19. In the process, he may have provided the comic relief the Braves needed to escape the crushing pressure of a losing streak and the impetus the team needed to get it back on track to a division title.

The Braves started the season with a major league record 13-game winning streak that put them in a commanding position to win their second division title in Atlanta. However, they fell into a miserable slump during which they lost 19 of 21 games going into August 19.

Pascual Perez

Pittinger, Togie

Beaneaters: 1900–04
Pitcher
Birthplace: Greencastle, Pennsylvania
B: January 12, 1872

D: January 14, 1909
Batted left, threw right
Ht. 6–2; **Wt.** 175

Togie (Charles) Pittinger is a good example of the adage that "the candle that burns brightest burns shortest."

Pittinger holds two of the most prestigious records in Braves history, yet he had an extremely short career with Boston and in the majors. The right-hander pitched only five years with the Beaneaters, yet set modern franchise records for most victories (27) and most shutouts (7) in a season. Those records have been tied but not broken.

In 1902, Pittinger was one of the National League's best pitchers even though the ranks included such names as the great Christy Mathewson, fellow Hall of Famers Jack Chesbro and "Iron Man" Joe McGinnity, and Pittinger's own Boston teammate Vic Willis.

Pittinger was 27–16 with seven shutouts and a 2.52 ERA. Willis also won 27 games that year, yet the Beaneaters finished in third place, 29 games behind Pittsburgh. The duo's 54 combined victories accounted for 74 percent of the team's 73 wins.

A true workhorse, Pittinger, who didn't debut in the majors until he was 28 years old, was second in the league to Willis that year in innings (389⅓), games (46), and complete games (36). In the last four of his five seasons in Boston, Pittinger averaged 339 innings per year. He had only the one 20-victory season with the Beaneaters, though he followed it with two 20-loss seasons.

After going 15–21 in 1904 for a team that finished seventh, 51 games out of first, Pittinger probably thought things couldn't get much worse. But he probably reassessed his thinking when he was traded to Philadelphia. The Phillies were the only team in the NL worse than Boston, finishing 53½ games behind the pennant-winning Giants.

The trade was a major one at the time. In exchange for Pittinger, Boston received pitcher Chick Fraser and team captain and star third baseman Harry Wolverton.

Pittinger and the Phillies were bolstered by the deal, while

The Braves acquired Perez from Pittsburgh early in the season. After he went 5–0 at Richmond he was promoted to Atlanta for the second half. It was Perez who was scheduled to start August 19 against Montreal. However, when game time arrived, Perez was nowhere to be found. Phil Niekro was forced to make the start.

Not until 10 minutes after the start of the game did the 25-year-old Dominican show up at Atlanta–Fulton County Stadium. He'd gotten his driver's license earlier that day and decided to drive to the park by himself for the first time. He circled I-285 "two or three times," running out of gas at one point. He finally discovered he had to take I-20 into the city to get to the stadium.

Well, the comedy of the situation seemed to allow the Braves to rise above the pressure they were feeling. They won that night, 5–4, and beat the Mets the next night, 2–1 in 10 innings, behind Perez's 9⅓ innings of work.

The next two years were the best of Perez's checkered career. He became one of the best right-handers in the league, winning 15 games in '83 and 14 in '84. In '83, he was second in the NL in winning percentage and made the All-Star team for the only time in his career.

After that, his career with the Braves went downhill in a hurry. He spent three stints on the disabled list in 1985 and another on the restricted list for missing a team flight. He finished 1–13 and was released by the club the following spring.

Perez, Pascual

Braves	W	L	Pct	G	GS	CG	ShO	IP	H	BB	SO	ERA	SV
1982	4	4	.500	16	11	0	0	79⅓	85	17	29	3.06	0
1983	15	8	.652	33	33	7	1	215⅓	213	51	144	3.43	0
1984	14	8	.636	30	30	4	1	211⅓	208	51	145	3.74	0
1985	1	13	.071	22	22	0	0	95⅓	115	57	57	6.14	0
Career	34	33	.507	101	96	11	2	601⅔	621	176	375	3.92	0

Togie Pittinger

Boston showed no improvement. The Beaneaters remained in seventh place in 1905, while the Phillies climbed past them and all the way to fourth. Pittinger was a big reason for that success. He had the only other 20-victory season of his career, and his 23 wins were second in the league to Mathewson's 31.

However, five consecutive seasons of averaging 339 innings were Pittinger's undoing. He pitched only two more years, not winning more than nine games in either one.

Pittinger, Togie

Beaneaters	W	L	Pct	G	GS	CG	ShO	IP	H	BB	SO	ERA	SV
1900	2	9	.182	18	13	8	0	114	135	54	27	5.13	0
1901	13	16	.448	34	33	27	1	281⅓	288	76	129	3.01	0
1902	27	16	.628	46	40	36	7	389⅓	360	128*	174	2.52	0
1903	18	22*	.450	44	39	35	3	351⅔	396*	143*	140	3.48	1
1904	15	21	.417	38	38	35	5	335⅓	298	144*	146	2.66	0
Career	75	84	.472	180	163	141	16	1,471⅓	1,477	545	616	3.08	1

Pocoroba, Biff

Braves: 1975–84
Catcher
Birthplace: Burbank, California

B: July 25, 1953
Batted both, threw right
Ht. 5–10; **Wt.** 180

Biff Pocoroba has one of the most memorable names in Atlanta Braves history, and for a few years he was one of the better catchers in the National League, too. He even made the National League All-Star team in 1978 and won the Gold Glove as the league's best defensive catcher that season.

Shortly after that All-Star Game appearance at age 25, though, Pocoroba's rise to stardom was halted by shoulder problems. He eventually underwent surgery that year to repair a tear in the rotator cuff. He never was a regular catcher again, though he was effective as a backup receiver and as a pinch hitter for several seasons.

Pocoroba jumped from Double-A to Atlanta in 1975. The switch-hitter's best season was 1977 when he hit .290 with eight home runs and 44 RBIs in a career-high 113 games. In 1980 he led the Braves with 15 pinch hits. When the Braves won the National League West in 1982, he was the team's backup catcher behind Bruce Benedict.

At age 30, Pocoroba was released in April 1984. He spent his entire career with the Braves, and afterward he started a sausage production business in suburban Atlanta.

Oh yes, about that name: His full given name is . . . Biff Pocoroba.

Pocoroba, Biff

Braves	G	AB	R	H	2B	3B	HR	RBI	SB	AVG	SLG
1975	67	188	15	48	7	1	1	22	0	.255	.319
1976	54	174	16	42	7	0	0	14	1	.241	.282
1977	113	321	46	93	24	1	8	44	3	.290	.445
1978	92	289	21	70	8	0	6	34	0	.242	.332
1979	28	38	6	12	4	0	0	4	1	.316	.421
1980	70	83	7	22	4	0	2	8	1	.265	.386
1981	57	122	4	22	4	0	0	8	0	.180	.213
1982	56	120	5	33	7	0	2	22	0	.275	.383
1983	55	120	11	32	6	0	2	16	0	.267	.367
1984	4	2	1	0	0	0	0	0	0	.000	.000
Career	596	1,457	132	374	71	2	21	172	6	.257	.351

Ramirez, Rafael

Braves: 1980–87
Shortstop
Birthplace: San Pedro de Macorís, Dominican Republic

B: February 18, 1959
Batted right, threw right
Ht. 6–0; **Wt.** 185

There were those who likened Rafael Ramirez early in his career to a young Davey Concepcion, shortstop of Cincinnati's Big Red Machine. You could hardly blame long-suffering Braves fans for thinking/hoping that their shortstop savior had finally arrived. Those high expectations, however, probably were Ramirez's biggest enemy during his eight years in Atlanta.

Indeed, Ramirez had a sustained run as one of the National League's best shortstops. But in a very respectable six-year stretch as Atlanta's regular shortstop, he never quite lived up to the high expectations placed on him.

Drafted as an outfielder, Ramirez was quickly converted to shortstop in his first pro season and made it to Atlanta in the middle of his fourth year. In his second full season, he found himself in the midst of a pennant race, and he seemed to blossom into maturity with the pressure of the situation.

The Braves and Dodgers battled down to the final day of

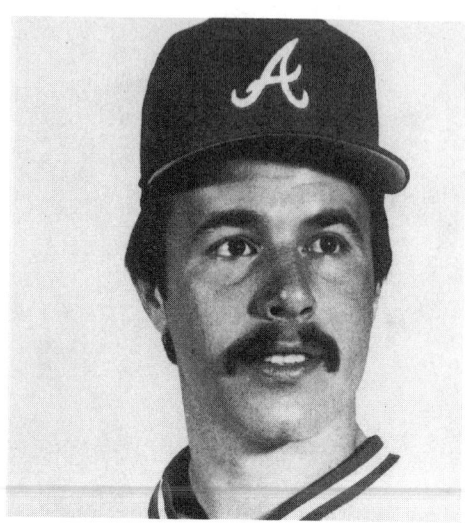

Biff Pocoroba

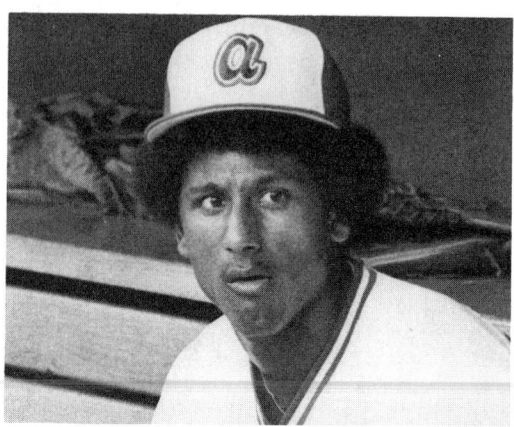

Rafael Ramirez

the 1982 schedule before Atlanta finally won the NL West. Ramirez was as big a reason for that success as any position player other than league MVP Dale Murphy. He outhit Bob Horner and Chris Chambliss, and even though those two players had better power production than Ramirez, the shortstop hit a career-high 10 home runs, played spectacular defense at times, and stole a career-high 27 bases. He led the team in hits and was second in steals and batting average.

The '82 Braves set a team record at that time of 186 double plays, and it was Ramirez and second baseman Glenn Hubbard who were at the heart of the infield making it happen. On June 27, Ramirez tied a National League record by assisting in six double plays at Cincinnati. But Ramirez's defensive lapses usually came on routine plays, something that would continue to haunt him in the future.

When Horner missed the last two weeks of the season with a hyperextended elbow, it was Ramirez, of all people, who helped pick up the offensive slack. On September 24, he hit two home runs and drove in five runs, allowing the Braves to beat the Padres, 11–6, and gain a crucial game on the Dodgers.

In 1983, Ramirez hit a career-high .297 and was third in the NL in hits. The following season he reached the pinnacle of his career. He was hitting .304 at the All-Star break and was selected for the NL All-Star team. He slumped in the second half, but his .266 average led NL shortstops. He also led the league in putouts, chances, and double plays at his position.

In 1985, Ramirez led NL shortstops in double plays for the fourth straight year, but in 1986 the Braves began to phase him out at the position, using him at third base and in the outfield to make room for Andres Thomas. Thomas took over as the regular shortstop in '87, and the Braves felt they saw enough potential in him to trade Ramirez to Houston that off-season.

Ramirez may not have been another Concepcion, but he was far better than Thomas ever turned out to be.

Ramirez, Rafael

Braves	G	AB	R	H	2B	3B	HR	RBI	SB	AVG	SLG
1980	50	165	17	44	6	1	2	11	2	.267	.352
1981	95	307	30	67	16	2	2	20	7	.218	.303
1982	157	609	74	169	24	4	10	52	27	.278	.379
1983	152	622	82	185	13	5	7	58	16	.297	.368
1984	145	591	51	157	22	4	2	48	14	.266	.327
1985	138	568	54	141	25	4	5	58	2	.248	.333
1986	134	496	57	119	21	1	8	33	19	.240	.335
1987	56	179	22	47	12	0	1	21	6	.263	.346
Career	927	3,537	387	929	139	21	37	301	93	.263	.345

Reardon, Jeff

Braves: 1992
Pitcher
Birthplace: Dalton, Massachusetts

B: October 1, 1955
Bats right, throws right
Ht. 6–0; **Wt.** 205

Jeff Reardon was the Braves' "rent-a-closer" in 1992. Just as John Schuerholz added Alejandro Pena for the stretch drive the previous year, he picked up Reardon on August 30, just in time to get him on the postseason roster. At the time, Reardon was the all-time career leader in saves, and the

Jeff Reardon

Braves were able to get him from Boston in exchange for two minor leaguers.

As Pena had been in '91, Reardon was nearly flawless through the playoffs. He gave up only two runs in 14 regular-season appearances, finishing with three victories and three saves. His third save gave him 30 for the season and 357 for his career. He joined Lee Smith as the only pitchers to have seven 30-save campaigns.

In the playoffs, Reardon picked up a win and a save and was unscored on in three games against the Pirates. However, his luck ran out in the World Series, creating controversy in decisive Game 6.

With the Braves leading Toronto, 4–3, in the ninth inning of Game 2 and on the verge of taking a 2–0 lead in games, Bobby Cox called on Reardon to get the final four outs. The veteran right-hander got out of the eighth, but with Atlanta two outs away from victory, he walked Derek Bell and gave up a two-run homer to pinch hitter Ed Sprague. That allowed Toronto to win the game and return home with a split of the first two games.

In Game 3, Cox again summoned Reardon, this time with one out and the score tied, 2–2, in the ninth. Though he wasn't charged with the loss, Reardon faced one batter and gave up the hit that drove in the deciding run and ended the game. With one out and the bases loaded, Cox brought in the veteran to face Candy Maldonado, who singled to right-center.

Cox obviously lost confidence in Reardon at that point, for he didn't use him again. With the entire Series on the line in the 11th inning of Game 6, Cox allowed left-hander Charlie Leibrandt, normally a starter, to face Toronto's right-handed sluggers Joe Carter and Dave Winfield.

Leibrandt retired Carter, but he gave up two-run double to Winfield, providing the Blue Jays with a 4–3 victory and the World Series championship. Reardon, ready in the bullpen, stood and watched.

Reardon, Jeff

Braves	W	L	Pct	G	GS	CG	ShO	IP	H	BB	SO	ERA	SV
1992	3	0	1.000	14	0	0	0	15⅔	14	2	7	1.15	3
Career	3	0	1.000	14	0	0	0	15⅔	14	2	7	1.15	3

Reed, Ron

Braves: 1966–75
Pitcher
Birthplace: La Porte, Indiana

B: November 2, 1942
Batted right, threw right
Ht. 6–6; Wt. 215

Reed, Ron													
Braves	**W**	**L**	**Pct**	**G**	**GS**	**CG**	**ShO**	**IP**	**H**	**BB**	**SO**	**ERA**	**SV**
1966	1	1	.500	2	2	0	0	8⅓	7	4	6	2.16	0
1967	1	1	.500	3	3	0	0	21⅓	21	3	11	2.95	0
1968	11	10	.524	35	28	6	1	201⅔	189	49	111	3.35	0
1969	18	10	.643	36	33	7	1	241⅓	227	56	160	3.47	0
1970	7	10	.412	21	18	6	0	134⅔	140	39	68	4.41	0
1971	13	14	.481	32	32	8	1	222⅓	221	54	129	3.73	0
1972	11	15	.423	31	30	11	1	213	222	60	111	3.93	0
1973	4	11	.267	20	19	2	0	116⅓	133	31	64	4.41	1
1974	10	11	.476	28	28	6	2	186	171	41	78	3.39	0
1975	4	5	.444	10	10	1	0	74⅔	93	16	40	4.22	0
Career	80	88	.476	218	203	47	6	1,419⅔	1,424	353	778	3.74	1

In 1969 the Braves brought the first major league title of any kind to the South by winning the National League West, and Ron Reed was a big reason it happened. The lanky right-hander was 18–10 in only his second full season in the majors. At age 26, it appeared he would be winning a lot of games for Atlanta for years to come.

Though Reed did have a long and relatively prosperous career, injuries prevented him from ever approaching an 18-victory season again. In fact, he broke his collarbone in spring training of 1970 when he tripped over first base and fell. He never had another winning season for the Braves.

Like Gene Conley before him and Deion Sanders after him, Reed was a two-sport professional athlete with the Braves. After a successful basketball career at Notre Dame, he signed a contract with the Detroit Pistons of the NBA in 1965. Bypassed in the baseball draft, he then signed as a free agent with the Milwaukee Braves. He started at the Class-A level but climbed all the way to the majors by the end of 1966.

Reed played only two seasons in the NBA before settling on baseball as his full-time occupation. He averaged 8.0 points per game as a forward. His quick rise through the Braves farm system convinced him that baseball provided the best career opportunity. He spent most of 1967 at Triple-A Richmond, then made the Atlanta starting rotation the following year.

In '68, Reed got off to a quick start, winning his first six decisions and going 8–3 in the first half. That was good enough to earn him a spot on the National League All-Star team, the first Atlanta rookie so honored. It was the only All-Star selection of his career.

Despite several other injuries, Reed remained a regular member of the Braves' starting rotation until he was traded to the Cardinals in May 1975. One of the highlights of his Atlanta career was being the winning pitcher against the Dodgers on April 8, 1974, when Hank Aaron hit No. 715.

Royster, Jerry

Braves: 1976–84, 1988
Infielder, outfielder
Birthplace: Sacramento, California

B: October 18, 1952
Batted right, threw right
Ht. 6–0; Wt. 165

Jerry Royster came to the Braves with just 29 games of big league experience. Nevertheless, he came with great expectations.

A highly regarded prospect in the Dodgers farm system, he was the key ingredient for the Braves in a six-player deal that sent Dusty Baker, still only 26 and already a productive player, to Los Angeles after the 1975 season. Atlanta also got Jimmy Wynn, Lee Lacy, and Tom Paciorek in the exchange and sent Ed Goodson to the Dodgers with Baker. Wynn was well on the downside of a fine career and was gone in a year; Lacy never fit in and was sent back to L.A. at midseason; and Paciorek was never more than a role player in two-plus years in Atlanta.

Royster was the Braves' justification for the trade. He was young (23) and highly regarded because of his speed, ability to play three infield positions, and offensive potential. He was coming off a season as the Pacific Coast League player of the year at Triple-A Albuquerque. To sum it up, he was viewed as the type of modern-day player many teams were building around but that the Braves lacked. He would be ex-

Ron Reed

Jerry Royster

citing, capable of taking over a game with his legs even when all else failed.

But while Baker went on to a great career with the Dodgers, Royster's 10 seasons in Atlanta deserve mixed reviews, at best. In many respects, he was a valuable asset, playing three infield positions and the outfield. But only in two seasons, 1976 (third base) and 1978 (shortstop) was he considered a regular. He led the team in steals his first five seasons as a Brave and still ranks as Atlanta's all-time stolen base leader (174). However, he batted only .246 in his Braves career. Perhaps his versatility worked against him, or maybe it was just a case of expectations being set too high.

The highlight of Royster's career was the role he played in helping the Braves win the 1982 NL West title. He hit a career-high .295 and was so much of a catalyst down the stretch that manager Joe Torre said he was the second-half MVP. That compliment came in spite of the fact that Dale Murphy was the league MVP.

Used sparingly the first four months of the season, Royster took over in left when Brett Butler struggled at the plate. From July 29 through the end of the season, Royster batted .326, scoring 30 runs and stealing 13 bases. He also put together a career-best 17-game hitting streak in August.

As the Braves tried to repeat in the NL West in 1983, Royster had another chance to fill a crucial need down the stretch. When Bob Horner broke his wrist in August, Royster took over at third base. However, an ankle injury three days later sidelined him for three weeks, and the Braves didn't win the division.

Royster, Jerry

Braves	G	AB	R	H	2B	3B	HR	RBI	SB	AVG	SLG
1976	149	533	65	132	13	1	5	45	24	.248	.304
1977	140	445	64	96	10	2	6	28	28	.216	.288
1978	140	529	67	137	17	8	2	35	27	.259	.333
1979	154	601	103	164	25	6	3	51	35	.273	.349
1980	123	392	42	95	17	5	1	20	22	.242	.319
1981	64	93	13	19	4	1	0	9	7	.204	.269
1982	108	261	43	77	13	2	2	25	14	.295	.383
1983	91	268	32	63	10	3	3	30	11	.235	.328
1984	81	227	22	47	13	2	1	21	6	.207	.295
1988	68	102	8	18	3	0	0	1	0	.176	.206
Career	1,118	3,451	459	848	125	30	23	265	174	.246	.319

Rudolph, Dick

Braves: 1913–20, 1922–23, 1927
Pitcher
Birthplace: New York City
B: August 25, 1887
D: October 20, 1949
Batted right, threw right
Ht. 5–9; **Wt.** 160

The Braves had many heroes who contributed to the "miracle" of 1914. But the chief architects of that unlikely pennant and World Series championship were starting pitchers Dick Rudolph, Bill James, and Lefty Tyler, of whom Rudolph was the biggest winner. Without Rudolph's stunning 26 regular season victories and two World Series wins, manager George Stallings probably never would have been known as "Miracle Man."

A native of the Bronx and a graduate of Fordham, Rudolph

Dick Rudolph

was small in stature and relied primarily on a superb curve, excellent control, and an unusually keen knowledge of hitters.

Because of his unimpressive physical stature and lack of a fastball, Rudolph spent several years laboring in the minors. Rudolph got a late-season tryout with the Giants in 1910 and made the club in the spring of the next season until being farmed out.

In 1912 he was 25–10 for Toronto, yet had to face a 25 percent pay cut in 1913 when salary restrictions were imposed by the International League. Though Rudolph signed, he quickly left the team, saying he was quitting baseball to enter law practice with his brother. It was an idle threat, but it worked. Toronto sold Rudolph May 4 to the Braves, who were trying to build during Stallings' first season. The price was $4,000 and washed-up right-hander Buster Brown.

Rudolph's first appearance was in relief and nearly earned him a ticket back to Toronto. Stallings, who had little patience with pitchers, especially those who couldn't throw strikes, brought in his 25-year-old right-hander with two on and two out. When Rudolph proceeded to walk the first batter, loading the bases, and to throw balls on the first three pitches to the next hitter, Stallings was fit to be tied. However, Rudolph then used three consecutive curves to record an inning-ending strikeout.

"He's got some guts," said an admiring Stallings, who quickly became a fan of Rudolph's.

In spite of his late start in 1913, the crafty Rudolph still won 14 games for a team that finished 13 games under .500. Stallings said he was one of the smartest pitchers he'd ever seen.

If Rudolph was smart in 1913, he was an absolute genius in 1914. At one point, he won 12 straight games en route to tying for the league lead in victories. The Braves pitchers were hot in the second half, leading the spirited climb from last place, and Rudolph was blistering. The team managed just one shutout prior to July 4 but 17 afterward. Six of those were by Rudolph, the third-best total in the league.

Rudolph finished second in the league in both innings and complete games.

In the World Series against the heavily favored Athletics of

Connie Mack, Rudolph was as masterful as he'd been during the regular season. In Game 1 he beat Philadelphia, 7–1, with a five-hitter. And he completed Boston's sweep by winning Game 4, 3–1. In 18 innings, he allowed just one earned run and 12 hits, striking out 15 and walking four.

Rudolph never had another season quite like 1914, but he did repeat as a 20-game winner in 1915 and remained one of the more durable and successful pitchers in the league through 1919.

Though the Braves finished second, seven games out, in 1915, Rudolph was second in the league in victories, innings, and complete games.

In 1916 he fell just one victory short of his third straight 20-win season.

The Braves became an inferior team by 1917, and the lack of support took its toll on Rudolph, who never won more than 13 games again. Yet as late as 1919 he still ranked among the league leaders in innings and complete games and had a 2.17 ERA.

That was his last productive season, and in 1921 he supposedly retired to become pitching coach for Fred Mitchell, who took over as manager for Stallings. Rudolph remained a coach through 1927, but on several occasions, when the Braves were short of pitching, he was called on to help bail out the staff.

"Rudolph was one of the smartest pitchers who ever toed the rubber," said Mitchell, a coach under Stallings before becoming manager. "He could almost read a batter's mind. I often sat on the bench with him and heard him tell whether or not the batter would hit or take. He made a real study of the profession."

Babe Ruth

Rudolph, Dick

Braves	W	L	Pct	G	GS	CG	ShO	IP	H	BB	SO	ERA	SV
1913	14	13	.519	33	22	17	2	249⅓	258	59	109	2.92	0
1914	26	10	.722	42	36	31	6	336⅓	288	61	138	2.35	0
1915	22	19*	.537	44	43*	30	3	341⅓	304*	64	147	2.37	1
1916	19	12	.613	41	38	27	5	312	266	38	133	2.16	3
1917	13	13	.500	31	30	22	5	242⅔	252	54	96	3.41	0
1918	9	10	.474	21	20	15	3	154	144	30	48	2.57	0
1919	13	18*	.419	37	32	24	2	273⅔	282*	54	76	2.17	2
1920	4	8	.333	18	12	3	0	89	104	24	24	4.04	0
1922	0	2	.000	3	3	1	0	16	22	5	3	5.06	0
1923	1	2	.333	4	4	1	1	19⅓	27	10	3	3.72	0
1927	0	0	—	1	0	0	0	1⅓	1	1	0	0.00	0
Career	121	107	.531	275	240	171	27	2,035	1,948	400	777	2.62	6

Ruth, Babe

Braves: 1935
Outfielder
Birthplace: Baltimore, Maryland
B: February 6, 1895

D: August 16, 1948
Batted left, threw left
Ht. 6–2; **Wt.** 215

Babe Ruth's career with the Braves lasted less than two months of the 1935 season, yet it offers a compelling chapter in both franchise history and in the life of the most magnificent sports figure of all time.

At age 40, Ruth was finished as a player, but he aspired to be a manager. The Yankees wanted no part of him in either role, yet because of his immense popularity, they were in a

quandary over what to do with the Sultan of Swat. Judge Emil Fuchs and his financially strapped Boston Braves provided the perfect solution.

Fuchs, the Braves' president, approached the Yankees about a plan that would allow them to drop Ruth gracefully. They would give The Bambino his release in order that he could pursue his managerial interest with the Braves. Fuchs already had a manager, Bill McKechnie, with whom he was happy, but he had to dangle a carrot in front of Ruth to get him to agree to play for the Braves.

The proposal Fuchs concocted called for Ruth to receive a salary of $25,000 not only to play for the Braves, but also to serve as "assistant manager" and second vice president of the club. He also offered Ruth a share of profits—if there were any—and a chance to purchase stock in what was a franchise in dire straits.

Of course, Fuchs convinced Ruth that with his gate appeal, the Braves would soon be raking in money at the box office. The Braves' president also gave Ruth the distinct impression that he'd replace McKechnie as manager within a year, with McKechnie moving into the front office as general manager.

Ruth, who started his career with the Red Sox, was extremely popular in Boston, and his return created a great deal of excitement in New England. He went to Boston to sign the contract, and thousands of fans braved frigid February temperatures to see him at the train station. A large banquet also was staged in his honor at the Copley Plaza.

When Ruth reported to spring training in St. Petersburg on March 4, he again was mobbed at the train station. Though he was overweight, out of shape, and not hitting, he attracted large crowds for exhibition games.

With true Ruthian drama, however, The Babe rose to the occasion for opening day, which drew a record crowd of 25,000 to Braves Field. Facing the great Carl Hubbell, he singled in a run in the first, scored the Braves' second run later in the inning, then capped the day with a two-run homer in the fifth. He had a hand in all of Boston's runs in a 4–2 victory over the Giants.

The city's baseball fans thought Ruth and their decrepit National League team had suddenly been reborn. But they quickly found neither to be true.

Slow, still out of shape, and suffering from a cold, Ruth struggled at the plate and didn't play full games. He also quickly soured on his deal with Fuchs. It was obvious the team was lousy and wasn't going to attract fans consistently; thus profits would be slim if any. Ruth seemed to have no duties or responsibilities as McKechnie's "assistant," and there was no indication he was valued as anything more than a prop to bolster attendance. Of course, that's exactly what he was.

In mid-May, Ruth tried to retire, but Fuchs talked him into making a road trip because several clubs were planning special events in his honor.

Ruth and the Braves continued to struggle, but on May 25 at Pittsburgh's spacious Forbes Field, The Babe gave one last, breathtaking display of his majesty. He homered in the first inning and in the third; singled in the fifth; and in the seventh, belted the 714th and last home run of his monumental career.

Fittingly, his third homer of the day was the first ball ever to clear Forbes' two-tiered grandstand roof in right field. In his biographical masterpiece *Babe*, author Robert W. Creamer reports that Gus Miller, the head usher at Forbes Field, measured the distance from home plate to where the ball was found as 600 feet.

After the third homer, Ruth came out of the game. He finished the day with six RBIs, but the Braves lost, 11–7. It was only the second time in Ruth's career that he hit three home runs in the same game. The next day, though, he went 0-for-4 with three strikeouts at Cincinnati in the only National League game he ever played from start to finish.

Four days later, on Memorial Day, Ruth started the first game of a doubleheader in Philadelphia. He struck out in the first inning, hurt his knee in the outfield in the bottom of the first, and left the game. He never played again.

On June 2 at Braves Field, Ruth, with his batting average at .181, announced his retirement. While Ruth was talking to the sports writers, Fuchs issued a statement saying the Braves had released The Babe as a player and assistant manager and fired him as an executive.

The Braves' relationship with Ruth was brief and tumultuous but momentous just the same. Ruth continued to express a desire to manage, but in the 13 years between his retirement and death, he never again had a full-time job in baseball.

Ruth, Babe											
Braves	G	AB	R	H	2B	3B	HR	RBI	SB	AVG	SLG
1935	28	72	13	13	0	0	6	12	0	.181	.431
Career	28	72	13	13	0	0	6	12	0	.181	.431

Sain, Johnny

Braves: 1942, 1946–51	**B:** September 25, 1917
Pitcher	**Batted right, threw right**
Birthplace: Havana, Arkansas	**Ht.** 6–2; **Wt.** 200

Few names are as deeply ingrained in Braves history as that of Johnny Sain. An outstanding pitcher who won 20 or more games four times from 1946 to 1950 with Boston, Sain later was a highly successful pitching coach who produced 16 20-game winners in 17 seasons. Yet it was a simple rhyme which spoke of the Braves' hopes for winning the 1948 pennant that has immortalized Sain.

"[Warren] Spahn and Sain and pray for rain," is still one of the most well-known lyrics in baseball lore. It appears in countless baseball histories and remains on the tongues of many fans even though it originated nearly half a century ago.

Desperate Braves fans hadn't known a pennant-winning team since 1914. So, their desire to see their aces, Spahn and Sain, pitch nearly every game down the 1948 stretch drive was somewhat understandable even though the Boston staff easily wound up with the best team ERA (3.37) in the league.

Spahn actually had one of his few subpar seasons in 1948, winning "just" 15 games and finishing with the highest ERA (3.71) he'd have in a full season until he was 43 years old. But Sain was at his best, leading the league with a career-high 24 victories and finishing third with a 2.60 ERA. From September 3 to 21, he started and won six times, allowing only 10 runs and fostering the poetic notion of a two-man rotation.

Sain was 31 years old when he reached the pinnacle of his career in the 1948 World Series by outdueling Cleveland's Bob Feller, 1–0, in Game 1 of what proved to be a six-game Series defeat for the Braves. Seldom has a player attained as much success as Sain enjoyed after having to endure so many setbacks in getting to the major leagues in the first place.

The right-hander from Arkansas literally had to beg for work in the low minors several times just to stay employed. He was told on many occasions that he had no future in the game, and his father, a former semipro pitcher, once tried to have Johnny converted to an outfielder in a last-ditch effort to have his son make an impression in pro ball.

Sain's father once persuaded Bill Dickey, the great Yan-

Johnny Sain

kees catcher who was from Arkansas, to watch Johnny pitch in high school. Afterward, Dickey refused to talk with the youngster "because I'd have to tell him he hasn't got it."

Sain's father finally got his son a contract to play for Troy in the Class-D Alabama State League, but the commissioner's office immediately ruled the pitcher a free agent because of a technicality. It took Sain two more years to find another job, this time with Osceola in the Class-D Northeast Arkansas League in 1937. He had a poor season and was released and told he'd be wise to find a real job.

In the off-season, Sain worked religiously on his curve, then in the spring talked himself into a tryout with the Giants, who were training in Fort Smith, Arkansas. The Giants, however, weren't interested either, but he landed a spot with Newport, a Detroit farm club, where he went 16–4 in 1938. He also played outfield, the result of a suggestion his father made to the Newport manager, and batted over .300. He won 18 for Newport in 1939 but afterward was made a free agent for the second time in his career, along with most of Detroit's farmhands, in a ruling by the commissioner's office.

Sain found a job with Nashville in 1940. He pitched there—and not particularly well—for two seasons. But the team's owner convinced the Braves to take a look at him on a trial basis during spring training in 1942. Braves manager Casey Stengel, saddled with a miserable lot of players, liked what he saw and bought the 24-year-old right-hander.

On opening day in Boston, Sain was brought in to relieve in the fifth inning with the Braves leading the Giants, 3–2, and slugger Johnny Mize coming to bat with two men on base. Sain struck out Mize, who was in the midst of a Hall of Fame career, and finished the game without allowing a run. Stengel liked Sain and brought him along slowly.

Used mainly in relief as a rookie, Sain performed well, winning four and saving six. After the season he enlisted in the navy's flight training program, along with other major leaguers such as Ted Williams and Johnny Pesky. While in preflight school, Sain pitched in a war charity game that attracted 40,000 fans to Yankee Stadium, and he was the last pitcher to face Babe Ruth.

Sain became a test pilot for the navy and was on the verge of being sent overseas when World War II ended. He was 28 years old when he reported for spring training in 1946. He had but four big league victories to his credit, but he was mature and in good condition, and he had learned a lot about pitching from other major leaguers in the service.

The 1946 Braves had a new manager, Billy Southworth, and were intent on finally making their presence felt in the National League. Sain was at the forefront of their plans. He was inserted in the starting rotation and responded by developing into one of the league's best pitchers. He finished second in the league with 20 wins and a 2.21 ERA. He also led the league in complete games and was third in strikeouts.

Among Sain's 20 victories was a near perfect game against Cincinnati in which the only base runner reached on a first-inning pop fly that dropped for a hit between an infielder and outfielder. He retired the final 25 Reds he faced.

Sain, who used to discuss hitting with Williams in navy flight school, also came back to the Braves ready to hit as well as to pitch. He batted .298 in 1946 and had 17 RBIs, nearly twice as many as any other pitcher in the league. By this time, Sain's curveball was recognized as one of the best in the game. In 1947 he was on the mound when Jackie Robinson

debuted with the Dodgers, and he also became the first Braves pitcher to win 20 games in successive seasons since Dick Rudolph in 1914–15. He batted .346 with 18 RBIs and had a 14-game hitting streak, too.

That performance set the stage for Sain's biggest season in 1948, when he not only led Boston to the pennant but also became the first Braves pitcher of the 20th century to post three straight 20-win seasons. For good measure, he became the first pitcher ever to lead the league in sacrifice bunts.

The Braves disintegrated in 1949, finishing four games under .500 and 22 out of first place. Sain was as much to blame as anyone. He won only 10 of 27 decisions and had the worst ERA (4.81) of his career except for his final season.

In 1950, Sain bounced back to win 20 again, finishing just one victory behind Spahn for the league lead. But the next year he struggled and was traded late in the season to the Yankees, where he was reunited with Stengel. In exchange, the Braves got a young right-hander named Lou Burdette and $50,000.

Sain played on World Series championship teams in 1951, '52, and '53. He made the All-Star team and won 14 games in 1953, then became a full-time reliever in 1954, leading the American League with 22 saves, though the statistic was not yet official.

Sain's playing career faded in 1955 after 139 victories. But he used the years of knowledge he gained fighting his way to the majors to forge another career as a coach. His first major league coaching job was with Kansas City in 1959. He eventually worked for the Yankees, Twins, Tigers, White Sox, and ultimately the Braves (1977 and 1985–86).

Sain, Johnny

Braves	W	L	Pct	G	GS	CG	ShO	IP	H	BB	SO	ERA	SV
1942	4	7	.364	40	3	0	0	97	79	63	68	3.90	6
1946	20	14	.588	37	34	24*	3	265	225	87	129	2.21	2
1947	21	12	.636	38	35	22	3	266	265*	79	132	3.52	1
1948	24*	15	.615	42	39*	28*	4	314⅔*	297*	83	137	2.60	1
1949	10	17	.370	37	36	16	1	243	285	75	73	4.81	0
1950	20	13	.606	37	37	25	3	278⅓	294*	70	96	3.94	0
1951	5	13	.278	26	22	6	1	160⅓	195	45	63	4.21	1
Career	104	91	.533	257	206	121	15	1,624⅓	1,640	502	698	3.49	11

Salvo, Manny

Bees, Braves: 1940–43	**B:** June 30, 1913
Pitcher	**Batted right, threw right**
Birthplace: Sacramento, California	**Ht.** 6–4; **Wt.** 210

Manny Salvo had only one winning season in a short big league career, but he managed to lead the majors in shutouts that year.

An outstanding minor league pitcher for several years, the big right-hander finally got a chance to prove himself in the majors with the Giants in 1939 when he was a highly regarded prospect. However, he was unimpressive and was traded to Boston on June 15, 1940, with Al Glossop for Tony Cuccinello.

Bees manager Casey Stengel, saddled with another poor ball club, pulled his new pitcher aside for some counseling and supposedly told Salvo that if he didn't produce, his next stop would not be in the major leagues.

Whether or not Stengel's words were the reason, the hard-

Manny Salvo

Red Schoendienst

throwing Salvo suddenly became one of the league's top pitchers. In little more than half the season, he won 10 games, half of them by shutout, for a team that finished 22 games under .500 and 34½ games out of first place.

His five shutouts tied Brooklyn's Whitlow Wyatt, who had the benefit of a full season, for the major league lead.

Giants manager Bill Terry, who had given up on Salvo the year before, said to him, "You never showed me that stuff you are putting out for the Bees." Salvo responded, "I give you my word I had more stuff with the Giants in 1939 than I have now. My winning is a puzzle to me as it may be to you."

Perhaps his puzzlement is the reason why he never had much success after that. Salvo pitched only three more seasons and recorded just four more shutouts.

In 1941 the high-kicking right-hander lost 10 in a row for another horrible team. The Braves scored only 17 runs in those 10 defeats, three of which were shutouts, including a 3–0, 12-inning loss to the Giants.

Salvo and Wyatt engaged in a memorable beanball battle in 1942, after which both pitchers were fined for inciting two bench-clearing brawls. The warring culminated in the eighth inning when Salvo hit Wyatt in the ribs with a pitch and the Dodgers pitcher responded by throwing his bat at his Boston counterpart. The Braves had the last say in a rare, 2–0, victory.

| Salvo, Manny | | | | | | | | | | | | | |
Bees, Braves	W	L	Pct	G	GS	CG	ShO	IP	H	BB	SO	ERA	SV
1940	10	9	.526	21	20	14	5*	160⅔	151	43	60	3.08	0
1941	7	16	.304	35	27	11	2	195	192	93	67	4.06	0
1942	7	8	.467	25	14	6	1	130⅔	129	41	25	3.03	0
1943	5	7	.417	21	14	5	1	98⅔	99	31	26	3.46	0
Career	29	40	.420	102	75	36	9	585	571	208	178	3.46	0

Schoendienst, Red

Braves: 1957–60
Second baseman, outfielder
Birthplace: Germantown, Illinois

B: February 2, 1923
Batted both, threw right
Ht. 6–0; **Wt.** 170

If not for Red Schoendienst, the Braves' last World Series championship might have come in 1914 rather than in 1957. Shudder the thought.

Make no mistake, Milwaukee had a powerful club in 1957 even before Schoendienst was acquired from New York at the June 15 trading deadline. Perhaps the Braves could have won

the pennant and the World Series without him, but his contributions were so great there is reason to believe otherwise.

Manager Fred Haney's club was never in serious trouble that year, but second base was its most glaring weakness, one that could have become debilitating later in the season if not for the acquisition of the 34-year-old Schoendienst. Not only did the veteran, who was obtained in exchange for Bobby Thomson, Danny O'Connell, and Ray Crone, stabilize the infield, but his offense helped offset the rash of injuries to key personnel that threatened to decimate the Braves at times.

When the Braves obtained Schoendienst, he'd already been a nine-time All-Star and led the league in defense five times at second base. A switch-hitter, he also batted over .300 four times in the previous five seasons. He proved to be just the spark the Braves needed, hitting .310 for Milwaukee (.309 overall) and leading the league with 200 hits. He was the first player to lead the league in hits when splitting the season with two teams.

In the World Series victory over the Yankees, Schoendienst also batted .278.

The following season, Schoendienst was limited to 106 games by pleurisy and a broken finger but still led the league's second basemen in fielding (.987) and hit .262 in the regular season and .300 in the World Series loss to the Yankees.

The Braves' pennant string was snapped at two in 1959, and it's probably no coincidence that Schoendienst missed nearly the entire season with tuberculosis. He was a part-time player in 1960 and was released after the season, returning to the Cardinals, his original team, as a player-coach.

A member of the Hall of Fame, Schoendienst was not a power hitter, but his home run in the 14th inning won the 1950 All-Star Game for the National League. He still holds the NL record for most years leading second basemen in fielding (7).

| Schoendienst, Red | | | | | | | | | | | |
Braves	G	AB	R	H	2B	3B	HR	RBI	SB	AVG	SLG
1957	93	394	56	122	23	4	6	32	2	.310	.434
1958	106	427	47	112	23	1	1	24	3	.262	.328
1959	5	3	0	0	0	0	0	0	0	.000	.000
1960	68	226	21	58	9	1	1	19	1	.257	.319
Career	272	1,050	124	292	55	6	8	75	6	.278	.365

Smith, Lonnie

Braves: 1988–92   **B:** December 22, 1955
Outfielder   **Bats right, throws right**
Birthplace: Chicago   **Ht.** 5-9; **Wt.** 195

The Braves couldn't have guessed how important Lonnie Smith would be to them when they signed him to a minor league contract in 1988. A 32-year-old veteran at the time, he began the season at Triple-A Richmond and wasn't called to Atlanta until July 28. He spent much of the next four and a half years in left field, though, batting over .300 in 1989 and '90 and providing critical offensive support to the pennant-winning efforts in 1991 and '92.

As is sometimes the case with successful players, though, Smith is remembered best by many for a crucial mistake. In his case, it was a baserunning error that was instrumental in the Braves' losing the 1991 World Series to Minnesota.

When Otis Nixon was suspended for the final two weeks of the (1991) regular season and the postseason, Ron Gant moved from left field to center, and Smith took over as the regular left fielder. He played well, hitting .254 in the last two weeks when the Braves outlasted the Dodgers for a very unlikely NL West title. During the playoffs, he batted .250. Then, he not only became the first player to appear in the Series with four different teams (Philadelphia, St. Louis, and Kansas City), but he also became the first National League player to hit a home run in three consecutive games (3, 4, and 5). Those three homers came in a span of just 10 at bats.

However, in Game 7, Smith seemingly could have scored what would have been the winning run had he not hesitated when rounding second base in the eighth inning. With the game scoreless, Smith led off the eighth with a single. Terry Pendleton followed with a double to left-center. Smith lost track of the ball and didn't pick up third base coach Jimy Williams, who was waving him on.

Smith's momentary delay at second forced Williams to hold him at third. Ron Gant grounded out, and after David Justice was walked, Sid Bream grounded into a double play, thwarting Atlanta's best scoring threat of the game.

Minnesota eventually scored the lone run of the game in the bottom of the 10th to win the Series.

"Why he stopped, I just don't know," Braves manager Bobby Cox said afterward.

Smith refused to explain himself after the game but later

said in the *Philadelphia Inquirer,* "What nobody realizes, I was going with the pitch on a delayed steal. I got about halfway, and I heard the sound of the bat. I made the mistake of not looking in [toward the batter] when I started running. I just assumed the ball would be hit on the ground.

"Before I had a chance to look back, I saw the two infielders trying to glove something [a decoy by Twins Chuck Knoblauch and Greg Gagne]. Then I looked up, and I happened to see [Dan] Gladden running toward the outfield [fence], and I saw Kirby [Puckett], and then I noticed the ball almost as it hit [the fence]. After I saw they weren't going to catch it, I started running as hard as I could."

"We should have won the game and should be world champions," said Braves general manager John Schuerholz.

Smith, by the way, never was a noted base runner despite decent speed. His habit of stumbling on the bases and in the outfield earned him the nickname "Skates."

Yes, it can be said that Smith cost the Braves their first World Series championship since 1957. But the bottom line is that they wouldn't have gotten as far as they did without his many contributions. His home runs in Games 3 and 4, alone, were instrumental in a pair of one-run victories that made Game 7 possible.

Just getting himself in position to play in the Series was a major achievement for Smith, since most teams considered him washed up in the spring of '88. Following his midseason promotion from Richmond that year, Smith returned in '89 to earn National League Comeback Player of the Year recognition from *The Sporting News.* He posted career highs in home runs (21) and RBIs (79) and stole 25 bases, joining Hank Aaron, Dusty Baker, and Dale Murphy as the only 20–20 men in Atlanta Braves history. He also led the NL in batting average with runners in scoring position (.427). His .315 batting average was third in the league, the best showing by a Brave since Ralph Garr won the 1974 batting crown.

Smith's overall numbers weren't nearly as impressive in 1990 as they were in '89, but he still became only the second Atlanta Brave to bat .300 in consecutive seasons (Garr in '71, '72) and only the third left fielder in franchise history to do so (Garr and Ed Brown in '26, '27).

Already having proven that adversity couldn't keep him down, Smith rebounded from a winter of criticism about his 1991 Series baserunning. A slow start left his final average at just .247, but he caught fire in late May and was at his best in the stretch drive to the division title. In 21 starts after August 13, he hit .302 with four homers and 18 RBIs.

Though he was reduced to a pinch-hitting role in the '92 NLCS, he made three World Series starts as the designated hitter and contributed a grand slam to Atlanta's 7–2 victory over Toronto in Game 5. The Braves did not offer him a contract for 1993.

Lonnie Smith

Smith, Lonnie

Braves	G	AB	R	H	2B	3B	HR	RBI	SB	AVG	SLG
1988	43	114	14	27	3	0	3	9	4	.237	.342
1989	134	482	89	152	34	4	21	79	25	.315	.533
1990	135	466	72	142	27	9	9	42	10	.305	.459
1991	122	353	58	97	19	1	7	44	9	.275	.394
1992	84	158	23	39	8	2	6	33	4	.247	.437
Career	518	1,573	256	457	91	16	46	207	52	.291	.456

Smoltz, John

Braves: 1988–
Pitcher
Birthplace: Warren, Michigan

B: May 15, 1967
Bats right, throws right
Ht. 6–3; **Wt.** 185

One of the most talented pitchers ever to wear a Braves uniform, John Smoltz also is one of the biggest enigmas in franchise history.

Blessed with the most overpowering pitches on the Atlanta staff in the early 1990s, Smoltz was a major contributor to the club's success in that period, yet he's never fully developed the potential as a big winner.

The best illustration of the right-hander's ability, as well as his unpredictability, is the entire 1991 season. In the first half of the season, Smoltz was 2–11 with a 5.16 ERA. He probably was on the verge of losing his job, but the counseling of sports psychologist Jack Lewellyn was credited with helping Smoltz overcome a tendency to let his emotions get out of control.

The result was an inspired second-half performance that enabled the Braves to drive to an improbable division title. After the All-Star break, Smoltz was 12–2 with a 2.62 ERA. As his confidence grew, Smoltz became almost untouchable the last two months when he was 8–1 with a 1.49 ERA in his last 13 starts with no home runs allowed. He won his last six decisions, including the division clincher when he beat Houston, 5–2, on the next-to-last day of the season.

Smoltz continued his stellar work in the postseason when he began to develop a reputation as the Braves' "big-game" pitcher. He won Games 3 and 7 of the League Championship Series, shutting out Pittsburgh, 4–0, in the final game to send the Braves to the World Series for the first time since 1958. His ERA was 1.76 in the two games—and it got even lower in the World Series.

Smoltz was lifted after giving up just two runs in seven innings of Game 3 of the Series against Minnesota. He came back again in Game 7, facing his boyhood idol, Jack Morris, and matched the Twins' ace pitch for pitch. However, after 7⅓ scoreless innings, Smoltz was relieved in a game the Braves finally lost, 1–0, in 10 innings. His ERA for the two Series

starts was 1.26. His combined postseason ERA was 1.52 in four starts.

Originally signed by the Detroit Tigers in 1985, Smoltz was still a minor leaguer when the Braves obtained him August 12, 1987, in exchange for right-hander Doyle Alexander.

The way Smoltz finished 1991 seemed to indicate he was blossoming into one of the game's great pitchers. In fact, many baseball observers, including some of his teammates, predicted he'd win the Cy Young Award in 1992.

While the 1992 season was a successful one for Smoltz and the Braves, the 25-year-old still finished just three games over .500 at 15–12. However, his dominating style showed in the fact that he became the first Brave since Phil Niekro in 1977 to lead the league in strikeouts.

On May 24, Smoltz tied a franchise record for a nine-inning game by striking out 15 in a 2–1 win at Montreal. The 15 strikeouts were a league high that season, as were the 29 consecutive scoreless innings he strung together in July.

Once again, Smoltz rose to the occasion in the postseason, going 2–0 in the NLCS with Pittsburgh and 1–0 in the World Series against Toronto. He won Games 1 and 4 against the Pirates and kept the Braves close enough in Game 7 that they were able to win on Francisco Cabrera's ninth-inning hit. He posted a 2.66 ERA and was named MVP of the League Championship Series.

In the World Series, he left without a decision in Game 2 and, with the Braves facing elimination, won Game 5, 7–2. His Series ERA was 2.70.

Smoltz had another productive season in 1993, matching his career high with 15 wins, yet still fell somewhat short of expectations. The Braves were only 18–17 in his 35 starts.

Nevertheless, Smoltz was named to the All-Star team for the third time in his career, finished second in the league in strikeouts, and tied for third in opponents' batting average (.230). Smoltz helped give the Braves their first foursome of 15-game winners (Tom Glavine, Greg Maddux, and Steve Avery) in history and the first in the National League since the Mets in 1986.

In the League Championship Series with Philadelphia, Smoltz suffered his first postseason loss ever despite not giving up an earned run in Game 4 when he was charged with the 2–1 defeat. His composite postseason record still was 6–1 with a 1.94 ERA in 10 games. He also set an NLCS record with 44 career strikeouts.

The strike-shortened 1994 season was not a memorable one for baseball, the Braves, and particularly Smoltz. He finished four games under .500 for one of the best teams in the game and had a 4.14 ERA. The reason for his ineffectiveness could have been a large bone spur that was removed from his right elbow in postseason surgery.

John Smoltz

| Smoltz, John | | | | | | | | | | | | |
Braves	W	L	Pct	G	GS	CG	ShO	IP	H	BB	SO	ERA	SV
1988	2	7	.222	12	12	0	0	64	74	33	37	5.48	0
1989	12	11	.522	29	29	5	0	208	160	72	168	2.94	0
1990	14	11	.560	34	34	6	2	231⅓	206	90*	170	3.85	0
1991	14	13	.519	36	36	5	0	229⅔	206	77	148	3.80	0
1992	15	12	.556	35	35*	9	3	246⅔	206	80	215*	2.85	0
1993	15	11	.577	35	35	3	1	243⅔	208	100	208	3.62	0
1994	6	10	.375	21	21	1	0	134⅔	120	48	113	4.14	0
Career	78	75	.510	202	202	29	6	1,358	1,180	500	1,059	3.59	0

Spahn, Warren

Braves: 1942, 1946–64   **B:** April 23, 1921
Pitcher   **Batted left, threw left**
Birthplace: Buffalo, New York **Ht.** 6–0; **Wt.** 175

Warren Spahn once offered the most succinct definition of pitching ever uttered: "Hitting is timing. Pitching is upsetting timing." Perhaps no other man in history has both understood and executed that doctrine with the consistency of the immortal left-hander with the classic, high-kicking motion.

Spahn, without question, was the best pitcher in Braves history. He still ranks as the winningest left-hander in the game, and an argument could be mounted that he was the greatest pitcher of the modern era . . . perhaps of all time.

His list of records and accomplishments is nearly endless. But the bottom line reads 363 victories, fifth all-time, and all but seven of those wins came with the Braves. Only Cy Young, Walter Johnson, Christy Mathewson, and Grover Cleveland Alexander won more. And Spahn didn't win a single game until he was 25 because he spent three years in the Army during World War II.

To put Spahn's achievements in perspective, consider that if a pitcher wins 20 games in a season today, it's usually regarded as the benchmark of his career. Spahn won 20 or more games 13 times in his 21-year career, a National League record.

The son of a Buffalo, New York, wallpaper hanger and weekend ballplayer, Warren Edward Spahn was named after President Warren Harding and Ed Spahn, his father.

The Braves signed him to his first pro contract out of high school for $150 and two suits of clothes. He debuted with the Braves in April 1942 but was farmed out after just 15⅔ innings. The reason? Manager Casey Stengel ordered the left-hander to throw at Brooklyn's Pee Wee Reese, but Spahn refused. Stengel concluded that his rookie didn't have the toughness required to pitch in the majors.

After finishing the season with the Braves' Hartford farm club, Spahn enlisted in the army. He was trained as a combat engineer, and in the fall of 1944 he was shipped to Europe to fight the Nazis. Staff Sergeant Spahn saw heavy action in several battles, including Remagen, where the Ludendorf bridge across the Rhine became a focal point for the Allied drive against Germany.

Spahn was slightly wounded in the foot and narrowly missed

Warren Spahn

One of the most stylish pitchers of all time, Warren Spahn also won more games than any other left-hander in history on his way to Cooperstown.

death while working on the bridge. His unit received the Distinguished Unit Emblem from the president, and Spahn was given a battlefield commission as second lieutenant. He is the only major league ballplayer ever to be so honored.

Years later, his battlefield experience would prove valuable when he made a guest appearance as a Nazi soldier on the popular TV series "Combat."

Spahn was able to return to the Braves in 1946, splitting time between starting and relieving with effectiveness but still showing little indication of the remarkable career on which he was embarking. Then, all of the sudden, at the age of 26, he became a big winner. In 1947, on the way to winning 21 games, he led the league in shutouts (7), innings, and ERA (2.33). He also made the National League All-Star team for the first of 14 times.

Spahn didn't have one of his better seasons in 1948, but he helped the Braves wake from a deep sleep to win their first NL pennant since 1914. In the process, he became forever linked to the Braves and the city of Boston by the famous battle cry "Spahn and Sain and pray for rain." It referred, somewhat erroneously, to the club's lack of pitching, implying that the best chance for winning the pennant was to exist on a rotation of Spahn, Johnny Sain, and bad weather.

In the World Series, won by Cleveland in six games, Spahn lost Game 2 to Bob Lemon, then won Game 5 with a brilliant, one-hit relief stint over the final five innings.

During the Braves' last four years in Boston, Spahn firmly established himself as one of the game's best pitchers. He won a total of 78 games, leading the league in victories in 1949 and '50, in shutouts in '51, and in strikeouts all four seasons. He also became a driving force in Boston behind the formation of the now well-known Jimmy Fund to fight cancer.

When the Braves moved to Milwaukee in 1953, Spahn had the honor of pitching the home opener against St. Louis, a game he won, 3–2, in 10 innings on Billy Bruton's home run.

That was the start of one of Spahn's finest campaigns. He led the league with a career-high 23 victories and a career-low 2.10 ERA.

The 20-victory habit continued in eight of the next 10 seasons, including a six-season run from 1956 to '61. It was broken only in 1955 and '62 when he won "only" 17 and 18 games, respectively. In 1957 he won the Cy Young Award as the best pitcher in baseball (there was only one award for both leagues at the time).

In the pennant-winning seasons of 1957 and '58, he led the NL in victories both times, a feat he repeated the following three years, as well. That five-year run atop the league's pitchers is a major league record, as is his eight seasons overall.

Spahn's good friend and colleague Lou Burdette was the hero of the '57 Series, winning three of the four games, but Spahn did chip in by winning Game 4, 7–5, in 10 innings. In '58 he won Games 1 and 4, pitching a 2-hit, 3–0 victory over Whitey Ford and Stengel's Yankees in Game 4. Unfortunately, that was the last Series in which he appeared.

During the 1950s, Spahn won 202 games, more than any other pitcher in the game. He turned 39 in the first month of the 1960 season, and everyone—including new Braves manager Charlie Dressen—expected him to be slowing down. Dressen announced he would cut down on the great left-hander's workload. Spahn's response was to lead the league in victories (21) and complete games.

He also led the league in complete games at age 40 . . . and 41 . . . and 42. His nine seasons of leading in complete games is a major league record, as is the seven consecutive from 1957 to '63.

Yet another testament to Spahn's staying power is the fact that he went most of his career without pitching a no-hitter, then pitched two in the space of six starts. The first came September 16, 1960, at age 39. The second came April 28, 1961, five days after his 40th birthday. Only Young (41), the winningest pitcher in history, and Nolan Ryan (43) pitched no-hitters at more advanced ages.

Just 6,117 fans showed up at County Stadium for Spahn's first no-hitter, which came on a rainy Friday evening when he was seeking his 20th victory of the season and the 287th of his career. His opponent was last-place Philadelphia. Spahn struck out six of the first nine men he faced and didn't allow a base runner until he walked outfielder Ken Walters with two out in the fourth. The only other base runner the Phillies managed came with one out in the fifth when catcher Cal Neeman drew a walk. Neither reached second.

Always playing practical jokes on teammates to help break the tension of the profession, Spahn played one on himself as he returned to the dugout after the fifth. "All right, just nobody say I've got a no-hitter going," he said, challenging the superstition that mentioning a no-hitter in progress will jinx the pitcher. Apparently, it doesn't apply to the pitcher's words.

With one out in the eighth and Milwaukee leading, 4–0, Philadelphia manager Gene Mauch sent up Tony Taylor and Lee Walls as pinch hitters. Spahn struck out both of them. To start the ninth, Mauch called on two more pinch hitters—Bobby Gene Smith and Bobby Del Greco—and Spahn struck out both of them, giving him four in a row and 15 total.

Weak-hitting second baseman Bobby Malkmus was Spahn's last hurdle, and Malkmus wound up hitting the hardest ball of the night. His liner up the middle was deflected by Spahn.

Shortstop Johnny Logan picked up the ball near second and threw quickly to Joe Adcock, who had to dig the ball out of the dirt for the final out.

Spahn not only had his first no-hitter, but also his 51st career shutout and a franchise-record 15-strikeout game.

It was impressive, to say the least, but what followed early the next season was even better. Facing the powerful, first-place San Francisco Giants on a chilly evening in Milwaukee, Spahn masterfully nursed a 1–0 lead he was given in the first inning against the likes of Willie Mays, Willie McCovey, Orlando Cepeda, and Felipe Alou. He allowed leadoff walks in the fourth and fifth innings but erased both base runners on double plays. When the game was over, he had faced the minimum of 27 batters, the last being pinch hitter Joey Amalfitano, who grounded to shortstop Roy McMillan.

The second no-hitter left the ageless wonder just 10 short of the coveted 300-victory plateau. That milestone was reached August 11, 1961, at County Stadium against the Cubs before a crowd of 40,775, eager to witness history.

The game was scoreless until the bottom of the fifth when Spahn broke the ice himself with a sacrifice fly. The Cubs tied it with a two-out run in the sixth, and the score remained 1–1 until the bottom of the eighth. That's when reserve outfielder Gino Cimoli struck the most prominent of three home runs he would contribute in his partial season as a Brave, providing the decisive run in a 2–1 game.

It was a monumental achievement for the Braves' left-hander, but he was far from finished. He won 21 times in 1961, his sixth consecutive 20-victory season and his fifth straight year leading the NL in wins. Lack of support resulted in those streaks being broken in 1962, but in 1963, at age 42, Spahn bounced back with an incredible season—perhaps the grandest of his astonishing career.

His 23 victories, matching his career high, gave him a nice, round 350 and made him the oldest pitcher in the modern (post-1900) era to win 20. He posted seven shutouts and a 2.60 ERA, walked only 1.7 batters per nine innings, and, of course, led the league in complete games for the seventh straight season. On July 2, 1963, he engaged in one of the most fabulous pitching duels in history, losing, 1–0, in 16 innings to 25-year-old Juan Marichal and the Giants at San Francisco.

All of this was for a second-division team. It would have been an appropriate place to retire. After all, what else was there to accomplish? But Spahn had 400 victories in his head, and who could blame him after what he did in '63?

Often a slow starter during his career, Spahn won five of his first nine decisions in 1964, so there was no glaring reason to believe he'd lost it at age 43. However, he would win only one more time as a Brave, No. 356 coming July 9 against Pittsburgh at Forbes Field. Even then, he was not sharp, leaving in the sixth.

Manager Bobby Bragan removed Spahn from the rotation after he was hit hard by the Mets July 26. He made just two more starts. At times, he pitched well in relief, even saving four games. However, he ended the year with a 5.29 ERA.

The end was at hand. On November 23, the Braves not only jettisoned Spahn, they sold him to the lowly Mets where he would pitch for Stengel, the manager who 23 years earlier said Spahn wasn't tough enough to be in the majors. He split his final major league season between the Mets, who released him July 19, and Giants, winning a total of seven games and posting a combined 4.01 ERA.

Stan Musial once said, "I don't think Spahn will ever get into the Hall of Fame. He'll never stop pitching."

That almost happened. Everyone knew Spahn was finished except Spahn. He went so far as to pitch three games in the Mexican League in 1966 to try and prove he still had it at age 45. It didn't work, and he finally retired—though he did pitch in three more games the following season when he was managing Tulsa of the Pacific Coast League.

Spahn managed Tulsa for four seasons, winning the pennant in 1968 when he was named Pacific Coast League Manager of the Year. He was a scout and minor league pitching instructor for the Cardinals in 1971, then returned to the majors in '72 for a two-year stint as a coach with the Cleveland Indians.

In 1973, Spahn was elected to the Hall of Fame in his first year of eligibility. He then stayed out of the game for a few years, returning for a four-year stint as a minor league pitching instructor for the California Angels in 1978.

A complete player, not just a great pitcher, Spahn hit 35 career home runs, a National League record for his position, and started 82 double plays, a major league record for a pitcher. His list of pitching records—club, league, and majors—is too extensive to detail. All you really need to know is that no left-hander ever won more games than his 363. When it comes to pitching, no Brave ever did it better or longer than Warren Spahn.

Eddie Stanky

Billy Southworth felt it crucial to add an experienced and reliable second baseman to their up-and-coming club for the 1948 season. The team was showing designs at making a run for first place, and with rookie Al Dark scheduled to play shortstop, the infield needed a sure hand.

That veteran infielder proved to be the pesky Eddie "The Brat" Stanky.

During spring training of 1948, the Braves sent utility man Bama Rowell, first baseman Ray Sanders, and $40,000 to the Dodgers in exchange for Stanky, who led National League second basemen in fielding (.985) the previous season. Brooklyn obviously was having cash flow problems. Neither Rowell nor Sanders ever played for the Dodgers. In fact, Sanders was sold back to Boston, and Rowell was sent to Philadelphia for the waiver price.

Though Stanky sustained a broken ankle July 8 sliding into Brooklyn's Bruce "The Bull" Edwards at third base, he provided the offensive spark and the steadying influence on defense the Braves needed to get started on their pennant-winning mission. Stanky was hitting .320, the best average of his career, when he was knocked out for the rest of the season. More importantly, his guidance helped Dark get comfortable at shortstop.

Stanky returned to the lineup in 1949 and had an excellent season, offensively and defensively. However, since the club slipped to fourth place, changes were deemed necessary to alter the chemistry of the team, which was working against Southworth. Both Dark and the cantankerous Stanky were sacrificed. They were sent to the Giants in exchange for outfielder Sid Gordon, shortstop Buddy Kerr, outfielder Willard Marshall, and right-hander Red Webb.

Spahn, Warren

Braves	W	L	Pct	G	GS	CG	ShO	IP	H	BB	SO	ERA	SV
1942	0	0	—	4	2	1	0	15⅔	25	11	7	5.74	0
1946	8	5	.615	24	16	8	0	125⅔	107	36	67	2.93	1
1947	21	10	.677	40	35	22	7*	289⅔*	245	84	123	2.33*	3
1948	15	12	.556	36	35	16	3	257	237	77	114	3.71	1
1949	21*	14	.600	38	38*	25*	4	302½*	283	86	151*	3.07	0
1950	21*	17	.553	41	39*	25	1	293	248	111	191*	3.16	1
1951	22	14	.611	39	36	26*	7*	310⅔	278	109*	164*	2.98	0
1952	14	19	.424	40	35	19	5	290	263	73	183*	2.98	3
1953	23*	7	.767	35	32	24	5	265⅔	211	70	148	2.10*	3
1954	21	12	.636	39	34	23	1	283⅓	262	86	136	3.14	3
1955	17	14	.548	39	32	16	1	245⅔	249	65	110	3.26	1
1956	20	11	.645	39	35	20	3	281⅓	249	52	128	2.78	3
1957	21*	11	.656	39	35	18*	4	271	241	78	111	2.69	3
1958	22*	11	.667	38	36	23*	2	290*	257	76	150	3.07	1
1959	21*	15	.583	40	36	21*	4*	292*	282	70	143	2.96	0
1960	21*	10	.677	40	33	18*	4	267⅔	254	74	154	3.50	2
1961	21*	13	.618	38	34	21*	4*	262⅔	236	64	115	3.02*	0
1962	18	14	.563	34	34	22*	0	269⅓	248	55	118	3.04	0
1963	23	7	.767	33	33	22*	7	259⅔	241	49	102	2.60	0
1964	6	13	.316	38	25	4	1	173⅔	204	52	78	5.29	4
Career	356	229	.609	714	635	374	63	5,046	4,620	1,378	2,493	3.05	29

Stanky, Eddie

Braves: 1948–49
Second baseman
Birthplace: Philadelphia

B: September 3, 1916
Batted right, threw right
Ht. 5–8; **Wt.** 170

One of the most critical ingredients in building a championship ball club is a talented middle infield. Without consistent play from the shortstop and second baseman, a team seldom will play the caliber of defense necessary to win a pennant.

For this reason, Braves owner Lou Perini and manager

Stanky, Eddie

Braves	G	AB	R	H	2B	3B	HR	RBI	SB	AVG	SLG
1948	67	247	49	79	14	2	2	29	3	.320	.417
1949	138	506	90	144	24	5	1	42	3	.285	.358
Career	205	753	139	223	38	7	3	71	6	.296	.377

Stivetts, Jack

Beaneaters: 1892–98
Pitcher, outfielder, first baseman,
    shortstop, third baseman,
    second baseman
Birthplace: Ashland, Pennsylvania

B: March 31, 1868
D: April 18, 1930
Batted right, threw right
Ht. 6–2; **Wt.** 185

Jack Stivetts wouldn't fit in today's "all-for-me" atmosphere in baseball. Called "Happy Jack" because of his pleasant demeanor, Stivetts was so selfless that he didn't care what position he played, as long as it helped the team.

In his career, Stivetts played every position except catcher, and played them well. He was primarily a pitcher, one of the best of the pre-1900 era. He also was one of the best hitting pitchers of all time, so he frequently played other positions, too.

Stivetts was a significant contributor to four of Boston's five pennant winners in the 1890s and holds the distinction of pitching the first no-hitter in franchise history.

After three seasons with St. Louis of the American Association, the hard-throwing Stivetts jumped to Boston in 1892 at the age of 24. He was coming off a 33-win season but would do even better for the Beaneaters, who were trying to win a second straight pennant in the new 12-team, split-season National League format.

Stivetts fit right into a rotation that included two future Hall of Famers, Kid Nichols and John Clarkson. In fact, he fit in so well that Clarkson became expendable by midseason and was released.

The highlight of Stivetts' season came in a two-game series at Brooklyn. On August 5 he was playing left field and broke up a scoreless pitching duel between Nichols and George Haddock with a two-run homer in the 12th inning. The next day, Stivetts pitched and didn't allow a hit in an 11–0 victory over the Bridegrooms. He also contributed a double and triple, driving in two runs and scoring two.

Later in the year, Stivetts pitched and won both games of a doubleheader with Louisville. Then, on the final day of the season, he pitched another no-hitter, though this one isn't in the record books. In winning his 35th game, he held Washington hitless for five innings before the game was called to allow Boston to catch a train for the championship series against the Cleveland Spiders, winners of the second half.

Two days later, Beaneaters manager Frank Selee sent Stivetts to the mound to oppose Cy Young in the first game of the best-of-nine series for the pennant. In a classic confrontation, Stivetts and Young battled through 11 scoreless innings before darkness forced the game to be called. Boston got just five hits off Young, and Cleveland got only four off Stivetts.

The Beaneaters eventually swept the series, with Stivetts winning two games to go with his scoreless tie.

Besides winning 35 games in the regular season, tying Nichols for third in the league, Stivetts also batted .296 and drove in 36 runs in 240 at bats.

In 1893, Boston made it three straight pennants. Stivetts struggled with the new pitching distance of 60 feet, six inches, winning "only" 20 games. He adjusted quickly, though, bouncing back in 1894 to win 26. He also posted career highs of eight home runs and 64 RBIs in just 244 at bats.

By 1897, Stivetts was pitching less and playing the outfield more frequently. He hit a career-high .367 in 1897, helping Boston to yet another pennant. The following season, his last with the Beaneaters, he batted .252 in the club's fifth pennant-winning effort in eight years under Selee.

Stivetts finished his career with 203 big league victories, an outstanding .606 winning percentage, and a lifetime batting average of .297. He is regarded as the first pitcher in history to hit a pinch-hit home run, a feat he accomplished three times.

Stivetts, Jack

Beaneaters	W	L	Pct	G	GS	CG	ShO	IP	H	BB	SO	ERA	SV
1892	35	16	.686	54	48	45	3	415⅔	346	171	180	3.03	1
1893	20	12	.625	38	34	29	1	283⅔	315	115	61	4.41	1
1894	26	14	.650	45	39	30	0	338	429	127	76	4.90	0
1895	17	17	.500	38	34	30	0	291	341	89	111	4.64	0
1896	22	14	.611	42	36	31	2	329	353	99	71	4.10	0
1897	11	4	.733	18	15	10	0	129⅓	147	43	27	3.41	0
1898	0	1	.000	2	1	1	0	12	17	7	1	8.25	0
Career	131	78	.627	237	207	176	6	1,798⅔	1,948	651	527	4.12	2

Beaneaters	G	AB	R	H	2B	3B	HR	RBI	SB	AVG	SLG
1892	71	240	40	71	14	2	3	36	8	.296	.408
1893	50	172	32	51	5	6	3	25	6	.297	.448
1894	68	244	55	80	12	7	8	64	3	.328	.533
1895	46	158	20	30	6	4	0	24	1	.190	.278
1896	67	221	42	76	9	6	3	49	4	.344	.480
1897	61	199	41	73	9	9	2	37	2	.367	.533
1898	41	111	16	28	1	1	2	16	1	.252	.333
Career	404	1,345	246	409	56	35	21	251	25	.304	.445

Jack Stivetts

Stone, George

Braves: 1967–72
Pitcher
Birthplace: Ruston, Louisiana

B: July 9, 1946
Batted left, threw left
Ht. 6–3; **Wt.** 205

There was nothing like a pennant race to bring out the best in George Stone. In an eight-year career with two teams, the left-hander had his two most productive seasons when his clubs won division titles.

In 1969 the Braves won their first title in Atlanta, beating the Giants by three games in the National League West. Stone was 13–10 for Luman Harris's team. Four years later, Stone was a member of the Mets' National League championship club, contributing a 12–3 record.

George Stone

The 25 games Stone won in those two seasons represent nearly 42 percent of his career total of 60 victories.

Signed out of Louisiana Tech in 1966, Stone actually made it to Atlanta the following year. In his second appearance and first start, he found himself in a 1–1 duel with future Hall of Famer Bob Gibson in which both pitchers were lifted after seven innings.

Stone began the '68 season in the minors before finally sticking with the Braves in the second half. That experience proved to be a good tune-up for his first pennant race. The Louisiana lefty was 7–4 with a 2.76 ERA, showing the Braves what they needed in order to count him in their plans for '69.

Phil Niekro (23 wins) and Ron Reed (18) were the two biggest winners in the Atlanta rotation en route to the '69 division title. However, Stone's career-high 13 wins were a big reason why the Braves climbed from fifth place in 1968 to first in '69. In the heat of the pennant drive, Stone even hit his lone major league home run September 12 to beat Houston, 4–3.

Stone won six of his first seven decisions in 1970, but arm problems began to plague him at that point. He won only five more times, then suffered consecutive losing seasons in 1971 and '72. The Braves lost confidence in him and traded him to the Mets in a four-player deal that would sour in a hurry.

In 1973, Stone's 12–3 record gave him the best winning percentage (.800) in the National League. He finished the year with an eight-game winning streak, helping the Mets beat the Cardinals by a game and a half in the NL East.

Stone, George

Braves	W	L	Pct	G	GS	CG	ShO	IP	H	BB	SO	ERA	SV
1967	0	0	—	2	1	0	0	7⅓	8	1	5	4.91	0
1968	7	4	.636	17	10	2	0	75	63	19	52	2.76	0
1969	13	10	.565	36	20	3	0	165⅓	166	48	102	3.65	3
1970	11	11	.500	35	30	9	2	207⅓	218	50	131	3.86	0
1971	6	8	.429	27	24	4	2	172⅔	186	35	110	3.60	0
1972	6	11	.353	31	16	2	1	111	143	44	63	5.51	1
Career	43	44	.494	148	101	20	5	738⅔	784	197	463	3.90	4

Sutter, Bruce

Braves: 1985–86, 1988
Pitcher
Birthplace: Lancaster, Pennsylvania

B: January 8, 1953
Batted right, threw right
Ht. 6–2; **Wt.** 190

Today, the split-fingered fastball seems to be nearly as common as the curveball, slider, and change-up. The man who popularized the pitch is Bruce Sutter, who terrorized hitters with it from 1977 through 1984 when he was the premier closer in the National League.

It seemed, when the Braves signed the 32-year-old right-hander to a six-year contract prior to the 1985 season, that they had added one of the game's ultimate weapons to their bullpen. However, as was the case with most players the team signed in the early years of free agency, something went wrong when Sutter pulled on the Atlanta uniform.

In 1984, Sutter set a National League record with 45 saves for the Cardinals. It was the fifth time in six years he'd led the league in saves. However, in 1985 the bearded reliever's save total was cut nearly in half, to 23, and his ERA ballooned to a career-high 4.48.

Unfortunately, 1985 proved to be Sutter's best year as a Brave. It turned out that his shoulder was damaged beyond repair, and he'd never again be the pitcher who won the 1979 NL Cy Young Award and was four times named the league's Fireman of the Year.

Sutter appeared in just 16 games in 1986 and had his shoulder operated on twice. He was forced to sit out the entire 1987 season, and after extensive rehabilitation, attempted a comeback in 1988. He managed 14 saves, but it was clear by his 4.76 ERA that his arm was no longer of big league caliber. He was forced to retire at age 35.

Sutter, Bruce

Braves	W	L	Pct	G	GS	CG	ShO	IP	H	BB	SO	ERA	SV
1985	7	7	.500	58	0	0	0	88⅓	91	29	52	4.48	23
1986	2	0	1.000	16	0	0	0	18¾	17	9	16	4.34	3
1988	1	4	.200	38	0	0	0	45⅓	49	11	40	4.76	14
Career	10	11	.476	112	0	0	0	152⅓	157	49	108	4.55	40

Bruce Sutter

Tenney, Fred

Beaneaters, Doves, Rustlers: 1894–1907, 1911
First baseman, outfielder, catcher, pitcher
Birthplace: Georgetown, Massachusetts

B: November 26, 1871
D: July 3, 1952
Batted left, threw left
Ht. 5–9; **Wt.** 155

Fred Tenney was one of the pioneers produced by the franchise in the game's early years, as well as one of the best defensive first basemen of all time.

Beaneaters manager Frank Selee had already won three pennants when he spotted Tenney, a rare prospect even then since he was a left-handed catcher. Tenney would help Selee win two more pennants, sealing Boston's status as the finest team of the 1890s.

One of the first college graduates to play in the majors, Tenney was attending the senior dinner at Brown University when he was summoned by Selee to the South End Grounds in June 1894. The Beaneaters were out of catchers because of injuries, and the Boston manager wanted him to catch the next day.

After getting very little sleep that night, Tenney took a train from Providence to Boston the following morning. He was put into the lineup that afternoon and played the entire game despite breaking a finger on his left hand in the fifth inning.

Tenney returned to Providence the next day for his graduation from Brown, then went right back to Boston. He agreed to play for the team in a month, once his finger healed.

Selee wasn't convinced Tenney could catch regularly. He used him off the bench for a year and a half, then farmed him out early in 1896 to work at first base, as well as catcher and outfield. Tenney was recalled at the end of May and was used mainly in the outfield.

The Beaneaters failed to win the pennant for the third straight year in 1896, and when they started slowly the following season, Selee shook up the club by benching popular veteran first baseman Tommy Tucker and moving Tenney to the position. The switch created some temporary unrest, but it quickly died when the team began to win.

Boston won pennants in 1897 and '98, and Tenney thus became a fixture at first base. Along with Jimmy Collins at third, Herman Long at shortstop, and Bobby Lowe at second, he gave Boston one of the greatest infields ever assembled in franchise history.

Not much of a power hitter or a big run producer, Tenney was consistent enough at the plate to produce a lifetime .294 average in 17 seasons, all but two with Boston. He hit over .300 five times as a regular and finished fifth in the league with a career-high 209 hits in 1899.

Tenney also revolutionized defensive play at first base. He positioned himself off the line and deep, as today's players do. He also introduced the first baseman's stretch and originated the 3-6-3 double play. Aggressive as well as smart, he once trapped future Hall of Famer Cap Anson off third and, instead of throwing the ball, ran across the diamond to tag him. He shocked opponents and thrilled crowds with such plays, which were unheard of at the time.

Tenney only led the league's first basemen in fielding percentage once (1902), but he still holds the major league record for most years leading his league in assists (8). In 1905 he made 152 assists, which stood as a National League record for first basemen until broken by Pittsburgh's Sid Bream in 1986.

Tenney, Fred

Beaneaters, Doves, Rustlers	G	AB	R	H	2B	3B	HR	RBI	SB	AVG	SLG
1894	27	86	23	34	7	1	2	21	6	.395	.570
1895	49	173	35	47	9	1	1	21	6	.272	.353
1896	88	348	64	117	14	3	2	49	18	.336	.411
1897	132	566	125	180	24	3	1	85	34	.318	.376
1898	117	488	106	160	25	5	0	62	23	.328	.400
1899	150	603	115	209	19	17	1	67	28	.347	.439
1900	112	437	77	122	13	5	1	56	17	.279	.339
1901	115	451	66	127	13	1	1	22	15	.282	.322
1902	134	489	88	154	18	3	2	30	21	.315	.376
1903	122	447	79	140	22	3	3	41	21	.313	.396
1904	147	533	76	144	17	9	1	37	17	.270	.341
1905	149	549	84	158	18	3	0	28	17	.288	.332
1906	143	544	61	154	12	8	1	28	17	.283	.340
1907	150	554	83	151	18	8	0	26	15	.273	.334
1911	102	369	52	97	13	4	1	36	5	.263	.328
Career	1,737	6,637	1,134	1,994	242	74	17	609	260	.300	.367

Thomson, Bobby

Braves: 1954–57
Outfielder
Birthplace: Glasgow, Scotland

B: October 25, 1923
Batted right, threw right
Ht. 6–2; **Wt.** 185

Bobby Thomson, the man who hit the heralded "Shot Heard Round the World" to win the National League pennant for the Giants in 1951, also played a major role in the history of the Braves franchise.

Thomson, of course, will always be remembered for his three-run home run off Brooklyn's Ralph Branca in the bottom of the ninth inning of the third and decisive game of a playoff for the National League flag. However, Braves fans have Thomson to thank for two distinct contributions, too, though the Scottish-born outfielder certainly wouldn't consider either to be personal highlights of his career.

Milwaukee, desperate for an outfielder with some power, acquired Thomson from New York just prior to spring training in 1954. It was a major trade because of Thomson's hero status in

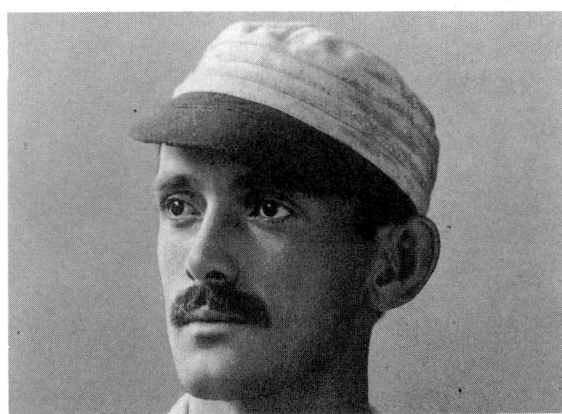

Fred Tenney

Bobby Thomson

Tobin, Jim

Bees, Braves: 1940–45   **D:** May 19, 1969
Pitcher, first baseman **Batted right, threw right**
Birthplace: Oakland, California **Ht.** 6–0; **Wt.** 185
B: December 27, 1912

Long before Phil Niekro came along, Jim Tobin was making the knuckleball an important part of franchise history. But Tobin could do more than baffle hitters with his knuckler. He also was quite a slugger.

Boston was in the midst of the bleakest period in franchise history when Tobin was acquired in a trade with Pittsburgh prior to the 1940 season, the last of five years the team answered to the nickname Bees.

Used as a starter and reliever in 1940, Tobin had the only winning record (7–3) in his six-year Boston career. But considering that the team finished an average of 37 games back during that period, it was to Tobin's credit that he wound up just 11 games under .500 lifetime as a Bee/Brave.

In 1941, Braves manager Casey Stengel began relying more and more on Tobin as a starter in an attempt to find some way to drag the club out of its doldrums. The team remained lousy, but Tobin quickly became Boston's most reliable pitcher. He led the club in wins four times and shutouts twice during the five-year period 1941–45.

In 1942, Tobin led the league in complete games and innings, as well as in losses (21). However, he also set a franchise record that's unlikely to be equaled.

A strong hitter who was frequently used as a pinch hitter, Tobin delivered a pinch homer against the Cubs May 12 at Braves Field. The next day, he pitched against the Cubs but made headlines with his bat.

In the third inning, Tobin hit a ball that was caught at the fence. In the fifth, he hit a solo homer to tie the game, 2–2. In the seventh, he tied the game again, 4–4, with another solo homer. Finally, with two out in the eighth, he hit a two-run homer to win the game, 6–5.

Including the pinch homer, Tobin hit four in five at bats. He became the first Brave since Babe Ruth in 1935 to hit three homers in a game and is the only pitcher in the 20th century to accomplish the feat. Tobin finished the season with six homers, one for every 19 at bats. The league leader, Hall of Famer Mel Ott with 30, hit one every 18.3 at bats.

In 1944, Tobin won a career-high 18 games, made the All-Star team, and led the league in complete games for the second time. He also etched his name in the Braves record book again, pitching the sixth no-hitter in franchise history.

New York and because the Braves gave up four players, including left-hander Johnny Antonelli. Antonelli would blossom that season, going 21–7 and winning the league ERA title.

On the other hand, Thomson broke his ankle in spring training and didn't play until July. The Braves appeared to be in deep trouble. They had little choice but to replace Thomson with a 20-year-old rookie with less than two years of professional experience. However, Hank Aaron did not disappoint.

After recovering from his broken ankle, Thomson played reasonably well for the Braves for the next three years. But he never again was the player he had been with the Giants, for whom he drove in 100 or more runs in four of five years before being traded to the Braves.

Thomson's career with the Braves ended in mid-1957. On June 15, with the Braves trying to put together the final pieces of a pennant-winning club, he was sent back to the Giants along with two other players in exchange for veteran second baseman Red Schoendienst. Well on his way to compiling Hall of Fame credentials, Schoendienst was credited by Milwaukee manager Fred Haney for supplying the infield leadership that helped the Braves win the pennant and World Series.

Thomson, Bobby

Braves	G	AB	R	H	2B	3B	HR	RBI	SB	AVG	SLG
1954	43	99	7	23	3	0	2	15	0	.232	.323
1955	101	343	40	88	12	3	12	56	2	.257	.414
1956	142	451	59	106	10	4	20	74	2	.235	.408
1957	41	148	15	35	5	3	4	23	2	.236	.392
Career	327	1,041	121	252	30	10	38	168	6	.242	.400

Jim Tobin

Tobin, whose warm-up routine included a knuckle massage by the trainer, opened the 1944 season with a one-hitter. Then in his second start of the year, on April 27 at Braves Field, he no-hit the Dodgers, 2–0. The only two Brooklyn base runners came in the first and ninth when the right-hander walked Paul Waner both times. To add even more drama to the event, Tobin hit a home run in the eighth inning, the first pitcher ever to homer in his no-hitter. Brooklyn manager Leo Durocher was so upset about the Dodgers' futile swings at Tobin's knuckleballs that he scolded them afterward.

In his first 18 innings of the season, Tobin allowed just one single, nearly matching Johnny Vander Meer's back-to-back no-hitters of 1938. Later in the season, Tobin did pitch a second "no-hitter," though it's not in the books because it came in the second game of a doubleheader against Philadelphia that was called after five innings because of darkness.

Tobin, Jim

Bees, Braves	W	L	Pct	G	GS	CG	ShO	IP	H	BB	SO	ERA	SV
1940	7	3	.700	15	11	9	0	96⅓	102	24	29	3.83	0
1941	12	12	.500	33	26	20	3	238	229	60	61	3.10	0
1942	12	21*	.364	37	33	28*	1	287⅔*	283	96	71	3.97	0
1943	14	14	.500	33	30	24	1	250	241	69	52	2.66	0
1944	18	19	.486	43	36	28*	5	299⅓	271	97	83	3.01	3
1945	9	14	.391	27	25	16	0	196⅔	220	56	38	3.84	0
Career	72	83	.465	188	161	125	10	1,368	1,346	402	334	3.34	3

Torgeson, Earl

Braves: 1947–52
First baseman, outfielder
Birthplace: Snohomish, Washington
B: January 1, 1924

D: November 8, 1990
Batted left, threw left
Ht. 6–3; **Wt.** 180

A much-ballyhooed prospect, Earl Torgeson joined the Braves in 1947 as a 23-year-old first baseman with an unusual blend of power and speed. He was an important part of Boston's pennant-winning club in 1948, and though he had a productive six seasons with the Braves, he never lived up to the expectations heaped on him by others.

When he first arrived in Boston, Torgeson was likened to Ted Williams and was seen as the Braves' best power-hitting prospect since Wally Berger. The spectacled left-handed hit-

Earl Torgeson

ter never approached the accomplishments of either man, but few others have either.

After the 1942 season with Seattle, Torgeson entered the army for three years. However, the Braves thought so much of him that general manager John Quinn purchased his contract in 1945. Torgeson came back from the service and played at Seattle again in 1946 before joining the Braves the next spring.

As a rookie, Torgeson showed plenty of promise, hitting .281 with 16 home runs, 78 RBIs, and 11 steals, which actually ranked fifth in the league. His production as a sophomore declined in most categories, though he stole 19 bases, again fifth in the league. And in the World Series against Cleveland, Torgeson was the leading hitter on either team with a .389 average.

Out with an injury most of 1949, Torgeson bounced back with his two best seasons in 1950 and '51. He hit a career-high .290 in 1950, led the league with 120 runs scored, and was fourth with 15 steals. The following season, he attained career highs in home runs (24), RBIs (92), and steals (20). Also in 1951, Torgeson tied a National League record shared by several players, including former Boston pitcher Kid Nichols, by getting seven RBIs in two consecutive innings.

However, when he slumped badly in 1952, the Braves sent Torgeson to Philadelphia in a four-team deal that ultimately brought Joe Adcock in for a long and prosperous tenure as the team's first baseman.

Torgeson, Earl

Braves	G	AB	R	H	2B	3B	HR	RBI	SB	AVG	SLG
1947	128	399	73	112	20	6	16	78	11	.281	.481
1948	134	438	70	111	23	5	10	67	19	.253	.397
1949	25	100	17	26	5	1	4	19	4	.260	.450
1950	156	576	120*	167	30	3	23	87	15	.290	.472
1951	155	581	99	153	21	4	24	92	20	.263	.437
1952	122	382	49	88	17	0	5	34	11	.230	.314
Career	720	2,476	428	657	116	19	82	377	80	.265	.427

Torre, Joe

Braves: 1960–68
Catcher, first baseman, outfielder
Birthplace: Brooklyn, New York

B: July 18, 1940
Batted right, threw right
Ht. 6–2; **Wt.** 212

In May 1961 veteran Braves All-Star catcher Del Crandall was reduced to nothing but pinch hitting for the rest of the season by a shoulder injury. To fill the vacancy, the club summoned a pudgy youngster still two months shy of his 21st birthday from its farm club at Louisville.

Joe Torre made his big league catching debut by working both ends of a doubleheader. He contributed a single, double, and home run and threw out three runners trying to steal.

Torre might not have looked like a big leaguer yet, but he already knew how to play like one. Part of the reason for that undoubtedly was his baseball roots. His father scouted for the Braves and Baltimore Orioles, and his older brother, Frank, was an outstanding defensive first baseman for Milwaukee's pennant winners in 1957 and '58.

A high school third baseman, Torre was moved behind the plate by the Braves because of his tendency to carry extra weight. He handled the challenge of the position remarkably well, spending parts of just two seasons in the minors before

Joe Torre

Turner, Jim

Bees: 1937–39
Pitcher
Birthplace: Antioch, Tennessee

B: August 6, 1903
Batted left, threw right
Ht. 6–0; **Wt.** 185

Jim Turner's performance for the Bees of 1937 provides one of the most compelling stories in franchise history and offers hope to all players who think they're stuck in the minor leagues.

A right-hander with a good curve and outstanding control, Turner spent 14 years in the minors before the lowly Braves went out on a limb for him. General manager Bob Quinn paid Indianapolis $1,000 down with another $9,000 to come if he made the club. It turned out to be some of the best money the organization ever spent.

At 33 years old, Turner was the oldest rookie in the majors when the 1937 season began. Most baseball people thought Quinn had made a poor investment, but Turner quickly proved otherwise. He and fellow rookie Lou Fette, who was 30, each won 20 games, becoming the first freshmen to win 20 since Hall of Famer Grover Cleveland Alexander in 1911. It was the only time in history that two rookies have won 20 games for the same team.

Turner and Fette tied for second in the league in victories behind future Hall of Famer Carl Hubbell. Turner also led the league in ERA (2.38) and complete games (24) and tied for the lead in shutouts (5). At one point, he strung together 31 consecutive scoreless innings.

Though Turner made the All-Star team the following season and won 14 games, he never had another year in which he remotely approached his success as a rookie.

Nicknamed "Milkman Jim" because his family was in the dairy business, Turner in 1940 was traded to Cincinnati, where he again won 14 games and helped his former Boston manager, Bill McKechnie, win the World Series. Two years later, he was back in the Series as a reliever with the Yankees.

establishing himself as one of the game's best offensive catchers. Torre, who caught Warren Spahn's 300th career win in 1961, went on to finish second to the Cubs' Billy Williams, a future Hall of Famer, as the league's Rookie of the Year.

Crandall returned in 1962 and had yet another All-Star season, but by 1963, he was a backup to Torre, and a year later he was traded to San Francisco. With the job entirely his in 1964, Torre became the first major league catcher since 1955 to hit .300 or better with at least 20 homers and 100 RBIs.

His .321 average ranked fourth in the National League. By driving in 109 runs, he set a club RBI record for catchers and also finished fourth in the league.

In 1965, Torre's 27 homers helped the Braves set a major league record by having six players (Eddie Mathews, Hank Aaron, Mack Jones, Felipe Alou, and Gene Oliver) with 20 or more home runs.

When the Braves moved to Atlanta in 1966, Torre repeated the unusual trifecta for catchers he originally achieved two years earlier, this time hitting .315 with a career-high 36 home runs and 101 RBIs. His home run total tied Willie McCovey for fourth in the league and established a Braves record for catchers. His homers included the first ever hit in a regular-season game at Atlanta Stadium.

Torre's zest for hearty dining and night life led to his departure from Atlanta in the spring of 1969 when he was sent to St. Louis in exchange for Orlando Cepeda.

Though Cepeda was aging and hobbled by bad knees, he helped lead the Braves to a division title that season. Torre began to take better care of himself, was moved to third base by the Cardinals, and developed into an even better player than he'd been for the Braves. The highlight of his career came in 1971 when he won the batting title and was voted the league's MVP.

Torre, Joe

Braves	G	AB	R	H	2B	3B	HR	RBI	SB	AVG	SLG
1960	2	2	0	1	0	0	0	0	0	.500	.500
1961	113	406	40	113	21	4	10	42	3	.278	.424
1962	80	220	23	62	8	1	5	26	1	.282	.395
1963	142	501	57	147	19	4	14	71	1	.293	.431
1964	154	601	87	193	36	5	20	109	2	.321	.498
1965	148	523	68	152	21	1	27	80	0	.291	.489
1966	148	546	83	172	20	3	36	101	0	.315	.560
1967	135	477	67	132	18	1	20	68	2	.277	.444
1968	115	424	45	115	11	2	10	55	1	.271	.377
Career	1,037	3,700	470	1,087	154	21	142	552	10	.294	.462

Jim Turner

Turner, Jim

Bees	W	L	Pct	G	GS	CG	ShO	IP	H	BB	SO	ERA	SV
1937	20	11	.645	33	30	24*	5*	256⅔	228	52	69	2.38*	1
1938	14	18	.438	35	34	22	3	268	267	54	71	3.46	0
1939	4	11	.267	25	22	9	0	157⅔	181	51	50	4.28	0
Career	38	40	.487	93	86	55	8	682⅓	676	157	190	3.24	1

Upshaw, Cecil

Braves: 1966–69, 1971–73
Pitcher
Birthplace: Spearsville, Louisiana
B: October 22, 1942

D: February 7, 1995
Batted right, threw right
Ht. 6–6; **Wt.** 205

The Braves thrilled Atlanta and much of the South in 1969, winning the National League West in only their fourth season since moving from Milwaukee. Cecil Upshaw was a big part of what the team did that summer, and since he was only 26 years old, it was reasonable to expect the big reliever to be a part of the team's future for quite some time.

However, in one of the most freakish accidents to befall a major league ballplayer, Upshaw nearly lost a finger on the second day of the 1970 season. He didn't appear in a game that year, and though he recovered to pitch five more seasons in the majors, he never again approached the effectiveness he enjoyed prior to the injury.

The sidearming Upshaw was 6–4 with a 2.91 ERA in 1969, and his 27 saves ranked second in the National League. Though the Braves were swept by the Mets in the playoffs, there was plenty of optimism for 1970. The mood was darkened considerably, though, by Upshaw's misfortune, which stemmed from horseplay among teammates as they returned to their hotel after the second game of the season.

A native of Louisiana, the 6–6 Upshaw was an All-American basketball player in both high school and college (Centenary). As he was strolling along the sidewalk that evening in San Diego, he decided to show some of the other Braves how to dunk a basketball. He leaped at the metal awning on a parking lot booth. The ring on his right ring finger caught on the awning, severing the nerves and artery.

Upshaw spent the next two months at the Stanford University Medical Center where he underwent five skin and nerve graft surgeries. At one point, gangrene set in, and amputation was considered. But the finger was saved, and so was the big right-hander's career.

On opening day of the 1971 season, he worked the final four innings to get credit for a 7–4 victory against Cincinnati. In many respects, he had an excellent season, posting an 11–6 record with 17 saves. His ERA, though, was 3.51, considerably higher than it had ever been prior to the accident. It became increasingly clear that Upshaw had lost some of his touch.

His once-promising career ended in 1975 when he was only 32. After recording 48 saves in three seasons prior to the accident, he had only 38 in five years afterward. Upshaw died in 1995 at age 52 from a heart attack.

Upshaw, Cecil

Braves	W	L	Pct	G	GS	CG	ShO	IP	H	BB	SO	ERA	SV
1966	0	0	—	1	0	0	0	3	0	3	2	0.00	0
1967	2	3	.400	30	0	0	0	45⅓	42	8	31	2.58	8
1968	8	7	.533	52	0	0	0	116⅔	98	24	74	2.47	13
1969	6	4	.600	62	0	0	0	105⅓	102	29	57	2.91	27
1971	11	6	.647	49	0	0	0	82	95	28	56	3.51	17
1972	3	5	.375	42	0	0	0	53⅔	50	19	23	3.69	13
1973	0	1	.000	5	0	0	0	3⅔	8	2	3	9.82	0
Career	30	26	.536	241	0	0	0	409⅔	395	113	246	3.01	78

Washington, Claudell

Braves: 1981–86
Outfielder
Birthplace: Los Angeles

B: August 31, 1954
Batted left, threw left
Ht. 6–0; **Wt.** 190

Claudell Washington was a talented ballplayer who contributed significantly to the Braves' division title in 1982. However, he was never fully accepted by Braves fans because of the high expectations created by his free-agent courtship

Cecil Upshaw

Claudell Washington

during the fall of 1980. He actually was one of the more productive free-agent signees in the early years of Ted Turner's ownership.

In Washington's five-and-a-half year stay with the Braves, his biggest moment came on April 21, 1982, when he delivered the winning hit in one of the most thrilling games ever played in Atlanta.

The 1982 Braves were the talk of baseball under new manager Joe Torre. On April 20 they set a major league record by winning their 12th consecutive game at the start of the season. It appeared the streak would end the next night when the Braves trailed, 3–2, and were down to their last out against the Cincinnati Reds. However, Washington delivered a bases-loaded single to center, giving the Braves a 4–3 victory.

That 13th straight victory was the last in the streak, but it was enough to propel Torre's club to the West title.

Washington, who led the team in hitting (.291) the previous year, contributed a career-high 80 RBIs and a then-career-best 16 home runs to the club's surprising title. And though his teammates failed to generate any offense in the League Championship Series, Washington led the Braves with a .333 average.

Strong-armed but sometimes inconsistent on defense, Washington continued to hit well, if not spectacularly, throughout his Braves career, even making the All-Star team in 1984 when he hit a career-high 17 home runs. He also averaged 22 steals in his five full seasons with the team.

Washington, Claudell

Braves	G	AB	R	H	2B	3B	HR	RBI	SB	AVG	SLG
1981	85	320	37	93	22	3	5	37	12	.291	.425
1982	150	563	94	150	24	6	16	80	33	.266	.416
1983	134	496	75	138	24	8	9	44	31	.278	.413
1984	120	416	62	119	21	2	17	61	21	.286	.469
1985	122	398	62	110	14	6	15	43	14	.276	.455
1986	40	137	17	37	11	0	5	14	4	.270	.460
Career	651	2,330	347	647	116	25	67	279	115	.278	.435

White, Deacon

Red Stockings: 1877
First baseman, outfielder, catcher
Birthplace: Caton, New York
B: December 7, 1847
D: July 7, 1939
Batted left, threw right
Ht. 5–11; **Wt.** 175

Deacon White only played one National League season with Boston, but he holds an honored position in team history. In 1877 he became the first player in franchise history to win the batting crown. Only eight others, including Hank Aaron twice, have won it since.

Not only did White lead the league in hitting with a .387 average in 1877—the second year the league had been in existence—but he nearly won the rare Triple Crown even though he hit only two home runs. He led the league in RBIs with 49 in the 61-game season, leading the Red Stockings to their first pennant in the new league. And his two home runs tied for third behind Cincinnati's Lip Pike, who hit but four to lead the league.

White, who played mainly first base and right field in 1877, was not a newcomer to the club, however. He was a member

Deacon White

of Boston's National Association pennant winners of 1873, '74, and '75 but jumped to Chicago in 1876 when the National League was formed. Since the White Stockings won the first NL pennant, White thus played on five consecutive championship teams in the two leagues. However, his string was broken in 1878 when he signed with Cincinnati and Boston won its second straight pennant.

A versatile and durable player, White had a long career that spanned five years in the National Association and 15 in the National League and didn't end until he was 42 years old.

White, Deacon

Red Stockings	G	AB	R	H	2B	3B	HR	RBI	SB	AVG	SLG
1877	59	266	51	103*	14	11*	2	49*	—	.387*	.545*
Career	59	266	51	103	14	11	2	49	—	.387	.545

Willey, Carl

Braves: 1958–62
Pitcher
Birthplace: Cherryfield, Maine
B: June 6, 1931
Batted right, threw right
Ht. 6–0; **Wt.** 175

Which Braves pitcher led the National League in shutouts when the club won its second consecutive pennant in 1958?

Warren Spahn? Lou Burdette? Bob Buhl? Gene Conley? Joey Jay?

No, it was 27-year-old rookie Carl Willey, who made only 19 starts and won just nine games. But the lanky New Englander held the opposition scoreless in four games, tops in the league.

Though the great Milwaukee teams probably are remembered more for hitting than pitching, it was pitching that carried them to the pennant in '58. The team ERA of 3.21 led the league by more than a third of a run. Burdette and Spahn ranked third and fourth in the league in ERA. Though Willey (2.70) beat them both, he didn't have enough innings to qualify for the league lead.

After 1958, Willey never had an ERA under 3.00 again, nor did he even post a winning record in the remaining seven seasons of his career.

Willey, whose big league debut was delayed by two years of

Carl Willey

Earl Williams

service in the Korean War, opened '58 in the Milwaukee bullpen but was quickly sent down to Wichita. Eight days after his demotion he pitched a no-hitter, and within a month he was back in the majors, this time in the Braves' starting rotation. In his first start, he shut out the slugging Giants in mid-June. In his next outing, he worked a complete-game victory against the Dodgers.

In August, Willey led the Braves' staff with five victories, including a 2–0 victory against Pittsburgh on the final day of the month. It was his fourth shutout in 14 big league starts. In his next start, he blanked the Pirates for nine innings, only to lose, 1–0, in the 10th.

The Sporting News named Willey its Rookie of the Year for '58. He would never win in double figures, though, and prior to the 1963 season Milwaukee sold him to the lowly New York Mets.

Willey, Carl

Braves	W	L	Pct	G	GS	CG	ShO	IP	H	BB	SO	ERA	SV
1958	9	7	.563	23	19	9	4*	140	110	53	74	2.70	0
1959	5	9	.357	26	15	5	2	117	126	31	51	4.15	0
1960	6	7	.462	28	21	2	1	144⅔	136	65	109	4.35	0
1961	6	12	.333	35	22	4	0	159⅔	147	65	91	3.83	0
1962	2	5	.286	30	6	0	0	73⅓	95	20	40	5.40	1
Career	28	40	.412	142	83	20	7	634⅔	614	234	365	3.94	1

Williams, Earl

Braves: 1970–72, 1975–76   **B:** July 14, 1948
Catcher, first baseman   **Batted right, threw right**
Birthplace: Newark, New Jersey   **Ht.** 6–3; **Wt.** 220

It once seemed that Earl Williams was destined to become one of the great sluggers in Braves history. To look at his career record and see that he played only eight seasons in the majors, ending in 1977 when he was just 29 years old, makes you think there must be a misprint. But that's not the case.

In 1971, Williams played like he was intent on being the next Yogi Berra. All he did was win National League Rookie of the Year by hitting .260 with 33 home runs and 87 RBIs. His home run total still ranks second in history for an NL

rookie to the 38 posted by Boston's Wally Berger in 1930 and Frank Robinson in 1956.

Maybe too much pressure was put on Williams. Perhaps the demands of learning to catch in the majors wore on him. Or maybe he was just intent on self-destructing. Whatever the reason, Williams stopped being compared to Hall of Famers just as quickly as he created such notions. He went from being one of the game's most exciting young talents to being an ex-ballplayer about as quickly as it can be done.

One thing for sure, Williams was no fluke in '71. In 1969 at Class-A Greenwood, he hit 33 home runs for the season, including eight in one seven-day span, two of which were grand slams. And he followed his brilliant rookie season with similar production (.258, 28 home runs, 92 RBIs) in 1972. He could hit all right, but somewhere between Atlanta and Cooperstown, something went terribly wrong.

The answer probably has to do with making a major position change in the big leagues and Williams' difficulty in controlling his weight. Little more than a season removed from their 1969 NL West title, the Braves of '71 were off to a slow start, creating pressure on manager Luman Harris. Displeased with the production of catchers Bob Didier and Hal King and looking for a way to bolster the offense, Harris decided to make Williams a catcher.

The 22-year-old rookie had never played the position before, and he wasn't real happy about learning. He had virtually no experience as a catcher. The Braves actually signed him as a pitcher, but they thought so much of his offensive potential that they brought him up through the farm system playing first base, third base, and outfield. In Williams' defense, it's almost impossible to think of a team trying to turn a player into a catcher overnight at the big league level. It's a tribute to the promise the organization saw in him that they'd even think about doing so.

Though Williams complained, he did an adequate job defensively. And he certainly didn't let his displeasure with his defensive duties bother his swing. On September 10, he even became the fourth—and last—man to hit a home run into the upper deck at Atlanta Stadium. He hit it against Gaylord Perry, a Hall of Famer. The only other Brave to reach that region was Hank Aaron.

However, Braves management grew weary of reading in the newspaper of Williams' complaints about catching. They also noticed his expanding waistline. Following the theory that it is better to trade a player too soon than too late, they put together a blockbuster deal with Baltimore following the '72 season.

Williams and prospect Taylor Duncan went to the Orioles in exchange for veteran pitcher Pat Dobson, highly regarded pitching prospect Roric Harrison, second baseman Dave Johnson, and catcher Johnny Oates. The Orioles returned him to the Braves in 1975, but he was only a part-time player for a year and a half and was out of the game shortly thereafter.

Williams, Earl

Braves	G	AB	R	H	2B	3B	HR	RBI	SB	AVG	SLG
1970	10	19	4	7	4	0	0	5	0	.368	.579
1971	145	497	64	129	14	1	33	87	0	.260	.491
1972	151	565	72	146	24	2	28	87	0	.258	.457
1975	111	383	42	92	13	0	11	50	0	.240	.360
1976	61	184	18	39	3	0	9	26	0	.212	.375
Career	478	1,648	200	413	58	3	81	255	0	.251	.437

Willis, Vic

Beaneaters: 1898–1905
Pitcher
Birthplace: Cecil County, Maryland
B: April 12, 1876

D: August 3, 1947
Batted right, threw right
Ht. 6–2; **Wt.** 185

The 1898 Beaneaters won the final pennant in a glorious period of franchise history that included eight of the first 23 championships in National League history. A big reason for winning the 1898 flag was the arrival of a rookie right-hander named Vic Willis.

The 22-year-old Willis teamed with Kid Nichols and Ted Lewis to give Boston a pitching threesome that was the envy of all baseball. Nichols, still at the height of his Hall of Fame career, led the league in victories (31), and Lewis and Willis were right behind with 26 and 25 wins, respectively.

When Nichols' career started to fade in 1899, Willis be-

Vic Willis

came the mainstay of the Boston pitching staff. He led the club in wins four times in the six-year period from 1899 through 1904. He also consistently ranked among the league leaders in most major pitching departments during that time, leading the league in shutouts in 1899 and 1901, in ERA in 1899, and in strikeouts in 1902.

Known as the "Delaware Peach" long before Ty Cobb was called the "Georgia Peach," Willis pitched the second no-hitter in franchise history. On August 7, 1899, he held Washington hitless in a 7–1 victory.

Willis also suffered quite a few losses for the Beaneaters, especially at the end of his Boston career when the team took a dive toward the bottom of the league. He was a three-time 20-game loser, leading the league in defeats in 1904 and '05, his last two seasons with the club. In 1995 he was elected to the Hall of Fame by the Veterans Committee.

Willis, Vic

Beaneaters	W	L	Pct	G	GS	CG	ShO	IP	H	BB	SO	ERA	SV
1898	25	13	.658	41	38	29	1	311	264	148	160	2.84	0
1899	27	8	.771	41	38	35	5*	342⅔	277	117	120	2.50*	2
1900	10	17	.370	32	29	22	2	236	258	106	53	4.19	0
1901	20	17	.541	38	35	33	6*	305⅓	262	78	133	2.36	0
1902	27	19	.587	51*	46*	45*	4	410*	372*	101	225*	2.20	3*
1903	12	17	.414	33	32	29	2	278	256	88	125	2.98	0
1904	18	25*	.419	43	43	39*	2	350	357	109	196	2.85	0
1905	11	29*	.275	41	41	36	4	342	340*	107	149	3.21	0
Career	150	145	.508	320	302	268	26	2,575	2,386	854	1,161	2.82	5

Wilson, Jim

Braves: 1951–54
Pitcher
Birthplace: San Diego, California
B: February 20, 1922

D: September 2, 1986
Batted right, threw right
Ht. 6–1; **Wt.** 200

That Jim Wilson was able to pitch the first no-hitter at Milwaukee County Stadium was a wonder—but it wasn't as astonishing as the fact that he was even healthy enough to be pitching in the majors at all in 1954.

As a highly regarded rookie with the Red Sox in 1945, Wilson survived a brush with death. The 23-year-old right-hander suffered a fractured skull when he was hit by a line drive off the bat of Hank Greenberg. Doctors feared for his life, and though he recovered, Wilson missed nearly all of the following season due to severe headaches caused by the accident.

Still on the comeback trail in 1947, he was KOed by yet another line drive, this one breaking his leg. Finally, in the spring of 1948, his hand was crushed in a trailer accident.

Most ballplayers would have given up and gone home, but Wilson kept plugging away, overcoming more physical adversity than most athletes could even imagine. He spent all of 1950 in the minors, then was purchased by the Braves.

Entering the 1951 season, the 29-year-old Wilson had pitched just 8⅓ innings in the majors since Greenberg's line drive sidetracked his career in 1945. In his first three seasons as a Brave, Wilson was in and out of the starting rotation, seldom impressing anyone yet winning 12 games with a lousy seventh-place club in 1952.

By 1954, though, the breaking-ball pitcher was a little-used reliever, and in May the Braves put him on waivers. However,

Jim Wilson

no team thought enough of him to claim him. When a doubleheader came up a week later, he was given a start and responded by beating Pittsburgh, 5–0.

Six days later, on June 12, manager Charlie Grimm gave him the ball again in an apparent mismatch with future Phillies Hall of Famer Robin Roberts. The result was a 2–0, no-hit victory by Wilson. It was the eighth no-hitter in franchise history and the first since Vern Bickford's in 1950.

Against all odds, Wilson continued to pitch well. He was 8–0 at one point and was named to the All-Star team. However, he was used infrequently in the second half, never won another game as a Brave, and was sold to Baltimore the following April.

Wilson, Jim

Braves	W	L	Pct	G	GS	CG	ShO	IP	H	BB	SO	ERA	SV
1951	7	7	.500	20	15	5	0	110	131	40	33	5.40	1
1952	12	14	.462	33	33	14	0	234	234	90	104	4.23	0
1953	4	9	.308	20	18	5	0	114	107	43	71	4.34	0
1954	8	2	.800	27	19	6	4	127⅔	129	36	52	3.52	0
Career	31	32	.492	100	85	30	4	585⅔	601	209	260	4.32	1

Woodward, Woody

Braves: 1963–68
Shortstop, second baseman
Birthplace: Miami

B: September 23, 1942
Batted right, threw right
Ht. 6–2; **Wt.** 185

Much more often than not, shortstop has been a source of deep concern since the Braves moved from Milwaukee. Many have tried and failed. Few have lasted over an extended period of time. Only with the signing of free agent Rafael Belliard and the development of Jeff Blauser did defensive stability come to the position in the early 1990s.

In retrospect, it seems it didn't have to be that way. For in

1965, the Braves' last season in Milwaukee, 22-year-old Woody Woodward fielded the position better than anyone else in the last half century of franchise history.

Woodward's .977 fielding percentage that season is the best compiled by a regular Braves shortstop in either Atlanta or Milwaukee history. To beat it, you have to go back to 1942 when Eddie Miller fielded at a .983 clip for Boston.

In Woodward, it appeared the Braves had someone capable of settling in at short for several seasons. However, the team was extremely offensive-minded in those days, and hitting was not a Woodward strength. He batted a mere .208 in 1965 with 11 RBIs.

Consequently, the Braves were more enamored with the possibilities of Denis Menke and later Sonny Jackson at short than they were with Woodward. In the team's first two years in Atlanta, Woodward spent most of his time at second base while Menke manned short. When the club decided in 1968 to go with the speedy Jackson at short and the promising Felix Millan at second, Woodward was traded to Cincinnati in a six-player deal.

Woodward's best offensive season for the Braves was 1966, the team's first in Atlanta, when he hit .264 with 43 RBIs, both career highs. He seldom approached such numbers, though, as his .236 lifetime average illustrates.

Perhaps the offensive highlight of Woodward's career came with the Reds in 1970 when he hit his only home run. And, as fate would have it, he hit it against the Braves.

Woodward now is vice president of baseball operations for the Seattle Mariners.

Woodward, Woody

Braves	G	AB	R	H	2B	3B	HR	RBI	SB	AVG	SLG
1963	10	2	1	0	0	0	0	0	0	.000	.000
1964	77	115	18	24	2	1	0	11	0	.209	.243
1965	112	265	17	55	7	4	0	11	2	.208	.264
1966	144	455	46	120	23	3	0	43	2	.264	.327
1967	136	429	30	97	15	2	0	25	0	.226	.270
1968	12	24	2	4	1	0	0	1	1	.167	.208
Career	491	1,290	114	300	48	10	0	91	5	.233	.285

Woody Woodward

All the Team's Men

Following are two lists containing the names and statistics of the nearly 1,500 men who have played for the Braves franchise in three cities and under various nicknames from the founding of the National League in 1876 through 1994.

The first list includes those players who broke in with the team prior to 1900. The second list includes players whose major league debut with the Braves came in 1900 or later.

All statistics refer only to the players' careers with the Braves organization and do not account for service with other major league teams. Figures in parentheses indicate years played with the Braves franchise.

Pre-1900 Players

A

Allen, Bob (1897) shortstop; outfielder; second baseman: 38-for-119, .319, in 34 games.

Allen, Myron (1886) second baseman: 0-for-3, .000, in one game.

Annis, Bill (1884) outfielder: 17-for-96, .177, in 27 games.

B

Bailey, Harvey (1899–1900) pitcher: 6–4 with 4.13 ERA in 16 games.

Banks, Bill (1895–96) pitcher: 1–3 with 8.10 ERA in five games.

Bannon, Jimmy (1894–96) outfielder; shortstop; second baseman; third baseman: 423-for-1,326, .319, in 340 games; pitcher: 0–0 with 3.60 ERA in two games, both relief.

Barnes, Ross (1881) shortstop; second baseman: 80-for-295, .271, in 69 games.

Barrett, Marty (1884) catcher: 0-for-6, .000, in three games.

Bennett, Charlie (1889–93) catcher: 235-for-1,089, .216, in 337 games.

Bergen, Marty (1896–99) catcher; first baseman; outfielder: 339-for-1,278, .265, in 344 games.

Bergh, John (1880) catcher: 8-for-40, .200, in 11 games.

Bond, Tommy (1877–81) pitcher: 149–87 with 2.21 ERA in 247 games; outfielder; third baseman; first baseman: 235-for-1,044, .225, in 264 games.

Borden, Joe (1876) pitcher: 11–12 with 2.89 ERA in 29 games; one save.

Bradley, Foghorn (1876) pitcher: 9–10 with 2.49 ERA in 22 games; one save.

Bransfield, Kitty (1898) catcher; first baseman: 2-for-9, .222, in five games.

Brodie, Steve (1890–91) outfielder: 288-for-1,037, .278, in 265 games.

Brouthers, Dan (1889) first baseman: 181-for-485, .373, in 126 games.

Brown, Lew (1876–77, 83) catcher; outfielder; first baseman: 110-for-470, .234, in 117 games.

Brown, Tom (1888–89) outfielder: 188-for-782, .240, in 197 games.

Brynan, Tod (1891) pitcher: 0–1 with 54.00 ERA in one game, start.

Buffinton, Charlie (1882–86) pitcher: 104–70 with 2.83 ERA in 104 games; outfielder; first baseman: 320-for-1,257, .255, in 314 games.

Burdock, Jack (1878–88) second baseman; third baseman; shortstop: 761-for-3,029, .251, in 760 games.

Burke, Dan (1892) catcher: 0-for-4, .000, in one game.

C

Carroll, Cliff (1893) outfielder: 98-for-438, .224, in 120 games.

Clarke, Boileryard (1899–1900) catcher; first baseman: 135-for-493, .274, in 141 games.

Clarkson, Dad (1892) pitcher: 1–0 with 1.29 ERA in one game, start.

Clarkson, John (1888–92) pitcher: 149–82 with 2.82 ERA in 242 games; four saves.

Cogswell, Ed (1879) first baseman: 76-for-236, .322, in 49 games.

Coliver, Bill (1885) outfielder: 0-for-4, .000, in one game.

Collins, Jimmy (1895–1900) third baseman; shortstop; outfielder: 821-for-2,653, .309, in 674 games.

Connaughton, Frank (1894, 1906) shortstop; outfielder; catcher; second baseman: 68-for-215, .316, in 58 games.

Connor, John (1884) pitcher: 1–4 with 3.15 ERA in seven games, all starts.

Conway, Dick (1887–88) pitcher: 13–17 with 4.22 ERA in 32 games, all starts.

Coyle, Bill (1893) pitcher: 0–1 with 9.00 ERA in two games.

Crowley, Bill (1881, 84) outfielder: 181-for-686, .264, in 180 games.

D

Daily, Con (1886–87) catcher; outfielder: 62-for-300, .207, in 86 games.

Daley, Bill (1889) pitcher: 3–3 with 4.31 ERA in nine games.

Daly, Joe (1892) catcher: 0-for-0, —, in one game.

Davis, Daisy (1894–95) pitcher: 6–9 with 5.17 ERA in 15 games, all starts.

Dealy, Pat (1885–86) catcher; third

Larvell "Sugar Bear" Blanks was the Braves' regular shortstop in 1975 and is one of nearly 1,500 men to have played for the oldest continuously operating sports franchise in America.

baseman; outfielder; shortstop; first baseman: 44-for-176, .250, in 50 games.

Deasley, Pat (1881–82) catcher; outfielder; shortstop; first baseman: 105-for-411, .255, in 110 games.

Dignan, Steve (1880) outfielder: 11-for-34, .324, in eight games.

Dolan, Cozy (1895–96, 05–06) pitcher: 12–13 with 4.44 ERA in 35 games; one save; outfielder; first baseman; second baseman: 277-for-1,079, .257, in 296 games.

Donovan, Patsy (1890) outfielder: 36-for-140, .257, in 32 games.

Duffy, Hugh (1892–1900) outfielder; third baseman; shortstop; second baseman; catcher; first baseman: 1,544-for-4,656, .332, in 1,152 games.

F

Foley, Curry (1879–80) pitcher: 23–23 with 3.33 ERA in 57 games; outfielder; first baseman: 143-for-478, .299, in 115 games.

Fox, John (1881) pitcher: 6–8 with 3.33 ERA in 17 games.

Frisbee, Charlie (1899) outfielder: 50-for-152, .329, in 42 games.

G

Ganzel, Charlie (1889–97) catcher; outfielder; first baseman; shortstop; third baseman; second baseman: 535-for-2,007, .267, in 535 games.

Garry, Jim (1893) pitcher: 0–1 with 63.00 ERA in one game, relief.

Gastright, Hank (1893) pitcher: 12–4 with 5.13 ERA in 19 games.

Getzien, Charlie (1890–91) pitcher: 27–22 with 3.32 ERA in 51 games.

Ging, Billy (1899) pitcher: 1–0 with 1.13 ERA in one game, start.

Glenn, Ed (1888) outfielder; third baseman: 10-for-65, .154, in 20 games.

Gunning, Tom (1884–86) catcher: 59-for-317, .186, in 87 games.

H

Hackett, Mert (1883–85) catcher; outfielder; third baseman: 118-for-562, .210, in 152 games.

Hackett, Walter (1885) second baseman; shortstop: 23-for-125, .184, in 35 games.

Hamilton, Billy (1896–1901) outfielder: 884-for-2,612, .338, in 690 games.

Hardie, Lou (1890) catcher; outfielder; third baseman; shortstop;

first baseman: 42-for-185, .227, in 47 games.

Harrington, Joe (1895–96) third baseman; second baseman; shortstop: 57-for-263, .217, in 72 games.

Hawes, Bill (1879) outfielder; catcher: 31-for-155, .200, in 38 games.

Hawley, Scott (1894) pitcher: 0–1 with 7.71 ERA in one game, start.

Hickey, Mike (1899) second baseman: 1-for-3, .333, in one game.

Hickman, Charlie (1897–99) pitcher: 7–2 with 3.87 ERA in 19 games; four saves; outfielder; first baseman: 42-for-124, .339, in 40 games.

Higgins, Bill (1888) second baseman: 10-for-54, .185, in 14 games.

Hines, Mike (1883–85, 88) catcher; outfielder: 90-for-435, .207, in 116 games.

Hines, Paul (1890) outfielder; first baseman: 72-for-273, .264, in 69 games.

Hodson, George (1894) pitcher: 4–4 with 5.84 ERA in 12 games.

Hornung, Joe (1881–88) outfielder; first baseman; third baseman: 810-for-3,077, .263, in 705 games.

Hotaling, Pete (1882) outfielder: 98-for-378, .259, in 84 games.

Houck, Sadie (1879–80) outfielder; shortstop: 102-for-403, .253, in 92 games.

Hurley, Jerry (1889) outfielder; catcher: 0-for-4, .000, in one game.

J

Johnston, Dick (1885–89) outfielder; shortstop: 552-for-2,155, .256, in 529 games.

Jones, Charley (1879–80) outfielder: 196-for-635, .309, in 149 games.

K

Keister, Bill (1898) shortstop; second baseman; outfielder: 5-for-30, .167, in 10 games.

Kelley, Joe (1891) outfielder: 70-for-273, .256, in 85 games.

Kelly, King (1887–89, 91–92) catcher; outfielder; second baseman; shortstop; third baseman; first baseman: 510-for-1,764, .289, in 442 games; pitcher: 1–0 with 2.84 ERA in four games, all relief.

Kiley, John (1891) pitcher: 0–1 with 6.75 ERA in one game, start.

Killen, Frank (1899) pitcher: 7–5 with 4.26 ERA in 12 games, all starts.

Klobedanz, Fred (1896–99, 1902) pitcher: 53–25 with 4.12 ERA in 89 games.

Klusman, Billy (1888) second baseman: 18-for-107, .168, in 28 games.

Kuhns, Charlie (1899) shortstop; third baseman: 5-for-18, .278, in seven games.

L

Ladd, Hil (1898) outfielder: 1-for-4, .250, in one game.

Lake, Fred (1891, 97, 1910) catcher; outfielder; pinch hitter: 16-for-70, .229, in 27 games.

Lampe, Henry (1894) pitcher: 0–1 with 11.81 ERA in two games.

Lawson, Al (1890) pitcher: 0–1 with 4.00 ERA in one game, start.

Leary, Jack (1880) outfielder: 0-for-3, .000, in one game; pitcher: 0–1 with 15.00 ERA in one game, start.

Leonard, Andy (1876–78) outfielder; shortstop; second baseman: 231-for-837, .276, in 182 games.

Lewis, Fred (1881) outfielder: 25-for-114, .219, in 27 games.

Lewis, Ted (1896–1900) pitcher: 78–47 with 3.53 ERA in 144 games; three saves.

Long, Herman (1890–1902) shortstop; outfielder; third baseman; second baseman; first baseman: 1,900-for-6,777, .280, in 1,646 games.

Lovett, Tom (1894) pitcher: 8–6 with 5.97 ERA in 15 games.

Lowe, Bobby (1890–1901) second baseman; shortstop; third baseman; outfielder: 1,606-for-5,617, .286, in 1,410 games; pitcher: 0–0 with 9.00 ERA in one game, relief.

M

Madden, Kid (1887–89) pitcher: 38–35 with 3.74 ERA in 79 games; one save.

Mahoney, Mike (1897) catcher: 1-for-2, .500, in two games; pitcher: 0–0 with 18.00 ERA in one game, relief.

Mains, Willard (1896) pitcher: 3–2 with 5.48 ERA in eight games; one save.

Manning, Jack (1876, 78) pitcher: 19–5 with 2.80 ERA in 37 games; five saves; outfielder; shortstop; second baseman: 139-for-536, .259, in 130 games.

Manning, Jim (1884–85) outfielder; shortstop; second baseman; third baseman: 146-for-651, .224, in 173 games.

Mathews, Bobby (1881–82) pitcher: 20–15 with 2.83 ERA in 39 games;

outfielder; shortstop: 50-for-240, .208, in 64 games.

McBride, Dick (1876) pitcher: 0–4 with 2.73 ERA in four games, all starts.

McCarthy, Tommy (1885, 92–95) outfielder; second baseman; shortstop: 652-for-2,204, .296, in 552 games; pitcher: 0–0 with 4.50 ERA in one game, relief.

McClure, Hall (1882) outfielder: 2-for-6, .333, in two games.

McGann, Dan (1896, 1908) second baseman; first baseman: 169-for-646, .262, in 178 games.

McGarr, Chippy (1890) third baseman; shortstop; outfielder: 115-for-487, .236, in 121 games.

McGinley, Tim (1876) outfielder; catcher: 6-for-40, .150, in nine games.

Meekin, Jouett (1899) pitcher: 7–6 with 2.83 ERA in 13 games, all starts.

Merritt, Bill (1893–94, 99) catcher; outfielder: 55-for-169, .325, in 50 games.

Moriarity, Gene (1884) outfielder: 1-for-16, .063, in four games.

Morrill, John (1876–88) first baseman; third baseman; second baseman; shortstop; outfielder; catcher: 1,247-for-4,759, .262, in 1,219 games; pitcher: 1–2 with 4.32 ERA in 17 games; three saves.

Murnane, Tim (1876–77) first baseman; outfielder; second baseman: 126-for-448, .281, in 104 games.

N

Nash, Billy (1885–89, 91–95) third baseman; second baseman; shortstop; outfielder: 1,283-for-4,561, .281, in 1,186 games; pitcher: 0–0 with 0.00 ERA in one game, relief.

Nichols, Kid (1890–1901) pitcher: 329–183 with 3.00 ERA in 556 games; 16 saves.

Nichols, Tricky (1876) pitcher: 1–0 with 1.00 ERA in one game, start.

Nyce, Charlie (1895) shortstop: 8-for-35, .229, in nine games.

O

O'Leary, Dan (1880) outfielder: 3-for-12, .250, in three games.

O'Rourke, Jim (1876–78, 80) outfielder; first baseman; catcher; third baseman; shortstop: 369-for-1,195, .309, in 352 games.

O'Rourke, John (1879–80) outfielder: 194-for-630, .308, in 153 games.

Jim O'Rourke

O'Rourke, Tom (1887–88) catcher; outfielder; third baseman: 25-for-152, .164, in 42 games.

P

Parks, Bill (1876) outfielder: 0-for-4, .000, in one game.

Parsons, Charlie (1886) pitcher: 0–2 with 3.94 ERA in two games, both starts.

Pickett, Dave (1898) outfielder: 12-for-43, .279, in 14 games.

Poorman, Tom (1885–86) outfielder: 151-for-598, .253, in 144 games.

Powers, Phil (1880) catcher; outfielder: 18-for-126, .143, in 37 games.

Purcell, Blondie (1885) outfielder: 19-for-87, .218, in 21 games.

Q

Quarles, Bill (1893) pitcher: 2–1 with 4.67 ERA in three games, all starts.

Quinn (1881) first baseman: 0-for-4, .000, in one game.

Quinn, Joe (1888–89, 91–92) second baseman; shortstop; third baseman: 401-for-1,640, .245, in 417 games.

R

Radbourn, Charley (1886–89) pitcher: 78–81 with 3.58 ERA in 165 games; outfielder; third baseman: 140-for-629, .223, in 176 games.

Radford, Paul (1883) outfielder: 53-for-258, .205, in 72 games.

Ray, Irv (1888–89) shortstop; second baseman; third baseman: 61-for-239, .255, in 59 games.

Richardson, Hardy (1889) second baseman; outfielder: 163-for-536, .304, in 132 games.

Richmond, John (1880–81) shortstop;

outfielder: 59-for-227, .260, in 59 games.

Richmond, Lee (1879) pitcher: 1–0 with 2.00 ERA in one game, start.

Rooks, George (1891) outfielder: 2-for-16, .125, in five games.

Rowen, Ed (1882) outfielder; catcher; shortstop; third baseman: 81-for-327, .248, in 83 games.

Ryan, Cyclone (1891) pitcher: 0–0 with 0.00 ERA in one game, relief.

Ryan, Jack (1894–96) catcher; first baseman; outfielder; second baseman: 112-for-422, .265, in 110 games.

S

Schafer, Harry (1876–78) third baseman; outfielder; shortstop: 112-for-435, .257, in 105 games.

Schellhase, Al (1890) outfielder; catcher; shortstop; third baseman: 4-for-29, .138, in nine games.

Sexton, Frank (1895) pitcher: 1–5 with 5.69 ERA in seven games.

Smith, Edgar (1883) outfielder; catcher: 25-for-115, .217, in 30 games.

Smith, Pop (1889–90) shortstop; second baseman: 160-for-671, .238, in 193 games.

Smith, Stub (1898) shortstop: 1-for-10, .100, in three games.

Smith, Tom (1894) pitcher: 0–0 with 15.00 ERA in two games, both relief; one save.

Snyder, Pop (1878–79, 81) catcher; outfielder; shortstop; second baseman: 176-for-774, .227, in 203 games.

Sommers, Pete (1888) catcher: 3-for-13, .231, in four games.

Sowders, Bill (1888–89) pitcher: 20–17 with 2.43 ERA in 43 games; two saves.

Stafford, General (1898–99) outfielder; first baseman; second baseman; shortstop: 87-for-305, .285, in 92 games.

Stahl, Chick (1897–1900) outfielder: 675-for-2,065, .327, in 523 games; pitcher: 0–0 with 9.00 ERA in one game, relief.

Staley, Harry (1891–94) pitcher: 72–38 with 4.21 ERA in 131 games.

Stemmeyer, Bill (1885–87) pitcher: 29–27 with 3.49 ERA in 58 games; one save.

Stivetts, Jack (1892–98) pitcher: 131–78 with 4.12 ERA in 237 games; two saves; outfielder; first baseman; third baseman; second baseman; shortstop: 409-for-1,345, .304, in 404 games.

Stocksdale, Otis (1895) pitcher: 2–2 with 5.87 ERA in four games, all starts.

Stovey, Harry (1891–92) outfielder; first baseman: 176-for-690, .255, in 172 games.

Streit, Oscar (1899) pitcher: 1–0 with 6.75 ERA in two games.

Stultz, George (1894) pitcher: 1–0 with 0.00 ERA in one game, start.

Sullivan, Billy (1899–1900) catcher; shortstop; second baseman: 85-for-312, .272, in 94 games.

Sullivan, Denny (1880) catcher: 1-for-4, .250, in one game.

Sullivan, Jim (1891, 95–97) pitcher: 26–26 with 4.35 ERA in 66 games; three saves.

Sullivan, Marty (1890–91) outfielder; third baseman: 159-for-572, .278, in 138 games.

Sullivan, Mike (1898–99) pitcher: 1–1 with 9.00 ERA in four games.

Sutton, Ezra (1877–88) shortstop; third baseman; outfielder; second baseman; first baseman: 1,161-for-4,045, .287, in 977 games.

T

Taber, John (1890) pitcher: 0–1 with 4.15 ERA in two games; one save.

Tate, Pop (1885–88) catcher; outfielder: 120-for-498, .241, in 136 games.

Tenney, Fred (1894–1907, 11) catcher; outfielder; first baseman: 1,994-for-6,637, .300, in 1,737 games; pitcher: 0–0 with 4.50 ERA in one game, relief.

Trott, Sam (1880) catcher; outfielder: 26-for-125, .208, in 39 games.

Tucker, Tommy (1890–97) first baseman; outfielder: 1,025-for-3,565, .288, in 916 games; pitcher: 0–0

with 9.00 ERA in one game, relief.

Tyng, Jim (1879) pitcher: 1–2 with 5.00 ERA in three games, all starts.

V

Van Dyke, Bill (1893) outfielder: 3-for-12, .250, in three games.

Viau, Lee (1892) pitcher: 1–0 with 0.00 ERA in one game, start.

Von Fricken, Tony (1890) pitcher: 0–1 with 10.13 ERA in one game, start.

W

Warner, John (1895) catcher: 1-for-7, .143, in three games.

West, Frank (1894) pitcher: 0–0 with 9.00 ERA in one game, relief.

Wheelock, Bobby (1887) outfielder; shortstop; second baseman: 42-for-166, .253, in 48 games.

White, Deacon Jim (1877) first baseman; outfielder; catcher: 103-for-266, .387, in 59 games.

White, Will (1877) pitcher: 2–1 with 3.00 ERA in three games, all starts.

Whiteley, Gurdon (1885) outfielder; catcher: 25-for-135, .185, in 33 games.

Whitney, Frank (1876) outfielder; second baseman: 33-for-139, .237, in 34 games.

Whitney, Jim (1881–85) pitcher: 133–121 with 2.49 ERA in 266 games; two saves; outfielder; first baseman; third baseman: 406-for-1,502, .270, in 370 games.

Willis, Vic (1898–1905) pitcher: 151–147 with 2.82 ERA in 320 games; five saves.

Wilson, Zeke (1895) pitcher: 2–4 with 5.20 ERA in six games, all starts.

Wise, Nick (1888) outfielder; catcher: 0-for-3, .000, in one game.

Wise, Sam (1882–88) shortstop; third

George Wright

baseman; second baseman; outfielder; first baseman: 755-for-2,825, .267, in 709 games.

Wright, George (1876–78, 80–81) shortstop; second baseman; 246-for-921, .267, in 198 games; pitcher: 0–0 with 0.00 ERA in one game, relief.

Wright, Harry (1876–77) outfielder: 0-for-7, .000, in two games.

Wright, Sam (1876, 81) shortstop: 2-for-12, .167, in three games.

Y

Yeager, George (1896–99) catcher; first baseman; outfielder; second baseman; third baseman; shortstop: 84-for-329, .255, in 103 games.

Yerrick, Bill (1895–96) pitcher: 1–3 with 8.10 ERA in five games.

Post-1900 Players

ATLANTA PLAYERS IN ALL CAPS

A

AARON, HANK (54–74) outfielder; first baseman; second baseman; third baseman: 3,600-for-11,628, .310, in 3,076 games.

AARON, TOMMIE (62–63, 65, 68–71) first baseman; outfielder;

third baseman; second baseman: 216-for-944, .229, in 437 games.

Abbaticchio, Ed (03–05, 10) second baseman; shortstop; outfielder: 473-for-1,856, .255, in 495 games.

ABERNATHY, TED (66) pitcher: 4–4 with 3.86 ERA in 38 games, all relief; four saves.

ACKER, JIM (86–89) pitcher: 7–27 with 3.71 ERA in 169 games; 16 saves.

Adcock, Joe (53–62) first baseman; outfielder: 1,206-for-4,232, .285, in 1,207 games.

Addis, Bob (50–51) outfielder: 62-for-227, .273, in 101 games.

Aderholt, Morrie (45) outfielder, sec-

Ted Abernathy

ond baseman: 34-for-102, .333, in 31 games.

AKER, JACK (74) pitcher: 0–1 with 3.78 ERA in 17 games, all relief.

Akers, Bill (32) third baseman; second baseman; shortstop: 24-for-93, .258, in 36 games.

ALDRICH, JAY (89) pitcher: 1–2 with 2.19 ERA in eight games, all relief.

ALEXANDER, DOYLE (80, 86–87) pitcher: 25–27 with 4.09 ERA in 68 games, all starts.

Allen, Frank (16–17) pitcher: 11–13 with 3.00 ERA in 48 games; one save.

ALOMAR, SANDY (64–66) shortstop; second baseman: 43-for-205, .210, in 117 games.

ALOU, FELIPE (64–69) outfielder; first baseman; third baseman; shortstop: 989-for-3,348, .295, in 841 games.

ALVAREZ, JOSE (81–82, 88–89) pitcher: 8–9 with 2.99 ERA in 98 games, all relief; five saves.

Anderson, Bill (25) pitcher: 0–0 with 10.13 ERA in two games, both relief.

Andrews, Nate (43–45) pitcher: 37–47 with 3.22 ERA in 94 games; two saves.

Andrews, Stan (39–40) catcher: 12-for-59, .203, in 32 games.

Antonelli, John (48–53, 61) pitcher: 18–22 with 3.88 ERA in 86 games.

Asmussen, Tom (07) catcher: 0-for-5, .000, in two games.

ASPROMONTE, BOB (69–70) outfielder; third baseman; shortstop; second baseman; first baseman: 77-for-325, .237, in 144 games.

Aspromonte, Ken (62) second baseman; third baseman: 23-for-79, .291, in 34 games.

ASSELSTINE, BRIAN (76–81) out-

Brian Asselstine

fielder: 146-for-574, .254, in 284 games.

ASSENMACHER, PAUL (86–89) pitcher: 17–14 with 3.46 ERA in 226 games, all relief; 14 saves.

Atwell, Toby (56) catcher: 5-for-30, .167, in 15 games.

Aubrey, Harry (03) shortstop; second baseman; outfielder: 69-for-325, .212, in 96 games.

AUTRY, AL (76) pitcher: 1–0 with 5.40 ERA in one game, start.

Autry, Chick (09) first baseman; outfielder: 39-for-199, .196, in 65 games.

Averill, Earl (41) outfielder: 2-for-17, .118, in eight games.

AVERY, STEVE (90–   ) current Braves pitcher.

Avila, Bobby (59) second baseman: 41-for-172, .238, in 51 games.

B

Babich, Johnny (36) pitcher: 0–0 with 10.50 ERA in three games, all relief.

Bagwell, Bill (23) outfielder: 27-for-93, .290, in 56 games.

Bailey, Ed (64) catcher: 71-for-271, .262, in 95 games.

Bailey, Fred (16–18) outfielder; pinch hitter: 23-for-124, .185, in 60 games.

Bailey, Gene (19–20) outfielder: 4-for-17, .083, in 13 games.

BAKER, DUSTY (68–75) outfielder: 616-for-2,216, .278, in 628 games.

Balas, Mike (38) pitcher: 0–0 with 6.75 ERA in one game, relief.

BALES, LEE (66) second baseman; third baseman: 1-for-16, .063, in 12 games.

Ball, Jim (07–08) catcher: 7-for-51, .137, in 16 games.

Bancroft, Dave (24–27) shortstop; third baseman; second baseman: 474-for-1,626, .292, in 445 games.

Barbare, Walter (21–22) shortstop; second baseman; third baseman;

first baseman: 252-for-923, .273, in 240 games.

BARBER, STEVE (70–72) pitcher: 3–2 with 4.96 ERA in 49 games; two saves.

Barberich, Frank (07) pitcher: 1–1 with 5.84 ERA in two games, both starts.

Barclay, George (04–05) outfielder: 40-for-201, .199, in 53 games.

BARKER, LEN (83–85) pitcher: 10–20 with 4.64 ERA in 47 games.

Barkley, Red (39) shortstop; third baseman: 0-for-11, .000, in 12 games.

Barnes, Jesse (15–17, 23–25) pitcher: 58–86 with 3.07 ERA in 192 games; four saves.

Barnes, Virgil (28) pitcher: 2–7 with 5.82 ERA in 16 games.

Barnicle, George (39–41) pitcher: 3–3 with 6.55 ERA in 20 games.

Barrett, Dick (34) pitcher: 1–3 with 6.68 ERA in 15 games.

Barrett, Frank (46) pitcher: 2–4 with 5.09 ERA in 23 games, all relief.

Barrett, Johnny (46) outfielder: 10-for-43, .233, in 24 games.

Barrett, Red (43–45, 47–49) pitcher: 42–58 with 3.74 ERA in 182 games; five saves.

Barron, Red (29) outfielder: 4-for-21, .190, in 10 games.

Barry, Shad (00–01) outfielder; shortstop; second baseman; first baseman; third baseman: 73-for-294, .248, in 92 games.

Bass, Doc (18) pinch hitter: 1-for-1, 1.000, in two games.

Batchelder, Joe (23–25) pitcher: 1–0 with 5.66 ERA in 11 games.

Bates, Johnny (06–09) outfielder: 426-for-1,632, .261, in 456 games.

BEALL, BOB (75, 78–79) first baseman; outfielder: 54-for-231, .234, in 145 games.

Virgil Barnes

BEARD, MIKE (74–77) pitcher: 4–2 with 3.74 ERA in 74 games.

BEAUCHAMP, JIM (65, 67) first baseman; pinch hitter: 0-for-6, .000, in 8 games.

Beaumont, Ginger (07–09) outfielder: 421-for-1,463, .288, in 398 games.

Beazley, Johnny (47–49) pitcher: 2–1 with 4.24 ERA in 13 games.

Beck, Fred (09–10) outfielder; first baseman: 223-for-905, .246, in 250 games.

Becker, Beals (08–09) outfielder: 185-for-733, .252, in 195 games.

Bedell, Howie (62) outfielder: 27-for-138, .196, in 58 games.

BEDROSIAN, STEVE (81–85, 93–95) pitcher: 40–45 with 3.26 ERA in 350 games; 41 saves.

BEHENNA, RICK (83) pitcher: 3–3 with 4.58 ERA in 14 games.

Bell, Gus (62–64) outfielder; pinch hitter: 62-for-220, .282, in 85 games.

Bell, Les (28–29) third baseman; second baseman; shortstop: 308-for-1,074, .287, in 292 games.

BELL, MIKE (90–91) first baseman: 15-for-53, .200, in 53 games.

BELL, TERRY (87) pinch hitter: 0-for-1, .000, in one game.

BELLIARD, RAFAEL (91–) current Braves player.

BELLOIR, ROB (75–78) shortstop; second baseman; third baseman: 36-for-167, .216, in 81 games.

BENEDICT, BRUCE (78–89) catcher: 696-for-2,878, .242, in 982 games.

Benge, Ray (36) pitcher: 7–9 with 5.79 ERA in 21 games.

Benton, Larry (23–27, 35) pitcher: 44–42 with 4.22 ERA in 179 games; three saves.

BERENGUER, JUAN (91–92) pitcher: 3–4 with 3.23 ERA in 77 games, all relief; 18 saves.

Berger, Wally (30–37) outfielder; first baseman: 1,263-for-4,153, .304, in 1,057 games.

Berres, Ray (40–41) catcher: 100-for-508, .197, in 205 games.

BERROA, GERONIMO (89–90) outfielder: 36-for-140, .257, in 88 games.

BERRYHILL, DAMON (91–93) catcher: 152-for-643, .236, in 217 games.

Betts, Huck (32–35) pitcher: 43–41 with 3.63 ERA in 150 games; eight saves.

Bickford, Vern (48–53) pitcher: 66–56 with 3.69 ERA in 181 games; two saves.

BIELECKI, MIKE (91–92, 94) pitcher: 4–4 with 2.88 ERA in 40 games.

Blackaby, Ethan (62–65) outfielder: 3-for-25, .120, in 15 games.

Blackburn, Earl (15–16) catcher: 31-for-116, .267, in 50 games.

Blackburne, Lena (19) third baseman; shortstop; first baseman; second baseman: 21-for-80, .262, in 31 games.

Blanchard, Johnny (65) outfielder: 1-for-10, .100, in 10 games.

Blanche, Al (35–36) pitcher: 0–1 with 3.78 ERA in 17 games, all relief.

BLANKENSHIP, KEVIN (88) pitcher: 0–1 with 3.38 ERA in two games, both starts.

BLANKS, LARVELL (72–75, 80) second baseman; shortstop; third baseman: 189-for-803, .235, in 282 games.

BLASINGAME, WADE (63–67) pitcher: 29–22 with 4.24 ERA in 94 games; three saves.

BLAUSER, JEFF (87–) current Braves players.

BLOCKER, TERRY (88–89) outfielder; pinch hitter: 49-for-229, .214, in 92 games; pitcher: 0–0 with 0.00 ERA in one game, relief.

Boeckel, Tony (19–23) third baseman; shortstop; second baseman: 717-for-2,509, .286, in 668 games.

BOEVER, JOE (87–90) pitcher: 6–16 with 4.24 ERA in 129 games, all relief; 30 saves.

Boggs, Ray (28) pitcher: 0–0 with 5.40 ERA in four games, all relief.

BOGGS, TOMMY (78–83) pitcher: 19–34 with 4.15 ERA in 91 games.

BOLLING, FRANK (61–66) second baseman: 654-for-2,647, .247, in 755 games.

BONNELL, BARRY (77–79) outfielder; third baseman: 278-for-1,039, .268, in 344 games.

Bonner, Frank (03) second baseman; shortstop: 38-for-173, .220, in 48 games.

Bool, Al (31) catcher: 16-for-85, .188, in 49 games.

Boone, Ray (59–60) catcher: 6-for-27, .222, in 20 games.

BORBON, PEDRO (92–) current Braves pitcher.

Boultes, Jake (07–09) pitcher: 8–14 with 2.96 ERA in 42 games.

BOUTON, JIM (78) pitcher: 1–3 with 4.97 ERA in five games, all starts.

Bowerman, Frank (08–09) catcher; first baseman: 79-for-353, .224, in 119 games.

Boyd, Bob (61) first baseman: 10-for-41, .244, in 36 games.

BOYER, CLETE (67–71) third baseman; shortstop: 467-for-1,914, .244, in 533 games.

Boyle, Buzz (29–30) outfielder: 15-for-58, .259, in 18 games.

BRADFORD, LARRY (77, 79–81) pitcher: 6–4 with 2.52 ERA in 104 games, all relief.

Brady, Bill (12) pitcher: 0–0 with 0.00 ERA in one game, relief.

Brady, Bob (46–47) catcher; pinch hitter: 1-for-6, .167, in four games.

Brady, King (12) pitcher: 0–0 with 20.25 ERA in one game, relief.

Brain, Dave (06–07) third baseman; outfielder: 273-for-1,034, .264, in 272 games.

Brandt, Ed (28–35) pitcher: 94–119 with 4.01 ERA in 283 games; 13 saves.

Braun, John (64) pitcher: 0–0 with 0.00 ERA in one game, relief.

Rafael Belliard

John Blanchard

Braxton, Garland (21–22) pitcher: 2–5 with 3.89 ERA in 42 games.

Bray, Buster (41) outfielder: 1-for-11, .091, in four games.

BREAM, SID (91–93) first baseman: 236-for-914, .258, in 333 games.

BREAZEALE, JIM (69, 71–72) first baseman; third baseman: 25-for-106, .236, in 64 games.

Bridwell, Al (06–07, 11–12) shortstop; outfielder: 293-for-1,256, .233, in 342 games.

BRITTON, JIM (67–69) pitcher: 11–13 with 3.62 ERA in 60 games; four saves.

BRIZZOLARA, TONY (79, 83–84) pitcher: 8–11 with 5.06 ERA in 44 games.

Broskie, Sig (40) catcher: 6-for-22, .273, in 11 games.

Brown, Bob (30–36) pitcher: 16–21 with 4.48 ERA in 79 games; one save.

Brown, Buster (09–13) pitcher: 25–64 with 3.54 ERA in 139 games; four saves.

Brown, Drummond (13) catcher: 11-for-34, .324, in 15 games.

Brown, Eddie (26–28) outfielder; first baseman: 512-for-1,693, .302, in 450 games.

Brown, Fred (01–02) outfielder: 4-for-20, .200, in nine games.

BROWN, JARVIS (94) outfielder: 2-for-15, .133, in 17 games.

BROWN, OSCAR (69–73) outfielder: 77-for-316, .244, in 160 games.

Brown, Sam (06–07) catcher; outfielder; third baseman; first baseman; second baseman: 88-for-439, .200, in 141 games.

Browne, George (08) outfielder: 122-for-536, .228, in 138 games.

Brubaker, Bill (43) third baseman; first baseman: 8-for-19, .421, in 13 games.

BRUCE, BOB (67) pitcher: 2–3 with 4.89 ERA in 12 games; one save.

Brunet, George (60–61) pitcher: 2–0 with 5.10 ERA in 22 games.

Brush, Robert (07) first baseman: 0-for-2, .000, in two games.

Bruton, Billy (53–60) outfielder: 1,126-for-4,079, .276, in 1,618 games.

Bues, Art (13) second baseman; third baseman: 0-for-1, .000, in two games.

Buhl, Bob (53–62) pitcher: 109–72 with 3.27 ERA in 282 games; five saves.

Burdette, Lou (51–63) pitcher: 179–120 with 3.53 ERA in 468 games; 23 saves.

Burg, Joe (10) third baseman; shortstop: 15-for-46, .326, in 13 games.

Burke, Billy (10–11) pitcher: 1–1 with 4.81 ERA in 21 games.

Burke, Frank (07) outfielder: 23-for-129, .178, in 43 games.

Burns, Joe (43) third baseman; outfielder: 28-for-135, .207, in 52 games.

Burris, Paul (48, 50, 52–53) catcher: 43-for-196, .219, in 69 games.

BURROUGHS, JEFF (77–80) outfielder: 466-for-1,742, .268, in 522 games.

Burrus, Dick (25–28) first baseman; outfielder: 438-for-1,431, .306, in 419 games.

Bush, Guy (36–37) pitcher: 12–20 with 3.49 ERA in 47 games; one save.

Butler, Art (11) third baseman; second baseman; shortstop: 12-for-68, .176, in 27 games.

BUTLER, BRETT (81–83) outfielder: 238-for-915, .260, in 280 games.

Butler, Cecil (62, 64) pitcher: 2–0 with 3.31 ERA in 11 games.

C

CABRERA, FRANCISCO (89–93) catcher, first baseman: 87-for-339, .257, in 193 games.

Calderone, Sam (54) catcher: 11-for-29, .379, in 22 games.

Calhoun, Bill (13) first baseman: 1-for-13, .077, in six games.

Callahan, Joe (39–40) pitcher: 1–2 with 6.40 ERA in 10 games.

Camelli, Hank (47) catcher: 29-for-150, .193, in 52 games.

Cameron, Jack (06) outfielder; pinch hitter: 11-for-61, .180, in 18 games; pitcher: 0–0 with 0.00 ERA in two games.

CAMP, RICK (76–78, 80–85) pitcher: 56–49 with 3.37 ERA in 414 games; 57 saves.

CAMPBELL, DAVE (77–78) pitcher: 4–10 with 3.82 ERA in 118 games; 14 saves.

Campbell, Vin (12) outfielder: 185-for-624, .296, in 145 games.

Canavan, Hugh (18) pitcher: 0–4 with 6.36 ERA in 11 games.

Cannell, Rip (04–05) outfielder: 221-for-913, .242, in 254 games.

Cantwell, Ben (28–36) pitcher: 74–106 with 3.87 ERA in 290 games.

CAPRA, BUZZ (74–77) pitcher: 26–27 with 3.73 ERA in 101 games; one save.

Capri, Pat (44) second baseman: 0-for-1, .000, in seven games.

CARABALLO, RAMON (93) second baseman: 0-for-0, —, in six games.

Cardoni, Ben (43–45) pitcher: 0–6 with 4.76 ERA in 36 games; one save.

CARDWELL, DON (70) pitcher: 2–1 with 9.00 ERA in 16 games.

Carnett, Eddie (41) pitcher: 0–0 with 20.25 ERA in two games, both relief.

Carney, Pat (01–04) outfielder; first baseman: 308-for-1,248, .247, in 338 games; pitcher: 4–10 with 4.69 ERA in 16 games.

CARROLL, CLAY (64–68) pitcher: 16–21 with 3.66 ERA in 155 games; 13 saves.

Carroll, Dixie (19) outfielder: 13-for-49, .265, in 15 games.

CARTY, RICO (63–72) outfielder; catcher; first baseman; third baseman; pinch hitter: 871-for-2,746, .317, in 829 games.

CARY, CHUCK (87–88) pitcher: 1–1 with 4.68 ERA in 20 games, all relief; one save.

CASANOVA, PAUL (72–74) catcher: 100-for-476, .210, in 173 games.

CASTILLA, VINNY (91–92) shortstop; third baseman: 5-for-21, .238, in 21 games.

Jim Britton

Brett Butler

CASTILLO, TONY (89–91) pitcher: 6–3 with 4.56 ERA in 71 games; one save.

Cather, Teddy (14–15) outfielder: 64-for-247, .259, in 90 games.

Causey, Red (19) pitcher: 4–5 with 4.57 ERA in 10 games, all starts.

CAUSEY, WAYNE (68) second baseman; shortstop; third baseman: 4-for-37, .108, in 16 games.

CEPEDA, ORLANDO (69–72) first baseman: 414-for-1,474, .281, in 401 games.

CERONE, RICK (85) catcher: 61-for-282, .216, in 96 games.

Chadbourne, Chet (18) outfielder: 27-for-104, .260, in 27 games.

Chambers, Rome (00) pitcher: 0–0 with 11.25 ERA in one game, relief.

CHAMBLISS, CHRIS (80–86) first baseman: 727-for-2,668, .272, in 886 games.

CHANEY, DARREL (76–79) shortstop; second baseman; third baseman; catcher: 241-for-1,067, .226, in 379 games.

Chaplin, Tiny (36) pitcher: 10–15 with 4.12 ERA in 40 games; two saves.

Chappell, Larry (16–17) outfielder: 12-for-55, .218, in 24 games.

Chappelle, Bill (08–09) pitcher: 3–5 with 1.81 ERA in 18 games.

Chatham, Buster (30–31) third baseman; shortstop: 118-for-448, .263, in 129 games.

CHEADLE, DAVE (73) pitcher: 0–1 with 18.00 ERA in two games, relief.

Cheney, Larry (19) pitcher: 0–2 with 3.55 ERA in eight games.

Chipman, Bob (50–52) pitcher: 12–11 with 4.22 ERA in 89 games; five saves.

Chrisley, Neil (61) pinch hitter: 2-for-9, .222, in 10 games.

Christenbury, Lloyd (19–22) outfielder; shortstop; second baseman; third baseman: 113-for-414, .273, in 205 games.

Cimoli, Gino (61) outfielder: 23-for-117, .197, in 37 games.

CLANCY, JIM (91) pitcher: 3–2 with 5.71 ERA in 24 games, all relief; three saves.

Clark, Earl (27–33) outfielder: 233-for-785, .297, in 280 games.

CLARK, GLEN (67) pinch hitter: 0-for-4, .000, in four games.

Clarke, Josh (11) outfielder: 28-for-120, .233, in 32 games.

Clarkson, Bill (28–29) pitcher: 0–3 with 7.34 ERA in 21 games.

Earl Clark

Clarkson, Buzz (52) shortstop; third baseman: 5-for-25, .200, in 14 games.

CLARY, MARTY (87, 89–90) pitcher: 5–14 with 4.48 ERA in 58 games.

Clemens, Chet (39, 44) outfielder: 8-for-40, .200, in 28 games.

Clements, Jack (00) catcher: 13-for-42, .310, in 16 games.

CLINE, TY (63–67) outfielder; first baseman: 136-for-589, .231, in 348 games.

CLONINGER, TONY (61–68) pitcher: 86–62 with 3.94 ERA in 225 games; five saves.

CLOSTER, ALAN (73) pitcher: 0–0 with 14.54 ERA in four games, all relief.

Clymer, Otis (13) outfielder: 12-for-37, .324, in 14 games.

Cocreham, Gene (13–15) pitcher: 3–5 with 5.27 ERA in 17 games.

Coffey, Jack (09) shortstop: 48-for-257, .187, in 73 games.

Coffman, Dick (40) pitcher: 1–5 with 5.40 ERA in 31 games, all relief; three saves.

COFFMAN, KEVIN (87–88) pitcher: 4–9 with 5.46 ERA in 23 games.

Cole, Dave (50–53) pitcher: 3–7 with 4.47 ERA in 59 games.

Ty Cline

Cole, Dick (57) outfielder: 1-for-14, .071, in 15 games.

Collins, Bill (10–11) outfielder; third baseman: 147-for-628, .234, in 168 games.

COLLINS, DON (77) pitcher: 3–9 with 5.09 ERA in 40 games; two saves.

Collins, Pat (29) catcher: 0-for-5, .000, in seven games.

Collins, Wilson (13–14) outfielder: 10-for-38, .263, in 43 games.

Collins, Zip (15–17) outfielder: 64-for-309, .207, in 107 games.

Compton, Pete (15–16) outfielder: 48-for-214, .224, in 69 games.

Conatser, Clint (48–49) outfielder: 102-for-376, .271, in 143 games.

Conley, Gene (52, 54–58) pitcher: 42–43 with 3.56 ERA in 146 games; six saves.

Conlon, Jocko (23) second baseman; shortstop; third baseman: 32-for-147, .218, in 59 games.

Connolly, Joe (13–16) outfielder: 358-for-1,241, .288, in 412 games.

Connor, Joe (00) catcher: 4-for-19, .211, in seven games.

Constable, Jim (62) pitcher: 1–1 with 2.00 ERA in three games; one save.

Conway, Rip (18) second baseman; third baseman: 4-for-24, .167, in 14 games.

Cooley, Duff (01–04) outfielder; first baseman: 511-for-1,808, .283, in 458 games.

Cooney, Bill (09–10) pinch hitter; outfielder; second baseman; shortstop: 6-for-22, .273, in 13 games; pitcher: 0–0 with 1.42 ERA in three games.

Cooney, Jimmy (28) shortstop; second baseman: 7-for-51, .137, in 18 games.

Cooney, Johnny (21–30, 38–42) pinch hitter; outfielder; first baseman: 676-for-2,360, .286, in 858 games; pitcher: 34–44 with 3.72 ERA in 159 games; six saves.

COOPER, GARY (80) outfielder: 0-for-2, .000, in 21 games.

Cooper, Mort (45–47) pitcher: 22–20 with 3.31 ERA in 58 games; two saves.

Cooper, Walker (50–52) catcher: 300-for-1,028, .292, in 313 games.

CORRELL, VIC (74–77) catcher: 193-for-871, .222, in 299 games.

Coscarart, Joe (35–36) third baseman;

Vic Correll

George Crowe

shortstop; second baseman: 157-for-651, .241, in 190 games.

Cottier, Chuck (59–60) second baseman: 55-for-253, .217, in 105 games.

Cottrell, Ensign (14) pitcher: 0–1 with 9.00 ERA in one game, start.

Courtney, Ernie (02) outfielder; shortstop: 36-for-165, .218, in 48 games.

Cousineau, Dee (23–25) catcher: 2-for-4, .500, in five games.

Covington, Sam (17–18) outfielder: 14-for-69, .203, in 20 games.

Covington, Wes (56–61) outfielder: 407-for-1,435, .284, in 468 games.

Cowan, Billy (65) outfielder: 5-for-27, .185, in 19 games.

COWLEY, JOE (82) pitcher: 1–2 with 4.47 ERA in 17 games.

Cozart, Charles (45) pitcher: 1–0 with 10.13 ERA in five games, all relief.

Crandall, Del (49–63) catcher; first baseman; outfielder: 1,176-for-4,583, .257, in 1,394 games.

Crandall, Doc (18) pinch hitter; outfielder: 8-for-28, .286, in 14 games; pitcher: 1–2 with 2.38 ERA in five games.

Creedon, Connie (43) pinch hitter: 1-for-4, .250, in five games.

Crolius, Fred (01) outfielder: 48-for-200, .240, in 49 games.

Crone, Ray (54–57) pitcher: 25–20 with 3.57 ERA in 98 games; three saves.

Cronin, Bill (28–31) catcher: 68-for-296, .230, in 126 games.

Crowe, George (52–53, 55) first baseman: 153-for-562, .272, in 224 games.

CROWLEY, TERRY (76) pinch hitter: 0-for-6, .000, in seven games.

Cruise, Walton (19–24) outfielder; first baseman; pinch hitter: 361-for-1,272, .284, in 406 games.

Crum, Cal (17–18) pitcher: 0–1 with 10.80 ERA in two games.

Crutcher, Dick (14–15) pitcher: 7–9 with 3.65 ERA in 47 games; two saves.

Cuccinello, Tony (36–40, 42–43) second baseman; third baseman: 627-for-2,254, .278, in 617 games.

Culler, Dick (44–47) shortstop; third baseman: 316-for-1,251, .253, in 355 games.

Cummings, Jack (29) catcher: 1-for-6, .167, in three games.

Cunningham, Bill (24) outfielder: 119-for-437, .272, in 114 games.

Cunningham, Bruce (29–32) pitcher: 13–24 with 4.64 ERA in 104 games; two saves.

Cuppy, Nig (00) pitcher: 8–4 with 3.08 ERA in 17 games; one save.

Curran, Sammy (02) pitcher: 0–0 with 1.35 ERA in one game, relief.

Curtis, Cliff (09–11) pitcher: 11–37 with 3.28 ERA in 65 games; three saves.

Curtis, Jack (62) pitcher: 4–4 with 4.16 ERA in 30 games; one save.

Cusick, Jack (52) shortstop; third baseman: 13-for-78, .167, in 49 games.

D

Dagenhard, John (43) pitcher: 1–0 with 0.00 ERA in two games.

Dahlen, William (08–09) shortstop; second baseman; third baseman: 171-for-721, .237, in 213 games.

Dahlgren, Babe (41) first baseman; third baseman: 39-for-166, .235, in 44 games.

DalCANTON, BRUCE (75–76) pitcher: 5–12 with 3.46 ERA in 68 games; four saves.

Dam, Bill (09) outfielder: 1-for-2, .500, in one game.

Daniels, Jack (52) outfielder: 41-for-219, .187, in 106 games.

Dark, Al (46, 48–49, 60) shortstop; outfielder; third baseman; second baseman; first baseman: 366-for-1,226, .299, in 332 games.

DAVEY, MIKE (77–78) pitcher: 0–0 with 4.34 ERA in 19 games, all relief; two saves.

DAVIDSON, TED (68) pitcher: 0–0 with 6.75 ERA in four games, all relief.

Davis, George (13–15) pitcher: 6–6 with 3.68 ERA in 26 games.

DAVIS, JODY (88–90) catcher; first baseman: 43-for-267, .161, in 92 games.

DAVIS, MARK (92) pitcher: 1–0 with 7.02 ERA in 14 games, all relief.

DAVIS, TRENCH (87) pinch hitter: 0-for-3, .000, in six games.

DAYLEY, KEN (82–84) pitcher: 10–17 with 4.48 ERA in 48 games.

Deal, Charlie (13–14) second baseman; third baseman; shortstop: 65-for-293, .222, in 89 games.

DEDMON, JEFF (83–87) pitcher: 19–16 with 3.77 ERA in 229 games; 11 saves.

Delahanty, Jim (04–05) pitcher: 0–0 with 1.69 ERA in two games.

de la HOZ, MIKE (64–67) second baseman; third baseman; shortstop; outfielder; first baseman: 153-for-618, .248, in 304 games.

Delaney, Art (28–29) pitcher: 12–22 with 4.44 ERA in 59 games; two saves.

Demaree, Al (19) pitcher: 6–6 with 3.80 ERA in 25 games; three saves.

Jody Davis

Mike de la Hoz

Demaree, Frank (41–42) outfielder: 68-for-300, .227, in 112 games.

DeMerit, John (57–59, 61) outfielder: 20-for-116, .172, in 79 games.

DeMontreville, Gene (01–02) second baseman; third baseman; shortstop: 298-for-1,058, .282, in 264 games.

DENSON, DREW (89) first baseman: 9-for-36, .250, in 12 games.

Dessau, Rube (07) pitcher: 0–1 with 10.61 ERA in two games, both starts.

Detweiler, Ducky (42, 46) third baseman; pinch hitter: 14-for-45, .311, in 13 games.

DEVINE, ADRIAN (73, 75–76, 78–79) pitcher: 14–15 with 4.40 ERA in 148 games; 16 saves.

Devlin, Art (12–13) first baseman; shortstop; third baseman; outfielder: 174-for-646, .269, in 197 games.

DeVogt, Rex (13) catcher: 0-for-6, .000, in three games.

Devore, Josh (14) outfielder: 29-for-128, .227, in 51 games.

Dexter, Charlie (02–03) shortstop; second baseman; outfielder; third baseman; catcher: 149-for-640, .233, in 171 games.

Frank Demaree

DIAZ, CARLOS (82) pitcher: 3–2 with 4.62 ERA in 19 games, all relief; one save.

Dickson, Walt (12–13) pitcher: 9–26 with 3.61 ERA in 55 games; one save.

DIDIER, BOB (69–72) catcher: 161-for-715, .225, in 235 games.

Diehl, Ernie (06, 09) outfielder; shortstop: 7-for-15, .467, in four games.

Diehl, George (42–43) pitcher: 0–0 with 3.52 ERA in two games, both relief.

DIETZ, DICK (73) catcher; first baseman: 41-for-139, .295, in 83 games.

Dillard, Don (63, 65) outfielder: 31-for-138, .225, in 87 games.

DiMaggio, Vince (37–38) outfielder; second baseman: 249-for-1,033, .241, in 282 games.

Dinneen, Bill (00–01) pitcher: 35–32 with 3.03 ERA in 77 games.

Dittmer, Jack (52–56) second baseman: 278-for-1,196, .232, in 379 games.

DOBSON, PAT (73) pitcher: 3–7 with 4.99 ERA in 12 games.

Doll, Art (36, 38) pitcher: 0–1 with 3.00 ERA in four games; catcher: 2-for-13, .154, in seven games.

Donlin, Mike (11) outfielder: 70-for-222, .315, in 56 games.

Donnelly, Blix (51) pitcher: 0–1 with 7.36 ERA in six games, all relief.

Donnelly, Ed (11–12) pitcher: 8–12 with 4.03 ERA in 42 games.

Donovan, Bill (42–43) pitcher: 4–6 with 3.20 ERA in 38 games.

Donovan, Dick (50–52) pitcher: 0–4 with 6.87 ERA in 25 games; one save.

Dorner, Gus (06–09) pitcher: 29–62 with 3.40 ERA in 113 games; one save.

DOYLE, PAUL (69) pitcher: 2–0 with 2.08 ERA in 36 games, all relief; four saves.

Drabowsky, Moe (61) pitcher: 0–2 with 4.62 ERA in 16 games, all relief; two saves.

Dreesen, Bill (31) third baseman: 40-for-180, .222, in 48 games.

Dresser, Bob (02) pitcher: 0–1 with 3.00 ERA in one game, start.

Drews, Frank (44–45) outfielder: 59-for-288, .205, in 95 games.

Dudra, John (41) second baseman; third baseman; first baseman; shortstop: 9-for-25, .360, in 14 games.

Dugan, Joe (29) third baseman; short-

stop; second baseman; outfielder: 38-for-125, .304, in 60 games.

Dugey, Oscar (13–14, 20) third baseman; second baseman; shortstop; outfielder; pinch runner: 23-for-117, .197, in 68 games.

Dunlap, Bill (29–30) outfielder: 14-for-58, .241, in 26 games.

E

Earley, Tom (38–42, 45) pitcher: 18–24 with 3.78 ERA in 91 games; five saves.

Eason, Mal (02) pitcher: 9–11 with 2.75 ERA in 27 games.

EASTERLY, JAMIE (74–79) pitcher: 8–20 with 5.72 ERA in 91 games; two saves.

EAVE, GARY (88–89) pitcher: 2–0 with 2.81 ERA in eight games.

Eayrs, Eddie (20–21) outfielder: 81-for-259, .313, in 102 games; pitcher: 1–2 with 7.26 ERA in nine games.

Eckhardt, Ox (32) pinch hitter: 2-for-8, .250, in eight games.

Edelman, John (55) pitcher: 0–0 with 11.12 ERA in five games, all relief.

EDEN, MIKE (76) second baseman: 0-for-8, .000, in five games.

Edwards, Foster (25–28) pitcher: 6–9 with 4.60 ERA in 54 games.

Egan, Dick (15–16) second baseman; shortstop; third baseman; outfielder; first baseman: 110-for-458, .240, in 166 games.

EICHELBERGER, JUAN (88) pitcher: 2–0 with 3.86 ERA in 20 games, all relief.

EICHHORN, MARK (89) pitcher: 5–5 with 4.35 ERA in 45 games, all relief.

Eilers, Dave (64–65) pitcher: 0–0 with 7.15 ERA in 12 games, all relief.

Elliott, Bob (47–51) third baseman: 763-for-2,588, .295, in 718 games.

Elliott, Glenn (47–49) pitcher: 4–5 with 4.08 ERA in 34 games; one save.

Elliott, Jumbo (34) pitcher: 1–1 with 5.87 ERA in seven games.

Elliott, Rowdy (10) catcher: 0-for-2, .000, in three games.

Emmerich, Bob (23) outfielder: 2-for-24, .083, in 13 games.

English, Gil (37–38) third baseman; shortstop; outfielder; second baseman: 119-for-434, .274, in 132 games.

Errickson, Dick (38–42) pitcher: 35–46 with 3.84 ERA in 155 games; 13 saves.

Dick Errickson

ESASKY, NICK (90) first baseman: 6-for-35, .171, in nine games.

Estock, George (51) pitcher: 0–1 with 4.33 ERA in 37 games; three saves.

Etchison, Buck (43–44) first baseman: 72-for-327, .220, in 119 games.

Evans, Chick (09–10) pitcher: 1–4 with 4.96 ERA in 17 games; two saves.

EVANS, DARRELL (69–76, 89) third baseman; outfielder; first baseman: 712-for-2,896, .246, in 866 games.

Evers, Johnny (14–17, 29) second baseman: 278-for-1,093, .254, in 318 games.

F

FALCONE, PETE (83–84) pitcher: 14–11 with 3.89 ERA in 68 games; two saves.

Fallenstein, Ed (33) pitcher: 2–1 with 3.60 ERA in nine games.

Farrell, Doc (27–29) shortstop; second baseman; third baseman: 229-for-915, .250, in 249 games.

Farrell, Kerby (43) first baseman: 75-for-280, .268, in 85 games; pitcher: 0–1 with 4.30 ERA in five games, all relief.

Felix, Gus (23–25) outfielder; second baseman; third baseman: 322-for-1,169, .275, in 319 games.

Ferguson, George (08–11) pitcher: 24–44 with 3.54 ERA in 105 games.

Fernandez, Nanny (42, 46–47) third baseman; outfielder; shortstop: 285-for-1,158, .246, in 343 games.

Ferrell, Wes (41) pitcher: 2–1 with 5.14 ERA in four games.

Fette, Lou (37–40, 45) pitcher: 41–40 with 3.17 ERA in 107 games; one save.

Fillingim, Dana (18–23) pitcher: 46–68 with 3.51 ERA in 187 games; five saves.

FISCHER, HANK (62–66) pitcher: 27–28 with 4.23 ERA in 142 games; six saves.

FISCHLIN, MIKE (87) pinch runner: 0-for-0, —, in one game.

Fisher, Tom (04) pitcher: 6–16 with 4.25 ERA in 31 games.

Fitzberger, Charlie (28) pinch hitter: 2-for-7, .286, in seven games.

Fitzpatrick, Ed (15–17) second baseman; outfielder; third baseman: 158-for-697, .227, in 251 games.

Flaherty, Patsy (07–08, 11) pitcher: 24–35 with 3.11 in 62 games; outfielder: 61-for-295, .207, in 111 games.

Fletcher, Elbie (34–35, 37–39, 49) first baseman: 448-for-1,739, .258, in 499 games.

Ford, Gene (36) pitcher: 0–0 with 13.50 ERA in two games.

Ford, Hod (19–23, 32–33) shortstop; second baseman; third baseman; first baseman: 493-for-1,845, .267, in 549 games.

FORD, WENTY (73) pitcher: 1–2 with 5.51 ERA in four games.

FORSTER, TERRY (83–85) pitcher: 7–5 with 2.29 ERA in 127 games, all relief; 19 saves.

FOSTER, LEO (71, 73–74) shortstop; second baseman; third baseman; outfielder: 23-for-128, .180, in 84 games.

Fournier, Jack (27) first baseman: 106-for-374, .283, in 122 games.

Fox, Terry (60) pitcher: 0–0 with 4.32 ERA in five games, all relief.

FRANCONA, TITO (67–69) first baseman; outfielder: 188-for-688, .273, in 255 games.

Frankhouse, Fred (30–35, 39) pitcher: 63–61 with 3.88 ERA in 233 games; eight saves.

Fraser, Chick (05) pitcher: 14–21 with 3.28 ERA in 39 games.

Hod Ford

Tito Francona

Frasier, Vic (37) pitcher: 0–0 with 5.63 ERA in three games, all relief.

Freeman, Buck (00) outfielder; first baseman: 126-for-418, .301, in 117 games.

FREEMAN, JIMMY (72–73) pitcher: 2–4 with 6.87 ERA in 19 games; one save.

FREEMAN, MARVIN (90–93) pitcher: 11–5 with 3.44 ERA in 122 games, all relief; four saves.

Freigau, Howard (28) shortstop; second baseman: 28-for-109, .257, in 52 games.

FRIAS, PEPE (79) shortstop: 123-for-475, .259, in 140 games.

FRISELLA, DANNY (73–74) pitcher: 4–6 with 4.67 ERA in 78 games; 14 saves.

Frock, Sam (07, 10–11) pitcher: 13–22 with 3.31 ERA in 54 games; two saves.

FULLER, JOHN (74) outfielder: 1-for-3, .333, in three games.

Funk, Frank (63) pitcher: 3–3 with 2.68 ERA in 25 games, all relief.

G

Gabler, Frank (37–38) pitcher: 4–7 with 5.42 ERA in 20 games; two saves.

Gabrielson, Len (60, 63–64) outfielder; first baseman; third baseman: 33-for-158, .209, in 74 games.

GALLAGHER, DAVE (94) outfielder: 34-for-152, .224, in 89 games.

Gallagher, Gil (22) shortstop: 1-for-22, .045, in seven games.

Gammons, Daff (01) outfielder; second baseman; third baseman: 18-for-93, .194, in 28 games.

GANT, RON (87–93) outfielder; second baseman; third baseman: 836-for-3,192, .262, in 858 games.

GARBER, GENE (78–87) pitcher: 53–73 with 3.34 ERA in 557 games; 141 saves.

GARCIA, DAMASO (88) second baseman: 7-for-60, .117, in 21 games.

Garms, Debs (37–39) outfielder; third baseman; second baseman: 412-for-1,419, .290, in 374 games.

GARR, RALPH (68–75) outfielder; pinch hitter: 1,022-for-3,222, .317, in 800 games.

GARRETT, ADRIAN (66) outfielder: 0-for-3, .000, in four games.

GARRIDO, GIL (68–72) shortstop; second baseman; third baseman: 205-for-847, .242, in 320 games.

GASTON, CITO (67, 75–78) outfielder; first baseman: 126-for-503, .250, in 258 games.

GATEWOOD, AUBREY (70) pitcher: 0–0 with 4.50 ERA in three games, all relief.

Gautreau, Doc (25–28) second baseman; shortstop: 207-for-799, .259, in 257 games.

Gearin, Dinty (24) pitcher: 0–1 with ∞ ERA in one game, start.

Geier, Phil (04) outfielder; third baseman; second baseman; shortstop: 141-for-580, .243, in 149 games.

GEIGER, GARY (66–67) outfielder: 52-for-243, .214, in 147 games.

Genewich, Joe (22–28) pitcher: 57–76 with 4.18 ERA in 207 games; five saves.

Gentile, Sam (43) pinch hitter: 1-for-4, .250, in eight games.

GENTRY, GARY (73–75) pitcher: 5–7 with 3.57 ERA in 26 games; one save.

George, Lefty (18) pitcher: 1–5 with 2.32 ERA in nine games.

Geraghty, Ben (43–44) second baseman; shortstop; third baseman: 4-for-17, .235, in 19 games.

Gervais, Lefty (13) pitcher: 0–1 with 5.74 ERA in five games.

Getz, Gus (09–10) third baseman; second baseman; outfielder; shortstop: 61-for-292, .209, in 94 games.

Gibson, Frank (21–27) catcher; first baseman; third baseman: 309-for-1,098, .281, in 448 games.

Giggie, Bob (59–60) pitcher: 1–0 with 4.07 ERA in 16 games, all relief; one save.

Gilbert, Larry (14–15) outfielder: 76-for-330, .230, in 117 games.

GILBREATH, ROD (72–78) second baseman; third baseman; shortstop: 356-for-1,436, .248, in 500 games.

Gillenwater, Carden (45–46) outfielder: 200-for-741, .270, in 243 games.

Gladu, Roland (44) third baseman; outfielder: 16-for-66, .242, in 21 games.

GLAVINE, TOM (87–) current Braves pitcher.

Glossop, Al (40) second baseman; third baseman; shortstop: 35-for-148, .236, in 60 games.

GOGGIN, CHUCK (73) second baseman; outfielder; shortstop; catcher: 26-for-90, .289, in 64 games.

Goldsmith, Hal (26–28) pitcher: 6–10 with 3.98 ERA in 45 games; one save.

GOMEZ, LUIS (80–81) shortstop; third baseman; second baseman: 60-for-313, .192, in 156 games; pitcher: 0–0 with 27.00 ERA in one game, relief.

Gonder, Jesse (65) catcher: 8-for-53, .151, in 31 games.

Gonzalez, Mike (12) catcher: 0-for-2, .000, in one game.

GONZALEZ, TONY (69–70) outfielder: 208-for-750, .277, in 212 games.

Good, Gene (06) outfielder: 18-for-119, .151, in 34 games.

Good, Ralph (10) pitcher: 0–0 with 2.00 ERA in two games, relief.

Good, Wilbur (10–11) outfielder: 73-for-251, .291, in 66 games.

GOODSON, ED (75) first baseman; third baseman: 16-for-76, .211, in 47 games.

Gordon, Sid (50–53) 582-for-2,017, .289, in 568 games.

Gorin, Charles (54–55) pitcher: 0–1 with 3.60 ERA in seven games, all relief.

Gowdy, Hank (11–17, 19–23, 29–30) catcher; first baseman: 595-for-2,290, .260, in 852 games.

Graham, Peaches (08–11) catcher; outfielder; third baseman; second baseman; first baseman; shortstop: 229-for-861, .266, in 310 games.

Graham, Skinny (24–26) pitcher: 10–19 with 4.89 ERA in 54 games; one save.

GRANT, MARK (90) pitcher: 1–2 with 4.64 ERA in 33 games; three saves.

Graves, Sid (27) outfielder: 5-for-20, .250, in seven games.

GREENE, TOMMY (89–90) pitcher: 2–2 with 5.35 ERA in nine games.

Greenfield, Kent (27–29) pitcher: 14–25 with 4.77 ERA in 65 games.

Ken Griffey

GREGG, TOMMY (88–92) outfielder; first baseman: 165-for-670, .246, in 327 games.

Gremminger, Ed (02–03) third baseman: 269-for-1,033, .260, in 280 games.

Gremp, Buddy (40–42) first baseman; second baseman; catcher; third baseman: 65-for-291, .223, in 113 games.

GRIFFEY, KEN (86–88) outfielder; first baseman: 252-for-884, .285, in 271 games.

Griffin, Hank (11–12) pitcher: 0–6 with 5.65 ERA in 18 games.

Griffith, Tommy (13–14) outfielder: 37-for-175, .211, in 53 games.

Grimes, Burleigh (30) pitcher: 3–5 with 7.35 ERA in 11 games.

Grossart, George (01) outfielder: 3-for-26, .115, in seven games.

GUINN, SKIP (68) pitcher: 0–0 with 3.60 ERA in three games, all relief.

Gyselman, Dick (33–34) third baseman; second baseman; shortstop: 43-for-191, .225, in 82 games.

H

Haas, Eddie (58, 60) outfielder: 12-for-46, .261, in 41 games.

Haefner, Mickey (50) pitcher: 0–2 with 5.63 ERA in eight games.

Haid, Hal (31) pitcher: 0–2 with 4.50 ERA in 27 games, all relief; one save.

Hale, Dad (02) pitcher: 1–4 with 6.32 ERA in eight games.

HALL, ALBERT (81–88) outfielder; pinch runner: 196-for-772, .254, in 355 games.

Hall, Bob (49–50) pitcher: 6–6 with 5.41 ERA in 52 games.

HALL, JIMMIE (70) outfielder: 10-for-47, .213, in 39 games.

Hanebrink, Harry (53, 57–58) third baseman; outfielder; second baseman: 46-for-220, .209, in 120 games.

HANNA, PRESTON (75–82) pitcher: 17–21 with 4.49 ERA in 133 games; one save.

Hannifin, Jack (08) third baseman; second baseman; shortstop; outfielder: 53-for-257, .206, in 90 games.

HARDIN, JIM (72) pitcher: 5–2 with 4.41 ERA in 26 games; two saves.

HARGAN, STEVE (77) pitcher: 0–3 with 6.87 ERA in 16 games.

Hargrave, Pinky (32–33) catcher: 70-for-290, .241, in 127 games.

Harley, Dick (05) pitcher: 2–5 with 4.66 ERA in nine games.

Harper, George (29) outfielder: 133-for-457, .291, in 136 games.

HARPER, TERRY (80–86) outfielder: 339-for-1,337, .254, in 473 games.

Harris, Dave (25, 28) outfielder: 92-for-357, .258, in 99 games.

HARRISON, RORIC (73–75) pitcher: 20–23 with 4.50 ERA in 73 games; six saves.

Hartman, Bob (59) pitcher: 0–0 with 27.00 ERA in three games, all relief.

Hartsfield, Roy (50–52) second baseman: 266-for-976, .273, in 265 games.

Haslin, Mickey (36) third baseman; second baseman: 29-for-104, .279, in 36 games.

Hassett, Buddy (39–41) first baseman; outfielder: 409-for-1,453, .281, in 389 games.

HAUSMAN, TOM (82) pitcher: 0–0 with 4.91 ERA in three games, all relief.

Hazle, Bob (57–58) outfielder: 64-for-190, .337, in 61 games.

Hearn, Bunn (18, 20) pitcher: 5–9 with 3.30 ERA in 28 games.

Hearn, Bunny (26–29) pitcher: 7–11 with 4.38 ERA in 59 games; two saves.

Heath, Jeff (48–49) outfielder: 150-for-475, .316, in 151 games.

HEATH, MIKE (91) catcher: 29-for-139, .209, in 49 games.

HEEP, DANNY (91) first baseman; outfielder: 5-for-12, .417, in 14 games.

Heltzel, Heinie (43) third baseman: 13-for-86, .151, in 29 games.

Roy Hartsfield

HENDERSON, KEN (76) outfielder: 114-for-435, .262, in 133 games.

Hendley, Bob (61–63) pitcher: 25–29 with 3.78 ERA in 95 games; four saves.

Hendrickson, Don (45–46) pitcher: 4–9 with 4.90 ERA in 39 games; five saves.

HENRY, DWAYNE (89–90) pitcher: 2–4 with 5.29 ERA in 46 games; one save.

Henry, John (18) catcher: 21-for-102, .206, in 43 games.

Henry, Snake (22–23) first baseman; pinch hitter: 14-for-75, .187, in 29 games.

HERBEL, RON (71) pitcher: 0–1 with 5.23 ERA in 25 games, all relief; one save.

Herman, Billy (46) second baseman; third baseman; first baseman: 77-for-252, .306, in 75 games.

Hermann, Albert (23–24) second baseman; third baseman; first baseman; pinch hitter: 22-for-94, .234, in 32 games.

HERMOSO, ANGEL (67) shortstop;

Billy Herman

second baseman: 8-for-26, .308, in 11 games.

HERNANDEZ, RAMON (67) pitcher: 0–2 with 4.18 ERA in 46 games, all relief; five saves.

HERRNSTEIN, JOHN (66) outfielder: 4-for-18, .222, in 17 games.

Hersh, Earl (56) outfielder: 3-for-13, .231, in seven games.

Hershey, Frank (05) pitcher: 0–1 with 6.75 ERA in one game, start.

Herzog, Buck (10–11, 18–19) third baseman; shortstop; second baseman; first baseman: 371-for-1,422, .261, in 376 games.

HESKETH, JOE (90) pitcher: 0–2 with 5.81 ERA in 31 games, all relief; five saves.

Hess, Otto (12–15) pitcher: 24–41 with 3.68 ERA in 80 games; one save; first baseman: 62-for-229, .271, in 104 games.

Heving, Joe (45) pitcher: 1–0 with 3.38 ERA in three games, all relief.

Hickey, Jim (42, 44) pitcher: 0–1 with 6.75 ERA in nine games.

High, Andy (25–27) third baseman; second baseman; shortstop: 320-for-1,079, .297, in 303 games.

HILL, GARRY (69) pitcher: 0–1 with 15.43 ERA in one game, start.

Buck Herzog

HILL, MILT (94) pitcher: 0–0 with 7.94 ERA in 10 games, all relief.

Hill, Oliver (39) pinch hitter: 1-for-2, .500, in two games.

Hinton, John (01) third baseman: 1-for-13, .077, in four games.

HIPPAUF, HERB (66) pitcher: 0–1 with 13.50 ERA in three games, all relief.

Hitchcock, Jim (38) shortstop; third baseman: 13-for-76, .171, in 28 games.

Hodgin, Ralph (39) outfielder: 10-for-48, .208, in 32 games.

Hoeft, Billy (64) pitcher: 4–0 with 3.80 ERA in 42 games, all relief; four saves.

HOERNER, JOE (72–73) pitcher: 3–5 with 6.50 ERA in 45 games, all relief; four saves.

Hofferth, Stew (44–46) catcher: 88-for-408, .216, in 136 games.

Hoffman, Izzy (07) outfielder: 24-for-86, .279, in 19 games.

Hogan, Shanty (25–27, 33–35) catcher; outfielder: 281-for-1,034, .272, in 331 games.

Hogg, Brad (11–12) pitcher: 1–4 with 6.83 ERA in 18 games; two saves.

Hogue, Bobby (48–51) pitcher: 13–9 with 3.74 ERA in 112 games; 12 saves.

Holke, Walter (19–22) first baseman: 579-for-2,043, .283, in 536 games.

Holland, Dutch (32–33) outfielder: 54-for-187, .289, in 52 games.

Hollingsworth, Bonnie (28) pitcher: 0–2 with 5.24 ERA in seven games.

Holmes, Tommy (42–51) outfielder: 1,503-for-4,956, .303, in 1,289 games.

Hood, Abie (25) second baseman: 6-for-21, .286, in five games.

Hoover, Dick (52) pitcher: 0–0 with 7.71 ERA in two games, relief.

Hopp, Johnny (46–47) outfielder; first baseman: 272-for-875, .311, in 263 games.

HORNER, BOB (78–86) third baseman; first baseman: 994-for-3,571, .278, in 960 games.

Hornsby, Rogers (28) second baseman: 188-for-486, .387, in 140 games.

HOUSE, TOM (71–75) pitcher: 18–11 with 3.06 ERA in 185 games; 28 saves.

Houser, Ben (11–12) first baseman: 113-for-403, .280, in 128 games.

Howard, Del (06–07) outfielder; second baseman; shortstop; first baseman: 193-for-732, .264, in 197 games.

HOWARD, LARRY (73) catcher: 1-for-8, .125, in four games.

HOWELL, JAY (93) pitcher: 3–3 with 2.31 ERA in 54 games, all relief.

HRABOSKY, AL (80–82) pitcher: 7–4 with 3.51 ERA in 100 games, all relief; seven saves.

HRINIAK, WALT (68–69) catcher: 10-for-33, .303, in 16 games.

HUBBARD, GLENN (78–87) second baseman: 983-for-4,016, .245, in 1,196 games.

Huber, Otto (39) second baseman; third baseman: 6-for-22, .273, in 11 games.

Hughes, Tom (14–18) pitcher: 39–22 with 2.22 ERA in 106 games; 14 saves.

Hulihan, Harry (22) pitcher: 2–3 with 3.15 ERA in seven games.

Hunnefield, Bill (31) third baseman; second baseman: 6-for-21, .286, in 11 games.

HUNTER, BRIAN (91–93) first baseman; outfielder: 136-for-589, .231, in 236 games.

Huston, Warren (44) third baseman; shortstop; second baseman: 11-for-55, .200, in 33 games.

Hutchings, Johnny (41–42, 44–46) pitcher: 10–17 with 4.01 ERA in 128 games; six saves.

Hutchinson, Ira (37–38, 44–45) pitcher: 24–24 with 3.59 ERA in 118 games; six saves.

I

INFANTE, ALEXIS (90) second baseman; third baseman; shortstop: 1-for-28, .036, in 20 games.

Ingerton, Scotty (11) third baseman; outfielder; first baseman; second baseman; shortstop: 130-for-521, .250, in 136 games.

J

Jacklitsch, Fred (17) catcher: 0-for-0, —, in one game.

Jackson, George (11–13) outfielder: 158-for-554, .285, in 152 games.

JACKSON, SONNY (68–74) shortstop; outfielder; third baseman: 459-for-1,890, .243, in 637 games.

JACOBY, BROOK (81, 83) third baseman: 2-for-18, .111, in 15 games.

James, Bernie (29–30) second baseman; outfielder: 33-for-112, .295, in 54 games.

James, Bill (13–19) pitcher: 37–21 with 2.28 ERA in 84 games; two saves.

JAMES, DION (87–89) outfielder: 297-for-1,050, .283, in 329 games.

JARVIS, PAT (66–72) pitcher: 83–72 with 3.59 ERA in 221 games; three saves.

JASTER, LARRY (70, 72) pitcher: 2–2 with 6.23 ERA in 19 games.

Javery, Al (40–46) pitcher: 53–74 with 3.80 ERA in 205 games; five saves.

JAY, JOEY (53–60, 66) pitcher: 24–28 with 3.39 ERA in 124 games; three saves.

Jeffcoat, George (43) pitcher: 1–2 with 3.06 ERA in eight games.

Jester, Virgil (52–53) pitcher: 3–5 with 3.84 ERA in 21 games.

Jethroe, Sam (50–52) outfielder: 460-for-1,762, .261, in 440 games.

JIMENEZ, GERMAN (88) pitcher: 1–6 with 5.01 ERA in 15 games.

Johnson, Arthur (40–42) pitcher: 7–16 with 3.68 ERA in 49 games; one save.

JOHNSON, BOB D. (77) pitcher: 0–1 with 7.25 ERA in 15 games, all relief.

JOHNSON, BOB W. (68) third baseman; second baseman: 49-for-187, .262, in 59 games.

JOHNSON, DAVEY (73–75) second baseman; first baseman; pinch hitter: 266-for-1,014, .262, in 294 games.

JOHNSON, DERON (68) first baseman; third baseman: 71-for-342, .208, in 127 games.

Johnson, Ernie (50, 52–58) pitcher: 36–22 with 3.74 ERA in 242 games; 18 saves.

JOHNSON, JOE (85–86) pitcher: 10–11 with 4.53 ERA in 32 games.

JOHNSON, KEN (65–69) pitcher: 45–34 with 3.22 ERA in 130 games; three saves.

Al Javery

Johnson, Lou (62) outfielder: 33-for-117, .282, in 61 games.

JOHNSON, RANDY (82–84) third baseman; second baseman: 129-for-484, .267, in 204 games.

Johnson, Roy (37–38) outfielder; third baseman: 77-for-289, .266, in 92 games.

Johnson, Si (46–47) pitcher: 12–10 with 3.45 ERA in 64 games; three saves.

Johnston, Jimmy (26) third baseman; second baseman; outfielder: 14-for-57, .246, in 23 games.

Jolly, David (53–57) pitcher: 16–14 with 3.77 ERA in 159 games; 19 saves.

Jones, Bill (11–12) outfielder; pinch hitter: 12-for-53, .226, in 27 games.

JONES, CHIPPER (93–) current Braves player.

Jones, Johnny (20) pitcher: 1–0 with 6.52 ERA in three games.

Jones, Ken (30) pitcher: 0–1 with 5.95 ERA in eight games.

JONES, MACK (61–63, 65–67) outfielder; first baseman: 516-for-2,040, .253, in 613 games.

Jones, Nippy (57) first baseman; outfielder: 21-for-79, .266, in 30 games.

Jones, Percy (29) pitcher: 7–15 with 4.64 ERA in 35 games.

Jones, Sheldon (52) pitcher: 1–4 with 4.76 ERA in 39 games; one save.

Joost, Eddie (43, 45) second baseman; third baseman; shortstop: 113-for-562, .201, in 159 games.

Jordan, Buck (32–37) first baseman; third baseman; outfielder; pinch hitter: 700-for-2,322, .301, in 601 games.

Mack Jones

Buck Jordan

JORGENSEN, MIKE (83–84) first baseman; outfielder: 19-for-74, .257, in 88 games.

JUSTICE, DAVID (89–) current Braves player.

K

Kahle, Bob (38) pinch hitter: 1-for-3, .333, in eight games.

Kahn, Owen (30) pinch runner: 0-for-0, —, in one game.

Kaiser, Al (11–12) outfielder: 40-for-210, .190, in 70 games.

Kamp, Ike (24–25) pitcher: 2–5 with 5.10 ERA in 25 games.

Kane, Tom (38) second baseman: 0-for-2, .000, in two games.

Karl, Andy (47) pitcher: 2–3 with 3.86 ERA in 27 games, all relief; three saves.

Keating, Ray (19) pitcher: 7–11 with 2.98 ERA in 22 games.

Kelleher, John (24) pinch hitter: 0-for-1, .000, in one game.

KELLEY, DICK (64–68) pitcher: 12–19 with 3.31 ERA in 113 games.

KELLEY, TOM (71–73) pitcher: 14–13 with 3.64 ERA in 62 games.

Kelly, Joe (17–19) outfielder: 144-for-664, .217, in 181 games.

KELLY, MIKE (94) outfielder: 73-for-255, .286, in 63 games.

KELLY, ROBERTO (94–) current Braves player.

Kenney, Art (38) pitcher: 0–0 with 15.43 ERA in two games, both relief.

KEOUGH, MARTY (66) first baseman; outfielder: 1-for-17, .059, in 17 games.

KERFELD, CHARLIE (90) pitcher: 3–1 with 5.58 ERA in 25 games, all relief; two saves.

Buddy Kerr

Kerr, Buddy (50–51) shortstop; second baseman: 147-for-679, .216, in 224 games.

KESTER, RICK (68–70) pitcher: 0–0 with 5.98 ERA in 21 games, all relief.

Kibbie, Hod (25) second baseman; shortstop: 11-for-41, .268, in 11 games.

KING, HAL (70–71) catcher: 94-for-402, .234, in 175 games.

King, Lee (19) pinch hitter: 0-for-1, .000, in two games.

Kirke, Jay (11–13) outfielder; first baseman; second baseman; shortstop; third baseman: 156-for-486, .321, in 141 games.

Kittridge, Malachi (01–03) catcher: 177-for-735, .241, in 226 games.

Klaus, Billy (52–53) shortstop: 0-for-6, .000, in nine games.

KLESKO, RYAN (92–) current Braves player.

Klimchock, Lou (62–65) second baseman; pinch hitter; first baseman; third baseman: 19-for-114, .167, in 76 games.

KLINE, RON (70) pitcher: 0–0 with 7.11 ERA in five games, all relief; one save.

KLINE, STEVE (77) pitcher: 0–0 with 6.64 ERA in 16 games, all relief; one save.

Kling, Johnny (11–12) catcher; third baseman: 134-for-493, .272, in 156 games.

Klopp, Stan (44) pitcher: 1–2 with 4.27 ERA in 24 games, all relief.

Kluttz, Clyde (42–45) catcher: 195-for-727, .268, in 244 games.

Knetzer, Elmer (16) pitcher: 0–2 with 7.20 ERA in two games, both relief.

Knight, Jack (27) pitcher: 0–0 with 15.00 ERA in three games, all relief.

Knothe, Fritz (32–33) third baseman; shortstop: 118-for-502, .235, in 133 games.

Knotts, Joe (07) catcher: 0-for-8, .000, in three games.

Kolb, Gary (64–65) outfielder; third baseman; second baseman; catcher: 19-for-91, .209, in 60 games.

KOMMINSK, BRAD (83–86) outfielder; third baseman: 139-for-642, .217, in 220 games.

Konetchy, Ed (16–18) first baseman; outfielder: 379-for-1,477, .257, in 407 games; pitcher: 0–1 with 6.75 ERA in one game, start.

Konstanty, Jim (46) pitcher: 0–1 with 5.28 ERA in 10 games.

KOPACZ, GEORGE (66) first baseman: 0-for-9, .000, in six games.

Kopf, Larry (22–23) shortstop; second baseman; third baseman: 162-for-604, .268, in 165 games.

Koppe, Joe (58) shortstop: 4-for-9, .444, in 16 games.

Koslo, Dave (54–55) pitcher: 1–2 with 3.63 ERA in 13 games, all relief; one save.

Kowalik, Fabian (36) pitcher: 0–1 with 8.00 ERA in one game, start.

Kraft, Clarence (14) first baseman: 1-for-3, .333, in three games.

KRAUSSE, LEW (74) pitcher: 4–3 with 4.18 ERA in 29 games.

KREMERS, JIMMY (90) catcher: 8-for-73, .110, in 29 games.

Kroh, Rube (12) pitcher: 0–0 with 5.68 ERA in three games.

Krsnich, Mike (60, 62) outfielder; first baseman; third baseman: 4-for-21, .190, in 15 games.

Kruger, Art (10) 0-for-1, .000, in one game.

Kuczek, Steve (49) pinch hitter: 1-for-1, 1.000, in one game.

L

LaCORTE, FRANK (75–79) pitcher: 4–24 with 6.23 ERA in 44 games.

LACY, LEE (76) second baseman; outfielder; third baseman: 49-for-180, .272, in 50 games.

Lakeman, Al (49) first baseman: 1-for-6, .167, in three games.

Lamanna, Hank (40–42) pitcher: 6–5 with 5.24 ERA in 45 games; one save.

Lane, Hunter (24) third baseman; second baseman: 1-for-15, .067, in seven games.

Lanfranconi, Walt (47) pitcher: 4–4 with 2.95 ERA in 36 games; one save.

Lanning, Johnny (36–39, 47) pitcher: 25–31 with 3.71 ERA in 132 games; six saves.

Lansing, Gene (22) pitcher: 0–1 with 5.98 ERA in 15 games.

Larker, Norm (63) first baseman: 26-for-147, .177, in 64 games.

Larsen, Swede (36) second baseman: 0-for-1, .000, in three games.

LaRUSSA, TONY (71) second baseman: 2-for-7, .286, in nine games.

Lary, Frank (64) pitcher: 1–0 with 4.38 ERA in five games.

LAU, CHARLIE (60–61, 67) catcher; pinch hitter: 36-for-180, .200, in 101 games.

Lauterborn, Bill (04–05) second baseman; third baseman; shortstop; outfielder: 56-for-269, .208, in 87 games.

Lawson, Bob (01) pitcher: 2–2 with 3.33 ERA in six games.

Leach, Freddy (32) outfielder: 55-for-223, .247, in 84 games.

Lee, Bill (45–46) pitcher: 16–12 with 3.58 ERA in 41 games.

Lee, Hal (33–36) outfielder; second baseman: 492-for-1,820, .270, in 491 games.

Lefler, Wade (24) pinch hitter: 0-for-1, .000, in one game.

Legett, Lou (29) catcher: 13-for-81, .160, in 39 games.

LEIBRANDT, CHARLIE (90–92) pitcher: 39–31 with 3.35 ERA in 92 games.

LEMASTER, DENNY (62–67) pitcher: 58–59 with 3.63 ERA in 192 games.

LEMKE, MARK (88–   ) current Braves player.

LEON, MAX (73–78) pitcher: 14–18 with 3.71 ERA in 162 games; 13 saves.

Leverett, Dixie (29) pitcher: 3–7 with 6.36 ERA in 24 games; one save.

Lewis, Bill (35–36) catcher: 19-for-66, .288, in 35 games.

Liddle, Don (53) pitcher: 7–6 with 3.08 ERA in 31 games; two saves.

Liese, Fred (10) pinch hitter: 0-for-4, .000, in five games.

LILLIQUIST, DEREK (89–90) pitcher: 10–18 with 4.59 ERA in 44 games.

LINARES, RUFINO (81–82, 84) outfielder: 136-for-502, .271, in 189 games.

Lindaman, Vive (06–09) pitcher: 36–60 with 2.92 ERA in 131 games; two saves.

Lindemann, Ernie (07) pitcher: 0–0 with 5.68 ERA in one game, start.

Linden, Walt (50) catcher: 2-for-5, .400, in three games.

Lindquist, Carl (43–44) pitcher: 0–2 with 4.98 ERA in seven games.

Littlefield, Dick (58) pitcher: 0–1 with 4.26 ERA in four games; one save.

Litwhiler, Danny (46–48) outfielder; third baseman: 140-for-506, .277, in 183 games.

Brad Komminsk

Charlie Lau

Rufino Linares

Danny Litwhiler

Livingston, Mickey (49) catcher: 15-for-64, .234, in 28 games.

Loane, Bob (40) outfielder: 5-for-22, .227, in 13 games.

Logan, Bob (45) pitcher: 7–11 with 3.18 ERA in 34 games; one save.

Logan, Johnny (51–61) shortstop: 1,329-for-4,931, .270, in 1,351 games.

Lombardi, Ernie (42) catcher: 102-for-309, .330, in 105 games.

Long, Red (02) pitcher: 0–0 with 1.13 ERA in one game, start.

Lopata, Stan (59–60) catcher; first baseman: 6-for-56, .107, in 32 games.

Lopez, Al (36–40) catcher; first baseman: 373-for-1,527, .244, in 471 games.

LOPEZ, JAVIER (92–) current Braves player.

Lord, Bris (13) outfielder: 59-for-235, .251, in 73 games.

Low, Fletcher (15) third baseman: 1-for-4, .250, in one game.

Lucas, Red (24–25) second baseman; third baseman: 14-for-53, .264, in

Javier Lopez

39 games; pitcher: 1–4 with 5.16 ERA in 27 games.

LUECKEN, RICK (90) pitcher: 1–4 with 5.77 ERA in 36 games, all relief; one save.

LUM, MIKE (67–75, 79–81) outfielder; first baseman: 773-for-3,089, .250, in 1,225 games.

Luque, Dolf (14–15) pitcher: 0–1 with 3.95 ERA in four games.

Lush, Billy (01–02) outfielder; third baseman: 97-for-440, .220, in 127 games.

Lyons, Al (48) pitcher: 1–0 with 7.82 ERA in seven games, all relief.

LYONS, STEVE (92) outfielder; second baseman: 1-for-14, .071, in 11 games.

M

MacFayden, Danny (35–39, 43) pitcher: 60–64 with 3.40 ERA in 169 games; two saves.

MACHA, MIKE (79) third baseman: 2-for-13, .154, in six games.

Mack, Joe (45) first baseman: 60-for-260, .231, in 66 games.

MacKenzie, Ken (60–61) pitcher: 0–2 with 5.87 ERA in 14 games, all relief.

Macon, Max (44, 47) pitcher: 0–0 with 12.60 ERA in two games, both relief; first baseman, outfielder: 100-for-367, .272, in 107 games.

MacPherson, Harry (44) pitcher: 0–0 with 0.00 ERA in one game, relief.

Madden, Tommy (06) outfielder: 4-for-15, .267, in four games.

MADDOX, JERRY (78) third baseman: 3-for-14, .214, in seven games.

MADDUX, GREG (93–) current Braves pitcher.

Magee, Sherry (15–17) outfielder; first baseman; shortstop: 324-for-1,236, .262, in 350 games.

Maggert, Harl (38) outfielder; third baseman: 25-for-89, .281, in 66 games.

Maguire, Freddie (29–31) second baseman; shortstop: 375-for-1,504, .249, in 432 games.

MAHLER, MICKEY (77–79) pitcher: 10–24 with 5.27 ERA in 65 games.

MAHLER, RICK (79–88, 91) pitcher: 79–89 with 4.00 ERA in 307 games; two saves.

Majeski, Hank (39–41) third baseman; pinch hitter: 108-for-425, .254, in 128 games.

Malarkey, John (02–03) pitcher:

19–26 with 2.89 ERA in 53 games; one save.

Malkmus, Bobby (57) second baseman: 2-for-22, .091, in 13 games.

Mallon, Les (34–35) second baseman; third baseman; outfielder: 162-for-578, .280, in 158 games.

Maloney, Charlie (08) pitcher: 0–0 with 4.50 ERA in one game, relief.

Mangum, Leo (32–35) pitcher: 9–6 with 4.61 ERA in 57 games; one save.

MANN, KELLY (89–90) catcher: 9-for-52, .173, in 18 games.

Mann, Les (13–14, 19–20, 24–27) outfielder: 504-for-1,846, .273, in 572 games.

Manno, Don (40–41) outfielder; third baseman; first baseman: 7-for-37, .189, in 25 games.

Mantilla, Felix (56–61) shortstop; second baseman; third baseman; outfielder: 220-for-953, .231, in 402 games.

Manville, Dick (50) pitcher: 0–0 with 0.00 ERA in one game, relief.

MARAK, PAUL (90) pitcher: 1–2 with 3.69 ERA in seven games, all starts.

Maranville, Rabbit (12–20, 29–33, 35) shortstop; second baseman; third baseman: 1,696-for-6,724, .252, in 1,795 games.

Marquard, Rube (22–25) pitcher: 25–39 with 4.44 ERA in 109 games; one save.

Marquez, Luis (51) outfielder: 24-for-122, .197, in 68 games.

Marriott, William (25) third baseman; outfielder: 99-for-370, .268, in 103 games.

Marshall, Doc (04) catcher; outfielder: 9-for-43, .209, in 13 games.

MARSHALL, MIKE (76–77) pitcher: 3–1 with 3.75 ERA in 28 games, all relief; six saves.

Marshall, Willard (50–52) outfielder: 217-for-833, .261, in 262 games.

Martel, Doc (10) first baseman: 4-for-31, .129, in 10 games.

Martin, Billy (14) shortstop: 0-for-3, .000, in one game.

Martin, Billy (61) pinch hitter: 0-for-6, .000, in six games.

Martin, Jack (14) third baseman; first baseman; second baseman: 18-for-85, .212, in 33 games.

Martin, Ray (43, 47–48) pitcher: 1–0 with 2.45 ERA in five games.

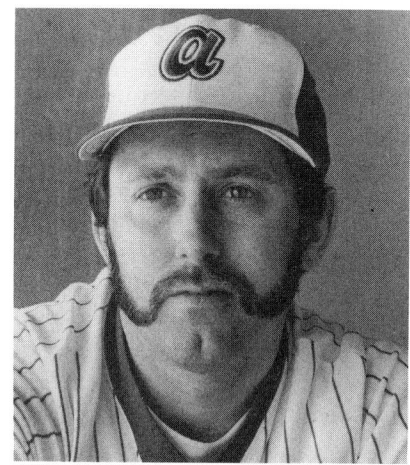
Mike Marshall

MARTINEZ, MARTY (67–68) short-stop; second baseman; third baseman; catcher; first baseman: 103-for-429, .240, in 157 games.

Masi, Phil (39–49) catcher; outfielder; third baseman; first baseman: 698-for-2,668, .262, in 945 games.

Massey, Mike (17) second baseman: 18-for-91, .198, in 31 games.

Massey, Red (18) outfielder; third baseman; first baseman; shortstop: 59-for-203, .291, in 66 games.

Mathes, Joe (16) second baseman: 0-for-0, —, in two games.

MATHEWS, EDDIE (52–66) third baseman; first baseman; outfielder: 2,201-for-8,049, .273, in 2,223 games.

Mattern, Al (08–12) pitcher: 36–58 with 3.37 ERA in 138 games; four saves.

MATTHEWS, GARY (77–80) outfielder: 643-for-2,231, .288, in 588 games.

Matthews, Joe (22) pitcher: 0–1 with 3.60 ERA in three games.

MATULA, RICK (79–81) pitcher: 19–23 with 4.41 ERA in 66 games.

Mauch, Gene (50–51) second baseman; third baseman; shortstop: 30-for-141, .213, in 67 games.

MAXIE, LARRY (69) pitcher: 0–0 with 3.00 ERA in two games, both relief.

MAY, DAVE (75–76) outfielder: 102-for-417, .245, in 187 games.

Maye, Lee (59–65) outfielder; third baseman: 568-for-2,028, .280, in 593 games.

Mayo, Eddie (37–38) third baseman; shortstop: 42-for-186, .226, in 73 games.

McAfee, William (31) pitcher: 0–1 with 6.37 ERA in 18 games.

McAuliffe, Gene (04) catcher: 1-for-2, .500, in one game.

McCarthy, Bill J. (05) catcher: 0-for-3, .000, in one game.

McCarthy, Bill T. (06) pitcher: 0–0 with 9.00 ERA in one game, relief.

McCarthy, Johnny (43, 46) first baseman: 96-for-320, .300, in 80 games.

McCarthy, Tom (08–09) pitcher: 7–8 with 2.24 ERA in 22 games.

McCleskey, Jeff (13) third baseman: 0-for-3, .000, in two games.

McCloskey, Jim (36) pitcher: 0–0 with 11.25 ERA in four games.

McCormick, Frank (47–48) first baseman: 120-for-392, .306, in 156 games.

McCormick, Mike (46–48) outfielder: 228-for-791, .288, in 266 games.

McCreery, Tom (03) outfielder: 18-for-83, .217, in 23 games.

McDonald, Ed (11–12) third baseman; shortstop: 155-for-634, .244, in 175 games.

McDonald, Tex (13) third baseman; second baseman; outfielder: 52-for-145, .359, in 62 games.

McDOWELL, ODDIBE (89–90) outfielder: 159-for-585, .272, in 189 games.

McElyea, Frank (42) outfielder: 0-for-4, .000, in seven games.

McGee, Dan (34) shortstop: 3-for-22, .136, in seven games.

McGowan, Beauty (37) outfielder: 1-for-12, .083, in nine games.

McGRIFF, FRED (93–) current Braves player.

McInnis, Stuffy (23–24) first baseman: 360-for-1,188, .303, in 300 games.

McKechnie, Bill (13) outfielder: 0-for-4, .000, in one game.

Oddibe McDowell

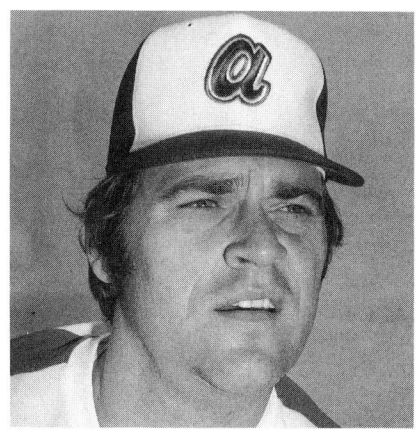
Denny McLain

McLAIN, DENNY (72) pitcher: 3–5 with 6.50 ERA in 15 games; one save.

McLAUGHLIN, BO (79) pitcher: 1–1 with 4.89 ERA in 37 games.

McLAUGHLIN, JOEY (77, 79) pitcher: 5–3 with 3.48 ERA in 40 games; five saves.

McLeod, Ralph (38) outfielder: 2-for-7, .286, in six games.

McMahon, Don (57–62) pitcher: 23–19 with 3.34 ERA in 233 games.

McManus, Marty (34) second baseman; third baseman: 120-for-435, .276, in 119 games.

McMICHAEL, GREG (93–) current Braves pitcher.

McMillan, Roy (61–64) shortstop: 310-for-1,306, .237, in 399 games.

McMURTRY, CRAIG (83–86) pitcher: 25–35 with 4.06 ERA in 127 games; one save.

McNamara, Dinny (27–28) outfielder: 1-for-13, .077, in 20 games.

McNamara, Tim (22–25) pitcher: 14–29 with 4.71 ERA in 92 games.

McNichol, Ed (04) pitcher: 2–12 with 4.28 ERA in 17 games.

McQUEEN, MIKE (69–72) pitcher: 5–11 with 4.60 ERA in 73 games; three saves.

McQuillan, Hugh (18–22, 27) pitcher: 35–50 with 4.01 ERA in 141 games; 11 saves.

McTigue, Bill (11–12) pitcher: 2–5 with 6.28 ERA in 24 games.

McWILLIAMS, LARRY (78–82, 87) pitcher: 25–24 with 4.53 ERA in 100 games.

Medwick, Joe (45) outfielder; first baseman: 62-for-218, .284, in 66 games.

MENKE, DENIS (62–67) second base-

Joe Medwick

man; shortstop; third baseman; first baseman; outfielder: 545-for-2,222, .245, in 685 games.

MERCKER, KENT (89–) current Braves pitcher.

MESSERSMITH, ANDY (76–77) pitcher: 16–15 with 3.49 ERA in 45 games; one save.

Metkovich, Catfish (54) first baseman; outfielder: 34-for-123, .276, in 68 games.

Meyers, Chief (17) catcher: 17-for-68, .250, in 25 games.

MILLAN, FELIX (66–72) second baseman; shortstop; third baseman: 874-for-3,114, .281, in 799 games.

Miller, Doc (10–12) outfielder: 239-for-778, .307, in 197 games.

MILLER, EDDIE L. (78–81) outfielder: 72-for-287, .251, in 94 games.

Denis Menke

Miller, Eddie R. (39–42) shortstop: 506-for-1,984, .255, in 524 games.

Miller, Frank (22–23) pitcher: 11–16 with 3.69 ERA in 39 games; two saves.

MILLER, NORM (73–74) outfielder: 10-for-49, .204, in 51 games.

MILLER, STU (68) pitcher: 0–0 with 27.00 ERA in two games, both relief.

Miller, Tom (18–19) pinch hitter: 2-for-8, .250, in nine games.

Mills, Art (27–28) pitcher: 0–1 with 5.36 ERA in 19 games.

Mitchell, Fred (13) pinch hitter: 1-for-3, .333, in four games.

MITCHELL, KEITH (91) outfielder: 21-for-66, .318, in 48 games.

MIZEROCK, JOHN (89) catcher: 6-for-27, .222, in 11 games.

Mogridge, George (26–27) pitcher: 12–14 with 4.30 ERA in 59 games; eight saves.

MONTANEZ, WILLIE (76–77) first baseman: 291-for-964, .302, in 239 games.

MONTEFUSCO, JOHN (81) pitcher: 2–3 with 3.49 ERA in 26 games; one save.

Montgomery, Al (41) catcher: 10-for-52, .192, in 42 games.

MOORE, DONNIE (82–84) pitcher: 9–9 with 3.47 ERA in 106 games, all relief; 23 saves.

Moore, Eddie (26–28) second baseman; shortstop; third baseman; outfielder: 224-for-810, .277, in 234 games.

Moore, Gene (36–38, 40–41) outfielder: 607-for-2,138, .284, in 585 games.

MOORE, JUNIOR (76–77) third baseman; second baseman; outfielder: 101-for-387, .261, in 132 games.

Moore, Randy (30–35) outfielder; third baseman; second baseman; first baseman; catcher: 590-for-2,060, .286, in 656 games.

Moran, Herbie (08–10, 14–15) outfielder: 148-for-700, .211, in 207 games.

Moran, Hiker (38–39) pitcher: 1–1 with 3.91 ERA in seven games.

Moran, Pat (01–05) catcher; first baseman; third baseman; outfielder; shortstop; second baseman: 354-for-1,485, .238, in 439 games.

MORDECAI, MIKE (94–) current Braves player.

More, Forrest (09) pitcher: 1–5 with 4.44 ERA in 10 games.

Morehead, Seth (61) pitcher: 1–0 with 6.46 ERA in 12 games, all relief.

MORENO, OMAR (86) outfielder: 84-for-359, .234, in 118 games.

MORET, ROGER (76) pitcher: 3–5 with 5.00 ERA in 27 games; one save.

Morgan, Cy (21–22) pitcher: 1–1 with 7.39 ERA in 19 games, all relief; one save.

Morgan, Joe (59) second baseman: 5-for-23, .217, in 13 games.

Moriarty, Ed (35–36) second baseman; pinch hitter: 12-for-40, .300, in 14 games.

Moroney, Jim (06) pitcher: 0–3 with 5.33 ERA in three games, all starts.

Morrison, Guy (27–28) pitcher: 1–2 with 5.06 ERA in 12 games.

MORRISON, JIM (88) third baseman; outfielder: 14-for-92, .152, in 51 games; pitcher: 0–0 with 0.00 ERA in three games, all relief.

Morton, Bubba (63) outfielder: 5-for-28, .179, in 15 games.

MORTON, CARL (73–76) pitcher: 52–47 with 3.47 ERA in 141 games.

Moss, Ray (31) pitcher: 1–3 with 4.60 ERA in 12 games.

MOTLEY, DARRYL (86–87) outfielder: 2-for-18, .111, in 11 games.

Mowry, Joe (33–35) outfielder; second baseman: 108-for-464, .233, in 192 games.

Mueller, Heinie (28–29) outfielder: 53-for-244, .217, in 88 games.

Mueller, Ray (35–38, 51) catcher: 159-for-699, .227, in 241 games.

Muich, Joe (24) pitcher: 0–0 with 11.00 ERA in three games, all relief.

Mulligan, Dick (46–47) pitcher: 1–0 with 3.12 ERA in five games, all relief.

Murff, Red (56–57) pitcher: 2–2 with 4.65 ERA in 26 games; three saves.

Carl Morton

Murphy, Buzz (18) outfielder: 12-for-32, .375, in nine games.

MURPHY, DALE (76–90) outfielder; catcher; first baseman: 1,901-for-7,098, .268, in 1,926 games.

Murphy, Dave (05) shortstop; third baseman: 2-for-11, .182, in three games.

Murphy, Frank (01) outfielder: 46-for-176, .261, in 45 games.

Murray, Amby (36) pitcher: 0–0 with 4.09 ERA in four games.

Murray, Jim (14) outfielder: 26-for-112, .232, in 39 games.

MURRELL, IVAN (74) outfielder; first baseman: 33-for-133, .248, in 73 games.

Murtaugh, Danny (47) second baseman; third baseman: 1-for-8, .125, in three games.

Myers, Hap (13) first baseman: 143-for-524, .273, in 140 games.

N

NAHORODNY, BILL (80–81) catcher; first baseman: 41-for-170, .241, in 73 games.

NASH, JIM (70–72) pitcher: 23–17 with 4.49 ERA in 77 games; three saves.

NAVARRO, JULIO (70) pitcher: 0–0 with 4.10 ERA in 17 games, all relief; one save.

Needham, Tom (04–07) catcher; outfielder; first baseman; second baseman; third baseman: 234-for-1,085, .216, in 336 games.

Nehf, Art (15–19) pitcher: 52–41 with 2.52 ERA in 126 games.

NEIBAUER, GARY (69–73) pitcher: 4–6 with 4.71 ERA in 66 games; one save.

Neill, Tommy (46–47) outfielder: 14-for-55, .255, in 20 games.

Neis, Bernie (25–26) outfielder: 121-for-448, .270, in 136 games.

Nelson, Tommy (45) third baseman; second baseman: 20-for-121, .165, in 40 games.

NETTLES, GRAIG (87) third baseman; first baseman: 37-for-177, .209, in 112 games.

Neun, Johnny (30–31) first baseman: 92-for-316, .291, in 160 games.

Nichols, Chet (51, 54–56) pitcher: 29–28 with 3.74 ERA in 104 games; four saves.

NICHOLSON, DAVE (67) outfielder: 5-for-25, .200, in 10 games.

Nicholson, Fred (21–22) outfielder; first baseman; second baseman: 136-for-467, .291, in 161 games.

NIED, DAVID (92) pitcher: 3–0 with 1.17 ERA in six games.

NIEKRO, JOE (73–74) pitcher: 5–6 with 3.76 ERA in 47 games; three saves.

NIEKRO, PHIL (64–83, 87) pitcher: 268–230 with 3.20 ERA in 740 games; 29 saves.

Nieman, Butch (43–45) outfielder: 269-for-1,050, .256, in 332 games.

NIEVES, MELVIN (92) outfielder: 4-for-19, .211, in 12 games.

Niggeling, Johnny (38, 46) pitcher: 3–5 with 3.45 ERA in 10 games.

Nixon, Al (21–23) outfielder: 205-for-777, .264, in 229 games.

NIXON, OTIS (91–93) outfielder: 377-for-1,318, .286, in 378 games.

NOLAN, JOE (75, 77–80) catcher: 136-for-551, .247, in 267 games.

North, Lou (24) pitcher: 1–2 with 5.35 ERA in nine games.

Northrop, Jake (18–19) pitcher: 6–6 with 2.91 ERA in 18 games.

Nottebart, Don (60–62) pitcher: 9–9 with 3.81 ERA in 82 games; six saves.

Noyes, Win (13) pitcher: 0–0 with 4.79 ERA in 11 games, all relief.

Nutter, Dizzy (19) outfielder: 11-for-52, .212, in 18 games.

O

OATES, JOHNNY (73–75) catcher: 149-for-631, .236, in 201 games.

OBERKFELL, KEN (84–88) third baseman; second baseman: 547-for-2,017, .271, in 590 games.

O'BRIEN, CHARLIE (94–   ) current Braves player.

O'Brien, Johnny (59) second baseman: 23-for-116, .198, in 44 games.

O'Connell, Danny (54–57) second baseman; third baseman; shortstop; first baseman: 415-for-1,675, .248, in 457 games.

O'Dea, Ken (46) catcher: 7-for-32, .219, in 12 games.

O'DELL, BILLY (65–66) pitcher: 12–9 with 2.24 ERA in 86 games; 24 saves.

ODOM, BLUE MOON (75) pitcher: 1–7 with 7.07 ERA in 15 games.

Odom, Dave (43) pitcher: 0–3 with 5.27 ERA in 22 games; two saves.

Oeschger, Joe (19–23) 50–65 with 4.10 ERA in 181 games; three saves.

OFFICE, ROWLAND (72, 74–79) outfielder: 540-for-2,076, .260, in 752 games.

Ogrodowski, Joe (25) pitcher: 0–0 with 54.00 ERA in one game, relief.

O'Hara, Kid (04) outfielder: 6-for-29, .207, in eight games.

OLIVA, JOSE (94–   ) current Braves player.

OLIVER, GENE (63–67) catcher; first baseman; outfielder: 304-for-1,209, .251, in 403 games.

OLIVO, CHI-CHI (61, 64–66) pitcher: 7–6 with 3.96 ERA in 96 games, all relief; 12 saves.

Olmo, Luis (50–51) outfielder; third baseman: 46-for-210, .219, in 90 games.

OLSON, GREG (90–93) catcher; third baseman: 308-for-1,273, .242, in 411 games.

OLSON, GREGG (94) pitcher: 0–2 with 9.20 ERA in 16 games; all relief; one save.

OLWINE, ED (86–88) pitcher: 0–1 with 4.52 ERA in 80 games; all relief; three saves.

O'NEAL, RANDY (87) pitcher: 4–2 with 5.61 ERA in 16 games.

O'Neil, Mickey (19–25) catcher; second baseman: 428-for-1,750, .245, in 576 games.

O'Neill, Jack (06) catcher; first baseman; outfielder: 30-for-167, .180, in 61 games.

Jim Nash

Jose Oliva

Orndorff, Jess (07) catcher: 2-for-17, .118, in five games.

O'Rourke, Frank (12) shortstop; third baseman: 24-for-196, .122, in 61 games.

Osborne, Wayne (36) pitcher: 1–1 with 5.85 ERA in five games.

Osinski, Dan (65) pitcher: 0–3 with 2.82 ERA in 61 games, all relief; six saves.

Outlaw, Jimmy (39) outfielder; third baseman: 35-for-133, .263, in 65 games.

OWEN, LARRY (81–83, 85) catcher: 20-for-107, .187, in 58 games.

P

PACIOREK, TOM (76–78) first baseman; outfielder; third baseman: 134-for-488, .275, in 188 games.

Padgett, Don (46) catcher: 25-for-98, .255, in 44 games.

Padgett, Ernie (23–25) shortstop; second baseman; third baseman: 208-for-769, .270, in 228 games.

Pafko, Andy (53–59) outfielder; third baseman: 521-for-1,897, .275, in 658 games.

PAGE, MIKE (68) outfielder: 5-for-28, .179, in 20 games.

Paine, Phil (51, 54–57) pitcher: 5–0 with 3.17 ERA in 49 games, all relief.

PALMER, DAVID (86–87) pitcher: 19–21 with 4.18 ERA in 63 games.

Palmero, Emilio (28) pitcher: 0–1 with 5.40 ERA in three games.

PANTHER, JIM (73) pitcher: 2–3 with 7.63 ERA in 23 games, all relief.

PAPPAS, MILT (68–70) pitcher: 18–20 with 3.41 ERA in 59 games.

PARRETT, JEFF (90–91) pitcher: 2–3 with 4.47 ERA in 38 games, all relief; two saves.

Parson, Jiggs (10–11) pitcher: 0–3 with 4.92 ERA in 17 games.

Patton, Gene (44) pinch runner: 0-for-0, —, in one game.

PAYNE, MIKE (84) pitcher: 0–1 with 6.35 ERA in three games.

PECOTA, BILL (93–94) third baseman; second baseman; outfielder: 44-for-174, .253, in 136 games.

Peery, Red (29) pitcher: 0–1 with 5.11 ERA in nine games.

PENA, ALEJANDRO (91–92, 95–) current Braves pitcher.

Pendleton, Jim (53–56) outfielder; shortstop; third baseman; first baseman; second baseman: 113-for-445, .254, in 213 games.

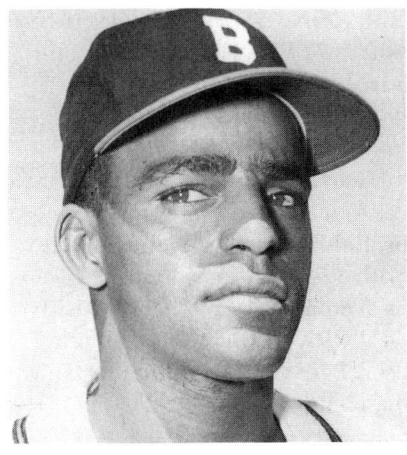
Jim Pendleton

PENDLETON, TERRY (91–94) third baseman: 636-for-2,168, .293, in 551 games.

PEPITONE, JOE (73) first baseman: 4-for-11, .364, in three games.

Peploski, Henry (29) third baseman: 2-for-10, .200, in six games.

Perdue, Hub (11–14) pitcher: 37–44 with 4.03 ERA in 108 games; five saves.

PEREZ, MARTY (71–76) shortstop; second baseman; third baseman: 594-for-2,394, .248, in 690 games.

PEREZ, PASCUAL (82–85) pitcher: 34–33 with 3.37 ERA in 101 games.

PERRY, GAYLORD (81) pitcher: 8–9 with 3.94 ERA in 23 games, all starts.

PERRY, GERALD (83–89) first baseman; outfielder: 551-for-2,040, .270, in 643 games.

PETRY, DAN (91) pitcher: 0–0 with 5.55 ERA in 10 games, all relief.

Pfeffer, Big Jeff (06–08, 11) pitcher: 26–35 with 3.45 ERA in 84 games; two saves; outfielder: 31-for-158, .196, in 60 games.

Phillips, Damon (44, 46) third baseman; shortstop; pinch hitter: 127-for-491, .259, in 142 games.

Phillips, Eddie (24) catcher: 0-for-3, .000, in three games.

Phillips, Taylor (56–57) pitcher: 8–5 with 3.75 ERA in 50 games; four saves.

Piatt, Wiley (03) pitcher: 9–14 with 3.18 ERA in 25 games.

Piche, Ron (60–63) pitcher: 9–10 with 3.88 ERA in 100 games; 10 saves.

Pick, Charlie (19–20) second baseman; third baseman; outfielder; first baseman: 134-for-497, .270, in 129 games.

Juan Pizarro

Pickrel, Clarence (34) pitcher: 0–0 with 5.06 ERA in 10 games.

Piechota, Al (40–41) pitcher: 2–5 with 5.66 ERA in 22 games.

PIERCE, JACK (73–74) first baseman: 2-for-29, .069, in 17 games.

Pierotti, Al (20–21) pitcher: 1–2 with 4.05 ERA in eight games.

Pilney, Andy (36) pinch hitter: 0-for-2, .000, in three games.

Pisoni, Jim (59) outfielder: 4-for-24, .167, in nine games.

Pittinger, Togie (00–04) pitcher: 75–84 with 3.08 ERA in 180 games; one save.

Pizarro, Juan (57–60) pitcher: 23–19 with 3.93 ERA in 90 games; one save.

POCOROBA, BIFF (75–84) catcher; third baseman; pinch hitter: 374-for-1,457, .257, in 596 games.

Poland, Hugh (43–44, 46) catcher: 31-for-170, .182, in 56 games.

PORTER, BOB (81–82) outfielder; first baseman; pinch hitter: 7-for-41, .171, in 41 games.

Posedel, Bill (39–41, 46) pitcher: 33–34 with 4.27 ERA in 105 games; five saves.

Potter, Nels (48–49) pitcher: 11–13 with 3.32 ERA in 59 games; nine saves.

Bill Posedel

Powell, Ray (17–24) outfielder: 890-for-3,324, .268, in 873 games.

Preibisch, Mel (40–41) outfielder: 9-for-44, .205, in 16 games.

Prendergast, Jim (48) pitcher: 1–1 with 10.26 ERA in 10 games; one save.

PRESLEY, JIM (90) third baseman; first baseman: 131-for-541, .242, in 140 games.

PRIDDY, BOB (69–71) pitcher: 9–14 with 4.79 ERA in 82 games, all relief; 12 saves.

Pruett, Hub (32) pitcher: 1–5 with 5.14 ERA in 18 games.

PULEO, CHARLIE (86–89) pitcher: 13–16 with 3.88 ERA in 108 games; one save.

Pyle, Ewald (45) pitcher: 0–1 with 7.24 ERA in four games.

Q

Queen, Billy (54) outfielder: 0-for-2, .000, in three games.

Quinn, Jack (13) pitcher: 4–3 with 2.40 ERA in eight games.

R

RABB, JOHN (85) outfielder: 0-for-2, .000, in three games.

Ragan, Pat (15–19) pitcher: 39–49 with 2.74 ERA in 125 games; one save.

RAKOW, ED (67) pitcher: 3–2 with 5.26 ERA in 17 games.

RAMIREZ, RAFAEL (80–87) shortstop; third baseman; outfielder: 929-for-3,537, .263, in 927 games.

Ramsey, Bill (45) outfielder: 40-for-137, .292, in 78 games.

Randall, Newt (07) outfielder: 55-for-258, .213, in 75 games.

Ranew, Merritt (64) catcher: 2-for-17, .118, in nine games.

Rariden, Bill (09–13) catcher; third baseman; second baseman: 206-for-918, .224, in 306 games.

Rawlings, Johnny (17–20) second baseman; shortstop; third baseman; outfielder: 250-for-1,059, .236, in 315 games.

Raymer, Fred (04–05) second baseman; first baseman; outfielder: 193-for-917, .210, in 251 games.

RAYMOND, CLAUDE (61–63, 67–69) pitcher: 19–19 with 3.86 ERA in 181 games, all relief; 33 saves.

REARDON, JEFF (92) pitcher: 3–0 with 1.15 ERA in 14 games, all relief; three saves.

Reed, Billy (52) second baseman: 13-for-52, .250, in 15 games.

REED, RON (66–75) pitcher: 80–88 with 3.74 ERA in 218 games; one save.

Rehg, Wally (17–18) outfielder: 124-for-474, .262, in 127 games.

Reid, Earl (46) pitcher: 1–0 with 3.00 ERA in two games, both relief.

Reis, Bobby (36–38) pitcher: 7–11 with 4.56 ERA in 55 games.

Reis, Tommy (38) pitcher: 0–0 with 7.11 ERA in four games, all relief.

Reiser, Pete (49–50) outfielder; third baseman: 76-for-299, .254, in 137 games.

Reulbach, Ed (16–17) pitcher: 7–7 with 2.53 ERA in 26 games.

REYNOSO, ARMANDO (91–92) pitcher: 3–1 with 5.81 ERA in nine games; one save.

Rhem, Flint (34–35) pitcher: 8–13 in 3.96 ERA in 35 games.

Rhiel, Billy (30) third baseman; second baseman: 8-for-47, .170, in 20 games.

Rice, Del (55–59) catcher: 120-for-553, .217, in 208 games.

Rich, Woody (44) pitcher: 1–1 with 5.76 ERA in seven games.

RICHARDS, RUSTY (89–90) pitcher: 0–0 with 6.97 ERA in three games.

Richbourg, Lance (27–31) outfielder: 758-for-2,434, .312, in 629 games.

Richie, Lew (09–10) pitcher: 7–10 with 2.37 ERA in 26 games; two saves.

Rickert, Joe (01) outfielder: 10-for-60, .167, in 13 games.

Rickert, Marv (48–49) outfielder; first baseman: 84-for-290, .290, in 103 games.

Rico, Art (16–17) catcher; outfielder: 4-for-18, .222, in 17 games.

Riconda, Harry (26) third baseman: 2-for-12, .167, in four games.

Pete Reiser

Riddle, Johnny (37–38) catcher: 16-for-60, .267, in 21 games.

Riggert, Joe (19) outfielder: 68-for-240, .283, in 63 games.

Riley, Jim (10) outfielder: 0-for-1, .000, in one game.

Ritchey, Claude (07–09) second baseman: 257-for-1,007, .255, in 295 games.

RITCHIE, JAY (66–67) pitcher: 4–7 with 3.44 ERA in 74 games, all relief; six saves.

RIVERA, BEN (92) pitcher: 0–1 with 4.70 ERA in eight games, all relief.

Roach, Mel (53–54, 57–61) second baseman; outfielder; third baseman; first baseman: 94-for-355, .265, in 139 games.

Roberge, Skippy (41–42, 46) third baseman; second baseman; shortstop: 112-for-508, .220, in 177 games.

Robertson, Charlie (27–28) pitcher: 9–22 with 4.89 ERA in 41 games; one save.

Robertson, Gene (29–30) third baseman; shortstop: 19-for-87, .218, in 29 games.

ROBINSON, BILL (66) outfielder: 3-for-11, .273, in six games.

ROBINSON, CRAIG (74–77) shortstop: 115-for-515, .223, in 197 games.

Robinson, Humberto (55–56, 58) pitcher: 5–5 with 2.98 ERA in 33 games; three saves.

ROCKETT, PAT (76–78) shortstop: 88-for-411, .214, in 152 games.

ROENICKE, GARY (87–88) outfielder; first baseman: 59-for-265, .223, in 116 games.

Rollings, Red (30) third baseman; second baseman: 29-for-123, .236, in 52 games.

ROMERO, ED (89) second baseman; shortstop; third baseman: 5-for-19, .263, in seven games.

Roof, Phil (61, 64) catcher: 0-for-2, .000, in two games.

ROSARIO, VICTOR (90) shortstop; second baseman: 1-for-7, .143, in nine games.

Roselli, Bob (55–56, 58) catcher: 3-for-12, .250, in 11 games.

Roser, Bunny (22) outfielder: 27-for-113, .239, in 32 games.

Roser, Steve (46) pitcher: 1–1 with 3.60 ERA in 14 games; one save.

Ross, Chet (39–44) outfielder: 316-for-1,309, .241, in 413 games.

Bama Rowell

Connie Ryan

ROSSY, RICO (91) shortstop: 0-for-1, .000, in five games.

Rowell, Bama (39–41, 46–47) second baseman; outfielder; third baseman: 476-for-1,705, .279, in 497 games.

Roy, Normie (50) pitcher: 4–3 with 5.13 ERA in 19 games; one save.

ROYSTER, JERRY (76–84, 88) shortstop; third baseman; outfielder; second baseman: 848-for-3,451, .246, in 1,118 games.

Rudolph, Dick (13–20, 22–23, 27) pitcher: 121–107 with 2.62 ERA in 275 games; six saves.

RUIZ, CHICO (78, 80) third baseman; second baseman; shortstop: 21-for-72, .292, in 43 games.

RUNGE, PAUL (81–88) third baseman; second baseman; shortstop: 80-for-345, .232, in 183 games.

Rush, Bob (58–60) pitcher: 17–12 with 3.07 ERA in 69 games.

Russell, Jim (48–49) outfielder: 181-for-737, .246, in 219 games.

RUSSELL, JOHN (89) catcher; outfielder; first baseman; third baseman: 29-for-159, .182, in 74 games;

pitcher: 0–0 with 0.00 ERA in one game, relief.

Ruth, Babe (35) outfielder: 13-for-72, .181, in 28 games.

RUTHVEN, DICK (76–78) pitcher: 23–36 with 4.19 ERA in 74 games.

Ryan, Connie (43–44, 46–50) second baseman; third baseman; shortstop; first baseman: 552-for-2,237, .247, in 669 games.

Ryan, Rosy (25–26) pitcher: 2–10 with 6.48 ERA in 44 games; two saves.

S

SADECKI, RAY (75) pitcher: 2–3 with 4.21 ERA in 25 games; one save.

Sadowski, Bob (63–65) pitcher: 19–26 with 3.74 ERA in 104 games; eight saves.

SADOWSKI, ED (66) catcher: 1-for-9, .111, in three games.

Sain, Johnny (42, 46–51) pitcher: 104–91 with 3.49 ERA in 257 games; 11 saves.

St. Claire, Ebba (51–53) catcher: 101-for-408, .248, in 144 games.

ST. CLAIRE, RANDY (91–92) pitcher: 0–0 with 4.70 ERA in 29 games, all relief.

Salkeld, Bill (48–49) catcher: 89-for-359, .248, in 144 games.

Salvo, Manny (40–43) pitcher: 29–40 with 3.46 ERA in 102 games.

SAMPLE, BILLY (86) outfielder; second baseman: 57-for-200, .285, in 92 games.

Samuel, Amado (62–63) shortstop; second baseman; third baseman: 46-for-226, .204, in 91 games.

SANDERS, DEION (91–94) outfielder: 275-for-1,056, .260, in 363 games.

Sanders, Ray (46, 48–49) first baseman; pinch hitter: 67-for-284, .236, in 94 games.

Sandlock, Mike (42, 44) third baseman; shortstop: 4-for-31, .129, in 32 games.

SANTORINI, AL (68) pitcher: 0–1 with 0.00 ERA in one game, start.

Sauer, Ed (49) outfielder: 57-for-214, .266, in 79 games.

Sawatski, Carl (57–58) catcher: 26-for-115, .226, in 68 games.

Scalzi, Johnny (31) pinch hitter: 0-for-1, .000, in two games.

Scarsella, Les (40) first baseman: 18-for-60, .300, in 18 games.

Schacht, Sid (51) pitcher: 0–2 with 1.93 ERA in five games, all relief.

Schacker, Hal (45) pitcher: 0–1 with 5.28 ERA in six games, all relief.

Schmidt, Butch (13–15) first baseman: 292-for-1,073, .272, in 296 games.

SCHNEIDER, DAN (63–64, 66) pitcher: 2–2 with 3.98 ERA in 57 games.

Schoendienst, Red (57–60) second baseman; outfielder: 292-for-1,050, .278, in 272 games.

Schreiber, Hank (17) shortstop; third baseman: 2-for-7, .286, in two games.

SCHUELER, RON (72–73) pitcher: 13–15 with 3.78 ERA in 76 games; four saves.

SCHULER, DAVE (85) pitcher: 0–0 with 6.75 ERA in nine games, all relief.

Schulmerich, Wes (31–33) outfielder: 227-for-816, .278, in 243 games.

Schulte, Jack (06) shortstop: 0-for-7, .000, in two games.

Schulte, Johnny (32) catcher: 2-for-9, .222, in 10 games.

Schultz, Joe (12–13) second baseman; outfielder: 7-for-30, .233, in 13 games.

Schuster, Bill (39) shortstop; third baseman: 0-for-3, .000, in two games.

SCHWALL, DON (66–67) pitcher: 3–3 with 4.30 ERA in 12 games.

Dick Ruthven

Ebba St. Claire

Schwind, Art (12) third baseman: 1-for-2, .500, in one game.

Scott, Jack (17, 19–21) pitcher: 32–42 with 3.42 ERA in 117 games; five saves.

Seibold, Socks (29–33) pitcher: 41–65 with 4.48 ERA in 141 games; four saves.

Sellers, Rube (10) outfielder: 5-for-32, .156, in 12 games.

Seymour, Cy (13) outfielder: 13-for-73, .178, in 39 games.

Shannon, Joe (15) outfielder; second baseman: 2-for-10, .200, in five games.

Shannon, Red (15) second baseman: 0-for-3, .000, in one game.

Sharpe, Bud (05, 10) first baseman; outfielder; catcher: 136-for-609, .223, in 161 games.

Shaw, Al (09) catcher: 4-for-41, .098, in 18 games.

Shaw, Bob (62–63) pitcher: 22–20 with 2.74 ERA in 86 games; 15 saves.

Shay, Marty (24) second baseman; shortstop: 16-for-68, .235, in 19 games.

Shean, Dave (09–10, 12) second baseman; shortstop: 199-for-820, .243, in 229 games.

Shearer, Ray (57) outfielder: 1-for-2, .500, in two games.

Sheely, Earl (31) first baseman: 147-for-538, .273, in 147 games.

Shemo, Steve (44–45) second baseman; third baseman; shortstop: 20-for-77, .260, in 35 games.

Sherdel, Bill (30–32) pitcher: 12–15 with 4.45 ERA in 49 games; one save.

SHIELDS, STEVE (85–86) pitcher: 1–2 with 5.47 ERA in 29 games.

Shires, Art (32) first baseman: 71-for-298, .238, in 82 games.

Shoffner, Milt (37–39) pitcher: 15–14

Socks Seibold

with 3.23 ERA in 57 games; three saves.

Shoun, Clyde (47–49) pitcher: 10–4 with 4.18 ERA in 63 games; five saves.

Shupe, Vince (45) first baseman: 76-for-283, .269, in 78 games.

Siemer, Oscar (25–26) catcher: 29-for-119, .244, in 47 games.

Simmons, Al (39) outfielder: 93-for-330, .282, in 93 games.

SIMMONS, TED (86–88) first baseman; catcher; third baseman: 102-for-411, .248, in 227 games.

SINATRO, MATT (81–84) catcher: 22-for-129, .171, in 58 games.

Siner, Hosea (09) third baseman; second baseman; shortstop: 3-for-23, .130, in 10 games.

Singleton, Elmer (45–46) pitcher: 1–5 with 4.31 ERA in 22 games; one save.

SISK, DOUG (90–91) pitcher: 2–1 with 4.86 ERA in 17 games, all relief.

Sisler, George (28–30) first baseman: 505-for-1,551, .326, in 388 games; pitcher: 0–0 with 0.00 ERA in one game, relief.

Sisti, Sibby (39–42, 46–54) third baseman; second baseman; shortstop; outfielder; first baseman: 732-for-2,999, .244, in 1,016 games.

SKOK, CRAIG (78–79) pitcher: 4–5 with 4.17 ERA in 87 games, all relief; four saves.

Slagle, James (01) outfielder: 69-for-255, .271, in 66 games.

Slaughter, Enos (59) outfielder: 3-for-18, .167, in 11 games.

Sleater, Lou (56) pitcher: 2–2 with 3.15 ERA in 25 games; two saves.

SMALL, HANK (78) first baseman: 0-for-4, .000, in one game.

Smalley, Roy (54) shortstop; second baseman; first baseman: 8-for-36, .222, in 25 games.

Smith, Bob (23–30, 33–37) shortstop; second baseman; outfielder; third baseman: 375-for-1,535, .244, in 647 games; pitcher: 83–120 with 4.06 ERA in 349 games; 36 saves.

Smith, Earl (23–24) catcher: 71-for-250, .284, in 105 games.

Smith, Elmer (01) outfielder: 10-for-57, .175, in 16 games.

Smith, Fred (13) third baseman; second baseman; shortstop; outfielder: 65-for-285, .228, in 92 games.

Smith, Harry (08–10) catcher: 86-for-390, .221, in 154 games.

Pete Smith

Smith, Jack (26–29) outfielder: 234-for-779, .300, in 295 games.

Smith, Jack H. (64) pitcher: 2–2 with 3.77 ERA in 22 games, all relief.

Smith, Jimmy (18) second baseman; shortstop; outfielder; third baseman: 23-for-102, .225, in 34 games.

SMITH, KEN (81–83) first baseman; outfielder: 15-for-56, .268, in 83 games.

SMITH, LONNIE (88–92) outfielder: 457-for-1,573, .291, in 518 games.

SMITH, PETE (87–93) pitcher: 30–48 with 4.10 ERA in 125 games.

Smith, Red (14–19) third baseman; outfielder: 678-for-2,440, .278, in 720 games.

SMITH, ZANE (84–89) pitcher: 39–58 with 4.06 ERA in 159 games; one save.

SMOLTZ, JOHN (88–   ) current Braves pitcher.

Snodgrass, Fred (15–16) outfielder; first baseman: 117-for-461, .254, in 135 games.

SOLOMON, EDDIE (77–79) pitcher: 17–26 with 4.26 ERA in 86 games; two saves.

SOSA, ELIAS (75–76) pitcher: 6–6

Zane Smith

with 4.79 ERA in 64 games, all relief; five saves.

Southworth, Bill (64) third baseman: 2-for-7, .286, in three games.

Southworth, Billy (21–23) outfielder; second baseman: 421-for-1,338, .315, in 337 games.

Spahn, Warren (42, 46–64) pitcher: 356–229 with 3.05 ERA in 714 games; 29 saves.

Spangler, Al (59–61) outfielder: 59-for-214, .276, in 175 games.

SPECK, CLIFF (86) pitcher: 2–1 with 4.13 ERA in 13 games.

Spencer, Chet (06) outfielder: 4-for-27, .148, in eight games.

Sperber, Ed (24–25) outfielder; pinch hitter: 17-for-61, .279, in 26 games.

SPIKES, CHARLIE (79–80) outfielder: 36-for-129, .279, in 107 games.

Spohrer, Al (28–35) catcher: 575-for-2,216, .259, in 754 games.

Spratt, Harry (11–12) shortstop; second baseman; outfielder; third baseman: 60-for-243, .247, in 89 games.

STAEHLE, MARV (71) second baseman; third baseman: 4-for-36, .111, in 22 games.

Stanky, Eddie (48–49) second baseman: 223-for-753, .296, in 205 games.

Stanley, Joe (03–04) outfielder; shortstop: 77-for-316, .244, in 89 games; pitcher: 0–0 with 9.00 ERA in one game, relief.

STANTON, MIKE (89–95) pitcher: 18–21 with 4.01 ERA in 304 games, all relief; 55 saves.

Starr, Charlie (09) second baseman; shortstop; third baseman: 48-for-216, .222, in 61 games.

Starr, Ray (33) pitcher: 0–1 with 3.86 ERA in nine games.

Al Spangler

Steinfeldt, Harry (11) third baseman: 16-for-63, .254, in 19 games.

Stem, Fred (08–09) first baseman: 71-for-317, .224, in 93 games.

Stengel, Casey (24–25) outfielder: 130-for-474, .274, in 143 games.

Stewart, Joe (04) pitcher: 0–0 with 9.64 ERA in two games, both relief.

STONE, GEORGE (67–72) pitcher: 43–44 with 3.90 ERA in 148 games; four saves.

Stout, Allyn (43) pitcher: 1–0 with 6.75 ERA in nine games, all relief; one save.

Strand, Paul (13–15) pitcher: 7–3 with 2.37 ERA in 29 games; two saves.

Street, Gabby (05) catcher: 2-for-12, .167, in three games.

Strincevich, Nick (40–41) pitcher: 4–8 with 5.66 ERA in 35 games; one save.

Stripp, Joe (38) third baseman: 63-for-229, .275, in 59 games.

Strobel, Allie (05–06) second baseman; shortstop; third baseman; outfielder: 66-for-336, .196, in 105 games.

Stryker, Dutch (24) pitcher: 3–8 with 6.01 ERA in 20 games.

Sturgeon, Bobby (48) second baseman; shortstop; third baseman: 17-for-78, .218, in 34 games.

Sullivan, Andy (04) shortstop: 0-for-1, .000, in one game.

Sullivan, Joe (39–41) pitcher: 18–25 with 3.67 ERA in 83 games; three saves.

Sullivan, John (20–21) outfielder; first baseman; pinch hitter: 74-for-255, .290, in 86 games.

Surkont, Max (50–53) pitcher: 40–36 with 3.90 ERA in 105 games.

Sutcliffe, Butch (38) catcher: 1-for-4, .250, in four games.

SUTTER, BRUCE (85–86, 88) pitcher: 10–11 with 4.55 ERA in 112 games, all relief; 40 saves.

Sweeney, Bill (07–13) second baseman; third baseman; shortstop; outfielder; first baseman: 902-for-3,219, .280, in 902 games.

Swift, Bill (40) pitcher: 1–1 with 2.89 ERA in four games, all relief; one save.

T

Taggert, Bob (18) outfielder: 48-for-146, .329, in 35 games.

Talcott, Roy (43) pitcher: 0–0 with 27.00 ERA in one game, relief.

Tanner, Chuck (55–57) outfielder: 92-for-375, .245, in 179 games.

TARASCO, TONY (93–94) outfielder: 44-for-167, .263, in 111 games.

Taylor, Ben (55) first baseman: 1-for-10, .100, in 12 games.

Taylor, Ed (26) third baseman; shortstop: 73-for-272, .268, in 92 games.

Taylor, Hawk (57–58, 61–63) catcher; outfielder: 20-for-111, .180, in 67 games.

Taylor, Zack (26–29) catcher: 258-for-1,028, .251, in 314 games.

TEPEDINO, FRANK (73–75) first baseman; pinch hitter: 84-for-324, .259, in 160 games.

Terry, Zeb (18) shortstop: 32-for-105, .305, in 28 games.

THEISS, DUANE (77–78) pitcher: 1–1 with 5.33 ERA in 20 games, all relief.

Thevenow, Tommy (37) shortstop; third baseman; second baseman: 4-for-34, .118, in 21 games.

Thiel, Bert (52) pitcher: 1–1 with 7.71 ERA in four games, all relief.

THOMAS, ANDRES (85–90) shortstop; third baseman: 493-for-2,103, .234, in 577 games.

Thomas, Frank (61, 65) outfielder; first baseman: 127-for-456, .279, in 139 games.

Thomas, Herb (24–25, 27) outfielder; second baseman; shortstop: 49-for-218, .225, in 61 games.

THOMAS, LEE (66) first baseman: 25-for-126, .198, in 39 games.

Thomas, Roy (09) outfielder: 74-for-281, .263, in 82 games.

Andres Thomas

Frank Thomas

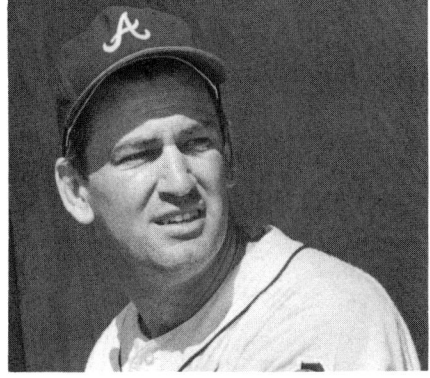

Bob Tillman

Jeff Treadway

Thomas, Walt (08) shortstop: 2-for-13, .154, in five games.

Thompson, Don (49) outfielder: 2-for-11, .182, in seven games.

Thompson, Fuller (11) pitcher: 0–0 with 3.86 ERA in three games, all relief.

THOMPSON, MIKE (74–75) pitcher: 0–6 with 4.69 ERA in 17 games.

THOMPSON, MILT (84–85) outfielder: 85-for-281, .302, in 98 games.

Thompson, Tommy (33–36) outfielder; first baseman: 266-for-1,003, .265, in 347 games.

Thomson, Bobby (54–57) outfielder; third baseman: 252-for-1,041, .242, in 327 games.

Thorpe, Bob (51–53) outfielder; pinch hitter: 83-for-331, .251, in 110 games.

Thorpe, Jim (19) outfielder; first baseman: 51-for-156, .327, in 60 games.

Tiefenauer, Bob (63–65) pitcher: 5–8 with 2.95 ERA in 64 games, all relief; 15 saves.

Tierney, Cotton (24) second baseman; third baseman: 131-for-505, .259, in 136 games.

TILLMAN, BOB (68–70) catcher: 142-for-649, .219, in 226 games.

Titus, John (12–13) outfielder: 192-for-614, .313, in 183 games.

Tobin, Jim (40–45) pitcher: 72–83 with 3.34 ERA in 188 games; three saves; first baseman: 122-for-560, .218, in 259 games.

Torgeson, Earl (47–52) first baseman; outfielder: 657-for-2,476, .265, in 720 games.

Torphy, Red (20) first baseman: 3-for-15, .200, in three games.

Torre, Frank (56–60) first baseman: 324-for-1,202, .270, in 514 games.

TORRE, JOE (60–68) catcher; first baseman; outfielder; pinch hitter: 1,087-for-3,700, .294, in 1,037 games.

TORREALBA, PABLO (75–76) pitcher: 0–3 with 3.32 ERA in 42 games, all relief; two saves.

Tost, Lou (42–43) pitcher: 10–11 with 3.62 ERA in 38 games.

Touchstone, Clay (28–29) pitcher: 0–0 with 7.60 ERA in six games, all relief.

Townsend, Ira (20–21) pitcher: 0–0 with 3.86 ERA in eight games.

Townsend, Leo (20–21) pitcher: 2–3 with 2.81 ERA in eight games.

Tragesser, Walt (13–19) catcher: 84-for-399, .211, in 175 games.

TREADWAY, JEFF (89–92) second baseman; third baseman: 391-for-1,379, .284, in 429 games.

TREVINO, ALEX (84) catcher: 65-for-266, .244, in 79 games.

Trowbridge, Bob (56–59) pitcher: 12–10 with 3.78 ERA in 94 games; three saves.

Tuckey, Tom (08–09) pitcher: 3–12 with 3.49 ERA in 25 games.

Turner, Jim (37–39) pitcher: 38–40 with 3.24 ERA in 93 games; one save.

Twombly, George (17) outfielder; first baseman: 19-for-102, .186, in 32 games.

Tyler, Fred (14) catcher: 2-for-19, .105, in six games.

Tyler, Johnnie (34–35) outfielder: 17-for-53, .321, in 16 games.

Tyler, Lefty (10–17) pitcher: 92–92 with 3.06 ERA in 247 games; six saves.

U

UECKER, BOB (62–63, 67) catcher: 43-for-238, .181, in 108 games.

Ulisney, Mike (45) catcher: 7-for-18, .389, in 11 games.

UMBACH, ARNIE (64, 66) pitcher: 1–2 with 3.12 ERA in 23 games.

Upham, Bill (18) pitcher: 1–1 with 5.23 ERA in three games.

UPSHAW, CECIL (66–73) pitcher:

Milt Thompson

Frank Torre

The Miracle Braves

The years 1914 and 1915 were two of the most exciting in Braves history. In 1914, the "Miracle" Braves stunned the sports world by not only rallying from last place on July 18 to win the pennant but also by sweeping four games from Connie Mack's heavily favored Philadelphia Athletics in the World Series. The Braves of "Miracle Man" George Stallings slipped to second place in 1915, but there still was tremendous interest in the team, much of it created by the mid-season opening of Braves Field, the largest ballpark in America at the time.

The centerpiece of this page is one of the most unique remnants of the 1914 season. It's the Indian blanket warmup coat worn by outfielder Les Mann, who hit .247 in 126 games in 1914 and scored the winning run in the 12th inning of Game 3 in the Series. The Braves had no insignia on their coats, which was common in that era, but Mann's name is embroidered inside the collar.

The Boston Herald page tells of the opening of Braves Field on August 18, 1915 and the raising of the 1914 pennant. Also shown is a Boston Garter advertisement featuring Braves second baseman Johnny Evers, the winner of the 1914 Chalmers Award as the National League MVP, and a "blanket" tobacco premium depicting righthander Hub Perdue, who pitched three and a half seasons for the Braves before being traded in mid-1914.

All-Star Tradition

The All-Star Game was born in 1933 when sports editor Arch Ward of the *Chicago Tribune* convinced club owners to stage a mid-season game at Comiskey Park during Chicago's Century of Progress Exposition. The only Brave selected to play for the National League was slugging outfielder Wally Berger, one of the greatest power hitters in franchise history.

The 1933 All-Stars were outfitted with special uniforms, and the one shown here is the actual one worn by Berger. The letter at the bottom, right is the notification Berger received from the National League office of his selection to the team.

Also shown: (top, right) a letter from Braves president Judge Emil Fuchs to Berger discussing his 1935 contract proposal; (center, right) Berger's 1935 contract for $12,000; a page from a scrapbook kept by Berger's wife; a 1935 scorecard showing Berger and Babe Ruth in the Braves lineup; and a belt buckle, tie clasp and metal luggage tag that belonged to Berger.

BERGER SLAMS $10,000 HOMER

Just Out of Sick Bed, He Pinch-Hits for Maranville With Three Men On---Smashing Drive Puts Team in World's Series Money---Every One of Braves to Get $400

Circuit Clout in Seventh Beats Phillies, 4 to 1---His Mates in Wild Frenzy of Joy

The Babe

Babe Ruth did more to popularize baseball than any other man in history. His larger-than-life feats, on and off the field, and his unmatched charisma made him one of the most recognized men in the world long before the advent of television. But the Sultan of Swat was on his last legs when he joined the Braves for the 1935 season. He played just 28 games for Boston but hit the last six of his 714 home runs for the Braves before retiring on June 2 at age 40.

This jersey is the last one worn by Ruth. His famous uniform No. 3 is stitched on the tail of the shirt. The photograph shows Ruth (left) crossing bats with fellow Braves slugger Wally Berger.

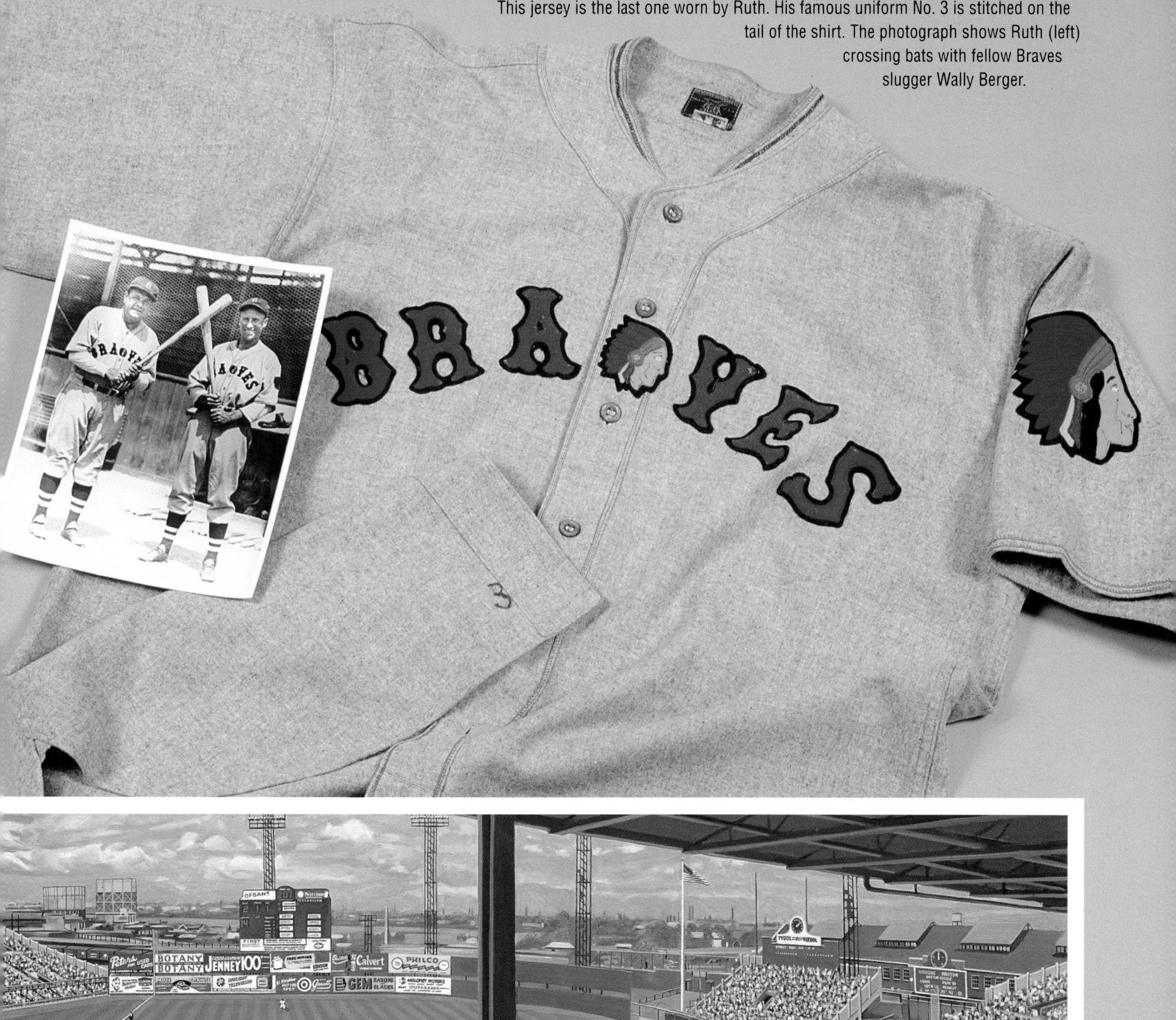

Braves Field Panorama by Andy Jurinko

Last Years in Boston

A. Clyde Shoun's 1947 satin jersey

B. Bill Voiselle's 1948 World Series jersey

C. Dr. Charles Lacks' trainer's shirt, circa 1946

D. 1948 National League champions pennant

E. 1930 Pilgrim hat replica patch worn for Boston's Tricentennial

F. 1949 Program

G. 1929 Scorecard

On To Milwaukee

A. 1958 World Series Pennant
B. Warren Spahn replica jersey
C. 1957 Commemorative World Series bat
D. Warren Spahn wood carving
E. 1954 Scorecard
F. 1955 Yearbook
G. 1961 Yearbook
H. 1963 Yearbook
I. 1965 Yearbook
J. 1957 World Series Booklet

County Stadium Classic by Andy Jurinko

Fading Milwaukee Memories

A. Hank Aaron replica jersey
B. 1964 Team photo
C. 1960s Pennant
D. The Sporting News, 1964 Cover

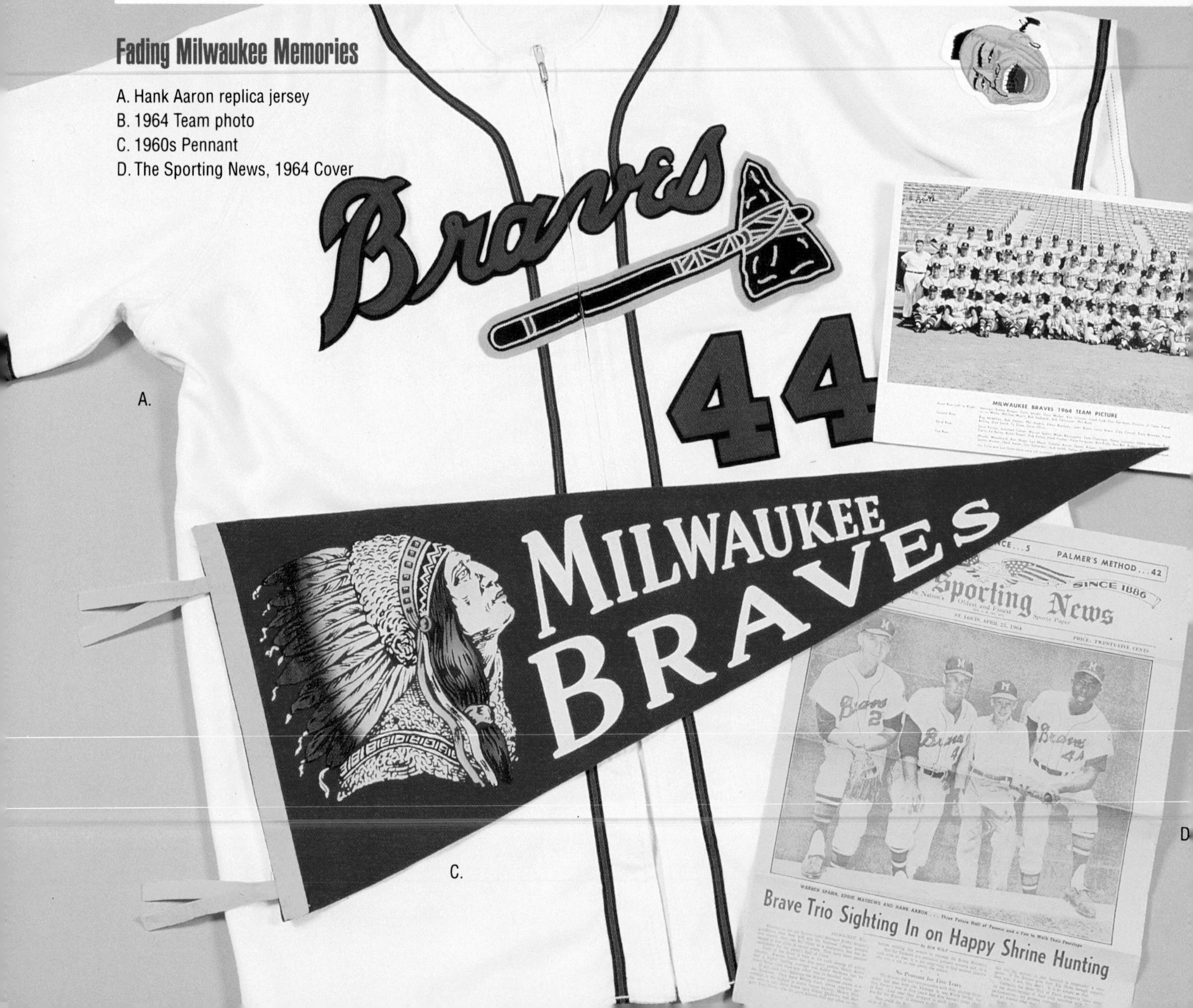

A.

C.

D

The Superstars

A. Phil Niekro's 1979 jersey
B. 1983 Yearbook
C. Flag bat used by Dale Murphy in a poster
D. Dale Murphy advertisement for Canon
E. Georgia license plate
F. Hartland statues (L–R): Warren Spahn, Eddie Mathews, Hank Aaron
G. Eddie Mathews' autobiography

Uniforms Through The Years

A. 1929 Jersey
B. Johnny Sain's 1948 World Series cap
C. 1935 Replica cap
D. Ed Wright's 1945 Jersey
E. Connie Ryan's 1948 warmup jacket
F. Jack Dittmer's 1956 warmup jacket
G. Eddie Mathews' 1957 World Series jersey
H. Eddie Mathews' cap
I. Terry Pendleton's 1991 World Series jersey
J. Dale Murphy's 1981 jersey
K. Hank Aaron's 1974 jersey
L. Dale Murphy's 1987 cap
M. Johnny Sain's cap as 1985 coach
N. 1948 World Series program
O. 1951 Program
P. 1958 Scorecard
Q. 1964 Yearbook
R. 1966 Scorecard
S. 1973 Yearbook
T. Ron Gant bat
U. Jeff Burroughs bat
V. Jeff Blauser bat

Uniforms and memorabilia on these and other pages of the color gallery courtesy of Tony Cocchi, Roger Pavey and Darrell O'Mary of Atlanta, the Atlanta Braves, and Mitchell & Ness Nostalgia Company, Philadelphia

Moving To The South

A. 1969 Division championship flag
B. 1969 NLCS ticket
C. 1969 NLCS program
D. 1969 Team photo
E. 1968 Team photo
F. 1967 Media guide
G. 1966 Yearbook
H. 1968 Yearbook
I. 1967 Yearbook
J. 1969 Yearbook
K. 1967 Scorebook
L. 1966 Team photo
M. Ticket to first game in Atlanta
N. "Phantom" tickets to 1969 World Series
O. Press pin and tie tack

A. Bobbing head doll
B. 1972 All-Star Game pennant
C. 1972 All-Star Game sticker
D. 1972 All-Star Game program
E. 1985 Uniform patch
F. 1982 NLCS program
G. 1982 NLCS tickets
H. 1983 Uniform patch
I. 1981 Scorebook
J. 1971 Scorebook
K. 1970 Media guide
L. 1973 Media guide
M. 1979 Yearbook
N. 1990 Uniform patch
O. 1972 All-Star Game pin
P. Anniversary books

Hank Aaron: The All-Time Home Run King

A. Aaron's 708th home run ball
B. Aaron cracked bat
C. 45 RPM record
D. T-shirt
E. Bumper sticker
F. Bust
G. 500th Home run card
H. 500th Home run button

A. Aaron media guides
B. 714th Home run certificate
C. 715th Home run certificate
D. Hank Aaron Day poster
E. Aaron pennant
F. 1974 Press pass
G. 715 Commemorative paper weight
H. Aaron autobiography

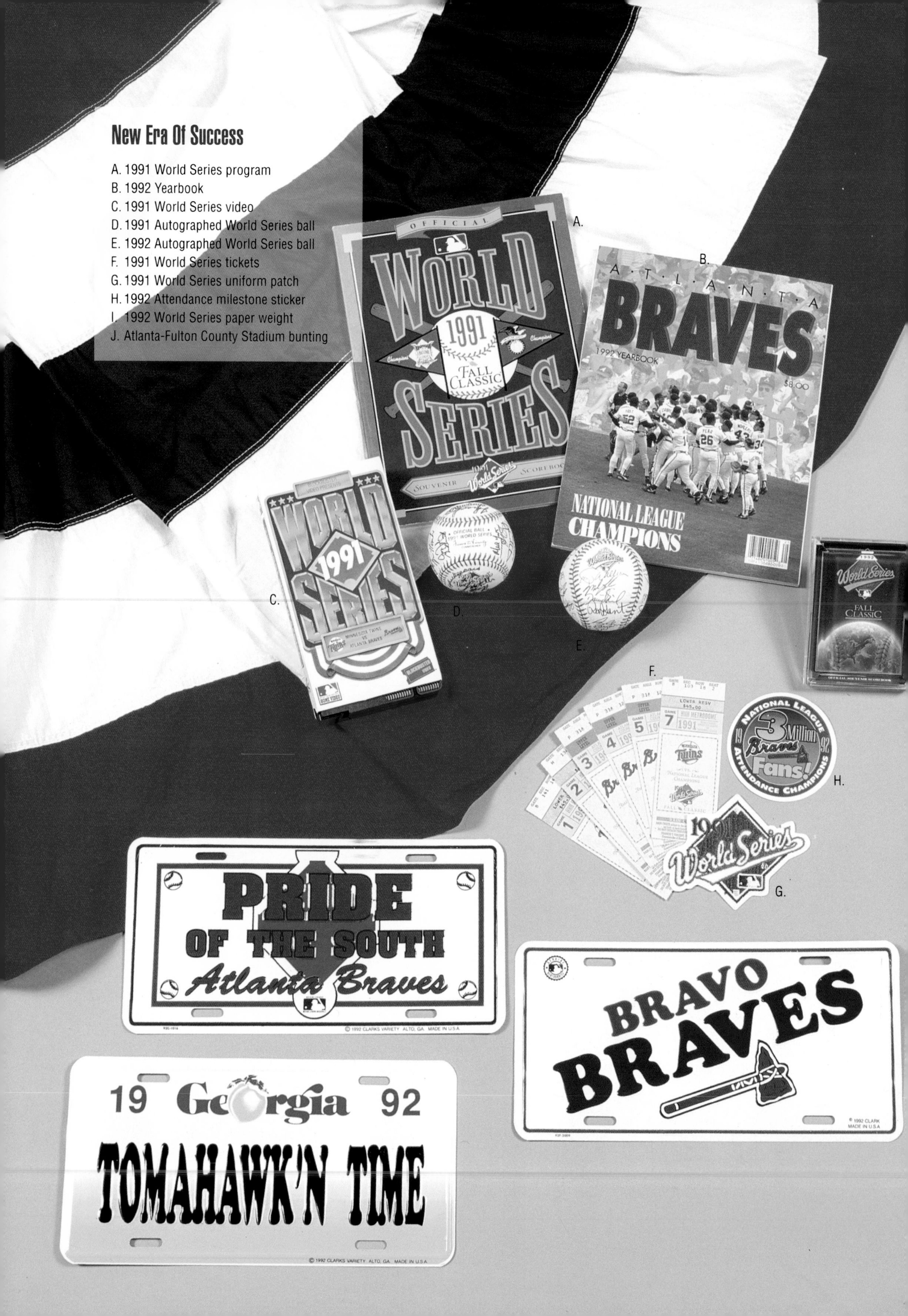

New Era Of Success

A. 1991 World Series program
B. 1992 Yearbook
C. 1991 World Series video
D. 1991 Autographed World Series ball
E. 1992 Autographed World Series ball
F. 1991 World Series tickets
G. 1991 World Series uniform patch
H. 1992 Attendance milestone sticker
I. 1992 World Series paper weight
J. Atlanta-Fulton County Stadium bunting

A. 1991 World Series balls
B. 1992 NLCS program
C. 1993 NLCS program
D. 1993 NLCS tickets
E. 1995 Uniform patch
F. 1992 World Series tickets
G. 1992 NLCS tickets
H. 1992 World Series uniform patch

Trading Card Roundup

A. 1991 Player pins
B. Tomahawk earrings
C. 1992 World Series press pin
D. Hank Aaron button
E. 1956 "Phantom" World Series press pin

Bob Uecker

30–26 with 3.01 ERA in 241 games, all relief; 78 saves.

Urban, Luke (27–28) catcher: 35-for-128, .273, in 50 games.

Urbanski, Billy (31–37) shortstop; third baseman; pinch hitter: 791-for-3,046, .260, in 763 games.

V

VALDESPINO, SANDY (68) outfielder: 20-for-86, .233, in 36 games.

VALDEZ, SERGIO (89–90) pitcher: 1–2 with 6.16 ERA in 25 games, all relief.

Vargas, Roberto (55) pitcher: 0–0 with 8.76 ERA in 25 games, all relief; two saves.

Vargus, Bill (25–26) pitcher: 1–1 with 3.89 ERA in 15 games.

VARNEY, PETE (76) catcher: 1-for-10, .100, in five games.

VATCHER, JIM (90) outfielder: 7-for-27, .259, in 21 games.

VAUGHAN, CHARLIE (66, 69) pitcher: 1–0 with 4.50 ERA in two games.

Veigel, Al (39) pitcher: 0–1 with 6.75 ERA in two games, both starts.

Emil Verban

Ozzie Virgil

VELAZQUEZ, FREDDIE (73) catcher: 8-for-23, .348, in 15 games.

Veltman, Pat (31) pinch hitter: 0-for-1, .000, in one game.

Verban, Emil (50) second baseman: 0-for-5, .000, in four games.

Vernon, Mickey (59) first baseman; outfielder: 20-for-91, .220, in 74 games.

VERSALLES, ZOILO (71) third baseman; shortstop; second baseman: 37-for-194, .191, in 66 games.

VIRGIL, OZZIE (86–88) catcher: 268-for-1,108, .242, in 344 games.

Voiselle, Bill (47–49) pitcher: 28–28 with 3.94 ERA in 89 games; three saves.

Volz, Jake (05) pitcher: 0–2 with 10.38 ERA in three games.

Voyles, Phil (29) outfielder: 16-for-68, .235, in 20 games.

Bob Walk

W

Wagner, Bill (18) catcher: 10-for-47, .213, in 13 games.

WALK, BOB (81–83) pitcher: 12–13 with 4.85 ERA in 36 games.

Wall, Murray (50) pitcher: 0–0 with 9.00 ERA in one game, relief.

Wallace, Lefty (42, 45–46) pitcher: 5–6 with 4.11 ERA in 51 games.

Wallen, Norm (45) third baseman: 2-for-15, .133, in four games.

Walsh, Ed (17) pitcher: 0–1 with 3.50 ERA in four games.

Walsh, Joe (38) shortstop: 0-for-8, .000, in four games.

Walters, Bucky (31–32, 50) third baseman; second baseman: 22-for-115, .191, in 32 games; pitcher: 0–0 with 4.50 ERA in one game, relief.

Waner, Lloyd (41) outfielder: 21-for-51, .412, in 19 games.

Waner, Paul (41–42) outfielder; first baseman: 168-for-627, .268, in 209 games.

WARD, DUANE (86) pitcher: 0–1 with 7.31 ERA in 10 games, all relief.

Warstler, Rabbit (36–40) shortstop; second baseman; third baseman: 391-for-1,725, .227, in 512 games.

Wasem, Link (37) catcher: 0-for-1, .000, in two games.

WASHINGTON, CLAUDELL (81–86) outfielder: 647-for-2,330, .278, in 651 games.

WATSON, BOB (82–84) first baseman; outfielder: 92-for-348, .264, in 171 games.

Watson, Mule (20–23) pitcher: 28–33 with 4.22 ERA in 109 games; four saves.

Weafer, Hal (36) pitcher: 0–0 with 12.00 ERA in one game, relief.

Rabbit Warstler

Weaver, Orlie (11) pitcher: 3–12 with 6.47 ERA in 27 games.

Weeden, Bert (11) pinch hitter: 0-for-1, .000, in one game.

Weir, Roy (36–39) pitcher: 6–4 with 3.55 ERA in 29 games.

Welsh, Jimmy (25–27, 29–30) outfielder; second baseman; first baseman: 600-for-2,079, .289, in 553 games.

Wentzel, Stan (45) outfielder: 4-for-19, .211, in four games.

Werts, Johnny (26–29) pitcher: 15–21 with 4.29 ERA in 88 games; two saves.

WESSINGER, JIM (79) second baseman: 0-for-7, .000, in 10 games.

West, Max (38–42, 46) outfielder; first baseman: 612-for-2,328, .263, in 665 games.

Westerberg, Oscar (07) shortstop: 2-for-6, .333, in two games.

Weston, Al (29) pinch hitter: 0-for-3, .000, in three games.

WETHERBY, JEFF (89) outfielder: 10-for-48, .208, in 52 games.

Whaling, Bert (13–15) catcher: 129-for-573, .225, in 211 games.

Whelan, Tom (20) first baseman: 0-for-1, .000, in one game.

Whisenant, Pete (52) outfielder: 10-for-52, .192, in 24 games.

WHISENTON, LARRY (77–79, 81–82) outfielder; pinch hitter: 48-for-205, .234, in 116 games.

Whitcher, Bob (45) pitcher: 0–2 with 2.87 ERA in six games.

White, Charlie (54–55) catcher: 29-for-123, .236, in 62 games.

White, Ernie (46–48) pitcher: 0–3 with 2.84 ERA in 28 games; two saves.

White, Jack (04) outfielder: 0-for-5, .000, in one game.

White, Kirby (09–10) pitcher: 7–15 with 2.94 ERA in 26 games.

White, Sam (19) catcher: 0-for-1, .000, in one game.

White, Sammy (61) catcher: 14-for-63, .222, in 21 games.

White, Steve (12) pitcher: 0–0 with 6.00 ERA in three games, all relief.

WHITED, ED (89) third baseman; first baseman: 12-for-74, .162, in 36 games.

Whitehouse, Gil (12) catcher: 0-for-3, .000, in two games.

Whitney, Pinky (33–36) third baseman; second baseman; shortstop: 372-for-1,443, .258, in 382 games.

Pinky Whitney

WHITT, ERNIE (90) catcher: 31-for-180, .172, in 67 games.

Whitted, Possum (14) outfielder; second baseman; first baseman; third baseman; shortstop: 57-for-218, .261, in 66 games.

Wickland, Al (18) outfielder: 87-for-332, .262, in 95 games.

Wietelmann, Whitey (39–46) shortstop; second baseman; third baseman: 379-for-1,634, .232, in 532 games; pitcher: 0–0 with 14.09 ERA in four games, all relief.

Wilborn, Claude (40) outfielder: 0-for-7, .000, in five games.

WILHELM, HOYT (69–71) pitcher: 8–4 with 3.10 ERA in 61 games, all relief; 17 saves.

Wilhelm, Kaiser (04–05) pitcher: 17–43 with 4.07 ERA in 73 games.

Wilhoit, Joe (16–17) outfielder: 139-for-569, .244, in 170 games.

WILLARD, JERRY (91–92) catcher: 11-for-37, .297, in 43 games.

Willey, Carlton (58–62) pitcher: 28–40 with 3.94 ERA in 142 games; one save.

Williams, Ace (40, 46) pitcher: 0–0 with 16.00 ERA in six games, all relief.

Williams, Earl B. (28) catcher: 0-for-2, .000, in three games.

WILLIAMS, EARL C. (70–72, 75–76) catcher; first baseman; third baseman: 413-for-1,648, .251, in 478 games.

Williams, Pop (03) pitcher: 4–5 with 4.12 ERA in 10 games, all starts.

Wilson, Art (18–20) catcher; first baseman; third baseman: 119-for-490, .243, in 176 games.

Wilson, Charlie (31) third baseman: 11-for-58, .190, in 16 games.

Wilson, Frank (24–26) outfielder: 120-for-482, .249, in 160 games.

Mark Wohlers

Wilson, Jim (51–54) pitcher: 31–32 with 4.32 ERA in 100 games; one save.

Wise, Casey (58–59) second baseman; shortstop; third baseman: 27-for-147, .184, in 53 games.

Witherup, Roy (06) pitcher: 0–3 with 6.26 ERA in eight games.

WOHLERS, MARK (91–   ) current Braves pitcher.

Wolverton, Harry (05) third baseman: 104-for-463, .225, in 122 games.

Womack, Sid (26) catcher: 0-for-3, .000, in one game.

WOODALL, BRAD (94–   ) current Braves player.

Woodend, George (44) pitcher: 0–0 with 13.50 ERA in three games, all relief.

WOODWARD, WOODY (63–68) shortstop; second baseman; third baseman; first baseman: 300-for-1,290, .233, in 491 games.

Workman, Chuck (43–46) outfielder; third baseman; first baseman: 389-for-1,595, .244, in 457 games.

Worthington, Red (31–34) outfielder: 298-for-1,036, .288, in 291 games.

Wright, Ab (44) outfielder: 50-for-195, .256, in 71 games.

Wright, Al (33) second baseman: 1-for-1, 1.000, in four games.

Wright, Ed (45–48) pitcher: 23–15 with 3.71 ERA in 77 games.

WYNN, JIM (76) outfielder: 93-for-449, .207, in 148 games.

Y

Yeargin, Al (22, 24) pitcher: 1–12 with 4.91 ERA in 33 games.

Young, Cy (11) pitcher: 4–5 with 3.71 ERA in 11 games, all starts.

Young, Harley (08) pitcher: 0–1 with 3.29 ERA in six games.

Young, Herman (11) third baseman; shortstop: 6-for-25, .240, in nine games.

Young, Irv (05–08) pitcher: 50–78 with 3.15 ERA in 142 games; one save.

Z

Zachary, Tom (30–34) pitcher: 42–42 with 3.48 ERA in 120 games; four saves.

ZIEM, STEVE (87) pitcher: 0–1 with 7.71 ERA in two games, both relief

Zinn, Guy (13) outfielder: 41-for-138, .297, in 36 games.

ZUVELLA, PAUL (82–85) shortstop; second baseman; third baseman: 53-for-221, .240, in 97 games.

Paul Zuvella

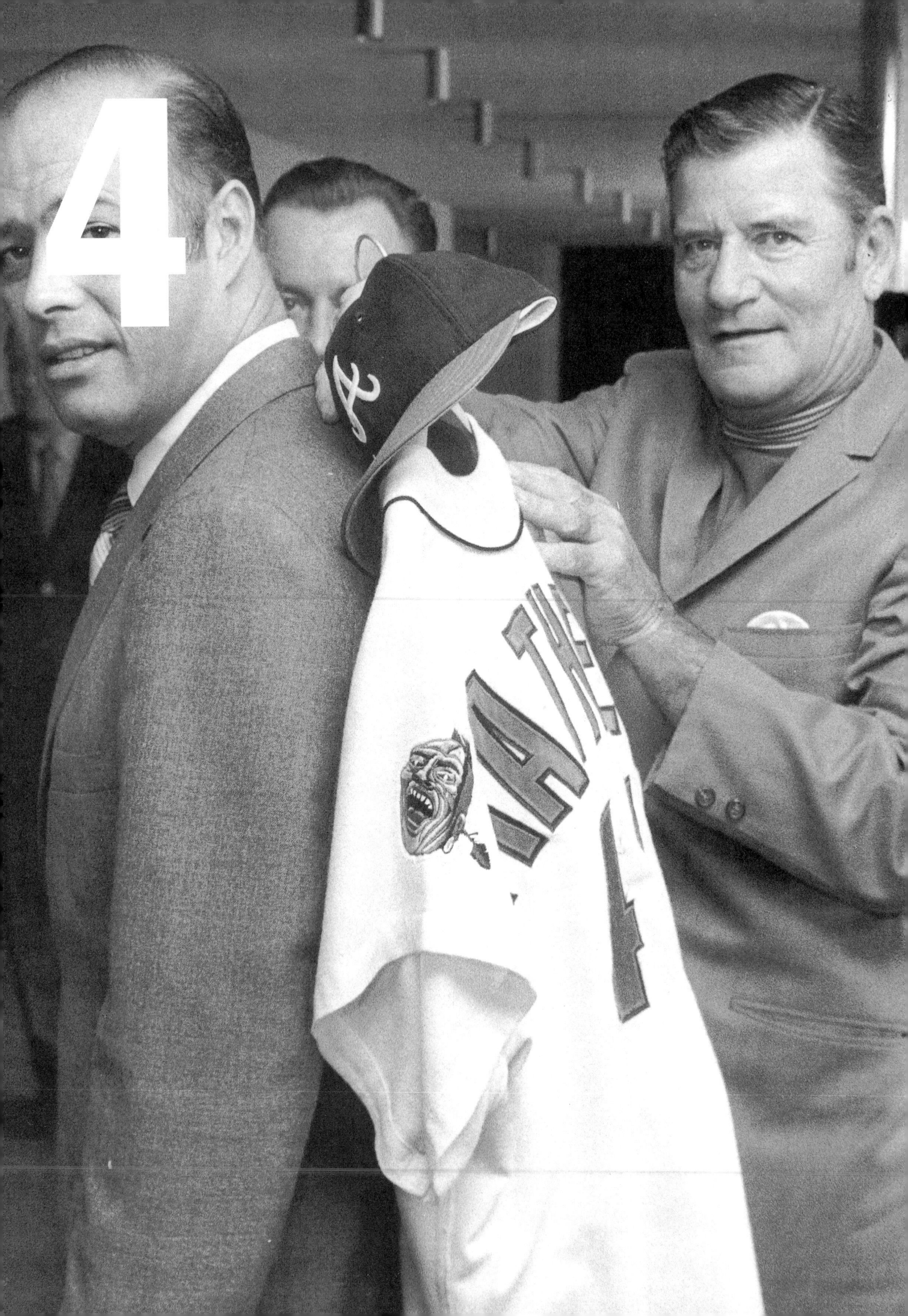

The Strategists

In 1949, six years after he last managed the Braves, Casey Stengel took the Yankees to the World Series championship in his first season with the Bronx Bombers. Afterward, he was named manager of the year, prompting him to remark to Pittsburgh's Billy Meyer, the 1948 manager of the year, "Ain't it funny, Bill, how all of a sudden I got so smart and you got so dumb?"

Managing the Braves did indeed make many managers, including the legendary Stengel, look pretty dumb. During six years in Boston, Stengel never got the team above fifth place and had only one winning season. But in 12 years with the Yankees, he won 10 pennants and seven World Series, for which he was voted into the Hall of Fame.

Of the 46 men who have managed the Braves—from Frank Selee who lasted 1,677 games to Ted Turner who sat in the dugout for just one game—Stengel wasn't the only one to suffer from a lack of talent. Though the franchise has enjoyed several periods of success and fostered many great players, there have been even more years when managers have had to suffer with resources that weren't adequate to compete for the pennant or even the first division.

Typical of the prospects that Boston managers encountered in the bleak period from 1922 through 1945 was an outfielder Stengel sent back to the minors with the assessment "That boy couldn't hit the ground if he fell out of an airplane."

Yet Stengel and many of the other managers who failed, as well as the few who have succeeded, compose a rich and entertaining chapter in the history of the longest continuously operating franchise in pro sports history.

Stengel is one of eight Hall of Famers to manage the Braves, and he's certainly not the only one to be stymied by the organization. Bill McKechnie (1930–37) made the Hall of Fame as the only manager to win pennants in three different cities. But all he could do in Boston was set the franchise record for losses (666).

The Braves have had 13 player-managers and two owner-managers—Turner and Judge Emil Fuchs. The roll call also includes Harry Wright, the "Father of Professional Baseball"; the profane and superstitious "Miracle Man" George Stallings; Fred Tenney, one of the first college graduates ever to play or manage in the majors; the tempestuous Rogers Hornsby, who won the last of his seven batting titles as player-manager; and Charlie Grimm, a left-handed banjo player.

It's interesting to note that Tenney's degree from Brown University, the same school Turner attended, didn't help him manage. His .334 percentage over four seasons is the worst among managers who lasted at least one year with the franchise. And Hornsby, who managed most of the 1928 season, actually had a batting average (.387) that was 67 points higher than his winning percentage (.320).

With 1,004 wins and five pennants, Selee easily ranks as the most successful of the group. His .607 winning percentage is the best for a manager who lasted more than one year at the job.

However, with 670 wins through 1994, Bobby Cox is the winningest Braves manager of the 20th century, and with only moderate success he could catch Selee if he manages into 1998.

Stallings, in 1914, and Fred Haney, in 1957, won the only two World Series championships owned by the franchise.

This chapter chronicles the careers of all 46 men who have managed the Braves since their birth as the Boston Red Stockings.

Luman Harris welcomed Eddie Mathews to his coaching staff in 1971, but the following year, Mathews replaced Harris as manager.

1876–81 / Wright, Harry

Record: 254–187 (.576)
Birthplace: Sheffield, England
B: January 10, 1835; **D:** October 3, 1895

What Orville and Wilbur Wright were to aviation, Harry and George Wright were to the Braves—and to professional baseball, too.

Harry, the older of baseball's two Wright brothers, organized the Cincinnati Red Stockings in 1869 as the game's first team composed entirely of openly salaried players. For his founding efforts, Wright is generally regarded as the "Father of Professional Baseball."

The Cincinnati club, with Harry managing and playing several positions and George as its star shortstop, was a barnstorming team. In the Red Stockings' first year and a half, the club traveled 21,000 miles and won its first 89 games before finally losing at Brooklyn. But by the end of 1870, the Cincinnati team was falling apart, destined to return to amateur status the next year. Harry Wright had other plans, though. He and George were off to Boston to form the team that lives today as the Atlanta Braves.

In 1871 professional league baseball was created with the formation of the National Association. The Boston club, managed by Harry Wright and bearing the same Red Stockings nickname as his Cincinnati team, was one of nine clubs to pay the $10 franchise fee. Not only did March 17, 1871, mark the birth of the Braves, but it also signaled the start of major league baseball.

Wright's Red Stockings didn't win the first National Association pennant, but they did win the next four. In 1871, Boston narrowly missed winning the championship, finishing two games behind Philadelphia. But backed by the pitching of Al Spalding, George Wright's superb play at shortstop, and Harry Wright's leadership, Boston won pennants in 1872, '73, '74, and '75.

In fact, the Red Stockings had attained such superiority by 1875 that they won the league by 15 games with an .899 winning percentage (71–8), which has never been surpassed. This imbalance in competition was one of the factors that led to the dissolution of the National Association at that point and the formation of the National League in 1876.

Spalding and three other Boston players jumped to Chicago in 1876, leaving Wright shorthanded and destined for a fourth-place finish. However, he reloaded in 1877, mainly by signing pitcher Tommy Bond from Hartford, and proceeded to win the second National League pennant. The Red Stockings repeated as NL champs in 1878, giving Wright six league titles in seven years. However, he'd never win another one.

The beginning of Wright's demise as Red Stockings manager came, interestingly enough, with the defection of three players, including his younger brother George, to Providence in 1879. George one-upped his older brother, leading Providence to the pennant by five games over Harry's Red Stockings. It was the only year George managed.

As for Harry, he lasted just two more years in Boston. The Red Stockings finished under .500 (.476) for the first time in 1880 and wound up in sixth place for the second straight season in 1881, prompting his dismissal.

Wright's managerial career was far from over, though. He managed Providence the next two years, then went to Philadelphia in 1884 and managed the Phillies for a decade. Wright nearly always had competitive teams. In 23 seasons, including five in the National Association, he won 1,225 of 2,145 games, a nifty .581 percentage.

Born in England, Wright was the son of a professional cricket player. He moved to the United States at an early age and was raised in New York. A jeweler by profession, Wright played cricket and was introduced to baseball by the New York Knickerbockers, for whom he debuted in 1858. Five years later, he moved to Cincinnati to serve as pro at the Union Cricket Club. In 1866 he helped organize the Cincinnati Red Stockings. When that team declared its professionalism in 1869, Wright was well on his way to being one of the game's most notable pioneers.

Wright's contributions to baseball are numerous. He is credited with developing flannel uniforms and the "knicker" style of pants. Referred to as a "baseball Edison," he originated team play by teaching his players to back each other up on defense, and he introduced pregame batting practice. He also was the first manager to use hand signals to direct his players.

At the meeting during which the National League was formed in February 1876, Wright was instrumental in developing the new organization's regulations. He also was the first to take his team on a foreign tour (England in 1874) and the first to have a "day" held in his honor at the ballpark. Perhaps most importantly, he constantly crusaded to keep the game clean by opposing the drinking, gambling, and carousing common among ballplayers of that era.

Following the 1893 season, the Phillies did not renew Wright's contract to manage. Because of his stature in the game, though, he was named the National League's first supervisor of umpires.

Wright died of pneumonia at age 60. In 1896, on "Harry Wright Day," some $3,000 was collected at ballparks for a monument to be erected at his grave. The marker in Philadelphia's West Laurel Hill Cemetery reads "Father of Professional Baseball." It also could read "Father of America's oldest continuously operating pro sports franchise—the Atlanta Braves."

Harry Wright

Wright, Harry

	W	L	T	Pct
1876	39	31	0	.557
1877	42	18	1	.700
1878	41	19	0	.683
1879	54	30	0	.643
1880	40	44	2	.476
1881	38	45	0	.458
Red Stockings	254	187	3	.576
Career	1,225	885	35	.581

1882, 1883–88 / Morrill, John

Record: 335–296 (.531)
Birthplace: Boston
B: February 19, 1855; **D:** April 2, 1932

When the Red Stockings' owners, headed by president Arthur H. Soden, decided to replace Harry Wright after the 1881 season, they chose one of the most popular men ever to wear the franchise uniform in Boston. John Morrill was a hometown product who had established himself as a versatile, dependable player with the club. He also was so well thought of that he was nicknamed "Honest John."

Morrill replaced George Wright as captain in 1879 when the younger of the club's Wright brothers departed for Providence. In replacing Harry Wright, 27-year-old "Honest John" became the club's first true player-manager in the National League, though Harry played center field and pitched in the old National Association.

At least in the first half of his managerial career, Morrill was able to get Boston back in the thick of contention in the National League. Following two straight sixth-place finishes under Wright, the Red Stockings climbed to third in 1882 for Morrill, who was the regular first baseman.

But in one of the stranger managerial moves in franchise history, Morrill turned the team over to second baseman Jack Burdock to start the 1883 season. The team, now known

John Morrill

as the Beaneaters, did not respond well to the change either, losing 11 of its first 15 games. That experience only set the stage for Morrill's eventual return as manager, as well as for one of the most thrilling turnarounds the team has ever known.

With the club in fourth place on July 22, Morrill replaced Burdock. Inspired by the move, Boston won 33 of its last 44 games (.750) and 14 of its final 15. After being in seventh place in June, the club claimed its first pennant since 1878 and its third in eight seasons of National League play. It also was Morrill's finest year as a player. He hit a career-high .319 and led the league's first basemen in fielding (.974).

That pennant was the highlight of Morrill's seven-year stay as manager. The Beaneaters played even better ball (.658) in 1884, yet finished second, a distant 10½ games behind Providence. From there, it was all downhill. After finishing fourth in 1888, Morrill was sold to Washington in the spring of 1889. Many fans and businessmen were upset about the move, but to no avail, of course.

Morrill became a sporting goods dealer and is credited with developing the football face mask and laced-front pants. He also dabbled in sports writing, composing articles about baseball for the *Boston Journal.*

Morrill, John

	W	L	T	Pct
1882	45	39	1	.536
1883	33	11	0	.750
1884	73	38	5	.658
1885	46	66	1	.411
1886	56	61	1	.479
1887	12	17	3	.414
1888	70	64	3	.522
Red Stockings, Beaneaters	335	296	14	.531
Career	348	334	14	.510

1883 / Burdock, Jack

Record: 30–24 (.556)
Birthplace: Brooklyn, New York
B: April, 1852; **D:** November 28, 1931

"Black Jack" Burdock was one of the best defensive second basemen in the formative years of the National League. But the spunk and competitiveness that made him a success as a player also were his undoing as a manager.

The 5–9, 158-pound Brooklyn native led National League second basemen in fielding five times in the first nine years of the league's existence. In 1882, Burdock recorded his fourth fielding title in six years, and the following spring he was promoted to Boston's manager, replacing first baseman John Morrill in a curious move.

Under Burdock in 1883, Boston struggled early, losing 11 of its first 15, then began to rally, climbing from seventh place in June to fourth by July 22. However, at that point, president Arthur H. Soden put Morrill back in charge of the team. Even though the club, now being called the Beaneaters, had won 26 of its last 39 after a slow start under Burdock, "Black Jack" had embarrassed the club and the league a few days earlier. After hitting a pop foul, he grabbed the opposing catcher to

Jack Burdock

prevent him from catching the ball. The umpire fined Burdock $20 on the spot, and the incident led to his removal as manager.

With Morrill in charge, the Beaneaters won 33 of their last 44 games, sprinting from fourth place to an unlikely pennant. Burdock, 31, played a major role in the team's success. Never a strong hitter, he batted a career-high .330, 86 points over his lifetime average of .244.

Burdock played 14 seasons in the National League, preceded by four in the National Association. The only managing he did, though, came in those first 54 games of 1883.

Burdock, Jack

	W	L	T	Pct
1883	30	24	0	.556
Beaneaters	30	24	0	.556
Career	30	24	0	.556

1887 / Kelly, King

Record: 49–43 (.533)
Birthplace: Troy, New York
B: December 31, 1857; **D:** November 8, 1894

King Kelly was never named manager of the Beaneaters, but as captain, he is credited with running the team for most of the 1887 season, his first in Boston. In the early years of baseball, the captain often was more powerful than the manager.

The biggest star of his era, Kelly was purchased from the White Sox for $10,000 in a transaction that shocked baseball and severely undermined the authority of manager John Morrill.

With the team languishing in fifth place and lacking direction under the carefree Kelly, Morrill regained control for the final month of the 1887 season. However, the team actually played worse for him than it did for Kelly and remained in fifth place.

A Hall of Fame player, Kelly jumped from the Beaneaters to the Boston franchise of the upstart Players League in 1890, managing the team to a pennant. The following year he managed Cincinnati of the American Association to sixth place, but he never managed again.

King Kelly

Kelly, King

	W	L	T	Pct
1887	49	43	3	.533
Beaneaters	49	43	3	.533
Career	173	148	9	.539

1889 / Hart, Jim

Record: 83–45 (.648)
Birthplace: Fairview, Pennsylvania
B: July 10, 1855; **D:** July 18, 1919

Jim Hart never played in the major leagues, and his misfortune of trying to run a team built around unruly superstar "King" Kelly led to a very short tenure as a National League manager.

Remarkably, Hart brought the Beaneaters home just one game out of first place in 1889, yet still lost his job. His .648 winning percentage is the best in franchise history for a one-season manager.

Hart's first job in professional baseball came in 1885. At age 28 he was appointed vice president and manager of Louisville in the American Association, which was regarded as a major league at the time. Known as a shrewd businessman and a conservative manager, Hart finished under .500 both seasons he ran the Louisville club, but he still turned a profit.

In 1887 he bought the minor league franchise in Milwaukee, which he ran for two years and sold. As a consequence, he was available when Boston suddenly found itself in need of a manager for the 1889 season.

Beaneaters president Arthur H. Soden, disenchanted with John Morrill, sold his manager and first baseman to Washing-

Jim Hart

ton just before the start of the season. The pickings for a new manager were limited at that point. Hart's availability made him an obvious choice to manage the talented ballclub.

Hart's conservative nature made him a good fit for the job, since he was content to allow Kelly, the premier showman of that era, to have center stage. That formula almost led to a pennant, but it wound up backfiring on Hart.

Boston led the league by a game over New York entering play on October 2, the next-to-last day of the season. But the Beaneaters suffered a 7–1 loss at Cleveland, a defeat that was particularly devastating because Kelly showed up drunk and was unable to play. At the same time, New York was winning and taking back first place by two percentage points.

New York clinched the pennant the next day with a victory. Hart was blamed for Kelly's drunkenness and ultimately became the scapegoat for Boston's failure to win the pennant. Though his dismissal may have been unfair, it created an opening for Frank Selee, who would become one of the most successful managers in franchise history. In fact, Selee's availability may have prompted Hart's brief tenure as much as anything.

Though Hart never managed again, he did just fine for himself. He went to Chicago to help Al Spalding run the White Stockings (now the Cubs) and became president of that club in 1891 when Spalding retired to run his sporting goods business.

Hart, Jim

	W	L	T	Pct
1889	83	45	5	.648
Beaneaters	83	45	5	.648
Career	202	174	7	.537

1890–1901 / Selee, Frank

Record: 1,004–649 (.607)
Birthplace: Amherst, New Hampshire
B: October 26, 1859; **D:** July 5, 1909

Frank Selee was the greatest manager in the history of what is now the Braves franchise. In 12 years as Boston's manager, he won five pennants, all within the eight-year period 1891–98. He holds franchise records for pennants, games (1,677), wins (1,004), full seasons (12), and percentage (.607) for managers with more than one year of service.

An absolute master at recognizing talent and building a team, Selee went to Chicago after wearing out his welcome in Boston and assembled the most dominating Cubs team in that franchise's history.

A New England native, Selee was the mild-mannered son of a Methodist minister. He had a very brief career as a pro player before taking his first managerial job in 1885 with Haverhill of the New England League. After two seasons there, he moved to Oshkosh of the Northwestern League and won his first pennant in 1887. He moved up to Omaha of the American Association in 1888 and won another pennant there in 1889.

It was at Omaha that William Conant, one of the three partners who owned the Beaneaters, met Selee while scouting a pitcher named Kid Nichols. In the process of recommending Nichols, Selee also tipped off Conant to a Milwaukee player named Bobby Lowe. Nichols and Lowe would become central figures in Boston's success under Selee, Nichols as a Hall of Famer pitcher and Lowe as a second baseman with a surprisingly potent bat.

After the talented Beaneaters fell one game short of the pennant in 1889, manager Jim Hart was dismissed. Not only did Boston sign Selee to manage, but the Beaneaters also purchased his star pitcher, Nichols, from Omaha for $3,500 and plucked Lowe from Milwaukee for just $700. Selee's ability to spot talent would soon become legendary, and the Beaneaters would prosper from it for a full decade.

Selee's first team didn't take the league by storm. In fact, Boston finished fifth in 1890 in spite of a fine 76–57 record. The next season, however, the Beaneaters won the first of three consecutive pennants, clearly establishing Selee's stature as one of the finest managers in the game.

Selee wasn't regarded as a brilliant strategist. In fact, once the game began, he gave the players great liberty to make their own decisions. However, that was because he made sure the Beaneaters had the best-prepared players in the game. They were fundamentally sound, mentally as well as physically, and were known for outthinking their opponents.

Frank Selee

The development of one of the game's most exciting offensive plays is credited to Selee. In a dead-ball era when advancing runners more than a base at a time proved difficult, he introduced what is known as the "hit-and-run." Boston often would start a runner from first, forcing either the second baseman or shortstop to cover second and opening a hole in the infield for the hitter to exploit. The maneuver thrilled fans who were not used to such daring and ingenuity.

After winning pennants in 1891, '92, and '93, Selee reloaded during a three-year period in which Boston finished third once and fourth twice but still played well over .500. Some of the young players he rebuilt the team around included third baseman Jimmy Collins, who would become a Hall of Famer, and a left-handed catcher from Brown University named Fred Tenney whom he turned into an outstanding first baseman.

The Beaneaters bounced back to win consecutive pennants in 1897 and '98 before settling for second in 1899. In 1900, Boston dropped to fourth, six games below .500. It was the only losing record Selee had in 12 years in Boston. He got the Beaneaters back to even .500 in 1901 even though he lost several key players to the upstart American League. But the front office, which refused to fight the new league for talent, took out the fifth-place finish on Selee by not offering him a contract.

In 12 years with Boston, Selee had 10 first-division teams and five pennant winners, and he won nearly 61 percent of his games. He never made more than $3,500 in a year, though he supplemented his income with ownership of a haberdashery.

As soon as the Beaneaters cut Selee loose, he was picked up by the man he'd replaced in Boston, Jim Hart, who'd become president of the Chicago Cubs. Selee inherited a horrible team, but within two years, he had them in contention. He assembled the famed infield of (Joe) Tinker to (Johnny) Evers to (Frank) Chance.

But in the midst of the 1905 season, with the Cubs on the verge of greatness, Selee was forced by poor health to take a leave of absence. He never returned. The Cubs he'd built, however, went on to win four pennants and finish second once in the next five years. Before that streak was fulfilled, Selee died of tuberculosis in 1909 at age 49.

In 16 seasons managing two franchises, he finished under .500 just twice and posted a composite winning percentage of .598, fourth best in history.

Selee, Frank

	W	L	T	Pct
1890	76	57	1	.571
1891	87	51	2	.630
1892	102	48	2	.680
1893	86	43	2	.667
1894	83	49	1	.629
1895	71	60	2	.542
1896	74	57	1	.565
1897	93	39	3	.705
1898	102	47	3	.685
1899	95	57	1	.625
1900	66	72	4	.478
1901	69	69	2	.500
Beaneaters	1,004	649	24	.607
Career	1,284	862	34	.598

1902–04 / Buckenberger, Al

Record: 186–242 (.435)
Birthplace: Detroit, Michigan
B: January 31, 1861; **D:** July 1, 1917

Bad decisions are a part of any business. But baseball fans and historians have a way of not letting major league clubs forget their mistakes.

The firing of Frank Selee took place nearly a century ago, yet anyone who peeks back into the history of the Braves can clearly see that his dismissal still ranks as one of the biggest blunders in franchise history. As if letting Selee get away wasn't enough, the ownership group headed by president Arthur Soden compounded this monumental bungling by hiring Albert (Al) C. Buckenberger as his replacement.

Buckenberger was only 41. A minor league second baseman, he began managing at age 23. He had considerable experience at the big league level for someone of his age. He managed Columbus of the American Association in 1889, then landed with Pittsburgh in 1892.

In 1893, Buckenberger brought the Pirates in second, just five games behind the Beaneaters. That achievement probably was still in the thoughts of Boston's ownership group when they began searching for Selee's successor. Pittsburgh's management was less impressed, though. They fired Buckenberger late the following season, replacing him with a young catcher named Connie Mack.

Buckenberger was picked up by St. Louis in 1895 but fired after just 50 games with the team in 11th place. He then returned to the minors, where he stayed until he was rescued from Rochester by the Beaneaters.

The club's new manager arrived in Boston at a crucial time and one that would lead to the first extended period of pathetic baseball in franchise history. The American League had been born the year before. Not only was the new league raiding quality players from the Beaneaters, but it was fielding an interesting, competitive team in Boston.

Buckenberger, who helped develop star Boston pitcher Vic Willis at Syracuse, said the exodus of talent was no concern to him. He claimed he could replace the defectors with comparable players from Rochester.

To his credit, Buckenberger coaxed the Beaneaters home in third place, nine games over .500, in 1902. But the team still lost the battle of Boston to the more entertaining Somersets.

Al Buckenberger

The next two seasons were disastrous, and after the Beaneaters finished with a miserable 55–98 (.359) record in 1904, 51 games out of first, Buckenberger was fired. Though he was just 43, he never managed in the majors again. And Boston's National League franchise would never dig itself out of the hole it had fallen into with its American League competitor.

Buckenberger, Al

	W	L	T	Pct
1902	73	64	5	.533
1903	58	80	2	.420
1904	55	98	2	.359
Beaneaters	186	242	9	.435
Career	488	539	16	.475

1905–07, 1911 / Tenney, Fred

Record: 202–402 (.334)
Birthplace: Georgetown, Massachusetts
B: November 26, 1871; **D:** July 3, 1952

Fred Tenney was proof that a college education isn't necessarily an advantage in managing a baseball team. Not that Tenney had much to work with, but his Brown University degree seems to have been quite useless in light of his team's ghastly .334 percentage in his four seasons as a player-manager.

Tenney was an excellent ballplayer and might even have been a decent manager if he'd come along at another time. But the turmoil created by competition with the American League and the flurry of ownership changes had brought the franchise to its knees. It's doubtful that any manager could have done significantly better than Tenney under the same circumstances.

Fred Tenney

A left-handed catcher at Brown, Tenney was signed right off the campus at graduation by Beaneaters manager Frank Selee, whose catching corps was crippled by injuries. Selee eventually turned Tenney into a first baseman.

When Tenney became Boston's manager in 1905, succeeding Al Buckenberger, ownership partners Arthur Soden and William Conant were on the run. They even told Tenney not to worry about winning games and promised him a bonus if he could help them avoid losing money. He went so far as to chase foul balls into the stands—and he got his bonus.

However, Tenney's first team finished 52 games under .500 and 54½ games out of first place. That was typical of Boston for a decade. Tenney's best team was the 1907 club, which was 58–90 (.392) and finished in seventh place, 47 games out of first. That's pretty good by comparison with his 1906 team, which was last in the league in hitting, pitching, and fielding and finished a franchise-record 66½ games out of first. It also was the first franchise representative to wind up in last place.

In 1908 the Dovey brothers, George and John, who bought the team the previous year, traded Tenney to New York. He was released after two seasons there and spent 1910 as a player-manager in the minors. But in 1911 the 39-year-old Tenney was brought back to Boston to manage by yet another new owner, William Russell. Tenney, well aware of what he was being asked to do, balked at first. He finally agreed when Russell promised to buy some stock in the club Tenney was trying to unload.

The 1911 team played to a .291 percentage (44–107), the second-worst showing in franchise history. Even though Tenney had another year remaining on his contract, he was fired at the end of the season.

Tenney, Fred

	W	L	T	Pct
1905	51	103	2	.331
1906	49	102	1	.325
1907	58	90	4	.392
1911	44	107	5	.291
Beaneaters, Doves, Rustlers	202	402	12	.334
Career	202	402	12	.334

1908 / Kelley, Joe

Record: 63–91 (.409)
Birthplace: Cambridge, Massachusetts
B: December 9, 1871; **D:** August 14, 1943

Joe Kelley was far from the most successful manager in franchise history, but he probably was the most vain. A Hall of Fame outfielder with a lifetime batting average of .317, Kelley had the unusual habit of carrying a mirror in his uniform pocket. It was not uncommon for him to pull it out on the field and take a quick look at himself.

Regarded as a charismatic player, he had great fan appeal, a factor that probably helped convince the struggling Doves to hire him as manager in 1908. He also was a local product, hailing from nearby Cambridge.

Kelley, who started his big league career with Boston in 1891, spent his best seasons with the great Baltimore teams

Joe Kelley

Frank Bowerman

of the 1890s. His first managerial experience came when he took over Cincinnati in the midst of the 1902 season. He continued as a player-manager for the Reds through 1905, never finishing higher than third but never failing to produce a winning record.

In 1906, Cincinnati replaced Kelley as manager but kept him as a player under his old Baltimore skipper, Ned Hanlon. But at age 34, he hit just .228 and was released. He managed in the minors in 1907 at Toronto, then was summoned to Boston to replace Fred Tenney in 1908.

Kelley got the club up to sixth place, its best finish since 1903, but his work was undermined by catcher Frank Bowerman, who fancied himself as the manager. Bowerman had the ear of team president George Dovey, who fired Kelley at the end of the season and turned the managing duties over to Bowerman.

Kelley, Joe

	W	L	T	Pct
1908	63	91	2	.409
Doves	63	91	2	.409
Career	338	321	10	.513

1909 / Bowerman, Frank

Record: 22–54 (.289)
Birthplace: Romeo, Michigan
B: December 5, 1868; **D:** November 30, 1948

It is difficult to judge Boston's managers in the first decade of the 20th century because the teams were so pitiful. But in all probability, it's safe to say Frank Bowerman was a better catcher/first baseman than he was a manager.

For that matter, he probably would have been a better politician than a manager, too. He only got to manage the Doves by talking his way into the job behind the back of Joe Kelley, a future Hall of Famer and a local product who lasted just one season as manager.

Team president George Dovey canned Kelley after the

1908 season and gave Bowerman exactly what he had been asking for—at least for 76 games. The 40-year-old Bowerman was in over his head. He continued to try to play as well as manage and was doing both so poorly that he was sent home to rest when he appeared on the verge of breaking. He returned to the team and immediately resigned in mid-July with a horrid 22–54 record.

Shortstop Bill Dahlen called the shots while Bowerman was gone, but it was catcher Harry Smith who took over the team upon Bowerman's resignation.

Bowerman, Frank

	W	L	T	Pct
1909	22	54	0	.289
Doves	22	54	0	.289
Career	22	54	0	.289

1909 / Smith, Harry

Record: 23–54 (.299)
Birthplace: Yorkshire, England
B: October 31, 1874; **D:** February 17, 1933

Harry Smith thought his playing career was through and that he'd been put out to pasture as a scout. At least that's how 1909 started for him, but by midseason he was back in the Boston dugout as player-manager.

Smith was a veteran backup catcher who never played much and spent most of his 10-year career with Pittsburgh. He was on a scouting mission in 1909 when manager Frank Bowerman, nearly cracking, left the Doves.

The 34-year-old Smith was summoned to shore up the catching in Bowerman's absence. He did exactly that, with shortstop Bill Dahlen running the club until Bowerman resigned at midseason. Then Smith was named manager for the remainder of the year.

Harry Smith

Boston was in last place when Smith took over and still in last when the season ended. Smith was not asked to manage again in 1910.

Smith, Harry

	W	L	T	Pct
1909	23	54	2	.299
Doves	23	54	2	.299
Career	23	54	2	.299

1910 / Lake, Fred

Record: 53–100 (.346)
Birthplace: Nova Scotia, Canada
B: October 16, 1866; **D:** November 24, 1931

Another year, another manager. Fred Lake made it five managers in four years—and he wasn't around long either.

Lake was a catcher who appeared in just 48 big league games, including 27 in three stints with Boston in 1891, in 1897, and finally as a 43-year-old manager in 1910.

In 1908 and 1909, Lake managed the Red Sox. And he probably would have been back in 1910 if he hadn't had the audacity to ask for a raise. When he requested more money, the Red Sox simply showed him the door.

Doves president George Dovey thought he sensed an opportunity to one-up the Red Sox, so he promptly hired Lake to replace Harry Smith. Of course, it mattered not. Boston again finished at the bottom of the National League barrel in 1910, 50½ games from the top.

Lake had another year left on his contract, but the club bought it out and brought Fred Tenney back to manage in 1911.

Lake, Fred

	W	L	T	Pct
1910	53	100	4	.346
Doves	53	100	4	.346
Career	163	180	6	.475

1912 / Kling, Johnny

Record: 52–101 (.340)
Birthplace: Kansas City, Missouri
B: February 25, 1875; **D:** January 31, 1947

In 1912 the Braves were finally born in name. Besides a new nickname, the club also had new ownership, which, not surprisingly, wanted its own manager. Even though Fred Tenney had a year remaining on his contract, he was ousted in favor of catcher Johnny Kling.

Kling was the catcher on the Cubs teams that won four pennants from 1906 to 1910. The only season in that five-year span they didn't win the pennant was 1909, when Kling won the world pocket billiard title, temporarily giving up baseball.

In 1906 and 1907 he led National League catchers in defense, and he compiled a lifetime batting average of .271 in 13 seasons.

Fred Lake

Johnny Kling

Kling came to Boston in a midseason trade in 1911. The following season, he became player-manager. And a year later, he was gone. Such was the fate of Boston managers in this period.

Under Kling, the Braves finished last for the fourth consecutive season, a feat that wasn't repeated until 1976–79.

Kling, Johnny

	W	L	T	Pct
1912	52	101	2	.340
Braves	52	101	2	.340
Career	52	101	2	.340

1913–20 / Stallings, George

Record: 579–597 (.492)
Birthplace: Augusta, Georgia
B: November 17, 1867; **D:** May 13, 1929

Only one manager in baseball history is known as "Miracle Man," and that is George Tweedy Stallings, who led the 1914 Braves to one of the most improbable World Series championships of all time.

In 13 years of managing, eight with the Braves, he won just that lone pennant and had a career winning percentage of only .495 with four teams. Stallings apparently used up his allotment of miracles in 1914, taking the Braves from last place on July 18 to the pennant and a World Series victory over the

George Stallings

highly favored Philadelphia Athletics. He ranks third in franchise history with 579 wins.

Superstitious, temperamental, brilliant, abusive, and profane—they all described Stallings, one of a few true "characters" to occupy the manager's seat during the colorful history of Braves baseball. Regarded as a gentleman off the field, he was anything but that on the field, doling out vicious tongue-lashings for the slightest slips.

A Georgia native, he graduated from Virginia Military Institute and studied medicine for two years at Baltimore's College of Physicians and Surgeons. During his college days, he was a good enough catcher to get a tryout with the Phillies in 1887. Harry Wright was managing the Phillies and convinced Stallings he should pass up medicine for baseball.

Stallings wasn't much of a player. His major league career consisted of four games with Brooklyn in 1890 and three more during his brief managerial stay with the Phillies in 1897–98.

In 1895, at age 27, he got his first minor league managing job with Nashville. He was at Detroit in the Western League the following season, then jumped quickly to the National League with the Phillies in 1897.

The Phillies players did not respond to Stallings' derisive coaxing. They not only played poorly, but they also rebelled against him, convincing management to can Stallings early in the second season of his three-year contract.

He managed Detroit to a third-place finish in 1901, the inaugural American League season, but was immediately replaced. He then spent several seasons in the minors until returning to the majors in 1909 with the New York Highlanders (now the Yankees). Despite having the team in the pennant race late in the 1910 season, Stallings was fired because of a dispute with star first baseman Hal Chase, who then took over as manager.

When the Braves hired Stallings in 1913, they were making their eighth managerial change in seven years. Not only had they finished last for four consecutive seasons, but they hadn't finished higher than sixth or played better than .420 baseball in the previous decade. They were at rock bottom.

While Stallings' harsh tactics didn't always work, they were just what the Braves needed to prod them into respectability. He was tough, but he built up the players' self-esteem and confidence. And if they didn't respond, he simply got rid of them. He used 46 players in 1913, constantly shuffling players on and off the roster in search of the type of men he felt were winners. And he found most of the regulars who made up the 1914 team.

Slowly but surely, the Braves began to believe in themselves and in Stallings. They finished in fifth place in 1913 with a .457 percentage, their best showing since 1902.

That, of course, set the stage for the remarkable 1914 season, which would have been quite a story even if the Braves had been respectable in recent seasons. But considering they hadn't had a winning record in 12 years, it was all the more astonishing.

The scrappy, on-the-field leadership of newly acquired second baseman Johnny Evers combined perfectly with Stallings' style to get the maximum out of a mediocre team supported by a suddenly dominant pitching staff. That probably surprised Stallings as much as anyone, since he hated pitchers, especially those who couldn't consistently throw the ball over the plate.

"Oh, those bases on balls!" he supposedly muttered on his deathbed when asked what caused his failing heart.

The National League standings were tightly bunched much of the 1914 season, and as a result the Braves were able to climb quickly once they got hot.

Stallings drove his players hard. He called them "boneheads." Once, when he wanted Hank Gowdy to pinch-hit, he turned to the bench and yelled, "Now you, Bonehead, get up there with a bat and see if you can hit the ball." Seven players supposedly went to the bat rack because they were all used to being called Bonehead.

Stallings was more than a taskmaster and psychologist, though. He knew the game and his players as thoroughly as any manager of his era, perhaps better than any other. He knew the "percentages," and he played them. He'd get his players together at the team hotel nearly every morning for "skull sessions" to discuss strategy.

Though he probably didn't invent platooning, Stallings was one of the first managers to use it extensively. And his success with it in the 1914 World Series popularized the practice of using right-handed hitters against left-handed pitching and vice versa.

Without Stallings' constant lineup juggling, it's doubtful the 1914 Braves could have performed their miracle. They had only one .300 hitter, outfielder Joe Connolly, and diminutive shortstop Rabbit Maranville often batted cleanup.

Often called "Chief" or "Big Daddy" by his players, Stallings didn't leave anything to chance. He was one of the most superstitious baseball men of all time.

Among other things, he thought loose scraps of paper and peanut shells were bad luck. Cubs infielder Heinie Zimmerman would torment Stallings by tearing up paper and scattering it in front of the Braves' dugout. Stallings once ate two slices of lemon meringue pie before a game. The Braves won, so he had the same pregame snack for the next nine days until they lost.

Stallings always sat with his legs crossed during a game, his top leg constantly bouncing up and down. He also slid up and down the bench continually. He wore out the seats of three pairs of pants per season—four in 1914.

But Stallings couldn't win another pennant for the Braves. The 1915 team played well (83–69) in spite of numerous injuries but still finished second, seven games behind the Phillies. And in 1916, Boston was six games better (89–63) yet slid to third place, though only four games out of first.

From there, the Braves went into a steep slide. There was nothing Stallings nor anyone else could do to stop it for 30 years.

After enduring two sixth-place finishes and two sevenths, Stallings resigned in November 1920. He was dissatisfied with the contract he was offered by new ownership and with the lack of money available to buy new players. A wealthy central Georgia plantation owner, he returned to his 6,000-acre spread to tend to his 80,000 peach trees and prize Hereford cattle.

Stallings wasn't ready to get out of baseball, though. He and a partner purchased the Rochester franchise of the International League. Stallings served as manager until he "fired himself" in the middle of the 1927 season. Two years later, he died.

Stallings, George

	W	L	T	Pct
1913	69	82	3	.457
1914	94	59	5	.614
1915	83	69	5	.546
1916	89	63	6	.586
1917	72	81	5	.471
1918	53	71	0	.427
1919	57	82	1	.410
1920	62	90	1	.408
Braves	579	597	26	.492
Career	879	898	36	.495

1921–23 / Mitchell, Fred

Record: 186–274 (.404)
Birthplace: Cambridge, Massachusetts
B: June 5, 1878; **D:** October 13, 1970

One of the first things George Stallings did when he was named Braves manager in 1913 was to hire Fred Mitchell as pitching and third base coach. And when Stallings resigned after the 1920 season, it was only natural that management would replace him with Mitchell, whom Stallings called "my right eye."

A native of Cambridge, Massachusetts, Mitchell left the Braves in 1916 to coach at Harvard. But a year later, he was lured back to the majors to manage the Cubs. In 1918 he led Chicago to the pennant but lost to the Red Sox in the World Series. He remained with the Cubs through 1920, then signed with his hometown Braves.

Originally a pitcher, Mitchell made his big league debut in 1901 by relieving Cy Young in the first game ever played by the Red Sox (then the Somersets). He pitched for five years, winning as many as 11 games for the Phillies in 1903. An arm injury ended his pitching career in 1905, but he became a catcher and returned to the majors briefly in 1910 with the New York Highlanders, who were managed by Stallings.

Mitchell's experience as both a pitcher and catcher helped

Fred Mitchell

him develop into what Stallings said was the best pitching coach ever.

Part Cherokee, Mitchell was a strict disciplinarian. He briefly revitalized the Braves in 1921, getting them up to fourth place and five games over .500. However, the team lost 100 games each of the next two seasons, prompting the end of his big league managerial career at age 45. He continued with the Braves as a scout and coached at Harvard.

Mitchell, Fred

	W	L	T	Pct
1921	79	74	0	.516
1922	53	100	1	.346
1923	54	100	1	.351
Braves	186	274	2	.404
Career	494	543	7	.476

1924–27 / Bancroft, Dave

Record: 249–363 (.407)
Birthplace: Sioux City, Iowa
B: April 20, 1891; **D:** October 9, 1972

Dave Bancroft was one of the greatest defensive shortstops of all time, as evidenced by his Hall of Fame plaque. He was not, however, much of a manager judging by his only big league experience, which came in a four-year stint as player-manager with the Braves.

Bancroft became a Brave in an unusual trade, one that involved three future Braves managers. Prior to the 1924 season he came to Boston from the Giants along with Casey Stengel, who also would have an unsuccessful term in the job. In exchange, the Giants got Billy Southworth, who would direct the Braves to the 1948 pennant.

Bancroft played well for the Braves, leading the league's shortstops in defense in 1925 and twice batting over .300. However, he never got the team over .500 or out of the second division.

After the 1927 season Bancroft was released and signed with Brooklyn. But he never managed again.

Bancroft, Dave

	W	L	T	Pct
1924	53	100	1	.346
1925	70	83	0	.458
1926	66	86	1	.434
1927	60	94	1	.390
Braves	249	363	3	.407
Career	249	363	3	.407

1928 / Slattery, Jack

Record: 11–20 (.355)
Birthplace: South Boston, Massachusetts
B: January 6, 1878; **D:** July 17, 1949

It's questionable if Jack Slattery would have lasted long as Braves manager under any circumstances, but with the bombastic Rogers Hornsby around, he didn't have a chance.

Slattery was a Braves coach under George Stallings in 1918 and 1919. A product of South Boston and a Fordham graduate, he then coached at Tufts College, Boston College, and Harvard before Braves president Judge Emil Fuchs asked him to manage the club in 1928.

Shortly afterward, Fuchs obtained Hornsby in a trade with the Giants. One of the greatest hitters the game has ever known, Hornsby also was a haughty, opinionated, overbearing presence who quickly wore out his welcome at most stops. He was not about to be "managed" by a college coach, as he viewed Slattery.

A former catcher/first baseman who appeared briefly in the majors with five clubs, Slattery was no match for the "Rajah," as Hornsby was so aptly nicknamed. Hornsby began undermining Slattery almost immediately in spring training. There was speculation the manager would be fired even before the season began. That didn't happen, but after a rough road trip and only 31 games, Slattery, who had a two-year contract, resigned with the Braves in seventh place.

Dave Bancroft

Jack Slattery

Slattery, Jack

	W	L	T	Pct
1928	11	20	0	.355
Braves	11	20	0	.355
Career	11	20	0	.355

1928 / Hornsby, Rogers

Record: 39–83 (.320)
Birthplace: Winters, Texas
B: April 27, 1896; **D:** January 5, 1963

It was Rogers Hornsby who was responsible for running off Jack Slattery as Braves manager in 1928. It's interesting that as bad as the Braves played under Slattery (.355), they actually played worse (.320) for his replacement—Hornsby, a man destined for the Hall of Fame.

Already a six-time batting champion when he was acquired by the Braves prior to the 1928 season, Hornsby also managed St. Louis to a World Series championship in 1926. For that feat, he was accorded godlike stature with the fans of St. Louis, yet he still was shipped to New York in the off-season because of his confrontational personality and three-year contract demand.

The Braves were his third team in three years, and a year later the Cubs became the fourth team in four years. Considering he was regarded as possibly the greatest right-handed hitter of all time, a reputation some might argue he deserves even today, it's clear Hornsby's condescending demeanor is what caused him to be shuffled from city to city like a second-rate player.

Hornsby began taking shots at Slattery in spring training and didn't let up until the former college coach resigned 31 games into the season. Team president Judge Emil Fuchs responded by putting Hornsby in charge. The added responsi-

Rogers Hornsby

bility and the team's lackluster performance didn't affect Hornsby's hitting. At age 32, he simply won his seventh and last batting title (.387).

The Braves finished seventh under Hornsby, the same position they held when he took over for Slattery. Still, Fuchs might have kept him around if not for the overwhelming offer of five players and $200,000 from the Cubs. The cash-strapped Braves couldn't turn down that kind of money.

Hornsby, Rogers

	W	L	T	Pct
1928	39	83	0	.320
Braves	39	83	0	.320
Career	701	812	17	.463

1929 / Fuchs, Emil

Record: 56–98 (.364)
Birthplace: Hamburg, Germany
B: April 17, 1878; **D:** December 5, 1961

Ted Turner only lasted one game as Braves manager in 1977, but Judge Emil Fuchs, who owned the club from 1923 to 1935, spent the entire 1929 season as manager.

Fuchs, who was born in Germany, graduated from the New York School of Law and was a New York City magistrate from 1915 to 1918; thus he was always called "Judge." He had no professional baseball experience as a player, coach, or manager when he decided to run the team on the field in 1929.

"The time has gone when a manager has to chew tobacco and talk from the side of his mouth," said Fuchs. "I don't think our club can do any worse with me as manager than it has done the last few years."

Sad, but true.

As was the case with the 1977 Braves Turner tried to manage, the 1929 team was so bad it wouldn't have mattered if the Ringling Brothers were running the show. And sometimes, it seemed as if that was the case. Boston finished last for Fuchs, even though the Braves somehow managed to win six more games than they did in 1928 when they were seventh under Jack Slattery and Rogers Hornsby.

But Johnny Evers, Fuchs' "assistant manager," actually ran the team. The Judge, who received a great deal of ridicule for his unusual decision to manage, was frequently out of town or at least out of the dugout on other business.

The team did win seven of its first nine games under his leadership, but it quickly settled into the losing pattern that had been customary for more than 20 years. The players didn't pay much attention to Fuchs when he was in the dugout. He simply added to the impression, which unfortunately was accurate, that this was not a ball club to be taken seriously.

Fuchs, Judge Emil

	W	L	T	Pct
1929	56	98	0	.364
Braves	56	98	0	.364
Career	56	98	0	.364

Judge Emil Fuchs

Bill McKechnie

1930–37 / McKechnie, Bill

Record: 560–666 (.457)
Birthplace: Wilkinsburg, Pennsylvania
B: August 7, 1886; **D:** October 29, 1965

Bill McKechnie is the only manager in big league history to win pennants in three different cities. Wouldn't you know, Boston was not one of them. Instead, McKechnie holds the distinction of losing more games (666) than any other manager in franchise history.

Nicknamed "Deacon Bill" because of his churchgoing ways, McKechnie managed in the majors for a quarter of a century, winning pennants at Pittsburgh (1925), St. Louis (1928), and Cincinnati (1939 and '40). But the best he could do with the Braves and Bees (1930–37) was consecutive fourth-place finishes in 1933–34. Those, however, were the Braves' only two first-division finishes in a 24-year period stretching from 1922 to 1945.

McKechnie must have been a genius. Whether he was or not, he was voted into the Hall of Fame—probably as much for his two fourths with the Braves as for his four pennants and two World Series titles. It certainly wasn't for his playing

ability, though he survived for 11 years as a utility man. He even played one game for the Braves in 1913 when manager George Stallings was sifting through 46 players in search of a few good men.

Regarded as one of the keenest baseball men in the business, McKechnie was so well regarded that he was named major league manager of the year in 1937 for leading a very bad Boston team to a winning record (79–73) and fifth-place finish. Probably figuring his luck had run out with such a shoddy franchise, he promptly packed his bags and moved to Cincinnati in 1938.

Besides winning the pennant for Pittsburgh in 1925, he helped the team make history by bringing the Pirates back from a 3–1 deficit in games to win the World Series against Washington. It was the first time such a comeback had been accomplished.

Nevertheless, McKechnie was fired a year later when the Pirates dipped to third. In 1928 the Cardinals made him manager, and he won the pennant in his first season. However, when his club was swept in the Series by the Yankees, he was demoted to Rochester in 1929 by Cardinals owner Sam Breadon. In the middle of the season Breadon recalled McKechnie, once again swapping him with Billy Southworth, who would one day manage the Braves, too.

Rightfully upset by the lack of respect he'd been shown, McKechnie ran for tax collector in his hometown of Wilkinsburg, Pennsylvania. He said he'd quit baseball if elected, but he lost. He turned down a two-year offer from the Cardinals to accept a three-year deal as Braves manager in 1930.

Against all odds, the conservative McKechnie actually posted four seasons of .500 or better in his eight years in Boston. However, he also suffered through a franchise-record 115 losses in 1935.

Among McKechnie's strengths was his ability to handle pitchers. Perhaps the best example came during his Boston stay when he helped geriatric rookies Jim Turner (age 34) and Lou Fette (30) each win 20 games in 1937.

McKechnie, who also helped the financially troubled Braves by occasionally passing on a paycheck, left the struggling franchise for a better contract with Cincinnati in 1938. The Reds, who finished eighth in 1937, climbed to fourth in

McKechnie's first season, then won the pennant in 1939 and the World Series in 1940.

McKechnie, Bill

	W	L	T	Pct
1930	70	84	0	.455
1931	64	90	2	.416
1932	77	77	1	.500
1933	83	71	2	.539
1934	78	73	1	.517
1935	38	115	0	.248
1936	71	83	3	.461
1937	79	73	0	.520
Braves, Bees	560	666	9	.457
Career	1,896	1,723	28	.524

1938–43 / Stengel, Casey

Record: 373–491 (.432)
Birthplace: Kansas City, Missouri
B: July 30, 1890; **D:** September 29, 1975

Casey Stengel went down in history as one of the greatest managers of all time for winning 10 pennants and seven World Series in a span of just 12 years with the Yankees. But the good fans of Brooklyn and Boston never would have bought that description in the late 1930s and early 1940s.

In his first nine seasons (1934–43) of managing, three with the Dodgers and six with the Braves, Stengel never finished in the first division and had but one winning team.

One of the most colorful men ever to be associated with the game, Stengel once said, "You judge a manager on where he finishes." In that case, he was a lousy manager who suddenly became a genius in New York.

Though Stengel was as entertaining as ever during his stay with the Braves, it was clear he had worn out his welcome by 1943, his last season in Boston. Two days before the season opener, he suffered a severely broken leg when he was hit by a car while crossing the street on a wet night. Stengel was in

Casey Stengel

traction for quite a while and missed the first two months of the season.

Coach Bob Coleman directed the team for the first 46 games and had the team in sixth place upon Stengel's return. That's where the Braves stayed, improving one notch after finishing seventh the previous four seasons.

A local sports writer nominated the cabdriver who hit Stengel as Boston's sportsman of the year.

"The man who did the most for baseball in Boston in 1943 was the motorist who ran Stengel down," wrote Dave Egan of the *Boston Record.*

Stengel, of course, proved his critics wrong, but the accident nearly prevented his later success. He made a slow recovery and considered retiring when new Braves owner Lou Perini decided to change managers for 1944. Stengel already was well off financially because of his investments in oil. But he stayed with baseball, managing five years in the minors before getting the Yankees job in 1949.

Charles Dillon Stengel was a native of Kansas City, the abbreviation of which was used to form the nickname by which millions eventually identified him. An above-average outfielder, Stengel compiled a lifetime batting average of .284 in 14 seasons, the last two with the Braves.

But his pranks and unique brand of double-talk known as "Stengelese" are what made him one of the most unforgettable characters ever to grace the sports scene.

Once when he was announced as the hitter for Pittsburgh in front of his old fans at Brooklyn, he doffed his cap and a sparrow flew out. During an exhibition game in the minors, he climbed down a manhole in the outfield, emerging just in time to catch a fly ball—much to the dismay of his manager and pitcher. He also practiced sliding into second base on his way to the outfield between innings. And he was known to pick up a stray newspaper in the outfield and read it to the fans.

Among Stengel's most-repeated lines was one he uttered in a barber's chair after a tough loss. The barber asked him if he wanted a shave, and Stengel replied, "Yes, but don't cut my throat. I may want to do that later myself."

On his policy of curfews for players, he said, "Being with a woman all night never hurt a professional ballplayer. It's staying up all night looking for a woman that does him in."

Such wit was a valuable commodity for a manager in entertaining writers after losses. And there certainly were plenty of those early in Stengel's managing career and again at the end when he supervised the Mets' baptism.

The Braves were responsible for starting Stengel's managerial escapades. They released him in 1925, ending his big league playing career, and sent him to Worcester of the Eastern League to serve as player-manager and club president.

Presented with the opportunity to manage Toledo in 1926, Stengel asked the Braves for his release. Judge Emil Fuchs, the Braves' president, wouldn't grant it. But Stengel was nobody's fool, in spite of his shenanigans. He released himself as a player, then wrote a letter from team president Stengel to manager Stengel, informing him he'd been fired. And finally, he resigned as president!

Commissioner Kenesaw Mountain Landis offered to step in and prevent Stengel from leaving, but Fuchs said to let him go.

Stengel managed Toledo of the American Association for six years, then returned to the majors as a coach with Brooklyn. In 1934 he succeeded Max Carey as the Dodgers' manager. When the club failed to show progress in three seasons under Stengel, he was fired with a year to go on his contract. He sat out 1937, collecting $15,000 from the Dodgers to do so, then was snapped up by Boston—answering to the nickname Bees at the time—for the 1938 season.

The Bees, like the Dodgers, didn't have the financial resources to be competitive. Stengel managed to keep the club two games over .500 in his first season, but he never got it close to .500 in the next five years. However, there was never a dull moment.

At the Polo Grounds late one afternoon, Boston was nursing a lead going to the ninth inning against the Giants, and darkness was setting in. Under Stengel's orders, the Braves were stalling, hoping to get the game called after eight innings. The umpires, just to spite Stengel, were determined to finish the game. When play was about to begin in the bottom of the ninth, Stengel protested, then stalled even more by talking to his pitcher. The umpire threatened to forfeit the game to the Giants. Finally, Stengel crawled across the ground, using a flashlight to point his way. Of course, he was ejected.

Stengel felt comfortable enough in Boston to buy stock in the ailing franchise. On the occasion of another ejection, he was reminded of that purchase by umpire Bill Klem, who said, "I always suspected you were crazy. But now I'm convinced you're crazy. I just heard you bought stock in this ball club. No sane man ever would do that."

In 1943 the Perini regime brought the end of Stengel's stay in Boston, but it probably was one of the best things ever to happen to him. When he resurfaced in the majors in 1949, he won the World Series with the Yankees. It was the first of a remarkable five consecutive Series championships. Stengel's lack of success in Boston was no longer an issue. He was the toast of baseball and retained that lofty status through four comical seasons with the Mets and right up to his death in 1975 as a wealthy man at age 86.

The marker on Stengel's grave in Glendale, California, appropriately reads, "There comes a time in every man's life, and I've had plenty of them."

Bob Coleman

manager when owner Lou Perini sent the Ol' Perfessor packing in 1944.

Perini had every intention of doing whatever it took to make the Braves contenders, but he had to wait out World War II to do so. Therefore, Coleman was viewed as little more than an interim manager.

A former catcher, Coleman played 116 games in a three-year big league career with Pittsburgh and Cleveland. Prior to joining the Braves, he'd served one-year stints as a coach with the Red Sox and Tigers, but mainly he was a career minor league manager. He spent 35 years managing in the minors, 23 of them before coming to the Braves. Among the players he sent to the majors were Hall of Fame slugger Hank Greenberg and Braves utility man Felix Mantilla.

He brought the Braves home sixth in 1944, then resigned late the next July with the club in seventh place and riding an eight-game losing streak.

Stengel, Casey

	W	L	T	Pct
1938	77	75	1	.507
1939	63	88	1	.417
1940	65	87	0	.428
1941	62	92	2	.403
1942	59	89	2	.399
1943	47	60	0	.439
Bees, Braves	373	491	6	.432
Career	1,905	1,842	19	.508

Coleman, Bob

	W	L	T	Pct
1943	21	25	0	.457
1944	65	89	1	.422
1945	42	51	1	.452
Braves	128	165	2	.437
Career	128	165	2	.437

1943, 1944–45 / Coleman, Bob

Record: 128–165 (.437)
Birthplace: Huntingburg, Indiana
B: September 26, 1890; **D:** July 16, 1959

Bob Coleman, a Braves coach who ran the team the first two months of 1943 when Casey Stengel was hospitalized with a broken leg, had the distinction of following Stengel as

1945 / Bissonette, Del

Record: 25–34 (.424)
Birthplace: Winthrop, Maine
B: September 6, 1899; **D:** June 9, 1972

Del Bissonette's only season coaching for the Braves was an eventful one. When Bob Coleman called it quits as manager in late July 1945, Bissonette was given the assignment of directing the team through the final 59 games.

Del Bissonette

The responsibility was new to the former Dodgers first baseman, but the pressure wasn't overbearing. The Braves were in seventh place at the time, and it had been decades since any serious expectations were placed on the club. By the end of the season, Bissonette had gotten the Braves to sixth place.

Billy Southworth took over as Boston manager in 1946, and Bissonette, who'd been a minor league manager for the Braves, went to Pittsburgh as a coach. It was his last year in the majors.

The Maine apple farmer was once a promising slugger, but injuries limited him to a five-year career in which he batted .305, had two 100-RBI seasons, and set what was then a Dodgers rookie record with 25 homers in 1928.

Bissonette, Del

	W	L	T	Pct
1945	25	34	1	.424
Braves	25	34	1	.424
Career	25	34	1	.424

1946–51 / Southworth, Billy

Record: 424–358 (.542)
Birthplace: Harvard, Nebraska
B: March 9, 1893; **D:** November 15, 1969

In 13 seasons managing the Cardinals and Braves, Billy Southworth won four pennants and nearly 60 percent of his games. No team he managed finished a season in the second division. It's an impressive record, yet he remains the only manager to win more than three pennants, be eligible for the Hall of Fame, and not make it.

Nevertheless, Southworth holds an important position in Braves history. It was Southworth who led the Braves out of the darkness of three of the worst decades of baseball imaginable, taking them to the 1948 World Series, their first postseason opportunity since the miracle of 1914.

When Lou Perini and two other Boston contractors bought the Braves in 1944, they made it clear they intended to build the Braves into a competitive franchise. They took many steps in that direction, with one of the boldest being the hiring of Southworth from the Cardinals.

Southworth won three consecutive pennants and two World Series in St. Louis in 1942–44. The Cardinals finished a strong second in 1945, then Perini made his move that fall.

The Braves put up a five-year contract offer for Southworth that included a $35,000 base salary and a bonus plan—$5,000 for fourth place, $10,000 for third, $15,000 for second, and $20,000 for the pennant. Cardinals owner Sam Breadon said he couldn't match it and wouldn't stand in Southworth's way. The Braves had a new manager and the attention of the baseball world.

As a player, Southworth was a speedy and dependable outfielder, leading the league in defense (.991) at his position in 1920 with Pittsburgh. The previous year, he tied for the league lead in triples (14), and from 1918 through 1921, his first season with the Braves, he averaged 22 steals per year. He batted over .300 all three seasons he played in Boston, though he missed most of 1922 with a knee injury.

In 1928, at age 35, Southworth was named manager of the Cardinals' Rochester farm club, which he led to the International League pennant. He was named player-manager with the Cardinals the following year, replacing Bill McKechnie, who'd won the pennant in 1928 but lost the Series. However, Southworth was returned to Rochester in July, and McKechnie was brought back from that farm club to run the Cardinals.

Southworth got back to the majors briefly in 1933 as a coach with the Giants but then was out of baseball for a year until the Cardinals gave him a minor league job in 1935. Early in the 1940 season, he made a triumphant return as

Billy Southworth

Cardinals manager. He was named manager of the year in 1941 and '42 and made St. Louis the class of the league. That's what attracted Perini's attention.

Southworth instilled discipline in the Braves, something they hadn't known for a long time. He ran rigid practices and he made players hustle.

With the assistance of Perini's willingness to buy players, Southworth was able to transform the Braves from perennial losers into contenders almost overnight. They finished fourth in his first season, 1946, with their best record since 1933. The next year, they moved up to third, the highest they'd finished since 1916. And in 1948 they won the pennant by 6½ games over Southworth's old Cardinals before losing the World Series in six games to Cleveland.

After the 1947 season, Southworth's base salary was increased to $50,000, the highest in baseball.

Almost as quickly as the Braves came together under Southworth, they began to fall apart. Many of the veterans began to resent their manager's strict rules, and dissension developed. Favored to repeat as pennant winners in 1949, the Braves stumbled all the way to fourth, finishing four games under .500. Southworth, who drove himself harder than he did his players, was so distraught he had to be sent home to rest in mid-August. Coach Johnny Cooney ran the team for 46 games in his absence.

The players voted Stallings only a half share of their fourth-place bonus money, though Commissioner Happy Chandler overruled them and made it a full share.

In 1950 the Braves got back in the race, finishing fourth again but just eight games out of first with an 83–71 record. But in 1951, with Boston in fifth place on June 19, Southworth was forced to resign for health reasons at age 58 even though he had a year and a half left on his contract. He never managed again.

Southworth, Billy

	W	L	T	Pct
1946	81	72	1	.529
1947	86	68	0	.558
1948	91	62	1	.595
1949	55	54	2	.505
1950	83	71	2	.539
1951	28	31	1	.475
Braves	424	358	7	.542
Career	1,044	704	22	.597

1949 / Cooney, Johnny

Record: 20–25 (.444)
Birthplace: Cranston, Rhode Island
B: March 18, 1901; **D:** July 8, 1986

Johnny Cooney never had the title of Braves manager, but he's given credit in official records for running the club as a coach late in the 1949 season when Billy Southworth was on leave for health reasons.

Cooney has the distinction of being the only man ever to play in both leagues, coach in both leagues, manage in both leagues, and umpire in one. His managerial duties in both leagues came under similar circumstances. During a coach-

Johnny Cooney

ing stint with the White Sox in the late 1950s and early 1960s, he ran the club for several games when manager Al Lopez was away from the team.

Cooney, Johnny

	W	L	T	Pct
1949	20	25	1	.444
Braves	20	25	1	.444
Career	20	25	1	.444

1951–52 / Holmes, Tommy

Record: 61–69 (.469)
Birthplace: Brooklyn, New York
B: March 29, 1917

Tommy Holmes was one of the finest and most well-liked players in Braves history. He also was one of the franchise's all-time nice guys. He was a popular choice among the players and fans to replace Billy Southworth as manager in June 1951, but unfortunately he was still "one of the guys" and never could get the proper distance a manager needs from his players.

Holmes, who set what was then a modern National League record by hitting in 37 straight games in 1945, began the 1951 season as player-manager of the Braves' farm club at Hartford. He was not prepared to manage in the majors, but when Southworth resigned on June 19, he was promoted to Boston anyway.

Tommy Holmes

The Braves didn't respond noticeably to new leadership. They were in fifth place, three games under .500 when Holmes took over and in fourth place, two games under .500 when the season ended.

The team got off slowly in 1952, its final year in Boston. The Braves won just 13 of their first 35 games and were mired in seventh place on May 31 when Holmes was fired and replaced by Charlie Grimm, who was promoted from the Braves' Milwaukee farm club.

Holmes finished the season as a pinch hitter with the Dodgers, the only portion of his big league career not spent in a Braves uniform. He managed in the minors for five years and worked as a scout for the Dodgers for one year before becoming director of the Greater New York Sandlot Baseball Foundation. In 1973 he joined the Mets' front office to work in community relations.

Holmes, Tommy

	W	L	T	Pct
1951	48	47	0	.505
1952	13	22	0	.371
Braves	61	69	0	.469
Career	61	69	0	.469

1952–56 / Grimm, Charlie

Record: 341–285 (.545)
Birthplace: St. Louis, Missouri
B: August 28, 1898; **D:** November 15, 1983

When the Braves moved from Boston to Milwaukee in 1953, they didn't have to introduce their manager to their new fans. Charlie Grimm, who took over the Braves from Tommy Holmes in 1952, had been a highly successful manager with Milwaukee's American Association club in the early 1940s, returned there in 1951, and left early the next season to manage in Boston.

Charlie Grimm

During Grimm's first stint in Milwaukee, he worked for promotional genius Bill Veeck. The two teamed not only to win a lot of games but also to fully entertain their patrons.

One season, as Grimm's birthday approached, someone asked the manager what he wanted for his birthday. "A left-handed pitcher," he said.

Veeck held a birthday celebration on the field, giving Grimm a $1,000 war bond and a huge cake. At the end of the ceremony, Julio Acosta, a left-handed pitcher who'd been secretly purchased from Norfolk, stepped out of the cake. Acosta pitched that day, striking out 17 but losing in extra innings. However, he eventually helped Milwaukee win the pennant.

There seldom was a dull moment when Grimm was around. An excellent first baseman who won seven fielding titles and batted .290 in a 20-year career spent mainly with the Cubs and Pirates, "Jolly Cholly," as he was known, developed quite a reputation as a free spirit and left-handed banjo player.

Grimm also was a pretty good manager, winning three pennants and nearly 55 percent of his games over 19 seasons with the Cubs and Braves. His managerial debut came in 1932 while still a regular player for the Cubs. With the team in second place late in the year and bristling under the direction of the dictatorial Rogers Hornsby, the Cubs fired Hornsby and made the affable Grimm player-manager. The club rallied with a 14-game winning streak in September to win the pennant.

In 1935 the Cubs won another pennant with Grimm as player-manager. His playing career ended in 1936, but he continued as manager until mid-1938. With the Cubs in third place, he resigned, saying he couldn't relate to the players.

After a couple of years in broadcasting, Grimm returned to the Cubs' dugout as a coach before joining Veeck in Milwaukee. He was called back to Wrigley Field to manage in 1944 and won the franchise's last pennant in 1945. The Cubs relieved Grimm of his managerial duties in 1949 but gave him a front office job. The next year, he was back managing in the minors where he stayed for two years before taking over the Braves in early 1952.

After playing out the string in Boston in rather uninspired fashion, the Braves arrived in Milwaukee with one of the game's most talented teams in 1953. They were the toast of the town and played exciting, entertaining baseball under Grimm for three seasons, finishing second in 1953 and '55 and third in '54. However, the club got off to a disappointing start in 1956, and Grimm was fired after 46 games with the Braves in fifth place. He was replaced by Fred Haney.

Grimm eventually returned to the Cubs and served them for 15 more years in various positions, including a very brief stint as manager in 1960. When he died at age 85, his ashes were scattered over Wrigley Field.

Grimm, Charlie

	W	L	T	Pct
1952	51	67	2	.432
1953	92	62	3	.597
1954	89	65	0	.578
1955	85	69	0	.552
1956	24	22	0	.522
Braves	341	285	5	.545
Career	1,287	1,067	14	.547

1956–59 / Haney, Fred

Record: 341–231 (.596)
Birthplace: Albuquerque, New Mexico
B: April 25, 1898; **D:** November 9, 1977

When Fred Haney was named to replace Charlie Grimm as manager of the Braves on June 16, 1956, he walked into a no-win situation. The Braves were expected to win—period. If they won the pennant, it was because they were loaded with superstars. And if they lost the pennant, it was because of poor managing. That's the nature of baseball, especially with a team as potent as the Braves of the late 1950s.

Haney managed the Braves for the last 109 games of 1956 and all of the next three seasons. In those three-plus seasons, Milwaukee won more games than any other team in baseball, including the Yankees. The Braves won two pennants and a World Series for Haney, lost the 1956 pennant on the last day of the season and the '59 flag in a playoff with the Dodgers.

In other words, Haney came within a couple of victories of four consecutive pennants. Nevertheless, he probably was second-guessed and criticized more in a four-year period than any other manager in franchise history. He was even hung in effigy in the midst of a pennant-winning season.

Nicknamed "Pudge" because of his short (5–6) stature, Haney had a seven-year career as a major league infielder, compiling a lifetime batting average of .275. He spent his first four seasons with Detroit, where he was a teammate of Ty Cobb.

Haney began managing in the minors at Toledo in 1936 when he was 38 years old. His first shot in the majors came in 1939 with the St. Louis Browns, who lost 111 games under his guidance. Somehow, he survived that season, only to be fired early in 1941. He was back at Toledo the next year, then spent the next six years as a broadcaster for the Hollywood Stars of the Pacific Coast League.

Haney was so smart in the booth that the Stars put him back on the field as manager for four seasons, two of which produced pennants. That got him another chance in the majors with Pittsburgh in 1953–55, but the Pirates finished last all three seasons.

In 1956, Charlie Grimm plucked Haney out of the unemployment line and hired him as a coach in Milwaukee. When the Braves went into a dive, losing nine of 13 in June and dropping to fifth place, Grimm was fired and Haney was offered the job. He hesitated at taking it, but did so when encouraged by Grimm.

The managerial change awakened a sleeping giant. The Braves won their first 11 games under Haney and moved into first place. By late July, Milwaukee had opened a 5½-game lead in just five weeks for their new manager. Unfortunately, the Braves gradually began to lose their momentum. They went into September still leading by 2½ games, but that margin was reduced to just one game by the final series of the year, three games at St. Louis. Haney's club lost the first two, and the Dodgers swept three from Pittsburgh to pass the Braves and win the pennant by one game.

With Hank Aaron, Eddie Mathews, Joe Adcock, and several other sluggers, the Braves had one of the most powerful lineups of that era. However, Haney often liked to play for one run. This conservative strategy on such an explosive team brought Haney criticism when the Braves failed to win the 1956 pennant, and the complaints continued throughout his term in Milwaukee.

The Braves were the class of baseball in 1957, finally winning the pennant and knocking off the Yankees in a seven-game World Series. They were on the verge of repeating that success in 1958 when they blew a 3–1 lead in games to the Yankees in the Series.

In 1959 the Braves played well in April, early May, and September, but in between they were barely mediocre. And it cost them. They finished the regular season tied with the Dodgers, forcing a best-of-three playoff. Los Angeles won the first two games, ending the Braves' brief run at a dynasty.

Five days after the playoff loss, Haney resigned at age 61. It was hard to argue with what he achieved in his three-plus seasons as Braves manager—but people did and still do it.

Haney, Fred				
	W	**L**	**T**	**Pct**
1956	68	40	1	.630
1957	95	59	1	.617
1958	92	62	0	.597
1959	86	70	1	.551
Braves	341	231	3	.596
Career	629	757	7	.454

1960–61 / Dressen, Charlie

Record: 159–124 (.562)
Birthplace: Decatur, Illinois
B: September 20, 1898; **D:** August 10, 1966

Why the Braves ever hired Charlie Dressen as manager probably will never be fully understood. Dressen liked his players to bunt, steal, and hit-and-run; but the Braves were a power team. Dressen was known as a disciplinarian; but the Braves were a team of fun-loving veterans who resented any attempt to clamp down on them.

Perhaps the talented Braves would have begun to disintegrate in 1960 anyway, but it seems certain that Dressen's arrival hastened the process.

At 5–5, Dressen was even smaller than Fred Haney, his predecessor. But unlike Haney, he was cocky and arrogant.

Fred Haney

Charlie Dressen

Dressen, Charlie

	W	L	T	Pct
1960	88	66	0	.571
1961	71	58	1	.550
Braves	159	124	1	.562
Career	1,008	973	9	.509

He never managed a ball game he didn't think he—not his players—could find a way to win. And perhaps he had good reason to be so confident.

Dressen, who dropped out of school at age 14 to pitch semipro ball, was a quarterback for a brief time in the early days of the NFL, playing for George Halas's Decatur Staleys, who became the Chicago Bears. He also was a third baseman for eight seasons in the majors, most of it with Cincinnati, compiling a .272 lifetime batting average.

After his playing career ended in 1933, Dressen was named Cincinnati's manager late the following season. He never got the Reds out of the second division and was fired in late 1937 with the team buried in last place.

In 1939, Dressen got a job coaching under Leo Durocher with the Dodgers. He stayed there through 1946, then moved to the Yankees for two seasons. In 1951 he was named the Dodgers' manager and would have won the pennant if not for Bobby Thomson's famous home run. Brooklyn did win the pennant the next two years, but when Dressen demanded a long-term contract, Walter O'Malley replaced him with Walter Alston in 1954.

After a year in the minors, Dressen resurfaced with the pathetic Washington Senators for three seasons, then was a coach with the Dodgers for two years before being hired by the Braves in 1960.

Against team policy at the time, the Braves gave Dressen a two-year contract. The team got off to a slow start under him and was stuck at .500 through the end of May. By the All-Star break Milwaukee was in second place, and on July 24 the Braves moved into first place. However, that lasted only a day. Pittsburgh stayed on top the rest of the season, winning the pennant by seven games over the runner-up Braves.

The 1961 season brought more of the same. The team appeared lifeless until August when it caught fire and won 20 of 29 games. With 25 games remaining and the Braves in third place, Dressen thought they still had a shot at the pennant. When he was summoned to the front office, he fully expected to be getting a new contract. Instead, he was fired and replaced by executive vice president Birdie Tebbetts.

The change did the Braves no good at all. They played a game under .500 the rest of the way and dropped to fourth place.

1961–62 / Tebbetts, Birdie

Record: 98–89 (.524)
Birthplace: Burlington, Vermont
B: November 10, 1912

When Birdie Tebbetts replaced Charlie Dressen late in the 1961 season, it appeared the Braves could still right themselves and make a run at the pennant. Not only was that expectation not fulfilled, but by the time Tebbetts left Milwaukee a year later, it was obvious most of the life had been sucked out of a once-great team.

George Robert Tebbetts acquired his nickname during his days at Providence College. It was due to his high-pitched voice and talkative nature.

Tebbetts had a 14-year career as a big league catcher, most of it with the Tigers and Red Sox. Despite missing three years during World War II, he was named to four All-Star teams and compiled a lifetime batting average of .270.

His playing career ended in 1952, but two years later, at age 41, Tebbetts was hired to manage Cincinnati. In nearly five seasons with the Reds, he got his team into the first division only in 1956 when Cincinnati finished third. He was dismissed in late 1958 with the Reds in last place.

The Braves' decision to hire Tebbetts as executive vice president in the fall of 1958 must have seemed rather curious to the Milwaukee players and fans. During Tebbetts' managing tour with Cincinnati, the Braves and Reds developed quite a rivalry, which included several beanball exchanges and brawls.

The Braves fizzled going down the stretch in 1961 when Tebbetts moved from the front office to the dugout. Given a full season to work with in 1962, he didn't do any better. Milwaukee finished fifth, their worst showing since 1952. Five days after the season ended, Tebbetts resigned to change tribes. He managed the Cleveland Indians for four seasons with little success.

Birdie Tebbetts

Tebbetts, Birdie

	W	L	T	Pct
1961	12	13	0	.480
1962	86	76	0	.531
Braves	98	89	0	.524
Career	748	705	2	.515

1963–66 / Bragan, Bobby

Record: 310–287 (.519)
Birthplace: Birmingham, Alabama
B: October 30, 1917

Milwaukee fans and players got a lot of practice learning to like their enemies. First, it was Birdie Tebbetts, who came to the Braves from Cincinnati. And right behind him, it was Bobby Bragan, no stranger to the boos at County Stadium—and a lot of other places, for that matter.

Bragan, who took over as Braves manager in 1963, was a boisterous, controversial individual. And that's putting it nicely. To many people, he was just plain "bush."

There were numerous incidents in Bragan's career that helped him earn such a reputation, but probably the most famous took place July 31, 1957, right in front of Braves fans at County Stadium.

Bragan was in the second unsuccessful year of his first big league managing job for Pittsburgh. The Pirates made an appeal play at second base, saying Milwaukee's Bob Buhl missed second base. When the umpire ruled in the Braves' favor, Bragan displayed his opinion by holding his nose. That prompted his ejection.

Bragan had one of his pitchers, Whammy Douglas, quickly slip into the stands to buy an orange drink. Sipping on the drink through one of two straws, Bragan paraded onto the field, confronting the umpires and also offering them a sip of his orange drink. When he was ordered off the field, Bragan threatened to throw the drink in the face of umpire Frank Secory. Only under the threat of forfeit did he finally leave.

Bragan was fined $100 and given a written reprimand by the league. Two days after the incident, he also was fired.

This is the man the front office brought back to County Stadium as the Braves' leader in 1963. It should be no surprise he received a lot of boos in his three-plus seasons at the

club's helm, especially considering that the team didn't play well.

Bragan, who came to the Braves from a coaching job with Houston in 1962, was supposed to serve as a coach under Tebbetts. But when Tebbetts resigned, Bragan suddenly found himself managing his third—and last—team.

The 1963 Braves finished sixth in a 10-team league. It was the first and only time in the team's 13-year Milwaukee history that they did not wind up in the first division. Though the Braves finished over .500 in each of Bragan's three full seasons, they never got above fifth place. In 1966, Bragan moved with the team to Atlanta. But on August 8, with the Braves not making a good impression on their new fans, he was fired with the club in seventh place, seven games under .500.

Bragan, Bobby

	W	L	T	Pct
1963	84	78	1	.519
1964	88	74	0	.543
1965	86	76	0	.531
1966	52	59	1	.468
Braves	310	287	2	.519
Career	443	478	6	.481

1966–67 / Hitchcock, Billy

Record: 110–100 (.524)
Birthplace: Inverness, Alabama
B: July 31, 1916

Usually, there's nothing all that special about a manager's first game with his team, except, of course, to the manager. But Billy Hitchcock's first game as the Braves' manager in 1966 still ranks as one of the most memorable games ever played in Atlanta.

A coach under Bobby Bragan when the club moved into its new home at Atlanta Stadium in 1966, Hitchcock assumed the managerial duties August 9. The Dodgers were in town, and a sellout crowd showed up to see the great Sandy Koufax pitch. His opponent was another left-hander, Denny Lemaster. The crowd was particularly upbeat because Hitchcock had Eddie Mathews, whom Bragan had benched, back in the starting lineup.

Bobby Bragan

Billy Hitchcock

The Braves were 52–59 and going nowhere. The Dodgers, on the other hand, were headed to the World Series. But the Braves gave Koufax and his teammates all they could handle this rainy evening.

Lemaster matched Koufax pitch for pitch. Both gave up solo home runs and survived a two-hour rain delay to enter the ninth inning tied, 1–1. Lemaster retired the Dodgers without incident in the ninth, setting the stage for a dramatic, game-ending home run by Mathews in the bottom of the inning.

The Braves, who were in seventh place when Bragan was fired, rallied under Hitchcock, winning 19 of 21 at one point and 33 of 51 overall. It was enough to get the team out of the second division and into fifth place.

Hitchcock was only supposed to be the interim manager, but the club played so well for him that he was brought back in 1967. The Braves were competitive most of the season but stumbled down the stretch, winning just 10 of their last 31 games and falling to seventh place. The slump caused Hitchcock to be relieved with three games remaining on the schedule.

Hitchcock, Billy

	W	L	T	Pct
1966	33	18	0	.647
1967	77	82	0	.484
Braves	110	100	0	.524
Career	274	261	0	.512

1967 / Silvestri, Ken

Record: 0–3 (.000)
Birthplace: Chicago, Illinois
B: May 3, 1916; **D:** March 31, 1992

Ken Silvestri, the Braves' longtime bullpen coach, had the unsavory task of getting the 1967 team to the finish line. When the club fell apart in September, Billy Hitchcock was fired with three games remaining. Silvestri was named interim manager and promptly lost those three games, not that they mattered. They were the only three games he ever man-

Ken Silvestri

aged in the majors.

Silvestri came to Atlanta with the Braves from Milwaukee. He was a coach with the club from 1963 to 1975. He also had coaching stints in the majors with the Phillies (1959–60) and the White Sox (1976, 1982).

As a player, Silvestri was a seldom-used catcher for the White Sox, Yankees, and Phillies, hitting .217 in an eight-year career that was interrupted by service in World War II.

Silvestri, Ken

	W	L	T	Pct
1967	0	3	0	.000
Braves	0	3	0	.000
Career	0	3	0	.000

1968–72 / Harris, Luman

Record: 379–373 (.504)
Birthplace: New Castle, Alabama
B: January 17, 1915

Luman "Lum" Harris has the distinction of being the first manager to lead the Atlanta Braves into postseason play. He also had the longest continuous tenure (nearly five seasons) of any manager in the team's history in the South until Bobby Cox passed him in 1995.

Luman Harris and a young fan

In 1938 the major leagues were still a dream to Harris, a 23-year-old pitcher for the Atlanta Crackers of the Southern Association. But he was a lot closer to the big time than he realized.

Harris's catcher, Paul Richards, was 29 years old and had already spent parts of four seasons in the majors. The two were minor league teammates for three years in Atlanta before baseball sent them in different directions. But the friendship fostered with the Crackers later brought them back together when Richards became a manager and front office executive.

Harris used a knuckleball and fastball to forge a six-year career in the majors, mostly with some very bad Philadelphia Athletics teams in the 1940s that were managed by the legendary Connie Mack. He was 35–63 lifetime with a 4.16 ERA. In 1943 he led the American League with 21 losses, including 13 in a row.

In 1951, Richards was named White Sox manager, and he promptly brought in his old buddy Harris as pitching coach. The two would work together much of the next two decades.

Harris was Richards' pitching coach for four seasons in Chicago, then the next seven years (1955–61) at Baltimore. Richards departed the Orioles late in the '61 season to become the first general manager of the expansion Houston Colt 45s in the National League. He left Harris in charge of the Orioles for the final 27 games, providing his protégé with his first managerial experience, then brought him to Houston as pitching coach for the Colt 45s inaugural season in 1962.

Late in 1964, Richards fired Harry Craft and named Harris the Astros' manager. But after one full season in which Houston lost 97 games and finished ninth, Harris shifted from the dugout to scouting.

Richards moved on to the Braves organization, and naturally, he took Harris with him. In 1967, Harris managed the Braves' farm club at Richmond to the International League pennant. That earned him the major league managing job, left vacant by Billy Hitchcock's firing.

Under the low-key Harris, who always seemed to have a fungo bat in his hands, the Braves finished fifth in 1968 with an 81–81 record. But the advent of divisional play and the acquisition of Orlando Cepeda in 1969 helped bring surprising prosperity to Harris and the Braves in 1969. They won the first National League West title by three games over San Francisco. Even though Atlanta's initial venture into postseason play ended quickly with three straight losses to the Mets, Harris's Braves had injected a much-needed charge into Southern baseball.

That division title raised expectations, though, and the Braves were unable to live up to them. They slid all the way to fifth, 10 games under .500, in 1970. The team rebounded a little to third in 1971, but the following season Harris was fired after 105 games, with Atlanta mired in fourth place.

Harris, Lum

	W	L	T	Pct
1968	81	81	1	.500
1969	93	69	0	.574
1970	76	86	0	.469
1971	82	80	0	.506
1972	47	57	1	.452
Braves	379	373	2	.504
Career	466	488	2	.488

1972–74 / Mathews, Eddie

Record: 149–161 (.481)
Birthplace: Texarkana, Texas
B: October 13, 1931

Eddie Mathews seemed to be a near-perfect fit for the role of Braves manager, a position he assumed in August 1972 when Luman Harris was dismissed.

One of the greatest players in franchise history, in fact the only Brave to play in Boston, Milwaukee, and Atlanta, Mathews joined the team as first base coach in 1971, two seasons after his playing career ended with Detroit.

Hard-nosed, fiery, competitive, and popular with the players and fans, Mathews seemed to have it all. Yet he lasted just one full season in the job, becoming one of many great players who were unsuccessful as managers.

In his 1994 book *Eddie Mathews and the National Pastime*, the Hall of Fame third baseman writes, "Drinking was a big contributing factor in my losing the manager's job in Atlanta." He also claims his successor, Clyde King, undermined him.

The Braves played well at times for Mathews but couldn't sustain it. They finished fifth, nine games under .500, in 1973, his only full season as manager. That club was the only one in history to have three players—Hank Aaron, Dave Johnson, and Darrell Evans—hit 40 or more home runs.

Mathews received much of the credit for helping Evans develop into a power hitter. The young third baseman, who'd never hit more than 19 home runs before, became a pull hitter under Mathews' guidance and even took on many of the mannerisms his tutor used in hitting 512 lifetime homers.

Of course, Mathews also was managing the Braves when Aaron broke Babe Ruth's career home run record in 1974. A longtime friend and teammate of Aaron's in Milwaukee and Atlanta, Mathews was in the midst of the turmoil created when the Braves announced Aaron would sit out the first three games of the season at Cincinnati, then try for the record in an 11-game home stand.

When Commissioner Bowie Kuhn pressured the Braves to play Aaron in Cincinnati, Mathews made the decision to do

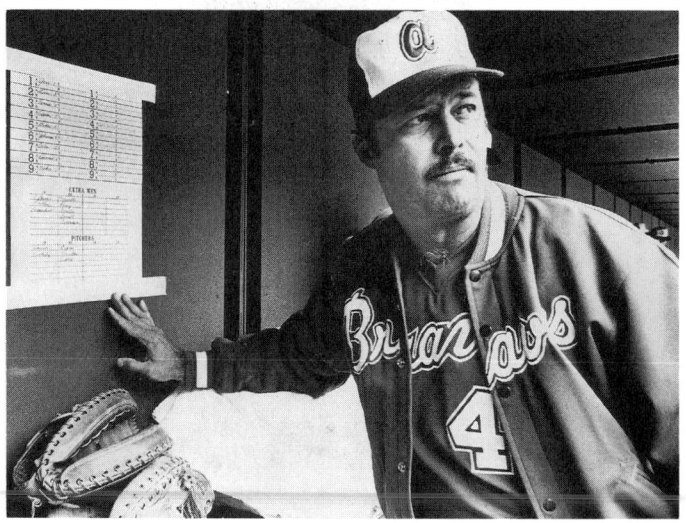

Eddie Mathews

so in the season opener in which Aaron tied Ruth. Before the second game of the series, Mathews announced he would hold Aaron out of the lineup until the Braves got to Atlanta. Aaron did not play in the second game, but when Kuhn threatened to suspend Mathews and Braves chairman Bill Bartholomay, Mathews played Aaron for the first seven innings of the final game of the series.

Perhaps inspired by Aaron's presence and accomplishment, the 1974 Braves began playing well for Mathews in mid-May. They won 26 of 34 and climbed to 10 games over .500 at 44–34. At that point, though, they went into a dive, losing 15 of 21 to fall to 50–49 on July 21 when Mathews was fired and replaced by King.

Mathews, Eddie

	W	L	T	Pct
1972	23	27	0	.460
1973	76	85	1	.472
1974	50	49	0	.505
Braves	149	161	1	.481
Career	149	161	1	.481

1974–75 / King, Clyde

Record: 96–101 (.487)
Birthplace: Goldsboro, North Carolina
B: May 23, 1925

Sportswriters covering the Braves during Clyde King's brief stay as Braves manager referred to him as "Saint Clyde" for his straitlaced demeanor. It was quite a contrast to that of the man he replaced, Eddie Mathews, who let those same reporters drink on his tab.

King was a reliever for the Dodgers in the mid-to-late 1940s and early 1950s. He pitched on pennant-winning teams in 1947 and '52 but didn't appear in either World Series. His best season was 1951, the year Bobby Thomson's home run cost Brooklyn the pennant. King led the league in relief wins that season with 13.

A one-time manager of the minor league Atlanta Crackers, King also was pitching coach for Cincinnati and Pittsburgh prior to his big league managing debut in 1969 at San Francisco. He directed the Giants to a near NL West title that

year, finishing second, three games back of Atlanta. But King was fired the next year, just 42 games into the season.

The bespectacled King joined the Braves as a special assignment scout prior to stepping in behind Mathews to manage in 1974. The Braves, who were just one game over .500 when King took over, actually played well for him. They were 38-25, moving up from fourth under Mathews to a final finish of third. But in 1975, with the club struggling to stay out of last place, King was fired with just 27 games left in the season.

King, Clyde

	W	L	T	Pct
1974	38	25	1	.603
1975	58	76	0	.433
Braves	96	101	1	.487
Career	234	229	1	.505

1975 / Ryan, Connie

Record: 9–18 (.333)
Birthplace: New Orleans, Louisiana
B: February 27, 1920

Connie Ryan was a rare three-city Brave. A slick-fielding second baseman for Boston in the 1940s, he represented the Braves on the 1944 All-Star team and played for the 1948 pennant winners. His playing career covered 12 seasons with five clubs, and he compiled a .248 lifetime batting average.

Ryan also was a coach on Milwaukee's World Series championship team in 1957 and later coached in Atlanta during the 1970s.

When Clyde King was dismissed late in the 1975 season, Ryan was named interim manager for the last 27 games. His only other major league managing came under similar circumstances in 1977 when he directed the Texas Rangers for six games.

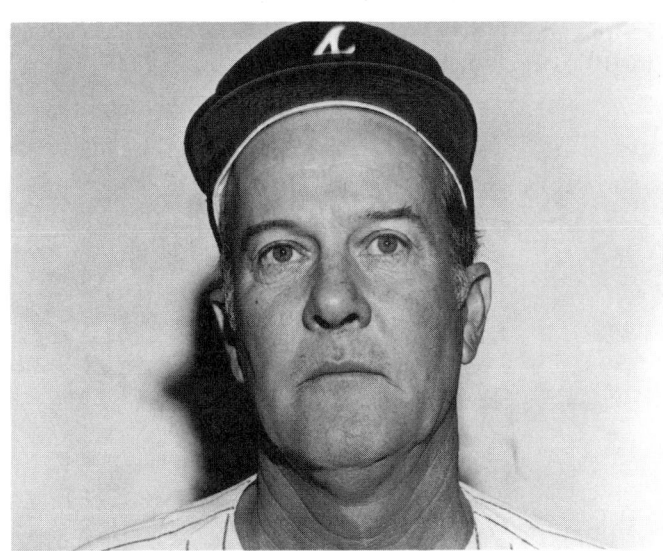

Connie Ryan

Clyde King

Ryan, Connie

	W	L	T	Pct
1975	9	18	0	.333
Braves	9	18	0	.333
Career	9	18	0	.333

1976–77 / Bristol, Dave

Record: 130–192 (.404)
Birthplace: Macon, Georgia
B: June 23, 1933

Dave Bristol was one of the fieriest managers in Braves history—and he had plenty to get riled about in his two-year stay in Atlanta.

To begin with, Bristol never seemed to get over his dismissal as Cincinnati's manager after a third-place finish in 1969. It's hard to blame him, considering that if he'd just been able to survive one more season, he could have been on his way to a long run of success with the Big Red Machine, one of the greatest teams of all time. Sparky Anderson came in after him, won a pennant in 1970, and won consecutive World Series titles in 1975 and '76. Bristol, meanwhile, was saddled with some horrible teams the rest of his career.

As a player, Bristol never made it to the majors, but he got there quickly as a manager, taking over the Reds in the second half of 1966 at age 33. He was there for another three full seasons while the groundwork was being put in place for the great Cincinnati teams of the 1970s.

From Cincinnati, Bristol went directly to Milwaukee, where he failed to get the Brewers out of the second division in two-plus seasons. He was a coach at Montreal from 1973 to 1975, once getting into a pregame argument with the Cardinals' Reggie Smith while exchanging lineup cards at home plate. Bristol then came to the Braves as manager at the start of Ted Turner's ownership of the club in 1976. The team was at rock bottom, and Bristol could do nothing to alter that course.

The Braves finished dead last in both 1976 and '77 under Bristol, and the '77 club played to a .377 percentage (61–101), the franchise's worst showing since 1935.

The 1976 Braves won eight of their first 13 games and led the NL West but then proceeded to lose the next 13 games, the team's longest losing streak since 1906.

The 1977 team also started 8–5 but then plummeted into an Atlanta-record 17-game losing streak. After the 16th straight loss, a distraught Turner sent Bristol on a "10-day scouting trip" and appointed himself manager. The Braves lost at Pittsburgh, 2–1, and National League president Chub Fenney ordered Turner out of the dugout. A thoroughly humiliated Bristol was reinstated and the Braves beat the Pirates, 6–1, the next day to end the losing streak. However, neither he nor the team could fully recover from the losing streak and Turner's intervention. Bristol was fired after the 1977 season.

Bristol, Dave

	W	L	T	Pct
1976	70	92	0	.432
1977	61	100	0	.379
Braves	131	192	0	.406
Career	658	764	3	.463

1977 / Turner, Ted

Record: 0–1 (.000)
Birthplace: Cincinnati, Ohio
B: November 19, 1938

Ted Turner's logic was hard to argue with under the circumstances. "When you're setting records for losing streaks, it doesn't hurt to change things," he said after his one-game stint as Braves manager in 1977 resulted in an Atlanta-record 17th consecutive defeat. "If things get sour in your love life, you get a new hairdo, don't you? Or you buy a new suit or dress?"

Such maneuvers and statements were typical of Turner in the early years after he purchased the Braves in 1976. He was

Dave Bristol

Ted Turner

more interested in making headlines and gaining fame than in winning games.

Dave Bristol, in his second and last season as manager, took the Braves to the first 16 losses in that 1977 streak. The team was mired in last place with an 8–21 record when Turner sent Bristol on a "10-day scouting trip" on May 11 and proceeded to take hold of the managerial reins himself—well, sort of.

The Braves owner was in the midst of a brief reprieve from a one-year suspension for "tampering" with former San Francisco outfielder Gary Matthews, who'd signed with the Braves as a free agent. The Braves were suing Commissioner Bowie Kuhn over the tampering ruling, and Turner was allowed to resume his association with the club during the litigation.

Turner named himself manager, pulled on a double-knit uniform, stuck a plug of tobacco in his cheek, and warmed up for his debut by running sprints in the outfield. During the game at Pittsburgh, Turner sat on the bench, but coach Vern Benson actually made strategic decisions. The Braves lost anyway, 2–1. National League president Chub Feeney, citing an obscure rule prohibiting a manager from having a financial stake in the team, immediately ordered Turner out of the dugout.

Turner, Ted

	W	L	T	Pct
1977	0	1	0	.000
Braves	0	1	0	.000
Career	0	1	0	.000

1978–81, 1990–   / Cox, Bobby

Record: 670–616 (.521)
Birthplace: Tulsa, Oklahoma
B: May 21, 1941

When Bobby Cox was named Braves manager on November 22, 1977, many fans wondered if there was a mistake in the announcement. Few had heard of *Bobby* Cox and wondered if the team's new manager might be Billy Cox, third baseman on the great Dodgers teams of the late 1940s and early '50s. But it was indeed Bobby Cox, who, at age 36, became the youngest manager in the National League.

It took two tours of duty in Atlanta, but Cox not only over-

Bobby Cox

came the identity crisis but eventually became one of the most successful and respected managers in franchise history.

The Yankees' first base coach in 1977, Cox was a once-promising infielder who had his career cut short by knee injuries. The Dodgers signed him in 1959 for a $40,000 bonus. He played seven years in the Dodgers' farm system, then was acquired by the Braves' farm system in 1966. After spending 1967 at Richmond, where he batted .297 and hit 14 home runs, Cox was traded to the Yankees for catcher Bob Tillman and pitcher Dale Roberts.

In the spring of 1968, Cox won the Yankees' starting job at third base. He hit just .229 yet was named to the Topps' Rookie All-Star Team. The following year, though, he lost his job to Bobby Murcer. Cox found himself back in the minors in 1970, and in 1971, at age 30, he retired and began his managerial career with the Yankees' Florida State League team at Fort Lauderdale.

Cox managed in the minors for six years, never finishing a season with a losing record. His West Haven team won the Eastern League pennant in 1972, and he followed that with four years managing the Yankees' top farm club at Syracuse. By 1977 he'd earned a promotion to the majors and a reputation as a top managerial prospect.

But no manager's reputation was safe with the Braves in those days, as Cox soon discovered.

The Braves began a youth movement, headed by Dale Murphy and Bob Horner, under Cox, but he wasn't around by the time the youngsters blossomed. His first two teams finished sixth, giving the Braves a string of four straight last-place finishes from 1976 to '79. Finally, in 1980, there was progress. The Braves were 81–80, their first season over .500 since 1974, and it seemed as if Cox's patience with his young players was finally paying dividends.

However, the 1981 season was interrupted by a players' strike, which also seemed to halt the Braves' progress. They were 25–29 in the first half and 25–27 in the second half of the split-season format.

With attendance down nearly 50 percent, owner Ted Turner felt the team had failed to show progress and fired Cox. At the same time, when asked what he would look for in Cox's replacement, Turner responded, "Well, if I hadn't just fired him, Bobby Cox would be the leading candidate. We need somebody like him."

Turner wasn't simply trying to soothe the wounds of the man he'd just fired. As he would demonstrate four years later, the Braves' owner had genuine respect for Cox.

Meanwhile, Cox landed on his feet as manager of the up-and-coming Toronto Blue Jays. In 1982 he led the Blue Jays to the best record (78–84) in their six-year existence. Toronto continued to show progress under his direction, too. The Jays were 89–73 in 1983 and again in 1984, when they climbed from fourth place to second in the American League East.

Then in 1985, Toronto won 99 games and the first division title in franchise history. In the playoffs, the Blue Jays won three of the first four games from Kansas City, only to lose the next three and fall one game short of the World Series.

Cox was bitterly disappointed by the playoff defeat, but he soon had plenty of good news to take his mind off it. He was named American League and Major League manager of the year, but even before he learned of those honors, he'd decided to give up his spikes for an office job—as general manager of the team that had fired him in 1981.

During his four years with the Blue Jays, Cox continued to make his permanent home in suburban Atlanta. He'd met his second wife, Pam, during an off-season promotional tour in North Georgia when he was still Braves manager, and he liked the area. That's why he was able to walk away from a good situation in Toronto to return to the Braves, who were once again in a rebuilding mode.

The Braves had fallen apart in 1985 under Eddie Haas, and Turner had already hired Chuck Tanner as manager a week before he convinced Cox to come back to Atlanta. The team was in complete disarray and played poorly for Tanner, who lasted just two-plus seasons. Tanner, who did well when managing veterans in Pittsburgh, was not suited for bringing along the young prospects the Braves were counting on, so Cox replaced him with Russ Nixon, who'd been managing in the Atlanta farm system.

Throughout his term as general manager, Cox maintained a devout policy of building from within through scouting, drafting, and signing top prospects, especially pitchers. By 1990, the Braves had one of the most highly regarded farm systems in baseball, and the big league club already was stocked with several top young players such as David Justice, Ron Gant, Tom Glavine, Jeff Blauser, and John Smoltz, who'd been obtained in a trade Cox made with Detroit.

However, the club continued to struggle in 1990. With the Braves' record at 25–40 on June 22, Nixon was fired and Cox moved back into the dugout for the remainder of the 1990 season. He retained his duties as general manager, too, but team president Stan Kasten made it clear Cox would be allowed to keep only one of the two positions for 1991.

Cox chose the dugout over the office. The Braves hired John Schuerholz as general manager, and he and Cox proved a very capable team.

Almost overnight, Cox went from managing a last-place team, which is where the 1990 club finished, to directing the franchise's greatest run of success since the 1950s.

The turnaround was evident almost immediately, and Cox soon found himself directing one of the most incredible reversals in baseball history. Patient, reserved, and unassuming, he had the perfect makeup for bringing along a team of talented young players mixed with a few veterans.

In 1991 the Braves won the division title and beat Pittsburgh in the National League Championship Series before falling to Minnesota, 1–0, in the 10th inning of the seventh game of the World Series.

Cox received several postseason awards, including Major League Manager of the Year by *The Sporting News,* making him the first man to win that honor in both leagues.

Many people speculated that the Braves would not repeat, saying their 1991 "miracle" was a fluke. But Cox led the team to yet another division title in 1992 with 98 victories, the most in the majors and a modern franchise record. Atlanta then beat the Pirates in the NLCS with a breathtaking seventh-game victory before another World Series setback, this one to Cox's former employer, Toronto.

Cox's 1993 team was favored to win a third consecutive pennant and nearly did so, winning the NL West but losing to Philadelphia in the playoffs. Nevertheless, the Braves put together a spirited stretch drive (54–19 after the All-Star

break) to win the division on the final day of the season. Their 104 victories set a franchise record, led the majors, and won National League manager of the year honors for Cox.

In 1994 the Braves moved to the NL East and finished second to Montreal in a season shortened to 114 games by a players' strike. Cox's patient, conservative style suddenly drew some criticism, but it was hard to argue with his record and accomplishments. In his last seven full seasons of managing, beginning with Toronto in 1983, Cox's record was 641–444 (.591) with four division titles, two runner-up finishes, and two pennants.

Cox entered the 1995 season as the winningest Braves manager of the modern era. The only manager in franchise history to win more games is Frank Selee, whose 1,004 victories came mainly in the 19th century.

Cox's return to the Braves after his 1981 firing was unusual in itself, and his success in that circumstance is unprecedented.

In the 20th century, only 10 men have had breaks in service in managing the same team. Just eight of those 10 managed other teams before returning to the scene. Cox is the only one of those eight to win a division title or pennant in his second time around the block. He's continued to prove that a manager can go home again.

Cox, Bobby

	W	L	T	Pct
1978	69	93	0	.426
1979	66	94	0	.412
1980	81	80	0	.503
1981	50	56	1	.472
1990	40	57	0	.412
1991	94	68	0	.580
1992	98	64	0	.605
1993	104	58	0	.642
1994	68	46	0	.596
Braves	670	616	1	.521
Career	1,025	908	1	.530

1982–84 / Torre, Joe

Record: 257–229 (.529)
Birthplace: Brooklyn, New York
B: July 18, 1940

Of the 14 men who managed the Braves for three or more seasons in the 20th century, only Fred Haney (.596), Bobby Cox (.546), and Charlie Grimm (.545) did so with more success than Joe Torre (.529). Yet management showed remarkably little patience with Torre, especially in light of his ability to interrupt more than a decade of mostly miserable baseball in Atlanta by winning the 1982 National League West title.

A five-time All-Star catcher for the Braves in the 1960s, Torre also won the National League MVP award and batting title in 1971 with the St. Louis Cardinals. In 18 seasons, he compiled a lifetime batting average of .297 with 252 home runs and five years of 100 or more RBIs.

Torre began his managerial career in May 1977 when, at age 36 and with no minor league experience, he replaced Joe Frazier as manager of the Mets. Torre was still a part-time player with the Mets at the time, but he retired 18 days later.

Joe Torre

In nearly five full seasons under Torre, the Mets never approached .500. Following the strike-divided 1981 season, he was fired at about the same time the Braves were parting ways with Bobby Cox. Undaunted by Torre's poor record in New York and influenced by his personable manner, Braves owner Ted Turner made the first man to hit a regular-season homer at Atlanta Stadium the team's next manager.

Whether Torre pushed the right buttons in spring training or simply was in the right place at the right time, the young Braves team of 1982 came out of the starting gate like no other club in history. Torre's team won its first 13 games, establishing a major league record for consecutive victories at the start of the season.

It was a thrilling two weeks for the Braves and their fans and quite a way for Torre to begin his new job. However, in some ways, those first 13 games were the highlight of his three years managing the team.

The Braves played only three games over .500 the rest of the season but still won the division on the strength of their record start. But in their first postseason play since 1969, the Braves were swept by the Cardinals in three games of what was then a best-of-five playoff for the pennant. In spite of the quick end to the season, Torre was named the league's manager of the year by Associated Press.

The 1983 Braves finished second, three games back of the Dodgers, with a record that was just one game worse than the previous year's division-winning team. In 1984, Torre again brought the Braves in second, but this time the club was 12 games out of first, and its record fell to two games under .500.

Citing the team's failure to progress, Turner fired Torre in spite of three seasons in which attendance averaged nearly 1.9 million and the club didn't finish lower than second. It

would be quite a while before the franchise next enjoyed that level of success.

Torre, Joe

	W	L	T	Pct
1982	89	73	0	.549
1983	88	74	0	.543
1984	80	82	0	.494
Braves	257	229	0	.529
Career	874	976	0	.472

1985 / Haas, Eddie

Record: 50–71 (.413)
Birthplace: Paducah, Kentucky
B: May 26, 1935

Few managers in Braves history were less suited for the job than was Eddie Haas. And many people within the organization thought he was the ideal man for the position when he was hired. In fact, Ted Turner had overruled the recommendation of his baseball advisers three years earlier when he chose Joe Torre over Haas to follow Bobby Cox.

It wasn't that Haas didn't know baseball or wasn't a devoted, hard-working employee. The Braves knew he was that and more, because he'd been a player, coach, minor league manager, scout, and batting instructor in the organization since 1958, playing briefly at the big league level as an outfielder in 1958 and '60.

If anyone deserved to be manager, it was Haas. But he didn't have the personality and makeup for the demands put on a big league manager. He couldn't handle the media. The more the team lost, the more reticent he became. The players, many of whom knew Haas well from coming through the farm system, sensed just how uncomfortable he was in the position and quickly grew just as uncomfortable playing for him.

On August 25, after only 121 games, Haas was fired with the team in fifth place.

Eddie Haas

Haas, Eddie

	W	L	T	Pct
1985	50	71	0	.413
Braves	50	71	0	.413
Career	50	71	0	.413

1985 / Wine, Bobby

Record: 16–25 (.390)
Birthplace: New York City
B: September 17, 1938

A classic good-field/no-hit infielder, Bobby Wine lasted 12 years in the majors, mostly with the Phillies, despite a lifetime batting average of .215. He won a Gold Glove in 1963 and led National League shortstops in fielding (.980) in 1967.

When his playing career ended in 1972, Wine moved directly into big league coaching at Philadelphia, where he stayed for 12 years. In 1985 he was hired by the Braves to serve on Eddie Haas's staff, and when Haas was fired, Wine took over for the final 41 games of the season.

For the next seven years, Wine continued with the Braves as a scout and coach. Then when the Mets hired Dallas Green as manager in 1993, Wine returned to his hometown of New York to be Green's bench coach.

Wine, Bobby

	W	L	T	Pct
1985	16	25	0	.390
Braves	16	25	0	.390
Career	16	25	0	.390

Bobby Wine

1986–88 / Tanner, Chuck

Record: 153–208 (.424)
Birthplace: New Castle, Pennsylvania
B: July 4, 1929

When the Braves hired Chuck Tanner as manager for 1986, he promised he'd someday lead a championship Braves team in a victory parade down Peachtree Street. Six years later, that parade was held, but Tanner was long gone from Atlanta.

A former Braves outfielder who hit a pinch-hit home run on the first major league pitch he saw in 1955, Tanner was used sparingly in an eight-year big league career in which he batted .261 with four teams.

His managing career was considerably longer, but the results weren't a great deal better. Known for his optimism and enthusiasm, Tanner managed four big league teams for a combined 19 seasons from 1970 to 1988. In 1979 he took Pittsburgh to the World Series championship, beating Baltimore in seven games. However, that was the only team he managed that finished a season in first place. He did have five runner-up finishes, though.

Tanner managed eight years in the minors before taking over the Chicago White Sox in 1970. In 1972 he brought the White Sox in second and was named major league manager of the year. But he was fired after finishing fifth in 1975.

He took Oakland to a runner-up finish in 1976; then colorful owner Charlie Finley traded him to Pittsburgh for catcher Manny Sanguillen and $100,000. Tanner managed the Pirates for nine years before being fired after back-to-back last-place finishes in 1984 and '85.

Ted Turner, who "managed" one game in 1977 against Pittsburgh, promptly hired Tanner. Tanner quipped, "I beat him. Maybe that's why he hired me."

In 1986, Tanner's optimism was sobered by a last-place finish—his third in a row with two teams. He got the Braves up to fifth in 1987, but with a record that was three games worse than the previous season's.

Just 39 games into the 1988 season, with the Braves again

Chuck Tanner

buried in the NL West basement, Tanner was fired, ending his run of 17 consecutive full seasons as a major league manager.

Tanner, Chuck

	W	L	T	Pct
1986	72	89	0	.447
1987	69	92	0	.429
1988	12	27	0	.308
Braves	153	208	0	.424
Career	1,352	1,381	5	.495

1988–90 / Nixon, Russ

Record: 130–216 (.376)
Birthplace: Cleves, Ohio
B: February 19, 1935

Russ Nixon nearly presided over the greatest story in Atlanta baseball history. It's a thought that probably still haunts him. Whether or not the 1991 team would have ascended from last place to pennant winners under Nixon rather than Bobby Cox is impossible to know, but the fact is that Nixon was fired less than a year before the Braves' turnaround.

A backup catcher often hampered by injuries, Nixon fashioned a 12-year big league career during which he appeared in 100 games just twice. His lifetime batting average with three teams was .268.

Nixon managed in the Cincinnati farm system from 1970 through 1975, then joined the Reds' major league coaching staff in 1976. In mid-1982, he replaced John McNamara as Cincinnati's manager but failed to get the club out of the last-place hole he inherited. His 1983 team improved by 13 games over the previous year but still finished last, prompting his dismissal.

Russ Nixon

In 1986, Nixon was hired as a Braves coach under Chuck Tanner after spending the previous two years coaching at Montreal. However, he was more general manager Bobby Cox's man than he was Tanner's, and he was viewed as an outsider on Tanner's staff. Nixon began the 1988 season managing the Braves' Greenville farm club, but when Tanner was fired 39 games into the season, Nixon was promoted to Atlanta.

In one full season and parts of two others, the often-outspoken Nixon failed to get the Braves out of last place. On June 22, 1990, he was fired and replaced by Cox. The Braves remained in last place the rest of the season before their stunning reversal in 1991.

Nixon, Russ

	W	L	T	Pct
1988	42	79	0	.347
1989	63	97	1	.394
1990	25	40	0	.385
Braves	130	216	1	.376
Career	231	347	1	.400

5

The Front Office

The presidents and general managers in Braves history have tried just about everything to make the franchise successful on the field and at the box office.

They've jumped from city to city to city in search of a strong fan base and changed the club's nickname in hope of fostering a better image. They've acquired many of the biggest names ever to play the game and shuffled hundreds of players and dozens of managers in search of the right chemistry.

Often, their efforts were in vain, but they never stopped trying. The result is that today's Braves franchise is considered among the strongest in baseball. This chapter profiles the major front office people who have shaped the course of the oldest continuously operating pro sports franchise in America.

The Presidents

1876 / Nathaniel T. Apollonio

Nathaniel T. Apollonio not only was the franchise's first president in National League history, but he preceded the new league by directing the club's affairs during its last two seasons in the National Association.

Described as a "public-spirited citizen" in Harold Kaese's *The Boston Braves,* Apollonio was elected team president December 3, 1873. Just over two years later, on February 2, 1876, he and Harry Wright represented the Red Stockings at the New York meeting that marked the formation of the National League.

Other clubs in attendance were Philadelphia, Chicago, Cincinnati, Hartford, Louisville, Brooklyn, and St. Louis.

Apollonio must not have been able to settle for anything less than first place. The Red Stockings won National Association pennants in his first two years as president, but after they finished fourth 1876, the inaugural National League season, he sold the team to a group headed by Arthur H. Soden.

1877–1906 / Arthur H. Soden

Arthur H. Soden, who became president of the franchise in its second year in the National League and served in that role for three decades, was one of the most influential men in the formative years of professional league baseball.

Soden, along with William Conant and James Billings, took control of the Boston Red Stockings prior to the 1877 season in an election among stockholders. Soden, who was chosen president, and Billings, who was voted treasurer, owned a majority of the stock. Conant was elected secretary. Together, the threesome was commonly referred to as the Triumvirs after Caesar, Pompey, and Crassus, the rulers of ancient Rome.

Soden's most notable contribution to baseball was creating the so-called reserve clause. It stabilized the game for years but led to great conflict between players and owners and eventually was overturned in 1976 by arbitrator Peter Seitz and the court system.

In 1879, Boston's prized shortstop George Wright and star outfielder "Orator" Jim O'Rourke jumped ship to play for rival Providence. Adding insult to injury, Wright also managed Providence to the pennant, beating older brother Harry Wright's Red Stockings by five games.

Players commonly jumped from team to team in that era when their contracts expired. Soden reasoned, "What man in his right mind will invest money in this kind of business? Today he has some assets. Tomorrow he may have none."

Soden's reserve clause bound four players to each team, but it ultimately grew to include all players and thus dictated the fabric of the game for close to a century.

Arthur H. Soden

General manager John Quinn (with manager Billy Southworth, left, at 1949 spring training) grew up on baseball, learning the game from his father Bob, the Bees'/Braves' president from 1936–44.

Born in Framingham, Massachusetts on April 23, 1843, Soden was a hospital steward during the Civil War. Afterward, he became a wholesale druggist, then got into the roofing business where he became wealthy.

Known as a man with unquestioned integrity, Soden typified the conservative, frugal stereotype of a New Englander. He brought his lunch to the office, and complimentary tickets to Red Stockings games were almost nonexistent. Even the players' wives had to pay admission.

The franchise won eight pennants while Soden was president, the most of any team in that period. But while his team was tearing through the league on the field, Soden often was holding it together in the boardrooms. He was a major force in leading the National League successfully through wars with three rival leagues—the Union Association (1884), the Players League (1890), and the American Association (1891).

When National League president William Hulbert died in the spring of 1882, Soden served in that capacity for the rest of the year until a successor was named. He often helped other clubs who were in financial trouble, once loaning the Giants $60,000.

Another contribution Soden and his partners made to the game was introducing the practice of buying players. After Boston won the 1883 pennant and finished second in 1884, the club fell on hard times, finishing fifth the next two seasons. Billings suggested to Soden that the team buy King Kelly, the most exciting player of the day, from Chicago.

It was a then-unheard-of method for acquiring talent, but the Triumvirs proceeded, purchasing Kelly for the incredible sum of $10,000. The move shocked all of baseball and initiated what became a common practice in baseball. And it was a method at which Soden's teams would continue to set the pace for several years.

The formation of an American League team in Boston in 1901 quickly eroded the Triumvirs' long run of success. The team, which had become known as the Beaneaters, struggled on the field and at the gate. After the 1906 season, Soden and Conant, who'd bought out Billings two years earlier, sold the team. The National League made both of them honorary members for the role they played in making the young league a success.

1907–09 / George B. Dovey

The role of Paducah, Kentucky, in franchise history is not a particularly memorable one. Not only did it produce Eddie Haas, the Braves' ill-suited manager of 1985, but it also contributed greatly to the imposition of the nickname "Doves" on the team for four years. True to that peaceful nickname, the team had four horrid seasons under the Dovey brothers.

George B. and John S. Dovey, natives of Philadelphia, played baseball as youths in Paducah for Barney Dreyfuss, who would become owner of the Louisville franchise in the National League and later of the Pittsburgh Pirates. The Doveys ran a coal mine until it was flooded. After that, they got into the railroad business and then teamed with John Harris of Pittsburgh and Beaneaters player-manager Fred Tenney in late 1906 to buy Boston's National League club from Arthur Soden for $75,000.

Harris was the chief investor, but he allowed the Doveys to run the club. Tenney actually played a significant role in setting up the transfer of ownership, as did the Dovey's old

George B. Dovey

friend Dreyfuss, who had turned the Pirates into a highly successful franchise. George Dovey was elected president and John Dovey business manager.

The Doveys made some improvements in the run-down South End Grounds, which the customers seemed to appreciate. The fans began referring to the team as the Doves, and the name stuck as long as the Doveys operated the franchise.

1909–10 / John S. Dovey

John S. Dovey succeeded his brother, George, as team president as a result of unfortunate circumstances.

During the 1909 season, George was on a train trip through the Ohio Valley when he died at age 48 from a hemorrhage of the lungs. The team president had visited chief investor John Harris in Pittsburgh, then traveled to Steubenville, Ohio, to scout players. On June 19, while on a train bound for Cincinnati, he died.

John, who was serving as business manager, replaced his brother as president, but he and Harris sold the team after the 1910 season and the club's second straight last-place finish. Fortunately, the nickname "Doves" went with them.

John S. Dovey

William H. Russell

John M. Ward

1911 / William Hepburn Russell

As bad as "Doves" was for a nickname, "Rustlers" might have been even worse. That's what the team was known as in 1911, during William Hepburn Russell's lone season as franchise president.

A New York attorney, Russell was a native of Hannibal, Missouri, and a boyhood friend of Mark Twain. He headed a group of investors that included Boston publishers Louis C. Page and George A. Page and Boston insurance executive Frederic J. Murphy. They bought the team for approximately $100,000.

The new owners brought back Fred Tenney as manager, but the team was horrible and finished with a worse record and deeper in last place than it had the previous season.

Russell, 54, was in poor health and gave up his law practice. The team's problems didn't help his health, and he died in November, prompting the sale of the franchise.

The biggest contribution Russell made to the team was keeping it in Boston. Ned Hanlon, who won five pennants from 1894 to 1900 managing Baltimore and Brooklyn, tried to buy the franchise with the intent of moving it to Baltimore. Russell, however, rejected the offer.

1912 / John M. Ward

John Montgomery Ward was one of the early stars of the National League. He pitched Providence to the 1879 pennant by five games over Boston, preventing the Red Stockings from winning their third straight flag.

After a Hall of Fame playing career that included some double duty as manager, Ward became a successful New York attorney. In late 1911 he joined New York political contractor James E. Gaffney in purchasing what was then known

as the Boston Rustlers of the National League for $177,000. Ward was elected president, but his association with the franchise was brief.

Ward was a winner, and the Rustlers—or Braves as they were renamed in 1912—were not. As much as anything, that poor record was what led Ward to resigning on July 31 of his first season as president.

Boston was coming off three straight last-place finishes and was well on its way to a fourth when Ward sold out to Gaffney, saying, "I'm getting out just in time by the looks of it. This club is driving me bughouse."

Ward was hardly used to such baseball. As a Providence rookie in 1878, he led the National League with a 1.51 ERA. In pitching the Grays to the pennant the following season, he led the NL with 47 wins and 239 strikeouts. During his first six seasons Ward averaged 27 victories, before his arm burned out and forced him to become an infielder. He led the league's shortstops in fielding in 1887 for New York and twice led the league in steals, including 111 in 1887. His career batting average was .275 over 17 seasons.

In 1890, Ward helped organize the players' union, known as the Brotherhood, and the Players League, which lasted just one season. He retired four years later, at age 34, but remained a member of the National League rules committee for a number of years.

1912–15 / James E. Gaffney

James Gaffney is one of the most important men in franchise history. If not for him, there's no telling what the Braves might be called today. Would they still be the Rustlers? Might they have reverted to the Doves, Beaneaters, or Red Stockings? Or would they be known as the Bees or be named after some other insect, animal, or mascot?

There's no telling, but if not for Gaffney's connections to

James E. Gaffney

the Tammany Hall politicians in New York, there's no reason to assume Boston's National League franchise would ever have been called the Braves.

The Tammany politicos were often referred to as "braves" because the Tammany Society was named after a Delaware Indian chief. Gaffney, a contractor with strong ties to the Tammanys, therefore renamed the team in their honor when he purchased it.

The profile of an Indian chief was added to the sleeve of the team's uniform jerseys, replacing the old English *B*. The nickname caught on and has been used since 1912 except for the five-year period 1936–40 when it was changed to Bees.

Gaffney and John Montgomery Ward purchased the club after William H. Russell died in late 1911. Ward served as president until the middle of the 1912 season when he became disenchanted and sold out to Gaffney, who assumed the presidency.

Besides changing the name of the team, Gaffney also refurbished the dilapidated South End Grounds. The grandstand was expanded, and the left-field bleachers were torn down so the fence could be moved back from 250 to 350 feet from home plate.

In 1914, Gaffney purchased the old Allston Golf Course and commenced building Braves Field, which opened August 18, 1915. It was the largest such structure in baseball at the time, seating 43,500, and was billed as the "World's Greatest Ballpark."

Also in 1914, Gaffney made the decision to sign second baseman Johnny Evers, who had been released by the Cubs. Evers proceeded to win the Chalmers Award as the league's MVP in leading the Braves to their "miracle" World Series championship.

Gaffney had been a policeman for a while but eventually got into contracting and became wealthy doing it. When he sold the Braves early in 1916, he continued to collect rent from the Braves on the ballpark he built and still owned.

1916–18 / Percy D. Haughton

Percy Haughton had one of the most unique backgrounds of any man to serve the Braves as president. Among other accomplishments, he was considered one of the great college football coaches in America during the early 20th century. However, he did not enjoy similar success with the Braves.

An 1899 Harvard graduate, Haughton won three letters in football as an All-America back/tackle and one of the finest punters and dropkick specialists of his era. He also earned four letters in baseball as a first baseman and second baseman.

Shortly after graduation, he accepted the head coaching position at Cornell. He stayed at Cornell two seasons, then worked as a bond salesman, before returning to his alma mater, where the football program was in a state of disorder.

Haughton coached Harvard's football team from 1908 to 1916, compiling a 71–7–5 record (.886), still the best in school history. During one stretch under Haughton, the Crimson put together a 33-game unbeaten streak that is referred to as the school's golden era.

"Here was a great coach, not merely a good one," Notre Dame coach Jesse Harper once said. "He was colder than an iceberg, harder than granite. But he was brilliant—a natural leader. He was to football what General Patton was to our armies."

Haughton headed a syndicate that purchased the Braves in early 1916. He continued to coach Harvard football that year, too, but the school suspended its program the next two seasons because of World War I.

One of Haughton's first moves as Braves president was to give "Miracle Man" George Stallings a new contract as manager. He then tried to bar profanity on the team—and might as well have confiscated all the balls, bats, and gloves, too. Stallings, perhaps the most profane manager in history, quickly broke the ban, and Haughton realized he was a long way from Harvard.

After finishing a strong third in 1916, the Braves slid to sixth and seventh the next two years, and Haughton's group sold the club.

Percy D. Haughton

Though he was 42 years old, Haughton enlisted in the Army after selling the Braves and served in France as a major in chemical warfare. After the war, he returned home to work as a securities broker. However, his love for sports lured him back to coaching in 1923 when he was appointed head coach at Columbia. But the following October, while dressing for practice, he became ill and died suddenly at the age of 48.

Haughton was skilled in several sports. In 1908 he won the U.S. tennis championship in singles, and in 1912 he won the national doubles title. He also authored a book titled *Foot Ball and How to Watch It.*

1919–22 / George Washington Grant

Were the Braves ever a "farm team" for the New York Giants? There were those who ventured that theory when George Washington Grant purchased the Braves in 1919, but it's doubtful the mighty Giants would stoop so low. That's how bad the Braves were.

Grant, who became a big baseball fan in his youth in Cincinnati, was a motion picture executive who pioneered the film industry in Europe. He was a New Yorker known to be a close friend of Giants owner Charles Stoneham and manager John McGraw, hence the "farm team" talk. The purchase price for the franchise was believed to be approximately $400,000.

Supporters of the "farm team" theory got all the ammunition they needed when the Braves sent their best pitcher, Art Nehf, to New York in August 1919 for four pitchers and $40,000. Nehf became a mainstay of McGraw's staff, helping the Giants to four straight pennants in 1921–24.

In Grant's four years as president, the Braves managed a winning record only in 1921. After they lost 100 games and fell to last place in 1922, he sold the club.

1923–25 / Christy Mathewson

When Judge Emil Fuchs purchased controlling interest in the Braves in 1923, he did so with the understanding that Christy Mathewson was part of the deal. Unfortunately, Mathewson's pitching days were history.

Fuchs had been the attorney for John McGraw's New York Giants, for whom Mathewson starred. The former New York magistrate bought the Braves from George Washington Grant, a friend of McGraw's, and it was McGraw who arranged a meeting between Mathewson and Fuchs.

Fuchs wanted Mathewson to serve as the Braves' president. Mathewson, who would become one of the original five

Christy Mathewson

George W. Grant (lower left) embarks on a spring training adventure which also included Commissioner Kenesaw Mountain Landis (lower right).

Hall of Fame inductees, was not in good health but gladly accepted the position.

It was a real coup for Fuchs, because Mathewson was one of the most idolized men ever to grace the American sports scene. Tall, handsome, college educated at Bucknell, and winner of 373 career games, his mere presence was enough to give Bostonians hope in their downtrodden National League franchise.

Unfortunately, Mathewson wasn't able to spend his full time and energy on the Braves. While serving in France during World War I, he'd inhaled poison gas during an accident in chemical warfare training. Eight men died, and Mathewson and others suffered lung damage.

Weakened by the accident, Mathewson contracted tuberculosis after returning home. His doctor told him that he would die within two years if he accepted the position with the Braves.

Nevertheless, Mathewson took the job but spent a great deal of time traveling to and from a sanatorium in Saranac Lake, New York. While attending the opening game of the 1925 World Series, Fuchs received word that Mathewson had died at Saranac Lake. He was just 45 years old.

1926–35 / Judge Emil E. Fuchs

Long before the Braves were owned by Ted Turner, they were owned by Judge Emil Fuchs. Unlike Turner, who has made millions while operating the team, Fuchs lost at least a million and eventually filed for bankruptcy. But Fuchs and Turner, both of whom ventured into the dugout to manage the Braves, share first place as the two biggest characters ever to serve as team president.

Among other things, Fuchs brought Babe Ruth, Rogers Hornsby, Christy Mathewson, Casey Stengel, and George Sisler to Boston, though none of those great names were successful in making the Braves winners. Like Turner in his early baseball years, Fuchs was a tireless promoter, holding the first Ladies Days in Boston, staging Knot Hole Days for kids, and sanctioning the first radio broadcast of a game in Boston. He wined and dined the writers who covered the team, calling them his "board of directors."

Judge Emil Fuchs

Born April 17, 1878, Fuchs was a graduate of New York University's law school and served as a New York City magistrate and deputy attorney general of New York state. He also was the attorney for the New York Giants, enabling him to stay close to the game he'd loved since his youth.

Fuchs' relationship with the Giants put him in position to buy the Braves in 1923 from George Washington Grant, a friend of Giants manager John McGraw. The first three seasons Fuchs owned the club, Christy Mathewson was president, but upon the death of the former Giants' pitching great in the fall of 1925, the short, round Fuchs assumed that position.

The Braves were in constant financial trouble during Fuchs' reign. The Red Sox were much more popular with Boston's baseball fans, and the Braves' inability to field a competitive team caused the franchise to dig itself a deeper hole each season.

A major hindrance to financial success was Boston's ban on Sunday games, which Fuchs fought with vigor—a little too much vigor the city decided. Sunday play was finally legalized in 1929, but Fuchs was charged with spending money to influence the vote. He pleaded no contest, and the Braves were fined $1,000 in municipal court.

The 1929 season was a big one for the judge. Not only were Sunday games instituted, but Fuchs named himself manager. Playing most of the previous season under the great Rogers Hornsby, the Braves had one of their worst records ever, posting a .327 percentage and finishing 44½ games out of first. Fuchs got a lucrative offer for Hornsby and unloaded him to the Cubs. Figuring the team couldn't do any worse no matter who was managing, the judge moved into the dugout.

The Braves did have a slightly better record in 1929 than they had the previous year, but they slipped from seventh place to last. After the first couple of weeks of the season, Fuchs didn't spend much time in the dugout, preferring to let "assistant manager" Johnny Evers run the club.

Fuchs hired a real manager, Bill McKechnie, in 1930, and the Braves actually began to improve on the field. The judge also had received financial backing from Boston businessman Charles F. Adams, who was named the team's vice president. However, with the onset of the Great Depression, there was little hope for turning around the team's fiscal problems—not that the judge quit trying.

By 1935 the nation's financial state was improving, but a still desperate Fuchs announced plans to hold dog races at Braves Field. He had to find a way to pay back $79,000 to Adams, or else he'd lose control of the team. However, the league was outraged over the thought of dog racing at one of its parks and nixed the idea.

When the estate of James Gaffney, which still controlled Braves Field, threatened to stage the dog races anyway, the league loaned Fuchs $7,500 for spring training and took over the lease on Braves Field, subletting it to the team at a reduced price. The Braves still needed to find a way to generate revenue, though, and Fuchs decided he'd take his chances with Babe Ruth, the biggest attraction the game had ever known.

The 40-year-old Ruth was at the end of the line, and the Yankees were trying to find a way to unload him diplomatically. Fuchs came to the rescue. The Yankees released Ruth to the Braves to allow him to accept a position as player, assistant manager, and second vice president.

Though Boston's fans were initially thrilled, they quickly discovered Ruth was finished. He was seldom effective and caused problems on the team by ignoring rules. The Braves were miserable and on their way to what was then a modern National League record of 115 losses. On June 2, Ruth retired, ending all doubts about Fuchs' fate. On July 31 the judge forfeited his majority share of the team, and 14 months later he filed for bankruptcy.

After the season, the league temporarily took over the team until it could be reorganized financially. Fuchs, who paid $550,000 for the team, was $300,000 in debt when he stepped down. However, he was able to resume his law practice and pay off his debts. He died in 1961 at age 83.

1936–44 / Bob Quinn

Charles F. Adams had two sporting passions, baseball and horse racing. Unfortunately for him, Commissioner Kenesaw Mountain Landis did not approve of anyone connected with the former having anything to do with the latter. Therefore, when Adams, who'd bailed out Judge Fuchs with a loan in 1929 and thus become vice president of the Braves, got involved with Suffolk Downs, the first horse track in Massachusetts, Landis steered Adams away from baseball.

The National League directed a financial reorganization of the Braves in late 1935. Adams was neither an officer nor a shareholder. However, since the club still owed him some $325,000, he remained in control of the ownership syndicate. In his absence, Adams sought an experienced baseball man with good business sense to serve as president. That man was Bob Quinn.

Quinn had worked as the Dodgers' business manager the previous two seasons, but he was no stranger to Boston baseball fans. Unfortunately, they associated him with the failures of the Red Sox. Quinn, born in 1870, was president of Boston's American League team from 1923 to 1932, a gruesome decade in which the Red Sox finished last eight times, seventh once, and sixth once. The syndicate he headed bought the team from Harry Frazee, the man who sold Babe Ruth to the Yankees and ran the franchise into the ground.

Bob Quinn

Quinn was noted for his honesty and stubbornness. His willingness to give Boston another try spoke of his courage.

Quinn was a driving force behind the formation of the American Association team in his hometown of Columbus, Ohio, where he worked for 17 years. In 1917 he got his first major league job as business manager of the St. Louis Browns. After five years there, he put together the syndicate that bought the Red Sox. It was Quinn and his partners who sold the franchise to longtime owner Tom Yawkey.

Despite his hard work and loyal service to the Braves, Quinn's second term in Boston wasn't a great deal more successful than his first. The team never reached the first division and had just two winning seasons.

In his 24-year association with three major league clubs, Quinn worked for only three winning teams, and just one— the third-place Browns of 1921—made the first division.

Quinn's legacy in Boston will always be that he changed the team's nickname from Braves to Bees for five years.

When he arrived in 1936, the club was coming off its worst season ever, having lost 115 games and finishing 61½ games out of first. Hoping to change the franchise's image and its luck, a contest was held in which fans were invited to select a new nickname. "Bees" won. Quinn even changed the name of Braves Field to National League Park but encouraged that it be called the Beehive.

In 1941, after five second-division finishes for the Bees, Quinn realized the nickname wasn't the problem and switched it back to Braves.

Constantly trying to find money to run the team properly and fighting interference from minority stockholders, Quinn persuaded several fans to form a new syndicate that purchased the team in 1941. That group included Lou Perini, who would soon emerge to lead a much-needed major overhaul in Braves baseball.

Quinn remained as president of the Braves until his 75th birthday in February 1945. Perini assumed the presidency, but Quinn's son John was promoted from farm director to general manager to handle the daily operations of the club.

At his son's urging, Bob Quinn stayed with the club one more year as farm director. He later was director of the Baseball Hall of Fame and Museum at Cooperstown for four years. Quinn died in 1954 at the age of 84.

1945–56 / Lou Perini

Lou Perini liked to build things. During World War II, he made a fortune building roads, tunnels, airports, ammunition dumps, piers, and wharves. And after the war, he used the profits to help build the Braves into one of the most powerful franchises in the National League.

Under Perini's ownership, the Braves won three pennants and a World Series in two cities from 1948 to 1958. His Milwaukee teams of the mid-to-late 1950s are still regarded as some of the finest ever assembled.

When Perini moved the Braves from Boston to Milwaukee in 1953, he spawned one of the greatest short-term success stories in baseball history. Milwaukee, one of the smallest markets in the game, fell head-over-heels in love with the Braves. From 1953 to 1959, attendance surpassed 2 million four times and averaged just under 2 million for the seven-year period.

In 1953, with virtually no advance sale because of the late

Lou Perini

announcement of the franchise shift, the second-place Braves attracted more than 1.8 million fans, a National League record. Not surprisingly, Perini was named major league executive of the year by *The Sporting News.*

Perini, who quit school after the 11th grade, started as a laborer in his father's construction company and eventually became president of what he and his two brothers turned into an international firm. He originally was in a group that tried to buy the Braves from Charles Adams in 1936. Finally, in 1941, he purchased a small interest in the club. He and two partners, Guido Rugo and Joe Maney, bought out the other stockholders after the 1943 season.

Since all three were contractors, they became known as the "Three Little Steam Shovels." Each promptly put an additional $250,000 into the club to pay off creditors and to provide operating funds.

"We want to give New England fans a pennant, and we intend to have one," said Perini, who was just 40 years old and the youngest of the new owners.

The energetic, candid Perini sat tight for a couple of years until the war ended, but then he swung into action like no other Braves owner, before or since.

When Perini and his partners bought the Braves, the club had one of the smallest farm systems in baseball. By 1947 they had 15 minor league teams, seven of which they owned outright. Perini, who traveled in a private plane himself, also put a plane at the disposal of farm director Harry Jenkins, a pilot, so he could keep an eye on all the prospects.

The lighting system at Braves Field was updated, and an extensive promotional plan was developed to bring in fans from outlying areas. But Perini knew he had to have a product to sell, too, so he proceeded to show the entire baseball world just how serious he was about turning around the Braves' fortunes.

While Perini was waiting for the Braves' improved farm system to sprout major league players, he went out and got some immediate reinforcements for a team that hadn't been in the first division since 1934.

The Cardinals were the best team in the league in the early 1940s, winning successive pennants in 1942, '43, and '44. Perini's philosophy seemed to be: If you can't beat 'em, acquire 'em.

He started in 1945 by trading for Mort Cooper, who'd averaged 22 wins in the three previous seasons. It was the biggest transaction in the league for several years. Even though Cooper soon developed a bad arm and was never as effective as he'd been in St. Louis, Perini wasn't deterred.

After the 1945 season, Perini made a move that clearly and firmly demonstrated the Braves' intentions. He approached the Cardinals for permission to talk with manager Billy Southworth and proceeded to lure him to Boston with a lucrative deal.

The Braves improved steadily under Southworth, and Perini continued to acquire players at the major league and minor league levels. The most significant transactions included trades to get third baseman Bob Elliott in 1947 and second baseman Eddie Stanky in 1948, the purchase of minor league first baseman Earl Torgeson for $100,000, and the signing of shortstop prospect Al Dark off the LSU campus.

It all paid off with a pennant in 1948, the first for the Braves since 1914. The team didn't sustain its success, but by the time Perini got it to Milwaukee, the club was well stocked with fresh talent for the upcoming decade.

Perini bought out Rugo in 1951 and Maney the following year, so that he owned all but four shares by the time he decided to uproot the franchise in 1953.

Braves attendance was less than 500,000 in 1951 and failed to reach 300,000 in 1952 when the club lost nearly $500,000. In early March 1953 only 420 season tickets had been sold.

The Braves had a farm team in Milwaukee, and there were reports in the spring of 1953 that the city was trying to get Perini to give up his territorial rights so Bill Veeck could move the St. Louis Browns to Wisconsin. However, Perini wouldn't do so. On March 13, *The Sporting News* ran a story saying the Braves were about to move to Milwaukee, and Perini refused to deny it. The next day the Braves president announced his intention, and on March 18 the National League approved the first shift of an established major league franchise in the modern era.

Perini's regime rode a crest of unbridled popularity during the first few years in Milwaukee, but the relationship with the fans eventually soured and deteriorated quickly.

Though Perini relinquished the team presidency in 1957, he didn't sell the franchise until after the 1962 season when the Chicago-based LaSalle Corporation purchased it for $6.2 million. Perini died in 1972 at age 68.

1957–61 / Joseph F. Cairnes

Joseph Cairnes was president of the Braves during the most successful era in franchise history, yet he was one of the more disliked men in Milwaukee during much of that time.

As popular as the Braves were with Milwaukeeans in the

Joseph F. Cairnes

1950s, the team still ranked behind Sudsville's favorite beverage when it came to loyalty. And Cairnes had the misfortune of directing the Braves' business operations at the time when that allegiance was tested with a decision that helped lead to suddenly tempered support for the franchise after 1958.

When owner Lou Perini relinquished his presidency of the team after the 1956 season, he turned the job over to Cairnes, an executive in his Boston construction firm. The Braves proceeded to win the World Series in 1957 and another pennant in 1958, then a bomb was dropped on the fans. They were no longer permitted to bring beer into County Stadium.

That, of course, is standard procedure at all stadiums today. But it wasn't then, and the Milwaukee fans, many of whom worked in breweries, resented the restriction. Attendance began to decline, and though the beer ban was lifted in mid-1962, crowds never really recovered. No one thought it was a coincidence.

Though Cairnes didn't come up with the beer ban on his own, he drew the ire of the fans since he was team president.

Born in Somerville, Massachusetts, in 1907, Cairnes headed the Massachusetts Public Works Commission in 1945–46. After becoming an associate of Perini's in the construction business, he was named executive vice president of the Braves in 1952, the team's last year in Boston.

1962–66 / John J. McHale

Warren Spahn, Eddie Mathews, Lou Burdette, Joe Adcock, Johnny Logan, Bob Buhl, Del Crandall, Billy Bruton, and Red Schoendienst were nine of the greatest players in franchise history and formed the heart of the dynamic Milwaukee teams of the 1950s. John McHale helped make them all ex-Braves.

Prior to being named team president in 1962, McHale was the Braves' general manager, a position that he assumed shortly after the 1958 World Series and that he kept in conjunction with his presidency. The record shows that the Braves

fell apart rather quickly after McHale began shuffling players. There is no denying he inherited a team with a lot of aging superstars, yet it's also clear he was unable to make the changes necessary to keep the team at or near the top of the standings.

Shortly after the Braves lost to the Dodgers in a playoff for the 1959 pennant and dropped to second place in 1960, McHale began dismantling the team that won the World Series in 1957 and another pennant in 1958.

In an attempt to bolster the infield defense, he traded young pitchers Joey Jay and Juan Pizarro to Cincinnati for shortstop Roy McMillan, and sent outfielder Billy Bruton to Detroit in exchange for second baseman Frank Bolling. Jay and Pizarro became All-Stars for the Reds and White Sox, respectively, and McMillan only lived up to his reputation as a good-field/no-hit player. Though Bruton played well for the Tigers, McHale got the better end of that deal since Bolling became a two-time All-Star and three-time NL fielding leader at second.

To make room for McMillan and Bolling in the middle of the infield, Schoendienst was released, and Logan, who was near the end of his career, was traded to Pittsburgh for journeyman outfielder Gino Cimoli. The transformation of a once-mighty team into mediocrity had only just begun.

Before McHale left the Braves in 1967 for a position as assistant commissioner to William Eckert, he sent Buhl to the Cubs in 1962 for left-hander Jack Curtis in a horrible deal for the Braves. He followed that with another ill-advised trade, sending Adcock, who still had some pop left in his bat, to Cleveland in a five-player transaction after the '62 season.

Burdette was the next to go. The hero of the '57 World Series still had some good innings left but was well on the downside of his career when McHale sent the right-hander to St. Louis in 1963 for catcher Gene Oliver and right-hander Bob Sadowski. After the '63 season, McHale made one of his better deals involving the team's stars when he traded Crandall to San Francisco in a seven-player transaction that brought Felipe Alou to Milwaukee.

The last to go were future Hall of Famers Spahn, who was sold to the Mets after the '64 season, and Mathews, who basically was given to Houston on New Year's Eve 1966 in a five-player trade. The Mathews deal actually was made by Paul Richards, who'd become vice president for baseball opera-

John J. McHale

tions, and helped lead to a rift with McHale that contributed to his departure from the Braves.

Because of the magnitude of the names involved, the success of the Braves in the 1950s, and the lack of same in the '60s, these deals don't look particularly good on McHale's resume. While none of the nine key players ever again approached the level of success they had with the Braves, in hindsight it is obvious McHale was late in pulling the trigger and seldom got much for the team's former stars.

Though McHale wasn't able to restore the Braves to serious contenders, the team never had a losing season under his direction. But in his last five seasons, including the team's first in Atlanta, the Braves finished fifth four times and sixth once.

McHale spent nearly half a century in professional baseball, starting as a first baseman in the Tigers organization in 1941. He signed off the Notre Dame campus and eventually earned the distinction of being the only major league executive to have played football and baseball at Yankee Stadium. He was a member of the Fighting Irish football team that played Army there in 1940 and appeared there several times with the Tigers.

After playing sparingly and hitting just .193 in parts of five seasons for Detroit, McHale retired as a player at age 27 in 1948 to become the team's assistant farm director. That decision and his quick rise weren't hurt by the fact that he married into the family of Tigers' owner Walter Briggs. In 1957, at age 35, McHale became the youngest general manager in the game.

When John Quinn left the Braves after the 1958 World Series to become general manager of the Phillies, the Braves replaced him with McHale. After eight seasons with the Braves, McHale moved into the commissioner's office for a year and a half, then went to Montreal to spearhead the formation of the expansion Expos. He was president and CEO of that franchise from its inception in 1969 through 1986. He also was the Expos' general manager for eight seasons, from 1977 to 1984.

In 1981, when Montreal took the Dodgers to the final game of the National League playoffs, McHale was named Major League Executive of the Year by *The Sporting News*.

1967–72 / Bill Bartholomay

Bill Bartholomay has been involved with the Braves as chairman of the board or president since the Chicago-based LaSalle Corporation, which he headed, purchased the franchise in 1962 and moved it to Atlanta in 1966.

He was president when the Braves won their first National League West title in 1969 and has been with the club through four subsequent division titles and two National League pennants. Bartholomay stepped down as Braves president prior to the 1973 season.

It was Bartholomay who signed 62-year-old Satchel Paige to a Braves contract in 1968. Paige, who was denied access to the majors during most of his playing career because of his race, thus was able to qualify for a major league pension.

Currently the Braves' chairman, Bartholomay was a director of the White Sox before he became involved with the Braves. In 1994 he chaired baseball's commissioner search committee and was active with the owners' negotiating group during the players' strike.

Bill Bartholomay

Bartholomay, an Illinois native, is a member of Major League Baseball's Ownership and Restructuring Committee and the Players Benefit Plan. In 1989 he was elected to a four-year term on the Commissioner's Executive Council, the first representative of the Atlanta Braves to serve in that capacity. He also is a past member of the National League Executive Committee.

1973–75 / Dan Donahue

Eddie Robinson traded Hank Aaron, but Dan Donahue made the decision to part with the all-time home run king.

The front office thought Aaron would retire after he broke Babe Ruth's record in 1974. However, "the Hammer"

Dan Donahue

decided he wanted to continue playing. The Braves were trying to rebuild with younger players and weren't interested in paying the high salary Aaron would command. Therefore, Donahue told Robinson, the Braves' vice president of baseball operations, to trade Aaron, who was sent to the Milwaukee Brewers for outfielder Dave May and pitcher Roger Alexander.

A native of Lowell, Massachusetts, Donahue had been a Braves fan since his youth. He saw his first game at Braves Field in 1932 when he was just eight years old.

Donahue was a graduate of Dartmouth and the Boston University law school. While president of the Atlanta/LaSalle Corporation, the Braves' parent company, in 1973, he also was elected president of the team at age 49.

1976–86 / Ted Turner

In the early years after Ted Turner bought the Braves on January 14, 1976, he was a constant presence around the ball club. He was obsessed with being part of the story, grabbing for headlines, and meddling in the baseball end of the operation, of which he had no knowledge or experience.

"One of my goals in life was to be surrounded by unpretentious, rich young men," he once said. "Then I bought the Braves and I was surrounded by 25 of them."

And he loved every minute of it, even though those 25 rich, young men seldom played respectable baseball.

Now, with the Braves among the most successful franchises in professional sports, Turner has long ago abandoned the team's front office operations. In the mid-1980s, he realized the error of his ways and brought back Bobby Cox as general manager to direct baseball matters. At the same time, he was more or less forced to step back from the

Ted Turner

Braves because of the enormous growth of Turner Broadcasting, his massive television and entertainment empire.

No more verbal and legal wranglings with the commissioner; no more wooing of baseball's biggest free agent names; no more hobnobbing with players and sports writers; no more sitting in the stands with his shirt off, a wad of tobacco in his cheek and a beer in his hand; no more pushing a baseball around the bases with his nose or participating in pregame ostrich races; no more threats to change the team nickname to Eagles; no more threats to move some home games to New Orleans and Washington, D.C.; and no more taking over as manager of the team.

The Ted Turner of the 1990s is a far different man from the "Captain Outrageous" Braves fans and the entire world learned to know in the late 1970s and early 1980s when his comments and actions seemed to make him a daily public spectacle.

Proof has come in many different ways, including his selection as Man of the Year in 1991 by *Time* magazine. The magazine gives such recognition to the person who, for better or worse, most influenced the course of world events in the previous 12 months. Turner received the designation mainly for the coverage of the Persian Gulf War by his Cable News Network.

Born in Cincinnati on November 19, 1938, Turner attended Brown University. He majored in economics but never graduated because he was expelled as a senior for having a woman in his room. He returned to Georgia to work in his father's billboard business, and in 1963 he took over and saved it after his father committed suicide.

In 1970 he bought Channel 17 in Atlanta, which in 1976 he turned into Superstation WTBS by transmitting the station's signal via satellite to cable systems across the United States. He also bought the Braves and the National Basketball Association's Atlanta Hawks in 1976. By eventually televising almost all Braves games on the Superstation, Turner created thousands of fans for the team from coast to coast, spawning the self-anointed nickname "America's Team."

When Turner bought the Braves, he didn't know anything about baseball. But that fact didn't stifle his enthusiasm for his new acquisition. At 37, he was the youngest owner in baseball, and he quickly shook up the establishment by signing the game's first free agent, pitcher Andy Messersmith. Turner gave Messersmith a three-year contract for $200,000 per season with a bonus of $400,000.

The $1 million package made the other owners gasp and served as the first notice that the game's economic fabric was about to be revolutionized.

When the 1976 Braves were introduced on opening night, Turner also was presented to the crowd. He leaped out of his seat by the dugout, bounded onto the field, and sprinted to the mound. When Ken Henderson hit the first Braves home run of the season, Turner again bolted onto the field to congratulate his employee. It was clear from the start that the team's new owner was anything but the typical stuffed shirt.

Controversy followed Turner like his shadow in 1977. He was fined $10,000 and suspended for a year by Commissioner Bowie Kuhn for tampering with Gary Matthews while the outfielder was still with the Giants. Turner signed the free agent anyway to a five-year, $1.2 million contract, and went to court to fight Kuhn over the suspension.

While the legality of the suspension was being tested,

Turner was able to resume his duties as team president. On May 11, with the Braves sinking in a 16-game losing streak, Turner sent manager Dave Bristol on a 10-day "scouting trip." He then donned a uniform, took over as manager, and proceeded to extend the losing streak to 17 games. National League President Chub Feeney immediately ordered him to retire as manager.

Even when Kuhn's suspension of Turner was upheld, the Braves' owner managed to make more news by spending the summer winning an America's Cup challenge as captain of the *Courageous*.

The Braves finished last in 1977 and again in 1978 and '79. The '78 season brought the arrival of rookie slugger Bob Horner directly from the campus of Arizona State. After Horner was named the league's rookie of the year, his agent, Bucky Woy, and Turner became embroiled in an ugly contract dispute played out in the newspapers.

Turner continued to pursue prominent free agents, winning some and losing some. He signed Al "the Mad Hungarian" Hrabosky in 1980, Claudell Washington in 1981, and Bruce Sutter in 1985. He also made serious but failed overtures to Pete Rose and Reggie Jackson.

In 1982 a long stretch of miserable baseball under Turner's reign was temporarily interrupted by a division title. And right in the midst of the locker-room celebration was Turner, gulping and wallowing in champagne.

The wild days were winding down, though. Turner would soon turn over responsibility for the Braves to Cox and new president Stan Kasten. Turner had launched CNN in 1980 and Headline News in 1982. Other subsidiaries of Turner Broadcasting followed, including Turner Network Television (TNT), SportSouth, Turner Program Services, Turner Entertainment Company, Turner Home Entertainment, and World Championship Wrestling. In 1986 he purchased the MGM/United Artists film library for $1.4 billion and also created the Goodwill Games, an international multisport event.

By the mid-1980s, Turner had pretty well retreated from his boisterous, oft-bizarre public persona. Recognized as a billionaire in 1989, Turner wed actress Jane Fonda in 1991.

1986–   / Stan Kasten

Stan Kasten is one of the most unique front office executives in sports history. He not only serves as president of the Braves but also holds the same position with the Ted

Stan Kasten

Turner–owned Atlanta Hawks of the National Basketball Association. He is the first man ever to simultaneously hold the presidency of two major sports franchises.

Kasten was named president of the Hawks in the spring of 1986 at age 34. The presidency of the Braves was added to his responsibilities later that year. He also serves as vice president of sports teams for Turner Broadcasting.

Kasten was named NBA executive of the year in 1986 and again in 1987. In baseball, his legal background and the financial expertise he gained working on the NBA's salary cap made him a valued member of the owners' negotiating committee during the 1994 players' strike.

Born February 1, 1952, Kasten was raised in New Jersey. He received an undergraduate degree from New York University and earned his law degree from Columbia Law School.

In 1976, Kasten was celebrating his graduation from law school by making a tour of major league ballparks. He met Turner at a Braves-Cardinals game in St. Louis, and shortly thereafter he was hired as legal counsel for the Braves and Hawks. He was the Hawks' assistant general manager for two years, and in 1979 he was named that team's general manager. At age 27, he was the youngest GM in NBA history. Kasten held that position until 1989.

Kasten's development allowed Turner to remove himself from direct involvement with his sports teams. The appointment of Kasten as Braves president in late 1986 was a significant factor in the development of the franchise into championship caliber because it freed general manager Bobby Cox to focus on player personnel.

The General Managers

1945–58 / John Quinn

You could say John Quinn was born into the Braves' front office. His father, Bob Quinn, was president of the franchise from 1936 to 1944, and when he retired in February 1945, John was promoted from farm director to general manager. In that capacity, he oversaw the daily operations of the club and made player transactions, while owner Lou Perini assumed the presidency.

During Quinn's 14 seasons as general manager, the

Braves won three pennants and a World Series, in large part because of the transactions he made.

At the end of the 1946 season, Quinn obtained third baseman Bob Elliott from Pittsburgh in a six-player trade that bordered on grand theft. Elliott was the league's MVP in 1947 and led the Braves to the World Series in 1948. Quinn's ability to acquire second baseman Eddie Stanky from Brooklyn in the spring of 1948 also contributed greatly to that pennant, the club's first since 1914.

In the summer of 1951, Quinn sent Johnny Sain, who'd been

John Quinn

a four-time 20-game winner for Boston, to the Yankees in exchange for $50,000 and a young pitcher named Lou Burdette. With just 1⅓ innings of big league service, Burdette was an unknown commodity but proved to be one of the all-time great Braves right-handers and the hero of the 1957 World Series.

Quinn also acquired slugging first baseman Joe Adcock from Cincinnati in 1953, picked up the fabled Bob "Hurricane" Hazle from the Reds in 1956, and in June 1957 brought in second baseman Red Schoendienst, who proved to be the stabilizing force on Milwaukee's pennant winners.

The biggest "stinker" on Quinn's record was the 1954 deal in which he sent left-hander Johnny Antonelli to the Giants. At age 24, Antonelli pitched New York to the '54 World Series championship and was a five-time All-Star for the Giants. The powerful Braves of the 1950s might have won three or four more pennants had Quinn not made that deal.

Quinn was born on April 1, 1908, in Columbus, Ohio, where his father was in the midst of a 17-year term of running that city's American Association franchise, which he had helped found. By the time Quinn was eight, his father was in the majors as business manager of the St. Louis Browns, so he was learning the inner workings of the game and meeting key baseball people while he was growing up.

Quinn attended Boston College when his father was president of the Red Sox, and after graduating in 1929, he immediately went to work for his father. Though the senior Quinn left Boston for two years with the Dodgers, John stayed with the Red Sox. The two hooked up again with the Braves in 1936. With his father as team president, John was secretary of the club and also held positions such as traveling secretary and farm director.

Still not quite 37 years old, Quinn "inherited" the general manager's position upon his father's retirement in 1945. As one of the game's youngest executives, he took over a miserable club that hadn't finished above fifth place since 1934. But with the acumen he'd picked up from being around the game his entire life and the influx of Perini's money, Quinn quickly built the Braves into the 1948 National League champions.

Though that team fell apart after the pennant, Quinn had constructed a powerhouse by the time the Braves moved to Milwaukee in 1953. With Warren Spahn, Burdette, Hank Aaron, Eddie Mathews, Adcock, Del Crandall, Johnny Logan, and others, the Braves took Milwaukee by storm, drawing in excess of 1 million fans in each of their first nine seasons in Wisconsin and going over 2 million from 1954 to 1957.

The Braves won the 1957 Series and had a 3–1 lead in games over the Yankees in 1958 before losing. By that time, Quinn was widely recognized as one of the best general managers in the game, and his services were in great demand. After the '58 Series, he was lured to Philadelphia with a lucrative salary and the title of vice president to go along with general manager.

1966–72 / Paul Richards

Shortly after the Braves moved to Atlanta, Paul Richards was hired to shape the fortunes of the South's first professional sports franchise. He was hired not only because he had an extensive background as a player, manager, and general manager, but also because he already was familiar to Atlanta's baseball fans.

Richards was a catcher for the Atlanta Crackers in the mid-1930s. He was named the team's player-manager in 1938 and proceeded to lead the Crackers to the Southern Association pennant. The Braves knew it wouldn't hurt their effort to sell their product to new customers if the customers could relate to a familiar face.

When Richards was hired by the Braves, he already was a legendary character for a career that began in 1926 when he was a 17-year-old out of Waxahachie, Texas. His work with the Braves served to further solidify the reputation of the lanky,

Paul Richards

crusty Richards, who was regarded as a pitching expert by some.

In six years as the Braves' vice president of baseball operations, Richards created quite a bit of controversy and made two deals that led directly to the team's 1969 division title, its first in Atlanta.

Never at a loss for a few biting words, Richards became embroiled in a contract dispute with All-Star catcher Joe Torre prior to the 1969 season. "No more than Torre did for us last season, I don't care if he holds out until Thanksgiving," said Richards, who proceeded to trade Torre to St. Louis for first baseman Orlando Cepeda that spring.

Cepeda was a driving force behind the Braves' NL West title in 1969, but he did little afterward. Torre, on the other hand, became an even bigger success with the Cardinals than he'd been with the Braves, winning the 1971 batting title and MVP.

The other acquisition Richards made that helped the Braves win in 1969 was picking up 46-year-old knuckleball specialist Hoyt Wilhelm on waivers from California. Acquired September 8, Wilhelm saved four games and won two others down the stretch.

In 1971, Richards and Clete Boyer got involved in a nasty verbal skirmish over the third baseman's displeasure with the team's curfew rule. Boyer, only 34 and still productive, wound up getting his release and had to go to Japan to find a job. It was a common theory that Richards "blackballed" Boyer from the majors.

Richards' worst trade came in June 1968 when he sent reliever Clay Carroll, right-hander Tony Cloninger, and infielder Woody Woodward to Cincinnati for right-hander Milt Pappas, left-hander Ted Davidson, and infielder Bob Johnson. Carroll helped the Reds win a pennant and three division titles and, in 1972, led the league in saves. Cloninger and Woodward also contributed in Cincinnati, but Pappas did little for the Braves, and Davidson and Johnson were useless.

There were those, including Braves president Bill Bartholomay, who felt Richards was losing his touch and was too tentative in making moves by 1972. In the middle of the season, farm director Eddie Robinson was promoted and given the power to make player transactions. At age 63, Richards was shuffled to the background, and his contract was not renewed at the end of the year.

Richards made many contributions to baseball. He is credited with inventing the oversized catcher's mitt for use with knuckleball pitchers. And shortly after becoming general manager of the Orioles late in 1954, he engineered a memorable trade with the Yankees in which 18 players changed teams.

Richards had an eight-year big league career as a good-field/no-hit catcher. A manager for the White Sox and Orioles from 1951 to 1961, Richards never won a pennant in that Yankees-dominated era, but he did take Baltimore to a runner-up finish in 1960 when he was chosen AL manager of the year.

Among other assignments, he was the first general manager of the expansion Houston Colt 45s.

1972–76 / Eddie Robinson

Sometimes trades work, and sometimes they don't. Anyone who serves as a major league general manager for any length of time has plenty of both kinds, and that was the case

Eddie Robinson

with Eddie Robinson, one of the more prolific deal makers in franchise history.

One thing about Robinson: He never got bashful. He knew that home run hitters strike out a lot, but they have to keep swinging. Robinson was always swinging in trade talks.

Promoted from Braves farm director to director of player personnel in June 1972, Robinson was then named vice president of baseball operations in January 1973. He was in power for four years.

Two of Robinson's worst trades came after the 1972 season when he was trying to assemble the first team that would have his stamp on it. He sent Rico Carty, one of the greatest pure hitters in franchise history, to Texas in October for reliever Jim Panther, one of the worst pitchers in franchise history. Less than a week later, he acquired pitchers Danny Frisella and Gary Gentry, both of whom were worthless to the Braves, for All-Star second baseman Felix Millan and left-hander George Stone, who played major roles in helping the Mets win the 1973 pennant.

Later that off-season, Robinson exchanged right-handers with Montreal in one of his better moves. The Expos got Pat Jarvis, who was finished, and the Braves received Carl Morton, who averaged 16 wins for the next three years.

In May 1973, Robinson made what could well be called the all-time stinker in franchise history. He sent a first base prospect named Andre Thornton to the Cubs in exchange for first baseman Joe Pepitone. Thornton was just 23 and had yet to make the majors. He wound up hitting 253 career homers, mostly for Cleveland. Pepitone, on the other hand, retired after three games with the Braves.

But the following year, Robinson obtained one of the biggest bargains the Braves have ever received, picking up right-hander Buzz Capra off waivers from the Mets. All Capra did was lead the league in ERA in 1974.

In 1975, Robinson made two poor decisions. In May he sent Ron Reed, a quality right-hander, to the Cardinals for Ray Sadecki and Elias Sosa, two pitchers who failed to help the Braves. Then in November he pulled off a blockbuster with the Dodgers, shipping Dusty Baker and Ed Goodson to Los Angeles for shortstop Jerry Royster, outfielders Tom Paciorek and Jimmy Wynn, and utility man Lee Lacy. While Baker became one of the great outfielders in Dodgers history, the Braves got substantial service out of only Royster, who wound up a utility man.

But the deal that Robinson will go down in history for making was neither good nor bad, just sad. It came in the fall of 1974 when he became the only man ever to trade the all-time home run king. Hank Aaron wanted to continue playing at age 41, so Robinson sent him back to Milwaukee in exchange for a decent outfielder named Dave May and Roger Alexander, a right-hander who never made it.

Robinson seemed to have an excellent background to become what in effect was the Braves' general manager, but he fell victim to new ownership. Shortly after Ted Turner bought the team in 1976, Robinson was demoted, prompting him to take a position with the Texas Rangers that led to his becoming general manager of that franchise in 1978.

A native Texan who liked to smoke big cigars, Robinson had an accomplished playing career. He was a well-traveled, slick first baseman in the American League for 13 years, leading the league in defense at his position for Cleveland in 1948, when he hit .300 in the World Series against the Braves. He made four All-Star teams and compiled a lifetime batting average of .268.

1976 / John Alevizos

In his 1991 book *We Could've Finished Last Without You,* former Braves public relations and promotions guru Bob Hope calls John Alevizos a "mystery man." To Braves fans, he remains just that, because he was gone before most people even realized he had arrived.

In May 1976, shortly after he purchased the Braves, Ted Turner hired Alevizos as executive vice president and general manager. Baseball people were stunned—as they were by many things Turner did in those days—because most had never heard of Alevizos. The reason was that he had no pure baseball experience, though he had worked for the Boston Red Sox the previous five years as vice president of administration.

Holder of a graduate degree in business from Harvard, Alevizos was involved in real estate ventures in the Boston area. He'd been part of a group of investors who tried to buy the Braves from the Chicago-based LaSalle Corporation, only to be beaten by Turner.

Four months after becoming the Braves' general manager, Alevizos, who was 55, abruptly "resigned," though there was speculation that Turner prompted his decision.

Alevizos conducted an evaluation of the Atlanta player development operation for Turner, which brought the hiring of several scouts and minor league instructors. He also made two player transactions, sending Darrell Evans and Marty Perez to San Francisco for four players, including first baseman Willie Montanez, and acquiring reliever Mike Marshall from the Dodgers for utility man Lee Lacy and reliever Elias Sosa.

Additionally, Alevizos helped set the groundwork for Hank Aaron to return to the Braves in a front office position after the all-time home run king retired from the Milwaukee Brewers as a player in 1976.

1976–79 / Bill Lucas

When the Houston Astros hired former Brave Bob Watson as general manager in 1994, the story across the nation was that he was the major leagues' first black GM. How quickly people forget!

Almost two decades earlier, in late 1976, Braves owner Ted Turner put that distinction on Bill Lucas.

No, Lucas's title wasn't general manager. It was director of player personnel and later vice president of player personnel. But he made trades and negotiated contracts. His responsibilities were the same as a GM's, and everyone, including other clubs, thought of him as the Atlanta GM. It's just that the Braves weren't using that title at the time. Neither Paul Richards nor Eddie Robinson was labeled "general manager" before Lucas, but that's what they were.

On September 19, 1976, Lucas became the highest-ranking black in baseball history at age 40. The promotion culminated a steady rise through the Braves organization for the former minor league infielder who was drafted by Milwaukee in 1956. However, Lucas died in May 1979 at age 43 of a massive brain hemorrhage and coronary arrest after only two full seasons as "general manager."

Raised in Jacksonville, Florida, Lucas actually started his baseball career at age 13 when he worked in the concession stand at the local minor league ballpark. He went on to become an NAIA All-American shortstop at Florida A&M, from where he graduated.

Lucas spent three years in the Army, then played six seasons in the Braves' farm system. A knee injury forced him to abandon his playing career in 1964. He taught school in Fort Meyers, Florida, for a short time, then became public rela-

John Alevizos

Bill Lucas

tions director for the minor league Atlanta Crackers in 1965. In 1966 he was part of the Braves' transition team for their move to Atlanta from Milwaukee, then was named assistant farm director in 1967.

Working under Robinson, Lucas moved up to farm director when his boss was named vice president of baseball operations in September 1972. Four years later, Lucas was calling the shots on the baseball side of the Braves' front office.

Since he'd been developing players in the Braves' farm system for a decade, Lucas chose to try to build the club from within by relying on players such as Dale Murphy and Glenn Hubbard. He acquired few players by trade, purchase, or free agency in his brief time in charge of player personnel.

However, he did make a couple of key acquisitions, including one in a big trade after he'd been on the job less than two months. In the winter of 1976, Lucas sent five players to Texas in exchange for outfielder Jeff Burroughs, a former American League MVP who had two excellent offensive seasons in Atlanta.

In 1978, Lucas traded volatile pitcher Dick Ruthven to Philadelphia for reliever Gene Garber, who became the Braves' all-time saves leader. It was Lucas, too, who agreed to let third baseman Bob Horner start his professional career at the major league level in 1978. Horner responded by hitting 23 home runs and being named National League Rookie of the Year.

Lucas's short term running the Braves also coincided with Turner's stormy early years as owner. The Gary Matthews tampering case, Turner's eventual suspension, Turner's day in the dugout as manager, and the nasty Bucky Woy ruckus over Horner's contract all took place in the Lucas years.

1979–1985 / John Mullen

Like Eddie Mathews, Ernie Johnson, Connie Ryan, and Donald Davidson, John Mullen was a rare three-city Brave. He started with the team at age 21 when he was a secretary for farm director Harry Jenkins in 1947. Some 32 years later he became general manager after the death of Bill Lucas.

Mullen made some significant moves to help put together the 1982 division championship team. However, he also completed a trade late the following season that backfired

John Mullen

and was blamed as a major reason the Braves went into a tailspin for several years.

Mullen brought first baseman Chris Chambliss, a leader on the 1982 team, to Atlanta in 1980 with a five-player trade that sent outfielder Barry Bonnell to Toronto. He also signed free-agent outfielder Claudell Washington in 1981, and in mid-1982 he acquired pitcher Pascual Perez from Pittsburgh. Perez won only four games that season, but the comic relief he provided with his pregame trip around I-285 made him a cult hero and helped lift some pressure from the team down the stretch.

But with the Braves trying to stay with the Dodgers late in 1983, Mullen sent three of Atlanta's best young players—Brett Butler, Brook Jacoby, and Rick Behenna—to Cleveland for right-hander Len Barker. The Braves didn't catch the Dodgers, Barker was a bust, and Butler and Jacoby developed into All-Stars.

In the six full seasons Mullen was general manager, the Braves had two second-place finishes to go with the '82 division title.

Mullen originally made his mark with the Braves as assistant farm director and then farm director. Among the players signed while he was in the minor league department were Hank Aaron, Eddie Mathews, and Phil Niekro.

In 1952, Mullen actually came within 10 minutes of costing the Braves Aaron. The team was under a time agreement with the Indianapolis Clowns, who owned Aaron's services, about whether or not to sign the youngster. The Giants were anxiously waiting for the time limit to expire so they could sign him. Boston decided to purchase Aaron's contract for $10,000, but Mullen forgot to wire the Clowns of the team's intent until just 10 minutes before the time agreement expired.

Mullen came to Atlanta with the Braves as farm director in 1966, but in September he left to become assistant general manager of the Houston Astros. He held that job for 13 years under three GMs—Grady Hatton, Spec Richardson, and Tal Smith—before returning to Atlanta in 1979.

A modest, quiet, unassuming man who was a dedicated employee, Mullen had no trouble taking a back seat in the fall of 1985 when Ted Turner hired Bobby Cox as general manager. Mullen was named assistant GM. He held that job until John Schuerholz was hired in 1990, at which time he was named vice president of baseball administration. Mullen died in 1991, and the Braves wore his initials, JWM, on their left uniform sleeve during that pennant-winning season.

1986–90 / Bobby Cox

John Schuerholz will always be remembered, and rightfully so, as the general manager who turned the Braves into champions in 1991. Likewise, Bobby Cox's legacy in franchise history will be as the manager of that "worst-to-first" saga in '91. What shouldn't be lost in history, though, is the role Cox played as general manager from 1986 to 1990 in setting up one of the most scintillating success stories baseball has ever witnessed.

Fired as Braves manager after the 1981 season, Cox was a big success in managing the Toronto Blue Jays the next four years. But after falling one game short of the American League pennant in 1985, he was lured back to Atlanta, where he'd maintained his residence, by Ted Turner. The man

Bobby Cox

1990– / John Schuerholz

In February 1991 the Braves ran a quarter-page season-ticket ad in the major Atlanta newspapers. It featured new general manager John Schuerholz in pleated slacks, dress shirt, tie, and his trademark suspenders pictured below the headline "Atlanta's in for some radical changes."

Little did anyone—including Schuerholz—know just how radical those changes would be and just how quickly they would occur.

Within eight months of that ad, a franchise that had long been ridiculed for ineptitude had set an Atlanta attendance record of 2.14 million and was on its way to the World Series for the first time since 1958. Shortly afterward, thousands of fans from all over the Southeast showed up on Peachtree Street to fete the team in a wild parade that bordered on chaos at times.

Imagine, just a year earlier, Commissioner Fay Vincent had expressed concern about the future of baseball in Atlanta.

The Braves' incredible "worst-to-first" fantasy in 1991 was the most radical change any baseball franchise has ever experienced, and Schuerholz was the major instigator of the tomahawk-chopping fervor that enveloped the entire Southeast. Not only did he make the deals that thrust the young team into contention, but he also changed forlorn attitudes inside and outside the organization and spruced up Atlanta–Fulton County Stadium, overhauling virtually every aspect of Braves baseball. In the process, he was honored as the National League Executive of the Year by UPI.

A native of Baltimore, Schuerholz attended Towson State University, where he played baseball and soccer and was the school's athlete of the year in 1962. After graduating, he was a junior high school teacher for four and one-half years before getting into baseball administration with the Orioles in 1966 as an assistant in the minor league and scouting departments.

In 1968, Schuerholz joined the expansion Kansas City Royals as an administrative assistant. Two years later, he was named assistant farm director, and in 1975 he became farm director. In 1979, Schuerholz was made vice president of player personnel, and in 1981, at age 41, he was named executive vice president and general manager of the Royals.

When Kansas City won the World Series in 1985, just 17

who'd fired Cox four years earlier brought him back in a more prestigious position—general manager.

Working in the office instead of on the field was a new experience for Cox, but he set a solid course for the franchise that even the most experienced and skilled executive would have been hard-pressed to match.

Cox's resolve was to build the Braves from within through scouting, signing, and developing young players, especially pitchers. He knew it would take time for the farm system to produce the players necessary to vault the Braves into contention, but he stayed the course through five bleak seasons that produced four last-place finishes and one fifth-place.

But through it all, prospects were being developed. Other organizations realized it and tried to pry some of the talent away from the Braves in trades, but Cox refused to bite. He stayed away from the free-agent market and used his budget in player development. When he made trades, most of them were nondescript. He refused to part with the prospects he felt would someday turn around the Braves' fortunes.

Cox's record as general manager speaks for itself. Draft picks during his five seasons in the front office included Steve Avery, Chipper Jones, Ryan Klesko, Kent Mercker, Mike Stanton, and Mark Wohlers. At the same time, Jeff Blauser, Ron Gant, Tom Glavine, David Justice, and Mark Lemke were being brought through the farm system and into the majors.

Javier Lopez and Tony Tarasco were signed as free agents. Lonnie Smith and Greg Olson were acquired as minor league free agents. Cox bought Jeff Treadway from Cincinnati in 1989, and he acquired John Smoltz, Charlie Leibrandt, Francisco Cabrera, and Pete Smith in trades.

Finally, in June 1990, Cox supplanted Russ Nixon as manager. He remained general manager, too, and six weeks later made a difficult but necessary trade, one that contributed greatly to the transformation the team was undergoing. It was Cox who sent the immensely popular Dale Murphy to Philadelphia on August 4 in a move that opened up right field for David Justice, whose emergence to stardom can be traced directly to that trade.

At the end of the season, Braves president Stan Kasten gave Cox the option of working in the dugout or front office. Cox's decision to manage allowed Kasten to hire Schuerholz, who expertly fine-tuned the roster in the winter.

John Schuerholz

seasons after the club's birth, Schuerholz was named major league executive of the year by *The Sporting News*. In Schuerholz's 22 years with Kansas City, the Royals won six division titles, two pennants, and a World Series.

With Bobby Cox electing to leave the Braves' front office and return to the dugout as manager in 1990, team president Stan Kasten was in need of a general manager. He wasted no time in hiring Schuerholz. The announcement came during the 1990 playoffs.

After two months of assessing the situation, Schuerholz swung into action to prepare the Braves for the 1991 season. Like Cox, he didn't touch the nucleus of young players already on the roster but instead chose to supplement their talent with the acquisition of several veteran free agents.

At the time Schuerholz started his shopping spree, his purchases seemed prudent but hardly spectacular. He stayed away from the big-name, high-priced free agents but chose solid, proven players.

First on the list was third baseman Terry Pendleton, a career .259 hitter who'd never hit more than 13 home runs in a season but was a quality defensive player.

In quick succession, Schuerholz added first baseman Sid Bream and shortstop Rafael Belliard, giving the Braves three-fourths of an entirely new infield. The next acquisitions were catcher Jeff Heath, reliever Juan Berenguer, and minor league free-agent outfielder Deion Sanders. Just prior to the start of the season, Schuerholz tinkered with the roster one more time, lifting center fielder Otis Nixon from the Expos' camp in a virtual steal of a trade.

The sum total of all the moves was that some interest in the Braves had been regenerated among the fans and media. But no one was expecting a miracle. Schuerholz even admitted he'd have been happy to finish with a .500 record with the club coming off a pitiful 65–97 season.

But suddenly, everything clicked. The Braves' young players blossomed, and Schuerholz's veterans fit in perfectly to give the team an exciting chemistry that eventually led to the World Series. The prize acquisition, of course, was Pendleton, who won the batting title and the league's MVP award. Another key acquisition Schuerholz made for the stretch run was Alejandro Pena, who was obtained from the Mets in a trade and proved invaluable as Cox's closer.

Schuerholz continued to make successful deals in 1992, when the Braves won another pennant, and in 1993 when they won their third straight division title. At the same time, the Braves were an unprecedented box office sensation, smashing the franchise attendance record by topping 3 million in 1992 and attracting nearly 3.9 million fans in 1993.

Among Schuerholz's key transactions were signing Cy Young Award winner Greg Maddux in 1993 and trading three minor league players for first baseman Fred McGriff in mid-1993.

Naturally, not all of Schuerholz's deals have worked as planned. The names of relievers Mark Davis (1992) and Gregg Olson (1994) rank at the top of his list of flops.

However, the contributions Schuerholz has made to the remarkable transformation of the Braves from a laughing-stock to a championship-caliber organization are innumerable, both on and off the field.

The Support Staff

If anyone ever proved you don't have to be big in stature to succeed in baseball, it was former Braves executive Donald Davidson. The 48-inch-tall Davidson served the club for nearly 40 years in three cities. He started as a mascot and errand boy in 1936, and by 1976, when he was fired by Ted Turner, he had risen to assistant to the president.

Davidson is one of hundreds of people who have worked behind the scenes for the franchise over the last 125 years. Without them, there could have been no big show.

Born in Boston in 1925, Davidson's growth was stunted at

Donald Davidson

age 6 by a form of sleeping sickness. It never handicapped him, though, and led to the beginning of his long association with the franchise. In 1936, Davidson was scrambling for autographs near the Boston dugout with other kids when catcher Ray Mueller spotted him. Mueller lifted Davidson, took him into the dugout, and introduced him to manager Bill McKechnie. McKechnie allowed Davidson to sit on the bench, and when the Bees won—a rare event—he asked the youngster back for the next game.

Davidson began shining players' shoes and running errands. Before long, his reputation spread, and he was doing the same thing for Red Sox players when the Bees were out of town. He continued doing clubhouse work for several years and eventually moved into the front office in 1948.

Davidson spent most of his career with the Braves as traveling secretary. His size and sassy personality made him one of the best-known front office employees in the game. His friends included most of the sport's biggest stars, including Babe Ruth, Ted Williams, and Casey Stengel, who nicknamed him "Duckbutt."

Davidson was used to doing things his way, so when the strong-willed and cost-conscious Turner bought the Braves in 1976, the two probably didn't have a chance of coexisting. Against Turner's orders, Davidson continued to travel first class, and that habit precipitated his firing. The next day he was hired by the Houston Astros as assistant to the president.

The man Davidson replaced as traveling secretary was Duffy Lewis, who was quite a story himself. From 1910 to 1914 with the Red Sox, Lewis was a member of what is con-

Duffy Lewis

sidered one of the finest defensive outfields in history. It consisted of Lewis in left and Hall of Famers Tris Speaker in center and Harry Hooper in right.

In Lewis's 11-year big league career, he batted .284 and played on three World Series champion Red Sox teams, including 1915 when he batted .444. He joined the Braves' coaching staff under McKechnie in 1931, then became traveling secretary in 1936 and held that position for 11 years. The players called him "Big Chief" because he would go to great lengths to look out for their best interests.

The Braves' best-known front office employee in Atlanta was a part-timer who worked for the club for 17 years. He was nearly as big a fixture at Atlanta Stadium as was Phil Niekro. That employee was Levi Walker, Jr., more commonly known as Chief Noc-a-Homa.

Walker, who says he is three-quarters Ottawa and one-quarter Cherokee, did a war dance on the mound, then sprinted to his tepee in the left-field stands before every home game. His war cries could be heard throughout the

Chief Noc-a-Homa

game, especially since attendance often was sparse during his mascot days, which ended in 1986.

Billy Sullivan, who gave Donald Davidson his job in the Braves' public relations department during the 1948 World Series, was one of the most advanced PR men of his era.

Sullivan, who went on to become president and part owner of pro football's Boston/New England Patriots, promoted the team in the late 1940s when owner Lou Perini turned a sad franchise into a proud one. He published the Braves' first sketch book, the forerunner of today's yearbooks, and also produced a promotional film, unique at the time. Sullivan had fireworks and concerts at Braves Field, too, and chartered planes and buses to bring in fans from outlying areas of New England.

Another publicity and promotions man who was quite adept at stirring up interest in the Braves was Bob Hope, who started as an usher when the team moved to Atlanta in 1966. Hope, who liked to characterize himself as the "village idiot," was the instigator of promotions ranging from a wet T-shirt contest to a bathtub race and an ostrich race in the 1970s. He also was one of Ted Turner's most valued employees in his early years of ownership.

One front office employee who didn't hang around long before going on to endeavors such as baseball broadcasting, movies, television sitcoms, beer commercials, and other such cut-up gigs is former catcher Bob Uecker. A lifetime .200 hitter who made a career out of making fun of himself, Uecker was director of the Braves speakers' bureau for a short time in the late 1960s.

The real unsung heroes of baseball are scouts, and the Braves have had some of the finest over the years. They have included Dewey Griggs, who signed Hank Aaron; Johnny Moore, who did some creative hustling to get Eddie Mathews under contract; and Jeff Jones, a Harvard graduate who scouted New England for many years and signed 25 major leaguers.

More recently, longtime scouts Paul Snyder, Bill Wight, and Fred Shaffer have won the prestigious Scout of the Year Award.

Bobby Dews, the minor league field coordinator, is a veteran of two decades with the organization who is responsible for supervising all instruction in the farm system. A former minor league infielder with the Cardinals, he joined the Braves in 1975 as manager at Class-A Greenwood. He's held a variety of positions, including farm director and two stints as a major league coach.

One of the more recognizable people in the Braves' dugout for longtime fans is trainer Dave Pursley. He has been with the organization since 1961.

Paul Snyder

6

The Ballparks

In the first 125 years of their existence, the Braves have played in but four permanent ballparks. That's barely more than the number of cities they've called home. But a fifth residence, which will bring special meaning to Opening Day 1997, is taking shape just out of the shadow of the club's current home, Atlanta–Fulton County Stadium.

When the franchise was born as the Boston Red Stockings in 1871, the inaugural season of the National Association, the team played at the South End Grounds, which was little more than an open field to which a wooden grandstand had been added.

The franchise played at the South End Grounds most of 44 seasons, the longest it stayed in any of its four permanent ballparks, and won 13 pennants—four in the National Association and nine in the National League.

A fire completely destroyed the South End Grounds in 1894, forcing the team to play at Boston's Congress Street Grounds for a short time until its home was rebuilt.

Not until 1915, the year after their "miracle" World Series championship, did the Braves finally move into their next home, Braves Field. The largest ballpark in America when it opened, 43,500-seat Braves Field was called "the last word in baseball parks" at its dedication by National League president John K. Tener. In 37 full seasons at Braves Field, the team won just a single pennant, and it waited until 1948 to do that.

Mostly, the spacious ballpark was known for a dearth of home runs and the ineptitude of its tenant. In fact, the Braves were so bad that the nickname was changed to Bees and the ballpark was renamed National League Park (or the Beehive) from 1936 to 1940 in an attempt to change the franchise's image.

On several occasions from 1913 through 1946, the Braves played a few games at Fenway Park, too, better known as the home of the American League's Red Sox. In turn, the Red Sox also played at larger Braves Field during the 1915 and 1916 World Series and on Sundays from 1929 to 1932.

When the Braves pulled up stakes and vacated Boston in the spring of 1953, they did so to take up residence at Milwaukee County Stadium, a recently completed structure that was the first building of its kind to be constructed entirely with public funds.

The Braves remained in Milwaukee only 13 seasons, but they won two pennants and a World Series at County Stadium and, at least for the first half of their stay, attracted fans in record-setting numbers.

Then it was off to Atlanta in 1966 where another new stadium and a virgin region awaited.

In 1974, Atlanta Stadium was the site of one of the greatest feats in sports history—Hank Aaron's 715th home run, which broke Babe Ruth's career record. It has seen many other memorable games and achievements, and in the early 1990s, it was awash in tomahawk-chopping fans who poured in from all over the Southeast in incredible numbers to watch the Braves win two pennants and three division titles.

The next home of the Braves promises to be the best yet. It is being built as an 85,000-seat arena to be used for track and field during the 1996 Olympic Games. Then, by opening day 1997, it will be converted into a 49,800-seat, state-of-the-art ballpark at which the Braves will continue their storied history as America's oldest continuously operating professional sports franchise.

The thrills of 1991 transformed Atlanta–Fulton County Stadium from an often-lifeless pit into the frenzied Chop Shop where capacity crowds constantly chanted and waved tomahawks in a boisterous show of support for the home team.

South End Grounds

Fenway Park and Braves Field are the two most famous ballparks in Boston baseball history. However, it is interesting to note that the South End Grounds, home of the Red Stockings in 1871 when the National Association was formed and five years later when the association was replaced by the National League, had the only double-decked grandstand of the parks that have been used over the years by the city's major league baseball teams.

The second deck to the pavilion was added in 1888 by the three owners known as the Triumvirs, headed by team president Arthur Soden. Soden and his partners were among the more progressive executives in the early years of professional baseball.

In 1887 the Triumvirs bought "King" Kelly from Chicago for a staggering price of $10,000. Kelly was one of the most accomplished and flamboyant players of the 19th century, and fans loved him.

The following year, the Beaneaters, as the team was being called, made another major purchase from the White Stockings. This time, the Triumvirs bought pitching great John Clarkson, a local product from Cambridge, for another $10,000.

Together, Kelly and Clarkson were known as the "$20,000 Battery." Fans clamored to see them, prompting the Triumvirs to build a second tier of seats at the wooden South End Grounds.

When the grandstand was double-decked at a cost of $75,000, it was referred to as the Grand Pavilion, a name also used in place of South End Grounds at times. It was the highest and most distinctive grandstand of its time. A large crowd of 12,000 attended the 1888 opener, proving that the Triumvirs had made wise investments in the ballpark and in Kelly and Clarkson.

Few ballparks have ever witnessed as much success as the South End Grounds, which was home for the franchise from 1871, when it was known as the Union Base Ball Ground, to late in the 1914 season. That near 44-year residency was significantly interrupted only for two months in 1894 when the grandstand burned down and was rebuilt.

In those 44 seasons the Red Stockings, who became the Beaneaters in 1883, won 13 league championships and one World Series. The club won the last four National Association titles in 1872–75, then won nine National League pennants (1877–78, 1883, 1891–93, 1897–98, and 1914).

In September 1914, the Braves moved their home games to Fenway Park to accommodate the large crowds who wanted to witness the "miracle" that was taking place. A Labor Day morning/afternoon doubleheader with the Giants drew 75,000 people.

Braves Field was being planned at the time, and when it wasn't completed for the opening of the 1915 season, the Braves continued playing some games at Fenway for the first half of the schedule. The last game at the South End Grounds was June 3, 1915. New York beat Boston, 10–3.

Home plate at the ballpark was located on Walpole Street, hence the name Walpole Street Grounds that was sometimes

The South End Grounds—or the Grand Pavilion—remains the only Boston ballpark with a two-tiered grandstand to be home to a major league team.

The second deck was added in 1888 to accommodate crowds eager to see Boston's "$20,000 Battery" of King Kelly and John Clarkson.

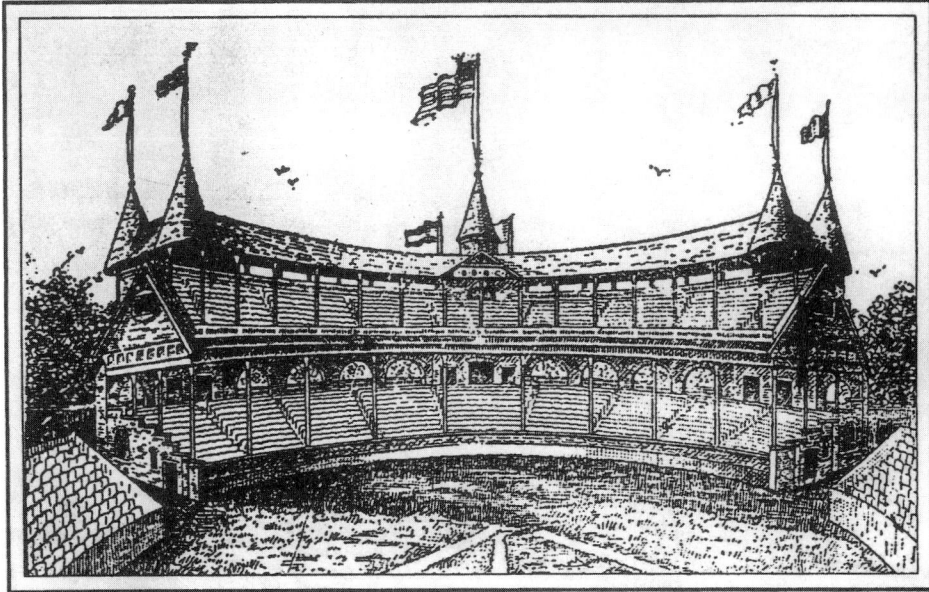

used. The most distinctive architectural feature was the spires atop the grandstand. Originally, there were six, but the number was reduced to two when the park was rebuilt.

The dimensions of the 11,000-seat South End Grounds were 250 feet down the left-field line, 255 down the right-field line, and 440 feet to the center-field fence. Despite the short foul lines, the park had a spacious outfield. The distance from home plate to left-center was 445; to right-center, 440. The deepest part of the park was a spot in left-center that was 450 feet away.

In the early years, much of the playing surface was simply dirt with patches of grass. But eventually the infield grass became so well developed that it was stripped and moved to Braves Field in 1915.

There were 50-cent bleachers running down the first-base line, and it was under these bleachers that a fire started during the third inning on May 15, 1894. Reports differ on how the blaze started. Some claim it was set by boys setting fire to trash underneath the seats. Others say it was set off by a lighted cigar falling into peanut shells.

The flames spread quickly, and the game was called in a 3–3 tie. The fire destroyed everything—the bleachers, the grandstand, and an estimated 170 buildings, including a school and a fire station, covering 12 acres around the park. The 1893 pennant also went up in flames. Estimates of the total damage were as high as $1 million, and some 1,000 people were left homeless.

Some of the team's home games were played on the road, but most were played at the Congress Street Grounds.

By July 20, the park had been rebuilt and the Beaneaters returned. However, the new South End Grounds was somewhat smaller than the original, which had been underinsured.

The ballpark was not maintained well, and its shabbiness became a bit of a sore spot with fans around the turn of the century, helping the new American League competition become entrenched in Boston. The Triumvirs, known for their distaste for spending a few bucks, ignored complaints. Thus in 1901 many fans decided to support the Somersets or Pilgrims, who would become the Red Sox, at the Huntington Avenue Baseball Grounds, and the National League game was put in an immediate hole from which it never really recovered.

When new ownership took over in 1907, the Dovey brothers, George and John, added a new scoreboard and some cushioned seats. Attendance did increase noticeably that year, from 143,280 to 203,221, but it remained well under half what the Red Sox were drawing.

James Gaffney, a contractor, bought the franchise in 1912, and immediately began looking for a site on which to build a new park. He also named the team Braves, and three and a half years later he welcomed Bostonians to Braves Field.

Though the South End Grounds was far from being a sports palace, it served the franchise for nearly half a century and was the scene of some of the great moments in team history.

The Braves' ancestors played most of 44 seasons at Boston's South End Grounds and won 13 pennants in the most successful period in franchise history.

The six spires on the roof were the most distinctive feature of the South End Grounds, but when the park burned in 1894 and was rebuilt, only two spires were used.

Congress Street Grounds

The Congress Street Grounds was only a temporary address for the Beaneaters, but it provided the site for one of the greatest offensive displays in franchise and baseball history.

When the South End Grounds burned May 15, 1894, manager Frank Selee's three-time defending National League champions were left homeless. The best available ballpark in which the Beaneaters could play their home games was the Congress Street Grounds, located adjacent to Boston Harbor.

The park also was referred to as the Brotherhood Grounds, because Boston's short-lived Union Association team played some games there in 1884, as did the Players League entry in 1890. The 1891 American Association Reds called it home, too. The Players League and American Association entries won pennants there.

A small wooden structure with a 250-foot left-field fence, the Congress Street Grounds proved a lifesaver for the Beaneaters and helped second baseman Bobby Lowe make history.

Just two weeks after the South End Grounds fire, Lowe took advantage of the Congress Street Grounds' short target in left to become the first player to hit four home runs in the same game. Only 11 others—two of them Braves—have accomplished it since then.

Boston was hosting Cincinnati in a morning/afternoon doubleheader on May 30, Memorial Day. Selee's team won the first game, 13–10, after trailing, 9–3, entering the eighth. Lowe took a break between games to eat a dinner of fresh seafood at a nearby restaurant. He returned to the Congress Street Grounds refreshed and ready to make history.

Not known as a power hitter, the 25-year-old Lowe was but 5–10 and 150 pounds, and he was batting leadoff. He struck out in his first at bat, then proceeded to hit home runs to left in his next four plate appearances. He closed the afternoon with a single, leading Boston to a 20–11 victory. Two of his homers came in the nine-run third inning.

Since many early ballparks were built with railroads and highways beyond the outfield fences, legends unfolded of "long-distance" home runs landing on a freight car or truck and being carried across the country. But lore has it that the "longest" homer of all was hit at the Congress Street Grounds. The ball landed on an Australia-bound ship in Boston Harbor and traveled halfway around the world!

Fenway Park

One of the most famous ballparks in history, Fenway Park is best known as the picturesque home of the Boston Red Sox, who still play there today. But Fenway also served as home for the Braves on several occasions, including the final two games of the "miracle" of 1914.

The irregularly shaped structure, which seats 33,871, was opened on April 20, 1912. Babe Ruth made his big league debut at Fenway as a Red Sox pitcher on July 11, 1914. The original wooden grandstands were replaced by a concrete and steel structure in 1934.

Located at the intersection of Lansdowne Street and what is now called Yawkey Way, Fenway remains famous for the left-field wall, known as the "Green Monster," which dominates the park. The wall is 37 feet high and is topped by a 23-foot screen. The wall used to be covered with advertisements but is now entirely green.

Fenway Park's "Green Monster" wall in left wasn't so green in 1914 when the "Miracle" Braves drew an overflow crowd for Game 3 of their World Series sweep of the Athletics.

The Braves first played at Fenway in 1913, when the Red Sox allowed them to use it for the Memorial Day doubleheader to accommodate large crowds. Once Braves Field, bigger than Fenway, was opened, the Braves returned the favor for the Red Sox home games in the 1915 and 1916 World Series.

The Braves also used Fenway during the last month of the 1914 season when the 11,000-seat South End Grounds couldn't handle the crowds eager to see George Stallings' club pull off one of the most improbable of all league championships. And after beating the heavily favored Athletics in the first two games of the World Series at Philadelphia, the Braves returned to Fenway to finish the "miracle" with victories in Games 3 and 4.

The Braves continuned to play some home games at Fenway in 1915 until Braves Field was christened on August 18, 1915. With what was then the largest ballpark in the United States, it seemed the Braves would never have to borrow Fenway again. However, 31 years later they had to return, if only for a couple of days.

The seats at Braves Field received a fresh coat of green paint for the 1946 opener. But the paint on some seats had not completely dried when the fans arrived. Consequently, many departed with green splotches on their clothes.

The Braves apologized and paid more than $6,000 in cleaning bills to some 5,000 fans. To make sure there weren't more paint problems, the opening series was finished at Fenway.

Braves Field

James Gaffney built Braves Field with the idea that it would be the "perfect ballpark." Obviously, he was a pitchers' owner.

The most distinctive feature of the park the defending World Series champion Braves moved into on August 18, 1915, was the vast expanse of outfield grass from foul line to foul line.

Just prior to the opening, the great Ty Cobb visited the site when the Tigers were in town to play the Red Sox. Standing at home plate, he surveyed the distant target and remarked, "No home run will ever go over that fence. This is the only field in the country on which you can play an absolutely fair game of ball without the interference of fences."

That's what Gaffney had in mind. He didn't dislike home runs. He just thought they should be of the inside-the-park variety, and he wanted the outfield to be designed so that a homer could be hit to any field without clearing the fence.

Ty Cobb once said no one would ever hit a ball out of Braves Field, and indeed it was nearly 10 years before Frank "Pancho" Snyder conquered the left field wall.

When it opened in 1915, Braves Field was the largest ballpark in the country and was hailed as "the last word in baseball parks" by National League president John Tener.

When Braves Field opened, the left- and right-field foul lines extended 402 feet from home plate. Straightaway center field was 520 feet, and deepest center—just to the right—was 550 feet. It was enormous. And to make matters even worse for power hitters, a stiff breeze usually was blowing in from center off the Charles River.

The outfield distance was changed numerous times in the 37-plus seasons the club played at Braves Field. But until it was significantly shortened in 1928, only seven over-the-fence home runs were hit compared to 209 inside-the-parkers. On August 29, 1922, when a strong wind gave Braves' outfielders fits, the New York Giants hit four inside-the-park home runs in one game.

Though Cobb's prediction wasn't quite right, it did take nearly two years for the first over-the-fence home run and almost a full decade for the first homer to clear the left-field fence.

On May 26, 1917, Cardinals outfielder Walton Cruise, who later played for the Braves, hit a ball into the right-field bleachers known as the Jury Box. But it wasn't until May 28, 1925, that New York Giants catcher Frank "Pancho" Snyder became the first player to clear the fence in left.

Braves Field was a vision Gaffney had from the time he purchased the team in 1912. A contractor, he explored various sites on which to build the park before settling in 1914 on the old Allston Golf Links on Commonwealth Avenue, a major street in Boston.

The property was deemed unsuitable for most building projects because of the cost of filling in a large hollow in the middle. But the valley formed a natural amphitheater and a low-cost spot for building a ballpark. The tiers of concrete and iron seating were built on the hillside, leaving the actual playing surface 17 feet below street level.

Nearly 1,000 laborers worked for five months to build Braves Field, with Gaffney himself overseeing the project. The cost was approximately $1 million, and it required 750 tons of steel and 8.2 million pounds of cement to complete the structure.

The covered one-level grandstand stretched from home plate, well past both first and third bases and roughly halfway down each foul line to the outfield corners. The back rows were so far from the field that fans sitting there felt detached from the game.

The rest of the foul lines were filled in with uncovered pavilion seating. There also was the well-known Jury Box in right field, home of as many as 2,000 very vocal fans. Capacity was 43,500. A 10-foot cement wall surrounded the park, and railroad tracks ran behind the left- and center-field fence.

Sporting Life noted that Braves Field had the latest in modern conveniences: "Clubhouses are under the grandstand and equipped with showers," and "retiring rooms have been located in the different sections of the field, making it the best laid out plant that has ever been arranged for."

This sign refers to a unique feature of Braves Field, a trolley line which dropped off and picked up passengers inside the ballpark.

Concessions included hot pastrami sandwiches, fried clams, and steamed clams with a little jug of baked beans on the side.

The Braves hosted the Cardinals for the first game on August 18, 1915, and much of baseball and a good portion of Boston's populace attended. Estimates of the total number of fans packed into the park ranged as high as 56,000, of whom 10,000 were children who were guests of the team. It was easily the largest crowd in baseball history at the time, and several thousand more people were turned away.

"It is the last word in baseball parks," proclaimed National League president John K. Tener, who helped raise the 1914 pennant. "Its building was the biggest single event in ten years time."

A justly proud Gaffney said, "We had the park with the smallest seating capacity in the National League a year ago. Now we have the park with the largest seating capacity. The last shall be first, you know.

"Nothing, however, is too good for the world's champions or for Boston, the best baseball city on the map."

Clark Griffith, manager of the Washington Senators and a close friend of Gaffney's, had the honor of throwing the first ball from the mound. Braves manager George Stallings was the catcher, and St. Louis manager Miller Huggins stood at the plate. Art Butler of St. Louis got the first hit, but Braves shortstop Rabbit Maranville drove in the first run, and Boston won, 3–1, behind the pitching of Dick Rudolph.

The Braves didn't repeat as National League champions in 1915. In fact, it would take them more than three decades of mostly miserable baseball to win their next pennant. However, Braves Field didn't have to wait for a World Series. The Braves loaned the park to the Red Sox for the 1915 and 1916 Series, both won by Boston, because Braves Field could hold some 6,000 more fans than Fenway Park.

After the Braves finished second in 1915 and third in 1916, the team's performance went into steep decline, and attendance at Braves Field followed suit. In 1918, a season shortened to 124 games by World War I, a record low of only 84,938 fans paid to see the team play. But even in peacetime, the Braves seldom were a good draw.

The first major alteration in the outfield distances took place in 1928 when team president Judge Emil Fuchs was trying to induce more home runs and more fan support. He had additional seats built in left and center, reducing the distance of the fence to 353 feet in left and 387 in center.

However, when the opponents were able to take more advantage of the shorter target than the Braves, Fuchs erected a tarp and began dismantling the seats in midseason. Before he did, though, third baseman Les Bell became the first 20th-century Brave to hit three homers in a game and also added a triple.

Various other changes were constantly being made, the last coming during a 1946 refurbishing that left the final fence distances at 337 down the left-field line, 370 to center, and 319 down the right-field line. The deepest part of the park was 390 feet in right-center.

Though the club was seldom in contention during its stay at Braves Field, the history of the park is filled with memorable and even historic moments, as well as the exploits of great players, great managers, and great characters.

In Game 2 of the 1916 World Series played at Braves Field, a young Red Sox left-hander named Babe Ruth gave up a first-inning run, then strung together 13 scoreless innings to beat Brooklyn, 2–1. Some 19 years later, Ruth began the final weeks of his career with a home run in his first game as a Brave at Braves Field.

On May 1, 1920, the Braves and Dodgers played to a 1–1 tie in a major league record 26 innings. Pitchers Joe Oeschger of Boston and Leon Cadore of Brooklyn each worked complete games.

Braves rookie shortstop Ernie Padgett turned the first unassisted triple play in the National League since 1878 in his second big league game in 1923.

In 1936, the Beehive, as it was being called, hosted the All-Star Game, which produced the first National League victory in the series. However, a record-low crowd of only 25,556 saw

The "Jury Box" bleachers in right field served as home to a rowdy group of fans who worshiped rightfielder Tommy Holmes.

An overflow crowd spilled into the outfield for this game in 1932.

it because many fans mistakenly thought the game was sold out.

In 1938 a game was ended by a hurricane; in 1942, Jim Tobin became the only pitcher in the 20th century to hit three homers in the same game; Tommy Holmes put together a then-National-League-record 37-game hitting streak in 1942, the same year Paul Waner got his 3,000th career hit; the first night game at Braves Field was played in 1946; and in 1950 outfielder Sam Jethroe broke the color line in Boston baseball.

In 1946 owner Lou Perini and his two partners, the "Three Little Steam Shovels," began making significant improvements in the ballclub and in the park, which received $500,000 worth of work. Among other things, skyboxes were installed on the roof. The fans responded in record numbers, nearly reaching 1 million for the year.

Attendance finally surpassed 1 million in 1947 and again in 1948 when the club won its first pennant since 1914 and attracted 1,455,439 patrons, a Boston Braves record.

In the Braves' first World Series game at their 33-year-old park, Sain outdueled Cleveland's Bob Feller, 1–0. But Boston lost Game 2 and two out of three at Cleveland. Down 3–2 in games, the Braves returned to Boston needing to beat the Indians twice in order to win the Series. However, they lost Game 6, 4–3.

For the third straight season attendance at Braves Field topped 1 million in 1949, but by 1951 it had fallen into a desperate decline. Only 281,278 walked through the Gaffney

Team president Judge Emil Fuchs (left of plaque) was at the end of his financial line in 1935, but with Babe Ruth in a Braves uniform, an optimistic crowd turned out to honor the man who controlled the club for 13 years.

Street turnstiles in 1952. The 8,822 who witnessed the final game of the season, an 8–2 loss to Brooklyn on September 21, comprised the second-largest crowd of the season. They had no idea they'd also watched the last official game the Braves would ever play in Boston.

The announcement of moving the franchise to Milwaukee in 1953 wasn't made until the Braves were in spring training.

Perini sold Braves Field to Boston University for $500,000, and parts of the park remain as Nickerson Field, where the school's football team plays. The Gaffney Street entrance remains and is marked by a plaque detailing the historical significance of the spot.

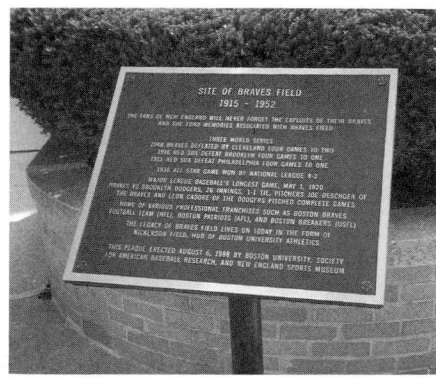

Memories of Braves Field linger today on the campus of Boston University.

Milwaukee County Stadium

Milwaukee County Stadium was the first major league ballpark financed entirely by public funds, and the good citizens of the county wasted no time in showing their approval of the house that beer and bratwurst built.

Not until March 18, 1953, three days after County Stadium was opened to the public for the first time, did Milwaukee learn that the Braves, formerly of Boston, were immediately moving to Wisconsin. Opening day was less than a month away, but one of the great fairy tales in baseball history had been born.

Despite no off-season promotion or ticket sales, Milwaukeeans welcomed the Braves with open arms and open wallets. The team that drew a pitiful 281,278 fans to Braves Field in 1952 attracted a then-National-League-record 1,826,397 to County Stadium in 1953.

Like most fairy tales, this one fizzled quickly. After just 13 years, the Braves went looking for more fertile ground once again. But while Milwaukee's infatuation with the Braves lasted, County Stadium played host to quite an adventure.

For years, city and county officials sought funds to build a modern ballpark, but not until 1947 did the county board finally approve construction of such a facility. In 1949 the Story Quarry site was chosen to be the location of the park, and on October 19, 1950, ground was finally broken just west of 44th Street adjacent to the Wood's Veterans Administration grounds.

A brief delay was caused by a federal restriction on the use of steel in new construction during the Korean War. By March 1953, though, the $5 million facility with a seating capacity of 36,011 was ready for occupancy by the Brewers, the Braves' top farm team. The Brewers were coming off two straight American Association pennants, so they had enjoyed considerably more recent success than their parent club, which had fallen on hard times since its 1948 pennant.

Milwaukee's citizens and its city officials undoubtedly hoped the presence of County Stadium would help lure a major league franchise to the suds capital. Little did they know, though, that it would happen within days of the ballpark's completion.

Milwaukee County Stadium was the first ballpark built with lights included and the first to be completely financed by public funds.

Prior to the construction of bleachers, patients at the Veterans Hospital located on a hill overlooking right field enjoyed this view.

As bad as Braves attendance was in 1952, it is doubtful whether team owner Lou Perini would have moved the franchise so quickly if not for Bill Veeck's interest in beating him to the punch by taking the St. Louis Browns to Milwaukee. But faced with virtually no advance sale in Boston and the prospect of County Stadium awaiting a big league tenant in a ripe market to which he already owned the territorial rights, Perini couldn't resist temptation.

The announcement that the Braves were on the way set off a wild celebration in Milwaukee, and it continued for much of the ensuing seven years.

When the Braves reached their new home, they found a ballpark that proved much to their liking. Built specifically for baseball, its dimensions were 320 feet down both lines, 404 to center, and 392 to left- and right-center. Originally, the outfield fence was just four feet high, but in 1957 it was increased to 10 feet, and in 1961 a wall was built.

County Stadium was the first ballpark built with lights included. There was a hill beyond the right-field fence from where the patients of the Veterans Hospital used to watch games. However, the addition of outfield bleachers eventually blocked the view. After the Braves' first season in Milwaukee, seating capacity was increased to 43,394.

A sellout crowd of 34,357 showed up for the first regular-season game at County Stadium on April 14 and cheered nearly every move by both teams. The Braves responded with a 3–2 victory over St. Louis by virtue of Billy Bruton's 10th-inning home run.

The entire season was like a dream. On May 20, in only their 13th home game, the Braves passed their 1952 season attendance of 281,278 in Boston. And after winning just 64 games in 1952, the Braves won 92 in 1953 and finished in second place.

Milwaukee was sold on the Braves. County Stadium attendance topped 2 million for the next four years, peaking at

Long before Atlanta introduced Chief Noc-a-Homa to Braves fans, County Stadium was home to a similar outfield attraction, complete with smoking tepee.

2,215,404 in the World Series championship season of 1957. That remained the all-time franchise record until it was surpassed in 1992.

As it turned out, the Braves were a team on the verge of greatness when they arrived in Milwaukee. Left-hander Warren Spahn already was one of the best pitchers in baseball. Third baseman Eddie Mathews, only a 21-year-old sophomore in 1953, led the league with 47 home runs. Hank Aaron would reach the scene in 1954.

Few ballparks have ever been home simultaneously for three such extraordinary players with so many productive years in front of them. And the supporting cast wasn't bad either.

In 13 seasons at County Stadium, the Braves never had a worse record than the 84–78 they posted in 1963. Besides winning two pennants, they finished second five times, including 1959 when they lost a playoff for the pennant to the Dodgers.

County Stadium witnessed many thrilling moments during the Braves' 13-year residence. One of the first was provided by burly right-hander Max Surkont in the team's second month at its new home. On May 25, 1953, Surkont struck out eight consecutive Cincinnati batters to set a modern major league record that stood until it was broken by Tom Seaver in 1970.

Milwaukee pitchers authored four no-hitters at County Stadium versus none for the opposition.

In 1955, County Stadium hosted the All-Star Game. Braves right-hander Gene Conley struck out the side (Al Kaline, Mickey Vernon, and Al Rosen) in the 12th inning to earn a 6–5 National League victory made possible by Stan Musial's home run.

One of the grandest events in Braves history and one of the biggest moments in Aaron's career took place at County Stadium on September 23, 1957. That's when Aaron hit what he's often called his "most memorable" home run, a two-run shot in the 11th, to beat St. Louis, 4–2, and clinch the Braves' first pennant since 1948.

In the 1957 World Series, the Braves lost Game 3 and won Games 4 and 5 at County Stadium before winning the championship at Yankee Stadium.

The Braves had the home-field advantage for the 1958 Se-

ries, and it appeared that edge would lead to their second straight championship when they beat the Yankees in the first two games at County Stadium.

But after taking a 3–1 lead in games, the Braves lost the last three, including Games 6 and 7 at County Stadium.

The Braves failed to win a third straight pennant in 1959, but County Stadium played host to one of the most incredible games in history. On May 26, Pittsburgh's Harvey Haddix pitched 12 perfect innings against one of the game's most potent lineups, only to lose the perfect game, the no-hitter, the shutout, and the game in the 13th.

On August 11, 1961, at County Stadium, a crowd of 40,775 gathered in anticipation of watching Spahn become the 13th man—and just the third lefty—to win 300 games. He didn't disappoint them, beating the Cubs, 2–1.

But once-rabid Milwaukeeans were staying home in droves. In 1960 attendance fell just shy of 1.5 million. In 1961 it barely reached 1.1 million. The Braves would never attract 1 million fans again to County Stadium.

After the 1962 season, during which attendance was just 766,921, Perini sold the Braves to a syndicate of seven Chicago businessmen. And by mid-1963 there was a report that the franchise was looking to leave Milwaukee for Atlanta.

One of the few things at County Stadium that hadn't changed was Spahn, who was on his way to a 23–7 season at the age of 42. On September 17, 1963, a crowd of 33,676 turned out for a night in honor of the immortal southpaw. It was the largest County Stadium crowd since Spahn won his 300th game more than two years earlier.

In 1964, County Stadium saw plenty of offense—five Braves hit 20 or more home runs—and a slight rejuvenation of fan interest. The club finished just five games out of first, but in fifth place, drawing 910,911 fans. However, Atlanta was building a stadium, and though it wasn't official, all indications pointed to the Braves as the future tenant.

After the 1964 season, the Braves' board voted to move to Atlanta, but a court injunction forced the team to remain in Milwaukee one more year to fulfill its County Stadium lease.

In 1965 a National League record six Braves hit 20 or more home runs, but only 555,584 came out to see the fire-

The Braves shattered National League attendance records at County Stadium, but Milwaukee's love affair with the team steadily declined after the World Series championship of 1957.

works. On September 20 in an afternoon makeup game against Houston, Aaron hit his last home run as a Milwaukee Brave (No. 398) before a mere 812 people. Two days later, County Stadium said farewell to the Braves. Just 12,577 witnessed the Braves' 7–6 loss to the Dodgers.

When the 1966 season opened, the Braves were playing in Atlanta in spite of the determined but futile legal efforts of Milwaukee County to keep the team in Wisconsin.

County Stadium remained without a full-time major league baseball team until 1970 when the Seattle Pilots moved to Milwaukee and became the Brewers. However, in 1968 and '69, the Chicago White Sox played a total of 20 "home" games at the park.

County Stadium also served as a part-time home for the Green Bay Packers of the National Football League from 1953 to 1994.

Atlanta–Fulton County Stadium

It's the stadium that introduced major league sports to the South. For years, it was commonly known as the Launching Pad, much to the dismay of pitchers everywhere. It's the ballpark Pascual Perez got lost trying to find and Chief Noc-a-Homa called home. It's where Pete Rose's 1978 hitting streak ended and the miracle of 1991 unfolded. And most of all, it's the house where Hank caught The Babe.

Atlanta Stadium, which became Atlanta–Fulton County Stadium in 1976, has been the site of some of the most thrilling and momentous events in Braves and baseball history. It has often been characterized by horrendous baseball and a sea of empty seats. But in recent seasons, it has been mobbed by frenzied, tomahawk-chopping hordes wallowing in one of the most prosperous periods in franchise history.

In the spring of 1965, construction of a new ballpark was being completed just south of the Georgia State Capitol Building near the merging of three interstate highways (20, 75, and 85).

The story of this new Atlanta Stadium began when Ivan Allen, Jr., whose family was in the office supply business, decided in 1961 to run for mayor. Then 50 years old, Allen was president of the Atlanta Chamber of Commerce. He said in his campaign that if elected, he would build a modern sports stadium. At the time major league sports had yet to invade the South, but the hope was that such a stadium would induce a team to try this fertile region.

When Allen was elected, he set out to fulfill his campaign promise, but he knew he'd have a difficult time getting the land and money for a modern stadium without a tenant to occupy it. At this point, Furman Bisher, sports editor of the *Atlanta Journal,* became a major player in helping make the stadium a reality.

Bisher had become acquainted with Charlie Finley, who purchased the Kansas City Athletics of the American League in 1960. It was known that Finley was looking for a new home for his ball club. At an Atlanta sports banquet in February 1962, Bisher suggested to Finley that he move the Athletics to the Georgia capitol. When Finley asked where his team would play, Bisher told him Allen was just waiting for a reason to build a stadium.

Finally, in the spring of 1963, Finley visited Atlanta and got the full-fledged dog-and-pony show from Allen, Bisher, and C&S Bank president Mills B. Lane. Included was a trip to the current site of Atlanta–Fulton County Stadium, which at the time was little more than vacant property, once a residential area, that was waiting to be redeveloped.

In Bisher's 1966 book *Miracle in Atlanta,* he wrote that Finley, standing about where second base would be located, said to Allen, "I can almost hear the crack of the bat. You build a stadium here, and I guarantee you Atlanta will get a major league franchise."

He was right, but it wasn't Finley's Athletics who would play at Atlanta Stadium. At about the same time, the syndicate of Chicago businessmen who had purchased the Braves from Lou Perini in the fall of 1962 was questioning whether Milwaukee could provide adequate support for their new investment.

Attendance had dived to 766,921 in 1962 from a Milwaukee high of over 2.2 million in 1957. Season ticket sales were de-

Atlanta Stadium gave Southerners their first taste of major league baseball.

Atlanta mayor Ivan Allen Jr., the driving force
behind the construction of Atlanta Sadium,
was justly proud at the topping off ceremony.

pressed, and the citizenship failed to respond to a public offering of stock. Before selling, Perini had his president and
general manager, John McHale, feel out Bisher about the possibility of moving the Braves to Atlanta. Perini sold the team
before he got that far, but the new owners had the same idea.

Allen was still trying to bring Finley's Athletics to Atlanta
in 1964 to play at old Ponce de Leon Park for a year while the
new stadium was under construction. But at the 1963 All-Star
Game in Cleveland, Finley was ordered by the American
League to stay in Kansas City.

A week and a half earlier, Delbert Coleman, one of the
new Braves partners, called a friend of his in Atlanta. That
friend was Arthur Montgomery, president of the Atlanta
Coca-Cola Bottling Company and head of Mayor Allen's Stadium Authority. Coleman told Montgomery the Braves were
interested in moving to Atlanta.

So, on the same day in Cleveland when Finley was told by
the rest of the American League owners to sit tight, Allen,

Georgia governor Carl Sanders, and the rest of the Atlanta
delegation met with some of the Braves owners. Though it
was a preliminary meeting, it became clear both sides were
serious about a relationship. All they needed was a stadium.

In September 1963, officials of the Braves met with the Atlanta group and agreed on the basic groundwork of the franchise shift to take place in 1964. But a week later, the deal
seemed to fall apart when a "Go to Bat for the Braves" effort
was launched in Milwaukee to appease the new owners. This
attempt to sell season tickets and sponsorships fell far short
of expectations, though, and the Braves' owners called Atlanta once again in early 1964 to say that the move was on
again for 1965.

On March 5, 1964, Allen announced he had an agreement with an "unidentified" major league team desirous of
moving to Atlanta. The next day the city approved the stadium site, and on March 31 a construction contract was
awarded for $18 million.

On April 15, 1964, ground was broken. Just fifty-one
weeks later, the Braves and Detroit Tigers played an exhibition game to dedicate Atlanta Stadium. The year between
the groundbreaking and that exhibition game began with
rumors of the Braves' intent to leave Milwaukee, leading to a
July story in *The Sporting News* that drew the same conclusion.

Not until October 21 did it become official, though. Following a meeting of the Braves' directors, team public relations man Ernie Johnson, a former Braves pitcher who would
become familiar to Atlantans as an announcer, read a statement that said, "The board of directors of the Milwaukee
Braves, Inc., voted today to request the permission of the National League to transfer their franchise to Atlanta, Georgia,
for 1965."

But in November, because of the threat of legal proceedings by Milwaukee County, the National League instructed
the Braves to fulfill their lease by playing the 1965 season at
County Stadium before moving to Atlanta in 1966.

As it turned out, Atlanta Stadium was used by the Crackers, the Braves' International League farm club, in 1965.

Before Atlanta Stadium was built, Atlantans
watched their baseball at Ponce de Leon Park; the
Sears building seen over the roof is now a City
Hall annex, and the magnolia tree which graced
center field still stands.

Braves chairman Bill Bartholomay reviews
plans during the construction of the stadium.

Meanwhile, the Braves played before barely half a million fans in Milwaukee.

Atlanta Stadium was typical in design of other circular concrete and steel ballparks being constructed in places such as Cincinnati, St. Louis, Philadelphia, and San Francisco during the same period. What was different was how quickly the Atlanta ballpark was completed. No other such facility had ever gone up in less than a year. But with the possibility of a major league tenant in 1965, Atlanta had no choice but to deliver.

When the stadium opened, the home run distances were 325 feet down the lines, 375 feet to the power alleys, and 402 feet to center field. It's now 330 to the foul poles and 385 in the power alleys, but the center-field fence remains 402 feet from home plate. Originally, a six-foot fence surrounded the outfield, but there's now a 10-foot wall.

Seating capacity at the three-tiered stadium has changed slightly at times but is now listed at 52,710. In September 1966 the National Football League's expansion Atlanta Falcons joined the Braves as tenants. The Falcons departed after the 1991 season to occupy the new Georgia Dome.

The Braves' first regular season game at Atlanta Stadium was played April 12, 1966, against Pittsburgh. A sellout crowd announced at 50,671 saw the Braves and Pirates battle through 12 innings tied at 1–1. In the 13th, future Hall of Famer Willie Stargell hit a two-run homer off Atlanta starter Tony Cloninger, giving the visitors a 3–1 edge. Joe Torre hit his second solo home run of the game in the bottom of the 13th, but the Braves lost, 3–2.

Some of the firsts: Matty Alou (batter), Gene Alley (hit), Torre (home run), Felipe Alou (Braves' batter), Rico Carty (Braves' hit), and Hank Aaron (Braves' steal).

The signature game of the first season was Denny Lemaster's 2–1 victory against the Dodgers and Sandy Koufax on August 9. A sellout crowd endured a rain delay of more than two hours in the fourth inning, but most stayed to see Eddie Mathews break a 1–1 tie with a game-winning home run off Koufax in the ninth.

The first Atlanta Braves finished fifth with an 85–77 record and attracted 1,539,801 fans to their new address, nearly 1 million more people than came to see them the previous year in Milwaukee.

One of the peculiarities about Atlanta Stadium was its early reputation as a home run hitter's paradise. Its fame as the "Launching Pad" came from the large number of home runs hit at the park. Indeed, plenty of home runs, many of the historic variety, have been hit at the park.

Many reasons—ranging from the number of power hitters the Braves have employed to the lack of pitching skill on the team's roster to the altitude of Atlanta and the configuration of the stadium—have been offered to explain the home runs. All probably have merit.

The most interesting is the altitude theory. Prior to the Colorado Rockies' coming into the league in 1993, Atlanta's altitude of 1,057 feet above sea level was the highest in the majors. However, when the Braves' pitching staff became one of the best in baseball in the 1990s, home runs by visiting teams became much less frequent.

Of course, the most famous home run of all was struck by Aaron on April 8, 1974. Coming in the fourth inning of the home opener off the Dodgers' Al Downing, it was the 715th of Aaron's career, breaking Babe Ruth's mighty record. A record crowd of 53,775 was at the stadium that night.

Talk about home runs, and the name of Atlanta Stadium nearly always enters the discussion. Aaron also hit his 500th (July 14, 1968), 600th (April 27, 1971), and 700th (July 21, 1973) home runs there. Hall of Famer Willie McCovey hit his 500th home run at Atlanta Stadium, too, on June 30, 1978.

In 1973, Aaron, Darrell Evans, and Dave Johnson became the first threesome of teammates to hit 40 or more home runs in the same season. As much as anything, Johnson's ability to hit 43 homers that year solidified Atlanta Stadium's reputation for home runs, since he'd never before been regarded as a power hitter.

All those homers kept Chief Noc-a-Homa dancing outside his left-field tepee. A full-blooded Native American, Levi Walker, Jr., performed for 17 seasons at the stadium, doing a pregame dance on the pitcher's mound and whooping it up after Atlanta home runs.

The National League split into two six-team divisions in 1969, and the Braves took advantage of it by winning the West and bringing postseason play to the South for the first time. Sellout crowds attended the first two games of the best-of-five playoff with the East division champion New York Mets. However, the Braves lost both games, 9–5 and 11–6, then were eliminated in the first game at Shea Stadium.

The team went into immediate decline after the playoff loss, and so did attendance, which barely exceeded 1 million in 1970 and '71. In 1972 it plunged to 752,973, and it didn't reach 1 million again until 1980. Not even the privilege of being able to watch Aaron pursue Ruth's record seemed to be much of an inducement to the fans. They wanted solid baseball and a contending team, and the Braves weren't providing either.

One bright moment came in 1972 when Atlanta Stadium played host to the All-Star Game. Aaron thrilled the full house with a sixth-inning home run, and the National League won, 4–3, in 10 innings.

The biggest reason for the Braves' shortcomings usually was a lack of pitching. The exception to the rule often was knuckleball specialist Phil Niekro, who became one of the most beloved athletes in Atlanta history. On August 5, 1973, at Atlanta Stadium, Niekro pitched the first no-hitter in the team's Southern history. He beat San Diego, 9–0, for the first no-hitter by a Brave since Warren Spahn in 1961.

In 1975, the team was so bad (67–94) that barely half a million people came to Atlanta Stadium to see it. On September 8, attendance bottomed out when only 737 people paid to get into the ballpark. Unfortunately, the team was about to get a lot worse, and it would be a dark seven years before the Braves could attract a decent crowd for anything other than the annual July 4 fireworks show.

In 1976 the stadium was renamed, Ted Turner bought the team, and a steady stream of free agents began to be imported. But noticeable improvement was foreign. The "highlight" of 1976 was San Francisco's John "the Count" Montefusco pitching a no-hitter against the Braves on September 29 in the final home game of the season.

The early Turner years didn't produce many victories or attract many fans to the stadium, but there was a constant array of offbeat promotions and stunts, many of which Turner participated in himself. One such event was "Wedlock and Headlock Night." Prior to the game 34 couples were married at home plate, and after the game the patrons were treated to a professional wrestling match.

One of the more memorable events at Atlanta–Fulton County Stadium occurred on June 16, 1978, when a pudgy third baseman named Bob Horner made his major league debut straight off the Arizona State campus. In only his third professional at bat, the 20-year-old Horner deposited a pitch from Pittsburgh veteran Bert Blyleven over the left-center fence. Just like that, the Braves had a new star. Horner and another young power hitter named Dale Murphy would soon lead the Braves out of their doldrums.

Also in 1978, the Braves played a major role in one of the most fascinating baseball stories of modern times. On July 31 at Atlanta–Fulton County Stadium, Cincinnati superstar Pete Rose hit safely in his 44th consecutive game, tying the all-time National League record set by "Wee" Willie Keeler in 1897. Rose's next target was Joe DiMaggio's major league record of 56 games, but the Braves quickly put a stop to that attempt when rookie Larry McWilliams and veteran Gene Garber held Rose hitless August 1.

In 1982, under new manager Joe Torre, the Braves won their second National League West title. They did so primarily by starting the season with a major league record 13-game winning streak.

On April 20 they set the record in Atlanta, winning their 12th straight, 4–2, over Cincinnati, when Claudell Washington tripled home the winning run. The next night, they extended the record to 13 games by beating the Reds again, 4–3.

But as was the case in 1969, the Braves had but a brief encounter with the postseason. They lost the first two games at St. Louis and were eliminated from the best-of-five playoffs, 6–2, in Game 3 at Atlanta Stadium before a capacity crowd.

A then-Atlanta record of more than 1.8 million fans watched the Braves in 1982. Entertaining baseball was back, at least for a while. Murphy was named the league's MVP in 1982 and repeated in 1983 when the Braves finished second but set another Atlanta attendance record of more than 2.1 million.

On July 6, 1986, at Atlanta–Fulton County, Horner became the 11th man in history and the third Brave to hit four home runs in one game, yet the Braves still lost to the Expos, 11–8. It was the first time in history that a four-homer performance had been in vain.

In 1991 the atmosphere at Atlanta–Fulton County Stadium changed considerably, as testified to by an Atlanta record 2,140,217 chopping and chanting fans. A new era in Braves baseball was launched, and the old ballpark was transformed from a baseball morgue into the liveliest stadium in America.

The Braves went from having the worst record in baseball in 1990 to the World Series in 1991. On September 11, with the Braves and Dodgers staring down each other daily in the standings, Kent Mercker, Mark Wohlers, and Alejandro Pena combined for a 1–0, no-hit victory over San Diego. It was the

Renamed Atlanta–Fulton County Stadium in 1976, the Braves' home was commonly referred to as the "Launching Pad" until strong pitching in the 1990s cut down the barrage of home runs.

second Braves' no-hitter in Atlanta and the first combined no-hitter in National League history.

The season came down to the final series, three games in Atlanta against the Astros. After winning the first game, the Braves cruised to a 5–2 victory behind John Smoltz in the next-to-last game of the season. That clinched a tie for the division title. The players then huddled on the field and thousands of fans remained in the stands to watch the end of the Dodgers' game on the center-field TV screen. When the Giants won, the Braves and their fans erupted in a wild celebration. The playoffs were coming to Atlanta for the third time.

The Braves hadn't won a postseason game since the 1958 World Series, but that fact didn't dampen Atlanta's enthusiasm for the 1991 National League Championship Series, especially after the Braves split the first two games in Pittsburgh.

The first playoff victory at Atlanta–Fulton County Stadium came October 12 when the Braves pounded the Pirates, 10–3, in Game 3 behind home runs by Ron Gant, Greg Olson, and Sid Bream. Pittsburgh, however, won the next two games, but the Braves bounced back to win Games 6 and 7 in Pittsburgh. Suddenly, the World Series was coming to the Southeast for the first time.

It was a home-field advantage Series. The Twins won the first two games in Minnesota, but the Braves swept all three at Atlanta–Fulton County Stadium. Atlanta was ecstatic, but Minnesota returned home to win two extra-inning, one-run decisions and the Series.

Nothing could match the thrills the Braves provided at their home park in 1991, but the 1992 season came close.

The Braves entered their July 25 game at Atlanta–Fulton County Stadium riding a 12-game winning streak and led the Pirates, 1–0, in the ninth inning. The streak appeared ready to end when Pittsburgh's Andy Van Slyke hit what looked like a two-run homer to right-center. But, at the last possible second, Otis Nixon leaped, stuck his glove over the wall, and pulled back Van Slyke's drive. The Braves won their 13th in a row, and Nixon's sensational play became known simply as "The Catch."

The Braves carried plenty of momentum into the playoffs against Pittsburgh for the second straight year. Much of that momentum was provided by the delirious fans who packed Atlanta–Fulton County Stadium to a franchise-record count of 3,077,400.

The Braves had the home-field advantage for both the

When Ted Turner married actress Jane Fonda, a bit of Hollywood began to frequent Braves games.

playoffs and the World Series this time, and they needed it. Smoltz beat the Pirates in Game 1 of the playoffs, 5–1, and the Braves rolled to a 13–5 romp in Game 2. However, the Pirates won two of three at Pittsburgh and whipped the Braves, 13–4, in Game 6 at Atlanta–Fulton County.

Down 2–0 entering the bottom of the ninth inning in Game 7, the Braves were on the verge of missing a second straight trip to the World Series. However, with one run in, the bases loaded, and two outs, pinch hitter Francisco Cabrera lined a single to left. David Justice scored the tying run, and Bream slid home just in front of Barry Bonds' throw, to end the game and cause the outbreak of instant pandemonium in Atlanta.

Unfortunately, the World Series did not provide such a happy ending. Tom Glavine pitched the Braves to a 3–1 victory over the Blue Jays in Game 1 at Atlanta, but Toronto won the next three games to take a commanding lead. The Braves won Game 5 to get the Series back to Atlanta–Fulton County. However, the Jays won Game 6, 4–3, in 11 innings despite the Braves' thrilling rally to tie the game, 2–2, in the ninth and another rally that fell a run short in the 11th.

The Braves weren't able to bring the World Series back to Atlanta in 1993, but they did provide their fans with one of the most scintillating pennant races of all time.

Despite signing free agent pitcher Greg Maddux, the Braves couldn't keep pace with the San Francisco Giants, who seemed to be running away with the division title in mid-July. That's when John Schuerholz acquired first baseman Fred McGriff from San Diego to bolster the Braves' offense.

On the evening of McGriff's debut as a Brave, July 20, one of the more bizarre incidents in the history of Atlanta–Fulton County Stadium took place. During batting practice, a fire erupted on the club level of the stadium in the press box area. The game was delayed for nearly two hours, and when it finally started, St. Louis jumped to a 5–0 lead. Spurred by a McGriff home run, though, the Braves rallied for an 8–5 victory.

Atlanta proceeded to play .754 baseball over the final 65 games to win the division—on the last day of the season. The Braves were at home against Colorado, and the Giants were playing the Dodgers at Los Angeles. Glavine's pitching and Justice's 40th home run were the key ingredients in a 5–3 victory over the Rockies, clinching a tie. Then, when the Dodgers knocked off the Giants, the Braves and their fans celebrated again at the stadium.

Bobby Cox's club was the first National League team ever to win three consecutive division titles. And don't think the fans didn't appreciate it. The franchise attendance record was shattered again with 3,884,720 fans filing through the Atlanta–Fulton County Stadium turnstiles in 1993.

Hosting the playoffs was becoming a tradition. However, the results weren't so gratifying this time. The Braves split the first two games at Philadelphia, then came home and whipped the Phillies, 9–4, in Game 3. It was the last victory for Atlanta, though. The Phillies won Games 4 and 5 at Atlanta–Fulton County and ended the Braves' run at a third straight pennant by winning Game 6 at Philadelphia.

The strike-shortened 1994 season wasn't without its memorable moments at Atlanta–Fulton County either. One of the biggest was a ceremony to officially retire Murphy's uniform number 3. It joined those of Spahn (21), Niekro (35), Mathews (41), and Aaron (44) on the club-level facade.

Other tributes at the stadium to the team's former greats

include a bust of Aaron inside the park and statues of Aaron and Niekro on the concourse outside the park, where a statue of Georgia native and Hall of Famer Ty Cobb can also be found.

The thrills at Atlanta–Fulton County Stadium surely didn't come to an end in 1994, but they were numbered. The construction of the new Olympic stadium just south of the current park signaled an imminent change. The Braves were scheduled to move into the new facility on opening day 1997. Atlanta–Fulton County Stadium was doomed to be leveled, but the many magic moments it provided will live on in the memories of Braves fans.

The plaza outside the ballpark has statues of Phil Niekro, Ty Cobb, and this one of Hank Aaron.

Centennial Olympic Stadium

For years, Braves fans knew it as a large asphalt slab where many parked their cars just south of Atlanta–Fulton County Stadium. Then in 1993 they saw it become a massive hole in the ground. By the start of the 1995 season, it was beginning to take shape as the anticipated home of the Braves in 1997.

The new facility on Ralph Abernathy Boulevard, within a home run of Atlanta–Fulton County, was intended to host the track and field competition during the 1996 Olympic Games, then to be converted to a baseball stadium for use by the Braves.

Known as Centennial Olympic Stadium during construction, the name of the 85,000-seat arena was to be changed when it becomes a 49,800-seat ballpark. The Braves had the prerogative to select that name.

The three-tiered stadium was designed to have 28,800 seats in the field level, 15,000 in the upper deck, and 6,000 on the club level. There also were slated to be 52 skyboxes with 12 to 16 seats, as well as a stadium club and bar in left field with another 600 seats.

The design called for minimal foul territory, placing the fans extremely close to the players. Additionally, all seats are angled to face the middle of the infield.

Other features include a Braves Museum and Hall of Fame in left field, a retail area, a large scoreboard in center field, and a spacious plaza where fans enter the park, which will include shops, restaurants, and entertainment. The Olympic cauldron and flame will be a permanent part of the complex.

REGULAR SEASON RECORD AT EACH BALLPARK

Park	Years	W	L	T	Pct
South End Grounds	1876–1914	1,431	1,045	44	.578
Congress Street Grounds	1894	21	10	0	.677
Braves Field	1915–52	1,411	1,430	23	.497
Fenway Park	1913–15, 1946	48	26	2	.649
Milwaukee County Stadium	1953–65	602	414	7	.593
Atlanta–Fulton County Stadium	1966–94	1,165	1,113	4	.511

The Hall of Famers

Of the 222 men in the National Baseball Hall of Fame, 46—better than one in five—wore a Braves uniform as a player, manager, or coach. These include Cy Young, the winningest pitcher of all time; Warren Spahn, the winningest left-hander; and Hank Aaron and Babe Ruth, the top home run hitters from each side of the plate. No other franchise can make such a claim.

Unfortunately, many of these men either spent far too little time with the Braves, or, quite often, their careers were in steep decline by the time they joined the club.

Of the 46 former Braves in the Hall of Fame, eight were elected to the Cooperstown shrine largely or exclusively for their accomplishments with the franchise. Four others established or enhanced their credentials with the team.

Aaron, Spahn, and their former Milwaukee teammate, Eddie Mathews, built their reputations and statistics almost exclusively with the Braves and are the only three franchise Hall of Fame players of the post–World War II era. The Wright brothers, George and Harry, were elected as pioneers for their work in establishing the Red Stockings as an original National League franchise. Hugh Duffy and Kid Nichols also were products of the pre-1900 era. Rabbit Maranville's long career began (1912), ended (1935), and was played predominantly as a Brave, though it included stints with four other teams.

John Clarkson, Jimmy Collins, Billy Hamilton, and Vic Willis spent large portions of their careers in baseball's early years with teams other than Boston, but accumulated a large portion of their credentials in the franchise's uniform.

Then there are the players such as Ruth and Young, two of the most accomplished in history, who simply passed through for the final days of their illustrious careers.

Hall of Fame managers Casey Stengel and Bill McKechnie combined to win 14 pennants in their careers, but neither could lead the Braves to better than a fourth-place finish in a 14-year stretch of the 1930s and '40s. Al Lopez also was elected to the Hall as a manager, though his service to the organization was as a catcher.

Five others—Luke Appling, Bob Gibson, Willie Stargell, Satchel Paige, and George Kelly—never played for or managed the Braves but served the team as coaches.

Each position on the field is represented among the 46 Braves Hall of Famers. The breakdown is as follows: pitchers (13), catchers (1), first basemen (4), second basemen (4), third basemen (2), shortstops (3), left fielders (4), center fielders (4), right fielders (6), managers (3), and pioneers/executives (2).

Two other Hall of Famers, bringing the total to 48, served the Braves as president but never wore the team's uniform: John Montgomery Ward in 1911–12 and Christy Mathewson in 1923–25.

Johnny Evers (R), the heart of the 1914 World Series championship team, had compiled his Hall of Fame credentials and returned to the Braves as a coach in 1929 when he posed for this picture with second baseman Freddie Maguire.

Henry Louis Aaron

HENRY "HANK" L. AARON
MILWAUKEE N.L., ATLANTA N.L., MILWAUKEE A.L. 1954-1976
HIT 755 HOME RUNS IN 23-YEAR CAREER TO BECOME MAJORS'ALL-TIME HOMER KING. HAD 20 OR MORE FOR 20 CONSECUTIVE YEARS, AT LEAST 30 IN 15 SEASONS AND 40 OR BETTER EIGHT TIMES. ALSO SET RECORD FOR GAMES PLAYED (3,298), AT-BATS (12,364), LONG HITS (1,477), TOTAL BASES (6,856), RUNS BATTED IN (2,297). PACED N.L. IN BATTING TWICE AND HOMERS, RUNS BATTED IN AND SLUGGING PCT FOUR TIMES EACH. WON MOST VALUABLE PLAYER AWARD IN N.L. IN 1957.

Right fielder
Braves: 1954–74
Major leagues: 1954–76
Elected: 1982
Birthplace: Mobile, Alabama
B: February 5, 1934
Batted right; threw right

	G	AB	H	BA	RBI	R	2B	3B	HR	SA	SB
Braves	3,076	11,628	3,600	.310	2,203	2,107	600	96	733	.567	240
Career	3,298	12,364	3,771	.305	2,298	2,174	624	98	755	.555	240

Hank Aaron will always be remembered as the man who supplanted Babe Ruth as the all-time home run king, but his legacy should be much more than that. In his prime, he was one of the finest—and smoothest—all-around outfielders ever to play the game. Now a senior vice president with the Braves, Aaron was the National League Most Valuable Player in 1957. He led the league in batting twice, led in home runs and RBIs four times each, played in 24 All-Star Games, and holds major league career records for home runs (755), RBIs (2,297), long hits (1,477), and total bases (6,856). "Hammerin' Hank" ranks second in lifetime at bats (12,364) and runs (2,174) and third in games (3,298) and hits (3,771). In 1970, Aaron became the first man to compile both 3,000 career hits and 500 home runs. He went on to break Ruth's lifetime home run record on April 8, 1974. All but the last 22 of Aaron's home runs were hit as a Brave, and those came in his final two seasons with the Milwaukee Brewers. The slugging outfielder missed being the first unanimous selection to the Hall of Fame by nine votes (97.8 percent). Only Ty Cobb and Tom Seaver have received a higher percentage.

Lucius Benjamin Appling

LUCIUS BENJAMIN APPLING
CHICAGO A.L. 1930-1950
A.L. BATTING CHAMPION IN 1936 AND 1943.
PLAYED 2,218 GAMES AT SHORTSTOP
FOR MAJOR LEAGUE MARK.
HAD 2,749 HITS.
LIFETIME BATTING AVERAGE OF .310.
LED A.L. IN ASSIST 7 YEARS.
HOLDS A.L. RECORD FOR CHANCES
ACCEPTED BY SHORTSTOP 11,569.

Coach
Braves: 1981, 1984
Major leagues: 1930–43, 1945–50
Elected: 1964
Birthplace: High Point, North Carolina
B: April 2, 1909
D: January 3, 1991
Batted right; threw right

	G	AB	H	BA	RBI	R	2B	3B	HR	SA	SB
Career	2,422	8,856	2,749	.310	1,116	1,319	440	102	45	.398	179

Luke Appling never played an inning for the Braves and spent only two years coaching at the major league level. However, as a hitting instructor in the farm system and at spring training, he played a significant role in helping develop many of the club's young stars of the early 1990s. Talkative and good-natured, he was well liked and well respected for the good cheer and knowledge he brought to the organization. Appling was one of the game's finest hitters in the 1930s and '40s during a 20-year career as the shortstop of the White Sox. He won American League batting titles in 1936 and 1943 and hit over .300 in all but four seasons. His .388 average in 1936 is the best by a shortstop in the 20th century. Appling struck out an average of just 30 times per season.

Howard Earl Averill

HOWARD EARL AVERILL
"ROCK"
CLEVELAND A.L.   DETROIT A.L.
BOSTON N.L.   1929-1941
COMPILED .318 CAREER BATTING AVERAGE
AND HIT 238 HOME RUNS. TWICE MADE
MORE THAN 200 HITS IN SEASON. PACING
LEAGUE WITH 232 IN 1936. DROVE IN
100 OR MORE RUNS FIVE TIMES. RAPPED
FOUR HOMERS, THREE CONSECUTIVELY
IN FIRST GAME AND BATTED IN 11 RUNS
IN 1930 TWIN-BILL.

Center fielder
Braves: 1941
Major leagues: 1929–41
Elected: 1975
Birthplace: Snohomish, Washington
B: May 21, 1902
D: August 16, 1983
Batted left; threw right

	G	AB	H	BA	RBI	R	2B	3B	HR	SA	SB
Braves	8	17	2	.118	2	2	0	0	0	.118	0
Career	1,668	6,353	2,019	.318	1,164	1,224	401	128	238	.534	70

Earl "Rock" Averill was a powerful hitter for his size (5–9, 172), but his strength and skills were eroded by the time he joined the Braves at the age of 39. Averill began his career with a home run in his first big league at bat for Cleveland in 1929. He batted .332 as a rookie with 18 home runs and 96 RBIs. In 1936, Averill led the American League with 232 hits. He batted over .300 eight times, including his first six seasons, and had season highs of 32 home runs and 143 RBIs. Averill also played a role in cutting short the career of Hall of Fame pitcher Dizzy Dean. It was his line drive that smashed the big toe of Dean's left foot in the 1937 All-Star Game. Dean tried to come back too soon, strained his shoulder, and was never the same pitcher again.

David James Bancroft

Shortstop–manager
Braves: 1924–27
Major leagues: 1915–30
Elected: 1971
Birthplace: Sioux City, Iowa
B: April 20, 1891
D: October 9, 1972
Batted left and right; threw right

	G	AB	H	BA	RBI	R	2B	3B	HR	SA	SB
Braves	445	1,626	474	.292	145	238	71	19	6	.370	19
Career	1,913	7,182	2,004	.279	591	1,048	320	77	32	.358	145

	G	W	L	Pct
Braves	612	249	363	.407
Career	612	249	363	.407

Dave Bancroft was a great shortstop but not much of a manager if you go by his four-year record as the Braves' player-manager. The franchise averaged 91 losses per season under Bancroft, but then no one else could do better with the Braves in this era. No one ever questioned Bancroft's skills at shortstop, though. He handled a major league record 984 chances in 1922. He was described as "scrappy" and "fiery," characteristics which he used to help the Phillies to a pennant in 1915 and the Giants to successive pennants in 1921, '22, and '23. A career .279 hitter, Bancroft had five .300 seasons, including 1925 and '26 with the Braves. He was called "Beauty" because of his habit of shouting that word as pitches to opposing hitters approached the plate.

Dennis Joseph Brouthers

First baseman
Beaneaters: 1889
Major leagues: 1879–96, 1904
Elected: 1945
Birthplace: Sylvan Lake, New York
B: May 8, 1858
D: August 3, 1932
Batted left; threw left

	G	AB	H	BA	RBI	R	2B	3B	HR	SA	SB
Beaneaters	126	485	181	.373	118	105	26	9	7	.507	22
Career	1,673	6,711	2,296	.342	1,296	1,523	460	205	106	.519	256

Dan Brouthers played only one season for Boston's National League franchise, but what a year it was. Signed when the Detroit Wolverines folded, he led the league with a .373 average in 1889 and nearly took the Beaneaters to the pennant. They finished one game behind the New York Giants that season. Brouthers was nicknamed "Big Dan" for good reason. At 6–2, 207 pounds, he'd be large even by today's standards, and he was known for hitting monstrous home runs in a "dead ball" era. Credited with originating the phrase, "Keep your eye on the ball," Brouthers also was the first man to win consecutive batting titles (1882–83). Regarded as the mightiest slugger of the 1800s, he won five batting crowns in his 19-year career, led the league in home runs and RBIs twice each, and posted a .342 career average.

John Gibson Clarkson

Pitcher
Beaneaters: 1888–92
Major leagues: 1882–94
Elected: 1963
Birthplace: Cambridge, Massachusetts
B: July 1, 1861
D: February 4, 1909
Batted right; threw right

	W	L	Pct	ERA	G	CG	IP	H	BB	SO	ShO
Beaneaters	149	82	.643	2.82	242	226	2,093	1,957	676	834	20
Career	328	178	.648	2.81	531	485	4,536	4,295	1,191	1,978	37

Don't think for a moment that talk of big money is a relatively new phenomenon to baseball. In fact, it has been a subject of controversy for as long as the pro game has existed. After the 1887 season, baseball was abuzz about the Beaneaters buying John Clarkson from the Chicago White Stockings for what was regarded as the incredible sum of $10,000. Clarkson became known as the "$10,000 Wonder," and he quickly proved he was worth the price and the nickname. He was 33–20 with a 2.76 ERA in his first season with Boston and led the league with 483 innings pitched. Actually, that probably was an "off" year for Clarkson. He led the league in innings four times—twice working at least 620. He also led the league in victories three times, including 49 for the Beaneaters in 1889 and 53 for Chicago in 1885.

James Joseph Collins

Third baseman
Beaneaters: 1895–1900
Major leagues: 1895–1908
Elected: 1945
Birthplace: Buffalo, New York
B: January 16, 1870
D: March 6, 1943
Batted right; threw right

	G	AB	H	BA	RBI	R	2B	3B	HR	SA	SB
Beaneaters	674	2,653	821	.309	484	470	129	43	34	.429	71
Career	1,726	6,796	2,000	.294	983	1,055	352	117	65	.409	194

A revolutionary defensive third baseman and a clutch hitter, Jimmy Collins was the Brooks Robinson of his day. A third baseman who can't charge, scoop up a bunt barehanded, and throw out the batter at first can't play in the majors today. But before Collins came along, no one was making that play. He was the first man to position himself well off the base and to move around according to the situation. Collins was a key member of two of the most accomplished teams in Braves history. In 1897 he batted .346 with 132 RBIs for the best team of record in franchise history. The next year Collins led the league in home runs with 15, and Boston won its second straight pennant. In 1901, Collins jumped to the new Boston franchise in the American League, and two years later he made a unique piece of history by managing that club to victory in the first modern World Series.

Hugh Duffy

Center fielder
Beaneaters: 1892–1900
Major leagues: 1888–1901, 1904–06
Elected: 1945
Birthplace: Cranston, Rhode Island
B: November 26, 1866
D: October 19, 1954
Batted right; threw right

	G	AB	H	BA	RBI	R	2B	3B	HR	SA	SB
Beaneaters	1,152	4,656	1,544	.332	926	997	220	72	69	.454	331
Career	1,737	7,042	2,282	.324	1,299	1,553	325	118	105	.448	574

In 1889, Chicago White Stockings great Cap Anson told Hugh Duffy to get lost, because, "We've got a bat boy." Five years later, the 5–7, 168-pound Duffy compiled the highest batting average of all time—.440—as an outfielder for the Beaneaters. Duffy also tied for the league lead in home runs (18) that year and led in RBIs (145 in 125 games) to capture the so-called Triple Crown. Besides being a lifetime .324 hitter who won two home run titles, he was regarded as a brilliant defensive outfielder and stole 574 bases in his 17-year career. In his nine-year career with the Beaneaters, the team won four pennants.

John Joseph Evers

Second baseman–coach
Braves: 1914–17, 1929–32
Major leagues: 1902–17, 1922, 1929
Elected: 1946
Birthplace: Troy, New York
B: July 22, 1883
D: March 28, 1947
Batted left; threw right

	G	AB	H	BA	RBI	R	2B	3B	HR	SA	SB
Braves	318	1,093	278	.254	77	157	28	5	2	.294	25
Career	1,784	6,137	1,659	.270	538	919	216	70	12	.334	324

Johnny Evers is best known in baseball history as the Cubs' second baseman in the Tinkers to Evers to Chance double-play combination immortalized in a poem by F. P. Adams. However, Braves fans should remember him as a vital cog on the renowned "Miracle" Braves of 1914. Traded to Boston that year, Evers teamed with shortstop Rabbit Maranville to spark the team's pennant drive. In fact, he was named Most Valuable Player even though he batted only .279. In the World Series, he batted .438 and drove in the winning run in the fourth and final game as the Braves swept Connie Mack's Philadelphia Athletics. That was the first modern World Series championship in franchise history. Evers played only two and a half more seasons with Boston before the Phillies picked him up on waivers.

Robert Gibson

Coach
Braves: 1982–84
Major leagues: 1959–75
Elected: 1981
Birthplace: Omaha, Nebraska
B: November 9, 1935
Batted right; threw right

	W	L	Pct	ERA	G	CG	IP	H	BB	SO	ShO
Career	251	174	.591	2.91	528	255	3,885	3,279	1,336	3,117	56

In 1968, Bob Gibson compiled one of the most dominating seasons any pitcher ever achieved. He had the lowest ERA (1.12) in National League history, pitched 13 shutouts en route to a 22–9 record, and struck out 35 Tigers in 27 innings in the World Series. Though he never pitched for any team other than the Cardinals in his 17-year career, he made a significant contribution to the Braves as a pitching coach for three seasons under manager Joe Torre. The Braves won the NL West in 1982 and finished second the next two seasons. Gibson's work with an unheralded pitching staff cannot be discounted. Known for his fiery competitive nature, he seemed to be able to transfer some of that intensity to his Braves staff. Among Gibson's many accomplishments as a player were two Cy Young Awards, one MVP, five 20-victory seasons, and a 7–2 record with a 1.89 ERA in World Series play.

Burleigh Arland Grimes

Pitcher
Braves: 1930
Major leagues: 1916–34
Elected: 1964
Birthplace: Emerald, Wisconsin
B: August 9, 1893
D: December 6, 1985
Batted right; threw right

	W	L	Pct	ERA	G	CG	IP	H	BB	SO	ShO
Braves	3	5	.375	7.35	11	1	49	72	22	15	0
Career	270	212	.560	3.53	616	314	4,179	4,412	1,295	1,512	35

Burleigh Grimes' career was in decline by the time he joined the Braves in 1930. At age 36, all five of his 20-victory seasons were behind him. The last of the legal spitball pitchers, Grimes still had some respectable work left in him, but he failed to show it in Boston. He got off to a slow start and was traded to St. Louis in mid-June. He was 13–6 for the Cardinals, salvaging a respectable 16–11 record for the season and helping St. Louis to the pennant. He also pitched on pennant winners the next two years, 1931 with the Cards and 1932 with the Cubs. His career ended in 1934 with 10 appearances for the Yankees, when he supposedly threw the last legal spitball, a pitch that was outlawed in 1920 but allowed by Grimes and a few others through a grandfather clause. His greatest years were with the Dodgers.

William Robert Hamilton

Center fielder
Beaneaters: 1896–1901
Major leagues: 1888–1901
Elected: 1961
Birthplace: Newark, New Jersey
B: February 16, 1866
D: December 16, 1940
Batted left; threw right

	G	AB	H	BA	RBI	R	2B	3B	HR	SA	SB
Beaneaters	690	2,612	884	.338	281	651	95	27	14	.412	274
Career	1,591	6,268	2,158	.344	736	1,690	242	94	40	.432	912

"Slidin' Billy" Hamilton was one of the most effective leadoff hitters and base stealers in history. He was traded to the Beaneaters in 1896 from the Phillies and promptly led the league in walks and on-base percentage. The next two seasons, he batted .343 and .369 to help Boston win back-to-back pennants. Hamilton stole 937 bases in his 14-year career and led his league seven times. His 117 steals in 1889 was the all-time record until Lou Brock broke it in 1974. It should be noted that stolen bases were awarded much more liberally in Hamilton's era than today, but he was a premier thief, nonetheless. "Slidin' Billy" remains the only man in history to have more runs scored than games played.

William Jennings Bryan Herman

Second baseman
Braves: 1946
Major leagues: 1931–43, 1946–47
Elected: 1975
Birthplace: New Albany, Indiana
B: July 7, 1909
Batted right, threw right

	G	AB	H	BA	RBI	R	2B	3B	HR	SA	SB
Braves	75	252	77	.306	22	32	23	1	3	.440	1
Career	1,922	7,707	2,345	.304	839	1,163	486	82	47	.407	67

Billy Herman was traded to the Braves from Brooklyn just before his 37th birthday in midseason 1946. Though he batted .306 in 75 games, his career was all but over. He was traded to Pittsburgh at the end of the season in the deal that brought the Braves third baseman Bob Elliott, a key figure on their 1948 pennant-winning club. Herman's greatest seasons were with the Cubs, for whom he followed Rogers Hornsby at second base in 1932. He played on three pennant winners in Chicago and another in Brooklyn. Herman led the NL with 227 hits and 57 doubles in 1935, his best season, when he batted .341.

Rogers Hornsby

Second baseman–manager
Braves: 1928
Major leagues: 1915–37
Elected: 1942
Birthplace: Winters, Texas
B: April 27, 1896
D: January 5, 1963
Batted right; threw right

	G	AB	H	BA	RBI	R	2B	3B	HR	SA	SB
Braves	140	486	188	.387	94	99	42	7	21	.632	5
Career	2,259	8,173	2,930	.358	1,584	1,579	541	169	301	.577	135

	G	W	L	Pct
Braves	122	39	83	.320
Career	1,530	701	812	.463

One of the greatest right-handed hitters of all time, Rogers Hornsby won the last of his seven NL batting titles in his only season with the Braves. He also managed the club most of that season, but with considerably less distinction. The Braves were 39–83 under his direction, finishing in seventh place. "Admired by many but liked by few" aptly sums up the "Rajah," an outspoken individual who managed to alienate most acquaintances, sooner or later. He refused to read, watch movies, or do anything else he felt would put a strain on his batting eye. It must have worked, since his .358 career average is second only to Ty Cobb's. In the five-year period 1921–25, his composite average was .402, and his .424 mark in 1924 is a record in the 20th century. Hornsby was named MVP twice and won two Triple Crowns. He also managed the 1926 Cardinals to the World Series championship.

Joseph James Kelley

Left fielder–manager
Beaneaters: 1891; **Doves:** 1908
Major leagues: 1891–1906, 1908
Elected: 1971
Birthplace: Cambridge, Massachusetts
B: December 9, 1871
D: August 14, 1943
Batted right; threw right

	G	AB	H	BA	RBI	R	2B	3B	HR	SA	SB
Beaneaters, Doves	85	273	70	.256	20	32	9	3	2	.333	5
Career	1,853	7,006	2,220	.317	1,194	1,421	358	194	65	.451	443

	G	W	L	Pct
Doves	154	63	91	.409
Career	669	338	321	.513

A native of Cambridge, Massachusetts, Joe Kelley played the first 12 games of his career and the last 73 with the hometown team, but his Hall of Fame credentials were achieved in 15 years with Baltimore, Brooklyn, and Cincinnati. A player-manager for Cincinnati in 1902–05, he had the same role for Boston in 1908 but never managed or played again. In the seven-year period 1894–1900, Kelley played on six NL pennant winners in Baltimore and Brooklyn. Though he never led the league in a major offensive category, the speedy, strong-armed outfielder had 11 consecutive .300 seasons, including a career-high .393 in 1894. He also had five straight 100-RBI campaigns and once went nine-for-nine in a doubleheader.

George L. Kelly

Coach
Bees, Braves: 1938–43
Major leagues: 1915–17, 1919–30, 1932
Elected: 1973
Birthplace: San Francisco, California
B: September 10, 1895
D: October 13, 1984
Batted right; threw right

	G	AB	H	BA	RBI	R	2B	3B	HR	SA	SB
Career	1,622	5,993	1,778	.297	1,020	819	337	76	148	.452	65

An accomplished first baseman for John McGraw's New York Giants, George Kelly never played for the Braves. However, he was a coach under manager Casey Stengel during a six-year period in which Boston failed to finish higher than fifth. Nicknamed "Highpockets" because of his 6–4, 190-pound frame, Kelly was an excellent clutch hitter. The great McGraw was quoted as saying Kelly delivered "more important hits" than any other player he ever managed. He led the league in home runs in 1921, led in RBIs in 1920 and '24, and strung together four years of 100 or more RBIs in New York's pennant-winning seasons of 1921–24. In 1924, he hit seven home runs in a six-game stretch, and he had six straight .300 seasons from 1921 through 1926.

Michael Joseph Kelly

Right fielder–catcher
Beaneaters: 1887–89, 1891–92
Major leagues: 1878–93
Elected: 1945
Birthplace: Troy, New York
B: December 31, 1857
D: November 8, 1894
Batted right; threw right

	G	AB	H	BA	RBI	R	2B	3B	HR	SA	SB
Beaneaters	442	1,764	510	.289	258	372	105	27	28	.427	238
Career	1,455	5,894	1,813	.308	950	1,357	359	102	69	.438	368

"King" Kelly was one of the most charismatic players in history. He was a member of the pennant-winning Beaneaters in 1891 and 1892, though his skills had eroded and he wasn't a regular. In an earlier stint with the Beaneaters, he was much more successful. He batted .322 and stole 84 bases in 1887 after Boston purchased him for $10,000 from the Chicago White Stockings, whom he helped to five pennants from 1880 to '86. A two-time NL batting champ, Kelly was the subject of the popular song "Slide, Kelly, Slide" because of his daring baserunning that sometimes included "shortcuts" around the bases when the umpire wasn't watching. Among other things, he was a bit of a pioneer. Cap Anson credited Kelly with being the first player to use the hit-and-run. He also was one of the first catchers to use finger signs, one of the first outfielders to back up infielders, and one of the first base runners to use the hook slide.

Ernesto Natali Lombardi

Catcher
Braves: 1942
Major leagues: 1931–47
Elected: 1986
Birthplace: Oakland, California
B: April 6, 1908
D: September 26, 1977
Batted right; threw right

	G	AB	H	BA	RBI	R	2B	3B	HR	SA	SB
Braves	105	309	102	.330	46	32	14	0	11	.482	1
Career	1,853	5,855	1,792	.306	990	601	277	27	190	.460	8

Possessing huge hands that he "locked" together in a golf-type grip on the bat, Lombardi was the National League MVP in 1938 with Cincinnati. He's the only catcher to lead the league in hitting twice, and he did so despite being one of the slowest runners ever to play the game. The Braves bought Lombardi from Cincinnati in 1942. He batted .330 to lead the league, but Boston still finished seventh and traded him to New York the following year. Legend has it that Lombardi's hands were so big that he'd occasionally snare a pitcher's errant delivery bare-handed to save a wild pitch. Not a noted defensive catcher, Lombardi did catch Johnny Vander Meer's back-to-back no-hitters in 1938 and was instrumental in Cincinnati's winning consecutive pennants in 1939 and '40.

Alfonso Ramon Lopez

Catcher
Bees: 1936–40
Major leagues: 1928, 1930–47
Elected: 1977
Birthplace: Tampa, Florida
B: August 20, 1908
Batted right; threw right

	G	AB	H	BA	RBI	R	2B	3B	HR	SA	SB
Bees	471	1,527	373	.244	168	148	54	9	21	.333	11
Career	1,950	5,916	1,547	.261	652	613	206	43	51	.337	46

Al Lopez's career in Boston coincided with the five-year period the club was known as the Bees. A smart, durable, and talented catcher, Lopez never would have made the Hall of Fame on his playing skills, even though he held the record for games caught until 1987. It was as a manager that he gained acclaim. If not for Lopez, the Yankees might have dominated the American League even more than they did in the 1950s and early '60s. From 1949 through 1964, he was the only non-Yankees manager to win the AL pennant. He won at Cleveland in 1956 with a record 111 victories, and he won again in 1959 with the White Sox, one of the weakest offensive teams ever to get to the World Series. Additionally, his teams finished second seven times between 1951 and '58 and either first or second 10 times in his 17-year career.

Walter James Vincent Maranville

Shortstop
Braves: 1912–20, 1929–33, 1935
Major leagues: 1912–33, 1935
Elected: 1954
Birthplace: Springfield, Massachusetts
B: November 11, 1891
D: January 5, 1954
Batted right; threw right

	G	AB	H	BA	RBI	R	2B	3B	HR	SA	SB
Braves	1,795	6,724	1,696	.252	558	801	244	103	23	.329	194
Career	2,670	10,078	2,605	.258	884	1,255	380	177	28	.340	291

Rabbit Maranville spent 15 of his 23 seasons in the majors with the Braves, both starting and ending his career with the club. He never batted .300 over a full season but is re-garded as one of the finest defensive shortstops in the game's history. In 1914, his second full season in the majors, he sparked Boston to such a dramatic and unexpected pennant that the team has forever been known as the "Miracle Braves." The 5-5, 155-pound bundle of spirit and determination batted just .246 that season but set a record at the time for chances at the position and teamed with Johnny Evers to lead the league in double plays. The Braves swept mighty Philadelphia in four straight games in the World Series, with Maranville hitting .308.

Richard William Marquard

Pitcher
Braves: 1922–25
Major leagues: 1908–25
Elected: 1971
Birthplace: Cleveland, Ohio
B: October 9, 1889
D: June 1, 1980
Batted left and right; threw left

	W	L	Pct	ERA	G	CG	IP	H	BB	SO	ShO
Braves	25	39	.391	4.44	109	19	545	658	171	164	4
Career	201	177	.532	3.07	536	197	3,309	3,231	858	1,593	31

Rube Marquard had his best years with the New York Giants and was a mere shadow of that greatness when he joined the Braves for the final four seasons of his career. He never had a winning record for Boston, but in his defense, he was pitching for some awful teams. He won 73 games for the Giants in 1911–13, including a league-high 26 in 1912, as New York won three straight pennants. Marquard also won his first 19 games in 1912. He pitched a no-hitter against the Dodgers in 1915, was traded to them later in the season, then helped them win a pennant in 1916 when he was 13–6.

Edwin Lee Mathews

Third baseman–coach–manager
Braves: 1952–66, 1971–74
Major leagues: 1952–68
Elected: 1978
Birthplace: Texarkana, Texas
B: October 13, 1931
Batted left; threw right

	G	AB	H	BA	RBI	R	2B	3B	HR	SA	SB
Braves	2,223	8,049	2,201	.273	1,388	1,452	338	70	493	.517	66
Career	2,391	8,537	2,315	.271	1,453	1,509	354	72	512	.509	68

	G	W	L	Pct
Braves	311	149	161	.481
Career	311	149	161	.481

Eddie Mathews was the only man to play for the Braves in all three cities the franchise has called home. He was the most prolific home-run-hitting third baseman in history until Mike Schmidt came along and also was the seventh man to join the 500-home-run club. In 1953, only his second season in the majors, he hit a league-high 47 homers, starting a string of nine years in which he hit 31 or more. He also led the NL with 46 home runs in 1959, the fourth and last time he reached 40. A mainstay of the great Milwaukee teams of the 1950s, Mathews had an excellent batting eye, leading the league in walks four times. He and Hank Aaron formed the greatest one-two home run punch in history. They hit 863 home runs while playing together. Mathews became a Braves coach under Luman Harris in 1971 and replaced Harris as manager in mid-1972.

Christopher Mathewson

President
Braves: 1923–25
Major leagues: 1900–16
Elected: 1936
Birthplace: Factoryville, Pennsylvania
B: August 12, 1880
D: October 7, 1925
Batted right; threw right

	W	L	Pct	G	GS	CG	ShO	IP	H	BB	SO	ERA	SV
Career	373	188	.665	635	551	434	79	4,780	4,218	844	2,502	2.13	28

There are those who regard Christy Mathewson as the greatest pitcher of all time. Unfortunately, he never pitched for the Braves, but he did serve as team president from 1923 until his death in 1925. A measure of his stature is that he was one of the original five inductees into the Hall of Fame in 1936. The other four were Ty Cobb, Babe Ruth, Honus Wagner, and Walter Johnson. Mathewson was idolized by the masses. Besides winning 373 games, third all-time, he was handsome, intelligent, and clean-cut. Known as "Matty" or "Big Six," the New York Giants right-hander had four seasons of 30 or more wins and 13 of 20 or more. He completed 434 of 551 career starts. He once worked 68 straight innings without allowing a walk and had a World Series ERA of 1.15 in 11 games. Despite poor health, he was persuaded to join the Braves' front office when Judge Emil Fuchs purchased controlling interest in the team. Mathew-

son continued to be plagued by illness and died at age 45 while serving as Braves president.

Thomas Francis Michael McCarthy

Right fielder
Beaneaters: 1885, 1892–95
Major leagues: 1884–96
Elected: 1946
Birthplace: Boston
B: July 24, 1863
D: August 5, 1922
Batted right; threw right

	G	AB	H	BA	RBI	R	2B	3B	HR	SA	SB
Beaneaters	552	2,204	652	.296	384	450	83	21	24	.385	160
Career	1,275	5,128	1,496	.292	666	1,069	192	53	44	.376	468

Tommy McCarthy teamed with Hugh Duffy to form Boston's so-called Heavenly Twins in the outfield. He played on the pennant-winning clubs of 1892–93, and though he was not a particularly strong or prolific hitter by Hall of Fame standards, he made his mark with defense, stolen bases, and "smarts." He was clever, perfecting the art of trapping fly balls to fool base runners, and he was an adept bunter and hit-and-run specialist. His arm was one of the best, too, accounting for an NL record 53 assists in 1893. McCarthy had four .300 seasons, including two of his finest for the Beaneaters in 1893 and '94 when he hit .346 and .349.

Bill McKechnie

Outfielder–manager
Braves: 1913, 1930–35; **Bees:** 1936–37
Major leagues: 1907, 1910–18, 1920
Elected: 1962
Birthplace: Wilkinsburg, Pennsylvania
B: August 7, 1886
D: October 29, 1965
Batted right and left; threw right

	G	AB	H	BA	RBI	R	2B	3B	HR	SA	SB
Braves	1	4	0	.000	0	1	0	0	0	.000	0
Career	846	2,843	713	.251	240	319	86	33	8	.313	127

	G	W	L	Pct
Braves, Bees	1,235	560	666	.453
Career	3,647	1,896	1,723	.524

Boston is the only National League team Bill McKechnie managed that didn't win a pennant under his direction. Yet it was his work for the Braves and Bees that solidified his reputation for managerial genius. In eight seasons as the Boston manager, his team never finished higher than fourth and was under .500 four times—including 1935 when the club was 38–115, finishing 61½ games out of first. Just two years later, he got the club up to fifth and was named Manager of the Year in his final season in Boston. In 25 years of managing, he had a .524 winning percentage despite the awful Boston teams he had to endure. He won pennants at Pittsburgh in 1925, St. Louis in 1928, and Cincinnati in 1939 and '40. He won the World Series in 1925 and '40. A light-hitting infielder, McKechnie also appeared in one game for the 1913 Braves before he was sent to the Yankees.

Joseph Michael Medwick

JOSEPH MICHAEL MEDWICK
"DUCKY WUCKY"
ST. LOUIS N.L. 1932 TO 1940, 1947, 1948
BROOKLYN N.L. 1940 TO 1943, 1946
NEW YORK N.L. 1943 TO 1945—BOSTON N.L. 1945
LED N.L. IN BATTING IN 1937 WITH .374
AVERAGE, BATTED .353 IN 1935, .351 IN 1936,
.332 IN 1939, LIFETIME TOTAL 2471 HITS,
BATTING AVERAGE .324, NAMED TO ALL STAR
TEAMS 1935-6-7-8-9. MOST VALUABLE PLAYER
N.L. 1937. LED N.L. IN RUNS BATTED IN
AND TWO BASE HITS 1936-7-8.
BATTED .300 OR MORE 15 TIMES.

Left fielder
Braves: 1945
Major leagues: 1932–48
Elected: 1968
Birthplace: Carteret, New Jersey
B: November 24, 1911
D: March 21, 1975
Batted right; threw right

	G	AB	H	BA	RBI	R	2B	3B	HR	SA	SB
Braves	66	218	62	.284	26	17	13	0	0	.344	3
Career	1,984	7,635	2,471	.324	1,383	1,198	540	113	205	.505	42

"Ducky" Medwick typified the St. Louis Cardinals' "Gas House Gang" of the 1930s with his rough, all-out style of play. By the time he joined the Braves in mid-1945, he had lost the skills that made him a Triple Crown winner and MVP in 1937. In his half season in Boston, Medwick played regularly as an outfielder and first baseman for a sixth-place team. Though his career lasted three more years in Brooklyn and St. Louis, he never again was an everyday player. Known for hitting bad pitches, Medwick led the NL in RBIs and doubles for three straight seasons, 1936–38. His Triple Crown numbers in 1937 were .374, 31, 154. In 1934 he helped spur the Cardinals to a World Series title by hitting .379. In the Cards' 11–0 rout in the decisive seventh game, he was ordered to leave the game by Commissioner Landis when Detroit fans pelted him with garbage because they felt he slid too hard into third.

Charles Augustus Nichols

CHARLES A.(KID) NICHOLS
RIGHT HANDED PITCHER WHO WON 30 OR
MORE GAMES FOR SEVEN CONSECUTIVE
YEARS (1891-97) AND WON AT LEAST 20
GAMES FOR TEN CONSECUTIVE SEASONS
(1890-99) WITH BOSTON N.L. ALSO PITCHED
FOR ST. LOUIS AND PHILADELPHIA N.L. ONE
OF FEW PITCHERS TO WIN MORE THAN 300
GAMES, HIS MAJOR LEAGUE RECORD BEING
360 VICTORIES, 202 DEFEATS.

Pitcher
Beaneaters: 1890–1901
Major leagues: 1890–1901, 1904–06
Elected: 1949
Birthplace: Madison, Wisconsin
B: September 14, 1869
D: April 11, 1953
Batted right and left; threw right

	W	L	Pct	ERA	G	CG	IP	H	BB	SO	ShO
Beaneaters	330	182	.645	2.99	557	477	4,542	4,434	1,159	1,667	44
Career	362	207	.636	2.95	621	533	5,061	4,912	1,268	1,868	48

Kid Nichols pitched without a windup, and considering his success, perhaps a few others ought to try such an approach. The most accomplished pre-1900 pitcher, he played a major role in winning five pennants for the Beaneaters from 1891 to 1898. He won 27 games as a rookie in 1890, then reeled off 30 or more victories in seven consecutive years. He had a dozen 20-victory seasons, all but the last for Boston. Nichols felt a windup was wasted motion and detrimental to control. He didn't have a curve and relied primarily on his fastball and excellent control. In only one season did he average more than 2.8 walks per nine innings, and twice he averaged 1.7 or less. He led the league in victories four times. His 533 complete games rank fourth all-time, and in 502 starts for Boston, he was relieved only 25 times.

James Henry O'Rourke

JAMES H. O'ROURKE
"ORATOR JIM" PLAYED BALL UNTIL HE
WAS PAST FIFTY, INCLUDING TWENTY-ONE
MAJOR LEAGUE SEASONS. AN OUTFIELDER
AND CATCHER FOR THE BOSTON RED
STOCKINGS OF 1873, HE LATER WORE
THE UNIFORMS OF THE CHAMPIONSHIP
PROVIDENCE TEAM OF 1879, BUFFALO
NEW YORK AND WASHINGTON.

Left fielder–catcher
Red Stockings: 1876–78, 1880
Major leagues: 1876–93, 1904
Elected: 1945
Birthplace: Bridgeport, Connecticut
B: August 24, 1852
D: January 8, 1919
Batted right; threw right

	G	AB	H	BA	RBI	R	2B	3B	HR	SA	SB
Red Stockings	277	1,195	369	.309	140	244	68	25	9	.430	
Career	1,774	7,435	2,304	.310	1,010	1,446	414	132	50	.421	191

Professional ballplayers were a rugged, generally uneducated group in the 19th century. "Orator" Jim O'Rourke was an exception, so nicknamed because of his Yale Law

School background and verbosity. O'Rourke played for Boston in the National Association for four seasons and continued with the club in the new National League, helping the Red Stockings win pennants in 1877 and '78. A consistent .300 hitter, he led the NL in home runs in 1890 with a grand total of six. He was the regular left fielder for the league champion New York Giants in 1888 and '89. He retired in 1893 at the age of 41, but in 1904, at age 52, he returned to catch the pennant-clinching game for the New York Giants. He even got a hit and scored a run. He also served the game as a manager, umpire, and minor league president.

Leroy Robert Paige

LEROY ROBERT PAIGE
"SATCHEL"
NEGRO LEAGUES   1926-1947
CLEVELAND A.L.   1948-1949
ST. LOUIS A.L.   1951-1953
KANSAS CITY A.L.   1965
PAIGE WAS ONE OF THE GREATEST STARS
TO PLAY IN THE NEGRO BASEBALL LEAGUES.
THRILLED MILLIONS OF PEOPLE AND WON
HUNDREDS OF GAMES. STRUCK OUT 21 MAJOR
LEAGUERS IN AN EXHIBITION GAME. HELPED
PITCH CLEVELAND INDIANS TO THE 1948
PENNANT IN HIS FIRST BIG LEAGUE YEAR
AT AGE 42. HIS PITCHING WAS A LEGEND
AMONG MAJOR LEAGUE HITTERS.

Coach
Braves: 1968–69
Major leagues: 1948–49, 1951–53, 1965
Elected: 1971
Birthplace: Mobile, Alabama
B: July 7, 1906
D: June 8, 1982
Batted right; threw right

	W	L	Pct	ERA	G	CG	IP	H	BB	SO	ShO
Career	28	31	.475	3.29	179	7	476	429	183	290	4

Denied access to the major leagues because of his race until he was 42 years old, Satchel Paige was a legend for his success in the Negro Leagues. The Braves brought him back into the game for a brief time as a coach in 1968 and '69 to help him qualify for a pension. In 1948, Bill Veeck signed Paige to help the Indians in their pennant drive. Given Veeck's reputation for promotion, it was understandable that many felt he was simply grabbing publicity by making Paige the oldest rookie in history. However, it didn't take long for people to realize Paige could still pitch. He was 6–1 with a 2.47 ERA in 21 games, seven of them starts. In his second start, he pitched a shutout. Veeck got some promotional value, too, since Paige drew 200,000 fans in his first three starts.

Gaylord Jackson Perry

GAYLORD JACKSON PERRY
SAN FRANCISCO, N.L.   1962-1971
CLEVELAND, A.L.   1972-1975
TEXAS, A.L.   1975-1977, 1980
SAN DIEGO, N.L.   1978-1979
NEW YORK, A.L.   1980
ATLANTA, N.L.   1981
SEATTLE, A.L.   1982-1983
KANSAS CITY, A.L.   1983
ACHIEVED PITCHERS' MAGIC NUMBERS WITH 314 WINS
AND 3,534 STRIKEOUTS. PLAYING MIND GAMES WITH
HITTERS THROUGH ARRAY OF RITUALS ON MOUND WAS
PART OF HIS ARSENAL. 20-GAME WINNER 5 TIMES WITH
LIFETIME ERA OF 3.10. NO-HIT CARDS FOR GIANTS
9/17/68. OUTSTANDING COMPETITOR. ONLY CY YOUNG WINNER
IN BOTH LEAGUES.

Pitcher
Braves: 1981
Major leagues: 1962–83
Elected: 1991
Birthplace: Williamston, North Carolina
B: September 15, 1938
Batted right; threw right

	W	L	Pct	ERA	G	CG	IP	H	BB	SO	ShO
Braves	8	9	.471	3.93	23	3	151	182	24	60	0
Career	314	265	.542	3.10	777	303	5,352	4,938	1,379	3,534	53

Gaylord Perry was 42 years old when the Braves signed him as a free agent for the 1981 season. He basically was hanging on in an attempt to win 300 games, which he did the following season for Seattle. He left Atlanta at 297. Though his skill was diminished, he still had his control, leading the NL that year with an average of just 1.4 walks per nine innings. The only man to win the Cy Young Award in both leagues, Perry was notorious for throwing a spitball, a reputation that kept both hitters and umpires on edge. He led the National League in victories twice and the American League once, and he had five 20-victory seasons despite the fact that he usually found himself on weak teams. After his playing days, he had a brief career as a coach at Limestone College in Gaffney, South Carolina. Perry's brother Jim won 215 games in a 17-year career.

Charles Gardner Radbourn

CHARLIE RADBOURNE
"OLD HOSS"
PROVIDENCE, BOSTON AND CINCINNATI
NATIONAL LEAGUE 1881 TO 1891. GREATEST
OF ALL 19TH CENTURY PITCHERS. WINNING
1884 PENNANT FOR PROVIDENCE, RADBOURNE
PITCHED LAST 27 GAMES OF SEASON, WON
26. WON 3 STRAIGHT IN WORLD SERIES.

Pitcher
Beaneaters: 1886–89
Major leagues: 1881–1891
Elected: 1939
Birthplace: Rochester, New York
B: December 11, 1854
D: February 5, 1897
Batted right; threw right

	W	L	Pct	ERA	G	CG	IP	H	BB	SO	ShO
Beaneaters	78	81	.491	3.58	165	157	1,418	1,495	361	468	6
Career	310	195	.614	2.68	528	489	4,535	4,335	875	1,830	34

"Ol' Hoss" Radbourn was a little tired by the time he got to Boston, but he still had three 20-victory seasons for the Beaneaters. Who could blame Radbourn for being a little burned out in 1886? Two years earlier, he single-handedly pitched Providence to the pennant. Talk about a "Hoss," he pitched 30 of his team's final 32 games, winning 26 of them, including 18 in a row at one point. Overall, he was 60–12 in 1884 with a 1.38 ERA in 679 innings! Though overhand pitching was legalized that season, he still threw underhand and boasted an incredible curve as well as a screwball. The pitching distance was only 50 feet, but the batter could request a high or low pitch. Radbourn had nine 20-victory seasons and totaled 310 career wins in just 11 seasons before his arm had given its all.

George Herman Ruth

Right fielder
Braves: 1935
Major leagues: 1914–35
Elected: 1936
Birthplace: Baltimore, Maryland
B: February 6, 1895
D: August 16, 1948
Batted left; threw left

	G	AB	H	BA	RBI	R	2B	3B	HR	SA	SB
Braves	28	72	13	.181	12	13	0	0	6	.431	0
Career	2,503	8,399	2,873	.342	2,213	2,174	506	136	714	.690	123

Babe Ruth hit his final six home runs as a Brave, including the last three in a fitting farewell at Pittsburgh's Forbes Field. He was out of shape, in poor health, and obviously not fit to play with the Braves, so he soon retired in the city where his remarkable career began as a pitcher with the Red Sox. Ruth changed the game forever with his power and brought it new popularity with skill and charisma that combined to make him one of the most famous people in history. He had potential Hall of Fame talent as a pitcher—twice winning 23 or more games, leading the AL in ERA in 1916, and working 29⅔ consecutive scoreless inning in the World Series for the Red Sox—before turning to full-time slugging. In 1919, his last year with the Red Sox before being sold to the Yankees, he set a major league record with 29 home runs while the "dead" ball was still in use. From 1918 through 1932, he won 12 AL home runs crowns in 15 years, crushing 40 or more 11 times. "The Bambino's" 60 home runs in 1927 stood as the single-season record until Roger Maris hit 61 in '61, and his 714 career homers weren't eclipsed until Hank Aaron did it in 1974. Ruth won six RBI titles and even led the league in batting average (.378) in 1924.

Albert Fred Schoendienst

Second baseman
Braves: 1957–60
Major leagues: 1945–63
Elected: 1989
Birthplace: Germantown, Illinois
B: February 2, 1923
Batted right and left; threw right

	G	AB	H	BA	RBI	R	2B	3B	HR	SA	SB
Braves	272	1,050	292	.278	75	124	55	6	8	.365	6
Career	2,216	8,479	2,449	.289	773	1,223	427	78	84	.387	89

When the Braves picked up Red Schoendienst from the Giants in June 1957, they acquired a crucial piece of the lineup that produced back-to-back National League pennants in 1957 and '58 and a World Series championship in '57. Schoendienst batted .310 over the final 93 games of 1957 and wound up leading the league with 200 hits. As a 34-year-old veteran who was a regular with the Cardinals' 1946 World Series champs, he stabilized the infield and provided the leadership manager Fred Haney credited with being instrumental in the team's success. Stricken by tuberculosis in 1959, Schoendienst saw his career as a regular end. He retired in 1963 as a reserve for St. Louis. He had seven .300 seasons and led NL second basemen in fielding the same number of times. He also had a long career as a manager and coach, managing St. Louis to pennants in 1967 and '68 and a World Series title in '67.

Aloysius Harry Simmons

Left fielder
Bees: 1939
Major leagues: 1924–41, 1943–44
Elected: 1953
Birthplace: Milwaukee, Wisconsin
B: May 22, 1902
D: May 26, 1956
Batted right; threw right

	G	AB	H	BA	RBI	R	2B	3B	HR	SA	SB
Bees	93	330	93	.282	43	39	17	5	7	.427	0
Career	2,215	8,759	2,927	.334	1,827	1,507	539	149	307	.535	87

Al Simmons is yet another Hall of Famer who spent a brief and rather uneventful period with the franchise during the twilight of his career. Sold to the Bees by Washington for $3,000 prior to the 1939 season, Simmons was sold to pennant-winning Cincinnati on August 31 so he would qualify for the World Series. "Bucketfoot Al," so-called because of his unusual "open" stance, fell just 73 hits shy of the coveted 3,000 mark and won back-to-back batting titles for the pennant-winning Athletics in 1930 and '31. He stormed into the major leagues in 1924, batting .308 with 102 RBIs as a rookie. He proceeded to hit .322 or better with at least 104 RBIs in each of the next 10 years. His 253 hits in 1925 rank second in AL history.

George Harold Sisler

First baseman–coach
Braves: 1928–30
Major leagues: 1915–30
Elected: 1939
Birthplace: Manchester, Ohio
B: March 24, 1893
D: March 26, 1973
Batted left; threw left

	G	AB	H	BA	RBI	R	2B	3B	HR	SA	SB
Braves	388	1,551	505	.326	214	192	81	19	9	.420	24
Career	2,055	8,267	2,812	.340	1,175	1,284	425	164	101	.468	375

George Sisler was called the "smartest hitter that ever lived" by Branch Rickey and the "nearest thing to a perfect ballplayer," by the crusty Ty Cobb. He played most of his final three seasons with the Braves, serving as a player-coach in 1930. Though he certainly was not the player he had been in his youth, he still had no trouble hitting .300 each year in Boston, as he did in all but one season (.290 in 1926) after his rookie year. Sisler won AL batting titles for St. Louis in 1920 and '22, hitting over .400 both times. His 257 hits in 1920 are still a record, and he put together a 41-game hitting streak in 1922. Sisler never hit more than 19 home runs, but he was an excellent defensive first baseman, led the league in steals four times, and had four 100-RBI seasons. His productivity suffered a noticeable drop after he sat out the entire 1923 season with a sinus infection that caused double vision.

Enos Bradsher Slaughter

Outfielder
Braves: 1959
Major leagues: 1938–42, 1946–59
Elected: 1985
Birthplace: Roxboro, North Carolina
B: April 27, 1916
Batted left; threw right

	G	AB	H	BA	RBI	R	2B	3B	HR	SA	SB
Braves	11	18	3	.167	1	0	0	0	0	.167	0
Career	2,380	7,946	2,383	.300	1,304	1,247	413	148	169	.453	71

When Enos "Country" Slaughter became a Brave in 1959, he was 43 years old and only a step from retirement. He was used mainly as a pinch hitter in a very brief and unproductive stint with Milwaukee. Fortunately, he called it quits in time to keep his lifetime batting average for 19 seasons at an even .300. Known for his hustling style of play, Slaughter was a mainstay of the great "Gas House Gang" St. Louis Cardinals teams of the 1940s. In 1942 he led the National League in hits (188) and batting (.318), then missed the next three years because of military service. He returned in 1946 to lead the league in RBIs (130). He also led the league in doubles (1939) and triples (1942, 1949), was an excellent defensive outfielder, and appeared in five World Series. The only losing World Series team he played on was the 1957 Yankees, who lost to the Braves.

Warren Edward Spahn

Pitcher
Braves: 1942, 1946–64
Major leagues: 1942, 1946–65
Elected: 1973
Birthplace: Buffalo, New York
B: April 23, 1921
Batted left; threw left

	W	L	Pct	ERA	G	CG	IP	H	BB	SO	ShO
Braves	356	229	.609	3.05	714	374	5,048	4,620	1,378	2,493	63
Career	363	245	.597	3.08	750	382	5,246	4,830	1,434	2,583	63

The winningest left-hander in history, Warren Spahn ranks fifth all-time in victories despite the fact he didn't record his first win until he was 25 years old and had served in combat in World War II. One of the most stylish pitchers ever with his classic leg kick, Spahn won all but his last seven games with the Braves. He had 13 20-victory seasons, including six in a row. His last came in 1963 at age 42 when he was 23–7 with a 2.60 ERA and a league-leading 22 complete games. The 1957 Cy Young Award winner, he led the NL in strikeouts four straight seasons early in his career. Spahn also led the league in victories eight times, complete games nine times, and ERA twice. His 63 shutouts are the most by an NL left-hander, and his 5,246 innings represent the NL record. In 1960, at the age of 39, he pitched his first no-hitter and followed it in 1961 with another at age 40. Among other things, Spahn also knew how to use the bat. He hit 35 career home runs, the NL record.

Wilver Dornel Stargell

Coach
Braves: 1986–88
Major leagues: 1962–82
Elected: 1988
Birthplace: Earlsboro, Oklahoma
B: March 6, 1940
Batted left; threw left

	G	AB	H	BA	RBI	R	2B	3B	HR	SA	SB
Career	2,360	7,927	2,232	.282	1,540	1,195	423	55	475	.529	17

Willie Stargell never played for the Braves, but his influence in developing some of the team's young hitting stars of the early 1990s played a big role in the club's success during that period. Brought to Atlanta as a major league coach by his former Pittsburgh manager, Chuck Tanner, Stargell became an inspirational hitting instructor in the Braves' farm system after Tanner was fired in 1988. Stargell played his entire 21-year career for the Pirates, twice leading the league in home runs and sparking the Bucs to six division titles and World Series championships in 1971 and '79. The slugging first baseman/outfielder swept three MVP awards in '79, tying with Keith Hernandez for the regular season honor and winning it in both the playoffs and Series.

Charles Dillon Stengel

Outfielder–manager
Braves: 1924–25, 1941–43; **Bees:** 1938–40
Major leagues: 1912–25
Elected: 1966
Birthplace: Kansas City, Missouri
B: July 30, 1889
D: September 29, 1975
Batted left; threw left

	G	AB	H	BA	RBI	R	2B	3B	HR	SA	SB
Braves	143	474	130	.274	41	57	20	6	5	.373	13
Career	1,277	4,288	1,219	.284	535	575	182	89	60	.410	131

	G	W	L	Pct
Braves, Bees	870	373	491	.429
Career	3,766	1,905	1,842	.508

One of the most fabled names in baseball history, Casey Stengel played for the Braves and managed the club as both the Braves and the Bees. However, he had little success at either effort in Boston. An outfielder with little power or speed, Stengel still managed to play 14 seasons in the majors, the last two with the Braves. It was as a manager, though, that he made the Hall of Fame—in spite of his six seasons in Boston. From 1938 through 1943, Boston had only one winning record under Stengel and never finished higher than fifth. He did, of course, go on to much greater things with the Yankees. With a considerably stronger supporting cast, he took the Yankees to 10 AL pennants and seven World Series championships in 12 years from 1949 through 1960.

Edward Augustine Walsh

Pitcher
Braves: 1917
Major leagues: 1904–17
Elected: 1946
Birthplace: Plains, Pennsylvania
B: May 14, 1881
D: May 26, 1959
Batted right; threw right

	W	L	Pct	ERA	G	CG	IP	H	BB	SO	ShO
Braves	0	1	.000	3.50	4	1	18	22	9	4	0
Career	195	126	.607	1.82	430	250	2,964	2,346	617	1,736	57

Regarded as the greatest spitball pitcher of all time because of his record low 1.82 lifetime ERA, Ed Walsh pitched all but his final four games for the Chicago White Sox. His arm gave out in 1913, and after repeated failed comebacks with Chicago, he made one final, futile bid to recover with the Braves in 1917. In the early 1900s, Walsh was as dominating for an extended period of time as any pitcher has ever been. From 1906 through 1912, he averaged 24 victories per season, going a lusty 40–15 in 1908. His ERA during that span was 1.88 or better five times and never strayed above 2.22. He led the AL in innings four times, including a post-1900 record 464 in 1908. In 1910 he was 18–20 for a sixth-place team and earned the distinction of being the only pitcher to lead the league in losses and ERA (1.26).

Note: Ed Walsh's middle name is incorrect on the Hall of Fame plaque.

Lloyd James Waner

Center fielder
Braves: 1941
Major leagues: 1927–42, 1944–45
Elected: 1967
Birthplace: Harrah, Oklahoma
B: March 16, 1906
D: July 22, 1982
Batted left; threw right

	G	AB	H	BA	RBI	R	2B	3B	HR	SA	SB
Braves	19	51	21	.412	4	7	1	0	0	.431	1
Career	1,993	7,772	2,459	.316	598	1,201	281	118	27	.393	67

Lloyd Waner spent most of his 18-year career with Pittsburgh playing in the same outfield as his older brother Paul from 1927 through 1940. Lloyd was a Brave for barely a month late in his career. The Pirates traded him to Boston on May 7, 1941. He managed to get into 19 games before the Braves turned around and shipped him to Cincinnati on June 12. Known as "Little Poison," the younger Waner was a speedy singles hitter, while his brother, who also spent a short time with Boston, had more power and was known as "Big Poison." Lloyd had a rookie record 223 hits in 1927, and 198 of them were singles, a major league record. He batted .300 or better in his first six seasons and 10 of his first 12. He covered enough ground to lead the league's outfielders in putouts four times.

Paul Glee Waner

Right fielder
Braves: 1941–42
Major leagues: 1926–45
Elected: 1952
Birthplace: Harrah, Oklahoma
B: April 16, 1903
D: August 29, 1965
Batted left; threw left

	G	AB	H	BA	RBI	R	2B	3B	HR	SA	SB
Braves	209	627	168	.268	85	83	27	3	3	.335	3
Career	2,549	9,459	3,152	.333	1,309	1,627	605	191	113	.473	104

The Waners didn't take long to make an impression. Paul, "Big Poison," broke into the majors in 1926, the year before Lloyd. And whereas Lloyd left his rookie signature with 223 hits in 1927, Paul led the league in triples (22) and on-base percentage (.413) as a freshman and was fifth in batting average (.336). He didn't slack off either, winning the batting title as a sophomore and two more times in his career en route to the elite 3,000-hit club. He had 12 consecutive .300 seasons and eight years of 200 or more hits. In 1927 his career-best and league-leading .380 average and 131 RBIs helped the Pirates into the World Series and earned Waner the National League MVP honors. He was at the end of the line when he joined the Braves but did get his 3,000th hit with Boston in 1942.

John Montgomery Ward

President
Braves: 1912
Major leagues: 1878–94
Elected: 1964
Birthplace: Bellefonte, Pennsylvania
B: March 3, 1860
D: March 4, 1925
Batted left; threw right

	W	L	Pct	G	GS	CG	SHO	IP	H	BB	SO	ERA	SV
Career	164	102	.617	292	261	244	24	2,461	2,317	253	920	2.10	3

	G	AB	H	BA	RBI	R	2B	3B	HR	SA	SB
Career	1,825	7,647	2,105	.275	867	1,408	231	96	26	.341	540

Like Christy Mathewson, John "Monte" Ward never played for the Braves but served the franchise as president—if only for a few months. Ward was a partner in purchasing the team in late 1911 and was president until resigning July 31, 1912. He was one of the finest and most versatile players in the early years of the National League. Originally a pitcher for Providence, he led the league in ERA (1.51) as an 18-year-old rookie and in wins (47) in his second season. In 1884 an arm injury forced him to abandon pitching, but he continued playing for another decade with New York and Brooklyn. He led the league's shortstops in fielding (.919) in 1887 and led the league in stolen bases in 1887 (111) and 1892 (88). Ward also was a player-manager his last five seasons. He's the only Hall of Famer to win more than 150 games as a pitcher and collect more than 2,000 hits.

James Hoyt Wilhelm

JAMES HOYT WILHELM
NEW YORK N.L. 1952-1956 ST. LOUIS N.L. 1957
CLEVELAND A.L. 1957-1958 BALTIMORE A.L. 1958-1962
CHICAGO A.L. 1963-1968 CALIFORNIA A.L. 1969
ATLANTA N.L. 1969-1970, 1971 CHICAGO N.L. 1970
LOS ANGELES N.L. 1971-1972
BASEBALL'S PREMIER RELIEF PITCHER. USED KNUCKLE
BALL TO WIN 143 GAMES (A RECORD 124 IN RELIEF)
AND AMASSED 227 SAVES OVER 21-YEAR CAREER.
NO-HIT YANKEES ON SEPT. 20, 1958 IN INFREQUENT
START FOR ORIOLES. PITCHED IN RECORD 1070
GAMES WITH LIFETIME ERA OF 2.52.

Pitcher
Braves: 1969–71
Major leagues: 1952–72
Elected: 1985
Birthplace: Huntersville, North Carolina
B: July 26, 1923
Batted right; threw right

	W	L	Pct	ERA	G	CG	IP	H	BB	SO	ShO
Braves	8	4	.667	3.13	61	0	92	87	44	82	0
Career	143	122	.540	2.52	1,070	20	2,254	1,757	778	1,610	5

Hoyt Wilhelm, who pitched in more games than anyone else in big league history, played a significant role in securing the Braves' first postseason appearance in Atlanta. In a heated pennant race in 1969, the Braves purchased the veteran knuckleball reliever, then 46 years old, from California on September 8. He couldn't have been more effective, appearing in eight games, going 2–0 with four saves and an 0.75 ERA. Wilhelm made his last appearance at age 48 for the Dodgers. He didn't debut in the majors until he was 28, because of service in World War II, and he hit a home run in his first at bat—the only one he ever hit. He popularized the knuckleball like no one before him and was the first relief pitcher to be inducted into the Hall of Fame.

Victor Gazaway Willis

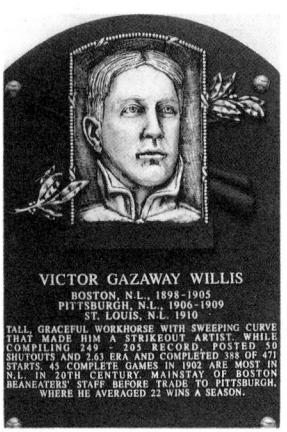

VICTOR GAZAWAY WILLIS
BOSTON, N.L. 1898-1905
PITTSBURGH, N.L. 1906-1909
ST. LOUIS, N.L. 1910
TALL, GRACEFUL WORKHORSE WITH SWEEPING CURVE
THAT MADE HIM A STRIKEOUT ARTIST. WHILE
COMPILING 249 - 205 RECORD, POSTED 50
SHUTOUTS AND 2.63 ERA AND COMPLETED 388 OF 471
STARTS. 45 COMPLETE GAMES IN 1902 ARE MOST IN
N.L. IN 20TH CENTURY. MAINSTAY OF BOSTON
BEANEATERS' STAFF BEFORE TRADE TO PITTSBURGH,
WHERE HE AVERAGED 22 WINS A SEASON.

Pitcher
Beaneaters: 1898–1905
Major leagues: 1898–1910
Elected: 1995
Birthplace: Cecil County, Maryland
B: April 12, 1876
D: August 3, 1947
Batted right; threw right

	W	L	Pct	ERA	G	CG	IP	H	BB	SO	ShO
Beaneaters	151	147	.507	2.82	320	268	2,575	2,386	854	1,161	26
Career	249	205	.548	2.63	513	388	3,996	3,621	1,212	1,651	50

Vic Willis was one of the earliest stars in franchise history, yet he's the most recent Brave—actually a Beaneater—to be elected to the Hall of Fame. The right-hander who holds the modern National League record for complete games (45 in 1902) and losses (29 in 1905) in a season was enshrined by the Veterans Committee in 1995. Ten years earlier, he earned enough votes for induction but had to be passed over because his vote total was third highest among the candidates and the Veterans Committee was limited to two selections (Enos Slaughter and Arky Vaughn). As a 22-year-old rookie in 1898, Willis was 25–13 for the pennant-winning Beaneaters. He had seven more 20-win seasons, three with Boston. In 1899 he pitched the second no-hitter in franchise history, beating Washington, 7–1.

George Wright

GEORGE WRIGHT
STAR OF BASEBALL'S FIRST
PROFESSIONAL TEAM, THE
CINCINNATI RED STOCKINGS OF 1869.
GREAT SHORTSTOP AND CAPTAIN OF
CHAMPION BOSTONS IN NATIONAL
LEAGUE'S PIONEER YEARS.

Shortstop
Red Stockings: 1876–78, 1880–81
Major leagues: 1876–82
Elected: 1937
Birthplace: Yonkers, New York
B: January 28, 1847
D: August 21, 1937
Batted right; threw right

	G	AB	H	BA	RBI	R	2B	3B	HR	SA	SB
Red Stockings	198	921	246	.267	81	171	38	8	1	.329	
Career	329	1,494	383	.256	132	264	54	20	2	.323	

The Wright brothers weren't to baseball what another couple of Wrights were to manned flight, but they were close. George, the younger brother of Harry, played shortstop for the 1869 Cincinnati Red Stockings, the first team composed entirely of paid players. The Red Stockings, organized by Harry Wright, moved to Boston in 1871 and became part of the new National Association, the predecessor to the National League. George was the first player to come to bat in the NL in 1876, and he grounded out to short. He batted .299 for Harry's team, which finished fourth in the league. The Wrights' Red Stockings won the next two NL pennants, though. George was the first shortstop to play beyond the baseline and was regarded as an excellent fielder.

William Henry Wright

HARRY WRIGHT
MANAGER AND CENTERFIELDER OF FAMOUS
CINCINNATI RED STOCKINGS, UNDEFEATED
IN 69 GAMES IN 1869-1870. FIRST MANAGER
TO WIN FOUR STRAIGHT PENNANTS WITH
BOSTON NATIONAL ASSOCIATION 1872-73-74-
75. BROTHER OF GEORGE WRIGHT. ALSO IN
HALL OF FAME. SPONSORED FIRST BASEBALL
TOUR TO ENGLAND IN 1876. INTRODUCED
KNICKER UNIFORMS. HIT 7 HOME RUNS IN
GAME AT NEWPORT, KY. IN 1867.

Outfielder–manager
Red Stockings: 1876–81
Major leagues: 1876–77
Elected: 1953
Birthplace: Sheffield, England
B: January 10, 1835
D: October 3, 1895
Batted right; threw right

	G	W	L	Pct
Red Stockings	444	254	187	.572
Career	2,145	1,225	885	.581

	W	L	Pct	ERA	G	CG	IP	H	BB	SO	ShO
Rustlers	4	5	.444	3.71	11	8	80	83	15	35	2
Career	511	316	.618	2.63	906	749	7,354	7,092	1,219	2,800	76

Known as the "Father of Professional Baseball," Harry Wright organized the 1869 Cincinnati Red Stockings, the first completely professional team. He moved that team to Boston two years later to join the new National Association. And it is that club to which the Atlanta Braves trace their roots, making them the only franchise to field a team every season of professional league baseball. Harry managed the Red Stockings to four pennants in the National Association and to National League flags in 1877 and '78. Among other things, Wright is credited with introducing the knicker-style pants still worn today, and he patented the first scorecard. An innovator, he suggested several changes in the game that were later made. They included overhand pitching, a cork-centered ball, and pregame practice. He had a 23-year managerial career, the last 10 with the Phillies.

It hardly seems proper that the pitcher who won more games than anyone else in history would end his career with a team named the Rustlers. But that's the nickname the franchise went by in 1911. The Rustlers acquired 44-year-old Cy Young from Cleveland for the waiver price in July. The Rustlers were en route to an eighth-place finish and the second-worst winning percentage (.291) in franchise history. Young made 11 starts and recorded the last four of his record 511 career victories. That total is the reason why the annual award for pitching excellence in each league is named after Young, who had 16 20-victory seasons, including 14 in a row, and five 30-win seasons. His career ERA was 2.63. He led his league in fewest walks and most strikeouts 11 times and averaged just 1.5 walks per nine innings. Young spent most of his 22-year career with the Cleveland Spiders and the Boston Red Sox.

Denton True Young

Pitcher
Rustlers: 1911
Major leagues: 1890–1911
Elected: 1937
Birthplace: Gilmore, Ohio
B: March 29, 1867
D: November 4, 1955
Batted right; threw right

Great Moments

The most memorable regular-season moments in Braves history have come in virtually all descriptions, from great hitting and pitching feats to pennant clinchers, the longest game ever played, and even the ruination of the most splendid game ever pitched.

For sure, there has been no shortage of highlights in the twisted but compelling history of America's oldest continuously operating professional sports franchise.

At the top of the list, of course, is Hank Aaron's 715th home run, an event of such magnitude that it transcended sports to rate among the epic achievements of the 20th century.

Though nothing else in franchise history can possibly rival in significance Aaron's passing of Babe Ruth on the all-time home run list, there have been many other events that nevertheless rank with the grandest moments baseball has produced since the birth of the National League in 1876.

This chapter includes the accounts of several of those moments, as well as box scores of many of the other most memorable regular-season games in Braves history.

Aaron Passes The Babe

The morning of April 8, 1974, dawned like almost any other in Atlanta. The bald rock of Stone Mountain hovered to the east, and the early-morning aroma of bacon and eggs emanated from the greasy spoons. But there was one big difference this Monday morning. As commuters hurried toward their offices, most shared the same thought: Will he do it tonight?

The Braves were opening their home season that evening at Atlanta Stadium in a game that played merely a supporting role to the grandest drama ever to unfold in baseball history. At the top of the all-time home run list, Hank Aaron, by virtue of his 714th career homer April 4 at Cincinnati, was perched in a tie with the most legendary hero in sports history, George Herman Ruth.

One more snap of Aaron's fabled wrists could bring "The Hammer's" glorious yet sometimes painful pursuit of "The Babe's" once-untouchable record to an end this evening. The world had been waiting and watching for months as the buildup reached gargantuan proportions. All eyes and ears were now focused on Atlanta for that one swing that would propel one of the most talented yet unassuming men ever to play the game into instant immortality.

The promotional minds in the Braves' front office made sure no one would underestimate the magnitude of the occasion. A huge outline of the United States filled with a pseudo American flag adorned the center-field grass. The 45-minute pregame ceremony turned into an event of its own with balloons, speeches, a band, a choir, and Pearl Bailey, who sang the national anthem. Aaron's parents were there, along with Sammy Davis, Jr., Georgia governor Jimmy Carter, and Atlanta mayor Maynard Jackson.

The center of all the attention was himself escorted onto the field at 7:47 P.M. through two lines of young girls dressed in shorts and Braves T-shirts and caps and holding bats high in a ceremonial arc.

A full house of 53,775, still a stadium record, was on hand, along with the visiting Los Angeles Dodgers, who sent veteran left-hander Al Downing to the mound attempting to delay Aaron's mission.

The crowd's attention, along with that of a national television audience, peaked when Aaron came to the plate to lead off the second inning. And Downing drew a cascade of boos by walking Aaron on five pitches, none of which attracted a swing. It seemed the Dodgers pitcher had no intention of becoming part of history if he could possibly avoid it.

Aaron scored later in the inning, breaking Willie Mays' National League record for runs. Not bad, but it wasn't what this night was all about.

In the fourth inning, Downing had his second meeting with Aaron, and this time there was no place to hide. With Darrell Evans on first base with no outs and the Dodgers leading, 3–1, Downing finally challenged Aaron.

After throwing the first pitch in the dirt and drawing more boos, the 32-year-old Dodger delivered a high fastball. With a mean whip of the bat, his first swing of the evening, Aaron sent the specially marked ball into the Braves' bullpen in left-center, approximately 400 feet from home plate, at 9:07 P.M. Left fielder Bill Buckner made a futile attempt to intercept history, but he had no chance to reach it. The large message board in left-center flashed "715," and just like that, Hank Aaron was the all-time home run king.

No. 715 came on Monday, April 8, 1974 when Hank Aaron sent a high fastball from Los Angeles left-hander Al Downing into the left-center field bullpen at Atlanta Stadium.

Pandemonium ensued. Fireworks exploded above the center-field roof.

As Aaron circled the bases, two young men jumped out of the stands and joined him briefly between second and third before security guards escorted them off the field. When Aaron rounded third, he broke into a wide grin at the sight of his teammates waiting for him at the plate. Braves reliever Tom House, who caught No. 715 in the bullpen, raced to greet Aaron and present him the ball. The crowd roared for a full 10 minutes as Aaron was mobbed by teammates, relatives, friends, and well-wishers.

Monte Irvin, representing commissioner Bowie Kuhn, who was in Cleveland attending a meeting of the Wahoo Club, congratulated Aaron. When Irvin mentioned Kuhn, the crowd booed lustily, showing their scorn that he was the one person who'd chosen to ignore the magnitude of Aaron's objective.

"I just thank God it's all over," said Aaron, who'd had to endure months of media interviews, near-constant scrutiny, and death threats and hate mail, all of which led to his own bodyguard and the need to find temporary living quarters in Atlanta and to register under a false name at hotels on the road.

Aaron played the entire game, which the Braves won, 7–4. In the bottom of the sixth, when many of the fans had headed for home, he even paused in the dugout to take a congratulatory phone call from President Richard Nixon.

Afterward, Aaron told hundreds of reporters, "The home run wouldn't have really meant that much to me if we hadn't won the game. Five years ago, I never thought I'd be in this position, but now that I am, I'm sure glad it's over with."

April 8, 1974
Braves 7, Dodgers 4

Los Angeles	AB	R	H	RBI
Lopes, 2b	2	1	0	0
Lacy, 2b	1	0	0	0
Buckner, lf	3	0	1	0
Wynn, cf	4	0	1	2
Ferguson, c	4	0	0	0
W Crawford, df	4	1	1	0
Cey, 3b	4	0	1	1
Garvey, 1b	4	1	1	0
Russell, ss	4	0	1	0
Downing, p	1	1	1	1
Marshall, p	1	0	0	0
Joshua, ph	1	0	0	0
Hough, p	0	0	0	0
Mota, ph	1	0	0	0
Totals	34	4	7	4

Atlanta	AB	R	H	RBI
Garr, rf	3	0	0	1
Lum, 1b	5	0	0	1
Evans, 3b	4	1	0	0
H Aaron, lf	3	2	1	2
Office, cf	0	0	0	0
Baker, cf	2	1	1	0
Da Johnson, 2b	3	1	1	0
Foster, 2b	0	0	0	0
Corell, c	4	1	0	0
C Robinson, ss	0	0	0	0
Tepedino, ph	0	0	0	1
M Perez, ss	2	1	1	0
Reed, p	2	0	0	0
Oates, ph	1	0	0	1
Capra, p	0	0	0	0
Totals	29	7	4	6

E—Buckner, Cey, Russell 2, Lopes, Ferguson, LOB—Los Angeles 5, Atlanta 7. 2B—Baker, Russell, Wynn. HR—H. Aaron (2). S—Garr. SF—Garr.

Los Angeles	0	0	3	0	0	1	0	0	0—4	
Atlanta	0	1	0	4	0	2	0	0	x—7	

Los Angeles	IP	H	R	ER	BB	SO
Downing L,0-1	3	2	5	2	4	2
Marshall	3	2	2	1	1	1
Hough	2	0	0	0	2	1

Atlanta	IP	H	R	ER	BB	SO
Reed W, 1-0	6	7	4	4	1	4
Capra	3	0	0	0	1	6

Save—Capra 1. WP—Reed. PB—Ferguson. T—2:27. A—53,775.

Smoltz Clinches "Worst to First"

The Braves had the worst record (65–97) in baseball in 1990. Though many observers felt they might be an improved team in 1991, no one could have foreseen the thoroughly astounding developments which unfolded that season.

No team in modern baseball history had ever gone from "worst to first"—until October 5, the next-to-last day of the 1991 season.

It was fitting that the Braves' starting pitcher for that Saturday afternoon game against Houston at Atlanta–Fulton County Stadium was John Smoltz. The dramatic turnaround the Braves were making was mirrored by the reversal Smoltz forged in the second half of the season. After a miserable first half in which he was 2–11 with a 5.16 ERA, the 24-year-old right-hander had gone 11–2 since the All-Star break and was trying to get his record over .500 in his last start of the year.

The Braves entered the October 5 game riding a seven-game winning streak that had given them a one-game lead over Los Angeles with two games remaining on the schedule for both clubs. The Dodgers were at Candlestick Park to play the Giants.

With a capacity crowd on hand in Atlanta, Smoltz held Houston scoreless through the first three innings while the Braves built a 4–0 lead.

Smoltz allowed Houston back in the game in the fourth with two runs to make it 4–2.

In the fifth, Ron Gant hit a solo home run, his 32nd of the season, to complete the afternoon's scoring. Meanwhile, Smoltz settled into a groove. He gave up a bunt single to Kenny Lofton leading off the fifth but picked off Lofton and allowed just one other base runner the remainder of the game.

The Braves and their fans were able to celebrate the improbable 1991 division title when John Smoltz beat Houston, 5–2, on the next-to-last day of the season, and moments later, the Dodgers lost to the Giants.

With the Braves holding a 5–2 advantage and Smoltz cruising, the anticipation of a most unlikely division title began mounting in the stadium, as well as throughout Atlanta and the South where millions of fans were following the culmination of this tomahawk-chopping season on television and radio. At the same time, everyone was being kept aware that the Dodgers were losing, 4–0, at San Francisco in a game that was nearing an end, too. A clinching party was imminent.

With two outs and one on in the ninth, Houston shortstop Andujar Cedeno hit a routine fly ball to David Justice in right field. The Braves had their eighth straight victory and were guaranteed at least a tie for the division title.

Justice thrust his left arm and index finger in the air, and

Greg Olson scampered from behind the plate and leaped into Smoltz's arms. The team began celebrating, then gathered in the middle of the field to watch the end of the Dodgers game on the center-field television screen. Just moments later, Eddie Murray grounded out, eliminating the Dodgers and sending the Braves to the playoffs for the first time since 1982.

The players immediately erupted in a full-scale celebration, and so did a stadium full of wildly chopping and chanting fans, who'd remained to bask in the glory of the most improbable moment in franchise history. After three consecutive last-place finishes and six straight seasons as baseball's laughingstock, the Braves suddenly were division champs.

October 5, 1991
Braves 5, Houston 2

Houston	AB	R	H	RBI
Lofton, cf	4	0	1	0
Finley, rf	4	0	1	0
Biggio, c	4	0	0	0
Bagwell, 1b	4	1	2	0
Gonzalez, lf	4	0	1	0
Caminiti, 3b	4	0	0	0
Cedeno, ss	4	1	2	1
Candaele, 2b	3	0	1	1
Portugal, p	1	0	0	0
Henry, p	0	0	0	0
Young, ph	1	0	0	0
Gardner, p	0	0	0	0
Ortiz, ph	1	0	0	0
Mallicoat, p	0	0	0	0
Totals	**34**	**2**	**8**	**2**

Braves	AB	R	H	RBI
L. Smith, lf	4	1	2	1
Mitchell, lf	0	0	0	0
Lemke, 2b	4	1	1	0
Pendleton, 3b	2	0	1	1
Justice, rf	4	0	0	0
Gant, cf	3	2	2	2
Bream, 1b	3	0	1	0
Olson, c	4	0	0	0
Belliard, ss	4	1	1	0
Smoltz, p	2	0	0	0
Totals	**30**	**5**	**8**	**4**

Houston	0	0	0	2	0	0	0	0	0—2
Braves	2	1	1	0	1	0	0	0	x—5

E—Cedeno 2. DP—Houston 2. LOB—Houston 5, Atlanta 6. 2B—Cedeno, L. Smith. HR—Gant (32). S—Smoltz. SF—Gant.

Houston	IP	H	R	ER	BB	SO
Portugal (L, 10–12)	2	7	4	3	2	0
Henry	1	0	0	0	0	0
Gardner	3	1	1	1	0	1
Mallicoat	2	0	0	0	1	2

Atlanta	IP	H	R	ER	BB	SO
Smoltz (W, 14–13)	9	8	2	2	0	2

Portugal pitched to 3 batters in 3rd.

T—2:17. A—44,994. Umpires—Williams, Marsh, Wendelstedt, Pulli.

The Longest Game Ever Played

One of the most fascinating games in major league history occurred in Boston on May 1, 1920, at Braves Field. The combatants on this cold, damp day were the Braves and the visiting Brooklyn Robins, ancestors of the Dodgers. At the end of the day, the two teams had played 26 innings, and the game was still tied, 1–1. It remains the longest game—by innings—in major league history.

In the next day's *Boston Post*, the game story began, "From 3 o'clock until nearly 7 in the evening, and until the fast gathering gloom made further play impossible, George Stallings' men, with big Joe Oeschger pitching the grandest battle of his career, held in check the powerful sluggers from the City of Churches and it was not until the end of the 26th inning, when the lights were appearing in the windows across the Charles, that Umpire McCormick called the game with both sides boasting a single run."

Brooklyn, headed for the pennant, got its run in the fifth inning when Ernie Krueger walked, advanced on an infield out, and scored on a single by Ivy Olson. Boston, on its way to seventh place in Stallings' last season as manager, tied the game in the sixth when Walton Cruise tripled and scored on a single by Tony Boeckel.

The story of the day, however, was the pitching of Oeschger and Brooklyn's Leon Cadore, both of whom worked the entire 26 innings.

Oeschger, 28, was a hard-throwing right-hander who was in his first full season with Boston. Cadore, 29, also was right-handed. More of a finesse pitcher, he was in the midst of the

best of his 10 big league seasons. Both men were considered big and strong for their era. Oeschger was 6–0, 190, and Cadore was 6–1, 190.

Braves right-hander Joe Oeschger held Brooklyn scoreless for the last 21 innings of a 1–1, 26-inning tie on May 1, 1920 in the longest game ever played.

By holding Brooklyn scoreless over the last 21 innings, Oeschger set a major league record that still stands. He retired the Robins in order in 16 of the 26 innings, giving up just nine hits and four walks while striking out seven. He didn't allow a single extra-base hit.

The Braves touched Cadore for 15 hits, including doubles by Oeschger and Rabbit Maranville as well as Cruise's triple. Cadore struck out seven and issued five walks.

The game, called because of darkness, lasted just three hours and 50 minutes, and only three balls were used.

Not surprisingly, both pitchers later complained of "dead" arms. Oeschger, who pitched a 20-inning tie the year before with Philadelphia, didn't seem to suffer any long-term effects, though. He won 15 games in 1920 and had a career-high 20 wins the next season when he tied for the league lead in shutouts (3). Cadore, however, may have been a little worse for the wear. Like Oeschger, he won 15 games in 1920 but slipped to 13 in 1921 and never won in double figures again.

May 1, 1920
Boston 1, Brooklyn 1

Brooklyn	AB	H	O	A	E
Olson, 2b	10	1	6	9	1
Neis, rf	10	1	6	9	1
Johnston, 3b	10	2	3	1	0
Wheat, lf	9	2	3	0	0
Myers, cf	2	1	2	0	0
Hood, cf	6	1	8	1	0
Koney, 1b	9	1	30	1	0
Ward, ss	10	0	5	3	1
Krueger, c	2	0	4	3	0
Elliott, c	7	0	7	3	0
Cadore, p	10	0	1	10	0
Totals	85	9	78	34	2

Boston	AB	H	O	A	E
Powell, cf	7	1	8	0	0
Pick, 2b	11	0	5	10	2
Mann, lf	10	2	6	0	0
Cruise, rf	9	1	4	0	0
Holke, 1b	10	2	43	1	0
Boeckel, 3b	11	3	1	7	0
Maranville, ss	10	3	1	9	0
O'Neil, c	2	0	4	3	0
*Christenbury	1	1	0	0	0
Gowdy, c	6	1	6	1	0
Oeschger, p	3	1	0	11	0
Totals	86	15	79	42	2

*Batted for O'Neil in ninth.

Brooklyn—
Boston
0 0 0 0 1 0 0 0 0 0 0 0 0 0 0 0 0 0 0 0 0 0 0 0 0 0—1
0 0 0 0 0 1 0 0 0 0 0 0 0 0 0 0 0 0 0 0 0 0 0 0 0 0—1

Called on account of darkness.

Two-base hits—Maranville, Oeschger. Three-base hit—Cruise. Stolen bases—Myers, Hood. Double plays—Olson and Konetchy: Oeschger, Gowdy, Holke and Gowdy. Bases on balls—Off Cadore 5, off Oeschger 4. Struck out—By Cadore 6, by Oeschger 7. Wild pitch—Oeschger.

Adcock Slugs Way to All-Time Record

Only 12 men in history have hit four home runs in the same game. Remarkably, three of them played for the Braves—one in each city the team has called home.

In 1894, Boston's Bobby Lowe became the first player to homer four times in a game. Bob Horner did it for Atlanta in 1986. And in between those two, Milwaukee's Joe Adcock put on a 1954 slugging display the likes of which had never been seen before or equaled since.

Playing at Brooklyn's Ebbets Field, a park in which Adcock thrived to an incredible extent throughout his career, the Braves' first baseman hit four home runs and a double to set what still ranks as the single-game major league record for total bases (18).

Entering that July 31 game, Adcock was hitting .442 for the year against Dodgers pitching and .467 at Ebbets Field. The previous evening, he had a single, double, and home run. But that was child's play compared to what he would do to the Dodgers on a hot Saturday afternoon.

Facing right-hander Don Newcombe in the second, Adcock led off the inning with a home run to left. He did it with a bat he'd borrowed from teammate Charlie White after breaking his the previous night.

In the fourth inning against right-handed reliever Erv Palica, Adcock doubled and later scored as the Braves took a 6–1 lead.

With Palica still pitching in the fifth, Adcock smashed a three-run homer into the upper deck in left-center, making it 9–1.

In the seventh inning, Adcock victimized right-hander Pete Wojey with a two-run homer to left, bringing the score to 11–2.

Finally, with left-hander Johnny Podres pitching in the ninth, Adcock unloaded with his fourth home run, this one to left-center, making the score 13–6. The final was 15–7.

At the time, Adcock was just the seventh man to hit four homers in a game and only the fifth to do so in nine innings.

But what he did went far beyond that. He saw just seven pitches in the five at bats, which produced four home runs and a double. The four homers came against four different pitchers. Then 26 years old, Adcock had seven RBIs, scored five times, and, of course, compiled a record 18 total bases.

Joe Adcock put his home run trot to good use July 31, 1954 when he set the major league total base record of 18 with four home runs and a double.

July 31, 1954
Braves 15, Dodgers 7

Milwaukee	AB	H	O	A
Bruton, cf	6	4	4	0
O'Connell, 2b	5	0	4	4
Mathews, 3b	4	2	3	2
Aaron, lf	5	2	0	0
Adcock, 1b	5	5	11	0
Pafko, rf	4	3	0	0
Pendleton, rf	1	0	0	0
Logan, ss	2	1	1	1
Smalley, ss	2	1	0	1
Crandall, c	4	0	2	1
Calderone, c	1	1	2	0
Wilson, p	1	0	0	0
Burdette, p	3	0	0	4
Buhl, p	0	0	0	0
Jolly, p	1	0	0	0
Totals	**44**	**19**	**27**	**13**

Brooklyn	AB	H	O	A
Gilliam, 2b	4	4	3	1
Reese, ss	3	1	1	2
Zimmer, ss	1	0	1	1
Snider, cf	4	1	0	0
Shuba, lf	1	0	0	0
Hodges, 1b	5	1	7	0
Amoros, lf	5	3	6	0
Robinson, 3b	0	0	0	0
Hoak, 3b	2	1	0	1
Furillo, rf	5	2	3	0
Walker, c	5	1	6	1
Newcombe, p	0	0	0	0
Labine, p	0	0	0	0
a-Moryn	1	0	0	0
Palica, p	0	0	0	0
Wojey, p	1	0	0	1
b-Podres, p	2	2	0	1
Totals	**39**	**16**	**27**	**8**

Milwaukee	1	3	2	0	3	0	3	0	3—15
Brooklyn	1	0	0	0	0	1	0	4	1— 7

Pitchers	IP	H	R	ER	BB	SO
Wilson	1*	5	1	1	0	0
Burdette (Winner 10–11)	6⅓	8	5	5	2	3
Buhl	0†	2	0	0	0	0
Jolly	1⅔	1	1	1	1	1
Newcombe (Loser 6–6)	1‡	4	4	4	0	0
Labine	1	1	0	0	0	0
Palica	2⅓	5	5	5	2	1
Wojey	2⅔	4	3	3	0	3
Podres	2	5	3	2	0	1

*Pitched to three batters in second.
†Pitched in two batters in eighth.
‡Pitched to three batters in second.

a-Grounded into a double play for Labine in second.
b-Singled for Wojey in seventh.
R—Mathews 3, Aaron 2, Adcock 5, Pafko 2, Pendleton, Logan, Smalley, Gilliam, Hodges, Amoros 2, Hoak, Walker, Furillo. E—Hoak. RBI—Mathews 2, Snider, Adcock 7, Logan, Bruton, Pafko 2. Hoak 2, Hodges, Furillo, Walker 2. 2B—Gilliam, Pafko, Bruton 3, Amoros, Adcock, Aaron. 3B—Amores. HR—Mathews 2, Adcock 4, Hoak, Pafko, Hodges, Walker. SH—O'Connell. SF—Hoak. DP—Mathews, O'Connell and Adcock; O'Connell, Logan and Adcock; Zimmer, Gilliam and Hodges. LOB—Milwaukee 5, Brooklyn 10. HP—Wilson (Robinson). WP—Podres. U—Boggess, Engeln, Stewart and Barlick. T—2:53. Attendance—12,263.

Bobby Lowe's Four Home Runs
May 30, 1894

Bostons	AB	R	B	TB	PO	A	E
Lowe, 2b	6	4	5	17	2	2	0
Long, ss	3	5	2	6	2	4	1
Duffy, cf	5	0	1	1	1	0	0
McCarthy, lf	6	2	3	4	3	0	0
Nash, 3b	4	3	3	3	1	1	0
Tucker, 1b	2	1	0	0	10	2	0
Bannon, rf	4	2	2	3	1	0	0
Ryan, c	5	2	2	3	5	0	0
Nichols, p	5	1	1	1	2	3	0
Totals	**40**	**20**	**19**	**38**	**27**	**12**	**1**

Cincinnatis	AB	R	B	TB	PO	A	E
Hoy, cf	6	1	1	1	3	0	0
McCarthy, 1b	5	2	3	3	9	1	1
Latham, 3b	4	3	3	5	0	3	2
Holliday, lf	4	3	2	8	1	0	0
McPhee, 2b	5	0	2	2	4	4	0
Vaughn, c	4	1	2	5	3	5	1
Canavan, rf	5	1	1	4	2	0	0
Smith, ss	5	0	1	2	1	4	1
Chamberlain, p	5	0	1	2	1	1	0
Totals	**43**	**11**	**16**	**32**	**24**	**18**	**5**

Innings	1	2	3	4	5	6	7	8	9
Bostons	2	0	9	0	1	5	2	1	x—20
Cincinnatis	2	0	0	0	4	0	0	0	5—11

Earned runs—Bostons 7, Cincinnatis 10. Two-base hits—Long, Bannon, Ryan, McCarthy, Latham 2. Smith, Chamberlain. Home runs—Lowe 4, Long, Holliday 2, Canavan, Vaughn. Sacrifice hit—Duffy. Stolen bases—Long 2, Duffy, Nash, Latham. First base on balls—Long 2, Nash 2, Tucker 3, Bannon, Latham, Holliday. First base on errors—Bostons 4, Cincinnatis 1. Struck out—Bannon, McCarthy, Ryan, Vaughn, Chamberlain, McPhee. Passed ball—Ryan. Wild pitch—Chamberlain. Hit by pitched ball—Long, Tucker. Time—2h.16m. Umpire—Swartwood.

Bob Horner's Four Home Runs
July 6, 1986

Montreal	AB	R	H	RBI
Webster, lf	6	2	5	3
Wright, cf	6	1	2	1
Dawson, rf	6	1	2	2
Brooks, ss	5	0	2	0
Wallach, 3b	2	1	0	0
Galarraga, 1b	2	0	0	0
Krenchicki, 1b	1	0	1	0
Reardon, p	0	0	0	0
Fitzgerald, c	3	3	1	2
Newman, 2b	4	3	2	2
McGaffigan, p	2	0	1	1
Burke, p	1	0	0	0
Law, 1b	1	0	0	0
Totals	**39**	**11**	**16**	**11**

Atlanta	AB	R	H	RBI
Moreno, rf	4	0	1	0
Simmons, 3b	1	0	0	0
Oberkfell, 3b	5	1	4	1
Murphy, cf	5	0	0	0
Horner, 1b	5	4	4	6
Griffey, lf	5	0	2	1
A Thomas, ss	4	0	1	0
Virgil, c	4	1	1	0
Hubbard, 2b	3	1	1	0
Chambliss, ph	0	0	0	0
Garber, p	0	0	0	0
Z Smith, p	1	0	0	0
Dedmon, p	0	1	0	0
Sample, ph	1	0	0	0
Assenmacher, p	0	0	0	0
Ramirez, rf	1	0	0	0
Totals	**39**	**8**	**14**	**8**

Montreal	0	0	1	3	6	0	1	0	0—11
Atlanta	0	1	0	1	5	0	0	0	1— 8

Game Winning RBI—Webster (5).
E—Horner, Wallach. DP—Montreal 2, Atlanta 2. LOB—Montreal 10, Atlanta 6. 2B—Dawson, Webster, Fitzgerald, Wright, Brooks, Virgil, Hubbard, Krenchicki. HR—Horner 4 (17), Newman (1), Dawson (13), Webster (5). SB—Webster (22), Griffey (1). S—McGaffigan, Dedmon, Krenchicki.

Montreal	IP	H	R	ER	BB	SO
McGaffigan	4⅔	8	7	4	0	2
Burke W, 6-2	2⅔	4	0	0	1	1
Reardon	1⅔	2	1	1	0	1

Atlanta	IP	H	R	ER	BB	SO
Z Smith L, 7-9	4	9	8	8	2	3
Dedmon	2	4	2	2	1	2
Assenmacher	2	2	1	1	2	1
Garber	1	1	0	0	0	0

Z Smith pitched to 4 batters in the 5th.
HBP—Galarraga by Dedmon, Fitzgerald by Dedmon. PB—Virgil.
Umpires—Home, Poncino; First, Gregg; Second, Davis; Third, Harvey.
T—3:06. A—18,153.

Haddix's Perfection Ruined In 13th

It is one of the most celebrated games in history and yet one of the most bizarre, too.

On May 26, 1959, at Milwaukee County Stadium, Pittsburgh left-hander Harvey Haddix was as perfect as a pitcher can be, not for nine innings, but for 12. But he still lost in the 13th to the Braves in one of the strangest endings a baseball game has ever known.

The 33-year-old Haddix, nicknamed "The Kitten," was but 5–9, 170 pounds, but on this night, at least, he was all heart and left arm. He entered the game with a 3–2 record and was feeling ill. The opposing Braves were coming off two straight pennants and were again entrenched in first place.

Haddix retired the powerful Milwaukee lineup in order for the first 12 innings, 36 men up and 36 down. No other pitcher in modern National League history had ever pitched a perfect game for nine innings at that time, let alone 12.

Meanwhile, the Pirates had plenty of scoring opportunities against Lou Burdette but couldn't cash in before the 19,194 fans who braved threatening weather and were rewarded by witnessing history.

In the bottom of the 13th, Felix Mantilla led off for Milwaukee by hitting a routine grounder to third. Pittsburgh's Don Hoak fielded it cleanly but threw low to first where Rocky Nelson failed to scoop it out of the dirt, ending the perfect game. Eddie Mathews sacrificed Mantilla to second, then Haddix walked Hank Aaron intentionally to set up a double play with slow-footed Joe Adcock coming to the plate.

However, Adcock spoiled the strategy and ruined Haddix's masterpiece by smashing a ball over the right-center fence. The game was over, but the confusion was just beginning.

Many fans left thinking the score was 3–0. However, Aaron was unaware that Adcock's drive had left the park. Af-

The bizarre end to Harvey Haddix's 12 perfect innings came when Joe Adcock (9) hit a "home run" but was called out for passing Hank Aaron on the bases.

ter he reached second and saw that Mantilla had scored, Aaron turned and trotted toward the dugout. Adcock kept circling the bases, and when he got to third, he was called out for "passing" Aaron. Umpire crew chief Frank Dascoli ruled that Adcock's hit was a double and that Aaron's run counted because he left the baseline voluntarily. The score, then, was 2–0. Or was it?

The next day, National League president Warren Giles ruled that since Adcock's hit was a double, Aaron could not advance beyond third. Therefore, the game went into the books as a 1–0 loss for Haddix. Burdette, who gave up 12 hits, was the winning pitcher.

For years, Haddix's superhuman effort was listed as the only perfect game of more than nine innings and the longest no-hitter in history. Now, however, because of new scoring rules, he's not listed as having pitched a no-hitter or a perfect game. The official rules, though, include a category where only Haddix is listed: "Perfect games for nine innings that were broken up in extra innings." Perhaps that's where this game belongs, for it certainly was one of a kind.

May 26, 1959
Braves 1, Pirates 0

Pittsburgh	AB	R	H	RBI
Schofield, ss	6	0	3	0
Virdon, cf	6	0	1	0
Burgess, c	5	0	0	0
Nelson, 1b	5	0	2	0
Skinner, lf	5	0	1	0
Mazeroski, 2b	5	0	1	0
Hoak, 3b	5	0	2	0
Mejias, rf	3	0	1	0
a-Stuart	1	0	0	0
Christopher, rf	1	0	0	0
Haddix, p	5	0	1	0
Totals	47	0	12	0

Milwaukee	AB	R	H	RBI
O'Brien, 2b	3	0	0	0
b-Rice	1	0	0	0
Mantilla, 2b	1	1	0	0
Mathews, 3b	4	0	0	0
Aaron, rf	4	0	0	0
Adcock, 1b	5	0	1	1
Covington, lf	4	0	0	0
Crandall, c	4	0	0	0
Pafko, cf	4	0	0	0
Logan, ss	4	0	0	0
Burdette, p	4	0	0	0
Totals	38	1	1	1

a-Flied out for Mejias in 10th;
b-Flied out for O'Brien in 10th.

Pittsburgh	0	0	0	0	0	0	0	0	0	0	0	0	0	0—0
Milwaukee	0	0	0	0	0	0	0	0	0	0	0	0	1	1—1

Two out when winning run scored.
E—Hoak. A—Pittsburgh 13, Milwaukee 21. DP—Logan and Adcock; Mathews, O'Brien, Adcock; Adcock, Logan. LOB—Pittsburgh 8, Milwaukee 1.
2B Hit—Adcock. Sacrifice—Mathews

Pitchers	IP	H	R	ER	BB	SO
Haddix (L, 3–3)	12⅔	1	2	1	0	8
Burdette (W, 8–2)	13	12	0	0	0	2

Umpires—Smith, Dascoli, Secory, Dixon.
Time—2:54. Attendance—19,194.

Cloninger Hits Two Grand Slams

The Fourth of July fireworks went off a little early in San Francisco in 1966, and Giants fans weren't too pleased with the year's display. Impressed, perhaps, but not happy.

In the first inning of the July 3 game at Candlestick Park between the Giants and the Braves, just recently transferred to Atlanta, the visitors touched starter Joe Gibbon and reliever Bob Priddy for seven runs. The most devastating blow was delivered by Braves pitcher Tony Cloninger. With two outs, the 25-year-old right-hander connected for a grand slam off Priddy.

The assault didn't stop there. When Cloninger came to bat in the fourth inning against Ray Sadecki, the bases were loaded again . . . and again he hit a grand slam. He also had a run-scoring single in the sixth inning to give him nine RBIs in the 17–3 victory before 27,002 fans. For the record, he also pitched a complete game 7-hitter, raising his record to 9–7.

Cloninger is still the only man in National League history to hit two grand slams in the same game. It wasn't necessarily a fluke, though. He had another two-home-run game earlier in the year and finished the season with five homers and 23 RBIs. He hit 11 career home runs.

Cloninger also set a major league record that day for most

RBIs in a game by a pitcher, and his nine RBIs still represent the all-time Braves single-game record. He became only the second National League pitcher (Don Newcombe was the other) to have two games with two homers in the same season, too.

A pitcher by trade, Tony Cloninger is still the only man in National League history to hit two grand slams in the same game.

July 3, 1966
Braves 17, Giants 3

Atlanta	AB	R	H	RBI
F. Alou, 1b	3	0	0	0
de la Hoz, 3b	2	0	0	0
M. Jones, cf	6	1	3	0
Aaron, rf	4	2	1	1
Geiger, rf	2	1	1	1
Carty, lf	4	3	3	1
Herrnstein, lf	1	0	0	0
Torre, c	6	2	3	3
Bolling, 2b	5	2	2	2
Woodward, ss	6	2	4	0
Menke, 3b	3	2	0	0
Cloninger, p	5	2	3	9
Totals	**47**	**17**	**20**	**17**

San Francisco	AB	R	H	RBI
J. Alou, rf	4	0	1	0
Haller, c	3	1	1	1
Mays, cf	1	1	0	0
Landrum, cf	2	0	0	0
McCovey, 1b	1	0	0	0
Dietz, c	3	0	0	0
Hart, 3b	3	0	1	0
Virgil, 3b	1	0	0	0
Gabrielson, lf	4	0	1	1
Davenport, ss	1	0	0	0
Mason, 2b	3	0	0	0
Lanier, 2b	4	0	2	0
Gibbon, p	0	0	0	0
Priddy, p	0	0	0	0
Sadecki, p	3	1	1	1
Peterson, ph	1	0	0	0
Totals	**34**	**3**	**7**	**3**

Errors—Cloninger, Hart, Lanier, Gabrielson.

Atlanta	7	1	0	5	1	0	0	1	2—17
San Francisco	0	0	0	1	1	0	0	1	0— 3

Double plays: Atlanta 1, San Francisco 1. Left on base: Atlanta 8, San Francisco 6. Two-base hits: Woodward 2, M. Jones, Geiger. Home runs: Torre (19), Cloninger 2 (4), Carty (3), Aaron (25), Sadecki (2), Haller (16). Sacrifice fly: Bolling.

Atlanta	IP	H	R	ER	BB	SO
Cloninger (W, 9–7)	9	7	3	3	2	5

San Francisco	IP	H	R	ER	BB	SO
Gibbon (L, 3–5)	⅔	5	5	5	0	0
Priddy	2	4	3	3	2	0
Sadecki	6⅓	11	9	5	2	4

Wild pitches: Cloninger, Sadecki. Attendance: 27,002. Playing time: 2:42.

The No-Hitters

Jack Stivetts pitched the first one in 1892. George Davis pitched his in the midst of a "miracle" and between classes at Harvard Law School. Jim Tobin was the first to hit a home run while pitching one. Warren Spahn waited until he was 39 years old to pitch one, then followed it with another at age 40. Kent Mercker, Mark Wohlers, and Alejandro Pena shared one. And Mercker was the first Brave to pitch one on the road.

Braves have pitched 14 no-hitters, most of which seem to have a life of their own for various reasons.

Stivetts pitched the first no-hitter in franchise history on August 5, 1892, in the midst of winning 35 games and helping Boston to the pennant. The 24-year-old right-hander, who hit a two-run, game-winning homer the day before while playing left field, issued five walks in beating Brooklyn, 11–0.

Vic Willis pitched the team's second no-hitter in just his second season in the majors. He beat Washington, 7–1, on August 7, 1899, during a season in which he led the league with five shutouts and a 2.50 ERA at the age of 23. Known as the "Delaware Peach," Willis is the only one of this group to be scored on during his no-hitter.

There have been several surprises to author no-hitters for the club, not the least of whom was Frank "Big Jeff" Pfeffer, who won just 31 games in a six-year career. In 1907, Pfeffer had only six victories, one of which was a 6–0 no-hitter against Cincinnati on May 8.

Davis pitched the fourth no-hitter in franchise history on September 9, 1914, in the midst of the "Miracle" Braves' rally from last place on July 4 to the pennant and World Series championship. Nicknamed "Iron" for his strength, Davis no-hit Philadelphia, 7–0, in the second game of a doubleheader. It was the only shutout of his career, which produced but seven wins before he was released at age 25. He finished law school and opened a practice in Buffalo.

Tom Hughes was used more as a reliever than as a starter in his nine-year career, but he no-hit Pittsburgh, 2–0, on June 16, 1916. The 32-year-old right-hander led the league in winning percentage (16–3, .842) that year but suffered a broken hand that cut short his season.

Phil Niekro wasn't the first Brave to rely primarily on a knuckleball to pitch a no-hitter. That distinction belongs to Tobin, a 31-year-old right-hander who held Brooklyn hitless in a 2–0 win April 27, 1944. His eighth-inning home run made him the first pitcher in history to enhance a no-hitter with a homer.

Vern Bickford was the first Brave to pitch a no-hitter at night. On August 11, 1950, he beat the Dodgers, 7–0, for the seventh no-hitter in franchise history and the only one in the majors that season.

The Braves tried to waive Jim Wilson in May 1954, but when no one took him, manager Charlie Grimm gave the 32-year-old right-hander a start in a doubleheader June 6. Wilson pitched a shutout, so Grimm started him again June 12, and he no-hit the Phillies, 2–0. It was the first no-hitter at Milwaukee County Stadium and propelled Wilson to an eight-game winning streak and selection to the All-Star team.

On August 18, 1960, "Fidgety" Lou Burdette no-hit Philadelphia, 1–0. The only base runner Burdette allowed

In 1944, Jim Tobin became the first man ever to hit a home run while pitching a no-hitter.

came in the fifth inning when he hit Tony Gonzalez with a pitch. However, Gonzalez was erased on a double play, so Burdette faced the minimum of 27 batters.

Not to be outdone by his teammate and close friend, Spahn, who'd gone nearly 16 seasons without a no-hitter, answered Burdette by also no-hitting the Phillies, 4–0, a month later on September 16. It was the first Braves' no-hitter by a left-hander, too.

Then Spahn did Burdette one better, pitching his second no-hitter, 1–0, over San Francisco, on April 28, 1961. It was the left-hander's second no-hitter in six starts and, at the time it made him the second-oldest man ever to pitch one.

Niekro joined the no-hit club August 5, 1973, beating San Diego, 9–0. It was the first no-hitter at Atlanta Stadium and the first by a Brave since the move South.

The 13th no-hitter in franchise history came September 11, 1991, in the midst of a heated pennant race. The 1–0 victory over San Diego was the first combined no-hitter in National League history, with Mercker working the first six innings, Wohlers the next two, and Pena the ninth.

Alejandro Pena, Kent Mercker and Mark Wohlers pitched the only combined no-hitter in National League history September 11, 1991.

Mercker, who won the so-called "fifth" spot in the Braves' starting rotation for the 1994 season, quickly showed why when he no-hit the Dodgers, 6–0, on April 8 at Los Angeles. It was the first complete game of the 26-year-old left-hander's career and the first Braves' no-hitter on the road in modern history.

Braves No-Hitters

Jack Stivetts, August 5, 1892
Boston at Brooklyn

Boston	AB	R	B	TB	PO	A	E
McCarthy, rf	4	3	2	2	1	0	0
Duffy, cf	4	1	2	4	0	0	0
Long, ss	5	1	1	2	1	4	0
Ganzel, c	5	0	1	1	7	0	1
Nash, 3b	5	0	0	0	2	6	0
Tucker, 1b	5	2	4	4	11	0	1
Stivetts, p	5	2	2	5	0	1	0
Quinn, 2b	4	1	2	2	3	2	0
Nichols, lf	5	1	1	1	2	0	1
Totals	42	11	15	21	27	13	3

Brooklyn	AB	R	B	TB	PO	A	E
Griffin, cf	3	0	0	0	3	0	1
Corcoran, ss	4	0	0	0	2	5	1
Ward, 2b	2	0	0	0	4	2	1
Brouthers, 1b	3	0	0	0	11	0	0
Burns, rf	4	0	0	0	2	0	0
Daly, 3b	4	0	0	0	1	1	0
O'Brien, lf	3	0	0	0	1	0	0
Kinslow, c	2	0	0	0	3	1	1
Stein, p	2	0	0	0	0	3	1
Kennedy, p	1	0	0	0	0	1	1
Totals	28	0	0	0	27	13	6

Boston	0	0	2	2	1	4	0	2	0—11
Brooklyn	0	0	0	0	0	0	0	0	0— 0

Earned runs—Bostons, 5. Two-base hits—Long, Stivetts. Three-base hits—Duffy (1), Stivetts (1). Sacrifice hits—Duffy (2), Ganzel (1). Corcoran. Stolen bases—Long (2), Nichols, Ward, Kennedy. First base on balls—By McCarthy, Duffy, Quinn, Griffin. Ward (2), Brouthers, Kinslow. First base on errors—Bostons, 3; Brooklyns, 2. Struck out—Nichols (2), Corcoran, Daly, O'Brien, Kinslow (2), Stein. Double play—Long, Quinn and Tucker. Passed balls—Kinslow, 1. Time—1h. 55m. Umpire—Lynch.

Vic Willis, August 7, 1899
Washington at Boston

Washington	AB	R	BH	TB	PO	A	E
Slagle, cf	4	0	0	0	2	0	0
O'Brien, lf	2	1	0	0	3	1	0
McGann, 1b	3	0	0	0	7	0	0
Bonner, 2b	3	0	0	0	2	2	1
Freeman, rf	2	0	0	0	0	0	1
Padden, ss	3	0	0	0	1	4	0
Atherton, 3b	2	0	0	0	1	1	0
Duncan, c	3	0	0	0	8	1	0
Dineen, p	3	0	0	1	0	1	0
Totals	25	1	0	1	24	10	2

Boston	AB	R	BH	TB	PO	A	E
Hamilton, cf	4	3	3	4	1	1	0
Tenney, 1b	4	1	2	2	15	0	0
Long, ss	5	1	2	4	4	2	0
Collins, 3b	5	1	3	3	0	4	1
Duffy, lf	5	1	3	3	0	0	0
Stahl, rf	4	0	1	1	1	0	0
Lowe, 2b	3	0	2	2	2	5	0
Bergen, c	5	0	0	0	3	4	1
Willis, p	3	0	1	2	1	0	0
Totals	38	7	17	21	27	16	2

Washington	1	0	0	0	0	0	0	0	0—1
Boston	3	0	0	0	0	1	0	3	x—7

Earned runs—Boston 6. Two-base hits—Hamilton, Willis. Three-base hit—Long. Sacrifice hit—Tenney. Stolen bases—Tenney, Long, Collins. First base on balls—Hamilton, Stahl, Lowe 2, Willis, O'Brien, McGann, Atherton. Left on bases—Boston 12, Washington 2. Struck out—Hamilton, Collins, Bergen 2, Long, Slagle, O'Brien, Bonner, Dineen 2. Double plays—Hamilton and Tenney; Long and Collins; Padden, Bonner and McGann. Passed ball—Bergen. Hit by pitched ball—Freeman. Time—2h. 5m. Umpires—Messrs. Lynch and Connolly. Attendance—2000.

Frank Pfeffer, May 8, 1907
Cincinnati at Boston

Cincinnati	AB	R	B	P	A	E
Huggins, 2b	4	0	0	5	4	2
Kane, 3b	4	0	0	0	3	1
Davis, cf	4	0	0	3	0	0
Lobert, ss	3	0	0	1	2	0
Cannell, 1b	2	0	0	10	2	0
Mitchell, rf	3	0	0	1	0	1
Kruger, lf	3	0	0	0	0	0
Schlei, c	2	0	0	3	2	0
Mason, p	2	0	0	1	3	0
Totals	27	0	0	24	16	4

Boston	AB	R	B	P	A	E
Bates, rf	3	1	1	1	0	0
Tenney, 1b	2	2	0	12	0	0
Beaumont, cf	4	1	2	3	0	0
Howard, 2b	3	0	0	2	3	0
Bridwell, ss	3	1	1	0	4	0
Burke, lf	4	0	1	2	0	0
Brain, 3b	3	0	1	2	3	1
Brown, c	3	1	1	5	0	0
Pfeffer, p	3	0	1	0	2	0
Totals	28	6	8	27	12	1

Cincinnati	0	0	0	0	0	0	0	0	0—0
Boston	0	0	1	1	2	0	0	2	x—6

Two-base hit—Pfeffer. Sacrifice hits—Tenney, Howard, Mason, Huggins. Stolen bases—Bridwell, Ganzel. Left on bases—Boston 4. Cincinnati 4. First on balls—Off Pfeffer 1, Mason 3. Hit by pitcher—Ganzel, Bridwell. Struck out—By Pfeffer 3, Mason 1. Umpire—Emslie. Time—1.45. Attendance—2696.

George Davis, September 9, 1914
Philadelphia at Boston

Philadelphia	AB	R	B	P	A	E
Lobert, 3b	4	0	0	3	2	0
Becker, lf	3	0	0	0	0	0
Magee, 1b	4	0	0	4	1	0
Hilley, rf	4	0	0	2	0	0
Byrne, 2b	3	0	0	3	0	0
Paskert, cf	1	0	0	5	0	1
Martin, ss	2	0	0	3	3	0
Burns, c	3	0	0	4	0	0
Tincup, p	1	0	0	0	0	0
Rixey, p	0	0	0	0	1	0
Oeschger, p	0	0	0	0	0	0
*Cravath	1	0	0	0	0	0
†Killifer	1	0	0	0	0	0
Totals	27	0	0	24	7	1

Boston	AB	R	B	P	A	E
Moran, cf	2	0	0	0	0	0
Mann, cf	2	1	2	1	0	0
Evers, 2b	4	0	0	2	2	0
Connolly, lf	2	0	0	0	0	0
Cather, lf	2	0	0	0	0	0
Whitted, rf	4	1	2	1	0	0
Schmidt, 1b	4	0	1	14	0	0
Smith, 3b	4	2	2	2	3	2
Maranville, ss	3	1	1	3	2	0
Gowdy, c	4	1	1	4	1	0
Davis, p	4	1	3	0	3	0
Totals	35	7	12	27	11	2

*Batted for Tincup in fifth inning.
†Batted for Rixey in eighth inning.

Philadelphia	0	0	0	0	0	0	0	0	0—0
Boston	0	2	0	2	0	0	1	2	x—7

Hits—Off Tincup 5 in 4 innings, Rixey 3 in 3 innings, Oeschger 3 in 1 inning. Three-base hit—Mann. Sacrifice hit—Evers. Stolen base—Whitted. Double plays—Maranville, Evers, Schmidt 2. Left on bases—Boston 7, Philadelphia 5. First on balls—Off Tincup 2, Davis 5. First on errors—Philadelphia 3. Struck out—By Rixey 3, Davis 4. Time—2.00. Umpires—Eason and Quigley.

Tom Hughes, June 16, 1916
Pittsburgh at Boston

Pittsburgh	AB	H	O	A	E
Carey, cf	4	0	2	0	0
Johnston, 1b	4	0	7	0	0
Wagner, ss	3	0	6	3	0
Hinchman, rf	2	0	0	0	0
Schultz, 3b	3	0	1	3	0
Barney, lf	3	0	0	0	0
Viox, 2b	3	0	0	1	0
Schmidt, c	3	0	7	6	0
Kantlehner, p	2	0	1	1	1
Harmon, p	0	0	0	1	0
*Costello	1	0	0	0	0
Totals	28	0	24	15	1

Boston	AB	H	O	A	E
Maranville, ss	1	0	4	1	0
Snodgrass, cf	4	3	0	0	0
Wilhoit, rf	4	0	5	0	0
Magee, lf	3	1	2	0	0
Koney, 1b	3	1	5	0	0
Smith, 3b	3	0	0	0	1
Egan, 2b	3	1	1	1	0
Tragressor, c	0	0	0	0	0
Gowdy, c	3	1	9	0	0
Hughes, p	3	0	1	1	0
Totals	27	7	27	3	1

*Batted for Kantlehner in eighth.

Pittsburgh	0	0	0	0	0	0	0	0	0—0
Boston	1	0	0	0	0	0	0	0	1 x—2

Two-base hit—Gowdy. Stolen bases—Wagner, Maranville, Snodgrass. Bases on balls—Off Kantlehner 2, off Harmon 1, off Hughes 2. Hits—Off Kantlehner 6 in 7 innings. Struck out—By Kantlehner 5, by Harmon 2, by Hughes 7. Umpires—Klem and Emslie.

Jim Tobin, April 27, 1944
Brooklyn at Boston

Brooklyn	AB	H	O	A
P. Waner, rf	2	0	5	0
Walker, lf	4	0	3	0
Olmo, 2b	3	0	2	3
Galan, cf	3	0	4	0
Schultz, 1b	3	0	6	1
English, 3b	3	0	1	2
Hart, ss	3	0	0	3
Owen, c	3	0	2	0
Ostermueller, p	2	0	1	0
*Bordagaray	1	0	0	0
Totals	27	0	24	9

Boston	AB	H	O	A
Ryan, 3b	4	2	1	3
Holmes, cf	4	0	2	0
Workman, rf	3	1	2	0
Ross, lf	3	0	2	0
Clemens, lf	0	0	0	0
Masi, c	3	0	7	0
Etchison, 1b	3	0	10	0
Wietelmann, ss	3	0	1	1
Shemo, 2b	3	1	2	4
Tobin, p	3	1	0	1
Totals	29	5	27	9

Brooklyn	0	0	0	0	0	0	0	0	0—0
Boston	0	0	1	0	0	0	0	1	x—2

*Batted for Ostermueller in ninth. Runs—Ryan, Tobin. Errors—Hart 2. Runs batted in—Workman, Tobin. Two base hits—Ryan 2. Home run—Tobin. Double play—Hart, Olmo and Schultz. Bases on balls—Off Tobin 2, off Ostermueller 2. Struck out—By Tobin 6, by Ostermueller 2. Umpires—Stewart, Jorda and Magerkuth. Attendance—1,447.

Vern Bickford, August 11, 1950
Brooklyn at Boston

Brooklyn	AB	R	H	O	A	E
Reese, ss	4	0	0	2	2	0
Hermanski, lf	2	0	0	0	0	0
Snider, cf	4	0	0	3	0	1
Robinson, 2b	3	0	0	2	4	0
Furillo, rf	3	0	0	4	0	0
Hodges, 1b	3	0	0	4	2	0
Campanella, c	2	0	0	7	0	0
Cox, 3b	3	0	0	1	1	0
Erskine, p	0	0	0	1	0	1
Hatten, p	1	0	0	0	0	1
*Abrams	1	0	0	0	0	0
Bankhead, p	0	0	0	0	2	0
†Russell	0	0	0	0	0	0
Totals	26	0	0	24	11	3

Boston	AB	R	H	O	A	E
Hartsfield, 2b	5	1	2	1	3	0
Jethroe, cf	4	1	2	2	0	0
Torgeson, 1b	4	2	1	12	0	0
Elliott, 3b	5	2	3	2	3	0
Cooper, c	4	1	1	4	0	0
Gordon, lf	3	0	2	1	0	0
Marshall, rf	2	0	0	2	0	0
Kerr, ss	4	0	0	3	5	0
Bickford, p	4	0	1	0	1	0
Totals	35	7	12	27	12	0

Brooklyn	0	0	0	0	0	0	0	0	0—0
Boston	3	1	0	0	1	0	2	0	x—7

Pitchers	IP	R	H	SO	BB
Bickford (W, 14–8)	9	0	0	3	4
Erskine (L, 0–1)	1⅔	4	5	4	1
Hatten	3⅓	1	3	2	2
Bankhead	3	2	4	2	2

*Flied out for Hatten in sixth.
†Walked for Bankhead in ninth.
Runs batted in—Elliott (2), Cooper (2), Gordon (2), Jethroe. Two-base hits—Elliott, Cooper. Double play—Kerr to Torgeson. Left on bases—Brooklyn 3, Boston 9. Umpires—Goetz, Dascoli and Jorda. Time of game 2:05. Attendance—29,008.

Jim Wilson, June 12, 1954
Philadelphia at Milwaukee

Philadelphia	AB	H	O	A
Jones, 3b	4	0	3	2
Ashburn, cf	1	0	0	0
Schell, cf	2	0	1	0
Torgeson, 1b	3	0	7	2
Ennis, lf	3	0	2	0
Hamner, 2b	3	0	3	1
Burgess, c	1	0	4	1
Wyrostek, rf	3	0	3	0
Morgan, ss	3	0	0	3
Roberts, p	2	0	1	2
a-Clark	1	0	0	0
Totals	26	0	24	11

Milwaukee	AB	H	O	A
Bruton, cf	4	2	2	0
Logan, ss	3	1	2	2
Aaron, lf	4	1	4	0
Mathews, 3b	3	0	0	2
Adcock, 1b	3	0	9	0
Pafko, rf	3	0	2	0
O'Connell, 2b	3	1	2	1
Crandall, c	3	1	6	1
Wilson, p	3	1	0	2
Totals	29	7	27	8

Philadelphia	0	0	0	0	0	0	0	0	0—0
Milwaukee	1	0	0	0	1	0	0	0	x—2

Pitchers	IP	H	R	ER	BB	SO
Wilson (Winner 2–0)	9	0	0	0	2	6
Roberts (Loser 7–7)	8	7	2	2	0	3

a-Fanned for Roberts in ninth.
R—Logan, Crandall. E—None. RBI—Logan, Crandall. 2B—Wilson. Hit—Logan, Crandall. SB—Bruton. SH—Logan. DP—Crandall and Logan. LOB—Philadelphia 1. Milwaukee 4. U—Pinelli. Boggess and Engelin. T—1:40. Attendance—28,218.

Lou Burdette, August 18, 1960
Philadelphia at Milwaukee

Philadelphia	B.Av.	AB	R	H	RBI	O	A	E
Callison, rf	.272	3	0	0	0	4	0	0
Taylor, 2b	.294	3	0	0	0	2	5	0
Curry, rf	.273	0	0	0	0	1	0	0
Herrera, 1b	.293	3	0	0	0	10	0	2
Gonzalez, cf	.265	2	0	0	0	1	0	0
Walls, 3b	.245	3	0	0	0	3	0	0
Malkmus, 3b	.151	0	0	0	0	0	0	0
Coker, c	.220	3	0	0	0	5	0	0
Amaro, ss	.249	2	0	0	0	1	2	0
a-Walters	.262	1	0	0	0	0	0	0
Conley, p	(7–10)	2	0	0	0	0	3	0
b-B. G. Smith	.270	1	0	0	0	0	0	0
Totals		26	0	0	0	24	13	2

Milwaukee	B.Av.	AB	R	H	RBI	O	A	E
Burton, cf	.289	4	0	1	1	3	0	0
Crandall, c	.276	4	0	2	0	3	0	0
Mathews, 3b	.271	4	0	1	0	1	4	0
Aaron, rf	.289	4	0	1	0	1	0	0
Covington, lf	.279	3	0	1	0	0	0	0
Spangler, lf	.231	0	0	0	0	0	0	0
Roach, 2b	.318	3	0	1	0	0	3	0
Cottier, 2b	.184	0	0	0	0	0	0	0
Adcock, 1b	.297	3	0	0	0	18	3	0
Logan, ss	.264	3	0	0	0	0	6	0
Burdette, p	(14–7)	3	1	2	0	1	3	0
Totals		31	1	9	1	27	19	0

a-Grounded out for Amaro in 9th;
b-Flied out for Conley in 9th.

Philadelphia	0	0	0	0	0	0	0	0	0—0
Milwaukee	0	0	0	0	0	0	0	0	x—1

2B—Burdette, Bruton. DP—Conley, Taylor and Herrera. LEFT—Philadelphia 0. Milwaukee 6.

Pitchers	IP	H	R	ER	BB	SO
Conley (L)	8	9	1	1	0	4
Burdette (W)	9	0	0	0	0	3

HBP—By Burdette (Gonzalez). U—Jackowski, Landes, Pelekoudas, Barlick. T—2:10. A—16,338.

Warren Spahn, September 16, 1960
Philadelphia at Milwaukee

Philadelphia	AB	R	H	RBI
Callison, lf	3	0	0	0
d-Del Greco	1	0	0	0
Malkmus, 2b	4	0	0	0
Walters, rf	2	0	0	0
Herrera, 1b	3	0	0	0
Gonzalez, cf	3	0	0	0
Neeman, c	2	0	0	0
Woods, 3b	2	0	0	0
a-Taylor	1	0	0	0
Amaro, ss	2	0	0	0
Lepcio, 3b	0	0	0	0
b-Walls	1	0	0	0
Koppe, ss	0	0	0	0
Buzhardt, p	2	0	0	0
c-Smith	1	0	0	0
Totals	**27**	**0**	**0**	**0**

Milwaukee	AB	R	H	RBI
Bruton, cf	3	1	2	0
Crandall, c	4	0	2	1
Mathews, 3b	4	0	2	1
Aaron, rf	3	1	1	0
Dark, lf	4	1	1	1
Adcock, 1b	2	0	1	1
Logan, ss	3	0	0	0
Cottier, 2b	3	0	0	0
Spahn, p	3	1	1	0
Totals	**29**	**4**	**10**	**4**

a-Struck out for Woods in 8th;
b-Struck out for Amaro in 8th;
c-Struck out for Buzhardt in 9th;
d-Struck out for Callison in 9th.

Philadelphia	0	0	0	0	0	0	0	0	0—0
Milwaukee	0	0	0	2	1	0	1	0	x—4

E—None. A—Philadelphia 12, Milwaukee 6. DP—Amaro, Malkmus, Herrera 2. LOB—Philadelphia 2, Milwaukee 6.
3B Hits—Dark. SB—Burton. Sacrifice—Logan. SF—Adcock.

Pitchers	IP	H	R	ER	BB	SO
Buzhardt (L, 4–16)	8	10	4	4	3	1
Spahn (W, 20–9)	9	0	0	0	2	15

Umpires—Gorman, Smith, Sudol, Boggess. Time—2:02.
Attendance—6,117.

Warren Spahn, April 28, 1961
San Francisco at Milwaukee

San Francisco	AB	R	H	RBI
Hiller, 2b	2	0	0	0
Kuenn, 3b	3	0	0	0
Mays, cf	3	0	0	0
McCovey, 1b	2	0	0	0
Cepeda, lf	3	0	0	0
F. Alou, rf	3	0	0	0
Bailey, c	3	0	0	0
Pagan, ss	2	0	0	0
a-M. Alou	1	0	0	0
S. Jones, p	2	0	0	0
b-Amalfitano	1	0	0	0
Totals	**25**	**0**	**0**	**0**

Milwaukee	AB	R	H	RBI
McMillan, ss	3	0	0	0
Bolling, 2b	3	1	2	0
Mathews, 3b	3	0	0	0
Aaron, cf	3	0	1	1
Roach, lf	4	0	1	0
Spangler, lf	0	0	0	0
Adcock, 1b	3	0	1	0
Lau, c	2	0	0	0
DeMerit, rf	4	0	0	0
Spahn, p	4	0	0	0
Totals	**29**	**1**	**5**	**1**

a-Grounded out for Pagan in 9th;
b-Grounded out for Jones in 9th.

San Francisco	0	0	0	0	0	0	0	0	0—0
Milwaukee	1	0	0	0	0	0	0	0	x—1

E—McCovey. A—San Francisco 3, Milwaukee 11. DP—Spahn, McMillan, Adcock 2. LOB—San Francisco 5, Milwaukee 11.
Sacrifice—McMillan.

Pitchers	IP	H	R	ER	BB	SO
Jones (L, 2–1)	8	5	1	0	5	9
Spahn (W, 2–1)	9	0	0	0	2	5

HBP—By Jones (Bolling). PB-Bailey 2. Umpires—Donatelli, Burkhardt, Pelekoudas, Forman, Conian. Time of game—2:16.
Attendance—8,518.

Phil Niekro, August 5, 1973
San Diego at Atlanta

San Diego	AB	R	H	RBI	E
Anderson, ss	3	0	0	0	0
Grubb, cf	4	0	0	0	0
Roberts, 3b	4	0	0	0	1
Colbert, 1b	3	0	0	0	0
Gaston, rf	4	0	0	0	0
Locklear, lf	3	0	0	0	0
Kendall, c	2	0	0	0	0
Corrales, c	0	0	0	0	0
R. Morales, 2b	3	0	0	0	0
Arlin, p	1	0	0	0	0
Romo, p	1	0	0	0	0
Winfield, ph	1	0	0	0	0
Ross, p	0	0	0	0	0
Totals	**29**	**0**	**0**	**0**	**1**

Atlanta	AB	R	H	RBI	E
Garr, rf	3	3	3	0	0
Jackson, rf	2	1	1	0	0
Lum, lf	4	1	1	1	0
Evans, 3b	0	2	0	1	1
Baker, cf	5	1	2	2	0
Johnson, 2b	3	0	1	0	0
Goggin, 2b	0	0	0	1	0
Tepedino, 1b	4	0	2	2	0
Perez, ss	4	0	1	0	1
Casanova, c	4	1	1	1	0
Niekro, p	3	0	0	0	0
Totals	**32**	**9**	**12**	**8**	**2**

San Diego	0	0	0	0	0	0	0	0	0—0
Atlanta	1	0	2	1	0	4	0	1	x—9

San Diego	IP	H	R	ER	BB	SO
Arlin (L, 6–10)	2*	5	3	3	2	1
Romo	5	6	5	2	5	2
Ross	1	1	1	0	1	0

Atlanta	IP	H	R	ER	BB	SO
Niekro (W, 11–5)	9	0	0	0	3	4

*Pitched to four batters in third.
DP—San Diego 2. LOB—San Diego 5, Atlanta 9. 2B—Garr 2. HR—Casanova (4). SB—Garr, Jackson. SF—Evans, Goggin. PB—Kendall, Corrales. U—Tata, Vargo, Pryor and Froeming. T—2:26. A—8,748.

Combined No-Hitter, September 11, 1991
San Diego at Atlanta

San Diego	AB	R	H	RBI
Fernandez, ss	4	0	0	0
Jackson, cf	4	0	0	0
Gwynn, rf	3	0	0	0
McGriff, 1b	3	0	0	0
Santiago, c	3	0	0	0
Teufel, 3b-2b	3	0	0	0
Clark, lf	2	0	0	0
Azocar, ph-lf	1	0	0	0
Shipley, 2b	1	0	0	0
Howell, ph-3b	1	0	0	0
Harris, p	1	0	0	0
Roberts, ph	1	0	0	0
Totals	**27**	**0**	**0**	**0**

Atlanta	AB	R	H	RBI
Nixon, lf	4	0	0	0
Treadway, 2b	4	0	1	0
Lemke, 2b	0	0	0	0
Pendleton, 3b	4	1	2	1
Justice, lf	4	0	0	0
Gant, cf	2	0	0	0
Bream, 1b	3	0	1	0
Mitchell, pr	0	0	0	0
Wohlers, p	0	0	0	0
L. Smith, ph	1	0	0	0
Rossy, pr	0	0	0	0
Pena, p	0	0	0	0
Olson, c	4	0	2	0
Bellard, ss	3	0	1	0
Mercker, p	2	0	0	0
Hunter, 1b	1	0	0	0
Totals	**32**	**1**	**7**	**1**

San Diego	0	0	0	0	0	0	0	0	0—0
Atlanta	0	0	0	0	1	0	0	0	x—1

E—Pendleton (20), Shipley (4). LOB—San Diego 3, Atlanta 9. 2B—Pendleton (27), Bellard (7) HR—Pendleton (20) S—Harris.

San Diego	IP	H	R	ER	BB	K
Harris (L 5–5)	8	7	1	1	2	7

Atlanta	IP	H	R	ER	BB	K
Mercker (W 5–3)	6	0	0	0	2	6
Wohlers (H. 1)	2	0	0	0	0	0
Pena (S. 8)	1	0	0	0	0	0

T—2:11 A—20,477. Umpires—HP. Wendelstedt, 1B. Pulli, 2B. Williams, 3B. Marsh.

Kent Mercker, April 8, 1994
Atlanta at Los Angeles

Braves	AB	R	H	RBI
Sanders, cf	4	0	1	0
Blauser, ss	4	0	0	0
Klesko, lf	3	0	0	0
Gallagher, lf	0	0	0	0
McGriff, 1b	3	2	1	1
Justice, rf	3	2	1	1
Pendleton, 3b	4	2	3	3
Lopez, c	3	0	0	1
Lemke, 2b	3	0	0	0
Mercker, p	4	0	0	0
Totals	**31**	**6**	**6**	**6**

Los Angeles	AB	R	H	RBI
DeShields, 2b	3	0	0	0
Butler, cf	2	0	0	0
Piazza, c	4	0	0	0
Karros, 1b	3	0	0	0
Wallach, 3b	3	0	0	0
Mondesi, rf	3	0	0	0
Ashley, lf	3	0	0	0
Offerman, ss	3	0	0	0
Astacio, p	2	0	0	0
Wayne, p	0	0	0	0
Webster, ph	1	0	0	0
Park, p	0	0	0	0
Totals	**27**	**0**	**0**	**0**

Braves	0	2	0	1	0	0	1	0	2—6
Los Angeles	0	0	0	0	0	0	0	0	0—0

2B—Pendleton. 3B—Pendleton. HR—McGriff (1st), Justice (1st), Pendleton (1st). SF—Lopez. SB—DeShields. LOB—Atlanta 3, Los Angeles 4. DP—Los Angeles.

Atlanta	IP	H	R	ER	BB	SO
Mercker (W, 1–0)	9	0	0	0	4	10

Los Angeles	IP	H	R	ER	BB	SO
Astacio (L, 0–1)	7⅔	5	4	4	2	11
Wayne	⅓	0	0	0	0	0
Park	1	1	2	2	2	2

T—2:26. A—36,546. Umpires—Rapuano, Pulli, West, Bonn.

Four Consecutive Home Runs

Twice within four days in 1994, the Braves hit three consecutive home runs, quite a slugging feat. But that still didn't measure up to what Milwaukee batters did June 8, 1961, at Crosley Field.

Entering the seventh inning, the Braves trailed Cincinnati right-hander Jim Maloney, 10–2. Milwaukee's Frank Bolling led off the inning with a single, and Eddie Mathews followed with a home run, bringing the score to 10–4. When Hank Aaron made it back-to-back home runs, Maloney was lifted in favor of left-hander Marshall "Sheriff" Bridges. Joe Adcock greeted Bridges with a home run, and Frank Thomas followed with yet another, cutting the deficit to 10–6.

There still were no outs, but Bridges got out of the inning without further damage, and the Braves lost the game, 10–8. However, the four straight home runs by Mathews, Aaron, Adcock, and Thomas was a major league first. It still ranks as a National League record, though the feat has been duplicated twice in the American League.

Milwaukee actually hit six home runs in that losing effort. Braves' starter Warren Spahn hit one in the third inning, and Mathews hit another in the eighth.

This game sent Braves hitters on a power rampage. The next day at Chicago's Wrigley Field, they hit four home runs, including a grand slam by Lee Maye, but lost, 11–10. On June 10, they hit four more homers, including one by pitcher Lou Burdette, in a 9–5 victory over the Cubs. That total tied what was then the three-game major league record of 14. It remains the National League record, accomplished on four occasions—three of those by the Braves.

Then on June 11 at Wrigley, the Braves added two more homers in the first game of a doubleheader, an 8–4 win, tying what was then the major league record of 16 in four games. The last home run in the streak was a three-run shot by Spahn, who also hit the first one. The 16 homers in four

Frank Thomas helped the Bravers accomplish a major league first in 1961 when he hit the fourth of four consecutive home runs, following Eddie Mathews, Hank Aaron, and Joe Adcock.

games remains the National League record, attained three times—all by the Braves.

The onslaught continued. In 15 games through June 24, the Braves hit 39 home runs. And by July 2, they had 46 in 21 games. Despite all that slugging, though, the 1961 Braves still finished in fourth place, their worst showing since leaving Boston in 1952.

June 8, 1961
Cincinnati 10, Braves 8

Braves	AB	R	H	RBI
Maye, rf	3	0	1	0
d-Demerit, rf	1	0	0	0
Bolling, 2b	5	2	1	0
Mathews, 3b	4	2	4	3
Aaron, cf	4	1	2	1
Adcock, 1b	5	1	1	2
Thomas, lf	5	1	2	1
Torre, c	4	0	1	0
McMillan, ss	4	0	0	0
Spahn, p	1	1	1	1
a-Lau	1	0	0	0
Drabowsky, p	0	0	0	0
b-Baylor	1	0	0	0
Brunet, p	0	0	0	0
Totals	38	8	13	8

Cincinnati	AB	R	H	RBI
Blasingame, 2b	5	1	2	1
Kasko, ss	4	1	1	0
Cardenas, ss	0	0	0	0
Pinson, cf	4	1	2	2
Robinson, rf	4	1	2	0
Freese, 3b	4	1	1	4
Post, lf	4	2	1	0
Coleman, 1b	4	2	3	2
Zimmerman, c	4	1	1	0
Maloney, p	2	0	1	0
Bridges, p	0	0	0	0
c-Gernert	1	0	0	0
Henry, p	0	0	0	0
Brosnan, p	1	0	0	0
Totals	37	10	14	9

a-Flied out for Spahn in 6th.
b-Struck out for Drabowsky in 7th.
c-Lined out for Bridges in 7th.
d-Grounded out for Maye in 8th.

Braves	0	0	2	0	0	0	5	1	0— 8
Cincinnati	0	1	1	3	1	4	0	0	x—10

E—Maye, McMillan. A—Milwaukee 7, Cincinnati 12. DP—Blasingame, Coleman; Freese, Blasingame, Coleman. LOB—Milwaukee 9, Cincinnati 11.
2B Hits—Mathews, Aaron, Post. HR—Mathews 2, Aaron, Adcock, Thomas, Spahn, Freese, Coleman. Sacrifice—Maloney. SF—Freese.

Pitchers	IP	H	R	ER	BB	SO
Spahn (L, 6–5)	5	8	6	5	4	2
Drabowsky	1	4	4	4	0	0
Brunet	2	2	0	0	2	0
*Maloney (W, 4–2)	6	8	5	5	5	2
Bridges	1	2	2	2	0	1
Henry	⅓	2	1	1	0	0
Brosnan	1⅔	1	0	0	0	1

* Faced 3 batters in 7th.
HBP—By Maloney (Spahn). Wild pitch—Spahn. Umpires—Donatelli, Conlan, Burkhart, Pelekoudas. Time—3:14. Attendance—5,149.

Surkont Sets Consecutive Strikeouts Record

Few Braves were as popular in the team's first season in Milwaukee as was right-hander Max Surkont. His pitching was nearly impeccable in the first two months of 1953, making him an immediate hit with everyone, and those fans who shared his Polish ancestry were particularly fond of him.

Surkont won nine of his first 10 decisions. He was at his best on the damp evening of May 25 when he raised his record to 6–0 by beating Cincinnati, 10–3, at County Stadium. The game took on added significance early when the burly pitcher began sending Cincinnati hitters back to the dugout with their bats in their hands.

Even with rain in the forecast, 24,445 fans showed up to watch Surkont pitch the second game of a doubleheader against the Redlegs, whom he'd beaten, 2–0, on opening day at Cincinnati in the first game the Braves ever played representing Milwaukee.

After winning the first game of the doubleheader, the Braves jumped on Cincinnati for six runs in the first inning of the second game. Surkont, who had a good but not overpowering fastball and above-average control, could thus just concentrate on throwing strikes.

The 30-year-old pitcher finished the second inning by striking out Cincinnati reliever Herm Wehmeier, certainly not a noteworthy accomplishment in itself. However, Surkont proceeded to strike out Rocky Bridges, Bobby Adams, and Gus Bell in order in the third inning and Willard Marshall, Bob Borkowski, and Grady Hatton in the fourth. That gave him seven consecutive strikeouts, which tied the modern major league record shared by Hooks Wiltse of the Giants and Dazzy Vance and Van Lingle Mungo of the Dodgers.

Rain had begun falling in the fourth inning, though, putting the game and Surkont's record in jeopardy, especially since the Redlegs were stalling in hopes of a postponement.

In the bottom of the fourth, with Surkont at bat, time was called, and the grounds crew covered the field with the tarp. But after a 33-minute delay, the game was resumed in light rain. The Braves were retired in the bottom of the fourth, then Surkont struck out Andy Seminick to open the fifth. That made it eight in a row, a new modern record—if the top of the fifth inning could be finished.

Immediately after Seminick struck out, time was called

Max Surkont was nearly untouchable the first half of the 1953 season, especially on May 25 when he struck out a then-record eight straight Cincinnati Redlegs.

again. Braves manager Charlie Grimm complained, and the umpires agreed to continue. Surkont retired the next two batters, making the game and the record official. Another 40-minute rain delay followed, but the game was eventually played to completion. Surkont went the distance, striking out 13 in a 10–3 victory.

The record stood until Hall of Famer Tom Seaver struck out 10 in a row in 1970. Unfortunately, Surkont's success didn't last anywhere near as long. On June 16, his 31st birthday, he was given a night in his honor at County Stadium. Surkont received a large amount of Polish sausage, his favorite food, from adoring fans and proceeded to eat it like there was no tomorrow. It surely was no coincidence that he was 9–1 up to the sausage barrage and 2–4 the rest of the season. He was traded during the winter and never had another winning season.

May 25, 1953
Milwaukee 10, Cincinnati 3

Cincinnati	AB	H	O	A
Bridges, 2b	4	0	4	2
Adams, 3b	3	0	1	3
Bell, cf	4	1	4	0
Marshall, rf	4	1	1	0
Borkowski, lf	4	2	1	0
Hatton, 1b	4	1	8	0
Landrith, c	0	0	1	0
Seminick, c	3	0	3	1
McMillan, ss	3	0	1	3
Perkowski, p	0	0	0	0
Wehmeier, p	1	0	0	1
Nevel, p	0	0	0	0
a-Marquis	1	0	0	0
Smith, p	1	0	0	1
Totals	32	5	24	11

Milwaukee	AB	H	O	A
Bruton, cf	3	2	2	0
Logan, ss	4	2	1	1
Mathews, 3b	4	2	1	0
Gordon, lf	4	3	0	0
Pafko, rf	3	0	2	0
Adcock, 1b	4	2	5	1
Dittmer, 2b	4	1	2	1
Cooper, c	4	1	13	1
Surkont, p	4	0	1	0
Totals	34	13	27	4

Cincinnati	0	1	0	0	0	0	0	0	2—	3
Milwaukee	6	0	1	3	0	0	0	0	x—	10

Pitchers	IP	H	R	ER	BB	SO
Surkont (Winner 6–0)	9	5	3	3	2	13
Perkowski (Loser 1–4)	0*	5	6	6	1	0
Wehmeier	3⅓	5	4	4	0	2
Nevel	⅔	1	0	0	0	0
Smith	4	2	0	0	0	2

*Pitched to six batters in first.

a-Grounded out for Nevel in fifth.
R—Bell, Marshall, Borkowski, Bruton 2, Logan 2, Mathews 2, Gordon 2, Pafko, Adcock. E—None. RBI—Hatton, Borkowski 2, Mathews 5, Adcock 2, Cooper, Pafko, Logan. 2B—Borkowski, Gordon, Adcock, Bruton. 3B—Adcock, Gordon. HR—Borowski, Matthews 2. DP—Smith, McMillan and Hatton; McMillan, Bridges and Hatton. LOB—Cincinnati 4, Milwaukee 2. HP—Smith (Bruton). U—Engeln, Stewart, Pinelli, and Boggess. T—2:06. Attendance—24,445.

The Duel by the Bay

There have been many classic pitching performances in Braves history, but never has there been a better duel between two such classic pitchers as there was the night of July 2, 1963.

The site was San Francisco's hostile Candlestick Park. The pitchers were Juan Marichal, the Giants' 25-year-old right-hander who was already showing why he would wind up in the Hall of Fame, and Warren Spahn, the Braves' 42-year-old left-hander whose Cooperstown plaque was awaiting only his final victory total.

Just 15,921 fans braved the night's elements to witness the matchup, but what they saw was one of the last of the truly great fight-to-the-end matchups in history. There'll never be another one like it, at least not based on the way the game is played now.

To add perspective to what took place that night, remember that Spahn and Marichal were pitching against two of the most potent lineups in the game. The Giants, who had the likes of Willie Mays, Willie McCovey, Felipe Alou, and Orlando Cepeda, were on their way to leading the league in home runs (197) and slugging percentage (.414) by wide margins. The Braves would finish second to San Francisco in home runs (139).

Yet the two great pitchers, one old enough to have fathered the other, cut through those lineups, inning after inning, like ships knifing through the thick fog building on the Bay. Marichal, the "Dominican Dandy," used the overpowering pitches that won 25 games for him that season, tying Sandy Koufax for the league lead. Spahn, who'd reached the magic 300-win club two years earlier, was reduced to using courage and cunning, yet he would finish right behind Marichal and Koufax with 23 wins. And both men featured signature high leg kicks which made them two of the most stylish pitchers of all time.

Slowly, the scoring opportunities withered and the innings mounted. Hank Aaron hit a ball that seemed destined for a home run in the fourth, but the bay breeze kept it in play for a long out. Later in the inning, Norm Larker tried to score from second on a single to center by Del Crandall, only to be thrown out by the glorious Mays. In the seventh, Spahn, always a threat at the plate, hit a ball off the top of the fence in right. It missed being a home run by inches, but Spahn had to settle for a double and was stranded at second.

The Milwaukee left-hander had the Giants under control until the ninth when McCovey smashed a ball into the right-field seats. However, it was ruled foul despite the Giants' objections, and the game remained scoreless as it moved into extra innings.

At age 42, Warren Spahn pitched 15⅓ straight scoreless innings against 25-year-old Juan Marichal before losing, 1–0, in the 16th on a home run by Willie Mays.

Neither pitcher was threatened through the 13th. In the 14th, Spahn gave up a leadoff bloop double to Harvey Kuenn with the Giants' sluggers to follow. He walked Mays intentionally—the first pass he'd issued in 31⅔ innings—then disposed of McCovey and Alou. But with two outs, Denis Menke, who'd replaced Eddie Mathews at third, booted what should have been an inning-ending grounder by Cepeda to load the bases. Spahn was up to the challenge, though, and got Ed Bailey to pop out, ending the inning.

The Braves could do nothing against Marichal. Finally, in the bottom of the 16th, the odds caught up to Spahn. With one out, he hung a screwball, and Mays sent it over the left-field fence and into the night, making the Braves 1–0 losers. The time was 12:25 A.M.

Spahn threw 201 pitches over 4 hours and 10 minutes, and all he had to show for it was the end of his personal string of 27⅓ scoreless innings. His gallantry, however, remains unmatched in franchise history.

July 2, 1963
San Francisco 1, Milwaukee 0

Braves	AB	R	H	RBI
Maye, cf	6	0	0	0
Bolling, 2b	7	0	2	0
H. Aaron, rf	6	0	0	0
Mathews, 3b	2	0	0	0
Menke, 3b	5	0	2	0
Larker, 1b	5	0	0	0
Jones, lf	5	0	1	0
b-Dillard, lf	1	0	0	0
Crandall, c	6	0	2	0
McMillan, ss	6	0	0	0
Spahn, p	6	0	1	0
Totals	55	0	8	0

Giants	AB	R	H	RBI
Kuenn, 3b	7	0	1	0
Mays, cf	6	1	1	1
McCovey, lf	6	0	1	0
F. Alou, rf	6	0	1	0
Cepeda, 1b	6	0	2	0
Bailey, c	6	0	1	0
Pagan, ss	2	0	0	0
a-Davenport	1	0	0	0
Bowman, ss	3	0	2	0
Hiller, 2b	6	0	0	0
Marichal, p	6	0	0	0
Totals	55	1	9	1

a-Flied out for Pagan in 7th;
b-Struck out for Jones in 14th.

Milwaukee	0	0	0	0	0	0	0	0	0	0	0	0	0	0	0	0—0
S. Francisco	0	0	0	0	0	0	0	0	0	0	0	0	0	0	0	1—1

E—Kuenn and Menke. PO-A—Milwaukee, 46-19 (one out when winning run scored); San Francisco, 48-14. LOB—Milwaukee, 11; San Francisco, 9. 2B—Spahn, Kuenn. HR—Mays. SB—Cepeda, Maye, Menke.

Pitchers	IP	H	R	ER	BB	SO
Spahn (L, 11–4)	15⅓	9	1	1	1	2
Marichal (W, 13–3)	16	8	0	0	4	10

U—Burkhart, Pelekoudas, Walsh, Conlan. T—4.10. A—15,921

12-Homer Barrage Sets NL Records

Fred Haney was shell-shocked. "That was the greatest demonstration of power I've ever seen," said the man who three years later would become the beneficiary of this power-laden Milwaukee lineup.

But on August 30, 1953, Haney was managing the Pirates and not the Braves. He'd just sat through 18 innings at Pittsburgh's Forbes Field while his team received one of the worst doubleheader bludgeonings ever administered. The Braves won the first game, 19–4, and the second, 11–5. In the process, they necessitated a major rewriting of the record books.

Before the day was over, Milwaukee's sluggers (Hank Aaron, remember, was still a year away from the majors) had accomplished the following:

- Hit eight home runs in the first game, tying the major league record and setting a National League single-game record that still stands.
- Hit 12 home runs in the doubleheader, establishing a National League record that still stands.
- Accumulated 73 total bases in the two games, still a National League doubleheader record.

Leading the slaughter were Eddie Mathews and Jim Pendleton, who hit three home runs apiece for the day. Mathews, still just 21 years old, was on his way to leading the league with 47 homers. He hit two in the first game and one in the second, giving him 28 for the season on the road, a new National League record. He hit two more away from home before the year was over, and his 30 still rank as the league record for a left-handed hitter on the road.

Rookie outfielder Jim Pendleton hit three home runs in the first game of a doubleheader August 30, 1953 at Pittsburgh in an awesome display of power by the Braves that has never been equaled.

Pendleton, a 29-year-old rookie with but one previous homer, hit all three of his in the first game, becoming just the second player to hit three in a game during his freshman season. Mathews had become the first a year earlier.

The final home run tally for the day read as follows: Mathews (3), Pendleton (3), Johnny Logan (2), Del Crandall, Jack Dittmer, Joe Adcock (inside-the-park), and Sid Gordon.

August 30, 1953
Braves 19, Pittsburgh 4
Braves 11, Pittsburgh 5

First Game

Braves	AB	R	H
Bruton, cf	5	2	2
Logan, ss	6	1	2
e-Sisti, ss	0	1	0
Mathews, 3b	5	2	2
Hanebrink, 3b	0	0	0
Adcock, 1b	5	1	3
Crowe, 1b	0	0	0
Crandall, c	5	2	2
St. Claire, c	0	0	0
Pendleton, rf	5	5	4
Gordon, lf	1	2	1
b-Thorpe, lf	2	0	0
Dittmer, 2b	5	2	3
Roach, 2b	1	0	0
Antonelli, p	5	1	1
Totals	45	19	20

Pittsburgh	AB	R	H
Bernier, lf	5	0	0
O'Connell, 3b	5	0	1
Abrams, rf	4	0	1
Thomas, cf	4	0	0
J. O'Brien, 2b	4	1	0
E. O'Brien, ss	4	1	2
Ward, 1b	4	1	1
Sandlock, c	2	1	1
c-Janowicz, c	2	0	0
Lindell, p	1	0	1
Hall, p	0	0	0
a-Pellagrini	1	0	0
Waugh, p	0	0	0
d-Cole	1	0	1
Bowman, p	0	0	0
f-Koback	1	0	1
Totals	38	4	9

Braves	0	1	1	3	4	2	4	4	0—19
Pittsburgh	0	0	1	0	0	0	2	1	0— 4

Pitchers	IP	H	R	ER	BB	SO
Antonelli (W, 11–9)	9	9	4	2	0	6
Lindell (L, 5–16)	3	6	5	5	4	2
Hall	2	5	4	1	1	1
Waugh	2	5	6	6	2	0
Bowman	2	4	4	4	1	1

a-Flied out for Hall in 5th.
b-Ran for Gordon in 6th.
c-Lined out for Sandlock in 7th.
d-Singled for Waugh in 7th.
e-Ran for Logan in 8th.
f-Tripled for Bowman in 9th.
E—Abrams, Hall, Pendleton, Bruton, Hanebrink. RBI—Dittmer 4, Mathews 4, Pendleton 5, Antonelli, Logan 4, Crandall, Lindell, Cole. 2B—Sandlock, Dittmer. 3B—Bruton, Koback. HR—Mathews 2, Pendleton 3, Logan, Crandall, Dittmer. SH—Antonelli. DP—Dittmer, Logan and Adcock. LOB—Milwaukee 8, Pittsburgh 7. T—2:41.

Second Game

Braves	AB	R	H
Bruton, cf	3	1	1
a-Crandall	1	0	0
Thorpe, rf	1	0	1
Logan, ss	5	2	3
Mathews, 3b	5	2	2
Adcock, 1b	4	1	1
Cooper, c	4	0	0
Pendleton, rf, cf	4	1	1
Gordon, lf	4	2	2
Dittmer, 2b	4	2	1
Buhl, p	1	0	0
Liddle, p	1	0	0
Totals	37	11	12

Pittsburgh	AB	R	H
Abrams, rf	3	1	0
O'Connell, 3b	5	1	2
Rice, lf	4	0	3
Thomas, cf	5	0	0
Ward, 1b	4	0	0
Atwell, c	4	1	3
J. O'Brien, 2b	5	1	3
E. O'Brien, ss	4	0	1
LaPalme, p	3	1	1
Hetki, p	0	0	0
b-Bernier	1	0	0
Friend, p	0	0	0
Totals	38	5	13

Braves	1	0	3	0	0	0	6	1	0—11
Pittsburgh	2	1	0	0	2	0	0	0	0— 5

Pitchers	IP	H	R	ER	BB	SO
Buhl	5	9	5	4	4	2
Liddle (W, 6–4)	4	4	0	0	2	3
LaPalme (L, 6–15)	6⅔	9	9	4	0	1
Hetki	1⅓	2	2	1	0	0
Friend	1	1	0	0	0	0

a-Flied out for Bruton in 7th.
b-Struck out for Hetki in 8th.
E—Mathews, Ward, E. O'Brien. RBI—Logan 2, Mathews 3, Crandall, Adcock 2, Gordon, Rice, J. O'Brien 2. 3B—Logan. HR—Logan, Mathews, J. O'Brien, Adcock, Gordon. SH—Buhl, Liddle. DP—Dittmer, Logan, and Adcock; Logan, Dittmer, and Adcock; E. O'Brien and Ward. LOB—Milwaukee 1, Pittsburgh 12. WP—LaPalme. U—Boggess, Engeln, Stewart, and Pinelli. T—2:16. Attendance—9,458.

Box Scores of Other Noteworthy Games

Hank Aaron's 3,000 Hit
May 17, 1970 (Second Game)

Atlanta	AB	R	H	RBI
Jackson, ss	7	0	1	0
Millan, 2b	6	3	2	0
H. Aaron, rf	5	2	3	3
Carty, lf	3	0	0	0
Gonzalez, lf	2	1	0	0
Cepeda, 1b	6	0	1	1
Lum, cf	6	0	0	0
Boyer, 3b	5	0	2	0
Didier, c	6	0	0	0
Stone, p	3	0	0	0
Wilhelm, p	0	0	0	0
Garr, ph	1	0	0	0
Kline, p	0	0	0	0
Jaster, p	1	0	0	0
King, ph	1	0	0	0
Neibauer, p	0	0	0	0
Totals	52	6	9	4

Cincinnati	AB	R	H	RBI
Rose, rf	7	1	1	1
Woodward, 2b	4	0	1	0
Chaney, 2b	3	0	1	0
Gullett, p	1	0	1	1
Perez, 3b	7	2	5	0
Bench, c	7	2	2	2
May, 1b	6	1	3	3
McRae, lf	3	0	0	0
Tolan, cf	3	0	1	0
Corrales, c	2	0	0	0
Stewart, 2b	3	0	0	0
Concepcion, ss	7	1	2	0
Simpson, p	2	0	0	0
Ward, ph	1	0	0	0
Granger, p	1	0	0	0
Helms, ph	1	0	0	0
Carroll, p	0	0	0	0
Bravo, ph-lf	1	0	0	0
Totals	59	7	17	7

Atlanta	1	0	2	0	0	0	0	0	3	0	0	0	0	0—6
Cincinnati	0	0	0	0	0	2	0	1	0	3	0	0	0	1—7

One out when winning run scored.

Atlanta	IP	H	R	ER	BB	SO
Stone	7*	9	3	3	1	9
Wilhelm	1	0	0	0	1	2
Kline	1†	3	3	3	0	0
Jaster	3	2	0	0	1	1
Neibauer (L, 0–2)	2⅓	3	1	1	2	1

Cincinnati	IP	H	R	ER	BB	SO
Simpson	7	4	3	2	2	2
Granger	3	4	3	1	4	1
Carroll	3	1	0	0	0	0
Gullett (W, 2–0)	2	0	0	0	2	4

*Pitched to three batters in eighth.
†Pitched to three batters in tenth.

E—Concepcion, Cepeda, Boyer, Chaney, Perez. DP—Atlanta 1, Cincinnati 3. LOB—Atlanta 11, Cincinnati 15. 2B—Perez, Tolan, May. 3B—Concepcion. HR—H. Aaron (16), Rose (6), Bench (11), May (11). SB—Perez, Tolan. SH—Millan, Bravo. HBP—By Simpson (Cepeda). U—Venzon, Secory, Engel and Wendelstedt. T—3:55. A—33,217.

Warren Spahn's 300th Win
August 11, 1961

Chicago	AB	R	H	RBI
Heist, cf	4	0	0	0
Zimmer, 2b	4	0	2	0
Santo, 3b	3	1	0	0
Altman, rf	4	0	1	0
Williams, lf	4	0	1	0
Rodgers, 1b	4	0	1	1
Kindall, ss	4	0	1	0
Bertell, c	3	0	0	0
a-Banks	1	0	0	0
Curtis, p	2	0	0	0
b-McAnany	1	0	0	0
Totals	34	1	6	1

Milwaukee	AB	R	H	RBI
Cimoli, cf	4	1	2	1
Bolling, 2b	4	0	0	0
Mathews, 3b	4	0	1	0
Aaron, rf	2	0	1	0
Adcock, 1b	2	0	0	0
Thomas, lf	3	0	1	0
Torre, c	3	1	0	0
McMillan, ss	3	0	1	0
Spahn, p	2	0	0	1
Totals	27	2	6	2

a-Safe on error for Beriell in 9th;
b-Flied out for Curtis in 9th.

Chicago	0	0	0	0	0	1	0	0	0—1
Milwaukee	0	0	0	1	0	0	0	1	x—2

E—Williams, Bolling, Mathews. A—Chicago 9, Milwaukee 10. DP—McMillan, Bolling, Adcock; Williams, Bertell, Zimmer. LOB—Chicago 8, MIlwaukee 4.
HR—Cimoli. SB—Aaron. Sacrifice—Santo. SF—Spahn.

Pitchers	IP	H	R	ER	BB	SO
Curtis (L, 7–7)	8	6	2	1	2	6
Spahn (W, 12–12)	9	6	1	1	1	5

Umpires—Crawford, Barlick, Jackowski, Varga. Time—2:25. Attendance—40,775.

Lemaster/Koufax Duel
August 9, 1966

Los Angeles	AB	R	H	RBI
W. Davis, cf	4	0	0	0
Wills, ss	4	0	0	0
Johnson, rf	3	0	0	0
T. Davis, lf	3	0	1	0
Stuart, 1b	4	0	0	0
Lefebvre, 2b	3	1	1	1
Roseboro, c	3	0	0	0
Kennedy, 3b	3	0	0	0
Koufax, p	3	0	1	0
Totals	30	1	3	1

Atlanta	AB	R	H	RBI
Alou, 1b	4	1	1	1
Mathews, 3b	4	1	1	1
Aaron, rf	3	0	0	0
Oliver, c	3	0	0	0
Carty, lf	3	0	0	0
Jones, cf	2	0	0	0
de la Hoz, ph	0	0	0	0
Cline, pr-cf	0	0	0	0
Menke, ss	2	0	0	0
Woodward, 2b	3	0	2	0
Lemaster, p	3	0	0	0
Totals	27	2	4	2

Los Angeles	0	0	0	0	0	0	0	1	0—1
Atlanta	1	0	0	0	0	0	0	0	1—2

One out when winning run scored.

Los Angeles	IP	H	R	ER	BB	SO
Koufax (L, 18–6)	8⅓	4	2	2	1	9

Atlanta	IP	H	R	ER	BB	SO
Lemaster (W, 10–8)	9	3	1	1	2	10

E—None. LOB—Los Angeles 4, Atlanta 2. 2B—Woodward, Koufax. HR—Alou (24), Lefebvre (18), Mathews (8). SH—Menke. T—2:19. A—52,270.

Tommy Holmes Hits in Record 37th
Straight Game
July 8, 1945 (Second Game)

Pittsburgh	AB	H	O	A
Coscarart, 2b	4	1	2	3
Saltzgaver, 2b	0	0	0	0
Handley, 3b	4	1	3	2
Russell, lf	2	0	2	0
Elliot, rf	3	0	1	0
Gionfriddo, rf	1	0	1	0
Dahlgren, 1b	4	0	5	1
Gustine, ss	3	0	4	1
Barnhart, ss	1	1	0	0
Barrett, cf	3	0	1	0
Davis, c	3	2	4	1
Butcher, p	1	0	0	2
Strincevich, p	0	0	0	0
*Waner	1	0	0	0
Rescigno, p	1	0	1	0
Totals	31	5	24	10

Boston	AB	H	O	A
Ramsey, lf	4	1	4	0
Culler, ss	4	3	0	0
Holmes, rf	5	1	1	0
Workman, 3b	4	2	2	3
Masi, c	5	2	3	0
Gillenwater, cf	5	3	9	0
Shupe, 1b	4	2	7	0
Drews, 2b	4	0	1	2
Tobin, p	4	0	0	0
Totals	39	14	27	5

Pittsburgh	1	0	0	0	0	0	0	0	0— 1
Boston	1	0	0	7	0	0	4	x—13

*Batted for Strincevich in fifth. R—Coscarart, Ramsey, Culler 2, Holmes, Workman 3, Masi 2, Gillenwater 2, Shupe, Tobin. E—Coscarart, Gustine 2, Russell. RBI—Coscarart, Workman, Tobin, Culler, Holmes 2, Masi 2, Gillenwater 2, Shupe. 2B—Davis, Masi. HR—Coscarart, Holmes, Workman. SB—Russell, Holmes, Workman, Drews. DP—Workman, Drews, and Shupe; Handley, Coscarart and Dahlgren. BB—Butcher 1, Rescigno 4, Tobin 1. SO—Rescigno 3, Tobin 2. Hits—Butcher 9 in 3⅔, Strincevich 0 in ⅓ (pitched to two batters). HP—Tobin 1, Butcher 1. Loser—Butcher. Umpires—Dunn and Sears. Attendance—25,317.

Jim Tobin's 3-HR Game
May 13, 1942

Chicago	AB	R	H	O	A
Gilbert, cf	4	0	0	3	0
Merullo, ss	4	1	0	3	3
Hack, 3b	4	1	1	1	2
Nicholson, rf	4	1	2	3	0
Novikoff, lf	4	0	0	2	0
Stringer, 2b	3	0	0	1	3
Cavarretta, 1b	2	1	0	9	0
McCullough, c	4	1	1	2	1
Mooty, p	3	0	0	0	1
Bithorn, p	0	0	0	0	1
*Russell	1	0	1	0	0
Totals	34	5	5	24	11

Boston	AB	R	H	O	A
Cooney,1b	5	0	1	11	0
Holmes, cf	3	1	1	2	1
Miller, ss	4	1	1	3	3
Fernandez, 3b	3	0	0	3	2
Lombardi, c	2	1	1	1	0
Masi, c	2	0	0	1	0
West, lf	3	0	1	0	0
Waner, rf	3	1	0	3	0
Sisti, 2b	4	0	0	3	2
Tobin, p	4	3	3	0	5
Totals	33	6	9	27	13

Chicago	0	0	2	0	0	2	0	0	1—5
Boston	0	0	0	1	1	0	2	2	x—6

*Batted for Bithorn in ninth. Errors—Mooty, Fernandez, Miller 2, Tobin. Runs batted in—Nicholson 3, Russell, Lombardi, Miller, Tobin 4. Two-base hits—Russell. Home runs—Nicholson, Lombardi, Tobin 3. Miller. Stolen bases—McCullough, Merullo. Bases on balls—Off Mooty 4. off Tobin 3. Struck out—By Mooty 1, by Bithorn 1. Hits—Off Mooty 7 in 6⅔ innings. Passed ball—Lombardi. Losing pitcher—Bithorn. Umpires—Ballanfant, Barlick, and Pinelli.

Ernie Padgett's Unassisted Triple Play
October 6, 1923 (Second Game)

Philadelphia	A	R	H	O	A
Sand, ss	3	0	1	0	3
Mokan, cf	2	0	0	0	0
Walker, rf	2	0	0	4	0
Tierney, 2b	2	0	1	3	2
Lee, lf	2	0	1	0	0
Holke, 1b	2	0	1	3	0
Woehr, 3b	2	0	1	1	1
Wilson, c	2	0	0	1	0
Weiner, p	0	0	0	0	0
Head, p	1	1	0	0	0
Totals	18	1	6	*12	6

Boston	A	R	H	O	A
Emmerich, cf	1	0	0	2	0
Nixon, rf	3	1	1	3	0
McInnis, 1b	1	0	1	0	1
Cooney, lf	1	0	1	2	0
Hermann, 3b	2	0	1	1	1
Padgett, ss	2	1	1	4	0
Conlon, 2b	2	1	1	2	2
Cousineau, c	2	1	2	0	0
Batchelder, p	1	0	0	1	0
Totals	18	4	8	15	4

*Game called after 4½ innings by agreement.

Philadelphia	0	0	1	0	0—1
Boston	1	3	0	0	x—4

Error—Lee. Two-base hit—Sand. Three-base hit—McInnis. Sacrifice—Mokan. Double plays—Sand, Tierney and Holke 2. Triple play—Padgett (unassisted). Left on base—Philadelphia 4, Boston 5. Bases on balls—Off Weinert 2, off Head 1. Struck out—By Weinert 1. Hits—Off Weinert, 5 in 2 innings; off Head 3 in 2 innings. Hit by pitcher—By Batchelder (Head).
Losing pitcher—Weinert. Umpires—Hart and McCormick. Time—45 minutes.

Warren Spahn's 18 Strikeouts
June 14, 1952

Chicago	AB	H	O	A
Miksis, 2b	6	3	2	4
Addis, cf	4	1	4	0
†Jackson	1	0	0	0
Jeffcoat, cf	2	1	2	0
Serena, 3b	7	1	0	3
Sauer, lf	6	0	3	0
Edwards, c	6	1	7	0
Fondy, 1b	6	2	16	2
Hermanski, rf	6	0	7	0
Smalley, ss	5	1	2	7
Ramsdell, p	2	0	1	1
*Pramesa	1	0	0	0
Klippstein, p	1	0	1	1
Totals	53	10	45	18

Boston	AB	H	O	A
Jethroe, cf	5	0	0	0
Daniels, rf	5	0	4	0
Crowe, 1b	6	1	9	1
Gordon, lf	2	0	1	0
Thorpe, lf	3	0	1	0
St. Claire, c	6	1	19	0
‡Hartsfield	0	0	0	0
Mathews, 3b	6	0	2	4
Sistl, 2b	4	0	4	4
§Clarkson	1	0	0	0
Logan, ss	5	1	5	2
Spahn, p	5	1	0	1
Totals	48	4	45	12

Chicago	0	0	0	0	0	0	0	0	1	0	0	0	0	0	2—3
Boston	0	0	0	0	0	1	0	0	0	0	0	0	0	0	0—1

Pitchers	IP	H	R	ER	BB	SO
Ramsdell	7	2	1	1	3	3
Klippstein (Winner 4–4)	8	2	0	0	0	3
Spahn (Loser 6–5)	15	10	3	3	2	18

*Flied out for Ramsdell in eighth.
†Struck out for Addis in tenth.
‡Ran for St. Claire in fifteenth.
§Grounded out for Sisti in fifteenth.
R—Miksis, Serena, Smalley, Spahn. E—None. RBI—Spahn, Serena, Jeffcoat 2. 2B—Miksis 2, Fondy, Smalley. 3B—Crowe, Jeffcoat. HR—Spahn, Serena. SH—Daniels, Klippstein 2. LOB—Chicago 9, Boston 6. WP—Spahn. U—Boggess, Pinelli, Engeln, and Jorda. T—8:14. Attendance—3,053.

Babe Ruth's Last Game
May 30, 1935 (First Game)

Boston	AB	R	H
Urbanski, ss	4	0	2
Thompson, rf	4	1	0
Ruth, lf	1	0	0
Lee, lf	4	1	3
Berger, cf	5	1	1
R. Moore, 1b	4	2	2
Mallon, 2b	3	1	2
Mowry, ph	1	0	0
Whitney, 3b	5	0	3
Spohrer, c	5	0	0
Frankhouse, p	4	0	1
Cantwell, p	0	0	0
Totals	40	6	14

Philadelphia	AB	R	H
Allen, cf	4	1	0
Watkins, lf	5	1	1
J. Moore, rf	3	2	1
Camilli, 1b	3	3	2
Haslin, ss	4	2	3
Chiozza, 2b	4	0	3
Todd, c	5	1	1
Vergez, 3b	3	1	0
Bivin, p	2	0	0
Boland, ph	1	0	0
Jorgens, p	0	0	0
Wilson, ph	1	0	1
C. Davis, p	0	0	0
Totals	35	11	12

Boston	0	1	1	0	2	1	1	0	0—6
Philadelphia	3	0	0	1	0	0	0	7	0—11

Errors: Urbanski, Berger, Mallon, Chiozza, Todd. Runs batted in: Berger, 1, R. Moore 2, Whitney 1, Haslin 3, Chiozza 4, Wilson 1, Watkins 1, Camilli 1. Two-base hits: Urbanski, Whitney, Lee, Haslin 2, Watkins. Three-base hits: Chiozza, R. Moore. Home runs: Berger, R. Moore. Sacrifices: Haslin, Mallon. Left on base: Boston 11. Phillies 8. Bases on balls: off Bivin 2, Jorgens 1, Frankhouse 6, Cantwell 1. Struck out by Bivin 3, Frankhouse 1. Hits: off Bivin 10 in 6 innings; off Jorgens 3 in 2 innings; off C. Davis 1 in 1 inning; off Frankhouse 11 in 7⅔ innings; off Cantwell 1 in ⅓ inning. Winning pitcher: Jorgens. Losing pitcher: Cantwell. Umpires: Quigley, Pfirman, and Moran. Time, 2:25.

13th Straight Win to Start Season
April 21, 1982

Cincinnati	AB	R	H	RBI
E. Molner, cf	4	0	1	0
Driessen, 1b	4	0	1	0
Oester, 2b	4	1	1	0
Concepcion, ss	3	1	0	0
Biittner, rf	4	1	2	3
Householder, ri	0	0	0	0
Vail, lf	4	0	1	0
Hurdie, lf	0	0	0	0
Krenchicki, 3b	4	0	2	0
OBerry, c	4	0	0	0
Soto, p	3	0	0	0
Hume, p	0	0	0	0
Shirley, p	1	0	1	0
Kern, p	0	0	0	0
Price, p	0	0	0	0
Totals	35	3	9	3

Atlanta	AB	R	H	RBI
Butler, cf	5	1	2	0
Hubbard, 2b	4	0	1	0
Pocoroba, ph	0	0	0	0
Washington, rf	4	0	2	2
Horner, 3b	3	0	0	0
Murphy, lf	4	1	2	0
Chambliss, 1b	4	1	2	1
Benedict, c	2	0	1	0
Royster, pr	0	0	0	0
Sinatro, c	0	0	0	0
Ramirez, ss	3	1	1	1
Mahler, p	1	0	0	0
Whisenton, ph	1	0	0	0
Hanna, p	0	0	0	0
Smith, ph	1	0	0	0
Camp, p	0	0	0	0
Linares, ph	1	0	0	0
Totals	33	4	11	4

Two out when winning run scored

Cincinnati	0	0	3	0	0	0	0	0—3
Atlanta	0	0	0	1	1	0	1	0	2—4

DP—Cincinnati 1, Atlanta 1. LOB—Cincinnati 7, Atlanta 9. 2B—Krenchicki, Murphy. HR—Biittner (1), Chambliss (3). SF—Ramirez.

Cincinnati	IP	H	R	ER	BB	SO
Solo	6⅓	7	2	2	1	7
Hume	1⅓	1	0	0	2	0
Shirley L, 0–1	1	2	2	2	1	1
Kern	0	0	0	0	1	0
Price	0	1	0	0	0	0

Atlanta	IP	H	R	ER	BB	SO
Mahler	5	7	3	3	1	3
Hanna	2	1	0	0	1	1
Camp W, 2–0	2	1	0	0	0	1

Kern pitched to 1 batter in the 9th. Price pitched to 1 batter in the 9th. WP—Kern. T—2:44. A—22,153.

End of Pete Rose's 44-Game Hitting Streak
August 1, 1978

Cincinnati	AB	R	H	RBI
Rose, 3b	4	1	0	0
Griffey, rf	4	1	2	0
Concepcion, ss	3	1	2	2
Foster, lf	4	0	0	0
Bench, c	4	1	1	2
Tomlin, p	0	0	0	0
K. Henderson, cf	3	0	0	0
Driessen, 1b	3	0	0	0
Kennedy, 2b	4	0	0	0
Norman, p	0	0	0	0
Borbon, p	2	0	1	0
Hume, p	0	0	0	0
D. Collins, ph	1	0	1	0
Sarmiento, p	0	0	0	0
Correll, c	1	0	0	0
Totals	33	4	7	4

Braves	AB	R	H	RBI
Royster, ss	5	2	2	0
Bonnell, lf	5	3	4	3
Matthews, rf	5	1	2	0
Burroughs, lf	2	1	1	1
Office, cf	1	2	0	0
Horner, 3b	5	4	3	4
Murphy, 1b	5	1	1	1
Gilbreath, 2b	5	1	3	3
Nolan, c	5	0	3	2
McWilliams, p	1	0	0	0
Beall, ph	1	1	1	0
Campbell, p	0	0	0	0
Ruiz, ph	1	0	0	0
Garber, p	2	0	1	0
Totals	43	16	21	14

Cincinnati	3	0	0	0	1	0	0	0	0—4
Braves	2	0	0	1	5	0	3	5	x—16

E—Horner, Griffey, Kennedy, Concepcion. DP—Cincinnati 2, Atlanta 1. LOB—Cincinnati 6, Atlanta 6. 2B—Griffey, Royster 2, Bonnell, Horner, Gilbreath. HR—Bench (16), Concepcion (5), Horner (10), Murphy (16), Bonnell (1). SB—Bonnell. S—Royster.

Cincinnati	IP	H	R	ER	BB	SO
Norman	0	4	2	2	0	0
Borbon (L, 5–2)	5	7	6	6	1	3
Hume	1	1	0	0	0	0
Sarmiento	1	4	3	3	1	1
Tomlin	1	5	5	1	0	2

Atlanta	IP	H	R	ER	BB	SO
McWilliams (W, 3–0)	5	4	4	4	3	2
Campbell	1	0	0	0	1	1
Garber	3	3	0	0	0	4

Save—Garber (16). WP—Borbon. T—2:55. A—31,159.

Red Barrett's 58-Pitch Game; Shortest Night Game in ML History
August 10, 1944

Cincinnati	AB	R	H
Williams, 2b	4	0	0
Criscola, rf	4	0	0
Walker, cf	3	0	1
McCormick, 1b	3	0	0
Mueller, c	3	0	0
Tipton, lf	3	0	0
Mesner, 3b	3	0	0
Miller, ss	3	0	1
Walters, p	2	0	0
*Crabtree	1	0	0
Totals	29	0	2

Braves	AB	R	H
Macon, lf	4	0	0
Holmes, cf	4	0	2
Workman, 3b	3	0	0
Nieman, rf	4	1	1
Hofferth, c	4	0	0
Etchison, 1b	3	0	0
Phillips, ss	4	1	3
Wietelmann, 2b	4	0	0
Barrett, p	3	0	0
Totals	33	2	6

Braves	0	1	0	0	1	0	0	0	0—2
Cincinnati	0	0	0	0	0	0	0	0	0—0

*Batted for Walters in 9th. E—Criscola. RBI—Phillips, Holmes. 2B—Phillips. BB—Walters 1. SO—Walters 1. Umpires—Conlan, Barr, and Sears. Attendance—7,783.

First National League Game
April 22, 1876

Boston	AB	R	H
G. Wright, ss	4	2	1
Leonard, 2b	4	0	2
O'Rourke, cf	5	1	2
Murnane, 1b	6	1	2
Schafer, 3b	5	1	1
McGinley, c	5	1	0
Manning, rf	4	0	0
Parks, lf	4	0	0
Josephs, p	3	0	0
Totals	40	6	8

Philadelphia	AB	R	H
Force, ss	5	0	1
Eggler, cf	5	0	0
Fisler, 1b	5	1	3
Meyerle, 2b	5	1	1
Sutton, 3b	5	0	0
Coons, c	4	2	2
Hall, lf	4	0	2
Fouser, rf	4	0	0
Knight, p	4	1	1
Totals	41	5	10

Red Stockings	0	1	2	0	1	0	0	2—6
Philadelphia	0	1	0	0	0	3	0	1—5

Runs earned—Athletics 2, Red Stockings 1. First base by errors—Athletics 3, Red Stockings 1. Bases on balls—Red Stockings 2, Athletics 1. Umpire—Wm. McLean. Time of game—2 hours, 5 minutes.

First Game at Braves Field
August 18, 1915

St. Louis	AB	R	B	P	A	E
Huggins, 2b	3	0	0	1	2	1
Butler, ss	4	0	1	1	4	0
Bescher, lf	4	1	2	0	0	0
Miller, 1b	4	0	0	13	0	0
Long, rf	4	0	2	2	0	0
Wilson, cf	4	0	2	1	0	0
Snyder, c	4	0	1	5	1	0
Betzel, 3b	3	0	0	1	0	0
Sallee, p	2	0	0	0	4	0
*Hyatt	1	0	0	0	0	0
Meadows, p	0	0	0	0	0	0
Totals	33	1	8	24	11	1

Last Game in Boston
September 21, 1952

Brooklyn	AB	H	O	A
Furillo, rf	5	2	0	0
Reese, ss	5	1	1	3
Snider, cf	5	1	4	0
Robinson, 2b	3	2	4	3
Pafko, lf	5	0	2	0
Campanella, c	5	2	8	2
Hodges, 1b	2	0	7	1
Cox, 3b	2	2	1	0
Black, p	4	1	0	0
Totals	36	11	27	9

Boston	AB	H	O	A
Jethroe, cf	4	0	2	0
Logan, ss	4	2	1	6
Mathews, 3b	4	1	1	3
Cooper, c	4	0	5	0
Gordon, lf	3	0	2	0
Torgeson, 1b	2	0	10	1
Dittmer, 2b	3	0	3	3
Daniels, rf	1	0	3	1
Wilson, p	1	0	0	2
Jester, p	0	0	0	0
*Spahn	1	0	0	0
Jones, p	0	0	0	0
Totals	27	3	27	16

Brooklyn	0	1	0	0	0	1	0	6	0—8
Boston	0	0	0	2	0	0	0	0	0—2

Pitchers	IP	H	R	ER	BB	SO
Black (Winner 15-3)	9	3	2	0	2	4
Wilson (Loser 12-13)	7⅔	8	7	7	3	8
Jester	⅓	2	1	1	0	0
Jones	1	1	0	0	0	0

*Grounded out for Jester in eighth. R—Furillo, Snider, Robinson, Campanella 2. Rodgers, Cox, Black, Logan, Mathews. E—Furillo. RBI—Campanella 2, Snider, Cox, Black 2, Furillo 2. 2B—Mathews, Furillo 2. HR—Campanella. SH—Wilson, Cox. DP—Torgeson, Daniels, Dittmer, Logan and Cooper; Dittmer, Logan and Torgeson. LOB—Brooklyn 7, Boston 2. U—Pinelli, Engeln, Boggess, and Jackowski. T—2:12. Attendance—8,822.

First Game in Milwaukee
April 14, 1953

St. Louis	AB	H	O	A
Hemus, ss	3	0	1	2
Schoendienst, 2b	4	0	4	2
Musial, lf-cf	5	0	1	0
Bilko, 1b	4	0	12	0
Slaughter, rf	3	0	1	0
Jablonski, 3b	4	2	0	2
b-Haddix	0	0	0	0
Johnson, 3b	0	0	0	0
Repulski, cf	3	1	2	0
c-Lowrey, lf	1	1	0	0
D. Rice, c	3	1	7	0
a-Benson	0	0	0	0
Fusselman, c	1	0	0	0
Staley, p	4	1	0	5
Totals	35	6d	28	11

Boston	AB	R	B	P	A	E
Moran, rf	4	0	0	0	0	0
Evers, 2b	3	0	1	3	2	0
Compton, cf	4	0	0	2	0	1
Magee, lf	3	1	1	5	0	0
Schmidt, 1b	2	0	1	8	1	0
Smith, 3b	3	1	1	0	3	0
Maranville, ss	4	1	2	2	4	0
Gowdy, c	3	0	1	7	1	0
Rudolph, p	3	0	0	0	0	0
Totals	29	3	7	27	11	1

*Batted for Sallee in eighth inning.

St. Louis	0	0	0	0	0	0	0	0	1—1
Boston	0	1	0	2	0	0	0	0	x—3

Two-base hits—Long, Gowdy. Stolen base—Smith. Sacrifice hit—Schmidt. Double plays—Huggins, Butler, Miller; Maranville, Evers, Schmidt. Left on bases—St. Louis 6, Boston 9. First on balls—Off Rudolph 1, Sallee 5, Meadows 1. Hits—Off Sallee 5, in 7 innings; Meadows 2, in 1 inning. Struck out—By Rudolph 6, Sallee 2, Meadows 1. Umpires—Klem and Emslie. Time—1:11.

Last Game in Milwaukee
September 22, 1965

Los Angeles	AB	R	H	RBI
Wills, ss	6	3	2	0
Gilliam, 3b	4	1	2	0
Davis, cf	5	1	2	2
L. Johnson, lf	5	0	1	2
Ferrara, rf	2	1	1	0
Fairly, rf	3	0	0	0
Lefebvre, 2b	5	1	3	3
Parker, 1b	5	0	1	0
Torborg, c	3	0	0	0
Roseboro, c	2	0	0	0
Koufax, p	1	0	0	0
Tracewski, ph	0	0	0	0
Perranoski, p	2	0	1	0
Drysdale, ph	1	0	0	0
Kennedy 3b	0	0	0	0
Totals	44	7	13	7

Milwaukee	AB	R	H	RBI
Cowan, lf	5	0	0	0
Dillard, ss	1	0	0	0
Jones, cf	5	1	2	1
Aaron, rf	6	0	2	0
Torre, c	4	1	1	0
Oliver, 1b	4	2	3	1
Mathews	4	1	2	0
Bolling, 2b	4	1	1	4
Woodward, ss	3	0	1	0
Thomas, ph	0	0	0	0
Alomar, ss	1	0	0	0
Blasingame, p	2	0	1	0
O'Dell, p	1	0	0	0
Alou, ph	1	0	0	0
Menke, ph	1	0	0	0
Totals	42	6	13	6

Los Angeles	1	0	0	2	3	0	0	0	0	1—7
Milwaukee	0	4	2	0	0	0	0	0	0	0—6

E—None. DP—Los Angeles 3, Milwaukee 1. LOB—Los Angeles 10, Milwaukee 9.
2B—Blasingame, Woodward. HR—Lefebvre (12), Bolling (7), Jones (29), Oliver (19). SB—Wills 3, Davis. S—Davis, Mathews.

Dodgers Pitching	IP	H	R	ER	BB	SO
Koufax	2	6	5	5	0	3
Reed	2	3	1	1	1	1
Perranoski, W, 5–6	6	3	0	0	4	3
Miller	1	1	0	0	0	0

Braves Pitching	IP	H	R	ER	BB	SO
Blasingame	4⅓	7	6	6	3	3
O'Dell	1⅔	0	0	0	0	2
Osinski	2	2	0	0	1	1
Niekro	2	2	0	0	0	1
Olivo L, 0–1	⅓	1	1	1	1	0
Kelley	⅔	1	0	0	0	0

Koufax, faced 2 men in 3d.
T—3:38. A—12,577.

Milwaukee	AB	H	O	A
Bruton, cf	5	3	5	0
Logan, ss	2	0	3	2
Mathews, 3b	3	0	2	6
Gordon, lf	4	1	4	1
Pafko, rf	4	0	4	0
Adcock, 1b	3	1	8	1
Crandall, c	3	1	3	2
Dittmer, 2b	4	0	1	1
Spahn, p	4	0	0	2
Totals	32	6	30	15

St. Louis	0	0	0	0	1	0	0	0	1	0—2
Milwaukee	0	1	0	0	0	0	0	1	0	1—3

Pitchers	IP	H	R	ER	BB	SO
Spahn (Winner 1–0)	10	6	2	2	3	2
Staley (Loser 0–1)	9⅓	6	3	2	2	6

a-Ran for D. Rice in eighth.
b-Ran for Jablonski in ninth.
c-Doubled for Repulski in ninth.
d-One out when winning run scored.
R—Slaughter, Haddix, Bruton 2, Adcock. E—Dittmer, Spahn, Jablonski. RBI—Jablonski, Lowrey, Gordon, Bruton. 2B—D. Rice, Lowrey. 3B—Bruton. HR—Bruton. SH—Schoendienst, Crandall, Logan. DP—Gordon and Mathews; Logan, Mathews and Dittmer. LOB—St. Louis 7, Milwaukee 6. HP—Staley (Logan). U—Conlan, Warneke, Donatelli, and Gorman. T—2:29. Attendance—34,357.

First Game in Atlanta
April 12, 1966

Pittsburgh	AB	R	H	RBI
M. Alou, cf	6	0	1	0
Alley, ss	6	0	2	0
Clemente, rf	6	1	2	0
Stargell, lf	6	1	1	2
Clendenon, 1b	4	0	0	0
Mazeroski, 2b	5	0	2	0
Bailey, 3b	4	0	0	0
Pagliaroni, c	5	1	2	1
Veale, p	3	0	0	0
Face, p	0	0	0	0
Lynch, ph	0	0	0	0
Mota, pr	0	0	0	0
Schwall, p	1	0	0	0
Totals	46	3	10	3

Atlanta	AB	R	H	RBI
F. Alou, cf	5	0	2	0
Mathews, 3b	6	0	0	0
Aaron, rf	6	0	1	0
Carty, lf	5	0	2	0
Torre, c	4	2	2	2
Menke, ss	3	0	0	0
Thomas, 1b	5	0	0	0
Bolling, 2b	5	0	1	0
Cloninger, p	3	0	0	0
Totals	42	2	8	2

Pittsburgh	0	0	0	0	0	0	1	0	0	0	0	2—3
Atlanta	0	0	0	0	1	0	0	0	0	0	0	1—2

Pittsburgh	IP	H	R	ER	BB	SO
Veale	8⅔	5	1	1	5	4
Face	⅓	0	0	0	0	0
Schwall (W, 1–0)	4	3	1	1	3	2

Atlanta	IP	H	R	ER	BB	SO
Cloninger (L, 0–1)	13	10	3	3	3	12

E—Menke. DP—Pittsburgh 2, Atlanta 2. LOB—Pittsburgh 8, Atlanta 11. HR—Torre 2 (2). Pagliaroni (1), Stargell (1). SB—Aaron. SH—Cloninger, Bailey, Torre. WP—Veale, Cloninger 2. T—3:37. A—50,671.

1914 Pennant Clincher
September 29

Chicago	AB	R	H
Leach, cf	4	0	1
Goode, rf	3	1	1
Saier, 1b	3	0	1
Zimmerman, 2b	4	0	1
Schulte, lf	3	1	0
Bues, 3b	2	0	1
Fisher, ss	3	0	0
Archer, c	3	0	0
Cheney, p	3	0	0
Totals	28	2	5

Braves	AB	R	H
Moran, rf	4	0	0
Evers, 2b	3	1	0
Connolly, lf	3	1	1
Whitted, cf	4	1	1
Schmidt, 1b	2	0	0
Smith, 3b	2	0	1
Maranville, ss	1	0	0
Whaling, c	2	0	0
Gowdy, c	1	0	0
Hughes, p	4	0	0
*Gilbert	1	0	0
Totals	27	3	3

One out when winning run scored.
*Batted for Whaling in 5th.

Chicago	1	0	0	1	0	0	0	0	0—2
Braves	0	0	0	0	2	0	0	0	1—3

Two-base hit—Whitted. Three-base hits—Zimmerman, Bues. Sacrifice hit—Maranville. Sacrifice fly—Saier. Stolen base—Connolly. Left on bases—Chicago 2, Boston 12. First on balls—Off Cheney 11, Hughes 2. First on errors—Chicago 2. Hit by pitcher—Maranville. Struck out—By Cheney 3, Hughes 8. Passed balls—Archer 2. Wild pitches—Hughes 2. Time 2:10. Umpires—O'Connor and Byron.

1948 Pennant Clincher
September 26

New York	AB	R	H
Lohrke, 2b	4	0	0
Lockman, cf	3	0	0
Gordon, 3b	4	0	1
Mize, 1b	3	0	1
Marshall, rf	4	0	0
Mueller, lf	4	1	1
Yvars, c	3	1	1
Kerr, ss	2	0	0
*McCarthy	1	0	1
†Bamberger	0	0	0
Rhawn, ss	0	0	0
Jansen, p	2	0	0
‡Frey	1	0	0
Hansen	0	0	0
Totals	31	2	5

Braves	AB	R	H
Holmes, rf	4	1	1
Dark, ss	4	1	1
Torgeson, 1b	4	0	0
Elliott, 3b	4	1	1
Heath, lf	4	0	0
Salkeld, c	3	0	0
Masi, c	0	0	0
M. McCormick, cf	3	0	1
Sisti, 2b	1	0	1
Bickford, p	3	0	0
Potter, p	0	0	0
Totals	30	3	6

New York	0	0	0	0	0	0	0	2	0—2
Braves	3	0	0	0	0	0	0	0	X—3

*Singled for Kerr in 8th.
†Ran for McCarthy in 8th.
‡Grounded out for Jansen in 8th.
E—Gordon, Potter. RBI—McCarthy, Frey, Elliott. 2B—M. McCormick. HR—Elliott. SB—Lockman. DP—Sisti, Dark, and Torgeson. BB—Jansen 2, Bickford 1, Potter 1. SO—Jansen 3, Hansen 2, Bickford 2. Hits—Bickford 5 in 7 (none out in 8th). Jansen 6 in 7. HP—Jansen 1. Winner—Bickford. Loser—Jansen. Umpires—Barr, Dascoli, Ballanfant, and Barlick. Attendance—31,172.

1957 Pennant Clincher
September 23

St. Louis	AB	R	H
Blasingame, 2b	5	0	0
Moon, cf	4	1	1
Musial, 1b	4	1	3
a-Schofield	0	0	0
Cunningham, 1b	1	0	0
Noren, rf	4	0	1
Ennis, lf	5	0	1
Dark, ss	5	0	1
Landrith, c	4	0	1
b-Boyer	0	0	0
H. Smith, c	1	0	0
Kasko, 3b	4	0	1
Mizell, p	0	0	0
Jackson, p	3	0	0
c-King	1	0	0
Muffett, p	0	0	0
Totals	41	2	9

Braves	AB	R	H
Schoendienst, 2b	6	1	2
Logan, ss	5	1	1
Mathews, 3b	6	0	1
Aaron, cf	4	2	3
Adcock, 1b	4	0	1
d-DeMerit	0	0	0
Conley, p	0	0	0
Pafko, rf	5	0	1
Covington, lf	4	0	2
Crandall, c	4	0	2
Burdette, p	4	0	1
e-Torre, 1b	1	0	0
Totals	43	4	14

St. Louis	0	0	0	0	0	2	0	0	0	0	0—2
Braves	0	1	0	0	0	0	1	0	0	0	2—4

Pitchers	IP	H	R	ER	BB	SO
Burdette	10	9	2	2	2	4
Conley (W, 9–9)	1	0	0	0	0	1
Mizell	1*	4	1	1	0	0
Jackson	7	7	1	1	2	1
Muffett (L, 3–2)	2⅔	3	2	2	2	1

*Pitched to four batters in second.
a-Ran for Musial in 8th.
b-Ran for Landrith in 9th.
c-Flied out for Jackson in 9th.
d-Ran for Adcock in 10th.
e-Hit into double play for Burdette in 10th.
(Two outs when winning run scored.) E—Moon, Dark, Kasko. RBI—Covington, Dark 2, Mathews, Aaron 2. 2B—Musial 2, Mathews. HR—Aaron. SH—Logan. SF—Covington. SB—Boyer. DP—Mizell, Blasingame, Dark, and Musial; Crandall and Logan; Dark and Musial; Dark, Blasingame, and Musial; Cunningham, H. Smith, and Cunningham. LOB—St. Louis 8, Braves 13. U—Ballanfani, Boggess, Dascoli, Gorman. T—3:33. Attendance—40,926.

1958 Pennant Clincher
September 21

Milwaukee	AB	R	H	RBI
Bruton, cf	5	1	2	0
Schoedienst, 2b	5	1	3	1
Mathews, 3b	4	1	0	0
Aaron, rf	3	2	2	4
Covington, lf	4	0	0	0
Pafko, lf	0	0	0	0
Torre, 1b	4	0	0	0
Crandall, c	4	0	1	0
Logan, ss	4	0	0	0
Spahn, p	5	1	2	0
McMahon, p	1	0	0	0
Totals	39	6	10	5

Cincinnati	AB	R	H	RBI
Grammas, 2b	2	0	1	0
e-Newcombe	1	0	1	0
f-Henrich, ss	0	0	0	0
i-Bailey	1	0	0	0
Lynch, rf	3	0	0	1
Whisenant, lf	3	0	0	0
g-Crowe	1	0	0	0
Pena, p	0	0	0	0
Robinson, 3b	4	1	1	1
Dotterer, c	4	0	1	0
Dropo, 1b	4	1	1	0
Bell, cf	4	1	1	0
McMillan, ss	2	0	0	0
b-Burgess	1	0	1	2
c-Miksis, 2b	0	1	0	0
h-Fondy	1	0	0	0
Lawrence, p	1	0	0	0
a-Thurman	1	0	0	0
Acker, p	0	0	0	0
d-Fridley, lf	2	1	1	1
Totals	35	5	7	5

a-Struck out for Lawrence in 5th;
b-Singled for McMillan in 7th;
c-Ran for Burgess in 7th;
d-Doubled for Acker in 7th;
e-Singled for Grammas in 7th;
f-Ran for Newcombe in 7th;
g-Fouled out for Whisenant in 7th;
h-Grounded out for Miksis in 9th;
i-Flied out for Henrich in 9th.

Milwaukee	0	0	0	0	4	0	2	0	0—6
Cincinnati	0	0	0	0	0	0	5	0	0—5

E—McMillan; Logan. A—Milwaukee 7, Cincinnati, 6. DP—Grammas, McMillan. LOB—Milwaukee 6, Cincinnati 5.
2B Hits—Spahn, Aaron, Crandall, Bell, Fridley. HR—Aaron, Robinson.

Pitchers	IP	H	R	ER	BB	SO
Spahn (W, 21–11)	6⅓	5	5	3	2	2
McMahon	2⅔	2	0	0	0	0
Lawrence (L, 8–13)	5	7	4	3	2	2
Acker	2	3	2	2	0	1
Pena	2	0	0	0	0	3

Umpires—Dascoll, Donatelli, Crawford, Smith. Time—2:46. Attendance—27,213.

Final Game of 1959 Playoff
September 29

Milwaukee	AB	R	H	RBI	PO	A	E
Bruton, cf	6	0	0	0	4	0	0
Mathews, 3b	4	2	2	1	2	2	0
Aaron, rf	4	1	2	0	3	0	0
Torre, 1b	3	0	1	2	10	2	0
Maye, lf	2	0	0	0	2	0	0
a-Pafko, lf	1	0	0	0	0	0	0
b-Slaughter	1	0	0	0	0	0	0
DeMerit, lf	0	0	0	0	1	0	0
i-Spangler, lf	0	0	0	0	3	0	0
Logan, ss	3	1	2	0	2	5	0
Schoendienst, 2b	1	0	0	0	0	0	0
d-Vernon	1	0	0	0	0	0	0
Cottier, 2b	0	0	0	0	0	0	0
k-Adcock	1	0	0	0	0	0	0
Avila, 2b	0	0	0	0	1	0	0
Crandall, c	6	1	1	0	6	1	0
Mantilla, 2b-ss	5	0	1	1	1	1	2
Burdette, p	4	0	1	0	0	2	0
McMahon, p	0	0	0	0	0	0	0
Spahn, p	0	0	0	0	0	0	0
Jay, p	1	0	0	0	0	0	0
Rush, p	1	0	0	0	0	0	0
Totals	**44**	**5**	**10**	**4**	**x35**	**13**	**2**

Los Angeles	AB	R	H	RBI	PO	A	E
Gilliam, 3b	5	0	1	0	4	3	0
Neal, 2b	6	2	2	1	3	2	1
Moon, rf-lf	6	1	3	1	3	1	0
Snider, cf	4	0	1	0	1	0	1
e-Lillis	0	1	0	0	0	0	0
Williams, p	2	0	0	0	0	0	0
Hodges, 1b	5	2	2	0	11	0	0
Larker, lf	4	0	2	2	2	0	0
f-Pignatano, c	1	0	1	0	3	0	0
Roseboro, c	3	0	0	0	5	1	0
g-Furillo, rf	2	0	2	1	0	0	0
Wills, ss	5	0	1	0	2	5	0
Drysdale, p	1	0	0	0	1	1	0
Podres, p	1	0	0	0	0	0	0
Churn, p	0	0	0	0	0	1	0
c-Demeter	1	0	0	0	0	0	0
Koufax, p	0	0	0	0	0	0	0
Labine, p	0	0	0	0	0	0	0
h-Essegian	0	0	0	0	0	0	0
i-Fairly, cf	2	0	0	0	1	0	0
Totals	48	6	15	5	36	14	2

a-Flied out for Maye in 5th.
b-Popped out for Palko in 7th.
c-Lined out for Churn in 8th.
d-Called out on strikes for Schoendienst in 9th.
e-Ran for Snider in 9th.
f-Ran for Larker in 9th.
g-Hit sacrifice fly for Roseboro in 9th.
h-Announced for Labine in 9th.
i-Hit into force out for Essegian in 9th.
j-Walked for DeMerit in 11th.
k-Hit into force out for Cottier in 11th.
x-Two out when winning run scored.

Milwaukee	2	1	0	0	1	0	0	1	0	0	0	0—5
Los Angeles	1	0	0	1	0	0	0	0	3	0	0	1—6

Double—Aaron. Triples—Crandall, Neal. Home Runs—Mathews, Neal. Sacrifice Flies—Furillo, Mantilla. Double Plays—Wills to Neal to Hodges, Torre to Logan to Torre. Passed Ball—Pignatano.

Milwaukee	IP	H	R	ER	BB	SO
Burdette	*8	10	5	5	0	4
McMahon	**0	1	0	0	0	0
Spahn	⅓	1	0	0	0	0
Jay	2⅓	1	0	0	1	1
Rush (L)	1	2	1	0	1	0
Los Angeles	**IP**	**H**	**R**	**ER**	**BB**	**SO**
Drysdale	4⅓	6	4	3	2	3
Podres	2⅓	3	0	0	1	1
Churn	1⅓	1	1	1	0	0
Koufax	⅔	0	0	0	3	1
Labine	⅓	0	0	0	0	1
Williams (W)	3	0	0	0	3	3

*Pitched to three batters in 9th.
**Pitched to one batter in 9th.

Hit by Pitcher—Pignatano (by Jay). Wild Pitch—Podres. Left on Bases—Milwaukee 13, Los Angeles 11. Umpires—Barlick, Boggess, Donatelli, Conlan, Jackowski, Gorman. Attendance—36,853. Time of Game—4:06.

1969 Division Clincher
September 30

Cincinnati	AB	R	H	RBI
Rose, rf	3	0	2	1
Helms, 2b	4	0	1	0
Tolan, cf	4	0	0	0
Perez, 3b	4	0	0	0
Bench, c	4	0	1	0
May, 1b	4	1	1	0
Stewart, lf	4	0	1	0
Woodward, ss	2	1	1	1
Johnson, ph	1	0	0	0
Nolan, p	2	0	0	0
Granger, p	0	0	0	0
Totals	**32**	**2**	**7**	**2**

Atlanta	AB	R	H	RBI
Millan, 2b	3	1	0	0
Gonzalez, cf	4	0	4	1
H. Aaron, rf	2	0	1	1
Carty, lf	3	0	1	1
Wilhelm, p	0	0	0	0
Cepeda, 1b	3	0	0	0
Boyer, 3b	4	0	0	0
Didier, c	4	0	0	0
Garrido, ss	2	0	0	0
Lum, ph-lf	2	0	1	0
Niekro, p	2	1	2	0
Garr, ph	0	1	0	0
Aspromonte, ss	1	0	0	0
Totals	**30**	**3**	**9**	**3**

Cincinnati	0	0	0	0	2	0	0	0	0—2
Atlanta	0	0	1	0	0	0	2	0	x—3

Pitchers	IP	H	R	ER	BB	SO
Nolan (L. 8-8)	6*	8	3	3	2	1
Granger	2	1	0	0	1	0
Niekro (W. 23-13)	7	7	2	2	1	6
Wilhelm (Save 4)	2	0	0	0	0	3

*Pitched to two batters in seventh.

E—Perez. DP—Cincinnati 1. LOB—Cincinnati 6, Atlanta 9. 2B—May. SH—Nolan, Woodward, Millan. SF—Carty. HBP—By Granger (Cepeda). U—Crawford, Pelekoudas, Harvey, and Dezelan. T—2:14. A—43,974.

1992 Division Clincher
September 29

San Francisco	AB	R	H	RBI
Felder, cf	4	0	2	0
Thompson, 2b	4	0	1	0
Clark, 1b	4	0	2	0
James, lf	4	0	0	0
Williams, 3b	4	0	1	0
Hosey, rf	4	0	0	0
Manwaring, c	4	0	2	0
Clayton, ss	3	0	0	0
Black, p	2	0	0	0
Reed, p	0	0	0	0
Jackson, p	0	0	0	0
Litton, ph	1	0	0	0
Burba, p	0	0	0	0
Patterson, ph	1	0	0	0
Totals	**35**	**0**	**8**	**0**

Braves	AB	R	H	RBI
Nixon, rf-cf	4	0	0	0
Blauser, ss	2	1	0	0
Belliard, ss	1	0	0	0
Pendleton, 3b	4	1	1	0
L. Smith, lf	2	1	1	1
Justice, rf	1	0	0	0
Gant, cf-lf	4	2	3	2
Hunter, 1b	4	1	1	1
Berryhill, c	3	0	2	2
Lemke, 2b	3	0	0	0
Leibrandt, p	3	0	0	0
Totals	**31**	**6**	**8**	**6**

San Francisco	0	0	0	0	0	0	0	0	0—0
Braves	0	1	0	4	1	0	0	0	x—6

2B—Pendleton, Berryhill. HR—Gant (17th). LOB—Houston 9, Atlanta 3.

San Francisco	IP	H	R	ER	BB	SO
Black (L, 10–12)	3⅓	3	5	5	2	1
Reed	⅔	1	0	0	0	1
Jackson	1	3	1	1	0	1
Burba	3	1	0	0	0	3
Atlanta	**IP**	**H**	**R**	**ER**	**BB**	**SO**
Leibrandt (W, 14–7)	9	8	0	0	1	4

Balk—Black. T—2:30. A—40,860. Umpires—Rapuano, West, Tata, Rippley.

1993 Division Clincher
October 3

Colorado	AB	R	H	RBI
Liriano, ss	4	1	1	0
E. Young, lf	4	0	1	0
Galarraga, 1b	4	0	0	0
Hayes, 3b	4	0	1	0
Clark, rf	3	1	1	0
Jones, cf	3	0	1	0
Boston, ph	1	0	0	0
Sheaffer, c	2	0	0	1
Mejia, 2b	3	1	1	1
Nied, p	1	0	0	0
Munoz, p	0	0	0	0
Wedge, ph	1	0	0	0
Ruffin, p	0	0	0	0
Tatum, ph	0	0	0	0
Cole, ph	1	0	0	0
Wayne, p	0	0	0	0
Blair, p	0	0	0	0
Painter, p	0	0	0	0
Totals	**31**	**3**	**6**	**2**

Braves	AB	R	H	RBI
Nixon, cf	4	2	2	0
Blauser, ss	4	1	2	0
Gant, lf	3	0	1	2
McGriff, 1b	4	1	1	1
Justice, rf	4	1	2	1
Pendleton, 3b	4	0	2	1
Berryhill, c	4	0	1	0
Lemke, 2b	3	0	1	0
McMichael, p	0	0	0	0
Glavine, p	3	0	0	0
Bedrosian, p	0	0	0	0
Belliard, 2b	1	0	0	0
Totals	**34**	**5**	**12**	**5**

Colorado	0	0	0	0	1	1	1	0	0—3
Braves	0	0	2	2	0	0	1	0	x—5

2B—Liriano, Jones. 3B—Gant. HR—Mejia (5th), Justice (40th). SF—Sheaffer. SB—Gant. LOB—Colorado 3, Atlanta 11. DP—Colorado 1, Atlanta 1.

Colorado	IP	H	R	ER	BB	SO
Nied (L, 5–9)	3⅔	7	4	4	5	2
Munoz	⅓	0	0	0	0	1
Ruffin	2	1	0	0	1	3
Wayne	0	1	1	1	0	0
Blair	1⅔	3	0	0	0	1
Painter	⅓	0	0	0	0	0
Atlanta	**IP**	**H**	**R**	**ER**	**BB**	**SO**
Glavine (W, 22–6)	6⅔	6	3	3	1	4
Bedrosian	⅓	0	0	0	0	1
McMichael (S, 19)	2	0	0	0	0	2

Wayne pitched to 1 batter in 7th. HBP—Lemke by Nied. WP—Painter. T—2:56. A—48,904. Umpires—Davidson, Poncino, Gorman, Hohn.

9

NORTHWEST
AIRLINES
FLIGHT
208

The Postseason

The modern World Series between the champions of the National and American Leagues wasn't born until 1903. Since then, the Braves have appeared in the World Series six times, winning in 1914 and 1957. The 1914 "Miracle Braves" accomplished the first four-game sweep in Series history, stunning the heavily favored Philadelphia Athletics of Connie Mack. The 1957 Milwaukee Braves defeated Casey Stengel's powerful Yankees in seven games.

The franchise's postseason history also includes five trips to the relatively new creation known as the National League Championship Series, which was devised to determine pennant winners when division play was implemented in 1969. The Braves won that very first National League West title but were swept by the Mets in the inaugural NLCS. Atlanta's two NLCS triumphs came in 1991 and 1992, both against Pittsburgh in seven games.

But the franchise's history also includes two postseason appearances in the 19th century when Boston's National League franchise, playing under the nicknames of Red Stockings and Beaneaters, won eight pennants in the first 23 years of National League history.

In 1892 the National League expanded from eight to 12 teams and adopted a split-season format for the only time until the strike-interrupted 1981 season. The Beaneaters of manager Frank Selee won the first half, and the Cleveland Spiders, featuring a 25-year-old right-hander named Cy Young, won the second half.

To determine the league championship, a best-of-nine series was held. After the two clubs played to an 11-inning scoreless tie in a duel between Young and Boston's Jack Stivetts, Boston swept the next five games. Stivetts and Hall of Famer Kid Nichols each won two games, and Boston defeated Young twice. The Beaneaters' Hugh Duffy was the offensive star, leading both teams with a .462 average and nine RBIs.

In 1894 a best-of-seven postseason series called the Temple Cup was instituted between the National League's top two teams. However, the Temple Cup was never accepted by the players or the fans and died after four years. It was the Beaneaters' misfortune to play in the final Temple Cup in 1897.

Selee's team, the best of record (.705) in franchise history, beat Baltimore by two games in the regular season and was not at all enthused about meeting the Orioles in the postseason series. As a result, Baltimore won in five games of what really was no more than an exhibition.

Though postseason appearances by the Braves in the 20th century have been limited, they have produced much excitement and plenty of memorable moments. This chapter is devoted to the franchise's modern history in the NLCS and World Series.

Braves versus Philadelphia Athletics World Series

1914

If ever one team did a psych job on another, the Braves did it to the mighty Philadelphia Athletics in the 1914 World Series.

Managed by the legendary Connie Mack, the Athletics with their vaunted "$100,000 infield" won the World Series in 1910, 1911, and 1913 and had the best record in baseball (99–53) in 1914. The Braves, on the other hand, were considered a fluke—a "miracle." They'd never won the Series, hadn't won a pennant since 1898, and prior to 1914 hadn't even posted a winning season since 1902. To make matters worse, the Braves had to play the Series without third baseman Red Smith, one of their best hitters, who suffered a broken leg on the last day of the season.

Most gamblers wouldn't even take a bet on what was considered a tremendous mismatch. But this ominous outlook played right into the hand of Braves manager George

Milwaukee's infatuation with the Braves was at its peak in 1957 when this group of fans flew to New York for the start of the World Series at Yankee Stadium.

Defensive specialist Charlie Deal (above) filled in ably at third base during the Series for Red Smith, who suffered a broken leg on the last day of the regular season.

Stallings, a master psychologist who'd prodded his team from last place on July 18 to winning the pennant by 10½ games. He knew his team had confidence and momentum, while the Athletics were sure to be overconfident.

Stallings orchestrated the situation like a magnificent conductor, resulting in one of the most phenomenal upsets in Series history. For not only did the Braves win, but they also pulled off the only four-game sweep in the first 23 years of Series history.

How did Stallings get the Braves mentally prepared for the heavily favored Athletics? Instead of showing respect and admiration for the defending Series champs, he displayed scorn. In fact, he actually predicted the Braves would win in four straight.

Stallings praised the Braves and said he wouldn't even bother to scout Mack's club. Then he secretly sent his assistants to do just that. Mack, on the other hand, assigned his ace pitcher, Chief Bender, to scout the Braves. But Bender

never bothered. "We don't need to scout that bush-league outfit," the pitcher told his manager.

Stallings also told his players not to talk to the Athletics unless it was to insult them, and he set the tone by getting into an argument with the gentlemanly Mack over practice time at Shibe Park. When the stadium announcer came to Stallings in Philadelphia to ask for Boston's lineup for the first game, the Braves manager chased him out of the dugout. Philadelphia outfielder Eddie Murphy greeted his friend Rabbit Maranville before the first game, only to find that Boston's fun-loving shortstop wouldn't say hello or even shake Murphy's hand.

The atmosphere only deteriorated from there. The Braves won no points for sportsmanship, but their superior gamesmanship shook up the Athletics and gave Boston the edge it needed. For example, Stallings and his men harassed Philadelphia's young catcher Wally Schang so badly that he had two passed balls and allowed nine stolen bases—still the record for a four-game Series.

Mack's team was led by five of the best pitchers in the American League, Bender (17–3), Bob Shawkey (16–8), Eddie Plank (15–7), Joe Bush (16–12), and Herb Pennock (11–4). The "$100,000 infield" consisted of first baseman Stuffy McInnis, second baseman Eddie Collins, third baseman Frank "Home Run" Baker, and shortstop Jack Barry. Collins led the AL in hitting (.344), and Baker led in homers (9).

The Braves boasted a spunky double-play combination of Maranville and Johnny Evers, who won the Chalmers Award as the league's MVP. But they had just one .300 hitter, outfielder Joe Connolly (.306).

It was the pitching of Dick Rudolph (26–10), Bill James (26–7), and Lefty Tyler (16–13) that led Boston to the 1914 pennant, and it was the same trio who mowed down the Athletics in the Series. Philadelphia scored a total of just six runs in the four games.

Game One

Braves president James Gaffney lost the coin toss for the home-field advantage, but that was all the Braves lost in the Series. It took Stallings' team but six innings to convince the Athletics they had their hands full, but by that time, it was too late for Mack's men to turn the tide that was about to engulf them.

Fans who couldn't get into Philadelphia's Shibe Park packed nearby rooftops to watch their heavily favored Athletics face the upstart Braves in the first game of the 1914 World Series.

Bender quickly discovered he did himself and his teammates a great disservice by failing to scout the Braves. Boston roughed him up for six runs in the first 5⅓ innings while Rudolph was breezing through the Philadelphia lineup. The rout was on.

The Braves got the only two runs they would need in the top of the second before a disappointed Shibe Park crowd of 20,562. Possum Whitted led off with a walk and scored on a one-out double by catcher Hank Gowdy, who proved to be the offensive star of the Series. Maranville, just starting his Hall of Fame career, then singled to right, scoring Gowdy.

The Athletics got a run back in the bottom of the second, thanks to an error by Boston right fielder Herbie Moran. But Rudolph put the Philadelphia hitters to sleep for the rest of the afternoon, facing just 25 men over the final seven innings.

The Braves went up 3–1 in the fifth on a leadoff triple by Gowdy and a single by Maranville. Then they chased Bender with three runs in the sixth, the key blow being a two-run triple by Whitted.

The Braves completed their scoring in the eighth off Weldon Wyckoff. Butch Schmidt and Gowdy singled to put runners at the corners with one out, at which point Stallings' troops added insult to injury. As Maranville struck out, Boston executed a perfect double steal by Schmidt and Gowdy, two of the slowest players on the team. When Schmidt slid across the plate under Collins' throw, the Braves whooped it up and needled the Athletics.

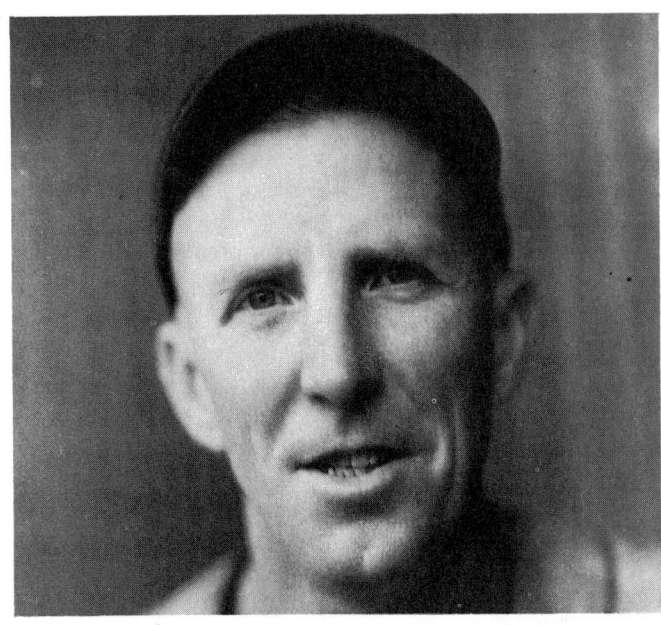

The batting star of the Series was Braves catcher Hank Gowdy, who led both teams with a .545 average.

Rudolph, who was in trouble only in the second inning, allowed five hits in the 7–1 victory. He walked three and struck out eight. Gowdy had a single, double, and triple in three at bats.

Game Two

The second game was a classic pitching duel between James, a 22-year-old right-hander, and Plank, a 39-year-old left-hander who was well on his way to Cooperstown. The Athletics could barely scratch against James, and though the Braves had numerous base runners, they failed time after time to get a clutch hit.

The game was scoreless through eight innings. After allowing a leadoff walk in the first, James didn't permit another base runner until Schang doubled with one out in the sixth for the Athletics' first hit. However, the mild threat ended when Schang was thrown out trying to take third on a pitch that got away from Gowdy.

Philadelphia's only other hit was a two-out infield single by Collins in the seventh, but James picked him off first base to end the inning.

The Braves had base runners against Plank in seven of the first eight innings but never got a man past second. Only in the seventh did the veteran left-hander retire Boston in order.

But with one out in the top of the ninth, Charlie Deal, who replaced the injured Smith at third base, hit a fly ball to center that Amos Strunk lost in the sun. Deal wound up with a cheap double that proved to be the undoing of the Athletics.

James struck out for the fourth time in the game, and on the third strike, Deal was trapped off second. Schang threw to second behind Deal, who broke for third and was ruled safe on a close play. Les Mann followed with a single to right-center, driving in the only run of the game.

In his two-hit, 1–0 masterpiece, James issued just three walks—two of them in the ninth—and struck out eight. Plank gave up seven hits, walked four, and struck out six.

When the Braves left for Boston with a 2–0 lead in games, Stallings ordered all the team's equipment—including its road uniforms—shipped home. "We won't be coming back," said the psych master.

Game Three

The Series moved to Boston for Games 3 and 4, but first the clubs rested on Sunday, October 10, because no ball playing was permitted on the Sabbath in Boston. With the South End Grounds in poor repair and seating only 11,000, the Braves gladly accepted the Red Sox' offer to play the games in new Fenway Park.

Some 300 fans camped out overnight to get tickets for the Monday afternoon game, and 35,520 packed Fenway for the affair. Prior to the game, Evers drove around the field in

the new Chalmers automobile he received for being named the league's MVP.

With their backs against the wall, the Athletics took their first lead in the Series by scoring a run in the first against Tyler. The Braves evened the score in the second with a two-out rally against Bush. Maranville walked and stole second, then scored when the red-hot Gowdy doubled to left.

Both teams got a run in the fourth. Philadelphia scored when McInnis doubled and Jimmy Walsh singled him home.

After the Braves won the first two games in Philadelphia, the scene shifted to Boston, where the big story was George Stallings, the architect of the "miracle" of 1914.

Boston answered when Schmidt singled with one out, took second on an infield out, and scored on Maranville's single to center.

The game stayed at 2–2 through nine innings with neither team getting a runner past second base from the fifth through the ninth. In the 10th, however, Philadelphia struck for two runs.

Bush had been cruising entering the 10th. He'd allowed just two hits since the fourth and had retired the last 10 Braves he'd faced. However, Gowdy, the Braves' eighth-place hitter, led off the bottom of the 10th with a home run to center, closing the gap to 4–3. Josh Devore batted for Tyler and struck out, but Moran drew a walk and Evers singled, giving Boston runners at the corners with one out. Connolly flied to center, allowing Moran to tag at third and score the tying run. Whitted popped to third to end the inning.

James, who two days earlier pitched a two-hit shutout in Game 2, was called on to relieve Tyler in the 11th. He retired the Athletics easily, but the Braves went down in order in the bottom of the inning, too.

In the 12th, James issued two walks, one intentional, but got out of the inning when McInnis grounded to Evers at second. Then Gowdy, who batted just .243 in the regular season, got the winning rally started with a leadoff double. Mann ran for Gowdy, and Larry Gilbert, batting for James, was walked intentionally. When Moran bunted, Bush fielded the ball and threw wildly to third, allowing Mann to score and ending the 5–4 game.

With the Series scheduled to shift back to Philadelphia for Game 5, if needed, Stallings canceled the Braves' train reservations.

Game Four

Rudolph, who pitched a complete-game victory in Game 1, drew the assignment of trying to close out the Athletics in Game 4. Mack had Bender, his ace who'd been hit hard in the opener, rested but chose instead to start Shawkey, a 23-year-old right-hander.

It looked like a good decision when the Braves were hitless through the first three innings. But with the game scoreless in the bottom of the fourth, Boston got on the board with a single run.

Manager George Stallings with his three starting pitchers, (L-R) Dick Rudolph, Lefty Tyler, and Bill James who held the mighty Athletics to a .172 team batting average in the Series.

Philadelphia tied it with a run in the fifth, but the Braves came right back with the decisive runs in the bottom of the fifth. With two outs and none on, Rudolph singled and Moran doubled, putting runners at second and third. Evers followed with a two-run single, providing Rudolph all the cushion he needed.

The Athletics didn't even get a hit over the final four innings, with Rudolph facing the minimum of 12 hitters. He allowed only a leadoff walk in the seventh to Walsh, who was later picked off second by Gowdy.

Philadelphia finally held Gowdy hitless, but it didn't matter. The Braves, behind outstanding pitching that limited Mack's team to a .172 batting average and five earned runs in four games, had pulled an upset of monumental proportions.

A wild celebration followed in which "Miracle Man" Stallings, Gowdy, who hit .545, and Maranville were the chief recipients of the affection of thousands of fans. Stallings and Maranville both made speeches, then a swarm of people, including many players, paraded around Fenway with a band and made their way through the streets of Boston.

The Braves received winning shares of $2,812.28 apiece and became a fabled chapter of baseball lore.

Game 1
Friday, October 9, at Philadelphia

Boston	AB	R	H	RBI
Moran, rf	5	0	0	0
Evers, 2b	4	1	1	0
Connolly, lf	3	1	1	0
Whitted, cf	3	2	1	2
Schmidt, 1b	4	1	2	1
Gowdy, c	3	2	3	1
Maranville, ss	4	0	2	2
Deal, 3b	4	0	0	0
Rudolph, p	4	0	1	0
Totals	34	7	11	6

Philadelphia	AB	R	H	RBI
Murphy, rf	4	0	1	0
Oldring, lf	3	0	0	0
Collins, 2b	3	0	0	0
Baker, 3b	4	0	1	0
McInnis, 1b	2	1	0	0
Strunk, cf	4	0	2	0
Barry, ss	4	0	0	0
Schang, c	2	0	0	0
Lapp, c	1	0	0	0
Bender, p	2	0	0	0
Wyckoff, p	1	0	1	0
Totals	30	1	5	0

```
Boston        0 2 0 0 1 3 0 1 0—7 11 2
Philadelphia  0 1 0 0 0 0 0 0 0—1  5 0
```

E—Evers, Moran. DP—Boston 1, Philadelphia 4. LOB—Boston 3, Philadelphia 6. 2B—Gowdy, Baker, Wyckoff. 3B—Gowdy, Whitted. HR—None. SF—None. SH—Oldring. SB—Moran, Schmidt, Gowdy. CS—None.

Boston	IP	H	R	ER	BB	K
Rudolph (W)	9	5	1	0	3	8

Philadelphia	IP	H	R	ER	BB	K
Bender (L)	5⅓	8	6	6	2	3
Wyckoff	3⅔	3	1	1	1	2

HBP—None. WP—None. T—1:58. A—20,562. Umpires—Dinneen, Klem, Byron, Hilderbrand.

Game 2
Saturday, October 10, at Philadelphia

Boston	AB	R	H	RBI
Mann, rf	5	0	2	1
Evers, 2b	4	0	2	0
Cather, lf	5	0	0	0
Whitted, cf	3	0	0	0
Schmidt, 1b	4	0	1	0
Gowdy, c	2	0	0	0
Maranville, ss	2	0	1	0
Deal, 3b	4	1	1	0
James, p	4	0	0	0
Totals	33	1	7	1

Philadelphia	AB	R	H	RBI
Murphy, rf	3	0	0	0
Oldring, lf	3	0	0	0
Collins, 2b	3	0	1	0
Baker, 3b	3	0	0	0
McInnis, 1b	3	0	0	0
Strunk, cf	3	0	0	0
Barry, ss	2	0	0	0
Schang, c	3	0	1	0
Plank, p	2	0	0	0
Walsh, ph	0	0	0	0
Totals	25	0	2	0

```
Boston        0 0 0 0 0 0 0 0 1—1 7 1
Philadelphia  0 0 0 0 0 0 0 0 0—0 2 1
```

E—Maranville, McInnis. DP—Boston 1. LOB—Boston 11, Philadelphia 1. 2B—Schang, Deal. 3B—Gowdy, Whitted. HR—None. SF—None. SH—Maranville. SB—Deal 2, Barry. CS—None.

Boston	IP	H	R	ER	BB	K
James (W)	9	2	0	0	3	8

Philadelphia	IP	H	R	ER	BB	K
Plank (L)	9	7	1	1	4	6

HBP—Maranville by Plank. PB—Schang. T—1:56. A—20,562. Umpires—Hilderbrand, Byron, Klem, Dinneen.

Game 3
Monday, October 12, at Boston

Philadelphia	AB	R	H	RBI
Murphy, rf	5	2	2	0
Oldring, lf	5	0	0	0
Collins, 2b	4	0	1	1
Baker, 3b	5	0	2	2
McInnis, 1b	5	1	1	0
Walsh, cf	4	0	1	1
Barry, ss	5	0	0	0
Schang, c	4	1	1	0
Bush, p	5	0	0	0
Totals	42	4	8	4

Boston	AB	R	H	RBI
Moran, rf	4	1	0	0
Evers, 2b	5	0	3	0
Connolly, lf	4	0	0	1
Whitted, cf	5	0	0	0
Schmidt, 1b	5	1	1	0
Deal, 3b	5	0	1	0
Maranville, ss	4	1	1	1
Gowdy, c	4	1	3	2
Mann, pr	0	1	0	0
Tyler, p	3	0	0	0
Devore, ph	1	0	0	0
James, p	0	0	0	0
Gilbert, ph	0	0	0	0
Totals	40	5	9	4

```
Philadelphia  1 0 0 1 0 0 0 0 0 2 0 0—4 8 2
Boston        0 1 0 1 0 0 0 0 0 2 0 1—5 9 1
```

E—Schang, Bush, Connolly. DP—Boston 1. LOB—Philadelphia 10, Boston 8. 2B—Murphy 2, Gowdy 2, McInnis, Deal, Baker. 3B—None. HR—Gowdy. SF—Collins, Connolly. SH—Oldring, Moran. SB—Collins, Evers, Maranville 2. CS—None.

Philadelphia	IP	H	R	ER	BB	K
Bush (L)	11	9	5	4	4	4

Boston	IP	H	R	ER	BB	K
Tyler	10	8	4	4	3	4
James (W)	2	0	0	0	3	1

HBP—None. WP—None. T—3:06. A—35,520. Umpires—Klem, Dinneen, Byron, Hilderbrand.

Game 4
Tuesday, October 13, at Boston

Philadelphia	AB	R	H	RBI
Murphy, rf	4	0	0	0
Oldring, lf	4	0	1	0
Collins, 2b	4	0	1	0
Baker, 3b	4	0	1	0
McInnis, 1b	4	0	1	0
Walsh, cf	2	0	1	0
Barry, ss	3	1	1	0
Schang, c	3	0	0	0
Shawkey, p	2	0	1	1
Pennock, p	1	0	0	0
Totals	31	1	7	1

Boston	AB	R	H	RBI
Moran, rf	4	1	1	0
Evers, 2b	3	1	1	2
Connolly, lf	2	0	0	0
Mann, lf	2	0	0	0
Whitted, cf	3	0	2	0
Schmidt, 1b	4	0	1	1
Gowdy, c	2	0	0	0
Maranville, ss	3	0	0	0
Deal, 3b	3	0	0	0
Rudolph, p	2	1	1	0
Totals	28	3	6	3

```
Philadelphia  0 0 0 0 1 0 0 0 0—1 7 0
Boston        0 0 0 1 2 0 0 0 x—3 6 0
```

E—None. DP—Boston 1. LOB—Philadelphia 4, Boston 5. 2B—Walsh, Shawkey, Moran. 3B—None. HR—None. SF—None. SH—None. SB—Whitted. CS—None.

Philadelphia	IP	H	R	ER	BB	K
Shawkey (L)	5	4	3	3	2	0
Pennock	3	2	0	0	2	3

Boston	IP	H	R	ER	BB	K
Rudolph (W)	9	7	1	1	1	7

HBP—None. WP—Rudolph. PB—Schang. T—1:49. A—34,365. Umpires—Byron, Hilderbrand, Klem, Dinneen.

COMPOSITE LINE SCORE

Boston Braves (N.L.)	0	3	0	2	3	3	0	1	1	2	0	1—16
Philadelphia Athletics (A.L.)	1	1	0	1	1	0	0	0	0	2	0	0— 6

COMPOSITE BATTING AND FIELDING STATISTICS

Boston Braves	G	AB	R	H	2B	3B	HR	RBI	BB	SO	SB	BA	SA	PO	A	E
Butch Schmidt, 1b	4	17	2	5	0	0	0	2	0	2	1	.294	.294	52	3	0
Johnny Evers, 2b	4	16	2	7	0	0	0	2	2	2	1	.438	.438	8	16	1
Rabbit Maranville, ss	4	13	1	4	0	0	0	3	1	1	2	.308	.308	7	13	1
Charlie Deal, 3b	4	16	1	2	2	0	0	0	0	0	2	.125	.250	6	11	0
Herbie Moran, rf	3	13	2	1	1	0	0	0	1	1	1	.077	.154	2	0	1
Possum Whitted, cf	4	14	2	3	0	1	0	2	3	1	1	.214	.357	5	0	0
Joe Connolly, lf	3	9	1	1	0	0	0	1	1	1	0	.111	.111	2	2	1
Hank Gowdy, c	4	11	3	6	3	1	1	3	5	1	1	.545	1.273	31	4	0
Les Mann, rf-pr-ph-lf	3	7	1	2	0	0	0	1	0	1	0	.286	.286	1	0	0
Ted Cather, lf	1	5	0	0	0	0	0	0	0	1	0	.000	.000	2	0	0
Josh Devore, ph	1	1	0	0	0	0	0	0	0	1	0	.000	.000			
Larry Gilbert, ph	1	0	0	0	0	0	0	0	1	0	0	—	—			
Red Smith	Did not play—broken ankle.															
Bert Whaling	Did not play															
Oscar Dugey	Did not play															
Billy Martin	Did not play															
Dick Rudolph, p	2	6	1	2	0	0	0	0	1	1	0	.333	.333	0	3	0
Bill James, p	2	4	0	0	0	0	0	0	0	4	0	.000	.000	0	5	0
Letty Tyler, p	1	3	0	0	0	0	0	0	0	1	0	.000	.000	1	5	0
Dick Crutcher	Did not play															
Otto Hess	Did not play															
Paul Strand	Did not play															
George Davis	Did not play															
Gene Cooreham	Did not play															
Dick Cottrell	Did not play															
team total	4	135	16	33	6	2	1	14	15	18	9	.244	.341	117	62	4

Double plays—4
Left on bases—27

Philadelphia Athletics	G	AB	R	H	2B	3B	HR	RBI	BB	SO	SB	BA	SA	PO	A	E
Stuffy McInnis, 1b	4	14	2	2	1	0	0	0	3	3	0	.143	.214	50	2	0
Eddie Collins, 2b	4	14	0	3	0	0	0	1	2	1	1	.214	.214	9	12	1
Jack Barry, ss	4	14	1	1	0	0	0	0	1	3	1	.071	.071	5	20	1
Frank Baker, 3b	4	16	0	4	2	0	0	2	1	3	0	.250	.375	10	15	0
Eddie Murphy, rf	4	16	2	3	2	0	0	0	2	2	0	.188	.313	4	0	0
Amos Strunk, cf	2	7	0	2	0	0	0	0	0	2	0	.286	.286	4	0	0
Rube Oldring, lf	4	15	0	1	0	0	0	0	0	5	0	.067	.067	6	0	0
Wally Schang, c	4	12	1	2	1	0	0	0	1	4	0	.167	.250	17	3	1
Jimmy Walsh, ph-cf	3	6	0	2	1	0	0	1	3	1	0	.333	.500	2	0	0
Jack Lapp, c	1	1	0	0	0	0	0	0	0	0	0	.000	.000	2	1	0
Larry Kopf	Did not play															
Chick Davies	Did not play															
Shag Thompson	Did not play															
Wickey McAvoy	Did not play															
Harry Davis	Did not play															
Ira Thomas	Did not play															
Bullet Joe Bush, p	1	5	0	0	0	0	0	0	0	2	0	.000	.000	0	5	1
Eddie Plank, p	1	2	0	0	0	0	0	0	0	1	0	.000	.000	0	1	0
Chief Bender, p	1	2	0	0	0	0	0	0	0	0	0	.000	.000	1	3	0
Bob Shawkey, p	1	2	0	1	1	0	0	1	0	1	0	.500	1.000	0	3	0
Weldon Wyckoff, p	1	1	0	1	1	0	0	0	0	0	0	1.000	2.000	1	0	0
Herb Pennock, p	1	1	0	0	0	0	0	0	0	0	0	.000	.000	0	0	0
Rube Bressier	Did not play															
Jack Coombs	Did not play															
team total	4	128	6	22	9	0	0	5	13	28	2	.172	.242	111	65	4

Double plays—4
Left on bases—21

COMPOSITE PITCHING STATISTICS

Boston Braves	G	GS	CG	IP	H	R	ER	BB	SO	W	L	SV	ERA
Dick Rudolph	2	2	2	18	12	2	1	4	15	2	0	0	0.50
Bill James	2	1	1	11	2	0	0	6	9	2	0	0	0.00
Letty Tyler	1	1	0	10	8	4	4	3	4	0	0	0	3.60
Dick Crutcher	Did not play												
Otto Hess	Did not play												
George Davis	Did not play												
Paul Strand	Did not play												
Gene Cocreham	Did not play												
Dick Cottrell	Did not play												
team total	4	4	3	39	22	6	5	13	28	4	0	0	1.15

Philadelphia Athletics	G	AB	R	H	2B	3B	HR	RBI	BB	SO	SB	BA	SA	PO	A	E
Bullet Joe Bush	1	1	1	11	9	5	4	4	4	0	1	0	3.27			
Eddie Plank	1	1	1	9	7	1	1	4	6	0	1	0	1.00			
Chief Bender	1	1	0	5⅓	8	6	6	2	3	0	1	0	10.13			
Bob Shawkey	1	1	0	5	4	3	2	2	0	0	1	0	3.60			
Weldon Wyckoff	1	0	0	3⅔	3	1	1	1	2	0	0	0	2.45			
Herb Pennock	1	0	0	3	2	0	0	2	3	0	0	0	0.00			
Rube Bressier	Did not play															
Chick Davies	Did not play															
Jack Coombs	Did not play															
team total	4	4	2	37	33	16	14	15	18	0	4	0	3.41			

Total Attendance—111,009 Average Attendance—27,752 Winning Player's Share—$2,812 Losing Player's Share—$2,032

Braves versus Cleveland Indians World Series

1948

The 1948 season was one of the most thrilling in history for Boston baseball fans. The "Spahn and Sain and pray for rain" Braves won the city's first National League pennant since 1914, and the Red Sox fought the Cleveland Indians to the wire for the American League pennant.

An all-Boston World Series was a very real possibility, especially when the Red Sox and Indians finished the regular season in a tie, forcing a one-game playoff, the first in AL history, at Fenway Park. However, Cleveland won that playoff, 8–3, prompting an all–Native American rather than an all-Boston Series.

The Braves of manager Billy Southworth had a formidable lineup, which included third baseman Bob Elliott, who won the 1947 National League MVP Award, "Jury Box" favorite Tommy Holmes, first baseman Earl Torgeson, and the double-play combination of shortstop Al Dark, the major league Rookie of the Year, and second baseman Eddie Stanky. How-ever, the Braves had to play the Series without hard-hitting outfielder Jeff Heath, who broke his ankle sliding four days before the end of the season.

The pitching wasn't all Spahn (15–12) and Sain (24–15) either. Rookie Vern Bickford (11–5) and Bill "Ninety-Six" Voiselle (13–13) were dependable starters, too.

Cleveland also had an excellent starting rotation with Bob Feller (19–15), Bob Lemon (20–14), and rookie knuckleball specialist Gene Bearden (20–7), who led the league with a 2.43 ERA.

The Indians also had a talented and potent infield, which included shortstop/manager Lou Boudreau, the AL MVP, third baseman Ken Keltner, second baseman Joe Gordon, and first baseman Eddie Robinson, who would become the Braves' general manager in 1972. The outfield was led by young Larry Doby, who was in his first full season in the majors but already was developing into one of the league's best players. And the Cleveland bullpen included the legendary Satchel Paige, a 42-year-old rookie.

It's questionable whether the Braves could have matched up

with the Indians even with Heath. But without the man who batted .319 with 20 homers and 76 RBIs and led NL outfielders in defense (.991), they were not able to generate the offense necessary to stay with the powerful Indians and lost the Series in six games. Except for Game 5, when Boston broke out for 11 runs, the Braves' hitters were stymied by the Cleveland staff.

The opposing managers in the 1948 World Series were Boston's Billy Southworth and Cleveland shortstop Lou Boudreau.

Game One

The Series opened at Braves Field, and a crowd of 40,135 was treated to quite a pitching duel between two right-handers. Cleveland offered the 29-year-old Feller, a hard-throwing strikeout king who was in the midst of a Hall of Fame career. Boston countered with Sain, the 31-year-old control artist who was having the best season of his out-standing career.

Sain was at his best, and he had to be. The two teams were locked in a scoreless duel until the bottom of the eighth when the Braves scored the only run of the game, and a tainted one at that.

Catcher Bill Salkeld drew a leadoff walk off Feller and was replaced by Phil Masi. Mike McCormick got Masi to second with a sacrifice bunt, and Stanky was intentionally walked to set up a double play.

Sibby Sisti ran for Stanky, and with Sain at bat, Feller whirled and threw to Boudreau in an attempt to pick Masi off second. The Braves' runner was called safe, though he appeared to be out, as photographs later seemed to prove. After Sain lined out, Holmes singled to left, scoring Masi. It was one of only two hits Feller allowed, but it was the one the Braves needed.

Sain was masterful, scattering four singles, not walking a bat-ter, and striking out six. He didn't allow more than one base runner in any inning and never let an Indian past second base. Feller, who struck out just two, gave up only the eighth-inning single to Holmes and another to Marv Rickert in the fifth.

Johnny Sain, who out-pitched Bob Feller in Game 1, chats with Jeff Heath, who broke his ankle the last week of the regular season.

The 1948 National League champion Boston Braves.

Game Two

Most pitchers would have been pleased to win 15 games, as 27-year-old Warren Spahn did in 1948. But it was one of the lesser seasons of the great left-hander's career. His shaky performance in Game 2 of the Series was another indicator that he was not at his best in 1948.

The Braves got on the board with a run in the first off 28-year-old Lemon, who led the AL with 10 shutouts that year, but it was their only run of the game and unearned at that. With one out, Dark reached on Gordon's error at second. Torgeson singled Dark to third, and Elliott singled to make it 1–0.

Spahn allowed only a hit and a walk in the first three innings, but in the fourth, Cleveland reached him for a pair of runs. That proved to be all the support Lemon needed, though the Indians added single runs in the fifth and ninth.

The Braves, meanwhile, had no luck with Lemon. They got runners at second and third with one out in the fourth, only to have Spahn tap to the mound and Holmes fly to left. And they had runners at first and second with one out in the sixth, but Stanky hit into an inning-ending double play.

The Indians' 4–1 victory evened the Series at one game apiece as the scene shifted to Cleveland.

Braves first baseman Earl Torgeson takes the throw to retire Indians player/manager Lou Boudreau.

Game Three

Cleveland's monstrous Municipal Stadium wasn't the best place to watch a ball game, but it did afford a lot of fans the opportunity to see the World Series in 1948. A throng of 70,306 witnessed Game 3, but that actually was the smallest crowd to attend the three games on the shore of Lake Erie.

The pitching matchup called for two 28-year-old rookies to face each other. Boston called on Bickford, a right-hander, and Cleveland started Bearden, a left-hander.

The Indians scored single runs in the third and fourth innings, driving Bickford from the game with the only scoring of the afternoon.

In the third, Bearden started a rally with a one-out double to right and Dale Mitchell walked. Doby then grounded to second for a potential inning-ending double play. But after forcing Mitchell, Dark threw wildly to first and Bearden scored.

The Indians made it 2–0 in the fourth on a leadoff walk to Keltner and one-out singles by Robinson and Jim Hegan.

The Braves' hitters could do nothing with Bearden's knuckleballs. They got five hits, the same number as Cleveland, but couldn't put together two in the same inning. Bearden retired the last eight hitters to give Cleveland a 2–1 edge in games.

Game Four

Steve Gromek, a 28-year-old right-hander who was 9–3 in 1948, mainly in relief, had the assignment of facing Sain in Game 4. Gromek made just nine starts that year, completing four of them, but he looked like a Cy Young Award winner against the Braves.

Sain pitched another masterful game but lost, 2–1, despite giving up just five hits and no walks.

With a record World Series crowd of 81,897 watching, the Indians broke on top early when Mitchell led off the first with a single and scored on Boudreau's one-out double.

In the third, Doby's two-out home run made it 2–0. The Braves got that run back in the seventh when Rickert led off with a home run, but that was the extent of the scoring.

Boston didn't have more than one hit in any inning except the seventh when Mike McCormick singled after Rickert's homer. The Braves went down in order in the ninth and trailed in games, 3–1.

Game Five

Needing three straight victories in order to win the Series, the Braves finally exploded at the plate in the third game at Municipal Stadium, which was played before another record crowd of 86,288.

Facing elimination, Southworth called on 37-year-old right-hander Nels Potter, who'd been used mainly in relief, to get the Braves back to Boston. His opponent was Feller, who'd been outdueled by Sain in Game 1.

It quickly became apparent that this game was going to have a different tone for the Braves than had the first four. Holmes and Dark opened with singles, and after Torgeson flied to right, Elliott hit a three-run homer. In one-third of an inning, Boston scored as many runs as in the first four games of the Series.

Mitchell led off the bottom of the first with a home run, making it 3–1, but the Braves got that run back in the third on another homer by Elliott.

Potter had little trouble with the Indians in the first three innings, but that changed quickly in the fourth when Cleveland took a 5–4 lead, the big blow being a three-run homer by Hegan.

However, Potter was lifted for Spahn at that point, and the Boston left-hander shut down Cleveland's hitters for the remainder of the game. He worked 5⅔ innings of one-hit, one-walk relief, striking out seven while the Boston hitters pounded Feller and four relievers.

In the sixth, the Braves tied the game, 5–5, on a one-out home run by Salkeld. The following inning, Boston drove Feller from the mound with a six-run outburst that accounted for the final score of 11–5.

Holmes led off with a single, Dark sacrificed, and Torgeson singled in a run, making it 6–5. Ed Klieman replaced Feller and faced three batters, giving up two walks around a single by Rickert and a throwing error by Doby. The score was 8–5 when Russ Christopher relieved Klieman.

Mike McCormick greeted Klieman with a run-scoring single and Stanky followed with another RBI single, making it 10–5. Spahn's sacrifice fly concluded the onslaught.

The victory relieved the frustration of the Boston hitters and allowed a return to Braves Field, where Southworth's club felt it could win the last two games.

Johnny Sain checks the strong left arm of Warren Spahn, who won Game 5 with 5⅔ innings of one-hit relief.

Game Six

Boudreau had Lemon, who'd handcuffed the Braves in Game 2, ready for Game 6. Southworth countered with Voiselle, the right-hander who'd worked 3⅔ innings of one-hit relief in Game 3.

Both pitchers were far from flawless, but they kept the game close into the late innings when the Indians, who never trailed in the game, rallied for a 4–3 victory and the Series championship.

Cleveland took a 1–0 lead in the third on doubles by Mitchell and Boudreau. The Braves got even in the fourth on an infield single by Elliott, a walk to Salkeld, and Mike McCormick's two-out single to center.

In the sixth, Gordon led off with a home run to break the tie, then the Indians added another run on a walk, a single by Robinson, and Hegan's infield grounder. The Indians padded their lead to 4–1 in the eighth.

The Braves were close to being KOed, but they rallied to chase Lemon with two runs in the eighth. Holmes led off with a single, and Torgeson delivered a one-out double. After Elliott drew a walk to load the bases, Lemon was relieved by Bearden. Pinch hitter Clint Conaster's sacrifice fly scored Holmes, then Masi delivered a pinch-hit double to left, scoring Torgeson and sending Elliott to third. However, with the tying run 90 feet away and the lead run in scoring position, Mike McCormick bounced back to the pitcher to end the inning.

In the ninth, Stanky drew a leadoff walk from Bearden, but Sisti, batting for Spahn, hit into a double play and Holmes flied to left to end the game and the Series.

There was no question that the Braves' inability to score runs was their downfall in the Series. However, they actually outhit Cleveland, .230 to .199 and scored the same number of runs as the Indians—17. Of course, 11 of the Braves' 17 runs came in one game.

Game 1
Wednesday, October 6, at Boston

Cleveland	AB	R	H	RBI
Mitchell, lf	4	0	0	0
Doby, cf	4	0	1	0
Boudreau, ss	4	0	0	0
Gordon, 2b	4	0	1	0
Keltner, 3b	4	0	1	0
Judnich, rf	4	0	0	0
Robinson, 1b	3	0	0	0
Hegan, c	3	0	1	0
Feller, p	2	0	0	0
Totals	**32**	**0**	**4**	**0**

Boston	AB	R	H	RBI
Holmes, rf	4	0	1	1
Dark, ss	4	0	0	0
Torgeson, 1b	2	0	0	0
Elliott, 3b	3	0	0	0
Rickert, lf	3	0	1	0
Salkeld, c	1	0	0	0
Masi, c	0	1	0	0
McCormick, cf	2	0	0	0
Stanky, 2b	2	0	0	0
Sisti, 2b	0	0	0	0
Sain, p	3	0	0	0
Totals	**24**	**1**	**2**	**1**

```
Cleveland   0  0  0  0  0  0  0  0  0—0   4  0
Boston      0  0  0  0  0  0  0  1  x—1   2  2
```

E—Elliott 2. DP—None. LOB—Cleveland 6, Boston 4. 2B—None. 3B—None. HR—None. SF—None. SH—Feller, Salkeld, McCormick. SB—Hegan, Gordon, Torgeson. CS—None.

Cleveland	IP	H	R	ER	BB	K
Feller (L)	8	2	1	1	3	2

Boston	IP	H	R	ER	BB	K
Sain (W)	9	4	0	0	0	6

HBP—None. WP—None. T—1:42. A—40,135. Umpires—Barr, Stewart, Brieve, Paparellia, Pinelli.

Game 2
Thursday, October 7, at Boston

Cleveland	AB	R	H	RBI
Mitchell, lf	5	1	1	0
Clark, rf	3	0	0	0
Kennedy, rf	1	0	1	1
Boudreau, ss	5	1	2	1
Gordon, 2b	4	1	1	1
Keltner, 3b	4	0	0	0
Doby, cf	4	0	2	1
Robinson, 1b	3	0	1	0
Hegan, c	3	1	0	0
Lemon, p	4	0	0	0
Totals	**36**	**4**	**8**	**4**

Boston	AB	R	H	RBI
Holmes, rf	4	0	0	0
Dark, ss	4	1	1	0
Torgeson, 1b	4	0	2	0
Elliott, 3b	4	0	1	1
Rickert, lf	4	0	0	0
Salkeld, c	1	0	1	0
Masi, c	1	0	0	0
McCormick, cf	4	0	2	0
Stanky, 2b	2	0	1	0
Spahn, p	2	0	0	0
Barrett, p	2	0	0	0
F. McCormick, ph	1	0	0	0
Potter, p	0	0	0	0
Sanders, ph	1	0	0	0
Totals	**32**	**1**	**8**	**1**

```
Cleveland   0  0  0  2  1  0  0  0  1—4   8  1
Boston      1  0  0  0  0  0  0  0  0—1   8  3
```

E—Gordon, Dark 2, Elliott. DP—Cleveland 2, Boston 1. LOB—Cleveland 8, Boston 8. 2B—Boudreau, Doby, Stanky. 3B—None. HR—None. SF—None. SH—Stanky, Clark. SB—None. CS—None.

Cleveland	IP	H	R	ER	BB	K
Lemon (W)	9	8	1	0	3	5

Boston	IP	H	R	ER	BB	K
Spahn (L)	4⅓	6	3	3	2	1
Barrett	2⅔	1	0	0	0	1
Potter	2	1	1	0	0	1

HBP—None. WP—None. T—2:14. A—39,633. Umpires—Summers, Stewart, Grieve, Barr, Pinelli, Paparella.

Game 3
Friday, October 8, at Cleveland

Boston	AB	R	H	RBI
Holmes, rf	4	0	0	0
Dark, ss	4	0	1	0
M. McCormick, lf	4	0	1	0
Elliott, 3b	3	0	1	0
F. McCormick, 1b	3	0	1	0
Conatser, cf	3	0	0	0
Masi, c	3	0	0	0
Stanky, 2b	3	0	1	0
Bickford, p	0	0	0	0
Voiselle, p	1	0	0	0
Ryan, ph	1	0	0	0
Barrett, p	0	0	0	0
Totals	**29**	**0**	**5**	**0**

Cleveland	AB	R	H	RBI
Mitchell, lf	3	0	0	0
Doby, cf	3	0	1	0
Boudreau, ss	3	0	0	0
Gordon, 2b	4	0	0	0
Keltner, 3b	3	1	0	0
Judnich, rf	3	0	0	0
Robinson, 1b	3	0	1	0
Hegan, c	1	0	1	1
Bearden, p	3	1	2	0
Totals	**28**	**2**	**5**	**1**

```
Boston      0  0  0  0  0  0  0  0  0—0   5  1
Cleveland   0  0  1  1  0  0  0  0  x—2   5  0
```

E—Dark. DP—Boston 1, Cleveland 2. LOB—Boston 3. Cleveland 7. 2B—Bearden, Dark. 3B—None. HR—None. SF—None. SH—Bickford. SB—None. CS—None.

Boston	IP	H	R	ER	BB	K
Bickford (L)	3⅓	4	2	1	5	1
Voiselle	3⅔	1	0	0	0	0
Barrett	1	0	0	0	0	0

Cleveland	IP	H	R	ER	BB	K
Beardon (W)	9	5	0	0	0	4

HBP—None. WP—None. T—1:36. A—70,306. Umpires—Grieve, Barr, Summers, Paparella, Pinelli.

Game 4
Saturday, October 9, at Cleveland

Boston	AB	R	H	RBI
Holmes, rf	4	0	0	0
Dark, ss	4	0	0	0
Torgeson, 1b	3	0	2	0
Elliott, 3b	4	0	0	0
Rickert, lf	4	1	2	1
M. McCormick, cf	4	0	1	0
Masi, c	3	0	0	0
Salkeld, ph	1	0	0	0
Stanky, 2b	3	0	1	0
Sain, p	2	0	1	0
Totals	**32**	**1**	**7**	**1**

Cleveland	AB	R	H	RBI
Mitchell, lf	4	1	1	0
Doby, cf	3	1	1	1
Boudreau, ss	3	0	1	1
Gordon, 2b	3	0	0	0
Keltner, 3b	3	0	0	0
Judnich, rf	3	0	0	0
Kennedy, rf	0	0	0	0
Robinson, 1b	3	0	2	0
Hegan, c	2	0	0	0
Gromek, p	3	0	0	0
Totals	**27**	**2**	**5**	**2**

```
Boston      0  0  0  0  0  0  1  0  0—1   7  0
Cleveland   1  0  1  0  0  0  0  0  x—2   5  0
```

E—None. DP—Cleveland 1. LOB—Boston 6, Cleveland 2. 2B—Torgeson 2, Boudreau. 3B—None. HR—Doby, Rickert. SF—None. SH—Sain, Hegan. SB—None. CS—None.

Boston	IP	H	R	ER	BB	K
Sain (L)	8	5	2	2	2	3

Cleveland	IP	H	R	ER	BB	K
Gromek (W)	9	7	1	1	1	2

HBP—None. WP—None. T—1:31. A—81,897. Umpires—Grieve, Barr, Summers, Stewart, Pinelli, Paparella.

Game 5
Sunday, October 10, at Cleveland

Boston	AB	R	H	RBI
Holmes, rf	5	2	2	0
Dark, ss	4	1	1	0
Torgeson, 1b	5	1	2	1
Elliott, 3b	4	3	2	4
Rickert, lf	5	1	1	1
Salkeld, c	4	2	1	1
M. McCormick, cf	5	1	1	1
Stanky, 2b	3	0	1	1
Potter, p	2	0	1	0
Spahn, p	2	0	0	0
Totals	**39**	**11**	**12**	**10**

Cleveland	AB	R	H	RBI
Mitchell, lf	3	1	1	1
Doby, cf	4	0	0	0
Boudreau, ss	4	0	2	0
Gordon, 2b	3	1	1	0
Keltner, 3b	3	1	0	0
Judnich, rf	3	1	1	1
Boone, ph	1	0	0	0
Peck, rf	0	0	0	0
Robinson, 1b	4	0	0	0
Hegan, c	4	1	1	3
Feller, p	2	0	0	0
Klieman, p	0	0	0	0
Christopher, p	0	0	0	0
Paige, p	0	0	0	0
Rosen, p	1	0	0	0
Muncrief, p	0	0	0	0
Tipton, ph	1	0	0	0
Totals	**33**	**5**	**6**	**5**

```
Boston      3  0  1  0  0  1  6  0  0—11  12  0
Cleveland   1  0  0  4  0  0  0  0  0—5    6  2
```

E—Doby, Keltner. DP—None. LOB—Boston 6, Cleveland 4. 2B—Boudreau. 3B—None. HR—Elliott 2, Mitchell, Hegan, Salkeld. SF—None. SH—Dark. SB—None. CS—None.

Boston	IP	H	R	ER	BB	K
Potter	3⅓	5	5	5	2	0
Spahn (W)	5⅔	1	0	0	1	7

Cleveland	IP	H	R	ER	BB	K
Feller (L)	6⅓	8	7	7	2	5
Klieman	0	1	3	3	2	0
Christopher	0	2	1	1	0	0
Paige	⅔	0	0	0	0	0
Muncrief	2	1	0	0	0	0

HBP—None. WP—None. Balk—Paige. T—2:39. A—86,288. Umpires—Barr, Summers, Stewart, Grieve, Paparella, Pinella.

Game 6
Monday, October 11, at Boston

Cleveland	AB	R	H	RBI
Mitchell, lf	4	1	1	0
Kennedy, lf	1	0	0	0
Doby, rf	4	0	2	0
Boudreau, ss	3	0	1	1
Gordon, 2b	4	1	1	1
Keltner, 3b	4	1	1	0
Tucker, cf	3	1	1	0
Robinson, 1b	4	0	2	1
Hegan, c	4	0	1	1
Lemon, p	3	0	0	0
Bearden, p	1	0	0	0
Totals	**35**	**4**	**10**	**4**

Boston	AB	R	H	RBI
Holmes, rf	5	1	2	0
Dark, ss	4	0	1	0
Torgeson, 1b	4	1	1	0
Elliott, 3b	3	1	3	0
Rickert, lf	3	0	0	0
Conatser, cf	1	0	0	1
Salkeld, c	2	0	0	0
Masi, c	1	0	1	1
M. McCormick, cf-lf	4	0	1	1
Stanky, 2b	1	0	0	0
Ryan, ph	0	0	0	0
Voiselle, p	1	0	0	0
F. McCormick, ph	1	0	0	0
Spahn, p	0	0	0	0
Sisti, ph	0	0	0	0
Totals	**31**	**3**	**9**	**3**

```
Cleveland   0 0 1 0 0 2 0 1 0—4  10  0
Boston      0 0 0 1 0 0 0 2 0—3   9  0
```

E—None. DP—Cleveland 4, Boston 1. LOB—Cleveland 7, Boston 7.
2B—Mitchell, Boudreau, Torgenson, Masi. 3B—None. HR—Gordon.
SF—None. SH—Voiselle. SB—None. CS—None.

Cleveland	IP	H	R	ER	BB	K
Lemon (W)	7⅓	8	3	3	4	1
Bearden	1⅔	1	0	0	1	0

Boston	IP	H	R	ER	BB	K
Voiselle (L)	7	7	3	3	2	2
Spahn	2	3	1	1	0	4

HBP—Boudreau by Voiselle. WP—None. Balk—Lemon. T—2:17. A—40,103. Umpires—Summers, Stewart, Grieve, Barr, Pinelli, Paparella.

COMPOSITE LINE SCORE

```
Cleveland Indians (A.L.)   2 0 3 7 1 2 0 1 1—17
Boston Braves (N.L.)       4 0 1 1 0 1 7 3 0—17
```

COMPOSITE BATTING AND FIELDING STATISTICS

Cleveland Indians	G	AB	R	H	2B	3B	HR	RBI	BB	SO	SB	BA	SA	PO	A	E
Eddie Robinson, 1b	6	20	0	6	0	0	0	1	1	0	0	.300	.300	60	7	0
Joe Gordon, 2b	6	22	3	4	0	0	1	2	1	2	1	.182	.318	15	13	1
Lou Boudreau, ss	6	22	1	6	4	0	0	3	1	1	0	.273	.455	11	14	0
Ken Keltner, 3b	6	21	3	2	0	0	0	0	2	3	0	.095	.095	3	11	1
Walt Judnich, rf	4	13	1	1	0	0	0	1	1	4	0	.077	.077	7	0	0
Larry Doby, cf-rf	6	22	1	7	1	0	1	2	2	4	0	.318	.500	11	0	1
Dale Mitchell, lf	6	23	4	4	1	0	1	1	2	0	0	.174	.348	13	0	0
Jim Hegan, c	6	19	2	4	0	0	1	5	1	4	1	.211	.368	25	5	0
Thurman Tucker, cf	1	3	1	1	0	0	0	0	1	0	0	.333	.333	3	1	0
Allie Clark, rf	1	3	0	0	0	0	0	0	0	1	0	.000	.000	2	0	0
Bob Kennedy, rf-lf	3	2	0	1	0	0	0	1	0	1	0	.500	.500	2	0	0
Hal Peck, rf	1	0	0	0	0	0	0	0	0	0	0	—	—	0	0	0
Ray Boone, ph	1	1	0	0	0	0	0	0	0	1	0	.000	.000			
Al Rosen, ph	1	1	0	0	0	0	0	0	0	0	0	.000	.000			
Joe Tipton, ph	1	1	0	0	0	0	0	0	0	1	0	.000	.000			
Johnny Berardino	Did not play															
Hank Edwards	Did not play															
Bob Lemon, p	2	7	0	0	0	0	0	0	0	0	0	.000	.000	3	9	0
Gene Bearden, p	2	4	1	2	1	0	0	0	0	1	0	.500	.750	0	7	0
Bob Feller, p	2	4	0	0	0	0	0	0	0	2	0	.000	.000	2	4	0
Steve Gromek, p	1	3	0	0	0	0	0	0	0	1	0	.000	.000	1	1	0
Russ Christopher, p	1	0	0	0	0	0	0	0	0	0	0	—	—	0	0	0
Eddie Klieman, p	1	0	0	0	0	0	0	0	0	0	0	—	—	0	0	0
Bob Muncriet, p	1	0	0	0	0	0	0	0	0	0	0	—	—	1	0	0
Satchel Paige, p	1	0	0	0	0	0	0	0	0	0	0	—	—	0	0	0
Sam Zoldak	Did not play															
Don Black	Did not play—injured															
team total	**6**	**191**	**17**	**38**	**7**	**0**	**4**	**16**	**12**	**26**	**2**	**.199**	**.298**	**159**	**72**	**3**

Double plays—9
Left on bases—34

Boston Braves	G	AB	R	H	2B	3B	HR	RBI	BB	SO	SB	BA	SA	PO	A	E
Earl Torgeson, 1b	5	18	2	7	3	0	0	1	2	1	1	.389	.556	44	5	0
Eddie Stanky, 2b	6	14	0	4	1	0	0	1	7	0	0	.286	.357	8	12	0
Al Dark, ss	6	24	2	4	1	0	0	0	0	2	0	.167	.208	7	12	3
Bob Elliott, 3b	6	21	4	7	0	0	2	5	2	2	0	.333	.619	11	14	3
Tommy Holmes, rf	6	26	3	5	0	0	0	1	0	0	0	.192	.192	10	2	0
Mike McCormick, cf-lf	6	23	1	6	0	0	0	2	0	4	0	.261	.261	17	0	0
Marv Rickert, lf	5	19	2	4	0	0	1	2	0	4	0	.211	.368	20	0	0
Bill Salkeld, c-ph	5	9	2	2	0	0	1	1	5	1	0	.222	.556	19	2	0
Phil Masi, pr-c-ph	5	8	1	1	1	0	0	1	0	0	0	.125	.250	10	1	0
Frank McCormick, ph-1b	3	5	0	1	0	0	0	0	0	2	0	.200	.200	5	1	0
Clint Conatser, cf	2	4	0	0	0	0	0	1	0	0	0	.000	.000	1	0	0
Sibby Sisti, pr-2b-ph	2	1	0	0	0	0	0	0	0	0	0	.000	.000	0	0	0
Connie Ryan, ph-pr	2	1	0	0	0	0	0	0	0	1	0	.000	.000			
Ray Sanders, ph	1	1	0	0	0	0	0	0	0	0	0	.000	.000			
Jeff Heath	Did not play—injured															
Jim Russell	Did not play—heart illness															
Bobby Sturgeon	Did not play															
Johnny Sain, p	2	5	0	1	0	0	0	0	0	0	0	.200	.200	2	2	0
Warren Spahn, p	3	4	0	0	0	0	0	1	0	1	0	.000	.000	0	3	0
Nels Potter, p	2	2	0	1	0	0	0	0	0	1	0	.500	.500	1	0	0
Bill Voiselle, p	2	2	0	0	0	0	0	0	0	0	0	.000	.000	1	0	0
Red Barrett, p	2	0	0	0	0	0	0	0	0	0	0	—	—	0	0	0
Vern Bickford, p	1	0	0	0	0	0	0	0	0	0	0	—	—	0	0	0
Bobby Hogue	Did not play															
Clyde Shoun	Did not play															
Al Lyons	Did not play															
Ernie White	Did not play															
team total	**6**	**187**	**17**	**43**	**6**	**0**	**4**	**16**	**16**	**19**	**1**	**.230**	**.326**	**156**	**54**	**6**

Double plays—3
Left on bases—34

COMPOSITE PITCHING STATISTICS

Cleveland Indians	G	GS	CG	IP	H	R	ER	BB	SO	W	L	SV	ERA
Bob Lemon	2	2	1	16⅓	16	4	3	7	6	2	0	0	1.65
Bob Feller	2	2	0	14⅓	10	8	8	5	7	0	2	0	5.02
Gene Bearden	2	1	1	10⅔	6	0	0	1	4	1	0	1	0.00
Steve Gromek	1	1	1	9	7	1	1	1	2	1	0	0	1.00
Bob Muhrief	1	0	0	2	1	0	0	0	0	0	0	0	0.00
Satchel Paige	1	0	0	⅔	0	0	0	0	0	0	0	0	0.00
Russ Christopher	1	0	0	0	2	1	1	0	0	0	0	0	∞
Eddie Klieman	1	0	0	1	3	3	2	0	0	0	0	0	∞
Sam Zoldak	Did not play												
Don Black	Did not play—injured												
team total	**7**	**6**	**4**	**53**	**43**	**17**	**16**	**16**	**19**	**4**	**2**	**1**	**2.72**

Boston Braves	G	GS	CG	IP	H	R	ER	BB	SO	W	L	SV	ERA
Johnny Sain	2	2	2	17	9	2	2	0	9	1	1	0	1.06
Warren Spahn	3	1	0	12	10	4	4	3	12	1	1	0	3.00
Bill Voiselle	2	1	0	10⅔	8	3	3	2	2	0	1	0	2.53
Nels Potter	2	1	0	5⅓	6	6	5	2	1	0	0	0	8.44
Red Barrett	2	0	0	3⅔	1	0	0	0	1	0	0	0	0.00
Vern Bickford	1	1	0	3⅓	4	2	1	5	1	0	1	0	2.70
Bobby Hogue	Did not play												
Clyde Shoun	Did not play												
Al Lyons	Did not play												
Ernie White	Did not play												
team total	**7**	**6**	**2**	**52**	**38**	**17**	**15**	**12**	**26**	**2**	**4**	**0**	**2.60**

Total Attendance—358,362. Average Attendance—59,727. Winning Player's Share—$6,772.07. Losing Player's Share—$4,570.73

Braves versus New York Yankees World Series

1957

The Braves narrowly missed bringing the World Series to Milwaukee for the first time in 1956, losing the pennant on the last day of the season. But the exceptionally talented 1957 team didn't let the opportunity to play in the Series escape, rewarding their zealous new fans by winning the pennant by eight games.

Even with slugging first baseman Joe Adcock missing two months with a broken leg and speedy center fielder Billy Bruton out for the second half because of a mangled knee, the '57 Braves were loaded.

Starting pitchers Warren Spahn, Lou Burdette, and Bob Buhl were three of the best in the business, and rookie Don McMahon was developing into quite a reliever. Eddie Mathews and Hank Aaron were in their prime and, like Spahn, were headed to the Hall of Fame. They'd be joined in Cooperstown by second baseman Red Schoendienst, acquired from St. Louis at the June 15 trading deadline. Del Crandall was the best catcher in the league, Johnny Logan was a quality shortstop, and rookie outfielder Bob "Hurricane" Hazle had the hottest bat in baseball the last two months.

It was a formidable Braves team that met the perennial American League champion Yankees in the World Series. The Yankees had won six of the last eight Series, including 1956. Led by former Braves/Bees manager Casey Stengel, the Bronx Bombers were loaded, too. Stengel had an array of starting pitchers that included Whitey Ford, Bob Turley, Tom Sturdivant, Bobby Shantz, and Don Larsen. Reliever Bob Grim led the AL in saves (19). And the lineup was chock-full of stars such as Hall of Famers Mickey Mantle and Yogi Berra, along with Elston Howard, Hank Bauer, Bill Skowron, Tony Kubek, and Gil McDougald.

Few World Series have ever been played between two teams with such talented rosters. Interestingly, the difference in the Series for the Braves would prove to be a Yankees castoff. In 1951, New York bought Johnny Sain from the then-Boston Braves to bolster their late-season pennant drive. The Yankees agreed to throw in a 24-year-old minor league right-hander by the name of Burdette.

But Burdette wasn't the only Brave to have a great Series. Aaron, just 23 years old and coming off a monster season for which he was named National League MVP, was the leading offensive force in the Series. He led both clubs in numerous departments, including hits (11), average (.393), home runs (3), and RBIs (7).

Hank Aaron had a great Series, hitting .393 with three home runs and seven RBIs.

The story of the Braves' 1957 World Series championship was Lou Burdette, who was 3-0 and shut out the Yankees in the last 24 innings he worked.

Game One

Played before a capacity Yankee Stadium crowd of 69,476, the opener featured a matchup of future Hall of Fame left-handers. Braves manager Fred Haney called on Spahn, the crafty 36-year-old veteran who'd led the National League with 21 wins. Stengel started the 28-year-old Ford, who was 11–5 in 1957.

The game was scoreless until the bottom of the fifth when a leadoff single by Gerry Coleman and a two-out double by Bauer gave New York a 1–0 lead.

The Yankees added to their margin in the sixth when they knocked out Spahn with two more runs.

Milwaukee got its lone run in the seventh on a leadoff double by Wes Covington and a two-out single by Schoendienst.

Ford went the distance in the 3–1 victory, limiting the Braves to just four singles and Covington's double. The Yankees had seven singles and two doubles against three Milwaukee pitchers.

Game Two

Haney called on the 30-year-old Burdette, who was coming off a 17–9 season, to get the Braves even before the Series moved to Milwaukee. The Yankees went with Shantz, the 5-6, 142-pound left-hander who was 11–5 in 1957 and led the AL in ERA (2.45).

The teams traded single runs in both the second and third innings, but the Braves were quite lucky to go into the fourth in a 2–2 tie.

Aaron led off the second with a triple over Mantle's head in center, then Adcock followed with a single to get the Braves on the board first. But in the bottom of the second, Enos Slaughter drew a one-out walk and Kubek singled to put runners at first and third with two outs. Coleman beat out a slow roller to third, which allowed Slaughter to score the tying run. Shantz then drilled a ball into the left-field corner that looked like a sure two-run, extra-base hit. However, Covington, regarded as a shaky defensive player, raced into the corner and made a backhanded catch while running at full speed to end the inning.

The two teams traded solo home runs in the third. Logan hit one for the Braves, and Bauer answered for the Yankees, making it 2–2.

In the fourth, Milwaukee gave Burdette the cushion he needed to even the Series. Adcock, Andy Pafko, and Covington started with successive singles for one run, and when Slaughter's throw from left on Covington's hit went through Kubek's legs at third, Pafko came all the way around to score an unearned run. That made it 4–2, and Burdette made it stand up.

The fidgety right-hander retired the Yankees in order only in the first, fourth, and eighth innings and allowed seven hits and three walks. As was his trademark, though, he was at his best with men on base.

Though Burdette was the hero of the day, without Covington's catch, it might have been an entirely different outcome. The split in New York gave the Braves the home-field advantage as the Series moved to Milwaukee.

Game Three

The debut of the World Series at County Stadium before 45,804 fans was not a pretty sight, except for the family and friends of Kubek, the Milwaukee native who was the AL's Rookie of the Year in 1957. Pumped up to play in his hometown, Kubek had three hits, two of them home runs, drove in four runs, and scored three to single-handedly account for more offense than the entire Braves team. New York won, 12–3, quickly dispelling any thoughts that the Braves might win the Series at home.

Milwaukee was never really in the game. Starter Bob Buhl was knocked out in the first inning when the Yankees scored three times.

The Braves had a chance to get back in the game in the second against Bob Turley but managed just one run. Hazle and Del Rice started the inning with singles. With one out,

Hazle took third on a wild pitch, then scored on a single by Schoendienst. After Logan struck out, Mathews walked, loading the bases. However, Aaron flied to right.

The Yankees got a two-run single by Jerry Lumpe in the third to make it 5–1. And Mantle hit a two-run homer in the fourth off Gene Conley for a 7–1 New York lead.

The Braves showed a little life in the fifth when they cut the Yankees' margin to 7–3 on a two-run homer by Aaron. However, Stengel's team put away the game by scoring their final five runs in the seventh, all with two outs.

Larsen, who relieved Turley in the second, picked up the win with 7⅓ innings of relief. The Yankees outhit the Braves only 9–8, but six Milwaukee pitchers issued 11 walks. Turley and Larsen combined to walk eight themselves, but the Braves stranded 14 runners, tying a Series record.

Game Four

The Yankees could have put the Braves in a nearly impossible situation by winning Game 4, and they almost did just that. But Haney's team rallied in what probably was the most anxious yet thrilling game of the Series to win, 7–5, behind Spahn.

The loser of Game 1, Spahn fell behind quickly when McDougald's two-out single scored Mantle, who'd reached on a fielder's choice in the first. Sturdivant, the Yankees' starter and regular-season leader with 16 wins, made that run stand up until the fourth. But Logan drew a walk to lead off the inning, then Mathews doubled and Aaron hit a three-run homer. One out later, Frank Torre hit a solo homer to give the Braves a 4–1 lead.

After giving up the first-inning run, Spahn breezed through the New York lineup, facing the minimum of 18 men from the second through the seventh with the help of a couple of double plays.

When Spahn retired the first two Yankees in the ninth, many fans headed for the exit gates. However, Berra and McDougald singled, bringing Howard to the plate as the potential tying run. The New York first baseman proceeded to hit a three-run homer, stunning the Braves and their fans.

Spahn retired Carey on a fly ball to right to end the inning, but the damage had been done. When the Braves went out in order in the bottom of the ninth against Tommy Byrne, the Yankees seemed to have a big edge in momentum.

Indeed, in the 10th, New York took a 5–4 lead with another two-out rally. This time, Kubek sneaked a single up the middle on a ball that Schoendienst flagged down but couldn't throw in time. Bauer followed with a triple over Aaron's head and off the center-field fence. The Braves were on the verge of allowing near-certain victory to slip into a grim defeat and a 3–1 deficit in games.

At this point, however, fate seemingly intervened. Nippy Jones, batting for Spahn to lead off the 10th, skipped away from an inside pitch by Byrne and complained that the ball struck his foot. Umpire Augie Donatelli disagreed, but at Jones's request asked for the ball. When Donatelli saw a black smudge, ostensibly shoe polish, he awarded Jones first base.

Jones was replaced by pinch runner Felix Mantilla, but he was immortalized in World Series lore when the "shoe-polish incident" led to a winning rally. Stengel brought in Grim, his ace reliever, and Schoendienst advanced Mantilla into scoring position with a sacrifice bunt. Logan then doubled into the left-field corner, tying the game and bringing Mathews to the plate. First base was open, but Mathews had just one hit in 11 at bats, so Stengel allowed Grim to pitch to the Milwaukee third baseman. Using a bat borrowed from Adcock, Mathews slammed a 2–2 pitch over the right-field fence, causing County Stadium to erupt with joy.

Milwaukee had witnessed its first World Series victory by its beloved Braves. More importantly, Haney's team had evened the score in games at 2–2.

Eddie Mathews hit a dramatic home run in the 10th inning of Game 4 which proved to be the turning point of the Series for the Braves.

The Braves congratulate Mathews after his game-ending home run tied the Series at two games for each team.

Game Five

The return to Yankee Stadium loomed as the Braves sent Burdette to the mound to face Ford in Game 5. Both men had already pitched masterful, complete-game victories, Ford in Game 1 and Burdette in Game 2.

Ford once again baffled Milwaukee's powerful lineup, but the 1957 World Series belonged to Selva Lewis Burdette.

Neither team mounted a serious scoring threat through the first five innings. The closest Burdette came to trouble

was in the fourth inning when McDougald led off with a drive to left that appeared headed for extra bases and possibly a home run. But Covington, just as he had in Game 2, saved Burdette by crashing into the fence and making the catch.

In the first five innings, the Braves managed just a walk and three singles, none in the same inning. In the sixth, however, Mathews beat out an infield hit with two outs. Aaron and Adcock followed with singles, and the Braves had what proved to be the only run of the game.

Over the final three innings, Burdette pitched like a true thoroughbred, facing just 10 men. He allowed seven singles in the game, never more than one in an inning, and didn't walk a batter. Ford and Turley, who pitched the eighth, were nearly as good, yielding just six singles and a walk.

The Braves were headed to New York, needing only a split of the two games to win their first World Series since 1914.

Lou Burdette, who shut out the Yankees, 1–0, in Game 5, greets Eddie Mathews after the final out gave the Braves a 3–2 edge.

Game Six

Buhl, who didn't make it through the first inning in Game 3, had the opportunity to redeem himself in Game 6 and win the Series. But he didn't last much longer this time. On the other hand, New York's Turley, who'd also been roughed up in Game 3, was at his best when the Yankees needed him most.

Both hard-throwing right-handers started the afternoon in dominating fashion. Turley struck out four Braves in the first three innings. Buhl struck out the side in the first, though the Yankees mixed in a walk and a single, and he notched a fourth strikeout in the second.

But in the bottom of the third, Slaughter coaxed a two-out walk, and Berra followed with a home run into the right-field seats. It was his 10th Series homer, second to Babe Ruth.

Torre led off the fifth with a home run, cutting the Braves' deficit to 2–1, and Aaron led off the seventh with a homer to tie the game.

In the bottom of the seventh, however, with Ernie Johnson still pitching in a near-flawless relief stint, Bauer hooked a one-out liner down the left-field line that caught the foul pole for a home run. That's the way it ended, the Yankees winning, 3–2, to send the Series to a seventh game.

Game Seven

Spahn was supposed to pitch Game 7, but he was weakened by a three-day bout with the flu. Though Burdette had just two days of rest, Haney decided to use his sly right-hander rather than give the assignment to Conley, Bob Trowbridge, or Juan Pizarro, all of whom had been ineffective in short relief stints.

Stengel countered with Larsen, who had made history with a perfect game in the 1956 Series and picked up the victory in Game 3 of this Series with 7⅓ innings of relief.

Both pitchers got through the first two innings without incident, but the Braves erupted for four runs in the third, sending Larsen to an early shower and giving Burdette plenty of breathing room.

With one out, Hazle singled to left. Logan grounded to third, but Kubek's throw pulled Coleman off second, putting runners at first and second. Mathews doubled to right for two runs, and Stengel pulled Larsen in favor of Shantz. Aaron greeted the little left-hander with a single, driving in Mathews for a 3–0 Milwaukee lead. Covington singled, the

Braves' fourth hit of the inning, to put runners at the corners, and Aaron scored the fourth run when Torre grounded into a force play.

The Braves added a fifth run in the eighth on a home run by Crandall, but by then, Burdette had the game well in hand. The Yankees did mount a final threat in the ninth, loading the bases with three singles, two coming with two outs. Then Skowron hit a smash down the third-base line that could have broken up the shutout. But Mathews was protecting the line. He made a nifty backhanded stab and stepped on the bag to force McDougald for the final out.

The Braves were World Series champions, and just as the team broke into immediate celebration, so, too, did thousands of fans back in Milwaukee. People poured into the streets to party and wave banners and signs.

Burdette gave up seven hits—six singles and a first-inning double—and walked just one. He retired New York in order four times and didn't allow more than one hit in an inning or a runner to get past second until the ninth inning.

Within roughly 72 hours, Burdette shut out the defending World Series champs and one of baseball's most potent line-ups twice. After allowing the Yankees single runs in the second and third innings of Game 2, he shut them out for 24 consecutive innings, posting a Series ERA of 0.67 to go with his 3–0 record. There was no question who was the Series MVP.

The Braves swarm over Lou Burdette after the final out of Game 7 at Yankee Stadium gave the franchise its first World Series championship since 1914.

Game 1
Wednesday, October 2, at New York

Milwaukee	AB	R	H	RBI
Schoendienst, 2b	4	0	1	1
Logan, ss	3	0	0	0
Mathews, 3b	2	0	0	0
Aaron, cf	4	0	1	0
Adcock, 1b	4	0	0	0
Torre, 1b	0	0	0	0
Pafko, rf	4	0	0	0
Covington, lf	4	1	2	0
Crandall, c	4	0	1	0
Spahn, p	1	0	0	0
Johnson, p	0	0	0	0
Jones, ph	1	0	0	0
McMahon, p	0	0	0	0
Totals	31	1	5	1

New York	AB	R	H	RBI
Bauer, rf	4	0	1	1
McDougald, ss	4	0	1	0
Mantle, cf	4	0	2	0
Skowron, 1b	1	0	0	0
Howard, 1b	2	1	1	0
Collins, 1b	1	0	0	0
Berra, c	3	1	1	0
Carey, 3b	3	0	1	1
Coleman, 2b	3	1	2	1
Kubek, lf	3	0	0	0
Ford, p	3	0	0	0
Totals	31	3	9	3

Milwaukee   0 0 0 0 0 0 1 0 0—1   5   0
New York   0 0 0 0 1 2 0 0 x—3   9   1

E—Howard. DP—Milwaukee 1, New York 1. LOB—Milwaukee 7, New York 7. 2B—Coleman, Bauer, Covington. 3B—None. HR—None. SF—None. SH—Coleman. SB—Hegan, Gordon, Torgeson. CS—None.

Milwaukee	IP	H	R	ER	BB	K
Spahn (L)	5⅓	7	3	3	1	0
Johnson	⅔	0	0	0	0	1
McMahon	2	2	0	0	1	3

New York	IP	H	R	ER	BB	K
Ford (W)	9	5	1	1	4	5

HBP—None. WP—None. T—2:10. A—69,476. Umpires—Paparella, Conlan, McKinley, Donatelli, Secory, Chylak.

Game 2
Thursday, October 3, at New York

Milwaukee	AB	R	H	RBI
Schoendienst, 2b	4	0	0	0
Logan, ss	3	1	1	1
Mathews, 3b	4	0	0	0
Aaron, cf	4	1	1	0
Adcock, 1b	4	1	2	1
Torre, 1b	0	0	0	0
Pafko, rf	4	1	1	0
Covington, lf	4	0	2	1
Crandall, c	3	0	1	0
Burdette, p	3	0	0	0
Totals	33	4	8	3

New York	AB	R	H	RBI
Bauer, rf	5	1	1	1
McDougald, ss	4	0	0	0
Mantle, cf	3	0	0	0
Berra, c	4	0	0	0
Slaughter, lf	3	1	1	0
Simpson, 1b	4	0	0	0
Kubek, 3b	4	0	2	0
Coleman, 2b	2	0	1	1
Collins, ph	1	0	0	0
Shantz, p	1	0	0	0
Ditmar, p	1	0	0	0
Lumpe, ph	1	0	1	0
Grim, p	1	0	0	0
Howard, ph	1	0	1	0
Richardson, pr	0	0	0	0
Totals	34	2	7	2

Milwaukee   0 1 1 2 0 0 0 0 0—4   8   0
New York   0 1 1 0 0 0 0 0 0—2   7   2

E—Mantle, Kubek. DP—New York 1. LOB—Milwaukee 5. New York 8. 2B—Slaughter. 3B—Aaron. HR—Logan, Bauer. SF—None. SH—Burdette. SB—None. CS—None.

Milwaukee	IP	H	R	ER	BB	K
Burdette (W)	9	7	2	2	3	5

New York	IP	H	R	ER	BB	K
Shantz (L)	3	6	4	3	1	3
Ditmar	4	1	0	0	0	1
Grim	2	1	0	0	0	2

HBP—Logan by Ditmar. WP—None. T—2:26. A—65,202. Umpires—Conlan, McKinely, Donatelli, Paparella, Secory, Chylax.

Game 3
Saturday, October 5, at Milwaukee

New York	AB	R	H	RBI
Bauer, rf	5	1	1	2
Kubek, lf	5	3	3	4
Mantle, cf	3	2	2	2
Berra, c	4	2	1	0
McDougald, ss	1	2	0	1
Simpson, 1b	1	0	1	1
Howard, ph-1b	2	0	0	0
Collins, 1b	1	0	0	0
Lumpe, 3b	5	0	1	2
Coleman, 2b	4	1	0	0
Turley, p	1	0	0	0
Larsen, p	2	1	0	0
Totals	34	12	9	12

Milwaukee	AB	R	H	RBI
Schoendienst, 2b	5	0	3	1
Logan, ss	4	1	2	0
Mathews, 3b	2	0	0	0
Aaron, cf	5	1	2	2
Covington, lf	3	0	0	0
Adcock, 1b	3	0	0	0
Trowbridge, p	0	0	0	0
Jones, ph	1	0	0	0
McMahon, p	0	0	0	0
Pafko, ph	0	0	0	0
Hazle, rf	4	1	0	0
Rice, c	3	0	1	0
DeMerit, ph	0	0	0	0
Crandall, c	1	0	0	0
Buhl, p	0	0	0	0
Pizarro, p	1	0	0	0
Conley, p	0	0	0	0
Sawatski, ph	1	0	0	0
Johnson, p	0	0	0	0
Torre, ph-1b	2	0	0	0
Totals	35	3	8	3

New York   3 0 2 2 0 0 5 0 0—12   9   0
Milwaukee   0 1 0 0 2 0 0 0 0— 3   8   1

E—Buhl. DP—Milwaukee 1. LOB—New York 7, Milwaukee 14. 2B—None. 3B—None. HR—Kubek 2, Mantle, Aaron. SF—McDougald. SH—None. SB—McDougald. CS—None.

New York	IP	H	R	ER	BB	K
Turley	1⅔	3	1	1	4	2
Larsen (W)	7⅓	5	2	2	4	4

Milwaukee	IP	H	R	ER	BB	K
Buhl (L)	⅔	2	3	2	2	0
Pizarro	1⅓	3	2	2	2	1
Conley	1⅔	2	2	2	1	0
Johnson	2	0	0	0	1	2
Trowbridge	1	2	5	5	3	1
McMahon	2	0	0	0	2	2

HBP—Pafko by Larsen. PB—Rice. WP—Turley. T—3:18. A—45,804. Umpires—McKinley, Donatelli, Paparella, Conlan, Chylax, Secory.

Game 4
Sunday, October 6, at Milwaukee

New York	AB	R	H	RBI
Kubek, lf-cf	5	1	2	0
Bauer, rf	5	0	1	1
Mantle, cf	5	1	0	0
Slaughter, lf	0	0	0	0
Berra, c	3	1	2	0
McDougald, ss	4	1	2	1
Howard, 1b	4	1	1	3
Collins, 1b	0	0	0	0
Carey, 3b	4	0	1	0
Coleman, 2b	4	0	1	0
Sturdivant, p	1	0	0	0
Simpson, ph	1	0	0	0
Shantz, p	0	0	0	0
Lumpe, ph	1	0	1	0
Kucks, p	0	0	0	0
Byrne, p	1	0	0	0
Grim, p	0	0	0	0
Totals	38	5	11	5

Milwaukee	AB	R	H	RBI
Schoendienst, 2b	4	0	1	0
Logan, ss	4	2	1	1
Mathews, 3b	4	2	2	2
Aaron, cf	3	1	2	3
Covington, lf	4	0	0	0
Torre, 1b	3	1	1	1
Adcock, ph-1b	1	0	0	0
Hazle, rf	2	0	0	0
Pafko, rf	2	0	0	0
Crandall, c	4	0	0	0
Spahn, p	3	0	0	0
Jones, ph	0	0	0	0
Mantilla, ph	0	1	0	0
Totals	34	7	7	7

```
New York    1 0 0  0 0 0  0 0 3  1—5 11 0
Milwaukee   0 0 0  4 0 0  0 0 0  3—7  7 0
```

E—None. DP—Milwaukee 3. LOB—New York 4, Milwaukee 4. 2B—Mathews, Carey, Schoendienst, Logan. 3B—Bauer. HR—Aaron, Torre, Howard, Mathews. SF—None. SH—Schoendienst. SB—Covington. CS—None.

New York	IP	H	R	ER	BB	K
Sturdivant	4	4	4	4	1	1
Shantz	3	0	0	0	1	4
Kucks	⅔	1	0	0	1	1
Byrne	1⅓	0	1	1	0	1
Grim (L)	½	2	2	2	0	0

Milwaukee	IP	H	R	ER	BB	K
Spahn (W)	10	11	5	5	1	2

HBP—Jones by Byrne. PB—None. WP—None. T—2:31. A—45,804. Umpires—Donatelli, Paparella, Conlan, McKinley, Chylak, Secory.

Game 5
Monday, October 7, at Milwaukee

New York	AB	R	H	RBI
Bauer, rf	4	0	2	0
Kubek, cf	3	0	0	0
McDougald, ss	4	0	1	0
Berra, c	4	0	1	0
Slaughter, lf	3	0	2	0
Simpson, 1b	3	0	0	0
Lumpe, 3b	3	0	0	0
Coleman, 2b	3	0	1	0
Mantle, ph	0	0	0	0
Turley, p	0	0	0	0
Ford, p	2	0	0	0
Howard, ph	1	0	0	0
Richardson, 2b	0	0	0	0
Totals	30	0	7	0

Milwaukee	AB	R	H	RBI
Schoendienst, 2b	1	0	0	0
Mantilla, 2b	3	0	0	0
Logan, ss	4	0	0	0
Mathews, 3b	3	1	1	0
Aaron, cf	3	0	2	0
Adcock, 1b	3	0	1	1
Torre, 1b	0	0	0	0
Pafko, rf	3	0	2	0
Covington, lf	2	0	0	0
Crandall, c	3	0	0	0
Burdette, p	3	0	0	0
Totals	28	1	6	1

```
New York    0 0 0  0 0 0  0 0 0—0 7 0
Milwaukee   0 0 0  0 0 1  0 0 x—1 6 1
```

E—Adcock. DP—New York 1, Milwaukee 3. LOB—New York 4, Milwaukee 5. 2B—None. 3B—None. HR—None. SF—None. SH—Kubek, Covington. SB—None. CS—None.

New York	IP	H	R	ER	BB	K
Ford (L)	7	6	1	1	1	2
Turley	1	0	0	0	0	2

Milwaukee	IP	H	R	ER	BB	K
Burdette (W)	9	7	0	0	0	5

HBP—None. WP—None. T—2:00. A—45,811. Umpires—Paparella, Conlan, McKinley, Donatelli, Chylak, Secory.

Game 6
Wednesday, October 9, at New York

Milwaukee	AB	R	H	RBI
Mantilla, 2b	3	0	0	0
Logan, ss	4	0	0	0
Mathews, 3b	3	0	1	0
Aaron, cf	4	1	1	1
Covington, lf	4	0	0	0
Torre, 1b	3	1	2	1
Hazle, rf	3	0	0	0
Rice, c	3	0	0	0
Buhl, p	1	0	0	0
Johnson, p	1	0	0	0
Sawatski, ph	1	0	0	0
McMahon, p	0	0	0	0
Totals	30	2	4	2

New York	AB	R	H	RBI
Bauer, rf	4	1	1	1
Kubek, cf	4	0	0	0
Slaughter, lf	2	1	0	0
Berra, c	4	1	3	2
McDougald, ss	3	0	1	0
Lumpe, 3b	3	0	1	0
Simpson, 1b	3	0	0	0
Collins, 1b	0	0	0	0
Coleman, 2b	2	0	1	0
Turley, p	3	0	0	0
Totals	28	3	7	3

```
Milwaukee   0 0 0  0 1 0  1 0 0—2 4 0
New York    0 0 2  0 0 0  1 0 x—3 7 0
```

E—None. DP—Milwaukee 2, New York 1. LOB—Milwaukee 3, New York 6. 2B—Mathews, Coleman, Berra. 3B—None. HR—Berra, Torre, Aaron, Bauer. SF—None. SH—McDougald. SB—None. CS—None.

Milwaukee	IP	H	R	ER	BB	K
Buhl	2⅔	4	2	2	4	4
Johnson (L)	4⅓	2	1	1	0	5
McMahon	1	1	0	0	0	0

New York	IP	H	R	ER	BB	K
Turley (W)	9	4	2	2	2	8

HBP—None. WP—Buhl. T—2:09. A—61,408. Umpires—Conlan, McKinley, Donatelli, Paparella, Secory, Chylak.

Game 7
Thursday, October 10, at New York

Milwaukee	AB	R	H	RBI
Hazle, rf	4	1	2	0
Pafko, ph-rf	1	0	0	0
Logan, ss	5	1	1	0
Mathews, 3b	4	1	1	2
Aaron, cf	5	1	2	1
Covington, lf	3	0	1	0
Torre, 1b	2	0	0	1
Mantilla, 2b	4	0	0	0
Crandall, c	4	1	2	1
Burdette, p	2	0	0	0
Totals	34	5	9	5

New York	AB	R	H	RBI
Bauer, rf	4	0	1	0
Slaughter, lf	4	0	0	0
Mantle, cf	4	0	1	0
Berra, c	3	0	0	0
McDougald, ss	4	0	1	0
Kubek, 3b	4	0	1	0
Coleman, 2b	4	0	2	0
Collins, 1b	2	0	0	0
Sturdivant, p	0	0	0	0
Howard, ph	1	0	0	0
Byrne, p	1	0	0	0
Larsen, p	0	0	0	0
Shantz, p	0	0	0	0
Lumpe, ph	1	0	0	0
Ditmar, p	0	0	0	0
Skowron, 1b	3	0	0	0
Totals	35	0	7	0

```
Milwaukee   0 0 4  0 0 0  1 0 0—5 9 1
New York    0 0 0  0 0 0  0 0 0—0 7 3
```

E—Mathews, Berra, McDougald, Kubek. DP—New York 1. LOB—Milwaukee 8, New York 9. 2B—Bauer, Mathews. 3B—None. HR—Crandall. SF—None. SH—Burdette, Mathews, Covington. SB—None. CS—None.

Milwaukee	IP	H	R	ER	BB	K
Burdette (W)	9	7	0	0	1	3

New York	IP	H	R	ER	BB	K
Larsen (L)	2⅓	3	3	2	1	2
Shantz	⅔	2	1	0	0	0
Ditmar	2	1	0	0	0	1
Sturdivant	2	2	0	0	0	1
Byrne	2	1	1	1	2	0

HBP—None. WP—None. T—2:34. A—61,207. Umpires—Conlan, McKinley, Donatelli, Paparella, Secory, Chylak.

COMPOSITE LINE SCORE

Milwaukee Braves (N.L.)	0	2	5	6	3	1	2	1	0	3—23	
New York Yankees (A.L.)	4	1	5	2	1	2	6	0	3	1—25	

COMPOSITE BATTING AND FIELDING STATISTICS

Milwaukee Braves	G	AB	R	H	2B	3B	HR	RBI	BB	SO	SB	BA	SA	PO	A	E
Joe Adcock, 1b-ph	5	15	1	3	0	0	0	2	0	2	0	.200	.200	38	2	1
Red Schoendienst, 2b	5	18	0	5	1	0	0	2	0	1	0	.278	.333	5	10	0
Johnny Logan, ss	7	27	5	5	1	0	1	2	3	6	0	.185	.333	13	25	0
Eddie Mathews, 3b	7	22	4	5	3	0	1	4	8	5	0	.227	.500	9	19	1
Andy Pafko, rf-ph	6	14	1	3	0	0	0	0	0	1	0	.214	.214	9	0	0
Hank Aaron, cf	7	28	5	11	0	1	3	7	1	6	0	.393	.786	11	0	0
Wes Covington, lf	7	24	1	5	1	0	0	1	2	6	1	.208	.250	13	1	0
Del Crandall, c	6	19	1	4	0	0	1	1	1	1	0	.211	.368	21	4	0
Bob Hazle, rf	4	13	2	2	0	0	0	0	1	2	0	.154	.154	6	0	0
Frank Torre, 1b-ph	7	10	2	3	0	0	2	3	2	0	0	.300	.900	37	2	0
Felix Mantilla, pr-2b	4	10	1	0	0	0	0	0	1	0	0	.000	.000	6	8	0
Del Rice, c	2	6	0	1	0	0	0	0	1	2	0	.167	.167	15	2	0
Nippy Jones, ph	3	2	0	0	0	0	0	0	0	0	0	.000	.000			
Carl Sawatski, ph	2	2	0	0	0	0	0	0	0	2	0	.000	.000			
John DeMerit, pr	1	0	0	0	0	0	0	0	0	0	0	—	—			
Mel Roach	Did not play															
Lou Burdette, p	3	8	0	0	0	0	0	0	1	2	0	.000	.000	0	9	0
Warren Spahn, p	2	4	0	0	0	0	0	0	1	2	0	.000	.000	1	3	0
Ernie Johnson, p	3	1	0	0	0	0	0	0	0	1	0	.000	.000	1	4	0
Bob Buhl, p	2	1	0	0	0	0	0	0	0	1	0	.000	.000	0	2	1
Juan Pizarro, p	1	1	0	0	0	0	0	0	0	0	0	.000	.000	0	0	0
Don McMahon, p	3	0	0	0	0	0	0	0	0	0	0	—	—	0	2	0
Gene Conley, p	1	0	0	0	0	0	0	0	0	0	0	—	—	1	0	0
Bob Trowbridge, p	1	0	0	0	0	0	0	0	0	0	0	—	—	0	0	0
Taylor Phillips	Did not play															
Dave Jolley	Did not play															
Team total	7	225	23	47	6	1	8	22	22	40	1	.209	.351	186	93	3

Double plays—10
Left on bases—46

New York Yankees	G	AB	R	H	2B	3B	HR	RBI	BB	SO	SB	BA	SA	PO	A	E
Elston Howard, 1b-ph	6	11	2	3	0	0	1	3	1	3	0	.273	.545	22	1	1
Jerry Coleman, 2b	7	22	2	8	2	0	0	2	3	1	0	.364	.455	16	17	1
Gil McDougald, ss	7	24	3	6	0	0	0	2	3	3	1	.250	.250	13	24	1
Jerry Lumpe, 3b-ph	6	14	0	4	0	0	0	2	1	1	0	.286	.286	3	6	0
Hank Bauer, rf	7	31	3	8	2	1	2	6	1	6	0	.258	.581	10	0	0
Mickey Mantle, cf-pr	6	19	3	5	0	0	1	2	3	1	0	.263	.421	8	0	1
Tony Kubek, lf-3b-cf	7	28	4	8	0	0	2	4	0	4	0	.286	.500	17	5	2
Yogi Berra, c	7	25	5	8	1	0	1	2	4	0	0	.320	.480	44	2	1
Enos Slaughter, lf	5	12	2	3	1	0	0	3	2	0	.250	.333	7	0	0	
Harry Simpson, 1b-ph	5	12	0	1	0	0	0	1	0	4	0	.083	.083	24	1	0
Andy Carey, 3b	2	7	0	2	1	0	0	1	1	0	0	.286	.429	3	6	0
Joe Collins, 1b-ph	6	5	0	0	0	0	0	0	0	3	0	.000	.000	12	2	0
Bill Skowron, 1b-ph	2	4	0	0	0	0	0	0	0	0	0	.000	.000	5	2	0
B. Richardson, pr-2b	2	0	0	0	0	0	0	0	0	0	0	—	—	0	0	0
Darrell Johnson	Did not play															
Whitey Ford, p	2	5	0	0	0	0	0	0	0	1	0	.000	.000	1	1	0
Bob Turley, p	3	4	0	0	0	0	0	0	0	2	0	.000	.000	2	2	0
Tommy Byrne, p	2	2	0	1	0	0	0	0	0	1	0	.500	.500	0	1	0
Don Larsen, p	2	2	1	0	0	0	0	0	2	1	0	.000	.000	0	1	0
Tom Sturdivant, p	2	1	0	0	0	0	0	0	0	0	0	.000	.000	0	1	0
Bobby Shantz, p	3	1	0	0	0	0	0	0	0	0	0	.000	.000	0	1	0
Art Ditmar, p	2	1	0	0	0	0	0	0	0	1	0	.000	.000	0	0	0
Bob Grim, p	2	0	0	0	0	0	0	0	0	0	0	—	—	0	0	0
Johnny Kucks, p	1	0	0	0	0	0	0	0	0	0	0	—	—	0	0	0
Al Cicotte	Did not play															
team total	7	230	25	57	7	1	7	25	22	34	1	.248	.378	187	72	6

Double plays—5
Left on bases—45

COMPOSITE PITCHING STATISTICS

Milwaukee Braves	G	GS	CG	IP	H	R	ER	BB	SO	W	L	SV	ERA
Lou Burdette	3	3	3	27	21	2	2	4	13	3	0	0	0.67
Warren Spahn	2	2	1	15⅓	18	8	8	2	2	1	1	0	4.70
Ernie Johnson	3	0	0	7	2	1	1	1	8	0	1	0	1.29
Don McMahon	3	0	0	5	3	0	0	3	5	0	0	0	0.00
Bob Buhl	2	2	0	3⅓	6	5	4	6	4	0	1	0	10.80
Juan Pizarro	1	0	0	1⅔	3	2	2	2	1	0	0	0	10.80
Gene Conley	1	0	0	1⅔	2	2	2	1	0	0	0	0	10.80
Bob Trowbridge	1	0	0	1	2	5	5	3	1	0	0	0	45.00
Taylor Phillips	Did not play												
Dave Jolley	Did not play												
team total	7	7	4	62	57	25	24	22	34	4	3	0	3.48

New York Yankees	G	GS	CG	IP	H	R	ER	BB	SO	W	L	SV	ERA
Whitey Ford	2	2	1	16	11	2	2	5	7	1	1	0	1.13
Bob Turley	3	2	1	11⅓	7	3	3	6	12	1	0	0	2.31
Don Larsen	2	1	0	9⅔	8	5	4	5	6	1	1	0	3.72
Bobby Shantz	3	1	0	6⅔	8	5	3	2	7	0	1	0	4.05
Art Ditmar	2	0	0	6	2	0	0	0	2	0	0	0	0.00
Tom Sturdivant	2	1	0	6	4	4	4	1	2	0	0	0	6.00
Tommy Byrne	2	0	0	3⅓	1	2	2	2	1	0	0	0	5.40
Bob Grim	2	0	0	2⅓	3	2	2	0	2	0	1	0	7.71
Johnny Kucks	1	0	0	⅔	1	0	0	1	1	0	0	0	0.00
Al Cicotte	Did not play												
team total	7	7	2	62⅓	47	23	20	22	40	3	4	0	2.89

Total Attendance—394,712. Average Attendance—56,387.
Winning Player's Share—$8,924. Losing Player's Share—$5,606

Milwaukee celebrated the Braves' 1957 success with a ticker-tape parade attended by thousands.

Braves versus New York Yankees World Series

1958

Even though they won just one World Series, the Milwaukee Braves of the 1950s are generally considered to have been one of the most talented assemblages of talent in history. Yet so much of their legacy is "what might have been." It's staggering to think of the regard in which they'd be held today if only they had won three more games.

Losers of the 1956 pennant on the last day of the season, the Braves bounced back to win the World Series in 1957. In 1959 they lost the pennant in a playoff. Then there's the 1958 World Series, the best example of the missed opportunities that still haunt this team's track record.

In a rematch of the '57 Series, the Braves, who won the National League by eight games, met the Yankees, who won the American League by 10 games. It was a clash of what were clearly the game's most powerful clubs.

Both teams had identical 92–62 records. Both had two pitching aces. Warren Spahn led the National League with 22 wins, and Lou Burdette was right behind with 20. Bob Turley won 21 games to pace the American League, and Whitey Ford, who was 14–7, led the league in ERA (2.01). The Braves had no relievers who reached double figures in saves, but New York's Ryne Duren led the AL with 20.

The Milwaukee offense, of course, was led by Hank Aaron and Eddie Mathews, who combined for 61 home runs, and Wes Covington, who added 24 in just 90 games. The Yankees had Mickey Mantle, who led the AL with 42 home runs, and Yogi Berra (22 homers), along with the usual supporting cast that included a bevy of capable hitters such as Bill Skowron, Elston Howard, Hank Bauer, and Gil McDougald. Surprisingly, neither team had a 100-RBI man, though Aaron, Mantle, and Berra all drove in 90 or more runs.

On paper, they were two extremely well matched teams. The Yankees had a .268 team batting average to .266 for the Braves. Milwaukee hit 167 home runs, just three more than New York. And the Braves' pitching staff had a 3.21 composite ERA to 3.22 for the Yankees.

Fred Haney's Braves enjoyed the home-field edge and took advantage of it by winning the first two games at County Stadium by the scores of 4–3 and 13–5. When they split the first two games at Yankee Stadium to take a commanding 3–1 lead in games, it appeared they would have no trouble capturing a second straight World Series—especially with the last two games, if needed, scheduled for Milwaukee.

But the Yankees were indeed too well matched with the Braves to be subdued with such little suspense. It remained for Casey Stengel's team to write the most telling chapter of the Braves' "what might have been" story.

Depending on how you look at it, Milwaukee's failure to repeat as World Series champs came down to poor hitting by the Braves or great pitching by the Yankees. Either way, Haney's club scored only five runs in the last three games, all losses.

Game One

Future Hall of Fame left-handers Spahn and Ford hooked up in the Series opener before 46,367 fans at County Stadium. The result was a tense duel that wasn't decided until the 10th inning when Spahn, in typical fashion, was still around to finish what he started and Ford had been relieved by Duren.

The game was scoreless until the fourth when Skowron lined a two-out solo home run just inside the left-field foul pole. The Braves answered in the bottom of the inning, though, to take a 2–1 lead. Aaron led off with a walk, advanced to second on a passed ball, and went to third on an infield grounder for the second out. Del Crandall singled to left to tie the game, then Andy Pafko and Spahn singled to get Crandall home.

The home run ball foiled Spahn again in the fifth. With one out, Ford walked and Bauer followed with a homer to left that allowed New York to regain the lead, 3–2.

That was all the scoring Spahn would allow, though. In the eighth, the Braves tied the game. Mathews drew a leadoff walk and went to third on Aaron's double to right. Duren replaced Ford and struck out Joe Adcock. But Covington drove a sacrifice fly to center, scoring Mathews to make it 3–3.

That's the way it stayed until the Braves won it in the bottom of the 10th with three singles by Adcock, Crandall, and Billy Bruton, who'd entered the game in the ninth as a pinch hitter. The last two hits came with two outs.

Game Two

Two 20-game winners, Burdette and Turley, were matched in the second game. And although Burdette wasn't as sharp as he had been in baffling the Yankees in 1957, he still raised his World Series record to 4–0 against the team that had traded him to the Braves.

Actually, Burdette didn't need to be very sharp, since the Braves chased Turley and reliever Duke Maas in the first inning with a seven-run outburst on the way to a 13–5 victory.

The Yankees nearly had a big inning of their own in the first when they loaded the bases with none out. But Burdette escaped with only a 1–0 deficit by getting Howard to hit into a force play and Berra to ground into a double play.

Bruton quickly evened the game by leading off the bottom of the first with a homer. Red Schoendienst followed with a double, and with one out, Aaron walked and Covington singled, scoring Schoendienst with the lead run and putting men at first and third. Stengel pulled Turley for Maas, who got Frank Torre to fly to left with Covington tagging and going to second. Crandall walked to load the bases, then the rout really began. Johnny Logan's single scored Aaron and Covington, and Burdette followed with a three-run homer to make it 7–1.

Burdette's homer was the first by a pitcher in the Series since 1940, and Milwaukee's seven-run explosion set a Series record for the first inning.

The Braves added a run in the second on a double by Mathews and a single by Covington. A leadoff homer by Mantle made it 8–2 in the fourth, and that's the way it stayed through the sixth.

In the seventh, the Braves used singles by Aaron, Covington, and Torre and a sacrifice fly by Crandall to increase their lead to 10–2. A walk to Bruton, a double by Schoendienst, and a two-run single by Mathews made it 12–2 in the eighth. Another single by Aaron and a sacrifice fly by Pafko made it 13–2 heading to the ninth.

The Yankees managed a bit of an uprising in the ninth, but it was far too late. Bauer led off with a home run, McDougald singled, and Mantle hit his second homer of the game to account for the 13–5 final.

Billy Bruton led off Game 2 of the 1958 World Series with a home run to spark a seven-run inning and lead the Braves to a 2–0 edge in games.

Game Three

The Series moved to Yankee Stadium for Game 3, which was played before a crowd of 71,599. The Braves sent 32-year-old right-hander Bob Rush, who was 10–6 in his first year with Milwaukee, to face Don Larsen, who was 9–6 and had been slowed by an elbow injury.

Just as Game 2 was all Braves, Game 3 was all Yankees. Larsen scattered six singles to shut out Milwaukee for seven innings, and Rush and reliever Don McMahon were hounded by control problems that led to New York's two scoring rallies.

The game was scoreless entering the bottom of the fifth when Rush loaded the bases with three walks, the last two with two outs. Bauer followed with a single to right, making it 2–0.

Again in the seventh, this time with McMahon pitching, the Yankees and Bauer struck after a walk, the sixth of seven Milwaukee pitchers would issue. With one out and Enos Slaughter on first courtesy of the free pass, Bauer homered to left, making it 4–0. It was Bauer's third home run of the Series and ended the scoring.

Game Four

Spahn, who pitched 10 strong innings to win Game 1, put on a pitching clinic in Game 4. Ford pitched well for the Yankees, too, but he couldn't keep the Braves from winning, 3–0, and taking a commanding 3–1 lead in games.

Spahn gave up harmless walks in the first and third innings, the only two he issued, but neither advanced past first. The Yankees' first hit and their lone scoring threat came in the fourth when Mantle slammed a one-out triple off the scoreboard in left-center. But Spahn retired Skowron on a grounder back to the mound and got Berra to line to Schoendienst. The Milwaukee second baseman leaped to knock down Berra's liner, recovered the ball, and threw to first barely in time for the third out.

Over the final five innings, Spahn was nearly flawless. The

lone New York base runner came in the seventh when Skowron got a one-out single to center, but he died at first when Berra fouled out and Howard was called out on strikes.

The Braves, meanwhile, strung together single runs in the sixth, seventh, and eighth with the help of some shaky play in left by Norm Siebern, starting in place of the injured Howard.

Schoendienst started the sixth with a fly to left that Siebern and Mantle watched drop between them for a triple. Logan followed with a grounder to short that Kubek let go through his legs for an error, making it 1–0.

In the seventh Crandall walked, and one out later Pafko doubled to put Braves at second and third. Spahn blooped a single to left, just in front of Siebern who got a late start on the ball. It was 2–0, and with the way Spahn was pitching, it almost felt comfortable.

Once again in the eighth, Siebern figured in the Braves' scoring. Logan opened the inning with a long fly that the New York left fielder lost in the sun. Siebern covered his head for protection, and the ball bounced into the stands for a double. Mathews followed with a double of his own, making it 3–0, prompting Stengel to pull Ford.

Spahn allowed only one ball to be hit out of the infield in the last two innings. Afterward, he said it was the best game he'd pitched in his career. The Braves led in games, 3–1, and looked like champs. After all, no team since the 1925 Pirates had come back from a 3–1 deficit to win the Series, and the Braves had their Yankee killer, Burdette, going in Game 5.

Warren Spahn pitched a brilliant two-hit shutout in Game 4 to give the Braves a 3–1 lead in games.

Game Five

How quickly things can change in baseball! How unexpectedly fortunes can turn just when it looks as if they're locked in one direction! How painfully a great team on the verge of its second straight World Series championship can suddenly hit the wall!

The Braves seemed to have everything going their way as they headed into Game 5 at Yankee Stadium. Even if they lost, they would go back to Milwaukee needing only a split of two games to win the Series. But with Burdette, the winner of Game 2, pitching against Turley, who hadn't survived the first inning of Milwaukee's 13–5 victory, it looked as if the Braves could wrap up the Series in New York, where they'd won the previous season.

The hard-throwing Turley was at his best, though, and the Yankees finally proved Burdette mortal.

The Milwaukee right-hander was flawless in the first two innings, retiring all six Yankees he faced. Even when he gave up a leadoff home run to McDougald in the third, he settled down to cruise through the fifth, trailing only 1–0.

But Turley was more than equal to the challenge. Through five innings, he allowed just one single. In the sixth, he gave up two hits but was helped by a double play. Then in the bottom of the sixth, his teammates solved Burdette in a big way—with six runs.

Turley never wavered, yielding just two harmless singles over the final three innings. He finished with a five-hitter, walking three and striking out 10 in a 7–0 victory that sent the Series back to Milwaukee.

Game Six

With just a little more support, Spahn could have duplicated Burdette's 1957 feat by beating the Yankees three times in the 1958 World Series. And, of course, if that had happened, Milwaukee Braves history wouldn't be filled with quite so much "what might have been."

Pitching with the World Series championship within grasp, Spahn was marvelous in Game 6. But so was the Yankees' bullpen.

The Braves had a chance to put the game out of reach early and did knock out Ford in the second inning. However, the Milwaukee offense failed to fully capitalize on its early opportunities and then went to sleep.

With 46,367 County Stadium fans ready to celebrate a World Series championship, the Yankees got on the board first when Bauer homered with two outs in the first. It was his fourth homer of the Series.

The Braves bounced right back to tie the game in the bottom of the inning. Schoendienst led off with a single, advanced on a sacrifice by Logan, and scored on Aaron's two-out single. Milwaukee quickly jumped ahead, 2–1, in the second on three straight one-out singles by Covington, Pafko, and Spahn. When Schoendienst followed with a walk, Stengel pulled Ford in favor of Art Ditmar. Logan then hit a rather short fly to left. Pafko tried to score but was cut down by Howard's throw to Berra.

It appeared Spahn would make the one-run lead stand up until one of Milwaukee's four errors in the game betrayed the great left-hander in the sixth. Mantle led off the inning with a single. When Howard followed with a single to center, Mantle was about to stop at second, but Bruton, who'd just replaced Pafko in center, bobbled the ball, permitting Mantle to take third. Berra's fly to center scored Mantle to tie the game at 2–2.

With New York relievers Ditmar and Duren mowing down the Braves with ease and Spahn doing the same to the Yankees, the game was still 2–2 at the end of nine innings. In the 10th, McDougald hit a leadoff home run to give Stengel's team a 3–2 lead. With two outs, Howard and Berra singled. McMahon relieved Spahn, and Skowron singled in Howard to make it 4–2.

The Braves didn't go down without a fight, though. Logan walked and took second when Duren used a full windup to strike out Mathews. Aaron drove in Logan with a single, cutting the deficit to 4–3. Adcock also singled, advancing Aaron to third. Stengel brought in Turley to face pinch hitter Torre, who popped to short. Suddenly, the Series was tied at three games apiece, and the Yankees had the momentum.

Hank Aaron drove in two runs with a pair of singles in Game 6, but he couldn't keep the Braves from losing, 4–3, in 10 innings, allowing the Yankees to tie the Series.

Game Seven

At least the Braves could put the decisive game in the hands of their Yankee killer, Burdette. But the hit-and-miss Milwaukee offense had to deal with Larsen, who'd shut them out for seven innings in Game 3.

The Braves jumped to a quick lead, much to the delight of the 46,367 fans who were on the edges of their County Stadium seats. Schoendienst led off the first with a single, and Bruton followed with a walk. Both runners advanced on a sacrifice by Torre, and Aaron walked to load the bases. The Braves got only one run, though, which scored when Covington grounded to first. Mathews was walked to load the bases again, and Crandall was called out on strikes to end the inning.

New York came right back to take a 2–1 lead in the second, thanks to a pair of unearned runs made possible by two errors by Torre, who'd led National League first basemen in defense that year.

Berra led off the inning with a walk. Howard sacrificed but was safe when Torre fielded his bunt and made a bad underhand toss to Burdette. On the very next play, the Yankees loaded the bases when Jerry Lumpe grounded to first and Torre made another bad throw to Burdette.

Considering the circumstances, Burdette did well to get out of the inning with only two runs scoring. He never did give up a hit in the inning. The Yankees tied the game when Skowron grounded into a force play, scoring Berra. And they took the lead, 2–1, on a sacrifice fly by Kubek.

The Braves mounted a threat in the third but came out of it without a run even though they knocked out Larsen. Singles by Bruton and Aaron put runners at first and second with one out. Stengel yanked Larsen for Turley, who had shut out the Braves in Game 5. He retired Covington on a tap in front of the plate that advanced the runners. After he walked Mathews to load the bases, Turley got out of the inning by inducing Crandall to ground out.

The game was still 2–1, New York, heading into the bottom of the sixth when Crandall hit a two-out home run off

Turley to tie the game. The World Series had come down to just three innings.

With two outs in the eighth, the roof fell in on Burdette and the Braves. Berra doubled and Howard singled to break the tie. Andy Carey got another single, and Skowron then delivered the crowning blow, a three-run homer to left-center.

It was 6–2 and the Braves were down to their final six outs. Turley retired Haney's team in order in the eighth. Mathews led off the ninth with a walk, but Crandall and Logan flied out. Adcock pinch-hit for McMahon and kept alive Milwaukee's slim hopes with a single. But Schoendienst lined to center.

A second consecutive World Series championship, once a victory away, was lost forever.

The Braves had Lou Burdette, their "Yankee killer," on the mound in Game 7 but still lost the Series.

Game 1
Wednesday, October 1, at Milwaukee

New York	AB	R	H	RBI
Bauer, rf	5	1	2	2
McDougald, 2b	4	0	2	0
Mantle, cf	3	0	0	0
Howard, lf	5	0	0	0
Berra, c	4	0	2	0
Skowron, 1b	4	1	2	1
Carey, 3b	4	0	0	0
Kubek, ss	4	0	0	0
Ford, p	2	1	0	0
Duren, p	1	0	0	0
Totals	36	3	8	3

Milwaukee	AB	R	H	RBI
Schoendienst, 2b	4	0	0	0
Logan, ss	4	0	1	0
Torre, ph	1	0	0	0
Mantilla, ss	0	0	0	0
Mathews, 3b	3	1	0	0
Aaron, rf	4	1	1	0
Adcock, 1b	5	1	2	0
Covington, lf	4	0	0	1
Crandall, c	5	1	2	1
Pafko, cf	3	0	1	0
Bruton, cf	2	0	1	1
Spahn, p	4	0	2	1
Totals	39	4	10	4

```
New York    0 0 0  1 2 0  0 0 0  0—3   8  1
Milwaukee   0 0 0  2 0 0  0 1 0  1—4  10  0
```

E—Kubek. DP—None. LOB—New York 7, Milwaukee 11. 2B—Logan, Berra, Aaron. 3B—None. HR—Skowron, Bauer. SF—Covington. SH—None. SB—None. CS—None.

New York	IP	H	R	ER	BB	K
Ford	7	6	3	3	3	8
Duren (L)	2	4	1	1	1	5

Milwaukee	IP	H	R	ER	BB	K
Spahn (W)	10	8	3	3	4	6

HBP—None. WP—Spahn. PB—Berra. T—3:09. A—46,367. Umpires—Barlick, Berry, Gorman, Flaherty, Jackowski, Umont.

Game 2
Thursday, October 2, at Milwaukee

New York	AB	R	H	RBI
Bauer, rf	4	2	2	1
McDougald, 2b	4	1	1	0
Mantle, cf	3	2	2	3
Howard, lf	3	0	1	0
Siebern, lf	3	0	1	0
Berra, c	4	0	0	0
Skowron, 1b	4	0	0	0
Carey, 3b	2	0	0	0
Slaughter, ph	1	0	0	0
Richardson, 3b	1	0	0	0
Kubek, ss	3	0	0	0
Turley, p	0	0	0	0
Maas, p	0	0	0	0
Kucks, p	0	0	0	0
Lumpe, ph	1	0	0	0
Dickson, p	0	0	0	0
Throneberry, ph	1	0	0	0
Monroe, p	0	0	0	0
Totals	33	5	7	5

Milwaukee	AB	R	H	RBI
Bruton, cf	4	2	3	1
Schoendienst, 2b	4	1	1	0
Mathews, 3b	5	2	2	2
Aaron, rf	4	2	2	0
Covington, lf	4	1	3	2
Mantilla, ph	0	1	0	0
Pafko, lf	0	0	0	1
Torre, 1b	5	0	1	1
Crandall, c	2	1	0	1
Logan, ss	4	1	1	2
Burdette, p	4	1	1	3
Totals	37	13	15	13

```
New York    1 0 0  1 0 0  0 0  3—5   7  0
Milwaukee   7 1 0  0 0 0  2 3  x—13 15  1
```

E—Mathews. DP—Milwaukee 2. LOB—New York 2, Milwaukee 5. 2B—Schoendienst 2, Mathews. 3B—None. HR—Bruton, Burdette, Mantle 2, Bauer. SF—Crandall, Pafko. SH—None. SB—Mathews. CS—None.

New York	IP	H	R	ER	BB	K
Turley (L)	⅓	3	4	4	1	1
Maas	⅓	2	3	3	1	0
Kucks	3⅓	3	1	1	0	0
Dickson	3	4	2	2	0	1
Monroe	1	3	3	3	1	1

Milwaukee	IP	H	R	ER	BB	K
Burdette (W)	9	7	5	4	1	5

HBP—None. WP—None. T—2:43. A—46,367. Umpires—Berry, Gorman, Flaherty, Barlick, Umont, Jackowski.

Game 3
Saturday, October 4, at New York

Milwaukee	AB	R	H	RBI
Bruton, cf	3	0	0	0
Schoendienst, 2b	4	0	2	0
Mathews, 3b	3	0	0	0
Aaron, rf	3	0	0	0
Covington, lf	3	0	1	0
Torre, 1b	4	0	2	0
Crandall, c	4	0	1	0
Logan, ss	3	0	0	0
Rush, p	2	0	0	0
Hanebrink, ph	1	0	0	0
McMahon, p	0	0	0	0
Wise, ph	1	0	0	0
Totals	31	0	6	0

New York	AB	R	H	RBI
Bauer, rf	4	1	3	4
Kubek, ss	4	0	0	0
Mantle, cf	2	0	0	0
Berra, c	4	0	0	0
Siebern, lf	2	1	0	0
Lumpe, 3b	3	0	1	0
Richardson, 3b	1	0	0	0
Skowron, 1b	4	0	0	0
McDougald, 2b	2	1	0	0
Larsen, p	1	0	0	0
Slaughter, ph	0	1	0	0
Duren, p	0	0	0	0
Totals	27	4	4	4

```
Milwaukee   0 0 0  0 0 0  0 0  0—0   6  0
New York    0 0 0  0 2 0  2 0  x—4   4  0
```

E—None. DP—Milwaukee 1, New York 1. LOB—Milwaukee 10, New York 6. 2B—None. 3B—None. HR—Bauer. SF—None. SH—None. SB—None. CS—None.

Milwaukee	IP	H	R	ER	BB	K
Rush (L)	6	3	2	2	5	2
McMahon	2	1	2	2	2	2

New York	IP	H	R	ER	BB	K
Larsen (W)	7	6	0	0	3	8
Duren	2	0	0	0	3	1

HBP—None. WP—Duren. T—2:42. A—71,599. Umpires—Gorman, Flaherty, Barlick, Berry, Jackowski, Umont.

Game 4
Sunday, October 5, at New York

Milwaukee	AB	R	H	RBI
Schoendienst, 2b	5	1	1	0
Logan, ss	5	1	1	0
Mathews, 3b	4	0	1	1
Aaron, cf-rf	4	0	2	0
Adcock, 1b	3	0	0	0
Torre, 1b	1	0	0	0
Crandall, c	3	1	2	0
Covington, lf	3	0	0	0
Bruton, cf	0	0	0	0
Pafko, rf-lf	4	0	1	0
Spahn, p	4	0	1	1
Totals	36	3	9	2

New York	AB	R	H	RBI
Siebern, lf	3	0	0	0
McDougald, 2b	4	0	0	0
Bauer, rf	4	0	0	0
Mantle, cf	4	0	1	0
Skowron, 1b	3	0	1	0
Berra, c	3	0	0	0
Richardson, 3b	2	0	0	0
Howard, ph	1	0	0	0
Carey, 3b	0	0	0	0
Kubek, ss	2	0	0	0
Slaughter, ph	1	0	0	0
Dickson, p	0	0	0	0
Ford, p	1	0	0	0
Kucks,	0	0	0	0
Lumpe, ss	1	0	0	0
Totals	29	0	2	0

Milwaukee	0	0	0	0	0	1	1	1	0—3	9	0
New York	0	0	0	0	0	0	0	0	0—0	2	1

E—Kubek. DP—New York 1. LOB—Milwaukee 8, New York 4. 2B—Aaron, Pafko, Logan, Mathews. 3B—Mantle, Schoendienst. HR—None. SF—None. SH—None. SB—None. CS—None.

Milwaukee	IP	H	R	ER	BB	K
Spahn (W)	9	2	0	0	2	7

New York	IP	H	R	ER	BB	K
Ford (L)	7	8	3	2	1	6
Kucks	1	1	0	0	1	0
Dickson	1	0	0	0	0	0

HBP—None. WP—Ford. T—2:17. A—71,563. Umpires—Flaherty, Barlick, Berry, Gorman, Umont, Jackowski.

Game 5
Monday, October 6, at New York

Milwaukee	AB	R	H	RBI
Bruton, cf	3	0	2	0
Schoendienst, 2b	3	0	1	0
Mathews, 3b	4	0	1	0
Aaron, rf	4	0	0	0
Covington, lf	4	0	1	0
Wise, ph	0	0	0	0
Torre, 1b	3	0	0	0
Crandall, c	3	0	0	0
Logan, ss	3	0	0	0
Burdette, p	2	0	0	0
Pizarro, p	0	0	0	0
Hanebrink, ph	1	0	0	0
Willey, p	0	0	0	0
Totals	30	0	5	0

New York	AB	R	H	RBI
Bauer, rf	4	1	1	0
Lumpe, 3b	3	0	1	0
Richardson, 3b	1	0	0	0
Mantle, cf	3	1	2	0
Berra, c	4	1	1	1
Howard, lf	3	1	0	0
Skowron, 1b	4	1	1	1
McDougald, 2b	4	2	2	3
Kubek, ss	4	0	1	0
Turley, p	3	0	1	2
Totals	33	7	10	7

Milwaukee	0	0	0	0	0	0	0	0	0—0	5	0
New York	0	0	1	0	0	6	0	0	x—7	10	0

E—None. DP—Milwaukee 1, New York 1. LOB—Milwaukee 7, New York 4. 2B—Berra, McDougald. 3B—None. HR—McDougald. SF—None. SH—Schoendienst. SB—None. CS—None.

Milwaukee	IP	H	R	ER	BB	K
Burdette (L)	5⅓	8	6	6	1	4
Pizarro	1⅔	2	1	1	1	3
Willey	1	0	0	0	0	2

New York	IP	H	R	ER	BB	K
Turley (W)	9	5	0	0	3	10

HBP—None. WP—Pizarro. T—2:19. A—65,279. Umpires—Flaherty, Barlick, Berry, Jackowski, Umont, Gorman.

Game 6
Wednesday, October 8, at Milwaukee

New York	AB	R	H	RBI
Carey, 3b	5	0	0	0
McDougald, 2b	5	1	2	1
Bauer, rf	5	1	2	1
Mantle, cf	5	1	1	0
Howard, lf	5	1	2	0
Berra, c	4	0	2	1
Skowron, 1b	4	0	1	1
Kubek, ss	2	0	0	0
Slaughter, ph	1	0	0	0
Duren, p	2	0	0	0
Turley, p	0	0	0	0
Ford, p	1	0	0	0
Ditmar, p	1	0	0	0
Lumpe, ph	1	0	0	0
Totals	41	4	10	4

Milwaukee	AB	R	H	RBI
Schoendienst, 2b	4	1	2	0
Logan, ss	2	1	0	0
Mathews, 3b	5	0	0	0
Aaron, rf	5	0	3	2
Adcock, 1b	4	0	1	0
Mantilla, ph	0	0	0	0
Crandall, c	4	0	0	0
Torre, ph	1	0	0	0
Covington, lf	4	1	2	0
Pafko, cf	2	0	1	0
Bruton, cf	2	0	0	0
Spahn, p	4	0	1	1
McMahon, p	0	0	0	0
Totals	37	3	10	3

New York	1	0	0	0	0	1	0	0	2—4	10	1
Milwaukee	1	1	0	0	0	0	0	0	1—3	10	4

E—Ditmar, Schoendienst, Logan 2, Bruton. DP—New York 1, Milwaukee 1. LOB—New York 10, Milwaukee 9. 2B—Schoendienst. 3B—None. HR—Bauer, McDougald. SF—Berra. SH—Logan 2. SB—None. CS—None.

New York	IP	H	R	ER	BB	K
Ford	1⅓	5	2	2	1	2
Ditmar	3⅔	2	0	0	0	2
Duren (W)	4⅔	3	1	1	2	8
Turley	⅓	0	0	0	0	0

Milwaukee	IP	H	R	ER	BB	K
Spahn (L)	9⅔	9	4	4	2	5
McMahon	⅓	0	0	0	0	1

HBP—None. WP—None. T—3:07. A—46,367. Umpires—Barlick, Berry, Gorman, Umont, Jackowski, Flaherty.

Game 7
Thursday, October 9, at Milwaukee

New York	AB	R	H	RBI
Bauer, rf	5	0	0	0
McDougald, 2b	5	0	2	0
Mantle, cf	4	0	0	0
Berra, c	4	2	1	0
Howard, lf	3	2	2	1
Lumpe, 3b	3	0	0	0
Carey, 3b	1	1	1	0
Skowron, 1b	4	1	2	4
Kubek, ss	2	0	0	1
Larsen, p	1	0	0	0
Turley, p	2	0	0	0
Totals	34	6	8	6

Milwaukee	AB	R	H	RBI
Schoendienst, 2b	5	1	1	0
Bruton, cf	3	0	1	0
Torre, 1b	2	0	0	0
Aaron, rf	3	0	1	0
Covington, lf	4	0	0	1
Mathews, 3b	1	0	0	0
Crandall, c	4	1	1	1
Logan, ss	4	0	0	0
Burdette, p	3	0	0	0
McMahon, p	0	0	0	0
Adcock, ph	1	0	1	0
Mantilla, pr	0	0	0	0
Totals	30	2	5	2

New York	0	2	0	0	0	0	4	0—6		8	0
Milwaukee	1	0	0	0	1	0	0	0—2		5	2

E—Torre 2. DP—New York 1. LOB—New York 7, Milwaukee 8. 2B—McDougald, Berra. 3B—None. HR—Crandall, Skowron. SF—Kubek. SH—Torre, Howard, Turley. SB—Howard. CS—None.

New York	IP	H	R	ER	BB	K
Larsen	2	3	1	1	3	1
Turley (W)	7	2	1	1	3	2

Milwaukee	IP	H	R	ER	BB	K
Burdette (L)	8	7	6	4	2	3
McMahon	1	1	0	0	1	2

HBP—None. WP—None. T—2:31. A—46,367. Umpires—Gorman, Flaherty, Barlick, Berry, Jackowski, Umont.

COMPOSITE LINE SCORE

New York Yankees (A.L.)	2	2	1	2	4	7	2	4	3	2—29	
Milwaukee Braves (N.L.)	9	2	0	2	0	2	3	5	0	2—25	

COMPOSITE BATTING AND FIELDING STATISTICS

New York Yankees	G	AB	R	H	2B	3B	HR	RBI	BB	SO	SB	BA	SA	PO	A	E
Bill Skowron, 1b	7	27	3	7	0	0	2	7	1	4	0	.259	.481	55	4	0
Gil McDougald, 2b	7	28	5	9	2	0	2	4	2	4	0	.321	.607	18	23	0
Tony Kubek, ss	7	21	0	1	0	0	0	1	1	7	0	.048	.048	9	15	2
Jerry Lumpe, 3b-ss-ph	6	12	0	2	0	0	0	0	1	2	0	.167	.167	2	5	0
Hank Bauer, rf	7	31	6	10	0	0	4	8	0	5	0	.323	.710	7	0	0
Mickey Mantle, cf	7	24	4	6	0	1	2	3	7	4	0	.250	.583	16	0	0
Elston Howard, lf-ph	6	18	4	4	0	0	0	2	1	4	1	.222	.222	14	2	0
Yogi Berra, c	7	27	3	6	3	0	0	2	1	0	0	.222	.333	60	6	0
Andy Carey, 3b	5	12	1	1	0	0	0	0	0	3	0	.083	.083	2	6	0
Norm Siebern, lf	3	8	1	1	0	0	0	3	2	0	.125	.125	5	0	0
Bobby Richardson, 3b	4	5	0	0	0	0	0	0	0	0	0	.000	.000	0	1	0
Enos Slaughter, ph	4	3	1	0	0	0	0	0	1	1	0	.000	.000			
Marv Throneberry, ph	1	1	0	0	0	0	0	0	0	1	0	.000	.000			
Darrell Johnson	Did not play															
Bob Turley, p	4	5	0	1	0	0	0	2	0	1	0	.200	.200	0	1	0
Whitey Ford, p	3	4	1	0	0	0	0	0	2	2	0	.000	.000	1	1	0
Ryne Duren, p	3	3	0	0	0	0	0	0	0	2	0	.000	.000	0	1	0
Don Larsen, p	2	2	0	0	0	0	0	0	1	0	0	.000	.000	1	0	0
Johnny Kucks, p	2	1	0	1	0	0	0	0	0	0	0	1.000	1.000	0	0	0
Art Ditmar, p	1	1	0	0	0	0	0	0	0	0	0	.000	.000	1	0	1
Murry Dickson, p	2	0	0	0	0	0	0	0	0	0	0	—	—	0	0	0
Duke Maas, p	1	0	0	0	0	0	0	0	0	0	0	—	—	0	0	0
Zack Monroe, p	1	0	0	0	0	0	0	0	0	0	0	—	—	0	0	0
Bobby Shantz	Did not play															
Tom Sturdivant	Did not play—sore arm															
team total	7	233	29	49	5	1	10	29	21	42	1	.210	.369	191	65	3

Double plays—5
Left on bases—40

Milwaukee Braves	G	AB	R	H	2B	3B	HR	RBI	BB	SO	SB	BA	SA	PO	A	E
Frank Torre, 1b-ph	7	17	0	3	0	0	0	1	2	0	0	.176	.176	40	2	2
Red Schoendienst, 2b	7	30	5	9	3	1	0	0	2	1	0	.300	.467	18	19	1
Johnny Logan, ss	7	25	3	3	2	0	0	2	2	4	0	.120	.200	10	24	2
Eddie Mathews, 3b	7	25	3	4	2	0	0	3	6	11	1	.160	.240	5	13	1
Hank Aaron, rf-cf	7	27	3	9	2	0	0	2	4	6	0	.333	.407	14	0	0
Bill Bruton, ph-cf-rf	7	17	2	7	0	0	1	2	5	5	0	.412	.588	12	0	1
Wes Covington, lf	7	26	2	7	0	0	0	4	2	4	0	.269	.269	11	1	0
Del Crandall, c	7	25	4	6	0	0	1	3	3	10	0	.240	.360	43	5	0
Joe Adcock, 1b-ph	4	13	1	4	0	0	0	0	1	3	0	.308	.308	23	2	0
Andy Pafko, cf-rf-lf	4	9	0	3	1	0	0	1	0	0	0	.333	.444	8	0	0
Felix Mantilla, ss-pr	4	0	1	0	0	0	0	0	0	0	0	—	—	0	0	0
Harry Hanebrink, ph	2	2	0	0	0	0	0	0	0	0	0	.000	.000			
Casey Wise, ph-pr	2	1	0	0	0	0	0	0	0	1	0	.000	.000			
Del Rice	Did not play															
Warren Spahn, p	3	12	0	4	0	0	0	3	0	6	0	.333	.333	2	6	0
Lou Burdette, p	3	9	1	1	0	0	1	3	0	3	0	.111	.444	2	2	0
Bob Rush, p	1	2	0	0	0	0	0	0	0	2	0	.000	.000	0	3	0
Don McMahon, p	3	0	0	0	0	0	0	0	0	0	0	—	—	1	0	0
Juan Pizarro, p	1	0	0	0	0	0	0	0	0	0	0	—	—	0	1	0
Carl Willey, p	1	0	0	0	0	0	0	0	0	0	0	—	—	0	0	0
Bob Buhl	Did not play—sore arm															
Ernie Johnson	Did not play															
Humberto Robinson	Did not play															
Bob Trowbridge	Did not play															
Gene Conley	Did not play—arm injury															
team total	7	240	25	60	10	1	3	24	27	56	1	.250	.296	189	78	7

Double plays—5
Left on bases—58

COMPOSITE PITCHING STATISTICS

New York Yankees	G	GS	CG	IP	H	R	ER	BB	SO	W	L	SV	ERA
Bob Turley	4	2	1	16⅓	10	5	5	7	13	2	1	1	2.76
Whitey Ford	3	3	0	15⅓	19	8	7	5	16	0	1	0	4.11
Don Larsen	2	2	0	9⅓	9	1	1	6	9	1	0	0	0.96
Ryne Duren	3	0	0	9⅓	7	2	2	6	14	1	1	1	1.93
Johnny Kucks	2	0	0	4⅓	4	1	1	1	0	0	0	0	2.08
Murry Dickson	2	0	0	4	4	2	2	0	1	0	0	0	4.56
Art Ditmar	1	0	0	3⅔	2	0	0	0	2	0	0	0	0.00
Zack Monroe	1	0	0	1	3	3	3	1	1	0	0	0	27.00
Duke Maas	1	0	0	⅓	2	3	3	1	0	0	0	0	81.00
Bobby Shantz	Did not play												
Tom Sturdivant	Did not play												
team total	7	7	1	63⅔	60	25	24	27	56	4	3	2	3.39

Milwaukee Braves	G	GS	CG	IP	H	R	ER	BB	SO	W	L	SV	ERA
Warren Spahn	3	3	2	28⅔	19	7	7	8	18	2	1	0	2.20
Lou Burdette	3	3	1	22⅓	22	17	14	4	12	1	2	0	5.64
Bob Rush	1	1	0	6	3	2	2	5	2	0	1	0	3.00
Don McMahon	3	0	0	3⅓	3	2	2	3	5	0	0	0	5.40
Juan Pizarro	1	0	0	1⅔	2	1	1	1	3	0	0	0	5.40
Carl Willey	1	0	0	1	0	0	0	0	2	0	0	0	0.00
Bob Buhl	Did not play—sore arm												
Ernie Johnson	Did not play												
Humberto Robinson	Did not play												
Bob Trowbridge	Did not play												
Gene Conley	Did not play—arm injury												
team total	7	7	3	63	49	29	26	21	42	3	4	0	3.71

Total Attendance—393,909. Average Attendance—56,273. Winning Player's Share—$8,759. Losing Player's Share—$5,896

Braves versus New York Mets
National League Championship Series

1969

The Braves picked the wrong year to win their first National League West title. Their opponent in the first NL Championship Series ever played was the New York Mets. If ever there was a true "team of destiny," it may have been the "Miracle Mets" of 1969, who swept Atlanta in three games and went on to beat the heavily favored Baltimore Orioles in a five-game World Series.

The unquestioned strength of manager Gil Hodges' team was pitching. The Mets, who had five last-place finishes and two ninths in their previous seven seasons of existence, won the NL East behind a staff that was led by Cy Young winner

Tom Seaver and that was at or near the top of the league in all major pitching departments.

Nevertheless, the Braves, paced by a record performance from Hank Aaron, pounded the Mets for 27 hits and 15 runs in three games, only to lose all three in what was then a best-of-five format.

The 35-year-old Aaron, making his first postseason appearance since 1958, provided enough offense himself to carry most teams through a three-game series. But the Atlanta pitching and defense didn't cooperate.

Aaron homered in each of the three games, had a pair of doubles, drove in seven runs, accumulated 16 total bases and batted a robust .357. His three homers and 16 total bases are still major league records for a three-game league championship series, and his seven RBIs remain the National League record for a three-game series. (The best-of-five format was used through 1984.)

And it's not like Aaron was the only Brave hitting. Five of Atlanta's eight regulars batted .300 or better in the series. First baseman Orlando Cepeda, the inspirational spark of the club, hit .455 with one homer and three RBIs. Center fielder Tony Gonzalez batted .357 with a home run. Second baseman Felix Millan checked in at .333, and left fielder Rico Carty batted .300. Yet the Braves couldn't win a single game, the first two of which were played in Atlanta.

A crowd of 50,122 turned out at Atlanta Stadium for the first postseason game ever played in the South. They were treated to a classic pitching matchup between the two biggest winners in the league. Seaver, 24, was 25–7, and Phil Niekro, the 30-year-old knuckleball specialist, was 23–13. By the end of the day, though, both pitchers were long gone in the face of the two teams combining for 14 runs and 20 hits.

The Braves held leads of 3–2 after three innings and 5–4 after seven, but the Mets struck for five off Niekro in the eighth to win, 9–5. But Niekro wasn't entirely at fault. His defense was charged with two errors and made a couple of other questionable plays. Five of the runs off Niekro were unearned.

Though Seaver gave up eight hits and five runs, he got the win, and Ron Taylor, who shut out the Braves in the final two innings, picked up the save.

Game 2 at Atlanta was another slugfest, featuring 17 runs and 22 hits from the two teams. Ron Reed started for Atlanta and Jerry Koosman for New York. Neither was around long in a game the Braves never led and lost, 11–6.

Reed didn't make it out of the second when the Mets scored three to lead 4–0. New York led 8–0 through 4½ innings and 9–1 through 5½, yet the Braves still managed to make the game interesting with a five-run fifth.

Nolan Ryan, a little-used but hard-throwing 22-year-old reliever, wound up as the star of the final game, a 7–4 Mets win before 53,195 frenzied fans at Shea Stadium.

Right-hander Pat Jarvis started for the Braves against New York's Gary Gentry, but in following the pattern of the series, neither was very effective. Two-run homers by Aaron and Cepeda gave the Braves a 4–3 lead through 4½ innings, but the Mets struck back with three runs in the bottom of the fifth, chasing Jarvis.

Ryan limited the Braves to three hits in seven innings, during which he struck out seven.

As well as the Braves hit in the three games, the Mets did much better, compiling a team batting average of .327 and outscoring Atlanta, 27–15. The ERAs of the Braves' starting pitchers told the story: Niekro, 4.50; Reed, 21.60; and Jarvis, 12.46.

Phil Niekro was roughed up by the Mets in Game 1 and the Braves never recovered.

Game 1
Saturday, October 4, at Atlanta

New York	AB	R	H	RBI
Agee, cf	5	0	0	0
Garrett, 3b	4	2	2	0
Jones, lf	5	1	1	1
Shamsky, rf	4	1	3	0
Weis, pr, 2b	0	0	0	0
Boswell, 2b	3	2	0	0
Gaspar, rf	0	0	0	0
Kranepool, 1b	4	2	1	0
Grote, c	3	1	1	1
Harrelson, ss	3	1	1	2
Seaver, p	3	0	0	0
Martin, ph	1	0	1	2
Taylor, p	0	0	0	0
Totals	35	9	10	6

Atlanta	AB	R	H	RBI
Millan, 2b	5	1	2	0
Gonzalez, cf	5	2	2	2
H. Aaron, rf	5	1	2	2
Carty, lf	3	1	1	0
Lum, lf	1	0	1	0
Cepeda, 1b	4	0	1	0
Boyer, 3b	1	0	0	1
Didier, c	4	0	0	0
Garrido, ss	4	0	1	0
Niekro, p	3	0	0	0
Aspromonte, ph	1	0	0	0
Upshaw, p	0	0	0	0
Totals	36	5	10	5

```
New York   0 2 0 2 0 0 0 5 0—9  10 1
Atlanta    0 1 2 0 1 0 1 0 0—5  10 2
```

E—Boswell, Cepeda, Gonzalez. DP—Atlanta (2). LOB—New York 3, Atlanta 9. 2B—Carty, Millan, Gonzalez, H. Aaron, Garrett, Lum. 3B—Harrelson. HR—Gonzalez, H. Aaron. SF—Boyer. SB—Cepeda, Jones. CS—None.

New York	IP	H	R	ER	BB	K
Seaver (W)	7	8	5	5	3	2
Taylor (S)	2	2	0	0	0	2

Atlanta	IP	H	R	ER	BB	K
Niekro (L)	8	9	9	4	4	4
Upshaw	1	1	0	0	0	1

HBP—Cepeda by Seaver. PB—Didier, Grote. T—2:37. A—50,122. Umpires—Barlick, Donatelli, Sudol, Vargo, Palekoudas, Steiner.

Game 2
Sunday, October 5, at Atlanta

New York	AB	R	H	RBI
Agee, cf	4	3	2	2
Garrett, 3b	5	1	2	1
Jones, lf	5	2	3	3
Shamsky, rf	5	1	3	1
Gaspar, pr, rf	0	0	0	0
Boswell, 2b	5	1	1	2
McGraw, p	0	0	0	0
Kranepool, 1b	4	0	1	1
Grote, c	5	1	0	0
Harrelson, ss	5	1	1	1
Koosman, p	2	1	0	0
Taylor, p	0	0	0	0
Martin, ph	1	0	0	0
Weis, 2b	1	0	0	0
Totals	42	11	13	11

Atlanta	AB	R	H	RBI
Millan, 2b	2	1	2	0
Gonzalez, cf	4	1	1	0
H. Aaron, rf	5	1	1	3
Carty, lf	4	2	1	0
Cepeda, 1b	4	1	2	1
Boyer, 3b	4	0	1	2
Didier, c	4	0	0	0
Garrido, ss	4	0	1	0
Reed, p	0	0	0	0
Doyle, p	0	0	0	0
Pappas, p	1	0	0	0
T. Aaron, ph	1	0	0	0
Britton, p	0	0	0	0
Upshaw, p	1	0	0	0
Aspromonte, ph	1	0	0	0
Neibauer, p	0	0	0	0
Totals	35	6	9	6

```
New York   1 3 2 2 1 0 2 0 0—11  13 1
Atlanta    0 0 0 1 5 0 0 0 0—6   9 3
```

E—H. Aaron, Cepeda, Harrelson, Boyer. DP—New York (2), Atlanta (1). LOB—New York 10, Atlanta 7. 2B—Jones, Harrelson, Carty, Garrett, Cepeda. 3B—None. HR—Agee, Boswell, H. Aaron, Jones. SB—Agee (2), Garrett, Jones. CS—None.

New York	IP	H	R	ER	BB	K
Koosman	4⅔	7	6	6	4	5
Taylor (W)	1⅓	1	0	0	0	2
McGraw (S)	3	1	0	0	1	1

Atlanta	IP	H	R	ER	BB	K
Reed (L)	1⅔	5	4	4	3	3
Doyle	1	2	2	0	1	3
Pappas	2⅓	4	3	3	0	4
Britton	⅓	0	0	0	1	0
Upshaw	2⅔	2	2	2	1	1
Neibauer	1	0	0	0	0	1

T—3:10. A—50,170. Umpires—Donatelli, Sudol, Vargo, Peiekoudas, Steiner, Barlick.

Game 3
Monday, October 6, at New York

Atlanta	AB	R	H	RBI
Millan, 2b	5	0	0	0
Gonzalez, cf	5	1	2	0
H. Aaron, rf	4	1	2	2
Carty, lf	3	1	1	0
Cepeda, 1b	3	1	2	2
Boyer, 3b	4	0	0	0
Didier, c	3	0	0	0
Lum, ph	1	0	1	0
Jackson, ss	0	0	0	0
Garrido, ss	2	0	0	0
Alou, ph	1	0	0	0
Tillman, c	0	0	0	0
Jarvis, p	2	0	0	0
Stone, p	1	0	0	0
Upshaw, p	0	0	0	0
Aspromonte, ph	1	0	0	0
Totals	35	4	8	4

New York	AB	R	H	RBI
Agee, cf	5	1	3	2
Garrett, 3b	4	1	1	2
Jones, lf	4	1	2	0
Shamsky, rf	4	1	1	0
Gaspar, pr, rf	0	0	0	0
Boswell, 2b	4	1	3	3
Weis, 2b	0	0	0	0
Kranepool, 1b	4	0	1	0
Grote, c	4	1	1	0
Harrelson, ss	3	0	0	0
Gentry, p	0	0	0	0
Ryan, p	4	1	2	0

```
Atlanta    2 0 0 0 2 0 0 0—4  8 1
New York   0 0 1 2 3 1 0 0 x—7  14 0
```

E—Millan. DP—Atlanta (1). LOB—Atlanta (7), New York (6). 2B—Cepeda, Agee, H. Aaron, Kranepool, Jones, Grote. 3B—None. HR—H. Aaron, Agee, Boswell, Cepeda, Garrett. SH—Harrelson. SB—None. CS—None.

Atlanta	IP	H	R	ER	BB	K
Jarvis (L)	4⅓	10	6	6	0	6
Stone	1	2	1	1	0	0
Upshaw	2⅔	2	0	0	0	2

New York	IP	H	R	ER	BB	K
Gentry	2	5	2	2	1	1
Ryan (W)	7	3	2	2	2	7

T—2:24. A—53,195. Umpires—Sudol, Vargo, Pelekoudas, Steiner, Barlick, Donatelli.

COMPOSITE LINE SCORE

```
New York   1  5  3  6  41  2  5  0—27
Atlanta    2  1  2  1   8  0 10  0—15
```

COMPOSITE BATTING AND FIELDING STATISTICS

New York Mets	G	AB	R	H	TB	2B	3B	HR	RBI	BA	PO	A	E	FA
Shamsky, rf	3	13	3	7	7	0	0	0	1	.538	3	0	0	1.000
Ryan, p	1	4	1	2	2	0	0	0	0	.500	1	0	0	1.000
Martin, ph	2	2	0	1	1	0	0	0	2	.500	0	0	0	.000
Jones, lf	3	14	4	6	11	2	0	1	4	.429	11	0	0	1.000
Garrett, 3b	3	13	3	5	10	2	0	1	3	.385	1	6	0	1.000
Agee, cf	3	14	4	5	12	1	0	2	4	.357	9	0	0	1.000
Boswell, 2b	3	12	4	4	10	0	0	2	5	.333	3	2	1	.833
Kranepool, 1b	3	12	2	3	4	1	0	0	1	.250	20	3	0	1.000
Harrelson, ss	3	11	2	2	5	1	1	0	3	.182	6	6	1	.923
Grote, c	3	12	3	2	3	1	0	0	1	.167	22	1	0	1.000
Gaspar, rf-pr	3	0	0	0	0	0	0	0	0	.000	0	0	0	.000
McGraw, p	1	0	0	0	0	0	0	0	0	.000	0	0	0	.000
Gentry, p	1	0	0	0	0	0	0	0	0	.000	0	0	0	.000
Taylor, p	2	0	0	0	0	0	0	0	0	.000	1	0	0	1.000
Weis, pr-2b	3	1	0	0	0	0	0	0	0	.000	1	3	0	1.000
Koosman, p	1	2	1	0	0	0	0	0	0	.000	0	0	0	.000
Seaver, p	1	3	0	0	0	0	0	0	0	.000	1	1	0	1.000
Totals	3	113	27	37	65	8	1	6	24	.327	81	23	2	.981

Atlanta Braves	G	AB	R	H	TB	2B	3B	HR	RBI	BA	PO	A	E	FA
Lum, lf-ph	2	2	0	2	3	1	0	0	0	1.000	0	0	0	.000
Cepeda, 1b	3	11	2	5	10	2	0	1	3	.455	29	1	2	.938
H. Aaron, rf	3	14	3	5	16	2	0	3	7	.357	4	1	1	.833
Gonzalez, cf	3	14	4	5	9	1	0	1	2	.357	3	1	1	.800
Millan, 2b	3	12	2	4	5	1	0	0	0	.333	3	9	1	.923
Carty, lf	3	10	4	3	5	2	0	0	0	.300	3	0	0	1.000
Garrido, ss	3	10	0	2	2	0	0	0	0	.200	4	8	0	1.000
Boyer, 3b	3	9	0	1	1	0	0	0	3	.111	4	8	1	.923
Tillman, c	1	0	0	0	0	0	0	0	0	.000	2	0	0	1.000
Reed, p	1	0	0	0	0	0	0	0	0	.000	0	1	0	1.000
Jackson, ss	1	0	0	0	0	0	0	0	0	.000	0	0	0	.000
Doyle, p	1	0	0	0	0	0	0	0	0	.000	0	0	0	.000
Britton, p	1	0	0	0	0	0	0	0	0	.000	0	0	0	.000
Neibauer, p	1	0	0	0	0	0	0	0	0	.000	0	0	0	.000
Stone, p	1	1	0	0	0	0	0	0	0	.000	1	1	0	1.000
Upshaw, p	3	1	0	0	0	0	0	0	0	.000	0	1	0	1.000
T. Aaron, ph	1	1	0	0	0	0	0	0	0	.000	0	0	0	.000
Alou, ph	1	1	0	0	0	0	0	0	0	.000	0	0	0	.000
Pappas, p	1	1	0	0	0	0	0	0	0	.000	0	0	0	.000
Jarvis, p	1	2	0	0	0	0	0	0	0	.000	1	2	0	1.000
Aspromonte, ph	3	3	0	0	0	0	0	0	0	.000	0	0	0	.000
Niekro, p	1	3	0	0	0	0	0	0	0	.000	0	3	0	1.000
Didier, c	3	11	0	0	0	0	0	0	0	.000	24	1	0	1.000
Totals	3	106	15	27	51	9	0	5	15	.255	78	37	6	.950

COMPOSITE PITCHING STATISTICS

New York Mets	G	GS	CG	IP	H	R	ER	SO	BB	HB	WP	W	L	PCT	ERA
Taylor	2	0	0	3⅓	3	0	0	4	0	0	0	1	0	1.000	0.00
McGraw	1	0	0	3	1	0	0	1	1	0	0	0	0	.000	0.00
Ryan	1	0	0	7	3	2	2	7	2	0	0	1	0	1.000	2.57
Seaver	1	1	0	7	8	5	5	2	3	1	0	1	0	1.000	6.43
Gentry	1	1	0	2	5	2	2	1	1	0	0	0	0	.000	9.00
Koosman	1	1	0	4⅔	7	6	6	5	4	0	0	0	0	.000	11.57
Totals	**3**	**3**	**0**	**27**	**27**	**15**	**15**	**20**	**11**	**1**	**0**	**3**	**0**	**1.000**	**5.00**

Saves—Taylor, McGraw.

Atlanta Braves	G	GS	CG	IP	H	R	ER	SO	BB	HB	WP	W	L	PCT	ERA
Neibauer	1	0	0	1	0	0	0	1	0	0	0	0	0	.000	0.00
Doyle	1	0	0	1	2	2	0	3	1	0	0	0	0	.000	0.00
Britton	1	0	0	⅓	0	0	0	0	1	0	0	0	0	.000	0.00
Upshaw	3	0	0	6⅓	5	2	2	4	1	0	0	0	0	.000	2.84
Niekro	1	1	0	8	9	9	4	4	4	0	0	0	1	.000	4.50
Stone	1	0	0	1	2	1	1	0	0	0	0	0	0	.000	9.00
Pappas	1	0	0	2⅓	4	3	3	4	0	0	0	0	0	.000	11.57
Jarvis	1	1	0	4⅓	10	6	6	6	0	0	0	0	1	.000	12.46
Reed	1	1	0	1⅔	5	4	4	3	3	0	0	0	1	.000	21.60
Totals	**3**	**3**	**0**	**26**	**37**	**27**	**20**	**25**	**10**	**0**	**0**	**0**	**3**	**.000**	**6.92**

Braves versus St. Louis Cardinals
National League Championship Series

1982

The 1982 Braves, behind the slugging of MVP Dale Murphy and Bob Horner, led the National League in home runs (146) and runs (739). But when manager Joe Torre's team made its first postseason appearance since 1969, that potent offense was nowhere to be found.

Atlanta used a major league record 13-game winning streak to open the season and coasted the rest of the way, losing 19 of 21 at one point before winning the division by a game, only when the Dodgers lost on the final day of the season. Then the Braves couldn't restart in time to avoid their second three-game sweep in two trips to the National League Championship Series.

The St. Louis Cardinals won the NL East with a team built around pitching, defense and speed. Whitey Herzog's club led the league in fielding percentage (.981) and steals (200) and finished third in ERA (3.37).

The opening of the playoffs in St. Louis gave Braves fans reason for hope but, in the end, only left them wondering how things might have been different if rain had stayed away from Busch Memorial Stadium. The Braves led, 1–0, behind Phil Niekro through 4½ innings when a storm wiped out the rest of the game just three outs short of being official. It was the first rainout at Busch since August 1976.

When the official first game was played the following evening, the Braves forgot to bring their bats. Right-hander Bob Forsch, opposed by Pascual Perez, humbled Atlanta, 7–0, with a three-hit shutout before 53,008 fans at St. Louis.

Forsch retired the last 11 Braves in order. Atlanta managed only singles by Claudell Washington in the third, Bruce Benedict in the fifth, and Washington in the sixth. On top of that, Forsch contributed two singles and a sacrifice fly to St. Louis's 13-hit attack.

Niekro, who was 17–4 at age 43, came back to start Game 2, which was delayed a day by more rain. His opponent was John Stuper, a 25-year-old rookie right-hander who was 9–7.

St. Louis scored a run in the first, but the Braves took a 3–1 lead with two in the third and one in the fifth, which proved to be the Braves' last run of the game.

The Cardinals scored in the sixth on an RBI double by Darrell Porter, on his way to being named MVP of the playoffs, to close within 3–2. And they tied it with a single run in the eighth.

The game was decided in the ninth. David Green got a leadoff single and advanced to second on a sacrifice bunt by Tom Herr. Ken Oberkfell, who was 6-for-10 lifetime against Garber, came to the plate with Bruce Sutter on deck. But Torre elected to let Gene Garber pitch to Oberkfell, who singled to center, ending the game.

The Braves had their tickets printed for the 1982 World Series, but the Cardinals had plans of their own.

Braves third baseman Bob Horner tagged out Darrell Porter trying to stretch a double into a triple, but the St. Louis catcher still batted .556 and was named MVP of the playoffs.

The series moved to Atlanta–Fulton County Stadium with the Braves on the verge of being swept for the second time in two playoff appearances. Though Atlanta's chances of winning the pennant were extremely slim, a crowd of 52,173 showed up at Atlanta–Fulton County Stadium, only to be quickly disappointed.

The Cardinals, behind Joaquin Andujar, scored four in the second inning off Rick Camp for all the runs they needed to reach the World Series.

Down 5–0 entering the bottom of the seventh, the Braves tried to rally, scoring twice on four singles. However, Sutter bailed out Andujar, retiring the final seven Braves in St. Louis's 6–2 victory.

The Braves scored just five runs in the three games and had only one extra-base hit, Benedict's double in the second game. Murphy, Horner, and Chris Chambliss, the heart of the Atlanta batting order, contributed a total of four singles and no RBIs in 32 at bats.

Bob Walk (left) and Tommy Boggs reflect the somber mood after the Braves were swept by St. Louis.

Game 1
Thursday, October 7, at St. Louis

Atlanta	AB	R	H	RBI
Washington, rf	4	0	2	0
Ramirez, ss	4	0	0	0
Murphy, cf	4	0	0	0
Chambliss, 1b	3	0	0	0
Horner, 3b	3	0	0	0
Royster, lf	3	0	0	0
Hubbard, 2b	3	0	0	0
Benedict, c	3	0	1	0
Perez, p	2	0	0	0
Bedrosian, p	0	0	0	0
Moore, p	0	0	0	0
Whisenton, ph	1	0	0	0
Walk, p	0	0	0	0
Totals	30	0	3	0

St. Louis	AB	R	H	RBI
Herr, 2b	5	0	2	0
Oberkfell, 3b	5	0	1	1
L. Smith, lf	3	1	1	1
Green, lf	0	0	0	0
Hernandez, 1b	4	1	1	0
Hendrick, rf	4	1	1	1
Porter, c	4	1	2	0
McGee, cf	4	2	2	1
O. Smith, ss	3	0	1	2
Forsch, p	3	1	2	1
Totals	35	7	13	7

Atlanta	0	0	0	0	0	0	0	0	0—0	3	0
St. Louis	0	0	1	0	0	5	0	1	x—7	13	1

E—Oberkfell. DP—None. LOB—Atlanta 3, St. Louis 11. 2B—Porter. 3B—McGee. HR—None. SF—O. Smith, Forsch, L. Smith. SH—None. SB—None. CS—Washington.

Atlanta	IP	H	R	ER	BB	K
Perez (L)	5	7	4	4	1	2
Bedrosian	⅔	3	2	2	1	1
Moore	1⅓	1	0	0	0	1
Walk	1	2	1	1	1	1

St. Louis	IP	H	R	ER	BB	K
Forsch (W)	9	3	0	0	0	6

HBP—Smith by Moore. WP—Bedrosian. T—2:25. A—53,008. Umpires—Williams, Engel, Wendelstedt, Froemming, Rennert, Runge.

Game 2
Saturday, October 9, at St. Louis

Atlanta	AB	R	H	RBI
Washington, rf	3	0	0	0
Ramirez, ss	4	1	1	1
Murphy, cf, lf	4	0	1	0
Chambliss, 1b	3	0	0	0
Horner, 3b	4	0	0	0
Butler, cf	0	0	0	0
Royster, lf, 3b	4	0	2	0
Hubbard, 2b	3	1	1	0
Benedict, c	2	1	1	0
Niekro, p	0	0	0	1
Pocoroba, ph	1	0	0	0
Garber, p	1	0	0	0
Totals	29	3	6	2

St. Louis	AB	R	H	RBI
Herr, 2b	3	0	0	0
Oberkfell, 3b	5	1	1	1
L. Smith, lf	4	0	1	0
Sutter, p	0	0	0	0
Hernandez, 1b	4	1	1	0
Porter, c	2	1	2	1
Hendrick, rf	4	0	2	0
McGee, cf	4	0	0	1
O. Smith, ss	2	0	1	0
Stuper, p	1	0	0	0
Braun, ph	1	0	0	0
Bair, p	0	0	0	0
Green, lf	1	1	1	0
Totals	31	4	9	3

Atlanta	0	0	2	0	1	0	0	0	0—3	6	0
St. Louis	1	0	0	0	0	1	0	1	1—4	9	1

E—McGee. DP—None. LOB—Atlanta 6, St. Louis 9. 2B—Porter (2), Benedict. 3B—None. HR—None. SF—Niekro. SH—Stuper, Niekro, Hubbard, Herr. SB—O. Smith, Murphy. CS—Murphy.

Atlanta	IP	H	R	ER	BB	K
Niekro	6	6	2	2	4	5
Garber (L)	2⅓	3	2	2	1	2

St. Louis	IP	H	R	ER	BB	K
Stuper	6	4	3	2	1	4
Bair	1	2	0	0	3	0
Sutter (W)	2	0	0	0	0	1

WP—Niekro. PB—Benedict. T—2:46. A—53,408. Umpires—Engel, Wendelstedt, Froemming, Rennert, Runge, Williams

Game 3
Sunday, October 10, at Atlanta

St. Louis	AB	R	H	RBI
Herr, 2b	5	1	1	0
Oberkfell, 3b	5	0	1	0
L. Smith, lf	4	0	1	0
Hernandez, 1b	4	1	2	1
Porter, c	3	1	1	0
Hendrick, rf	5	1	1	1
McGee, cf	5	2	2	3
O. Smith, ss	4	0	3	1
Andujar, p	1	0	0	0
Sutter, p	1	0	0	0
Totals	37	6	12	6

Atlanta	AB	R	H	RBI
Ramirez, ss	3	0	1	0
Royster, lf	4	0	0	0
Washington, rf	2	0	1	0
Harper, pr, rf	1	1	0	0
Horner, 3b	4	0	1	0
Chambliss, 1b	4	0	0	0
Murphy, cf	3	1	2	0
Hubbard, 2b	3	0	1	1
Benedict, c	3	0	0	0
Camp, p	0	0	0	0
Perez, p	1	0	0	0
Moore, p	0	0	0	0
Whisenton, ph	1	0	0	0
Mahler, p	0	0	0	0
Bedrosian, p	0	0	0	0
Butler, ph	1	0	0	0
Garber, p	0	0	0	0
Totals	30	2	6	1

St. Louis	0	4	0	0	1	0	0	0	1—6	12	0
Atlanta	0	0	0	0	0	0	2	0	0—2	6	1

E—Ramirez. DP—St. Louis (3). LOB—St. Louis 11, Atlanta 3. 2B—Herr. 3B—McGee. HR—McGee. SH—Andujar 2, L. Smith. SB—None. CS—None.

St. Louis	IP	H	R	ER	BB	K
Andujar (W)	6⅔	6	2	2	2	4
Sutter (S)	2⅓	0	0	0	0	0

Atlanta	IP	H	R	ER	BB	K
Camp (L)	1	4	4	4	1	0
Perez	3⅓	3	1	1	1	2
Moore	1⅓	1	0	0	0	0
Mahler	1⅓	3	0	0	2	0
Bedrosian	⅓	0	0	0	0	1
Garber	1	1	1	1	0	1

Balk—Andujar. WP—Andujar 2. T—2:51. A—52,173. Umpires—Wendelstedt, Froemming, Rennert, Runge, Williams, Engel.

COMPOSITE BATTING STATISTICS

St. Louis Cardinals	AVG	G	AB	R	H	2B	3B	HR	RBI	BB	SO	SB
Joaquin Andujar, p	.000	1	1	0	0	0	0	0	0	0	1	0
Doug Bair, p	.000	1	0	0	0	0	0	0	0	0	0	0
Steve Braun, ph	.000	1	1	0	0	0	0	0	0	0	0	0
Bob Forsch, p	.667	1	3	1	2	0	0	0	1	0	0	0
David Green, of	1.000	2	1	1	1	0	0	0	0	0	0	0
George Hendrick, of	.308	3	13	2	4	0	0	0	2	1	2	0
Keith Hernandez, 1b	.333	3	12	3	4	0	0	0	1	2	3	0
Tommy Herr, 2b	.231	3	13	1	3	1	0	0	0	1	2	0
Willie McGee, of	.308	3	13	4	4	0	2	1	5	0	5	0
Ken Oberkfell, 3b	.200	3	15	1	3	0	0	0	2	0	0	0
Darrell Porter, c	.556	3	9	3	5	3	0	0	1	5	2	0
Lonnie Smith, of	.273	3	11	1	3	0	0	0	1	0	1	0
Ozzie Smith, ss	.556	3	9	0	5	0	0	0	3	3	0	1
John Stuper, p	.000	1	1	0	0	0	0	0	0	0	0	0
Bruce Sutter, p	.000	2	1	0	0	0	0	0	0	0	0	0
Totals	**.330**		**103**	**17**	**34**	**4**	**2**	**1**	**16**	**12**	**16**	**1**

Atlanta Braves	AVG	G	AB	R	H	2B	3B	HR	RBI	BB	SO	SB
Steve Bedrosian, p	.000	2	0	0	0	0	0	0	0	0	0	0
Bruce Benedict, c	.250	3	8	1	2	1	0	0	0	2	1	0
Brett Butler, of	.000	2	1	0	0	0	0	0	0	0	0	0
Rick Camp, p	.000	1	0	0	0	0	0	0	0	0	0	0
Chris Chambliss, 1b	.000	3	10	0	0	0	0	0	0	1	0	0
Gene Garber, p	.000	2	1	0	0	0	0	0	0	0	0	0
Terry Harper, of	.000	1	1	0	0	0	0	0	0	0	0	0
Bob Horner, 3b	.091	3	11	0	1	0	0	0	0	0	2	0
Glenn Hubbard, 2b	.222	3	9	1	2	0	0	0	1	0	3	0
Rick Mahler, p	.000	1	0	0	0	0	0	0	0	0	0	0
Donnie Moore, p	.000	2	0	0	0	0	0	0	0	0	0	0
Dale Murphy, of	.273	3	11	1	3	0	0	0	0	0	2	1
Phil Niekro, p	.000	1	0	0	0	0	0	0	1	0	0	0
Pascual Perez, p	.000	2	3	0	0	0	0	0	0	0	1	0
Biff Pocoroba, ph	.000	1	1	0	0	0	0	0	0	0	0	0
Rafael Ramirez, ss	.182	3	11	1	2	0	0	0	1	1	1	0
Jerry Royster, of, 3b-1	.182	3	11	0	2	0	0	0	0	0	2	0
Bob Walk, p	.000	1	0	0	0	0	0	0	0	0	0	0
Claudell Washington, of	.333	3	9	0	3	0	0	0	0	2	2	0
Larry Whisenton, ph	.000	2	2	0	0	0	0	0	0	0	1	0
Totals	**.169**		**89**	**5**	**15**	**1**	**0**	**0**	**3**	**6**	**15**	**1**

COMPOSITE PITCHING STATISTICS

St. Louis Cardinals	W	L	ERA	G	GS	CG	SV	SHO	IP	H	ER	BB	SO
Joaquin Andujar	1	0	2.70	1	1	0	0	0	6⅔	6	2	2	4
Doug Bair	0	0	0.00	1	0	0	0	0	1.0	2	0	3	0
Bob Forsch	1	0	0.00	1	1	1	0	1	9.0	3	0	0	6
John Stuper	0	0	3.00	1	1	0	0	0	6.0	4	2	1	4
Bruce Sutter	1	0	0.00	2	0	0	1	0	4⅓	0	0	0	1
Totals	**3**	**0**	**1.33**	**6**	**3**	**1**	**1**	**1**	**27.0**	**15**	**4**	**6**	**15**

Atlanta Braves	W	L	ERA	G	GS	CG	SV	SHO	IP	H	ER	BB	SO
Steve Bedrosian	0	0	18.00	2	0	0	0	0	1.0	3	2	1	2
Rick Camp	0	1	36.00	1	1	0	0	0	1.0	4	4	1	0
Gene Garber	0	1	8.10	2	0	0	0	0	3⅓	4	3	1	3
Rick Mahler	0	0	0.00	1	0	0	0	0	1⅔	3	0	2	0
Donnie Moore	0	0	0.00	2	0	0	0	0	2⅔	2	0	0	1
Phil Niekro	0	0	3.00	1	1	0	0	0	6.0	6	2	4	5
Pascual Perez	0	1	5.19	2	1	0	0	0	8⅔	10	5	2	4
Bob Walk	0	0	9.00	1	0	0	0	0	1.0	2	1	1	1
Totals	**0**	**3**	**6.04**	**12**	**3**	**0**	**0**	**0**	**25⅓**	**34**	**17**	**12**	**16**

Braves versus Pittsburgh Pirates National League Championship Series

1991

After the Braves' totally unexpected and completely exhilarating charge to the National League West division title in the second half of 1991, it wouldn't have been surprising if Bobby Cox's team had been emotionally drained. Fortunately, that was not the case. The fun had just begun.

The script for the National League Championship Series was supposed to have Pittsburgh, who'd won its second straight East division title, primed and poised for a trip to the World Series. The Braves, the first team in modern history to go from having baseball's worst record one season to first place the next, were just supposed to be happy to be playing.

But Atlanta had already shown it wasn't too keen on following form. These Braves broke the mold that had cast the franchise in mediocrity, disappointment, and much worse since the late 1950s.

Paced by a talented young starting rotation that included Tom Glavine, who was headed for the Cy Young Award, John Smoltz, and Steve Avery, as well as veteran Charlie Leibrandt, Cox's team was no fluke but rather an emerging power. The offense was led by third baseman Terry Pendleton, who'd won the batting title (.319) and would later be named the league's MVP. Outfielders Ron Gant (32 homers, 34 steals) and David Justice (21 homers, 87 RBIs) were two of the most exciting young hitters in the league. But the Braves were forced to play the postseason without speedy center fielder Otis Nixon, who was suspended for substance abuse.

Pittsburgh's lineup included Barry Bonds, one of the game's premier players, Bobby Bonilla, the league leader in doubles, and multitalented center fielder Andy Van Slyke. Right-hander Doug Drabek (15–14) and left-hander John Smiley (20–8) were regarded as two of the league's best pitchers. And one of the Pirates' biggest assets was manager Jim Leyland, a master at platooning and getting the maximum out of his entire roster.

Both teams were talented, but the Pirates had the home-field advantage, as well as postseason experience. Nevertheless, it was the Braves who prevailed, on the strength of a pitching staff that posted a 1.57 ERA in the seven games, limiting Pittsburgh to 12 runs—none in the last two games—and a .224 batting average.

By winning the last two games of the best-of-seven series at Pittsburgh, the Braves returned to the World Series for the first time since 1958 and brought the event to the South for the first time ever. Avery, who won Games 2 and 6 by 1–0 scores and worked 16⅓ scoreless innings, was named MVP of the NLCS.

In Game 1 at Three Rivers Stadium, Pittsburgh extended the Braves' playoff losing streak to seven straight games and postseason losing streak to 10, dating back to Game 4 of the 1958 World Series.

Drabek and Bob Walk combined to pitch a five-hitter, beating Glavine, 5–1, before a crowd of 57,347. The Braves didn't manage an extra-base hit or a run until the ninth inning when Justice led off with a home run.

Avery, with ninth-inning help from Alejandro Pena,

Lonnie Smith, who filled in for the suspended Otis Nixon, slides safely into third.

evened the playoffs at one game apiece and ended the franchise's long stretch of postseason futility with a six-hitter in a 1–0 victory in Game 2.

Former Braves left-hander Zane Smith was nearly as stingy for Pittsburgh. He allowed the game's lone run in the sixth. Justice led off with a single, advanced to second on an infield out, and scored on a two-out double by Mark Lemke.

With 50,905 fans chopping and chanting for Game 3 at Atlanta–Fulton County Stadium, Cox's team erupted for four runs in the first inning en route to a 10–3 victory behind Smoltz and three relievers.

Pittsburgh actually opened the scoring when Orlando Merced led off the game with a home run. But the Braves erased that in a hurry against Smiley. With two outs and none on, Gant, Justice, and Brian Hunter strung together three successive doubles to give the Braves a 2–1 lead they never relinquished. Greg Olson followed with a home run to make it 4–1 heading to the second inning.

Gant added a solo home run in the seventh, and Sid Bream hit a three-run homer in the eighth, en route to the 10–3 final. The five home runs in the game tied the major league record for a playoff, but the statistic that was most important was the Braves' 2–1 lead in games.

Left-handers Dave Tomlin and Leibrandt faced each other in Game 4, but neither was around for the decision, a 3–2, 10-inning Pittsburgh victory that evened the NLCS at two games for each team.

The Braves' offense started quickly and died just as suddenly. Lonnie Smith opened the first inning with a double, advanced to third when Pendleton lined to right, and scored

on Gant's grounder to short. Justice, Hunter, and Olson then strung together singles for a 2–0 lead.

Pittsburgh nicked Leibrandt for a run in the second and another in the fifth to tie the game. The game remained 2–2 until the top of the 10th when Kent Mercker entered the game for the Braves. He immediately walked Van Slyke but retired Bonilla and Bonds. But Van Slyke stole second, then Steve Buechele walked. Cox pulled Mercker for rookie right-hander Mark Wohlers, and Leyland sent in left-handed batter Mike LaValliere to pinch-hit for Don Slaught. LaValliere singled on an 0–2 pitch, and Pittsburgh had a 3–2 lead.

From the second inning through the 10th, Atlanta managed but three singles. The result was a tie in the series.

Once again, the Braves' offense failed to materialize for Game 5, putting Atlanta in the precarious position of having to win two straight at Pittsburgh in order to go to the World Series.

Smith, who'd pitched well in Game 2 but lost to Avery, outdueled Glavine, 1–0, in Game 5, giving the Pirates a 3–2 lead in games. The only run was scored in the fifth when Buechele drew a one-out walk that was followed by singles from Slaught and Jose Lind.

Atlanta outhit Pittsburgh, 9–6, but blew a couple of excellent scoring opportunities with some very unusual methods.

In the second inning, the Braves loaded the bases with no outs but then couldn't even make contact. Rafael Belliard struck out, then Glavine did the same. On strike three, Glavine missed the squeeze-bunt sign, leaving Hunter trapped off third, where he was tagged to end the inning.

The fourth inning was even wackier. Justice reached on a two-base throwing error by Gary Redus to start the inning. With two outs, Lemke delivered a single to left that appeared to score Justice. However, Justice was ruled out for missing third base, ending the inning.

On the verge of elimination and returning to Pittsburgh, the Braves turned their hopes over to the baby-faced Avery, who had shut out the Pirates in Game 2. By the time Game 6 was over, the 21-year-old left-hander had earned his second 1–0 victory of the series, as well as the nickname "Poison Avery."

Drabek, who pitched six shutout innings in Game 1, matched Avery pitch for pitch through eight innings, only to lose in the ninth. With one out, Gant walked, and with two outs, he stole second. Olson followed with a double for the only run of the game.

Ron Gant's home run in Game 3 helped the Braves take a 2–1 lead in games.

Steve Avery (L) was named MVP of the 1991 National League Championship Series for beating Pittsburgh twice by 1–0 scores, but it was his buddy Deion Sanders who did the talking.

The National League pennant and a trip to the World Series came down to Game 7. The pitching matchup was Smoltz, the winner of Game 3 as well as Atlanta's division clincher, against Smiley, who was pounded in Game 3—and did even worse this time.

The erratic Atlanta offense jumped on Smiley for three runs in the first inning, driving him from the game and giving Smoltz all the support he needed. Hunter's two-run homer was the big blow.

The only other run of the game came in the top of the fifth. With two outs, Gant walked and stole second, his record seventh steal of the NLCS. After Justice also walked, Hunter doubled, making it 4–0.

Smoltz pitched a neat six-hitter, allowing only one extra-base hit in his first shutout of the year.

The Braves gained a World Series berth against Minnesota by becoming only the third National League team to win the last two playoff games on the road. Atlanta pitchers held the Pirates scoreless in the last 22 innings of the NLCS and the last 27 innings at Three Rivers Stadium.

The two teams scored a total of only 31 runs, a record low

The Braves chopped up a big myth with their success in 1991.

for a seven-game National League playoff. The only Brave to play in more than five games and hit over .300 was Olson, who played in all seven games and batted .333. For Pittsburgh, Jay Bell batted .414, but the Pirates' big gun, Bonds, batted just .148 with no RBIs.

Game 1
Wednesday, October 9, at Pittsburgh

Atlanta	AB	R	H	RBI
Smith, lf	4	0	0	0
Lemke, 2b	4	0	0	0
Pendleton, 3b	3	0	0	0
Justice, rf	3	1	2	1
Gant, cf	4	0	0	0
Bream, 1b	4	0	2	0
Olson, c	4	0	0	0
Belliard, ss	2	0	0	0
Willard, ph	1	0	0	0
Blauser, ss	0	0	0	0
Glavine, p	2	0	1	0
Gregg, ph	1	0	0	0
Wohlers, p	0	0	0	0
Stanton, p	0	0	0	0
Totals	32	1	5	1

Pittsburgh	AB	R	H	RBI
Redus, 1b	4	0	1	0
Bell, ss	3	1	1	0
Van Slyke, cf	4	2	2	2
Bonilla, rf	3	1	2	1
Bonds, lf	2	0	0	0
Buechele, 3b	3	1	1	0
Slaught, c	3	0	0	0
Lind, 2b	3	0	0	1
Drabek, p	3	0	1	1
Walk, p	0	0	0	0
Totals	29	5	8	5

Atlanta	0	0	0	0	0	0	0	0	1—1	5	1
Pittsburgh	1	0	2	0	0	1	0	1	x—5	8	1

E—Belliard, Redus. DP—Atlanta 1. LOB—Atlanta 6, Pittsburgh 7. 2B—Drabek, Buechele, Van Slyke. 3B—None. HR—Van Slyke, Justice. SF—Lind. SH—Bell. SB—Redus. CS—None.

Atlanta	IP	H	R	ER	BB	K
Glavine (L)	6	6	4	4	3	4
Wohlers	1	1	0	0	0	0
Stanton	1	1	1	1	2	1

Pittsburgh	IP	H	R	ER	BB	K
Drabek (W)	6	3	0	0	2	5
Walk	3	2	1	1	0	2

HBP—None. WP—None. T—2:52. A—57,347. Umpires—Harvey, Pulli, DeMuth, Gregg, Davidson, Froemming.

Game 2
Thursday, October 10, at Pittsburgh

Atlanta	AB	R	H	RBI
Smith, lf	3	0	0	0
Mitchell, pr-lf	1	0	0	0
Pendleton, 3b	4	0	0	0
Gant, cf	3	0	2	0
Justice, rf	4	1	1	0
Hunter, 1b	4	0	1	0
Olson, c	4	0	2	0
Lemke, 2b	4	0	2	1
Belliard, ss	3	0	0	0
Avery, p	4	0	0	0
Pena, p	0	0	0	0
Totals	34	1	8	1

Pittsburgh	AB	R	H	RBI
Redus, 1b	3	0	1	0
Bell, ss	4	0	1	0
Van Slyke, cf	4	0	0	0
Bonilla, rf	4	0	2	0
Bonds, lf	4	0	1	0
Buechele, 3b	3	0	0	0
Slaught, c	3	0	0	0
Wilkerson, ph	1	0	0	0
Lind, 2b	3	0	1	0
Z. Smith, p	2	0	0	0
Mason, p	0	0	0	0
McClendon, ph	1	0	0	0
Belinda, p	0	0	0	0
Totals	32	0	6	0

Atlanta	0	0	0	0	1	0	0	0	0—1	8	0
Pittsburgh	0	0	0	0	0	0	0	0	0—0	6	0

E—None. DP—Atlanta 1, Pittsburgh 1. LOB—Atlanta 9, Pittsburgh 7. 2B—Lemke, Bonilla. 3B—None. HR—None. SF—None. SH—None. SB—Gant 3, Redus, Bonds 2. CS—None.

Atlanta	IP	H	R	ER	BB	K
Avery (W)	8⅓	6	0	0	2	9
Pena (S)	⅔	0	0	0	0	1

Pittsburgh	IP	H	R	ER	BB	K
Z. Smith (L)	7	8	1	1	2	5
Mason	1	0	0	0	0	1
Belinda	1	0	0	0	0	1

HBP—Gant, by Z. Smith. WP—Pena. T—2:46. A—57,533. Umpires—Pulli, DeMuth, Gregg, Davidson, Froemming, Harvey.

Game 3
Saturday, October 12, at Atlanta

Pittsburgh	AB	R	H	RBI
Merced, 1b	5	1	1	1
Rodriguez, p	0	0	0	0
Bell, ss	5	1	3	1
Van Slyke, cf	3	0	1	0
Bonilla, rf	5	0	0	0
Bonds, lf	5	1	1	0
Buechele, 3b	4	0	2	0
LaValliere, c	2	0	0	0
Slaught, ph-c	1	0	1	0
Lind, 2b	4	0	1	1
Smiley, p	0	0	0	0
Espy, ph	1	0	0	0
Landrum, p	0	0	0	0
Varsho, ph	1	0	0	0
Patterson, p	0	0	0	0
Wilkerson, ph	1	0	0	0
Kipper, p	0	0	0	0
McClendon, ph-1b	0	0	0	0
Totals	37	3	10	3

Atlanta	AB	R	H	RBI
Smith, lf	3	1	0	0
Mitchell, lf	1	0	0	0
Pendleton, 3b	5	0	2	1
Gant, cf	5	2	2	1
Justice, rf	3	1	1	1
Hunter, 1b	4	1	1	1
Pena, p	0	0	0	0
Olson, c	3	3	2	2
Lemke, 2b	2	1	0	0
Belliard, ss	3	0	1	1
Smoltz, p	3	0	1	0
Stanton, p	0	0	0	0
Wohlers, p	0	0	0	0
Bream, 1b	1	1	1	3
Totals	33	10	11	10

Pittsburgh	1	0	0	1	0	0	1	0	0—3	10	2
Atlanta	4	1	1	0	0	0	1	3	x—10	11	0

E—Merced, Bell. DP—None. LOB—Pittsburgh 11, Atlanta 5. 2B—Bell, Buechele, Pendleton, Gant, Justice, Hunter. 3B—None. HR—Gant, Olson, Bream, Merced, Bell. SF—None. SH—Belliard. SB—Bonds, Olson, Smoltz. CS—Smith, Justice.

Pittsburgh	IP	H	R	ER	BB	K
Smiley (L)	2	5	5	4	0	2
Landrum	1	2	1	1	2	2
Patterson	2	1	0	0	0	3
Kipper	2	2	1	1	0	1
Rodriguez	1	1	3	3	2	1

Atlanta	IP	H	R	ER	BB	K
Smoltz (W)	6⅓	8	3	3	2	7
Stanton	⅔	1	0	0	1	0
Wohlers	⅓	1	0	0	1	1
Pena (S)	1⅔	0	0	0	0	1

HBP—Smith by Smiley. WP—Stanton. T—3:22. A—50,905. Umpires—DeMuth, Gregg, Davidson, Froemming, Harvey, Pulli.

Game 4
Sunday, October 13, at Atlanta

Pittsburgh	AB	R	H	RBI
Redus, 1b	5	1	1	0
Bell, ss	5	0	3	0
Van Slyke, cf	3	1	0	0
Bonilla, rf	3	1	1	0
Bonds, lf	5	0	1	0
Buechele, 3b	3	0	3	0
Slaught, c	4	0	1	1
LaValliere, ph-c	1	0	1	1
Lind, 2b	4	0	0	0
Tomlin, p	2	0	0	0
Wilkerson, ph	1	0	0	0
Walk, p	0	0	0	0
McClendon, ph	1	0	0	0
Belinda, p	0	0	0	0
Totals	37	3	11	2

Atlanta	AB	R	H	RBI
Smith, lf	4	1	2	0
Pendleton, 3b	5	0	1	0
Gant, cf	5	0	0	1
Justice, rf	4	1	1	0
Hunter, 1b	3	0	1	0
Bream, ph-1b	1	0	0	0
Olson, c	3	0	1	1
Lemke, 2b	3	0	0	0
Belliard, ss	3	0	1	0
Leibrandt, p	1	0	0	0
Clancy, p	0	0	0	0
Gregg, ph	1	0	0	0
Stanton, p	0	0	0	0
Willard, ph	1	0	0	0
Mercker, p	0	0	0	0
Wohlers, p	0	0	0	0
Totals	34	2	7	2

```
Pittsburgh  0 1 0 0 1 0 0 0 1—3  11  1
Atlanta     2 0 0 0 0 0 0 0 0—2   7  1
```

E—Bonds, Justice. DP—Atlanta 1. LOB—Pittsburgh 10, Atlanta 7. 2B—Smith. 3B—None. HR—None. SF—None. SH—Belliard, Leibrandt, Buechele. SB—None. CS—Bell, Bonilla.

Pittsburgh	IP	H	R	ER	BB	K
Tomlin	6	6	2	2	2	1
Walk	2	1	0	0	0	0
Belinda (W)	2	0	0	0	1	1

Atlanta	IP	H	R	ER	BB	K
Leibrandt	6⅔	8	2	1	3	6
Clancy	⅓	0	0	0	0	0
Stanton	2	2	0	0	0	2
Mercker (L)	⅔	0	1	1	2	0
Wohlers	⅓	1	0	0	0	0

HBP—None. WP—Stanton. T—3:43. A—51,109. Umpires—Gregg, Davidson, Froemming, Harvey, Pulli, DeMuth.

Game 5
Monday, October 14, at Atlanta

Pittsburgh	AB	R	H	RBI
Redus, 1b	4	0	0	0
Bell, ss	4	0	2	0
Van Slyke, cf	4	0	1	0
Bonilla, rf	2	0	1	0
Bonds, lf	4	0	0	0
Buechele, 3b	3	1	0	0
Slaught, c	3	0	1	0
Lind, 2b	4	0	1	1
Z. Smith, p	3	0	0	0
Mason, p	1	0	0	0
Totals	32	1	6	1

Atlanta	AB	R	H	RBI
Smith, lf	4	0	2	0
Pena, p	0	0	0	0
Pendleton, 3b	4	0	1	0
Gant, cf	4	0	1	0
Justice, rf	4	0	0	0
Hunter, 1b	3	0	1	0
Gregg, ph	1	0	1	0
Olson, c	3	0	1	0
Lemke, 2b	4	0	2	0
Belliard, ss	2	0	0	0
Blauser, ph-ss	2	0	0	0
Glavine, p	2	0	0	0
Mitchell, ph-lf	1	0	0	0
Totals	34	0	9	0

```
Pittsburgh  0 0 0 0 1 0 0 0 0—1  6  2
Atlanta     0 0 0 0 0 0 0 0 0—0  9  1
```

E—Redus, Lind, Blauser. DP—Pittsburgh 2, Atlanta 1. LOB—Pittsburgh 8, Atlanta 8. 2B—Bell, Van Slyke, Bonilla. 3B—Pendleton. HR—None. SF—None. SH—Slaught. SB—Gant, L. Smith. CS—Hunter.

Pittsburgh	IP	H	R	ER	BB	K
Z. Smith (W)	7⅔	7	0	0	1	5
Mason (S)	1⅓	2	0	0	0	1

Atlanta	IP	H	R	ER	BB	K
Glavine (L)	8	6	1	1	3	7
Pena	1	0	0	0	0	1

HBP—None. WP—None. T—2:51. A—51,109. Umpires—Davidson, Froemming, Harvey, Pulli, DeMuth, Gregg.

Game 6
Wednesday, October 16, at Pittsburgh

Atlanta	AB	R	H	RBI
Smith, lf	3	0	2	0
Mitchell, lf	0	0	0	0
Treadway, 2b	3	0	1	0
Lemke, 2b	0	0	0	0
Pendleton, 3b	4	0	0	0
Justice, rf	4	0	0	0
Gant, cf	3	1	1	0
Bream, 1b	4	0	0	0
Olson, c	4	0	1	1
Belliard, ss	3	0	1	0
Avery, p	3	0	1	0
Gregg, ph	1	0	0	0
Pena, p	0	0	0	0
Totals	32	1	7	1

Pittsburgh	AB	R	H	RBI
Redus, 1b	3	0	0	0
Merced, ph	0	0	0	0
Bell, ss	4	0	0	0
Van Slyke, cf	3	0	0	0
Bonilla, rf	2	0	0	0
Bonds, lf	3	0	0	0
Buechele, 3b	3	0	1	0
Slaught, c	3	0	1	0
Lind, 2b	3	0	1	0
Drabek, p	2	0	0	0
Varsho, ph	1	0	1	0
Totals	27	0	4	0

```
Atlanta     0 0 0 0 0 0 0 0 1—1  7  0
Pittsburgh  0 0 0 0 0 0 0 0 0—0  4  0
```

E—None. DP—Atlanta 2. LOB—Atlanta 8, Pittsburgh 3. 2B—L. Smith 2, Olson. 3B—None. HR—None. SF—None. SH—Treadway, Merced. SB—Gant 2. CS—L. Smith.

Atlanta	IP	H	R	ER	BB	K
Avery (W)	8	3	0	0	2	8
Pena (S)	1	1	0	0	0	1

Pittsburgh	IP	H	R	ER	BB	K
Drabek (L)	9	7	1	1	3	5

HBP—None. WP—Pena. T—3:09. A—54,508. Umpires—Froemming, Harvey, Pulli, DeMuth, Gregg, Davidson.

Game 7
Thursday, October 17, at Pittsburgh

Atlanta	AB	R	H	RBI
Smith, lf	3	1	0	0
Mitchell, lf	1	0	0	0
Pendleton, 3b	5	1	1	0
Gant, cf	3	1	1	1
Justice, rf	3	0	0	0
Hunter, 1b	4	1	2	3
Olson, c	3	0	1	0
Lemke, 2b	3	0	0	0
Belliard, ss	3	0	1	0
Smoltz, p	2	0	0	0
Totals	30	4	6	4

Pittsburgh	AB	R	H	RBI
Merced, 1b	4	0	1	0
Bell, ss	4	0	2	0
Van Slyke, cf	4	0	0	0
Bonilla, rf	4	0	1	0
Bonds, lf	4	0	1	0
Buechele, 3b	4	0	0	0
LaValliere, c	3	0	1	0
Lind, 2b	4	0	0	0
Smiley, p	0	0	0	0
Walk, p	1	0	0	0
Espy, ph	1	0	0	0
Mason, p	0	0	0	0
Wilkerson, ph	1	0	0	0
Belinda, p	0	0	0	0
Totals	34	0	6	0

```
Atlanta     3 0 0 0 1 0 0 0 0—4  6  1
Pittsburgh  0 0 0 0 0 0 0 0 0—0  6  0
```

E—Lemke. DP—None. LOB—Atlanta 8, Pittsburgh 8. 2B—Hunter, Bonds. 3B—None. HR—Hunter. SF—Gant. SH—Smoltz. SB—Gant. CS—None.

Atlanta	IP	H	R	ER	BB	K
Smoltz (W)	9	6	0	0	1	8

Pittsburgh	IP	H	R	ER	BB	K
Smiley (L)	⅔	3	3	3	1	1
Walk	4⅓	2	1	1	3	3
Mason	2	1	0	0	1	0
Belinda	2	0	0	0	2	2

HBP—None. WP—None. Balk—Walk. T—3:04. A—46,932. Umpires—Harvey, Pulli, DeMuth, Gregg, Davidson, Froemming.

COMPOSITE BATTING STATISTICS

Atlanta Braves	AVG	G	AB	R	H	2B	3B	HR	RB	BB	SO	SB
Steve Avery, p	.143	2	7	0	1	0	0	0	0	0	4	0
Rafael Belliard, ss	.211	7	19	0	4	0	0	0	1	3	3	0
Jeff Blauser, ss	.000	2	2	0	0	0	0	0	0	0	0	0
Sid Bream, 1b	.300	4	10	1	3	0	0	1	3	0	1	0
Jim Clancy, p	.000	1	0	0	0	0	0	0	0	0	0	0
Ron Gant, of	.259	7	27	4	7	1	0	1	3	2	4	7
Tom Glavine, p	.250	2	4	0	1	0	0	0	0	0	2	0
Tommy Gregg, ph	.250	4	4	0	1	0	0	0	0	0	2	0
Brian Hunter, 1b	.333	5	18	2	6	2	0	1	4	0	2	0
David Justice, of	.200	7	25	4	5	1	0	1	2	3	7	0
Charlie Leibrandt, p	.000	1	1	0	0	0	0	0	0	0	0	0
Mark Lemke, 2b	.200	7	20	1	4	1	0	0	1	4	0	0
Kent Mercker, p	.000	1	0	0	0	0	0	0	0	0	0	0
Keith Mitchell, of	.000	5	4	0	0	0	0	0	0	0	1	0
Greg Olson, c	.333	7	24	3	8	1	0	1	4	4	3	1
Alejandro Pena, p	.000	4	0	0	0	0	0	0	0	0	0	0
Terry Pendleton, 3b	.167	7	30	1	5	1	1	0	1	1	3	0
Lonnie Smith, of	.250	7	24	3	6	3	0	0	0	4	5	2
John Smoltz, p	.200	2	5	0	1	0	0	0	0	1	4	1
Mike Stanton, p	.000	3	0	0	0	0	0	0	0	0	0	0
Jeff Treadway, 2b	.333	1	3	0	1	0	0	0	0	0	0	0
Jerry Willard, ph	.000	2	2	0	0	0	0	0	0	0	1	0
Mark Wohlers, p	.000	3	0	0	0	0	0	0	0	0	0	0
Totals	.231		229	19	53	10	1	5	19	22	42	11

Pittsburgh Pirates	AVG	G	AB	R	H	2B	3B	HR	RB	BB	SO	SB
Stan Belinda, p	.000	3	0	0	0	0	0	0	0	0	0	0
Jay Bell, ss	.414	7	29	2	12	2	0	1	1	0	10	0
Barry Bonds, of	.148	7	27	1	4	1	0	0	0	2	4	3
Bobby Bonilla, of	.304	7	23	2	7	2	0	0	1	6	2	0
Steve Buechele, 3b	.304	7	23	2	7	2	0	0	0	4	6	0
Doug Drabek, p	.200	2	5	0	1	1	0	0	1	0	2	0
Cecil Espy, ph	.000	2	2	0	0	0	0	0	0	0	2	0
Bob Kipper, p	.000	1	0	0	0	0	0	0	0	0	0	0
Bill Landrum, p	.000	1	0	0	0	0	0	0	0	0	0	0
Mike La Valliere, c	.333	3	6	0	2	0	0	0	1	2	0	0
Jose Lind, 2b	.160	7	25	0	4	0	0	0	3	0	6	0
Roger Mason, p	.000	3	1	0	0	0	0	0	0	0	1	0
Lloyd McClendon, 1b-1	.000	5	4	0	0	0	0	0	0	1	0	0
Orlando Merced, 1b-2	.222	3	9	1	2	0	0	1	1	0	1	0
Bob Patterson, p	.000	1	0	0	0	0	0	0	0	0	0	0
Gary Redus, 1b	.158	5	19	1	3	0	0	0	0	1	4	2
Rosario Rodriguez, p	.000	1	0	0	0	0	0	0	0	0	0	0
Don Slaught, c	.235	6	17	0	4	0	0	0	1	1	4	0
John Smiley, p	.000	2	0	0	0	0	0	0	0	0	0	0
Zane Smith, p	.000	2	5	0	0	0	0	0	0	0	4	0
Randy Tomlin, p	.000	1	2	0	0	0	0	0	0	0	0	0
Andy Van Slyke, of	.150	7	25	3	4	2	0	1	2	5	5	1
Gary Varsho, ph	.500	2	2	0	1	0	0	0	0	0	1	0
Bob Walk, p	.000	3	2	0	0	0	0	0	0	0	2	0
Curtis Wilkerson, ph	.000	4	4	0	0	0	0	0	0	0	3	0
Totals	.224		228	12	51	10	0	3	11	22	57	6

COMPOSITE PITCHING STATISTICS

Atlanta Braves	W	L	ERA	G	GS	CG	SV	SHO	IP	H	ER	BB	SO
Steve Avery	2	0	0.00	2	2	0	0	0	16⅓	9	0	4	17
Jim Clancy	0	0	0.00	1	0	0	0	0	⅓	0	0	0	0
Tom Glavine	0	2	3.21	2	2	0	0	0	14.0	12	5	6	11
Charlie Leibrandt	0	0	1.35	1	1	0	0	0	6⅔	8	1	3	6
Kent Mercker	0	1	13.50	1	0	0	0	0	⅔	0	1	2	0
Alejandro Pena	0	0	0.00	4	0	0	3	0	4⅓	1	0	0	4
John Smoltz	2	0	1.76	2	2	1	0	1	15⅓	14	3	3	15
Mike Stanton	0	0	2.45	3	0	0	0	0	3⅔	4	1	3	3
Mark Wohlers	0	0	0.00	3	0	0	0	0	1⅓	3	0	1	1
Totals	4	3	1.57	19	7	1	3	1	63.0	51	11	22	57

Pittsburgh Pirates	W	L	ERA	G	GS	CG	SV	SHO	IP	H	ER	BB	SO
Stan Belinda	1	0	0.00	3	0	0	0	0	5.0	0	0	3	4
Doug Drabek	1	1	0.60	2	2	1	0	0	15.0	10	1	5	10
Bob Kipper	0	0	4.50	1	0	0	0	0	2.0	2	1	0	1
Bill Landrum	0	0	9.00	1	0	0	0	0	1.0	2	1	2	2
Roger Mason	0	0	0.00	3	0	0	1	0	4⅓	3	0	1	2
Bob Patterson	0	0	0.00	1	0	0	0	0	2.0	1	0	0	3
Rosario Rodriguez	0	0	27.00	1	0	0	0	0	1.0	1	3	2	1
John Smiley	0	2	23.63	2	2	0	0	0	2⅔	8	7	1	3
Zane Smith	1	1	0.61	2	2	0	0	0	14⅔	15	1	3	10
Randy Tomlin	0	0	3.00	1	1	0	0	0	6.0	6	2	2	1
Bob Walk	0	0	1.93	3	0	0	1	0	9⅓	5	2	3	5
Totals	3	4	2.57	20	7	1	2	0	63.0	53	18	22	42

Braves versus Minnesota Twins World Series

1991

Atlanta's opponent in the World Series, the Minnesota Twins, pulled off an achievement similar to the Braves' "worst to first" turnaround. They went from last place in the American League West in 1990 to winning the division and the pennant in 1991. The two Series foes offered quite a bit of inspiration to the downtrodden everywhere—and they also combined to produce one of the most entertaining World Series ever played.

The Twins, who beat Toronto in a five-game American League Championship Series, featured a pitching staff anchored by 36-year-old right-hander Jack Morris (18–12) and 23-year-old right-hander Scott Erickson, who tied for the AL lead in wins (20–8). Manager Tom Kelly's lineup included center fielder Kirby Puckett, one of the best players in the game, and second baseman Chuck Knoblauch, the American League Rookie of the Year, as well as slugging first baseman Kent Hrbek.

The Twins led the AL in batting average (.280) and defense (.985), but the two biggest things they had going for them in the Series were (1) Morris and (2) the Hubert H. Humphrey Metrodome. Some cynics might add a third: the Braves' bullpen.

The Series went the full seven games, with Minnesota finally winning in the 10th inning. Both teams swept the games at their home parks, but since the Series opened in the American League city, that trend did not benefit Atlanta. Morris, who was named the Series MVP, won Games 1 and 7 and pitched well in Game 4. He had a 2–0 record and a 1.17 ERA, allowing just three earned runs in 23 innings.

The Braves, playing in their first World Series since 1958, outhit the Twins, .253 to .232, and outscored them, 29–24, but a major portion of that offense was generated in a 14–5 rout in Game 5.

The biggest surprise of the Series was its offensive star—Atlanta second baseman Mark Lemke, who batted .417 to lead both clubs. He had 10 hits, including a double and three triples, and drove in four runs.

Game One

In the Series opener before 55,108 fans at the noisy Metrodome, Bobby Cox stuck with the rotation he established in the playoffs and started Charlie Leibrandt against Morris. That decision didn't look good when Leibrandt got in trouble in the first inning and stayed in it until he was finally lifted in the fifth with the Braves trailing, 4–0.

The Braves got on the board in the sixth with singles by Jeff Treadway, David Justice, and Ron Gant. But the Twins got the run right back in the bottom of the inning when Hrbek homered to make it 5–1.

In the eighth, the Braves finally got Morris out of the game but had to settle for just one run. Lonnie Smith and Treadway opened the inning with walks, prompting Kelly to pull Morris for Mark Guthrie. Pendleton grounded into a double play, with Smith going to third. Justice walked to put runners at the corners, then Rick Aguilera relieved Guthrie. Gant delivered a single, his third hit of the game, making it 5–2 and putting runners at first and third again. But Sid Bream, representing the tying run, flied to center to end the threat.

Aguilera retired Atlanta in order in the ninth, giving the Twins the early edge in the Series. By picking up the win, Morris raised his World Series record to 6–1.

Game Two

The advantage the Twins enjoyed by having four of the seven Series games in their indoor arena showed itself quickly in Game 2. In the bottom of the first, Dan Gladden lifted a pop-up into short right-center. Both Lemke and Justice could have made the play, but they wound up colliding and letting the ball drop. Justice was charged with a two-base error.

Afterward, Lemke and Justice explained that they couldn't hear each other over the Metrodome noise and they were afraid to take their eyes off the ball to check on their proximity for fear of not being able to pick up the ball again in the white ceiling.

Perhaps shaken by the play, Glavine then walked Knoblauch. Puckett grounded into a double play, but Minnesota was still alive because of the dropped pop-up. Chili Davis took advantage of that extra out by hitting a two-run homer.

The Braves fought back for a run in the second off Kevin Tapani on a sacrifice fly by Brian Hunter.

A controversial call by first base umpire Drew Coble ended an Atlanta scoring opportunity in the third. With one out, Smith reached on an error. After Pendleton flied out, Gant singled, sending Smith to third. But Gant made a wide turn at first and Tapani threw behind him to Hrbek. Gant appeared to hold the bag, and Hrbek seemed to lift Gant's right leg. Coble, under heated protest from the Braves, ruled Gant out with Justice waiting to hit.

Glavine settled down and retired 15 in a row and 17 of 19 until Brian Harper singled with one out in the seventh for Minnesota's second hit of the game.

Meanwhile, the Braves tied the game in the fifth. Greg Olson led off with a double, took third on an infield out, and scored on a sacrifice fly by Rafael Belliard.

The score remained 2–2 until the bottom of the eighth when Scott Leius hit the first pitch of the inning for a home run, which was decisive in the Twins' 3–2 victory.

The good news was that the Braves were going home to host the first World Series game in their 26-year Atlanta history. But it was difficult to get very excited with Minnesota holding a two-game advantage.

Game Three

If Braves fans were distressed by their team's two losses at Minnesota, they didn't show it. A capacity crowd of 50,878, ready to chop, chant, and party, showed up for the South's first World Series game, and it didn't leave disappointed.

In a classic game, the Braves opened an early 4–1 lead, allowed Minnesota to tie it in the eighth, then won it, 5–4, in the 12th on a close play at the plate.

The pitching matchup was Erickson for Minnesota against Avery, the Braves' precocious left-hander who was MVP of the playoffs. Avery outpitched the Twins' 20-game winner, but both were gone way before the longest night game in Series history had been decided.

Before many fans had settled into their seats, Minnesota led 1–0 on the strength of a leadoff triple by Gladden and a sacrifice fly by Knoblauch. Gladden's triple was somewhat tainted because Gant and Justice got tangled up chasing the ball.

But the Braves quickly tied the game in the second. Olson drew a two-out walk and scored when Lemke and Belliard followed with singles.

Justice led off the fourth with a home run to give Atlanta the lead. Then in the fifth, Lonnie Smith hit a one-out home run, making it 3–1. The Braves added another run in the inning when David West relieved Erickson and walked Olson with the bases loaded.

It looked as if the 4–1 lead would be more than enough for Avery, who retired 15 in a row and 18 of 20 after Gladden's triple. But in the seventh, Puckett led off with a home run to make the score 4–2. And in the eighth, the Twins finally got even. Harper pinch-hit for Junior Ortiz and reached on Pendleton's error. Cox immediately pulled Avery for Alejandro Pena, who hadn't blown a save in 14 opportunities since joining the Braves. But Davis, pinch-hitting for reliever Steve Bedrosian, promptly homered to tie the game.

The game remained tied at 4–4 entering the 12th when Minnesota mounted a rally against Mark Wohlers. Gladden got a one-out single, then Knoblauch reached on Lemke's error, with Gladden going to third. Cox brought in Mercker to pitch to Hrbek, who struck out. Then Jim Clancy replaced Mercker and intentionally walked Puckett to load the bases.

Kelly was out of position players, so he called on Aguilera to bat for Guthrie. Clancy retired him on a fly to center to end the threat.

Then in the bottom of the 12th, Justice got a one-out single off Aguilera and, with two outs, stole second. After Olson walked, Lemke singled to left, and Justice—making sure to touch third this time—slid across home, barely avoiding the tag by Harper.

The two teams used a Series-record 42 players, including all nonpitchers and a record 12 pinch hitters. Aguilera became the first pitcher used as a pinch hitter in the Series since Don Drysdale in 1965.

Game Four

Mark Lemke entered the World Series known mainly by Braves fans for his defense. By the time the Series was over, he'd become known nationwide for the surprising offensive display he put on against Minnesota.

After winning Game 3 with an RBI single in the 12th inning, Lemke came back some 19 hours later to win Game 4 with his bat, too. This time, he delivered a one-out triple in the bottom of the ninth and scored on Jerry Willard's sacrifice fly to give the Braves a 3–2 win, evening the Series at two games for each team.

Both starting pitchers acquitted themselves well. Morris left in the middle of the seventh with Minnesota leading, 2–1, and Smoltz departed a half inning later after Atlanta had tied the game, 2–2.

The Twins opened the scoring in the second when Harper led off with a double and Mike Pagliarulo delivered a one-out single. Atlanta tied it in the third on Pendleton's two-out home run, his first in 117 career postseason at bats.

The game remained 1–1 entering the seventh when the clubs traded runs. Pagliarulo hit a one-out homer in the top of the inning off Smoltz, and Smith hit a two-out shot in the bottom of the inning off reliever Carl Willis.

In the ninth, with Willis still pitching, Olson grounded out, then Lemke tripled to left-center for his third hit of the game and his first three-hit game of the season. Jeff Blauser was walked intentionally to set up a double-play situation with relief pitcher Mike Stanton due to bat.

Kelly then called on Bedrosian, a former and future Brave, to relieve Willis. Cox countered by inserting Willard, who spent most of the year in the minors, to bat for Stanton. Willard hit Bedrosian's first pitch to medium right field, where Shane Mack caught it and threw to the plate. Lemke seemed to get a late start at third but slid around Harper's tag.

The Braves had rallied to tie the Series, and the drums were beating throughout Atlanta, where tomahawk chopping had broken out on every street corner.

Game Five

After the first two games of the Series, the Braves' chances looked quite bleak. But after five games, they appeared quite bright. That's how much three days in Atlanta did for Bobby Cox's team.

Not only did the Braves win Game 5, but they did so in such convincing fashion—14–5—that it gave the team's fans the illusion that winning one of two at Minnesota wouldn't be difficult at all. At least that's the way it seemed.

In a rematch of the pitchers who started Game 2, a 3–2 Minnesota win, Glavine started for the Braves and Tapani for the Twins. But it was the Atlanta offense that stole the show.

The game actually was scoreless entering the bottom of the fourth when the Braves erupted for four runs. Gant led off with a single and Justice followed with a home run for the first two. Then the bottom of the order produced the other two runs. Lemke got his second triple in two games to drive in Olson, and Belliard delivered a double to make it 4–0.

Singles by Pendleton and Gant in the fifth and an infield out by Justice upped the score to 5–0. Minnesota showed life in the sixth by scoring three times to knock out Glavine, who suddenly couldn't find the plate.

But in the seventh, Atlanta put six runs on the board to go ahead 11–3. Smith led off the inning with a home run, his third in three games, making him the fifth player to do so in a World Series, but the first non-Yankee. The big blow in the inning was a two-run triple by Lemke—his second of the game and third in his last four at bats.

Minnesota scored once in the eighth, then the Braves got three more in their half of the inning, making it 14–4. The Twins closed the scoring with a run in the ninth.

The Braves pounded out 17 hits, eight for extra bases, off five pitchers for the most lopsided World Series game in four years. The 14 runs were the most by one team in a Series game since the Yankees beat Pittsburgh, 16–3, in 1960. Every

Atlanta starter except Glavine had at least one hit and scored at least one run. Justice had five RBIs, the 14th time a player has had at least that many in a Series game.

The Braves were only one win away from the third World Series championship in franchise history and the first since 1957. But the Metrodome and Morris awaited.

After pitching well and losing in Game 2, Tom Glavine was shaky in Game 5 yet won, thanks to the Braves' 14-run outburst.

Braves fans came to Game 5 ready to sweep the Twins out of Atlanta.

Game Six

The Twins won the 1987 World Series against St. Louis in seven games by winning only their four home games. They undoubtedly kept that victory in mind as they prepared for Games 6 and 7 against the Braves at the Metrodome.

It took 11 innings to decide Game 6, and when Puckett finally sent everyone home with a leadoff home run, breaking a 3–3 tie, Cox was left to explain why he'd chosen Leibrandt, who hadn't worked in relief for two years, to pitch the 11th.

"Why not Leibrandt?" Cox responded when asked the obvious question. "We'd be pretty stupid if we are resistant in bringing in a 15-game winner. He's faced Puckett before. He just got the ball up, and Puckett hit it hard."

Terry Pendleton had a big Series, hitting .367 with two home runs.

Puckett's home run was only the ninth game-ending homer in Series history. It made Game 6 the third game of this Series to be decided on the final pitch. Interestingly, Leibrandt struck out Puckett the two times he faced him in Game 1.

The Twins scored twice off Avery in the first inning without hitting the ball hard.

Puckett kept Atlanta off the scoreboard in the third when he climbed the wall in left-center to rob Gant of an RBI double. But the Braves tied the game in the fifth on a two-run homer by Pendleton off Erickson.

Minnesota came right back in the bottom of the fifth to regain the lead without benefit of a hit. Gladden walked, stole second, took third on a fly ball to right, and scored on a sacrifice fly by Puckett.

In the seventh, Lemke led off with a single, which chased Erickson for Guthrie, who struck out Blauser. Lemke advanced to second on a wild pitch, then Smith walked and Pendleton singled to load the bases. Gant grounded into a force, allowing Lemke to score the tying run.

Neither team mounted a serious scoring threat through the 10th. In the 11th, the Braves got a leadoff single from Bream, but pinch runner Keith Mitchell was thrown out trying to steal. Hunter fouled out and Olson popped out against Aguilera to end the inning, setting the stage for Puckett's home run on the third pitch by Leibrandt.

Game Seven

When John Smoltz was a teenager growing up in Michigan, Jack Morris was in the midst of an All-Star career with the Detroit Tigers. It was only natural that Smoltz, a hard-throwing right-hander who would soon develop into a professional prospect, would chose as his idol the pitcher who helped lead the Tigers to the 1984 World Series championship. In fact, when Morris beat San Diego, 4–2, in Game 4 of that Series, Smoltz, then 17, and his father were at Tiger Stadium.

So, it was indeed a poignant moment for a 24-year-old Smoltz to find himself matched against a 36-year-old Morris in the decisive game of the 1991 World Series. But if Smoltz's emotions were touched by this close encounter with Morris, he showed no sense of awe in the way he pitched.

With the division-clinching victory and the pennant clincher already on his résumé, Smoltz matched Morris pitch for pitch in a valiant attempt to add the decisive Series game to his record. However, in the eighth inning, with Smoltz and Morris locked in a scoreless duel in one of the tensest Game 7s in history, Cox pulled his young pitcher. But Morris, the hardened veteran, went the distance in Minnesota's 1–0, 10-inning victory and was named MVP of the Series.

Both teams had several opportunities to score before the Twins ended the game in the 10th.

The Braves' best chance, one that was foiled in a rather bizarre manner, took place in the eighth inning. Smith led off with a single, then Pendleton followed with a drive into the left-center gap. Smith should have scored easily, and Braves third base coach Jimy Williams was waving at him to do just that. However, the Atlanta designated hitter made the most costly baserunning mistake in franchise history when he hesitated for no apparent reason when rounding second and had to stop at third.

Instead of having a run home and Pendleton at second or possibly third, the Braves had men at second and third. Still, there were no outs, but Gant proceeded to ground out to first with the runners holding. Justice was then intentionally walked to load the bases, and Bream grounded into a double play, ending the inning.

The Braves went out in order in the ninth, but the Twins had runners at first and second with no outs before Pena came on to get out of the jam. Morris also retired Atlanta in order in the 10th, setting the stage for Minnesota's winning rally.

Not known for his offense, Mark Lemke nearly carried the Braves to the 1991 World Series championship by hitting .417 with three triples.

Gladden led off with a broken-bat double against Pena, and he took third on a sacrifice by Knoblauch. Puckett and Hrbek were intentionally walked to set up a double play, but pinch hitter Gene Larkin, batting for Jarvis Brown, lofted Pena's first pitch over the head of a drawn-in Hunter in left for a Series-ending single.

For only the second time in history, all seven games were won by the home team, and Minnesota was the Series winner both times. Morris was extraordinary, limiting the Braves to seven hits and two walks while striking out eight. In his three Series starts, he had a 1.17 ERA over 23 innings. Smoltz, who didn't have a decision in the Series, posted a 1.26 ERA in two starts covering 14⅓ innings.

Four of the seven games were decided on the final pitch, five in the last inning, five by one run, and three—including the last two—in extra innings. This was the first Game 7 to end 1–0 since 1962, the first to go extra innings since 1924, and the fourth to be decided on the final swing of the bat.

An estimated 750,000 people flooded downtown Atlanta for a parade to bathe the Braves in appreciation and affection. The nearly two-hour celebration was televised live by Atlanta's three major TV stations, and city officials said it was the largest downtown gathering in history.

Sid Bream, who had a poor Series at the plate, grounded into an eighth-inning double play in Game 7 which ended an excellent scoring opportunity.

Ron Gant and Jeff Blauser ride through Atlanta in the post-Series parade which attracted a throng estimated as high as 750,000 people.

Game 1
Saturday, October 19, at Minnesota

Atlanta	AB	R	H	RBI
Smith, dh	3	1	0	0
Treadway, 2b	3	1	1	0
Pendleton, 3b	4	0	0	0
Justice, lf	2	0	1	0
Gant, cf	4	0	3	2
Bream, 1b	4	0	0	0
Hunter, lf	4	0	0	0
Olson, c	3	0	1	0
Belliard, ss	1	0	0	0
Blauser, ph-ss	2	0	0	0
Leibrandt, p	0	0	0	0
Clancy, p	0	0	0	0
Wohlers, p	0	0	0	0
Stanton, p	0	0	0	0
Totals	30	2	6	2

Minnesota	AB	R	H	RBI
Gladden, lf	2	1	0	0
Knoblauch, 2b	3	0	3	1
Puckett, cf	4	0	0	0
Davis, dh	3	0	0	0
Harper, c	4	0	2	0
Mack, rf	4	0	0	0
Hrbek, 1b	4	2	2	1
Leius, 3b	2	1	1	0
Pagliarulo, ph-3b	1	0	0	0
Gagne, ss	3	1	1	3
Morris, p	0	0	0	0
Guthrie, p	0	0	0	0
Aguilera, p	0	0	0	0
Totals	30	5	9	5

```
Atlanta     0 0 0 0 0 1 0 1 0—2 6 1
Minnesota   0 0 1 0 3 1 0 0 x—5 9 1
```

E—Treadway, Gladden. DP—Atlanta 2, Minnesota 2. LOB—Atlanta 7, Minnesota 5. 2B—Harper, Hrbek. 3B—None. HR—Gagne, Hrbek. SF—None. SH—Belliard. SB—Gladden, Knoblauch 2. CS—Gladden.

Atlanta	IP	H	R	ER	BB	K
Leibrandt (L)	4	7	4	4	1	3
Clancy	2	1	1	1	2	0
Wohlers	1	1	0	0	1	1
Stanton	1	0	0	0	0	2

Minnesota	IP	H	R	ER	BB	K
Morris (W)	7	5	2	2	4	3
Guthrie	⅔	0	0	0	1	0
Aguilera (S)	1⅓	1	0	0	0	0

HBP—None. WP—None. PB—None. T—3:00. A—55,108. Umpires—Denkinger, Wendelstedt, Coble, Tata, Reed, Montague.

Game 2
Sunday, October 20, at Minnesota

Atlanta	AB	R	H	RBI
Smith, dh	3	0	0	0
Pendleton, 3b	4	0	2	0
Gant, cf	4	0	1	0
Justice, rf	4	1	1	0
Bream, 1b	4	0	1	0
Hunter, lf	3	0	1	1
Olson, c	4	1	1	0
Lemke, 2b	3	0	0	0
Gregg, ph	1	0	0	0
Belliard, ss	2	0	1	1
Glavine, p	0	0	0	0
Totals	32	2	8	2

Minnesota	AB	R	H	RBI
Gladden, lf	4	0	0	0
Knoblauch, 2b	3	1	0	0
Puckett, cf	4	0	0	0
Davis, dh	3	1	1	2
Harper, c	2	0	1	0
Mack, rf	3	0	0	0
Hrbek, 1b	2	0	0	0
Leius, 3b	3	1	1	1
Gagne, ss	3	0	1	0
Tapani, p	0	0	0	0
Aguilera, p	0	0	0	0
Totals	27	3	4	3

```
Atlanta     0 1 0 0 1 0 0 0 0—2 8 1
Minnesota   2 0 0 0 0 0 0 1 x—3 4 1
```

E—Justice, Leius. DP—Atlanta 2. LOB—Atlanta 6, Minnesota 3. 2B—Bream, Olson. 3B—None. HR—Davis, Leius. SF—Hunter, Belliard. SH—Smith. SB—None. CS—None.

Atlanta	IP	H	R	ER	BB	K
Glavine (L)	8	4	3	1	3	6

Minnesota	IP	H	R	ER	BB	K
Tapani (W)	8	7	2	2	0	3
Aguilera (S)	1	1	0	0	0	3

HBP—None. WP—None. Balk—Glavine. T—2:37. A—55,145. Umpires—Wendelstedt, Coble, Tata, Reed, Montague, Denkinger.

Game 3
Tuesday, October 22, at Atlanta

Minnesota	AB	R	H	RBI
Gladden, lf	6	1	3	0
Knoblauch, 2b	5	0	1	1
Hrbek, 1b	6	0	1	0
Puckett, cf	4	1	1	1
Mack, rf	4	0	0	0
Willis, p	0	0	0	0
Sorrento, ph	1	0	0	0
Guthrie, p	0	0	0	0
Aguilera, p	1	0	0	0
Leius, 3b	3	0	0	0
Pagliarulo, ph-3b	1	0	0	0
Newman, ph-3b	1	0	0	0
Gagne, ss	5	0	0	0
Ortiz, c	2	0	1	0
Harper, ph-c	3	1	1	0
Erickson, p	1	0	0	0
West, p	0	0	0	0
Leach, p	0	0	0	0
Larkin, ph	1	0	1	0
Bedrosian, p	0	0	0	0
Davis, ph	1	1	1	2
Brown, rf	0	0	0	0
Bush, ph-rf	2	0	0	0
Totals	47	4	10	4

Atlanta	AB	R	H	RBI
Smith, lf	4	1	1	1
Mitchell, lf	2	0	0	0
Pendleton, 3b	4	1	0	0
Gant, cf	6	0	0	0
Justice, rf	6	2	2	1
Bream, 1b	3	0	1	0
Hunter, ph-1b	2	0	0	0
Olson, c	3	1	1	1
Lemke, 2b	5	0	2	1
Belliard, ss	3	0	1	1
Blauser, ph-ss	1	0	0	0
Avery, p	3	0	0	0
Pena, p	0	0	0	0
Treadway, ph	0	0	0	0
Stanton, p	0	0	0	0
Cabrera, ph	1	0	0	0
Wohlers, p	0	0	0	0
Mercker, p	0	0	0	0
Clancy, p	0	0	0	0
Totals	43	5	8	5

```
Minnesota   1 0 0 0 0 0 1 2 0 0 0 0—4 10 1
Atlanta     0 1 0 1 2 0 0 0 0 0 0 1—5  8 2
```

E—Knoblauch, Pendleton, Lemke. DP—None. LOB—Minnesota 10, Atlanta 12. 2B—Bream, Olson. 3B—Gladden. HR—Justice, Smith, Puckett, Davis. SF—Knoblauch. SH—Treadway. SB—Knoblauch, Justice. CS—None.

Minnesota	IP	H	R	ER	BB	K
Erickson	4⅔	5	4	3	2	3
West	0	0	0	0	2	0
Leach	⅓	0	0	0	0	1
Bedrosian	2	0	0	0	0	1
Willis	2	0	0	0	2	0
Guthrie	2	1	0	0	1	1
Aguilera (L)	⅔	2	1	1	1	0

Atlanta	IP	H	R	ER	BB	K
Avery	7	4	3	2	0	5
Pena	2	4	1	1	0	4
Stanton	2	1	0	0	1	3
Wohlers	⅓	1	0	0	0	0
Mercker	⅓	0	0	0	0	1
Clancy (W)	⅓	0	0	0	1	0

HBP—None. WP—None. T—4:04. A—50,878. Umpires—Coble, Tata, Reed, Montague, Denkinger, Wendelstedt.

Game 4
Wednesday, October 23, at Atlanta

Minnesota	AB	R	H	RBI
Gladden, lf	4	0	0	0
Knoblauch, 2b	3	0	1	0
Puckett, cf	4	0	1	0
Hrbek, 1b	4	0	0	0
Harper, c	4	1	2	0
Mack, rf	4	0	0	0
Pagliarulo, 3b	3	1	3	2
Leius, ph-3b	1	0	0	0
Bedrosian, p	0	0	0	0
Gagne, ss	3	0	0	0
Morris, p	2	0	0	0
Larkin, ph	1	0	0	0
Willis, p	0	0	0	0
Guthrie, p	0	0	0	0
Newman, 3b	0	0	0	0
Totals	33	2	7	2

Atlanta	AB	R	H	RBI
Smith, lf	4	1	2	1
Pendleton, 3b	4	1	2	1
Gant, cf	3	0	1	0
Justice, rf	3	0	0	0
Bream, 1b	3	0	0	0
Hunter, ph-1b	1	0	0	0
Olson, c	3	0	0	0
Lemke, 2b	4	1	3	0
Belliard, ss	2	0	0	0
Treadway, ph	1	0	0	0
Blauser, ss	0	0	0	0
Smoltz, p	2	0	0	0
Gregg, ph	1	0	0	0
Wohlers, p	0	0	0	0
Stanton, p	0	0	0	0
Cabrera, ph	0	0	0	0
Willard, ph	0	0	0	1
Totals	31	3	8	3

```
Minnesota   0 1 0 0 0 1 0 0—2 7 0
Atlanta     0 0 1 0 0 1 0 1—3 8 0
```

E—None. DP—None. LOB—Minnesota 5, Atlanta 7. 2B—Knoblauch, Harper, Pendleton, Lemke. 3B—Lemke. HR—Pendleton, Pagliarulo, Smith. SF—Willard. SH—None. SB—Gant, Smith, Knoblauch. CS—Mack.

Minnesota	IP	H	R	ER	BB	K
Morris	6	6	1	1	3	4
Willis	1	1	1	1	0	1
Guthrie (L)	1	1	1	1	1	1
Bedrosian	⅓	0	0	0	0	0

Atlanta	IP	H	R	ER	BB	K
Smoltz	7	7	2	2	0	7
Wohlers	⅓	0	0	0	1	0
Stanton (W)	1⅔	0	0	0	0	1

HBP—None. WP—Morris. T—2:57. A—50,878. Umpires—Tata, Reed, Montague, Denkinger, Wendelstedt, Coble.

Game 5
Thursday, October 24, at Atlanta

Minnesota	AB	R	H	RBI
Gladden, lf	5	1	1	0
Knoblauch, 2b	3	1	1	0
Bedrosian, p	0	0	0	0
Ortiz, c	1	0	0	1
Puckett, cf	2	1	1	0
Brown, ph-cf	2	0	0	0
Davis, rf	3	2	1	0
Willis, p	0	0	0	0
Harper, c	2	0	0	1
Bush, ph-rf	1	0	0	0
Leius, 3b	2	0	1	1
West, p	0	0	0	0
Newman, 2b	1	0	1	1
Hrbek, 1b	3	0	0	1
Sorrento, ph-1b	0	0	0	0
Gagne, ss	4	0	1	0
Tapani, p	1	0	0	0
Larkin, ph	1	0	0	0
Leach, p	0	0	0	0
Pagliarulo, ph-3b	2	0	0	0
Totals	33	5	7	5

Atlanta	AB	R	H	RBI
Smith, lf	5	1	1	1
Mitchell, lf	0	0	0	0
Pendleton, 3b	4	3	2	0
Gant, cf	4	3	3	1
Justice, rf	5	2	2	5
Bream, 1b	2	0	0	0
Hunter, ph-1b	2	2	2	2
Olson, c	5	1	3	0
St. Claire, p	0	0	0	0
Lemke, 2b	4	2	2	3
Belliard, ss	4	0	2	2
Glavine, p	2	0	0	0
Mercker, p	0	0	0	0
Gregg, ph	1	0	0	0
Clancy, p	1	0	0	0
Cabrera, ph	0	0	0	0
Totals	39	14	17	14

```
Minnesota   0  0  0  0  0  3  0  1  1—5   7  1
Atlanta     0  0  0  4  1  0  6  3  x—14 17  1
```

E—Harper, Pendleton. DP—Minnesota 1. LOB—Minnesota 7, Atlanta 5. 2B—Gagne, Belliard, Pendleton. 3B—Lemke 2, Newman, Gant, Gladden. HR—Justice, Smith, Hunter. SF—None. SH—Puckett. SB—Justice, Olson. CS—Leius.

Minnesota	IP	H	R	ER	BB	K
Tapani (L)	4	6	4	4	2	4
Leach	2	2	1	1	0	1
West	0	2	4	4	2	0
Bedrosian	1	3	2	2	0	1
Willis	1	4	3	3	0	0

Atlanta	IP	H	R	ER	BB	K
Glavine (W)	5⅓	4	3	3	4	2
Mercker	⅔	0	0	0	0	0
Clancy	2	2	1	1	1	2
St. Claire	1	1	1	1	0	0

HBP—None. WP—Bedrosian. PB—None. T—2:59. A—50,878. Umpires—Denkinger, Wendelstedt, Coble, Tata, Reed, Montague.

Game 6
Saturday, October 26, at Minnesota

Atlanta	AB	R	H	RBI
Smith, dh	3	1	0	0
Pendleton, 3b	5	1	4	2
Gant, cf	5	0	0	1
Justice, rf	4	0	0	0
Bream, 1b	4	0	1	0
Mitchell, ph-lf	0	0	0	0
Hunter, lf-1b	5	0	0	0
Olson, c	5	0	0	0
Lemke, 2b	4	1	2	0
Belliard, ss	2	0	1	0
Gregg, ph	0	0	0	0
Blauser, ph-ss	2	0	1	0
Avery, p	0	0	0	0
Stanton, p	0	0	0	0
Pena, p	0	0	0	0
Leibrandt, p	0	0	0	0
Totals	39	3	9	3

Minnesota	AB	R	H	RBI
Gladden, lf	4	1	0	0
Knoblauch, 2b	5	1	1	0
Puckett, cf	4	2	3	3
Davis, dh	4	0	0	0
Mack, rf	4	0	2	1
Leius, 3b	3	0	2	0
Pagliarulo, 3b	1	0	0	0
Hrbek, 1b	4	0	0	0
Ortiz, c	2	0	0	0
Harper, ph-c	2	0	0	0
Gagne, ss	4	0	1	0
Erickson, p	0	0	0	0
Guthrie, p	0	0	0	0
Willis, p	0	0	0	0
Aguilera, p	0	0	0	0
Totals	37	4	9	4

```
Atlanta     0  0  0  0  2  0  1  0  0  0—3  9  0
Minnesota   2  0  0  0  1  0  0  0  0  1—4  9  1
```

E—Harper. DP—Atlanta 2, Minnesota 2. LOB—Atlanta 7, Minnesota 5. 2B—Mack. 3B—Puckett. HR—Pendleton, Puckett. SF—Puckett. SH—None. SB—Gladden, Puckett. CS—Mitchell.

Atlanta	IP	H	R	ER	BB	K
Avery	6	6	3	3	1	3
Stanton	2	2	0	0	0	1
Pena	2	0	0	0	0	2
Leibrandt (L)	0	1	1	1	0	0

Minnesota	IP	H	R	ER	BB	K
Erickson	6	5	3	3	2	2
Guthrie	⅓	1	0	0	1	1
Willis	2⅔	1	0	0	0	1
Aguilera (W)	2	2	0	0	0	0

HBP—Smith by Erickson. WP—Guthrie. PB—None. T—3:36. A—55,155. Umpires—Montague, Denkinger, Wendelstedt, Coble, Tata, Reed.

Game 7
Sunday, October 27, at Minnesota

Atlanta	AB	R	H	RBI
Smith, dh	4	0	2	0
Pendleton, 3b	5	0	1	0
Gant, cf	4	0	0	0
Justice, rf	3	0	1	0
Bream, 1b	4	0	0	0
Hunter, lf	4	0	1	0
Olson, c	4	0	0	0
Lemke, 2b	4	0	1	0
Belliard, ss	2	0	1	0
Blauser, ph-ss	1	0	0	0
Smoltz, p	0	0	0	0
Stanton, p	0	0	0	0
Pena, p	0	0	0	0
Totals	35	0	7	0

Minnesota	AB	R	H	RBI
Gladden, lf	5	1	3	0
Knoblauch, 2b	4	0	1	0
Puckett, cf	2	0	0	0
Hrbek, 1b	3	0	0	0
Davis, dh	4	0	1	0
Brown, ph	0	0	0	0
Larkin, ph	1	0	1	1
Harper, c	4	0	2	0
Mack, rf	4	0	1	0
Pagliarulo, 3b	3	0	0	0
Gagne, ss	2	0	0	0
Bush, ph	1	0	1	0
Newman, ss	0	0	0	0
Sorrento, ph	1	0	0	0
Leius, ss	0	0	0	0
Morris, p	0	0	0	0
Totals	34	1	10	1

```
Atlanta     0  0  0  0  0  0  0  0  0  0—0  7  0
Minnesota   0  0  0  0  0  0  0  0  0  1—1 10  0
```

E—None. DP—Atlanta 3, Minnesota 1. LOB—Atlanta 8, Minnesota 12. 2B—Gladden, Hunter, Pendleton. 3B—None. HR—None. SF—None. SH—Belliard, Knoblauch. SB—None. CS—None.

Atlanta	IP	H	R	ER	BB	K
Smoltz	7⅓	6	0	0	1	4
Stanton	⅔	2	0	0	1	0
Pena (L)	1⅓	2	1	1	3	1

Minnesota	IP	H	R	ER	BB	K
Morris (W)	10	7	0	0	2	8

HBP—Hrbek by Smoltz. WP—None. PB—Harper. T—3:23. A—55,118. Umpires—Denkinger, Wendelstedt, Coble, Tata, Reed, Montague.

COMPOSITE LINE SCORE

Minnesota	5	1	1	0	4	4	2	4	1	1	1	0	—24
Atlanta	0	2	1	5	6	1	8	4	1	0	0	1	—29

COMPOSITE BATTING AND FIELDING STATISTICS

Minnesota Twins	G	AB	R	H	TB	2B	3B	HR	RBI	BB	IBB	SO	AVG	PO	A	E	AVG
Larkin, ph	4	4	0	2	2	0	0	0	1	0	0	0	.500	0	0	0	.000
Newman, ph-3b-2b-pr-ss	4	2	0	1	3	0	1	0	1	0	0	0	.500	0	2	0	1.000
Harper, c-ph	7	21	2	8	10	2	0	0	1	2	0	2	.381	33	5	2	.950
Leius, 3b-ph-ss	7	14	2	5	8	0	0	1	2	1	0	2	.357	5	8	1	.929
Knoblauch, 2b	7	26	3	8	9	1	0	0	2	4	0	2	.308	15	14	1	.957
Pagliarulo, ph-3b	6	11	1	3	6	0	0	1	2	1	1	2	.273	3	3	0	1.000
Puckett, cf	7	24	4	6	14	0	1	2	4	5	4	7	.250	16	1	0	1.000
Bush, ph-rf	3	4	0	1	1	0	0	0	0	0	0	1	.250	0	0	0	.000
Gladden, lf	7	30	5	7	13	2	2	0	0	3	0	4	.233	25	1	1	.963
Davis, dh-ph-rf	6	18	4	4	10	0	0	2	4	2	1	3	.222	1	0	0	1.000
Ortiz, c	3	5	0	1	1	0	0	0	1	0	0	1	.200	9	0	0	1.000
Gagne, ss	7	24	1	4	8	1	0	1	3	0	0	7	.167	13	24	0	1.000
Mack, rf	6	23	0	3	4	1	0	0	1	0	0	7	.130	11	0	0	1.000
Hrbek, 1b	7	26	2	3	7	1	0	1	2	2	1	6	.115	66	8	0	1.000
Bedrosian, p	3	0	0	0	0	0	0	0	0	0	0	0	.000	0	1	0	1.000
Leach, p	2	0	0	0	0	0	0	0	0	0	0	0	.000	0	0	0	.000
Guthrie, p	4	0	0	0	0	0	0	0	0	0	0	0	.000	0	1	0	1.000
West, p	2	0	0	0	0	0	0	0	0	0	0	0	.000	0	0	0	.000
Willis, p	4	0	0	0	0	0	0	0	0	0	0	0	.000	1	0	0	1.000
Aguilera, p-ph	4	1	0	0	0	0	0	0	0	0	0	0	.000	0	0	0	.000
Erickson, p	2	1	0	0	0	0	0	0	0	0	0	1	.000	1	0	0	1.000
Tapani, p	2	1	0	0	0	0	0	0	0	0	0	0	.000	0	2	0	1.000
Brown, rf-ph-cf-pr	3	2	0	0	0	0	0	0	0	0	0	0	.000	0	0	0	.000
Morris, p	3	2	0	0	0	0	0	0	0	0	0	1	.000	2	4	0	1.000
Sorrento, ph-1b	3	2	0	0	0	0	0	0	0	1	0	2	.000	1	0	0	1.000
Totals	7	241	24	56	96	8	4	8	24	21	7	48	.232	202	75	5	.982

Atlanta Braves	G	AB	R	H	TB	2B	3B	HR	RBI	BB	IBB	SO	AVG	PO	A	E	AVG
Lemke, 2b	6	24	4	10	17	1	3	0	4	2	0	4	.417	14	19	1	.971
Belliard, ss	7	16	0	6	7	1	0	0	4	1	0	2	.375	8	21	0	1.000
Pendleton, 3b	7	30	6	11	20	3	0	2	3	3	1	1	.367	3	20	2	.920
Gant, cf	7	30	3	8	10	0	1	0	4	2	0	3	.267	19	0	0	1.000
Justice, rf	7	27	5	7	13	0	0	2	6	5	1	5	.258	21	1	1	.957
Treadway, 2b-ph	3	4	1	1	1	0	0	0	0	1	0	2	.250	1	3	1	.800
Smith, dh-lf	7	26	5	6	15	0	0	3	3	3	0	4	.231	2	0	0	1.000
Olson, c	7	27	3	6	8	2	0	0	1	5	0	4	.222	47	6	0	1.000
Hunter, lf-ph-1b	7	21	2	4	8	1	0	1	3	0	0	2	.190	6	1	0	1.000
Blauser, ph-ss	5	6	0	1	1	0	0	0	0	1	1	1	.167	3	3	0	1.000
Bream, 1b	7	24	0	3	5	2	0	0	3	0	0	4	.125	69	7	0	1.000
Leibrandt, p	2	0	0	0	0	0	0	0	0	0	0	0	.000	0	1	0	1.000
Mercker, p	2	0	0	0	0	0	0	0	0	0	0	0	.000	0	0	0	.000
Pena, p	3	0	0	0	0	0	0	0	0	0	0	0	.000	0	0	0	.000
St. Claire, p	1	0	0	0	0	0	0	0	0	0	0	0	.000	0	0	0	.000
Stanton, p	5	0	0	0	0	0	0	0	0	0	0	0	.000	0	0	0	.000
Willard, ph	1	0	0	0	0	0	0	0	0	1	0	0	.000	0	0	0	.000
Wohlers, p	3	0	0	0	0	0	0	0	0	0	0	0	.000	0	0	0	.000
Cabrera, ph-c	3	1	0	0	0	0	0	0	0	0	0	0	.000	0	0	0	.000
Clancy, p	3	1	0	0	0	0	0	0	0	0	0	1	.000	0	0	0	.000
Glavine, p	2	2	0	0	0	0	0	0	0	0	0	0	.000	0	3	0	1.000
Mitchell, lf-pr	3	2	0	0	0	0	0	0	0	0	0	0	.000	0	0	0	.000
Smoltz, p	2	2	0	0	0	0	0	0	0	0	0	1	.000	2	1	0	1.000
Avery, p	2	3	0	0	0	0	0	0	0	0	0	2	.000	1	0	0	1.000
Gregg, ph	4	3	0	0	0	0	0	0	0	0	0	2	.000	0	0	0	.000
Totals	7	249	29	63	105	10	4	8	29	26	3	39	.253	196	86	5	.983

COMPOSITE PITCHING STATISTICS

Minnesota Twins	G	GS	CG	IP	H	R	ER	HR	BB	IBB	SO	HB	WP	W	L	PCT	ERA
Morris	3	3	1	23	18	3	3	1	9	1	15	0	1	2	0	1.000	1.17
Aguilera	4	0	0	5	6	1	1	0	1	0	3	0	0	1	1	.500	1.80
Guthrie	4	0	0	4	3	1	1	0	4	1	3	0	1	0	1	.000	2.25
Leach	2	0	0	2⅓	2	1	1	0	0	0	2	0	0	0	0	.000	3.86
Tapani	2	2	0	12	13	6	6	1	2	0	7	0	1	1	1	.500	4.50
Erickson	2	2	0	10⅔	10	7	6	3	4	0	5	1	0	0	0	.000	5.06
Willis	4	0	0	7	6	4	4	2	2	1	2	0	0	0	0	.000	5.14
Bedrosian	3	0	0	3⅓	3	2	2	0	0	0	2	0	1	0	0	.000	5.40
West	2	0	0	*0	2	4	4	1	4	0	0	0	0	0	0	.000	∞
Totals	7	7	1	87⅓	63	29	28	8	26	3	39	1	3	4	3	.571	3.74

*Pitched to two batters in fifth inning of third game and four batters in seventh inning of fifth game.
Shutout—Morris. Saves—Aguilera 2.

Atlanta Braves	G	GS	CG	IP	H	R	ER	HR	BB	IBB	SO	HB	WP	W	L	PCT	ERA
Stanton	5	0	0	7⅓	5	0	0	0	2	2	7	0	0	1	0	1.000	0.00
Wohlers	3	0	0	1⅔	2	0	0	0	2	0	1	0	0	0	0	.000	0.00
Mercker	2	0	0	1	0	0	0	0	0	1	0	0	0	0	0	.000	0.00
Smoltz	2	2	0	14⅓	13	2	2	1	1	0	11	1	0	0	0	.000	1.26
Glavine	2	2	1	13⅓	8	6	4	2	7	0	8	0	0	1	1	.500	2.70
Pena	3	0	0	5⅓	6	2	2	1	3	3	7	0	0	0	1	.000	3.38
Avery	2	2	0	13	10	6	5	1	1	0	8	0	0	0	0	.000	3.46
Clancy	3	0	0	4⅓	3	2	2	1	4	2	2	0	0	1	0	1.000	4.15
St. Claire	1	0	0	1	1	1	1	0	0	0	0	0	0	0	0	.000	9.00
Leibrandt	2	1	0	4	8	5	5	2	1	0	3	0	0	0	2	.000	11.25
Totals	7	7	1	65⅓	56	24	21	8	21	7	48	1	0	3	4	.429	2.89

No shutouts or saves.

Braves versus Pittsburgh Pirates
National League Championship Series

1992

For the third straight year, Pittsburgh was back in the National League Championship Series in 1992, and for the second consecutive season, the Braves provided the competition for Jim Leyland's team.

After two failed attempts, it looked as if the Pirates were finally going to the World Series when they led the Braves, 2–0, entering the bottom of the ninth inning of Game 7. Pittsburgh ace Doug Drabek had baffled the Braves over the first eight innings, allowing just five hits and one walk. But once again, the Braves provided another dose of the enchantment that made the early 1990s a magical period in the club's history.

With an Atlanta–Fulton County Stadium crowd of 51,975 watching as time stood still in the most breathtaking moment in Braves and NLCS history, pinch hitter Francisco Cabrera lined a 2–1 pitch to left, driving in David Justice and a sliding Sid Bream to turn a 2–1 defeat into a 3–2 victory. For the first time in postseason history, a team went from losing to winning on the final pitch of the decisive game. The Braves literally stole the playoffs from Pittsburgh and were off to the World Series again.

The Braves and Pirates of 1992 naturally were quite simi-lar to the teams that met in the previous year's NLCS, though Leyland's team had gone through more changes than had Bobby Cox's club.

Pittsburgh no longer had John Smiley in its starting rotation, perhaps a benefit considering how the Braves pounded the left-hander in the previous NLCS. Another left-hander, Danny Jackson, had taken his place. Additionally, Leyland's staff was bolstered by the addition of Tim Wakefield, a rookie who was 8–1 down the stretch, primarily with a knuckleball.

Offensively, the Pirates continued to be led by Barry Bonds, who would be named the league's MVP for the second time in three seasons. But Bobby Bonilla, a key cog in the 1991 attack, had departed via free agency, forcing Leyland to rely even more on crafty maneuvering of his troops.

The Braves had the use of center fielder and leadoff batter Otis Nixon, who sat out the 1991 playoffs on suspension. However, they did not have catcher Greg Olson, who suffered a broken leg and mangled ankle September 18 in a collision at home plate. Damon Berryhill, who platooned with Olson during the season, took over full-time in the NLCS. Jeff Blauser had taken over the starting shortstop job from Rafael Belliard, and Jeff Reardon had replaced Alejandro Pena as the late-season "hired closer."

The Braves got off to an efficient start in Game 1 by beating

With Greg Olson out of action with a broken leg, Damon Berryhill became the Braves' regular catcher in the post-season.

Ron Gant hit a grand slam in Game 2 and added another home run in Game 3.

the Pirates, 5–1, behind the pitching of John Smoltz. In eight innings, Smoltz allowed just four hits, and the only one that hurt him was a leadoff home run by Jose Lind in the eighth. By that time, though, the Braves had built a 5–0 lead before another frenzied tomahawk-chopping crowd at Atlanta–Fulton County Stadium.

In the second inning against Drabek, the Braves got on the board when Mark Lemke singled with two outs to drive in Sid Bream, who had singled earlier in the inning. Atlanta got two more runs in the fourth to go up, 3–0. Blauser homered in the fifth to make it 4–0, and the Braves completed their scoring in the seventh when Nixon led off with an infield single, stole second, and scored on a single by Terry Pendleton.

When Lind finally homered in the eighth, he broke Smoltz's personal streaks of 16 consecutive scoreless innings in the NLCS and 14⅓ straight in postseason play. It also was the first run Pittsburgh had scored in the last 29 innings of NLCS play, dating to the fifth inning of Game 5 in 1991. The performance lowered Smoltz's career postseason ERA to 1.43.

Game 2 was reminiscent of Game 5 of the 1991 World Series in which Atlanta beat the Twins, 14–5. With Steve Avery starting, the Braves KOed Jackson in the second inning and went on to a 13–5 rout of the Pirates behind Gant's fifth-inning grand slam. It was the fourth grand slam in NLCS history and the first of Gant's career.

Until the Pirates got to Avery for four runs in the seventh, he'd strung together a League Championship record 22⅓ consecutive scoreless innings over two years.

With Atlanta hitting .319 to Pittsburgh's .188 in the first two games, it appeared the Braves might have an easy time with the Pirates. But nothing could have been further from the truth. The biggest reason for the Braves' difficulties turned out to be Wakefield, who was an infielder until mid-1989 and opened the '92 season at Buffalo.

In Game 3, the 26-year-old knuckleball pitcher limited the Braves to five hits in the game of his life, a 3–2 victory before 56,610 fans at Pittsburgh's Three Rivers Stadium. Tom Glavine pitched well for Atlanta, too, but he and the Braves' hitters were overmatched this time.

The game was scoreless through three innings until Bream, a former Pirate, hit a solo homer with two outs in the fourth. Pittsburgh answered in the fifth with a solo home run by Don Slaught. And in the sixth, the Pirates took a 2–1 lead on doubles by Andy Van Slyke and Jeff King.

With two outs in the seventh, Gant hit a solo home run to tie the game, but the Pirates came right back in the bottom of the inning with the game-winning score. With one out, Mike Stanton relieved Glavine and gave up a sacrifice fly to Van Slyke that decided the game.

Glavine fell to 0–3 in NLCS play, and Wakefield became the first rookie to start and complete an NLCS game since Philadelphia's Charles Hudson in 1983.

In Game 4, Nixon, perhaps making up for time lost in 1991, tied a playoff record with four hits to lead the Braves to a 6–4 victory and a 3–1 edge in games. Smoltz, not as dominant as in his past playoff starts, still was good enough to earn his second victory of the series.

Smoltz and Nixon delivered RBI-singles in the second in-

John Smoltz won Games 1 and 4 and pitched well in Game 7 to earn MVP honors in the 1992 National League Championship Series.

ning to get the Braves on the board first. But Pittsburgh came right back with two in the bottom of the inning and another in the third to forge a 3–2 lead.

Atlanta got two in the fifth on an RBI single by Justice and a throwing error by King, then scored two more in the sixth for a 6–3 advantage. With two outs, Smoltz started a rally with a single and stole second. He then scored what proved to be the winning run when Nixon doubled. Blauser singled home Nixon for Atlanta's final run.

Nifty relief work by Stanton and Reardon gave the Braves a very commanding 3–1 lead in the series. Smoltz raised his career NLCS record to 4–0, tying Steve Carlton's record for wins. Most importantly, Atlanta pitchers continued to give Bonds fits, striking him out twice to make him 1-for-11 in the playoffs.

Facing elimination as well as humiliation against their home fans, the Pirates pulled themselves together to win Game 5, 7–1, routing Avery in the process. Bob Walk pitched a complete-game three-hitter for Pittsburgh, while Avery didn't even survive the first inning in the shortest outing of his career. Walk had only one complete game during the regular season and hadn't pitched a three-hitter since 1980.

If there ever were any thoughts of the Braves making short order of the Pirates, they were quashed in Game 6. The scene returned to Atlanta, but there wasn't much for the 51,975 fans to chop about during Pittsburgh's 13–4 romp over Glavine.

Wakefield continued to stump Braves hitters. Though he gave up nine hits and four walks in his second complete game of the playoffs, he had a 13–2 lead entering the ninth when he gave up a meaningless two-run homer to Justice.

All of a sudden, the Braves were in trouble, and Pittsburgh was trying to become the first team in NLCS history to win the pennant after losing three of the first four games.

If the Braves' situation was beginning to look somewhat insecure after Game 6, it was appearing downright catastrophic as Game 7 progressed. The capacity crowd at Atlanta–Fulton County Stadium didn't know whether to chop or drop.

Cox had his big-game pitcher going, but Smoltz was nicked for a run in the first. Alex Cole led off with a walk and Van Slyke delivered a one-out double. Bonds was intentionally passed to load the bases, and a sacrifice fly by Orlando

Merced made it 1–0. Smoltz escaped further damage when King popped foul to Berryhill.

Pittsburgh went ahead, 2–0, in the sixth on a leadoff double by Bell and a single by Van Slyke. The Pirates had the bases loaded in the seventh, but Cox brought in Avery, who got the final out by inducing Van Slyke to fly to center. Pittsburgh tried again to stretch its lead in the eighth. Merced, who'd reached on a fielder's choice, attempted to score on a one-out double by King but was cut down at the plate on a throw from Justice to Berryhill.

It didn't seem to matter, though, when Drabek retired the Braves in the eighth without even allowing a fair ball.

After leading in games, 3–1, the Braves were one inning away from blowing the pennant. However, the team that had provided its fans so many unexpected thrills over the previous two seasons still had its biggest surprise left.

Pendleton started the rally with a leadoff double. Then came the key play of the inning. Justice grounded to second, but Lind, who'd made only six errors all year, couldn't handle the routine play. Apparently rattled, Drabek, who'd issued only one walk all night, passed Bream on four pitches to load the bases.

Leyland pulled his starting pitcher in favor of his ace reliever, Stan Belinda. Gant's sacrifice fly to left scored Pendleton to make it 2–1 with one out. Berryhill then drew a walk to reload the bases. Hunter pinch-hit for Belliard and popped to second. The Braves were down to their last out, and with Reardon, who'd worked the ninth, due to hit, Cox called on Cabrera, who'd spent most of the season in the minors.

On a 2–1 pitch, Cabrera lashed a clean single to left, easily scoring Justice with the tying run. The gimpy Bream plodded around third and raced for the plate, trying to outrun the throw from Bonds in left. The runner and the ball ar-

After being suspended for the 1991 playoffs, Otis Nixon came back the next year to have a productive NLCS against Pittsburgh.

When Francisco Cabrera delivered a two-out, two-run single in the bottom of the ninth inning of Game 7, Sid Bream slid past Mike LaValliere to score the winning run in the most breath-taking moment in Braves history.

rived at virtually the same time, but the throw was slightly to the first base side of the plate. As Pittsburgh catcher Mike Lavalliere swiped his tag across the plate, Bream slid across its third base corner, barely avoiding the mitt.

Pandemonium immediately broke out. The ecstatic Braves piled on top of Bream, while many of the Pirates were frozen in shock at their positions. The fans, of course, chopped and chanted well into the wee hours.

Pinch-hitter Francisco Cabrera sent the Braves to the World Series for the second straight year with his clutch hit off the Pirates' Stan Belinda in Game 7.

Game 1
Tuesday, October 6, at Atlanta

Pittsburgh	AB	R	H	RBI
Cole, rf	4	0	1	0
Bell, ss	3	0	0	0
Van Slyke, cf	4	0	1	0
Bonds, lf	3	0	0	0
King, 3b	4	0	1	0
Merced, 1b	3	0	0	0
LaValliere, c	3	0	0	0
Lind, 2b	3	1	2	1
Drabek, p	2	0	0	0
Patterson, p	0	0	0	0
Neagle, p	0	0	0	0
Varsho, ph	1	0	0	0
Cox, p	0	0	0	0
Totals	**30**	**1**	**5**	**1**

Atlanta	AB	R	H	RBI
Nixon, cf	5	1	1	0
Blauser, ss	3	1	1	1
Belliard, pr-ss	0	0	0	0
Pendleton, 3b	4	0	1	1
Justice, rf	3	1	1	0
Bream, 1b	4	2	2	1
Gant, lf	3	0	0	0
Berryhill, c	3	0	0	0
Lemke, 2b	3	0	2	1
Smoltz, p	3	0	0	0
L. Smith, ph	1	0	0	0
Stanton, p	0	0	0	0
Totals	**32**	**5**	**8**	**4**

Pittsburgh	0	0	0	0	0	0	1	0—1	5	1
Atlanta	0	1	0	2	1	0	1	0	x—5	8	0

E—Merced. DP—Atlanta 1. LOB—Pittsburgh 5, Atlanta 8. 2B—King, Justice, Bream. 3B—None. HR—Blauser, Lind. SF—None. SH—Gant. SB—Gant, Nixon. CS—Merced.

Pittsburgh	IP	H	R	ER	BB	K
Drabek (L)	4⅔	5	4	3	2	4
Patterson	1⅓	3	1	1	1	1
Neagle	1	0	0	0	0	0
Cox	1	0	0	0	1	1

Atlanta	IP	H	R	ER	BB	K
Smoltz (W)	8	4	1	1	3	6
Stanton	1	1	0	0	0	2

HBP—None. WP—None. T—3:00. A—51,971. Umpires—McSherry, Marsh, Rippley, Darling, Davis, Montague.

Game 2
Wednesday, October 7, at Atlanta

Pittsburgh	AB	R	H	RBI
Redus, 1b	3	0	0	0
Merced, ph, 1b	1	0	0	0
Bell, ss	4	0	1	0
Van Slyke, cf	5	0	0	0
Bonds, lf	3	2	1	0
King, 3b	4	0	0	0
McClendon, rf	3	1	2	1
Cole, ph-rf	0	0	0	0
Slaught, c	3	1	1	1
Lind, 2b	4	1	1	2
Belinda, p	0	0	0	0
Jackson, p	0	0	0	0
Mason, p	0	0	0	0
Wehner, ph	1	0	0	0
Tomlin, p	0	0	0	0
Espy, ph	1	0	1	0
Neagle, p	0	0	0	0
Patterson, p	0	0	0	0
Garcia, 2b	1	0	0	0
Totals	**34**	**5**	**7**	**4**

Atlanta	AB	R	H	RBI
Nixon, cf	4	2	1	0
Blauser, ss	2	1	1	1
Belliard, ss	1	1	0	0
Pendleton, 3b	5	1	2	2
Justice, rf	3	1	1	2
Hunter, 1b	2	1	1	0
L. Smith, ph	1	0	0	0
Bream, 1b	1	0	0	0
Gant, lf	4	3	2	4
Reardon, p	0	0	0	0
Berryhill, c	5	1	2	1
Lemke, 2b	5	1	3	1
Avery, p	2	0	1	1
Freeman, p	0	0	0	0
Stanton, p	1	1	1	1
Wohlers, p	0	0	0	0
Sanders, ph-lf	1	0	0	0
Totals	**37**	**13**	**14**	**13**

Pittsburgh	0	0	0	0	0	0	4	1	0—5	7	0
Atlanta	0	4	0	0	4	0	5	0	x—13	14	0

E—None. LOB—Pittsburgh 7, Atlanta 9. 2B—McClendon, Pendleton, Stanton. 3B—Lind, Blauser. HR—Gant. SF—Avery. SH—None. SB—Nixon. CS—None.

Pittsburgh	IP	H	R	ER	BB	K
Jackson (L)	1⅓	4	4	4	2	0
Mason	⅓	0	0	0	0	0
Walk	2⅔	3	4	4	2	4
Tomlin	1⅓	2	0	0	1	0
Neagle	⅔	4	5	5	3	0
Patterson	⅓	0	0	0	0	0
Belinda	1	1	0	0	0	2

Atlanta	IP	H	R	ER	BB	K
Avery (W)	6⅓	6	4	4	2	3
Freeman	⅓	1	0	0	0	1
Stanton	⅓	0	1	0	1	0
Wohlers	1	0	0	0	1	0
Reardon	1	0	0	0	1	0

WP—Avery. PB—Berryhill. T—3:20. A—51,975. Umpires—Marsh, Rippley, Darling, Davis, Montague, McSherry.

Game 3
Friday, October 9, at Pittsburgh

Atlanta	AB	R	H	RBI
Nixon, cf	3	0	1	0
Blauser, ss	4	0	0	0
Pendleton, 3b	4	0	0	0
Justice, rf	4	0	1	0
Bream, 1b	4	1	1	1
Gant, lf	3	1	1	1
Berryhill, c	3	0	0	0
Lemke, 2b	3	0	1	0
Glavine, p	2	0	0	0
Stanton, p	0	0	0	0
L. Smith, ph	1	0	0	0
Wohlers, p	0	0	0	0
Totals	**31**	**2**	**5**	**2**

Pittsburgh	AB	R	H	RBI
Redus, 1b	3	1	3	0
Bell, ss	4	0	1	0
Van Slyke, cf	3	1	1	1
Bonds, lf	3	0	0	0
King, 3b	4	0	1	1
McClendon, rf	2	0	0	0
Espy, ph-rf	1	0	1	0
Slaught, c	3	1	1	1
Lind, 2b	4	0	0	0
Wakefield, p	3	0	0	0
Totals	**30**	**3**	**8**	**3**

Atlanta	0	0	0	1	0	0	1	0	0—2	5	0
Pittsburgh	0	0	0	0	1	1	1	0	x—3	8	1

E—Lind. DP—Atlanta 1, Pittsburgh 2. LOB—Atlanta 3, Pittsburgh 8. 2B—Nixon, Lemke, Redus, Bell, Van Slyke, King. 3B—Redus. HR—Bream, Slaught, Gant. SF—Van Slyke. SH—None. SB—None. CS—None.

Atlanta	IP	H	R	ER	BB	K
Glavine (L)	6⅓	7	3	3	3	2
Stanton	⅔	0	0	0	0	0
Wohlers	1	1	0	0	0	0

Pittsburgh	IP	H	R	ER	BB	K
Wakefield (W)	9	5	2	2	1	3

HBP—Bonds by Glavine. T—2:37. A—56,610. Umpires—Rippley, Darling, Davis, Montague, McSherry, Marsh.

Game 4
Saturday, October 10, at Pittsburgh

Atlanta	AB	R	H	RBI
Nixon, cf	5	2	4	2
Blauser, ss	3	1	2	1
Belliard, ss	1	0	0	0
Pendleton, 3b	5	0	0	0
Justice, rf	4	0	1	1
Bream, 1b	2	0	0	0
Hunter, ph-1b	2	0	0	0
Gant, lf	4	1	1	0
Stanton, p	0	0	0	0
Reardon, p	0	0	0	0
Berryhill, c	3	0	1	0
Lemke, 2b	2	1	0	0
Smoltz, p	3	1	2	1
Sanders, lf	1	0	0	0
Totals	35	6	11	5

Pittsburgh	AB	R	H	RBI
Cole, rf	4	1	1	1
Bell, ss	5	0	0	0
Van Slyke, cf	4	0	2	1
Bonds, lf	2	0	0	0
King, 3b	4	1	0	0
Merced, 1b	3	0	1	1
Redus, ph-1b	1	0	0	0
LaValliere, c	3	1	1	0
Slaught, ph-c	1	0	0	0
Lind, 2b	3	1	1	0
Drabek, p	1	0	0	0
Tomlin, p	0	0	0	0
Cox, p	0	0	0	0
Wehner, ph	1	0	0	0
Mason, p	0	0	0	0
Espy, ph	1	0	0	0
Totals	33	4	6	3

```
Atlanta      0 2 0 0 2 2 0 0 0—6 11 1
Pittsburgh   0 2 1 0 0 0 1 0 0—4  6 1
```

E—Blauser, King. DP—Pittsburgh 3. LOB—Atlanta 7, Pittsburgh 7. 2B—Nixon, Van Slyke, Merced. 3B—Van Slyke. HR—None. SF—None. SH—Blauser. SB—Nixon, Smoltz. CS—None.

Atlanta	IP	H	R	ER	BB	K
Smoltz (W)	6⅓	6	4	3	5	9
Stanton	1⅔	0	0	0	0	3
Reardon (S)	1	0	0	0	0	2

Pittsburgh	IP	H	R	ER	BB	K
Drabek (L)	4⅓	7	4	3	2	1
Tomlin	1⅓	3	2	2	0	0
Cox	⅓	1	0	0	0	0
Mason	3	0	0	0	2	1

HBP—None. WP—None. T—3:10. A—57,164. Umpires—Darling, Davis, Montague, McSherry, Marsh, Rippley.

Game 5
Sunday, October 11, at Pittsburgh

Atlanta	AB	R	H	RBI
Nixon, cf	4	0	0	0
Blauser, ss	3	0	0	1
Pendleton, 3b	4	0	1	0
Justice, rf	2	0	0	0
Bream, 1b	4	0	1	0
Gant, lf	3	0	0	0
Berryhill, c	4	0	0	0
Lemke, 2b	3	0	0	0
Avery, p	0	0	0	0
P. Smith, p	1	0	0	0
Treadway, ph	1	0	0	0
Leibrandt, p	0	0	0	0
Freeman, p	0	0	0	0
L. Smith, ph	1	1	1	0
Mercker, p	0	0	0	0
Totals	30	1	3	1

Pittsburgh	AB	R	H	RBI
Redus, 1b	4	1	2	1
Bell, ss	5	1	1	1
Van Slyke, cf	5	0	1	0
Bonds, lf	5	2	2	1
King, 3b	4	2	3	1
McClendon, rf	3	0	3	2
Slaught, c	1	1	1	1
Lind, 2b	4	0	0	0
Walk, p	4	0	0	0
Totals	35	7	13	7

```
Atlanta      0 0 0 0 0 0 0 1 0—1  3 0
Pittsburgh   4 0 1 0 0 1 1 0 x—7 13 0
```

E—None. DP—None. LOB—Atlanta 7, Pittsburgh 9. 2B—Bream, Redus 2, Bonds, King, McClendon. 3B—L. Smith. HR—None. SF—None. SH—None. SB—Bonds. CS—King.

Atlanta	IP	H	R	ER	BB	K
Avery (L)	⅓	5	4	4	0	0
P. Smith	3⅔	2	1	1	2	3
Leibrandt	1⅔	2	1	1	1	0
Freeman	1⅔	3	1	1	0	0
Mercker	1	1	0	0	1	0

Pittsburgh	IP	H	R	ER	BB	K
Walk (W)	9	3	1	1	5	2

HBP—None. WP—None. T—2:52. A—52,929. Umpires—Davis, Montague, McSherry, Marsh, Rippley, Darling.

Game 6
Tuesday, October 13, at Atlanta

Pittsburgh	AB	R	H	RBI
Redus, 1b	5	2	2	2
Bell, ss	4	0	1	1
Van Slyke, cf	4	0	1	1
Bonds, lf	4	1	2	1
King, 3b	5	1	1	0
McClendon, rf	3	3	3	1
Varsho, ph-rf	1	0	1	0
Slaught, c	4	2	1	2
Lind, 2b	5	2	1	2
Wakefield, p	3	1	0	0
Totals	38	13	13	12

Atlanta	AB	R	H	RBI
Nixon, cf	3	0	0	0
Mercker, p	0	0	0	0
Wohlers, p	0	0	0	0
Cabrera, ph	1	0	0	0
Blauser, ss	5	0	1	0
Pendleton, 3b	4	0	2	0
Treadway, 2b	1	1	1	0
Justice, rf	5	2	3	3
Bream, 1b	4	1	1	0
Gant, lf	3	0	0	0
Berryhill, c	3	0	0	0
Lopez, c	1	0	0	0
Lemke, 2b-3b	3	0	0	0
Glavine, p	0	0	0	0
Leibrandt, p	1	0	0	0
L. Smith, ph	1	0	1	1
Freeman, p	0	0	0	0
Sanders, ph-cf	2	0	0	0
Totals	37	4	9	4

```
Pittsburgh   0 8 0 0 4 1 0 0 0—13 13 1
Atlanta      0 0 0 1 0 0 1 0 2— 4  9 1
```

E—Bell, Blauser. DP—Atlanta 1. LOB—Pittsburgh 5, Atlanta 10. 2B—Redus, Slaught, Lind. 3B—None. HR—Bonds, Bell, McClendon, Justice 2. SF—None. SH—Wakefield 2. SB—None. CS—None.

Pittsburgh	IP	H	R	ER	BB	K
Wakefield (W)	9	9	4	4	4	4

Atlanta	IP	H	R	ER	BB	K
Glavine (L)	1	6	8	7	0	0
Leibrandt	3	2	0	0	2	3
Freeman	2	4	5	5	2	0
Mercker	2	0	0	0	0	1
Wohlers	1	1	0	0	0	2

HBP—Bell by Glavine. WP—Wakefield. PB—Slaught 2. T—2:50. A—51,975. Umpires—Montague, McSherry, Marsh, Rippley, Darling, Davis.

Game 7
Wednesday, October 14, at Atlanta

Pittsburgh	AB	R	H	RBI
Cole, rf	2	1	0	0
McClendon ph-rf	0	0	0	0
Espy, pr-rf	0	0	0	0
Bell, ss	4	1	1	0
Van Slyke, cf	4	0	2	1
Bonds, lf	3	0	1	0
Merced, 1b	3	0	0	1
King, 3b	4	0	1	0
LaValliere, c	4	0	1	0
Lind, 2b	4	0	1	0
Drabek, p	3	0	0	0
Belinda, p	0	0	0	0
Totals	31	2	7	2

Atlanta	AB	R	H	RBI
Nixon, cf	4	0	1	0
Blauser, ss	4	0	0	0
Pendleton, 3b	4	1	1	0
Justice, rf	4	1	0	0
Bream, 1b	3	1	1	0
Gant, lf	2	0	0	1
Berryhill, c	3	0	1	0
Lemke, 2b	2	0	1	0
L. Smith, ph	1	0	0	0
Belliard, 2b	0	0	0	0
Hunter, ph	1	0	0	0
Smoltz, p	1	0	0	0
Treadway, ph	1	0	1	0
Stanton, p	0	0	0	0
P. Smith, p	0	0	0	0
Avery, p	0	0	0	0
Sanders, ph	1	0	0	0
Reardon, p	0	0	0	0
Cabrera, ph	1	0	1	2
Totals	32	3	7	3

```
Pittsburgh   1 0 0 0 0 1 0 0 0—2 7 1
Atlanta      0 0 0 0 0 0 0 0 3—3 7 0
```

E—Lind. DP—Pittsburgh 1. LOB—Pittsburgh 9, Atlanta 7. 2B—Bell, Van Slyke, King, Lind, Pendleton, Bream, Berryhill. 3B—None. HR—None. SF—Merced, Gant. SH—Drabek. SB—Nixon. CS—None.

Pittsburgh	IP	H	R	ER	BB	K
Drabek (L)	8	6	3	1	2	5
Belinda	⅔	1	0	0	1	0

Atlanta	IP	H	R	ER	BB	K
Smoltz	6	4	2	2	2	4
Stanton	⅔	1	0	0	1	0
P. Smith	0	0	0	0	1	0
Avery	1⅓	2	0	0	0	0
Reardon (W)	1	0	0	0	1	1

HBP—None. WP—Reardon. T—3:22. A—51,975. Umpires—McSherry, Marsh, Rippley, Darling, Davis, Montague.

COMPOSITE BATTING STATISTICS

Atlanta Braves	AVG	G	AB	R	H	2B	3B	HR	RB	BB	SO	SB
Steve Avery, p	.000	3	2	0	0	0	0	0	1	0	1	0
R. Belliard, ss-3,2b-1	.000	4	2	1	0	0	0	0	0	1	0	0
Damon Berryhill, c	.167	7	24	1	4	1	0	0	1	3	2	0
Jeff Blauser, ss	.208	7	24	3	5	0	1	1	4	3	2	0
Sid Bream, 1b	.273	7	22	5	6	3	0	1	2	3	0	0
Francisco Cabrera, ph	.500	2	2	0	1	0	0	0	2	0	0	0
Marvin Freeman, p	.000	3	0	0	0	0	0	0	0	0	0	0
Ron Gant, of	.182	7	22	5	4	0	0	2	6	4	4	1
Tom Glavine, p	.000	2	2	0	0	0	0	0	0	0	0	0
Brian Hunter, 1b-2	.200	3	5	1	1	0	0	0	0	0	1	0
David Justice, of	.280	7	25	5	7	1	0	2	6	6	2	0
Charlie Leibrandt, p	.000	2	1	0	0	0	0	0	0	0	1	0
Mark Lemke, 2b-7,3b-1	.333	7	21	2	7	1	0	0	2	5	3	0
Javier Lopez, c	.000	1	1	0	0	0	0	0	0	0	0	0
Kent Mercker, p	.000	2	0	0	0	0	0	0	0	0	0	0
Otis Nixon, of	.286	7	28	5	8	2	0	0	2	4	4	3
Terry Pendleton, 3b	.233	7	30	2	7	2	0	0	3	0	2	0
Jeff Reardon, p	.000	3	0	0	0	0	0	0	0	0	0	0
Deion Sanders, of-3	.000	4	5	0	0	0	0	0	0	0	3	0
Lonnie Smith, ph	.333	6	6	1	2	0	1	0	1	0	0	0
Pete Smith, p	.000	2	1	0	0	0	0	0	0	0	0	0
John Smoltz, p	.286	3	7	1	2	0	0	0	1	0	2	1
Mike Stanton, p	1.000	5	1	1	1	1	0	0	1	0	0	0
Jeff Treadway, 2b-1	.667	3	3	1	2	0	0	0	0	0	1	0
Mark Wohlers, p	.000	3	0	0	0	0	0	0	0	0	0	0
Totals	.244	7	234	34	57	11	2	6	32	29	28	5

Pittsburgh Pirates	AVG	G	AB	R	H	2B	3B	HR	RB	BB	SO	SB
Stan Belinda, p	.000	2	0	0	0	0	0	0	0	0	0	0
Jay Bell, ss	.172	7	29	3	5	2	0	1	4	3	4	0
Barry Bonds, of	.261	7	23	5	6	1	0	1	2	6	4	1
Alex Cole, of	.200	4	10	2	2	0	0	0	1	3	2	0
Danny Cox, p	.000	2	0	0	0	0	0	0	0	0	0	0
Doug Drabek, p	.000	3	6	0	0	0	0	0	0	1	4	0
Cecil Espy, of-2	.667	4	3	0	2	0	0	0	0	0	1	0
Carlos Garcia, 2b	.000	1	1	0	0	0	0	0	0	0	0	0
Danny Jackson, p	.000	1	0	0	0	0	0	0	0	0	0	0
Jeff King, 3b	.241	7	29	4	7	4	0	0	2	0	1	0
Mike LaValliere, c	.200	3	10	1	2	0	0	0	0	0	3	0
Jose Lind, 2b	.222	7	27	5	6	2	1	1	5	1	4	0
Roger Mason, p	.000	2	0	0	0	0	0	0	0	0	0	0
Lloyd McClendon, of	.727	5	11	4	8	2	0	1	4	4	1	0
Orlando Merced, 1b	.100	4	10	0	1	1	0	0	2	2	4	0
Denny Neagle, p	.000	2	0	0	0	0	0	0	0	0	0	0
Bob Patterson, p	.000	2	0	0	0	0	0	0	0	0	0	0
Gary Redus, 1b	.438	5	16	4	7	4	1	0	3	2	3	0
Don Slaught, c	.333	5	12	5	4	1	0	1	5	6	3	0
Randy Tomlin, p	.000	2	0	0	0	0	0	0	0	0	0	0
Andy Van Slyke, of	.276	7	29	1	8	3	1	0	4	1	5	0
Gary Varsho, of-1	.500	2	2	0	1	0	0	0	0	0	0	0
Tim Wakefield, p	.000	2	6	1	0	0	0	0	0	0	1	0
Bob Walk, p	.000	2	5	0	0	0	0	0	0	0	1	0
John Wehner, ph	.000	2	2	0	0	0	0	0	0	0	2	0
Totals	.255	7	231	35	59	20	3	5	32	29	42	1

COMPOSITE PITCHING STATISTICS

Atlanta Braves	W	L	ERA	G	GS	CG	SV	SHO	IP	H	ER	BB	SO
Steve Avery	1	1	9.00	3	2	0	0	0	8.0	13	8	2	3
Marvin Freeman	0	0	14.73	3	0	0	0	0	3⅔	8	6	2	1
Tom Glavine	0	2	12.27	2	2	0	0	0	7⅓	13	10	3	2
Charlie Leibrandt	0	0	1.93	2	0	0	0	0	4⅔	4	1	3	3
Kent Mercker	0	0	0.00	2	0	0	0	0	3.0	1	0	1	1
Jeff Reardon	1	0	0.00	3	0	0	1	0	3.0	0	0	2	3
Pete Smith	0	0	2.45	2	0	0	0	0	3⅔	2	1	3	3
John Smoltz	2	0	2.66	3	3	0	0	0	20⅓	14	6	10	19
Mike Stanton	0	0	0.00	5	0	0	0	0	4⅓	2	0	2	5
Mark Wohlers	0	0	0.00	3	0	0	0	0	3.0	2	0	1	2
Totals	4	3	4.72	28	7	0	1	0	61.0	59	32	29	42

Pittsburgh Pirates	W	L	ERA	G	GS	CG	SV	SHO	IP	H	ER	BB	SO
Stan Belinda	0	0	0.00	2	0	0	0	0	1⅓	2	0	0	2
Danny Cox	0	0	0.00	2	0	0	0	0	1⅓	1	0	1	1
Doug Drabek	0	3	3.71	3	3	0	0	0	17.0	18	7	7	10
Danny Jackson	0	1	21.60	1	1	0	0	0	1⅔	4	4	2	0
Roger Mason	0	0	0.00	2	0	0	0	0	3⅓	0	0	2	1
Denny Neagle	0	0	27.00	2	0	0	0	0	1⅓	4	5	3	0
Bob Patterson	0	0	5.40	2	0	0	0	0	1⅔	3	1	1	1
Randy Tomlin	0	0	6.75	2	0	0	0	0	2⅔	5	2	1	0
Tim Wakefield	2	0	3.00	2	2	2	0	0	18.0	14	6	5	7
Bob Walk	1	0	3.86	2	1	1	0	0	11⅔	6	5	7	6
Totals	3	4	4.45	20	7	3	0	0	60⅔	57	30	29	28

Braves versus Toronto Blue Jays World Series

1992

When Bobby Cox returned to the downtrodden Braves as general manager after the 1985 season, he left a job as manager of one of baseball's finest franchises, one filled with talent and promise, the Toronto Blue Jays. Just seven years later, Cox had helped build the Braves into the same type of organization and ironically found himself back in the dugout managing against the Blue Jays in the World Series.

Cox's challenge was to win the Braves' first Series championship since 1957. His counterpart, Toronto manager Cito Gaston, himself a former Braves outfielder, was attempting to lead his club to the first Series championship by a Canadian-based team.

Toronto's starting rotation included a familiar arm to the Braves—right-hander Jack Morris, who'd been their nemesis in the '91 Series with Minnesota. Morris used free agency to sign with the Blue Jays and proceeded to tie for the American League lead with 21 wins. Toronto's staff also included Juan Guzman, fourth in the AL with a 2.64 ERA, hard-throwing David Cone, who'd been obtained from the Mets late in the season, and Tom Henke, one of the game's best relievers.

Offensively, the Jays featured the power of outfielder/first baseman Joe Carter, who ranked second in the AL with 119 RBIs and fourth with 34 home runs. Outfielder Dave Winfield, though 41, was still a threat, as shown by his 26 homers and 108 RBIs.

Second baseman Roberto Alomar was coming off an excellent season in which he ranked among the league leaders in numerous departments, including runs (3rd), on-base percentage (4th), and stolen bases (5th). Speedy Devon White was one of the game's best defensive center fielders and represented a constant threat on the basepaths.

It proved to be an evenly matched Series. Yet in spite of outscoring Toronto, 20–16, the Braves dropped four one-run games and the Series in six games.

Game One

No one did more to keep the Braves from winning the 1991 World Series than Morris, who was 2–0 with a 1.17 ERA to earn MVP honors. But Tom Glavine and Damon Berryhill combined in Game 1 to make sure the 37-year-old right-hander wouldn't ruin Atlanta's championship aspirations in 1992.

Before a crowd of 51,763 at Atlanta–Fulton County Stadium, Glavine pitched an efficient four-hitter and Berryhill smacked a three-run homer in the sixth inning to propel the Braves to a 3–1 victory.

The Glavine-Morris matchup was the first time 20-game winners had faced each other in Game 1 since the Mets' Tom Seaver and Baltimore's Mike Cuellar met in 1969. And both Glavine and Morris pitched well. In fact, each made only one bad pitch. Fortunately for the Braves, Morris's came with two runners on base.

Glavine gave up only two harmless singles in the first three innings, but Carter led off the fourth with a home run to left-center to put the Blue Jays on top.

Morris was even better. Entering the sixth, he was mowing down the Braves just as effectively as he'd done the previous year for Minnesota. Through five innings, he'd allowed just a leadoff single by Otis Nixon in the first. But with one out in the sixth, Morris walked David Justice and gave up a single to Sid Bream. Ron Gant grounded to short, forcing Bream at second and sending Justice to third. After Gant stole second, Berryhill, who hit 10 homers in the regular season, made it 3–1 with one swing of his bat.

At the same time, the Braves' catcher shattered Morris's streak of 18 consecutive scoreless innings against Atlanta in the World Series. It was the longest such streak since Bob Gibson strung together 19 against Boston in 1967.

The rest of the game was all Glavine. He retired Toronto in order in six of the nine innings, including the ninth, and didn't issue a walk. The two teams combined for just eight hits, the lowest in a Series game since 1972 when Cincinnati and Oakland had seven in Game 3.

Damon Berryhill's three-run homer off Jack Morris gave the Braves all the offense they needed in Game 1.

Pitching coach Leo Mazzone greeted Tom Glavine with a big hug after the lefthander beat the Blue Jays, 3–1, in Game 1.

Game Two

As Jeff Reardon stood on the mound in the ninth inning of Game 2, he ranked as the all-time leader in saves with 357. The Braves picked him up in a trade to bolster the bullpen for the stretch run, and he had done just that. However, the bottom was about to drop out for the 37-year-old bearded right-hander.

Through seven innings, the Braves had a 4–2 lead, but Toronto mounted a rally in the eighth, scoring another run before Reardon was summoned to squelch the Jays' uprising and preserve the Atlanta lead. He struck out Kelly Gruber to end the eighth with runners at first and third, but the ninth inning was a different story.

With one out, Reardon walked Derek Bell, bringing the potential winning run to the plate. Reliever Duane Ward was scheduled to bat, but Gaston inserted 25-year-old Ed Sprague as a pinch hitter. Sprague, who spent most of the year in the minors and had just one big league home run, sent Reardon's first pitch over the left-field wall for a 5–4 Toronto lead, the first time the Jays had led all evening.

Sprague's home run provided a major shift in momentum. Instead of heading for Toronto with a 2–0 lead in games, the Braves were only even and journeying into a strange American League domed stadium for the next three games. They never really recovered from the Game 2 setback, in which they lost despite going 5-for-5 in stolen base attempts.

Game Three

Once again, the Braves' failure to hold a late-inning lead resulted in a 3–2 loss in Game 3, allowing the Jays to capture the Series lead. And once again, it was Reardon who threw the fateful pitch.

With 51,813 at the Skydome for the first World Series game played outside the United States, Carter opened the scoring with a solo home run in the fourth off Avery. The Braves got even in the sixth against Guzman on a double by Deion Sanders and singles by Terry Pendleton and Justice.

In the eighth, Atlanta took a 2–1 lead. Nixon reached on Gruber's error, stole second, took third on an infield out, and scored on a two-out single by Lonnie Smith.

But Toronto tied the game in the bottom of the inning when Gruber, who'd set a record by failing to hit in his last 23 postseason at bats, led off with a home run against Avery.

The Braves managed only a leadoff single by Bream in the ninth, but pinch runner Brian Hunter was thrown out attempting to steal. That unsuccesful attempt ended a streak of nine straight steals by Atlanta in the Series and a postseason record 14 straight.

When Alomar opened the bottom of the ninth with a single, Cox lifted Avery for Mark Wohlers. Alomar stole second, and Carter was then walked intentionally. Winfield advanced both runners with a sacrifice bunt, and Cox brought in Mike Stanton to face Jon Olerud. When Gaston replaced Olerud with Sprague, Cox ordered a walk to load the bases and summoned Reardon to pitch to Candy Maldonado, who was hitless in seven Series at bats. With an 0–2 count on Maldonado, Reardon served a game-winning single, and the Blue Jays led 2–1 in games.

The turning point in the game came in the top of the fourth when Sanders and Pendleton singled to put runners at first and second with none out. Justice then drilled a pitch that seemed destined for extra bases in deep center. But White made a sensational, leaping catch against the wall, nearly leading to a triple play.

Making the loss even harder to swallow for the Braves was the fact that it was their fifth straight one-run defeat in Series play.

Game Four

Glavine turned in his second excellent performance of the Series in Game 4, but a malfunctioning Atlanta offense failed to support him. The result was that Toronto took a commanding 3–1 lead in games with a 2–1 victory behind left-hander Jimmy Key.

A Pat Borders home run in the third gave the Jays a 1–0 lead. And they got their other run in the seventh when Gruber drew a leadoff walk, took second on an infield out, and scored on a two-out single by White.

The Braves' lone run came in the eighth. Gant led off with a double, breaking an 0-for-17 postseason slump. Hunter followed with a single to put runners at the corners. Berryhill,

for reasons known only to himself, tried to bunt for a hit but popped out. Then Lemke hit a ball off Key that Gruber retrieved and threw to first for an out, allowing Gant to score and Hunter to take second.

With two outs and the score 2–1, Ward replaced Key, and the Braves got a big break. Nixon struck out, but when the ball got away from Borders, Nixon was safe at first, and Hunter advanced to third. With Blauser at the plate, Nixon stole second. However, Blauser grounded to first, ending the inning and Atlanta's impersonation of offense for the night.

Suddenly, the Braves were facing the prospect of not even getting the Series back to Atlanta.

Game Five

The Braves, batting a combined .185 in the first four games, entered Game 5 in desperate need of some offense. Veteran Lonnie Smith, in the lineup only because of the designated hitter rule in the American League park, supplied just that with a fifth-inning grand slam that carried Atlanta to a 7–2 victory.

With Smoltz and Morris, the foes in Game 7 of the 1991 Series, locked in a 2–2 tie through four innings, Atlanta finally broke loose in the fifth with a five-run uprising.

With two outs and none on, Nixon singled, stole second, and scored on a single by Sanders for a 3–2 Atlanta lead. Pendleton doubled, and Justice was intentionally walked to load the bases. Smith followed with a drive over the right-center fence for the first World Series grand slam ever by a

DH. It was sweet vindication for Smith, who was considered the goat of the 1991 Series because of a baserunning blunder in Game 7.

Smoltz and Stanton combined to shut out the Blue Jays over the final five innings, giving the Braves their first Series win on the road since 1958 and the first Series victory by an NL team in an AL domed stadium in 11 games dating back to 1987.

With the way the Braves had rallied against incredible odds for two straight seasons, no one was discounting the possibility they might become the sixth team in history to come back from a 3–1 deficit to win the World Series, especially with the last two games scheduled in Atlanta.

Game Six

Nixon and Smith found a measure of redemption in the 1992 World Series, but not so for Charlie Leibrandt.

Despite two heroic, last-ditch rallies, the Braves lost Game 6, 4–3, in 11 innings, allowing Toronto to become the first team based outside the United States to win the World Series.

Leibrandt, who gave up a game-ending home run to Kirby Puckett in Game 6 a year earlier, yielded a two-run double to Winfield in the top of the 11th that proved to be the decisive hit of the Series. The loss made Leibrandt 0–4 lifetime in the Series and made the Braves the first team since the 1972 Reds to lose four one-run games in the same Series.

The Blue Jays took a 1–0 lead in the first. But Atlanta tied it in the third against Cone, using a double and stolen base by Sanders and a sacrifice fly by Pendleton.

With Avery struggling, the Blue Jays took a 2–1 lead in the fourth when Maldonado stroked a leadoff home run. It looked as if that score might stand up when the Braves entered the ninth still needing a run to stay alive. And that's what they got.

Facing Henke, the Jays' ace closer, Blauser led off with a single and advanced on Berryhill's sacrifice. Smith, the hero of Game 5, then batted for Lemke and drew a walk. Hoping lightning could strike twice, Cox called on NLCS hero Francisco Cabrera to bat for Wohlers, but he lined to left for the second out.

That brought up Nixon, who was having an excellent Series. He promptly slapped a single to left, scoring Blauser to tie the game. With runners at second and third, though, Gant flied out to send the game to extra innings. It was the Braves' first run of the Series in 15⅔ innings against the Jays' bullpen.

Leibrandt eased through the 10th, but with one out in the 11th, he hit White with a pitch. Alomar followed with a single, and after Carter flied to center, Winfield grounded a ball past third for a two-run double and a 4–2 Toronto lead.

Still, the Braves weren't finished. With Key pitching in relief, Blauser opened the 10th with a single, just as he had to start the ninth-inning rally. Berryhill grounded to short, but Alfredo Griffin failed to field the ball, giving Atlanta runners

Otis Nixon sent Game 6 into extra innings with an RBI single in the ninth, but with the tying run at third in the 11th, he made the final out of the Series when he failed to beat out a bunt.

at first and third with no outs. Smoltz ran for Berryhill and advanced to second on a sacrifice bunt by Rafael Belliard. Hunter pinch-hit for Leibrandt and grounded to first, scoring Blauser and sending Smoltz to third with the potential tying run.

Gaston called on 26-year-old right-hander Mike Timlin to relieve Key and face Nixon, who represented Atlanta's last hope, just as he had in the ninth inning when he delivered a game-tying single. This time, the speedy Nixon chose to bunt down the first-base line. Timlin fielded the ball and flipped to Carter, retiring Nixon by a step and ending the Series.

Of the Braves' eight losses in back-to-back World Series, the last seven were by one run, and three came in extra innings. Atlanta became the first team to lose consecutive Series since the 1977–78 Dodgers.

The Braves came home for Game 6 trailing Toronto 3–2 in games, but Atlanta fans still had hopes of a World Series championship.

Jeff Blauser started scoring rallies in the ninth and 11th innings of Game 6 with singles.

Game 1
Saturday, October 17, at Atlanta

Toronto	AB	R	H	RBI
White, cf	4	0	0	0
Alomar, 2b	4	0	0	0
Carter, 1b	4	1	1	1
Winfield, rf	3	0	1	0
Maldonado, lf	3	0	0	0
Gruber, 3b	3	0	0	0
Borders, c	3	0	2	0
Lee, ss	3	0	0	0
Morris, p	2	0	0	0
Stottlemyre, p	0	0	0	0
Tabler, ph	1	0	0	0
Wells, p	0	0	0	0
Totals	30	1	4	1

Atlanta	AB	R	H	RBI
Nixon, cf	3	0	1	0
Blauser, ss	4	0	0	0
Belliard, ss	0	0	0	0
Pendleton, 3b	4	0	0	0
Justice, rf	2	1	0	0
Bream, 1b	3	0	1	0
Gant, lf	3	1	0	0
Berryhill, c	4	1	1	3
Lemke, 2b	3	0	1	0
Glavine, p	2	0	0	0
Totals	28	3	4	3

Toronto	0	0	0	1	0	0	0	0	0—1	4	0
Atlanta	0	0	0	0	0	3	0	0	x—3	4	0

E—None. DP—Atlanta 1. LOB—Toronto 2, Atlanta 7. 2B—None. 3B—None. HR—Berryhill, Carter. SF—None. SH—None. SB—Nixon, Gant. CS—None.

Toronto	IP	H	R	ER	BB	K
Morris (L, 0–1)	6	4	3	3	5	7
Stottlemyre	1	0	0	0	0	2
Wells	1	0	0	0	1	1

Atlanta	IP	H	R	ER	BB	K
Glavine (W, 1–0)	9	4	1	1	0	6

WP—Morris. T—2:37. A—51,763. Umpires—Crawford, Reilly, West, Morrison, Davidson, Shulock.

Game 2
Sunday, October 18, at Atlanta

Toronto	AB	R	H	RBI
White, cf	5	0	1	1
Alomar, 2b	4	1	1	0
Carter, lf	3	0	1	0
Winfield, rf	4	0	1	1
Olerud, 1b	4	0	0	0
Gruber, 3b	4	0	0	0
Borders, c	3	1	1	0
Lee, ss	3	1	1	0
Bell, ph	0	1	0	0
Griffin, ss	0	0	0	0
Cone, p	2	0	2	1
Wells, p	0	0	0	0
Maldonado, ph	1	0	0	0
Stottlemyre, p	0	0	0	0
Ward, p	0	0	0	0
Sprague, ph	1	1	1	2
Henke, p	0	0	0	0
Totals	34	5	9	5

Atlanta	AB	R	H	RBI
Nixon, cf	5	0	0	0
Sanders, lf	3	1	1	0
Pendleton, 3b	4	1	1	0
Justice, rf	3	1	1	1
Bream, 1b	1	1	0	0
Hunter, ph-1b	1	0	0	1
Blauser, ss	3	0	1	0
Belliard, ss	0	0	0	0
Berryhill, c	3	0	0	0
Lemke, 2b	4	0	1	1
Smoltz, p	3	0	0	0
Stanton, p	0	0	0	0
Reardon, p	0	0	0	0
L. Smith, ph	0	0	0	0
Gant, pr	0	0	0	0
Totals	30	4	5	3

Toronto	0	0	0	0	2	0	0	1	2—5	9	2
Atlanta	0	1	0	1	2	0	0	0	0—4	5	1

E—Borders, Lee, Bream. DP—Toronto 2, Atlanta 1. LOB—Toronto 6, Atlanta 8. 2B—Alomar, Borders. 3B—None. HR—Sprague. SF—Hunter. SH—None. SB—Sanders 2, Justice, Blauser, Gant. CS—None.

Toronto	IP	H	R	ER	BB	K
Cone	4⅓	5	4	3	5	2
Wells	1⅔	0	0	0	1	2
Stottlemyre	1	0	0	0	0	0
Ward (W, 1–0)	1	0	0	0	0	2
Henke (S, 1)	1	0	0	0	1	0

Atlanta	IP	H	R	ER	BB	K
Smoltz	7⅓	8	3	2	3	8
Stanton	⅓	0	0	0	0	0
Reardon (L, 0–1)	1⅓	1	2	2	1	1

HBP—Smith by Henke. T—3:30. A—51,763. Umpires—Reilly, West, Morrison, Davidson, Shulock, Crawford.

Game 3
Tuesday, October 20, at Toronto

Atlanta	AB	R	H	RBI
Nixon, cf	4	1	0	0
Sanders, lf	4	1	3	0
Pendleton, 3b	4	0	2	0
Justice, rf	3	0	1	1
L. Smith, dh	4	0	1	1
Bream, 1b	4	0	2	0
Hunter, pr-1b	0	0	0	0
Blauser, ss	4	0	0	0
Berryhill, c	4	0	0	0
Lemke, 2b	3	0	0	0
Totals	34	2	9	2

Toronto	AB	R	H	RBI
White, cf	4	0	0	0
Alomar, 2b	4	1	1	0
Carter, rf	3	1	1	1
Winfield, dh	3	0	1	0
Olerud, 1b	3	0	0	0
Sprague, ph	0	0	0	0
Maldonodo, lf	4	0	1	0
Gruber, 3b	2	1	1	1
Borders, c	3	0	1	0
Lee, ss	3	0	0	0
Totals	29	3	6	3

Atlanta	0	0	0	0	0	1	0	1	0—2	9	0
Toronto	0	0	0	1	0	0	0	1	1—3	6	1

E—Gruber. DP—Atlanta 1, Toronto 2. LOB—Atlanta 6, Toronto 5. 2B—Sanders. 3B—None. HR—Carter, Gruber. SF—None. SH—None. SB—Nixon, Sanders, Alomar, Gruber. CS—Hunter.

Atlanta	IP	H	R	ER	BB	K
Avery (L, 0–1)	8	5	3	3	1	9
Wohlers	⅓	0	0	0	1	0
Stanton	0	0	0	0	1	0
Reardon	0	1	0	0	0	0

Toronto	IP	H	R	ER	BB	K
Guzman	8	8	2	1	1	7
Ward (W, 2–0)	1	1	0	0	0	2

HBP—Carter by Wohlers, Sprague by Stanton, Justice by Guzman. T—2:49. A—51,813. Umpires—West, Morrison, Davidson, Shulock, Crawford, Reilly.

Game 4
Wednesday, October 21, at Toronto

Atlanta	AB	R	H	RBI
Nixon, cf	4	0	2	0
Blauser, ss	4	0	1	0
Pendleton, 3b	4	0	0	0
L. Smith, dh	4	0	0	0
Justice, rf	4	0	0	0
Gant, lf	3	1	1	0
Hunter, 1b	3	0	1	0
Berryhill, c	3	0	0	0
Lemke, 2b	3	0	0	1
Totals	32	1	5	1

Toronto	AB	R	H	RBI
White, cf	4	0	3	1
Alomar, 2b	3	0	0	0
Carter, rf	3	0	0	0
Winfield, dh	3	0	0	0
Olerud, 1b	3	0	2	0
Maldonado, lf	3	0	0	0
Gruber, 3b	2	1	0	0
Borders, c	3	1	1	1
Lee, ss	3	0	0	0
Totals	27	2	6	2

Atlanta	0	0	0	0	0	0	1	0—1	5	0
Toronto	0	0	1	0	0	0	1	0	x—2	6	0

E—None. DP—Atlanta 2. LOB—Atlanta 4, Toronto 5. 2B—Gant, White. 3B—None. HR—Borders. SF—None. SH—None. SB—Nixon, Blauser, Alomar. CS—None. PO—Nixon.

Atlanta	IP	H	R	ER	BB	K
Glavine (L, 1–1)	8	6	2	2	4	2

Toronto	IP	H	R	ER	BB	K
Key (W, 1–0)	7⅔	5	1	1	0	6
Ward	⅓	0	0	0	0	1
Henke (S, 2)	1	0	0	0	1	1

WP—Ward. T—2:21. A—52,090. Umpires—Morrison, Davidson, Shulock, Crawford, Reilly, West.

Game 5
Thursday, October 22, at Toronto

Atlanta	AB	R	H	RBI
Nixon, cf	5	2	3	0
Sanders, lf	5	1	2	1
Pendleton, 3b	5	1	2	1
Justice, rf	3	2	1	1
L. Smith, dh	4	1	1	4
Bream, 1b	4	0	0	0
Blauser, ss	4	0	1	0
Belliard, ss	0	0	0	0
Berryhill, c	4	0	1	0
Lemke, 2b	4	0	2	0
Totals	38	7	13	7

Toronto	AB	R	H	RBI
White, cf	4	0	0	0
Alomar, 2b	3	0	0	0
Carter, rf	4	0	1	0
Winfield, dh	4	0	0	0
Olerud, 1b	3	2	2	0
Sprague, ph-1b	1	0	0	0
Maldonado, lf	2	0	0	0
Gruber, 3b	4	0	0	0
Borders, c	4	0	2	2
Lee, ss	3	0	1	0
Totals	32	2	6	2

Atlanta	1	0	0	1	5	0	0	0	0—7	13	0
Toronto	0	1	0	1	0	0	0	0	0—2	6	0

E—None. DP—Atlanta 1, Toronto 1. LOB—Atlanta 5, Toronto 7. 2B—Nixon, Pendleton 2, Borders. 3B—None. HR—Justice, L. Smith. SF—None. SH—None. SB—Nixon 2. CS—Blauser.

Atlanta	IP	H	R	ER	BB	K
Smoltz (W, 1–0)	6	5	2	2	4	4
Stanton (S, 1)	3	1	0	0	0	1

Toronto	IP	H	R	ER	BB	K
Morris (L, 0–2)	4⅔	9	7	7	1	5
Wells	1⅓	1	0	0	0	0
Timlin	1	0	0	0	0	0
Eichhorn	1	0	0	0	1	1
Stottlemyre	1	3	0	0	1	0

HBP—Justice by Morris. T—3:05. A—52,268. Umpires—Davidson, Shulock, Crawford, Reilly, West, Morrison.

Game 6
Saturday, October 24, at Atlanta

Toronto	AB	R	H	RBI
White, cf	5	2	2	0
Alomar, 2b	6	1	3	0
Carter, 1b	5	0	2	1
Winfield, rf	5	0	1	2
Maldonado, lf	6	1	2	1
Gruber, 3b	4	0	1	0
Borders, c	4	0	2	0
Lee, ss	4	0	1	0
Tabler, ph	1	0	0	0
Griffin, ss	2	0	0	0
Cone, p	2	0	0	0
Stottlemyre, p	0	0	0	0
Wells, p	0	0	0	0
Bell, ph	1	0	0	0
Ward, p	0	0	0	0
Henke, p	0	0	0	0
Key, p	1	0	0	0
Timlin, p	0	0	0	0
Totals	**44**	**4**	**14**	**4**

Atlanta	AB	R	H	RBI
Nixon, cf	6	0	2	1
Sanders, lf	3	1	2	0
Gant, ph-lf	2	0	0	0
Pendleton, 3b	4	0	1	1
Justice, rf	4	0	0	0
Bream, 1b	3	0	0	0
Blauser, ss	5	2	3	0
Berryhill, c	4	0	0	0
Smoltz, pr	0	0	0	0
Lemke, 2b	2	0	0	0
L. Smith, ph	0	0	0	0
Belliard, 2b	0	0	0	0
Avery, p	1	0	0	0
P. Smith, p	1	0	0	0
Treadway, ph	1	0	0	0
Stanton, p	0	0	0	0
Wohlers, p	0	0	0	0
Cabrera, ph	1	0	0	0
Leibrandt, p	0	0	0	0
Hunter, ph	1	0	0	0
Totals	**38**	**3**	**8**	**3**

Toronto	1	0	0	1	0	0	0	0	0	0	2—4	14	1
Atlanta	0	0	1	0	0	0	0	0	1	0	1—3	8	1

E—Griffin, Justice. DP—Atlanta 1. LOB—Toronto 13, Atlanta 10. 2B—Carter 2, Winfield, Borders, Sanders. 3B—None. HR—Maldonado. SF—Carter, Pendleton. SH—Gruber, Berryhill, Belliard. SB—White, Alomar, Sanders 2. CS—Nixon.

Toronto	IP	H	R	ER	BB	K
Cone	6	4	1	1	3	6
Stottlemyre	⅔	1	0	0	0	1
Wells	⅓	0	0	0	0	0
Ward	1	0	0	0	1	1
Henke	1⅓	2	1	1	1	0
Key (W, 2–0)	1⅓	1	1	0	0	0
Timlin (S, 1)	⅓	0	0	0	0	0

Atlanta	IP	H	R	ER	BB	K
Avery	4	6	2	2	2	2
P. Smith	3	3	0	0	0	0
Stanton	1⅔	2	0	0	1	0
Wohlers	⅓	0	0	0	0	0
Leibrandt (L, 0–1)	2	3	2	2	0	0

HBP—White by Leibrandt, Borders by Stanton. T—4:07. A—51,763. Umpires—Shulock, Crawford, Reilly, West, Morrison, Davidson.

COMPOSITE LINE SCORE

Atlanta	1	1	1	2	7	4	0	2	1	0	1—20	
Toronto	1	1	1	4	0	1	1	2	3	0	2—16	

COMPOSITE BATTING STATISTICS

Atlanta Braves	AVG	G	AB	R	H	2B	3B	HR	RBI	BB	SO
Avery	.000	2	1	0	0	0	0	0	0	0	1
Belliard	.000	4	0	0	0	0	0	0	0	0	0
Berryhill	.091	6	22	1	2	0	0	1	3	1	11
Blauser	.250	6	24		6	0	0	0	0	1	9
Bream	.200	5	15	1	3	0	0	0	0	0	0
Cabrera	.000	1	1	0	0	0	0	0	0	0	0
Gant	.125	4	8	2	1	1	0	0	0	1	2
Glavine	.000	2	2	0	0	0	0	0	0	1	0
Hunter	.200	4	5	0	1	0	0	0	2	0	1
Justice	.158	6	19	4	3	0	0	1	3	6	5
Lemke	.211	6	19	0	4	0	0	0	2	1	3
Lopez	.000	0	0	0	0	0	0	0	0	0	0
Nixon	.296	6	27	3	8	1	0	0	1	1	3
Pendleton	.240	6	25	2	6	2	0	0	2	1	5
Sanders	.533	4	15	4	8	2	0	0	1	2	1
L. Smith	.167	5	12	1	2	0	0	1	5	1	4
P. Smith	.000		1	0	0	0	0	0	0	0	1
Smoltz	.000		3	0	0	0	0	0	0	0	2
Treadway	.000	1	1	0	0	0	0	0	0	0	0
Totals	**.220**	**6**	**200**	**20**	**44**	**6**	**0**	**3**	**19**	**20**	**48**

Toronto Blue Jays	AVG	G	AB	R	H	2B	3B	HR	RBI	BB	SO
Alomar	.208	6	24	3	5	1	0	0	0	3	3
Bell	.000	2	1	1	0	0	0	0	0	1	0
Borders	.450	6	20	2	9	3	0	1	3	1	1
Carter	.273	6	22	2	6	2	0	2	3	3	2
Cone	.500	2	4	0	2	0	0	0	1	1	0
Griffin	.000	2	0	0	0	0	0	0	0	0	0
Gruber	.105	6	19	2	2	0	0	1	1	2	5
Key	.000	2	1	0	0	0	0	0	0	0	0
Knott	.000	0	0	0	0	0	0	0	0	0	0
Lee	.105	6	19	1	2	0	0	0	0	1	2
Maldonado	.158	6	19	1	3	0	0	1	2	2	5
Morris	.000	2	2	0	0	0	0	0	0	0	2
Mulliniks	.000	0	0	0	0	0	0	0	0	0	0
Olerud	.308	4	13	2	4	0	0	0	0	0	4
Sprague	.500	3	2	1	1	0	0	1	2	1	0
Tabler	.000	2	2	0	0	0	0	0	0	0	0
White	.231	6	26	2	6	1	0	0	2	0	6
Winfield	.227	6	22	0	5	1	0	0	3	2	3
Totals	**.230**	**6**	**196**	**17**	**45**	**8**	**0**	**6**	**17**	**18**	**33**

COMPOSITE PITCHING STATISTICS

Atlanta Braves	W–L–S	ERA	G	GS	IP	H	R	ER	BB	K
Avery	0–1–0	3.75	2	2	12	11	5	5	3	11
Glavine	1–1–0	1.59	2	2	17	10	3	3	4	8
Leibrandt	0–1–0	9.00	1	0	2	3	2	2	0	0
Reardon	0–1–0	13.50	2	0	1⅓	2	2	2	1	1
P. Smith	0–0–0	0.00	1	0	3.0	3	0	0	0	0
Smoltz	1–0–0	2.70	2	2	13⅓	13	5	4	7	12
Stanton	0–0–1	0.00	4	0	5	3	0	0	2	1
Wohlers	0–0–0	0.00	2	0	⅔	0	0	0	1	0
Totals	**2–4–1**	**2.65**	**6**	**6**	**54⅓**	**45**	**17**	**16**	**18**	**33**

Toronto Blue Jays	W–L–S	ERA	G	GS	IP	H	R	ER	BB	K
Cone	0–0–0	3.48	2	2	10⅓	9	5	4	8	8
Eichhorn	0–0–0	0.00	1	0	1	0	0	0	0	1
Guzman	0–0–0	1.13	1	1	8	8	2	1	1	7
Henke	0–0–2	2.70	3	0	3⅓	2	1	1	2	1
Key	2–0–0	1.00	2	1	9	6	2	1	0	6
Morris	0–2–0	8.44	2	2	10⅔	13	10	10	6	12
Stottlemyre	0–0–0	0.00	4	0	3⅔	4	0	0	0	4
Timlin	0–0–1	0.00	2	0	1⅓	0	0	0	0	0
Ward	2–0–0	0.00	4	0	3⅓	1	0	0	1	5
Wells	0–0–0	0.00	4	0	4⅓	1	0	0	2	3
Totals	**4–2–3**	**2.78**	**6**	**6**	**55**	**44**	**20**	**17**	**20**	**48**

Braves versus Philadelphia Phillies
National League Championship Series

1993

All the pieces supposedly were in place in 1992 for the Braves to finally win their first World Series since 1957.

Right-hander Greg Maddux was signed via free agency and put together his second straight Cy Young season (20–10, 2.36). He combined with Tom Glavine, John Smoltz, and Steve Avery to give Atlanta the best starting rotation in the game. And slugging first baseman Fred McGriff (.310 as a

Brave with 19 of his 37 home runs) was acquired by trade from San Diego at midseason to put the final touch on the offense. The Braves were 51–17 (.750) after his July 20 arrival.

Ron Gant and David Justice had big years, too. Justice finished third in the league's MVP voting, followed by McGriff in fourth place and Gant in fifth.

Bobby Cox's team still lacked a dominant closer yet put on a spirited second-half drive to win a franchise-record 104 games and the division title on the final day of the season over the surprisingly spunky Giants. But a not-so-funny thing happened to the Braves on the way to the World Series. They ran into the upstart Philadelphia Phillies, who had their own designs on the pennant.

As the Braves and Twins had done in 1991 when they won their divisions after finishing last the previous year, the Phillies also pulled a last-to-first routine from 1992 to 1993. Manager Jim Fregosi's free-spirited ballclub won 97 games after losing 92 the year before.

The Philadelphia offense led the league in runs scored (877) with 69 more than the next closest team. The Phils also led the league in hits, doubles, and RBIs, were second in batting average (.274), and ranked near the top in nearly every other major hitting department.

Pesky center fielder Lenny Dykstra finished second in the league's MVP race to Barry Bonds. Dykstra led the league in runs (143), hits (194), and walks (129) and was second in doubles (44) and 10th in steals (37). First baseman John Kruk was among the league leaders in batting average all year and finished eighth (.316). Catcher Darren Daulton was sixth in RBIs (105) and hit 24 home runs, tied for the team lead with left fielder Pete Incaviglia.

Fregosi's pitching staff, though not spectacular, was sixth in the league in ERA (3.95) and led in strikeouts and complete games. All five starters won 12 or more games, including former Braves Tommy Greene (16–4) and Ben Rivera (13–9), as well as Curt Schilling (16–7), who tied Greene for the staff lead in wins. The bullpen was the domain of Mitch "Wild Thing" Williams, fourth in the league with 43 saves.

Still, the Braves were favored to become the first National League team to win three straight pennants since the Cardinals of 1942–44. But Cox's team didn't even get to the seventh game.

Atlanta outscored Philadelphia, 33–23, outhit them, .274 to .227, and outpitched them, 3.15 ERA to 4.75. Those statistics are misleading, though, because Atlanta did most of its scoring in Games 2 and 3. And, as they'd done in the World Series in 1991 and '92, the Braves lost the close ones, dropping three one-run games. The playoff collapse left the team, its fans, and even outside observers wondering if perhaps the Braves had used up their energy, emotions, and breaks in catching the Giants in the regular season.

The Phillies wasted no time in serving notice they intended to upset the Braves. Behind the strong pitching of Schilling, they thrilled 62,012 fans at Veterans Stadium by winning Game 1, 4–3, in 10 innings.

Schilling, a strong 26-year-old right-hander, set a League Championship Series record by striking out the first five Braves he faced. Before leaving after the eighth inning with a 3–2 lead, he struck out 10.

Trailing by a run entering the ninth, Atlanta tied the game with an unearned run off Williams. Kim Batiste, a Phillies defensive replacement at third base, threw away a potential double-play ball in the ninth, leading to Otis Nixon's RBI grounder to tie the game.

But Batiste redeemed himself by winning the game in the bottom of the 10th. Kruk started the Philadelphia rally with a one-out double off Greg McMichael and Batiste followed with a single to left, scoring Kruk and ending the game.

Atlanta came back in Game 2 at the Vet to make a statement with a 14–3 rout behind the pitching of Maddux and a four-homer barrage by McGriff, Jeff Blauser, Damon Berry-

The Phillies rallied against reliever Greg McMichael to win Game 1.

hill, and Terry Pendleton. McGriff started the assault with a monstrous first-inning homer off Greene, who was 10–0 at home during the regular season. McGriff's 438-foot shot, which staked Maddux to a 2–0 lead, was only the seventh homer in the 23-year history of Veterans Stadium to reach the upper deck in right field.

Atlanta wrapped up the game with a six-run third that included six consecutive hits and made it an 8–0 game. Blauser hit a solo home run, Pendleton contributed a two-run single, and Berryhill hit a three-run homer to cap the scoring.

In Game 3, the Braves started slowly against left-hander Terry Mullholland but put together a middle innings assault that produced a 9–4 victory and a 2–1 advantage in games.

Before 52,032 at Atlanta–Fulton County Stadium, the Braves fell behind 2–0 through five and a half innings, then took control, 9–2, by virtue of a five-run sixth and a four-run seventh. However, that two-inning outburst produced more runs than the Braves would score in the following three games.

Mullholland was rolling along through five innings but suddenly lost everything in the sixth. He faced five hitters

Fred McGriff's monstrous home run into the upper deck at Veterans Stadium started the Braves on their way to a 14–3 rout in Game 2 of the 1993 NLCS.

and didn't retire any of them, giving up a walk, three singles, and a two-run double by Justice. Roger Mason came on to get the Phillies out of the inning, but the Braves went right back to work in the seventh against Larry Anderson and David West. The big hit was a three-run double by Mark Lemke.

Glavine, who was 0–4 in the 1991 and '92 NLCS, finally got a playoff victory with seven strong innings in which he gave up only six hits and didn't issue a walk.

With a 2–1 edge in games following two dominating victories, the Braves appeared to be in control with the next two games at home. However, appearances can be deceiving.

Danny Jackson, who was fodder for the Atlanta offense in the Braves' 13–5 victory over Pittsburgh in Game 2 of the 1992 NLCS, was nearly unsolvable in Game 4. He pitched the Phillies to a 2–1 victory over Smoltz and evened the playoffs at 2–2.

The Braves touched Jackson for nine hits and two walks in 7⅔ innings but could manage only a single second-inning run en route to stranding 11 base runners. To add insult to injury, Jackson also drove in the winning run with an RBI single in the fourth.

The Phillies evened the NLCS despite striking out 15 times and stranding 15 base runners.

Game 5 featured another of the Braves' celebrated last-minute rallies, one that might have become part of their growing list of legendary wonderments. But the Phillies just would not be had.

Completely baffled and blown away by Schilling, the Braves trailed 3–0 entering the bottom of the ninth in spite of a strong outing by Avery, who allowed just two runs, one earned, in seven innings.

After Blauser walked to start the ninth and Gant reached on an error by Batiste, Schilling was lifted for Williams. And, as usual, Williams proceeded to complicate matters for the Phillies. McGriff singled to drive in the Braves' first run, and Justice followed with a sacrifice fly, making it 3–2. Pendleton and Francisco Cabrera also singled to tie the game. But with the potential winning run just 90 feet from scoring and only one out, Lemke struck out and Bill Pecota flied out to send the game into extra innings.

The Atlanta bullpen was not equal to the challenge. McMichael, who'd given up a solo home run to Daulton in the ninth, was replaced by Mark Wohlers, who proceeded to serve a game-winning home run to Dykstra. The Braves could do nothing against Anderson in the bottom of the 10th and headed for Philadelphia needing to win Games 6 and 7 in order to return to the World Series.

With Maddux and Glavine scheduled to pitch, that cer-

The Braves needed Greg Maddux to be at his best in Game 6, but he was far from it after being hit in the leg by a ball off the bat of Mickey Morandini.

tainly didn't seem like an insurmountable task—but Atlanta never even got to the second half of that 20-win tandem.

The Braves' offense, so productive in Games 2 and 3, struggled again in Game 6 against Greene and two Philadelphia relievers. And Maddux, who was struck in the leg by a hard smash off the bat of Mickey Morandini, was far from himself in a game where his best performance was needed.

Daulton got the Phillies on the board first with a two-run double in the third, and Fregosi's club was never headed. Blauser, who drove in all three Atlanta runs, hit a solo home run in the fifth, but Hollins answered with a two-run homer in the bottom of the inning to make it 4–1. In the sixth, a two-run triple by Morandini made it 6–1, and the Braves found themselves three innings away from going home instead of to the Series.

Blauser made it 6–3 with a two-run single in the seventh, but West and Williams each worked a perfect inning of relief to provide the Phillies their first pennant since 1983 and the fifth in their long history. Philadelphia also became the first East division team to win the pennant since St. Louis in 1987. Schilling, who had a 1.69 ERA and 19 strikeouts in 16 innings, was named MVP of the playoffs even though he didn't get a decision.

Game 1
Wednesday, October 6, at Philadelphia

Atlanta	AB	R	H	RBI	PO	A
Nixon, cf	4	0	2	2	2	0
Blauser, ss	4	0	0	0	1	1
Gant, lf	4	1	1	0	0	1
McMichael, p	0	0	0	0	0	1
McGriff, 1b	5	0	1	0	10	0
Justice, rf	4	0	0	1	3	0
Pendleton, 3b	5	0	1	0	3	2
Berryhill, c	3	0	0	0	8	0
Pecota, ph	0	1	0	0	0	0
Olson, c	1	0	1	0	0	0
Lemke, 2b	4	0	1	0	1	6
Tarasco, pr-lf	1	0	0	0	0	0
Avery, p	2	1	2	0	0	0
Sanders, ph	1	0	0	0	0	0
Mercker, p	0	0	0	0	0	0
Belliard, ph-2b	0	0	0	0	0	0
Totals	**38**	**3**	**9**	**3**	**28**	**11**

Philadelphia	AB	R	H	RBI	PO	A
Dykstra, cf	4	1	1	0	3	0
Duncan, 2b	5	0	1	0	3	0
Kruk, 1b	4	2	1	1	4	1
Hollins, 3b	4	0	1	0	2	1
Batiste, 3b	1	0	1	1	0	0
Daulton, c	3	0	0	0	12	0
Incaviglia, lf	4	1	2	1	3	0
Thompson, pr-lf	0	0	0	0	1	0
Chamberlain, rf	3	0	2	0	0	0
Mit. Williams, p	0	0	0	0	0	0
Stocker, ss	3	0	0	0	2	3
Schilling, p	3	0	0	0	0	0
Eisenreich, rf	1	0	0	0	0	0
Totals	**35**	**4**	**9**	**3**	**30**	**5**

Atlanta	0	0	1	1	0	0	0	0	1	0—3
Philadelphia	1	0	0	1	0	1	0	0	0	1—4

One out when winning run scored.

Atlanta	IP	H	R	ER	BB	SO
Avery	6	5	3	3	4	5
Mercker	2	2	0	0	1	2
McMichael (L)	1⅓	2	1	1	0	0

Philadelphia	IP	H	R	ER	BB	SO
Schilling	8	7	2	2	2	10
Mit Williams (W)	2	2	1	0	2	2

E—Batiste. DP—Atlanta 1. LOB—Atlanta 11, Philadelphia 8. 2B—Nixon, Olson, Avery, Dykstra, Kruk, Hollins, Chamberlain 2. HR—Incaviglia. SH—Belliard. SF—Justice. WP—Avery. U—Froemming, plate; Pulli, first; Tata, second; Quick, third; Crawford, left field; West, right field. T—3:33. A—62,012.

Game 2
Thursday, October 7, at Philadelphia

Atlanta	AB	R	H	RBI	PO	A
Nixon, cf	4	2	3	2	3	0
Wohlers, p	0	0	0	0	0	0
Blauser, ss	5	1	2	1	1	0
Belliard, pr-ss	1	1	0	0	0	0
Gant, lf	5	1	2	3	1	0
McGriff, 1b	5	2	3	2	5	2
Stanton, p	0	0	0	0	0	0
Tarasco, rf	0	0	0	0	0	0
Justice, rf	3	1	0	0	1	0
Sanders, cf	0	0	0	0	0	0
Pendleton, 3b	5	2	3	3	1	0
Berryhill, c	5	1	1	3	11	0
Lemke, 2b	5	1	0	0	0	2
Maddux, p	4	1	1	0	3	2
Bream, 1b	1	1	1	0	1	0
Totals	43	14	16	14	27	6

Philadelphia	AB	R	H	RBI	PO	A
Dykstra, cf	4	1	1	1	1	0
Morandini, 2b	5	0	1	0	1	5
Kruk, 1b	3	1	2	0	10	0
Hollins, 3b	3	1	1	2	0	0
Daulton, c	4	0	1	0	8	1
Andersen, p	0	0	0	0	0	0
Eisenreich, rf	4	0	0	0	3	0
Thompson, lf	4	0	0	0	2	0
Stocker, ss	4	0	1	0	1	1
Greene, p	0	0	0	0	0	0
Thigpen, p	0	0	0	0	0	0
Longmire, ph	1	0	0	0	0	0
Rivera, p	0	0	0	0	0	0
Chamberlain, ph	1	0	0	0	0	0
Mason, p	0	0	0	0	0	0
Jordan, ph	0	0	0	0	0	0
West, p	0	0	0	0	0	0
Pratt, c	1	0	0	0	1	0
Totals	34	3	7	3	27	7

Atlanta	2	0	6	0	1	0	0	4	1—14	16	0
Philadelphia	0	0	0	2	0	0	0	0	1—3	7	2

Atlanta	IP	H	R	ER	BB	SO
Maddux (W)	7	5	2	2	3	0
Stanton	1	1	0	0	1	0
Wohlers	1	1	1	1	0	3

Philadelphia	IP	H	R	ER	BB	SO
Greene (L)	2⅓	7	7	7	2	2
Thigpen	⅔	1	1	1	0	1
Rivera	2	1	1	1	1	2
Mason	2	1	0	0	0	1
West	1	4	4	3	1	2
Andersen	1	2	1	1	0	1

E—Stocker, Morandini. LOB—Atlanta 6, Philadelphia 8. 2B—Nixon, Gant 2. HR—McGriff, Blauser, Berryhill, Hollins, Pendelton, Dykstra. SB—Morandini. CS—Nixon. PB—Daulton. U—Pulli, plate; Tata, first; Quick, second; Crawford, third; West, left field; Froemming, right field. T—3:14. A—62,436.

Game 3
Saturday, October 9, at Atlanta

Philadelphia	AB	R	H	RBI	PO	A
Dykstra, cf	5	0	1	0	1	0
Duncan, 2b	5	2	2	0	1	4
Kruk, 1b	4	1	2	3	10	0
Hollins, 3b	3	0	0	0	1	0
Daulton, c	4	0	0	0	7	1
Incaviglia, lf	4	0	0	0	2	0
Chamberlain, lf	4	1	1	0	1	0
Stocker, ss	4	0	3	0	1	1
Mulholland, p	2	0	0	0	0	2
Mason, p	0	0	0	0	0	0
Thompson, ph	1	0	0	0	0	0
Andersen, p	0	0	0	0	0	1
West, p	0	0	0	0	0	0
Thigpen, p	0	0	0	0	0	0
Eisenreich, ph	1	0	1	1	0	0
Totals	37	4	10	4	24	9

Game 4
Sunday October 10, at Atlanta

Philadelphia	AB	R	H	RBI	PO	A
Dykstra, cf	3	0	2	0	2	0
Morandini, 2b	5	0	2	0	5	1
Kruk, 1b	5	0	0	0	6	1
Hollins, 3b	4	0	1	0	1	1
Batiste, 3b	0	0	0	0	1	0
Daulton, c	1	1	0	0	6	1
Eisenreich, rf	5	0	1	0	2	0
Thompson, lf	4	1	1	0	3	0
Stocker, ss	4	0	0	1	1	4
Jackson, p	4	0	1	1	0	0
Mit. Williams, p	0	0	0	0	0	1
Totals	35	2	8	2	27	9

Atlanta	AB	R	H	RBI	PO	A
Nixon, cf	3	0	1	0	1	0
Blauser, ss	4	0	0	0	2	1
Gant, lf	5	0	0	0	4	0
McGriff, 1b	4	1	2	0	3	1
Pendleton, 3b	4	0	1	0	0	0
Justice, rf	4	0	2	0	1	0
Olson, c	2	0	0	0	10	0
Berryhill, ph-c	1	0	1	0	5	0
Lemke, 2b	4	0	1	1	1	2
Smoltz, p	1	0	0	0	0	0
Mercker, p	0	0	0	0	0	0
Cabrera, ph	1	0	1	0	0	0
Sanders, pr	0	0	0	0	0	0
Wohlers, p	0	0	0	0	0	0
Pecota, ph	1	0	1	0	0	0
Totals	34	1	10	1	27	4

Philadelphia	0	0	0	2	0	0	0	0	0—2	8	1
Atlanta	0	1	0	0	0	0	0	0	0—1	10	1

Philadelphia	IP	H	R	ER	BB	SO
Jackson (W)	7⅔	9	1	1	2	4
Mit. Williams (S)	1⅓	1	0	0	0	0

Atlanta	IP	H	R	ER	BB	SO
Smoltz (L)	6⅓	8	2	0	5	10
Mercker	⅔	0	0	0	0	0
Wohlers	2	0	0	0	3	5

E—Mit. Williams, Lemke. DP—Philadelphia 1. LOB—Philadelphia 15, Atlanta 11. 2B—Thompson, McGriff, Pendleton, Lemke. CS—Gant. SH—Nixon 2. SF—Stocker. HBP—By Jackson (Olson). WP—Wohlers. U—Quick, plate; Crawford, first; West, second; Froemming, third; Pulli, left field; Tata, right field. T—3:33. A—52,032.

Atlanta	AB	R	H	RBI	PO	A
Nixon, cf	5	0	1	0	2	0
Blauser, ss	4	2	2	0	0	4
Gant, lf	4	1	1	0	2	0
McGriff, 1b	4	2	2	1	14	0
Pendleton, 3b	4	2	2	2	1	2
Justice, rf	4	1	1	2	2	0
Berryhill, c	3	1	1	0	6	0
Lemke, 2b	4	0	2	3	0	4
Glavine, p	3	0	0	0	0	3
Cabrera, ph	1	0	0	0	0	0
Mercker, p	0	0	0	0	0	0
McMichael, p	0	0	0	0	0	0
Totals	36	9	12	8	27	13

Philadelphia	0	0	0	1	0	1	0	1	1—4	10	1
Atlanta	0	0	0	0	0	5	4	0	x—9	12	0

Philadelphia	IP	H	R	ER	BB	SO
Mulholland (L)	*5	9	5	4	1	2
Mason	1	0	0	0	0	1
Andersen	⅓	2	3	3	1	0
West	⅔	1	1	1	1	2
Thigpen	1	0	0	0	1	2

Atlanta	IP	H	R	ER	BB	SO
Glavine (W)	7	6	2	2	0	5
Mercker	1	1	1	1	1	0
McMichael	1	3	1	1	0	1

*Pitched to five batters in sixth.

E—Duncan. LOB—Philadelphia 7, Atlanta 7. 2B—Chamberlain, Stocker, Eisenreich, Blauser, Gant, McGriff, Justice, Lemke. 3B—Duncan 2, Kruk. HR—Kruk. SB—Hollins, CS—Nixon. U—Tata, plate; Quick, first; Crawford, second; West, third; Froemming, left field; Pulli, right field. T—2:44. A—52,032.

Game 5
Monday, October 11, at Atlanta

Philadelphia	AB	R	H	RBI	PO	A
Dykstra, cf	5	1	1	1	2	0
Duncan, 2b	5	1	1	0	1	2
Andersen, p	0	0	0	0	0	0
Kruk, 1b	4	0	1	1	6	0
Hollins, 3b	4	0	0	0	0	1
Batiste, 3b	0	0	0	0	1	0
Daulton, c	3	1	2	1	13	0
Incaviglia, lf	4	1	0	0	3	0
Chamberlain, lf	3	0	1	1	1	2
Eisenreich, rf	4	0	0	0	1	0
Stocker, ss	4	0	0	0	1	3
Schilling, p	2	0	0	0	0	0
Mit. Williams, p	0	0	0	0	0	0
Morandini, ph-2b	1	0	0	0	0	0
Totals	35	4	6	4	30	8

Atlanta	AB	R	H	RBI	PO	A
Nixon, cf	4	0	0	0	4	0
Blauser, ss	4	1	1	0	0	3
Gant, lf	5	1	1	0	1	0
McGriff, 1b	4	1	2	1	8	0
Justice, rf	2	0	1	0	6	0
Pendleton, 3b	4	0	1	0	1	1
Berryhill, c	3	0	1	0	7	0
Cabrera, ph-c	1	0	1	1	1	0
Lemke, 2b	4	0	0	0	2	2
Avery, p	2	0	0	0	0	2
Mercker, p	0	0	0	0	0	0
Sanders, ph	1	0	0	0	0	0
McMichael, p	0	0	0	0	0	0
Pecota, ph	1	0	0	0	0	0
Wohlers, p	0	0	0	0	0	0
Totals	35	3	7	3	30	8

Philadelphia	1	0	0	1	0	0	0	0	1	1—4	6	1
Atlanta	0	0	0	0	0	0	0	3	0—3	7	1

Philadelphia	IP	H	R	ER	BB	SO
Schilling	*8	4	2	1	3	9
Mit. Williams (W)	1	3	1	1	0	1
Andersen (S)	1	0	0	0	0	2

Atlanta	IP	H	R	ER	BB	SO
Avery	7	4	2	1	2	5
Mercker	1	0	0	0	0	2
McMichael	1	1	1	1	0	0
Wohlers (L)	1	1	1	1	0	1

*Pitched to two batters in ninth.

E—Batiste, Gant. LOB—Philadelphia 5, Atlanta 6. 2B—Kruk. HR—Daulton, Dykstra. SH—Schilling. SF—Chamberlain, Justice. WP—Avery. U—Crawford, plate; West, first; Fremming, second; Pulli, third; Tata, left field; Quick, right field. T—3:21. A—52,032.

Game 6
Wednesday, October 13, at Philadelphia

Atlanta	AB	R	H	RBI	PO	A
Nixon, cf	2	1	1	0	1	0
Blauser, ss	4	1	2	3	2	5
Gant, lf	4	0	0	0	2	0
McGriff, 1b	1	0	0	0	9	1
Justice, rf	4	0	0	0	1	0
Pendleton, 3b	4	0	1	0	1	0
Berryhill, c	4	0	0	0	5	0
Lemke, 2b	3	1	1	0	2	3
Maddux, p	0	0	0	0	1	3
Mercker, p	0	0	0	0	0	0
Sanders, ph	1	0	0	0	0	0
McMichael, p	0	0	0	0	0	0
Wohlers, p	0	0	0	0	0	0
Pacota, ph	1	0	0	0	0	0
Totals	28	3	5	3	24	12

Philadelphia	AB	R	H	RBI	PO	A
Dykstra, cf	4	2	1	0	4	0
Morandini, 2b	5	1	1	2	2	3
Kruk, 1b	4	0	0	0	7	0
Hollins, 3b	2	1	1	2	1	1
Batiste, 3b	0	0	0	0	0	1
Daulton, c	4	0	2	2	8	0
Eisenreich, rf	4	0	0	0	0	1
Thompson, lf	4	1	2	0	1	0
Stocker, ss	3	0	0	0	4	1
Greene, p	0	1	0	0	0	1
Jordan, ph	1	0	0	0	0	0
West, p	0	0	0	0	0	1
Mit. Williams, p	0	0	0	0	0	0
Totals	31	6	7	6	27	9

Atlanta	0	0	0	0	1	0	2	0	0—3	5	3
Philadelphia	0	0	2	0	2	2	0	0	x—6	7	1

Atlanta	IP	H	R	ER	BB	SO
Maddux (L)	5⅔	6	6	5	4	3
Mercker	⅓	0	0	0	0	0
McMichael	⅔	1	0	0	2	0
Wohlers	1⅓	0	0	0	0	1

Philadelphia	IP	H	R	ER	BB	SO
Greene (W)	7	5	3	3	6	6
West	1	0	0	0	0	1
Mit. Williams (S)	1	0	0	0	0	2

E—Justice, Lemke, Maddux, Thompson. DP—Philadelphia 1. LOB—Atlanta 6, Philadelphia 9. 2B—Daulton. 3B—Morandini. HR—Hollins, Blauser. SH—Maddux 2, Greene 2. PB—Daulton. U—West, plate; Froemming, first; Pulli, second; Tata, third; Quick, left field; Crawford, right field. T—3:04. A—62,602.

COMPOSITE LINE SCORE

Philadelphia	2	0	2	7	2	4	0	1	3	2—23	47	7
Atlanta	2	1	7	1	2	5	6	4	5	0—33	59	5

COMPOSITE BATTING STATISTICS

Philadelphia Phillies

	AVG	G	AB	R	H	2B	3B	HR	RBI	SH	SF	HB	BB	SO	SB	CS	E
Batiste, K	1.000	4	1	0	1	0	0	0	1	0	0	0	0	0	0	0	2
Chamberlain, W	.364	4	11	1	4	3	0	0	1	0	1	0	1	3	0	0	0
Daulton, D	.263	6	19	2	5	1	0	1	3	0	0	0	6	3	0	0	0
Duncan, M	.267	3	15	3	4	0	2	0	0	0	0	0	0	5	0	0	1
Dykstra, L	.280	6	25	5	7	1	0	2	2	0	0	0	5	8	0	0	0
Eisenreich, J	.133	6	15	0	2	1	0	0	1	0	0	0	0	2	0	0	0
Hollins, D	.200	6	20	2	4	1	0	2	4	0	0	0	5	4	1	0	0
RIGHT	.091	—	11	—	1	1	0	0	0	0	0	0	2	1	—	—	—
LEFT	.333	—	9	—	3	0	0	2	4	0	0	0	3	3	—	—	—
Incaviglia, P	.167	3	12	2	2	0	0	1	1	0	0	0	3	0	0	0	0
Jordan, R	.000	2	1	0	0	0	0	0	0	0	0	0	1	0	0	0	0
Kruk, J	.250	6	24	4	6	2	1	1	5	0	0	0	4	5	0	0	0
Longmire, T	.000	1	1	0	0	0	0	0	0	0	0	0	1	0	0	0	0
Morandini, M	.250	4	16	1	4	0	1	0	2	0	0	0	0	3	1	0	1
Pratt, T	.000	1	1	0	0	0	0	0	0	0	0	0	0	1	0	0	0
Stocker, K	.182	6	22	0	4	1	0	0	1	0	1	0	2	5	0	0	1
RIGHT	.222	—	9	—	2	1	0	0	0	0	0	0	1	0	—	—	—
LEFT	.154	—	13	—	2	0	0	0	1	0	1	0	1	5	—	—	—
Thompson, M	.231	6	13	2	3	1	0	0	0	0	0	0	1	2	0	0	1
Greene, T	.000	2	0	1	0	0	0	0	0	2	0	0	1	0	0	0	0
Jackson, D	.250	1	4	0	1	0	0	0	1	0	0	0	0	3	0	0	0
Mullholland, T	.000	1	2	0	0	0	0	0	0	0	0	0	0	1	0	0	0
Schilling, C	.000	2	5	0	0	0	0	0	0	1	0	0	0	2	0	0	0
Williams, M	.000	4	0	0	0	0	0	0	0	0	0	0	0	0	0	0	1
Totals	.227	6	207	23	47	11	4	7	22	3	2	0	26	51	2	0	7

Atlanta Braves

	AVG	G	AB	R	H	2B	3B	HR	RBI	SH	SF	HB	BB	SO	SB	CS	E
Belliard, R	.000	2	1	0	0	0	0	0	0	1	0	0	0	1	0	0	0
Berryhill, D	.211	6	19	2	4	0	0	1	3	0	0	0	1	5	0	0	0
RIGHT	.400	—	5	—	2	0	0	0	0	0	0	0	1	2	—	—	—
LEFT	.143	—	14	—	2	0	0	1	3	0	0	0	0	3	—	—	—
Blauser, J	.280	6	25	5	7	1	0	2	4	0	0	0	4	7	0	0	0
Bream, S	1.000	1	1	1	1	0	0	0	0	0	0	0	0	0	0	0	0
Cabrera, F	.667	3	3	0	2	0	0	0	1	0	0	0	0	1	0	0	0
Gant, R	.185	6	27	4	5	3	0	0	3	0	0	0	2	9	0	1	1
Justice, D	.143	6	21	2	3	1	0	0	4	0	2	0	3	3	0	0	1
Lemke, M	.208	6	24	2	5	2	0	0	4	0	0	0	1	6	0	0	2
RIGHT	.273	—	11	—	3	2	0	0	4	0	0	0	0	2	—	—	—
LEFT	.154	—	13	—	2	0	0	0	0	0	0	0	1	4	—	—	—
McGriff, F	.435	6	23	6	10	2	0	1	4	0	0	0	4	7	0	0	0
Nixon, O	.348	6	23	3	8	2	0	0	4	2	0	0	5	6	0	2	0
RIGHT	.375	—	8	—	3	0	0	0	2	2	0	0	1	—	—	—	—
LEFT	.333	—	15	—	5	2	0	0	2	0	0	0	5	5	—	—	—
Olson, G	.333	2	3	0	1	0	0	0	0	0	0	1	0	1	0	0	0
Pecota, B	.333	4	3	1	1	0	0	0	0	0	0	0	1	1	0	0	0
Pendleton, T	.346	6	26	4	9	1	0	1	5	0	0	0	2	0	0	0	0
RIGHT	.364	—	11	—	4	1	0	0	1	0	0	0	1	—	—	—	—
LEFT	.333	—	15	—	5	0	0	1	4	0	0	0	1	—	—	—	—
Sanders, D	.000	5	3	0	0	0	0	0	0	0	0	0	0	1	0	0	0
Tarasco, T	.000	2	1	0	0	0	0	0	0	0	0	0	0	1	0	0	0
Avery, S	.500	2	4	1	2	1	0	0	0	0	0	0	0	1	0	0	0
Glavine, T	.000	1	3	0	0	0	0	0	0	0	0	0	0	0	0	0	0
Maddux, G	.250	2	4	1	1	0	0	0	0	2	0	0	0	1	0	0	1
Smoltz, J	.000	1	1	0	0	0	0	0	0	0	0	0	1	1	0	0	0
Totals	.274	6	215	33	59	14	0	5	32	5	2	1	22	54	0	3	5

COMPOSITE PITCHING STATISTICS

Philadelphia Phillies

	W	L	ERA	G	GS	CG	SHO	SV	IP	H	R	ER	HR	HB	BB	SO	WP
Andersen, L (R)	0	0	15.43	3	0	0	0	1	2⅓	4	4	4	0	0	1	3	0
Greene, T (R)	1	1	9.64	2	2	0	0	0	9⅓	12	10	10	3	0	7	7	0
Jackson, D (L)	1	0	1.17	1	1	0	0	0	7⅔	9	1	1	0	1	2	6	0
Mason, R (R)	0	0	0.00	2	0	0	0	0	3	1	0	0	0	0	0	2	0
Mulholland, T (L)	0	1	7.20	1	1	0	0	0	5	9	5	4	0	0	1	2	0
Rivera, B (R)	0	0	4.50	1	0	0	0	0	2	1	1	1	0	1	2	0	0
Schilling, C (R)	0	0	1.69	2	2	0	0	0	16	11	4	3	0	0	5	19	0
Thigpen, B (R)	0	0	5.40	2	0	0	0	0	1⅔	1	1	1	1	0	1	3	0
West, D (L)	0	0	13.50	3	0	0	0	0	2⅔	5	5	4	0	0	2	5	0
Williams, M (L)	2	0	1.69	4	0	0	0	2	5⅓	6	2	1	0	0	2	5	0
Totals	4	2	4.75	6	6	0	0	3	55	59	33	29	5	1	22	54	0

Atlanta Braves

	W	L	ERA	G	GS	CG	SHO	SV	IP	H	R	ER	HR	HB	BB	SO	WP
Avery, S (L)	0	0	2.77	2	2	0	0	0	13	9	5	4	1	0	6	10	2
Bedrosian, S (R)	0	0	—	0	0	0	0	0	0	0	0	0	0	0	0	0	0
Glavine, T (L)	1	0	2.57	1	1	0	0	0	7	6	2	2	1	0	5	5	0
Howell, J (R)	0	0	—	0	0	0	0	0	0	0	0	0	0	0	0	0	0
Maddux, G (R)	1	1	4.97	2	2	0	0	0	12⅔	11	8	7	2	0	7	11	0
McMichael, G (R)	0	1	6.75	4	0	0	0	0	4	7	3	3	1	0	2	1	0
Mercker, K (L)	0	0	1.80	5	0	0	0	0	5	3	1	1	0	0	2	4	0
Smoltz, J (R)	0	1	0.00	1	1	0	0	0	6⅓	8	2	0	0	0	5	10	0
Stanton, M (L)	0	0	0.00	1	0	0	0	0	1	1	0	0	0	0	1	0	0
Wohlers, M (R)	0	1	3.38	6	0	0	0	0	5⅓	2	2	2	2	0	3	10	1
Totals	2	4	3.15	6	6	0	0	0	54⅓	47	23	19	7	0	26	51	3

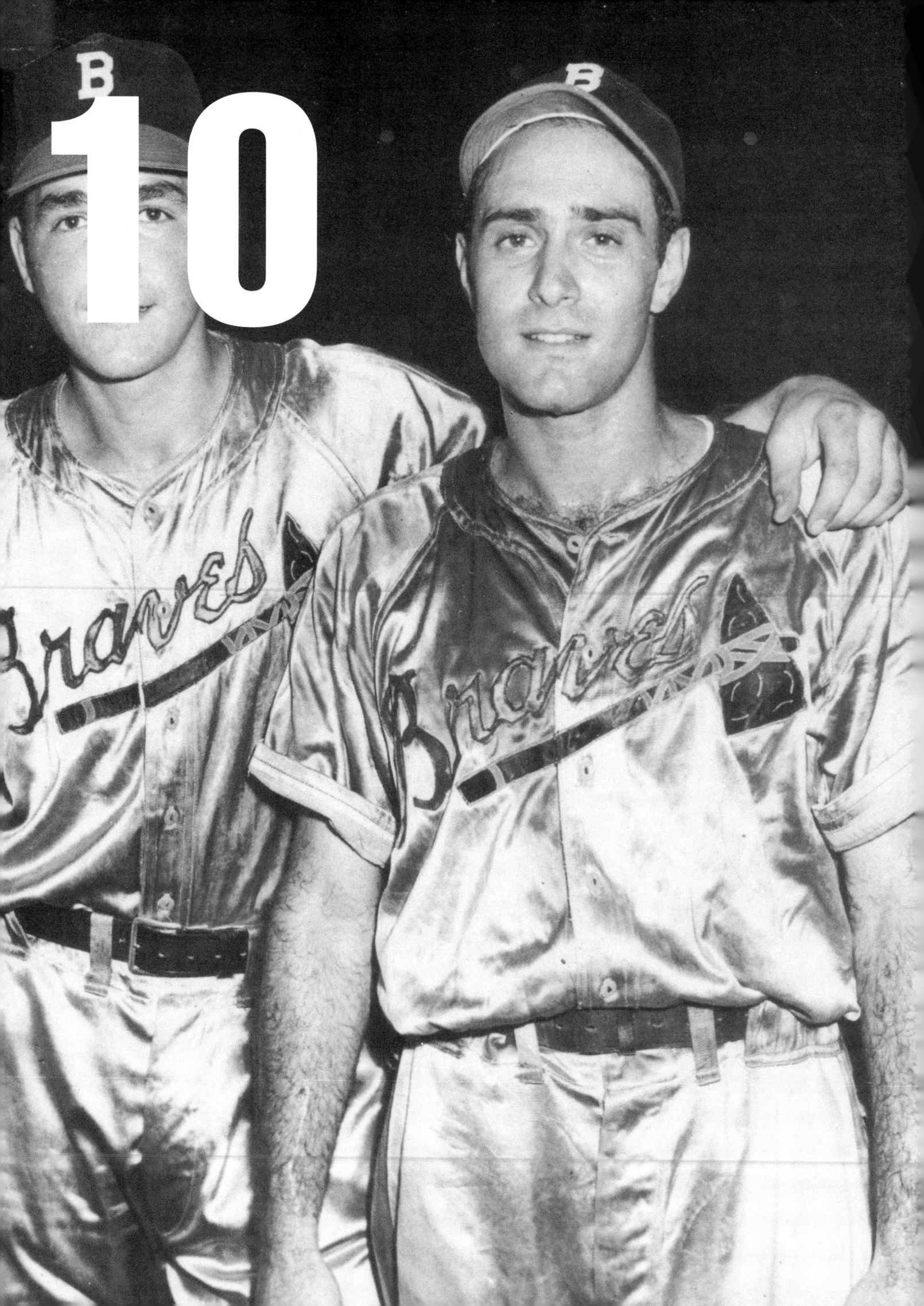

10

Off the Wall

The history of the oldest continuously operating sports franchise in America is a compendium of many of the most colorful anecdotes and notes in baseball history. The subject matter ranges from the humorous to the tragic, and the stories come in all lengths and descriptions.

This chapter is a collection of items that didn't fit anywhere else in *The Braves Encyclopedia* but nevertheless are indispensable (to varying degrees) pieces of franchise history.

No. 756

Nearly any serious baseball fan knows that Hank Aaron's all-time record home run total is 755. But what many don't realize is that the total would be 756 except for an umpire named Chris Pelekoudas.

On August 18, 1965, the Braves were playing the Cardinals at Busch Stadium. Aaron had 393 career home runs at the time, not that anyone was keeping a close count. He hit what appeared to be No. 394 in the eighth inning against veteran left-hander Curt Simmons. However, when Aaron arrived at home plate after circling the bases, he was flabbergasted to learn that Pelekoudas had ruled him out for stepping out of the front of the batter's box as he swung.

Braves manager Bobby Bragan went ballistic over the highly unusual call and was ejected. He played the game under protest, but since Milwaukee won anyway, it didn't matter.

Bureaucratic Nightmare

There have been plenty of embarrassing moments in Braves history. Leading the list of snafus may well be the team's action in the major league draft at the 1988 winter meetings. To make matters worse, the mix-up came in front of the home folks, since the meetings were held in Atlanta that year.

The Braves finished in last place in the National League West in 1988, earning the first selection in the draft of players with at least three years of pro experience who were left unprotected on 40-man rosters. With that number-one selection, the Braves made history by selecting their own player!

Through an oversight, the Braves left 19-year-old right-hander Ben Rivera unprotected. Rather than risk allowing another team to take their prospect, the Braves drafted him themselves.

"It's a little embarrassing," said Bobby Cox, who was in his third year as general manager. "We just messed up. Six of us cross-checked everything, but this went by us."

Asked what his reaction would have been if Rivera had been lost, Cox cracked, "I would have committed suicide."

Rivera didn't make it to the majors until 1992, and then he pitched only 15⅓ innings before the Braves traded him to Philadelphia in May for minor league right-hander Donnie Elliott. Rivera wound up pitching two innings against the Braves in the 1993 National League Championship Series.

A front office mistake forced the Braves to draft their own player, pitcher Ben Rivera, in 1988.

Johnny Antonelli (L) and Sibby Sisti (R) model the satin uniforms the Braves wore for night games in 1946.

Bennett's Tragedy

In the winter between the 1893 and 1894 seasons, John Clarkson, a former Boston great then employed by Cleveland, went on a hunting trip with friend Charlie Bennett, a catcher for the pennant-winning Beaneaters. When their train stopped at Wellesville, Kansas, the 38-year-old Bennett got off, then tried to reboard as the train began to move. He slipped on the icy platform, and his legs were crushed beneath the train's wheels. Although Bennett survived the accident, he lost both legs.

Bennett was one of the game's finest defensive catchers. He led his position in fielding seven times, three with Boston and four for Detroit. He was so well thought of in Detroit that the first American League field there was named after him.

A benefit game was held for Bennett at Boston's Congress Street Grounds in 1894. Heavyweight boxing champion "Gentleman" Jim Corbett played several innings, and the $6,000 in receipts was given to Bennett. He used the money to open a pottery in Detroit and lived to be 72.

Popular catcher Charlie Bennett lost both legs when he slipped under a train after the pennant-winning season of 1893.

Unassisted Triple Play

There have been just eight unassisted triple plays in modern (post-1900) major league history. The only one in Braves history occurred October 6, 1923. It was the first in the National League since 1878.

The play was made by an unlikely individual. Ernie "Red" Padgett was a 24-year-old shortstop who was appearing in only his second big league game.

The Braves were at home for a doubleheader against Philadelphia. In the fourth inning of the second game, the visitors had Cliff Lee at first base and Cotton Tierney at second with no outs. Walter Holke hit a line drive at Padgett, who caught the ball, touched second to retire Tierney and tagged the unsuspecting Lee between first and second.

Boston won the game, shortened to 4½ innings by darkness, 4–1. The play was the highlight of Padgett's five-year career, which consisted of only 271 games.

Ernie "Red" Padgett made the only unassisted triple play in Braves history in 1923.

All Dressed Up

The Braves have worn a variety of uniforms over the years—some of the best-looking designs in history as well as some of the ugliest. By far the most unique were the special satin uniforms that made their debut May 11, 1946, for the team's first night game at Braves Field.

The Braves were one of the last teams to install lights, so when they finally did, it was a big occasion in Boston. A crowd of 37,407, the largest at Braves Field in 13 years, turned out for the event. Though they saw the home team lose to the Giants, 5–1, they also were treated to the distinctive satin uniforms that were supposed to reflect the artificial light.

The jerseys featured the script "Braves" underlined by a tomahawk that today's fans have become accustomed to seeing. The 1946 season was the first year the tomahawk was used. The satin jerseys, brought out only for night games, also had heavy red piping running from collar to elbow.

The popular tomahawk remained on the Braves' jerseys through the 1962 season, then was revived in 1987.

The early Boston National League clubs wore only the city's name or an old English B on their jerseys. When the Braves nickname was adopted in 1912, the profile of an Indian chief in full headdress was added to the left sleeve.

Through the years, the chief came and went, then was replaced by a screaming Indian in the 1950s and '60s.

The Braves began wearing their names on the back of their uniform jerseys in 1963, the year the tomahawk disappeared.

The dawning of the double-knit era in the 1970s brought many changes, most for the worse. For several seasons, the jersey sleeves featured feathers that resembled tulips, and the Braves often looked more like a softball team than a major league baseball club.

Fortunately, a sense of style and taste prevailed with the return of the classic tomahawk jerseys in 1987.

A Motley Crew

In 1916, Braves business manager Walter Hapgood devised a moneymaking scheme that created a mutiny on the team and nearly landed the players in jail.

The Braves trained in Miami that spring. When teams broke camp and headed north by train in that era, they usually played exhibition games along the way to help pay expenses. Hapgood, however, went a little too far by arranging a schedule that required the players to sleep on trains for 20 straight nights.

After a week, the players, including Hall of Famer Rabbit Maranville, decided that if they were going to be treated like hoboes, they'd look like them, too. They stopped shaving and began wearing work shirts, gaudy ties, and funky caps. A shop owner in Georgia saw them and called the sheriff to report the presence of jail breakers in town. Hapgood got the message and changed the schedule.

Two Sweet Deals

Larvell Blanks, a utility infielder with the Braves from 1972 to 1975 and again in 1980, was known as "Sugar Bear" because he supposedly looked like the character on the cereal box that carried the same name.

Blanks was the Braves' regular shortstop in 1975, but on December 12, 1975, he was traded to the White Sox, along with Ralph Garr, for outfielder Ken Henderson and pitchers Dick Ruthven and Danny Osburn.

Talk about not feeling wanted . . . the White Sox immediately traded Blanks to Cleveland for pitcher Jack Brohamer. "Sugar Bear" had been traded twice in the same day—and sweet deals they were.

Near Braves Experiences

The Braves have had a lot of great players . . . and they've almost had a few more.

Would you believe Tom Seaver? Rube Waddell? Johnny Vander Meer? Luis Tiant? Richie/Dick Allen? Rip Sewell?

Those are six prominent names in baseball history, all of whom could have been Braves at the peak of their careers but instead never played a single game for the team.

Seaver, one of the great right-handed pitchers of all time, very nearly became a Brave right out of the University of Southern California in 1966, the year the Braves moved to Atlanta.

In January the Braves drafted Seaver. However, they lost him because of a technicality. When Seaver signed his contract in February, Southern Cal had already begun its season with an exhibition game that wasn't listed on the schedule and that the Braves didn't know about. Therefore, Seaver was ineligible to sign a contract, and Commissioner William Eckert voided it. Since Seaver had signed a contract, he could not pitch in college either.

Therefore, Eckert ruled that Seaver was a free agent and the right to his services would be determined in a lottery of teams willing to offer a bonus equal to the Braves' $40,000—but the Braves could not participate. Five teams entered the drawing, and the Mets won. Seaver turned the Mets franchise around, won 311 career games, and was inducted into the Hall of Fame in 1991.

In the spring of 1901, Waddell was a 24-year-old left-hander with Pittsburgh. The Pirates grew weary of his eccentricities and salary demands and offered him to Boston. The Beaneaters accepted Waddell on March 28, hoping they could sign him. They couldn't. A month later, the Pirates gave up and shipped Waddell to the Cubs. In 1902, Philadelphia's Connie Mack acquired Waddell and turned him into a Hall of Famer for the Athletics.

Vander Meer, the only man ever to pitch back-to-back no-hitters, became Braves property after the 1935 season when he was purchased from Scranton of the Eastern League. Then an unknown, 21-year-old left-hander, Vander Meer was sent to Nashville in 1936. A year later he was sold to Cincinnati, and in 1938 he pitched the first of his two no-hitters against Boston.

On April 16, 1971, the Braves signed Tiant, a 30-year-old right-hander who was experiencing arm problems and was assumed to be washed up by most teams. The Braves assigned Tiant to their Richmond farm club but released him a month later. Tiant was picked up by the Red Sox, and the next year he led the American League with a 1.91 ERA. From 1972 to 1976, Tiant averaged 19 wins, made two All-Star teams, and helped Boston win the 1975 pennant.

At age 32, the enigmatic Allen quit the White Sox in September 1974, two years after he'd been the American League MVP. When he opted for an early end to the season, Allen had 32 home runs, which held up as tops in the league. Chicago finally gave up on Allen (as Philadelphia had before) and traded him to the Braves that December for a player to be named. The Braves felt they could get Allen to report, but they were wrong.

In May 1975, Atlanta assigned Allen and catcher Johnny Oates to Philadelphia for catcher Jim Essian and outfielder Barry Bonnell. Essian was then sent to Chicago as the player

Richie/Dick Allen refused to join the Braves after a trade in December 1974.

to be named in the original deal. Allen did report to the Phillies and played three more seasons.

Then there's the case of Sewell, who was purchased by Boston from Buffalo of the International League. The 29-year-old right-hander didn't impress manager Bill McKechnie at spring training in 1937 and was returned to Buffalo. Beginning in 1939, Sewell won 143 games in 11 seasons with Pittsburgh. He won 21 games in 1943 and 1944 and pitched in three All-Star games with his famed "eephus" blooper pitch.

National Hero

Wenty Ford was the first native of the Bahamas to play for the Braves. He signed as a 19-year-old free agent in February 1966. In 1967 he pitched a 1–0 perfect game for West Palm Beach of the Florida State League and singled in the game's only run. After a solid year at Richmond (10–5, 2.42) in 1973, the 5–11 right-hander finally made it to Atlanta when rosters were expanded in September.

Ford made his major league debut on September 10, 1973, against San Francisco. He pitched a complete-game five-hitter, winning 10–4. But his performance was overshad-

owed by Davey Johnson's 40th home run of the season and Hank Aaron's 710th of his career. Ford made three more appearances, two in relief, and finished with a 1–2 record and 5.51 ERA.

Ford never made it back to the majors. He left the Braves organization after the 1975 season and returned to his home in Nassau, where he was a hero who assisted in the rise of baseball popularity on the islands through his work with children. In 1980, at age 33, Ford died in an auto accident and was buried as a hero before thousands of mourners in Nassau.

Late for Dinner

Warren Spahn didn't make many mistakes in his Hall of Fame career, which produced 363 victories. But one of his more ill-advised moves came in 1952 when he began construction of a restaurant right across the street from Braves Field. The diner was to be completed in time for the opening of the 1953 season.

However, during the spring of 1953, Spahn discovered he'd be summering in Milwaukee—not Boston.

The great left-hander found out about the Braves' move while filming a commercial for Gillette in St. Petersburg. Teammate Sibby Sisti, who'd finished his portion of the com-

mercial, left the set and happened upon a tickertape machine that was breaking the story of the Braves' move. Sisti went back to the set and told the director that the *B* on Spahn's cap was "no good." When asked to explain, Sisti said the cap now needed an *M*. Rather than shooting the commercial again, the announcer described Spahn as "formerly of the Boston Braves, now with the Milwaukee Braves."

Spahn's restaurant opened, as planned. A neon sign said, "Eat with Warren Spahn," and place mats carried the slogan "The Best in Baseball, the Best in Food" and showed the pitcher in his Boston Braves uniform. But Spahn soon sold out.

Rumble in the Garden

One of the more bizarre incidents in Braves history took place January 10, 1930, at Boston Garden when 17,000 customers paid to see Braves catcher Al Spohrer box Art "the Great" Shires, a first baseman for the White Sox.

There have been plenty of baseball fights on the field, in the clubhouse, under the stands, in bars, in hotels, and plenty of other places. But this was the first—and only—time when two ballplayers squared off with gloves in public for a profit.

Shires, who fancied himself a boxer, had the size advantage. He stood 6–1 and weighed 195. Spohrer, much more serious about baseball than was his foe, stood 5–10 and weighed 175.

Spohrer went down for the count of nine in the second round but rallied for a short time. The end came in the fourth round when Shires left Spohrer in a daze, forcing his seconds to throw in the towel for a TKO.

Buoyed by his victory, Shires wanted to fight Hack Wilson of the Cubs, but Commissioner Kenesaw Mountain Landis refused to allow it.

As baseball fate would have it, Shires and Spohrer became Braves teammates in 1932. Shires was picked up to be Boston's starting first baseman, but he injured his knee, missed the second half of the season, and never played in the majors again. He batted .291 in four big league seasons.

Spohrer spent most of his eight-year career with the Braves, compiling a lifetime .259 batting average.

Braves catcher Al Spohrer (L) squared off in a boxing match with Art Shires (R) at Boston Garden in 1930.

Double Duty

The Braves have had several two-sport athletes in their history. The most recent, of course, was outfielder Deion Sanders, who also played cornerback for the NFL's Atlanta Falcons while with the Braves.

Others have included Jim Thorpe, Gene Conley, George Crowe, Ron Reed, and Buddy Hassett.

Thorpe, who won the Olympic decathlon in 1912 and was widely regarded as the greatest athlete of his time, played six years of major league baseball, including 1919 with the Braves. He left his career as an outfielder in 1920 when the American Professional Football League, which became the NFL, was formed. In fact, he was the league's first president, mainly for promotional purposes, and played halfback for several teams through 1928.

Conley, a Braves pitcher from 1952 to 1958, played in the NBA with the Boston Celtics in 1952–53 and 1958–61 and later with the New York Knicks.

George Crowe, one of the game's great pinch hitters who broke in with the Braves in 1952–53 and 1955, was a pro basketball player before signing with the Braves. He played for New York of the World Basketball Tournament in 1946–48 and for Dayton of the National Basketball League in 1948–49.

Reed, who pitched for the Braves their first 10 years in Atlanta, had a brief run in the NBA, playing for the Detroit Pistons in 1966–67.

And Hassett, a Boston first baseman from 1939 to 1941, played for Union City (1933–34) and Jersey (1934–35) of the American Basketball League.

Distinguished Graduates

In May 1992 former Braves outfielder/first baseman Felipe Alou made history by becoming the first native of the Dominican Republic to manage a major league baseball team. Just two years later, Alou's Montreal Expos finished the strike-shortened 1994 season with the best record in baseball—and six games ahead of the Braves in the National League East.

Alou, a two-time All-Star as a Brave, is just one of many former franchise players who are still in the game. The original Atlanta Braves of 1966, of which Alou was a member, are unusually well represented among the game's hierarchy on and off the field.

Hank Aaron has held various positions with the Braves,

the latest being senior vice president. Two of the '66 Braves, Woody Woodward (Seattle) and Lee Thomas (Philadelphia) are general managers. And two, Alou and Joe Torre (St. Louis) are managers. Additionally, Denis Menke (Philadelphia) and Tony Cloninger (Yankees) are coaches; Felix Millan is an instructor and Latin American coordinator for the Mets; and 1966 manager Bobby Bragan is a VP with the Texas Rangers.

Other former Braves in prominent roles in 1995 included general managers Ron Schueler (White Sox) and Bob Watson (Houston), and managers Dusty Baker (San Francisco), Cito Gaston (Toronto), Dave Johnson (Cincinnati), Tony LaRussa (Oakland), and Johnny Oates (Texas).

Former Braves (L-R) Lee Thomas, Ron Schueler, and Bob Watson are now big league general managers.

Borrowed Players

In the early years of major league baseball, contract structures were not as well defined as they are now. Teams were allowed to "try out" players for up to three games without a contract. (The rules varied, but this was the most common one.) These loose rules led to some interesting "tryouts," a couple of examples of which follow.

In 1904 the Brooklyn Superbas, ancestors of the Dodgers, decided to test the ban on Sunday baseball in Brooklyn with a game against the Beaneaters. Boston first baseman Fred Tenney refused to play on Sundays, and outfielder Dick Cooley was ill, so outfielder John White was "borrowed" from Toronto of the Eastern League.

The Brooklyn police entered the ballpark right before game time and arrested the Brooklyn pitcher and catcher after the first pitch to Boston's Phil Geier. They confiscated Geier's bat and arrested the scorecard seller, too. The game went on, but White, after going 0-for-5, was returned to Toronto and never played in the majors again.

In an August 1906 series in Cincinnati, the Beaneaters came in crippled. Tenney still refused to play on Sundays, and shortstop Al Bridwell, third baseman Allie Strobel, and outfielder Johnny Bates were all injured. Two local amateurs were asked to help.

Jack Schulte played shortstop in the August 19 doubleheader, and Ernie Diehl played left field in both games and shortstop on August 20. Diehl was a prominent councilman and wealthy distiller in Cincinnati. He came out of his three-game trial with a .455 batting average but could not afford to play professionally and take a salary cut.

Let's Play Two . . . Teams

The Braves played—and won—an unusual doubleheader at Milwaukee County Stadium on September 24, 1954. In the first game the Braves beat the Reds, 4–3, and in the second game they beat the Cardinals, 4–2.

It ranks as one of the most unusual doubleheader sweeps of all time, and here's how it happened.

On September 22, the Braves beat Cincinnati, 3–1, in what was supposed to be the final game of the season between the two clubs. However, the Reds protested a ninth-inning decision that cost them two runs.

League president Warren Giles ruled in Cincinnati's favor. Since the Braves were involved in the pennant race, Giles ordered the Reds to return to Milwaukee to complete the game on September 24. Play was resumed with two Reds on base and two outs in the top of the ninth. Cincinnati tied the game, but the Braves scored in the bottom of the ninth to win.

Meanwhile, St. Louis was waiting to play the regularly scheduled game. Milwaukee won it, too, but unfortunately all the fuss was for nothing. The Braves still finished the season in third place.

Odds and Ends

* Hank Aaron's uniform number 44 is one of the most famous in baseball history. However, Aaron didn't don number 44 until his second season. He wore number 5 as a rookie.

* Speaking of numbers, Bill Voiselle, a right-hander who won 13 games for the National League champion Braves of 1948, was the only major leaguer to wear the name of his hometown on his uniform. Voiselle hailed from Ninety-Six, South Carolina, and wore uniform number 96.

* On July 13, 1961, Braves rookie outfielder Mack Jones made his big league debut and collected four hits, tying a record held by two Hall of Famers, Casey Stengel and Willie McCovey.

* Clarence "Cito" Gaston, a little-used outfielder with the Braves in 1967 and again in 1975–78, came back to haunt his former team in the 1992 World Series. As the first black to manage in the postseason, he led the Toronto Blue Jays to the Series championship in six games over Atlanta.

* Bill Dinneen was a 20-game winner for the Beaneaters of 1900, one of two seasons he pitched for the club. Dinneen had several other unique accomplishments in baseball. In 1903 for the Red Sox, he became the first pitcher to win three games in a World Series. In 1905 he pitched a no-hitter for the Red Sox. And after retiring as a player in 1909, he moved directly into umpiring in the American League, a job he held for 29 years, working 45 World Series games.

Hank Aaron didn't always wear No. 44 as this photo from his rookie season shows.

* Al Montgomery, a catcher who played sparingly for the 1941 Braves, appeared in the movie *Pride of the Yankees* as the masked catcher for several teams. Montgomery was killed in an auto accident in 1942 at the age of 21.

* Milo Hamilton, a long-time Braves announcer who called Hank Aaron's 715th home run in 1974, received the

In 1961, rookie Mack Jones tied a record by getting four hits in his first game.

1992 Ford C. Frick Award, which is presented annually by the Hall of Fame to a broadcaster who has made major contributions to baseball. Hamilton, an announcer with the Houston Astros in 1995, began broadcasting major league baseball in 1953.

* In the National League expansion draft to stock the Colorado Rockies and Florida Marlins for the 1993 season, Braves right-hander David Nied was the very first selection. Nied, who was 3–0 with a 1.17 ERA in a late-1992 callup from Richmond, was taken by Colorado. The Braves also lost shortstop Vinny Castilla and right-hander Armando Reynoso to the Rockies.

* For a period in the 1960s and '70s it was fashionable for major league clubs to drive relief pitchers to the mound, usually in a modified golf cart. The custom began on June 23, 1958, when Braves reliever Don McMahon was delivered to his assignment at Milwaukee County Stadium in a motorcycle sidecar.

* George Brunet, a left-hander who pitched 15 years in the majors, including 1960–61 with the Braves, also pitched in the Mexican League until he was 50 years old and set a minor league record with 3,175 strikeouts.

* Right-hander Humberto Robinson, who debuted with the Braves in 1955 and pitched for them for three seasons, was the first native of Panama to reach the majors.

* The smallest man ever to play for the Braves was Walter "Doc" Gautreau, also known as "Punk" for obvious reasons. A reserve second baseman from 1925 to 1928, Gautreau stood 5–4 and weighed 129 pounds. In 1927 he stole home twice in one game to tie a major league record.

* Bob Didier was the catcher on the Braves' 1969 division-winning club. The son of Mel Didier, a longtime scout, he was named to the Topps Major League Rookie All-Star Team that year but never played as a regular again and was out of the majors by 1974.

* Francis Ouimet gained sporting fame by winning the U.S. Open golf tournament as a 19-year-old amateur in 1913. He also holds a place in Braves history. He used to play golf at Boston's Allston Golf Links before Braves president James Gaffney purchased the site and turned it into Braves Field.

Ouimet also was elected vice president of the Braves in 1941.

* Shanty Hogan, a catcher who had two terms with the Braves, missed three days of spring training in 1933 because of sunburn. Later that year, he started a string of 121 errorless games behind the plate that extended into 1934.

* Sam Jethroe became the first black to play for the Braves in 1950 and went on to be selected the National League Rookie of the Year. However, he was not the first black signed by the organization. That distinction belongs to second baseman Waldon Williams. An 18-year-old from New York City, Williams signed with the Braves in December 1948 but never got to the majors.

* In 1953 right-hander Phil Paine, who pitched for the Braves in 1951, became the first former major leaguer to play in Japan. Paine, who was stationed in Japan with the U.S. Air Force, was 4–3 with a 1.77 ERA for the Nishitetsu Lions. He returned to the Braves for the 1954–57 seasons.

* The Braves have two players in the Canadian Baseball Hall of Fame. They are Jeff Heath, an outfielder with the 1948 pennant winners, and Claude Raymond, a reliever with Milwaukee (1961–63) and Atlanta (1967–69).

* On September 25, 1979, brothers Rick and Mickey Mahler pitched in the same game for the Braves, who lost to Houston, 8–0.

* Mort Cooper, who won 65 games in pitching St. Louis to pennants in 1942–44 before joining the Braves in 1945, used to chew aspirin on the mound to relieve his sore arm. Cooper was never the same as a Brave, though he did win 13 games and make the All-Star team in 1946.

* Fred Brown, an outfielder, had a big league career that consisted of only nine games for the Beaneaters in 1901–02. He then went on to a more successful career in politics. In 1913 he was elected the first Democratic governor of New Hampshire in 65 years. He later served as a U.S. senator from that state in 1933–39, then was appointed comptroller general of the United States.

* In 1959, Hank Aaron became the first player ever selected to the All-Star team by unanimous vote of his fellow players.

* Outfielder Terry Harper sustained the most unusual on-field injury by a Brave. In 1982 he dislocated his left shoulder while standing near the plate and waving a runner home.

Phil Paine became the first major leaguer to play in Japan while he was on military duty in 1953.

Claude Raymond, who pitched for the Braves in Milwaukee and Atlanta, will never get to Cooperstown but he's in the Canadian Baseball Hall of Fame.

* The Braves had a knack for getting Hall of Famers at the end of their careers. One of those was Yankees great Lefty Gomez, who was released by New York after the 1942 season and went to spring training with the Braves in 1943. He was carried on the roster in April but never pitched.

* In 1990, Braves pitcher Derek Lilliquist hit two home runs in the same game, the first pitcher to do so since Jim Gott in 1985.

* Right-hander Joe Cowley was a bust (1–2, 4.47) in his only season (1982) as a Brave, but in 1986 he set the American League record for most consecutive strikeouts to start a game. Pitching for the White Sox, he struck out the first seven Texas Rangers he faced. Later that year, Cowley also pitched a no-hitter against California, though he walked seven. A year later, he was out of the majors at age 29.

* Les Mann, a light-hitting outfielder with the 1914 "Miracle" Braves, came to the team from Springfield College, where he once returned a punt 75 yards in the closing minutes to beat Vermont. After his playing career, he pro-

moted baseball by speaking to kids. Commissioner Kenesaw Mountain Landis called Mann the "ambassador of American baseball."

* Outfielder Earl Clark played seven seasons (1927–33) for the Braves but never appeared in more than 84 games in any one year. However, on May 10, 1929, he set a major league record that still stands. He had 12 putouts and one assist for 13 total chances, the record for a nine-inning game.

* Patsy Flaherty, a left-hander who pitched for Boston in 1907–08 and 1911, was so adept at "quick-pitching" batters that he's given much of the credit for implementation of the rule against the practice.

* In 1994 the city of Eau Claire in northwest Wisconsin unveiled a bronze statue of Hank Aaron as he looked in 1952, when at age 18 he made his debut in organized baseball there at Carson Park.

* Tony Boeckel, who drove in the Braves' only run in the 26-inning marathon of 1920 and was the team's starting third baseman in 1923 when he hit .298, was killed in an accident prior to the 1924 season. He stopped his car to assist the victim of another accident on a highway in California and was struck by a passing truck and killed instantly.

* Buster Brown, a right-hander for the Braves from 1909 to 1913, was the all-time hard-luck pitcher. A product of Ames College, he pitched nine years in the majors. Despite a lifetime 3.21 ERA, he was 51–103 for three teams and never had a winning record. In 1909 for the Braves, he was 9–23 with a 2.67 ERA.

* Cecil Ferguson, a right-hander who won 24 games for Boston from 1908 to 1911, also was a pioneer in sports medicine. He went to medical school during the off-seasons and became well-known for working with the Dodgers, as well as athletes at Notre Dame and the University of Illinois.

* Of Hank Aaron's 755 home runs, 399 were hit with the bases empty, 243 with one man on, 97 with two on, and 16 with the bases full. He hit 385 homers on the road, 370 at home, and 13 in extra innings. Aaron hit more home runs (17) off Dodgers Hall of Famer Don Drysdale than off any other pitcher.

* When the spitball was outlawed in 1920, eight established pitchers were allowed to continue throwing it. One of

Mort Cooper used to chew aspirin when he pitched to relive a sore arm.

Milo Hamilton called Hank Aaron's 715th home run and later received the Ford C. Frick Award from the Hall of Fame.

Derek Lilliquist is the last Braves pitcher to hit two home runs in a game.

those was Braves right-hander Dana Fillingim. The hitters didn't approve, because Fillingim was 15–10 in 1921 and tied for the league lead in shutouts (3) before developing a sore arm that cut short his career.

* The last of the legal spitball pitchers was Hall of Famer Burleigh Grimes, who spent part of the 1930 season with the Braves. He was nicknamed "Ol' Stubblebeard" because he never shaved on the day he pitched. The reason was that the slippery elm he chewed to increase saliva irritated his skin.

* Guy Bush, who was pitching for the Pirates in 1935, gave up home runs Nos. 713 and 714 to Babe Ruth, then playing for the Braves. The next year, Bush became a Brave, too.

* Hod Ford was still a student at Tufts University when he broke in with the Braves as an infielder in 1919.

* Walt Cruise, an outfielder who scored the Braves' only run in the 26-inning, 1–1 tie of 1920, was married between games of a doubleheader at Cincinnati and did not play in the second game.

* Pat "Doc" Carney's big league career lasted four years (1901–04), all with Boston. He tried his hand at both pitching (4–10, 4.69) and playing the outfield (.247) but soon decided his career opportunities were better elsewhere. He returned to his alma mater, Holy Cross, to coach the baseball team for four years and then became a physician.

* William "Boileryard" Clarke, a catcher on two Baltimore pennant winners in the 19th century and then with Boston in 1899–1900, later became baseball coach at Princeton.

* In 1946, Braves center fielder Carden Gillenwater tied the major league record for putouts by an outfielder with 12 in a 17-inning game.

* Al Demaree's eight-year pitching career came to a close with the 1919 Braves. He then became a syndicated sports cartoonist, and his work appeared in The Sporting News for over 30 years.

* Bunny Hearn, a pitcher for the Braves in 1918 and 1920, coached baseball at the University of North Carolina for 27 years.

* Mike Lum, an outfielder who debuted with the Braves in 1967, became the first native Hawaiian to play in the majors since the islands gained statehood. Lum played 12 years with the Braves and hit home runs in three consecutive at bats on July 3, 1970, against San Diego.

* In 1949, Braves infielder Connie Ryan was the victim of

one of the most unusual ejections in franchise history. Ryan, who later was a Braves coach in both Milwaukee and Atlanta, was thrown out of a game against the Dodgers because he was wearing a yellow raincoat in the on-deck circle to protest the soggy playing conditions.

* The most unusual holdout in Braves history was reserve catcher Frank Gibson, who had a career batting average of .274 but played in more than 90 games just once. Gibson, who was with the Braves from 1921 to 1927, held out one spring not for more money, but for more work.

* James "Doc" Crandall, who appeared briefly with the Braves in 1918, is regarded as the first pitcher to be used as a regular reliever. He gained that reputation and his nickname with the New York Giants because famed writer Damon Runyon said he was the "physician of the pitching emergency."

* Mike de la Hoz, a Braves utility man from 1964 to 1967, didn't get much playing time, so he had to make the most of his opportunities. On July 8, 1965, he did just that. He entered the game in the eighth inning and delivered a pinch-hit home run. In the ninth, de la Hoz singled home the tying run, and in the 12th, he singled and scored the decisive run in a 9–8 victory over Houston.

* Roy Hartsfield, a native Georgian who played second base for the Boston Braves from 1950 to 1952, became the first manager of the expansion Toronto Blue Jays in 1977.

* In 1939, 19-year-old infielder Sibby Sisti played 63 games in the majors for the Braves and batted .228. Sisti spent his entire 13-year big league career with the Braves. Sisti also had a brief acting career, appearing as the "opposing" team's manager in the classic movie The Natural, which starred Robert Redford.

* Doc Farrell, the Braves' regular shortstop in 1927–28, was a dentist in the off-season.

* Clarence Jones, a coach with the Braves since 1984, became the first American to win the home run crown in Japan when he hit 38 for the Kintetsu Buffaloes in 1974. He won again in 1976 with 36 homers.

* Whitey Wietelmann, a Bees/Braves infielder from 1939 to 1946, once had the little finger on his left hand shattered by a line drive when he was pitching batting practice. He had to have part of the finger amputated.

* In 1962 the Braves signed Peter Marchegiano, brother of heavyweight boxing champ Rocky Marciano, to a minor league contract. He never made it to the majors.

Sibby Sisti had a role as a manager in the movie "The Natural," which starred Robert Redford.

11

Trades, Acquisitions, and Sales

Perhaps nothing else in sports attracts interest like trades and prospective trades. Just as "everyone thinks he's a comedian," every baseball fan thinks he's a general manager.

Therefore, this book wouldn't be complete without a discussion of the best and worst trades in franchise history. There certainly have been plenty of both.

The Braves have won just two World Series championships—1914 and 1957—and trades played a key role in both. They acquired second baseman Johnny Evers just before the 1914 season, and he led manager George Stallings' team to a "miracle" that year. In 1957 the acquisition of second baseman Red Schoendienst at the June 15 trading deadline helped get Fred Haney's team over the hump.

But the key to winning the World Series in 1957 was right-hander Lou Burdette, who beat the Yankees three times. The 1951 deal that brought Burdette to the Braves from the Yankees in exchange for Johnny Sain ranks as the best trade in franchise history.

The worst trade in Braves history? How about the 1973 deal that sent farmhand Andre Thornton to the Cubs for a washed-up Joe Pepitone? Thornton hit 253 career home runs, more than all but three men—Hank Aaron, Eddie Mathews, and Dale Murphy—hit as Braves.

Rating trades, of course, is completely subjective. Everyone has their own opinion. That's what makes it so much fun.

10 Best Trades

1. August 30, 1951

Right-hander Lou Burdette acquired from Yankees for right-hander Johnny Sain.

This deal involved two of the greatest pitchers in franchise history, and the Braves caught them both going the right way. Burdette had only 1⅓ innings of big league experience but became the fourth-winningest pitcher in franchise history and the hero of the 1957 World Series championship. Sain was well past his peak, though he did give the Yankees some good bullpen work for three years.

2. September 30, 1946

Third baseman Bob Elliott and catcher Hank Camelli acquired from Pittsburgh for third baseman Bill Herman, right-hander Elmer Singleton, outfielder Stan Wentzel, and infielder Whitey Wietelmann.

Grand theft. The Pirates wanted Herman to be their manager. He lasted one season, which produced a last-place finish. Elliott won the 1947 MVP Award, helped lead the Braves to the pennant the following year, and gave the club five solid seasons. None of the other players on either side of the deal were productive.

3. February 16, 1953

Right-hander Russ Meyer acquired from Philadelphia for first baseman Earl Torgeson; infielder Rocky Bridges and outfielder Jim Pendleton acquired from Brooklyn for Meyer; and first baseman Joe Adcock acquired from Cincinnati for Bridges.

The Braves had high hopes for Earl Torgeson, and though he gave them four good seasons, he never was the first baseman they expected. He certainly was no Adcock. This four-team trade basically was Torgeson for Adcock and Jim Pendleton. Given a chance to play full-time, Adcock developed into one of the game's legendary sluggers. Torgeson played nine more seasons but never as well as he had in Boston.

4. December 9, 1941

Outfielder Tommy Holmes acquired from New York Yankees for first baseman Buddy Hassett and outfielder Gene Moore.

Talk about a steal. Hassett was finished, and though Moore helped the Browns win the 1944 American League pennant, he was well on the downside of his career. Holmes, of course, was the victim of the talent backed up in the Yankees' system and became one of the great players in Braves history.

5. August 13, 1987

Right-hander John Smoltz acquired from Detroit for right-hander Doyle Alexander.

The Tigers mortgaged the future and helped make the Braves'. Alexander was 9–0 down the stretch to enable Detroit to win a division title. But Smoltz developed into a central figure in the Braves' success of the 1990s as Bobby Cox's big-game pitcher.

The Braves mortgaged the future for Len Barker, who was supposed to win the 1983 division title for them but proved virtually useless.

6. April 1, 1991

Outfielder Otis Nixon and third baseman Boi Rodriguez acquired from Montreal for catcher Jimmy Kremers and right-hander Keith Morrison.

This deal didn't get much attention when it was made, but it was one of John Schuerholz's best. Nixon was a major contributor to two pennants and three division titles. He batted .286 as a Brave, averaged over 53 steals per season, and provided excellent defense—including "The Catch." Best of all, he came virtually free of charge.

7. November 13, 1895

Outfielder "Slidin' " Billy Hamilton acquired from Phillies for third baseman Billy Nash.

Though Hamilton was past his peak, he had plenty left, including five .300 seasons. He was a key member of the pennant-winning Beaneaters of 1897 on his way to the Hall of Fame. Nash, who'd served Boston well, played poorly in Philadelphia and managed even worse in a one-year stint.

8. June 15, 1957

Second baseman Red Schoendienst acquired from New York Giants for right-hander Ray Crone, second base-

man Danny O'Connell, and outfielder Bobby Thomson.

The Braves might have won the 1957 pennant and World Series without Schoendienst, but it's very questionable. His acquisition at the trading deadline plugged the team's biggest hole. His leadership and league-leading 200 hits were invaluable. Thomson and O'Connell were well past their prime, and Crone was a bust.

9. February 11, 1914

Second baseman Johnny Evers acquired from Chicago Cubs for second baseman Bill Sweeney.

In 1991 the Braves signed a free-agent third baseman named Terry Pendleton who won the National League's MVP Award and led the team to a pennant. Seventy-seven years earlier, they made a similar transaction. Evers' career was in decline, but he had one great season left. He captained the Braves to their 1914 "miracle" and won the Chalmers Award as the league's MVP. Sweeney, who'd served the Braves well, had a poor season for the Cubs and never played in the majors again.

10. December 3, 1963

Outfielder Felipe Alou, catcher Ed Bailey, left-hander Billy Hoeft, and in-

After coming to Boston from Philadelphia, "Slidin' " Billy Hamilton had five .300 seasons and led the league in hits in 1897.

fielder Ernie Bowman acquired from the Giants for catcher Del Crandall, left-hander Bob Hendley, and right-hander Bob Shaw.

The Braves made few wise decisions when breaking up their championship team of the 1950s, but this was one of them. Alou became one of the club's best players, leading the league in hits twice in six seasons and providing power, too. Crandall was finished, and Hendley and Shaw each had only one decent season left.

10 Worst Trades

1. May 19, 1973

First baseman Andre Thornton sent to Cubs for first baseman Joe Pepitone.

Pepitone went to bat 11 times for the Braves and never played again. Thornton, who was 23 at the time of the deal and had yet to make the majors, went on to hit 253 career home runs, mostly with Cleveland.

2. February 1, 1954

Left-handers Johnny Antonelli and Don Liddle, third baseman Bobby Klaus, and catcher Ebba St. Claire sent to the Giants for catcher Sam Calderone and outfielder Bobby Thomson.

It's staggering to think how much more the Braves of the 1950s might have accomplished if they'd held onto Antonelli, who was an All-Star in five of the first six years after he was traded and av-

eraged 17 wins in that period. They thought they needed a power-hitting outfielder—Thomson—when Hank Aaron proved quite ready to fill that slot.

3. June 15, 1939

First baseman Elbie Fletcher sent to Pittsburgh for first baseman Bill Schuster.

Schuster played exactly two games for the Braves and only 123 in his career. Though Fletcher lacked power, he was a slick fielder who led the league in on-base percentage three straight seasons for the Pirates.

4. August 29, 1983

Outfielder Brett Butler, third baseman Brook Jacoby, and right-hander Rick Behenna sent to Cleveland for right-hander Len Barker.

This was the most controversial trade in the Braves' Atlanta history because it mortgaged the future in a failed attempt to win a division title. Barker's arm was fried. He won just 10 games in two-plus seasons. However, Butler and Jacoby turned into All-Stars. The deal helped plunge the Braves into a depression for several seasons.

5. November 17, 1975

Outfielder Dusty Baker and first baseman Ed Goodsen sent to Dodgers for utility man Lee Lacy, outfielders Jimmy Wynn and Tom Paciorek, and shortstop Jerry Royster.

This was supposed to be a blockbuster for the Braves, but all it did was give the Dodgers one of the best outfielders in their storied history. Baker seemed to be struggling trying to fill the shoes of Hank Aaron, but he blossomed in Los

Angeles. Royster failed to live up to his promise, and the other players the Braves received were insignificant acquisitions.

6. December 15, 1960

Right-hander Joey Jay and left-hander Juan Pizarro sent to Cincinnati for shortstop Roy McMillan.

Judging pitching talent was not a strong point of the Braves' brain trust in the 1950s. They had Warren Spahn and Lou Burdette, but they could have had so much more. McMillan provided a couple of good years of defense at shortstop, but his presence did not lead to an improved team. Jay and Pizarro, meanwhile, developed into All-Stars given the opportunity to pitch.

7. November 1, 1972

Second baseman Felix Millan and left-hander George Stone sent to Mets for right-handers Danny Frisella and Gary Gentry.

They celebrated this deal at Shea Stadium for quite a while. In need of pitchers, the Braves thought they'd acquired a couple who were hidden in the Mets' overstock. But Frisella and Gentry failed to produce, while Millan and Stone contributed greatly to the Mets' pennant in '73.

8. December 10, 1985

Right-hander Steve Bedrosian and outfielder Milt Thompson sent to Philadelphia for catcher Ozzie Virgil and right-hander Pete Smith.

Returned to the bullpen by the Phillies, Bedrosian became a Cy Young Award winner within two years. Virgil and Smith both had their moments as Braves, but neither provided anywhere near the sustained production Bedrosian did after the trade.

9. May 28, 1975

Right-hander Ron Reed and outfielder Wayne Nordhagen sent to St. Louis for left-hander Ray Sadecki and right-hander Elias Sosa.

Sadecki and Sosa were virtually useless to the Braves. However, Reed remained one of the better pitchers in the league for several seasons, especially after the Phillies moved him to the bullpen in 1976.

10. April 30, 1962

Right-hander Bob Buhl sent to Cubs for left-hander Jack Curtis.

This deal is another example of what a poor job the Braves did in breaking up their great team of the 1950s. Though Buhl's career was in decline, he averaged 13 wins for four seasons working in cozy Wrigley Field. Curtis won four games for the Braves—the last four victories of his career.

Major Trades and Acquisitions

Following is a list of the significant trades, sales, purchases, and free-agent signings in franchise history, dating from the formation of the National League in 1876.

1895, November 13
Outfielder Billy Hamilton acquired from Philadelphia Phillies for third baseman Billy Nash.

1904, December 14
Right-hander Chick Fraser and third baseman Harry Wolverton acquired

The Beaneaters gave up on Vic Willis after the 1905 season and traded him to Pittsburgh, where he had four straight 20-win seasons.

from Philadelphia Phillies for right-hander Togie Pittinger.

1905, December 13
Third baseman Dave Brain, first baseman Del Howard, and right-hander Vive Lindaman acquired from Pittsburgh for right-hander Vic Willis. Catcher Jack O'Neill and right-hander Big Jeff Pfeffer acquired from Chicago (NL) for catcher Pat Moran.

1906, January 25
Shortstop Al Bridwell acquired from Cincinnati for outfielder Jim Delahanty.

1906, May 7
Right-hander Gus Dorner acquired from Cincinnati for right-hander Chick Fraser.

1906, December 11
Left-hander Patsy Flaherty, second baseman Claude Ritchey, and outfielder Ginger Beaumont acquired from Pittsburgh for shortstop Ed Abbaticchio.

1907, June 20
Outfielder Newt Randall and infielder Bill Sweeney acquired from Chicago (NL) for outfielder Del Howard.

1907, December 13
Catcher Frank Bowerman, outfielder George Browne, shortstop Bill Dahlen,

right-hander George Ferguson, and first baseman Dan McGann acquired from New York (NL) for shortstop Al Bridwell, catcher Tom Needham, and first baseman Fred Tenney.

1908, June 17
Right-handers Tom McCarthy and Harley Young acquired from Pittsburgh for left-hander Irv Young.

1909, July 16
Right-handers Buster Brown and Lew Richie and second baseman Dave Shean acquired from Philadelphia (NL) for outfielder Johnny Bates and infielder Charlie Starr.

1910, February 1
Outfielder Fred Liese acquired from Chicago (NL) for outfielder Ginger Beaumont.

1910, April 4
Outfielder Wilson Collins and third baseman Buck Herzog acquired from New York (NL) for outfielder Beals Becker.

1910, April 28
Right-hander Sam Frock and first baseman Bud Sharpe acquired from Pittsburgh for right-hander Kirby White.

1910, May 13
Outfielder Doc Miller acquired from Chicago (NL) for right-hander Lew Richie.

1911, February 25
Third baseman Scotty Ingerton and right-hander Big Jeff Pfeffer acquired from Chicago (NL) for second baseman Dave Shean.

1911, June 10
Right-hander Hank Griffin, outfielder Al Kaiser, catcher Johnny Kling, and right-hander Orlie Weaver acquired from Chicago (NL) for outfielders Bill Collins and Wilbur Good, right-hander Cliff Curtis, and catcher Peaches Graham.

1911, July 21
Shortstop Al Bridwell and catcher Hank Gowdy acquired from New York (NL) for infielder Buck Herzog.

1912, February 20
Outfielder Vin Campbell acquired from Pittsburgh for outfielder Mike Donlin.

1912, June 21
Outfielder John Titus acquired from Philadelphia (NL) for outfielder Doc Miller.

1913, May 1
Third baseman Tex McDonald acquired from Cincinnati for catcher Johnny Kling.

1914, February 11
Second baseman Johnny Evers acquired from Chicago (NL) for second baseman Bill Sweeney.

1914, June 29
Outfielder Ted Cather and infielder Possum Whitted acquired from St. Louis (NL) for right-hander Hub Perdue.

1914, July 3
Outfielder Josh Devore acquired from Philadelphia (NL) for infielder Jack Martin.

1914, December 24
Outfielder Sherry Magee acquired from Philadelphia (NL) for infielder Oscar Dugey and utility man Possum Whitted.

1916, December 14
Outfielder Joe Kelly acquired from Chicago (NL) for coach Fred Mitchell.

1918, January 4
Second baseman Larry Doyle and catcher Art Wilson acquired from Chicago (NL) for left-hander Lefty Tyler.

1918, January 8
Second baseman Buck Herzog and infielder Jimmy Smith acquired from New York (NL) for right-hander Jesse Barnes and second baseman Larry Doyle.

1919, January 30
Infielder Lena Blackburne acquired from Cincinnati for outfielder Wally Rehg.

1919, February 22
First baseman Walter Holke acquired from New York (NL) for infielder Jimmy Smith.

1919, August 1
Right-handers Red Causey, Johnny Jones, and Joe Oeschger, and catcher Mickey O'Neil acquired from New York (NL) for left-hander Art Nehf.

1919, August 2
Outfielder Les Mann and second baseman Charlie Pick acquired from Chicago (NL) for second baseman Buck Herzog.

1921, January 23
Infielder Walter Barbare and outfielders Fred Nicholson and Billy Southworth acquired from Pittsburgh for shortstop Rabbit Maranville.

1922, February 18
Infielder Larry Kopf and left-hander Rube Marquard acquired from Cincinnati for right-hander Jack Scott.

1922, July 30
Right-handers Larry Benton, Harry Hulihan, and Fred Toney acquired from New York (NL) for right-hander Hugh McQuillan.

1923, June 7
Catcher Earl Smith acquired from New York (NL) for catcher Hank Gowdy; right-hander Jesse Barnes acquired from New York (NL) for right-hander Mule Watson.

1923, November 12
Shortstop Dave Bancroft and outfielders Bill Cunningham and Casey Stengel acquired from New York (NL) for right-hander Joe Oeschger and outfielder Billy Southworth.

Boston obtained outfielder Casey Stengel from the Giants in a deal that involved three future Braves managers.

1923, December 13
Second baseman Cotton Tierney acquired from Philadelphia (NL) for shortstop Hod Ford and outfielder Ray Powell. (Powell later replaced by outfielder Al Nixon.)

1925, February 4
Outfielder Bernie Neis acquired from Brooklyn for outfielder Cotton Tierney.

1925, April 17
Right-hander Rosy Ryan acquired from New York (NL) for right-hander Tim McNamara.

1925, October 6
Outfielder Eddie Brown, infielder Jimmy Johnston, and catcher Zack Taylor acquired from Brooklyn for right-hander Jesse Barnes, outfielder Gus Felix, and catcher Mickey O'Neil.

1927, June 12
Outfielder Doc Farrell and right-handers Kent Greenfield and Hugh McQuillan acquired from New York (NL) for right-hander Larry Benton, catcher Zack Taylor, and shortstop Herb Thomas.

1928, January 10
Second baseman Rogers Hornsby acquired from New York (NL) for catcher Shanty Hogan and outfielder Jimmy Welsh.

1928, March 20
Third baseman Les Bell acquired from St. Louis (NL) for third baseman Andy High.

1928, June 15
Right-handers Virgil Barnes, Ben Cantwell, and Bill Clarkson and catcher Al Spohrer acquired from New York (NL) for right-hander Joe Genewich.

1928, November 7
Right-handers Socks Seibold and Bruce Cunningham, left-hander Percy Jones, outfielder Lou Legett, and second baseman Freddie Maguire acquired from Chicago (NL) for second baseman Rogers Hornsby.

1929, June 14
Outfielder Jimmy Welsh acquired from New York (NL) for outfielder Doc Farrell.

1930, April 9
Right-hander Burleigh Grimes acquired from Pittsburgh for left-hander Percy Jones.

1930, June 16
Right-hander Fred Frankhouse and left-hander Bill Sherdel acquired from St. Louis (NL) for right-hander Burleigh Grimes.

1930, October 14
Right-hander Bill McAfee acquired from Chicago (NL) for right-hander Bob Smith.

1933 June 15
Outfielder Hal Lee and third baseman Pinky Whitney acquired from Philadelphia (NL) for outfielder Wes Schulmerich and third baseman Fritz Knothe.

1935, December 12
Right-handers Ray Benge and Bobby Reis, second baseman Tony Cuccinello, and catcher Al Lopez acquired from Brooklyn for left-hander Ed Brandt and outfielder Randy Moore.

Boston acquired All-Star second baseman Tony Cuccinello from Brooklyn in a six-player trade.

1936, February 6
Right-hander Johnny Babich and outfielder Gene Moore acquired from Brooklyn for right-hander Fred Frankhouse.

1936, April 30
Infielder Mickey Haslin acquired from Philadelphia (NL) for third baseman Pinky Whitney.

1936, December 4
Infielder Eddie Mayo acquired from New York (NL) for infielder Mickey Haslin.

1937, June 15
Right-hander Frank Gabler acquired from New York (NL) for outfielder Wally Berger.

1938, December 13
First baseman Buddy Hassett and outfielder Jimmy Outlaw acquired from Brooklyn for right-hander Ira Hutchinson and outfielder Gene Moore; right-hander Fred Frankhouse acquired from Brooklyn for third baseman Joe Stripp.

1938, December 16
Outfielder Johnny Dickshot and catcher Al Todd acquired from Pittsburgh (NL) for catcher Ray Mueller.

1939, March 31
Right-hander Bill Posedel acquired from Brooklyn for catcher Al Todd.

1939, June 15
Shortstop Bill Schuster acquired from Pittsburgh for first baseman Elbie Fletcher.

1939, December 6
First baseman Les Scarsella acquired from Cincinnati for right-hander Jim Turner; right-hander Jim Tobin acquired from Pittsburgh for right-hander Johnny Lanning.

1939, December 8
Right-hander Bill Swift acquired from Pittsburgh for right-hander Danny MacFayden.

1940, June 15
Infielder Al Glossop and right-hander Manny Salvo acquired from New York (NL) for second baseman Tony Cuccinello.

1941, May 7
Outfielder Lloyd Waner acquired from Pittsburgh for right-hander Nick Strincevich.

Buddy Hassett batted .308 for the 1939 Bees after being acquired from Brooklyn.

1941, June 12
Right-hander John Hutchings acquired from Cincinnati for outfielder Lloyd Waner.

1941, June 15
Catcher Al Montgomery acquired from Chicago (NL) for first baseman Babe Dahlgren.

1941, December 9
Outfielder Tommy Holmes acquired from New York (AL) for first baseman Buddy Hassett and outfielder Gene Moore.

A trade with Pittsburgh brought Lloyd "Little Poison" Waner to the Braves, where he was reunited with brother Paul "Big Poison" Waner for a short time.

One of the Braves' best trades brought outfielder Tommy Holmes to Boston from the Yankees.

1942, December 4
Right-hander Nate Andrews and shortstop Eddie Joost acquired from Cincinnati for shortstop Eddie Miller.

1943, April 27
Catcher Hugh Poland and second baseman Connie Ryan acquired from New York (NL) for catcher Ernie Lombardi.

1945, May 23
Right-hander Mort Cooper acquired from St. Louis (NL) for right-hander Red Barrett.

1945, June 14
Outfielder Joe Medwick and left-hander Ewald Pyle acquired from New York (NL) for catcher Clyde Kluttz.

1946, February 5
Outfielder Johnny Hopp acquired from St. Louis (NL) for shortstop Eddie Joost.

1946, April 18
Right-hander Jim Konstanty acquired from Cincinnati for outfielder Max West.

The Braves got Jim Konstanty from Cincinnati but didn't give him much of a chance before sending him to Philadelphia, where he helped pitch the Phillies to a pennant in 1950.

1946, June 12
Outfielder Johnny Barrett acquired from Pittsburgh for outfielder Chuck Workman.

1946, June 15
Second baseman Billy Herman acquired from Brooklyn for catcher Stew Hofferth.

1946, September 30
Catcher Hank Camelli and third baseman Bob Elliott acquired from Pittsburgh for third baseman Bill Herman, right-hander Elmer Singleton, outfielder Stan Wentzel, and infielder Whitey Wietelmann.

1947, March 29
Right-hander Andy Karl acquired from Philadelphia (NL) for catcher Don Padgett.

1947, June 13
Right-hander Bill Voiselle acquired from New York (NL) for right-hander Mort Cooper.

1947, November 18
Right-hander Al Lyons, outfielder Jim Russell, and catcher Bill Salkeld acquired from Pittsburgh for outfielder Johnny Hopp and second baseman Danny Murtaugh.

1948, February 28
Infielder Bobby Sturgeon acquired from Chicago (NL) for shortstop Dick Culler and right-hander Walt Lanfranconi.

1948, March 6
Second baseman Eddie Stanky acquired from Brooklyn for outfielder Bama Rowell and first baseman Ray Sanders.

1948, May 11
Outfielder Marv Rickert acquired from Cincinnati for outfielder Danny Litwhiler.

1948, December 15
Outfielder Pete Reiser acquired from Brooklyn for shortstop Nanny Fernandez and outfielder Mike McCormick.

1949, June 15
Outfielder Ed Sauer acquired from Pittsburgh for catcher Phil Masi.

1949, December 13
Infielder Gene Mauch acquired from Chicago (NL) for right-hander Bill Voiselle.

The Braves traded Danny Murtaugh to Pittsburgh, where he became known more for his work as a manager than as a second baseman.

1949, December 14
Outfielders Sid Gordon and Willard Marshall, shortstop Buddy Kerr, and right-hander Red Webb acquired from New York (NL) for shortstop Alvin Dark and second baseman Eddie Stanky.

1949, December 24
Outfielder Luis Olmo acquired from Brooklyn for outfielders Jim Russell and Ed Sauer.

1950, May 10
Catcher Walker Cooper acquired from Cincinnati for second baseman Connie Ryan.

1951, August 30
Right-hander Lou Burdette acquired from New York (AL) for right-hander Johnny Sain.

Sid Gordon was among the four players the Braves got from the Giants in exchange for Eddie Stanky and Al Dark.

Shortly after Andy Pafko was acquired from Brooklyn, the Braves moved to Milwaukee where he became a fan favorite.

1951, October 11
Shortstop Jack Cusick acquired from Chicago (NL) for outfielder Bob Addis.

1952, April 9
Right-hander Sheldon Jones acquired from New York (NL) for third baseman Bob Elliott.

1952, December 20
Right-hander Monk Dubiel acquired from Chicago (NL) for right-hander Sheldon Jones.

1953, January 17
Outfielder Andy Pafko acquired from Brooklyn for second baseman Roy Hartsfield.

1953, February 16
Right-hander Russ Meyer acquired from Philadelphia (NL) for first baseman Earl Torgeson; infielder Rocky Bridges and outfielder Jim Pendleton acquired from Brooklyn for right-hander Russ Meyer; first baseman Joe Adcock acquired from Cincinnati for infielder Rocky Bridges.

1953, December 26
Second baseman Danny O'Connell acquired from Pittsburgh for outfielders Sid Gordon and Sam Jethroe, left-handers Larry LaSalle and Fred Waters, and right-handers Curt Raydon and Max Surkont.

1954, February 1
Catcher Sam Calderone and outfielder Bobby Thomson acquired from New York (NL) for left-hander Johnny Antonelli, third baseman Bobby Klaus, left-hander Don Liddle, and catcher Ebba St. Claire.

1954, February 10
Catcher Charlie White acquired from Baltimore for right-hander Vern Bickford.

1954, March 21
Shortstop Roy Smalley acquired from Chicago (NL) for right-hander Dave Cole.

1955, June 3
Catcher Del Rice acquired from St. Louis (NL) for outfielder Pete Whisenant.

1956, April 9
Outfielder Bob Hazle and right-hander Corky Valentine acquired from Cincinnati for first baseman George Crowe.

1957, February 12
Outfielder Charlie King acquired from Detroit for second baseman Jack Dittmer.

1957, April 3
Infielder Dick Cole acquired from Pittsburgh for outfielder Jim Pendleton.

1957, June 15
Second baseman Red Schoendienst acquired from New York (NL) for right-hander Ray Crone, second baseman Danny O'Connell, and outfielder Bobby Thomson.

1957, November 16
Shortstop Casey Wise acquired from Chicago (NL) for outfielder Charlie King and right-handers Ben Johnson and Len Williams.

1957, December 5
Outfielder Eddie Haas and right-handers Don Kaiser and Bob Rush acquired from Chicago (NL) for left-hander Taylor Phillips and catcher Sammy Taylor.

1958, June 13
Catcher Joe Lonnett acquired from Philadelphia (NL) for catcher Carl Sawatski.

1959, March 31
Infielder Ted Kazanski, catcher Stan Lopata, and second baseman Johnny O'Brien acquired from Philadelphia (NL) for right-hander Gene Conley, infielder Harry Hanebrink, and shortstop Joe Koppe.

1959, April 11
First baseman Mickey Vernon acquired from Cleveland for right-hander Humberto Robinson.

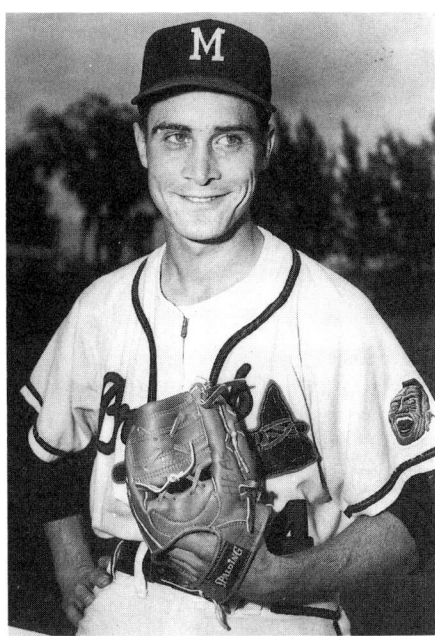

When the Braves acquired outfielder Eddie Haas from the Cubs, they had no idea he'd be their manager nearly 30 years later.

1959, October 16
Catcher Charlie Lau and right-hander Don Lee acquired from Detroit for right-hander Don Kaiser, catcher Mike Roarke, and shortstop Casey Wise.

1960, May 11
Left-hander George Brunet acquired from Kansas City for right-hander Bob Giggie.

1960, May 17
First baseman Ron Jackson acquired from Boston for first baseman Ray Boone.

1960, June 22
Third baseman Alvin Dark acquired from Philadelphia for infielder Joe Morgan.

1960, October 31
Infielder Andre Rodgers acquired from San Francisco for third baseman Alvin Dark.

1960, December 7
Second baseman Frank Bolling and outfielder Neil Chrisley acquired from Detroit for catcher Dick Brown, outfielder Billy Bruton, second baseman Chuck Cottier, and right-hander Terry Fox.

1960, December 15
Shortstop Roy McMillan acquired from Cincinnati for right-hander Joey Jay and left-hander Juan Pizarro.

1961, March 31
Right-hander Moe Drabowsky and left-hander Seth Morehead acquired from Chicago (NL) for infielders Andre Rodgers and Daryl Robertson.

1961, May 9
Outfielder Frank Thomas acquired from Chicago (NL) for utility man Mel Roach.

1961, June 1
Infielder Billy Consolo acquired from Minnesota for second baseman Billy Martin.

1961, June 15
Outfielder Gino Cimoli acquired from Pittsburgh for shortstop Johnny Logan.

1961, November 28
Outfielder Frank Thomas traded to New York (NL) for outfielder Gus Bell.

1961, December 15
Infielder Lou Klimchock and right-hander Bob Shaw acquired from Kansas City for catcher Jose Azcue, infielder Ed Charles, and outfielder Manny Jimenez.

1962, April 30
Left-hander Jack Curtis acquired from Chicago (NL) for right-hander Bob Buhl.

1962, November 27
Outfielder Don Dillard, right-hander Frank Funk, and outfielder Ty Cline acquired from Cleveland for first baseman Joe Adcock and left-hander Jack Curtis.

1962, November 30
First baseman Norm Larker acquired from Houston for outfielder Jim Bolger and right-hander Connie Grob.

1963, June 15
Catcher/first baseman Gene Oliver and right-hander Bob Sadowski acquired from St. Louis for right-hander Lou Burdette.

1963, December 3
Outfielder Felipe Alou, catcher Ed Bailey, left-hander Billy Hoeft, and infielder Ernie Bowman acquired from San Francisco for catcher Del Crandall, left-hander Bob Hendley, and right-hander Bob Shaw.

1964, April 9
Outfielder Gary Kolb and catcher Jimmie Coker acquired from St. Louis for catcher Bob Uecker.

Milwaukee obtained Gene Oliver from St. Louis in the Lou Burdette trade.

1964, May 8
Right-hander Jay Hook and outfielder Adrian Garrett acquired from New York (NL) for shortstop Roy McMillan.

1964, June 3
Outfielder Len Gabrielson traded to Chicago (NL) for catcher Merritt Ranew.

1964, August 8
Right-hander Frank Lary acquired from New York (NL) for right-hander Dennis Ribant.

1964, October 21
Right-hander Ron Piche and catcher Phil Roof traded to Los Angeles (AL) for right-hander Dan Osinski.

1965, February 1
Left-hander Billy O'Dell acquired from San Francisco for catcher Ed Bailey.

1965, May 23
Right-hander Ken Johnson and outfielder/first baseman Jim Beauchamp acquired from Houston for outfielder Lee Maye.

1965, December 15
Left-hander Arnie Earley, first baseman Lee Thomas, and right-hander Jay Ritchie acquired from Boston for right-handers Dan Osinski and Bob Sadowski.

1966, May 28
Right-hander Ted Abernathy acquired from Chicago (NL) for first baseman Lee Thomas.

1966, May 29
First baseman/outfielder John Herrnstein acquired from Chicago (NL) for first baseman/outfielder Marty Keough and left-hander Arnie Earley.

1966, June 15
Right-hander Joey Jay acquired from Cincinnati for right-hander Hank Fischer; right-hander Don Schwall acquired from Pittsburgh for left-hander Billy O'Dell.

1966, October 14
Catcher John Hoffman, shortstop Ed Pacheco, and outfielder Gene Ratliff acquired from Houston for second baseman Wes Bales, right-hander Tom Dukes, and left-hander Dan Schneider.

1966, November 29
Third baseman Clete Boyer acquired from New York (AL) for outfielder Bill Robinson and right-hander Chi Chi Olivo.

1966, December 31
Right-hander Bob Bruce and outfielder Dave Nicholson acquired from Houston for third baseman Eddie Mathews, right-hander Arnie Umbach, and infielder Sandy Alomar.

1967, June 6
Catcher Bob Uecker acquired from Philadelphia for catcher/first baseman Gene Oliver.

1967, June 15
Right-hander Claude Raymond acquired from Houston for left-hander Wade Blasingame.

1967, October 8
Shortstop Sonny Jackson and first baseman Chuck Harrison acquired from Houston for left-hander Denny Lemaster and shortstop Denis Menke.

1967, October 10
First baseman Deron Johnson acquired from Cincinnati for outfielder Mack Jones, right-hander Jay Ritchie, and first baseman/outfielder Jim Beauchamp.

The Braves parted with Chi Chi Olivo (above) to get Clete Boyer from the Yankees.

1967, December 7
Left-hander Dale Roberts and catcher Bob Tillman acquired from New York (AL) for third baseman Bobby Cox.

1968, June 11
Left-hander Ted Davidson, infielder Bob Johnson, and right-hander Milt Pappas acquired from Cincinnati for right-handers Clay Carroll and Tony Cloninger and infielder Woody Woodward.

1968, December 4
Third baseman Bob Aspromonte acquired from Houston for infielder Marty Martinez.

1969, March 17
First baseman Orlando Cepeda acquired from St. Louis for catcher/first baseman Joe Torre.

1969, March 25
Catcher Dave Adlesh acquired from St. Louis for infielder Bob Johnson.

1969, June 13
Outfielder Tony Gonzalez acquired from San Diego for catcher Walt Hriniak, outfielder Andy Finlay, and infielder Van Kelly.

1969, December 2
Left-hander Larry Jaster acquired from Montreal for right-hander Jim Britton and catcher Don Johnson.

1969, December 3
Right-hander Jim Nash acquired from Oakland for outfielder Felipe Alou.

1970, October 21
Shortstop Marty Perez acquired from California for catcher John Burns.

1970, November 30
Right-hander Hoyt Wilhelm acquired

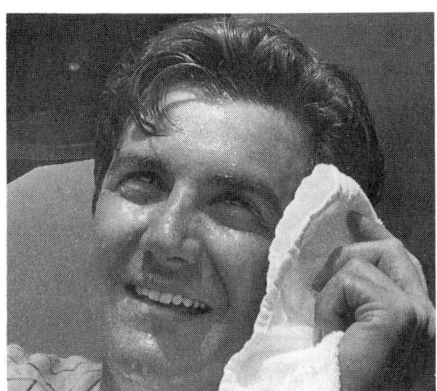

Bob Aspromonte spent two seasons with the Braves as a utilityman after being acquired from Houston.

Paul Casanova spent three years with the Braves after a long stint with the Washington Senators.

from Chicago (NL) for first baseman Hal Breeden.

1970, December 1
Right-hander Ron Herbel acquired from New York (NL) for third baseman Bob Aspromonte.

1970, December 2
Outfielder Hank Allen, right-hander Paul Click, and infielder John Ryan acquired from Milwaukee for catcher Bob Tillman.

1971, December 2
Catcher Paul Casanova acquired from Texas for catcher Hal King.

1972, June 15
Left-hander Joe Hoerner and first baseman Andre Thornton acquired from Philadelphia for right-handers Jim Nash and Gary Neibauer.

1972, October 27
Right-hander Jim Panther acquired from Texas for outfielder Rico Carty.

1972, November 1
Right-handers Danny Frisella and Gary Gentry acquired from New York (NL) for second baseman Felix Millan and left-hander George Stone.

1972, December 1
Right-handers Pat Dobson and Roric Harrison, second baseman Dave Johnson, and catcher Johnny Oates acquired from Baltimore for catcher/first

Roric Harrison (L) and Pat Dobson were supposed to bolster Braves pitching after their acquisition from Baltimore but they failed to do so.

baseman Earl Williams and shortstop Taylor Duncan.

1973, February 28
Right-hander Carl Morton acquired from Montreal for right-hander Pat Jarvis.

1973, April 22
Outfielder Norm Miller acquired from Houston for right-hander Cecil Upshaw.

1973, May 19
First baseman Joe Pepitone acquired from Chicago (NL) for first baseman Andre Thornton.

1973, June 7
First baseman Frank Tepedino, outfielder Wayne Nordhagen, and left-handers Alan Closter and Dave Cheadle acquired from New York (AL) for right-hander Pat Dobson.

1973, December 3
Right-hander Barry Lersch and shortstop Craig Robinson acquired from Philadelphia for right-hander Ron Schueler.

1974, March 26
Catcher Vic Correll acquired from Boston for second baseman Chuck Goggin.

The Braves traded Andre Thornton before he hit the first of his 253 career home runs.

This is Dave May, the man the Braves got from the Brewers for all-time home-run king Hank Aaron.

1974, November 2
Outfielder Dave May and right-hander Roger Alexander acquired from Milwaukee for outfielder Hank Aaron.

1974, November 7
Outfielder Clarence Gaston acquired from San Diego for right-hander Danny Frisella.

1974, December 3
First baseman Dick Allen acquired from Chicago (AL) for catcher Jim Essian.

1975, March 29
First baseman Reggie Sanders acquired from Detroit for first baseman Jack Pierce.

1975, April 17
First baseman/catcher Earl Williams acquired from Baltimore for left-hander Jimmy Freeman.

1975, May 7
Catcher Jim Essian and outfielder Barry Bonnell acquired from Philadelphia for first baseman Dick Allen and catcher Johnny Oates.

1975, May 28
Left-hander Ray Sadecki and right-hander Elias Sosa acquired from St. Louis for right-hander Ron Reed and outfielder Wayne Nordhagen.

1975, June 7
Right-hander Johnny Odom and short-stop Rob Belloir acquired from Cleveland for right-hander Roric Harrison.

1975, June 11
First baseman Ed Goodson acquired from San Francisco for shortstop Craig Robinson.

1975, September 4
Left-hander Norm Angelini and right-hander Al Autry acquired from Kansas City for left-hander Ray Sadecki.

1975, November 17
Utility man Lee Lacy, outfielders Jimmy Wynn and Tom Paciorek, and shortstop Jerry Royster acquired from Los Angeles for outfielder Dusty Baker and first baseman Ed Goodson.

1975, December 12
Shortstop Darrel Chaney acquired from Cincinnati for outfielder/first baseman Mike Lum; left-hander Rogelio Moret acquired from Boston for left-hander Tom House; outfielder Ken Henderson and right-handers Danny Osborn and Dick Ruthven acquired from Chicago (AL) for infielder Larvell Blanks and outfielder Ralph Garr.

1976, June 13
First baseman Willie Montanez, short-stop Craig Robinson, second baseman Mike Eden, and infielder Jake Brown acquired from San Francisco for first baseman Darrell Evans and shortstop Marty Perez.

1976, June 23
Right-hander Mike Marshall acquired from Los Angeles for utility man Lee Lacy and right-hander Elias Sosa.

1976, December 9
Outfielder Jeff Burroughs acquired from Texas for right-hander Adrian Devine, outfielders Ken Henderson and Dave May, left-hander Rogelio Moret, and right-hander Carl Morton.

1977, May 24
Right-hander Eddie Solomon acquired from St. Louis for left-hander Mike Beard.

1977, December 8
Right-handers Tommy Boggs and Adrian Devine and outfielder Eddie Miller acquired from Texas for first baseman Willie Montanez.

1978, June 15
Right-hander Gene Garber acquired from Philadelphia for right-hander Dick Ruthven.

1979, March 31
Shortstop Pepe Frias acquired from Montreal for right-hander Dave Campbell.

1979, May 25
Right-hander Bo McLaughlin acquired from Houston for right-hander Frank LaCorte.

1979, December 3
Catcher Bill Nahorodny acquired from Chicago (AL) for right-hander Rick Wieters.

1979, December 6
First baseman Chris Chambliss and shortstop Luis Gomez acquired from Toronto for outfielder Barry Bonnell, shortstop Pat Rockett, and right-hander Joey McLaughlin.

1979, December 7
Right-hander Doyle Alexander and shortstop Larvell Blanks acquired from Texas for right-hander Adrian Devine and shortstop Pepe Frias.

1980, February 16
Right-hander Gary Melson acquired from Cleveland for left-hander Don Collins.

1980, March 28
Right-hander Buddy Solomon traded to Pittsburgh for right-hander Greg Field.

1980, December 12
Outfielder Craig Landis and right-hander John Montefusco acquired from San Francisco for right-hander Doyle Alexander.

1981, March 7
Left-hander Carlos Diaz acquired from Seattle for outfielder Jeff Burroughs.

1981, March 25
Right-hander Bob Walk acquired from Philadelphia for outfielder Gary Matthews.

1982, February 1
Right-hander Donnie Moore acquired

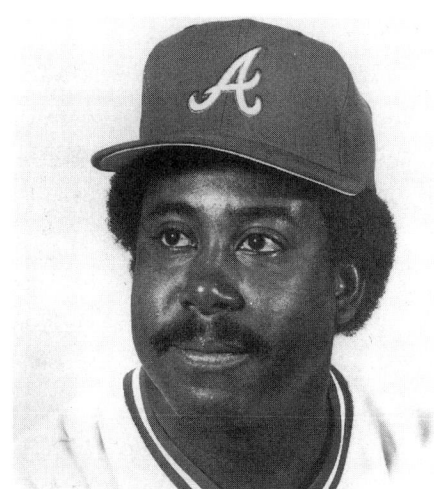

Donnie Moore developed into a good reliever after the Braves got him from St. Louis, but the pressure of baseball was attributed to his suicide in 1989.

Brook Jacoby became a two-time All-Star third baseman in Cleveland after the Braves traded him in the Len Barker deal.

from St. Louis for left-hander Dan Morogiello.

1982, March 23

Right-hander Roger Weaver acquired from Detroit for outfielder Eddie Miller.

1982, April 23

First baseman Bob Watson acquired from New York (AL) for right-hander Scott Patterson.

1982, June 29

Right-hander Pascual Perez and shortstop Carlos Rios acquired from Pittsburgh for left-hander Larry McWilliams.

1982, September 10

Right-hander Tom Hausman acquired from New York (NL) for left-hander Carlos Diaz.

1983, August 29

Right-hander Len Barker acquired from Cleveland for right-hander Rick Behenna, outfielder Brett Butler, and third baseman Brook Jacoby.

1984, June 15

Third baseman Ken Oberkfell acquired from St. Louis for first baseman Mike Jorgensen and left-hander Ken Dayley.

1984, December 5

Catcher Rick Cerone acquired from New York (AL) for right-hander Brian Fisher.

1985, April 17

Outfielder Johnny Rabb acquired from San Francisco for catcher Alex Trevino.

1985, December 6

Outfielder Billy Sample acquired from New York (AL) for shortstop Miguel Sosa.

1985, December 10

Catcher Ozzie Virgil and right-hander Pete Smith acquired from Philadelphia for right-hander Steve Bedrosian and outfielder Milt Thompson.

1986, March 5

Catcher/first baseman Ted Simmons acquired from Milwaukee for catcher Rick Cerone, right-hander David Clay, and shortstop Flavio Alfaro.

1986, June 29

Outfielder Ken Griffey and shortstop Andre Robertson acquired from New York (AL) for outfielder Claudell Washington and shortstop Paul Zuvella.

1986, July 5

Right-hander Doyle Alexander acquired from Toronto for right-hander Duane Ward.

1986, July 6

Right-hander Jim Acker acquired from Toronto for right-hander Joe Johnson.

1986, September 23

Outfielder Darryl Motley acquired from Kansas City for right-hander Steve Shields.

1987, January 19

Outfielder Dion James acquired from Milwaukee for outfielder Brad Komminsk.

1987, January 27

Left-hander Chuck Cary and right-hander Randy O'Neal acquired from Detroit for outfielder Terry Harper and outfielder Freddy Tiburcio.

1987, February 2

Second baseman Damaso Garcia acquired from Toronto for right-hander Craig McMurtry.

1987, July 24

Right-hander Joe Boever acquired from St. Louis for right-hander Randy O'Neal.

1987, August 13

Right-hander John Smoltz acquired from Detroit for right-hander Doyle Alexander.

1987, August 30

Right-hander Gene Garber traded to Kansas City for catcher Terry Bell.

1987, November 11

Outfielder Terry Blocker acquired from New York (NL) for left-hander Kevin Brown.

1987, December 8

Third baseman Ed Whited and right-

The Braves obtained Joe Boever from the Cardinals.

hander Mike Stoker acquired from Houston for shortstop Rafael Ramirez.

1988, March 28

Right-hander Jeff Dedmon traded to Cleveland for right-hander Tommy Kurczewski.

1988, August 28

Third baseman Ken Oberkfell traded to Pittsburgh for outfielder Tommy Gregg.

1988, September 29

Catcher Jody Davis acquired from Chicago (NL) for right-handers Kevin Blankenship and Kevin Coffman.

1989, March 30

Right-hander Dwayne Henry acquired from Texas for right-hander Dave Miller.

1989, July 2

Outfielder Oddibe McDowell acquired from Cleveland for outfielder Dion James; right-handers Sergio Valdez and Nate Minchey and outfielder Kevin

Ken Oberkfell served the Braves for five seasons before being traded to Pittsburgh.

Dean acquired from Montreal for left-hander Zane Smith.

1989, August 23
Shortstop Ed Romero traded to Milwaukee for right-hander Jay Aldrich.

1989, August 24
Left-hander Paul Assenmacher traded to Chicago (NL) for left-hander Pat Gomez and catcher Kelly Mann; left-hander Tony Castillo and catcher Francisco Cabrera acquired from Toronto for right-hander Jim Acker.

1989, December 15
Left-hander Charlie Leibrandt and right-hander Rick Luecken acquired from Kansas City for first baseman Gerald Perry and right-hander Jim Lemasters.

1989, December 17
Catcher Ernie Whitt and outfielder Kevin Batiste acquired from Toronto for right-hander Ricky Trlicek.

1990, January 24
Third baseman Jim Presley acquired from Seattle for right-hander Gary Eave and third baseman Ken Pennington.

1990, April 28
Right-hander Charley Kerfeld acquired from Houston for outfielder Kevin Dean and right-hander Lee Johnson.

1990, July 12
Right-hander Mark Grant acquired from San Diego for left-hander Derek Lilliquist.

1990, July 22
Right-hander Doug Sisk acquired from New York (NL) for right-hander Tony Valle.

1990, July 23
Right-hander Marvin Freeman ac-

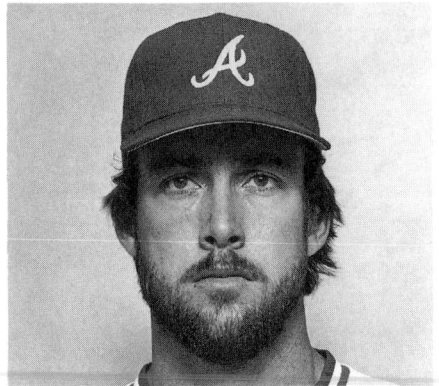

The Braves traded Jim Acker to Toronto in the deal that made Francisco Cabrera a Brave.

Jeff Parrett was one of three players the Braves obtained from the Phillies in the Dale Murphy trade.

quired from Philadelphia for right-hander Joe Boever.

1990, August 4
Right-hander Jeff Parrett, outfielder Jim Vatcher, and shortstop Victor Rosario acquired from Philadelphia for outfielder Dale Murphy and right-hander Tommy Greene.

1990, December 10
Right-hander Scott Taylor acquired from Seattle for outfielder Dennis Hood.

1991, April 1
Outfielder Otis Nixon and third baseman Boi Rodriguez acquired from Montreal for catcher Jimmy Kremers and right-hander Keith Morrison.

1991, June 25
Right-hander Dan Petry acquired from Detroit for shortstop Victor Rosario.

1991, July 31
Right-hander Jim Clancy acquired from Houston for right-handers Matt Turner and Earl Sanders.

1991, August 29
Right-hander Alejandro Pena acquired from New York (NL) for left-hander Tony Castillo and right-hander Joe Roa.

1991, September 29
Catcher Damon Berryhill and right-hander Mike Bielecki acquired from Chicago (NL) for left-hander Yorkis Perez and right-hander Turk Wendell.

1992, May 28
Right-hander Donnie Elliott acquired from Philadelphia for right-hander Ben Rivera.

1992, July 21
Left-hander Mark Davis acquired from Kansas City for right-hander Juan Berenguer.

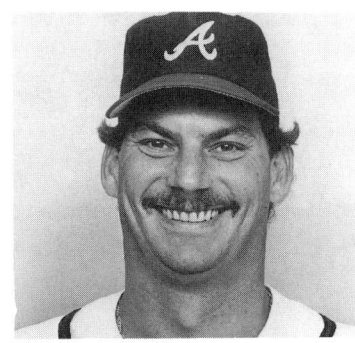

The Braves acquired Jim Clancy from Houston to help in the bullpen down the stretch in 1991.

1992, August 30
Right-hander Jeff Reardon acquired from Boston for right-hander Nate Minchey and outfielder Sean Ross.

1992, December 9
Third baseman Jose Oliva acquired from Texas for left-handers Charlie Leibrandt and Pat Gomez.

1993, July 18
First baseman Fred McGriff acquired from San Diego for right-hander Donnie Elliott and outfielders Vince Moore and Mel Nieves.

1993, November 17
First baseman/outfielder Brian Hunter traded to Pittsburgh for shortstop Jose Delgado.

1993, November 24
Outfielder Dave Gallagher acquired from New York (NL) for right-hander Pete Smith.

1994, May 29
Outfielder Roberto Kelly and right-hander Roger Etheridge acquired from Cincinnati for outfielder Deion Sanders.

1995, April 6
Outfielder Marquis Grissom acquired from Montreal for outfielders Roberto Kelly and Tony Tarasco and right-hander Esteban Yan.

The Braves acquired former Cy Young Award winner Mark Davis from Kansas City in 1992, but he couldn't regain his curveball magic.

Major Purchases and Other Acquisitions

1887, February 14
Catcher King Kelly from Chicago.

1888, April 3
Right-hander John Clarkson from Chicago.

1900, February 9
Utility man Shad Barry, right-hander Bill Dinneen, and outfielder Buck Freeman from Washington (NL).

1900, May 23
Right-hander Nig Cuppy from St. Louis (NL).

1901, March 28
Left-hander Rube Waddell from Pittsburgh.

1904, February 21
Shortstop Joe Bean from Pittsburgh.

1908, April 27
Utility man Jack Hannifin from New York (NL).

1909, February 26
Infielder Charlie Starr from Pittsburgh.

1909, April 17
Outfielder Jimmy Slagle from Chicago (NL).

1909, June 9
First baseman Chick Autry from Cincinnati (NL).

1909, June 19
Outfielder Roy Thomas from Pittsburgh.

1909, July 1
Right-hander Forrest More from St. Louis (NL).

1910, May 9
Right-hander Jiggs Parson from New York (NL).

1910, July 1
Shortstop Ed Abbaticchio from Pittsburgh.

1910, July 19
Outfielder Art Krueger from Cleveland.

1910, September 12
Third baseman Pete Burg from Chicago (AL).

1911, August 1
Outfielder Mike Donlin from New York (NL).

1912, April 10
Third baseman Art Devlin from New York (NL).

1913, March 17
Outfielder Allen Scheer from Washington.

1913, March 30
Outfielder Joe Connolly from Washington.

1913, July 3
Outfielder Otis Clymer from Chicago (NL).

1913, October 20
Right-hander George Beck from Philadelphia (NL).

1914, April 21
First baseman Clarence Kraft from Brooklyn.

1914, August 8
Third baseman Red Smith from Brooklyn.

1914, August 23
Outfielder Herbie Moran from Cincinnati.

1915, April 23
Infielder Dick Egan from Brooklyn.

1915, April 28
Right-hander Pat Ragan from Brooklyn.

1915, September 27
Outfielder Zip Collins from Pittsburgh.

1916, February 9
Left-hander Frank Allen, right-hander Elmer Knetzer, and first baseman Ed Konetchy from Pittsburgh.

1919, March 6
Right-hander Ray Keating from New York (AL).

1919, May 17
Outfielder Walt Cruise from St. Louis (NL).

1919, May 21
Outfielder Jim Thorpe from New York (NL).

1919, June 16
Third baseman Tony Boeckel from Pittsburgh.

1919, June 28
Right-hander Larry Cheney from Brooklyn.

1920, March 18
Right-hander Frank Miller from Pittsburgh.

1920, June 30
Right-hander Mule Watson from Pittsburgh.

1923, January 16
Catcher Dee Cousineau from New York (NL).

1923, December 13
Infielder John Kelleher from Chicago (NL).

1924, May 15
Left-hander Dinty Gearin from New York (NL).

1924, June 7
Outfielder Les Mann from Cincinnati.

1924, June 12
Right-hander Lou North from St. Louis (NL).

1925, July 12
Second baseman Doc Gautreau from Philadelphia (AL).

1925, July 25
Outfielder Andy High from Brooklyn.

1926, February 15
Left-hander George Mogridge from New York (AL).

1926, April 19
Right-hander Jack Smith from St. Louis.

1926, July 20
Infielder Eddie Moore from Pittsburgh.

1926, November 3
Right-hander Jack Knight from Philadelphia (NL).

1928, February 4
Shortstop Jimmy Cooney from St. Louis (NL).

1928, February 28
Catcher Zack Taylor from New York (NL).

1928, May 27
First baseman George Sisler from Washington.

1928, June 25
Infielder Howard Freigau from Brooklyn.

1928, December 8
Outfielder George Harper and shortstop Rabbit Maranville from St. Louis (NL).

1928, December 13
Catcher Pat Collins from New York (AL).

1928, December 24
Third baseman Joe Dugan from New York (AL).

1929, July 15
Catcher Jack Cummings from New York (NL).

1929, September 17
Third baseman Gene Robertson from New York (AL).

1930, March 12
Infielder Billy Rhiel from Brooklyn.

1930, May 12
Right-hander Tom Zachary from New York (AL).

1930, November 12
Catcher Al Bool from Pittsburgh.

1931, May 23
Right-hander Ray Moss from Brooklyn.

1931, May 28
Infielder Bill Hunnefield from Cleveland.

1932, March 19
Outfielder Fred Leach from New York (NL).

1932, December 29
Catcher Shanty Hogan from New York (NL).

1933, June 15
Right-hander Ray Starr from New York (NL).

1933, July 31
Right-hander Bob Smith from Cincinnati.

1934, February 13
Right-hander Steve Swetonic from Pittsburgh.

1934, April 11
Second baseman Marty McManus from Brooklyn.

Ray Starr appeared in only nine games after the Braves bought him from the Giants.

Rabbit Warstler was the Bees' starting shortstop in the late 1930s.

1934, May 13
Left-hander Jim Elliott from Philadelphia (NL).

1935, June 4
Right-hander Danny MacFayden from New York (AL).

1936, January 11
Left-hander Jim McCloskey from Brooklyn.

1936, January 17
Right-hander Tiny Chaplin and left-hander Sharkey Eiland from New York (NL).

1936, April 2
Right-hander Wayne Osborne from Brooklyn.

1936, July 6
Shortstop Rabbit Warstler from Philadelphia (AL).

1936, September 6
Right-hander Fabian Kowalik from Philadelphia (NL).

1937, May 1
Infielder Tommy Thevenow from Brooklyn.

1937, May 11
Outfielder Roy Johnson from New York (AL).

1937, June 4
Third baseman Gil English from Detroit.

1938, May 23
Right-hander Tommy Reis from Philadelphia (NL).

1938, August 1
Third baseman Joe Stripp from St. Louis (NL).

1938, December 29
Outfielder Al Simmons from Washington.

1939, December 5
Outfielder Bud Bates from Philadelphia (NL).

1940, May 29
Outfielder Gene Moore from Brooklyn.

1941, February 25
First baseman Babe Dahlgren from New York (AL).

1941, July 21
Outfielder Frank Demaree from New York (NL).

1942, February 7
Catcher Ernie Lombardi from Cincinnati.

1942, February 26
Right-hander George Washburn from New York (AL).

1943, January 26
Left-hander Lefty Gomez from New York (AL).

1943, May 15
Right-hander Manny Salvo from Philadelphia (NL).

1944, September 23
Infielder Tony York from Chicago (NL).

1945, February 24
Outfielder Carden Gillenwater from Brooklyn.

1945, July 14
Right-hander Bill Lee from Philadelphia (NL).

1945, August 1
Outfielder Morrie Aderholt from Brooklyn.

1946, April 15
First baseman Ray Sanders and right-hander Max Surkont from St. Louis (NL).

1946, May 3
Right-hander Steve Roser from New York (AL).

1946, June 2
Outfielder Mike McCormick from Cincinnati.

1946, June 9
Outfielder Danny Litwhiler from St. Louis (NL).

1946, June 12
Catcher Don Padgett from Brooklyn.

1946, July 8
Catcher Ken O'Dea from St. Louis (NL).

1946, September 19
Left-hander Dick Mulligan from Philadelphia (NL).

1946, December 7
Right-hander Red Barrett from St. Louis (NL).

1947, April 18
Right-hander Johnny Beazley from St. Louis (NL).

1947, June 7
Left-hander Clyde Shoun from Cincinnati.

1947, December 4
Outfielder Jeff Heath from St. Louis (AL).

1949, June 14
Catcher Mickey Livingston from New York (NL).

1950, April 10
Right-hander Charlie Bicknell from Philadelphia (NL).

1950, April 17
Left-hander Bob Chipman from Chicago (NL).

1950, August 8
Left-hander Mickey Haefner from Chicago (AL).

1950, September 13
Second baseman Emil Verban from Chicago (NL).

1951, April 16
Right-hander Blix Donnelly from Philadelphia (NL).

1951, May 13
Right-hander Sid Schacht from St. Louis (AL).

1953, December 7
Outfielder George Metkovich from Chicago (NL).

1958, March 30
Left-hander Dick Littlefield from Chicago (NL).

1959, July 21
Second baseman Bobby Avila from Boston.

1959, August 19
First baseman Ray Boone from Kansas City.

1959, September 11
Outfielder Enos Slaughter from New York (AL).

1960, November 28
Catcher Dick Brown from Chicago (AL).

1960, December 3
Second baseman Billy Martin from Cincinnati.

1961, June 9
First baseman Bob Boyd from Kansas City.

1961, June 15
Catcher Sammy White from Boston.

1961, July 4
Left-hander Johnny Antonelli from Cleveland.

1962, July 1
Second baseman Ken Aspromonte from Cleveland.

1963, May 4
Outfielder Bubba Morton from Detroit.

1964, April 1
Infielder Mike de la Hoz from Cleveland.

1965, July 20
Catcher Jesse Gonder from New York (NL).

1965, September 9
Outfielder/catcher Johnny Blanchard from Kansas City.

1966, April 4
First baseman/outfielder Marty Keough from Cincinnati.

1967, May 31
Catcher Charlie Lau from Baltimore.

"Big Bill" Lee, a big winner in his prime with the Cubs, was nearly 36 years old when the Braves bought him.

The purchase of Jeff Heath from the Browns prior to the 1948 season helped turn the Braves into pennant winners.

1967, June 11
First baseman/outfielder Tito Francona from Philadelphia.

1968, July 29
Second baseman Wayne Causey from California.

1969, September 8
Right-hander Hoyt Wilhelm from California.

1969, October 29
Outfielder Bobby Mitchell from New York (AL).

1970, June 29
Outfielder Jimmie Hall from Chicago (NL).

1970, July 11
Right-hander Don Cardwell from New York (NL).

1971, April 3
Infielder Marv Staehle from Montreal.

1972, June 29
Right-hander Denny McLain from Oakland.

1973, March 27
Catcher Dick Dietz from Los Angeles.

1973, May 22
Catcher Larry Howard from Houston.

1973, May 24
Second baseman Chuck Goggin from Pittsburgh.

1974, March 26
Right-hander Buzz Capra from New York (NL).

1974, April 1
Outfielder Ivan Murrell from San Diego.

1975, June 30
Right-hander Bruce DalCanton from Kansas City.

1976, April 10
Right-hander Andy Messersmith signed as a free agent.

1976, November 18
Outfielder Gary Matthews signed as a free agent.

1977, June 16
Right-hander Steve Hargan from Texas.

1979, February 15
Outfielder/first baseman Mike Lum signed as a free agent.

1979, November 17
Left-hander Al Hrabosky signed as a free agent.

1980, November 15
Outfielder Claudell Washington signed as a free agent.

1981, January 12
Right-hander Gaylord Perry signed as a free agent.

1982, December 2
Left-hander Terry Forster signed as a free agent.

1983, January 25
Left-hander Pete Falcone signed as a free agent.

1983, June 15
First baseman Mike Jorgensen from New York (NL).

1984, April 24
Catcher Alex Trevino from Cincinnati.

1984, December 7
Right-hander Bruce Sutter signed as a free agent.

1986, January 7
Right-hander David Palmer signed as a free agent.

1987, January 21
Outfielder Gary Roenicke signed as a free agent.

1989, March 25
Catcher John Russell from Philadelphia; second baseman Jeff Treadway from Cincinnati.

1989, March 29
Right-hander Mark Eichhorn from Toronto.

1989, August 11
Shortstop Ed Romero from Boston.

1989, November 17
First baseman Nick Esasky signed as a free agent.

Free agent signings like this one of Gaylord Perry became standard fare under the ownership of Ted Turner.

1989, November 20
Shortstop Alexis Infante from Toronto.

1990, April 6
Catcher Phil Lombardi from New York (NL).

1990, April 30
Left-hander Joe Hesketh from Montreal.

1990, September 24
Left-hander Nate Cromwell from Toronto.

1990, December 3
Third baseman Terry Pendleton signed as a free agent.

1990, December 5
First baseman Sid Bream signed as a free agent.

1990, December 18
Shortstop Rafael Belliard signed as a free agent.

1991, January 22
Catcher Mike Heath signed as a free agent.

1991, January 29
Right-hander Juan Berenguer signed as a free agent.

1991, June 15
Right-hander Rick Mahler from Montreal.

1992, January 9
Utility man Steve Lyons signed as a free agent.

1992, December 9
Right-hander Greg Maddux signed as a free agent.

1993, January 4
Infielder Bill Pecota signed as a free agent.

1993, October 5
Right-hander Milt Hill from Cincinnati.

1993, November 18
Outfielder Jarvis Brown from San Diego.

1993, November 26
Catcher Charlie O'Brien signed as a free agent.

1994, February 8
Right-hander Gregg Olson signed as a free agent.

1995, April 12
Outfielder Dwight Smith signed as a free agent.

Major Sales

1895, May 20
Outfielder Jimmie Collins to Louisville.

1895, November 14
Outfielder Tommy McCarthy to Brooklyn.

1897, June 3
First baseman Tommy Tucker to Washington.

1898, August 13
Right-hander Jack Stivetts to St. Louis.

1900, March 22
Outfielder Charlie Frisbee and right-hander/outfielder Charlie Hickman to New York.

1901, May 3
Left-hander Rube Waddell to Chicago (NL).

1901, May 13
Outfielder Shad Barry to Philadelphia (NL).

1908, May 16
Third baseman Dave Brain to Cincinnati.

1909, February 16
Outfielder George Browne to Chicago (NL).

1909, March 1
Catcher Mike Simon to Pittsburgh.

1909, May 21
Right-hander Bill Chappelle to Cincinnati.

1910, September 21
Catcher Harry Smith to Brooklyn.

1911, February 6
Outfielder/first baseman Fred Beck to Cincinnati.

1913, April 15
Infielder Bill McKechnie to New York (AL).

1914, May 4
Right-hander George Beck to Cleveland.

1915, April 6
Left-hander Ensign Cottrell to New York (AL).

1916, April 30
Right-hander Elmer Knetzer to Cincinnati.

1917, April 9
Catcher Earl Blackburn to Chicago (NL).

1917, July 10
Outfielder Joe Wilhoit to Pittsburgh.

1917, July 12
Second baseman Johnny Evers to Philadelphia (NL).

1917, August 1
Outfielder Sherry Magee to Cincinnati.

1919, April 19
First baseman Ed Konetchy to Brooklyn.

1919, May 16
Catcher John Henry to Boston.

1919, May 30
Right-hander Pat Ragan to New York (NL).

1919, July 9
Shortstop Lena Blackburne to Philadelphia (NL).

1919, July 15
Catcher Walt Tragesser on waivers to Philadelphia (NL).

1919, August 16
Right-hander Larry Cheney to Philadelphia (NL).

1920, March 9
Right-hander Red Causey to Philadelphia (NL).

1920, May 27
Right-hander Mule Watson to Pittsburgh.

1920, June 8
Second baseman Johnny Rawlings to Philadelphia (NL).

1920, July 4
Outfielder Gene Bailey to Boston.

1920, November 9
Outfielder Les Mann to St. Louis (NL).

1921, May 11
Outfielder John Sullivan to Chicago (NL).

1921, August 31
Left-hander Eddie Eayrs to Brooklyn.

1922, August 17
Right-hander Fred Toney to St. Louis (NL).

1922, December 12
First baseman Walter Holke to Philadelphia (NL).

1923, April 30
Infielder John Kelleher to Pittsburgh.

1924, July 14
Catcher Earl Smith to Pittsburgh.

1926, April 6
Infielder Ernie Padgett to Cleveland.

1926, June 29
Infielder Jimmy Johnston to New York (NL).

1927, October 14
Manager/shortstop Dave Bancroft to Brooklyn.

1927, December 14
Catcher Frank Gibson to St. Louis (NL).

1929, June 29
Right-hander Kent Greenfield to Brooklyn.

1929, July 6
Catcher Zack Taylor to Chicago (NL).

1929, October 27
Outfielder Les Bell to Chicago (NL).

1931, June 30
Infielder Bill Hunnefield to New York (NL).

1931, August 3
Right-hander Ray Moss to St. Louis (NL).

1931, December 11
Outfielder Lance Richbourg to Chicago (NL).

1933, April 19
First baseman Art Shires to St. Louis (NL).

1934, September 11
Outfielder Bob Worthington to St. Louis (NL).

1936, July 26
Right-hander Ray Benge to Philadelphia (NL).

1937, May 12
First baseman Buck Jordan to Cincinnati.

1938, February 5
Right-hander Guy Bush to St. Louis (NL).

1938, May 1
Right-hander Frank Gabler to Chicago (AL).

1939, August 19
Left-hander Milt Shoffner to Cincinnati.

1939, August 31
Outfielder Al Simmons to Cincinnati.

1940, March 3
Outfielder Debs Garms to Pittsburgh.

1940, May 8
Left-hander Bill Weir to Philadelphia (AL).

1940, June 21
Right-hander Lou Fette to Brooklyn.

1940, July 23
Infielder Rabbit Warstler to Chicago (NL).

1941, June 20
Left-hander Joe Sullivan to Pittsburgh.

1942, July 22
Right-hander Dick Errickson to Chicago (NL).

1943, May 12
Right-hander Manny Salvo to Philadelphia (NL).

1944, September 29
Right-hander George Woodend to Chicago (NL).

1945, March 1
Infielder Mike Sabena to Brooklyn.

1945, August 9
Right-hander Jim Tobin to Detroit.

1945, August 22
Right-hander Nate Andrews to Cincinnati.

1947, March 26
Left-handers Jack Christensen and Lou Tost to Pittsburgh.

1949, May 11
Left-hander Clyde Shoun to Chicago (AL).

1949, September 26
Right-hander Nels Potter to Cincinnati; catcher Bill Salkeld to Chicago (AL).

1949, December 13
Outfielder Marv Rickert to Pittsburgh.

1950, May 1
Infielder Robert Ries to Cincinnati.

1951, May 13
Right-hander Bobby Hogue to St. Louis (AL).

1952, June 3
Outfielder Willard Marshall to Cincinnati.

1955, April 13
Right-hander Jim Wilson to Baltimore.

1955, April 30
Shortstop Roy Smalley to Philadelphia (NL).

1957, June 8
Outfielder Chuck Tanner to Chicago (NL).

1957, October 16
Right-hander Dave Jolly to San Francisco.

1958, April 19
Right-hander Phil Paine to St. Louis.

1958, May 24
Outfielder Bob Hazle to Detroit.

1959, October 12
Right-hander Bob Trowbridge to Kansas City.

1960, June 11
Right-hander Bob Rush to Chicago (AL).

1961, May 10
Outfielder Wes Covington to Chicago (AL).

1961, October 13
Left-handers Johnny Antonelli and Ken MacKenzie to New York (NL).

1961, October 17
Right-hander Bob Botz to New York (NL).

1962, May 9
Right-hander Don McMahon to Houston.

1962, November 30
Right-hander Don Nottebart to Houston.

1963, March 22
Right-hander Carl Willey to New York (NL).

1963, August 8
First baseman Norm Larker to San Francisco.

1963, October 15
Infielder Amado Samuel to New York (NL).

1963, December 2
Outfielder Hawk Taylor to New York (NL).

1964, November 23
Left-hander Warren Spahn to New York (NL).

1965, March 28
Right-hander Frank Lary to New York (NL).

1965, July 20
Outfielder Gary Kolb to New York (NL).

1965, August 18
Right-hander Dave Eilers to New York (NL).

1967, May 31
Outfielder Ty Cline to San Francisco.

1968, December 3
First baseman Deron Johnson to Philadelphia.

1969, June 10
Right-hander Ken Johnson to New York (AL).

1969, August 19
Right-hander Claude Raymond to Montreal.

1969, August 22
Outfielder Tito Francona to Oakland.

1969, November 26
Left-hander Paul Doyle to California.

1970, June 25
Right-hander Milt Pappas to Chicago (NL).

1970, August 31
Outfielder Tony Gonzalez to California.

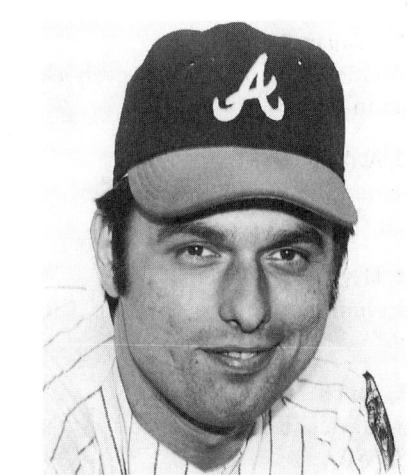

The Braves sold right-hander Milt Pappas to the Cubs.

1970, September 22
Right-hander Hoyt Wilhelm to Chicago (NL).

1972, June 29
First baseman Orlando Cepeda to Oakland.

1973, July 18
Left-hander Joe Hoerner to Kansas City.

1974, June 14
Right-hander Jack Aker to New York (NL).

1976, July 24
First baseman/catcher Earl Williams to Montreal.

1976, November 30
Outfielder Jimmy Wynn to New York (AL).

1977, March 29
Left-hander Pablo Torrealba to Oakland.

1977, May 1
Right-hander Mike Marshall to Texas.

1977, December 8
Right-hander Andy Messersmith to New York (AL).

1978, September 22
Outfielder Clarence Gaston to Pittsburgh.

1979, October 17
Left-hander Jamie Easterly to Montreal.

1990, April 30
Right-hander Sergio Valdez to Cleveland.

1990, September 24
Right-hander Rick Luecken to Toronto.

1990, November 16
Third baseman Tom Redington to San Diego.

1991, February 8
Outfielder Jim Vatcher to San Diego.

1992, December 1
Outfielder Tommy Gregg to Cincinnati.

1994, June 6
Right-hander Milt Hill to Seattle.

Milestones, Honors, and Other Facts

Baseball and statistics are inseparable. No other sport has a history as rich as baseball's, and that history is most often conveyed from fan to fan and generation to generation by these stats.

Following are numerous statistics and lists of various other data and information pertaining to the history of the Braves, including the eras during which they were known by other nicknames (Red Stockings, Beaneaters, Doves, Rustlers, and Bees). A thorough examination of the oldest continuously operating pro sports franchise in America would not be complete without them.

Special thanks to Rick Benner for compiling much of the information in this chapter and for contributing data for other portions of the encyclopedia.

Braves in the Hall of Fame

Name	Years with Braves	Year Selected	Name	Years with Braves	Year Selected	Name	Years with Braves	Year Selected
Players			Joe Medwick	1945	1968	Ed Walsh	1917	1946
Hank Aaron	1954–74	1982	Jim O'Rourke	1876–78, '80	1945	Hoyt Wilhelm	1969–71	1985
Earl Averill	1941	1975	Babe Ruth	1935	1936	Vic Willis	1898–1905	1995
Dave Bancroft	1924–27	1971	Red Schoendienst	1957–60	1989	Cy Young	1911	1937
Dan Brouthers	1889	1945						
Jimmy Collins	1895–1900	1945	Al Simmons	1939	1953	**Managers**		
Hugh Duffy	1892–1900	1945	George Sisler	1928–30	1939	Bill McKechnie	1930–37	1962
Johnny Evers	1914–17, '29	1946	Enos Slaughter	1959	1985	Casey Stengel	1938–43	1966
Billy Hamilton	1896–1901	1961	Lloyd Waner	1941	1967	Harry Wright	1876–81	1953
Billy Herman	1946	1975	Paul Waner	1941–42	1952			
Rogers Hornsby	1928	1942	George Wright	1876–78, '80–81	1937	**Coaches**		
Joe Kelley	1891, 1908	1971				Luke Appling	1981, '84	1964
King Kelly	1887–89, '91–92	1945				Bob Gibson	1982–84	1981
			Pitchers			George Kelly	1938–43	1973
Ernie Lombardi	1942	1986	John Clarkson	1888–92	1963	Satchel Paige	1969	1971
Al Lopez	1936–40	1977	Burleigh Grimes	1930	1964	Willie Stargell	1986–88	1988
Rabbit Maranville	1912–20, '29–35	1954	Rube Marquard	1922–25	1971			
Eddie Mathews	1952–66	1978	Kid Nichols	1890–1901	1949	**Team President**		
Tommy McCarthy	1885, '92–95	1946	Gaylord Perry	1981	1991	Christy Mathewson	1923, '25	1936
			Charlie Radbourn	1886–89	1939	John "Monte" Ward	1912	1964
			Warren Spahn	1942, '46–64	1973			

Major Braves Award Winners

MOST VALUABLE PLAYER, NL (Chalmers): Johnny Evers, 1914.
MOST VALUABLE PLAYER, NL (Baseball Writers Association of America, BBWAA): Bob Elliott, 1947;

Hank Aaron, 1957; Dale Murphy, 1982, 1983; Terry Pendleton, 1991.
MOST VALUABLE PLAYER, NL (*The Sporting News*): Tommy Holmes, 1945.

MAJOR LEAGUE PLAYER OF THE YEAR (*The Sporting News*): Hank Aaron, 1956; Dale Murphy, 1982, 1983.
CY YOUNG AWARD, NL (BBWAA):

Fred McGriff was named MVP of the 1994 All-Star Game for his two-run, pinch-hit homer in the ninth inning which tied the game the National League then won in the 10th.

In 1991, Tom Glavine (left) became the first Brave to win the Cy Young Award since Warren Spahn in 1957.

Craig McMurtry was National League Rookie Pitcher of the Year in 1983.

Warren Spahn, 1957; Tom Glavine, 1991; Greg Maddux, 1993, 1994.

MAJOR LEAGUE PITCHER OF THE YEAR (*The Sporting News*): Johnny Sain, 1948; Warren Spahn, 1953, 1957, 1958, 1961, 1963; Tom Glavine, 1991; Greg Maddux, 1993, 1994.

ROOKIE OF THE YEAR, NL (BBWAA): Alvin Dark, 1948; Sam Jethroe, 1950; Earl Williams, 1971; Bob Horner, 1978; David Justice, 1990.

ROOKIE OF THE YEAR, NL (*The Sporting News*): Earl Williams, 1971;

Greg Maddux won his first Cy Young Award as a Cub in 1992, then followed with two more as a Brave to become the first man ever to win three in a row.

Bob Horner, 1978; David Justice, 1990.

ROOKIE PITCHER OF THE YEAR, NL (*The Sporting News*): Carlton Willey, 1958; Steve Bedrosian, 1982; Craig McMurtry, 1983.

COMEBACK PLAYER OF THE YEAR, NL (*The Sporting News*): Dave Johnson, 1973; Lonnie Smith, 1989; Terry Pendleton, 1991.

COMEBACK PLAYER OF THE YEAR, NL (United Press International): Ron Gant, 1990.

MAJOR LEAGUE MANAGER OF THE YEAR (*The Sporting News*): Bill McKechnie, 1937.

MANAGER OF THE YEAR, NL (BBWAA): Bobby Cox, 1991.

MANAGER OF THE YEAR, NL (*The Sporting News*): Bobby Cox, 1991, 1993.

Felix Millan receives the 1967 Topps Minor League Player of the Year Award from Braves broadcaster Milo Hamilton.

MANAGER OF THE YEAR, NL (Associated Press): Joe Torre, 1982; Bobby Cox, 1991.

MAJOR LEAGUE EXECUTIVE OF THE YEAR (*The Sporting News*): Lou Perini, 1953.

EXECUTIVE OF THE YEAR, NL (United Press International): John Schuerholz, 1991.

LOU GEHRIG MEMORIAL AWARD (Phi Delta Theta): Dale Murphy, 1985.

ROBERTO CLEMENTE AWARD (Major League Baseball): Dale Murphy, 1988.

MOST VALUABLE PLAYER, LEAGUE CHAMPIONSHIP SERIES (National League): Steve Avery (1991), John Smoltz (1992).

MOST VALUABLE PLAYER, WORLD SERIES (*Sport* magazine): Lou Burdette (1957).

MOST VALUABLE PLAYER, ALL-STAR GAME: Fred McGriff (1994).

Gold Glove Award Winners

Hank Aaron, of	1958, 1959, 1960
Clete Boyer, 3b	1969
Del Crandall, c	1958, 1959, 1960, 1962
Greg Maddux, p	1993, 1994
Felix Millan, 2b	1969, 1972
Dale Murphy, of	1982, 1983, 1984, 1985, 1986
Phil Niekro, p	1978, 1979, 1980, 1982, 1983
Terry Pendleton, 3b	1992
Joe Torre, c	1965

Dale Murphy was a five-time Gold Glove winner.

The 1992 Gold Glove was one of many honors Terry Pendleton won with the Braves.

Silver Slugger Award Winners

Ron Gant (of)	1991	Fred McGriff (1b)	1993
Tom Glavine (p)	1991	Dale Murphy (of)	1982, 1983, 1984, 1985
David Justice (of)	1993		

Major League All-Star Team *(The Sporting News)*

1928	Rogers Hornsby, 2b	1956	Hank Aaron, of	1959	Eddie Mathews, 3b
1933	Wally Berger, of	1957	Red Schoendienst, 2b		Hank Aaron, of
1945	Tommy Holmes, of		Eddie Mathews, 3b	1960	Eddie Mathews, 3b
1948	Bob Elliott, 3b		Warren Spahn, p		Del Crandall, c
	Johnny Sain, p	1958	Hank Aaron, of		Warren Spahn, p
1953	Warren Spahn, p		Del Crandall, c		
1955	Eddie Mathews, 3b		Warren Spahn, p		

National League All-Star Team *(The Sporting News)*

1961	Frank Bolling, 2b	1969	Hank Aaron, of	1985	Dale Murphy, of
	Warren Spahn, p	1970	Hank Aaron, of	1991	Tom Glavine, p
1962	Del Crandall, c	1971	Hank Aaron, of		Ron Gant, of
1963	Hank Aaron, of	1973	Dave Johnson, 2b		Terry Pendleton, 3b
1964	Joe Torre, c		Darrell Evans, 3b	1992	Tom Glavine, p
1965	Hank Aaron, of	1976	Willie Montanez, 1b		Steve Avery, p
	Joe Torre, c	1982	Dale Murphy, of	1993	Greg Maddux, p
1966	Felipe Alou, of	1983	Glenn Hubbard, 2b		David Justice, of
	Joe Torre, c		Dale Murphy, of		Fred McGriff, 1b
1967	Hank Aaron, of	1984	Dale Murphy, of	1994	Greg Maddux, p

All-Star Game Selections

1933	Wally Berger, of		Warren Spahn, p	1969	Hank Aaron, of
1934	Wally Berger, of		Jim Wilson, p		Felix Millan, 2b
	Fred Frankhouse, p	1955	Hank Aaron, of		Phil Niekro, p
1935	Wally Berger, of		Gene Conley, p	1970	Hank Aaron, of
1936	Wally Berger, of		Del Crandall, c		Rico Carty, of
1937	Gene Moore, of		Johnny Logan, ss		Hoyt Wilhelm, p
1938	Tony Cuccinello, 2b		Eddie Mathews, 3b	1971	Hank Aaron, of
	Jim Turner, p	1956	Hank Aaron, of		Felix Millan, 2b
1939	Lou Fette, p		Del Crandall, c	1972	Hank Aaron, of
1940	Max West, of		Eddie Mathews, 3b	1973	Hank Aaron, of
1941	Eddie Miller, ss		Warren Spahn, p		Darrell Evans, 3b
1942	Ernie Lombardi, c	1957	Hank Aaron, of		Dave Johnson, 2b
	Eddie Miller, ss		Lou Burdette, p	1974	Hank Aaron, of
1943	Al Javery, p		Johnny Logan, ss		Buzz Capra, p
1944	Nate Andrews, p		Eddie Mathews, 3b		Ralph Garr, of
	Al Javery, p		Red Schoendienst, 2b	1975	Phil Niekro, p
	Connie Ryan, 2b		Warren Spahn, p	1976	Dick Ruthven, p
1945	No game	1958	Hank Aaron, of	1977	Willie Montanez, 1b
1946	Mort Cooper, p		Del Crandall, c	1978	Jeff Burroughs, of
	Johnny Hopp, of		Johnny Logan, ss		Phil Niekro, p
	Phil Masi, c		Eddie Mathews, 3b		Biff Pocoroba, c
1947	Bob Elliott, 3b		Don McMahon, p	1979	Gary Matthews, of
	Phil Masi, c		Warren Spahn, p	1980	Dale Murphy, of
	Johnny Sain, p	1959	Hank Aaron, of	1981	Bruce Benedict, c
	Warren Spahn, p		Lou Burdette, p	1982	Bob Horner, 3b
1948	Bob Elliott, 3b		Del Crandall, c		Dale Murphy, of
	Tommy Holmes, of		Johnny Logan, ss		Phil Niekro, p
	Phil Masi, c		Eddie Mathews, 3b	1983	Bruce Benedict, c
	Johnny Sain, p		Warren Spahn, p		Glenn Hubbard, 2b
	Eddie Stanky, 2b	1960	Hank Aaron, of		Dale Murphy, of
1949	Vern Bickford, p		Joe Adcock, 1b		Pascual Perez, p
	Warren Spahn, p		Bob Buhl, p	1984	Dale Murphy, of
1950	Walker Cooper, p		Del Crandall, c		Rafael Ramirez, ss
	Warren Spahn, p		Eddie Mathews, 3b		Claudell Washington, of
1951	Bob Elliott, 3b	1961	Hank Aaron, of	1985	Dale Murphy, of
	Warren Spahn, p		Frank Bolling, 2b	1986	Dale Murphy, of
1952	Warren Spahn, p		Eddie Mathews, 3b	1987	Dale Murphy, of
1953	Del Crandall, c		Warren Spahn, p		Ozzie Virgil, c
	Eddie Mathews, 3b	1962	Hank Aaron, of	1988	Gerald Perry, 1b
	Warren Spahn, p		Frank Bolling, 2b	1989	John Smoltz, p
1954	Gene Conley, p		Del Crandall, c	1990	Greg Olson, c
	Del Crandall, c		Eddie Mathews, 3b	1991	Tom Glavine, p
			Bob Shaw, p	1992	Ron Gant, of
			Warren Spahn, p		Tom Glavine, p
		1963	Hank Aaron, of		Terry Pendleton, 3b
			Warren Spahn, p		John Smoltz, p
			Joe Torre, c	1993	Steve Avery, p
		1964	Hank Aaron, of		Jeff Blauser, ss
			Joe Torre, c		Tom Glavine, p
		1965	Hank Aaron, of		David Justice, of
			Joe Torre, c		John Smoltz, p
		1966	Hank Aaron, of	1994	David Justice, of
			Felipe Alou, of		Greg Maddux, p
			Joe Torre, c		Fred McGriff, 1b
		1967	Hank Aaron, of	1995	Greg Maddux, p
			Denny Lemaster, p		Fred McGriff, 1b
			Joe Torre, c		

Phil Masi made three All-Star teams in his 11 seasons with the Braves.

1968   Hank Aaron, of
Felipe Alou, of
Ron Reed, p

Winning pitcher:
Warren Spahn, 1953 (Crosley Field)
Gene Conley, 1955 (County Stadium)

Home runs:

Max West, 1940 (Sportsman's Park)
Bob Elliott, 1951 (Briggs Stadium)
Eddie Mathews, 1959 (Forbes Field)
Del Crandall, 1960 (Kansas City Municipal Stadium)

Eddie Mathews, 1960 (Yankee Stadium)
Joe Torre, 1965 (Metropolitan Stadium)
Hank Aaron, 1971 (Tiger Stadium)
Hank Aaron, 1972 (Atlanta Stadium)

Dale Murphy, 1984 (Candlestick Park)
Fred McGriff, 1994 (Three Rivers Stadium)
Most Valuable Player: Fred McGriff, 1994

Massachusetts-Born Boston Braves

Bill Anderson, Boston	1925	Elbie Fletcher, Milton	1934–39, '49	Ray Martin, Norwood	1943, '47–48
Stan Andrews, Lynn	1939–40	John Fox, Roxbury	1881	Eddie Mayo, Holyoke	1937–38
Bill Annis, Stoneham	1884	Daff Gammons, New Bedford	1901	Gene McAuliffe, Randolph	1904
Mike Balas, Lowell	1938	Jim Garry, Great Barrington	1893	Bill McCarthy, Ashland	1906
Jimmy Bannon, Amesbury	1894–96	Doc Gautreau, Cambridge	1925–28	Tommy McCarthy, Boston	1885, '92–95
Johnny Barrett, Lowell	1946	Sam Gentile, Charlestown	1943		
Joe Batchelder, Wenham	1923–25	Gene Good, Roxbury	1906	Chippy McGarr, Worcester	1890
Marty Bergen, North Brookfield	1896–99	Sid Graves, Marblehead	1927	Stuffy McInnis, Gloucester	1923–24
John Bergh, Boston	1880	Mert Hackett, Cambridge	1883–85	Ralph McLeod, North Quincy	1938
Al Blanche, Somerville	1935–36	Walter Hackett, Cambridge	1885	Dinny McNamara, Lexington	1927–28
Frank Bonner, Lowell	1903	Jack Hannifin, Holyoke	1908	Tim McNamara, Millville	1922–25
Foghorn Bradley, Milford	1876	Joe Harrington, Fall River	1895–96	Bill Merritt, Lowell	1893–94, '99
Kitty Bransfield, Worcester	1898	John Henry, Amherst	1918		
Bob Brown, Dorchester	1930–36	Jim Hickey, North Abington	1942, '44	Fred Mitchell, Cambridge	1913
Lew Brown, Leominster	1876–77, '83	Mike Hickey, Chicopee	1899	Pat Moran, Fitchburg	1901–05
Charlie Buffinton, Fall River	1882–86	Shanty Hogan, Somerville	1925–27, '33–35	Cy Morgan, Lakeville	1921–22
Billy Burke, Clinton	1910–11	Bill Hunnefield, Dedham	1931	Ed Moriarty, Holyoke	1935–36
Dan Burke, Abington	1892	Jerry Hurley, Boston	1889	Jim Moroney, Boston	1906
Art Butler, Fall River	1911	Warren Huston, Newtonville	1944	John Morrill, Boston	1876–88
Joe Callahan, East Boston	1939–40	Al Javery, Worcester	1940–46	Dave Murphy, Adams	1905
Hank Camelli, Gloucester	1947	Art Johnson, Winchester	1940–42	Ambrose Murray, Fall River	1936
Hugh Canavan, Worcester	1918	Ike Kamp, Roxbury	1924–25	Eddie Phillips, Worcester	1924
Pat Carney, Holyoke	1901–04	John Kelleher, Brookline	1924	Dave Pickett, Brookline	1898
Dad Clarkson, Cambridge	1892	Joe Kelley, Cambridge	1891, 1908	Al Pierotti, Boston	1920–21
John Clarkson, Cambridge	1888–92	Art Kenney, Milford	1938	Paul Radford, Roxbury	1883
Art Conlon, Woburn	1923	John Kiley, South Dedham	1891	Art Rico, Roxbury	1916–17
Frank Connaughton, Clinton	1894, 1906	Lee King, Waltham	1919	Skippy Roberge, Lowell	1941–42, '46
Dick Conway, Lowell	1887–88	Mal Kittridge, Clinton	1901–03		
Bill Cooney, Boston	1909–10	Henry Lampe, Boston	1894	Norm Roy, Newton	1950
Dee Cousineau, Watertown	1923–25	Fletcher Low, Essex	1915	Jack Ryan, Haverhill	1894–96
Connie Creeden, Danvers	1943	Danny MacFayden, North Truro	1935–39, '43	Rosy Ryan, Worcester	1925–26
Bill Cronin, West Newton	1928–31			Frank Sexton, Brockton	1895
Sam Curran, Dorchester	1902	Harry MacPherson, North Andover	1944	Marty Shay, Boston	1924
Con Daily, Blackstone	1886–87	Freddie Maguire, Roxbury	1929–31	Dave Shean, Arlington	1909–10, '12
Bill Dam, Cambridge	1909	Mike Mahoney, Boston	1897		
John "Daisy" Davis, Boston	1884–85	Charlie Maloney, Cambridge	1908	Tom Smith, Boston	1894
Steve Dignan, Boston	1880	Jack Manning, Braintree	1876, '78	Jim Stafford, Webster	1898–99
Cozy Dolan, Cambridge	1895–96, 1905–06	Jimmy Manning, Braintree	1884–85	Allie Strobel, Boston	1905–06
Dick Donovan, Boston	1950–52	Rabbit Maranville, Springfield	1912–20, '29–35	Andy Sullivan, Southborough	1904
Bob Dresser, Newton	1902			Denny Sullivan, Boston	1880
Bill Dunlap, Palmer	1929–30	Marty Martel, Weymouth	1910	Jim Sullivan, Charlestown	1891, '95–97
Tom Earley, Roxbury	1938–42, '45				
Eddie Eayrs, Blackstone	1920–21				

Marty Sullivan, Lowell	1890–91	George Twombly, Boston	1917	Steve White, Dorchester	1912
Mike Sullivan, Boston	1898–99	Luke Urban, Fall River	1927–28	Gil Whitehouse,	
Butch Sutcliffe, Fall River	1938	Bill Vargus, North Scituate	1925–26	Somerville	1912
John Taber, Acushnet	1890	Joe Walsh, Roxbury	1938	Frank Whitney, Brockton	1876
Roy Talcott, Brookline	1943	Hal Weafer, Woburn	1936	Frank Wilson, Malden	1924–26
Fred Tenney, Georgetown	1894–1907, '11	Al Weston, Lynn	1929	Nick Wise, Boston	1888
		Bobby Wheelock,		Herman Young, Boston	1911
Red Torphy, Fall River	1920	Charlestown	1887		
Tommy Tucker, Holyoke	1890–97	Tom Whelan, Lynn	1920		

Wisconsin-Born Milwaukee Braves

John Braun, Madison	1964	Billy Hoeft, Oshkosh	1964	Bill Southworth,	
John DeMerit,		Dave Koslo, Menasha	1954–55	Madison	1964
West Bend	1957–61	Mike Krsnich, West Allis	1960, '62	Bob Uecker, Milwaukee	1962–63, '67
Bob Hartman, Kenosha	1959	Andy Pafko, Boyceville	1953–59		

Georgia-Born Atlanta Braves

Rick Camp, Trion	1976–85	Mack Jones, Atlanta	1961–67
Don Collins, Lyons	1977	Johnny "Blue Moon"	
Gary Cooper, Savannah	1980	Odom, Macon	1975
Jody Davis, Gainesville	1988–90	Gerald Perry, Savannah	1983–89
Marquis Grissom, Atlanta	1995–	Hank Small, Atlanta	1978
Terry Harper,		Eddie Solomon, Perry	1977–79
Douglasville	1980–86	Jeff Treadway, Columbus	1990–92
Milt Hill, Atlanta	1994	Brad Woodall, Atlanta	1994–

Trion native Rick Camp is one of several Atlanta Braves who were born and raised in Georgia.

Played with Both Boston Braves and Boston Red Sox

	Years with Braves	Years with Red Sox		Years with Braves	Years with Red Sox
Gene Bailey	1919–20	1920	Buck Freeman	1900	1901–07
Walter Barbare	1921–22	1918	Joe Heving	1945	1938–40
Frank Barberich	1907	1910	Charlie Hickman	1897–99	1902
Frank Barrett	1946	1944–45	Roy Johnson	1937–38	1932–35
King Brady	1912	1908	Eddie Joost	1943–45	1955
Chet Chadbourne	1918	1906–07	Andy Karl	1947	1943
Jack Coffey	1909	1918	Billy Klaus	1952–53	1955–58
Jimmy Collins	1895–1900	1901–07	Rube Kroh	1912	1906–07
Gene Conley	1952–58	1961–63	Lou Legett	1929	1933–35
Jimmy Cooney	1928	1917	Ted Lewis	1896–1900	1901
Nig Cuppy	1900	1901	Danny MacFayden	1935–39, '43	1926–32
Babe Dahlgren	1941	1935–36	Gene Mauch	1950–51	1956–57
Bill Dinneen	1900–01	1902–07	Stuffy McInnis	1923–24	1918–21
Joe Dugan	1929	1922	Marty McManus	1934	1931–33
Doc Farrell	1927–29	1935	Fred Mitchell	1901–02	1913
Wes Ferrell	1941	1934–37	Hap Myers	1913	1910–11

	Years with Braves	Years with Red Sox		Years with Braves	Years with Red Sox
Chet Nichols	1951–56	1960–63	Dave Shean	1909–10, '12	1918–19
Frank O'Rourke	1912	1922	Al Simmons	1939	1943
Nels Potter	1948–49	1941	Chick Stahl	1897–1900	1901–06
Jack Quinn	1913	1922–25	Jake Volz	1905	1901
Wally Rehg	1917–18	1913–15	Murray Wall	1950	1957–59
Woody Rich	1944	1939–41	Bucky Walters	1931–32, '50	1933–34
Joe Riggert	1919	1911	John Warner	1895	1902
Red Rollings	1930	1927–28	Rabbit Warstler	1936–40	1930–33
Babe Ruth	1935	1914–19	Joe Wilhoit	1916–17	1919
Red Shannon	1915	1919	Jim Wilson	1951–54	1945–46
Al Shaw	1909	1907	Cy Young	1911	1901–08

Played with Milwaukee Braves and Milwaukee Brewers

	Years with Braves	Years with Brewers		Years with Braves	Years with Brewers
Hank Aaron	1954–74	1975–76	Phil Roof	1961, '64	1970–71
Felipe Alou	1964–65	1974			

Most Years as a Regular Starter by Position

Position	Player	Years	Position	Player	Years
RHP	Phil Niekro	17 (1967–83)	3B	Eddie Mathews	15 (1952–66)
LHP	Warren Spahn	19 (1946–64)	SS	Herman Long	13 (1890–1902)
C	Del Crandall	9 (1953–60, 1962)	LF	Ralph Garr	5 (1971–75)
1B	Fred Tenney	12 (1897–1907, 1911)	CF	Billy Bruton	8 (1953–60)
2B	Glenn Hubbard	9 (1979–87)	RF	Hank Aaron	15 (1955–60, 1963–70, 1973)

Most Years with Braves

21	Hank Aaron	1954–74		Kid Nichols	1890–1901
	Phil Niekro	1964–83, '87		Mike Lum	1967–75, '79–81
20	Warren Spahn	1942, '46–64		Bruce Benedict	1978–89
15	Fred Tenney	1894–1907, '11	11	Jack Burdock	1878–88
	Rabbit Maranville	1912–20, '29–33, '35		Dick Rudolph	1913–20, '22–23, '27
	Johnny Cooney	1921–30, '38–42		Phil Masi	1939–49
	Eddie Mathews	1952–66		Johnny Logan	1951–61
	Dale Murphy	1976–90		Rick Mahler	1979–88, '91
14	Hank Gowdy	1911–17, '19–23, '29–30	10	Billy Nash	1885–89, '91–95
13	John Morrill	1876–88		Tommy Holmes	1942–51
	Herman Long	1890–1902		Joe Adcock	1953–62
	Bob Smith	1923–30, '33–37		Bob Buhl	1953–62
	Sibby Sisti	1939–42, '46–54		Ron Reed	1966–75
	Del Crandall	1949–50, '53–63		Biff Pocoroba	1975–84
	Lou Burdette	1951–63		Jerry Royster	1976–84, '88
12	Ezra Sutton	1877–88		Gene Garber	1978–87
	Bobby Lowe	1890–1901		Glenn Hubbard	1978–87

Players with Braves Three Times

Player	First Time	Second Time	Third Time
Fred Lake	1891	1897	1910
Les Mann	1913–14	1919–20	1924–27

Outfielder Les Mann is one of only two players to have had three terms of service with the Braves.

Players with Braves Two Times

Player	First Time	Second Time
Ed Abbaticchio	1903–05	1910
Doyle Alexander	1980	1986–87
Johnny Antonelli	1948–50, '53	1961
Jesse Barnes	1915–17	1923–25
Red Barrett	1943–45	1947–49
Steve Bedrosian	1981–85	1993–
Larry Benton	1923–27	1935
Mike Bielecki	1991–92	1994
Larvell Blanks	1972–75	1980
Al Bridwell	1906–07	1911–12
Lew Brown	1876–77	1883
Frank Connaughton	1894	1906
Johnny Cooney	1921–30	1938–42
Tony Cuccinello	1936–40	1942–43
Al Dark	1946, 1948–49	1960
Adrian Devine	1973, 1975–76	1978–79
Cozy Dolan	1895–96	1905–06
Oscar Dugey	1913–14	1920
Darrell Evans	1969–76	1989
Johnny Evers	1914–17	1929
Lou Fette	1937–40	1945
Patsy Flaherty	1907–08	1911
Elbie Fletcher	1934–35, 1937–39	1949
Hod Ford	1919–23	1932–33
Fred Frankhouse	1930–35	1939
Sam Frock	1907	1910–11
Clarence (Cito) Gaston	1967	1975–78
Hank Gowdy	1911–17, 1919–23	1929–30
Buck Herzog	1910–11	1918–19
Mike Hines	1883–85	1888
Shanty Hogan	1925–27	1933–35
Ira Hutchinson	1937–38	1944–45
Joey Jay	1953–55, 1957–60	1966
Joe Kelley	1891	1908
King Kelly	1887–89	1891–92

Player	First Time	Second Time
Johnny Lanning	1936–39	1947
Charlie Lau	1960–61	1967
Mike Lum	1967–75	1979–81
Danny MacFayden	1935–39	1943
Rick Mahler	1979–88	1991
Jack Manning	1876	1878
Rabbit Maranville	1912–20	1929–33, 1935
Tommy McCarthy	1885	1892–95
Dan McGann	1896	1908
Hugh McQuillan	1918–22	1927
Larry McWilliams	1978–82	1987
Bill Merritt	1893–94	1899
Gene Moore	1936–38	1940–41
Herbie Moran	1908–10	1914–15
Ray Mueller	1935–38	1951
Billy Nash	1885–89	1891–95
Phil Niekro	1964–83	1987
Johnny Niggeling	1938	1946
Jim O'Rourke	1876–78	1880
Alejandro Pena	1991–92	1995
Jeff Pfeffer	1906–08	1911
Joe Quinn	1888–89	1891–92
Claude Raymond	1961–63	1967–69
Jerry Royster	1976–84	1988
Dave Shean	1909–10	1912
Bob Smith	1923–30	1933–37
Jim Sullivan	1891	1895–97
Fred Tenney	1894–1907	1911
Frank Thomas	1961	1965
Bob Uecker	1962–63	1967
Bucky Walters	1931–32	1950
Jimmy Welsh	1925–27	1929–30
Earl Williams	1970–72	1975–76
George Wright	1876–78	1880–81
Sam Wright	1876	1881

Brothers Who Played with the Braves

Hank (1954–74) and Tommie (1962–63, '65, '68–71) Aaron

Bob (1969–70) and Ken (1962) Aspromonte

Jesse (1915–17, '23–25) and Virgil (1928) Barnes

Dad (1892) and John (1888–92) Clarkson

Jimmy (1928) and Johnny (1921–30, '38–42) Cooney

Mort (1945–47) and Walker (1950–53) Cooper

Mert (1883–85) and Walter (1885) Hackett

Mickey (1977–79) and Rick (1979–88, '91) Mahler

Joe (1973–74) and Phil (1964–83, '87) Niekro

Jim (1876–78, '80) and John (1879–80) O'Rourke

Joe (1915) and Red (1915) Shannon

Frank (1956–60) and Joe (1960–68) Torre

Fred (1914) and Lefty (1910–17) Tyler

Lloyd (1941) and Paul (1941–42) Waner

George (1876–78, '80–81), Harry (1876–77), and Sam (1876, '81) Wright

Notes

Hank and Tommie Aaron homered in the same game three times: June 12, 1962, versus Los Angeles; July 12, 1962, versus St. Louis (same inning); and August 14, 1962, versus Cincinnati.

Joe and Red Shannon were twins.

Clete (1967–71) and Cloyd (1978–81 as a coach) Boyer.

Billy (1966–67 as a coach and manager) and Jim (1938) Hitchcock.

Father and Son Who Played for the Braves

Ebba (1951–53) and Randy (1991–92) St. Claire

Braves with the Shortest Careers

Hitters	Position	Year	Average
1 game, 0 at bats:			
Daly, Joe	C	1892	.000
Fischlin, Mike	SS (PR)	1987	.000
Jacklitsch, Fred	C	1917	.000
Kahn, Owen	1B (PR)	1930	.000
Kelleher, John	IF (PH)	1924	.000
Patton, Gene	SS (PR)	1944	.000
1 game, 1 at bat, 1 hit:			
Kuczek, Steve	SS (PH)	1949	1.000 (double)
1 game, 1 at bat, 0 hits:			
Bell, Terry	C (PH)	1987	.000
Kruger, Art	OF (PH)	1910	.000
Lefler, Wade	OF (PH)	1924	.000
Veltman, Art	C (PH)	1931	.000
Weeden, Bert	C (PH)	1911	.000
White, Sam	C	1919	.000

Notes

Jim Riley (1910–OF), Andy Sullivan (1904–SS), and Tom Whelan (1920–1B) each played 1 game and had 1 official at bat with no hits, but each also drew a walk.

Pitchers	L/R	Year	G	W–L	IP	H	BB	SO	ERA
Brady, Bill	R	1912	1	0–0	1	2	0	0	0.00
Brynan, Charlie	R	1891	1	0–1	1	4	3	0	54.00
Cottrell, Ensign	L	1914	1	0–1	1	2	3	1	9.00
Garry, Jim	L	1893	1	0–1	1	5	4	2	63.00
Gearin, Dinty	L	1924	1	0–1	0	3	2	0	∞
MacPherson, Harry	R	1944	1	0–0	1	0	1	1	0.00

Pitchers	L/R	Year	G	W–L	IP	H	BB	SO	ERA
Ogrodowski, Joe	R	1925	1	0–0	1	6	3	0	54.00
Talcott, Roy	R	1943	1	0–0	⅓	1	2	0	27.00

1 Game Played

Hitters	Pos	Year	AB	R	H	Avg
Allen, Myron	2B	1886	3	0	0	.000
Bell, Terry	C (PH)	1987	1	0	0	.000
Burke, Dan	C	1892	4	0	0	.000
Coliver, Bill	OF	1885	4	0	0	.000
Daly, Joe	C	1892	0	0	0	.000
Dam, Bill	OF	1909	2	1	1	.500 (2B)
Fischlin, Mike	SS (PR)	1987	0	0	0	.000
Gonzalez, Mike	C	1912	2	0	0	.000
Hickey, Mike	2B	1899	3	0	1	.333
Hurley, Jerry	C	1889	4	0	0	.000
Jacklitsch, Fred	C	1917	0	0	0	.000
Kahn, Owen	1B (PR)	1930	0	1	0	.000
Kelleher, John	IF (PH)	1924	1	0	0	.000
Kruger, Art	OF (PH)	1910	1	0	0	.000
Kuczek, Steve	SS (PH)	1949	1	0	1	1.000 (2B)
Ladd, Hi	OF	1898	4	1	1	.250
Lefler, Wade	OF (PH)	1924	1	0	0	.000
Low, Fletcher	3B	1915	4	1	1	.250 (3B/RBI)
Martin, Bill	SS	1914	3	0	0	.000
McAuliffe, Gene	C	1904	2	0	1	.500
McCarthy, Bill	C	1905	3	0	0	.000
Parks, Bill	OF	1876	4	0	0	.000
Patton, Gene	SS (PR)	1944	0	0	0	.000
Quinn,—	1B	1881	4	0	0	.000
Riley, Jim	OF	1910	1	0	0	.000
Schwind, Art	3B	1912	2	0	1	.500

Hitters	Pos	Year	AB	R	H	Avg
Shannon, Red	2B	1915	3	0	0	.000
Small, Hank	1B	1978	4	0	0	.000
Sullivan, Andy	SS	1904	1	0	0	.000
Sullivan, Denny	C	1880	4	1	1	.250 (RBI)
Veltman, Art	C (PH)	1931	1	0	0	.000
Weeden, Bert	C (PH)	1911	1	0	0	.000
Whelan, Tom	1B	1920	1	0	0	.000
White, John	OF	1904	5	1	0	.000
White, Sam	C	1919	1	0	0	.000
Wise, Nick	OF	1888	3	0	0	.000
Womack, Sid	C	1926	3	0	0	.000

Pitchers	L/R	Year	W–L	IP	H	BB	SO	ERA
Autry, Al	R	1976	1–0	5	4	3	3	5.40
Balas, Mike	R	1938	0–0	⅓	3	0	0	6.75
Brady, Bill	R	1912	0–0	1	2	0	0	0.00
Brady, King	R	1912	0–0	⅔	5	3	0	20.25
Braun, John	R	1964	0–0	2	2	1	1	0.00
Brynan, Charlie	R	1891	0–1	1	4	3	0	54.00
Chambers, Jerome	L	1900	0–0	4	5	5	2	11.25
Clarkson, Dad	R	1892	1–0	7	5	3	0	1.29 (CG)
Cottrell, Ensign	L	1914	0–1	1	2	3	1	9.00
Curran, Sammy	—	1902	0–0	6⅔	6	0	3	1.35
Dresser, Bob	L	1902	0–1	9	12	0	8	3.00 (CG)
Garry, Jim	L	1893	0–1	1	5	4	2	63.00
Gearin, Dinty	L	1924	0–1	0	3	2	0	∞

Pitchers	L/R	Year	W–L	IP	H	BB	SO	ERA
Ging, Billy	R	1899	1–0	8	5	5	2	1.13 (CG)
Hawley, Scott	—	1894	0–1	7	10	7	1	7.71 (CG)
Hershey, Frank	R	1905	0–1	4	5	2	1	6.75
Hill, Garry	R	1969	0–1	2⅓	6	1	2	15.43
Kiley, John	L	1891	0–1	8	13	5	1	6.75 (CG)
Lawson, Al	R	1890	0–1	9	12	4	1	9.00 (CG)
Leary, Jack	L	1880	0–1	3	8	0	1	15.00
Lindemann, Ernie	R	1907	0–0	6⅓	6	4	3	5.68
Long, Red	R	1902	0–0	8	4	3	5	1.13 (CG)
MacPherson, Harry	R	1944	0–0	1	0	1	1	0.00
Maloney, Charlie	R	1908	0–0	2	3	1	0	4.50
Manville, Dick	R	1950	0–0	2	0	3	2	0.00
McCarthy, Bill	R	1906	0–0	2	2	3	0	9.00
Nichols, Tricky	R	1876	1–0	9	7	0	0	1.00 (CG)
Ogrodowski, Joe	R	1925	0–0	1	6	3	0	54.00
Richmond, Lee	L	1879	1–0	9	4	1	11	2.00 (CG)
Ryan, Cyclone	R	1891	0–0	3	2	1	0	0.00
Santorini, Al	R	1968	0–1	3	4	0	0	0.00
Stultz, George	—	1894	1–0	9	4	5	1	0.00 (CG)
Talcott, Roy	R	1943	0–0	⅔	1	2	0	27.00
Viau, Lee	R	1892	1–0	9	5	4	1	0.00 (CG)
Von Fricken, Anthony	R	1890	0–1	8	23	8	2	10.13 (CG)
Wall, Murray	R	1950	0–0	4	6	2	2	9.00
Weafer, Hal	R	1936	0–0	3	6	3	0	12.00
West, Frank	—	1894	0–0	3	5	2	1	9.00

Youngest Players to Debut with the Braves

Age					
Years	Months	Days	Name	Birth Date	Debut
17	06	14	Frank O'Rourke	11–28–94	06–11–12
17	11	06	Joey Jay	08–15–35	07–21–53
17	11	09	Gene Patton	07–08–26	06–17–44
18	02	06	Hawk Taylor	04–03–39	06–09–57
18	02	22	Johnny Antonelli	04–12–30	07–04–48
18	03	15	Ray Martin	03–13–25	07–02–43
18	04	16	Lew Brown	02–01–58	06–17–76
18	04	19	Joe Shannon	02–11–97	06–30–15
18	05	07	Joe Ogrodowski	11–20–06	04–27–25
18	05	29	Elbie Fletcher	03–18–16	09–16–34
18	07	25	Doc Bass	12–04–99	07–29–18
18	07	26	Red Shannon	02–11–97	10–07–15
18	10	22	Bill Southworth	11–10–45	10–02–64
18	10	28	Charley Vaughan	10–06–47	09–03–66
18	11	25	Sibby Sisti	07–26–20	07–21–39
19	00	20	Bob Brown	04–01–11	04–21–30
19	01	02	Mike McQueen	08–30–50	10–02–69
19	02	03	Joe Schultz	07–24–93	09–27–12
19	02	23	Dusty Baker	06–15–49	09–07–68
19	03	02	Shanty Hogan	03–21–06	06–23–25
19	03	12	Del Crandall	03–05–30	06–17–49
19	04	26	Paul Strand	12–19–93	05–15–13
19	05	00	Mickey O'Neil	04–12–00	09–12–19
19	05	12	Les Mann	11–18–93	04–30–13
19	07	18	Joe Kelley	12–09–1871	07–27–91
19	08	24	Rod Gilbreath	09–24–52	06–17–72
19	09	11	Earl Clark	11–06–07	08–17–27
19	09	11	Rowland Office	10–25–52	08–05–72
19	09	18	Roy Witherup	07–26–86	05–14–06
19	09	26	Wade Blasingame	11–22–43	09–17–63
19	10	06	John Edelman	07–27–35	06–02–55
19	11	04	Chick Evans	10–15–89	09–19–09
19	11	10	Jim Breazeale	10–03–49	09–13–69

Bonus baby Johnny Antonelli was barely 18 when he debuted with the Braves.

Braves Who Served in the Military

Player	Dates of Service (when known)	Player	Dates of Service (when known)
World War I		Connie Ryan	July 1944–January 1946
Hank Gowdy	June 1917–April 1919	Damon Phillips	September 1944–September 1946
Hank Schreiber	October 1917–January 1919	Max Macon	September 1944–November 1946
Rabbit Maranville	November 1917–April 1919	Gene Patton	November 1944–December 1945
Art Rico	December 1917–1918	Hugh Poland	February 1945–October 1945
Bill James	May 1918–1918	Chet Ross	February 1945–March 1946
Fred Bailey	May 1918–1919		
Rip Conway	June 1918–1918	**Korean War**	
Walt Tragesser	July 1918–1918	Bob Buhl	January 1951–January 1953
Dana Fillingim	July 1918–1918	Pete Whisenant	January 1951–November 1951
Joe Kelly	July 1918–1918	Johnny Antonelli	March 1951–March 1953
Ray Powell	July 1918–1918	Del Crandall	March 1951–March 1953
Wally Rehg	July 1918–1918	Phil Paine	November 1951–November 1953
Hugh Canavan	July 1917–February 1919	Chet Nichols	April 1952–February 1954
World War II		**Cold War**	
Bama Rowell	December 1941–October 1945	Bob Roselli	January 1954–August 1955
Bill Posedel	January 1941–October 1945	Mel Roach	July 1955–April 1957
Ace Williams	April 1942–March 1946	Bob Giggie	July 1956–April 1958
Lefty Wallace	July 1942–September 1944	Eddie Haas	December 1957–April 1958
Johnny Sain	August 1942–November 1945	Merritt Ranew	1960–1961
Warren Spahn	October 1942–June 1946	Hawk Taylor	October 1960–April 1961;
Buddy Gremp	December 1942–December 1945		November 1961–August 1962
Art Johnson	December 1942–November 1945	Joe Torre	September 1962–November 1962
Skippy Roberge	January 1943–February 1946	Denis Menke	October 1962–March 1963
Ducky Detweiler	January 1943–January 1946	Wade Blasingame	October 1964–March 1965
Tom Earley	January 1943–December 1944	Lee Bales	September 1965–March 1966
Hank Lamanna	March 1943–March 1946	Jim Britton	1965–1966; October 1969–March 1970
Max West	March 1943–January 1946	Gary Neibauer	February 1968–July 1968
Nanny Fernandez	May 1943–January 1946	Dusty Baker	January 1969–April 1969
Lou Tost	July 1943–December 1945		
Ray Martin	October 1943–April 1946	**Reserve Duty**	
Earl Reid	December 1943–February 1946	Jim Britton	August 11–25, 1968; June 7–22, 1969
Johnny McCarthy	January 1944–December 1945	Mike McQueen	June 30–July 11, 1971
Sam Gentile	April 1944–May 1946	Oscar Brown	July 9–24, 1971
John Dagenhard	May 1944, retired to manage a war plant	Dusty Baker	June 17–July 3, 1972
		Darrell Evans	June 17–July 3, 1972

STREAKS

Hitting

37—Tommy Holmes, 1945*
31—Rico Carty, 1970*
29—Rowland Office, 1976*
26—Hugh Duffy, 1894
26—Bill Sweeney, 1911*
25—Hank Aaron, 1956*
25—Hank Aaron, 1962*
23—Gene DeMontreville, 1901†
23—Al Dark, 1948†
23—Red Schoendienst, 1957
22—Earl Torgeson, 1950
22—Hank Aaron, 1959
22—Felipe Alou, 1968
22—Hank Aaron, 1971

22—Ralph Garr, 1971
20—Tommy Holmes, 1946*
20—Tommy Holmes, 1949*
20—Andy Pafko, 1953
20—Joe Adcock, 1959
20—Bob Horner, 1979
20—Otis Nixon, 1991
* Led league
† Tied for league lead

Pitching, Wins

13—Charlie Buffinton, 1884
13—Fred Klobedanz, 1897
13—Ted Lewis, 1898
13—Tom Glavine, 1992

12—Dick Rudolph, 1914
11—Warren Spahn, 1954
10—Dick Rudolph, 1916
10—Warren Spahn, 1961
10—Greg Maddux, 1995

Pitching, Losses

18—Cliff Curtis, 1910
14—Buster Brown, 1911
13—Joe Oeschger, 1922
13—Ben Cantwell, 1935
11—Irv Young, 1907
11—George Ferguson, 1909
11—Jim Yeargin, 1924
10—Joe Oeschger, 1923
10—Manny Salvo, 1941

Braves in Pro Basketball

Gene Conley, rhp, 1952, '54–58—Boston/New York (NBA) 1953–64

George Crowe, 1b, 1952–53, '55—Dayton (NBL) 1949

Buddy Hassett, 1b, 1939–41—Union City/Jersey (ABL) 1933–35

Ron Reed, rhp, 1966–75—Detroit (NBA) 1966–68

Del Rice, c, 1955–59—Rochester (NBL) 1946

Braves in Pro Football

Deion Sanders, of, 1991–94—Atlanta Falcons/San Francisco 49ers (NFL) 1989–

Jim Thorpe, of, 1919—Canton/Cleveland/Oorang/Rock Isle/New York Giants/Chicago Cardinals (NFL) 1915–28

Composite Finishes Since 1876

Position	Times
First	17
Second	13
Third	8
Fourth	15
Fifth	21

Position	Times
Sixth	20
Seventh	16
Eighth	9

(There have been 17 last-place finishes in franchise history.)

Year by Year

BOSTON

Year	Manager	Finish	Won	Lost	Pct.	Attendance
1876	Harry Wright	4	39	31	.557	—
1877	Harry Wright	1	42	18	.700	—
1878	Harry Wright	1	41	18	.683	—
1879	Harry Wright	2	54	30	.643	—
1880	Harry Wright	6	40	44	.476	—
1881	Harry Wright	6	38	45	.458	—
1882	John Morrill	3	45	39	.536	—
1883	Jack Burdock;					
	John Morrill	1	63	35	.643	—
1884	John Morrill	2	73	38	.658	—
1885	John Morrill	5	46	66	.411	—
1886	John Morrill	5	56	61	.479	—
1887	John Morrill;					
	King Kelly	5	61	60	.504	—
1888	John Morrill	4	70	64	.522	—
1889	Jim Hart	2	83	45	.648	—
1890	Frank Selee	5	76	57	.571	—
1891	Frank Selee	1	87	51	.630	—
1892	Frank Selee	1*	102	48	.680	—
1893	Frank Selee	1	86	43	.667	—
1894	Frank Selee	3	83	49	.629	—
1895	Frank Selee	T–4	71	60	.542	—
1896	Frank Selee	4	74	57	.565	—
1897	Frank Selee	1	93	39	.705	—
1898	Frank Selee	1	102	47	.685	—
1899	Frank Selee	2	95	57	.625	—
1900	Frank Selee	4	66	72	.478	—
1901	Frank Selee	5	69	69	.500	146,502
1902	Al Buckenberger	3	73	64	.533	116,960
1903	Al Buckenberger	6	58	80	.420	143,155
1904	Al Buckenberger	7	55	98	.359	140,694

BOSTON

Year	Manager	Finish	Won	Lost	Pct.	Attendance
1905	Fred Tenney	7	51	103	.331	150,003
1906	Fred Tenney	8	49	102	.325	143,280
1907	Fred Tenney	7	58	90	.392	203,221
1908	Joe Kelley	6	63	91	.409	253,750
1909	Frank Bowerman;					
	Harry Smith	8	45	108	.295	195,188
1910	Fred Lake	8	53	100	.346	149,027
1911	Fred Tenney	8	44	107	.291	116,000
1912	Johnny Kling	8	52	101	.340	121,000
1913	George Stallings	5	69	82	.457	208,000
1914	George Stallings	1	94	59	.614	382,913
1915	George Stallings	2	83	69	.546	376,283
1916	George Stallings	3	89	63	.586	313,495
1917	George Stallings	6	72	81	.471	174,253
1918	George Stallings	7	53	71	.427	84,938
1919	George Stallings	6	57	82	.410	167,401
1920	George Stallings	7	62	90	.408	162,483
1921	Fred Mitchell	4	79	74	.516	318,627
1922	Fred Mitchell	8	53	100	.346	167,965
1923	Fred Mitchell	7	54	100	.351	227,802
1924	Dave Bancroft	8	53	100	.346	117,478
1925	Dave Bancroft	5	70	83	.458	313,528
1926	Dave Bancroft	7	66	86	.277	303,598
1927	Dave Bancroft	7	60	94	.390	288,685
1928	Jack Slattery;					
	Rogers Hornsby	7	50	103	.327	227,001
1929	Judge Emil Fuchs	8	56	98	.364	372,351
1930	Bill McKechnie	6	70	84	.455	464,835
1931	Bill McKechnie	7	64	90	.416	515,005
1932	Bill McKechnie	5	77	77	.500	507,606
1933	Bill McKechnie	4	83	71	.539	517,803

BOSTON

Year	Manager	Finish	Won	Lost	Pct.	Attendance
1934	Bill McKechnie	4	78	73	.517	303,205
1935	Bill McKechnie	8	38	115	.248	232,754
1936	Bill McKechnie	6	71	83	.461	340,585
1937	Bill McKechnie	5	79	73	.520	385,339
1938	Casey Stengel	5	77	75	.507	341,149
1939	Casey Stengel	7	63	88	.417	285,994
1940	Casey Stengel	7	65	87	.428	241,616
1941	Casey Stengel	7	62	92	.403	263,680
1942	Casey Stengel	7	59	89	.399	285,332
1943	Bob Coleman,					
	Casey Stengel	6	68	85	.444	271,289
1944	Bob Coleman	6	65	89	.422	208,691
1945	Bob Coleman;					
	Del Bissonette	6	67	85	.441	374,178
1946	Billy Southworth	4	81	72	.529	969,673
1947	Billy Southworth	3	88	68	.558	1,277,361
1948	Billy Southworth	1	91	62	.595	1,455,439
1949	Billy Southworth,					
	Johnny Cooney	4	75	79	.487	1,081,795
1950	Billy Southworth	4	83	71	.539	944,391
1951	Billy Southworth;					
	Tommy Holmes	4	76	78	.494	487,475
1952	Tommy Holmes;					
	Charlie Grimm	7	64	89	.418	281,278

MILWAUKEE

1953	Charlie Grimm	2	92	62	.597	1,826,397
1954	Charlie Grimm	3	89	65	.578	2,131,388
1955	Charlie Grimm	2	85	69	.552	2,005,836
1956	Charlie Grimm;					
	Fred Haney	2	92	62	.597	2,046,331
1957	Fred Haney	1	95	59	.617	2,215,404
1958	Fred Haney	1	92	62	.597	1,971,101
1959	Fred Haney	2†	86	70	.551	1,749,112
1960	Fred Haney;					
	Charlie Dressen	2	88	66	.571	1,497,799
1961	Charlie Dressen;					
	Birdie Tebbetts	4	83	71	.539	1,101,441
1962	Birdie Tebbetts	5	86	76	.531	766,921
1963	Bobby Bragan	6	84	78	.519	773,018
1964	Bobby Bragan	5	88	74	.543	910,911
1965	Bobby Bragan	5	86	76	.531	555,584

ATLANTA

1966	Bobby Bragan;					
	Billy Hitchcock	5	85	77	.525	1,539,801
1967	Billy Hitchcock;					
	Ken Silvestri	7	77	85	.475	1,389,222
1968	Luman Harris	5	81	81	.550	1,126,540
1969	Luman Harris	1 West‡	93	69	.574	1,458,320
1970	Luman Harris	5	76	86	.469	1,078,848
1971	Luman Harris	3	82	80	.506	1,006,320
1972	Luman Harris;					
	Eddie Mathews	4	70	84	.455	752,973
1973	Eddie Mathews	5	76	85	.472	800,655

During his first tour of duty as Braves manager, Bobby Cox ran into Miz Lillian Carter on the campaign trail.

1974	Eddie Mathews;					
	Clyde King	3	88	74	.543	981,085
1975	Clyde King;					
	Connie Ryan	5	67	94	.416	534,672
1976	Dave Bristol	6	70	92	.432	818,179
1977	Dave Bristol;					
	Ted Turner	6	61	101	.371	872,464
1978	Bobby Cox	6	69	93	.426	904,494
1979	Bobby Cox	6	66	94	.413	769,465
1980	Bobby Cox	4	81	80	.503	1,048,411
1981	Bobby Cox	5**	50	56	.472	535,418
1982	Joe Torre	1‡	89	73	.549	1,801,985
1983	Joe Torre	2	88	74	.543	2,119,935
1984	Joe Torre	T–2	80	82	.494	1,724,892
1985	Eddie Haas;					
	Bobby Wine	5	66	96	.407	1,350,137
1986	Chuck Tanner	6	72	89	.447	1,387,181
1987	Chuck Tanner	5	69	92	.426	1,217,402
1988	Chuck Tanner;					
	Russ Nixon	6	54	106	.338	848,089
1989	Russ Nixon	6	63	97	.394	984,930
1990	Russ Nixon;					
	Bobby Cox	6	65	97	.401	980,129
1991	Bobby Cox	1	94	68	.580	2,140,217
1992	Bobby Cox	1	98	64	.605	3,077,400
1993	Bobby Cox	1‡	104	58	.642	3,884,720
1994	Bobby Cox	2 East††	68	46	.596	2,539,240

* First in 1st half (52–22); second in 2nd half (50–26).
† Lost playoff for pennant.
‡ Won division; lost National League Championship Series.
** Fourth in 1st half (25–29); fifth in 2nd half (25–27).
†† Season ended August 11 by players' strike.

13-Game Winning Streak to Open 1982

Game	Date	Opponent	Score	Winning Pitcher	Game	Date	Opponent	Score	Winning Pitcher
1.	April 6	at San Diego	1–0	Rick Mahler	8.	April 14	at Cincinnati	5–2	Rick Camp
2.	April 7	at San Diego	6–4	Bob Walk	9.	April 16	at Houston	5–3	Larry McWilliams
3.	April 9	Houston	6–2	Tommy Boggs	10.	April 17	at Houston	2–1	Preston Hanna
4.	April 10	Houston	8–6	Larry McWilliams	11.	April 18	at Houston	6–5	Al Hrabosky
5.	April 11	Houston	5–0	Rick Mahler	12.	April 20	Cincinnati	4–2	Steve Bedrosian
6.	April 12	at Cincinnati	6–1	Bob Walk	13.	April 21	Cincinnati	4–3	Rick Camp
7.	April 13	at Cincinnati	8–5	Gene Garber					

Braves' Biggest Innings

Runs	Inning	Date	Opponent	Runs	Inning	Date	Opponent
16	1	June 18, 1895	Baltimore	13	2	September 20, 1972	Houston
13	1	July 25, 1900	St. Louis				

Record Against Opponents (1900–94)

Franchise	W	L	Pct.	Franchise	W	L	Pct.
Brooklyn/Los Angeles	850	1,050	.447	New York/San Francisco	850	1,052	.447
Chicago	790	981	.446	New York Mets	228	201	.531
Cincinnati	892	1,023	.466	Philadelphia	910	861	.514
Colorado	21	2	.913	San Diego	245	203	.547
Florida	15	9	.625	St. Louis	805	969	.454
Houston	300	267	.529	Pittsburgh	795	974	.449
Montreal	139	165	.457				

Spring Training Sites

Municipal Stadium in West Palm Beach, the Braves' long-time Florida spring training camp.

1901	Norfolk, Virginia
1902–04	Thomasville, Georgia
1905	Charleston, South Carolina
1906	Jacksonville, Florida
1907	Thomasville, Georgia
1908–12	Augusta, Georgia
1913	Athens, Georgia
1914–15	Macon, Georgia
1916–18	Miami, Florida
1919–20	Columbus, Georgia
1921	Galveston, Texas
1922–37	St. Petersburg, Florida
1938–40	Bradenton, Florida
1941	San Antonio, Texas
1942	Sanford, Florida
1943–44	Wallingford, Connecticut
1945	Washington, D.C.
1946–47	Ft. Lauderdale, Florida
1948–61	Bradenton, Florida
1962	Palmetto, Florida
1963–	West Palm Beach, Florida

Braves-Pilgrims (Red Sox) City Series

Year	Champion	W–L
1905*	Pilgrims	6–1

* Postseason

Managers and Their Records

Years	Name	Games	W	L	T	Pct.	Years	Name	Games	W	L	T	Pct.
1876–81	Harry Wright	444	254	187	3	.576	1946–51	Billy Southworth	789	424	358	7	.542
1882, 1883–88	John Morrill	645	335	296	14	.531	1949	Johnny Cooney	46	20	25	1	.444
1883	Jack Burdock	54	30	24	0	.556	1951–52	Tommy Holmes	130	61	69	0	.469
1887	King Kelly	95	49	43	3	.533	1952–56	Charlie Grimm	631	341	285	5	.545
1889	Jim Hart	133	83	45	5	.648	1956–59	Fred Haney	575	341	231	3	.596
1890–1901	Frank Selee	1,677	1,004	649	24	.607	1960–61	Charlie Dressen	284	159	124	1	.562
1902–04	Al Buckenberger	437	186	242	9	.435	1961–62	Birdie Tebbetts	187	98	89	0	.524
1905–07, '11	Fred Tenney	616	202	402	12	.334	1963–66	Bobby Bragan	599	310	287	2	.519
1908	Joe Kelley	156	63	91	2	.409	1966–67	Billy Hitchcock	210	110	100	0	.524
1909	Frank Bowerman	76	22	54	0	.289	1967	Ken Silvestri	3	0	3	0	.000
1909	Harry Smith	79	23	54	2	.299	1968–72	Luman Harris	754	379	373	2	.504
1910	Fred Lake	157	53	100	4	.346	1972–74	Eddie Mathews	311	149	161	1	.481
1912	Johnny Kling	155	52	101	2	.340	1974–75	Clyde King	198	96	101	1	.487
1913–20	George Stallings	1,202	579	597	26	.492	1975	Connie Ryan	27	9	18	0	.333
1921–23	Fred Mitchell	462	186	274	2	.404	1976–77	Dave Bristol	322	130	192	0	.404
1924–27	Dave Bancroft	615	249	363	3	.407	1977	Ted Turner	1	0	1	0	.000
1928	Jack Slattery	31	11	20	0	.355	1978–81, '90–	Bobby Cox	1,287	670	616	1	.521
1928	Rogers Hornsby	122	39	83	0	.320	1982–84	Joe Torre	486	257	229	0	.529
1929	Emil Fuchs	154	56	98	0	.364	1985	Eddie Haas	121	50	71	0	.413
1930–37	Bill McKechnie	1,235	560	666	9	.457	1985	Bobby Wine	41	16	25	0	.390
1938–43	Casey Stengel	870	373	491	6	.432	1986–88	Chuck Tanner	361	153	208	0	.424
1943, '44–45	Bob Coleman	295	128	165	2	.437	1988–90	Russ Nixon	347	130	216	1	.376
1945	Del Bissonette	60	25	34	1	.424							

Braves Playing Managers

	Years as Manager	Years as Player/Manager	Positions		Years as Manager	Years as Player/Manager	Positions
Harry Wright*	1876–81	1876–77	OF	Harry Smith	1909	1909	C
John Morrill	1882, '83–88	1882, '83–88	1B, SS, 2B, OF, 3B, P	Fred Lake	1910	1910	PH
				Johnny Kling	1912	1912	C
Jack Burdock	1883	1883	2B	Dave Bancroft	1924–27	1924–27	SS, 3B
King Kelly	1887	1887	OF, 2B, C, P, SS, 3B	Rogers Hornsby	1928	1928	2B
				Tommy Holmes	1951–52	1951	OF
Fred Tenney	1905–07, '11	1905–07, '11	1B, P, OF				
Joe Kelley	1908	1908	OF, 1B	* Played only one game in each of two seasons.			
Frank Bowerman	1909	1909	C				

Braves Who Managed in the Major Leagues

	Games	Team (League), Year		Games	Team (League), Year
Joe Adcock	162	Cleveland (A), 1967	Dave Bancroft	615	Boston (N), 1924–27
Bob Allen	179	Philadelphia (N), 1890; Cincinnati (N), 1900	Lena Blackburne	232	Chicago (A), 1928–29
			Tommy Bond	6	Worcester (N), 1882
Felipe Alou	402	Montreal (N), 1992–	Frank Bowerman	76	Boston (N), 1909
Ken Aspromonte	480	Cleveland (A) 1972–74	Tom Brown	137	Washington (N), 1897–98
Dusty Baker	227	San Francisco (N), 1993–	Charlie Buffinton	116	Philadelphia (P), 1890

	Games	Team (League), Year		Games	Team (League), Year
Jack Burdock	54	Boston (N), 1883	Jack Manning	20	Cincinnati (N), 1877
Jack Clements	19	Philadelphia (N), 1890	Jimmy Manning	138	Washington (A), 1901
Jimmy Collins	842	Boston (A), 1901–06	Rabbit Maranville	53	Chicago (N), 1925
Johnny Cooney	46	Boston (N), 1949	Billy Martin	2,267	Minnesota (A), 1969;
Chuck Cottier	217	Seattle (A), 1984–86			Detroit (A), 1971–73;
Del Crandall	833	Milwaukee (A), 1972–75;			Texas (A), 1973–75;
		Seattle (A), 1983–84			New York (A), 1975–79, '83,
Bill Dahlen	615	Brooklyn (N), 1910–13			'85, '88;
Alvin Dark	1,950	San Francisco (N), 1961–64;			Oakland (A), 1980–82
		Kansas City (A), 1966–67;	Marty Martinez	1	Seattle (A), 1986
		Cleveland (A), 1968–71;	Eddie Mathews	311	Atlanta (N), 1972–74
		Oakland (A), 1974–75;	Gene Mauch	3,942	Philadelphia (N), 1960–68;
		San Diego (N), 1977			Montreal (N), 1969–75;
Patsy Donovan	1,597	Pittsburgh (N), 1897, '99;			Minnesota (A), 1976–80;
		St. Louis (N), 1901–03;			California (A), 1981–82,
		Washington (A), 1904;			'85–87
		Brooklyn (N), 1906–08;	Tommy McCarthy	27	St. Louis (AA), 1890
		Boston (A), 1910–11	Stuffy McInnis	155	Philadelphia (N), 1927
Hugh Duffy	1,221	Milwaukee (A), 1901;	Bill McKechnie	3,647	Newark (F), 1915;
		Philadelphia (N), 1904–06;			Pittsburgh (N), 1922–26;
		Chicago (A), 1910–11;			St. Louis (N), 1928–29;
		Boston (A), 1921–22			Boston (N), 1930–37;
Bob Elliott	155	Kansas City (A), 1960			Cincinnati (N), 1938–46
Johnny Evers	375	Chicago (N), 1913, '21;	Marty McManus	248	Boston (A), 1932–33
		Chicago (A), 1924	Roy McMillan	55	Milwaukee (A), 1972;
Kerby Farrell	153	Cleveland (A), 1957			New York (N), 1975
Cito Gaston	856	Toronto (A), 1989–	Fred Mitchell	1,044	Chicago (N), 1917–20;
Mike Gonzalez	23	St. Louis (N), 1938, '40			Boston (N), 1921–23
Hank Gowdy	4	Cincinnati (N), 1946	Pat Moran	1,344	Philadelphia (N), 1915–18;
Burleigh Grimes	306	Brooklyn (N), 1937–38			Cincinnati (N), 1919–23
Eddie Haas	121	Atlanta (N), 1985	Joe Morgan	563	Boston (A), 1988–91
Roy Hartsfield	484	Toronto (A), 1977–79	John Morrill	696	Boston (N), 1882–88;
Billy Herman	465	Pittsburgh (N), 1947;			Washington (N), 1889
		Boston (A), 1964–66	Tim Murnane	111	Boston (U), 1884
Buck Herzog	401	Cincinnati (N), 1914–16	Danny Murtaugh	2,068	Pittsburgh (N), 1957–64,
Tommy Holmes	130	Boston (N), 1951–52			'67, '70–71, '73–76
Rogers Hornsby	1,530	St. Louis (N), 1925–26;	Billy Nash	130	Philadelphia (N), 1896
		New York (N), 1927;	Johnny Neun	268	New York (A), 1946;
		Boston (N), 1928;			Cincinnati (N), 1947–48
		Chicago (N), 1930–32;	Kid Nichols	169	St. Louis (N), 1904–05
		St. Louis (A), 1933–37, '52;	Johnny Oates	561	Baltimore (A), 1991–94;
		Cincinnati (N), 1952–53			Texas (A) 1995–
Dave Johnson	1,244	New York (N), 1984–90;	Dan O'Leary	35	Cincinnati (U), 1884
		Cincinnati (N), 1993–	Jim O'Rourke	510	Buffalo (N), 1881–84,
Eddie Joost	156	Philadelphia (A), 1954			Washington (N), 1893
Joe Kelley	669	Cincinnati (N), 1902–05;	Blondie Purcell	82	Philadelphia (N), 1883
		Boston (N), 1908	Joe Quinn	156	St. Louis (N), 1895;
King Kelly	330	Boston (N), 1887;			Cleveland (N), 1899
		Boston (P), 1890;	Del Rice	155	California (A), 1972
		Cincinnati (AA),1891	Connie Ryan	33	Atlanta (N), 1975;
Mal Kittridge	18	Washington (A), 1904			Texas (A), 1977
Johnny Kling	155	Boston (N), 1912	Red Schoendienst	1,999	St. Louis (N), 1965–76, '80,
Fred Lake	349	Boston (A), 1908–09;			'90
		Boston (N), 1910	George Sisler	462	St. Louis (A), 1924–26
Tony LaRussa	2,359	Chicago (A), 1979–86;	Harry Smith	79	Boston (N), 1909
		Oakland (A), 1986–	Pop Snyder	288	Cincinnati (AA), 1882–84,
Al Lopez	2,425	Cleveland (A), 1951–56;			Washington (AA), 1891
		Chicago (A), 1957–65,	Billy Southworth	1,770	St. Louis (N), 1929, '40–45;
		'68–69			Boston (N), 1946–51
Bobby Lowe	78	Detroit (A), 1904			

Braves who became managers include (L–R, top row) Joe Adcock, Al Dark, Kerby Farrell, (center row) Dave Johnson, Eddie Joost, Clarence "Cito" Gaston, (bottom row) Tony LaRussa, Gene Mauch, and Johnny Oates.

	Games	Team (League), Year
Chick Stahl	40	Boston (A), 1906
Eddie Stanky	906	St. Louis (N), 1952–55; Chicago (A), 1966–68; Texas (A), 1977
Casey Stengel	3,766	Brooklyn (N), 1934–36; Boston (N), 1938–43; New York (A), 1949–60; New York (N), 1962–65
Harry Stovey	140	Worcester (N), 1881; Philadelphia (AA), 1885
Gabby Street	702	St. Louis (N), 1929–33; St. Louis (A), 1938
Billy Sullivan	159	Chicago (A), 1909
Chuck Tanner	2,738	Chicago (A), 1970–75; Oakland (A), 1976; Pittsburgh (N), 1977–85; Atlanta (N), 1986–88
Zack Taylor	649	St. Louis (A), 1946, '48–51
Fred Tenney	616	Boston (N), 1905–07, '11

	Games	Team (League), Year
Joe Torre	1,895	New York (N), 1977–81; Atlanta (N), 1982–84; St. Louis (N), 1990–95
Sam Trott	12	Washington (AA), 1891
Mickey Vernon	363	Washington (A), 1961–63
Ed Walsh	3	Chicago (A), 1924
Bucky Walters	206	Cincinnati (N), 1948–49
Deacon White	18	Cincinnati (N), 1879
Will White	72	Cincinnati (AA), 1884
Kaiser Wilhelm	221	Philadelphia (N), 1921–22
Harry Wolverton	153	New York (A), 1912
George Wright	85	Providence (N), 1879
Harry Wright	1,853	Boston (N), 1876–81; Providence (N), 1882–83; Philadelphia (N), 1885–93
Cy Young	6	Boston (A), 1907

Leagues: A=American; N=National; P=Players; AA=American Association; F=Federal; U=Union Association.

All-Time Coaches Roster

Tommie Aaron	1979–84	Roy Hartsfield	1973	Brian Snitker	1985, '88–90
Bill Adair	1962, '67	Billy Herman	1958–59	Allan Sothoron	1928
King Bader	Spring 1926*	Billy Hitchcock	1966	Willie Stargell	1986–88
Tony Bartirome	1986–88	Sonny Jackson	1982–83	Herm Starrette	1974–76
Jim Beauchamp	1991–	Clarence Jones	1985, '88–	John Sullivan	1980–81
Benny Bengough	1944–45	Bob Keely	1946–57	George Susce	1958–59
Vern Benson	1976–77	George Kelly	1938–43	Dixie Walker	1963–65
Ray Berres	1947	Mike Kelly	1938–39	Rube Walker	1982–84
Del Bissonette	1945	Bob Kennedy	1967	Bucky Walters	1950–55
Cloyd Boyer	1978–81	Duffy Lewis	1931–35	Pete Ward	1978
Jimmy Brown	1949–51	Roy Majtyka	1988–90	Ernie White	1947–48
Lou Burdette	1972–73	Eddie Mathews	1970–72	Jo-Jo White	1963–66
Tommy Burgess	1978	Dal Maxvill	1982–84	Jimy Williams	1990–
Jim Busby	1968–75	Leo Mazzone	1985, '90–	Bobby Wine	1985, '88–90
Chris Cannizzaro	1976–78	Fred Mitchell	1913–16	Whit Wyatt	1958–67
Bob Coleman	1943	Al Monchak	1986–88	Ned Yost	1991–
Johnny Cooney	1940–42, '46–55	Rich Morales	1986–87		
Pat Corrales	1990–	George Myatt	1960–61	* Resigned to become manager at Lynn (NEL).	
Bruce DalCanton	1987–90	Phil Niekro	1990		
Art Devlin	1928	Russ Nixon	1986–87	† Resigned to head Major League Scouting Bureau.	
Bobby Dews	1979–81, '85	Andy Pafko	1960–62		
Harry Dorish	1968–71	Satchel Paige	1969		
Oscar Dugey	1920	Joe Pignatano	1982–84		
Jimmy Dykes	1962	Grover Resinger	1966		
Jewel Ens	1934	Del Rice	1959		
Johnny Evers	1929	Johnny Riddle	1956–57		
Jim Fanning	1967–68†	Charlie Root	1956–57		
John Fitzpatrick	1958–59	Dick Rudolph	1921–27		
Freddy Fitzsimmons	1948	Connie Ryan	1957, '71, '73–74		
Jake Flowers	1946				
Bob Gibson	1982–84	Johnny Sain	1977, '85–86		
Billy Goodman	1968–70	Bob Scheffing	1960		
Hank Gowdy	1929–37	Tom Sheehan	1944		
Alex Grammas	1979	Ken Silvestri	1963–75		
Eddie Haas	1974–77, '84	Bob Skinner	1986–88		
Fred Haney	1956	Jack Slattery	1918–19		

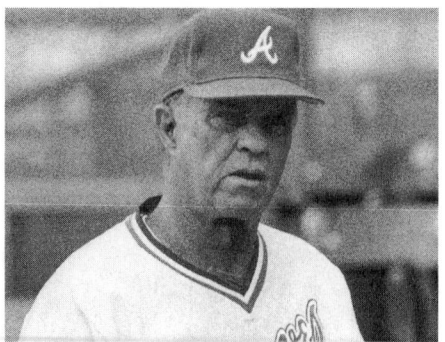

A great pitcher and a renowned pitching coach, Johnny Sain.

Braves Presidents

1876	Nathaniel T. Apollonio	1926–35	Judge Emil E. Fuchs
1877–1906	Arthur H. Soden	1936–44	Bob Quinn
1907–09	George B. Dovey	1945–56	Lou Perini
1909–10	John S. Dovey	1957–61	Joseph F. Cairnes
1911	William Hepburn Russell	1962–66	John J. McHale
1912	John M. Ward	1967–72	Bill Bartholomay
1912–15	James E. Gaffney	1973–75	Dan Donahue
1916–18	Percy D. Haughton	1976–86	Ted Turner
1919–22	George Washington Grant	1986–	Stan Kasten
1923–25	Christy Mathewson		

Hall of Fame pitcher Christy Mathewson (L) served as Braves president until his death, then Judge Emil Fuchs (R) took over.

General Managers

1945–58	John Quinn	1976	John Alevizos	1986–90	Bobby Cox
1966–72	Paul Richards	1976–79	Bill Lucas	1990–	John Schuerholz
1972–76	Eddie Robinson	1979–85	John Mullen		

Team Hitting, Pitching, Fielding

	HITTING			PITCHING		FIELDING		
Year	R	HR	BA/Rank	CG	ERA/Rank	E	DP	FA/Rank
1876	471	9*	.266/3	49	2.51/5	442	42	.860/5
1877	419*	4	.296/1	61*	2.15/1	290	36	.889/3
1878	298	2	.241/5	58	2.32/T-2	228*	48*	.914/1
1879	562	20*	.274/2	80	2.19/2	319*	58	.913/1
1880	416	20*	.253/2	70	3.08/7	367	54	.901/5
1881	349	5	.251/7	72	2.71/5	325	54	.909/3
1882	472	15	.264/3	81	2.80/4	314*	37	.910/T-1
1883	669	34*	.276/2	89	2.55/3	409	58	.901/3
1884	684	36	.254/4	109	2.47/2	384*	46	.922/1
1885	528	22	.232/5	111*	3.03/6	478	79	.901/T-6
1886	657	24	.260/4	116	3.24/T-5	465	63	.905/8
1887	831	53	.277/3	123	4.41/7	522	94	.905/8
1888	669	56	.245/3	134	2.61/3	494	91	.917/7
1889	826	42	.270/3	121	3.36/1	413	105	.926/T-3
1890	763	31	.258/6	132*	2.93/2	359	77	.935/3
1891	847*	54	.255/T-3	126*	2.76/1	358*	96	.938/1
1892	862	34	.250/6	142	2.86/2	454	127	.929/T-6
1893	1,008	65	.290/5	114*	4.43/5	353	118	.936/5
1894	1,220	103*	.331/3	108	5.41/5	415	120	.925/T-6
1895	907	54	.290/T-6	116	4.27/4	364	104	.934/4
1896	860	36	.300/3	110	3.78/4	368	94	.934/T-8
1897	1,025*	45*	.319/2	115	3.65/3	272	80	.951/T-1
1898	872	53*	.290/2	127	2.98/3	310	102	.950/T-2
1899	858	39	.287/5	138	3.26/2	303*	124	.952/1
1900	778	48*	.283/4	116	3.72/3	273*	86	.953/1
1901	531	28	.249/8	128	2.90/3	282	89	.952/2
1902	572	14	.249/6	124	2.61/3	240*	90	.959/1
1903	578	25	.245/8	125	3.34/5	361	89	.939/8
1904	491	24	.237/7	136	3.43/8	353	91	.945/T-6
1905	468	17	.234/8	139*	3.52/6	325	89	.951/7
1906	408	16	.226/8	137*	3.14/8	337	102	.947/8

Year	HITTING			PITCHING		FIELDING		
	R	HR	BA/Rank	CG	ERA/Rank	E	DP	FA/Rank
1907	502	22	.243/5	121	3.33/8	249	128*	.961/4
1908	537	17	.239/5	92	2.79/8	253	90*	.962/T-4
1909	435	15	.223/8	98	3.20/7	342	101	.948/8
1910	495	31	.246/7	72	3.22/7	305	137*	.954/8
1911	699	37	.267/2	73	5.08/8	347	110	.947/8
1912	693	35	.273/4	88	4.17/8	297	129*	.954/8
1913	641	32	.256/7	105*	3.19/6	273	82	.957/8
1914	657	35	.251/4	104*	2.74/4	246	143*	.963/3
1915	582	17	.240/8	95	2.57/2	213*	115	.966/T-1
1916	542	22	.233/8	97*	2.19/2	212*	124	.967/1
1917	536	22	.246/6	105*	2.77/5	224	122	.966/4
1918	424	13	.244/T-6	96*	2.90/5	184	89	.965/4
1919	465	24	.253/6	79	3.17/6	204	111	.966/4
1920	523	23	.260/7	93	3.54/7	239	125	.964/T-6
1921	721	61	.290/4	74	3.90/6	199	122	.969/T-4
1922	596	32	.263/8	63	4.37/6	215	121	.965/T-6
1923	636	32	.273/8	54	4.21/7	230	157	.964/6
1924	520	25	.256/8	66	4.46/7	168*	154	.973/1
1925	708	41	.292/5	77	4.39/5	221	145	.964/T-7
1926	624	16	.277/7	60	4.01/7	208	150	.967/5
1927	651	37	.279/5	52	4.22/7	231	130	.963/T-7
1928	631	52	.275/6	54	4.83/7	193	141	.969/6
1929	657	33	.280/8	78	5.12/7	204	146	.967/8
1930	693	66	.281/T-7	71	4.91/5	178	167	.971/5
1931	533	34	.258/8	78	3.90/5	170	141	.973/T-3
1932	649	63	.265/7	72	3.53/2	152*	145	.976/1
1933	552	54	.252/7	85	2.96/3	138*	148	.978/1
1934	683	83	.272/7	62	4.11/4	169	120	.972/T-3
1935	575	75	.263/8	54	4.93/8	197	101	.967/6
1936	631	67	.265/8	61	3.94/4	189	175*	.971/4
1937	579	63	.247/8	85*	3.22/1	157	128	.975/T-1
1938	561	54	.250/8	83*	3.40/2	173	136	.972/5
1939	572	56	.264/7	68	3.71/4	181	178*	.971/T-5
1940	623	59	.256/7	76	4.36/T-6	184	169*	.970/T-4
1941	592	48	.251/6	62	3.95/7	191	174*	.969/T-6
1942	515	68	.240/6	68	3.76/7	142	138	.976/3
1943	465	39	.233/8	87	3.25/4	176	139	.972/T-6
1944	593	79	.246/8	70	3.67/6	182	160	.971/T-4
1945	721	101	.267/T-5	57	4.04/6	193	160*	.969/6
1946	630	44	.264/2	73	3.35/5	169	129	.972/T-6
1947	701	85	.275/1	74*	3.62/2	153	124	.974/T-6
1948	739	95	.275/1	70*	3.37/1	143	132	.976/3
1949	706	103	.258/6	68*	3.99/5	148	144	.976T-4
1950	785	148	.263/4	88*	4.14/5	182	146	.970/7
1951	723	130	.262/3	73*	3.75/3	145	157	.976/5
1952	569	110	.233/7	63	3.78/6	154	143	.975/T-5
1953	738	156	.266/4	72	3.30/1	143	169	.976/4
1954	670	139	.265/4	63	3.19/2	116*	171	.981/1
1955	743	182	.261/T-3	61*	3.85/3	152	155	.975/T-5
1956	709	177	.259/3	64*	3.11/1	130	159	.979/3
1957	772*	199*	.269/T-2	60*	3.47/2	120	173	.981/2
1958	675	167	.266/T-1	72*	3.21/1	120	152	.980/2
1959	724	177*	.265/3	69*	3.51/2	127	138	.979/2
1960	724	170	.265/2	55*	3.76/5	141	137	.976/T-5
1961	712	188*	.258/6	57*	3.89/4	111*	152	.982/1
1962	730	181	.252/8	59	3.68/4	124*	154	.980/1
1963	677	139	.244/7	56*	3.27/5	129*	161	.980/1
1964	803*	159	.272/1	45	4.12/9	143	139	.977/2
1965	708	196*	.256/3	43	3.52/4	140	145	.978/4

	HITTING			PITCHING		FIELDING		
Year	R	HR	BA/Rank	CG	ERA/Rank	E	DP	FA/Rank
1966	782*	207*	.263/2	37	3.68/6	154	139	.976/6
1967	631	158*	.240/8	35	3.47/6	138	148	.978/T-4
1968	514	80	.252/T-2	44	2.92/6	125	139	.980/T-2
1969	691	141	.258/3	38	3.53/6	115*	114	.981/1
1970	736	160	.270/T-1	45	4.33/9	141	118	.977/T-7
1971	643	153	.257/5	40	3.75/10	146	180*	.977/9
1972	628	144	.258/T-3	40	4.27/12	156	130	.974/T-10
1973	799*	206*	.266/1	34	4.25/12	166	142	.974/T-9
1974	661	120	.249/10	46	3.05/2	132	161	.979/T-2
1975	583	107	.244/T-10	32	3.91/10	175	147	.972/T-10
1976	620	82	.245/11	33	3.86/10	167	151	.973/T-10
1977	678	139	.254/T-8	28	4.85/12	175	127	.972/T-10
1978	600	123	.244/12	29	4.08/12	153	126	.975/T-10
1979	669	126	.256/T-8	32	4.18/12	183	139	.970/12
1980	630	144	.250/11	29	3.77/8	162	156	.975/T-9
1981	395	64	.243/11	11	3.45/5	102	93	.976/10
1982	739*	146*	.256/8	15	3.82/10	137	186*	.979/T-6
1983	746*	130	.272/1	18	3.67/7	137	176*	.978/6
1984	632	111	.247/10	17	3.57/6	139	153	.978/T-6
1985	632	126	.246/10	9	4.19/11	159	197*	.976/T-9
1986	615	138	.250/T-10	17	3.97/10	141	181*	.978/T-5
1987	747	152	.258/9	16	4.63/12	116*	170	.982/T-1
1988	555	96	.242/11	14	4.09/11	151	138	.976/T-11
1989	584	128	.234/12	15	3.70/10	152	124	.976/T-10
1990	682	162	.250/T-10	17	4.58/12	158	133	.974/12
1991	749	141	.258/T-2	18*	3.49/3	138	122	.978/10
1992	682	138*	.254/T-5	26	3.14/1	109	121	.982/T-4
1993	767	169*	.262/9	18	3.14/1	108	146	.983/T-2
1994	542	137	.267/7	16	3.57/2	81	85	.982/T-4

* Led league.

League Leaders in Hitting

Average

1877	Deacon White	.387
1889	Dan Brouthers	.373
1894	Hugh Duffy	.440
1928	Rogers Hornsby	.387
1942	Ernie Lombardi	.330
1956	Hank Aaron	.328
1959	Hank Aaron	.355
1970	Rico Carty	.366
1974	Ralph Garr	.353
1991	Terry Pendleton	.319

Runs

1877	Jim O'Rourke	68
1879	Charley Jones	85
1883	Joe Hornung	107
1897	Billy Hamilton	152
1950	Earl Torgeson	120
1957	Hank Aaron	118
1960	Billy Bruton	112
1963	Hank Aaron	121
1966	Felipe Alou	122
1967	Hank Aaron	113*
1985	Dale Murphy	118

Hits

1877	Deacon White	103
1884	Ezra Sutton	162*
1894	Hugh Duffy	237
1907	Ginger Beaumont	187
1911	Doc Miller	192
1926	Eddie Brown	201
1945	Tommy Holmes	224
1947	Tommy Holmes	191
1956	Hank Aaron	200
1957	Red Schoendienst	200†
1959	Hank Aaron	223
1966	Felipe Alou	218
1968	Felipe Alou	210*
1974	Ralph Garr	214
1991	Terry Pendleton	187
1992	Terry Pendleton	199*

Doubles

1894	Hugh Duffy	51
1945	Tommy Holmes	47
1955	Hank Aaron	37*
	Johnny Logan	37*
1956	Hank Aaron	34

1961	Hank Aaron	39
1964	Lee Maye	44
1965	Hank Aaron	40

Triples

1877	Deacon White	11
1888	Dick Johnston	18
1891	Harry Stovey	20
1921	Ray Powell	18*
1956	Billy Bruton	15
1960	Billy Bruton	13
1974	Ralph Garr	17

Ralph Garr didn't have the muscle of Baltimore's Boog Powell but he still won the National League batting title in 1974.

Brett Butler led the league in triples in 1983.

Dale Murphy tied for the National League home run title in 1984 and won it outright in 1985.

| 1984 | Dale Murphy | 332 |
| 1991 | Terry Pendleton | 303* |

Slugging Average

1877	Deacon White	.545
1879	John O'Rourke	.521
1891	Harry Stovey	.498
1894	Hugh Duffy	.694
1928	Rogers Hornsby	.632
1945	Tommy Holmes	.577
1959	Hank Aaron	.636
1967	Hank Aaron	.573
1971	Hank Aaron	.669
1983	Dale Murphy	.540
1984	Dale Murphy	.547

Base On Balls

1877	Jim O'Rourke	20
1879	Charley Jones	29
1896	Billy Hamilton	110
1897	Billy Hamilton	105
1928	Rogers Hornsby	107
1948	Bob Elliott	131
1955	Eddie Mathews	109
1961	Eddie Mathews	93
1962	Eddie Mathews	101
1963	Eddie Mathews	124
1973	Darrell Evans	124
1974	Darrell Evans	126
1976	Jimmy Wynn	127
1978	Jeff Burroughs	117
1985	Dale Murphy	90

*Tied for league lead.
†Started season with New York, NL.

1975	Ralph Garr	11
1983	Brett Butler	13
1992	Deion Sanders	14

Home Runs

1879	Charley Jones	9
1880	Jim O'Rourke	6*
1891	Harry Stovey	16*
1894	Hugh Duffy	18
1897	Hugh Duffy	11
1898	Jimmy Collins	15
1900	Herman Long	12
1907	Dave Brain	10
1910	Fred Beck	10*
1935	Wally Berger	34
1945	Tommy Holmes	28
1953	Eddie Mathews	47
1957	Hank Aaron	44
1959	Eddie Mathews	46
1963	Hank Aaron	44*
1966	Hank Aaron	44
1967	Hank Aaron	39
1984	Dale Murphy	36*
1985	Dale Murphy	37

Runs Batted In

1877	Deacon White	49
1879	Charley Jones	62*
	John O'Rourke	62*
1894	Hugh Duffy	145

1935	Wally Berger	130
1957	Hank Aaron	132
1960	Hank Aaron	126
1963	Hank Aaron	130
1966	Hank Aaron	127
1982	Dale Murphy	109*
1983	Dale Murphy	121

Stolen Bases

1950	Sam Jethroe	35
1951	Sam Jethroe	35
1953	Billy Bruton	26
1954	Billy Bruton	34
1955	Billy Bruton	25

Total Bases

1877	Deacon White	145
1891	Harry Stovey	271
1894	Hugh Duffy	374
1898	Jimmy Collins	286
1945	Tommy Holmes	367
1956	Hank Aaron	340
1957	Hank Aaron	369
1959	Hank Aaron	400
1960	Hank Aaron	334
1961	Hank Aaron	358
1963	Hank Aaron	370
1966	Felipe Alou	355
1967	Hank Aaron	344
1969	Hank Aaron	332

Darrell Evans twice led the league in walks.

All-Time Braves Hitting Leaders

Games Played

Hank Aaron	3,076
Eddie Mathews	2,223
Dale Murphy	1,926
Rabbit Maranville	1,795

Fred Tenney	1,737
Herman Long	1,646
Bobby Lowe	1,410
Del Crandall	1,394
Johnny Logan	1,351
Tommy Holmes	1,289

At Bats

Hank Aaron	11,628
Eddie Mathews	8,049
Dale Murphy	7,098
Herman Long	6,777

Johnny Logan ranks ninth on the Braves' all-time list for games played.

Rabbit Maranville	6,724
Fred Tenney	6,637
Bobby Lowe	5,617
Tommy Holmes	4,956
Johnny Logan	4,931
John Morrill	4,759

Hits

Hank Aaron	3,600
Eddie Mathews	2,201
Fred Tenney	1,994
Dale Murphy	1,901
Herman Long	1,900
Rabbit Maranville	1,696
Bobby Lowe	1,606
Hugh Duffy	1,544
Tommy Holmes	1,503

Doubles

Hank Aaron	600
Eddie Mathews	338
Dale Murphy	306
Herman Long	295
Tommy Holmes	291
Wally Berger	248
Rabbit Maranville	244
Fred Tenney	242
John Morrill	234
Hugh Duffy	220

Triples

Rabbit Maranville	103
Hank Aaron	96
Herman Long	90
John Morrill	80
Billy Bruton	79
Fred Tenney	74
Hugh Duffy	73

Bobby Lowe	71
Sam Wise	71
Eddie Mathews	70

Home Runs

Hank Aaron	733
Eddie Mathews	493
Dale Murphy	371
Joe Adcock	239
Bob Horner	215
Wally Berger	199
Del Crandall	170
Ron Gant	147
Joe Torre	142
Darrell Evans	131

Extra-Base Hits

Hank Aaron	1,429
Eddie Mathews	901
Dale Murphy	714
Wally Berger	499
Herman Long	474
Joe Adcock	458
Tommy Holmes	426
Bob Horner	382
Rabbit Maranville	370
Hugh Duffy	362

Total Bases

Hank Aaron	6,591
Eddie Mathews	4,158
Dale Murphy	3,394
Herman Long	2,642
Fred Tenney	2,435
Rabbit Maranville	2,215
Wally Berger	2,212
Joe Adcock	2,164
Tommy Holmes	2,152
Bobby Lowe	2,144

Runs Scored

Hank Aaron	2,107
Eddie Mathews	1,452
Herman Long	1,291
Fred Tenney	1,134
Dale Murphy	1,103
Bobby Lowe	999
Hugh Duffy	996
Billy Nash	855
Rabbit Maranville	801
John Morrill	800

Runs Batted In

Hank Aaron	2,202
Eddie Mathews	1,388

Eddie Mathews and Hank Aaron combined to hit more home runs than any other two teammates in history.

Dale Murphy	1,143
Herman Long	964
Hugh Duffy	927
Bobby Lowe	872
Billy Nash	809
Wally Berger	746
Bob Horner	652
Del Crandall	628

Batting Average (min. 2,500 AB)

Billy Hamilton	.338
Hugh Duffy	.332
Ralph Garr	.317
Rico Carty	.317
Hank Aaron	.310
Jimmy Collins	.309
Wally Berger	.304
Tommy Holmes	.303
Fred Tenney	.300

Slugging Percentage (min. 2,500 AB)

Hank Aaron	.567
Wally Berger	.533
Eddie Mathews	.517
Joe Adcock	.511
Bob Horner	.507
Rico Carty	.496
Bob Elliott	.485
Dale Murphy	.478
Ron Gant	.466
Joe Torre	.462

Stolen Bases

Herman Long	431
Hugh Duffy	331
Billy Hamilton	274
Bobby Lowe	260
Fred Tenney	260
Hank Aaron	240
King Kelly	238
Billy Nash	232
Rabbit Maranville	194

Braves Triple-Crown Leaders

Player	Year	AVG	HR	RBI	Player	Year	AVG	HR	RBI
Jim O'Rourke	1876	.327	2	43	Eddie Mathews	1953	.302	47 (1)	135 (2)
Deacon White	1877	.387 (1)	2 (T-3)	49 (1)	Hank Aaron	1957	.322 (4)	44 (1)	132 (1)
Jim O'Rourke	1878	.278	1	29	Hank Aaron	1962	.323 (5)	45 (2)	128 (4)
Hugh Duffy	1894	.440 (1)	18 (1)	145 (1)	Hank Aaron	1963	.319 (4)	44 (T-1)	130 (1)
Gene DeMontreville	1901	.305	5	72	Hank Aaron	1967	.307	39 (1)	109 (3)
Ginger Beaumont	1907	.322 (3)	4	62	Hank Aaron	1969	.300	44 (2)	97
Doc Miller	1911	.333 (2)	7	91	Bob Horner	1979	.314 (5)	33 (4)	98
Rogers Hornsby	1928	.387 (1)	21 (5)	94	Dale Murphy	1982	.281	36 (2)	109 (T-1)
Wally Berger	1931	.323	19 (3)	84	Dale Murphy	1984	.290	36 (T-1)	100 (3)
Wally Berger	1932	.307	17	73	Dale Murphy	1985	.300	37 (1)	111 (2)
Wally Berger	1933	.313	27 (2)	106 (2)	Terry Pendleton	1992	.311	21	105 (2)
Tommy Holmes	1945	.352 (2)	28 (1)	117 (2)	Fred McGriff	1994	.318	34 (4)	94
Bob Elliott	1947	.317 (2)	22	113 (4)					
Sid Gordon	1952	.289	25 (T-4)	75	( ) = Ranking in league.				

Season Batting Leaders by Position

Average

C—Ernie Lombari .330 (1942)
1B—Dick Burrus .340 (1925)
      George Sisler .340 (1928)
2B—Rogers Hornsby .387 (1928)
3B—Terry Pendleton .319 (1991)
SS—Al Dark .322 (1948)
LF—Rico Carty .366 (1970)
CF—Hank Aaron .327 (1961)
RF—Hank Aaron .355 (1959)

Home Runs

C—Joe Torre 36 (1966)
1B—Hank Aaron 47 (1971)
2B—Dave Johnson 43 (1973)

3B—Eddie Mathews 47 (1953)
SS—Denis Menke 20 (1964)
LF—Wally Berger 38 (1930)
CF—Hank Aaron 45 (1962)
RF—Hank Aaron 44 (1957, '63, '66, '69)
      Dale Murphy 44 (1987)

Runs Batted In

C—Joe Torre 109 (1964)
1B—Hank Aaron 118 (1971)
2B—Dave Johnson 99 (1973)
3B—Eddie Mathews 135 (1953)
SS—Johnny Logan 83 (1955)
LF—Wally Berger 119 (1930)
CF—Wally Berger 130 (1935)
RF—Hank Aaron 132 (1957)

Dave Johnson was named National League Player of the Month for August 1973 en route to finishing with 43 home runs.

.300 Hitters in Season

1876	Jim O'Rourke	.327	1892	Hugh Duffy	.301		Jimmy Collins	.346
1877	Deacon White	.387	1893	Hugh Duffy	.363		Billy Hamilton	.343
	Jim O'Rourke	.362		Tommy McCarthy	.346		Hugh Duffy	.340
	John Morrill	.302	1894	Hugh Duffy	.440		Herman Long	.322
1879	John O'Rourke	.341		Tommy McCarthy	.349		Fred Tenney	.318
	Charley Jones	.315		Bobby Lowe	.346		Bobby Lowe	.309
1882	Joe Hornung	.302		Jimmy Bannon	.336	1898	Billy Hamilton	.369
1883	Jack Burdock	.330		Tommy Tucker	.330		Jimmy Collins	.328
	Ezra Sutton	.324		Herman Long	.324		Fred Tenney	.328
	John Morrill	.319	1895	Hugh Duffy	.352		Chick Stahl	.309
1884	Ezra Sutton	.346		Jimmy Bannon	.350	1899	Chick Stahl	.351
1885	Ezra Sutton	.313		Herman Long	.316		Fred Tenney	.347
1887	Sam Wise	.334	1896	Billy Hamilton	.365	1900	Billy Hamilton	.333
	King Kelly	.332		Herman Long	.343		Jimmy Collins	.304
1888	King Kelly	.318		Tommy Tucker	.304		Buck Freeman	.301
1889	Dan Brouthers	.378		Hugh Duffy	.300	1901	Fred Tenney	.305
	Hardy Richardson	.304	1897	Chick Stahl	.354	1902	Fred Tenney	.314

1903	Fred Tenney	.313	1941	Johnny Cooney	.319	
1907	Ginger Beaumont	.322	1944	Tommy Holmes	.309	
1911	Doc Miller	.333	1945	Tommy Holmes	.352	
	Bill Sweeney	.314	1946	Johnny Hopp	.333	
1912	Bill Sweeney	.344		Tommy Holmes	.310	
1921	Tony Boeckel	.313	1947	Bob Elliott	.317	
	Billy Southworth	.308		Tommy Holmes	.309	
	Ray Powell	.306		Phil Masi	.304	
	Walter Barbare	.302	1948	Tommy Holmes	.325	
1923	Billy Southworth	.319		Alvin Dark	.322	
	Stuffy McInnis	.315	1950	Bob Elliott	.305	
1925	Dick Burrus	.340		Sid Gordon	.304	
	Dave Bancroft	.319	1953	Eddie Mathews	.302	
	Jimmy Welsh	.312	1954	Joe Adcock	.308	
	Gus Felix	.307	1955	Hank Aaron	.314	
1926	Eddie Brown	.328	1956	Hank Aaron	.328	
	Dave Bancroft	.311	1957	Hank Aaron	.322	
1927	Lance Richbourg	.309	1958	Hank Aaron	.326	
	Eddie Brown	.306	1959	Hank Aaron	.355	
	Eddie Moore	.302		Eddie Mathews	.306	
1928	Rogers Hornsby	.387	1961	Hank Aaron	.327	
	George Sisler	.340		Eddie Mathews	.306	
	Lance Richbourg	.337	1962	Hank Aaron	.323	
1929	George Sisler	.326	1963	Hank Aaron	.319	
	Lance Richbourg	.305	1964	Rico Carty	.330	
1930	Wally Berger	.310		Hank Aaron	.328	
	George Sisler	.309		Joe Torre	.321	
	Lance Richbourg	.304		Lee Maye	.304	
1931	Wally Berger	.323	1965	Hank Aaron	.318	
1932	Wally Berger	.307	1966	Felipe Alou	.327	
	Red Worthington	.303		Rico Carty	.326	
1933	Wally Berger	.313		Joe Torre	.315	
	Randy Moore	.302	1967	Hank Aaron	.307	
1934	Buck Jordan	.311	1968	Felipe Alou	.317	
1935	Hal Lee	.303	1969	Hank Aaron	.300	
1936	Buck Jordan	.323	1970	Rico Carty	.366	
	Tony Cuccinello	.308		Felix Millan	.310	
1938	Debs Garms	.315		Orlando Cepeda	.305	
1939	Buddy Hassett	.308	1971	Ralph Garr	.343	
1940	Bama Rowell	.305		Hank Aaron	.327	

Dusty Baker (left) and Ralph Garr both made the .300 club in 1972.

1972	Ralph Garr	.325
	Dusty Baker	.321
1974	Ralph Garr	.353
1976	Willie Montanez	.321
1978	Jeff Burroughs	.301
1979	Bob Horner	.314
	Gary Matthews	.304
1983	Dale Murphy	.302
1985	Dale Murphy	.300
1987	Dion James	.312
1988	Gerald Perry	.300
1989	Lonnie Smith	.315
1990	Lonnie Smith	.305
	Ron Gant	.303
1991	Terry Pendleton	.319
1992	Terry Pendleton	.311
1993	Jeff Blauser	.305
1994	Fred McGriff	.318
	David Justice	.313

30 or More Home Runs in One Season

47	Eddie Mathews	1953	39	Eddie Mathews	1960	34	Hank Aaron	1972
47	Hank Aaron	1971	39	Hank Aaron	1967	34	Fred McGriff	1994
46	Eddie Mathews	1959	38	Wally Berger	1930	33	Earl Williams	1971
45	Hank Aaron	1962	38	Joe Adcock	1956	33	Bob Horner	1979
41	Eddie Mathews	1955	38	Hank Aaron	1970	33	Dale Murphy	1980
44	Hank Aaron	1957	37	Eddie Mathews	1956	32	Eddie Mathews	1957
44	Hank Aaron	1963	37	Dale Murphy	1985	32	Eddie Mathews	1961
44	Hank Aaron	1966	36	Joe Torre	1966	32	Hank Aaron	1965
44	Hank Aaron	1969	36	Dale Murphy	1982	32	Eddie Mathews	1965
44	Dale Murphy	1987	36	Dale Murphy	1983	32	Bob Horner	1982
43	Dave Johnson	1973	36	Dale Murphy	1984	32	Ron Gant	1990
41	Darrell Evans	1973	36	Ron Gant	1993	32	Ron Gant	1991
41	Jeff Burroughs	1977	35	Joe Adcock	1961	31	Eddie Mathews	1958
40	Eddie Mathews	1954	35	Bob Horner	1980	31	Mack Jones	1965
40	Hank Aaron	1960	34	Wally Berger	1934	31	Felipe Alou	1966
40	Hank Aaron	1973	34	Wally Berger	1935	30	Hank Aaron	1958
40	David Justice	1993	34	Hank Aaron	1961			
39	Hank Aaron	1959	34	Orlando Cepeda	1970			

Two Home Runs in One Inning

Charley Jones   June 10, 1880   8th   Bobby Lowe   May 30, 1894   3rd   Dale Murphy   July 27, 1989   6th

Most Extra-Base Hits in One Game

Player	Date	2B	3B	HR	Total
Joe Adcock	July 31, 1954	1	0	4	5
John O'Rourke	September 15, 1880	4	0	0	4
Sam Wise	June 30, 1885	2	2	0	4
Sam Wise	May 21, 1887	2	2	0	4
Tommy McCarthy	October 7, 1892	1	1	2	4
Tommy Tucker	July 22, 1893	4	0	0	4
Bobby Lowe	May 30, 1894	0	0	4	4
Hugh Duffy	September 18, 1894	1	3	0	4
Billy Southworth	August 4, 1921	3	0	1	4

Player	Date	2B	3B	HR	Total
Les Bell	June 2, 1928	0	1	3	4
Wally Berger	August 11, 1935	2	1	1	4
Jim Russell	June 7, 1948	2	0	2	4
Hank Aaron	May 3, 1962	1	1	2	4
Rico Carty	August 24, 1964	3	0	1	4
Felipe Alou	April 26, 1966	2	0	2	4
Bob Horner	July 7, 1985	2	1	1	4
Rafael Ramirez	May 21, 1986	4	0	0	4
Bob Horner	July 6, 1986	0	0	4	4

Most Total Bases in One Game

18	Joe Adcock	July 31, 1954		16	Bob Horner	July 6, 1986
17	Bobby Lowe	May 30, 1894		15	Les Bell	June 2, 1928

Career Grand Slams

16 Hank Aaron
9 Joe Adcock
8 Eddie Mathews
5 Wally Berger
4 Orlando Cepeda, Del Crandall, Hugh Duffy, Sid Gordon, Dale Murphy, Bobby Thomson
3 Sid Bream, Jeff Burroughs, Darrell Evans, Hank Gowdy, Bobby Lowe, Joe Torre
2 Jimmy Bannon, Les Bell, Bruce Benedict, Clete Boyer, Francisco Cabrera, Chris Chambliss, Tony Cloninger, Vic Correll, Bob Elliott, Rod Gilbreath, Glenn Hubbard, Dave Johnson, Hal King, Johnny Logan, Herman Long, Mike Lum, Rabbit Maranville, Gary Matthews, Denis Menke, Eddie Miller, Gene Moore, Billy Nash, Gene Oliver, Biff Pocoroba, Jim Russell, Earl Torgeson, Earl Williams
1 Tommie Aaron, Felipe Alou, Bobby Avila, Ed Bailey, Jeff Blauser, Tony Boeckel, Frank Bolling, Barry Bonnell, Frank Bonner, Billy Bruton, Lou Burdette, Rico Carty, Jimmy Collins, Joe Connolly, Duff Cooley, Walker Cooper, Wes Covington, George Ferguson, Patsy Flaherty, Elbie Fletcher, Hod Ford, Ron Gant, Ralph Garr, Tony Gonzalez, Ken Griffey, Terry Harper, Jeff Heath, Dutch Holland, Bob Horner, Ben Houser, Dion James, Sam Jethroe, Mack Jones, David Justice, Brad Komminsk, Al Lopez, Sherry Magee, Harl Maggert, Hank Majeski, Don Manno, Phil Masi, Dave May, Lee Maye,

Tommy McCarthy, Fred McGriff, Stuffy McInnis, Marty McManus, Felix Millan, Junior Moore, Pat Moran, Ray Mueller, Graig Nettles, Kid Nichols, Butch Nieman, Greg Olson, Tom Paciorek, Terry Pendleton, Joe Quinn, Bill Rariden, Pete Reiser, Lance Richbourg, Chet Ross, Connie Ryan, Ted Simmons, Sibby Sisti, Lonnie Smith, Red Smith, Chick Stahl, Harry Staley, Joe Stanley, Andres Thomas, Frank Thomas, Tommy Thompson, Bob Tillman, Frank Torre, Tommy Tucker, Bob Uecker, Paul Waner, Possum Whitted

Sid Bream hit three grand slams in his three years with the Braves.

Most Grand Slams in One Season

4   Sid Gordon, 1950   3   Del Crandall, 1955   3   Hank Aaron, 1962

Pinch-Hit Grand Slams

Player	Date	Opponent	Pitcher
Pat Moran	August 12, 1903	Chicago	Jocko Menefee
Les Bell	May 26, 1929	New York	Carl Hubbell
Wally Berger	October 1, 1933	Philadelphia	Reggie Grabowski
Harl Maggert	April 30, 1938	Philadelphia	Claude Passeau
Butch Nieman	July 6, 1945	Pittsburgh	Xavier Rescigno
Sibby Sisti	June 30, 1950	New York	Dave Koslo
Biff Pocoroba	May 17, 1977	Montreal	Bill Atkinson
Ted Simmons	June 3, 1986	Pittsburgh	Cecilio Guante
Graig Nettles	May 2, 1987	Houston	Aurelio Lopez

Graig Nettles delivered a pinch-hit grand slam in 1987.

Four Home Runs in One Game

May 30, 1894	Bobby Lowe, 2B	versus Cincinnati
July 31, 1954	Joe Adcock, 1B	at Brooklyn
July 6, 1986	Bob Horner, 1B	versus Montreal

Bob Horner is one of three Braves to hit four home runs in a game.

Three Home Runs in One Game

June 2, 1928	Les Bell, 3B	July 30, 1969	Bob Tillman, C
July 6, 1934	Hal Lee, OF	May 31, 1970	Rico Carty, OF
May 25, 1935	Babe Ruth, OF	July 3, 1970	Mike Lum, OF
May 13, 1942	Jim Tobin, RHP	July 26, 1970	Orlando Cepeda, 1B
September 27, 1952	Eddie Mathews, 3B	May 18, 1979	Dale Murphy, OF
August 30, 1953	Jim Pendleton, OF	July 22, 1986	Ken Griffey, OF
June 21, 1959	Hank Aaron, OF	May 26, 1990	Jeff Treadway, 2B
July 30, 1966	Gene Oliver, C	July 12, 1992	Jeff Blauser, SS

Hitting for the Cycle

| June 20, 1904 | Dick Cooley, OF | October 6, 1910 | Bill Collins, OF |
| April 26, 1907 | Johnny Bates, OF | September 23, 1987 | Albert Hall, OF |

Switch-Hit Home Runs in One Game

Jim Russell   June 7, 1948

Four Consecutive Home Runs

June 8, 1961   7th   Eddie Mathews, Hank Aaron, Joe Adcock, Frank Thomas

Three Consecutive Home Runs

July 9, 1938	3rd	Tony Cuccinello, Max West, Elbie Fletcher	August 14, 1978	3rd	Gary Matthews, Jeff Burroughs, Bob Horner
May 30, 1956	1st	Eddie Mathews, Hank Aaron, Bobby Thomson	Sept. 20, 1992	6th	David Justice, Brian Hunter, Ron Gant
June 26, 1957	5th	Hank Aaron, Eddie Mathews, Wes Covington	April 15, 1994	1st	Fred McGriff, Terry Pendleton, Tony Tarasco
May 31, 1958	1st	Hank Aaron, Eddie Mathews, Wes Covington	April 18, 1994	1st	Ryan Klesko, Fred McGriff, David Justice
June 18, 1961	3rd	Hank Aaron, Joe Adcock, Frank Thomas			

Most Home Runs in One Inning

| 4 | June 8, 1961 | 7th | Eddie Mathews, Hank Aaron, Joe Adcock, Frank Thomas | 4 | June 21, 1971 | 8th | Mike Lum, Hal King, Hank Aaron, Darrell Evans |
| 4 | June 8, 1965 | 10th | Joe Torre, Eddie Mathews, Hank Aaron, Gene Oliver | 4 | September 20, 1992 | 6th | David Justice, Brian Hunter, Ron Gant, Mark Lemke |

Home Runs by First Two Batters in Game

Roy Johnson and Rabbit Warstler, August 6, 1937, versus Chicago (Tex Carleton)

Leadoff Home Runs in Two Consecutive Games

Denis Menke	July 26 and 27, 1964	versus Cincinnati
Felipe Alou	July 26 and 27, 1965	versus Houston
Felipe Alou	August 9 and 10, 1966	versus Los Angeles

Twice in his Braves career, Felipe Alou led off consecutive games with home runs.

Home Run in First Big League At Bat

Johnny Bates	April 12, 1906	*Pinch-hitter
Chuck Tanner	April 12, 1955*†	†First pitch

No Home Runs, Season

(Since 1920, 500 or more at bats)

Player	Year	Games	At Bats	Player	Year	Games	At Bats
Rabbit Maranville	1929	145	560	Billy Urbanski	1933	144	566
Freddie Maguire	1930	146	516	Whitey Wietelmann	1943	153	534
Rabbit Maranville	1932	149	571				

20 Home Runs and 20 Stolen Bases in One Season

		HR	SB			HR	SB
1951	Earl Torgeson	24	20	1973	Dusty Baker	21	24
1961	Hank Aaron	34	21	1982	Dale Murphy	36	23
1963	Hank Aaron	44	31	1983	Dale Murphy	36	30
1964	Hank Aaron	24	22	1989	Lonnie Smith	21	25
1965	Hank Aaron	32	24	1990	Ron Gant	32	33
1966	Hank Aaron	44	21	1991	Ron Gant	32	34
1968	Hank Aaron	29	28	1993	Ron Gant	36	26

Hank Aaron's 733 Home Runs as a Brave

No.	Date	Opponent	Pitcher	No.	Date	Opponent	Pitcher
1954				5.	May 25	at Cincinnati	Herm Wehmeier
1.	April 23	at St. Louis	Vic Raschi	6.	June 15	at Brooklyn	Russ Meyer
2.	April 25	at St. Louis	Stu Miller	7.	June 17	at Brooklyn	Johnny Podres
3.	May 21	at Chicago	Hal Jeffcoat	8.	June 22	at New York	Johnny Antonelli
4.	May 22 (2nd)	at Chicago	Warren Hacker	9.	June 26	at Philadelphia	Robin Roberts

No.	Date	Opponent	Pitcher
10.	July 2	Cincinnati	Corky Valentine
11.	July 8	at Chicago	Warren Hacker
12.	July 29	at Pittsburgh	Johnny Hetki
13.	August 10	at St. Louis	Vic Raschi

1955

No.	Date	Opponent	Pitcher
14.	April 17	at Cincinnati	Gerry Staley
15.	April 27	at New York	Hoyt Wilhelm
16.	April 30	at Philadelphia	Thornton Kipper
17.	May 7	at St. Louis	Herb Moford
18.	May 8	at St. Louis	Harvey Haddix
19.	May 10	Pittsburgh	Max Surkont
20.	May 12	Brooklyn	Carl Erskine
21.	May 19	New York	Jim Hearn
22.	May 28	at Chicago	Warren Hacker
23.	June 7	at New York	Johnny Antonelli
24.	June 17	New York	Johnny Antonelli
25.	June 24	Brooklyn	Carl Erskine
26.	June 28	Chicago	Sam Jones
27.	June 29	Chicago	John Andre
28.	June 29	Chicago	John Andre
29.	July 2	at Cincinnati	Jackie Collum
30.	July 8 (2nd)	Cincinnati	Rudy Minarcin
31.	July 14	at Philadelphia	Bob Miller
32.	July 16	at New York	Sal Maglie
33.	July 21	at Pittsburgh	Lino Donoso
34.	July 22	at Brooklyn	Roger Craig
35.	July 24 (2nd)	at Brooklyn	Ed Roebuck
36.	August 7 (1st)	Pittsburgh	Lino Donoso
37.	August 9	St. Louis	Larry Jackson
38.	August 19	Chicago	Warren Hacker
39.	September 4	Cincinnati	Johnny Klippstein
40.	September 4	Cincinnati	Joe Black

1956

No.	Date	Opponent	Pitcher
41.	April 17	Chicago	Bob Rush
42.	April 22 (2nd)	at St. Louis	Larry Jackson
43.	May 7	Brooklyn	Ed Roebuck
44.	May 22	at Brooklyn	Carl Erskine
45.	May 30 (1st)	at Chicago	Russ Meyer
46.	May 30 (2nd)	at Chicago	Warren Hacker
47.	June 6	Brooklyn	Don Newcombe
48.	June 27	at Philadelphia	Harvey Haddix
49.	July 4 (2nd)	St. Louis	Herm Wehmeier
50.	July 6	Chicago	Don Kaiser
51.	July 16	Pittsburgh	Ron Kline
52.	July 17	New York	Windy McCall
53.	July 20	Philadelphia	Stu Miller
54.	July 22 (1st)	Philadelphia	Ben Flowers
55.	July 26	at New York	Johnny Antonelli
56.	July 30	at Brooklyn	Ken Lehman
57.	August 5	at Pittsburgh	Ron Kline
58.	August 19	at Cincinnati	Tom Acker
59.	August 23	Philadelphia	Curt Simmons
60.	August 26	Brooklyn	Roger Craig
61.	September 1	St. Louis	Wilmer Mizell
62.	September 3 (1st)	Cincinnati	Johnny Klippstein
63.	September 3 (1st)	Cincinnati	Johnny Klippstein
64.	September 3 (2nd)	Cincinnati	Brooks Lawrence
65.	September 13 (2nd)	at Philadelphia	Robin Roberts
66.	September 15	at Philadelphia	Bob Miller

1957

No.	Date	Opponent	Pitcher
67.	April 18	Cincinnati	Hal Jeffcoat
68.	April 22	Chicago	Bob Rush
69.	April 24	St. Louis	Herm Wehmeier
70.	April 27	at Cincinnati	Warren Hacker
71.	May 3	at Pittsburgh	Bob Friend
72.	May 5	at Brooklyn	Don Bessent
73.	May 11	at St. Louis	Willard Schmidt
74.	May 12 (1st)	at St. Louis	Murry Dickson
75.	May 12 (2nd)	at St. Louis	Herm Wehmeier
76.	May 18	Pittsburgh	Vernon Law
77.	May 18	Pittsburgh	Bob Smith
78.	May 27	Cincinnati	Johnny Klippstein
79.	June 4	at New York	Stu Miller
80.	June 9 (1st)	at Pittsburgh	Bob Friend
81.	June 9 (2nd)	at Pittsburgh	Ron Kline
82.	June 12	at Brooklyn	Ed Roebuck
83.	June 14	at Philadelphia	Don Cardwell
84.	June 15	at Philadelphia	Harvey Haddix
85.	June 19	New York	Ruben Gomez
86.	June 26	Brooklyn	Don Newcombe
87.	June 29	Pittsburgh	Johnny O'Brien
88.	June 30 (1st)	Pittsburgh	Vernon Law
89.	June 30 (2nd)	Pittsburgh	Joe Trimble
90.	July 1	at St. Louis	Murry Dickson
91.	July 3	at Cincinnati	Hal Jeffcoat
92.	July 4	at Cincinnati	Don Gross
93.	July 5	Chicago	Don Elston
94.	July 12	at Pittsburgh	Vernon Law
95.	July 16	at Philadelphia	Harvey Haddix
96.	July 25	Philadelphia	Robin Roberts
97.	August 4	Brooklyn	Carl Erskine
98.	August 9	at St. Louis	Lindy McDaniel
99.	August 15	at Cincinnati	Hal Jeffcoat
100.	August 15	at Cincinnati	Don Gross
101.	August 22	at Brooklyn	Sal Maglie
102.	August 23	at Brooklyn	Sandy Koufax
103.	August 24	at Brooklyn	Johnny Podres
104.	August 31	at Cincinnati	Joe Nuxhall
105.	September 3	at Chicago	Dick Littlefield
106.	September 10	Pittsburgh	Whammy Douglas
107.	September 17	New York	Curt Barclay
108.	September 22	at Chicago	Dick Drott
109.	September 23	St. Louis	Billy Muffett
110.	September 24	St. Louis	Sam Jones

1958

No.	Date	Opponent	Pitcher
111.	April 20	at Philadelphia	Robin Roberts
112.	April 22	at Pittsburgh	Ron Kline
113.	April 24	at Cincinnati	Brooks Lawrence
114.	April 24	at Cincinnati	Charlie Rabe
115.	May 13	at Philadelphia	Robin Roberts
116.	May 31	at Pittsburgh	Ron Kline
117.	June 3	at San Francisco	Ruben Gomez

No.	Date	Opponent	Pitcher
118.	June 3	at San Francisco	Marv Grissom
119.	June 8	at Los Angeles	Johnny Podres
120.	June 10	at Chicago	Dick Drott
121.	June 20	St. Louis	Billy Muffett
122.	June 27	Los Angeles	Sandy Koufax
123.	June 28	Los Angeles	Carl Erskine
124.	June 29	Los Angeles	Don Drysdale
125.	July 12	at San Francisco	Johnny Antonelli
126.	July 15	at St. Louis	Sal Maglie
127.	July 15	at St. Louis	Sal Maglie
128.	July 16	at St. Louis	Chuck Stobbs
129.	July 18	at Chicago	John Briggs
130.	July 19	at Chicago	Moe Drabowsky
131.	July 25 (2nd)	Chicago	Don Elston
132.	July 27	Chicago	Dave Hillman
133.	July 31	Los Angeles	Johnny Podres
134.	August 2	San Francisco	Ramon Monzant
135.	August 6	at Pittsburgh	Vernon Law
136.	August 19	at Los Angeles	Johnny Podres
137.	August 21	at Los Angeles	Sandy Koufax
138.	August 24	at San Francisco	Al Worthington
139.	September 12	St. Louis	Bob Mabe
140.	September 21	at Cincinnati	Tom Acker

1959

No.	Date	Opponent	Pitcher
141.	April 11	at Pittsburgh	Vernon Law
142.	April 18	Pittsburgh	Vernon Law
143.	April 23	at Philadelphia	Ray Semproch
144.	April 26	at Cincinnati	Hal Jeffcoat
145.	April 29	at St. Louis	Bob Blaylock
146.	April 30	at St. Louis	Alex Kellner
147.	May 3	San Francisco	Johnny Antonelli
148.	May 3	San Francisco	Johnny Antonelli
149.	May 16	at Los Angeles	Danny McDevitt
150.	May 16	at Los Angeles	Sandy Koufax
151.	May 17	at Los Angeles	Don Drysdale
152.	May 20	at San Francisco	Mike McCormick
153.	May 22	at Philadelphia	Robin Roberts
154.	May 30	Philadelphia	Don Cardwell
155.	June 3	San Francisco	Al Worthington
156.	June 10	at St. Louis	Alex Kellner
157.	June 21	at San Francisco	Johnny Antonelli
158.	June 21	at San Francisco	Stu Miller
159.	June 21	at San Francisco	Gordon Jones
160.	June 24	at St. Louis	Dick Ricketts
161.	June 25	St. Louis	Wilmer Mizell
162.	July 3	at Pittsburgh	George Witt
163.	July 11	Los Angeles	Don Drysdale
164.	July 14	at Chicago	Bill Henry
165.	July 29	Chicago	Dave Hillman
166.	July 29	Chicago	Dave Hillman
167.	July 30	Chicago	Art Ceccarelli
168.	July 31	St. Louis	Hal Jeffcoat
169.	August 1	St. Louis	Ernie Broglio
170.	August 12	at Cincinnati	Jim O'Toole
171.	August 17 (1st)	Los Angeles	Clem Labine
172.	August 18	Los Angeles	Don Drysdale
173.	August 18	Los Angeles	Don Drysdale
174.	August 28	at Chicago	John Buzhardt
175.	August 29	at Chicago	Bill Henry

No.	Date	Opponent	Pitcher
176.	August 29	at Chicago	Don Elston
177.	September 2	Philadelphia	Robin Roberts
178.	September 7 (1st)	Pittsburgh	Bob Friend
179.	September 20	at Philadelphia	Robin Roberts

1960

No.	Date	Opponent	Pitcher
180.	April 14	at Philadelphia	Curt Simmons
181.	April 16	at Philadelphia	Ruben Gomez
182.	April 22	at Pittsburgh	Bob Friend
183.	April 27	at Cincinnati	Jay Hook
184.	May 5	at Los Angeles	Johnny Podres
185.	May 13	Pittsburgh	Bob Friend
186.	May 15 (1st)	Pittsburgh	Harvey Haddix
187.	May 15 (2nd)	Pittsburgh	Bennie Daniels
188.	May 17	Los Angeles	Don Drysdale
189.	June 2	at Philadelphia	Ruben Gomez
190.	June 3	Cincinnati	Jay Hook
191.	June 4	Cincinnati	Don Newcombe
192.	June 12	at San Francisco	Bud Byerly
193.	June 20	Los Angeles	Don Drysdale
194.	June 20	Los Angeles	Don Drysdale
195.	June 21 (1st)	San Francisco	Mike McCormick
196.	June 24	Los Angeles	Sandy Koufax
197.	June 29 (2nd)	at Chicago	Bob Anderson
198.	July 1 (2nd)	at St. Louis	Curt Simmons
199.	July 3	at St. Louis	Ron Kline
200.	July 3	at St. Louis	Ron Kline
201.	July 4 (1st)	Pittsburgh	Bob Friend
202.	July 7	Philadelphia	Chris Short
203.	July 8	Cincinnati	Jay Hook
204.	July 19	St. Louis	Ron Kline
205.	July 20	St. Louis	Ernie Broglio
206.	July 22	at Chicago	Don Elston
207.	July 23	at Chicago	Don Cardwell
208.	August 4	at St. Louis	Ray Sadecki
209.	August 5	Chicago	Bob Morehead
210.	August 16	at Cincinnati	Jay Hook
211.	August 17	at Cincinnati	Jim Brosnan
212.	August 23	at Los Angeles	Ed Roebuck
213.	August 30	St. Louis	Ed Bauta
214.	September 8	San Francisco	Mike McCormick
215.	September 9	Los Angeles	Stan Williams
216.	September 10	Los Angeles	Roger Craig
217.	September 21	Cincinnati	Jim O'Toole
218.	September 30	at Pittsburgh	Vernon Law
219.	September 30	at Pittsburgh	Diomedes Olivo

1961

No.	Date	Opponent	Pitcher
220.	April 14	at Chicago	Bob Anderson
221.	April 30	San Francisco	Billy Loes
222.	April 30	San Francisco	Billy Loes
223.	May 12	at San Francisco	Sam Jones
224.	May 13	at San Francisco	Juan Marichal
225.	May 21 (2nd)	at Cincinnati	Jim Maloney
226.	May 26	Los Angeles	Turk Farrell
227.	May 28	Los Angeles	Roger Craig
228.	May 31	at Pittsburgh	Joe Gibbon
229.	June 8	at Cincinnati	Jim Maloney
230.	June 18	Los Angeles	Don Drysdale

No.	Date	Opponent	Pitcher	No.	Date	Opponent	Pitcher
231.	June 20	San Francisco	Mike McCormick	289.	August 29	at San Francisco	Billy O'Dell
232.	June 22	San Francisco	Juan Marichal	290.	September 7	Philadelphia	Dennis Bennett
233.	June 23	Chicago	Jack Curtis	291.	September 9	Philadelphia	Dennis Bennett
234.	July 1	Cincinnati	Jay Hook	292.	September 10	at New York	Bob Miller
235.	July 2 (1st)	Cincinnati	Jim O'Toole	293.	September 18	Los Angeles	Johnny Podres
236.	July 4	Los Angeles	Turk Farrell	294.	September 22	at Pittsburgh	Tommie Sisk
237.	July 5	Philadelphia	Art Mahaffey	295.	September 23	at Pittsburgh	Bob Friend
238.	July 7	Pittsburgh	Harvey Haddix	296.	September 23	at Pittsburgh	Bob Friend
239.	July 7	Pittsburgh	Harvey Haddix	297.	September 25	New York	Jay Hook
240.	July 21	at Pittsburgh	Bob Friend	298.	September 26	New York	Roger Craig
241.	July 21	at Pittsburgh	Bob Friend				
242.	July 23 (1st)	at Pittsburgh	Harvey Haddix	**1963**			
243.	July 25	Cincinnati	Ken Hunt	299.	April 11	New York	Don Rowe
244.	July 26	Cincinnati	Ken Johnson	300.	April 19	at New York	Roger Craig
245.	July 28	St. Louis	Larry Jackson	301.	April 21 (1st)	at New York	Jay Hook
246.	August 2 (2nd)	at Chicago	Bob Anderson	302.	April 22	at Los Angeles	Don Drysdale
247.	August 4	at San Francisco	Mike McCormick	303.	April 23	at Los Angeles	Ron Perranoski
248.	August 4	at San Francisco	Mike McCormick	304.	April 26	at San Francisco	Al Stanek
249.	August 12	Chicago	Don Cardwell	305.	April 28	at San Francisco	Don Larsen
250.	August 15	Pittsburgh	Joe Gibbon	306.	May 2	at Cincinnati	Joey Jay
251.	August 25 (1st)	at Philadelphia	John Buzhardt	307.	May 3	Chicago	Bob Buhl
252.	September 3 (2nd)	at Chicago	Dick Ellsworth	308.	May 7	San Francisco	Juan Marichal
				309.	May 11	at Philadelphia	Art Mahaffey
253.	September 25	St. Louis	Ray Wasburn	310.	May 18	at Chicago	Lindy McDaniel
				311.	May 19 (1st)	at Chicago	Dick Ellsworth
1962				312.	May 24	Pittsburgh	Bob Friend
254.	April 15	at Los Angeles	Sandy Koufax	313.	May 30	Los Angeles	Don Drysdale
255.	April 18	at San Francisco	Jack Sanford	314.	May 31	Houston	Ken Johnson
256.	May 3	at Philadelphia	Art Mahaffey	315.	June 7	at Pittsburgh	Tommie Sisk
257.	May 3	at Philadelphia	Jack Baldschun	316.	June 12	New York	Galen Cisco
258.	May 12 (2nd)	at New York	Bob Moorhead	317.	June 17	Pittsburgh	Don Cardwell
259.	May 18	New York	Roger Craig	318.	June 19	Pittsburgh	Earl Francis
260.	May 25	at St. Louis	Curt Simmons	319.	June 23	San Francisco	Jack Sanford
261.	May 25	at St. Louis	Ray Washburn	320.	June 30	at Los Angeles	Nick Willhite
262.	May 28	at Chicago	Glen Hobbie	321.	July 3	at San Francisco	Jack Sanford
263.	May 31	Cincinnati	Bob Purkey	322.	July 4	at San Francisco	Jack Fisher
264.	June 12	Los Angeles	Phil Ortega	323.	July 11 (1st)	at St. Louis	Ernie Broglio
265.	June 14	Los Angeles	Stan Williams	324.	July 13	at St. Louis	Curt Simmons
266.	June 15	at Pittsburgh	Diomedes Olivo	325.	July 19	Los Angeles	Don Drysdale
267.	June 18	at New York	Jay Hook	326.	July 21 (1st)	Los Angeles	Ed Roebuck
268.	June 20 (2nd)	at New York	Willard Hunter	327.	July 28	Cincinnati	Jim Maloney
269.	June 20 (2nd)	at New York	Willard Hunter	328.	July 29	Cincinnati	John Tsitouris
270.	June 25	at Los Angeles	Joe Moeller	329.	August 2	New York	Al Jackson
271.	June 30	Chicago	Dick Ellsworth	330.	August 14	Los Angeles	Don Drysdale
272.	July 3	at St. Louis	Bob Gibson	331.	August 23	at Los Angeles	Larry Sherry
273.	July 6	at Chicago	Dick Cardwell	332.	August 26	at Houston	Hal Brown
274.	July 8 (1st)	at Chicago	Dick Ellsworth	333.	August 27	at Houston	Don Nottebart
275.	July 12	St. Louis	Lindy McDaniel	334.	September 2	Philadelphia	Cal McLish
276.	July 17	San Francisco	Billy O'Dell	335.	September 6	at Philadelphia	Cal McLish
277.	July 19	San Francisco	Mike McCormick	336.	September 7	at Philadelphia	Ray Culp
278.	July 20	at Philadelphia	Art Mahaffey	337.	September 9	at Cincinnati	Joey Jay
279.	July 22 (1st)	at Philadelphia	Bill Smith	338.	September 10	at Cincinnati	John Tsitouris
280.	July 26	New York	Craig Anderson	339.	September 10	at Cincinnati	John Tsitouris
281.	July 29	at Cincinnati	Bob Purkey	340.	September 15	at St. Louis	Lou Burdette
282.	July 29	at Cincinnati	Bob Purkey	341.	September 25	Cincinnati	Jim O'Toole
283.	August 7	Chicago	Cal Koonce	342.	September 29	Chicago	Bob Buhl
284.	August 14	Cincinnati	Ted Wills				
285.	August 19	San Francisco	Billy O'Dell	**1964**			
286.	August 19	San Francisco	Billy O'Dell	343.	April 16	at Houston	Jim Owens
287.	August 24	at Chicago	Bob Buhl	344.	May 10 (1st)	at Pittsburgh	Bob Friend
288.	August 25	at Chicago	Don Cardwell	345.	May 23	St. Louis	Ron Taylor

No.	Date	Opponent	Pitcher	No.	Date	Opponent	Pitcher
346.	May 24	St. Louis	Bobby Shantz	401.	April 25	at San Francisco	Bob Priddy
347.	May 30 (1st)	at Chicago	Bob Buhl	402.	April 26	at San Francisco	Bob Bolin
348.	June 7	Chicago	Bob Buhl	403.	April 27	at Los Angeles	Don Sutton
349.	June 8	at Houston	Hal Brown	404.	April 28	at Los Angeles	Don Drysdale
350.	June 14 (1st)	at Los Angeles	Ron Perranoski	405.	April 29	Houston	Carroll Sembera
351.	June 22	Los Angeles	Phil Ortega	406.	May 1	Houston	Mike Cuellar
352.	June 27	New York	Carl Willey	407.	May 8	at Houston	Mike Cuellar
353.	June 28 (2nd)	New York	Frank Lary	408.	May 11	Cincinnati	Sammy Ellis
354.	June 30	at St. Louis	Roger Craig	409.	May 11	Cincinnati	Sammy Ellis
355.	July 16	San Francisco	Gaylord Perry	410.	May 17	at St. Louis	Curt Simmons
356.	July 26 (1st)	at New York	Al Jackson	411.	May 18	at Pittsburgh	Vernon Law
357.	July 26 (2nd)	at New York	Willard Hunter	412.	May 20	Chicago	Bill Faul
358.	July 31	at Chicago	Lindy McDaniel	413.	May 21	Chicago	Ferguson Jenkins
359.	August 1	at Chicago	Lou Burdette	414.	May 27	at Chicago	Ernie Broglio
360.	August 6	at Cincinnati	Joey Jay	415.	June 1	San Francisco	Ron Herbel
361.	August 11	Houston	Ken Johnson	416.	June 3	St. Louis	Bob Gibson
362.	August 11	Houston	Hal Woodeshick	417.	June 8	at New York	Jack Fisher
363.	August 15	at San Francisco	Jim Duffalo	418.	June 8	at New York	Jack Fisher
364.	August 24	Philadelphia	Dennis Bennett	419.	June 14	at Philadelphia	Roger Craig
365.	August 30 (2nd)	San Francisco	Ron Herbel	420.	June 18	Pittsburgh	Vernon Law
				421.	June 19	Pittsburgh	Bob Veale
366.	September 3	at St. Louis	Roger Craig	422.	June 21	Philadelphia	Larry Jackson
				423.	July 3	at San Francisco	Ray Sadecki
1965				424.	July 9	at Los Angeles	Sandy Koufax
367.	April 29	St. Louis	Ron Taylor	425.	July 17	Cincinnati	Don Nottebart
368.	May 2 (2nd)	Philadelphia	Bo Belinsky	426.	July 21	at St. Louis	Al Jackson
369.	May 4	Houston	Larry Dierker	427.	July 24 (2nd)	at Cincinnati	Sammy Ellis
370.	May 4	Houston	Danny Coombs	428.	July 26	St. Louis	Al Jackson
371.	May 16	at Philadelphia	Chris Short	429.	August 2	at Chicago	Robin Roberts
372.	May 30	at Houston	Larry Dierker	430.	August 13 (2nd)	Philadelphia	Ray Culp
373.	June 1	at Houston	Hal Woodeshick	431.	August 14	Philadelphia	Bob Buhl
374.	June 8	at Chicago	Bob Hendley	432.	August 22	at Los Angeles	Don Drysdale
375.	June 10	at Chicago	Larry Jackson	433.	August 26	New York	Tug McGraw
376.	June 12	at St. Louis	Bob Gibson	434.	August 30	Chicago	Ken Holtzman
377.	June 19	St. Louis	Ray Sadecki	435.	September 5 (2nd)	at Pittsburgh	Don Cardwell
378.	June 20	St. Louis	Bob Purkey				
379.	June 29	at New York	Tug McGraw	436.	September 13	at Chicago	Ken Holtzman
380.	July 5	Houston	Turk Farrell	437.	September 13	at Chicago	Ken Holtzman
381.	July 7	Houston	Ron Taylor	438.	September 22	Pittsburgh	Don Cardwell
382.	July 8	Houston	Don Nottebart	439.	September 25	Pittsburgh	Tommie Sisk
383.	July 11	at Cincinnati	Sammy Ellis	440.	September 25	Pittsburgh	Al McBean
384.	July 19	New York	Jack Fisher	441.	September 27	San Francisco	Ray Sadecki
385.	July 20	New York	Larry Miller	442.	October 1 (2nd)	at Cincinnati	Jim O'Toole
386.	July 21	at Los Angeles	Claude Osteen				
387.	July 22	at Los Angeles	Bob Miller				
388.	August 4 (1st)	Los Angeles	Don Drysdale				
389.	August 4 (2nd)	Los Angeles	Claude Osteen	**1967**			
390.	August 11	St. Louis	Ray Washburn	443.	April 19	Houston	Dave Giusti
391.	August 11	St. Louis	Ray Washburn	444.	April 19	Houston	Dave Giusti
392.	August 15	at Chicago	Larry Jackson	445.	April 28	Philadelphia	Dick Ellsworth
393.	August 17	at St. Louis	Tracy Stallard	446.	April 30	Philadelphia	Bob Buhl
394.	August 31 (1st)	at Cincinnati	Joey Jay	447.	May 5	Cincinnati	Sammy Ellis
395.	September 8	Philadelphia	Ray Culp	448.	May 10 (1st)	at Philadelphia	Jim Bunning
396.	September 17	San Francisco	Juan Marichal	449.	May 10 (2nd)	at Philadelphia	Larry Jackson
397.	September 17	San Francisco	Juan Marichal	450.	May 14	at Pittsburgh	Dennis Ribant
398.	September 20	Philadelphia	Ray Culp	451.	May 17	New York	Tom Seaver
				452.	May 21	Pittsburgh	Steve Blass
1966				453.	May 21	Pittsburgh	Pete Mikkelsen
399.	April 20	at Philadelphia	Ray Culp	454.	June 1	at St. Louis	Ray Washburn
400.	April 20	at Philadelphia	Bo Belinsky	455.	June 2	at Cincinnati	Sammy Ellis

No.	Date	Opponent	Pitcher
456.	June 3	at Cincinnati	Billy McCool
457.	June 4	at Cincinnati	Jim Maloney
458.	June 12	at Philadelphia	Dick Ellsworth
459.	June 14	at Philadelphia	Dallas Green
460.	June 22 (2nd)	at San Francisco	Frank Linzy
461.	June 27	Houston	Wade Blasingame
462.	June 27	Houston	Dan Schneider
463.	July 5	Chicago	John Hartenstein
464.	July 9	at New York	Jack Fisher
465.	July 14	Philadelphia	Rick Wise
466.	July 21	at St. Louis	Nelson Briles
467.	July 22	at St. Louis	Dick Hughes
468.	July 27	Cincinnati	Sammy Ellis
469.	August 3	at Chicago	Curt Simmons
470.	August 12 (2nd)	Houston	Mike Cuellar
471.	August 13	Houston	Carroll Sembera
472.	August 16	San Francisco	Bob Bolin
473.	August 19	at Los Angeles	Claude Osteen
474.	August 29	Pittsburgh	Tommie Sisk
475.	August 31	Los Angeles	Claude Osteen
476.	September 3	Los Angeles	Don Drysdale
477.	September 4 (1st)	Philadelphia	Rick Wise
478.	September 12	New York	Jack Fisher
479.	September 14	New York	Danny Frisella
480.	September 20	Cincinnati	Milt Pappas
481.	September 26	at Cincinnati	Milt Pappas

1968

No.	Date	Opponent	Pitcher
482.	April 15	St. Louis	Bob Gibson
483.	April 17	Chicago	Billy Hands
484.	April 19	at Cincinnati	John Tsitouris
485.	April 21	at Cincinnati	Milt Pappas
486.	April 23	at Chicago	Joe Niekro
487.	April 28	Philadelphia	Rick Wise
488.	May 11	Los Angeles	Claude Osteen
489.	May 11	Los Angeles	Claude Osteen
490.	May 14	at Philadelphia	Larry Jackson
491.	June 9 (2nd)	at Chicago	Billy Hands

No.	Date	Opponent	Pitcher
492.	June 12	St. Louis	Nelson Briles
493.	June 17	Cincinnati	Jim Maloney
494.	June 21	at St. Louis	Ron Willis
495.	June 27	Philadelphia	Chris Short
496.	June 28	at Los Angeles	Mike Kekich
497.	July 5	Houston	Mike Cuellar
498.	July 7	Houston	Larry Dierker
499.	July 7	Houston	Larry Dierker
500.	July 14	San Francisco	Mike McCormick
501.	July 26 (1st)	at Philadelphia	Grant Jackson
502.	August 6	Chicago	Joe Niekro
503.	August 21 (2nd)	at Chicago	Rich Nye
504.	August 23	Philadelphia	Rick Wise
505.	August 25	Philadelphia	Larry Jackson
506.	August 28 (2nd)	at Philadelphia	Jerry Johnson
507.	August 29	at Philadelphia	Larry Jackson
508.	September 11	San Francisco	Juan Marichal
509.	September 22	at San Francisco	Bob Bolin
510.	September 29	Los Angeles	Bill Singer

1969

No.	Date	Opponent	Pitcher
511.	April 12	Cincinnati	Gary Nolan
512.	April 16	at Houston	Denny Lemaster
513.	April 28	Houston	Larry Dierker
514.	May 3	Los Angeles	Claude Osteen
515.	May 13	at New York	Gary Gentry
516.	May 15	at New York	Don Cardwell
517.	May 15	at New York	Cal Kounce
518.	May 18	at Montreal	Roy Face
519.	May 22	New York	Tug McGraw
520.	May 31	at Chicago	Ferguson Jenkins
521.	June 1	at Chicago	Ken Holtzman
522.	June 2	at St. Louis	Gary Waslewski
523.	June 3	at St. Louis	Steve Carlton
524.	June 6	Pittsburgh	Dock Ellis
525.	June 8 (1st)	Pittsburgh	John Hartenstein
526.	June 11	Chicago	Rich Nye
527.	June 12	Chicago	Dick Selma

Memories of a couple of major milestones in Hank Aaron's climb up the home run ladder.

No.	Date	Opponent	Pitcher
528.	June 17	Houston	Jack Billingham
529.	June 25	Los Angeles	Claude Osteen
530.	June 27	at Houston	Denny Lemaster
531.	June 30	Cincinnati	Tony Cloninger
532.	July 7	at Los Angeles	Alan Foster
533.	July 8 (1st)	at Los Angeles	Claude Osteen
534.	July 15 (1st)	at Cincinnati	Clay Carroll
535.	July 24	Montreal	Dick Radatz
536.	July 25	Montreal	Howie Reed
537.	July 30 (1st)	at Philadelphia	Grant Jackson
538.	July 30 (1st)	at Philadelphia	Lowell Palmer
539.	August 9	New York	Tom Seaver
540.	August 13 (1st)	Philadelphia	John Boozer
541.	August 13 (1st)	Philadelphia	John Boozer
542.	August 17	St. Louis	Steve Carlton
543.	August 21	at Chicago	Billy Hands
544.	August 24	at St. Louis	Mudcat Grant
545.	August 28	at Pittsburgh	Steve Blass
546.	August 28	at Pittsburgh	Bruce DalCanton
547.	August 30	Chicago	Ken Johnson
548.	September 5	at Cincinnati	Jim Merritt
549.	September 7	at Cincinnati	Dennis Ribant
550.	September 10	San Francisco	Ron Bryant
551.	September 11	San Francisco	Mike McCormick
552.	September 17	at Los Angeles	Ray Lamb
553.	September 21	at San Diego	Tom Dukes
554.	September 26	San Diego	Mike Corkins

1970

No.	Date	Opponent	Pitcher
555.	April 9	at San Diego	Clay Kirby
556.	April 10	at Houston	Mike Griffin
557.	April 13	San Francisco	Frank Reberger
558.	April 14	San Francisco	Frank Reberger
559.	April 18	Los Angeles	Don Sutton
560.	April 23	at Pittsburgh	Luke Walker
561.	April 28	at St. Louis	Mike Torrez
562.	April 30	Chicago	Jim Cosman
563.	May 1	Chicago	Joe Decker
564.	May 5	Pittsburgh	Bob Moose
565.	May 6	Pittsburgh	Dock Ellis
566.	May 8	St. Louis	Bob Gibson
567.	May 9	St. Louis	George Culver
568.	May 11	at Chicago	Archie Reynolds
569.	May 15	at Cincinnati	Gary Nolan
570.	May 17 (2nd)	at Cincinnati	Wayne Simpson
571.	June 2	New York	Gary Gentry
572.	June 18	at Montreal	Steve Renko
573.	June 19 (2nd)	Houston	Denny Lemaster
574.	June 20	Houston	Mike Griffin
575.	June 21	Houston	Larry Dierker
576.	June 21	Houston	Larry Dierker
577.	June 30	at Cincinnati	Jim McGlothlin
578.	July 3 (2nd)	San Diego	Pat Dobson
579.	July 17	at St. Louis	Nelson Briles
580.	July 25	at Chicago	Ferguson Jenkins
581.	July 29	St. Louis	Mike Torrez
582.	July 29	St. Louis	Frank Linzy
583.	August 1	Pittsburgh	Bruce DalCanton

No.	Date	Opponent	Pitcher
584.	August 1	Pittsburgh	Orlando Pena
585.	August 2	Pittsburgh	Dock Ellis
586.	August 7 (1st)	at San Diego	Dave Roberts
587.	August 9	at San Diego	Pat Dobson
588.	August 12	Montreal	Bill Stoneman
589.	August 26	at New York	Gary Gentry
590.	September 3	Los Angeles	Alan Foster
591.	September 5 (2nd)	San Francisco	Rich Robertson
592.	October 1	at Cincinnati	Ray Washburn

1971

No.	Date	Opponent	Pitcher
593.	April 7	at Cincinnati	Jim McGlothlin
594.	April 10	Pittsburgh	Steve Blass
595.	April 13	Cincinnati	Don Gullett
596.	April 14	Cincinnati	Tony Cloninger
597.	April 14	Cincinnati	Tony Cloninger
598.	April 20	at Pittsburgh	Bob Moose
599.	April 25 (1st)	San Diego	Dave Roberts
600.	April 27	San Francisco	Gaylord Perry
601.	May 1	Los Angeles	Claude Osteen
602.	May 1	Los Angeles	Pete Mikkelson
603.	May 2	Los Angeles	Jim Brewer
604.	May 8	at San Francisco	Jerry Johnson
605.	May 18	New York	Jim McAndrew
606.	May 21	at New York	Nolan Ryan
607.	May 27	at Montreal	Ernie McAnally
608.	June 1	Houston	Wade Blasingame
609.	June 6	Chicago	Billy Hands
610.	June 8	St. Louis	Steve Carlton
611.	June 13	at Houston	Don Wilson
612.	June 21 (1st)	Montreal	Claude Raymond
613.	June 27	Cincinnati	Gary Nolan
614.	June 27	Cincinnati	Wayne Granger
615.	July 4	at New York	Tom Seaver
616.	July 10	at Pittsburgh	Steve Blass
617.	July 17	at Los Angeles	Doyle Alexander
618.	July 20	San Diego	Dave Roberts
619.	July 21 (1st)	San Diego	Steve Arlin
620.	July 21 (1st)	San Diego	Steve Arlin
621.	July 24	at Los Angeles	Claude Osteen
622.	July 31	at San Diego	Fred Norman
623.	August 3	at Philadelphia	Chris Short
624.	August 15	Houston	Ken Forsch
625.	August 20	St. Louis	Reggie Cleveland
626.	August 21	St. Louis	Steve Carlton
627.	August 21	St. Louis	Steve Carlton
628.	August 23 (1st)	Pittsburgh	Steve Blass
629.	August 24	Pittsburgh	Bob Veale
630.	August 25	Pittsburgh	Bruce Kison
631.	August 29	Pittsburgh	Bob Veale
632.	September 10	San Francisco	Jerry Johnson
633.	September 11	San Francisco	Don Carrithers
634.	September 14	at Cincinnati	Don Gullett
635.	September 14	at Cincinnati	Don Gullett
636.	September 15	at Houston	Jack Billingham
637.	September 17	at Los Angeles	Claude Osteen
638.	September 21	San Diego	Jay Franklin
639.	September 26	Los Angeles	Claude Osteen

No.	Date	Opponent	Pitcher
1972			
640.	April 22	Cincinnati	Don Gullett
641.	April 23	Cincinnati	Jack Billingham
642.	April 25	St. Louis	Bob Gibson
643.	April 26	St. Louis	Rick Wise
644.	May 5	at St. Louis	Bob Gibson
645.	May 6	at St. Louis	Rick Wise
646.	May 26	San Francisco	Juan Marichal
647.	May 28 (1st)	San Francisco	Ron Bryant
648.	May 31	San Diego	Fred Norman
649.	June 10	at Philadelphia	Wayne Twitchell
650.	June 13	New York	Danny Frisella
651.	June 14	New York	Jon Matlack
652.	June 24 (2nd)	at Los Angeles	Jim Brewer
653.	June 28 (1st)	at San Diego	Mike Corkins
654.	June 29	at San Diego	Mike Caldwell
655.	July 2	at Houston	Dave Roberts
656.	July 3	at Houston	Jim York
657.	July 9	Pittsburgh	Nelson Briles
658.	July 11	at St. Louis	Al Santorini
659.	July 19	at Pittsburgh	Nelson Briles
660.	August 6	at Cincinnati	Wayne Simpson
661.	August 6	at Cincinnati	Don Gullett
662.	August 9	Houston	Jerry Reuss
663.	August 13	Cincinnati	Tom Hall
664.	August 16	at New York	Gary Gentry
665.	August 29	Montreal	Balor Moore
666.	September 2	Philadelphia	Bucky Brandon
667.	September 2	Philadelphia	Mac Scarce
668.	September 13	Cincinnati	Tom Hall
669.	September 13	Cincinnati	Tom Hall
670.	September 17	San Francisco	Ron Bryant
671.	September 26	at Cincinnati	Don Gullett
672.	September 27	at Cincinnati	Ross Grimsley
673.	October 3	Los Angeles	Don Sutton
1973			
674.	April 11	at San Diego	Rich Troedson
675.	April 12	at San Diego	Fred Norman
676.	April 15	at Los Angeles	Al Downing
677.	April 20	at Cincinnati	Don Gullett
678.	April 27	New York	Tom Seaver
679.	May 1	Montreal	Balor Moore
680.	May 1	Montreal	John Strohmayer
681.	May 5	at Philadelphia	Steve Carlton
682.	May 13	San Diego	Bill Greif
683.	May 13	San Diego	Fred Norman
684.	May 16	at Houston	Jerry Reuss
685.	May 22	San Francisco	Juan Marichal
686.	May 27	at St. Louis	Reggie Cleveland

No.	Date	Opponent	Pitcher
687.	June 9	St. Louis	Scipio Spinks
688.	June 9	St. Louis	John Andrews
689.	June 11	Pittsburgh	Jim Rooker
690.	June 15	Chicago	Bill Bonham
691.	June 16	Chicago	Rick Reuschel
692.	June 22	at San Diego	Randy Jones
693.	June 29	Los Angeles	Charlie Hough
694.	July 2	San Francisco	Jim Barr
695.	July 8	at New York	George Stone
696.	July 8	at New York	George Stone
697.	July 13	Montreal	Bill Stoneman
698.	July 17	New York	Tug McGraw
699.	July 20	Philadelphia	Ken Brett
700.	July 21	Philadelphia	Ken Brett
701.	July 31	Cincinnati	Pedro Borbon
702.	August 16	at Chicago	Jack Aker
703.	August 17	at Montreal	Steve Renko
704.	August 18	at Montreal	Steve Rogers
705.	August 22	St. Louis	Reggie Cleveland
706.	August 28	Chicago	Milt Pappas
707.	September 3	at San Diego	Clay Kirby
708.	September 3	at San Diego	Vicente Romo
709.	September 8	Cincinnati	Jack Billingham
710.	September 10	San Francisco	Don Carrithers
711.	September 17	San Diego	Gary Ross
712.	September 22	at Houston	Dave Roberts
713.	September 29	Houston	Jerry Reuss
1974			
714.	April 4	at Cincinnati	Jack Billingham
715.	April 8	Los Angeles	Al Downing
716.	April 11	Los Angeles	Charlie Hough
717.	April 21	at Houston	Mike Griffin
718.	April 25	Pittsburgh	Jerry Reuss
719.	April 26	Chicago	Ray Burris
720.	April 30	at St. Louis	Lynn McGlothlen
721.	May 12 (1st)	San Francisco	Charlie Williams
722.	May 28	Philadelphia	Jim Lonborg
723.	June 4	at Philadelphia	Eddie Watt
724.	June 14	St. Louis	Bob Gibson
725.	July 7	at Chicago	Rick Reuschel
726.	July 27	Los Angeles	Rex Hudson
727.	August 6	at San Diego	Bill Greif
728.	August 6	at San Diego	Bill Greif
729.	August 14	Montreal	Chuck Taylor
730.	August 19	St. Louis	Claude Osteen
731.	September 14	at San Diego	Dave Freisleben
732.	September 18	at San Francisco	John Montefusco
733.	October 2	Cincinnati	Rawly Eastwick

Most RBIs in One Game

9	Harry Staley	June 1, 1893	9	Tony Cloninger	July 3, 1966	8	Joe Adcock	July 19, 1956

200 Hits in One Season

237	Hugh Duffy, 1894	210	Felipe Alou, 1968	201	Eddie Brown, 1926
224	Tommy Holmes, 1945	209	Fred Tenney, 1899	201	Hank Aaron, 1963
223	Hank Aaron, 1959	206	Lance Richbourg, 1928	200	Dick Burrus, 1925
219	Ralph Garr, 1971	205	George Sisler, 1929	200	Hank Aaron, 1956
218	Felipe Alou, 1966	204	Bill Sweeney, 1912	200	Ralph Garr, 1973
214	Ralph Garr, 1974	203	Hugh Duffy, 1893		
212	Bobby Lowe, 1894	202	Chick Stahl, 1899		

Most Hits in One Game

Hits	Player	Date	AB	2B	3B	HR	Innings
6	Sam Wise	June 20, 1883	7	1	1	0	9
6	King Kelly	August 27, 1887	7	1	0	1	9
6	Bobby Lowe	June 11, 1891	6	1	0	1	9
6	Fred Tenney	May 31, 1897	8	1	0	0	9
6	Chick Stahl	May 31, 1899	6	0	0	0	9
6	Felix Millan	July 6, 1970	6	1	1	0	9

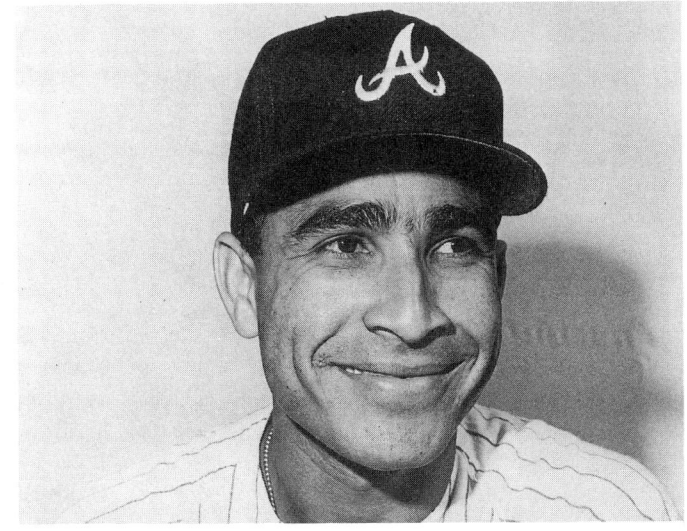

Felix Millan is one of half a dozen Braves to collect six hits in one game.

Most Consecutive Hits

10	Buddy Hassett	1940	8	Sid Gordon	1952	8	Jeff Burroughs	1978

Two Doubles in One Inning

Tommy Tucker	July 22, 1893	Jimmy Collins	September 27, 1897	Bob Thorpe	June 5, 1952
Hugh Duffy	July 10, 1894	Buck Jordan	August 25, 1936	Rico Carty	May 20, 1965
Hugh Duffy	September 27, 1896	Tony Cuccinello	August 25, 1936		
Herman Long	September 27, 1897	Gene Moore	August 25, 1936		

Most Triples in One Game

3	Hugh Duffy	September 18, 1894	3	Lance Richbourg	July 31, 1929
3	Pat Moran	August 10, 1905	3	Danny O'Connell	June 13, 1956
3	Ray Powell	September 27, 1921			

Two Triples in One Inning

Joe Hornung	May 6, 1882	8th	Buck Freeman	July 25, 1900	1st

Most Runs in One Game

6	Jim Whitney	June 9, 1883		5	Bob Elliott	July 20, 1951
6	King Kelly	August 27, 1887		5	Jim Pendleton	August 30, 1953
6	Ezra Sutton	August 27, 1887		5	Joe Adcock	July 31, 1954
6	Bobby Lowe	May 3, 1895		5	Rico Carty	August 24, 1964
6	Frank Torre	September 2, 1957		5	Lonnie Smith	May 6, 1989
5	Rabbit Maranville	June 10, 1931				

Most RBIs in One Inning

6	Dale Murphy	July 27, 1989	6th	5	Felix Millan	September 20, 1972	2nd

Grounded into Most Double Plays in One Game

3	Walt Cruise	September 18, 1921	versus Cincinnati
3	Joe Adcock	July 20, 1955	versus Pittsburgh

100 RBIs in One Season

145	Hugh Duffy, 1894	118	Hugh Duffy, 1893	107	Bob Elliott, 1950
135	Eddie Mathews, 1953	118	Hank Aaron, 1970	106	Bobby Lowe, 1897
132	Jimmy Collins, 1897	118	Hank Aaron, 1971	106	Wally Berger, 1933
132	Hank Aaron, 1957	117	Tommy Holmes, 1945	106	Hank Aaron, 1955
130	Wally Berger, 1935	117	Ron Gant, 1993	105	Dale Murphy, 1987
130	Hank Aaron, 1963	115	Bobby Lowe, 1894	105	Ron Gant, 1991
129	Hugh Duffy, 1897	114	Jimmy Bannon, 1894	105	Terry Pendleton, 1992
128	Hank Aaron, 1962	114	Eddie Mathews, 1959	104	Darrell Evans, 1973
127	Hank Aaron, 1966	114	Jeff Burroughs, 1977	103	Sid Gordon, 1950
126	Tommy McCarthy, 1894	113	Hugh Duffy, 1896	103	Eddie Mathews, 1954
126	Hank Aaron, 1960	113	Bob Elliott, 1947	103	Joe Adcock, 1956
124	Eddie Mathews, 1960	111	Tommy McCarthy, 1893	102	Hugh Duffy, 1899
123	Billy Nash, 1893	111	Jimmy Collins, 1898	101	Eddie Mathews, 1955
123	Hank Aaron, 1959	111	Orlando Cepeda, 1970	101	Joe Torre, 1966
121	Wally Berger, 1934	111	Dale Murphy, 1985	101	Rico Carty, 1970
121	Dale Murphy, 1983	109	Sid Gordon, 1951	100	Tommy Tucker, 1894
120	Hank Aaron, 1961	109	Joe Torre, 1964	100	Hugh Duffy, 1895
120	David Justice, 1993	109	Hank Aaron, 1967	100	Herman Long, 1896
119	Wally Berger, 1930	109	Dale Murphy, 1982	100	Herman Long, 1899
118	Dan Brouthers, 1889	108	Billy Nash, 1895	100	Bill Sweeney, 1912
		108	Hugh Duffy, 1898	100	Bob Elliott, 1948
		108	Joe Adcock, 1961	100	Dale Murphy, 1984

100 Runs Scored in One Season

160	Hugh Duffy, 1894	129	Herman Long, 1891	119	Joe Hornung, 1884
158	Bobby Lowe, 1894	127	Hank Aaron, 1962	119	Tommy McCarthy, 1892
152	Billy Hamilton, 1896	125	Hugh Duffy, 1892	118	Harry Stovey, 1891
152	Billy Hamilton, 1897	125	Fred Tenney, 1897	118	Tommy McCarthy, 1894
149	Herman Long, 1893	125	Tommy Holmes, 1945	118	Hank Aaron, 1957
147	Hugh Duffy, 1893	122	Hardy Richardson, 1889	118	Eddie Mathews, 1959
136	Herman Long, 1894	122	Chick Stahl, 1899	118	Dale Murphy, 1985
132	Billy Nash, 1894	122	Felipe Alou, 1966	117	Hank Aaron, 1966
131	Dale Murphy, 1983	121	Hank Aaron, 1963	116	Hank Aaron, 1959
130	Bobby Lowe, 1893	120	King Kelly, 1887	115	Herman Long, 1892
130	Jimmy Bannon, 1894	120	King Kelly, 1889	115	Billy Nash, 1893
130	Hugh Duffy, 1897	120	Earl Torgeson, 1950	115	Fred Tenney, 1899

115	Hank Aaron, 1961	107	Tommy McCarthy, 1893	103	Eddie Mathews, 1961
115	Dale Murphy, 1987	107	Jimmy Collins, 1898	103	Hank Aaron, 1964
114	Ray Powell, 1921	107	Ron Gant, 1990	103	Hank Aaron, 1970
114	Darrell Evans, 1973	106	Fred Tenney, 1898	103	Jerry Royster, 1979
113	Hank Aaron, 1967	106	Bill Bruton, 1955	102	Ezra Sutton, 1884
113	Dale Murphy, 1982	106	Hank Aaron, 1956	102	Dick Johnston, 1888
113	Ron Gant, 1993	106	Eddie Mathews, 1962	102	Vin Campbell, 1912
112	Tommy Tucker, 1894	105	Dan Brouthers, 1889	102	Eddie Mathews, 1960
112	Chick Stahl, 1897	105	Herman Long, 1896	101	Jimmy Bannon, 1895
112	Bill Bruton, 1960	105	Lance Richbourg, 1928	101	Bobby Lowe, 1895
110	Hugh Duffy, 1895	105	Hank Aaron, 1955	101	Sam Jethroe, 1951
110	Billy Hamilton, 1898	104	Tommy Tucker, 1890	101	Ralph Garr, 1971
110	Eddie Mathews, 1953	104	Jimmy Collins, 1900	101	Dusty Baker, 1973
110	Jeff Blauser, 1993	104	Bill Urbanski, 1934	101	Ron Gant, 1991
109	Herman Long, 1895	103	Sam Wise, 1887	100	Billy Nash, 1887
109	Eddie Mathews, 1957	103	Tommy Tucker, 1891	100	Sam Jethroe, 1950
109	Hank Aaron, 1958	103	Jimmy Collins, 1897	100	Johnny Logan, 1953
109	Hank Aaron, 1965	103	Hugh Duffy, 1899	100	Hank Aaron, 1969
108	Eddie Mathews, 1955	103	Billy Hamilton, 1900	100	Felix Millan, 1970
108	Eddie Mathews, 1960	103	Eddie Mathews, 1956		

300 Total Bases in One Season

400	Hank Aaron, 1959	332	Dale Murphy, 1984	309	Eddie Mathews, 1957
374	Hugh Duffy, 1894	332	Dale Murphy, 1985	309	Ron Gant, 1993
370	Hank Aaron, 1963	331	Hank Aaron, 1971	308	Orlando Cepeda, 1970
369	Hank Aaron, 1957	331	Darrell Evans, 1973	307	Rogers Hornsby, 1928
367	Tommy Holmes, 1945	328	Hank Aaron, 1958	306	Eddie Mathews, 1961
366	Hank Aaron, 1962	328	Dale Murphy, 1987	305	Dave Johnson, 1973
363	Eddie Mathews, 1953	325	Hank Aaron, 1955	305	Ralph Garr, 1974
358	Hank Aaron, 1961	325	Hank Aaron, 1966	303	Dale Murphy, 1982
355	Felipe Alou, 1966	323	Wally Berger, 1935	303	Terry Pendleton, 1991
344	Hank Aaron, 1967	319	Bobby Lowe, 1894	303	Terry Pendleton, 1992
341	Wally Berger, 1930	319	Hank Aaron, 1965	302	Eddie Mathews, 1960
340	Hank Aaron, 1956	318	Dale Murphy, 1983	302	Hank Aaron, 1968
336	Wally Berger, 1934	317	Gary Matthews, 1979	301	Jeff Burroughs, 1977
334	Hank Aaron, 1960	316	Wally Berger, 1931	301	David Justice, 1993
332	Hank Aaron, 1969	310	Ron Gant, 1990	300	Eddie Mathews, 1955

10 Doubles, Triples, Home Runs, and Stolen Bases in One Season

		2B	3B	HR	SB			2B	3B	HR	SB
1888	Dick Johnston	31	18	12	35	1921	Tony Boeckel	20	13	10	20
1891	Harry Stovey	31	20	16	57	1937	Gene Moore	29	10	16	11
1894	Jimmy Bannon	29	10	13	47	1951	Sam Jethroe	29	10	18	35
1894	Hugh Duffy	51	16	18	48	1960	Hank Aaron	20	11	40	16
1894	Herman Long	28	11	12	24	1960	Bill Bruton	27	13	12	22
1894	Bobby Lowe	34	11	17	23	1961	Hank Aaron	39	10	34	21
1897	Hugh Duffy	25	10	11	41	1974	Ralph Garr	24	17	11	26

75 Extra-Base Hits in One Season

92	Hank Aaron, 1959	79	Wally Berger, 1930	77	Hank Aaron, 1957
86	Eddie Mathews, 1953	79	Hank Aaron, 1962	77	Hank Aaron, 1963
85	Hugh Duffy, 1894	79	Hank Aaron, 1967	77	Hank Aaron, 1969
83	Hank Aaron, 1961	77	Wally Berger, 1934	76	Dale Murphy, 1984
81	Tommy Holmes, 1945	77	Wally Berger, 1935		

150 Singles in One Season

180	Ralph Garr, 1971	159	Bill Sweeney, 1912	151	Felix Millan, 1970
172	Fred Tenney, 1899	157	Stuffy McInnis, 1923	151	Ralph Garr, 1973
167	Hugh Duffy, 1893	157	Felipe Alou, 1968	150	Bobby Lowe, 1894
166	Lance Richbourg, 1928	155	Billy Hamilton, 1896	150	Gene Demontreville, 1901
162	Buddy Hassett, 1939	155	George Sisler, 1929	150	Ginger Beaumont, 1907
162	Ralph Garr, 1974	153	Chick Stahl, 1899	150	Dick Burrus, 1925
160	Eddie Brown, 1926	152	Hugh Duffy, 1894		
160	Rafael Ramirez, 1983	152	Fred Tenney, 1897		

30 Doubles in One Season

51	Hugh Duffy, 1894	35	Wally Berger, 1934	33	Orlando Cepeda, 1970
47	Tommy Holmes, 1945	35	Tommy Holmes, 1946	33	Glenn Hubbard, 1987
46	Hank Aaron, 1959	35	Bob Elliott, 1947	33	Terry Pendleton, 1993
44	Wally Berger, 1931	35	Tommy Holmes, 1948	32	John Morrill, 1887
44	Lee Maye, 1964	35	Dusty Baker, 1974	32	Herman Long, 1897
42	Rogers Hornsby, 1928	35	Gerald Perry, 1987	32	Fred Beck, 1910
42	Tommy Holmes, 1944	35	Dale Murphy, 1988	32	Vin Campbell, 1912
41	King Kelly, 1889	35	Ron Gant, 1991	32	Tony Boeckel, 1923
41	Dick Burrus, 1925	34	King Kelly, 1887	32	Felipe Alou, 1966
40	George Sisler, 1929	34	Bobby Lowe, 1894	32	Ralph Garr, 1973
40	Hank Aaron, 1965	34	Sherry Magee, 1915	32	Dale Murphy, 1984
39	Wally Berger, 1935	34	Red Smith, 1915	32	Dale Murphy, 1985
39	Alvin Dark, 1948	34	Wally Berger, 1932	31	Dick Johnston, 1888
39	Hank Aaron, 1961	34	Hank Aaron, 1956	31	Harry Stovey, 1891
39	Terry Pendleton, 1992	34	Hank Aaron, 1958	31	Bill Sweeney, 1912
38	Gene Moore, 1936	34	Gary Matthews, 1979	31	Red Smith, 1917
37	Wally Berger, 1933	34	Lonnie Smith, 1989	31	Eddie Brown, 1926
37	Hank Aaron, 1955	34	Ron Gant, 1990	31	Eddie Mathews, 1953
37	Johnny Logan, 1955	34	Jim Presley, 1990	31	Willie Montanez, 1977
37	Hank Aaron, 1967	34	Terry Pendleton, 1991	30	Hugh Duffy, 1895
37	Felipe Alou, 1968	33	John Morrill, 1883	30	Chick Stahl, 1897
37	Chris Chambliss, 1980	33	Hardy Richardson, 1889	30	Herman Long, 1899
37	Dion James, 1987	33	Herman Long, 1892	30	Bill Urbanski, 1934
36	Doc Miller, 1911	33	Bill Sweeney, 1911	30	Damon Phillips, 1944
36	Les Bell, 1928	33	Eddie Miller, 1940	30	Earl Torgeson, 1950
36	Tony Cuccinello, 1937	33	Tommy Holmes, 1943	30	Bill Bruton, 1955
36	Joe Torre, 1964	33	Tommy Holmes, 1947	30	Hank Aaron, 1964
35	Jimmy Bannon, 1895	33	Connie Ryan, 1947	30	Hank Aaron, 1969
35	Jimmy Collins, 1898	33	Sid Gordon, 1950	30	Jeff Burroughs, 1978
35	Eddie Brown, 1927	33	Joe Adcock, 1953		
35	Red Worthington, 1932	33	Hank Aaron, 1968		

10 Triples in One Season

20	Dick Johnston, 1887	15	Ezra Sutton, 1883	13	Jimmy Collins, 1897
20	Harry Stovey, 1891	15	Billy Nash, 1888	13	Chick Stahl, 1897
19	Chick Stahl, 1899	15	Walter Maranville, 1920	13	Buck Freeman, 1900
18	Dick Johnston, 1888	15	Billy Southworth, 1921	13	Bill Sweeney, 1912
18	Ray Powell, 1921	15	Bill Bruton, 1956	13	Ed Konetchy, 1916
17	Sam Wise, 1887	14	Ginger Beaumont, 1907	13	Rabbit Maranville, 1916
17	Fred Tenney, 1899	14	Wally Berger, 1930	13	Ed Konetchy, 1917
17	Ralph Garr, 1974	14	Chet Ross, 1940	13	Rabbit Maranville, 1917
16	John Morrill, 1883	14	Bill Bruton, 1953	13	Tony Boeckel, 1921
16	Hugh Duffy, 1894	14	Hank Aaron, 1956	13	Lance Richbourg, 1929
16	Chick Stahl, 1900	14	Deion Sanders, 1992	13	Bill Bruton, 1960
16	Billy Southworth, 1923	13	Joe Hornung, 1883	13	Brett Butler, 1983

12	Sam Wise, 1886	11	King Kelly, 1888	10	Jimmy Bannon, 1894
12	Billy Nash, 1887	11	Herman Long, 1891	10	Herman Long, 1895
12	Sam Wise, 1888	11	Herman Long, 1894	10	Hugh Duffy, 1897
12	Pop Smith, 1890	11	Bobby Lowe, 1894	10	Herman Long, 1898
12	Hugh Duffy, 1892	11	Jimmy Collins, 1899	10	Dick Cooley, 1903
12	Ed Gremminger, 1902	11	Joe Connolly, 1913	10	Ed Abbaticchio, 1904
12	Ed Abbaticchio, 1905	11	Les Mann, 1914	10	Joe Connolly, 1914
12	Johnny Bates, 1907	11	Walter Holke, 1920	10	Rabbit Maranville, 1919
12	Sherry Magee, 1915	11	Jimmy Welsh, 1926	10	Walter Holke, 1921
12	Ray Powell, 1919	11	Ray Powell, 1922	10	Walton Cruise, 1922
12	Ray Powell, 1920	11	Buster Chatham, 1930	10	Andy High, 1926
12	Lance Richbourg, 1928	11	Hank Aaron, 1960	10	Rabbit Maranville, 1929
12	Gene Moore, 1936	11	Ralph Garr, 1975	10	Red Worthington, 1931
12	Bill Bruton, 1955	10	Jim Whitney, 1883	10	Gene Moore, 1937
11	Jim O'Rourke, 1880	10	Joe Hornung, 1884	10	Tommy Holmes, 1943
11	Joe Hornung, 1882	10	Sam Wise, 1885	10	Sam Jethroe, 1951
11	John Morrill, 1882	10	Hardy Richardson, 1889	10	Hank Aaron, 1961
11	King Kelly, 1887	10	Joe Quinn, 1891		

Most Pinch Hits in One Season

20	Chris Chambliss	1986
18	Tommy Gregg	1990
17	Mike Lum	1979
16	Charlie Spikes	1979
15	Biff Pocoroba	1980

Chris Chambliss holds the Braves' season pinch-hit record with 20 in 1986.

Most Consecutive Pinch Hits

5	Rowland Office	1975

30 Stolen Bases in One Season

84	King Kelly, 1887	57	Herman Long, 1892	48	Hugh Duffy, 1894
83	Billy Hamilton, 1896	57	Hap Myers, 1913	47	Hardy Richardson, 1889
72	Otis Nixon, 1991	56	King Kelly, 1888	47	Jimmy Bannon, 1894
68	King Kelly, 1889	54	Billy Hamilton, 1898	47	Otis Nixon, 1993
66	Billy Hamilton, 1897	53	Tommy McCarthy, 1892	46	Tom Brown, 1888
63	Tom Brown, 1889	52	Dick Johnston, 1887	46	Tommy McCarthy, 1893
60	Herman Long, 1891	51	Hugh Duffy, 1892	44	Hugh Duffy, 1893
57	Harry Stovey, 1891	49	Herman Long, 1890	43	Billy Nash, 1887

43	Sam Wise, 1887	35	Dick Johnston, 1888	33	Ron Gant, 1990
43	Tommy Tucker, 1890	35	Herman Long, 1895	32	Billy Hamilton, 1900
43	Bobby Lowe, 1891	35	Sam Jethroe, 1950	32	Charlie Dexter, 1903
43	Tommy McCarthy, 1894	35	Sam Jethroe, 1951	32	Doc Miller, 1911
42	Hugh Duffy, 1895	35	Ralph Garr, 1973	32	Rabbit Maranville, 1916
42	Gerald Perry, 1987	35	Jerry Royster, 1979	32	Ron Gant, 1992
41	Joe Hornung, 1887	34	Dick Johnston, 1889	31	Sam Wise, 1886
41	Hugh Duffy, 1897	34	Fred Tenney, 1897	31	Billy Nash, 1892
41	Otis Nixon, 1992	34	Bill Bruton, 1954	31	Hank Aaron, 1963
39	Chippy McGarr, 1890	34	Ron Gant, 1991	31	Claudell Washington, 1983
39	Pop Smith, 1890	33	Sam Wise, 1888	30	Billy Nash, 1893
39	Hugh Duffy, 1896	33	Marty Sullivan, 1890	30	Billy Lush, 1902
39	Brett Butler, 1983	33	Chick Stahl, 1899	30	Ed Abbaticchio, 1905
38	Herman Long, 1893	33	Bill Sweeney, 1911	30	Ralph Garr, 1971
36	Bobby Lowe, 1892	33	Claudell Washington, 1982	30	Dale Murphy, 1983
36	Herman Long, 1896	33	Albert Hall, 1987		

Most Stolen Bases in One Game

6	Otis Nixon	June 16, 1991

Most Times Caught Stealing in One Game

3	Rabbit Maranville	June 6, 1913

100 Bases on Balls in One Season

131	Bob Elliott, 1948	115	Dale Murphy, 1987	107	Rogers Hornsby, 1928
127	Jimmy Wynn, 1976	113	Eddie Stanky, 1949	105	Billy Hamilton, 1897
126	Darrell Evans, 1974	113	Eddie Mathews, 1954	105	Darrell Evans, 1975
124	Eddie Mathews, 1963	111	Eddie Mathews, 1960	102	Earl Torgeson, 1951
124	Darrell Evans, 1973	110	Billy Hamilton, 1896	101	Eddie Mathews, 1962
119	Earl Torgeson, 1950	109	Eddie Mathews, 1955		
117	Jeff Burroughs, 1978	107	Billy Hamilton, 1900		

Most Times Walked in One Game

5	Pop Smith	April 17, 1890	5	Hank Aaron	September 3, 1960	5	Dale Murphy	April 22, 1983
5	Fred Tenney	August 16, 1907	5	Hank Aaron	July 11, 1972	5	Dale Murphy	May 23, 1987

Two Walks in One Inning

Hugh Duffy	June 18, 1894	1st	Jesse Barnes	October 2, 1917	2nd	Otis Nixon	September 9, 1992	1st

Most Times Struck Out in One Game

5	Harry Stovey	June 30, 1891*
5	Bob Sadowski	April 20, 1964

*10 innings

Pitcher Bob Sadowski is the only Brave to strike out five times in the same game during the 20th century.

Struck Out Twice in One Inning

Larry McWilliams   April 22, 1979   4th

Braves Who Played in All of Team's Games

Hank Aaron (OF)—1961
Joe Adcock (1B)—1953
Les Bell (3B)—1928
Wally Berger (OF)—1931
Tony Boeckel (3B)—1920, 1921
Eddie Brown (OF)—1926, 1927
Jack Burdock (2B)—1878, 1879, 1880
Chris Chambliss (1B)—1981
Jimmy Collins (3B)—1898, 1900
Tony Cuccinello (2B)—1937
Gene DeMontreville (2B)—1901
Cozy Dolan (OF)—1905
Hugh Duffy (OF)—1893, 1898
Ed Gremminger (3B)—1903
Tommy Holmes (OF)—1944, 1945

Joe Hornung (OF)—1881, 1882, 1883
Dick Johnston (OF)—1887
Ed Konetchy (1B)—1916
Andy Leonard (OF)—1878
Johnny Logan (SS)—1954, 1955
Bobby Lowe (2B)—1894
Jack Manning (OF)—1876, 1878
Eddie Mathews (3B)—1953
Tommy McCarthy (OF)—1892
Felix Millan (2B)—1969
John Morrill (3B, 1B)—1877, 1878, 1879, 1880, 1887
Dale Murphy (OF)—1982, 1983, 1984, 1985
Billy Nash (3B)—1891, 1895

Jim O'Rourke (OF)—1876, 1877, 1878, 1880
Harry Schafer (3B)—1876
George Sisler (1B)—1929
Pop Smith (2B)—1890
Red Smith (3B)—1915
Pop Snyder (C)—1878
Ezra Sutton (3B, SS)—1878, 1879, 1881
Bill Sweeney (2B)—1912
Earl Torgeson (1B)—1950, 1951
Tommy Tucker (1B)—1891
Whitey Wietelmann (SS)—1943
Chuck Workman (OF)—1943
George Wright (SS)—1876, 1877

All-Time Braves Pitching Leaders

Games Pitched

Phil Niekro	740
Warren Spahn	714
Gene Garber	557
Kid Nichols	556
Lou Burdette	468
Rick Camp	414
Bob Smith	349
Vic Willis	320
Rick Mahler	307
Ben Cantwell	290

Innings Pitched

Warren Spahn	5,046
Phil Niekro	4,622⅔
Kid Nichols	4,538
Lou Burdette	2,638

Vic Willis	2,575
Jim Whitney	2,263⅔
Tommy Bond	2,127⅓
John Clarkson	2,092⅔
Dick Rudolph	2,035
Bob Smith	1,813⅓

Games Won

Warren Spahn	356
Kid Nichols	329
Phil Niekro	268
Lou Burdette	179
Vic Willis	150
Tommy Bond	149
John Clarkson	149
Vic Willis	149
Jim Whitney	133
Jack Stivetts	131

Games Lost

Phil Niekro	230
Warren Spahn	229
Kid Nichols	183
Vic Willis	145
Jim Whitney	121
Lou Burdette	120
Bob Smith	120
Ed Brandt	119
Dick Rudolph	107
Ben Cantwell	106

Winning Percentage (mininum 100 decisions)

	W–L	Pct.
Harry Staley	72–38	.655
John Clarkson	149–82	.645
Kid Nichols	329–183	.643
Tommy Bond	149–87	.631
Jack Stivetts	131–78	.627
Ted Lewis	78–47	.624
Warren Spahn	356–229	.609
Bob Buhl	109–72	.602
Lou Burdette	179–120	.599
Charlie Buffinton	104–70	.598

Complete Games

Kid Nichols	475
Warren Spahn	374
Vic Willis	268
Jim Whitney	242
Tommy Bond	230
John Clarkson	226
Phil Niekro	226
Jack Stivetts	176
Dick Rudolph	171
Charlie Buffinton	166

Shutouts

Warren Spahn	63
Kid Nichols	44
Phil Niekro	43
Lou Burdette	30
Tommy Bond	29
Dick Rudolph	27
Vic Willis	26
Lefty Tyler	22
John Clarkson	20
Charlie Buffinton	19

Strikeouts

Phil Niekro	2,912
Warren Spahn	2,493
Kid Nichols	1,667
Vic Willis	1,161
Jim Whitney	1,157
John Smoltz	1,059
Lou Burdette	923
Charlie Buffinton	911
Tom Glavine	904
Denny Lemaster	842
John Clarkson	834
Tony Cloninger	834

Earned Run Average (minimum 1,000 innings)

Tommy Bond	2.21
Jim Whitney	2.49
Dick Rudolph	2.62
John Clarkson	2.82
Vic Willis	2.82
Charlie Buffinton	2.83
Kid Nichols	3.00
Warren Spahn	3.05
Lefty Tyler	3.06
Jesse Barnes	3.07

Saves

Gene Garber	141
Cecil Upshaw	78
Rick Camp	57
Mike Stanton	54
Don McMahon	50
Steve Bedrosian	41
Greg McMichael	40
Bruce Sutter	40
Bob Smith	36
Claude Raymond	33
Joe Boever	30

John Smoltz ranks sixth on the Braves' all-time strikeout list.

League Leaders in Pitching

Games Pitched

1878	Tommy Bond	59
1881	Jim Whitney	66
1889	John Clarkson	73
1897	Kid Nichols	46*
1898	Kid Nichols	50*
1902	Vic Willis	51
1910	Al Mattern	51
1915	Tom Hughes	50
1921	Jack Scott	47
1966	Clay Carroll	73

Innings Pitched

1878	Tommy Bond	532⅔
1881	Jim Whitney	552⅓
1888	John Clarkson	483⅓
1889	John Clarkson	620
1897	Kid Nichols	368
1902	Vic Willis	410
1905	Irv Young	378
1906	Irv Young	358⅓
1942	Jim Tobin	287⅔
1943	Al Javery	303
1947	Warren Spahn	289⅔
1948	Johnny Sain	314⅔
1949	Warren Spahn	302⅓
1950	Vern Bickford	311⅔
1958	Warren Spahn	290
1959	Warren Spahn	292
1961	Lou Burdette	272⅓
1974	Phil Niekro	302⅓
1977	Phil Niekro	330⅓
1978	Phil Niekro	334⅓
1979	Phil Niekro	342
1993	Greg Maddux	267
1994	Greg Maddux	202

Wins

1877	Tommy Bond	40
1878	Tommy Bond	40

Reliever Clay Carroll led the league with 73 appearances in 1966.

1881	Jim Whitney	31*
1889	John Clarkson	49
1896	Kid Nichols	30*
1897	Kid Nichols	31
1898	Kid Nichols	31
1948	Johnny Sain	24
1949	Warren Spahn	21
1950	Warren Spahn	21
1953	Warren Spahn	23*
1957	Warren Spahn	21
1958	Warren Spahn	22*
1959	Warren Spahn	21*
	Lou Burdette	21*
1960	Warren Spahn	21*
1961	Warren Spahn	21*
1974	Phil Niekro	20*
1979	Phil Niekro	21*
1991	Tom Glavine	20*
1992	Tom Glavine	20*
1993	Tom Glavine	22*
1994	Greg Maddux	16*

Winning Percentage

1877	Tommy Bond	.702
1878	Tommy Bond	.678
1889	John Clarkson	.721
1897	Fred Klobedanz	.788
1898	Ted Lewis	.733
1914	Bill James	.788
1916	Tom Hughes	.842
1933	Ben Cantwell	.667
1957	Bob Buhl	.720
1958	Warren Spahn	.667*
	Lou Burdette	.667*
1982	Phil Niekro	.810

Losses

1881	Jim Whitney	33
1885	Jim Whitney	32
1903	Togie Pittinger	22
1904	Vic Willis	25
1905	Vic Willis	29
1906	Gus Dorner	26
1909	George Ferguson	23
1912	Lefty Tyler	22
1915	Dick Rudolph	19
1917	Jesse Barnes	21
1919	Dick Rudolph	18
1924	Jesse Barnes	20
1928	Ed Brandt	21
1935	Ben Cantwell	25
1942	Jim Tobin	21
1943	Nate Andrews	20
1976	Dick Ruthven	17
1977	Phil Niekro	20
1978	Phil Niekro	18
1979	Phil Niekro	20
1980	Phil Niekro	18

1986	Rick Mahler	18
1988	Tom Glavine	17

Complete Games

1878	Tommy Bond	57
1881	Jim Whitney	57*
1889	John Clarkson	68
1902	Vic Willis	45
1904	Vic Willis	39*
1905	Irv Young	41
1906	Irv Young	37
1913	Lefty Tyler	28
1918	Art Nehf	28
1937	Jim Turner	24
1942	Jim Tobin	28
1944	Jim Tobin	28
1946	Johnny Sain	24
1948	Johnny Sain	28
1949	Warren Spahn	25
1950	Vern Bickford	27
1951	Warren Spahn	26
1957	Warren Spahn	18
1958	Warren Spahn	23
1959	Warren Spahn	21
1960	Lou Burdette	18*
	Warren Spahn	18*
1961	Warren Spahn	21
1962	Warren Spahn	22
1963	Warren Spahn	22
1974	Phil Niekro	18
1977	Phil Niekro	20
1978	Phil Niekro	22
1979	Phil Niekro	23
1991	Tom Glavine	9*
1993	Greg Maddux	8
1994	Greg Maddux	10

Shutouts

1877	Tommy Bond	6
1878	Tommy Bond	9
1879	Tommy Bond	11
1889	John Clarkson	8
1890	Kid Nichols	7
1894	Kid Nichols	3*
1899	Vic Willis	5
1900	Kid Nichols	4
1901	Vic Willis	6*
1910	Al Mattern	6*
1921	Dana Fillingim	3*
	Joe Oeschger	3*
1924	Jesse Barnes	4*
1937	Lou Fette	5*
	Jim Turner	5*
1939	Lou Fette	6
1940	Manny Salvo	5*
1947	Warren Spahn	7
1951	Warren Spahn	7
1956	Lou Burdette	6

1958	Carlton Willey	4
1959	Bob Buhl	4*
	Lou Burdette	4*
	Warren Spahn	4*
1961	Warren Spahn	4*
1992	Tom Glavine	5*
1994	Greg Maddux	3*

Strikeouts

1877	Tommy Bond	170
1878	Tommy Bond	182
1883	Jim Whitney	345
1889	John Clarkson	284
1902	Vic Willis	225
1949	Warren Spahn	151

Bob Buhl (R), here with Ernie Johnson, tied for the league lead in shutouts in 1959.

1950	Warren Spahn	191
1951	Warren Spahn	164*
1952	Warren Spahn	183
1977	Phil Niekro	262
1992	John Smoltz	215

Earned Run Average

1877	Tommy Bond	2.11
1879	Tommy Bond	1.96
1889	John Clarkson	2.73
1899	Vic Willis	2.50
1937	Jim Turner	2.38
1947	Warren Spahn	2.33
1951	Chet Nichols	2.88
1953	Warren Spahn	2.10
1956	Lou Burdette	2.70
1961	Warren Spahn	3.02
1967	Phil Niekro	1.87
1974	Buzz Capra	2.28
1993	Greg Maddux	2.36
1994	Greg Maddux	1.56

Saves

1876	Jack Manning	5
1881	Bobby Mathews	2
1883	Jim Whitney	2*
1884	John Morrill	2
1887	Bill Stemmeyer	1*
1889	Bill Sowders	2*

Buzz Capra put it all together for one year and led the league in ERA in 1974.

1891	John Clarkson	3*
	Kid Nichols	3*
1895	Kid Nichols	3*
1897	Kid Nichols	3*
1898	Kid Nichols	4
1902	Vic Willis	3
1915	Tom Hughes	9
1959	Don McMahon	15*

*Tied for league lead.

20 Games Won in One Season

49	John Clarkson, 1889		26	Jack Stivetts, 1894		22	Tom Glavine, 1993
48	Charlie Buffinton, 1884		26	Kid Nichols, 1895		21	Kid Madden, 1887
43	Tommy Bond, 1879		26	Fred Klobedanz, 1897		21	Ted Lewis, 1897
40	Tommy Bond, 1877		26	Ted Lewis, 1898		21	Kid Nichols, 1899
40	Tommy Bond, 1878		26	Bill James, 1914		21	Johnny Sain, 1947
37	Jim Whitney, 1883		26	Dick Rudolph, 1914		21	Warren Spahn, 1947
35	Kid Nichols, 1892		25	Charlie Buffinton, 1883		21	Warren Spahn, 1949
35	Jack Stivetts, 1892		25	Vic Willis, 1898		21	Warren Spahn, 1950
34	Kid Nichols, 1893		24	Jim Whitney, 1882		21	Warren Spahn, 1954
33	John Clarkson, 1888		24	Charley Radbourn, 1887		21	Warren Spahn, 1957
33	John Clarkson, 1891		24	Johnny Sain, 1948		21	Lou Burdette, 1959
32	Kid Nichols, 1894		24	Tony Cloninger, 1965		21	Warren Spahn, 1959
31	Jim Whitney, 1881		23	Jim Whitney, 1884		21	Warren Spahn, 1960
31	Kid Nichols, 1897		23	Charlie Getzein, 1890		21	Warren Spahn, 1961
31	Kid Nichols, 1898		23	Warren Spahn, 1953		21	Phil Niekro, 1979
30	Kid Nichols, 1891		23	Warren Spahn, 1963		20	Charley Radbourn, 1889
30	Kid Nichols, 1896		23	Phil Niekro, 1969		20	Harry Staley, 1891
27	Charley Radbourn, 1886		22	Charlie Buffinton, 1885		20	Bill Dinneen, 1900
27	Kid Nichols, 1890		22	Bill Stemmeyer, 1886		20	Vic Willis, 1901
27	Vic Willis, 1899		22	Harry Staley, 1892		20	Irv Young, 1905
27	Togie Pittinger, 1902		22	Jack Stivetts, 1896		20	Joe Oeschger, 1921
27	Vic Willis, 1902		22	Dick Rudolph, 1915		20	Ben Cantwell, 1933
26	Tommy Bond, 1880		22	Warren Spahn, 1951		20	Lou Fette, 1937
26	John Clarkson, 1890		22	Warren Spahn, 1958		20	Jim Turner, 1937

20	Johnny Sain, 1946	20	Lou Burdette, 1958	20	Tom Glavine, 1992
20	Johnny Sain, 1950	20	Phil Niekro, 1974	20	Greg Maddux, 1993
20	Warren Spahn, 1956	20	Tom Glavine, 1991		

No-Hitters by Braves Pitchers

August 6, 1892	Jack Stivetts, 11–0, versus Brooklyn
August 7, 1899	Vic Willis, 7–1, versus Washington
May 8, 1907	Big Jeff Pfeffer, 6–0, versus Cincinnati
September 9, 1914	George Davis, 7–0, versus Philadelphia
June 16, 1916	Tom Hughes, 2–0, versus Pittsburgh
April 27, 1944	Jim Tobin, 2–0, versus Brooklyn
August 11, 1950	Vern Bickford, 7–0, versus Brooklyn
June 12, 1954	Jim Wilson, 2–0, versus Philadelphia
August 18, 1960	Lou Burdette, 1–0, versus Philadelphia
September 16, 1960	Warren Spahn, 4–0, versus Philadelphia
April 28, 1961	Warren Spahn, 1–0, versus San Francisco
August 5, 1973	Phil Niekro, 9–0, versus San Diego
September 11, 1991	Kent Mercker (6 innings), Mark Wohler (2), Alejandro Pena (1), 1–0, versus San Diego
April 8, 1994	Kent Mercker, 6–0, at Los Angeles

Jim Wilson pitched the eighth no-hitter in franchise history.

No-Hitters Pitched against Braves

August 19, 1880	Larry Corcoran, 6–0, at Chicago
April 22, 1898	Jim Hughes, 8–0, at Baltimore
July 8, 1898	Red Donahue, 5–0, at Philadelphia
September 5, 1908	Nap Rucker, 6–0, at Brooklyn
July 17, 1924	Jesse Haines, 5–0, at St. Louis
June 11, 1938*	Johnny Vander Meer, 3–0, at Cincinnati
May 15, 1944	Clyde Shoun, 1–0, at Cincinnati
April 23, 1946	Ed Head, 5–0, at Brooklyn
June 18, 1947	Ewell Blackwell, 6–0, at Cincinnati
May 6, 1951	Cliff Chambers, 3–0, versus Pittsburgh
June 18, 1967	Don Wilson, 2–0, at Houston
August 19, 1969	Ken Holtzman, 3–0, at Chicago
September 29, 1976	John Montefusco, 9–0, versus San Francisco
April 7, 1979	Ken Forsch, 6–0, at Houston

*First of two consecutive no-hitters by Vander Meer

Most Relief Wins in Season

12	Ben Cantwell	1932	11	Dave Jolly	1954	11	Cecil Upshaw	1971

Most Relief Losses in Season

16	Gene Garber	1979	11	Joe Boever	1989	10	Steve Bedrosian	1983
11	Nels Potter	1949	10	Gene Garber	1982	10	Gene Garber	1987

Two Complete Game Wins in One Day

John Clarkson	September 12, 1889	3–2, 5–0	versus Cleveland
Mule Watson	August 13, 1921	4–3, 8–0	versus Philadelphia

Most Innings Pitched in One Game

Innings	Pitcher	Date	Opponent	Hits	Runs
26	Joe Oeschger	May 1, 1920	Brooklyn	9	1
22	Bob Smith	May 17, 1927	Chicago	20	4
21	Art Nehf	August 1, 1918	Pittsburgh	12	2
19	Otto Hess	July 31, 1912	Pittsburgh	14	7
19	Dana Fillingim	May 3, 1920	Brooklyn	12	1

Four Strikeouts in One Inning

Pitcher	Date	Inning	Opponent
Phil Niekro	July 29, 1977	6th	Pittsburgh
Paul Assenmacher	August 22, 1989	5th	St. Louis

Paul Assenmacher is one of two Braves to record four strikeouts in one inning.

Three Strikeouts on Nine Pitches in One Inning

Joe Oeschger	September 8, 1921	4th	Philadelphia

Most Strikeouts in Nine-Inning Game

17	Charlie Buffinton	September 2, 1884	versus Cleveland
16	Jim Whitney	June 14, 1883	versus Chicago
16	Charlie Buffinton	July 30, 1885	versus Detroit
15	Danny MacFayden	September 28, 1935	versus New York
15	Warren Spahn	September 16, 1960	versus Philadelphia
15	John Smoltz	May 24, 1992	versus Montreal

Most Walks in One Game

14	Piano Legs Hickman	August 16, 1899	versus Louisville
13	Mal Eason	September 3, 1902	versus Pittsburgh
12	Wiley Piatt	June 10, 1903	versus Chicago
12	Wiley Piatt	August 14, 1903	versus Chicago
12	Red Causey	September 8, 1919	versus Pittsburgh
12	Bob Smith	September 28, 1928	versus St. Louis*
11	Kid Nichols	July 9, 1890	versus Pittsburgh
10	Togie Pittinger	May 8, 1903	versus Brooklyn
10	Dana Fillingim	June 4, 1922	versus New York

*15 innings

.650 Winning Percentage in One Season

.842	Tom Hughes, 16–3, 1916
.810	Phil Niekro, 17–4, 1982
.788	Fred Klobedanz, 26–7, 1897
.788	Bill James, 26–7, 1914
.786	Tom Glavine, 22–6, 1993
.783	Jack Manning, 18–5, 1876
.771	Vic Willis, 27–8, 1899
.767	Warren Spahn, 23–7, 1953
.767	Warren Spahn, 23–7, 1963
.765	Ted Lewis, 26–8, 1898
.750	Charlie Buffinton, 48–16, 1884
.750	Steve Avery, 18–6, 1993
.750	Lou Burdette, 15–5, 1953
.750	Hank Gastright, 12–4, 1893
.738	Kid Nichols, 31–11, 1897
.727	Greg Maddux, 16–6, 1994
.722	Dick Rudolph, 26–10, 1914
.721	Kid Nichols, 31–12, 1898
.721	John Clarkson, 49–19, 1889
.720	Bob Buhl, 18–7, 1957
.714	Harry Staley, 20–8, 1891
.714	Tom Glavine, 20–8, 1992
.711	Kid Nichols, 32–13, 1894
.708	Kid Nichols, 34–14, 1893
.702	Tommy Bond, 40–17, 1877
.694	Tommy Bond, 43–19, 1879
.692	Bob Buhl, 18–8, 1956
.692	Steve Avery, 18–8, 1991
.688	Harry Staley, 22–10, 1892
.688	Tom Zachary, 11–5, 1930
.688	Vern Bickford, 11–5, 1948
.688	Max Surkont, 11–5, 1953
.686	Kid Nichols, 35–16, 1892
.686	Jack Stivetts, 35–16, 1892
.686	Tony Cloninger, 24–11, 1965
.682	Kid Nichols, 30–14, 1896
.682	Charlie Leibrandt, 15–7, 1992
.680	Art Nehf, 17–8, 1917
.678	Tommy Bond, 40–19, 1878
.677	Warren Spahn, 21–10, 1947
.677	Warren Spahn, 21–10, 1960
.667	Warren Spahn, 22–11, 1958
.667	Ben Cantwell, 20–10, 1933
.667	Lou Fette, 20–10, 1937
.667	Lou Burdette, 20–10, 1958
.667	Greg Maddux, 20–10, 1993
.667	Buzz Capra, 16–8, 1974
.667	Larry Benton, 14–7, 1925
.667	Bob Brown, 14–7, 1932
.658	Vic Willis, 25–13, 1898
.656	Warren Spahn, 21–11, 1957
.655	Fred Klobedanz, 19–10, 1898
.655	Lou Burdette, 19–10, 1956
.654	Lefty Tyler, 17–9, 1916
.654	Fred Frankhouse, 17–9, 1934
.654	Lou Burdette, 17–9, 1957
.652	Pascual Perez, 15–8, 1983

300 Innings Pitched in One Season

620	John Clarkson, 1889
587	Charlie Buffinton, 1884
555⅓	Tommy Bond, 1879
552⅓	Jim Whitney, 1881
532⅔	Tommy Bond, 1878
521	Tommy Bond, 1877
514	Jim Whitney, 1883
509⅓	Charley Radbourn, 1886
483⅓	John Clarkson, 1888
460⅔	John Clarkson, 1891
453	Kid Nichols, 1892
441⅓	Jim Whitney, 1885
434⅓	Charlie Buffinton, 1885
425⅓	Kid Nichols, 1891
425	Charley Radbourn, 1887
425	Kid Nichols, 1893
424	Kid Nichols, 1890
420	Jim Whitney, 1882
415⅔	Jack Stivetts, 1892
410	Vic Willis, 1902
407	Kid Nichols, 1894
389⅓	Togie Pittinger, 1902
388	Kid Nichols, 1898
383	John Clarkson, 1890
379⅔	Kid Nichols, 1895
378	Irv Young, 1905
372⅓	Kid Nichols, 1896
368	Kid Nichols, 1897
358⅓	Irv Young, 1906
351⅔	Togie Pittinger, 1903
350	Charlie Getzein, 1890
350	Vic Willis, 1904
348⅔	Bill Stemmeyer, 1886
343⅓	Kid Nichols, 1899
342⅔	Vic Willis, 1899
342	Vic Willis, 1905
342	Phil Niekro, 1979
341⅓	Dick Rudolph, 1915
338	Jack Stivetts, 1894
336⅓	Dick Rudolph, 1914
336	Jim Whitney, 1884
335⅓	Togie Pittinger, 1904
334⅓	Chick Fraser, 1905
334⅓	Phil Niekro, 1978
333	Charlie Buffinton, 1883
332⅓	Bill James, 1914
330⅓	Phil Niekro, 1977
329	Jack Stivetts, 1896
321	Kid Madden, 1887
320⅔	Bill Dinneen, 1900
317	Bill Sowders, 1888
316⅓	Al Mattern, 1909
314⅔	Johnny Sain, 1948
313⅓	Ted Lewis, 1898
312	Dick Rudolph, 1916
311⅔	Vern Bickford, 1950
311	Vic Willis, 1898

310⅔	Warren Spahn, 1951	305⅓	Vic Willis, 1901	302⅓	Warren Spahn, 1949
309⅓	Fred Klobedanz, 1897	305	Al Mattern, 1910	302⅓	Phil Niekro, 1974
309⅓	Bill Dinneen, 1901	303	Al Javery, 1943		
307⅓	Vive Lindaman, 1906	302⅓	Big Jeff Pfeffer, 1906		

200 Strikeouts in One Season

417	Charlie Buffinton, 1884	242	Charlie Buffinton, 1885	218	Charley Radbourn, 1886
345	Jim Whitney, 1883	240	Kid Nichols, 1891	215	John Smoltz, 1992
284	John Clarkson, 1889	239	Bill Stemmeyer, 1886	211	Tony Cloninger, 1965
270	Jim Whitney, 1884	225	Vic Willis, 1902	208	Phil Niekro, 1979
262	Phil Niekro, 1977	223	John Clarkson, 1888	208	John Smoltz, 1993
248	Phil Niekro, 1978	222	Kid Nichols, 1890	200	Jim Whitney, 1885

Shutout in First Big League Start

Pitcher	Date	Score	Opponent	Pitcher	Date	Score	Opponent
Bill Stemmeyer	October 3, 1885	18–0	Buffalo*	Cliff Curtis	September 2, 1909	1–0	Pittsburgh
Vive Lindaman	April 14, 1906	1–0	Brooklyn	Carl Willey	June 23, 1958	7–0	San Francisco
Tom Tuckey	August 11, 1908	2–0	St. Louis	*Six innings			

10 Saves in One Season

Gene Garber holds Braves records for saves in a season and in a career.

30	Gene Garber, 1982	19	Steve Bedrosian, 1983	10	Dave Jolly, 1954
27	Cecil Upshaw, 1969	19	Greg McMichael, 1993	10	Don McMahon, 1960
27	Mike Stanton, 1993	18	Billy O'Dell, 1965	10	Claude Raymond, 1962
25	Gene Garber, 1979	17	Cecil Upshaw, 1971	10	Claude Raymond, 1968
24	Gene Garber, 1986	17	Rick Camp, 1981	10	Rick Camp, 1977
23	Bruce Sutter, 1985	17	Juan Berenguer, 1991	10	Gene Garber, 1987
22	Gene Garber, 1978	16	Donnie Moore, 1984		
22	Rick Camp, 1980	15	Don McMahon, 1959		
21	Joe Boever, 1989	15	Alejandro Pena, 1992		
		14	Jim Acker, 1987		
		14	Bruce Sutter, 1988		
		13	Bob Shaw, 1963		
		13	Bobby Tiefenauer, 1964		
		13	Cecil Upshaw, 1968		
		13	Hoyt Wilhelm, 1970		
		13	Cecil Upshaw, 1972		
		13	Dave Campbell, 1977		
		13	Terry Forster, 1983		
		11	Clay Carroll, 1966		
		11	Tom House, 1974		
		11	Tom House, 1975		
		11	Steve Bedrosian, 1982		
		11	Steve Bedrosian, 1984		
		11	Gene Garber, 1984		
		11	Alejandro Pena, 1991		

Steve Bedrosian and Gene Garber accept the 1982 award for the best team bullpen.

Highest Batting Average by a Pitcher (minimum 40 at bats)

Pitcher, Year	H	AB	AVG	Pitcher, Year	H	AB	AVG
Johnny Sain, 1947	37	107	.346	Kid Nichols, 1894	50	170	.294
Jack Stivetts, 1896	76	221	.344	Kid Madden, 1889	25	86	.291
Jack Scott, 1921	30	88	.341	Charlie Buffinton, 1886	51	176	.290
Warren Spahn, 1958	36	108	.333	Socks Seibold, 1929	20	70	.286
Jack Stivetts, 1894	80	244	.328	Ben Cantwell, 1935	19	67	.284
Fred Klobedanz, 1897	48	148	.324	Ted Lewis, 1898	37	131	.282
Jim Whitney, 1882	81	251	.323	Kid Nichols, 1901	46	163	.282
Fred Klobedanz, 1896	13	41	.317	Jim Whitney, 1883	115	409	.281
Otto Hess, 1913	26	83	.313	Jim Tobin, 1943	30	107	.280
Ed Brandt, 1933	30	97	.309	Bill Dinneen, 1900	35	125	.280
Ed Wright, 1946	18	59	.305	Ben Cantwell, 1932	14	50	.280
Bill Sherdel, 1931	14	46	.304	Ben Cantwell, 1934	12	43	.279
Ben Cantwell, 1930	19	63	.302	Jim Tobin, 1940	12	43	.279
Johnny Sain, 1946	28	94	.298	Bill Stemmeyer, 1886	41	148	.277
Bob Smith, 1926	25	84	.298	Ed Donnelly, 1912	19	69	.275
Jack Stivetts, 1893	51	172	.297	Tom Zachary, 1932	21	77	.273
Jack Stivetts, 1892	71	240	.296	Joe Genewich, 1925	15	55	.273
Rick Mahler, 1984	21	71	.296	Bob Smith, 1935	17	63	.270

Most Home Runs in One Game, Pitcher

3	Jim Tobin	May 13, 1942	2	Lou Burdette	August 13, 1957	2	Tony Cloninger	July 3, 1966
2	Harry Staley	June 1, 1893	2	Lou Burdette	July 10, 1958	2	Derek Lilliquist	May 1, 1990
2	Jack Stivetts	June 12, 1896	2	Tony Cloninger	June 16, 1966			

Most Home Runs in One Season, Pitcher

6	Jim Tobin	1942	5	Jim Tobin	1945	5	Tony Cloninger	1966

Nonpitchers Who Pitched

Player (position)	L/R	Years	G	W–L	IP	H	BB	SO	ERA
Bannon, Jimmy (of)	R	1894–95	2	0–0	5	8	3	1	3.60
Blocker, Terry (of)	L	1989	1	0–0	1	0	2	0	0.00
Delahanty, Jim (3b)	R	1904–05	2	0–0	5⅓	10	1	0	1.69
Dolan, Cozy (of)	L	1905–06	4	0–2	16	19	7	8	5.63
Farrell, Kerby (1b)	L	1943	5	0–1	23	24	9	4	4.30
Gomez, Luis (ss)	R	1981	1	0–0	1	3	2	0	27.00
Kelly, King (c)	R	1887, '92	4	1–0	19	25	18	0	2.84
Konetchy, Ed (1b)	R	1918	1	0–1	8	14	2	3	6.75
Lowe, Bobby (2b)	R	1891	1	0–0	1	3	1	0	9.00
Macon, Max (1b)	L	1944, '47	5	0–0	5	11	2	2	12.60
McCarthy, Tommy (of)	R	1894	1	0–0	2	1	3	0	4.50
Morrill, John (1b)	R	1880–86	17	1–2	58⅓	75	12	22	4.32
Morrison, John (3b)	R	1988	3	0–0	3⅔	3	2	1	0.00
Nash, Billy (3b)	R	1889	1	0–0	1	0	1	0	0.00
Russell, John (c)	R	1989	1	0–0	⅓	0	0	0	0.00

Player (position)	L/R	Years	G	W–L	IP	H	BB	SO	ERA
Sisler, George (1b)	L	1928	1	0–0	1	0	1	0	0.00
Stahl, Chick (of)	L	1899	1	0–0	2	2	3	0	9.00
Stanley, Joe (of)	R	1903	1	0–0	4	4	4	4	9.00
Tenney, Fred (1b)	L	1905	1	0–0	2	5	1	0	4.50
Tucker, Tommy (1b)	R	1891	1	0–0	1	3	0	0	9.00
Wietelmann, W. (ss)	R	1945–46	4	0–0	7⅔	15	6	2	14.09
Wright, George (ss)	R	1876	1	0–0	1	1	0	1	0.00

Club Fielding Records

Catcher

.996—Del Crandall, 1956; Joe Torre, 1968

First Base

.997—Walter Holke, 1921; Joe Adcock, 1962; Chris Chambliss, 1981

Second Base

.994—Mark Lemke, 1994

Third Base

.981—Clete Boyer, 1968

Shortstop

.983—Eddie Miller, 1942

Outfield

1.000—Willard Marshall, 1951

Mark Lemke set the Braves' season record for defensive percentage at second base in 1994.

Most No-Hitters Caught

3	Del Crandall	Jim Wilson	June 12, 1954
		Lou Burdette	August 18, 1960
		Warren Spahn	September 16, 1960

Del Crandall caught three no-hitters in his distinguished Braves career.

Rookie Records

Home Runs		
Wally Berger	38	1930
Earl Williams	33	1971

Batting Average		
Chick Stahl	.354	1897

Hits, First Game		
Mack Jones	4	July 13, 1961

Doubles		
Al Dark	39	1948
Gene Moore	38	1936

RBIs		
Wally Berger	119	1930

Wins		
Lou Fette	20	1937
Jim Turner	20	1937
Irv Young	20	1905

Innings (since 1900)		
Irv Young	378	1905

Complete Games (since 1900)		
Irv Young	41	1905

Shutouts (since 1900)		
Irv Young	7	1905
Lou Fette	5	1937
Jim Turner	5	1937

Most Lopsided Win Since 1900

20–1 September 18, 1915   versus St. Louis

Most Runs in One Game

Since 1900		
23	September 2, 1957	versus Chicago

Pre-1900		
30	June 9, 1883	versus Detroit

Most Hits in One Game

Since 1900		
26	September 2, 1957	versus Chicago
25	April 10, 1900	versus Philadelphia
25	June 25, 1900	versus Philadelphia

Pre-1900		
30	September 3, 1896	versus St. Louis

Sources

Aaron to Zuverink by Rich Marazzi and Len Fiorito
Atlanta Braves: The First 25 Years
Atlanta Constitution
The Atlanta Journal
Babe: The Legend Comes To Life by Robert W. Creamer
The Ballplayers edited by Mike Shatzkin
The Baseball Chronology edited by James Charlton
The Baseball Encyclopedia, Joseph L. Reichler, editor
Baseball Registers by *The Sporting News*
Baseball's Greatest Quotations by Paul Dickson
Baseball Uniforms of the 20th Century by Marc Okkonen
The Bill James Historical Baseball Abstract
Biographical Dictionary of American Sports: Baseball edited by David L. Porter
Boston American
The Boston Braves by Harold Kaese
Boston Globe
Boston Herald
Boston Post
Braves media guides
Braves yearbooks
The Braves: The Pick and the Shovel by Al Hirshberg
Caught Short by Donald Davidson with Jesse Outlar
ChopTalk
The Complete Baseball Record Book by *The Sporting News*
Crimson in Triumph by Joe Bertagna
Eddie Mathews and the National Pastime by Eddie Mathews and Bob Buege
Green Cathedrals by Philip J. Lowry
The Great All-Time Baseball Record Book, Joseph L. Reichler, editor; revised by Ken
   Samelson
The Milwaukee Braves: A Baseball Eulogy by Bob Buege
Milwaukee Journal
Milwaukee Sentinel
Miracle in Atlanta by Furman Bisher
National Baseball Hall of Fame and Museum Yearbook
The National Baseball Library and Archive at Cooperstown, New York
National League Green Book
The New Phillies Encyclopedia by Rich Westcott and Frank Bilovsky
The New York Times
Official Baseball Guides by *The Sporting News*
The Sporting News
Sport Magazine
Sports Illustrated
Stengel: His Life and Times by Robert W. Creamer
Take Me Out to the Ballpark by Lowell Reidenbaugh
Tomahawk
Total Baseball edited by John Thorn and Pete Palmer
The Ultimate Baseball Book by Daniel Okrent and Harris Levine
Warren Spahn: Immortal Southpaw by Al Silverman
We Could've Finished Last Without You by Bob Hope
Who's Who in Professional Baseball by Gene Karst and Martin J. Jones, Jr.

Photo Credits

Photos courtesy of the Atlanta Braves, the Atlanta Historical Center, the *Atlanta Journal-Constitution,* the Boston Braves Historical Association, the Bostonian Society/Old State House, the Boston Public Library, the Harvard University Archives, the Library of Congress, the *Milwaukee Journal,* the National Baseball Library and Archive, Cooperstown, N.Y., the *Pittsburgh Post-Gazette,* Transcendental Graphics,

John Alevizos, Al Blanche, George Brace, Bob Brady, Bob Buege, Jimmy Cribb, Phil Davis, Michael Gagna, Joe Gerson, Chris Hamilton, Ernie Johnson, Sr., Randall Richards, Jim Rowe, Roger Pavey, Michael Pugh, Joe Sebo, Bill Setliff, Sibby Sisti, Bud Skinner, and Rich Westcott.

Acknowledgments

This encyclopedia would not have been complete without the special assistance of Rick Benner, Bob Brady, and Bill Setliff. The author also wishes to thank the following people for their contributions and support in making this volume possible: Ed Baker, Ann Boston, Thurman Brooks, Bob Browning, Carol Carter, Lane Caruso, Tony Cocchi, Morris Fostoff, Andy Jurinko, Roger Pavey, Glen Serra, and Rich Westcott, and all the folks at Temple University Press, P. M. Gordon Associates, Inc., and the National Baseball Library and Archive. Special thanks to Peter Capolino of Mitchell and Ness Nostalgia Co. and Virgil, Marty, and Shane Stadler.

About the Author

Gary Caruso is editor of *ChopTalk,* a monthly magazine that covers the Braves. He has been an avid follower of the Braves since his early youth and has spent most of his professional career covering the team as a reporter and editor. Caruso was on the staff of the *Atlanta Journal and Constitution* for 10 years, working the Braves beat in 1977–78 and serving as executive sports editor in 1982–85. He also has been a senior editor and writer for *The National Sports Daily* and has been a correspondent for *The Sporting News.*

A native of East Liverpool, Ohio, Caruso is a graduate of Marietta (Ohio) College. He is a member of the society for American Baseball Research (SABR) and the Boston Braves Historical Association. He and his wife, Lane, live in Avondale Estates, Georgia—8 miles due east of Atlanta–Fulton County Stadium.